D1098188

MINERALS OF CALIFORNIA

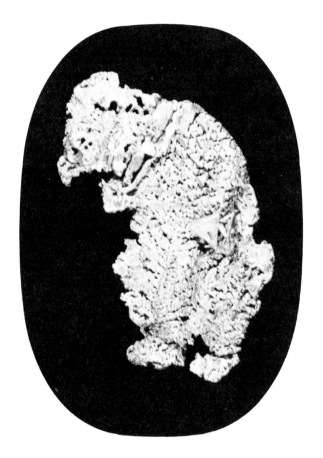

THE GOLDEN BEAR NUGGET

The Golden Bear Nugget is said to have been found in the mining town of Yankee Jim, Placer County, California, in 1871 by a small girl who kept the nugget in her possession throughout her lifetime. The lost identity of the nugget's finder, and the lack of record of her lifetime and death, are part of the mystery that surrounds many famous gems and nuggets.

The nugget was acquired by the California Federation of Mineralogical Societies by undetermined means in 1939, and became the organization's insignia on April 20, 1940. The nugget has been on display in the California Division of Mines and Geology mineral exhibit in San Francisco since 1952.

MINERALS OF CALIFORNIA
CENTENNIAL VOLUME (1866–1966)

by JOSEPH MURDOCH
University of California, Los Angeles

and

ROBERT WALLACE WEBB
University of California, Santa Barbara

With sections by
Ian Campbell and Eleanor M. Learned

BULLETIN 189

California Division of Mines and Geology
Ferry Building, San Francisco, CA 94111

1966

STATE OF CALIFORNIA
RONALD REAGAN, Governor

THE RESOURCES AGENCY
NORMAN B. LIVERMORE, JR., Administrator

DEPARTMENT OF CONSERVATION
JAMES G. STEARNS, Director

DIVISION OF MINES AND GEOLOGY
IAN CAMPBELL, STATE GEOLOGIST

BULLETIN 189
Price $5.00

Manuscript received December 31, 1965

CONTENTS

PREFACE TO THE CENTENNIAL VOLUME—1866-1966

Since 1914, the California Division of Mines and Geology has followed the policy of publishing, at approximately ten-year intervals, catalogs with commentaries on the minerals of California. This volume commemorates the publication in 1866 of the first systematic record of California minerals by W. P. Blake (9). In this Centennial volume, the writers have scrutinized all information included in volumes covering 1866–1954. They have modernized and updated information reported earlier which has been superseded by studies of the past decade. In addition, the publication of data on new minerals (which surprisingly are still found in ever-increasing numbers) and additions to the literature indicated by the restudy of old, established localities, are reported for the decade 1954–1964. Several new sections have been added. Tributes to serious students of California mineralogy are included in the form of photographs and brief biographies, acknowledging the indebtedness to pioneer contributors on mineralogical studies in the state. Revisions and additions make the Centennial volume an historical as well as a scientific record of California mineralogy. The interest of laymen and scientists in the past publications is recognized; the format and organization of the Centennial volume continues the attempt to provide for the interests of both. The bibliography has been updated and expanded. County lists published by Collins (1) pp. 40–64, in Murdoch and Webb (40), have been revised and are presented in this Centennial volume as a separate chapter. Codification has been attempted to reduce the confusion resulting from references to the geographic term "Mining District," especially in the pre-1920 literature.

Widespread interest in California minerals and mineral resources began early in the history of the state and has continued to increase to the present time. It has received a great impetus from the organization of many mineral societies, which have multiplied in number and now have large memberships in California. Recognition of the contribution of such groups to California mineralogy is contained in the chapter in this volume on the California Federation of Mineral Societies. The increasing number of minerals and mineral occurrences which are still being reported reflects this growing interest and is shown in the increasing size of successive catalogs of California minerals.

The first catalog was W. P. Blake's, (9) 1866, listing 77 mineral species in a small pamphlet of 31 pages. It was followed in 1884 and 1886 by a list compiled by H. G. Hanks (12), (15), then State Mineralogist, with about 135 species. In 1914, A. S. Eakle (12) compiled a comprehensive list of minerals found in California, including 352 species, which was published in Bulletin 67 of the California Division of Mines and Geology (henceforth referred to as CDMG). A second volume by the same author in 1923, Eakle (22), increased the number of known species to 417. Professor Adolf Pabst, University of California, Berkeley, issued in 1938 Bulletin 113 of the CDMG, Pabst (4), in which the number of known species increased to 446.

In 1948, Professors Joseph Murdoch and Robert Webb published a completely reorganized catalog, CDMG Bulletin 136, Murdoch and Webb (21), in which it was endeavored to provide written or, at least authoritative verbal validation of all mineral occurrences already listed, of all new entries representing old occurrences not previously mentioned, and of occurrences discovered since 1938, up to and including 1945. This was not possible in all cases because many earlier references were apparently not documented and represented verbal information from some unrecorded source, personal observation, or hearsay. This is particularly the case with entries in Eakle (12), (22); he undoubtedly added many items from his own extensive investigations throughout the state and rarely indicated which these were.

In the preparation of Bulletin 136 in 1948, the writers personally scanned all the literature dealing in any way with California minerals, and many publications of a nongeologic nature which were suspected of carrying mineralogical information. In this search, nearly 160 serials were consulted, in most cases from their earliest numbers. Besides these, many individual publications were studied. From these sources, references to thousands of individual occurrences were accumulated and compiled, resulting in the addition of some 70 species to the catalog and increasing the total for the state to about 516 minerals and many subspecies or varieties. In 1956, CDMG Bulletin 173 (Murdoch and Webb (39)) increased the total to 523, even with the discrediting of several minerals noted earlier. The present volume has over 5,200 individual entries of mineral occurrences, of which 678 are new since 1954. Only 196 remain invalidated. Up to December 31, 1964, 57 previously known and 22 entirely new minerals have been added to the Bulletin 173 list, making a current total of 602, of which 74 are new minerals, first discovered and described in California. A list of these with the dates of their published descriptions, follows.

Partzite, 1867	Arcanite, 1908	Woodhouseite, 1935
Melonite, 1867	Joaquinite, 1909	Ellestadite, 1937
Mariposite, 1868	*Neocolemanite, 1911	Teepleite, 1938
Calaverite, 1868	*Palaite, 1912	Veatchite, 1938
Metacinnabar, 1870	Salmonsite, 1912	*Nuevite, 1946
Aragotite, 1873	Sicklerite, 1912	Sahamalite, 1954
*Trautwinite, 1873	Stewartite, 1912	Galeite, 1955
Stibioferrite, 1873	Inyoite, 1914	Gerstleyite, 1956
Roscoelite, 1875	Meyerhofferite, 1914	*Lesserite, 1956
Posepnyte, 1877	Searlesite, 1914	Gowerite, 1959
*Sonomaite, 1877	Wilkeite, 1914	Haiweeite, 1959
Ionite, 1878	*Crestmoreite, 1917	Metahaiweeite, 1959
Tincalconite, 1878	*Eakleite, 1917	Schuetteite, 1959
Colemanite, 1883	*Griffithite, 1917	Tunellite, 1959
Hanksite, 1884	§Riversideite, 1917	*Woodfordite, 1959
Napalite, 1888	Plazolite, 1920	Nobleite, 1961
Sulphohalite, 1888	Vonsenite, 1920	Redledgeite, 1961
Knoxvillite, 1890	*Jurupaite, 1921	Wightmanite, 1962
Redingtonite, 1890	Merwinite, 1921	Deerite, 1964
‡Iddingsite, 1893	Kempite, 1924	Fresnoite, 1964
†Crossite, 1894	Foshagite, 1925	Greigite, 1964
Lawsonite, 1895	Kernite, 1927	Howieite, 1964
Northupite, 1895	*Chromrutile, 1928	Krauskopfite, 1964
Pirssonite, 1896	Probertite, 1929	Macdonaldite, 1964
*Palacheite, 1903	Curtisite, 1930	Muirite, 1964
Bakerite, 1903	Krausite, 1931	Traskite, 1964
Boothite, 1903	Sanbornite, 1931	Verplanckite, 1964
Tychite, 1905	Schairerite, 1931	Walstromite, 1964
Benitoite, 1907	Tilleyite, 1933	Zussmanite, 1964
*Carlosite, 1907	Burkeite, 1935	

* Discredited mineral.
† Described as a new species, but in fact a variety of glaucophane.
‡ Validity doubtful.
§ Discredited but suggested for reinstatement.

As has been observed in earlier editions, special interest in certain minerals or particular elements has almost always resulted in the finding of new minerals or new occurrences of minerals, sometimes in the reworking of old deposits or in the intensified prospecting for new localities. An instance of this is the detailed study of the borate deposits of the Mojave Desert area and of Death Valley by a group of U.S. Geological Survey workers, with the collaboration of the California Division of Mines and Geology. As a result, a number of new borate minerals have been found, primarily in the Boron area, but also in the Death Valley region. Another example is a recent study of the glaucophane schists which has resulted in the discovery of several new silicate minerals (Agrell, Brown, and McKie: Am. Mineral. 50, p. 278).

Hand in hand with the discovery of new minerals or localities goes the attrition of older ones. Prime examples of this are the Leona rhyolite locality in Alameda County and the lawsonite type locality in Marin County, which have been completely overrun by housing developments. Another is the famous Crestmore quarry, where the cement production has almost destroyed the collecting area, at least so far as the public is concerned. Besides these examples of loss due to progress, there are also some localities where the natural wear and tear of continued collecting has removed practically all available material.

In CDMG Bulletin 136, the introductory portion was considerably enlarged to include historical and geologic sketches of famous mineral localities—the Mother Lode, Crestmore, Searles Lake, Pala, Mesa Grande, and others—which contributed many minerals found for the first time in California. This was continued in CDMG Bulletin 173 in somewhat fuller fashion.

In the present volume, as in earlier ones, minerals are arranged in alphabetical order, so that only the name of the mineral need be known to find it immediately. A very complete system of cross-referencing has been employed so that varietal names (such as chrysotile) are referred to the main entry (serpentine). It is recognized that this arrangement separates minerals which belong to common groups, but the convenience of the alphabetical scheme is thought to outweigh this scattering of groups.

Occurrences of each mineral are listed by counties, and those of particular importance or interest are accompanied by a brief description of their geologic setting. For each occurrence, whenever possible, one or more references to the literature are given, so that the user may turn to the original description, which is ordinarily more detailed than can be given here. Occurrences marked "(N.R.)" which still lack written or even adequate verbal documentation have also been summarized in a separate appendix. The writers will be glad to have any reference to or confirmation of such cases drawn to their attention. Occurrences verified by personal communication are marked "(p.c.)", and a list of the names of the individuals supplying this verification is given in a separate appendix. Those represented by specimens in the exhibit of the CDMG at San Francisco carry the letters CDMG and the specimen number, as, "CDMG (5158)."

Species first discovered in California are marked by an asterisk (*), and followed by the date of the first published description. Discredited species are marked by a dagger (†).

The bibliography, containing nearly 2,500 titles, does not, of course, cover *all* notices of California minerals; but it is by far the most comprehensive yet assembled on California mineral occurrences. It lists all important publications in the field and practially all those of lesser importance.

Special note should be made that this volume does not purport to include all references in the literature of California to minerals that are also mineral resources and mineral commodities. As an example, barite occurs widely throughout California, but no attempt has been made to systematically report occurrences of the mineral wherever it is mentioned in the literature. Some localities of minor importance and of little general mineralogical interest are noted because they have been carried in early editions of *Minerals of California*. The authors consider it wise to retain these as part of the historical record, but newer and more important localities of the mineral as a mineral resource have not necessarily been added, and literature citations to articles on such localities have not necessarily been included. It is emphasized that validation of correct mineral identification in the literature has not been undertaken, so early identifications may be incorrect.

Occurrences noted since December 31, 1964, are being currently accumulated and filed for future supplements to the Centennial volume; corrections and information on new or omitted occurrences are solicited. Such items should be sent to the California Division of Mines and Geology, San Francisco.

It would be impracticable to acknowledge the services of all who have cooperated in the preparation of this and earlier volumes, but the writers wish to express their thanks to the following, who have made important contributions to the work: Professor Adolf Pabst, University of California, Berkeley; Professor A. O. Woodford, Pomona College; the late Professor Charles Palache, Harvard University; Dr. W. T. Schaller, U.S. Geological Survey; the late Dr. W. F. Foshag, U.S. National Museum; the late Mr. M. Vonsen, Petaluma, California; the member Societies of the California Federation of Mineralogical Societies; Professor George Tunell, University of California, Riverside; Professor C. Douglas Woodhouse, University of California, Santa Barbara; and the many individuals who generously wrote comments and criticisms.

Thanks are also due to the past and present members of the staff of the California Division of Mines and Geology, including State Mineralogists W. W. Bradley and Olaf P. Jenkins.

Special acknowledgment for direction on the Centennial volume are due Dr. Ian Campbell, Chief, CDMG, and California State Geologist. Mr. Charles W. Chesterman, Mr. Tom Gay, Dr. Eugene B. Gross, and Mr. Melvin Stinson, of the CDMG, offered many constructive suggestions in the preparation of the manuscript. Mrs. Mary Gill and Miss Shirley Henderson of the Department of Geology, University of California, Santa Barbara, offered expert stenographic and technical assistance. These services are gratefully acknowledged, but the writers assume full responsibility for errors and omissions.

Financial support for the project was received, from time to time, from the State Department of Conservation through the CDMG. Acknowledgment should also be made of subsidies received during the period 1936 to 1942 for the study of mineral localities in California, from the Committee on Research, University of California, Los Angeles, and 1950–1964, University of California, Santa Barbara. The results of these studies, although published elsewhere, have contributed to the accuracy and completeness of this volume.

JOSEPH MURDOCH
ROBERT W. WEBB

University of California
Los Angeles and Santa Barbara, California
December 31, 1965

INTRODUCTION

by IAN CAMPBELL, State Geologist

Viewed from the perspective of geologic time, one hundred years, a centennial, is scarcely discernible, even with the most modern of scanning techniques! Viewed from the perspective of recorded history, a centennial is still only a minute mark in the inexorable march (hopefully, a forward march) of time and civilization. Yet, viewed from the perspective of California's history—even more so from the perspective of California's statehood—a centennial looms large indeed.

Moreover, from the beginning of geologic history minerals have played an essential role—perhaps *the* essential role—in the building blocks of our earth (if not, indeed, of our universe also); they played a most significant role in California's early history as a state; and they continue to fulfill an essential role in today's economy.

Thus it is that, to those who have any interest—whether historic, scientific, esthetic or economic—in California's minerals, the appearance of a centennial edition of *Minerals of California* is an EVENT and deserves appropriate recognition and commemoration. It is in view of these considerations that the Division of Mines and Geology has, with the collaboration of the authors, Doctors Joseph Murdoch and Robert W. Webb, brought out this volume to commemorate the publication, one hundred years ago, of the first official list of minerals produced from California, the prototype "Minerals of California".

Entitled "Annotated Catalog of the Principal Mineral Species Hitherto Recognized in California, and the adjoining States and Territories," this list was prepared by Professor William P. Blake as a report to the California State Board of Agriculture, for whom Blake acted as geologist, besides being professor of mineralogy, geology, and mining at the "College of California", parent to the University of California, Berkeley. Not counting synonyms, 77 mineral species appear on this list.

From the earliest days that California was known to the western world, mineral wealth had been mentioned among the various accounts of the natural bounties of this region. Mineral riches—gold and silver, mainly—were among the chief attractions that brought the Spanish and other explorers to the western edge of the New World. For example, one early listing of some California rocks and minerals appeared as an appendix in Otto von Kotzebue's account of his visit aboard the vessel *Rurik* to San Francisco Bay in 1816.

Blake's "Annotated Catalog", modest as it was, marked a real achievement. California, as a state, was less than sixteen years old. Yet in the very first year of her statehood, the Legislature had established the post of State Geologist and had filled it with an able scientist, Dr. John B. Trask,* a physician whose wide-ranging interests included both mineralogy and geology, who authored some of the very first reports on the mineralogy of the State, and who was a leader in organizing the California Academy of Sciences. Unfortunately, funds for Dr. Trask's one-man survey were continued for only three years

---

*It deserves to be mentioned that, in 1965, Dr. Trask was honored by having a newly discovered mineral—one, so far, unique to California—named for him. Traskite is a hydrous barium silicate.

(1851–54), certainly not time enough to plan and carry through any report with so ambitious a title as "Minerals of California".

In 1860, the Legislature—again recognizing the importance of geology to the young State—appropriated funds to reestablish a Geologic Survey and appointed to the post of State Geologist a scientist of national reputation, Josiah D. Whitney. Prof. Whitney, partly by virtue of his own reputation and partly by virtue of the scientific attractions already coming to be recognized in the geology of California, was soon able to assemble a small group of scientists who, in their ability and dedication, immediately placed the California Survey in the front rank, if not perhaps in the top spot, among all the State Surveys of that time. Whitney numbered among his assistants such men as Clarence King (later to become the first Director of the U.S. Geological Survey), Arnold Hoffman (later to become Chief Topographer of the USGS), W. H. Brewer (later to become a professor at Yale and to be recognized as "the father of soil science"), and W. H. Dall (later to become one of the country's foremost paleontologists and Director of the Philadelphia Academy of Sciences). The Whitney Survey continued—with some ups and downs—until 1873, when, largely because of hard times and partly for other reasons related to personalities, funds were cut off. Not until 1880 was a somewhat equivalent agency reestablished and at that time designated as "The State Mining Bureau" and placed in charge of a "State Mineralogist", an office first filled by Henry Hanks, for whom the distinctive mineral hanksite was long ago named.

So much for that early history. Let us review briefly the contents of that first list of minerals of California. Of 111 entries, 19 are synonyms, and 15 occur only in "adjoining States and Territories", so actually only 77 mineral species are reported from California. These are nearly evenly divided between metallic ore minerals (37) and nonmetallic minerals (40). About half (22) of the nonmetallic species are "commercial" minerals, such as asbestos, gypsum, and fluorspar. And it was noted by Blake that altogether 59 of the 77 species listed could be categorized as "useful minerals".

Not surprisingly, the longest lists of localities were for gold, copper, quicksilver, and silver, because of the many active mines. Among the nonmetallic minerals, interestingly enough, there is a reference to diamonds ("well formed, highly modified crystals, from one-eighth to three-sixteenths of an inch in diameter, and generally of a pale straw color"—from Cherokee Flat, Butte County); and to borax ("Lake County, in large crystals in the clay of the Borax lake; Boracic acid, Clear Lake, Lake County"—this is the total entry!). No hint foreshadows the subsequent discovery of immense deposits of borate minerals elsewhere in California leading to the State's current multi-million dollar borax industry; while further finds of diamonds were to be limited to a few specimens and chips of little significance or value, and only from the one locality.

Likewise, no clue appears in that early list to the future development of the State's dominant cement, clay, diatomite, or gypsum industries. As to petroleum, although "the localities are numerous in the counties of San Luis Obispo, Santa Barbara, Tulare, and Los Angeles", Blake notes that "The purest and most limpid natural oils have thus far been obtained from the localities north of San Francisco, in Humboldt and Colusa counties." It is difficult to imagine what Professor Blake might think if he could see the trends in commercial minerals that have developed in the century following the publication of his hard-won list. What stronger lesson should be grasped from this hundred-year perspective than never to limit the search and reporting of minerals to only those that happen to be currently in strong demand: the least significant-appearing mineral described today may some day provide just the right answers to some yet-to-be-imagined future need!

Space does not permit equivalent comment on the successive editions of "Minerals of California". It must suffice here merely to present the following table, which provides some interesting statistical comparisons.

TABLE 1

Reference *Minerals of California*	Year	Number of mineral species described	Total mineral production in California for that year
Blake (9)	1866	77	$30,986,530 (1865)
Hanks (12, 15)	1884, 1886	135	$21,000,000 (est. 1887)
Eakle (12) CDMG Bull. 67	1914	352	$93,314,773
Eakle (22) CDMG Bull. 91	1923	417	$344,024,678
Pabst (4) CDMG Bull. 113	1938	446	$380,444,976
Murdoch and Webb (21) CDMG Bull. 136	1948	516	$1,174,674,000
Murdoch and Webb (39) CDMG Bull. 173	1956	523	$1,551,524,133
Murdoch and Webb CDMG Bull. 189	1966	602	$1,700,000,000 (est.)

Is it a coincidence or a correlation that explains the rough parallelism between the increasing number of minerals recorded in the State and the increasing value of the State's mineral production? To what degree did the publication of these successively more informative volumes serve to enhance mineral production; to what degree did the expanding mineral economy contribute to the increased data and increased demand for the successive volumes? These things we may never know precisely. But that there has been more than coincidence—in all probability, a definite correlation—between the published volumes and the production figures seems altogether likely.

Up-to-date indices to a state's known mineral occurrences constitute one of two principal guides to resource development that a forward-looking agency should supply to the public and to industry interested in the continued enhancement of such a basic factor in the economy as is the mineral industry. The other index, which likewise must be kept up

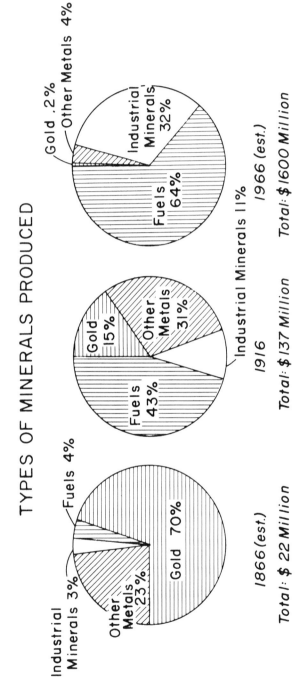

FIGURE 1. Mineral Production in California, at 50-year intervals (1866, 1916, 1966) showing shift in value of mineral commodities produced. (Data from U.S. Geological Survey, U.S. Bureau of Mines, and Division of Mines and Geology statistical reports.)

to date, is the geologic map. The first permits reasoning from the particular to the more general; the second, from the general to the particular. To be more specific: as our knowledge and understanding of minerals increase, we find that minerals provide ever more precise indices to the physical-chemical environment in which ore deposits are formed, and later (hopefully) found. Research on mineral relationships makes possible some tentative predictions: for example that, just from the occurrence of one species, conditions at that locality are favorable for finding certain other specific minerals—perhaps needed by our expanding economy. At the same time, the construction of increasingly accurate geologic maps and increasing knowledge of geologic factors, are enabling predictions to be made that in such-and-such a formation, or in this-or-that kind of rock, or adjoining a certain kind of contact, is a favorable environment for an ore deposit and is an area that particularly deserves detailed study and prospecting for certain specific minerals.

It is therefore with some pride, and with a high degree of confidence for the future of California's mineral industry that the Division of Mines and Geology brings out this centennial edition of *Minerals of California* which, imperfect as it doubtless is in a number of respects,* nevertheless provides more details on more minerals within our State than have ever been brought together before. Coincidentally, the Division takes pride in pointing to the near-completion of the Geologic Atlas of California which—imperfect as it also may be—nevertheless presents a far more complete picture of the geology of the State than has ever before been assembled.

These two items—important as they are—constitute only the record. Let us look a little more closely at some of the essentials. It has been well said that past history provides the best guide to the future. California's mineral history has been encapsulated in Table 1, above. Any projection based on this record of 100 years, predicts increasing demand, increasing development, and increasing production of minerals in this exceptionally favored State. And it is with good reason that California is referred to as an exceptionally favored State. From being a "one crop" (albeit what a crop!) State, mineralwise, during the gold-rush years, California has subsequently expanded her mineral production so that, although she is no longer the number one gold producer in the nation, she ranks number one in *diversity* of mineral commodities produced, and number one in the production of more individual mineral commodities than any other state. Mineralogists know, of course, that California has long been the number one State in the number of minerals occurring in the State and in the number of minerals found only within the State.

Why should California be so fortunate? There is no simple answer. But it is well to recall the remarks of a distinguished engineer that "A mineral deposit is an accident of geology". And California's geologic setting is such as to provide opportunity for more of such fortunate accidents than anywhere else in these United States. Her

---

*All users of this volume would do well to read the preface in order to know the "ground rules" that of necessity the authors felt should be followed in compiling this list of minerals. Thereby they will become aware of this volume's capabilities *and* of its limitations as a guide to mineral occurrences—and particularly to "ore deposits"

position, adjoining the circum-Pacific earthquake and volcanic belt guarantees a degree of geologic activity not found elsewhere in the conterminous United States. Her great variety of rocks, ranging in age from Precambrian to the Recent, and including a wide variety of sedimentary, igneous, and metamorphic types, provides the setting in which "geologic accidents" develop and mineral deposits are formed.

Largely because of these factors, "the law of diminishing returns" seems not yet to have taken any real toll from California's mineral production. In this connection it should suffice to point to three notable developments in the mineral economy of the State that have transpired very largely since just the last edition of Minerals of California (Bull. 173, 1956). 1) The bastnaesite deposit at Mountain Pass had been discovered a few years previously, development was underway, but returns at that time were somewhat disappointing. It took the subsequent discovery of practical methods for refining the rare earths and producing relatively pure europium oxide, as well as the discovery of the application of this rare earth to color television, to make the Mountain Pass deposit the bonanza that it is fast becoming. 2) In 1956, production of asbestos in California received only the barest mention in the U.S. Bureau of Mines Minerals Yearbook. In 1966 it will be reported as a multimillion dollar industry, with plans for expansion and enormous reserves of ore. This has come about partly through recognition that the curious "mountain leather" of the Coalinga area was not tremolite, after all, but a true chrysotile fibre in an unusual habit; partly through technological success in learning how to process this material; and partly through the economic opportunities conferred by growth of population. 3) In 1956 "geothermal steam" was a commercial oddity reported only from Italy and beginning to be talked about in New Zealand. Today, the successful harnessing of geothermal energy in the last four years to produce electric power at The Geysers represents a "first" in this field in terms of the entire North American continent. And developments in the Niland area of the Imperial Valley presage the possibility of producing not only power, but potash!

How fortunate can we be? Has California not been already more than sufficiently favored? Yet there *is* more to this "success story". A mineral is a mineral; but for a mineral to be useful, man must enter on the scene. California has attracted more mineralogists (whether measured in the somewhat restricted scientific terms of numbers of Fellows of the Mineralogical Society of America, or in the broader and more popular terms of number of members of the Federated Mineral Societies) than has any other state. Moreover, California has attracted more top flight scientists in all fields than most other states. The juxtaposition (if one may put it that way) of a wide variety of minerals in a diversity of geologic settings, and of numbers of imaginative scientists in general and mineralogists in particular, virtually guarantees that there will be more and perhaps bigger new discoveries, both of minerals and of useful application for minerals, than any we have yet seen.

Probably no current reader of this volume—unless geriatrics succeeds soon in significantly prolonging human life—will be around one hundred years hence to make the kind of comparisons we are making now between California's mineral "empire" as we see it in this current volume and as it was portrayed in Blake's modest catalog of 1866. But if man continues to gain mineralogic and geologic knowledge and if he succeeds in applying this knowledge wisely, there is little doubt in the mind of this State Geologist that the 2066 edition of "Minerals of California" will transcend this 1966 volume by an even greater amount than this Murdoch and Webb volume has transcended Professor Blake's catalog of 77 species. So let us then be on to new discoveries and, above all, to new wisdom!

JOSEPH MURDOCH

Joseph Murdoch, professor of geology emeritus, University of California, Los Angeles, has been actively involved in the study of minerals of California since his appointment in 1928 to the faculty at UCLA. The Centennial Volume is the third volume of *Minerals of California* under Dr. Murdoch's name following Bulletins 136 (1948), 173 (1956), and several supplements, in the intervening years. Each of the volumes and supplements were joint efforts with Robert W. Webb.

Dr. Murdoch was born in Massachusetts in 1890. He was educated at Harvard University, receiving the A.B. degree in 1911, the S.M. in 1912, and the Ph.D. in 1915, each in geology and mineralogy. After over a decade in the business world, he joined the UCLA geology faculty in 1928, and rose successively to professor of geology in 1949. His specializations involve ore mineral microscopy, including pioneer published works on opaque minerals, and studies on the crystal chemistry of several rare minerals, especially those of Crestmore, Riverside County, California, and pegmatite minerals. His extensive bibliography includes 45 articles on California minerals and several articles on Brazilian and Norwegian pegmatite minerals. Dr. Murdoch served as president of the Mineralogical Society of America in 1959–1960. He became professor emeritus in 1959.

JOSEPH MURDOCH

ROBERT WALLACE WEBB

Dr. Robert W. Webb, professor of geology at the University of California at Santa Barbara and co-author of this Centennial Volume, is one of the justly famous (especially among California mineralogists) team of "Murdoch and Webb." Since 1940, this team has been responsible for continuing the important series of reference catalogs of California's minerals, begun in 1866 by W. P. Blake. During the last 25 years, Murdoch and Webb have compiled three bulletins and numerous supplements for publication by the California Division of Mines and Geology.

Born in Los Angeles in 1909, Bob Webb became interested in minerals while still in high school—an interest that led him to major in geology at UCLA where he earned a bachelor's degree in 1931. He then started a graduate program, while serving as assistant and associate in geology at UCLA, at the California Institute of Technology where he received an M.S. degree in 1932, and a Ph.D. in 1937. Starting then as an instructor in geology and mineralogy at UCLA, he rose through the academic grades to full professor in 1951. In 1948 he transferred to the newly developing campus of UC at Santa Barbara where he served as chairman of the Department of Physical Sciences from 1953 to 1959 and where he was largely instrumental in establishing in 1954 a major in geology, leading to the establishment of a Department of Geology in 1960.

In the course of his 40 years of continuous association with the University of California, he has served as coordinator of the Army specialized training program (1943–44), as associate dean of the college of letters and sciences (1946–47), and as coordinator of veterans affairs for the UCLA campus and the statewide University of California (1944–1952) ; as Executive Secretary of the Division of Geology and Geography (now Earth Sciences) of the National Research Council and as Executive Director of the American Geological Institute (1953) ; as Director of the Ford Foundation experimental program for college instructors in California (1960–1963) ; and as visiting professor of geology for summer sessions at the Universities of New Mexico (1952), Maine (1956), Columbia University (1959, 1960), University of Massachusetts (1964), and Northeastern University (1965).

His bibliography comprises some 65 papers, many of which deal with the geology and mineralogy of California.

ROBERT W. WEBB

HISTORICAL AND GEOLOGICAL SKETCHES

ABORIGINAL AND INDIAN MINERALS

A number of minerals were known and used for one purpose or another by prehistoric races and by the later Indians of California. Many references are to be found in the following: C. C. Abbott (1) ; Haldeman (1) ; Heizer and Treganza (1) who give an extensive bibliography, with a list of minerals and occurrences; Kunz (24) ; Schumacher (1) ; E. F. Walker (1) ; W. V. Wells (1) ; Woodward (1) ; L. G. Yates (1), (3), (4), (5) ; others have also supplied information on this subject.

The earliest known mineral used was apparently turquoise, which was mined by aboriginal tribes in the northeast corner of San Bernardino County in prehistoric times. The old workings here were rediscovered in 1897 by T. C. Bassett, who found in them a couple of stone hammers and called his claim the Stone Hammer mine. This find aroused so much interest that the *San Francisco Call*, in 1898, sent out an expedition conducted by Dr. Gustav Eisen of the California Academy of Sciences to explore the mines. His account was published [Eisen (1)] in an extensive article in the *Call* of March 18, 1898, and led to further investigation of the area. The following extracts from Kunz (24), pp. 107–109, provide a good description of the find and of the general character of the area, which is the Turquoise Mountains (T. 16 N., R. 10 and 11 E., S.B.) :

"Mr. T. C. Bassett had observed in this neighborhood a small hillock where the float rock was seamed and stained with blue. On digging down a few feet, he found a vein of turquoise—a white talcose material inclosing nodules and small masses of the mineral, which at a depth of 20 feet showed fine gem color. Two aboriginal stone hammers were met with, as usual at all the turquoise localities in the southwest, and from this circumstance the location was named the Stone Hammer mine.

"The State Mining Bureau reported at about the same time that turquoise had been found in the desert region between Death Valley and Goff's Mining District, nearer the former, and that good samples were in the museum of the Bureau. * * *

"The turquoise district, as described by Mr. Eisen and others of the party, occupies an area of 30 or 40 miles in extent, but the best mines are in a smaller section, about 15 miles long by 3 or 4 in width. The region is conspicuously volcanic in aspect, being largely covered with outflows of trap or basaltic rock reaching outward from a central group of extinct craters. These flows extend for many miles in all directions, and appear as long, low ridges, separated by valleys and cañons of the wildest character. Among these basaltic rocks and in the valleys are found smaller areas of low, rounded hills of decomposed sandstones and porphyries, traversed at times by ledges of harder crystalline rocks, quartzites, and schists. In the cañons and on the sides of these hills are the old turquoise mines, appearing as saucer-like pits, from 15 to 30 feet across and of half that depth, but generally much filled up with debris. They are scattered about everywhere. Around them the ground consists of disintegrated quartz rocks like sand or gravel, full of fragments and little nodules of turquoise. Whenever the quartzite ledges outcrop distinctly they show the blue veins of turquoise, sometimes in narrow seams, sometimes in nodules or in pockets. The mode of occurrence appears closely to resemble that at Turquoise Mountain, Arizone. * * * Stone tools are abundant in the old workings, and the indications are plain that this locality was exploited on a great scale and probably for a long period, and must have been an important source of the turquoise used among the ancient Mexicans. From an archaeological point of view this locality possesses remarkable interest. The cañon walls are full of caverns, now filled up to a depth of several feet with apparently wind-blown sand and dust, but whose blackened roofs and rudely sculptured walls indicate that they were occupied for a long time by the people who worked the mines. In the blown sand were found stone implements and pottery fragments of rude type, incised but not painted. The openings to these caves are partially closed by roughly built walls composed of trap blocks piled upon one another with no attempt at fitting and no cement, but evidently made as a mere rude protection

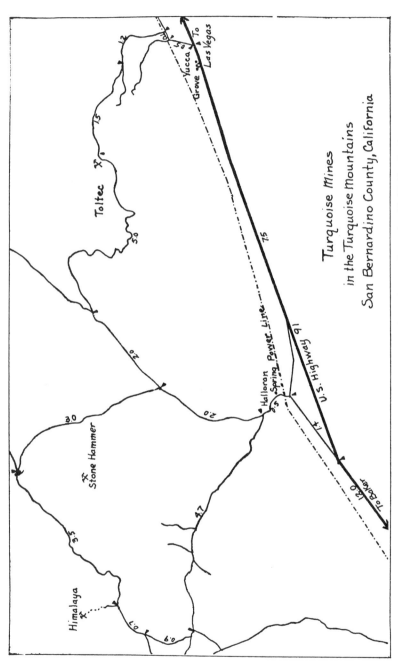

FIGURE 2. Positions of mines plotted by H. Earl Pemberton [see also H. E. Pemberton (3)] on Halloran Springs Quadrangle, United States Geological Survey, 1956.

against weather and wild beasts. The tools, found partly in the caves and largely in the mine pits are carefully wrought and polished from hard basalt or trap, chiefly hammers and adzes or axes, generally grooved for a handle and often of large size. Some are beautifully perfect, others much worn and battered by use.

"The most impressive feature, however, is the abundance of rock carvings in the whole region. These are very varied, conspicuous, and peculiar, while elsewhere they are very rare. Some are recognizable as 'Aztec water signs,' pointing the way to springs; but most of them are unlike any others known, and furnish a most interesting problem to American archaeologists. They are numbered by many thousands, carved in the hard basalt of the cliffs, or, more frequently, on large blocks of the same rock that have fallen and lie on the sides of the valleys. Some are combinations of lines, dots, and curves into various devices; others represent animals and men; a third and very peculiar type is that of the 'shield figures,' in which complex patterns of lines, circles, cross hatchings, etc., are inscribed within a shield-like outline perhaps 3 or 4 feet high.

"One curious legend still exists among the neighboring Indians that is no way improbable or inconsistent with the facts. The story was told Mr. Eisen by 'Indian Johnny,' son of the Piute chief, Tecopah, who died recently at a great age, and who in turn had received it from his father. Thousands of years ago, says the tale, this region was the home of the Desert Mojaves. Among them suddenly appeared, from the west or south, a strange tribe searching for precious stones among the rocks, who made friends with the Mojaves, learned about these mines, and worked them and got great quantities of stones. These people were unlike any other Indians, with lighter complexions and hair, very peaceable and industrious, and possessed of many curious arts. They made these rock carvings and taught the Mojaves the same things. This alarmed and excited the Piutes, who distrusted such strange novelties, and thought them some form of insanity or 'bad medicine,' and resolved on a war of extermination. After a long desperate conflict, most of the strangers and Mojaves were slain, since which time, perhaps a thousand years ago, the mines have been abandoned."

Other minerals were known to the Piute and other Indian tribes of more recent times. Cinnabar, hematite, and manganese oxides were used as color pigments, and talc in some cases as white. Talc in the form of steatite was formed into cooking vessels, beads or other ornaments, arrow straighteners, pipes, or finger rings. Fluorite was occasionally made into beads. Quartz crystals were collected, perhaps for their appearance, or as part of the medicine man's equipment. Mica plates served occasionally as ornaments. Magnesite was made into tokens with value for exchange.

Of these, talc, or steatite, was most commonly known. Practically all the old Indian sites have yielded steatite receptacles. The mineral was mined in a number of localities, of which the most important was on Santa Catalina Island. Steatite bowls or vessels partly carved out of the bed rock, and attached by a stem, which was later to be broken off and smoothed away, have been described as still remaining in the quarries at this place. Other localities for steatite are listed by Heizer and Treganza, (1) p. 307, as follows: Klamath River, two localities; 1 mile east of Tuolumne; 4 miles east of Lindsay, Tulare County; near mouth of Carrizo Gorge, San Diego County; west side of Williams Valley, Mendocino County; Santa Ynez Mountains; Santiago Canyon near Mount Pinos, Ventura County; Table Mountain, Madera County; Fish Creek Mountain, Fresno County; northeast of Cloverdale, Sonoma County; near Burnt Ranch, north fork of Trinity River, Trinity County.

Cinnabar was mined in at least two places in the State. One, the most important, was the famous New Almaden mine, near San Jose, and the other, Last Chance Peak, north of Death Valley. The New Almaden locality was known in very early times, and Indians came to it from as far away as Oregon and Washington. An interesting account of the locality is given by Downer, (1) p. 221.

"We are still three hundred and thirty-three feet below the summit, where in 1845 a shaft was sunk, and mining first commenced. This point had been the resort of the aborigines not only of this State, but from as far as the Columbia River, to attain the paint (vermillion) found in the cinnabar, and which they used in the decoration of their persons. How long this had been known to them cannot be ascertained; probably a long time, as they had worked into the mountain some fifty or sixty feet, with what implements can only be conjectured. A quantity of round stones, evidently from the brook, was found in a passage, with a number of skeletons; the destruction of life having been caused, undoubtedly, by the sudden caving of the earth burying the unskilled savages in the midst of their labors."

Quartz crystals appear in large numbers in Indian sites and were perhaps collected for their magical properties. One arrowhead, chipped out of a clear quartz crystal, is in the museum, CDMG (11562), but, in general, the cystals were untouched or occasionally pasted on one end with asphaltum, apparently so that they could be slung by a cord.

Mica plates, several inches across, and perforated, have been found, apparently used as ornaments.

Fluorite beads, from an unknown source, were found in some of the sites near Santa Barbara, San Luis Obispo, and along the north shore of Buena Vista Lake.

Magnesite from near Sulphur Bank, in Lake County, was shaped into cylindrical forms, and baked, to produce reddish, creamy, or black coloration, then polished, perforated, and used as money.

THE DISCOVERY OF GOLD IN CALIFORNIA

The history of gold in California far antedates James Marshall's famous discovery in 1848, although the early accounts are often vague or uncertain. In Hakluyt's Voyages, Drake in 1579 is said to mention the probability of gold here: "There is no part of the earth here to be taken up wherein there is not some special likelihood of gold or silver." Since he did not go inland, it is a trifle difficult to see how he could have had more than wishful thinking as a basis for his comment. This may well have been the source of the statement in 1816 by Jameson (1) p. 13: "On the coast of California there is a plain of 14 leagues in extent, covered with an alluvial deposite, in which lumps of gold are dispersed."

After Drake, there were many Spanish expeditions based on Mexico, but the journals of these make little or no mention of gold. A most entertaining story is told by Captain George Shelvocke, (1) p. 401, a British privateer, in his account of "A Voyage around the World by way of the Great South Sea, perform'd in the years 1719, '20, '21, '22 in the Speedwell of London" published in 1726. This does not concern our own state, but lower California, just north of Cape San Lucas. It is, however, of sufficient interest to quote briefly:

"The soil about *Puerto Seguro* (and very likely in most of the vallies) is a rich black mould, which, as you turn it fresh up to the sun, appears as if intermingled with golddust, some of which we endeavor'd to wash and purify from the dirt; but tho we were a little prejudiced against the thoughts that it could be possible that this metal should be so promiscuously and universally mingled with the common earth, yet we endeavour'd to cleanse and wash the earth from some of it, and the more we did, the more it appeared like gold, but in order to be farther satisfied, I brought away some of it, which we lost in our confusions in China."

Presumably his "gold" flakes were flakes of mica; but such an account might easily have formed the foundation for later, supposedly authentic tales.

The next account is more trustworthy, reporting placers worked in the "Carga Muchacha" area near Yuma, in 1775, Hanks (12) p. 217, and at St. Isadore [San Isidro] near San Diego in 1825, Wyld (2) p. 37, or in 1828, W. W. Jenkins (1) p. 70. Gold was reported from California in 1818 by Teschemacher (3) p. 287. Wyld (2) p. 37 also records a "small thread of gold worked in the Saint Barbara district in 1840." The San Francisco *Alta Californian* about 1868 (?) carried a letter from Abel Stearns relating the discovery of gold at San Francisquito in 1842, by Francisco Lopez, some of which gold he sent to the United States Mint in 1843. Duflot de Mofras (1) p. 186, an emissary of the French government, notes the discovery of a "* * * gold vein at San Francisquito, 6 leagues beyond San Fernando, in 1842, with pieces up to 2 or 3 ounces in weight." These two are apparently the same, and presumably refer to Placerita Canyon. Rickard (3) pp. 14, 15, quotes the report of Manuel Casteñares to the King of Spain in 1844 on the same locality: "Gold placers discovered in the course of the last year have attracted the greatest attention, for they extend nearly 30 leagues." These were near San Fernando Mission [Placerita Canyon again] discovered by Francisco Lopez, March 9, 1842, and worked by him in company with Charles Barec.

Rather surprisingly these reports either did not reach the east coast of America, or made very little impression on the public there, as it was not until after Marshall's discovery at Coloma in 1848, that the gold-rush excitement broke.

The accounts of the discovery of gold at Coloma by James Marshall, are, as is usually the case, conflicting in detail, even those purporting to be eye-witness reports. They are all in general agreement that the discovery was made by Marshall in the mill-race at Coloma in January or February 1848. W. W. Jenkins (1) p. 72 gives the date as January 19 without quoting any specific authority. J. Ross Browne and James W. Taylor (1) p. 14, state that on January 19, 1848, Marshall found some gold in the mill-race at Coloma. The first printed notice occurred on March 15, in the newspaper printed in San Francisco. Hittel (4) p. 529 quotes the diary of Henry W. Bigler, one of Marshall's fellow workers, which gives the date as January 24. He prints a facsimile reproduction of Bigler's diary. Marshall took the gold to Sutter's 4 days after the discovery, where it was tested.

George M. Evans (1) p. 385 notes the recovery of specks of gold from the bank of the San Joaquin river near Stockton, in September 1846, and reports the news of *abundant* gold near San Diego and the river Gila in August, 1847. He then goes on to make the following statement:

"On the 9th of February 1848, I with Henderson Cox, Beardsley Beers, two Shepards, and a number more were in the lower end of the mill-race [at Coloma] when Marshall, the overseer, and his little girl came in, and the child picked up a pretty stone as she called it, and showed it to her father, who pronounced it gold. He was so excited about it that he saddled his horse and that day rode to Sutter's Fort to tell Captain Sutter—but he did not believe it worth notice, and for a while the idea died away."

Evans also mentions a very early reference to gold supposedly made by one Lyola Cavello (or Cabello), a priest at "San José Mission on the bay of San Francisco," in *Recordado en Historia el California Alta* printed in Spain in 1690. This mentions small quantities of gold in "placeros" of streams to the north. There are various reasons for doubting the validity of this quotation. There were no missions in California as early as 1690; the title of the publication is not as it should be in Spanish; "Lyola" is not a given name, and should probably be "Loyola" in any case; and California was not known as Alta California until much later. There is probably some basis of truth behind this quotation, but in its present form it is quite valueless. It has been mentioned here as a matter of interest and to illustrate the general vagueness and unreliability of early reports.

In those days of slow travel, the news of Marshall's discovery was a long time reaching the east, and it was not until late in 1848 and early in 1849, that letters began coming in. One of the earliest records was a letter written by T. L. Hasse, September 26, 1848, from New York to a correspondent in Germany announcing the discovery, Berg-u. Hutt. Zt. (1) p. 791. The first official record was a report to the War Department by R. B. Mason, (1) p. 528. After this time there was a flood of letters and reports about California gold. One early report, R. M. Patterson (1) p. 61, tells of the finding of a 15-pound nugget, perhaps the same as that picked up by a soldier of Stevenson's regiment on the Mokelumne River in 1848, and is of interest as recording for the first time the presence of platinum in the gold sands.

A most unusual and spectacular story is told of an occurrence of gold in California, along the beach at Gold Bluff, Humboldt County, by S. Johnson (1), pp. 534–537. According to this account, a party of men travelling south from Oregon, in the year 1850, was forced by thick timber to turn out towards the shore. Reaching it, to their amazement, the beach appeared to be literally paved with gold. They could not believe their eyes, but on closer examination, found that the waves had accomplished a perfect job of panning, and had spread the gold particles almost uniformly over the surface of the sands. They scraped off some handfuls from the surface, but as they were short of provisions, and travel-weary, pushed on to their destination. The samples proved to be nearly half gold, and an expedition was immediately organized to exploit the beach. Unfortunately, but as was to be expected, by the time the party reached the beach once more, the waves and tide had completely dispersed the gold, so that the sands were no longer concentrates, and of no particular value.

BORAX

Discovery in California

The discovery of borax in California is interestingly described by Dr. John A. Veatch, in a letter to the Borax Company of California, dated June 28, 1857, and quoted in J. R. Browne and Taylor (1) pp. 179–185. The following quotations have been taken from this letter:

"I believe I was the first to detect the borates in mineral waters in this State, and perhaps, as yet, the only observer of their localities. My attention was first drawn to this subject by noticing crystals of bi-borate of soda in the artificially concentrated water of a mineral spring which I chanced at the time to be examining for other matters. This water was from one of the several springs since known as the Tuscan springs, and which have gained some fame, and very justly, I believe, as medicinal waters. The spot has been described by Dr. Trask under the name of the Lick Springs, and is so designated on Britton and Rey's late map; lying on the north part of Tehama county, eight miles east of Red Bluff. The crystals alluded to were observed on the eighth day of January, 1856. Several pounds were subsequently extracted by evaporating the water to a certain degree of concentration and allowing the borax to crystallize. The pioneer specimens of this product were deposited in the museum of the California Academy of Natural Sciences, as an evidence of the existence of a new and important link in the chain of our mineralogical productions, showing that along with the rich productions of the noble and useful metals, we have also that mineral substance so essential to their easy application to the purposes of man. * * *

"My mind being now alive to the subject, I learned, upon inquiry, of other localities which I supposed might yield the borates. One of these, near the mouth of Pitt river, forty miles north of the Tuscan springs, I had the pleasure of visiting in company with Dr. Wm. O. Ayres, in April, 1856. Specimens there obtained yielded the borate salts; and, from a subsequent examination of the intermediate country, several similar localities were found. The quantity was too small to be of any practical importance, but the prevalence of the salt gave encouragement to further search. A reconnoissance of the 'coast range' of mountains, from the neighborhood of Shasta over a length of some thirty miles towards the south, brought to light borates in the numerous small springs abounding in that region, but only in minute quantities. These springs were found almost exclusively in the sandstone, or in the magnesium limestone overlaying it; and the borates seemed to abound in localities bearing indications of volcanic disturbance. Thus a kind of guide was obtained in the prosecution of further explorations. I began to entertain hopes of finding streams with stronger impregnations, or accumulations, of the borates in salt lagoons said to exist in Colusi county, where the sandstone formation was largely developed, the adjacent foot-hills presenting volcanic features. Hunters told tales of mineral springs of sulphurous and bitter waters; of lakes of soda, and alkaline plains, white with efflorescent matters, in that region. Not being in a situation immediately to visit those inviting localities, I had, for the time, to content myself with pointing out to the hunters and others occasionally passing through that country such appearances as I wished particularly to be noted. Their reports, together with specimens sometimes furnished, were all corroborative of the correctness of my theory. Colonel Joel Lewis, of Sacramento City, who occasionally visited the coast range on hunting excursions, and to whom I explained the object of my search, and who, although not a scientific man, is an intelligent observer, had the kindness to look, in his peregrinations, for certain indications. He subsequently informed me by letter that he had met with an Irishman, living in Bear valley, who had found a 'lake of borax,' as it was pronounced by an Englishman who lived with the Irishman, and who had been at one time employed in a borax manufactory in England, and therefore assumed to speak knowingly on the subject. He also informed me in the same letter that a Major Vanbibber, of Antelope valley, had discovered large quantities of nitre in the same neighborhood. These glowing reports led me to hasten the excursion I had so long contemplated. In a personal interview with the colonel he told me of an enormous mass, of a white, pulverulent substance, he had himself observed near the margin of Clear lake, of the nature of which he was ignorant. Mr. Charles Fairfax, who was with the colonel at the time, stated to me that a small rivulet running at the base of the white hillock was an intensely impregnated mineral water, totally undrinkable, as he had accidently discovered by attempting to slake his thirst with it. From the meagre information gathered from these gentlemen, I was led to hope the 'hill of white powder,' as they termed it, might prove to be borate of lime. I determined to satisfy myself by personal examination at once, and I finally induced Colonel Lewis to act as my guide by furnishing him with a horse and paying expenses. It was some time in the early part of September of last year that he and I left Sacramento for the localities that had so much excited my hopes. At the town of Colusi, which we reached by steamer, horses were obtained, and we proceeded in a westerly direction across the Sacramento valley to the foot-hills of the coast mountains, a distance of about twenty miles. That portion of the plains skirting the hills gave unmistakable evidence of a heavy charge of mineral salts, and the exceedingly contorted and interrupted state of the hill strata enabled me at one to predict the presence of the beloved borates, which chemical trial on some efflorescent matter taken from a ravine proved to be the case in a slight degree. At this point we entered 'Fresh-water cañon,' which cuts the hills and forms a passway into Antelope and Bear valleys. Here I received information from a settler of a hot sulphur spring a few miles south of Bear valley, on one of the trails leading to Clear lake. This spring we succeeded in finding on the following day. It was with no small pleasure that I observed the outcropping magnesian limestone in the hills surrounding the valley of the springs. The strong smell of sulphurated hydrogen, and the appearance of a whitish efflorescence on the rocks, manifested, even at a distance, almost the certainty of finding the mineral I sought. The indications were not deceptive. The efflorescence proved to be boracic acid, in part, while the hot, sulphurous water held borate of soda in solution, together with chlorides and sulphates. There are three hot springs at this place, and several cold ones, all alike strongly impregnated with common salt and borax. * * * The same phenomenon occurs here that is observed at the Tuscan springs, viz., free boracic acid in the efflorescence on the margin of the springs, while the water itself shows a decided alkaline reaction. * * *

"The following day we reached the 'Hill of White Powder,' the goal of our hopes, on the margin of Clear Lake. This 'White Powder Hill,' the goal of our hopes, proved an illustration of how little the recollections of mere casual observers are to be depended upon. The hill, in place of consisting of materials in a state of disintegration, so as to admit of being 'shoveled up,' as my friend supposed, proved to be a concrete volcanic mass, bleached white by sulphurous fumes, and looking, at a little distance, like a huge mass of slaked lime, which the inattentive observer might readily suppose to be a 'hill of white powder.' The hope of a treasure in the form of borate of lime vanished forever.

"The road had been rather toilsome, the weather exceedingly hot, and my guide not very well; and as he had gone the full length of the contemplated journey, and felt somewhat disgusted at the result so far, and had nothing more to draw his attention in this direction, he proposed to return at once by the way of the Irishman's 'borax lake' and Vanbibber's nitre placer. This was agreed upon; so, collecting a few specimens of efflorescent matters from the ground, and filling a bottle with the water in the ravine, I closed the examination of the 'Hill of White Powder.' The ravine I afterwards called the 'boracic acid ravine,' and the white hill is now called 'Sulphur Bank.' Of these I shall have occasion to speak hereafter.

"Before leaving the neighborhood I determined, however, to know something more of its surroundings. I learned, upon inquiry of Mr. Hawkins, who lives near the spot, that a place not far off, known by the name of 'Alkali lake,' presented a rather peculiar appearance. Hawkins consented to act as my guide. After travelling a short distance, and clambering to the narrow edge of an almost precipitous mountain ridge, we looked down the opposite slope, equally steep, on a small muddy lake that sent up, even to our elevated position, no pleasant perfumes. Thus, on one of the hottest days September ever produced, without a breath of air to dilute the exquisite scent exhaled from two hundred acres of fragrant mud, of an untold depth, I slid down the mountain side into 'Alkali lake,' waded knee-deep into its soapy margin, and filled a bottle with the most diabolical watery compound this side the Dead Sea. Gathering a few specimens of the matter encrusting the shore, I hastened to escape from a spot very far from being attractive at the time, but which I have since learned to have no prejudice against. Of this place I shall have occasion to say more. * * *

"From Colusi my guide returned to Sacramento and I to Red Bluff; from there I came again to San Francisco, for the purpose of testing my specimens more critically than I was able to do in the country.

"Convinced of the richness of my 'Alkali lake' specimens, it remained to be seen whether the quantity was sufficient to justify the hope of making it available for practical purposes. A further and more strict examination was necessary. I felt, too, the propriety of a thorough exploration betwixt the Bluff and Clear lake, and more thence to the bay of San Francisco, thus rendering continuous the reconnaissance from Pitt river to the last-named point, a distance, in a direct line, of two hundred miles. After a hard struggle for the funds requisite, I returned to Red Bluff; and from thence, in company with my son, commenced a pretty thorough examination of the coast range and the adjoining edge of the Sacramento valley. * * *

"In due time I again reached the 'white hill.' The disgust of the first disappointment had worn off, and I felt disposed to re-examine the locality more critically. I now discovered, for the first time, that the 'white hill' was mostly a mass of sulphur, fused by volcanic heat. The external dust, composed of sulphur, mixed with sand and earthy impurities, and formed a concrete covering of a whitish appearance, hiding the nature of the mass beneath. On breaking the crust, numerous fissures and small cavities, lined with sulphur crystals of great beauty, were brought to light. Through the fissures, which seemed to communicate with the depth below, hot aqueous vapors and sulphurous fumes constantly escape. The fused mass, covering many acres and exhibiting a bluff front some forty feet high, is exceedingly compact and ponderous in structure; of various shades, from yellow to almost black. It seems to be very pure sulphur. The quantity is enormous, and at no distant day may be made available.

"From the 'sulphur bank' I again turned my attention to the ravine. The water, as I had before ascertained, was strongly impregnated with boracic acid, in a free state. The stream is small, yielding only about three gallons per minute, and is soon lost in the sandy soil, in its progress toward the margin of the lake. From the porous nature of the ground surrounding the spring, and saturated with the same kind of acid water, it is probable a large quantity escapes without making its appearance on the surface. The soil for some yards on either side of the ravine is, to the depth of an inch or two impregnated with boracic acid in summer. Sulphurretted hydrogen escapes in continued bubbles through the water, a feature common to all the borax localities I have yet found; in some places, however, the carburetted takes the place of the sulphuretted hydrogen. The head of this ravine is about three hundred yards from the margin of Clear Lake, winding around the base of the 'sulphur bank,' receiving some small springs in its course, which seem to have their origin beneath the sulphur. The flat land bordering the lake, some eight acres in extent, through which the ravine runs, shows a strong impregnation of boracic acid in its soil. The point where the ravine enters the lake is marked by a large quantity of water of a boiling temperature, issuing through the sand, a little within the margin of the lake. This percolation of hot water covers an area of one hundred and fifty by seventy-five feet. This fact I observed on my second visit, but not until the third or fourth visit did I ascertain that the water contained a considerable quantity of borax, along with an excess of boracic acid. From a gallon I obtained four hundred and eighty-eight grains of solid matter, consisting of borax, boracic acid, and a small portion of siliceous and other earthy impurities. On digging to a slight depth just outside the lake, the hot water burst up and ran off freely. From one of these places a stream issued of sixty gallons per minute. I have estimated the entire quantity at three hundred gallons per minute, and feel very confident of being largely within bounds. The stream seems to come from the direction of the sulphur bank, and it would probably be easy to intercept it before it enters the lake, by digging a little above high-water mark. It may be well to note here, that the difference between high and low water marks in Clear Lake is never more than three feet.

"The enormous amount of borax these springs are capable of yielding would equal half the quantity of that article consumed both in England and America. The large quantity of water in which it is dissolved would, of course, involve the necessity of extensive works for evaporation. Graduation, as a cheap and effective method of evaporation, would be exceedingly applicable here, from the continued prevalence of winds throughout the entire year. These winds blowing almost unceasingly from the west, form a peculiar feature of the country about Clear lake.

"There is nothing to hinder the manufacture of many million pounds of borax per annum, at a cost but little beyond that of producing salt by graduation. Fuel for final evaporation could be had in any quantities from the extensive oak forest in the immediate vicinity. With these observations I dismiss this locality, adding, however, that Mr. Joseph G. Baldwin located this with a four hundred and eighty acre school land warrant, for the benefit of a borax company.

"Having wandered from my story of my second visit to the 'sulphur bank,' and blended with it observations made in several subsequent examinations, I now turn to my second visit to 'Alkali lake,' or Lake Kaysa, as the Indians call it. I need only say, however, I became fully satisfied of the great value of the locality, the extent of which has only been recently developed. I observed that the lake itself contained but little water, but that wells dug anywhere near its margin immediately filled with the same kind of water; the conclusion, therefore, was, that an almost inexhaustible supply was obtainable. I learned, too, that what seemed to be mud at the margin and shelving off and covering the entire bottom to the depth of some feet, was a peculiar jelly-like substance of a soapy feel and smell. This matter I found to be so rich in borax, that I supposed it might be advantageously used for the extraction of the mineral. Thus satisfied of the value of the lake, I little thought that within a few yards of me lay an additional value in the form of millions of pounds of pure borax crystals, hidden by the jelly-like substance I was then contemplating. This important fact was not observed until some six months afterwards.

"This locality is by far the most important of any I have yet discovered. It is situated * * * in the angle formed by the two prongs into which Clear lake is divided at its eastern extremity. The elevated hill land that fills the angle separates into two sharp ridges, each following its division of the lake and leaving a valley between, of a triangular shape, near the apex of which lies Alkali lake. Clear lake is, therefore, on two sides of it, distant to the north about a mile, and to the south about half the distance. The open part of the triangular plain looks to the east, and expands into an extensive valley, from which it is cut off, partially, by a low volcanic ridge running across from one hill to the other, and thus enclosing the triangle.

"This ridge is composed of huge masses of rock resembling pumice-stone, which float like cork in water. A thin stratum of ashy-looking soil, scattered over with obsidian fragments, covers the ridge and affords foot to a stunted growth of manzanita shrubs.

"The whole neighborhood bears marks of comparatively recent volcanic action. Indeed, the action has not ceased entirely yet; hot sulphurous fumes issue from several places on the edge of the ridge just named, on the side next Alkali lake.

"The 'lake,' as it is called, is rather a marsh than a lake. In winter it covers some two hundred acres, with about three feet depth of water. In the dry portion of the year it shrinks to some fifty or sixty acres, with a depth of only a few inches. The 'soapy matter' covers the entire extent with a depth of nearly four feet, the upper part, for a foot in depth, being in a state of semi-fluidity, the lower having the consistency of stiff mortar. Beneath this is a rather tenacious blue clay. This water was nearly as highly charged with solid matter as that of the lake in its highest summer concentration; the proportion of borax to other substances being greater. The soapy or gelatinous matter, however, presents the greatest feature of attraction, being filled with the prismatic crystals of pure borax. They vary from a microscopic size up to the weight of several ounces. These crystals are semi-transparent, of a whitish or yellowish color. The form is an oblique rhomboidal prism, with replaced edges and truncated angles. In some cases the edges are bevelled, and in others the unmodified hexahedral prism exists. Beneath the gelatinous matter, and on the surface of the blue clay, and from sixteen to eighteen inches in it, crystals of a similar form, but much larger, are found. They weigh from an ounce, and seem to have been formed under different circumstances from the other crystals. My first impression was that they had been formed in the upper-stratum, and, sinking by their own gravity, had found their present position. An examination proves, however, that they were formed where they lie, as particles of the blue clay are found enclosed in their centers, which could not have been the case had the upper crystals been their nuclea, for no blue matter is ever found in them."

Following this discovery, very vigorous prospecting for borax was carried on all through the desert regions of California. The famous deposits of Death Valley were found in its playas in 1873, and less extensive ones in the Searles Lake basin in 1862. A number of other localities, of lesser importance, were also recorded, even in the early days.

Later (1882) the discovery was made of the immensely rich colemanite beds in Death Valley, along Furnace Creek; in the following year colemanite was found near Calico. Other important deposits of this mineral were discovered as time went on at Frazier Mountain, Ventura County (1898), Tick Canyon, Los Angeles County (1909), and in the Kramer region, Kern County (1913). These deposits were the principal source of borax until the discovery of kernite near Kramer (Boron) in 1927. This area, with Searles Lake, now (1964) produces practically all the borax in California.

Searles Lake Deposits

Discovery of the Searles Lake borax deposits is described in the following quotations from De Groot (3) p. 534 and H. S. Gale (13) p. 309.

"This extensive and valuable deposit of borax was discovered by John W. Searles, first observed signs of this salt when crossing the marsh that now bears his name, in 1862, at which time he was engaged in prospecting for gold in the Slate Range, lying to the east. Being unacquainted with the nature of the substance, he did not at the time pay much attention to it. Afterward, however, when borax began to be an object of general inquiry, he recognized in some samples of this salt shown him the stuff he had noticed while crossing this alkaline flat several years before. Satisfied on this point, he at once took proper steps for locating such portions of the marsh as he considered most valuable." De Groot (3) p. 534.

"The deposit is reported to have been located by J. W. Searles and E. M. Skillings on February 14, 1873. Borax was then obtained from the surface scrapings over the mud deposits about the margin of the main salt area * * * ." H. S. Gale (13) p. 309.

In his report, H. S. Gale (13) pp. 271, 272, describes the geologic setting and character of the deposits as follows:

"The most distinctive feature of this desert basin is the immense sheet of solid white salts that lies exposed in its bottom. It is to this salt deposit that the name Searles Lake (Searles Dry Lake *) has generally been applied. So far as known at present the deposit is unique in this country in the variety of its saline minerals * * *."

"The surface of the main or central salt deposit is a firm crust of salt crystals, mostly cubic halite, so hard and compact that it will support the weight of a * * * heavy drill rig. The surface shows a tendency to crack along irregular lines, so that it is divided into cakes or blocks. Flooding and re-solution tend to level inequalities that arise and the cakes and fractures are not so pronounced a feature here as they are on some salt surfaces of similar type elsewhere."

The following early description of the mineralogy of the Searles Lake deposits is also drawn from Gales's report (13) pp. 296, 297:

"Of the commoner minerals characteristic of desert-basin salines generally, probably the greater number are represented in the Searles Lake deposits, except ulexite, which is reported to be absent.

"The deep well at Searles Lake, which was begun in 1887 and completed in 1896 * * * has proved a veritable treasure house of unusual and entirely new minerals, including several that have never been found at any other place. The less soluble minerals were mostly found embedded in the muds or clay at the margin or underlying the main saline deposit. Several are characteristically found in small but distinctly formed crystals, many of which are unattached, as if they had grown within the mud. In places, however, layers of the crystalline material (as pirssonite) have become so consolidated as to present hard strata, offering considerable difficulty in drilling. Many of the specimens obtained as drill samples are fractured masses or even finely granulated material, but much perfectly preserved crystalline material has also been obtained in this way."

A more recent and comprehensive study of Searles Lake gives a detailed stratigraphic section of the beds in the deposit, a map showing the location of drill-holes, a discussion of the mineralogy of the deposit, and descriptions of the minerals present [G. I. Smith and Haines (3), pp. P5-P44]. The list of minerals reported from this deposit, amended to December 31, 1964, is as follows:

*Footnote in G. I. Smith and Haines (3) p. P3: "Searles Lake has been known by several other names which are used in older records. The commonest synonyms are Slate Range Lake, Alkali Flat, Borax Lake, and Searles Flat. The name Borax Lake has caused confusion in geologic literature because it is commonly not distinguished from Borax Lake in Lake County, California, which was the site of the earliest borax mining in the State."

Adularia (orthoclase)
Analcime
Anhydrite
Aphthitalite
Aragonite
Borax
Burkeite
Calcite
Celestite (San
 Bernardino
 County (17))
Cerargyrite (Inyo
 County (8))
Dolomite

Embolite (San
 Bernardino
 County (8))
Galeite
Gay-lussite
Glauberite
Gypsum
Halite
Hanksite
Mirabilite
Nahcolite
Natron
Northupite

Phillipsite
Pirssonite
Quartz
Realgar (N.R.)
Schairerite
Searlesite
Sulphohalite
Sulphur
Teepleite
Thenardite
Tincalconite
Trona
Tychite

In addition, colemanite, niter, and ulexite have been mentioned by hearsay from Searles Lake, but it is improbable that these minerals have as yet been identified. Celestite, cerargyrite, embolite, realgar, and gold have been reported "from Searles Lake." It is likely that these are from mines near Searles Lake, not from the lake itself.

CRESTMORE

The cement quarries at Crestmore, near Riverside in Riverside County, are the site of one of the famous mineral localities of the world. Here, in a contact metamorphic zone, have been found (through 1964) more than 148 minerals, many of them new to science, some of them found nowhere else in California, and all in a complex grouping of species. Eakle (11), (15), in 1917, first described systematically the Crestmore suite and thus initiated the study of this locality by mineralogists from all quarters of the globe, a study which has been pursued vigorously to the present day.

The quarries form a cluster about the Chino and Sky Blue Hills (Wet Weather, Lone Star, Chino, Commercial); excavations have developed these hills so that Sky Blue Hill stands as a narrow, fin-like projection above the surrounding country. The following abstract from Woodford (11), p. 333, outlines some of the early history of the locality:

"A cement plant was started in 1909 at Crestmore, near Riverside, 50 miles east of Los Angeles. Crystalline limestone and other rocks were quarried from the twin Crestmore Hills for use in the manufacture of cement and for other purposes.

"In 1914 Professor A. S. Eakle of the University of California called the attention of mineralogists to the numerous contact minerals which were being found at this promising locality. In the next two or three years Professor Eakle, Professor A. F. Rogers of Stanford, Mr. R. M. Wilke of Palo Alto, and especially Mr. L. J. Childs of Rialto, collected many fine specimens of grossularite, diopside, wollastonite, idocrase, and other minerals from the limestone contact zone. In 1914 Eakle and Rogers described the complex new mineral wilkeite, in 1917 Eakle published a general paper on the locality, and in 1918 Rogers reported periclase. The first period of good collecting came to an end in 1916 or 1917.

"Important Crestmore discoveries were made by W. F. Foshag and E. S. Larsen in the twenties, including spurrite, thaumasite, centrallasite and the new minerals merwinite and plazolite. In the thirties M. A. Peacock distinguished parawollastonite, using Crestmore material, Duncan McConnell reported on members of the apatite group, recognizing ellestadite as a new end-member, and Larsen and Dunham described the new mineral tilleyite.

"In 1938 new quarrying in the principal contact zone exposed not only minerals previously listed from the locality, but also many others. Part of the new finds are from the limestone contact and part are from the white dikes of intrusive pegmatite. A report on these finds was made in the *American Mineralogist* (Woodford, Crippen, and Garner, 1941)."

HENRY GARBER HANKS
(1826–1907)

Henry Garber Hanks was the first State Mineralogist of California. He headed the State Mining Bureau (State Division of Mines and Geology today), from 1880–1886, and published contributions to California mineralogy as late as 1905. Hanks continued the mineral catalogs for the state as begun by Blake and described several interesting new California mineral localities.

The mineral hanksite, described as a new mineral from California in 1884, was named in his honor.

George F. Becker was a pioneer California geologist, whose early studies defined the mineralogy of California's mercury deposits. His paper "Geology of the quicksilver deposits of the Pacific Slope" is classic. He began his geological career in California on the University of California (Berkeley) faculty in mining and metallurgy. His primary interest was in economic geology; he studied western mining regions as a member of the U. S. Geological Survey from 1879–1919. *Photo courtesy U.S. Geological Survey.*

GEORGE FERDINAND BECKER
(1847–1919)

GEORGE F. KUNZ
(1856–1932)

George Frederick Kunz was a distinguished self-taught mineralogist who, for more than a half-century, was the gem expert for Tiffany and Company, New York. He joined the U.S. Geological Survey staff in 1883, and published gem reports for the United States through 1909. He was a prolific writer, and his descriptions of gem finds in California, especially those from the pegmatites of San Diego and Riverside Counties, popularized California as a gem state. The gemstone kunzite, a variety of lilac spodumene, described from Pala, San Diego County, commemorates Kunz's contributions to California mineralogy. *Photo from American Mineralogist.*

Waldemar Lindgren was an economic geologist of international repute. Professor at the Massachusetts Institute of Technology (1912–1933) and geologist for the U.S. Geological Survey, he early became expert on the Sierra Nevada Mother Lode. His paper "The Tertiary gravels of the Sierra Nevada of California" is a standard reference. In addition, he wrote many folios of the Geological Atlas of the United States on areas in the Sierra Nevada, and reported many early California mineral localities. *Photo from American Mineralogist.*

WALDEMAR LINDGREN
(1860–1939)

ANDREW COWPER LAWSON
(1861–1952)

As professor of geology at the University of California, Berkeley, appointed in 1892, Andrew Cowper Lawson pioneered geological and mineralogical studies in many parts of the state. He inspired and directed the education of some of the most distinguished professional workers in the geological and mineralogical fields. With George Davis Louderback, he helped build one of the outstanding departments of geology and mineralogy in North America. Lawson's professional life spanned nearly seven decades, during which he described several new California minerals. Lawsonite, a new mineral from the California Coast Ranges, was named in his honor. *Photo courtesy A. O. Woodford.*

Arthur S. Eakle was professor of mineralogy at the University of California (Berkeley) for many years. Eakle began publication on California minerals in 1901, and his contributions were continuous until his retirement. He described the new minerals vonsenite, foshagite, and probertite from California localities. Eakle revived in 1914 the catalog "Minerals of California," first published by W. P. Blake in 1866, and continued by Hanks in 1884 and 1886. Eakle's volumes on California minerals are the ones on which this Centennial Volume is based. Eakle also pioneered study of the world famous Crestmore quarries and first defined a large number of the nearly 150 minerals reported from this locality. *Photo from American Mineralogist.*

ARTHUR STARR EAKLE
(1862–1931)

FREDERICK LESLIE RANSOME
(1868–1935)

Frederick Leslie Ransome was awarded the Ph.D. degree from the University of California, Berkeley, in 1896. During his career with the U.S. Geological Survey, he published many papers on the mineralogy and economic geology of California, in particular on the Mother Lode. In 1923, Dr. Ransome was appointed professor of economic geology at the University of Arizona. He transferred in 1927 to the faculty of the California Institute of Technology, holding a professorship in economic geology at the time of his death. Ransome discovered and named the new mineral from California, lawsonite, in 1895. *Photo from Geographical Society of America.*

Native son of California, Charles Palache received his Ph.D. from the University of California, Berkeley, in 1894. He joined the faculty of Harvard University in 1896, where he remained until his retirement in 1941. Author of many papers on mineralogy, and a crystallographer of note, Dr. Palache discovered many new minerals. His revision of Dana's "System of mineralogy" with Harvard coworkers, although incomplete at the time of his death, is the American standard for mineralogists.

CHARLES PALACHE
(1869–1954)

GEORGE DAVIS LOUDERBACK
(1874–1957)

George Davis Louderback was born in California, and educated at the University of California, Berkeley (Ph.D., 1899). After a brief interlude as professor of geology at the University of Nevada (1900–1906), he joined the faculty at the University of California. He retired from the University officially in 1944, but was active until his death in University of California geological and, academic affairs. Dr. Louderback served his native California with distinction in mineralogy, geology, seismology, and as a civic and academic leader. In 1907, he discovered and described the new and still rare mineral benitoite. *Photo from American Mineralogist.*

William Foshag had a distinguished career in mineralogy, terminated by his untimely death. He received his baccalaureate degree in chemistry from the University of California (Berkeley), but became fascinated by mineralogy through study of the Crestmore quarries with Professor Arthur Eakle. Foshag received his Ph.D. in geology in 1923, also from the University of California, and served as Curator of Mineralogy in the U. S. National Museum starting in 1919. Foshag described plazolite (1921), schairerite (1931), krausite (1931), and burkeite (1935), all new minerals from California. In addition, he contributed substantially to the knowledge of other California mineral localities and mineral suites through his writings that included more than 30 titles. The mineral foshagite, discovered in California and described in 1925, was named in his honor. *Photo from American Mineralogist.*

WILLIAM FREDERIC FOSHAG
(1894–1956)

Hoyt S. Gale was educated at Harvard University and upon graduation almost immediately began geological studies for the U. S. Geological Survey (1903). His early assignments were almost exclusively in the west, where he became involved in the pre-World War I search for nitrate, potash, and borax, in which his mineralogical interest grew. His papers on the saline lakes that followed the Pleistocene glacial lake sequences in the Mojave Desert and Basin Ranges, defined the history of mineral suites in such basins as Searles Lake. Gale maintained his interest in saline deposits, even after he resigned from the Geological Survey in 1920 to enter the petroleum industry. His last two contributions, published in 1946 and 1951, dealt with borate deposits at Kramer in Kern County, and saline deposits of Bristol Dry Lake in San Bernardino County. Galeite, a new mineral discovered at Searles Lake, in 1955, commemorates his contributions to California mineralogy. *Photo from Geological Society of America.*

HOYT STODDARD GALE
(1876–1952)

AUSTIN FLINT ROGERS
(1877–1957)

Dr. Austin Flint Rogers was professor of mineralogy at Stanford University for 40 years (1902–1942). He contributed 53 papers on minerals from California localities. He described the new minerals kempite and sanbornite and defined the crystallographic and mineralogic characteristics of many minerals from California localities. *Photo from American Mineralogist.*

E. S. Larsen (Jr.) was born in Oregon but received his academic degrees from the University of California, Berkeley (Ph.D. in 1918), after he had already distinguished himself as a mineralogist. Following service on the staff of the Carnegie Institution of Washington, and the U. S. Geological Survey, he became professor of petrography at Harvard University. He was widely acclaimed for his studies of properties of minerals. He described several new minerals from California, particularly from Searles Lake and Crestmore. Dr. Larsen's method for determining the age of minerals in batholiths from radioactive isotopic components of rarer accessory minerals is a standard today. *Photo from American Mineralogist.*

ESPER SIGNIUS LARSEN
(1878–1961)

ADOLPH KNOPF
(1882–1966)

Adolph Knopf, born in San Francisco in 1882, completed his academic preparation at the University of California, Berkeley, (Ph.D., 1909), after earning earlier degrees also at that university. His first published contribution, in 1905, dealt with the geology and mineralogy of Mineral King. In 1920 he joined the faculty at Yale University, where he taught until his first retirement in 1951. Moving back to California, he joined the geological faculty of Stanford University, an affiliation which continued until his death.

His association with the U. S. Geological Survey took him widely over North America, but he regularly contributed to California's geological and mineralogical knowledge by field and laboratory reports extending almost to the close of his distinguished career. Dr. Knopf's papers on the Mother Lode (1929) and the eastern Sierra Nevada (1918) are classics.

Vigorous proponent of mineral development and collection in California, Woodhouse joined the faculty of the Santa Barbara State College in 1938, after a career that included mine management and mineral exploration. In his years as a member of the faculty of Santa Barbara State College and the University of California, Santa Barbara, from which he became Professor Emeritus in 1955, Woodhouse built one of the best private collections of minerals in the United States. He fostered mineralogical study in the Santa Barbara Museum of Natural History, taught stimulating courses in geology and mineralogy, and has been a personal benefactor of his department, his students, and the science of mineralogy. He discovered many minerals new to California. The mineral woodhouseite was named in his honor.

CHARLES DOUGLAS WOODHOUSE
(1888–   )

Professor of geology at Pomona College since 1916, Dr. Woodford was born and reared in southern California. Versatile student of Professor A. C. Lawson, under whom he earned his Ph.D. in 1923, he returned to his alma mater, Pomona College, to found the department of geology. Dr. Woodford has followed in his mentor's footsteps and has inspired many students to enter mineralogical and geological careers. Dr. Woodford made substantial contributions to mineralogical studies of the famous Crestmore quarries, and to the mineralogy and geology of metamorphic minerals.

ALFRED OSWALD WOODFORD
(1890–   )

Waldemar T. Schaller was born in California in 1882 and received his baccalaureate degree from the University of California, Berkeley. Dr. Schaller's published record of California minerals exceeds that of any mineralogist to date. He discovered and described the minerals boothite (1903), salmonsite, sickerite, and stewartite (1912), inyoite and meyerhofferite (1914), kernite (1927), and he defined and clarified many aspects of California mineral localities. He was a staff member of the U. S. Geological Survey as chemist and mineralogist for over 50 years, and received the highest awards the field of mineralogy can confer.

WALDEMAR T. SCHALLER
(1882–1967)

ADOLF PABST
(1899–   )

Adolf Pabst is professor of mineralogy at the University of California, Berkeley, where he has been a staff member since 1927. After a baccalaureate degree from the University of Illinois, Pabst reecived his Ph.D. from the University of California in 1928. He has published widely on the mineralogy of California, and has been responsible for identifying several new minerals. He was the author of the 1938 volume of "Minerals of California". In 1965, he was honored by American mineralogists as the recipient of the Roebling Medal for distinguished contributions to crystallography and mineralogy.

From 1942 through 1964, many new minerals have been found in the course of continued collecting, and additions will probably continue as additional study proceeds.

The following generalizations concerning the occurrence have been drawn largely from Woodford (11) and C. Wayne Burnham (1). Woodford in particular has published a complete list of minerals found here up to 1941, and a full bibliography, while Burnham has discussed the probable conditions of formation of the minerals.

The contact metamorphic rocks occur between magnesian marbles and quartz diorite, and between the same marbles and a later quartz monzonite porphyry. The marbles occur as two roughly lenticular bodies, 400 to 500 feet in thickness, both composed of predazzite (brucite marble) and coarsely crystalline calcite, and are essentially free from silica, alumina, iron, and alkalies. The contact effects of the quartz diorite are minor, resulting in a narrow zone with diopside, wollastonite, and garnet (sometimes also epidote). In the course of this intrusion, the originally magnesium portions of the marbles were converted to periclase-rich rocks which in turn became predazzite rocks (with the brucite as pseudomorphs after periclase).

The quartz monzonite intrusive, on the other hand, was intensively contaminated by assimilation of the marble; the contact aureole is much more in evidence than that of the quartz diorite, and may be as much as 50 feet in thickness. In this aureole are found most of the complex mineral assemblages. Here is shown a well-defined zonal distribution of mineral groups, listed outward from the intrusive: 1) mainly garnet, with lesser wollastonite and diopside; 2) mainly idocrase; 3) primarily monticellite, but characterized by the presence of a considerable variety of minerals such as clinohumite, cuspidine, ellestadite, merwinite, perovskite, spurrite, tilleyite, and a host of calcium silicate-hydrates. In this region there is a tendency for the indefinite development of subzones: a silica-poor, calcite-rich outer portion (clinohumite, spurrite, etc.) and a silica-rich inner portion (merwinite, cuspidine, etc.). Textural relationships indicate also a sequence in which the more highly metasomatized assemblages have been formed at the expense of the less highly metasomatized. To quote the conclusion of C. Wayne Burnham (1), p. 879:

"Available evidence indicates that: (1) the contact metamorphic assemblages at Crestmore and their zonation are largely the compositionally controlled products of silica, alumina and iron metasomatism of relatively pure magnesian limestones; (2) temperatures of 625° C. or higher were reached prior to the introduction of silica into the present monticellite-zone rocks; and (3) the so-called "high temperature" assemblages, such as monticellite, spurrite and melilite, formed directly from the magnesian marbles without the intervention of "lower temperature" steps that involve diopside, wollastonite, and grossularite. Therefore it is proposed that contact metamorphism at Crestmore should be viewed as progressive metasomatism with consequent decarbonation at elevated temperatures rather than as progressive decarbonation attendant simply upon rising temperature."

The following is a list, complete through December 31, 1964, of known minerals from the Crestmore quarries. The list does not include new but as yet incompletely described species.

1. Actinolite
2. Afwillite
3. Albite
4. Allanite
   (Treanorite)
5. Andradite garnet
6. Andesine
7. Anglesite
8. Apatite
9. Apophyllite
10. Aragonite
11. Arsenopyrite
12. Augite
13. Axinite
14. Azurite
15. Bayldonite
16. Biotite
17. Bornite
18. Brucite
19. Bultfonteinite
20. Bytownite-anorthite
21. Calcite
22. Cassiterite
23. Centrallasite
24. Cerussite
25. Chalocite
26. Chalcopyrite
27. Chlorite
28. Chondrodite
29. Chrysocolla
30. Clinochlore
31. Clinohumite
32. Clinozoisite
    # Crestmoreite
    (see Tobermorite)
33. Cuprite
34. Cuspidine
    (Custerite)
35. Danburite
36. Datolite
37. Deweylite
38. Diallage
39. Diopside
40. Dolomite
41. Ellestadite
42. Epidote
43. Ettringite
44. Fluoborite
45. Forsterite
46. Foshagite
47. Galena
48. Gehlenite
49. Geikielite
50. Gonnardite
51. Graphite
52. Greenockite (var.
    Xanthochroite)
53. Grossularite
    garnet

54. Gypsum
    (Selenite)
55. Hawleyite
56. Hematite
57. Hemimorphite
58. Hillebrandite
59. Hornblende
60. Huntite
61. Hydromagnesite
62. Hydrotroilite
63. Hypersthene
64. Idocrase
    (Vesuvianite)
    Jurupaite (see
    Xonotlite)
65. Kaolinite (?)
66. Labradorite
67. Laumontite
    (Leonhardite)
68. Limonite
69. Löllingite
70. Ludwigite (?)
71. Magnesioferrite
72. Magnesite (?)
73. Magnetite
74. Malachite
75. Manganite (?)
76. Margarite
77. Melilite
78. Merwinite
79. Microcline
80. Mimetite
81. Molybdenite
82. Monticellite
83. Montmorillonite
    Mordenite (see
    Ptilolite)
84. Mottramite
85. Muscovite
86. Nasonite
87. Nekoite
88. Nontronite
89. Oligoclase
90. Opal (common
    and hyalite)
91. Orthoclase
92. Paigeite (?)
93. Pargasite (?)
94. Periclase
95. Perovskite
96. Phillipsite
97. Phlogopite
98. Plazolite
99. Plombierite
100. Prehnite
101. Pseudowollastonite
     (Parawollastonite)
102. Ptilolite
     (Mordenite)

103. Pyrite
104. Pyromorphite
105. Pyrrhotite
106. Quartz
107. Realgar
108. Riversideite
109. Rutile
110. Scapolite
111. Scawtite
112. Scolecite
     Schorl (see
     Tourmaline)
113. Sepiolite
114. Serendibite
115. Sericite
116. Serpentine
117. Siderite
118. Smithsonite
119. Sphalerite
120. Sphene
121. Spinel
122. Spurrite
123. Sternbergite
124. Stibnite
125. Stilbite
126. Strontianite
127. Szaibelyite
128. Talc (?)
129. Tetrahedrite
130. Thaumasite
131. Thomsonite
132. Thorite (var.
     Orangeite)
133. Tilleyite
134. Tobermorite
135. Tourmaline
     (brown)
136. Tourmaline
     (var. Schorl)
137. Tremolite (?)
138. Uralite
139. Uvarovite
140. Vermiculite
141. Vesuvianite
     (see Idocrase)
142. Wightmanite
143. Wilkeite
144. Wollastonite
     Woodfordite
     (see Ettringite)
145. Xanthophyllite
146. Xonotlite
147. Zinnwaldite
148. Zircon
149. Zoisite
     (var. Thulite)

PEGMATITE GEM AREA OF SOUTHERN CALIFORNIA

Over a considerable area in southern California, extending from San Jacinto Mountain to the Mexican line, the pegmatite dikes are in many cases distinguished by a relatively high concentration of lithium, with the result that many lithium minerals are present, such as spodumene, amblygonite, lepidolite, and the lithia-rich variety of tourmaline. This variety of tourmaline is typically more or less transparent, colorless, blue, pink, or green, and when clear becomes of value as a source of gem material. A relatively small percent of the pegmatites in this area are lithia-bearing, but even so, there are a considerable number which have produced gem tourmaline, sometimes in fairly large amount. Associated with the tourmaline are other gem minerals, such as beryl, topaz, kunzite (the transparent lilac spodumene) and occasionally clear garnet, and some of the not inconsiderable gem production has come from these varieties.

Minerals new to California and occasional new species are still being reported from the pegmatites even though mining activity has been curtailed for nearly half a century.

In general, the pegmatites are more or less irregular dikes in form, intruded into igneous rocks of the granodiorite type, or into schists closely associated with such rocks. They are not large, at least in the case of the gem-bearing dikes. Fifteen feet is probably near the maximum thickness, and many are considerably narrower. Mineralogically, they are composed mainly of quartz, albite and microcline, with minor amounts of garnet, muscovite or biotite, and occasional concentrations of lithia minerals. Those carrying gem minerals are often characterized by cavities, in which quartz, tourmaline, topaz, etc., have had opportunity to crystallize freely. It is suggested by various writers that these gem-bearing dikes have been re-worked by later lithia-rich solutions, after their original intrusion as common pegmatites. In a few cases, notably at Pala, Rincon, and Ramona, the pegmatites show a curious "line" structure, which gives the effect of stratification roughly parallel to the dike walls. This pattern has not been satisfactorily explained as to its origin, but it is produced by the concentration of tiny garnet crystals in sheets in a fine-grained facies of the dikes.

The details of individual pegmatites have been well treated by Kunz (24), and the following has largely been quoted or abstracted from this source.

The gem-producing localities are as follows: near the summit of the San Jacinto Range, in Riverside County; Coahuila Mountain, Aguanga Mountain, Pala, Mesa Grande, and Ramona; also minor occurrences east of Julian, and in the Chihuahua Valley. In addition, gem-quality garnet was found in the Jacumba area.

"The first discovery of colored gem-tourmaline in the State goes back as far as 1872, when Mr. Henry Hamilton, in June of that year, obtained and recognized this mineral in Riverside County, on the southeast slope of Thomas Mountain. These colored tourmalines, now found at a number of points, were not encountered by Professor Goodyear, who particularly noted the black tourmalines in the pegmatite veins, in his geological tour through San Diego County, in the same year, referred to above; but his reconnaissance was a little south of the gem-tourmaline belt. Some mining was done at this point, and fine gems were obtained. In the course of years, three localities were opened and more or less worked in this vicinity; so that in the author's report on American gem-production for 1893, the following statement appeared:

" 'Tourmalines are mined at the California gem mine, the San Jacinto gem mine, and the Columbian gem mine, near Riverside, California. These three mining claims cover the ground on which the tourmaline is found, and are situated in the San Jacinto range of mountains in Riverside County, California, at an altitude of 6500 feet, overlooking the Hemet Valley and Cahuila Valley, and 27 miles from the railroad. The formation in which the crystals are found is a vein from 40 to 50 feet wide running almost north and south through the old crystalline rocks which make up the mountain range. The vein in some places consists of pure feldspar, or else feldspar with quartz, in others all mica, and in others rose-quartz and smoky quartz. The tourmalines vary in size from almost micrograins to crystals 4 inches in diameter. They are most plentiful in the feldspar, but are found in other portions of the vein, sometimes in pockets and sometimes isolated. The larger crystals generally have a green exterior and are red or pink in the center. Some of the crystals contain green, red, pink, black, and intermediate colors; others again are all of uniform tint—red, pink, colorless, or blue. Associated with the tourmalines are rose-quartz, smoky quartz, asteriated quartz, and fluorite, and some of the quartz was penetrated with fine, hair-like crystals of tourmaline, strikingly like a similar occurrence of rutile.'

"It may seem remarkable that this locality of gem-tourmalines should have been unrecorded in the earlier lists of California minerals given by such authorities as Professor Blake and Mr. Hanks in the reports of the State Mining Bureau for 1882 and 1884. But the parties who knew of the occurrence did not make it public for some years, and the earlier specimens were taken out quietly and their locality not divulged. The writer had positive knowledge as to the facts, however, and possesses a fine specimen obtained prior to 1873.

"The second important discovery in this region was made, or at least announced, twenty years later, in 1892, by Mr. C. R. Orcutt—the great locality of lithia minerals at Pala. Some allusions to red tourmaline from uncertain sources in this part of the State had appeared before, but nothing very specific. In the list of California minerals prepared by Prof. William P. Blake in 1880–82, and also quoted in that of Mr. Henry G. Hanks, published in 1884, references are made to the recent discovery of rubellite, for the first time in the State, associated with lepidolite, 'in the San Bernardino range, southern California.' The general description is precisely that of the Pala specimens, but the location is very indefinite. Mr. Hanks refers to the same association under lepidolite, and mentions a specimen in the State Mineral Bureau, from San Diego County, and remarks that 'this may at some future time be found profitable to extract lithium from it'—a prediction abundantly verified now. Mr. Orcutt, however, was the first to make the locality known. It was noted by the author in his report for 1893 where the following account was given:

" 'Mr. Charles Russell Orcutt has announced a new and remarkable occurrence of pink Tourmaline in lepidolite, similar to that of Rumford, Maine, 12 miles south of Temecula, near San Lus Rey River, in San Diego County, the southern county of California, and it has already become celebrated from the abundance and beauty of the specimens yielded, as much as twenty tons having been sent East for sale.'

"In regard to the early history of this locality, Mr. F. M. Sickler, who grew up in the vicinity and has explored for mines and minerals thereabout a great deal, relates the following curious and somewhat romantic circumstances, in an article in the Kansas City *Jeweler and Optician*, of May, 1904. He states that the Pala lepidolite deposit had very long been known to the Indians, but that it was first brought to the notice of the whites by an Indian deer-hunter named Vensuelada. He found the spot while hunting and broke off pieces showing the beautiful pink rubellite in its matrix of pearl-colored lepidolite, and brought them to Pala. Henry Magee, an old miner and prospector, took the rubellite crystals for cinnabar, and located the property as a quicksilver mine. Failing to get any mercury from it, he nevertheless believed that the peculiar mineral must have some value, and sent samples to various chemists, but no one recognized it as a lithia compound of any importance. Weary of his poor success, Magee gave it up and failed to do the annual assessment work on the claim. Later, one Thomas Alvarado relocated the property as a marble quarry! Magee claimed that some interest in the mine was rightfully due to himself, but Alvarado refused to give him any. Upon this, Magee pointed eastward to the ridge now called Heriart Mountain, and said, 'If this stuff is of any value, I know where there are thousands of tons of it over there.' Magee died, however, and his secret died with him; but certain it is that several mines, with lepidolite and tourmaline, have lately been located on that very ridge. * * *

"In Pala, a little west of Smith's Mountain, in the Peninsula range, * * * a ledge of lepidolite containing rubellite has been traced for over a mile. It consists of a coarse granite, penetrating a norite rock, and including masses of pegmatite. Small garnets occur in the granite, and black tourmaline, with a little green tourmaline. The lepidolite appears in the southern portion, finally forming a definite vein which at one point is twenty yards wide. The rubellite is chiefly in clusters and radiations, several inches in diameter, also occasionally as single crystals, and the specimens of deep pink tourmaline in the pale lilac mica are remarkably elegant. About eighteen tons were mined during 1892.

"The next important discovery was made six years later, in 1898; this was the wonderful Mesa Grande locality, some 20 miles southeast of Pala. There are various stories about the Indians having known it for many years, and the most familiar account follows:

"The first discovery in San Diego County is thought to have been made about twenty-five years ago [1880], when some Indian children, at play in a camp near what is now Mesa Grande postoffice, picked up an oddly shaped stone, six-sided like a quartz crystal, about three inches long and a little thicker than a common lead-pencil. On cleaning it off and rubbing it with a bit of hide, it was seen to be of a beautiful blue color, bright and partially clear, almost like a sapphire. The natives had no idea of its nature, but were attracted by its beauty and singularity. Subsequently, other highly colored stones of like character—some blue, others green, others red—were picked up in the same vicinity by Indians and cowboys, but no one realized that they had any actual value. * * *

"The fact that some of the highly colored crystals are found in Indian graves in the vicinity, suggests that they may have been known and valued perhaps for a very long time. The ledge in which they occur is exposed by erosion on the side of the mountain; and the natives had certainly learned where to find crystals, and had them in their possession for some years before the whites knew anything about them. It is even said that they had learned to do a little rude blasting, and thus to reach the cavities in which the minerals occur. It was not until 1898, however, that this now famous locality was made known to the world. * * *

"For several years, these above noted were the only gem mines of this region, and their product was highly esteemed. But in 1902 began a succession of new discoveries that have attracted great attention. On Pala Chief Mountain and on Heriart Mountain began to be found not only fine-colored tourmalines, but the novel and remarkable gem-spodumene, designated as kunzite. This last-named mineral was found by Mr. Frederick M. Sickler, at which is now known as the White Queen mine, on Heriart Mountain, east of Pala, early in 1902; it is claimed, indeed, that he had obtained one or two pieces some time before, but it was not identified. In July 1902, Mr. Sickler visited San Diego and Los Angeles, and showed specimens to local jewelers and collectors, none of whom recognized it. The first determination was made by the writer, from specimens sent by Mr. Sickler early in 1903.

"The great Pala Chief mine, which has given its name to the middle one of the three ridges or mountains at Pala, and has yielded magnificent tourmalines and the largest and finest gem-spodumene crystals, was located in May, 1903, by Frank A. Salmons, John Giddens, Pedro Peiletch, and Bernardo Heriart. The actual discoverers were probably the two last named, the Basque prospectors who had already been working and locating mines with the two Sicklers, father and son, on Heriart Mountain, the ridge a little to the east. Mr. Salmons has been the principal operator, however, of this very notable mine."

In connection with the tourmaline mines at Mesa Grande, the following interesting bit of information has been supplied by Mr. John C. Snidecor of Santa Barbara. He states that the Big and Little Himalaya mines were bought in the early days (year unknown) by the grandfather of Mrs. Kong, a Santa Barbara gift shop owner. In 1912 or 1913 some of the tourmaline was shipped to China to be used in making "Empress of China" perfume bottles. As a matter of fact, much of the tourmaline mined in California found its way to China for this or similar purposes. Mrs. Kong sold the properties in 1951.

CERRO GORDO

The Cerro Gordo Mining district lies near the summit of the Inyo Range, 5½ miles by air line and 8 miles by a steep mountain road from Keeler, on the shore of Owens Lake. The mine was discovered by Mexican prospectors in the early sixties (1861 or 1866), but no great production was reached until the area was taken over by Americans in 1869. During the next eight years the total production was estimated at anywhere from $6,500,000 to $20,000,000, with the probable truth somewhat near the lower figure. In this period, the bonanza silver-lead ores were worked out, and mining lapsed until the discovery of extensive zinc-carbonate ores about 1911, which led to a revival of activity. It is interesting to note that in 1871–72 a small steamer on Owens Lake (?) carried bullion from the Swansea smelter across to the south shore, thus saving a long trip around by road, R. W. Raymond (6) p. 21. The region consists of a series of westward dipping Carboniferous rocks (mainly limestone) with intrusive dikes of diorite and monzonite, nearly parallel to the bedding. An underlying mass of monzonite porphyry outcrops to the north of the mines. At Cerro Gordo itself, the mines are the Union and Santa Maria. Other nearby mines in the district include the Ignacio and Ventura, to the west and south.

The primary ores were mainly argentiferous galena, with a very little dark sphalerite. The rich ores worked in the early days consisted of lenticular masses of massive cerussite, 5 or 6 feet across, in the limestone. These masses were concentrically banded, and usually had a small core of unaltered galena. The zinc from the sphalerite was concentrated as large masses of relatively pure smithsonite, also in the limestone. In one primary vein, tetrahedrite and pyrite were prominent.

The uncommon minerals for which the area is noted were formed by the oxidation of the original minerals. Some of these secondary minerals, such as linarite, azurite, and caledonite are bright colored and showy. Others, including some of the rarer varieties, are less conspicuous. A good description of the geology and minerals of the area may be found in A. Knopf (5) and (8), C. W. Merriam (1).

The following list includes all species recorded from the Cerro Gordo:

Anglesite	Chrysocolla	Mixite
Anhydrite	Duftite	Plumbogummite (?)
Argentite	Galena	Pyrite
Atacamite	Halloysite	Quartz
Aurichalcite	Hemimorphite	Silver
Azurite	Hydrozincite	Smithsonite
Barite	Leadhillite	Sphalerite
Bindheimite	Limonite	Stibnite
Calcite	Linarite	Tetrahedrite
Caledonite	Lironconite (?)	Willemite
Cerargyrite	Malachite	Wulfenite
Cerussite	Mimetite	

The following list includes occurrences in the other mines of the Cerro Gordo Mining District:

Bournonite	Goethite	Pyromorphite
Cervantite	Greenockite (?)	Realgar
Dufrenoysite	Jamesonite	Stromeyerite
Fluorite		Tetradymite

Cinnabar and metacinnabar were wrongly reported from this Cerro Gordo mine through confusion with another Cerro Gordo mine in San Benito County. Probably realgar likewise is incorrect.

Some of the minerals supposedly from this locality may have been from some distance away, since the smelter to which Cerro Gordo ore was shipped treated ores from outside the Cerro Gordo Mining District; specimens of these may easily have been confused with true Cerro Gordo material.

ERNEST WILLIAM CHAPMAN
(1894–1947)

Ernest William Chapman was born October 9, 1894, at Dunstable, Massachusetts. After serving in World War I, he moved to the Pacific Northwest and finally to Southern California in 1920. Mr. Chapman had an intense interest in rocks and minerals; in 1923 he started a collection of minerals, specializing in crystals. He was the second president of the Mineralogical Society of Southern California, and was very active in the organization of the California Federation of Mineralogical Societies, of which he was president from 1939 to 1940. Mr. Chapman was an enthusiastic and enjoyable speaker and therefore was much in demand by the mineral societies. *Photo courtesy of Mrs. John J. Mahanna.*

William Burton Pitts was born in Thomasville, Georgia, in 1867. For ten years he worked as a prescription clerk in an Atlanta drug store, then sold mineral water and salts from Germany's Carlsbad Springs. Traveling in California, Pitts' purchase of a bloodstone started him on the career which earned for him the affectionate title of "Dean of Amateur Lapidaries". In 1920, a Smithsonian Institution brochure on gem stones stirred him to duplicating the material pictured. His famous collection of flats, cabochons, rough gem material and transparencies was donated to the California Academy of Sciences in Golden Gate Park, San Francisco, California.

Until 1958, "Uncle Billy" Pitts alternated his time between the California Academy of Sciences (where he spent nearly every day of the week making his famed transparencies) and his native state of Georgia. He was an honorary member of the California Federation of Mineralogical Societies and honorary curator of gem minerals at the California Academy of Sciences. *Photo courtesy California Academy of Sciences.*

WILLIAM BURTON PITTS
(1867–1959)

JOHN RENSHAW
(1888–1951)

John Renshaw was born in Pittsburgh, Pennsylvania, October 14, 1888. He studied mineralogy under Professor Edwin V. Van Amringe at the Pasadena Junior College (now Pasadena City College) and attended the famous Van Amringe field trips. During a field trip to the Natural Soda Products Company, Keeler, California, the host and plant manager, David B. Scott, suggested the formation of a local mineral club. Influenced favorably by this suggestion, Renshaw and Van Amringe called a meeting at the Pasadena City Library June 23, 1931. John Renshaw was elected president and on September 1, 1931, with 175 people present, a constitution was adopted. This group became known as the Mineralogical Society of Southern California and has the distinction of being the first organized mineral society in the State of California.

Henry H. Symons was born in 1894, and spent his school days at Butte, Montana. He earned his mining engineering degree from Montana School of Mines at Butte in 1922, although his college career was interrupted by service in the Armed Forces in World War I and by work on a surveying crew for the Milwaukee Railroad. The year after he received his degree he came to California, where he held several jobs, including draftsman and millman before joining what is now the California Division of Mines and Geology in February, 1928. Mr. Symons is the author of many professional works, including papers on mining equipment, mineral statistics and fluorescent minerals. In 1937, as a member of the Northern California Mineralogical Society (now San Francisco Gem and Mineral Society, Inc.), he published the first issue of "Mineral Notes and News" for the newly organized California Federation of Mineralogical Societies, and acted as editor of this magazine until 1939. Henry Symons retired from the California Division of Mines and Geology in February 1960.

HENRY H. SYMONS
(1894–   )

Edwin Verne Van Amringe was born in Oakland, California, on August 24, 1899. He was educated in Oakland public schools and received a bachelor's degree in chemistry (1921) and a master's in education (1923) from the University of California. In 1924 when the Pasadena Junior College (now Pasadena City College) was founded, he became a faculty member to teach industrial chemistry and later geology. His comprehensive field-trip program at the college earned for him the respect of many students over the years, who profited greatly through intensive, informative teaching. In 1931, Mr. Van Amringe, with other amateur and professional mineralogists, organized the Mineralogical Society of Southern California, the first on the west coast. After serving as Secretary, Bulletin Editor, and President, he was selected to Honorary Life Membership.

In 1951, he was appointed Chairman of the Department of Physical Sciences, at Pasadena City College, but continued his annual Easter field trips until his death in 1956.

EDWIN VERNE VAN AMRINGE
(1899–1956)

PAUL VANDEREIKE
(1871–1956)

Paul VanderEike was born in Wisconsin on October 21, 1871. He earned an A.B. degree from Minnesota State University in 1911, and took further work in geology at that institution. From 1908 to 1911 he was Superintendent of the State Prison Night School, Stillwater, Minnesota.

In 1911, Mr. VanderEike became a faculty member of the Kern County Union High School District, Bakersfield, California. He also served as teacher and administrator for Bakersfield College, when a department of the high school for junior college students was established in 1913.

Mr. VanderEike was proprietor of a county newspaper from 1903–1906 and owned a flower shop, 1920–21. He had considerable interest in mineralogy and was editor and publisher of "Mineral Notes and News," a monthly magazine for "rockhounds" and "pebblepups" issued periodically for some years. Mr. VanderEike died August 1, 1956.

MAGNUS VONSEN
(1879–1954)

Magnus Vonsen was an amateur mineralogist whose interests led him to prepare himself on his own and by association with Professors Arthur Eakle of California, and Austin Rogers of Stanford, to become highly proficient in mineralogy. A long time and ardent collector, Vonsen was especially successful in finding mineral localities and unusual specimen materials in the northern Coast Ranges. Most of his life was spent in Petaluma. He had a special interest in borate minerals, and was the discoverer of the borate mineral from Riverside County that was named in his honor by Professor Eakle. He also first discovered teepleite in Clear Lake, and reported several new localities of pumpellyite and lawsonite in the glaucophane schists of the Coast Ranges. Mr. Vonsen had one of the fine private mineral collections in the United States, donated at his death to the California Academy of Sciences, San Francisco. *Photo courtesy American Mineralogist.*

John Melhase, B. S., E. M., was born in Hannibal, Missouri in 1885. After graduating in 1908 from Oregon State College, he entered the service of the Southern Pacific Company, where his career covered a lifetime of exemplary service. Beginning in 1912, he spent time in mineral surveys of railroad lands and oil fields geology throughout the Coast States, Arizona, Nevada, Utah and New Mexico. This work culminated in 1929 with his appointment as Chief of the San Francisco branch, which had headquarters in Houston, Texas. In 1923, he became Assistant Geologist at the main office, a position he held until his death.

In 1938, John Melhase became the first president of the newly formed California Federation of Mineralogical Societies. He was a charter member of the Northern California Mineral Society (now The San Francisco Gem and Mineral Society, Inc.) and contributed much to the advancement of several of the early San Francisco Bay Area groups. While doing geological field work, John Melhase died suddenly at Redding, California.

NO PHOTO
AVAILABLE

JOHN MELHASE
(1885–1938)

HISTORY AND DEVELOPMENT OF THE CALIFORNIA FEDERATION OF MINERALOGICAL SOCIETIES

By Eleanor M. Learned*

The history of earth science organizations, in general, and in California in particular, is one of rapid growth. Whether a group is labeled gem, mineral, lapidary, geology, or fossil, the keen, inquiring interest among the members is the same.

Although mineral clubs had been formed as early as 1885 (Brooklyn Institute Mineral Club and Spencer Blair Mineralogical Society, Philadelphia) and 1886 (New York City Mineral Club) in the eastern United States, it was not until 1931 that the first society in California was organized. This distinction belongs to the Mineralogical Society of Southern California in Pasadena, which was organized June 23, 1931, with the John Renshaw as the first president and Edwin V. Van Amringe the first secretary.

From the beginning of earth science organizations in California, the membership rolls of the majority of societies, particularly the urban ones and those close to educational facilities, contained the names of professional men and women willing to share their wealth of mineralogical knowledge with the "amateurs." From the records, it is evident that they gave unstintingly of their time and selves to develop good programs and classes in the related earth sciences and gemology and lapidary. How well they succeeded in laying good foundations is reflected in the many strong societies now geared to providing learning and sharing opportunities in nearly every phase of earth sciences or lapidary.

The phenomenal growth from 1931 to 1964 is reflected in the following figures: California now has over 200 gem and mineral societies with a total membership of nearly 16,000. The smallest and newest societies have fewer than 50 members and the largest in the state has more than 675!

Representatives of the several California societies met on June 16, 1935, a day which had been declared "Mineral Day" at the San Diego exposition, to formulate the development of a California Federation of Mineralogical Societies. E. W. Chapman, president of the Mineralogical Society of Southern California, was chairman. The objective was "a meeting planned in anticipation of the formation of a State Organization and an annual conference of the Mineralogical Societies of the Pacific Coast States." On January 4 and 5, 1936, the first convention of the Mineralogical Societies of California was held at the American Legion Club House in Riverside. Seven societies sent representatives, who organized The California Federation of Mineralogical Societies. The eight charter societies and their inception dates are: Mineralogical Society of Southern California (June 23, 1931, at Pasadena) ; Los Angeles Mineralogical Society (September 23, 1932, at Los Angeles) ; Orange Belt Mineralogical Society (April 6, 1933, at San Bernardino) ; San Diego Mineral Society (March 1934 at San Diego) ; West Coast Mineralogical Society (May 1934 at Fullerton) ; Northern California Mineral Society—now The San Francisco Gem and Mineral Society, Inc. (January 16, 1935, at San Francisco) ; Southwest Mineralogists (Janu-

*Federation Director and Past President, San Francisco Gem and Mineral Society.

ary 1935, at Los Angeles) ; Kern County Mineral Society (March 18, 1935, at Bakersfield). The present day results of federation and society activities is a lasting, growing tribute to those far-sighted individuals!

Annual conventions were held with the various societies serving as hosts until war conditions in 1942 necessitated the cancelling of the show scheduled at Pasadena with the Mineralogical Society of Southern California as host. At that time, the earth science organizations numbered about 30, the majority being affiliated with the California Federation.

The "Golden Bear Nugget" purchased by the Federation for $300 became the organization's insignia on April 20th, 1940. Since 1952 the Golden Bear Nugget has been on loan to the Division of Mines and Geology in San Francisco where it has been on public display, except during the annual Federation shows where it is displayed in its own special case.

John Melhase, a consulting mining engineer, mineralogist, and geologist for the Southern Pacific Railway Company and a member of the board of directors of the Northern California Mineral Society, was the first California Federation of Mineralogical Societies president. Mr. Melhase lectured extensively among the early societies and wrote many articles on mineralogy. The April 1940 issue of *The Mineralogist Magazine*, edited by Dr. H. C. Dake of Oregon, was a Memorial Issue for Mr. Melhase, who died April 9, 1938. But a greater memorial to his intense interest in mineral societies and federations can be found in the Federation Bulletin which he suggested. William B. Pitts (Uncle Billy), formerly Honorary Curator of Gem Stones at the California Academy of Sciences in Golden Gate Park, San Francisco, and a charter and honorary member of the Northern California Mineral Society and the East Bay Mineral Society, assisted John Melhase with the Bulletin. C. W. Marwedel Company (Norton abrasives agent) printed and distributed the Bulletin to the member societies of the Federation for a year free of charge for the privilege of including advertising. Henry H. Symons, Mining Engineer (retired) with the California Division of Mines and Geology and also a member of the San Francisco group, issued, in March 1937, *Mineral Notes and News*, *Bulletin No. 1* for the California Federation. He acted as editor until April 1939 when Paul Vander-Eike, 1937 president of the Kern County Mineral Society, took over the editorial duties. Paul Vander-Eike continued to do this through the war years until, editorship and teaching proving to be too much, he gave up teaching and devoted his time to editing the magazine. It was subsidized in June 1949 by the Federation, which then became its sole owner. Paul Vander-Eike resigned as editor in June 1950 and the job was given to Don MacLachlan and Ralph Dietz as co-editors under a contract with the Federation officers that took effect June 1952, at which time the magazine became known as *Gems and Minerals*. At the 1964 annual meeting of the California Federation of Mineralogical Societies held at Vallejo, Don MacLachlan and the Federation signed a contract whereby GEMEC Corporation and Don MacLachlan became sole owners of *Gems and Minerals* with the original and better benefits accruing to the California Federation.

The current list of honorary members of the California Federation of Mineralogical Societies includes Dr. Austin Flint Rogers (deceased),

William B. Pitts (deceased), Paul Vander-Eike (deceased), Orlin Bell (deceased), Charles S. Knowlton (deceased), Victor Arciniega, Carroll F. Chatham, Don MacLachlan, Dorothy Craig, and Vincent Morgan.

It has often been asked what are the values of a federation of mineralogical societies or of an individual society. Intangibles are somewhat hard to define and are understood only by those who are firm believers. But a hard-to-convince questioner can't argue with the worth of tangibles such as those offered by the many hard-working federation committees—many a new society has been helped during the formative period of growth, worthwhile programs of speakers and slides have been provided, society bulletin editors and field trip chairmen have learned much and given more through yearly working symposiums, show chairmen have found their chores made easier through help offered when asked for, lists of mineral, lapidary, and fossil judges have aided societies having competitive shows, societies and individuals are given the opportunity to help others through the American Federation of Mineralogical Societies Scholarship Fund; yearly Federation shows with competitive and noncompetitive exhibits have upgraded individual and society collections to a point beyond that of amateur standing, society officers and chairmen have found help and encouragement from their Federation counterparts, safety programs and anti-litter campaigns have gained wide respect for all Federation members from the general public, an all-inclusive insurance program has been offered to societies wishing to take advantage of excellent savings, a nomenclature committee has done much to improve the education of society members and those who attend their annual shows; and last, but of much importance, mutual respect and working agreements have been effected with the California Division of Mines and Geology, the California Academy of Sciences in San Francisco, the various junior and senior State Colleges and Universities, the Los Angeles County Museum, the Santa Barbara County Museum, California Institute of Technology, local schools, museums, and libraries, local officials, newspapers, and radio and TV stations.

The member societies and the California Federation of Mineralogical Societies are nonprofit organizations organized to disseminate knowledge of mineralogy and the earth sciences and to maintain the highest possible standards of conduct at all times. Every member is fully aware of the public image and strives toward the betterment of societies and federations.

In many instances the amateur has contributed much by his field work and discoveries that has helped the professional worker as well as the amateur. Many new minerals, and minerals new to the State of California, have been found by the amateur, and identified cooperatively for him by professional staffs. During the war, mineral hobbyists aided materially in the discovery of vital mineral deposits.

The steady growth of the mineral societies is a tribute to the faith and foresight of the early founders; very few societies have ceased to function. To the contrary, all have a history of almost spectacular membership increase, and boast of men and women from all walks of life, age, and intellect with the common bond of a thirst for knowledge and an eager desire to create beauty from the vast mineral storehouse provided in the State of California. Many an amateur has progressed to an almost professional stage of mineralogical knowledge as attested by those who are members of the Mineralogical Society of America and the more than professional ability of those who hold degrees in the American and British Gemological Institutes. Even the smaller societies conduct classes for their members in lapidary, silversmithing, intarsia, micro-mounting, gemology, thumbnailing, mineral identification, geology, sight identification, jewelry design, fossil identification, carving, and faceting. There are also junior activities in many of the aforementioned classes.

Competitions and general pride in excellence of achievement have created groups of people in many societies attesting to the fact that mineral societies occupy a most enviable place in our culture today. This so-called ''hobby'' is one of the highest creativity and knowledge, and the many active members are secure in the belief that gem and mineral groups will continue to grow!

DESCRIPTION OF CALIFORNIA MINERALS AND MINERAL LOCALITIES *

ADAMITE
Basic zinc arsenate, $Zn_2AsO_4(OH)$

Inyo County: **1,** Adamite occurs as small, colorless equant crystals on fracture surfaces of limestone at Chloride Cliff in the Amargosa Range (T. 30 N., R. 1 E., S.B.). Crystals were measured by Murdoch (5) p. 811.

San Bernardino County: **1,** Colorless, yellow and green crystals of Adamite were reported from the Mohawk mine, Crippen (p.c. '51).

Santa Cruz County: **1,** Adamite has been identified in the mineral suite from the Pacific Limestone Products (Kalkar) quarry, Santa Cruz, Chesterman (p.c. '64).

AENIGMATITE
A titano-silicate of iron and sodium, $Na_4(Fe^{2+},Fe^{3+},Ti)_{13}Si_{12}O_{42}$

Sonoma County: **1,** Aenigmatite is found as minute prismatic phenocrysts in lavas (sec. 13, T. 7 N., R. 8 W., M.D., and sec. 17, T. 7 N., R. 7 W., M.D.), Rose (p.c. '50).

AFWILLITE
Hydrous calcium silicate, $Ca_3(SiO_3 \cdot OH)_2 \cdot 2H_2O$

Riverside County: **1,** Crystals and massive afwillite occur in veins in complex contact rocks composed largely of merwinite, gehlenite, spurrite, calcite, etc., on the 910' level, Commercial quarry, Crestmore, Switzer and Bailey (8) p. 629, Murdoch (30) p. 1347.

ALABANDITE
Manganese sulphide, MnS

Manganese occurs usually as oxides or oxygen compounds, but the sulphide is found occasionally as a vein mineral in metallic sulphide deposits, especially with sulphides of copper.

San Diego County: **1,** Specimens of alabandite have come from this county, perhaps from the Julian Mining District (N.R.).

Santa Clara County: **1,** Alabandite was one of the manganese minerals in the boulder at Alum Rock Park, associated with hausmannite, tephroite, and others, A. F. Rogers (27) p. 206.

ALLANITE—Orthite
Basic calcium/cerium/lanthanum/sodium/aluminum/iron/manganese/beryllium/magnesium silicate, $(Ca,Ce,La,Na)_2(Al,Fe,Mn,Be,Mg)_3(SiO_4)_3OH$

Treanorite is considered identical with allanite.

Allanite is a minor constituent of granitic rocks. As such, it is reported frequently in microscopic proportions from many localities. The listings that follow do not represent every report in the literature of California. Some of the early references may actually be chromite,

* Species first discovered in California are marked by an asterisk and followed by date of first published description. Species first discovered in California which have been subsequently discredited are noted and a dagger (†) placed before the asterisk.

(59)

ilmenite, or magnetite since allanite is often confused with other common minerals, and validation of the accuracy of identification in published reports has not been systematically undertaken in the compilation of this volume.

Calaveras County: **1**, Microscopic brown crystals of allanite were found on the 300-foot level of the Ford mine, half a mile east of San Andreas, A. Knopf (11) p. 35.

Inyo County: **1**, Coarse-grained allanite occurs in a pegmatite, about 4500 ft. S. 30° W. of Jackass Spring, on Hunter Mt., Ubehebe quadrangle, McAllister (4) p. 52.

Kern County: **1**, Allanite is reported as a minor constituent of pegmatite dikes in the Kern River uranium area, MacKevett (2) pp. 191, 197.

Los Angeles County: **1**, Abundant rough tabular crystals and grains of allanite as much as 2 to 3 inches in size occur in a pegmatite with zircon and apatite, in Pacoima Canyon (sec. 17, T. 3 N., R. 13 W., S.B.), Neuerburg (2) p. 833. P. F. Patchick (2) p. 237 gives detailed location diagrams. **2**, Allanite, probably of clastic origin, has been observed in the Pelona schist, Ehlig (1) p. 170.

Riverside County: **1**, Microscopic crystals and grains of allanite occur in the gneiss of the Eagle Mountain iron deposit, Harder (6) p. 28. **2**, Allanite is found with serendibite and associated minerals in the new City quarry, 2 miles south of Riverside, Richmond (1) p. 725. **3**, Treanorite occurs in tabular, black crystals at Crestmore in pegmatites, Woodford et al. (10) and in black needles, Murdoch (p.c. '54).

San Bernardino County: **1**, Allanite occurs at Mountain Pass, Olson et al. (3) p. 36. **2**, Allanite is found in the border of a quartz mass in the Pomona Tile quarry on the road between Old Woman Spring and Yucca Valley, Hewett and Glass (3) p. 1048.

San Diego County: **1**, Allanite is found as black masses in quartz veins about 2 miles northwest of Pala on the hill about half a mile west of the road, Schaller (p.c. '25). **2**, Large rough crystals of allanite occur in a pegmatite on the N. S. Weaver Ranch 3 miles north of Pala, Wilke (p.c. '36).

Santa Barbara County: **1**, Irelan (4) p. 47 reported allanite from Santa Barbara and the Channel Islands, CDMG (10974). **2**, Allanite is reported from an unspecified locality in the county, L. G. Yates (2) p. 11.

Tulare County: **1**, Allanite in pegmatite, with rose quartz, occurs on the D. F. Gassenberger Ranch, northeast of Exeter, CDMG (19659).

Tuolumne County: **1**, Talus blocks from a pegmatite at the foot of Eagle Peak, on the northwest side of Yosemite Valley, carried small amounts of allanite, Ries (1) p. 229. **2**, Crystals as much as 15 mm in size occur in a pegmatite in Lang Gulch, Hutton (3) p. 233. **3**, Talus blocks of the Ragged Peak scree carry crystals up to 45 mm in size, ibid. (3) p. 236.

ALLEGHANYITE
Basic manganese silicate, $Mn_5Si_2O_8(OH)_2$
Alleghanyite may be identical with tephroite.

Amador County: **1**, Alleghanyite occurs with tephroite and other manganese minerals at the Germolis prospect near Fiddletown (SE ¼ sec. 9, T. 7 N., R. 11 E., M.D.), Hewett et al. (6) p. 49. **2**, Alleghanyite is reported from the Lubanko prospect (SE ¼ sec. 10, T. 7 N., R. 11 E., M.D.), Hewett et al. (6) p. 49.

Santa Clara County: **1**, A. F. Rogers (21) p. 443 reports this mineral from the Alum Rock Park manganese boulder. The identity of alleghanyite with tephroite is suggested by C. S. Ross and Kerr (2) p. 13.

ALLOPHANE
Amorphous silica alumina gel, Al₂O₃~35%·SiO₂22 to 28%

San Bernardino County: **1**, Allophane occurs in the veins of the California Rand silver mine, Hulin (1) p. 97.

San Luis Obispo County: **1**, A specimen has come from Arroyo Grande (N.R.).

ALSTONITE—Bromlite
Barium calcium carbonate, BaCa(CO₃)₂

Mariposa County: **1**, Alstonite reported from the sanbornite locality near Incline, may be witherite, A. F. Rogers (39) p. 171.

ALTAITE
Lead telluride, PbTe

Altaite is found associated with hessite, petzite, and gold tellurides in a few localities.

Calaveras County: **1**, The Stanislaus mines on Carson Hill carry large masses of altaite with calaverite and hessite (T. 2 N., R. 13 E., M.D.), Genth (5) p. 312. **2**, Altaite is also reported from the Morgan mine, Hanks (12) p. 68, and **3**, from the Frenchwood mine near Robinson's Ferry with other tellurides (sec. 25, T. 2 N., R. 13 E., M.D.), Hanks (12) p. 388.

Madera County: **1**, W. W. Bradley (29) p. 311 reports altaite about 200 yards east of the Chiquito trail and half a mile north of Fish Creek, in the North Fork Mining District.

Nevada County: **1**, Altaite is one of the minerals at the Providence mine, Nevada City, occurring in bunches in the Ural vein intergrown with native gold and associated with quartz, pyrite, and galena, Lindgren (12) p. 117. **2**, The ore of the Champion mine carries altaite, W. D. Johnston, Jr. (3) p. 27. **3**, From the 5000-foot level of the Empire mine, in Grass Valley, W. D. Johnston, Jr. (4) p. 44 reports the presence of altaite.

Tuolumne County: **1**, Hanks (12) p. 68 reports the occurrence of altaite in the Golden Rule mine near Tuttletown. **2**, Crystals cemented by gold came from the Barney Pocket mine, Sawmill Flat near Columbia, Eakle (1) p. 324. **3**, Clusters of crystallized gold and altaite in parallel grouping were found in the Bonanza and O'Hara mines near Sonora, Sharwood (5) p. 26. **4**, Altaite is reported from the Adelaide mine by Hanks (12) pp. 68, 388, and **5**, from the Sell mine (sec. 30, T. 2 N., R. 15 E., M.D.) as gray crystals on crystallized gold, Foshag (p.c. '35).

ALUNITE
Basic potassium aluminum sulphate, KAl₃(SO₄)₂(OH)₆

Calaveras County: **1**, Small crystals are found at Railroad Flat, W. W. Bradley (32) p. 565.

Colusa County: **1,** Massive alunite carrying gold was collected at Sulphur Creek, Woodhouse (p.c. '46).

Inyo County: **1,** Soda-bearing alunite has been analyzed from a deposit in the Funeral Range, Wherry (1) p. 83. **2,** A specimen, CDMG (20833), comes from the Cactus Range, W. W. Bradley (26) p. 85.

Kern County: **1,** Abundant stringers of coarsely crystalline alunite were collected by J. W. Bradley (p.c. '45) at Middle Buttes, near Mojave.

Lake County: **1,** Some alunite is reported at Sulphur Bank, D. E. White and Roberson (2) p. 406.

Mariposa County: **1,** Alunite occurs as a constituent of a quartzite at Tres Cerritos, southwest of Indian Gulch, H. W. Turner (19) p. 424.

Mono County: **1,** Massive pink and brown alunite occurs with andalusite at the andalusite deposit in the White Mountains, 7 miles east of Mocalno, north of Bishop, Kerr (3) p. 629. An analysis by A. Rautenberg, Lemmon (p.c. '36), shows that a flesh-colored material is natro-alunite. **2,** Alunite is a rare constituent of the clays in Little Antelope Valley, Cleveland (1) p. 19.

Orange County: **1,** Alunite occurs as chalky nodular masses associated with gypsum in schist, exposed in a road cut at San Juan Capistrano Point, Woodford (p.c. '36).

San Bernardino County: **1,** Alunite is abundant with krausite and other sulphates in the "sulphur hole", below the old borax mines, Calico Hills, Foshag (19) p. 352. **2,** Minor greenish-yellow crusts occur on limestone in a barite deposit southwest of Lead Mountain (T. 10 N., R. 1 W., S.B.), Murdoch (p.c. '45).

Shasta County: **1,** Isolated crystals and aggregates of alunite are common in the muds of the hot springs south of Lassen Peak, A. L. Day and Allen (1) p. 120, C. A. Anderson (8) p. 242.

Sonoma County: **1,** Alunite is common at The Geysers, Vonsen (6) p. 290; **2,** it is also abundant in Hooker Canyon (E ½ sec. 1, T. 6 N., R. 6 W., M.D.), in a breccia, and filling seams up to several feet in width, Laizure (9) p. 56.

ALUNOGEN
Hydrous aluminum sulphate, $Al_2(SO_4)_3 \cdot 18H_2O$

Alameda County: **1,** White powder at the Alma mine, Leona Heights, is alunogen, Schaller (1) p. 216.

Inyo County: **1,** Alunogen occurs in fibrous masses with epsomite in clay at the mine of the American Magnesium Company near Ballarat, Hewett et al. (1) p. 96.

Marin County: **1,** Fibrous tufts of alunogen are found with gypsum in shale at the road tunnel near Fort Barry, Vonsen (p.c. '32).

Mariposa County: **1,** Fibrous masses of alunogen occur with graphite on quartzite at the P and L mine, 2½ miles south of El Portal, W. W. Bradley (28) p. 343.

Nevada County: **1,** Blue alunogen occurs in the Providence mine, Nevada City, Lindgren (12) p. 120.

Placer County: **1,** W. W. Bradley (29) p. 107 reports alunogen from the Kilaga mine, 3 miles east of Lincoln.

San Luis Obispo County: **1,** A white powder found near Paso Robles is alunogen, Schrader et al. (1) p. 42.

Shasta County: **1,** Incrustations of alunogen appear around the hot springs in the Mount Lassen area, A. L. Day and Allen (1) p. 118.

Sonoma County: **1,** Alunogen is present in abundance at The Geysers, near Cloverdale, E. T. Allen and Day (2) p. 45, Vonsen (6) p. 290.

AMARANTITE
Basic hydrous iron sulphate, $Fe^{3+}SO_4(OH) \cdot 3H_2O$

Riverside County: **1,** Amarantite occurs with magnesium copiapite in the Santa Maria Mountains near Blythe, E. S. Dana (6) p. 612, Schairer and Lawson (1) p. 242.

AMBER
An oxygenated hydrocarbon

Ventura County: **1,** The occurrence of amber in minor amounts in Eocene beds on the northeast side of Simi Valley has been described by Murdoch (1) p. 309.

AMBLYGONITE
Lithium sodium aluminum fluophosphate, $(Li,Na)AlPO_4(F,OH)$

Amblygonite is an important lithia mineral, but only a few deposits are known in the state.

Riverside County: **1,** Amblygonite is found at the Fano mine (sec. 33, T. 6 S., R. 2 E., S.B.), on the north side of Coahuila Mountain in a pegmatite with kunzite, tourmaline, and lepidolite, Kunz (24) p. 122, (25), p. 968.

San Bernardino County: **1,** White, massive amblygonite is reported from Turtle Mountain, W. W. Bradley (26) p. 106.

San Diego County: **1,** A large mass of white massive amblygonite occurred at the Stewart mine, Pala, in pegmatite carrying rubellite and lepidolite, Kunz (18) p. 259, (24) p. 125, Schaller (8) p. 122. **2,** Amblygonite occurs also in the Caterina mine and others near Pala, Kunz (24) p. 86. **3,** On Aguanga Mountain, at the Mountain Lily mine, amblygonite is associated with cassiterite and blue tourmaline, CDMG (18625). **4,** Some white cleavable fragments of amblygonite were found at the Victor mine at Rincon, A. F. Rogers (4) p. 217. **5,** Kunz (24) p. 135 reported amblygonite from the Himalaya mine at Mesa Grande. **6,** The mineral occurs with lepidolite at the Royal mine, on the northeast slope of Granite Peak, (probably NW $\frac{1}{4}$ sec. 18, T. 13 S., R. 5 E., S.B.), Kunz (23) p. 314. A further reference for the Pala region is Jahns and Wright (5) pp. 19, 40.

AMMONIOJAROSITE
Basic ammonium iron sulphate, $NH_4Fe^{3+}_3(SO_4)_2(OH)_6$

Lake County: **1,** Ammoniojarosite has been tentatively reported from the Sulphur Bank mercury deposits, with buddingtonite and other minerals, Erd et al. (6) p. 833. This is the first report of this mineral in California.

AMPHIBOLES

In this group are a series of complex silicates of magnesium, iron, calcium, sodium and aluminum, or varying combinations of these elements. They are very common rock-forming minerals, and are found in both igneous and metamorphic rocks. They are so widespread that only the most interesting occurrences can be mentioned.

Validity of varietal names in this group is sometimes subject to debate.

The identification of the varieties of amphibole in the older literature was often based on physical inspection. Confirmation of identification requires optical, chemical, or crystallographic data. Validation of identification in locality reports has not been undertaken in the entries given below.

ACTINOLITE
Basic silicate of calcium magnesium and iron with fluorine,
$$Ca_2(Mg,Fe^{2+}{}_5[Si_8O_{22}](OH,F)_2$$

Alameda and Contra Costa Counties: **1,** Actinolite schists are common in the region around Berkeley and San Pablo. Boulders have been found with radiating crystals up to 10 cm in length, Hanks (12) p. 69, Blasdale (1) pp. 328, 333.

Kern County: **1,** Actinolite schists are widespread in the Rand formation, Hulin (1) p. 24. **2,** Crystals of actinolite have been found in a contact deposit a quarter of a mile east of Hobo Hot Springs, associated with molybdenite and garnet, W. D. O'Guinn (p.c. '35).

Madera County: **1,** Coarsely crystalline actinolite occurs with epidote and garnet on Shadow and Johnston Creeks at the Iron Mountain magnetite deposit, in the Ritter Range, Erwin (1) p. 67.

Marin County: **1,** Actinolite and lawsonite are found in the schists half a mile east of Reed Station, F. L. Ransome (3) p. 311, and **2,** large nests of crystals of actinolite occur in talcose rocks east of Sausalito Harbor, J. D. Dana (2) p. 634.

Mendocino County: **1,** Large and beautiful prisms of actinolite were found in a road cut on the Cloverdale Highway, 3 miles northwest of Pieta Creek, Vonsen (p.c. '45). **2,** Good actinolite prisms in large masses occur near Potter Valley (N.R.).

Riverside County: **1,** Actinolite occurs at Crestmore in secondary veins and as a weathering product of other minerals, Woodford (11) p. 350.

San Benito County: **1,** Actinolite is one of the vein minerals at the benitoite locality, near the headwaters of the San Benito River, Louderback and Blasdale (6) p. 360.

San Bernardino County: **1,** Actinolite has been found in the Hillis marble quarry 17 miles east of Victorville, The Mineralogist (3) p. 20. **2,** The mineral is found in the gravels at Cajon Pass, as pebbles of actinolite schist, Webb (p.c. '45). **3,** An additional locality in alluvium, near Wrightwood, is reported by Berkholz (16) p. 21.

Siskiyou County: **1,** Massive bladed actinolite occurs near the mouth of Black Gulch on the South Fork, Salmon River, Goudey (p.c. '36).

ANTHOPHYLLITE
Basic silicate of magnesium and iron with fluorine, $(Mg,Fe^{2+})_7Si_8O_{22}(OH,F)_2$

Anthophyllite is a metamorphic mineral that occurs in schists and gneisses.

Contra Costa County: **1,** Fibrous masses of anthophyllite occur in the schists near San Pablo, and the mineral has been analyzed by Blasdale (1) p. 343.

Riverside County: **1,** Anthophyllite occurs with tremolite and actinolite in the Eagle Mountains (N.R.).

San Bernardino County: **1,** Hanks (12) p. 67 reports anthophyllite in the Slate Range.

Shasta County: **1,** The mineral at the Stock asbestos mine, 3 miles east of Sims Station, is apparently anthophyllite asbestos, E. Sampson (2) p. 317.

Trinity County: **1,** At Coffee Creek, 1 mile north of Carrville, dark, soda-rich anthophyllite occurs as cross-fiber asbestos veins up to 5 cm in width in serpentine, Laudermilk and Woodford (1) p. 259.

CUMMINGTONITE
Basic silicate of magnesium and iron, $(Mg,Fe^{2+})_7Si_8O_{22}(OH)_2$

Cummingtonite occurs in brown fibrous or lamellar masses.

San Bernardino County: **1,** Cummingtonite has been reported from Daggett, CDMG (11381).

HORNBLENDE
Including edenite, pargasite, basaltic hornblende
Basic silicate of calcium/sodium/magnesium/iron/aluminum with fluorine,
$$Ca_2Na_{0-1}(Mg,Fe^{2+})_{3-5}(Al,Fe^{3+})_{2-0}[Si_{6-8}Al_{2-0}O_{22}](O,OH,F)_2$$

Hornblende is a very common constituent of igneous rocks, and of gneisses, and schists. In only a relatively few places does it occur with particular mineralogical uniqueness.

Calaveras County: **1,** Coarsely crystalline rock, made up almost exclusively of hornblende, has been found in considerable volume at Carson Hill, Moss (1) p. 1011. **2,** A large mass of hornblende rock occurs just west of Vallecito on the road to Angels Camp, Wilke (p.c. '36).

El Dorado County: **1,** Large cleavage masses of black hornblende occur with orthoclase, sulphides, and axinite at the old Cosumnes copper mine near Fairplay (N.R.).

Fresno County: **1,** Pargasite in fine light-brown prisms occurs in crystalline limestone with spinel and diaspore, in the Twin Lakes region on the trail from the easternmost of the Twin Lakes to Potter Pass, Chesterman (1) p. 274.

Inyo County: **1,** Hornblende occurs in large prismatic crystals up to 2.5 inches long in pegmatite near Little Dodd Spring, Panamint Range, McAllister (4) p. 52.

Mono County: **1,** Long, slender crystals of hornblende have been found with tridymite in cavities of lava 8 miles west of Bridgeport, Schaller (8) p. 128.

Plumas County: **1,** The variety edenite is one of the constituents of the plumasite at Spanish Peak, A. C. Lawson (5) p. 225.

Riverside County: **1,** Good, dark-green crystals of hornblende up to 1 inch in length were found in a pegmatite just west of the Jensen quarry, 4 miles west of Riverside, J. W. Clark (p.c. '36). **2,** Hornblende, common variety, and pargasite are reported from the Crestmore quarries sometimes in large crystals, Woodford (11) pp. 351-252. Uralite is also reported by J. W. Daly (1) p. 638.

San Bernardino County: **1,** Poorly formed crystals of basaltic hornblende are found in the volcanic ash deposits at Siberia crater, near Amboy. Occasionally these hornblendes form the cores of small volcanic bombs, Brady and Webb (1) p. 406. **2,** Pargasite occurs in coarsely crystalline masses in a diorite pegmatite, 4 miles southeast of Camp Irwin in the Mojave Desert (SE ¼ Sec. 11, T. 13 N., R. 3 E., S.B.), R. D. Allen and Kramer (3) p. 527.

Siskiyou County: **1,** Hornblende occurs as prominent black crystals in andesite at Sugar Loaf, Diller et al. (15) p. 61.

Tulare County: **1,** C. Durrell (4) p. 160 reports hornblende crystals up to several inches in length, in a hornblende gabbro near Woodlake (sec. 9, T. 17 S., R. 26 E., M.D.), and **2,** crystals up to 10 inches in Yokohl Valley (NW¼ sec. 17, T. 18 S., R. 28 E., M. D.).

<h3 style="text-align:center">NEPHRITE</h3>

The variety nephrite is tremolite or actinolite in compactly fibrous form, and is very similar in appearance to jadeite.

Marin County: **1,** Veins and lenses of nephrite have been found in massive serpentine at Massa Hill (sec. 19, T. 5 N., 7 W., M.D.), Chesterman (3) p. 3, (4) p. 1517.

Mariposa County: **1,** Nephrite jade has been found over a considerable area in the vicinity of Bagby, between David and Flyaway Gulches, Anon. (50) p. 21.

Mendocino County: **1,** Nephrite occurs in boulders at Williams Creek, about 6 miles east of Covelo, Chesterman (p.c. '51). **2,** Nephrite with crocidolite and jadeite has been reported from boulders in the stream bed, on the north fork, Eel River, near Mina, Anon. (12) p. 2.

Monterey County: **1,** Good jade quality nephrite has been found in serpentine in the western Santa Lucia Range, between Point Sur and Salmon Creek Ranger Station, mostly as rolled pebbles and boulders, A. F. Rogers (47) p. 1941. **2,** Beach boulders and nodules of nephrite in mylonite occur at Plaskett and Willow Creeks (secs. 19, 31, T. 23 S., R. 5 E., M.D.), Crippen (2) pp. 1–14.

Riverside County: **1,** Dark green nephrite occurs associated with magnetite and epidote at the contact between dolomite and quartz monzonite porphyry in the western part of the Eagle Mountains, Chesterman (p.c. '64). **2,** Nephrite, semi-opaque and jet-black to green in color, has been reported from the Storm Jade Mt. mines, Lost Mayan jade mines, Chiriaco summit, near Indio, Anon. (17) p. 590. The occurrence is associated with serpentine in dolomite (ophicalcite).

Santa Barbara County: **1,** A boulder of nephrite was found near Los Olivos in a creek bed, on the south slope of Figueroa Mountain, Woodhouse (p.c. '51).

Siskiyou County: **1,** Nephrite was found at Chan jade mine, Indian Creek, near Happy Camp, some with flecks of gold, Kraft (1) pp. 34, 35. CDMG (21119) from this locality, misidentified in 1943 as California jade, is nephrite of good quality, containing flecks of gold, Crippen (p.c. '55).

Trinity County: **1,** Stream boulders of jadeite with nephrite are reported from the north fork of the Eel River, Anon. (8) p. 16.

Tulare County: **1,** Masses of nephrite, some of cutting quality, occur in serpentine at Lewis Hill, 2 miles north of Porterville, Anon. (11) p. 1, Anon. (12) p. 2, Crippen (2) p. 4.

PALYGORSKITE
Hydrous basic silicate of calcium and aluminum, near
$Mg_2Al_2Si_3O_{20}(OH_2)_4(OH)_2 \cdot 4H_2O$

A fibrous amphibole. The occurrences reported below were originally described as attapulgite, which has been shown by Huggins et al. (1) p. 15 to be a short-fiber palygorskite.

Kern County: **1,** Veins in sediments in the Four Corners area have been identified as the clay mineral attapulgite, associated with montmorillonite, Droste and Gates (1). See San Bernardino County **(1).**

San Bernardino County: **1,** Veins in sediments in the Four Corners area have been identified as the clay mineral attapulgite, associated with montmorillonite, Droste and Gates (1). See Kern County **(1).**

TREMOLITE
Basic silicate of calcium and magnesium with fluorine, $Ca_2Mg_5Si_8O_{22}(OH,F)_2$

Mountain leather and *mountain cork* are flexible sheets of interlaced fibers of tremolite.

Amador County: **1,** Fibrous sheets of tremolite in the form of mountain leather and mountain cork have been found at the Little Grass Valley mine, Pine Grove Mining District, Hanks (12) p. 70.

Calaveras County: **1,** Slip-fiber veins of amphibole asbestos are common in basic rocks in the Calaveritas quadrangle. Hand specimens with fibers up to 2 inches were collected 200 ft. west of the triangulation station (SW ¼ sec. 1, T. 3 N., R. 13 E., M.D.), L. D. Clark (1) p. 17.

Contra Costa County: **1,** Tremolite is abundant with actinolite, in the schists near San Pablo, Blasdale (1) p. 333.

Fresno County: **1,** One- to two-inch crystals of tremolite have been found in contact zones in crystalline limestones in the Twin Lakes region, Chesterman (1) p. 254.

Inyo County: **1,** Tremolite occurs in altered carbonate rocks in the Quartz Spring area, McAllister (3) p. 36. **2,** Tremolite is found in radial clusters near the Lippincott mine, Ubehebe Mining District, McAllister (4) p. 52.

Kern County: **1,** Large columnar, brittle tremolite occurs at Tollgate Canyon, north of Tehachapi (N.R.).

Madera County: **1,** White fibrous asbestos is found in piemontite schist near Shadow Lake, A. M. Short (1) p. 493. **2,** An extensive area of asbestos occurs at the Savannah mine, near Grub Gulch, W. W. Bradley and R. P. McLaughlin (3) p. 538.

Marin County: **1,** Tremolite is found with wollastonite in the schists on the shore of Tomales Bay, F. M. Anderson (1) p. 132.

Placer County: **1,** White "slip-fiber" asbestos up to 8 inches was found a quarter of a mile east of Iowa Hill (sec. 28, T. 15 N., R. 10 E., M.D.), L. L. Root (5) p. 237. **2,** Tremolite occurs in long gray-green, silky fibers at the Morgan mine south of Towle (sec. 12, T. 15 N., R. 10 E., M.D.), C. A. Waring (4) p. 321.

Plumas County: **1,** Asbestos is found on the west slope of Fales Hill (sec. 25 ?, T. 25 N., R. 7 E., M.D.), Logan (20) p. 85. **2,** Tremolite occurs at Rich Bar, Indian Creek, northwest of Meadow Valley, E. S. Dana (5) p. 1096.

Riverside County: **1,** Slip-fiber asbestos has been reported southwest of Palm Springs, a quarter of a mile southwest of benchmark 3871 (secs. 4, 5, T. 7 S., R. 6 E., S.B.), southwest of Piñon Flat, F. J. H. Merrill (2) p. 550. **2,** Small amounts of white asbestiform tremolite occur in the crystalline limestone at the Jensen quarry, 4 miles west of Riverside, E. H. Peebles (p.c. '45). **3,** Prismatic aggregates of tremolite occur in the contact limestone at the new City quarry, Riverside, G. M. Richmond (1) p. 725. **4,** Well-formed small crystals of tremolite occur in limestone, with phlogopite, etc., at the Midland mine of the U.S. Gypsum Company, in the Little Maria Mountains, Ian Campbell (p.c. '36). **5,** Mountain cork is reported in whitish, cork-like masses from Blythe, Anon. (5) p. 496. **6,** Amphibole asbestos in fibers sometimes a foot or more in length, is found in an extensive zone $1\frac{1}{2}$ miles due east of Toro Peak (sec. 31, T. 7 S., R. 6 E., S.B.), Durrell (p.c. '54). **7,** Tremolite is reported with questionable identification from the Crestmore quarry, Woodford (11) p. 353.

San Bernardino County: **1,** Tremolite occurs as residual grains in a large talc deposit 7 miles northeast of Silver Lake, Wicks (1) p. 319. **2,** Crystals up to several inches in length occur in the Furnace limestone, Furnace Canyon, Baker (1) p. 337, Woodford and Harriss (4) p. 268. **3,** A pale blue soda-tremolite occurs with diopside near the mouth of Cascade Canyon, R. H. Merriam and Laudermilk (1) p. 716. **4,** Coarse-fibered tremolite occurs at the Scorpion mine, $2\frac{1}{2}$ miles from the Mojave River and 14 miles north from Oro Grande. Crossman (2) p. 236. **5,** Gold-bearing tremolite was found in the Wild Rose group, 30 miles southeast of Victorville, H. W. Turner (31) p. 835.

San Diego County: **1,** Asbestos fibers up to 6 inches in length come from 3 miles east of Warner Hot Springs. Goodyear (5) p. 148.

Santa Cruz County: **1,** Mountain leather is reported from near Santa Cruz, Fitch (1) p. 9.

Sierra County: **1,** Fibers of asbestos 5 to 6 inches long were collected from Goodyear Creek, half a mile from Goodyear Bar, Crawford (1) p. 406. **2,** Long slip-fiber asbestos occurs at the Green and Fair prospects (sec. 33, T. 20 N., R. 12 E., M.D.), Logan (13) p. 154. **3,** Leathery asbestos came from the Plumbago mine, Alleghany Mining District, Ferguson and Gannett (6) p. 48.

Sonoma County: **1,** Lenticular masses of slender prisms occur in the Culver-Baer area, Kramm (1) p. 344.

Trinity County: **1,** Asbestos occurs at several localities—near Castella, Trinity Center and Weaverville, G. C. Brown (2) pp. 876, 877.

Tulare County: **1,** Small occurrences of asbestos are found near Porterville, Frazier Valley, etc., Tucker (3) p. 905.

Tuolumne County: **1,** White fibrous tremolite occurs in the marble near Columbia, Hanks (12) p. 70.

Yuba County: **1,** Small amounts of slip-fiber asbestos occur south of Challenge, and in T. 19 and 20 N., R. 7 and 8 E., M.D., C. A. Waring (4) pp. 423, 424.

ALKALI AMPHIBOLES
BARKEVIKITE
$$Ca_2(NaK)(Fe^{2+},Mg,Mn^{3+},Mn)_5[Si_{6.5}Al_{1.5}O_{22}](OH,F)_2$$

Amphibole rich in ferrous iron and alkalies

Fresno County: **1,** Barkevikite occurs near the head of White Creek (SE $\frac{1}{4}$ sec. 4, T. 19 S., R. 13 E., M.D.), northwest of Coalinga, as crystals in cavities of a soda-syenite, accompanied by analcime, albite, and aegirite, Arnold and Anderson (8) p. 158.

Los Angeles County: **1,** Abundant barkevikite occurs in small dikes along South Riverside Drive at the north end of Griffith Park, Neuerburg (p.c. '50).

San Benito County: **1,** A mass of barkevikite syenite occurs near the gem mine (secs. 25, 26, T. 18 S., R. 12 E., M.D.), Eckel and Meyers (2) p. 91.

* CROSSITE, 1894
Intermediate between glaucophane and riebeckite

Crossite was described as a new mineral by Palache (3) pp. 181–192, belonging to the amphibole family. It has subsequently been placed in the family as a varietal sub-species of glaucophane.

Contra Costa County: **1,** Crossite was found in a boulder north of Berkeley, and described by Palache (3) p. 185, as a new amphibole; analysis by Blasdale, Washington (1) pp. 49, 50.

Los Angeles County: **1,** Microscopic crystals of crossite in schist were discovered in the San Pedro Hills near Malaga Cove, Woodford (1) p. 54, and **2,** from Santa Catalina Island, ibid.

Mendocino County: **1,** Prismatic grains of crossite occur in the Franciscan schist near the headwaters of Jumpoff Creek, near Covelo, S. G. Clark (p.c. '35).

Orange County: **1,** Crossite has been found abundantly in the San Onofre breccia at Dana Point, Jenni (p.c. '57).

San Diego County: **1,** Crossite occurs in schist boulders of the San Onofre breccia, with glaucophane, Woodford (2) p. 186, R. D. Reed (5) p. 347.

GLAUCOPHANE
Basic sodium/magnesium/aluminum silicate
$Na_2Mg_3Al_2Si_8O_{22}(OH,F)_2$

Glaucophane is a widespread constituent of the schists of the Coast Ranges, from Mendocino County to San Diego County.

Alameda County: **1,** A general study of glaucophane-bearing schists of Berkeley Hills has been published by Brothers (1) p. 614.

Calaveras County: **1,** A specimen from the Collier mine, 6 miles northeast of Murphys, was identified as glaucophane by Michael-Levy, Hanks (12) p. 183, CDMG (4259).

Lake County: **1,** Glaucophane was described from Sulphur Lake by Becker (4) p. 102. **2,** From the Wall Street quicksilver mine, Hanks (12) p. 183, CDMG (4720), reports glaucophane.

Los Angeles County: **1,** Glaucophane was found with crossite at Malaga Cove, Redondo Beach, R. D. Reed (5) p. 347. **2,** W. S. T. Smith (1) p. 1 reports glaucophane from Little Harbor, on Santa Catalina Island.

Marin County: **1,** Glaucophane occurs with lawsonite near Reed Station, on the Tiburon Peninsula, F. L. Ransome (3) p. 311. **2,** Extremely fine blue needles of glaucophane were found on Angel Island, F. L. Ransome (2) p. 206. **3,** An outcrop of glaucophane schist with abundant yellowish epidote has been observed on the north side of Tiburon Peninsula, Watters (p.c. '58).

San Benito County: **1,** Glaucophane occurs at the benitoite locality, near the headwaters of the San Benito River, Louderback and Blasdale (5) p. 360.

San Diego County: **1,** Glaucophane is found in schist boulders of the San Onofre breccia, with crossite, Woodford (2), p. 186. **2,** Glaucophane (*gastaldite*) occurs as silky fibers in diorite at the contact of a pegmatite dike at Rincon (secs. 25, 36, T. 10 S., R. 1 W., S.B.), Murdoch and Webb (6) p. 353.

Santa Clara County: **1,** Glaucophane occurs in eclogite and schists at the north end of Calaveras Valley, Nutter and Barber (1) p. 742. **2,** In the Oak Hill area, Carey and Miller (1) p. 166 report glaucophane. **3,** Holway (1) p. 347 reports glaucophane as seams and segregations in eclogite on Coyote Creek 6 miles north of San Martin.

Sonoma County: **1,** Glaucophane is found 2 miles southwest of Healdsburg, Nutter and Barber (1) p. 740, and **2,** at Camp Meeker, in crystalline schists, ibid. (1) p. 741. **3,** Blue crystals of glaucophane occur with lawsonite and clinozoisite $2\frac{1}{2}$ miles east of Valley Ford, CDMG (21318).

Mendocino County: **1,** A quarry 5.1 miles north of Longvale on U.S. 101 has furnished glaucophane schist with associated lawsonite, stilpnomelane, and riebeckite, Watters (p.c. '58).

RIEBECKITE

Basic silicate of sodium and iron with flourine, $Na_2Fe^{2+}_3Fe^{3+}_2Si_8O_{22}(OH,F)_2$

Crocidolite is the finely fibrous form ("blue asbestos") of riebeckite.

Lake County: **1,** CDMG (11464) from near Lakeport is crocidolite.

Mendocino County: **1,** Crocidolite, with nephrite and jadeite, occurs in boulders on the north fork, Eel River, near Mina, Anon. (12), p. 2. **2,** Patches of prismatic riebeckite crystals occur in glaucophane schist in a quarry 5.1 miles north of Longvale on Highway 101, associated with stilpnomelane and lawsonite, Watters (p.c. '58).

Santa Clara County: **1,** Crocidolite is reported by A. F. Rogers (7) p. 377, from a locality east of Hamilton.

Sonoma County: **1,** A specimen of crocidolite, CDMG (19626), is from Pine Flat. **2,** Riebeckite is found with aegirite in cavities of soda rhyolite near Glen Ellen on the east side of Sonoma Valley, Chesterman (p.c. '51).

Tulare County: **1,** Clusters of riebeckite needles as much as a quarter of an inch in length, are found along a serpentine contact, in quartz-albite schist, southeast of Rocky Hill, Durrell (2) p. 93.

Tuolumne County: **1,** Microscopic radiating tufts of riebeckite needles are found in albitite, at the Clio mine half a mile east of Jacksonville, A. Knopf (11) pp. 21, 40.

ANALCIME—Analcite

Hydrous sodium aluminum silicate, $NaAlSi_2O_6 \cdot H_2O$

Analcime is a zeolite occurring as a secondary mineral in volcanic rocks, often in large, well-formed crystals. It is also found as an original constituent in some diabases and basalts.

Alameda County: **1,** Analcime occurs in brilliant crystals, and massive, in amygdules of andesite in the Berkeley Hills, Lawson and Palache (4) p. 418.

Fresno County: **1,** Albite, aegirite, and barkevikite with analcime are found in cavities in a soda-syenite near the head of White Creek (SE ¼ sec. 4, T. 19 S., R. 13 E., M.D.), Arnold and Anderson (8) p. 158. It appears that this may be the occurrence referred to under San Benito County **(1)** as White Creek.

Inyo County: **1,** Amygdules of a basalt near the Russell borax mine, Mt. Blanco, are filled with crystals of analcime associated with radiating natrolite, Foshag (10) p. 10. **2,** Analcime is one of the minerals formed in Owens Lake beds by post-depositional reactions, Hay and Moiola (2) p. 76. **3,** A specimen of analcime lining vugs in basalt at Ryan is in the Smithsonian Institution collections. The specimen was donated by Rasor about 1927. This may be the same locality as **(1).**

Kern County: **1,** The lava flows of Red Rock Canyon carry associated analcime, natrolite, calcite, and occasionally opal, as amygdules, Murdoch and Webb (14) p. 330. **2,** Analcime has been identified along with other zeolites and gay-lussite, in clay and tuff layers in China Lake, Moiola and Hay (1) p. 47, Hay and Moiola (2) p. 76.

Los Angeles County: **1,** Crystals up to ⅜-inch in diameter appear in seams of basalt near Lake Malibu, Schwartz (1) p. 414. **2,** Analcime occurs with natrolite in cavities of "dolerite" on Mulholland Drive, Schürmann (1) p. 12. **3,** Analcime, with natrolite, prehnite, and apophyllite, is found in veins and cavity fillings in basalt in the Pacific Electric quarry in Brush Canyon, locality 3, Neuerburg (1) p. 158. **4,** Small crystals occur with natrolite in cavities in lava at the head of Tick Canyon, near Lang, Anon. (20) p. 382. **5,** A specimen of analcime crystals perched on a drusy crust of bakerite has been collected from the Stirling Borax mine, Tick Canyon, H. E. Pemberton (p.c. '58). This is an unusual mode of occurrence for this mineral.

Mono County: **1,** Small crystals of analcime are found in volcanic rock from Leavitt Meadows, W. W. Bradley (32) p. 565.

Plumas County: **1,** Analcime occurs as druses in pegmatites, and as an accessory in the igneous rocks at the Engels mine, H. W. Turner and Rogers (32) p. 373, Graton and McLaughlin (4) p. 18.

San Benito County: **1,** Crystals of analcime occur in seams of barkevikite syenite on White Creek (San Benito River?) (secs. 25, 26, T. 18 S., R. 12 E., M.D.), Watters (p.c. '51). See also Fresno County **(1).**

San Bernardino County: **1,** Analcime was observed in a single poor specimen from the Calico Mts., A. R. Palmer (1) p. 241. **2,** Analcime in minute crystals has been found at several horizons in the mud layers at Searles Lake, G. I. Smith and Haines (3) p. 25, Hay and Moiola (1) p. 323.

San Mateo County: **1,** Glassy crystals of analcime occur in amygdules of basaltic rock at Langley Hill, Haehl and Arnold (1) p. 39.

San Luis Obispo County: **1,** Cavities carrying analcime are found in augite-teschenite dikes on the north side of Cuyama Valley. The crystals are water-clear grains up to 6 mm disseminated through the rock, Fairbanks (12) p. 277.

Santa Barbara County: **1,** Analcime is reported in large grains, and as inclusions in augite grains, in an augite-teschenite rock at Point Sal, Fairbanks (14) p. 21.

Santa Clara County: **1,** Analcime occurs on Coyote Creek, near the Cochran(e) Ranch, Kartchner (1) p. 18.

Shasta County: **1,** Chabazite, natrolite, analcime and tridymite are associated in an amygdaloidal basalt 7 miles east of Round Mountain, Melhase (3) no. 6, p. 1.

Trinity County: **1,** Analcime is reported in crystals more than $1\frac{1}{2}$ inches in diameter from a placer mine in this county, Bixby (2) p. 168.

Ventura County: 1, H. S. Gale (11) p. 439 found analcime and natrolite in amygdules in basalt in the Frazier Mountain borax area.

ANAPAITE
Hydrous calcium iron phosphate, $Ca_2Fe^{2+}(PO_4)_2 \cdot 4H_2O$

Kings County: **1,** Layers of pale green crystals of anapaite were found at a depth of 500 feet in a core from the Lewis well (sec. 23, T. 21 S., R. 21 E., M.D.), Melhase (3) no. 7, p. 7.

ANATASE—Octahedrite
Titanium dioxide, TiO_2

This form of titanium dioxide is rarer than rutile, and is found only in minute crystals.

Coast Range Counties: Anatase is often present in weathered quartz diorites of the Coast Range batholith, Spotts (1) p. 237.

El Dorado County: **1,** Minute crystals of anatase with brookite were found on quartz crystals near Placerville, Kunz (5) p. 329, (6) p. 395, (7) p. 207, (15) p. 394.

Lake County: **1,** Anatase is reported in minor amounts as an associate of buddingtonite, in the altered pyroxene andesite of the Sulphur Bank mercury deposits, with stibnite, mercury minerals, and possibly ammoniojarosite, Erd et al. (6) p. 833, D. E. White and Roberson (2) p. 407.

Nevada County: **1,** Crystals of anatase have been reported in placer gravels near North Bloomfield, Crippen (p.c. '51).

Riverside County: **1,** Anatase occurs as a minor constituent of tonalite, in the tunnel south of Val Verde, R. W. Wilson (1) p. 124.

San Benito County: **1,** A few minute pale-brown crystals of anatase were found in the benitoite vein, Palache (6) p. 398, Louderback and Blasdale (5) p. 380.

San Bernardino County: **1,** Niobian anatase, in numerous flat tetragonal crystals, occurs in masses of soft greenish mica in a pegmatite in the Cady Mountains, north of Hector, Hewett and Glass (3) p. 1044.

ANAUXITE
A variety of Kaolinite
Basic aluminum silicate, $Al_2Si_3O_7(OH)_4$ Si:Al to 3:1

Alameda County: **1,** Anauxite is a constituent of the sedimentary rocks near Tesla (secs. 11, 12, T. 3 S., R. 3 E., M.D.), V. T. Allen (5) p. 274.

Amador County: **1,** A characteristic constituent of the Ione sandstone, especially on the Mokelumne River, 1 mile west of Lancha Plana, is anauxite, V. T. Allen (2) p. 145. **2,** Anauxite from the Newman pit near Ione was analyzed by Fairchild, R. C. Wells (3) p. 97. Brindley (2) p. 84, showed this occurrence to be kaolinite.

Contra Costa County: **1,** Some sedimentary layers in the Brentwood area, east of Mount Diablo (T. 1 N., R. 2 and 3 E., M.D.) carry up to 60 percent anauxite, V. T. Allen (5) p. 280.

Fresno County: **1,** Occasional layers of the sediments in the Panoche Hills are anauxite, V. T. Allen (5) p. 277.

Plumas County: **1,** A. F. Rogers (38) p. 160 identified as anauxite minute pale-brown tabular crystals in cavities of a pyroxene andesite at Drakesbad.

Tuolumne County: **1,** Thin brown crystals of anauxite occur in cavities of an augite andesite, near Jamestown, A. F. Rogers (36) p. 160.

ANDALUSITE
Aluminum silicate, Al_2SiO_5

Chiastolite is andalusite with symmetrically arranged black inclusions. Andalusite occurs as a constituent of gneisses and schists, quartz veins, and pegmatites. It is usually associated with kyanite, sillimanite, and staurolite.

Alpine County: **1,** Andalusite is found in some abundance, with lazulite, ilmenite, and rutile, in metamorphic rocks about 10 miles south-southwest from Markleeville, Woodhouse (p.c. '45).

Butte County: **1,** Andalusite crystals as much as 2 cm in size occur in andalusite schists, $1\frac{1}{2}$ miles southeast of Big Bear Lookout (locality 415), Hietanen (1) p. 575.

Fresno County: **1,** Large crystals of andalusite were found in pegmatite in Clarks Valley, 9 miles east of Sanger, Melhase (6) p. 22. **2,** Radiating masses and prismatic crystals up to 10 by 15 cm of a pink to dark-reddish-violet andalusite, were found in a narrow pegmatite about $1\frac{1}{2}$ miles southeast of Sharpsville (S. $\frac{1}{2}$ sec. 20, T. 11 S., R. 22 E., M.D.), G. A. Macdonald and Merriam (1) p. 588.

Imperial County: **1,** Excellent crystals of andalusite in mica schists were discovered in a lens as pale brown crystals at the Foster Bluebird mine 3 miles north of the abandoned station of Ogilby on the Southern Pacific Railroad, in the Cargo Muchacho Mts., Foster (p.c. '58).

Inyo County: **1,** The variety chiastolite occurs widely in the Rest Spring shale. An accessible occurrence is along San Lucas Canyon, near junction with the road to Cerro Gordo mine, McAllister (4) p. 53.

Kern County: **1,** Chiastolite schists occur on Walker Creek southeast of Bakersfield, R. J. Sampson and Tucker (4) p. 453.

Los Angeles County: **1,** The "spotted" (cordierite) slates at the junction of Franklin and Coldwater Canyons, Santa Monica Mountains, carry fair-sized chiastolite crystals, Funk (1) p. 33. **2,** Chiastolite crystals are prominent in the Santa Monica "slate" at localities 14, 15, 16, 17, in Nichols, Coldwater, and Franklin Canyons, Neuerburg (1) p. 159.

Madera County: **1,** Chiastolite was first noted by W. P. Blake (7) p. 304, along the Chowchilla River, notably at Chowchilla Crossing on the old Fort Miller road, Hanks (12) p. 70. **2,** Crystals of andalusite up to 1 cm in length, in a muscovite matrix, were found half a mile below the junction of Bench Creek and the North Fork, San Joaquin River, Erwin (1) p. 29. **3,** Large crystals (3 inches by ½ inch) were found at the Ne Plus Ultra mine, near Daulton's Ranch (sec. 35, T. 9 S., R. 18 E., M.D.) Hanks (12) p. 70, H. W. Turner (4) p. 455, Logan (24) p. 42. **4,** Fine specimens, up to 3 by 1¼ inches, showing a rich black cross pattern on white or salmon-colored background were described by W. W. Jefferis from this county, but the exact locality is not known, Kunz (24) pp. 88–89).

Mariposa County: **1,** Small crystals in slate are found at Miller's Ranch near Hornitos, Hanks (12) p. 70. **2,** Chiastolite is found on Moores Flat, ibid. p. 70. **3,** Colorless to pink glassy crystals 3–6 mm by 20 mm occur in slates (SW ¼ sec. 17, T. 6 S., R. 16 E., M.D.) in what is known as the Southwest of Three Buttes deposit. It is undeveloped, Bowen and Gray (2) p. 202. **4,** Andalusite occurs in pegmatites at May Lake, Yosemite National Park, R. L. 'Rose (1) p. 635.

Mono County: **1,** A large commercial deposit of andalusite, which carries corundum, pyrophyllite, and many other minerals in small amounts, was worked at the mine of Champion Sillimanite Incorporated, on the western slope of the White Mountains about 7 miles east of Mocalno, north of Bishop, A. Knopf (7) p. 550, Peck (1) p. 123, Jeffery and Woodhouse (3) p. 461, Kerr (3) p. 621, Woodhouse (5) p. 486. **2,** Andalusite occurs with lazulite, etc., in metamorphic rocks 1 mile west of Green Lake (sec. 28?, T. 3 N., R. 24 E., M.D.), Woodhouse (p.c. '45).

Nevada County: **1,** Andalusite has been reported from Grass Valley by Lindgren (12) p. 92.

Riverside County: **1,** Opaque pink andalusite occurs near Coahuila, Kunz (24) p. 99. **2,** Pink crystals in a small pegmatite cutting the magnesite deposit near Winchester have been described by Murdoch (3) p. 68. **3,** Giant pink crystals occur in pegmatite on Coahuila Mountain (sec. 29, T. 6 W., R. 2 E., S.B.), Webb (11) p. 581. It may be that this is the locality from which Kunz reports andalusite, see locality (1). **4,** An occurrence of andalusite north of Winchester (sec. 12, T. 5 S., R. 2 E., S.B.) is also reported by Webb (11) p. 581.

San Diego County: **1,** Pink radiating masses of andalusite are found in a quartz vein about 3 miles northeast of Pala (sec. 12, T. 9 S., R. 2 W., S.B.), Schaller (p.c. '46). **2,** Masses of andalusite as much as 3 inches in diameter are found in the northern parts of the Queen and Chief mines at Pala, Jahns and Wright (5) p. 42.

Tulare County: **1,** Crystals up to 5 cm long were found on the west side of the valley of Sheep Creek (NW ¼ sec. 34, T. 11 S., R. 28 E., M.D.), Durrell (p.c. '35).

ANDORITE
Lead/silver/antimony sulphide, $PbAgSb_3S_6$

Inyo County: **1,** Thin tabular crystals of andorite in the rich silver ore of the Thompson mine, Darwin Mining District, are reported by Hall and MacKevett (1) p. 17, (2) p. 59.

ANGLESITE
Lead sulphate, $PbSO_4$

Anglesite is a common oxidation product of galena, and is often found in lead deposits in small amounts. The mineral is readily confused with cerussite from which it often cannot be separated in field inspection. Localities entered below have not had the reported identification validated, and all occurrences known in the State are not included.

Inyo County: **1,** At the Modoc mine, anglesite is associated with bindheimite and azurite, as an oxidation product of galena, Hanks (12) p. 71. **2,** In the mines of Cerro Gordo Mining District anglesite occurred as large masses and crystalline crusts enclosing cores of galena, Silliman (12) p. 131, R. W. Raymond (5) p. 30, Charles W. Merriam (1) p. 43. **3,** In the Ubehebe Mining District anglesite occurs with cerussite as alteration from galena, C. A. Waring and Huguenin (2) p. 109. **4,** Anglesite is sparingly present in the Darwin mines, A. Knopf (4) p. 7. **5,** In the Panamint Mining District, Murphy (2) p. 322 reports anglesite. **6,** Anglesite is abundant as an ore mineral in the Minietta and Modoc mining areas, Argus Range, Woodhouse (p.c. '54).

Madera County: **1,** Anglesite is reported as an alteration of galena in the Minarets Mining District on Shadow Creek, and with linarite in the Bliss claims, North Fork Basin, Erwin (1) pp. 67, 70.

Mono County: **1,** Anglesite is widely distributed in moderate quantity in the Blind Spring Mining District, A. L. Ransome (2) p. 192. Crystals a third of an inch in diameter were reported by W. J. Hoffman (1) p. 732.

Plumas County: **1,** Wulfenite and anglesite are associated in gold ores from the Granite Basin Mining District, H. W. Turner (12) p. 589.

Riverside County: **1,** A very small amount of anglesite has been found at the Crestmore quarry, Eakle (15) p. 353. **2,** Anglesite occurs with carbonates and vanadates, at the Black Eagle mine, in the northern part of the Eagle Mountains, Tucker (8) p. 195.

San Bernardino County: **1,** Anglesite, massive and in crystals, occurs at the Ibex mine in the Black Mountains, 6 miles north of Saratoga Springs, Cloudman et al. (1) p. 821. **2,** The mineral also occurs in small amounts in the western part of the Calico Mining District, Weeks (2) p. 762; **3,** in the Imperial lode, Lava Beds Mining District, with wulfenite, Tucker and Sampson (17) p. 351.

ANHYDRITE
Calcium sulphate, CaSO₄

Imperial County: **1,** Anhydrite is reported from the Fish Creek Mountains, Min. Inf. Serv. (22) p. 1.

Inyo County: **1,** Anhydrite is found in small amounts in the Panamint and Funeral Ranges, Kunz (24) p. 103. **2,** Anhydrite is present with gypsum in drill cores from the Panamint Basin, G. I. Smith and Pratt (2) p. 40.

Mono County: **1,** In the mountains south of Mono Lake, Kunz (24) p. 103, reports anhydrite.

Orange County: **1,** The mineral was found sparingly near Anaheim, probably half a mile south of Santa Ana, Hanks (12) p. 72, Goodyear (3) p. 339.

Riverside County: **1,** Anhydrite occurs interlayered with gypsum in the Palen Mountains, A. F. Rogers (14) p. 134. **2,** Massive white crystalline anhydrite occurs at the Midland mine in the Little Maria Mountains, CDMG (20112), Anon. (23) p. 1.

San Bernardino County: **1,** Anhydrite is one of the many minerals found in small amounts at Searles Lake, De Groot (2) p. 537; and **2,** in the Owl Mountains near Owl Springs; **3,** in the Avawatz Mountains near the Amargosa River, Kunz (24) p. 103. and **4,** in the "sulphur pit" with krausite and other sulphates near Borate, in the Calico Mountains, Foshag (19) p. 352.

Shasta County: **1,** In the deep levels of the Bully Hill and Rising Star mines, anhydrite is found partly altered to gypsum, A. F. Rogers (14) p. 132, Albers and Robertson (3) p. 74.

ANKERITE
Carbonate of calcium/magnesium/and iron, $Ca(Mg,Fe)(CO_3)_2$

Ankerite is widely distributed in the Mother Lode Belt, and is especially prominent in the mines of Mariposa County.

The reader is reminded that validation of identification in reported occurrences in the following entries has not been systematically undertaken. Since ankerite is not readily separated physically from other members of the calcite group, some occurrences may in fact be in error.

Amador County: **1,** Ankerite occurs as incrustations on slate in the Plymouth mine, A Knopf (11) p. 35.

Calaveras County: **1,** Ankerite is abundant at Carson Hill, A. Knopf (11) p. 35; **2,** it occurs at the Golden Gate mine, 1 mile north of San Andreas, Tucker (1) p. 82.

El Dorado County: **1,** One of the gangue minerals in gold quartz veins at the Larkin mine, 1 mile east of Diamond Springs is ankerite, Logan (16) p. 30.

Mariposa County: **1,** Ankerite was first reported as an associate of mariposite on the Mariposa Estate, Silliman (7) p. 350. **2,** An enormous, massive belt of coarse white carbonate 300 to 500 feet wide, just west of Coulterville, is ankerite, A. Knopf (11) p. 35.

Nevada County: **1,** Ankerite is abundant in the veins of the mines at Grass Valley, W. D. Johnston, Jr. (4) p. 34.

Plumas County: **1,** Flat crystals of ankerite associated with pyrite and fine albite crystals in vugs, occur at the Shady Run mine, 8 miles east of Dutch Flat, Reid (1) p. 280.

San Bernardino County: **1,** Ankerite is found in the scheelite veins, as part of the gangue, at Atolia, Hulin (1) p. 73.

Tuolumne County: **1,** Ankerite is widespread as a gangue mineral in the Mother Lode mines of this county, Storms (9) p. 131.

ANNABERGITE—Nickel Bloom
Hydrous nickel arsenate, $Ni_3As_2O_8 \cdot 8H_2O$

Coatings of annabergite are an indication of the presence of nickel minerals that have been oxidized, and it is often associated with erythrite (cobalt bloom).

Inyo County: **1,** Annabergite is associated with erythrite, smaltite, and argentite in the claims of the Bishop Silver and Cobalt Mining Company, east of Long Lake (sec. 14, T. 9 S., R. 31 E., M.D.), Tucker and Sampson (25) p. 378.

Lassen County: **1,** A specimen, associated with smaltite and erythrite (?), from this county is in the California Division of Mines and Geology Museum (9981), but no detail of the locality is available.

Los Angeles County: **1,** Annabergite has been found with siderite and pyrrhotite in Pacoima Canyon, D'Arcy (3) p. 269; **2,** it occurs with erythrite, smaltite, and native silver at the old Kelsey mine in San Gabriel Canyon, Storms (4) p. 244.

Santa Cruz County: **1,** Annabergite (magnesian rich) is reported from the Pacific Limestone Products (Kalkar) quarry, as small, well-formed crystals, as well as fibers, E. H. Oyler (p.c. '59).

Tulare County: **1,** Specimens of annabergite have come from near Porterville, Noren (p.c. '54).

ANTIMONY
Native antimony, Sb.

Native antimony occurs in metal-bearing veins with silver, antimony, and arsenic ores, especially with stibnite. It has been found at a few localities in the State. Many references to "antimony" in the literature are to the sulphide stibnite, but there are some authentic occurrences.

Butte County: **1,** Native antimony is reported with bournonite in the gold ores of the Surcease mine (T. 21, N., R. 4 E., M.D.), O'Brien (6) p. 431.

El Dorado County: **1,** Native antimony has been reported from Pleasant Valley (N.R.)

Kern County: Antimony has been found in a number of localities in the Havilah and Kernville areas, associated with stibnite. Notable occurrences are as follows: **1,** On Erskine Creek, 4 miles south of Hot Springs, nodular masses up to 300 pounds have been found, Watts (2) p. 237. **2,** The Rayo mine (sec. 36, T. 26 S., R. 33 E., M.D.), and **3,** Erskine Creek (Tom Moore) mine (sec. 24, T. 27 S., R. 33 E., M.D.) have furnished specimens associated with stibnite, W. W. Bradley (11) pp. 21, 22, Behre (1) p. 332. Troxel and Morton (2) p. 31 report native antimony with oxides of antimony and stibnite from a quartz vein at the Tom Moore mine. **4,** Antimony was found at Little Caliente Spring, south of Piute, with stibiconite, CDMG (11671). **5,** Antimony has also been reported from the old San Emigdio mine (N.R.). **6,** Tucker (p.c. '36) reported antimony from Antimony Peak, 12 miles southwest of Sunset and 5 miles northwest of Cuddy Valley. **7,** In Jawbone Canyon (secs. 5, 6, T. 30 S., R. 36 E., M.D.) antimony is presumed to occur (N.R.). **8,** Native antimony has been found in small quantity, with stibnite, in the Calf Creek area, Greenhorn Summit tungsten mining region, Troxel and Morton (2) p. 37.

Riverside County: **1,** Antimony is reported from "South Riverside", E. S. Dana (7) p. 133.

ANTLERITE
Basic copper suphate, $Cu_3(SO_4)(OH)_4$

Antlerite is a secondary mineral found in the oxidized zone of copper deposits in arid regions.

Inyo County: **1,** Antlerite is listed by Hall and MacKevett (1) p. 16, as one of the supergene minerals identified from the Darwin Mining District; see also ibid (2) p. 64.

Madera County: **1,** A specimen of antlerite, CDMG (21752), is from the Buchanan mine near Knowles.

Shasta County: **1,** Antlerite is reported as coatings on fractures from the Old Mine ore body, Kinkel et al. (2) p. 89.

APATITE

Calcium phosphate, with other elements

Fluorapatite, $Ca_5(PO_4)_3F$

Chlorapatite, $Ca_5(PO_4)_3Cl$

Hydroxylapatite, $Ca_5(PO_4)_3(OH)$

Carbonate apatite, $Ca_5(PO_4)_3(CO_3)H_2O$

Validity of varietal names in this group is sometimes subject to debate.

Voelckerite, francolite, and *fluor-collophane* are fluorapatite. *Dahllite* and most *collophane* are carbonate apatite. A variety of voelckerite with little fluorine seems to be characteristic of the glaucophane schists in the Coast Ranges. *Collophane* is the chief constituent of phosphorite and bone phosphate. Its general occurrence in Pacific coastal waters has been discussed by Emery and Dietz (3) p. 8. Apatite has been observed as small crystals in many of the rocks of the State.

Amador County: **1,** Apatite was the principal gangue mineral in some of the deep-level ore of the Kennedy mine at Jackson, Hulin (3) p. 348.

Contra Costa County: **1,** The variety voelckerite was found in tabular honey-yellow crystals, in a boulder of glaucophane schist west of the Berkeley Country Club, Coats (p.c. '36).

Fresno County: **1,** Apatite, in crystals up to 1 inch, was reported with andalusite in a pegmatite in Clarks Valley, 9 miles east of Sanger, Melhase (6) p. 22. **2,** Galliher (1) p. 258, has analyzed impure granular collophane from sediments penetrated by Pacific Western well KOC No. 27. **3,** Apatite pseudomorphous after fossil wood has been found in nodules of the Moreno formation at the head of Escarpado Canyon (NW $\frac{1}{4}$ sec. 7, T. 15 S., R. 12 E. MD), Gulbrandsen et al. (1) p. 101.

Humboldt County: **1,** Collophane occurs with dahllite near Yager (Stanford Museum specimen).

Inyo County: **1,** A small amount of apatite has been found in the contact zone in the Darwin Mining District, Kelley (4) p. 540. **2,** The mineral is found 9 miles southeast of Keeler, W. W. Bradley (29) p. 106.

Kern County: **1,** Minor amounts of apatite occur in the cassiterite ores of the Gorman area, Troxel and Morton (2) p. 294. **2,** Thorium-bearing fluorapatite (francolite) has been found in radioactive bones in the northeastern part of the county, Troxel and Morton (2) p. 290. **3,** Massive blue apatite occurs associated with chalcedony, calcite, and wollastonite at the Jimmie Mack claim, Piute Mountain, Green Mountain Mining District, (CDMG identification, '64).

Mono County: **1,** Small white tabular crystals of apatite are associated with lazulite and pyrophyllite at the andalusite deposit in the White Mountains, Peacock and Moddle (1) p. 105.

Monterey County: **1,** Collophane occurs in beds of phosphate rock in Vaquero Canyon, Reed (3) p. 196; and **2,** as concretionary pellets in shale in Reliz Canyon, Galliher (1) p. 266.

Plumas County: **1,** Large crystals of apatite accompanying abundant sphene occur in the country rock of the Superior mine near Engels, Graton and McLaughlin (4) p. 34. **2,** Apatite is also found at the Engels mine with magnetite, ibid. p. 11. **3,** White apatite with black tourmaline is reported from Thompson Peak, Williams (p.c. '49).

Riverside County: **1,** Greenish-blue apatite occurred as granular masses in white calcite at the Crestmore quarry, Eakle (15) p. 348, and **2,** a small amount was found in the contact zone at the new City quarry in Riverside, G. M. Richmond (1) p. 725. **3,** Apatite occurs in a scapolite-pyroxene dike at the eastern end of the iron-ore belt in the Eagle Mountains, Harder (6) p. 54.

San Benito County: **1,** Light green apatite crystals occur in a vein with orthoclase, near the Gem mine, Cureton (p.c. '62).

San Bernardino County: **1,** Small opaque crystals of apatite were found in limestone at the eastern end of the Kingston Range, Kunz (24) p. 102. **2,** Apatite is a minor constituent in the bastnaesite occurrence at Mountain Pass, Olson et al. (3) p. 38.

San Diego County: **1,** Apatite is a minor constituent of the dumortierite pegmatite near Dehesa, Schaller (7) p. 211. **2,** Violet and pale-pink tabular crystals of apatite occurred at the old Mack mine, and pale dirty green crystals at the Victor mine, both near Rincon, A. F. Rogers (4) p. 217. **3,** Thick tabular yellowish-green crystals of apatite up to 1 cm occur in spodumene-petalite rock in the Clark dike, in the same locality, Murdoch (p.c. '45). **4,** Apatite occurs in pegmatite on Smith Mountain, Schrader et al. (1) p. 42. **5,** The mineral occurs at Mesa Grande, sometimes colored red-violet due to the presence of neodymium, Wherry (2) p. 146. **6,** Apatite from the Gem mine No. 1 near Aguanga is in tabular crystals up to 1 inch across, Wilke (p.c. '36), and pure violet in color from the Mountain Lily, Wherry (2) p. 146. **7,** Apatite is found in pegmatite at Dos Cabezas mine near Jacumba, Kunz (24) p. 102, and **8,** near Grapevine Camp (sec. 26, T. 11 S., R. 4 E., S.B.), F. J. H. Merrill (1) p. 717. **9,** Apatite has been reported from the pegmatites of Pala, Kunz (23) p. 942, and tabular crystals, as much as a quarter of an inch in diameter, pink-violet or purple have been found in the Queen mine and on Heriart Mountain at Pala, Jahns and Wright (5) p. 41. **10,** Minute prisms of francolite, pale flesh-colored, occur filling fractures in massive amblygonite at the Stewart mine, Pala, Murdoch (p.c. '45). **11,** Francolite is abundant in nodules dredged from the sea bottom off the southern California coast, Dietz and Emery (1) p. 1878, Dietz et al. (2) p. 818.

Santa Barbara County: **1,** Apatite occurs as small concretionary masses in shale near Santa Barbara, Galliher (1) p. 266.

Santa Clara County: **1,** The variety voelckerite occurs as veinlike patches in glaucophane rock in Calaveras Valley, A. F. Rogers (9) p. 160.

Sierra County: **1,** White prismatic crystals up to three-quarters of an inch in length occur in cavities in the magnetite ore of the Sierra iron mine at Upper Spencer Lake, Durrell (p.c. '45).

Trinity County: **1,** Phosphate-bearing rocks near Hyampom have been found to contain hydroxylapatite and whitlockite, together with tridymite and cristobalite and an unknown mineral near $AlPO_4$. The locality is (sec. 13, T. 3 N., R. 6 E., H.), Lydon (2) p. 67. This is the first report of this variety of apatite from California.

Tulare County: **1,** Massive light blue apatite occurs in irregular layers up to 1 inch thick in marble at the Consolidated Tungsten mine, Drum Valley (sec. 11, T. 15 S., R. 26 E., M.D.). The apatite is associated with wollastonite and blue calcite, (CDMG 21868), John T. Alfors (p.c. '64).

APHTHITALITE—Glaserite
Potassium sodium sulphate, $(K,Na)_2SO_4$

Inyo County: **1,** Aphthitalite is reported as saline crusts and effflorescences from Deep Spring Lake, B. F. Jones (1) p. B200, ibid. (2) p. 88A.

San Bernardino County: **1,** Colorless tabular crystals of trigonal aspect associated with octahedral halite and massive borax, came from well G. 75 at Searles Lake, Foshag (5) p. 367; see also G. I. Smith and Pratt (2) p. 27. G. I. Smith and Haines (3) p. 9, describe the occurrence as chiefly from the central facies of the Upper Salt. The mineral is found as colorless or yellowish-orange groups of bladed or tabular crystals, or fine-grained aggregates, and is associated with trona, borax and hanksite.

APOPHYLLITE
Basic hydrous calcium potassium silicate with fluorine, $KCa_4Si_8O_{20}(F,OH) \cdot 8H_2O$

Apophyllite is a secondary mineral found in cavities of volcanic rock.

Los Angeles County: **1,** Thin tabular crystals of apophyllite up to the size of a silver dollar, associated with natrolite, analcime, and prehnite, occur as coatings on joints of basalt, in the Pacific Electric quarry, Brush Canyon (sec. 35, T. 1 N., R. 14 W., S.B.), Neuerburg (1) p. 158, confirming Murdoch (p.c. '45).

Marin County: **1,** Clear glassy crystals of apophyllite 1 to 2 mm in size occur with wollastonite and calcite in fissures of a quartzite, $1\frac{1}{2}$ miles northwest of Inverness on the west side of Tomales Bay, Vonsen (p.c. '37).

Plumas County: **1,** Crystals of apophyllite occur in cavities in basalt at the Buckeye mine near Onion Valley, Kunz (24) p. 97.

Riverside County: **1,** Cavities in limestone or in massive wollastonite in the Crestmore quarry are lined with small clear pyramidal crystals of apophyllite, Eakle (15) p. 350, Woodford et al. (1) p. 370. **2,** Skeletal crystals up to 3 mm across have been found in the new City quarry, Riverside, E. H. Bailey (3) p. 565. **3,** Similar skeletonized crystals were were also found with prehnite at Crestmore, ibid.

San Francisco County: **1,** Very minute colorless crystals of apophyllite were found with gyrolite at Fort Point in San Francisco, Schaller (8) p. 126.

San Mateo County: **1,** A little apophyllite was found near La Honda, Sanford and Stone (1) p. 24.

Santa Barbara County: **1,** Apophyllite is reported from basic intrusive rocks at Point Sal, C. D. Woodhouse, (p.c. '63).

Santa Clara County: **1,** Well-developed crystals of apophyllite with gyrolite and bituminous matter were found lining crevices in the rock at the New Almaden mine, F. W. Clarke (4) p. 22. **2,** Quartz pseudomorphous after apophyllite has been found at Mine Hill in the New Almaden area, E. H. Bailey and Everhart (12) p. 102.

ARAGONITE
Calcium carbonate, CaCO₃

Flos-ferri is a fine snow-white branching stalactitic form of aragonite. Much of the banded onyx marble of the state has been erroneously called aragonite instead of calcite.

Alameda County: **1,** Coarsely crystalline aragonite in radiating prismatic masses occurs in a limestone quarry on the Patterson Grade, 7 miles east of Livermore, A. F. Rogers (p.c. '36).

Calaveras County: **1,** Stalactites of flos-ferri have come from a cave near Murphy, CDMG (13702). **2,** CDMG (13684) is from Coyote Creek near Vallecitos.

Colusa County: **1,** Rich, deep-brown veins of aragonite up to 5 inches across, and banded masses occur at the head of Sulphur Creek, Fairbanks (6) p. 120, Goodyear (4) p. 159. **2,** Beautiful snow-white and transparent crystals of aragonite have come from the Candace copper mine, Hanks (12) p. 73. **3,** Aragonite has come from Stony Ford, CDMG (12796). **4,** The mineral occurs near Smithville, Hanks (12) p. 74.

Fresno County: **1,** Beautiful clusters of acicular crystals of aragonite have been found coating fracture surfaces of serpentine at the Holman chrome mine (sec. 34, T. 18 S., R. 13 E., M.D.), Murdoch (p.c. '54).

Inyo County: **1,** Showy aggregates of aragonite crystals have been collected from an abandoned mine near the ghost town of Leadfield at the head of Titus Canyon, W. W. Bradley (24) p. 253. **2,** Aragonite has been found at the Whiteside mine, Mazourka Canyon (T. 12 S., R. 36 E., M.D.), D'Arcy (2) p. 74. **3,** Aragonite associated with halite has been collected at Bad Water in Death Valley, Vonsen (p.c. '45). **4,** White to colorless crystals of aragonite as much as half an inch in length, line fissures in some of the workings of the Lippincott mine, McAllister (4) p. 53. **5,** Slender crystals of aragonite have been formed in the muds of Deep Spring Lake, M. N. A. Peterson et al. (1) p. 6494, B. F. Jones (1) p. 201.

Kern County: **1,** Concretionary crystalline masses of aragonite occur with gypsum in a bed near the south end of the Kettleman Hills (sec. 10, T. 25 S., R. 10 E., M.D.), Reed (2) p. 830.

Lake County: **1,** Acicular crystals of aragonite occur with opal in basalt at Sulphur Bank, C. A. Anderson (9) p. 650, D. E. White and Roberson (2) p. 406.

Los Angeles County: **1,** Aragonite was found in Silver Canyon on Santa Catalina Island, CDMG (12415). **2,** Rosettes of aragonite prisms occur on fractures in basalt, accompanied by natrolite and analcime, at locality 7, west of Laurel Canyon, Neuerburg (1) p. 151.

Madera County: **1,** Acicular crystals of aragonite are found in the copper deposit at Beck's Lakes, Goudey (1) p. 7.

Merced County: **1,** Aragonite occurs in veins and replacement patches in the Franciscan rocks in the vicinity of Pacheco Pass. It is sometimes associated with lawsonite, pumpellyite and stipnomelane, B. McKee (2) p. 382. See also Santa Clara County **(2)**.

Mono County: **1,** Aragonite, with low- and high-magnesium calcite, form the pinnacles in Mono Lake, Scholl and Taft (1) p. 56.

Monterey County: **1,** Aragonite specimens from the cliff north of the mouth of Willow Creek are represented by CDMG (21307).

Orange County: **1,** A specimen, CDMG (12658), comes from Coal Canyon, on the west side of Mount Downey (Sugarloaf Mountain).

Placer County: **1,** Aragonite has been doubtfully reported from Gold Run, Hanks (12) p. 73.

Riverside County: **1,** A small amount of fibrous aragonite occurred at Crestmore, Eakle (15) p. 348, and prismatic crystals occur on fracture surfaces of contact rock, Commercial quarry, Murdoch (p.c. '54). **2,** Aragonite in a magnesian calcite-aragonite-huntite assemblage as an incrustation on calcite-monticellite rock at Crestmore, has been described by A. B. Carpenter (1) p. 146.

San Benito County: **1,** Aragonite occurs as bunches and stringers in the country rock of the benitoite vein near the headwaters of the San Benito River, Louderback and Blasdale (5) p. 363.

San Bernardino County: **1,** Aragonite was reported as probable by Silliman (12) p. 130, near Calico. It is likely that the mineral is strontianite, which occurs here rather abundantly. **2,** Clusters of prismatic crystals have been found in the upper quarries near Oro Grande (T. 6 N., R. 4 W., S.B.), Huguenin et al. (3) p. 878. **3,** Aragonite is reported from Holcomb Valley north and east of Big Bear Lake, Mary F. Berkholz (19), p. 14. **4,** Aragonite occurs in very fine-grained nearly pure beds in the Parling Mud, lower salt and mixed layer, at Searles Lake, G. I. Smith and Haines (3) p. 25.

San Diego County: **1,** A cluster of slender prisms, associated with calcite and stilbite, was found in a cavity of the volcanic rock at the Calavera quarry, Murdoch (p.c. '45).

San Francisco County: **1,** Slender colorless prisms of aragonite were found in seams of the serpentine at Fort Point, Eakle (1) p. 316.

San Luis Obispo County: **1,** Aragonite is reported in a road cut on state highway 466, 6.9 miles from Morro Bay, Mary F. Berkholz (15b) p. 25, (CDMG 21586).

Santa Barbara County: **1,** Aragonite occurs in small crystals with chromite in many of the chrome prospects in Happy Canyon, C. D. Woodhouse (p.c. '63).

Santa Clara County: **1,** Aragonite occurs sparingly in the New Almaden area, E. H. Bailey and Everhart (12) p. 102. **2,** Aragonite occurs in veins and replacement patches in the Franciscan rocks in the vicinity of Pacheco Pass. It is sometimes associated with lawsonite, pumpellyite and stipnomelane, B. McKee (2) p. 382. See also Merced County **(1)**.

Siskiyou County: **1,** Aragonite has come from a mineral spring near the Soda Springs Hotel, Hanks (12) p. 73.

Solano County: **1,** Aragonite was reported at Tolenas Springs, Watts (1) p. 668.

Sonoma County: **1,** Needle-like crystals and crusts of aragonite were found in the Helen mine, Kramm (1) p. 345. **2,** Aragonite has been reported as a metamorphic mineral in Franciscan schists near Cazadero (SW ¼ NE ¼, sec. 18, T. 8 N., R. 11 W., M.D.), Coleman and Lee (2) p. 578, ibid., (3) p. 16.

Tehama County: **1,** Crystals of aragonite occur in fracture surfaces of chromite at the Grau pit on Elder Creek, CDMG (21143). **2,** CDMG (11876) is aragonite from Tuscan mineral spring.

Tulare County: **1,** Aragonite specimens have been collected from near Tulare, CDMG (11643), and **2,** from Three Rivers, CDMG (9907).

Tuolumne County: **1,** Aragonite is reported from Table Mountain (N.R.).

†*ARAGOTITE, 1873
A hydrocarbon

This material, no longer recognized by Dana as a mineral species, has been reported from several cinnabar mines. It is related to idrialite.

Napa County: **1,** Aragotite occurred on cinnabar at the Redington mine, Knoxville, Durand (2) p. 218, Hanks (12) p. 289, (20) p. 674. **2,** Hanks (20) p. 674, reports aragotite from the Aetna mine, and gives a partial analysis.

Santa Clara County: **1,** Aragotite was first observed at the New Almaden mine impregating siliceous dolomite, and was described by Durand (2) p. 218, Hanks (12) p. 289, (20) p. 674.

Yolo County: **1,** A specimen of aragotite from the California mine is reported by Hanks (12) p. 289.

*ARCANITE, 1908
Potassium sulphate, K_2SO_4

Orange County: **1,** Eakle (9) p. 233, reported arcanite as a new mineral in yellow crystals from Tunnel No. 1 of the Santa Ana Tin Mining Company in Trabuco Canyon. These are pseudo-hexagonal due to twinning, and apparently are actually orthorhombic; thus the mineral is different from aphthitalite, which it closely resembles. This is the first recorded natural occurrence of this mineral although the artificial compound was known earlier.

ARGENTITE
Silver sulphide, Ag_2S

Alpine County: **1,** Argentite occurs sparingly in a number of mines in the Monitor area, south of Markleeville, associated with polybasite, pyrargyrite, and other sulpho-salts, Conkling (1) p. 184, Eakle (16) p. 13.

Imperial County: **1,** The mineral argentite is reported in a gold-quartz vein, with some silver, in the Mary Lode mine (secs. 14, 15, T. 12 S., R. 18 E., S.B.), R. J. Sampson and Tucker (18) p. 122. **2,** Tucker (11) p. 267, reports argentite from several mines 3 miles southeast of Midway Well.

Inyo County: **1,** Argentite was found with tetrahedrite and stephanite in the Belmont mine, Cerro Gordo Mining District, Tucker (4) p. 283, and **2,** it occurred with stephanite at the Oriental mine in Deep Spring Valley, Hanks (15) p. 93. **3,** The mineral was found at the Cliff mine, Goodyear (3) p. 237, and **4,** it was an important mineral in the Minietta Belle mine, Hanks (15) p. 93. **5,** Argentite with native silver was collected on the southwest border of Saline Valley, T. Warner (1) p. 938. **6,** Masses of argentite are reported from the Darwin Mining District, Kelley (4) p. 543. **7,** Crystals were reported by Aaron from the Kearsarge Mining District, Hanks (12) p. 75. **8,** Ragged masses, matted with quartz crystals and gold, came from the Silver Sprout vein, also from the Kearsarge Mining District, W. P. Blake (14) p. 125. **9,** Argentite is associated with cerargyrite in the Wild Rose Mining District, DeGroot (2) p. 213, and **10,** it is found in the Lee mine 18 miles east of Keeler, Tucker (11) p. 488. **11,** At the Sunrise mine in the Panamint Mining District, Stetefeldt (1) p. 259, reports argentite, and **12,** small amounts of the mineral occur with nickel and cobalt minerals at Long Lake (sec. 14, T. 9 S., R. 31 E., M.D.), Tucker and Sampson (25) p. 378.

Kern County: **1,** Argentite occurs with tetrahedrite and pyrargyrite at the Amalie mine, Crawford (2) p. 605, and **2,** it is found in several mines on Soledad (Butte) Mountain, in the Mojave Mining District, Bateson (1) p. 176, Hamilton and Root (5) p. 157, Tucker and Sampson (21), p. 298, Troxel and Morton (2) pp. 46–109.

Los Angeles County: **1,** Argentite occurred with native silver and arsenates at the Kelsey and O.K. mines, in San Gabriel Canyon 8 miles from Azusa, Irelan (4) p. 47, Storms (4) p. 244.

Mariposa County: **1,** Argentite occurs with pyrargyrite and proustite at the Silver Bar (Bryant) mine 6 miles southeast of Mariposa (sec. 15, T. 6 S., R. 19 E., M.D.), Laizure (6) p. 123, (8) p. 44.

Mono County: **1,** Small amounts of argentite are reported in the Bodie Mining District, Whiting (1) p. 389; and **2,** in the Blind Spring Mining District, Hanks (12) p. 75, with native silver and gold, and **3,** at the Silverado mine in the Patterson Mining District, Sweetwater Range, argentite occurs with gold, native silver and cerargyrite in quartz, Whiting (1) p. 359.

Napa County: **1,** Argentite is reported at the Palisade mine (sec. 24, T. 9 N., R. 7 W., M.D.), northeast of Calistoga, W. W. Bradley (1) p. 270, and **2,** at the Mount St. Helena mine in the same area with cerargyrite, Boalich (4) p. 159.

Nevada County: **1,** Argentite occurs with pyrargyrite and stephanite at the Allison Ranch mine, 2½ miles south of Grass Valley, Lindgren (12) p. 119, and **2,** it was found at the Banner mine, 5 miles east of Grass Valley, Chandler (1) p. 4.

Orange County: **1,** Argentite is reported with argentiferous galena at Silverado (N.R.).

Placer County: **1,** Argentite occurs in gold quartz with a little galena and tellurides, at the Alabama mine 1 mile east of Penryn, Logan (17) p. 11, and **2,** at the Eclipse mine (NW ¼ sec. 17, T. 12 N., R. 8 E., M.D.), ibid. p. 22.

Riverside County: **1,** Argentite was found with carbonates in the Palen Mountains, F. J. H. Merrill (2) p. 526.

San Bernardino County: **1,** Argentite occurs, usually with cerargyrite, in the mines in the New York Mountains, Tucker and Sampson (16) p. 276. **2,** Argentite is reported from the Lava Beds Mining District (T. 7 N., R. 4 and 5 E., S.B.), DeGroot (2) p. 529; **3,** in the mines at Calico, Weeks (2) p. 762, and **4,** found with sulphides in the

Goldstone area, 33 miles north of Barstow, Cloudman et al. (1) p. 805. **5**, Tucker (4) p. 366, reports argentite with cerargyrite at the War Eagle mine 9 miles north of Bagdad.

Shasta County: **1**, Argentite is found with native silver, freibergite and other silver minerals at the Big Dike mine, in the South Fork area (secs. 17, 18, T. 31 N., R. 6 W., M.D.), Laizure (1) p. 526, and **2**, at the Silver King mine, Middletown (sec. 8, T. 31 N., R. 5 W., M.D.), ibid. (1) p. 528.

Tuolumne County: **1**, Argentite occurs with sphalerite in quartz at Frazer's mine, J. B. Trask (1) p. 23.

ARGENTOJAROSITE
Basic silver iron sulphate, $AgFe_3(SO_4)_2(OH)_6$

Kern County: **1**, Argentojarosite is locally abundant in the oxidized zone of the Cactus Queen mine, Mojave Mining District, Troxel and Morton (2) p. 104.

ARSENIC
Native arsenic, As

Inyo County: **1**, Richthofen (3) p. 46, reported native arsenic from the Owens River.

Monterey County: **1**, Arsenic was recorded from the old Alisal silver mine, about 8 miles southeast from Salinas, by W. P. Blake (7) p. 301.

Nevada County: **1**, CDMG (19841) from the Alcalde mine at Dead-man Flat, 4 miles southwest of Grass Valley, carries native arsenic and gold in calcite. **2**, W. D. Johnston, Jr. (2) p. 340, (4) p. 36, observed botryoidal pieces of arsenic, some with free gold, on the 1600 foot level of the Empire mine at Grass Valley.

ARSENIOSIDERITE
Basic hydrous calcium iron arsenate, $Ca_3Fe_4(AsO_4)_4(OH)_6 \cdot 3H_2O$

San Bernardino County: **1**, Arseniosiderite was found by B. N. Moore at the Gallinger-Root (Lee Yim) mine 2 miles northwest of Ludlow, and analyzed by Charles Milton, R. C. Wells (3) p. 117.

ARSENOLITE—White Arsenic
Arsenic trioxide, As_2O_3

Alpine County: **1**, Arsenolite crystals up to half an inch in diameter were formed on the dumps of the Exchequer mine by the addition of water to burning enargite ore, Hanks (12) p. 76. **2**, Arsenolite was also found in small white octahedrons with realgar at the Monitor mine, ibid. p. 344.

San Bernardino County: **1**, Large masses of arsenolite were found at the Amargosa mines, in the sink of the Amargosa River (T. 18 N., R. 7 E., S.B.), W. P. Blake (9) p. 8, (30) p. 292.

Trinity County: **1**, Re-examination of specimens from the pyrrhotite deposit at Island Mountain shows claudetite reported by Landon (1) p. 279 to be in all probability arsenolite; some of the octahedral crystals are as much as 1 mm in size, Switzer (p.c. '49).

ARSENOPYRITE
Iron arsenic sulphide, FeAsS

Danaite is cobalt-bearing arsenopyrite.

Arsenopyrite is very widespread in the gold-quartz veins of the state, usually as one of the minor gangue minerals, often associated with pyrite and chalcopyrite. It is impracticable to list all occurrences, but the mineral is common in the Mother Lode ores, and in the gold deposits of Siskiyou, Shasta and Trinity Counties.

Alpine County: **1,** Well-formed crystals are reported from the old Morning Star mine, near Markleeville, Nichols (1) p. 172.

Amador County: **1,** At the Gwin mine, near Jackson, arsenopyrite was found ". . . in both large and small crystals. The former are particularly prized as they enclose aborescent masses of crystallized gold," F. L. Ransome (9) p. 8.

Calaveras County: **1,** A cobaltiferous variety of arsenopyrite occurs on the Hauselt Patent, 2 miles southeast of Sheepranch (NW $\frac{1}{4}$ NW $\frac{1}{4}$ sec. 22, T. 4 N., R. 14 E., M.D.). It is fine-grained, and on exposure to the air becomes coated with erythrite, Hess (19) p. 451.

Del Norte County: **1,** Arsenopyrite is found in the gold-quartz veins of several mines along Shelley Creek and upper Monkey Creek, Maxson (1) pp. 143, 144.

El Dorado County: **1,** Many of the Mother Lode mines carry some arsenopyrite, Logan (16) p. 34.

Fresno County: **1,** Arsenopyrite is abundant in the Jenny claim (NW $\frac{1}{4}$ sec. 16, T. 13 S., R. 27 E., M.D.), W. W. Bradley (2) p. 446.

Imperial County: **1,** Arsenopyrite is found in the Cargo Muchacho Mining District, Hanks (12) p. 240.

Inyo County: **1,** Arsenopyrite occurs with löllingite, pyrrhotite, and other sulphides in the Wilshire gold mine at the headwaters of Bishop Creek, Schroter (2) p. 53; **2,** with cobalt and silver minerals at Long Lake, Tucker and Sampson (2) p. 378, and **3,** in the Panamint Mining District at the head of Happy Canyon, Murphy (2) p. 317. **4,** Arsenopyrite is a minor mineral in the Darwin ores, Hall and MacKevett (4) p. 59.

Kern County: **1,** Numerous localities in and near the Green Mountain Mining District carry arsenopyrite, Tucker and Sampson (21) pp. 299, 304, 310, 325. **2,** The mineral is common at the Yellow Aster and neighboring mines near Randsburg, Hulin (1) p. 83. **3,** A vein 6 to 12 inches in width was mined for arsenic at the Contact mine (sec. 10, T. 10 N., R. 15 W., S.B.), Tucker (8) p. 368.

Mariposa County: **1,** The cobaltiferous variety, danaite, occurs with erythrite and mariposite at the Josephine mine, Bear Valley, H. W. Turner (12) p. 679.

Mono County: **1,** Arsenopyrite is common in the gold ores of the Sierra Nevada in this county, Mayo (4) pp. 83, 85.

Monterey County: **1,** Arsenopyrite occurs in gold-quartz veins in Los Burros Mining District, Hill (4) p. 327, and **2,** at the head of Chualar Canyon, Laizure (3) p. 28.

Napa County: **1,** Arsenopyrite is found at the Palisades mine 2 miles north of Calistoga, Hulin (p.c. '36).

Nevada County: **1,** The variety danaite occurs in well-formed brilliant crystals up to a quarter of an inch in size, at Meadow Lake, W. P. Blake (14) p. 298. **2,** Arsenopyrite is common but irregularly distributed in the gold veins of Grass Valley and Nevada City, Lindgren (12) p. 118. **3,** Laur (1) p. 1099, observed "pyrite blanche" in radial concretions at Grass Valley.

Placer County: **1,** Arsenopyrite occurs in the Ophir Mining District, Lindgren (7) p. 273; **2,** in the Canada Hill and Dutch Flat Mining Districts, C. A. Waring (4) pp. 340, 350, and **3,** at the Metallic mine near Cisco, it is associated with cobaltite, CDMG (1901).

Riverside County: **1,** Arsenopyrite occurs in crystals replacing löllingite at Crestmore, Kelley (2) p. 141. **2,** The mineral is found in the ore with barite and fluorite at the Cajalco tin mine, West (3) p. 132. **3,** Excellent crystals of arsenopyrite have been collected from a prospect hole near the old Good Hope mine west of Perris, Knowlton (p.c. '57).

San Bernardino County: **1,** Arsenopyrite occurs at the Grand View and other mines in the Ord Mountains, Gardner (1) p. 261. **2,** The mineral sometimes is found in considerable amount in the California Rand mine, Hulin (1) p. 83. **3,** At the American mine (sec. 19, T. 4 N., R. 11 E., S.B.), Tucker and Sampson (27) p. 54 report arsenopyrite.

San Diego County: **1,** Arsenopyrite is found with quartz and pyrrhotite in the gold veins of the Julian Mining District, Donnelly (1) p. 359. **2,** Abundant arsenopyrite occurs in quartz veins of the Willhite group 9 miles east of Descanso, Tucker and Reed (26) p. 12. **3,** Lenses of massive arsenopyrite occur in veins at the Black Mountain mine (sec. 5, T. 14 S., R. 2 W., S.B.), Tucker (10) p. 329.

Santa Clara County: **1,** Minor amounts of arsenopyrite are found in the mercury ores of the New Almaden mine, W. P. Blake (1) p. 439. This report of the presence of arsenopyrite in the New Almaden ores is probably erroneous, E. H. Bailey and Everhart (12) p. 98.

Santa Cruz County: **1,** Small crystals of arsenopyrite are abundantly disseminated in crystalline limestone, at the Pacific Limestone Products (Kalkar) quarry at Santa Cruz, Vonsen (p.c. '36).

Shasta County: **1,** Arsenopyrite is found in the gold ores at a number of localities near the western edge of the county, Averill (4) pp. 12, 50, 57 (cf. Trinity County).

Sierra County: **1,** Arsenopyrite is the principal vein sulphide in the gold ores of the Alleghany Mining District, Ferguson (2) p. 163. **2,** Arsenopyrite rich in gold comes from the Eagle mine, Kanaka Creek, CDMG (7768); **3,** it is associated with tellurides at the North Fork claim, Forest City, Hanks (12) p. 77.

Siskiyou County: **1,** Arsenopyrite is plentiful with pyrite in the massive ore of the Dewey mine near Gazelle, Mining and Scientific Press (29) p. 9.

Trinity County: **1,** Along the eastern edge of the county, near the Weaverville area, arsenopyrite is a moderately common mineral in the gold ores, Averill (10) pp. 28, 42, 64 (cf. Shasta County).

Tulare County: **1,** Arsenopyrite is a minor ore mineral in the mines of the Mineral King Mining District, Goodyear (3) p. 646, Franke (1) p. 436.

Tuolumne County: **1,** The variety danaite is found with erythrite at the Josephine mine, Logan (16) p. 189.

Yuba County: **1,** Arsenopyrite occurs in a gold vein, with chalco-pyrite and tellurides at the California M Lode, in the Dobbins Mining District, 2 miles northwest of Dobbins (T. 18 N., R. 7 E., M.D.), C. A. Waring (4) p. 446.

Additional references to minor occurrences are as follows: *Amador,* F. L. Ransome (9) p. 8; *Calaveras,* Tucker (1) p. 74, Franke and Logan (4) p. 239; *Kern,* Goodyear (3) p. 321, Tucker and Sampson (21) pp. 299, 304, 310, 325; *Mariposa,* R. W. Raymond (8) p. 52; *Nevada,* J. B. Trask (5) p. 86; *Placer,* Hanks (12) p. 77, W. W. Bradley (22) p. 18; *Riverside,* R. J. Sampson (9) p. 513; *Siskiyou,* Averill (5) p. 280; *Trinity,* Averill (4) p. 26.

ARTINITE
Hydrous basic magnesium carbonate, $Mg_2(CO_3)(OH)_2 \cdot 3H_2O$

Fresno County: **1,** Artinite occurs in fine tufts on serpentine rock along White Creek east of Condon Peak, C. A. Noren (p.c. '60).

San Benito County: **1,** Acicular crystals of artinite occur on frac-tures in serpentine at a chrome prospect near New Idria, Dickson and Murdoch (p.c. '54). **2,** Artinite is reported from the Alpine mine, CDMG (21729), (21750). **3,** Artinite also occurs as fibrous aggregates on serpentine from the vicinity of the Florence Mack mine, Oyler (p.c. '59). **4,** Artinite is also found on Clear Creek, Oyler (p.c. '59), CDMG (21730).

ATACAMITE
Basic copper chloride, $Cu_2Cl(OH)_3$

Inyo County: **1,** J. D. Dana (4) p. 786, recorded atacamite from this county. As the Cerro Gordo mine was the best known for rare minerals, it may perhaps have come from this mine. H. E. Pemberton (p.c. '64) points out that Cerro Gordo was not visited by Americans apparently until 1868. This report of atacamite is in an 1868 publica-tion. It is therefore unlikely that the specimen is from this locality.

Kings County: **1,** Atacamite has been reported from Avenal Creek (T. 23 S., R. 16 E., M. D.), W. W. Bradley (29) p. 456. This is a doubtful occurrence.

San Bernardino County: **1,** A specimen from 2 miles southeast of Goffs carried small crystals of atacamite in a vug. This is represented by CDMG (19428), and was identified by Foshag (p.c. '46).

AUGELITE
Basic aluminum phosphate, $Al_2PO_4(OH)_3$

Mono County: **1,** Crystals of this rare mineral up to three-quarters of an inch or more in size have been found in the andalusite ore body of the Champion Sillimanite Company, on the west slope of the White Mountains, Lemmon (1) p. 664. Complex crystals have been described by Pough (1) p. 536, and the x-ray structure has been worked out by Peacock and Moddle (1) pp. 111–113.

AURICHALCITE
Basic carbonate of zinc and copper, $(Zn,Cu)_5(CO_3)_2(OH)_6$

Inyo County: **1,** Aurichalcite occurs with hemimorphite and hydrozincite at the Cerro Gordo mine, A. F. Rogers (7) p. 374, C. W. Merriam (1) p. 43. **2,** It is found in the Defiance mine, in the Darwin Mining District, as fibrous radiating clusters and coatings, with linarite, and is often coated with heminorphite, Murdoch and Webb (14) p. 323, Hall and MacKevett (4) p. 64. **3,** Specimen CDMG (21321) came from one mile east of Dodd Spring, Ubehebe Mining District. **4,** Aurichalcite occurs in blue spherulitic globules on matrix from the War Eagle mine, near Tecopa, Woodhouse (p.c. '54).

Kern County: **1,** Aurichalcite is one of the ore minerals found near Loraine in the Blackhawk mine (SW ¼ sec. 5 T. 31 S., R. 33 E., M.D.) with other lead, copper and zinc minerals, Troxel and Morton (2) pp. 41, 345.

Mono County: **1,** Aurichalcite is found as pale-green fissure fillings in magnetite containing sphalerite, near Topaz. There is no written description of this occurrence except a statement by Eakle (22) p. 143, but it is probably an authentic occurrence.

AUTUNITE
Hydrous calcium uranium phosphate, $Ca(UO_2)_2(PO_4)_2 \cdot 10-12H_2O$

Meta-autunite I ($8H_2O$) and meta-autunite II (zero H_2O to $6\frac{1}{2}H_2O$) are not known in nature.

Imperial County: **1,** Autunite or torbernite is reported from a prospect 10 miles NE of Glamis, in metamorphic rocks, G. W. Walker et al. (5) pp. 10, 26.

Inyo County: **1,** Autunite is reported as occurring disseminated in clay beds, on the Green Valley claim (N ½ sec. 25, T. 19 S., R. 37 E., M.D.), Anon. (27) p. 5. New information on this occurrence shows the claim to be the "Green Velvet", and to have autunite coating conchoidal fracture surfaces in light gray clay, in beds of clay and tuffaceous sandstone, G. W. Walker et al. (5) pp. 10, 35. **2,** Autunite is reported from near Olancha (CDMG 21634). **3,** A little autunite has been found in Zinc Hill, Darwin area, Hall and MacKevett (4) p. 64.

Kern County: **1,** A specimen showing crusts of autunite from the Summit Diggings is in the University of California collections at Berkeley, and is probably the same as the one referred to by Hanks (15) p. 8, as from the Randsburg area; see also Anon. (25) p. 14. Additional data confirm the identity of this occurrence as the Chilson property in the Summit Range, 6 miles north of Randsburg (sec. 36 (?), T. 28 S., R. 40 E., M.D.). The autunite occurs as yellow crystals on joint surfaces and in small cavities in the Red Mt. volcanics, with torbernite, G. W. Walker et al. (5) p. 19. **2,** Autunite and meta-autunite occur at the Rosamond prospect (N ½ sec. 25, T. 10 N., R. 13 W., S.B.), 10 miles south of Mojave, G. W. Walker (1) p. 3. **3,** Autunite and torbernite have been found on the property of the Miracle Mining Company, near Miracle Hot Springs, in Kern Canyon, Anon. (26) p. 18, Troxel and Morton (2) p. 333. **4,** Autunite is reported in iron oxides from the Bluett property (NE ¼ sec. 9, T. 10 N., R. 13 W., S.B.), G. W.

Walker et al. (5), p. 17. **5,** Autunite with gummite (?), iron and manganese oxides, quartz and clay is found in a fault zone 6 miles SSE of Tehachapi (Buster Tom claims, sec. 8, T. 11 N., R. 14 W., S.B.), G. W. Walker et al. (5) p. 17. **6,** The mineral is found 1½ miles west of the Miracle mine and 3 miles west of Miracle Hot Springs (sec. 25 (?), T. 27 S., R. 31 E., M.D.). The autunite is carried in an iron-stained breccia zone, and is similar to the autunite from the Miracle mine, locality **(3)**. The prospect is known as the Wayne Case property, G. W. Walker et al. (5) p. 30, MacKevett (2). **7,** From the Kergon group of claims (sec. 20, T. 27 S., R. 32 E., M.D.) autunite is reported with fluorite and a molybdenum-bearing mineral in faults and fractures in granodiorite, G. W. Walker et al. (5) pp. 11, 30, MacKevett (2). In this property, autunite is the principal uranium mineral, Troxel and Morton (2) p. 330. **8,** From the Kervin claim, near Penyon Creek, CDMG (21611), autunite occurs in minor amounts. The material is found in a shear zone on a granite-metasedimentary contact, 9½ miles SE of Weldon (sec. 23, T. 27 S., R. 35 E., M.D.), with torbernite, G. W. Walker et al. (5) p. 31, MacKevitt (2), (CDMG 21612). **9,** Autunite sparsely coats fracture surfaces in altered rhyolite in the Middle Butte mine, 8 miles SW of Mojave (sec. 16, T. 10 N., R. 13 W., S.B.), in a former gold mine, G. W. Walker et al. (5) p. 17. **10,** Autunite was found after an aerial survey of the Mojave Mining District where an anomaly appeared in section 10. A shaft was sunk in which autunite coatings were found on fracture surfaces in an andesite porphyry dike and in quartz monzonite, G. W. Walker et al. (5) p. 15. **11,** The mineral has been identified from the Stillwell property (sec. 35, T. 10 N., R. 13 W., S.B.), 5 miles NW of Rosamond, G. W. Walker et al. (5) p. 15. **12,** Specimens from the Surprise claim, near McKittrick (CDMG 21649, and CDMG 21631). This property is briefly described by G. W. Walker et al. (5) p. 33 (sec. 3, T. 30 S., R. 21 E., M.D., called Surprise No. 1 claim), as carrying "honey-yellow secondary, uranium minerals" but the identity as autunite is not confirmed. **13,** Meta-autunite, coating fractures in granodiorite, is reported in the Verdi Development Company property (sec. 36, T. 10 N., R. 13 E., S.B.), G. W. Walker et al. (5) p. 15. **14,** Autunite is found with gummite (?) in fractures in rhyolite, at the Jumpin claim (secs. 9, 10, T. 9 N., R. 13 W., S.B.), 5¼ miles WNW of Rosamond, G. W. Walker et al. (5) p. 15. **15,** Autunite is reported from the Breckinridge area, (CDMG 21612). **16,** Autunite occurs at the Monte Cristo prospect with carnotite, MacKevett (2) p. 213. **17,** Autunite is the principal uranium mineral at the Owen group of claims (sec. 4, T. 32 S., R. 22 E., M.D.) in the Temblor Range, Troxel and Morton (2) p. 335. **18,** Autunite occurs in the Miller Ranch deposit 6 miles north of Cantil (SE ¼ sec. 1, T. 30 S., R. 36 E., M.D.), Troxel and Morton (2) p. 333.

Lassen County: **1,** Autunite comes from Siskon Mining Lease near Doyle, (CDMG 21658).

Los Angeles County: **1,** Autunite, with other secondary uranium minerals, occurs as fracture coatings in deeply weathered granite on the Rafferty property, 25 miles east of Lancaster (sec. 26, T. 7 N., R. 8 W., S.B.), G. W. Walker et al. (5) p. 20.

Riverside County: **1,** Autunite is reported from Joanna No. 2 mine, near Blythe, (CDMG 21628).

San Bernardino County: **1,** Specimens of yellow autunite with green plates of torbernite are reported to have come from the northeastern part of the county. There is not written description of this occurrence beyond a statement in Eakle (22) p. 238, but it is probably authentic. **2,** Autunite is reported from near Barstow, (CDMG 21647). **3,** The mineral is reported, probably with carnotite, as coatings and fractures in lake beds from the Harvard Hills (T. 10 N., R. 3 E., S.B.), 9 miles east of Yermo, G. W. Walker et al. (5) p. 20. It is probable that localities (**2**) and (**3**) are the same.

San Luis Obispo County: **1,** Autunite specimens come from the Wakefield property near Pozo, (CDMG 21623); **2,** from near Fellows, (CDMG 21651); **3,** from Sunset claim, near Taft, (CDMG 21648); **4,** from the Geeslin and Fiscus property, 3 miles SSW of Taft, with secondary uranium minerals as coatings on siltstones and shale, (sec. 34 (?), T. 32 S., R. 23 E., M.D.), G. W. Walker et al. (5) p. 34.

Trinity County: **1,** Autunite is reported from the county, (CDMG 21622).

Tulare County: **1,** Goodwin (1) p. 369, states: ". . . uranium- and thorium-bearing minerals which have been identified in Tulare County include xenotime, euxenite, torbernite, autunite, and uraninite."

Tuolumne County: **1,** Autunite has been observed from Sonora Pass area, CDMG (21644).

AWARUITE—Terrestrial Nickel-Iron
Native alloy of nickel and iron, with greater than 60% nickel

Del Norte County: **1,** Awaruite has been found as small (0.15–1.5 mm) rounded grains in the heavy residues of sands of the South Fork, Smith River, Jamieson (1) p. 414.

AXINITE
Basic aluminum calcium borosilicate with iron and manganese,
$Ca_2(Mn,Fe)Al_2BSi_4O_{15}(OH)$

Amador County: **1,** Crystals to 1 inch long were found in a vein cutting limestone in a quarry on the Allen Ranch, 4 miles west of Martell, Bowen (p.c. '55).

Butte County: **1,** Abundant loose crystals of axinite and clusters of crystals, plum-colored and of the usual platy habit, were found in the gold placers of Yankee Hill, Wilke (p.c. '36).

El Dorado County: **1,** Small clear brown crystals of axinite with many faces were found on epidote at the old Cosumnes copper mine 3 miles northeast from Fairplay, Schaller (18) p. 42. **2,** Thin-bladed masses of violet-colored axinite occur in veins on the northeast side of Lily Lake (T. 12 N., R. 17 W., M.D.), Clark (p.c. '36).

Inyo County: **1,** Axinite was reported from the Funeral Range, Kunz (24) p. 96. **2,** Perfectly formed small white crystals of axinite were found with smithsonite at the Ubehebe mine, Eakle (22) p. 188. **3,** A specimen of axinite, with well-developed crystals, in epidote (CDMG 21320) comes from the south end of Hidden (Butte) Valley, Ubehebe

Mining District. Additional data from McAllister (4) p. 53 on localities (2) and (3) suggest that ". . . Butte Valley is another name for Hidden Valley . . . the locality of the later find (3) is perhaps the same . . . but is probably not at Ubehebe mine, which is 6 miles toward the northwest and in other mountains." **4,** Axinite has been doubtfully reported from Sheppard Canyon, 14 miles west of Ballarat, (CDMG 21192). **5,** Coarse-grained axinite occurs in calcite marble very near a contact with intrusive quartz monzonite, west of Hidden Valley, as purplish aggregates of platy crystals up to an inch in length, McAllister (4) p. 53.

Kern County: **1,** Bladed subhedral crystals of plum- to brownish-blue axinite occur in a contact zone on the south fork of Erskine Creek (sec. 6, T. 28 S., R. 33 E., M.D.), Murdoch and Webb (11) p. 552. **2,** Small plum-colored crystals of axinite with massive wollastonite are found in a contact deposit on the Rademacher-Terese siding of the Owens Valley Branch of the Southern Pacific Railroad (T. 27 S., R. 39 E., M.D.), Murdoch and Webb (11) p. 553.

Madera County: **1,** Large violet-colored crystals, some of gem quality, with accessory sphene, occur in a small pegmatite about 5 miles northeast of Coarse Gold, W. W. Bradley (29) p. 310, Over (p.c. '45).

Marin County: **1,** Crystals of axinite with associated prehnite are found in the hills around the Stinson Ranch, Vonsen (p.c. '45).

Mono County: **1,** Plum-colored crystals up to 1 inch in size occur in vugs and fissures in metamorphic rock 200 yards northwest of the southern shore of a large unmapped lake at the southeast base of Mount Baldwin, Chelikowsky (p.c., '36).

Monterey County: **1,** Pale lavender crystals of axinite occur with epidote and quartz in metamorphosed serpentine, at Lime Kiln Creek, Chesterman (p.c. '51).

Placer County: **1,** Massive crystalline axinite in epidote rock has come from the north summit point of a ridge south of Five Lakes (sec. 7 (?), T. 15 N., R. 16 E., M.D.), Wood (p.c. '36).

Riverside County: **1,** Very large purple crystals have been collected from the old City quarry, North Hill, Riverside, A. F. Rogers (7) p. 378. **2,** Thin purple blades of axinite have been found in some of the Crestmore pegmatites, Woodford et al. (10) p. 358.

San Bernardino County: **1,** Axinite has been collected in the Owl (Owl Hole) Mountains, Kunz (24) p. 96. **2,** Axinite occurs with zoisite in the Henshaw quarry (SE ¼ sec. 33, T. 1 S., R. 5 W., S.B.), Cooney (p.c. '53).

San Diego County: **1,** Smoky pink crystals of axinite, brilliant and perfectly transparent, occurred in pockets of a pegmatite (?) with crystalline quartz, at the Freeman mine, near Bonsall (E ½ sec. 27, T. 10 S., R. 3 W., S.B.), Schaller (18) p. 37.

Siskiyou County: **1,** Big, pale-pinkish crystals of axinite occur in a 2- to 6-inch vein, in a road cut near the crossing of the Klamath River, between Yreka and Hornbrook, Vonsen (p.c. '45). **2,** CDMG (20825) is from the Humbug mining area northwest of Yreka, W. W. Bradley (23) p. 85.

Tulare County: **1,** Crystals of axinite up to three-quarters of an inch across occur with epidote at the Consolidated tungsten mine, Drum Valley, Noren (p.c. '54).

AZURITE
Basic copper carbonate, $Cu_3(CO_3)_2(OH)_2$

Azurite, chrysocolla, malachite, and other blue, blue-green, and green minerals, mostly copper-bearing, are widespread in stringers, coatings, and alterations associated with other copper minerals referenced in this volume. No systematic effort to report all occurrences of these minerals is practical. However, many minor occurrences are reported, and others omitted, because early literature was often to minor localities, and they have been retained for clarity of the historic record.

Although not as common as malachite, azurite is nevertheless widespread in its occurrence, often merely as blue stains or coatings in deposits of copper, or with ores containing even traces of copper minerals.

Calaveras County: **1,** Fine specimens of azurite and malachite have come from the Hughes mine, W. P. Blake (9) p. 8. **2,** Azurite has been found in the mines at and near Copperopolis, Hanks (12) p. 77, Reid (3) p. 398, and in other mines of the county.

El Dorado County: **1,** Good specimens of azurite have been found at the Alabaster Cave, Consumnes, and other mines in the Foothill copper belt, Aubury (4) p. 213, Tucker (3) pp. 276–278.

Imperial County: **1,** Azurite occurs with malachite at the Volunteer and Cave Man mines (secs. 23, 26, T. 12 S., R. 20 E., S.B.), Tucker (11) p. 252. **2,** Azurite is found in the Cargo Muchacho Mining District, Henshaw (1) p. 185.

Inyo County: **1,** Azurite has been found with oxide, silicate and green carbonate of copper at Greenwater, Black Mountains, south of Furnace Creek, C. A. Waring and Huguenin (2) p. 70. **2,** A little azurite was found in the Panamint Mining District, Murphy (2) p. 322. **3,** Azurite occurs with anglesite, bindheimite, and malachite at the Modoc mine, Hanks (12) p. 71, and **4,** in the Cerro Gordo Mining District, ibid. p. 71. **5,** Azurite is one of the oxidized copper minerals in the Darwin Mining District, Hall and MacKevett (4) p. 64.

Kern County: **1,** Azurite is found with sulphides and oxides at the Greenback mine, near Woody, Storms (13) p. 635.

Lake County: **1,** Azurite occurs with malachite at the Copper Prince mine 4 miles northwest of Middletown (sec. 19, T. 11 N., R. 7 W., S.B.), Aubury (1) p. 138.

Los Angeles County: **1,** Azurite was discovered on the east end of Santa Catalina Island, Mining and Scientific Press (5) p. 263.

Madera County: **1,** Azurite is found at the old Buchanan and Ne Plus Ultra mines near Daulton (T. 8 and 9 S., R. 18 E., M.D.), Aubury (11) pp. 218, 220.

Mariposa County: **1,** Many mines in the county carry minor amounts of azurite, J. R. Browne (4) p. 27, Aubury (1) pp. 204–213, Liebenam (1) p. 543. **2,** Fine crystals have been reported from the Hawlington area (N.R.).

Mendocino County: **1,** Azurite is reported from the Redwood Copper Queen (secs. 17, 20, T. 12 N., R. 13 W., M.D.), Aubury (1) p. 137.

Modoc County: **1,** Azurite is found at the Seitz mine, 7 miles southwest of Fort Bidwell, Tucker (3) p. 241.

Mono County: **1,** Aggregates of small crystals of azurite came from the Diana mine, A. W. Jackson (3) p. 371. **2,** The mineral was reported from the Detroit mine, Jordan Mining District, with malachite and cuprite, Whiting (1) p. 364. **3,** Azurite occurs sparingly at the Kerrick mine, Blind Spring Hill, A. L. Ransome (2) p. 190, and **4,** at Copper Mountain, 16 miles southwest of Bodie, ibid. p. 120.

Monterey County: **1,** Azurite is found with arsenopyrite on the Riley Ranch at the head of Chualar Canyon, Laizure (3) p. 28.

Nevada County: **1,** Azurite occurs with malachite at the Zinc House mine, near Empire Ranch, Aubury (1) p. 27.

Placer County: **1,** Azurite is reported from the Algol mine (sec. 9, T. 13 N., R. 7 E., M.D.), near Auburn, Aubury (1) p. 173. **2,** The mineral was found by Silliman (7) p. 351, with oxides and sulphates in the Valley View mine at Whiskey Hill, near Lincoln.

Plumas County: **1,** Azurite is found at various properties near Taylorsville (secs. 1, 11, 12, T. 24 N., R. 11 E., M.D.), Averill (8) p. 93.

Riverside County: **1,** Azurite is found at Crestmore in small amount, Eakle (15) p. 353. **2,** In the McCoy Mountains and Palen Mountains, F. J. H. Merrill (2) p. 525, reports azurite. The mineral occurs **3,** at the Black Eagle mine, Eagle Mountains, Tucker (8) p. 195, and **4,** at the Lost mine, Pacific mining area, Orcutt (2) p. 903.

San Bernardino County: **1,** Azurite is abundant with chrysocolla in the silver ores of the Calico Mining District, Weeks (2) p. 762. **2,** The mineral occurs in many of the mining areas of the county, in small amounts: Clark Mountains, Tucker (4) p. 339; Ord Mountains, Tucker and Sampson (28) p. 237; Signal, Old Dad Mountain, and Bumper claims, Cloudman et al. (1) p. 785; Whipple Mountains, Calarivada, and Halloran Springs, Tucker and Sampson (17) pp. 266, 269, 273; Shadow Mountain, Tucker (4) p. 341. **3,** Azurite crystals occur in druses in the Brilliant claim at the Ord Mountain mine, Weber (3) p. 27.

San Diego County: **1,** Azurite occurs with chalcopyrite and malachite at the Daley mine (sec. 11, T. 13 S., R. 1 E., S.B.), Tucker (8) p. 370.

Santa Barbara County: **1,** A small amount of azurite was found at the Laguna Ranch mine (3 miles west of sec. 5, T. 7 N., R. 29 W., S.B.), Cloudman et al. (1) p. 735.

Santa Clara County: **1,** Azurite occurs at the Hooker Creek mine, 7 miles south of Los Gatos, Huguenin and Castello (4) p. 184; **2,** it occurred with crystallized cinnabar in calcite at the Guadalupe mine, Kunz (24) p. 107.

Shasta County: **1,** Native copper, sulphides and azurite are reported in the Greenhorn mine, French Gulch Mining District (sec. 6, T. 32 N., R. 7 W., M.D.), Tucker (9) p. 433; **2,** at Bully Hill, Diller (7) p. 128, and **3,** at the Peck mine, Copper Hill, CDMG (800).

Siskiyou County: **1,** Azurite is found in minor amounts in gold veins of the Bonanza mine near Honolulu, Logan (8) p. 433; **2,** in the cliffs above the glacier on the north side of Mount Caesar, at the head of Little South Fork, Salmon River, Goudey (p.c. '36).

Sonoma County: **1,** Small amounts of azurite are present at the Cornucopia mine (secs. 33, 34, T. 12 N., R. 9 W., M.D.), W. W. Bradley (1)

p. 320; **2**, at Altamont (sec. 17, T. 7 N., R. 10 W., M.D.), Aubury (4) p. 167, and **3**, small perfect crystals have been reported 8 miles northeast of Cazadero (N.R.).

Trinity County: **1**, Azurite occurs in small amounts at Island Mountain, Vonsen (p.c. '45).

Tulare County: **1**, Azurite was found with "silver sulphides" at the Deer Creek silver mine 11 miles south of Porterville, Franke (1) p. 462; **2**, at the Hart prospect (sec. 2, T. 15 S., R. 28 E., M.D.), in the Redwood Canyon region, ibid. p. 435.

Tuolumne County: **1**, Azurite is found at the McKay Ranch (sec. 28, T. 1 N., R. 14 E., M.D.), Aubury (1) p. 201.

Ventura County: **1**, Azurite is reported from the Prospect mine near Triunfo, Carter (p.c. '36), and **2**, in the Ventura mine (T. 1 N., R. 18 W., S.B.) at the foot of the south slope of Simi Peak, associated with millerite and pentlandite, Tucker and Sampson (20) p. 257. (Localities (**1**) and (**2**) may be the same.)

*BAKERITE, 1903
Hydrous basic calcium borosilicate, $Ca_4B_4(BO_4)(SiO_4)_3(OH)_3H_2O$

General reference: Kramer and Allen (5).

Inyo County: **1**, Bakerite has been found in a small prospect hole at the entrance to Corkscrew Canyon, in Death Valley, Larsen (11) p. 43, and in many of the side gulches in Corkscrew Canyon, Murdoch (p.c. '54).

Los Angeles County: **1**, A finely crystalline crust on cavities in shale at the Sterling borax mine, Tick Canyon, has been shown by x-ray examination to be bakerite, Murdoch (p.c. '50). The bakerite is covered in part by celestite crystals. Further exploration produced bakerite crystals that were measured on the goniometer, confirming the identity, Murdoch (42) p. 919. Also, well-formed minute crystals of bakerite of two distinct crystal habits have been found associated with howlite masses at the Sterling borax mine, Tick Canyon, Murdoch (p.c. '57).

San Bernardino County: **1**, Bakerite, associated with howlite, was described and named by Giles (2) p. 353, with analyses, from the Borax Consolidated Company mines, at Borate, in the Calico Mountains.

BARITE—Heavy Spar
Barium sulphate, $BaSO_4$

Barite is widespread in many parts of the state. Occurrences of the mineral are very numerous, but few have mineralogical significance. As a mineral resource, barite occurs in considerable quantity in many deposits. In the localities referenced below, no attempt has been made to systematically report commodity occurrences, nor to report the mineral wherever it is mentioned in the literature. Some localities of minor importance and of little general mineralogical interest are noted because they have been carried in early editions of *Minerals of California.* The authors consider it wise to retain these as part of the historical record, but newer and more important localities of the mineral as a mineral resource have not been added, and literature citations to articles on such localities have not necessarily been included. It is emphasized that validation of correct mineral identification in the literature has not been undertaken, so early identifications may be incorrect.

An attempt has been made in the following citations to include at least all localities of unusual mineralogical interest as reported in the literature. A general recent reference to barite in California is F. H. Weber (2).

Alameda County: 1, Crystals of barite from the Leona Heights deposit are in the Stanford University Collections.

Alpine County: 1, Barite is one of the gangue minerals in the Morning Star mine, Hanks (12) p. 78.

Butte County: 1, Auriferous barite was found at the Pinkston mine half a mile south of Big Bend (sec. 8, T. 21 N., R. 4 E., M.D.), H. W. Turner (12) p. 588.

Calaveras County: Barite is found in a number of the gold mines of the county: 1, Satellite Copper mine, Hanks (15) p. 94. 2, Barite is the principal gangue mineral in the Quail Hill (Eagle Copper and Silver) mine, W. B. Clark and Lydon (4) p. 32; granular masses from this locality were reported in early literature, Cronise (1) p. 592, Silliman (7) p. 351 and Huttl (1) p. 62.

Contra Costa County: 1, CDMG (10330) is from Mount Diablo.

El Dorado County: 1, Barite "10 miles above Georgetown" is represented by CDMG (5991).

Fresno County: 1, Drusy barite occurs as fracture or vein fillings in quartzite near Rush Creek (sec. 16, T. 11 S., R. 25 E., M.D.), CDMG (21896).

Humboldt County: 1, Barite occurs in white crystalline veins up to a foot in width at Liscom Hill 8 miles northeast of Arcata, Laizure (3) p. 300. 2, The mineral occurs near Hoopa, CDMG (20938).

Imperial County: 1, In the Paymaster area mines, the mineral occurs as the principal gangue, with argentite (T. 12 S., R. 20 E., S.B.) Tucker (11) p. 267. 2, Small concretions of barite, sometimes hollow and lined with crystals, come from Coolidge Spring, a few miles south of Fish Springs and west of the old highway, Murdoch (p.c. '45).

Inyo County: 1, Veins of barite occur in the Alabama Hills, near Independence, Hanks (12) p. 78, (15) p. 94, W. W. Bradley (12) p. 6. 2, Barite occurs with free sulphur at the Defiance mine, Darwin, CDMG (7601). 3, CDMG (7201) came from Bishop Creek. 4, Barite occurs as pure white veins 2 to 5 feet wide in schists and slates in Gunter Canyon, 6 miles northeast of Laws, Tucker (11) p. 512, W. W. Bradley (12) p. 6, Tucker and Sampson (25) p. 481, Bateman (3) p. 83. 5, The mineral occurs as gangue in the copper ores near Greenwater, with one 40-foot ledge at Ramsey, Zalinski (1) pp. 81, 82. 6, Barite occurs in a 6- to 8-foot outcrop in Warm Springs Canyon, Tucker and Sampson (25) p. 482. 7, The mineral occurs with quartz as gangue at the Furnace Creek copper mine, Nicholas (1) p. 1087. 8, The mineral is found at the American mine, west of Zabriskie, C. A. Waring and Huguenin (2) p. 71. 9, Barite is found as gangue in a vein with sulphides and arsenates on Long Lake (sec. 14, T. 9 S., R. 31 E., M.D.), Tucker and Sampson (25) p. 378. 10, Coarse-grained barite is reported by McAllister (4) p. 53, from a vein up to 1 foot in thickness, 1400

feet S. 85° W. of the high point of a ridge behind the Lippincott mine.
11, Barite is an associated gangue mineral in the Darwin ores, Hall and
MacKevett (4) p. 62. **12,** Barite is an important mineral in the quartz
veins of the San Felipe and Santa Maria mines, Cerro Gordo Mining
District, C. W. Merriam (1) p. 60.

Kern County: **1,** Good crystals have been collected from Pine Canyon, north of Mojave, Murdoch (p.c. '45). **2,** Compact, fine grained
barite occurs in the Ritter Ranch (Iron Blossom) deposit (SW ¼ sec. 4,
T. 31 S., R. 33 E., M.D.), Troxel and Morton (2) p. 60.

Los Angeles County: **1,** Barite is the principal gangue mineral of the
silver-cobalt ore in the Kelsey mine, San Gabriel Canyon, Storms (4)
p. 244. **2,** A large outcrop of barite occurs (sec. 23, T. 1 N., R. 9 W.,
S.B.) on the west fork of San Dimas Canyon, F. J. H. Merrill (2)
p. 480. **3,** The mineral is found at the Renton and Black Jack mines
on Santa Catalina Island, Gieser (1) p. 245. **4,** Barite is present in
minor amounts in Felix fluorite mine north of Azusa, CDMG (13031).
5, Extensive veins of barite, with many small crystals and aggregates
appear in the sea cliffs of the Palos Verdes Hills, Rocks and Minerals
(1) p. 120, Schwartz (2) p. 8.

Mariposa County: **1,** Barite with tetrahedrite and triboluminescent
sphalerite occurs in the Fitch mine (sec. 9, 10, T. 4 W., R. 15 E., M.D.),
Eakle (5) p. 30. **2,** A large deposit of barite has been mined about 2
miles west of El Portal, Fitch (2) p. 461, O. E. Bowen and Gray (2)
p. 205. **3,** A large deposit occurs near Jerseydale (sec. 17, T. 4 S., R.
20 E., M.D.), W. W. Bradley (12) p. 7.

Mono County: **1,** Trenching exposed four feet of barite in the Mammoth Lake area (T. 4 S., R. 27 E., M.D.), R. J. Sampson (14) p. 132.
2, Large handsome crystals of barite have been found at the andalusite
deposit in the White Mountains, Woodhouse (p.c. '45). **3,** At the extreme northern tip of the county, near Coleville, a sizable deposit of
barite occurs, Eakle and McLaughlin (17) p. 141.

Napa County: **1,** Pseudomorphs of quartz after barite have been
found at the Redington mine, Durand (1) p. 211.

Nevada County: There are several large deposits of barite in the
county, as well as some occurrences in gold veins, Hanks (15) p. 94,
Eakle (7) p. 90, Pabst (4) p. 173. **1,** A 15-foot vein has been mined
commercially at the Democrat barytes mine (sec. 24, T. 16 N., R. 10 E.,
M.D.), E. MacBoyle (1) p. 71. **2,** Massive white to creamy barite occurs
at the Spanish barite deposit (NW ¼ sec. 19, T. 18 N., R. 11 E., M.D.),
Logan (20) p. 378. **3,** A large deposit occurs north of the old Spanish
mine, 6 miles from Washington, Logan (7) p. 12. **4,** An extensive deposit is found on the Maguire property at Liberty Hill, 5 miles from
Alta, Stose (1) p. 338. **5,** Barite with gold has been found at the
Malakoff mine, Hanks (12) p. 78. **6,** The mineral occurs at Pine Hill,
as seams in diabase, E. MacBoyle (1) p. 59.

Orange County: **1,** A large deposit of crystalline barite occurs as the
gangue mineral of the cinnabar deposit at Red Hill, Fairbanks (4) p.
118, F. J. H. Merrill (2) p. 516, W. W. Bradley (12) p. 8.

Placer County: **1,** Barite occurs as one of the gangue minerals at
Whiskey Hill, near Lincoln (sec. 26, T. 13 N., R. 8 E., M.D.), Silliman
(7) p. 351.

Plumas County: **1,** Several large lenses of barite occur in slate 5 miles from Almanor (Ohio and Ohio Extension claims) (sec. 5, T. 26 N., R. 8 E., and sec. 32, T. 27 N., R. 8 E., M.D.), Averill (8) p. 92. **2,** Barite was reported by Edman in lead and copper ores in the north arm of Indian Valley, Hanks (12) p. 78. **3,** A vein 2 to 3 feet wide of fine granular barite occurs at the Pinkston Ledge, half a mile south of the highest point of Big Bend Mountain, in the Bidwell Bar area, H. W. Turner (12) p. 558; **4,** from the Diadem lode, ibid., p. 587.

Riverside County: **1,** Barite is one of the gangue minerals, with fluorite and arsenopyrite, in the tin ores at the Cajalco tin mine, West (3) p. 132.

San Benito County: **1,** Veins of barite up to 6 feet in width have been exploited at the Bardin Ranch, on the southwest flank of Gabilan (Fremont) Peak, W. W. Bradley and Logan (7) p. 625, O. E. Bowen and Gray (2) p. 40.

San Bernardino County: **1,** Barite occurs as gangue in the silver ores of the Calico Mining District, Tucker and Sampson (17) p. 358, Lindgren (1) pp. 721, 725. **2,** The mineral is abundant in veins in and around Lead Mountain (T. 10 N., R. 1 W., S.B.), near Barstow, Tucker (4) p. 334, (8) p. 199, Durrell (7) p. 7. **3,** Barite occurs north and northwest of Barstow, Tucker and Sampson (17) p. 371, (9) p. 254. **4,** Microscopic crystals of barite have been found in the bones of the fossil beds, 6 miles northeast of Barstow, Howard (1) p. 120. **5,** A series of parallel veins of barite occur in basalt 3 miles north of Ludlow in the Hansen deposit (T. 8 N., R. 8 E., S.B.), W. W. Bradley (12) p. 54, Durrell (7) p. 5. **6,** A 3-foot vein of barite occurs in limestone 12 miles east of Victorville (T. 6 N., R. 2 W., S.B.), Tucker and Sampson (17) p. 279. **7,** Nodular barite with celestite in clay shales comes from Owl Holes (sec. 23, T. 18 N., R. 3 E., S.B.), Murdoch and Webb (11) p. 550. **8,** Stringers up to 12 inches occur at Foshay Pass, 26 miles southeast of Kelso, Tucker (4) p. 334. **9,** Barite occurs with calcite as the gangue of lead ores in the Lava Beds Mining District, Tucker and Sampson (17) p. 351. **10,** Two- to six-inch stringers of barite on a limestone schist contact are found 2 miles southeast of Afton, Tucker (4) p. 334. **11,** Barite, largely massive, forms a large proportion of the minerals of the bastnaesite locality at Mountain Pass, Olson et al. (3) p. 34. **12,** Barite is abundant as a gangue mineral in the Josephine Ledge, the Brilliant Ledge and in other mines in the Ord Mountains, F. H. Weber (3) p. 25.

San Francisco County: **1,** Tabular crystals occur in seams in the serpentine of Fort Point, San Francisco, Eakle (1) p. 316.

San Luis Obispo County: **1,** A one- to two-foot vein of barite occurs on the Fugler Ranch, 6 miles southeast of Arroyo Grande, Franks (2) p. 410. **2,** Rosettes of "sand barite" crystals have been found in limey sandstone in the Cuyama Valley, J. W. Eggleston (p.c. '36). A specimen from the Caliente Range about 10 miles south of Taylor Springs, CDMG (21298), is from this occurrence.

Santa Barbara County: **1,** A 20-foot vein of white barite occurs on the north fork of La Brea Creek (secs. 5, 6, T. 10 N., R. 30 W., S.B.), about 20 miles northeast of Sisquoc, W. W. Bradley (12) p. 55. **2,** Another deposit has been reported on the Sisquoc about 15 miles southeast of Santa Maria, Crawford (1) p. 406.

Santa Clara County: **1,** Barite crystals of unusual habit occurred in seams in the manganese boulder of Alum Rock Park, A. F. Rogers (21) p. 447. **2,** Barite is reported from New Almaden, E. H. Bailey and Everhart (12) p. 102.

Shasta County: **1,** Barite occurs as a gangue mineral in the mines of the Bully Hill Mining District (T. 34 N., R. 4 W., M.D.), Aubury (1) 60, Logan (7) p. 7, Tucker (8) p. 429; **2,** at the Glidden (Loftus) barytes, Tom Neal Creek (sec. 19, T. 38 N., R. 3 W., M.D.), Laizure (1) p. 515, F. F. Davis (8) p. 5; **3,** at the Exposed Treasure No. 1 and 2 claims, 12 miles north of Montgomery Creek (sec. 33, T. 36 N., R. 3 W., M.D.), Logan (9) p. 129, and **4,** near Baird (sec. 29, T. 34 N., R. 3 W., M.D.), ibid., p. 129. In general, barite is an important gangue mineral in the sulphide ores of the East Shasta Copper Zinc area, Albers and Robertson (3) p. 70.

Siskiyou County: **1,** Barite is one of the vein minerals with galena, 3 miles from Callahan on Boulder Creek, Logan (7) p. 181.

Trinity County: **1,** Dark-gray barite comes from about 15 miles below Hay Fork Post Office on the Hay Fork of Trinity River, CDMG (13716). **2,** Barite is found also at the Delta mine, Ferguson (1) p. 43. **3,** Coarsely crystalline barite is mined at the Alwood mine, Denny, F. F. David (8) p. 5.

Tulare County: **1,** An extensive deposit of barite occurs at the Paso Baryta Mines, Ltd., deposit in the southeastern part of the county (secs. 23, 24, T. 24 S., R. 36 E., M.D.), Tucker and Sampson (25) p. 481; **2,** the mineral is found on the Bauman Ranch, 15 miles east of Exeter, Franke (1) p. 431, and **3,** at the Bald Mountain deposit near Rattlesnake Creek on the upper Kern River, Franke (1) p. 431. **4,** Barite was found near Springville, Stoddard (5) p. 1129.

BASSANITE
Hydrous calcium sulphate, $2CaSO_4 \cdot H_2O$

Fresno County: **1,** Bassanite is reported in some nodules of fossilized wood from the Moreno formation, at the head of Escarpado Canyon (NW $\frac{1}{4}$ sec. 7, T. 15 S., R. 12 E., M.D.), Gulbrandsen et al. (1) p. 101.

Inyo County: **1,** Bassanite occurs as thin layers in unconsolidated beds at a depth of 360 feet, in the dry lake near Ballarat, Panamint Valley, in long, snow-white fibers, R. D. Allen and Kramer (1), p. 1266.

San Bernardino County: **1,** Bassanite, in snowy-white, long fibers, is found in drill holes at depths of 365 and 510 feet, in unconsolidated sediments in Danby dry lake (T. 1, 2 N., R. 17, 18 E., S.B.), R. D. Allen and Kramer (1) p. 1266. **2,** Bassanite was identified by x-ray analyses of fossiliferous nodules from the Calico Mts., A. R. Palmer (1) p. 241.

BASTNAESITE
Essentially cerium fluocarbonate, $(Ce,La)(CO_3)F$

San Bernardino County: **1,** Bastnaesite occurs in relative abundance, largely in dolomite breccias associated with syenitic intrusives, along an extensive zone at Mountain Pass, Pray and Sharp (1) p. 1519, Olson and Sharp (1) p. 1467, Anon. (15) p. 1, and (13) p. 2, Glass et al. (5). A comprehensive report on the minerals of the Mountain Pass region is found in Olson et al. (3).

BAVENITE
Basic calcium beryllium aluminum silicate, $Ca_4(Be,Al)_4Si_9(O,OH)_{28}$

San Diego County: **1,** Jahns and Wright (5) p. 31, report bavenite from Pala in very minor amounts. This is presumably the same occurrence reported in 1932 by Schaller and Fairchild (48) p. 409, as pseudomorphous after beryl. A cavity in the pseudomorph is lined with bavenite crystals.

BAYLDONITE
Basic arsenate of lead and copper, $(Pb,Cu)_7(AsO_4)_4(OH)_2 \cdot H_2O$

Riverside County: **1,** Some of the yellow-green coatings from the Commercial quarry, Crestmore, have been identified as near bayldonite, Murdoch (p.c., '56).

San Bernardino County: **1,** Some thin crusts of a yellowish-green mineral on limestone, associated with barite veins 1 mile southwest of Lead Mountain, suspected of being hedyphane, have been shown by x-ray study to be bayldonite, Murdoch and Webb (14) p. 327, Murdoch (p.c. '54).

†BECHILITE
Hydrous calcium borate, $CaB_4O_7 \cdot 4H_2O$

Shasta County: **1,** An incrustation at Lick Springs was called "borocalcite of Hayes," by J. B. Trask (7) p. 61. It may be bechilite or perhaps ulexite. No compound of the composition of bechilite has been found, Palache et al. (11) pp. 347, 365.

BEIDELLITE
Basic hydrous aluminum sodium silicate,
$Al_{2.17}[(OH)_2|Al_{0.83}Si_{3.17}O_{10}]^{0.32-}Na_{0.62}(H_2O)_4$

Los Angeles County: **1,** Beidellite occurs in graphitic schists with sillimanite in the upper part of Elizabeth Lake Canyon, near its junction with San Andreas rift valley, as patches and fracture fillings in feldspar, Beverly (1) p. 352).

Sierra County: **1,** Ferguson and Gannett (6) p. 45, describe as beidellite gray, clayey, microscopically crystalline masses in cavities in veins in the Alleghany Mining District.

BEMENTITE
Basic manganese silicate, $Mn_5Si_4O_{10}(OH)_6$

Manganese minerals like bementite, braunite, hausmannite, inesite, manganite, neotocite, psilomelane, pyrolusite, wad, and others are often not separable by field methods. It is apparent to the authors of this volume that many citations in the literature, especially those prior to 1940, may be incorrect identifications. Abundance of manganese minerals in the State in hundreds of localities makes systematic recording of all localities mentioned in the literature impractical. The following listings therefore may be incomplete, and many that are included are important only to reflect adequately the historic record.

Bementite ". . . . is found with both rhodochrosite and rhodonite, and is in some deposits the main manganese mineral. This mineral varies in color from dark honey yellow to reddish brown to straw color. When coarsely crystalline it is bladed, but most California bementite is finely crystalline and has a waxy luster, which is characteristic, but which inexperienced persons may have difficulty recognizing. The best way to find bementite is to look for weathered fragments of a waxy yellow or brown rock that cannot be scratched with a knife and that grades outward into black oxide,'' P. D. Trask et al. (4) p. 70. Bementite has been reported as one of the chief minerals in primary manganese ore from 19 counties in the state, ibid. p. 68, and the following specific localities are noted:

Alameda County: **1,** Bementite is found in the Arroyo Mocho manganese ore (N.R.), and **2,** at the Bailey mine with inesite and gray rhodochrosite (N.R.).

Calaveras County: **1,** Bementite occurs with rhodochrosite at the Big Little Bear (sec. 24, T. 3 N., R. 11 E., M.D.) and Kellogg (sec. 4, T. 2 N., R. 12 E., M.D.) properties, P. D. Trask et al. (4) p. 60.

Humboldt County: **1,** Bementite occurs with brown neotocite and rhodochrosite, at the Woods (Charles Mountain) mine, 12 miles north of Blocksburg (N.R.).

Mariposa County: **1,** Bementite occurs with oxides and carbonates near Coulterville, P. D. Trask et al. (4) p. 80.

Mendocino County: **1,** Granular pale-brown bementite occurs with neotocite at the Thomas mine, 6 miles northeast of Redwood (N.R.); **2,** it was found with inesite and neotocite at the Mount Sanhedrin deposits, especially in the Rhodochrosite claim at Impassable Rock (N.R.).

Riverside County: **1,** Bementite is found at the Beal-McClellan (SW ¼ sec. 23, T. 5 S., R. 4 W., S.B.) and Elsinore (same, secs. 23, 24) properties, P. D. Trask et al. (4) p. 83.

San Benito County: **1,** Manganiferous chert at the Hawkins mine (sec. 35, T. 11 S., R. 6 E., M.D.) is known to contain bementite, P. D. Trask et al. (4) p. 83.

San Joaquin County: **1,** The Old Ladd mine at Corral Hollow (secs. 2, 11, T. 4 S., R. 4 E., M.D.) carries bementite and hausmannite, W. W. Bradley (32) p. 98.

Santa Clara County: **1,** Bementite occurs at the Jones (NW ¼ sec. 27, T. 6 S., R. 5 E., M.D.) and other properties, mostly in the northeastern portion of the county, with rhodochrosite and oxides, P. D. Trask et al. (4) p. 87.

Stanislaus County: **1,** Bementite is a constituent of the ore from the Cummings lease on the Winship property, where it occurs as granular masses, mixed with gray rhodochrosite and rose-red inesite (N.R.).

Trinity County: **1,** Bementite occurs at the Hale Creek mine (NW ¼ sec. 23, T. 1 S., R. 1 E., H.) in Mad River Valley with inesite, P. D. Trask et al. (4) p. 59; **2,** at the Manganese Queen, Spider, and Lucky Bill properties (sec. 27, T. 30 N., R. 12 W., M.D.), ibid. p. 60, and **3,** with rhodonite and rhodochrosite (sec. 9, T. 26 N., R. 11 W., M.D.), ibid. p. 60.

Tuolumne County: **1,** Bementite occurs with rhodochrosite at the Hughes mine (sec. 17, T. 2 S., R. 15 E., M.D.), P. D. Trask et al. (4) p. 91.

* BENITOITE, 1907
Barium titano-silicate, $BaTiSi_3O_9$

Benitoite was discovered as a new mineral in San Benito County in 1907. It has also been reported as occurring in Belgium in sands in the Owithe Valley, Anten (1) p. B331, and in southwest Texas in Eocene sands, Lonsdale et al. (1) p. 79.

Fresno County: **1,** White benitoite occurs as a minor constituent in a section of drill core taken near Rush Creek (sec. 16, T. 11 S., R. 25 E., M. D.), CDMG (21897). Identification of benitoite was verified by x-ray diffraction and x-ray microprobe analyses of CDMG. Sanbornite, quartz, celsian, witherite, pyrrhotite, and diopside are associated minerals.

Kern County: **1,** Benitoite was found as detrital grains in the heavy mineral fractions from a drill-hole in the Lazard area, Lost Hills (southeast corner T. 27 S., R. 20 E., M.D.), with some piemontite, dumortierite and other minerals, R. D. Reed and Bailey (4) p. 363.

San Benito County: **1,** Colorless and sapphire-blue crystals of this mineral were discovered in 1907 near the headwaters of the San Benito River (sec. 25, T. 18 S., R. 12 E., M.D.). They were originally thought to be sapphire, but were found to be a new mineral and named by Louderback and Blasdale (2) p. 149, (5) p. 331. The crystals occur in a zone of narrow veins of natrolite in serpentine, and are associated with neptunite and joaquinite. The mineral represents the first natural occurrence of the trigonal class, hexagonal system, and its crystals have been studied and measured by various authors: A. F. Rogers (2) p. 616; Palache (6) p. 398; Hlawatsch (1) p. 178, (3) p. 602, (4) p. 293; Baumhauer (2) p. 592; Valeton (1) p. 92. **2,** A second locality for benitoite, close to the original discovery, has been reported, Mineral Notes and News (1) p. 3, Pabst (11) p. 479.

BERTHIERITE
Iron antimony sulphide, $FeSb_2S_4$

Kern County: **1,** Berthierite is reported as fibrous material associated with colemanite from Boron, H. E. Pemberton et al. (1) p. 34.

Tuolumne County: **1,** A dark-colored ore from the southeast slope of Mount Gibbs may contain an impure berthierite with galena and other sulphides, H. W. Turner (12) p. 714. This is a rather dubious occurrence, and it is more than possible that it is not authentic.

BERTRANDITE
Basic beryllium silicate, $Be_4Si_2O_7(OH)_2$

Bertrandite is a rare mineral found in pegmatites associated with beryl.

San Diego County: **1,** Tabular white to light-gray crystals of bertrandite are reported as occurring very rarely on Heriart and Chief Mountains, in the Pala pegmatites, Jahns and Wright (5) p. 31.

BERYL
Beryllium aluminum silicate, $Be_3Al_2Si_6O_{18}$

Aquamarine is a pale-blue to pale-green beryl. *Emerald* is a transparent green beryl. *Morganite* is pink. Beryl is found as crystals, some of which attain great size, in granite pegmatites. Synthetic emerald has been made in California, A. F. Rogers (49) p. 762.

Fresno County: **1,** Beryl has been reported 5 miles northeast of Trimmer (sec. 34, T. 11 S., R. 25 E., M.D.) with topaz, apparently in a pegmatite, W. W. Bradley (2) p. 438; **2,** it has been found in pegmatite just east of Academy (T. 12 S., R. 22 E., M.D.), Noren (p.c. '45).

Inyo County: **1,** Narrow veins with small crystals of opaque blue beryl are found cutting granite about $1\frac{1}{2}$ miles southeast of Lone Pine station, Webb and Murdoch (p.c. '45). This is probably the same locality reported by Sterrett (10) p. 312, as "in the desert between Barstow and Lone Pine," in pale- to dark-blue crystals up to half an inch in diameter. See also M. B. Strong (4) p. 20. **2,** Beryl has also been found with fluorite 3 miles west of Lone Pine, W. W. Bradley (23) p. 396, CDMG (20687).

Lassen County: **1,** Beryl is found with tourmaline and mica at the Mount Thompson gem mine (T. 28 N., R. 13 E., M.D.), north and east of Milford, Melhase (p.c. '40).

Riverside County: **1,** Yellow and pale-green beryl have been found at the Fano mine (NW $\frac{1}{4}$ SW $\frac{1}{4}$ sec. 33, T. 6 S., R. 2 E., S.B.), on the north side of Coahuila Mountain, Kunz (24) p. 49, Fisher (1) p. 68, Tucker and Sampson (35) p. 1965. **2,** The rose-colored variety, morganite, was found near Hemet, Kunz (25) p. 942. **3,** Blue and green crystals of beryl up to half an inch in length occur in a small pegmatite just west of the Jensen quarry 4 miles west of Riverside, Clark (p.c. '36). **4,** A considerable quantity of blue-green beryl, some of gem quality, is found 2 miles east of Riverside on the Mears property at the base of Box Springs Mountain, Sterrett (3) p. 799. **5,** Beryl, some of it aquamarine, has been collected from the S. P. Silica quarry near Nuevo, Knowlton (p.c. '57).

San Diego County: Beryl, sometimes in large and beautiful crystals, has been found in most of the gem-pegmatite dikes of this county. **1,** A pale rose crystal (morganite) came from a pegmatite mine on Aguanga Mountain near Oak Grove (probably the Mountain Lily), and measured 11 by $7\frac{1}{2}$ by $6\frac{1}{2}$ cm, Kunz (24) p. 49. Pink beryl from here showed 1.60 percent cesium oxide on analysis, F. W. Clarke (10) p. 309. **2,** Morganite was found in the Katerina (Catherina) and other mines on Heriart Hill, Pala, Kunz (23) p. 942, (24) p. 81, (26) p. 1345. This beryl carried 0.57 percent of cesium oxide, W. E. Ford (6) p. 128, Jahns and Wright (5) p. 37. **3,** At Mesa Grande, the Himalaya and Esmeralda mines produced pink, golden, and aquamarine beryl, Kunz (24) p. 49. One group of pink beryl from the Esmeralda mine showed tabular crystals $1\frac{1}{2}$ inches across, Kunz (26) p. 1340. **4,** At the Mack mine, Rincon (sec. 25, T. 10 S., R. 1 W., S.B.), there were pink and deep opaque blue beryls, Kunz (24) p. 49, and some clear, complexly etched crystals, Eakle (7) p. 89, A. F. Rogers (4) p. 212, Hanley (3) p. 14. **5,** At Ramona, in the A.B.C., Surprise, and other mines, variously colored beryl has been found, including morganite, Kunz (24) p. 49, Eakle (6) p. 89. W. E. Ford (4) p. 217, has observed some remarkable etching on yellow crystals from this locality. **6,** Pink and green beryls associated with essonite garnets are reported from the Crystal mine $8\frac{1}{2}$ miles northwest from Jacumba, Kunz (24) p. 49. **7,** Beryl in crystals up to two feet were discovered near Tule Mountain in pegmatite dikes which also carry purpurite (?), Weber (1) p. 8.

Trinity County: **1,** Pink crystals have been found in placer deposits near Hamburg, Smith (p.c. '36), CDMG (20685), and have been identified as beryl by Sperisen and Melhase. **2,** Emerald-green crystals have come from J. Carr's mine, Coffee Mining District, CDMG (15550).

Tuolumne County: **1,** Several small green beryl crystals, one doubly terminated, were found 3 or 4 miles from Jamestown, W. P. Blake (3) p. 84, Petar (1) p. 90.

BETAFITE
Basic oxide of uranium calcium niobium tantalum titanium and other rare earth elements, (Ca,Ce,Y,U,Cb) $(Nb,Ti,Ta)_2(O,OH)_7$

San Bernardino County: **1,** Betafite occurs as small octahedral crystals, associated with cyrtolite, in a mass of dark minerals, mostly biotite and magnetite, in a pegmatite in the Cady Mountains, north of Hector, Hewett and Glass (3) p. 1048. The crystals, some of which are 6 mm in diameter, are partially altered, with a crust of an unidentified mineral; see also G. W. Walker et al. (5) p. 21

BETA-URANOPHANE—Beta-uranotil
Hydrous basic calcium uranium silicate, $Ca(UO_2)_2(SiO_3)_2(OH)_2 \cdot 5H_2O$

Inyo County: **1,** Beta-uranophane (reported as beta-uranotil) is found in the county, CDMG (21645).

San Bernardino County: **1,** Beta-uranophane (reported as beta-uranotil) is recorded with uranophane from the New Method mine (Hope uranium prospect) Bristol Mts., near Amboy, Chesterman and Bowen (6) p. 1679.

BEYERITE
Carbonate of bismuth and calcium, $Ca(BiO)_2(CO_3)_2$

San Diego County: **1,** Compact masses of greenish-gray beyerite, as an alteration product of an earlier bismuth mineral, were found in the Stewart mine at Pala, Frondel (3) p. 533.

BIEBERITE
Hydrous cobalt sulphate, $CoSO_4 \cdot 7H_2O$

. San Luis Obispo County: **1,** Bieberite occurs as an alteration of Linnaeite in the Klau quicksilver mine, Santa Lucia Range (sec. 33, T. 26 S., R. 10 E., M.D.), Woodhouse and Norris (6) p. 114.

Trinity County: **1,** Small amounts of bieberite as a pale rose-red powder, occur with other alteration products on pyrrhotite at the Island Mountain deposit, Landon (1) p. 279.

BINDHEIMITE
Hydrous basic oxide of lead and antimony, $Pb_{2-y}Sb_{2-x}(O,OH,H_2O)_{6-7}$

Bindheimite is very widely distributed in oxidized ores and is much more abundant than was commonly believed in antimony-bearing ores of lead and silver, Shannon (1) p. 88.

Fresno County: **1,** Brown bindheimite has been described from this county, Larsen (11) p. 47, and a green opal-like specimen is in the University of California Collections at Berkeley.

Inyo County: **1,** Bindheimite is a common oxidation product in lead ores at the Cerro Gordo mine, Hanks (12) p. 71, A. Knopf (8) p. 114, C. W. Merriam (1) p. 43. **2,** Murphy (2) p. 322, has found bindheimite in the Panamint Mining District. **3,** Bindheimite is mentioned in a listing of minerals from the Darwin Mining District, Hall and Mac-Kevett (1) p. 16, ibid., (4) p. 64. **4,** Bindheimite is present in the ores of the Big Four and Defense mines in the Lookout (Modoc) Mining District, Hall and Stephens (3) pp. 24, 26.

San Bernardino County: **1,** Indistinctly fibrous material from this county, probably pseudomorphous after jamesonite, was analyzed by Shannon (1) p. 93. No detail of locality is given.

Santa Cruz County: **1,** Bindheimite has been confirmed in the suite of minerals found at the Pacific Limestone Products (Kalkar) quarry at Santa Cruz, C. W. Chesterman and Gross (p.c. '64).

BIOTITE
Basic potassium magnesium iron aluminum silicate, $K(Mg,Fe)_3(Al,Si_3O_{10})(OH)_2$

Biotite is the commonest of all the micas. It is a prominent con-stituent of many igneous rocks, and also of pegmatites, gneisses and schists. It is present as a rock-forming mineral in every county. Only a few occurrences are of sufficient interest to record.

Kern County: **1,** Biotite in a pegmatite in granite appears to be radioactive, and is under claim as the Dancing Devil No. 16 (sec. 23, T. 27 S., R. 31 E., M.D.), 7 miles west of Miracle Hot Springs, G. W. Walker et al. (5) p. 30.

Riverside County: **1,** Large, blade-like plates of biotite make a spec-tacular showing on the wall of the Southern Pacific silica quarry near Nuevo, Murdoch (p.c. '45). **2,** Woodford (11) p. 350, records biotite as occurring in the Crestmore quarries in the country rock, in the limestone predazzite rock, and as a constituent mineral of the contact rocks.

San Diego County: **1,** Occasionally large plates of biotite are found in the gem pegmatites at Pala, Schaller (p.c. '36). Some of the biotite from Pala shows cesium and rubidium on analysis, Stevens and Schal-ler (3) p. 528. **2,** Broad plates of biotite are present in the pegmatites at Rincon, A. F. Rogers (4) p. 216.

BISMITE
Bismuth trioxide, Bi_2O_3

San Diego County: **1,** Bismite has been reported at Pala, Kunz (20) p. 398, but Schaller (25) p. 230, considers yellow material from the Stewart mine to have been a mixture of $BiVO_4$ and $Bi(OH)_2$, while the gray material is $Bi_2O_3 \cdot 3H_2O$, hydrous bismuth trioxide. **2,** A yel-low oxidation product of bismuth, at the Victor mine, Rincon, was described by A. F. Rogers (4) p. 208 as including some microscopic crystals. These crystals were shown by Frondel (3) p. 523 to be Bi_2O_3, or true bismite, although the presence of vanadium in the ocherous material here too, was shown by Schaller (25) p. 165, indicating the presence of pucherite, Palache et al. (10) p. 600.

BISMUTH
Native bismuth, Bi

Crystals and veinlets of metallic bismuth sometimes accompany ores of bismuth, cobalt, silver, and gold. Bismuth is also occasionally found in pegmatitic veins.

Inyo County: **1,** Bismuth was found at Antelope Springs, Deep Spring Valley (N.R.), and **2,** doubtfully, at Big Pine Creek (N.R.). **3,** Native bismuth is reported in the silver ore from the Thompson mine, Darwin Mining District, Hall and MacKevett (1) p. 17, ibid., (4) p. 59.

Kern County: **1,** Knowlton (p.c. '57) reports a specimen of native bismuth from a locality between Jawbone Canyon and Havilah.

Mono County: **1,** Bismuth is reported from Oasis (N.R.).

Nevada County: **1,** A notable amount of bismuth was detected in the concentrates of the Providence mine, Nevada City Mining District, Lindgren (12) p. 117.

Riverside County: **1,** Bismuth has been reported from veins southeast of Banning, Sanford and Stone (1) p. 25. This occurrence is doubtful.

San Diego County: **1,** Long irregular crystals of bismuth, sometimes capping tourmaline, have been found at the Stewart mine, Pala, Kunz (20) p. 398; **2,** small bright cleavages occur in lepidolite at the Victor mine, Rincon, A. F. Rogers (4) p. 208. **3,** F. J. H. Merrill (1) p. 670, has reported bismuth from a locality near Jacumba.

Santa Cruz County: **1,** Bismuth is one of the associated minerals in the suite of minerals described from the Pacific Limestone Products (Kalkar) quarry at Santa Cruz, Chesterman (p.c. '64).

Sierra County: **1,** A specimen in the Stanford University Collections is from Slug Canyon.

BISMUTH-GOLD—Maldonite
Au₂Bi

El Dorado County: **1,** A natural alloy, 60 percent gold and 40 percent bismuth, came from the Coon Hollow hydraulic mine near Placerville in 1899, CDMG (15391).

BISMUTHINITE
Bismuth sulphide, Bi_2S_3

Bismuth has frequently been detected in the concentrates from several gold and copper regions, but the form in which it occurs has not in general been determined. Bismuthinite as a distinct mineral has been noticed in only a few localities.

Fresno County: **1,** Some small pieces of bismuthinite and bismutite were found at the Second Sierra and Lot One mines, in the Kings Creek area, CDMG (12856, 12857). **2,** Bismuthinite is reported from about 20 miles north of Trimmer on the Kings River (N.R.).

Inyo County: **1,** A specimen of bismuthinite has come from the Kearsarge Mountains, near Independence, CDMG (14253). **2,** The mineral occurs with barite and scheelite in bismutite from the Fernando mine, Darwin Mining District, L. K. Wilson (1) p. 553; **3,** it occurs also with bismutite from the Tungsten Hills, west of Bishop, Woodhouse (p.c. '46). **4,** Bismuthinite occurs as ocherous masses in a prospect on the west side of Panamint Valley in the Argus Range, near the mouth of Surprise Canyon. Alteration to oxides and carbonates is almost complete, Woodhouse (p.c. '54). **5,** Hall and MacKevett (1) p. 63 and (4) pp. 59, 77, report crystals of bismuthinite up to two inches long in calcite from the Fernando mine.

Kern County: **1,** Bismuthinite has been found in the Big Blue group of mines near Kernville (T. 25 S., R. 33 E., M.D.), Prout (1) p. 413, Troxel and Morton (2) p. 99.

Madera County: **1,** H. W. Turner (12) p. 714, records bismuthinite from Sierra gold and silver mine in the Minarets Mining District.

Mono County: **1,** A specimen from Oasis, CDMG (11467), is bismuthinite with bismutite. **2,** A little bismuthinite occurs in quartz veins with brannerite, 7 miles south of Coleville, in the canyon of the West Walker River, Pabst (13) p. 109. **3,** Bismuthinite has been found in small amount in the Scheelore mine, Rinehart and Ross (2) p. 97.

Riverside County: **1,** Bismuthinite is found at the Lost Horse mine (N.R.).

San Bernardino County: **1,** A few pounds of bismuthinite were found in the United Tungsten copper mine, in the Morongo Mining District (sec. 27, T. 2 N., R. 3 E., S.B.), Hamilton and Root (5) p. 114, Newman (1) p. 241; **2,** it occurs in quartz at the Gold Eagle mine, Morongo Mining District, Tucker and Sampson (17) p. 297.

San Diego County: **1,** A 5-pound mass of bismuthinite was found at Pala, G. A. Waring (2) p. 363.

BISMUTITE
Bismuth carbonate, $(BiO)_2CO_3$

Bismutite is of secondary origin, being derived chiefly from the alteration of bismuthinite and native bismuth. It is sometimes called bismuth ocher. Bismutosphaerite, originally described as a separate species, has been shown to be identical with bismutite, Frondel (3) p. 521.

Fresno County: **1,** Some small specimens of bismuthinite and bismutite came from the Second Sierra and Lot One mines in the Kings Creek area, CDMG (12856, 12857).

Inyo County: **1,** A little bismutite was found in the gold placers of Big Pine Creek, Hanks (12) p. 79. **2,** "Rich ores of bismuth, chiefly carbonate" come from Antelope Spring, on the northwest side of Deep Spring Valley, Goodyear (3) p. 236, Irelan (4) p. 46. **3,** Fibrous to crypto-crystalline specimens of bismutite were found near Lone Pine, Larsen (11) p. 48. There is a specimen from this locality in the University of California Collections at Berkeley. **4,** Bismutite occurs on bismuthinite at the Fernando mine, Darwin Mining District, L. K. Wilson (1) p. 553. Pseudomorphs of bismutite after bismuthinite are reported from the Fernando mine, Hall and MacKevett (1) pp. 63, 64. **5,** Bismutite has been found with tetradymite in a brecciated quartz vein in the Cerro Gordo Mining District, Webb (2) p. 399; **6,** it occurs with bismuthinite from the Tungsten Hills west of Bishop, Woodhouse (p.c. '46).

Los Angeles County: **1,** White earthy bismutite from somewhere in this county is represented by CDMG (16343).

Mono County: **1,** Bismutite occurs with bismuthinite near Oasis, CDMG (11467).

San Bernardino County: **1,** Green needles of bismuth carbonate, up to ⅛ by ¾ of an inch were found at the United Tungsten copper mine, in the Morongo Mining District (sec. 27, T. 2 N., R. 3 E., S.B.), Hess and Larsen (17) p. 261, Tucker (4) p. 374.

San Diego County: **1,** Bismutite was found at Pala as an alteration product of bismuth, Schaller (5) p. 267; and **2,** at the Victor mine, Rincon, it was found with bismite and pucherite, Sanford and Stone (1) p. 25, Palache et al. (10) p. 600.

BLÖDITE
Hydrous sodium magnesium sulphate, $Na_2Mg(SO_4)_2 \cdot 4H_2O$

Imperial County: **1,** A layer of blödite, 6 to 12 inches thick, occurs inter-stratified with thenardite and clay at the Bertram sodium sulphate deposits (N. ½ sec. 19, S. ½ sec. 13, T. 9 S., R. 12 E., S.B.), R. J. Sampson and Tucker (18) p. 140, Ver Planck (3) p. 5.

Inyo County: **1,** Blödite is found as a constituent of saline crusts in Deep Spring Lake, B. F. Jones (1) p. B200.

San Luis Obispo County: **1,** Very large crystals of blödite were found in the mud of Soda Lake, Carrizo Plain (T. 31 S., R. 20 and 21 E., M.D.), H. S. Gale (10) p. 430; the crystals were described by Schaller (32) p. 148.

BÖHMITE
Hydrous aluminum oxide, $Al_2O_3 \cdot H_2O$

Riverside County: **1,** Böhmite occurs at the Alberhill clay pits, associated with gibbsite, V. T. Allen (7) p. 1173.

BOLTWOODITE
Hydrous potassium uranyl silicate, near $K_2(UO_2)_2(SiO_3)_2(OH)_2 \cdot 5H_2O$

San Bernardino County: **1,** Boltwoodite is found very sparingly in the New Method mine (Hope uranium prospect), 6 miles east of Amboy, and 3 miles north of Highway U.S. 66 on the road to Kelso. Uranophane is also found on this property, but it is not in association with boltwoodite, W. C. Oke (p.c. '61).

*BOOTHITE, 1903
Hydrous cupric sulphate, $CuSO_4 \cdot 7H_2O$

Alameda County: **1,** Boothite was discovered as a new mineral with other sulphates of iron and copper at the Alma mine, Leona Heights, Schaller (1) p. 207. The mineral was analyzed by Schaller (8) p. 123.

Calaveras County: **1,** Massive boothite and crystals came from Campo Seco, Schaller (3) p. 192, (8) p. 122.

Santa Barbara County: **1,** Boothite is present in the veins of a small gold prospect near the Tunnel Ranch, Figueroa Mt., C. D. Woodhouse (p.c. '63).

BORACITE
Magnesium borate with chlorine, $Mg_6Cl_2B_{14}O_{26}$

San Bernardino County: **1,** Boracite has been reported from Otis, W. B. Wainewright (1) p. 158.

BORAX
Hydrous sodium borate, $Na_2B_4O_7 \cdot 10H_2O$

The mineral borax, usually accompanied by sulphates of lime and soda, is common at many of the depressions or sinks of the California deserts.

Inyo County: **1**, Borax occurs in many of the playas of the Death Valley area at and near Furnace Creek, **2**, at Resting Springs (T 21 N., R. 6 and 8 E., S.B.), and **3**, Tecopa (approximately T. 20 N., R. 9 E., S.B.), G. E. Bailey (2) pp. 48, 49, Hanks (11) pp. 36, 37. **4**, Borax also is found at Ash Meadows, close to the Nevada line in the southeast corner of the county, Yale (2) p. 1022. **5**, Borax was found in Saline Valley, in 1874, as a borax crust 6 to 24 inches in thickness, Fleming (1) p. 248, Waring and Huguenin (2) p. 62; **6**, the mineral occurs near Fish Slough, in the Bishop Creek area (T. 6 S., R. 33 E., M.D.), 5 to 6 miles from the bridge across the Owens River, Engineering and Mining Journal (5) p. 183. **7**, Some of the muds near Big Pine were reported to carry borax crystals, Yale (2) p. 1023.

Kern County: **1**, Abundant and valuable deposits of massive borax, in layers up to 10 feet in thickness, are found in the Suckow mine at Kramer, and in the mines of the Pacific Coast and Western Borax Companies, associated with colemanite, ulexite, probertite (kramerite), and other borates, with occasional particles of realgar, Schaller (45) p. 164. **2**, At Indian Springs, which is probably the same as Indian Wells (T. 26 S., R. 38 E., M.D.), described as "near Walker's Pass," borax has been found in the playa, G. E. Bailey (2) p. 50, Silliman (12) p. 130. **3**, Borax is reported from Rodriquez Lake (Rogers Lake or Muroc Lake) in the southeast corner of the county, Yale and Gale (4) p. 840, and **4**, also in China Lake (T. 25 S., R. 40 and 41 E., M.D.) partly in San Bernardino County, G. E. Bailey (2) p. 50.

Lake County: **1**, Although the first published record of borax in California was from Borax Lake in 1865, as crystals in the lake muds, Harris (1) p. 450, the compound was detected in the waters of Tuscan Springs in Tehama County, near the mouth of the Pit River, and in the waters of Borax Lake, as early as 1856, by Dr. John A. Veatch, reported by him in a letter to the Borax Company of California dated June 28, 1857, and quoted in J. R. Browne and Taylor (1) p. 179. Here he states that in March 1857, he had found crystals of borax in the underlying muds of the lake bed, ibid., p. 184. **2**, Abundant borax was also found, in solution in the waters of Lake Hachinhama, 4 miles west of Borax Lake, G. E. Bailey (2) p. 52.

San Bernardino County: **1**, A very important source of borax is the basin of Searles Lake, where the mineral is found as an efflorescence on the surface, and in large crystals in drill cores, associated with many unusual saline minerals, H. S. Gale (13) p. 285, G. I. Smith and Haines (2) p. 9. **2**, The mineral has also been detected at Soda Lake, in the sink of the Mojave River (T. 11, 12, and 13 N., R. 8 and 9 W., S.B.), G. E. Bailey (2) p. 62. **3**, A little borax occurs in the playa of Palma Lake 6 miles from Twenty-Nine Palms (secs. 5, 6, 29, 31, 32, T. 22 N., R. 9 E., S.B.), G. E. Bailey (2) p. 62, and **4**, it was found at Borate, in the Calico Hills, G. E. Bailey (2) p. 56.

Siskiyou County: **1,** Borax occurs as an efflorescence, and also in solution at Antelope Creek in the upper Sacramento Valley (T. 44 N., R. 1 W., M.D., approximate), J. B. Trask (7) p. 22.

Tehama County: **1,** Borax was apparently first recorded from California in the waters of Tuscan Springs, John A. Veatch in J. R. Browne and Taylor (1) p. 179.

BORNITE—Erubescite—Peacock Ore
A sulphide of copper and iron, Cu_5FeS_4

Bornite is not as widespread as chalcopyrite, but it does occur abundantly in some copper ores, and in minor amounts in many localities.

Bornite, chalcocite, chalcopyrite, cuprite, galena, marcasite, pyrite, pyrrhotite, stibnite, tenorite, tetrahedrite, and many other antimony, copper, iron, lead and zinc sulfides, and oxides are found in traces or in minor amounts in many localities. The entries listed reflect either mineralogical or historic interest, and the listings are not complete nor is all literature which mentions these minerals referenced.

Calaveras County: **1,** Bornite is found in small amounts in the ores at Copperopolis and Campo Seco, Hanks (12) p. 94.

Contra Costa County: **1,** Bornite occurs in small quantities with chalcopyrite and gold in Mitchell Canyon, Mount Diablo, H. W. Turner (1) p. 391.

Del Norte County: **1,** In the mines at the head of Copper Creek, bornite occurs in minor amounts, Laizure (3) p. 288, Maxson (1) p. 148.

El Dorado County: **1,** In the old Cosumnes mine, near Fairplay (sec. 25, T. 9 N., R. 12 E., M.D.) massive bornite occurred with molybdenite in a coarse pegmatite, Aubury (1) p. 180; **2,** small amounts were found at the Alabaster Cave mine, near Pilot Hill, Aubury (4) p. 211. **3,** A specimen, CDMG (7470) from the Boston mine at Latrobe, shows bornite pseudomorphous after picrolite. **4,** Small flakes of bornite occur scattered though serpentine near Shingle Springs, C. Y. Knight (1) p. 242. **5,** Small amounts of bornite are found at the Pioneer (Lilyama extension) mine, Aubury (4) p. 213, and **6,** at the Voss (Camel Back) mine, (sec. 11, T. 11 N., R. 8 E., M.D.), ibid., p. 407 and **7,** $4\frac{1}{2}$ miles west of Placerville (sec. 15, T. 10 N., R. 10 E., M.D.), Mining and Scientific Press (42) p. 840.

Fresno County: **1,** Bornite occurs with magnetite and free gold in the Uncle Sam mine, on the Kings River opposite Tehipite Dome, Hanks (12) p. 94, W. W. Bradley (2) p. 438.

Humboldt County: **1,** Bornite with native copper was recorded as float at the Red Cap Creek mine (sec. 29, T. 10 N., R. 6 E., H.), Crawford (1) p. 66; **2,** it occurs in schist at the Horse Mountain mine (secs. 33, 34, T. 6 N., R. 4 E., H.), Laizure (3) p. 306.

Imperial County: **1,** Deposits in discharge pipes of a deep well near Niland, show a powder pattern which is possibly that of bornite, D. E. White et al. (1) p. 919.

Inyo County: **1,** Bornite is found sparingly in the mines of the Ubehebe group, Aubury (1) p. 245; **2,** minor amounts are associated with other sulphides at the Bishop Creek mine, Schroter (2) p. 53. **3,** Bornite occurs with tetrahedrite at the Ashford (Golden Treasure) mine west of Shoshone on the east side of Death Valley, Tucker and

Sampson (25) p. 383; **4,** some bornite was reported from the New Discovery mine (T. 20 S., R. 44 E., M.D:), in the Panamint Range, ibid., p. 413. **5,** Minor amounts of bornite occur in the Pine Creek tungsten mine, Bateman (1) p. 238. **6,** A little bornite has been reported in the Darwin ores, Hall and MacKevett (4) p. 59.

Kern County: A little bornite was found with other sulphides at the following properties: **1,** Greenback, Woody Mining District, Storms (13) p. 635; **2,** Exposed Treasure, Mojave Mining District, Simpson (1) p. 409; **3,** Yellow Treasure mine in the Rademacher Mining District, 5½ miles north of Searles, Tucker and Sampson (21) p. 339.

Lake County: **1,** A little bornite has been found in the T.B.M. prospect (sec. 16, T. 12 N., R. 9 W., M.D.), L. L. Root (2) p. 85.

Los Angeles County: **1,** Bornite occurs with molybdenite, and other sulphides, in the Winter Creek group (T. 1 N., R. 11 W., S.B.) on Santa Anita Creek, R. J. Sampson (10) p. 176.

Madera County: **1,** A little bornite ccurs in the Minarets Mining District, Erwin (1) p. 70.

Mariposa County: **1,** Bornite is found sparingly in Cowan and Victoria mines, Hershey (5) p. 592.

Mendocino County: **1,** Considerable bornite was found with lawsonite in a road cut on the new Covelo road, Vonsen (p.c. '36).

Mono County: **1,** Minor amounts of bornite occur in the Tioga, Blind Spring (Benton) and Lake Mining Districts **2,** and in the Sweetwater Range, Whiting (1) pp. 373, 374, 378.

Nevada County: **1,** Bornite occurs with chalcocite and covellite in the Mineral Hill area, Dry Creek (T. 15 N., R. 6 E., M.D.), Forstner (4) p. 745. **2,** Minor amounts of the mineral are found at the Great Eastern (California) mine (T. 18 N., R. 13 E., M.D.) in the Meadow Lake Mining District, Logan (7) p. 359.

Plumas County: **1,** Important amounts of bornite, some forming a microscopic "graphic intergrowth" with chalcocite, are present in the ore of the Engels and Superior mines, Diller (9) p. 47, H. W. Turner and Rogers (32) p. 377, A. F. Rogers (17) p. 587. **2,** A narrow vein of massive bornite was found on A. J. Ford's claim, in Lights Canyon, Hanks (12) p. 94, and **3,** at Surprise Creek (T. 24, 27 N., R. 10 to 12 E., M.D.), Hanks (12) p. 94, Logan (4) p. 462.

Riverside County: **1,** Bornite is one of the many minor minerals at Crestmore, Eakle (15) p. 352.

San Bernardino County: Small occurrences of bornite are widely distributed through the county. Occurrences are represented from: **1,** Calico, Weeks (4) p. 534; **2,** Lava Beds, Storms (4) p. 356; **3,** Ord Mountain, **4,** Monumental, and **5,** Ivanpah Range, Tucker and Sampson (17) pp. 275, 277, 267; **6,** Signal, and **7,** Oro Grande, Cloudman et al. (1) pp. 785, 878; **8,** Dale, Tucker and Sampson (27) p. 79; **9,** Fremont, L. L. Root (2) p. 172, L. A. Wright et al. (5) p. 62. **10,** Bornite occurs as veinlets in quartz vein fragments of the Central Tunnel, Ord Mountain, Weber (3) p. 25.

Santa Clara County: **1,** Hanks (12) p. 94, reports bornite from near Lexington. **2,** One or two occurrences of bornite are reported in the New Almaden ores, E. H. Bailey and Everhart (12) p. 98.

Shasta County: **1,** A little bornite has been found in the Bully Hill, Afterthought, and other mines of the county, Diller (10) p. 12, Tucker

(9) p. 426. **2,** Bornite is a minor mineral in the ores of the East Shasta copper-zinc area, Albers and Robertson (3) pp. 70, 76.

Siskiyou County: **1,** Some bornite was found at the Richie mine on Boulder Creek, $3\frac{1}{2}$ miles southwest of Callahan, Crawford (2) p. 64. **2,** Bornite occurs with minor amounts of covellite and some chalcopyrite at the Preston Peak mine (sec. 22, T. 17 N., R. 5 E., H.), J. C. O'Brien (4) p. 428.

Trinity County: **1,** Some bornite occurs in the pyrrhotite body at Island Mountain, Stinson (1) p. 25.

Tulare County: Several small occurrences of bornite are noted in the county: **1,** Hart prospect (sec. 2, T. 15 S., R. 28 E., M.D.), Franke (1) p. 435; **2,** Powell copper (sec. 30, T. 19 S., R. 31 E., M.D.), Tucker (3) p. 909; **3,** Round Valley, $2\frac{1}{2}$ miles east of Lindsay, ibid., p. 910 and **4,** Oakland mine, Copper Canyon, 12 miles north of Mineral King, ibid., p. 910.

Tuolumne County: **1,** Bornite occurs with cinnabar on the slope of the ridge east of Horseshoe Bend, H. W. Turner and Ransome (15) p. 7. **2,** Bornite occurs with other sulphides in the lower levels of the Oak Hill mine (sec. 30, T. 2 S., R. 14 E., M.D.), Logan (23) p. 54.

BOTRYOGEN
Hydrous basic iron magnesium sulphate, $MgFe^{3+}(SO_4)_2OH \cdot 7H_2O$

Napa County: **1,** Minute aggregates of small bright-red crystals with copiapite, were discovered at the Redington mine, and described by Eakle (3) p. 231 as a new mineral, "palacheite." He later established its identity as crystallized botryogen, Eakle (4) p. 379. **2,** Hulin (p.c. '36) found botryogen at the Palisades mine, 2 miles north of Calistoga.

BOULANGERITE
Lead antimony sulphide, $Pb_5Sb_4S_{11}$

Inyo County: **1,** What has been tentatively identified as boulangerite from the Defiance mine, Darwin Mining District, is represented by a specimen in the University of California Collections at Berkeley.

Mono County: **1,** Boulangerite is found as slender prismatic crystals, with wollastonite and idocrase, in a crystalline limestone on the property of Elias Bushati (S $\frac{1}{2}$ sec. 13, T. 1 N., R. 25 E., M.D.), on the north side of Lee Vining Canyon, Milton (p.c. '44).

Santa Cruz County: **1,** Boulangerite occurs at the Pacific Limestone Products (Kalkar) quarry near Santa Cruz, E. H. Oyler (p.c. '60).

BOURNONITE
A lead copper antimony sulphide, $PbCuSbS_3$

Butte County: **1,** Bournonite is reported with native antimony at the Surcease mine (T. 21 N., R. 4 E., M.D.), J. C. O'Brien (6) p. 431.

Inyo County: **1,** Massive bournonite was found at Cerro Gordo, in the Inyo Range, Reid (2) p. 81.

Kern County: **1,** A mineral doubtfully identified as bournonite has been found in the Mojave Mining District, Schroter (1) p. 187. However, it is suggested that this might be jamesonite rather than bournonite.

BOUSSINGAULTITE—Cerbolite
Hydrous ammonium magnesium sulphate, $(NH_4)_2Mg(SO_4)_2 \cdot 6H_2O$

Sonoma County: **1,** Boussingaultite is abundant among the sulphate minerals as crusts and stalactites at The Geysers, near Cloverdale, Goldsmith (7) p. 264, E. T. Allen and Day (2) p. 45, Vonsen (6) p. 289.

Ventura County: **1,** Boussingaultite was found at South Mountain coating crevices of sandstones and shales. It was formed by the escape of heated gases, E. S. Larsen and Shannon (9) p. 127.

BRANNERITE
A rare earth oxide $(U,Ca,Fe,Y,Th)_3Ti_5O_{16}(?)$

Mono County: **1,** A few grains of brannerite have been found distributed in quartz veins (secs. 4 and 9, T. 7 N., R. 23 E., M.D.), 7 miles south of Coleville, in the canyon of the West Walker River, Pabst (13) p. 109. The mineral occurs as slender prismatic crystals up to one centimeter in length, solidly embedded in quartz.

Plumas County: **1,** Brannerite in broken crystals is associated with gold at the Little Nell property (SE ¼ sec. 35, R. 8 E., T. 23 N., M.D.), Pabst and Stinson (18) p. 2071.

San Bernardino County: **1,** This rare mineral is reported in very minor amounts as nodular masses in biotite in granitic gneisses, and in shear zones in the gneiss. It is associated with several other uncommon minerals, including euxenite. The occurrence is in a canyon on the north side of the San Bernardino Range, near Old Woman Springs (approx. sec. 22, T. 3 N., R. 3 E., S.B.), Hewett et al. (4) p. 30.

BRAUNITE
Manganese silicate, $Mn^{2+}Mn_6^{3+}SiO_{12}$

Manganese minerals like bementite, braunite, hausmannite, inesite, manganite, neotocite, psilomelane, pyrolusite, wad, and others are often not separable by field methods. It is apparent to the authors of this volume that many citations in the literature, especially those prior to 1940, may be incorrect identifications. Abundance of manganese minerals in the State in hundreds of localities makes systematic recording of all localities mentioned in the literature impractical. The following listings therefore may be incomplete, and many that are included are important only to reflect adequately the historic record.

This mineral is probably rather widespread in the siliceous manganese ores of the State. It has been recognized from the following localities:

Humboldt County: **1,** Braunite forms the primary ore mineral at the Fort Seward mine (sec. 15, T. 3 S., R. 4 E., H.), P. D. Trask et al. (4) p. 59.

Plumas County: **1,** Braunite has been found in the Braito mine (sec. 27, T. 26 N., R. 9 E., M.D.), P. D. Trask et al. (4) p. 71.

Santa Clara County: **1,** Braunite was identified by x-ray study of "psilomelane" from Santa Clara, Ramsdell (1) p. 147.

Stanislaus County: **1,** A specimen from the Buckeye mine (secs. 2, 3, T. 5 S., R. 5 E., M.D.) was studied by Fleischer and Richmond (1) p. 283.

Trinity County: **1,** Vonsen (p.c. '45) reported braunite with rhodo-chrosite from the Shellview mine (sec. 17, T. 4 S., R. 6 E., H.); see also P. D. Trask et al. (4) p. 90. **2,** Braunite occurs with other man-ganese minerals including rhodonite, bementite, and rhodochrosite in a deposit (sec. 26, T. 30 N., R. 12 W., M.D.) in sediments, Hewett et al. (6) p. 45.

BREWSTERITE
Hydrous strontium barium aluminum silicate, $(Sr,Ba)Al_2Si_6O_{16} \cdot 5H_2O$

Mendocino County: **1,** Brewsterite was found with edingtonite on Ash Creek, 1 mile northeast of the highway. The locality is not certain, and may be in Sonoma County, Vonsen (p.c. '45).

BROCHANTITE
Basic sulphate of copper, $Cu_4SO_4(OH)_6$

Calaveras County: **1,** Brochantite was found as druses of small dark-green crystals at Copperopolis, A. F. Rogers (7) p. 376.

Inyo County: **1,** Brochantite occurs with caledonite and linarite at the Cerro Gordo mine, Eakle (9) p. 228. **2,** Bottle-green radial crystals of brochantite in brown jasper and chrysocolla were found near the headwaters of Cottonwood Creek in the Panamint Mountains, Ball (2) p. 211. **3,** Brochantite is found in oxidized copper ores in the Darwin Mining District, Hall and MacKevett (1) p. 18, ibid. (4) p. 64.

Plumas County: **1,** Crystals of brochantite have been reported from the Engels mine (N.R.).

San Bernardino County: **1,** Brochantite was observed as coatings on breccia at Stagg (N.R.). **2,** Brochantite occurs in oxidized ores with linarite at a prospect in the Soda Lake Mountains near Baker, Murdoch (p.c. '49). **3,** Small crystals and crusts of brochantite are found in veins with chrysocolla 2 miles southwest of the Sidewinder mine, O. E. Bowen (1) p. 123.

BROMYRITE
Silver bromide, AgBr

Kern County: **1,** Bromyrite was reported as abundant in the Karma vein, at Soledad Mountain, near Mojave, but this occurrence is uncon-firmed, Bateson (1) p. 173. **2,** Bromyrite is reported with cerargyrite and other silver minerals from the Amalie (NW ¼ sec. 22, T. 30 S., R. 33 E., M.D.), Gold Peak (SW ¼ sec. 28, T. 30 S., R. 33 E., M.D.) and Cowboy (NE ¼ sec. 28, T. 30 S., R. 33 E., M.D.) mines in the Loraine area, Troxel and Morton (2) pp. 93, 281, 41.

BROOKITE
Titanium dioxide, TiO_2

El Dorado County: **1,** Small tabular crystals of brookite associated with anatase, occur on quartz, at Placerville, Kunz (5) p. 329, (15) p. 394, (24) p. 106.

Kern County: **1,** Minute spear-like crystals of brookite have been found in cavities of lava east of the highway in Red Rock Canyon, Murdoch (p.c. '47).

BRUCITE
Magnesium hydroxide, Mg(OH)$_2$

Fresno County: **1,** Chesterman (1) p. 272, found brucite in irregular masses and rounded pellets in contact metamorphic limestone in the Twin Lakes region.

Riverside County: **1,** Brucite is a product of alteration of periclase in the predazzite rock at Crestmore, Eakle (15) pp. 327, 332, A. F. Rogers (31) p. 463; **2,** it was found similarly in the new City quarry, 2 miles south of Riverside, Richmond (1) p. 725. **3,** A. F. Rogers (19) p. 581, reports brucite as an alteration of periclase, at the old City quarry at North Hill, Riverside. **4,** Brucite, pseudomorphous after periclase, is abundant at the Jensen quarry, Murdoch (p.c. '47).

San Benito County: **1,** Near the Florence Mack mine, brucite occurs as crusts of minute flat crystals on long slender calcite, in serpentine, E. H. Oyler (p.c. '59).

San Bernardino County: **1,** Brucite altering to hydromagnesite is found in marbles in Lucerne Valley (SE ¼ SE ¼ sec. 15, T. 6 N., R. 1 W., S.B.), Ian Campbell (1) p. 3.

San Francisco County: **1,** Brucite and xonotlite in serpentine, were found in cuts made by the Western Pacific Railroad on Army Street, San Francisco, Pabst (p.c. '44). **2,** Fibrous brucite in fine stellated white crystals is reported from the serpentines of the San Francisco Peninsula, Gibbs, quoted in Mining and Scientific Press (19) p. 28.

BULTFONTEINITE
Basic calcium silicate with fluorine, Ca$_2$SiO$_2$(OH,F)$_4$

Riverside County: **1,** Minute grains of bultfonteinite have been found as sugary streaks in veins of massive afwillite and scawtite on the 910' level of the Commercial quarry, Crestmore, Murdoch (30) p. 1347, ibid. (32) p. 900.

*BUDDINGTONITE, 1964
Hydrous ammonium aluminum silicate, NH$_4$AlSi$_3$O$_8$·½H$_2$O

Lake County: **1,** The new mineral, buddingtonite, has been described from the well-known Sulphur Bank mercury deposit. It occurs as a hydrothermal product presumably formed from feldspar. This is the first ammonium aluminum silicate found in nature. The mineral occurs as pseudomorphs after plagioclase, largely in compact masses, but occasionally as crystals of small size lining cavities, Erd et al. (6) p. 831. The origin of minerals of the "buddingtonite type" is considered more fully by Barker (1) p. 851.

*BURKEITE, 1935
Sodium sulpho-carbonate, Na$_6$SO$_4$(CO$_3$)$_2$

Burkeite was discovered in California in 1935. Burkeite or a member of the burkeite series, has recently (1962) been identified in Carbonate Lake, in Grant County, Washington, Bennett (1) p. 12.

Inyo County: **1,** Burkeite occurs in muds, and as efflorescences and saline crusts, at Deep Spring Lake, B. F. Jones (1) p. B200, ibid. (2) p. 88A.

San Bernardino County: **1,** Cross-shaped crystals of this new mineral, up to 4 mm in diameter, were found at a depth of 115 to 130 feet in well G 75, at Searles Lake. The mineral was described and named by Foshag (21) p. 50; see also G. I. Smith and Pratt (2) p. 29. The Searles Lake burkeite has been further studied by G. I. Smith and Haines (3) p. 50. The mineral is next in abundance to hanksite among the sulphate minerals of Searles Lake. It is present principally in the Lower Salt, massive or in vuggy layers, sometimes up to a foot thick, pure, or with intermixed trona.

BUSTAMITE
Calcium manganese silicate, $CaMn(SiO_3)_2$

Inyo County: **1,** Bustamite was reported from this county, Murdoch and Webb (4) p. 69, but the identification was in error, and the mineral was later correctly identified as zoisite, variety thulite, by Schaller and Glass (54) p. 519.

Madera County: **1,** Massive pale-pink bustamite is common at the Agnew Meadow manganese prospect about 0.1 mile south of Agnew Meadows. Identification is confirmed by x-ray diffraction and x-ray spectrochemical analysis at the CDMG Laboratory, John T. Alfors (p.c. '64).

*CALAVERITE, 1868
Gold telluride, $AuTe_2$

Calaveras County: **1,** Calaverite was discovered at the old Stanislaus mine on Carson Hill. It was analyzed and named by Genth (5) p. 314. **2,** Calaverite is also found in the Melones mine, ibid., p. 314, and **3,** at the Morgan mine on Carson Hill, with sylvanite and petzite, ibid., p. 314. **4,** The mineral occurs with altaite and petzite at the Frenchwood mine, Robinsons Ferry (sec. 28, T. 2 N., R. 13 E., M.D.), Hanks (12) p. 68.

El Dorado County: **1,** Calaverite was reported from the Darling mine near Rock Creek, about 3 miles northeast of American Flat, Palache et al. (10) p. 336.

Siskiyou County: **1,** Calaverite was doubtfully reported with gold and petzite from the northern part of the county (N.R.)

Tuolumne County: **1,** Calaverite occurred at the Golden Rule mine, Hanks (12) p. 104.

CALCIOVOLBORTHITE
Basic copper calcium vanadate, $CuCa(VO_4)OH$

San Bernardino County: **1,** Calciovolborthite has been reported to occur at Camp Signal, near Goffs, Schrader et al. (1) p. 46.

CALCITE
Calcium carbonate $CaCO_3$

The perfectly colorless transparent form is called *iceland spar.*

Calcite is widespread in many parts of the state. Occurrences of the mineral are very numerous, but few have mineralogical significance. As a mineral resource, calcite occurs in considerable quantity in many deposits. In the localities referenced below, no attempt has been made to systematically report commodity occurrences, nor to report the mineral wherever it is mentioned in the literature. Some localities of minor importance and of little general mineralogical interest are noted because they have been carried in early editions of *Minerals of California*. The authors consider it wise to retain these as part of the historical record, but newer and more important localities of the mineral as a mineral resource have not been added, and literature citations to articles on such localities have not necessarily been included. For commercial occurrences of limestone and marble, the reader is referred to Bulletin 138 of the CDMG, Forstner et al. (3).

Alameda County: **1**, Pseudomorphs of calcite after aragonite are found near Patterson Pass, east of Livermore, A. F. Rogers (3) p. 18. **2**, A fine grade of lithographic limestone occurs on the Crocker-Winship properties, south of Danville (N.R.).

Alpine County: **1**, Fine groups of calcite rhombohedrons have come from the Pennsylvania mine (N.R.).

Calaveras County: **1**, Fine stalactites occur in Mercers Cave, $1\frac{1}{4}$ miles northwest of Murphy (N.R.).

El Dorado County: **1**, Fine calcite stalactites occur at the Alabaster Cave (N.R.). **2**, Good crystals of calcite were found at the Cosumnes mine (N.R.).

Fresno County: **1**, Veins of fluorescent calcite with cinnabar were found on Avenal Creek, Melhase (4) p. 38.

Imperial County: **1**, Calcite occurs as inverted "stalactites" originally identified as aragonite, in the area surrounding the mud volcanos near Niland, Hanks (9) p. 232.

Inyo County: **1**, Good iceland spar has been found in the Darwin Mining District, Hanks (12) p. 114, CDMG (3709). **2**, Blue calcite with idocrase has been sent to the CDMG reportedly from the North Fork of Shepard Creek, half a mile north of the Crystal Dome mine (T. 22 S., R. 42, 43 E., M.D.), W. W. Bradley (26) p. 195. This locality is questionable, but the material does not look like that from Crestmore. **3**, Calcite crystals are present in mud layers of Deep Spring Lake, B. F. Jones (1) p. 201.

Kern County: **1**, "Sand calcite" crystals are found north of Ricardo, at the junction of Old Highway U.S. 6 and the Dove Springs road, Murdoch and Webb (11) p. 551. **2**, Fluorescent calcite is reported at the Hercules mine, Randsburg, The Mineralogist (2) p. 23.

Lake County: **1**, Calcite occurs, but is rare, at Sulphur Bank, D. E. White and Roberson (2) p. 408.

Los Angeles County: **1**, Well-formed crystals of calcite occur in the borate deposit in Tick Canyon, Eakle (10) p. 189. **2**, Rhombohedral crystals are found in veins in Franklin Canyon, Funk (1) p. 33 and **3**, at the Small Hill mine, on Santa Catalina Island, CDMG (4069). **4**, Crystal-lined vugs are found in dikes of limestone and breccia half a mile north of Vicente Point, San Pedro Hills, G. A. Macdonald (2) p. 331.

Madera County: **1**, Abundant crystals of calcite come from Kaiser Mountain $1\frac{1}{2}$ miles from the Huntington Lake road, Laizure (2) p. 102.

Marin County: **1**, Flat, thin-edged rhombohedrons of manganocalcite occur in a trachyte on the Burdell Ranch. They turn black on weathering or on being heated (N.R.).

Merced County: **1,** Strontiancalcite is reported from Delhi, CDMG (16326).

Modoc County: **1,** Optical quality iceland spar in masses up to 60 or 80 pounds occurred in veins in basalt near Cedarville in the Warner Range. This deposit produced some commercial material but is now worked out, Hughes (1) p. 6.

Mono County: **1,** Pseudomorphs of calcite, called "thinolite," after original steep tetragonal pyramids of an unknown mineral, have been found about Mono Lake, E. S. Dana (1) p. 19, I. C. Russell (1) pp. 315, 316. These pseudomorphs are frequently formed of imbricated groups of pyramids, packed one within the other to make prismatic forms up to 8 or 10 inches in length. Low- and high-magnesian calcite, and aragonite form pinnacled masses of tufa at Mono Lake, Scholl and Taft (1) p. 56. These pinnacles may be the same as those described as "thinolite." **2,** Large lenses or druses of iceland spar, some of optical quality, showing cleavage fragments up to 1 foot, occur in the upper Convict Basin, near Mammoth Lakes, Mayo (4) p. 84.

Monterey County: **1,** "Sand-calcite" crystals have been described by A. F. Rogers and Reed (28) p. 23, from the Cholame Hills (sec. 14, T. 23 S., R. 13 E., M.D.). In these the proportions are 65 percent sand, 35 percent calcite.

Nevada County: **1,** Fine scalenohedrons (dog-tooth spar) have come from the Pittsburg mine (N.R.). **2,** Crystals of calcite are associated with kämmererite at the Red Ledge mine near Washington (N.R.).

Riverside County: **1,** Coarsely crystalline blue calcite is very abundant at Crestmore, Eakle (15) p. 334. The blue color of calcite at Crestmore is discussed by Rosenholtz and Smith (1) p. 1049. **2,** Iceland spar occurs with fluorite and clear quartz at the Fluorspar group, 1 mile southwest of Packards Well, Palen Mountains, Aubury (1) p. 258. **3,** A magnesian calcite-aragonite-huntite assemblage, as an incrustation on calcite-monticellite rock at Crestmore, has been described by A. B. Carpenter (1) p. 146.

San Bernardino County: **1,** Calcite is found sparingly as minute, ivory-colored crystals at the base of the Upper Salt, Foshag (21) p. 51, G. I. Smith and Haines (2) p. 25, and at several other horizons in the Parting and Bottom Mud, ibid., pp. 25-26. The calcite is associated with adularia, aragonite, searlesite, thenardite and gay-lussite. **2,** Nodular concretions with radiating structure are found in a clay shale half a mile north of Mojave Water Camp, east of Daggett, Rocks and Minerals (1) p. 140, Murdoch and Webb (11) p. 551.

San Diego County: **1,** At the mine of Calcite Operators, Inc., (sec. 14, T. 10 S., R. 8 E., S.B.), broad flat plates of calcite, up to one foot across, and of optical quality, have been mined for gun-sights, Bramlette (p.c. '43), Durrell (p.c. '44).

San Francisco County: **1,** Calcite showing uncommon faces, in crystals up to several cm in size, came from Fort Point, San Francisco, Schaller (17) p. 103. They were associated with pectolite, datolite, and gyrolite.

Santa Barbara County: **1,** Large rhombohedra of calcite occur on Big Pine Mountain, C. D. Woodhouse (p.c. '63).

Santa Cruz County: **1,** Well-developed calcite crystals have been found in the Vicente Creek tunnel near Davenport (N.R.).

Shasta County: **1,** Stalactitic and tubular forms of calcite have been found in Potters Cave, near Baird, Eakle (7) p. 89. **2,** Fossil pearls, altered from the original aragonite, occur along the north side of the road in Oak Run Valley, near the contact of the Chico and Ione formations, R. D. Russell (1) p. 419.

Tulare County: **1,** Massive blue crystalline calcite, associated with scheelite, has been reported from the Consolidated tungsten mine, Drum Valley, C. Knowlton (p.c. '46).

Tuolumne County: **1,** Calcite showing scarlet triboluminescence occurs near Columbia, Melhase (4) p. 38.

Ventura County: **1,** Calcite is reported from San Nicolas Island, in seams varying from almost microscopic fineness up to two or three inches in thickness, sometimes showing good crystals, Bowers (3) p. 57.

CALEDONITE
Basic copper lead carbonate sulphate, $Cu_2Pb_5(SO_4)_3CO_3(OH)_6$

Inyo County: **1,** Caledonite was found with linarite and leadhillite at the Cerro Gordo mines, A. F. Rogers (1) p. 46, Eakle (9) p. 227, C. W. Merriam (1) p. 43. Guild (1) p. 330, described bright-green crystals from this locality. **2,** Caledonite was found with linarite at the Wonder prospect, Darwin Mining District, A. Knopf (4) p. 17; **3,** it occurs with linarite and crystallized cerussite in the Monster mine, northwest of Saline Valley, on the east flank of the Inyo Range, A. Knopf (5) p. 111. **4,** Caledonite and linarite came from the Reward mine, 2 miles east of Manzanar. A Knopf (5) p. 118. **5,** Caledonite is sparingly found in the Big Four and Modoc Mines, on the east flank of the Argus Range, west side of Panamint Valley, Hall and Stephens (3) pp. 26, 34.

Mono County: **1,** Caledonite was reported in the Blind Spring Mining District, Hulin (p.c. '36).

San Bernardino County: **1,** Caledonite occurs with linarite and dioptase at a mine in the Soda Lake Mountains near Baker, Murdoch (p.c. '49), (CDMG 31250).

CALOMEL
Mercurous chloride, HgCl

Napa County: **1,** White coatings of calomel on metacinnabar were found in the Redington (Boston) quicksilver mine on Oat Hill, CDMG (16284).

Orange County: **1,** A persistent amount of chlorine in analyses of metacinnabar from Red Hill, indicates the presence of calomel, although this mineral was not otherwise recorded from this locality, Genth and Penfield (10) p. 383.

San Benito County: **1,** Calomel is reported with cinnabar, native mercury, and montroydite, in silicate-carbonate rock, 3 miles south of the New Idria mine, E. H. Oyler (p.c. '62).

San Mateo County: **1,** Small amounts of calomel, native mercury, cinnabar and eglestonite occur on the Corte de Madera Rancho (?), 5 miles west of Palo Alto, A. F. Rogers (5) p. 48. **2,** Calomel, with eglestonite, montroydite, native mercury, and cinnabar is found in joints and fissures in a siliceous rock replacing serpentine, about 2 miles west of Redwood City, C. D. Woodhouse (3) p. 603.

†* CARLOSITE, 1907
See neptunite

Carlosite was described as a new mineral with benitoite from San Benito County in 1907 by Louderback and Blasdale. Subsequently the identity as neptunite was established, Louderback and Blasdale (2) p. 354.

CARNOTITE
Hydrous potassium uranyl vanadate, $K_2(UO_2)_2(VO_4)_2.1\text{-}3H_2O$

El Dorado County: **1,** Carnotite is reported from near Placerville, CDMG (21635).

Imperial County: **1,** G. W. Walker et al. (5) pp. 10, 26 reports carnotite in a metamorphic terrain intruded by felsic dikes and plugs. The carnotite is in the altered felsic rocks associated with torbernite or autunite, in talc-bearing metamorphic rocks. The locality is 10 miles northeast of Glamis (sec. 36(?), T. 12 S., R. 19 E., S.B.).

Kern County: **1,** Carnotite is found in thin-bedded sandy limestones at the Fiend claim (sec. 15, T. 9 N., R. 6 W., S.B.), on the south end of the Kramer Hills, G. W. Walker et al. (5) p. 20. **2,** The mineral is reported with opal as fracture coatings in sandy clay of the Ricardo formation in the Vanuray claim $2\frac{1}{2}$ mi. NW of Boron (sec. 26, T. 11 N., R. 8 W., S.B.), G. W. Walker et al. (5) p. 19. **3,** Carnotite comes from the Loperna property near McKittrick, CDMG (21614). This property is described by G. W. Walker et al. (5) p. 33 (sec. 2, T. 30 S., R. 21 E., M.D.), but the yellow coatings on fractures in altered and brecciated shale are called "secondary uranium minerals," and the identity as carnotite is not confirmed. **4,** Carnotite is reported from Knoll prospect, Verdi Development Company, Rosamond, CDMG (21632). **5,** Carnotite may occur with autunite in the ores of the Miracle mine, MacKevett (2) p. 211. **6,** Carnotite with autunite occurs coating calcite crystals, in vugs and veins from the Monte Cristo prospect, Kern River uranium area, MacKevett (2) p. 213. **7,** Carnotite (?) occurs in the Miracle mine (SE ¼ sec. 7, T. 27 S., R. 32 E., M.D.), Troxel and Morton (2) p. 333.

Lassen County: **1,** Carnotite is reported from Madonna Mia group near Chilcoot, CDMG (21650).

Mono County: **1,** Carnotite is reported from near Masonic, CDMG (21624).

Monterey County: **1,** From Pennington claim, near Parkfield, CDMG (21615 and 21616) confirms the occurrence of carnotite.

Nevada County: **1,** The Easter mine, near Floriston, CDMG (21657), carries carnotite.

Riverside County: **1,** Carnotite is reported from near Desert Center, CDMG (21627).

San Bernardino County: **1,** Carnotite comes from near Amboy, CDMG (21641). **2,** The mineral is found with copper minerals in the Jeep No. 2 claim 6 miles NW of Clark Mt. Peak (sec. 10, T. 17 N., R. 12 E., S.B.), G. W. Walker et al. (5) p. 22. **3,** Prospects in the Kramer Hills (secs. 12, 14, T. 9 N., R. 6 W., S.B.) carry yellow stains of carnotite, G. W. Walker et al. (5) p. 19. It is likely that localities represented by CDMG (21609) and (21652) are identical with this locality.

CASSITERITE—Tin Stone
Tin dioxide, SnO₂

Amador County: **1,** A 5-foot "vein of tin" reported on the Mokelumne River below Big Bar by W. P. Blake (28) p. 615, is most probably garnet.

Butte County: **1,** Cassiterite was reported from Goat Flat, Engineering and Mining Journal (19) p. 855.

Inyo County: **1,** There is an unverified report in the Mining and Scientific Press for 1901, of cassiterite nuggets from Bishop Creek, Segerstrom (1) p. 550.

Kern County: **1,** Nodules and stringers of cassiterite, some up to 3 tons weight, in limonite gossan, occur at the Meeke (Hogan) tin mine 4 miles north of Quail Lake, near Gorman, Mallery (2) no. 2, p. 8, Wiese and Page (1) p. 39, Page (3) p. 202, Wiese (2), p. 46, Troxel and Morton (2) p. 290.

Napa County: **1,** Cassiterite was doubtfully reported from the lower end of Chiles Valley, L. L. Palmer (1) p. 28.

Orange County: **1,** Cassiterite was found at the Trabuco tin mine, Trabuco Canyon, Mining and Scientific Press (30) p. 117, Segerstrom (1) p. 550.

Placer County: **1,** One nugget of cassiterite was found in the Middle Fork, Feather River, 3 miles above Big Bar, W. P. Blake (23) p. 376, (24) p. 208.

Riverside County: **1,** The most important deposit of cassiterite in the state was discovered in the Temescal area (the Cajalco mine) (secs. 2, 3, 10, 11, T. 4 S., R. 6 W., S.B.), C. T. Jackson (1) p. 152. According to Benedict (1) p. 450, the Indians knew of the presence of tin here as early as 1840. There are many references to this deposit, of which the more important are: Hanks (12) p. 120, Kunz (24) p. 105, Fairbanks (18) pp. 39–42. Besides the principal occurrences, there were other smaller deposits in the general vicinity. One of the more important of these is the Chief of the Hills (sec. 4 T. 6 S., R. 4 W., S.B.), 2 miles northeast of Elsinore, R. J. Sampson (9) p. 516, Segerstrom (1) p. 551.

San Bernardino County: **1,** Crystals of cassiterite occur with scheelite in a vein in dolomitic limestone at the Evening Star mine (sec. 30, T. 15 N., R. 14 E., S.B.), Tucker and Sampson (34) p. 498.

San Diego County: **1,** Cassiterite occurs with other pegmatite minerals in the Himalaya mine at Mesa Grande, Schaller (36) p. 352, and **2,** with topaz in Little Three mine near Ramona, ibid., p. 352. **3,** A little cassiterite was found with columbite, tourmaline, etc., in a pegmatite in the Chihuahua Valley (SW ¼ sec. 12, T. 9 S., R. 3 E., S.B.), ibid., p. 351. **4,** The mineral is found in a pegmatite with lepidolite and amblygonite, on Granite Mountain, about 3 miles southeast of Banner (NW ¼ sec. 18, T. 13 S., R. 5 E., S.B.), Schaller (p.c. '46). **5,** Sanford and Stone (1) p. 26, report cassiterite from Pala [doubtful]. **6,** Placer tin was supposedly found on the east slope of Laguna Mountain, F. J. H. Merrill (1) p. 669. **8,** F. J. H. Merrill (1) p. 669 also reports other possible occurrences in Pine Valley, **9,** at the south end of Viejas Mountain east of Alpine, and **10,** in the Defiance copper area, west of the Santa Margarita grant. These are all doubtful.

Santa Barbara County: **1,** Some cassiterite was found as float by Captain Stoddon in the San Rafael Mountains, Angel (2) p. 596.

Santa Clara County: **1,** Fine large crystals of cassiterite were reported from the eclogites, quartzite, and diorite of Oak Hill, near San José, Schrader et al. (1) p. 46.

Santa Cruz County: **1,** Cassiterite has been found in the suite of minerals at the Pacific Limestone Products (Kalkar) quarry at Santa Cruz, Chesterman and Gross (p.c. '64).

Siskiyou County: **1,** Cassiterite was found as float in Hungry Creek, Hess and Graton (1) p. 165. **2,** Stream tin is found in the gravels at Sawyers Bar (N.R.).

Sonoma County: **1,** A sample of stream tin, CDMG (18306), came from this county.

Trinity County: **1,** One large specimen of cassiterite was found in the soil near Weaverville, J. D. Whitney (6) p. 181, and several other small nuggets have been found near-by, Segerstrom (1) p. 552.

CELADONITE
Hydrous iron magnesium potassium and aluminum silicate,
$K(Mg,Fe^{2+})(Al,Fe^{3+})Si_4O_{10}(OH)_2 \cdot$ [Wise and Eugster (2) p. 1031]

Kern County: **1,** Green crystalline linings of cavities in basalt at Red Rock Canyon, have been identified by x-ray photographs as celadonite. It had previously been tentatively called "corundophilite", Murdoch (p.c. '53).

San Mateo County: **1,** CDMG (8961) is celadonite and comes from the San Gregorio Ranch, near San Mateo, Irelan (4) p. 46.

CELESTITE
Strontium sulphate, $SrSO_4$

"Baryto-celestite" is barium celestite.

Imperial County: **1,** B. N. Moore (1) p. 365, described celestite from "Fish Mts." The locality is in San Diego County **(1)**.

Inyo County: **1,** Slender bluish crystals of celestite occur with colemanite in Death Valley, Eakle (9) p. 230. **2,** Celestite occurs with analcime in vugs of a basalt at Ryan. A specimen was collected by C. N. Rasor about 1927.

Los Angeles County: **1,** Minute celestite crystals occur on a crust of bakerite at the Sterling borax mine, Tick Canyon, Murdoch (p.c. '49).

San Benito County: **1,** A 3-inch vein of celestite was found in old workings of the Butts quicksilver mine near Pine Rock, Tucker (11) p. 247.

San Bernardino County: **1,** Geodes in the colemanite ores at Borate, in the Calico Hills, are lined with strontianite and light-blue to colorless celestite crystals up to 4 cm in length, Eakle (9) p. 230, Foshag (9) p. 208. D. J. Henry (1) p. 231, reports pseudomorphs of celestite after satin spar. **2,** Slender pointed crystals of celestite occur in open fissures in the old Owens borax mine, at the north base of Lead Mountain, near Barstow, H. S. Gale (17) p. 10, Durrell (8) p. 9. **3,** In the Mud Hills and Strontium Hills, north of Barstow (T. 11 N., R. 1, 2 W.; sec. 20, T. 11 N., R. 1 W., S.B.), celestite occurs with strontianite in glassy aggregates or slender prismatic crystals, A. Knopf (9) p. 263,

Durrell (8) p. 23. **4,** An extensive zone of impure celestite associated with gypsum is found (T. 17, 18 N., R. 4, 5, 6 E., S.B.), 10 miles northwest of Silver Lake in the Avawatz Mountains, Phalen (3) p. 526, B. N. Moore (1) p. 359. **5,** Extensive beds of massive celestite 10 to 20 feet thick, occur 4 miles northwest of Ludlow (secs. 29, 30, T. 8 N., R. 7 E., S.B.), Mallery (1) p. 952, Tucker (4) p. 367, B. N. Moore (1) p. 357, Durrell (8) p. 37. **6,** An extensive deposit of celestite as concretions of massive material is found on the southwest margin of Bristol Dry Lake, south of Amboy (S ½ sec. 6, T. 4 N., R. 12 E., S.B.), H. S. Gale (17) p. 10, confirming Durrell (p.c. '45). **7,** Celestite is one of the minerals occasionally found at Searles Lake, Hanks (17) p. 63, DeGroot (3) p. 537. **8,** Celestite occurs in shales with nodular barite at Owl Holes (sec. 23, T. 18 N., R. 3 E., S.B.), Murdoch and Webb (11) p. 550, Durrell (8) p. 15. **9,** Barian celestite (barytocelestite) has been tentatively identified in the bastnaesite occurrence at Mountain Pass, Pray and Sharp (1) p. 1519.

San Diego County: **1,** Finely crystalline celestite underlain by gypsum occurs in the Fish Creek area, described as "Fish Mts." by B. N. Moore (1) p. 365, and located in Imperial County. Durrell (8) p. 5, corrects the location and describes the deposit.

CENTRALLASITE
Hydrous basic calcium silicate, $Ca_2Si_3O_7(OH)_2 \cdot H_2O$

Riverside County: **1,** Centrallasite was described by Foshag (12) p. 88, as occurring in platy to compact masses between feldspars, and associated with prehnite and datolite, in a pegmatite in the Wet Weather quarry at Crestmore. The identity of centrallasite has been questioned and it has been referred by some workers as identical with gyrolite. Flint et al. (1) p. 619, consider the species valid.

CERARGYRITE [1]—Horn Silver
Silver chloride, AgCl

Calaveras County: **1,** Thin crusts of cerargyrite on quartz were reported by W. P. Blake (14) p. 124, from the Morgan mine at Carson Hill.

Inyo County: Cerargyrite was fairly abundant in some of the mines of the Argus and Coso Ranges and in the Inyo Range, with lesser occurrences in the Panamint Mts. and other ranges to the southward. **1,** Argus Range: Tucker and Sampson (25) p. 445, in fine microscopic crystals at the Modoc mine (sec. 34, T. 19 S. R., 42 E. M.D.). **2,** Coso Range: De Groot (2) p. 213, Crawford (1) p. 374, Tucker (11) p. 488, Murphy (2) p. 322. **3,** The mineral was abundant in the upper workings at the Darwin mines, Tucker and Sampson (25) p. 546. Cerargyrite was found as euhedral crystals in the Lee mine, Darwin Mining District, Hall and MacKevett (1) p. 18, ibid. (4) p. 64. **4,** Inyo Range: massive cerargyrite was fairly abundant in the upper levels of the Cerro Gordo mine, Woodhouse (p.c. '45). **5,** Cerargyrite was found associated with argentite and wulfenite in the Kearsarge Mining District, 8 miles from Independence, G. M. Wheeler (1) p. 45. **6,** The min-

---

[1] International committee on mineral names recommends chlorargyrite as accepted usage, Anon. (55) p. 223.

eral was found as crusts in the Tecopa region, Woodhouse (p.c. '45). **7,** Cerargyrite was reported from the Chrysopolis area, Engineering and Mining Journal (15) p. 1176. **8,** The mineral was also reported from the Slate Range, Hanks (12) p. 124, and **9,** at the Minietta mines, Argus Range, Woodhouse (p.c. '54).

Kern County: **1,** Cerargyrite occurred at the Amalie mine with proustite and argentite (T. 31 S., R. 36 E., M.D.), Dyke (1) p. 764. The mineral was reported in the ores of the Gold Peak and Cowboy mines, near the Amalie mine in the Loraine area, Troxel and Morton (2) p. 281. Bromyrite, argentite, tetrahedrite and proustite are associated minerals, ibid. p. 41. **2,** Several of the mines in the Mojave Mining District carried a little cerargyrite with argentite in the gold veins, Bateson (1) p. 171, Tucker and Sampson (21) p. 298; Lodestar or Morningstar mine, Tucker (37) p. 221; Cactus Queen mine, Troxel and Morton (2) pp. 44, 109.

Mono County: **1,** Cerargyrite was found sparingly in the Blind Spring Mining District near Benton, Whiting (1) p. 378, **2,** with native silver near Bodie, ibid. p. 389, and **3,** at the Silverado mine (sec. 19, T. 7 N., R. 25 E., M.D.), in the Patterson Mining District, Sweetwater Range, ibid., p. 359, Eakle and McLaughlin (17) p. 166. **4,** A little cerargyrite was found with cuprite and chrysocolla at Lundy, Hanks (12) p. 139, CDMG (5158).

Napa County: **1,** "Silver chlorides" were reported from the Mount St. Helena (Silverado) mine, with sulphides and free gold, Boalich (4) p. 159.

Placer County: **1,** A mass of ore with wire silver and cerargyrite was discovered in 1871 in the Elizabeth lode in the Ophir Mining District, Mining and Scientific Press (14) p. 241. **2,** Cerargyrite was found abundantly in other veins in the Mother Lode gold region, Lindgren (7) p. 272. **3,** Beautiful specimens of cerargyrite have come from the Whitlach mine in Marshall Canyon, Engineering and Mining Journal (1) p. 66.

San Bernardino County: Many localities in this county have produced small amounts of cerargyrite, and it has been found abundantly in several places. **1,** Cerargyrite was the principal silver ore in the old Calico Mining District, associated with embolite, wulfenite, etc., Cloudman et al. (1) p. 829, Lindgren (1) pp. 721–728, Storms (2) p. 382. **2,** Cerargyrite was the most important mineral in the oxidized zone of the California Rand mine, and others in the area, Hulin (1) p. 98. **3,** Small deposits of rich ore were found in the Ord Mining District (T. 7 N., R. 2 E., S.B.), Cloudman et al. (1) p. 809. **4,** Crystals of cerargyrite came from the Blackhawk (Silver Reef) Mining District 40 miles east of Victorville, Storms (4) p. 366. Other minor occurrences are **5,** Trojan (Providence) Mining District, De Groot (2) p. 532; **6,** Lava Beds Mining District (T. 7 N., R. 4, 5 E., S.B.), ibid., p. 528; **7,** Dale area, Tucker and Sampson (27) p. 61; **8,** Kingston Range (T. 18 N., R. 13 E., S.B.), Tucker (8) p. 94; **9,** Grapevine Mining District (T. 10 N., R. 1 W., S.B.), Tucker and Sampson (28) p. 245; **10,** 9 miles north of Bagdad, Tucker (8) p. 97; **11,** Halloran Springs (T. 14 N., R. 10 E., S.B.), Tucker and Sampson (17) p. 273; **12,** Ivanpah Mining District, Loew (2) p. 186, Tucker (8) p. 94; **13,** Old Woman Mountains (T. 1 N., R. 21 E., S.B.), Irelan (4) p. 217; **14,** 3 miles east of Cima, New York

Mountains, Tucker and Sampson (16) p. 276; **15**, at the Black Metal mine, 3 miles west of the Colorado River and 50 miles southeast of Needles, Tucker and Sampson (17) p. 266; **16**, Calarivada mine (T. 18 N., R. 13 E., S.B.), ibid. p. 266; **17**, a little was found at Searles Lake, De Groot (2) p. 537, and **18**, Waterman mine (sec. 13, T. 10 N., R. 2 W., S.B.), L. A. Wright et al. (5) p. 139.

San Diego County: **1**, Cerargyrite was found 3 miles south of Julian, in ore with copper minerals, CDMG (9979).

Shasta County: **1**, Small perfect crystals of cerargyrite were found at the Silver King mine, 4 miles west of Redding, Hanks (15) p. 98.

CERITE
Hydrous silicate of the rare earth elements, near $(Ce,Y,Pr,Ca)_4Si_3O_{12} \cdot H_2O$

San Bernardino County: **1**, Cerite is reported with bastnaesite from the Mountain Pass deposit 30 miles east of Baker, Glass et al. (4) p. 665, ibid. (5), p. 460. The crystallography of this occurrence has been presented by P. Gay (1) p. 429.

CERUSSITE
Lead carbonate, $PbCO_3$

The mineral is readily confused with anglesite from which it often cannot be separated in field inspection. Localities entered below have not had the reported identification validated, and all occurrences known in the State are not included.

Imperial County: **1**, Cerussite was found with argentiferous galena, in small veins and pockets at the Mayflower mine (sec. 11, T. 14 S., R. 22 E., S.B.), F. J. H. Merrill (1) p. 732; **2**, it was also found in (T. 11 S., R. 19, 20 E., S.B.), Tucker (11) p. 262.

Inyo County: More than 30 occurrences are recorded from this county, most of them relatively unimportant. **1**, Large crystals came from the Union mine in the Russ Mining District (sec. 14, T. 6 S., R. 30 E., M.D.), Hanks (12) p. 124. **2**, Cerussite was an important mineral at the Cerro Gordo mine, ibid., p. 124, C. W. Merriam (1) p. 43. **3**, Cerussite was relatively common in the Darwin Mining District, A. Knopf (4) p. 7, Hall and MacKevett (4) p. 13. **4**, The principal ore mineral at the Carbonate mine near the base of the east slope of the Panamint Mountains was cerussite, C. A. Waring and Huguenin (2) p. 89. **5**, Fine crystals came from the Modoc mine (sec. 34, T. 19 S., R. 42 E., M.D.), Hanks (12) p. 124, Hall and Stephens (3) pp. 24–36. **6**, Well-crystallized cerussite with linarite and caledonite were found in the Monster mine, northwest of Saline Valley, A. Knopf (5) p. 111. **7**, Cerussite with wulfenite was found at the Empire mine (T. 21 S., R. 45 E., M.D.), W. P. Blake (14) p. 125. **8**, Cerussite is found at the Santa Rosa mine, Hall and MacKevett (4) p. 76. Minor occurrences are reported from the Panamint Range, Argus and Slate Ranges, northern end of the Inyo Range, Tecopa and Resting Springs area, Chloride Cliff, etc.: Stetefeldt (1) p. 259; Ball (1) p. 73; Tucker (4) pp. 286, 291, etc.; Tucker (11) pp. 453–530; Macallister (2) and others.

Madera County: **1**, Cerussite is reported in some of the lead ores on Shadow and Johnson Creeks, Minaret Mining District, Goudey (1) p. 7.

Mono County: **1,** Cerussite is common in veins rich in galena, in the Blind Spring Mining District, Whiting (1) p. 378, A. L. Ransome (2) p. 190; **2,** it was found on the west slope of the White Mountains, between Coldwater and Piute Canyons (T. 5 S., R. 33 or 34 E., M.D.), R. J. Sampson (14) p. 139.

Monterey County: **1,** A little cerussite came from the Alisal Rancho, in cavities of galena, associated with a small quantity of native arsenic, W. P. Blake (4) p. 301.

Orange County: **1,** Cerussite occurs sparingly at "Carbonate Hill" in Santiago Canyon, Bowers (4) p. 403.

Riverside County: **1,** Cerussite occurs with galena in the Free Coinage mine, Hodges Mountain (T. 7, 8 S., R. 21 E., S.B.), F. J. H. Merrill (2) p. 541, and **2,** also in the Steele mine near Pinacate (SE ¼ sec. 32, T. 4 S., R. 4 W., S.B.), ibid. p. 532. **3,** The mineral was found with vanadinite and sulphides at the Black Eagle mine (sec. 30, T. 3 S., R. 14 E., S.B.), Tucker (8) p. 195. **4,** Cerussite is found as an alteration of galena in the Crestmore quarries, Woodford (11) p. 352.

San Bernardino County: **1,** Massive cerussite occurs with chrysocolla in the Total Wreck mine and Langtry lode half a mile west of Calico. The mineral occurs sparingly elsewhere in the region, Lindgren (1) p. 727, Storms (3) p. 383. **2,** Cerussite is prominent in the mines 5 miles west of Oro Grande, Storms (4) p. 364, and **3,** it occurs with linarite, smithsonite, etc., in the Ibex mine, 6 miles north of Saratoga Springs, Cloudman et al. (1) p. 821. **4,** Cerussite is found with smithsonite and hydrozincite at the Carbonate mine (sec. 32, T. 16 N., R. 14 E., S.B.), Ivanpah Mining District, Tucker (4) p. 363, Tucker and Sampson (33) p. 128. **5,** The mineral occurs in the Lava Beds Mining District with wulfenite, anglesite, etc., Tucker and Sampson (17) p. 351, and **6,** it was found with vanadinite and cuprodescloizite at Signal, near Goffs, Schaller (24) p. 149. Cerussite was also reported in small amounts from **7,** Grapevine (T. 10 N., R. 1 W., S.B.), Tucker and Sampson (28) p. 245; **8,** Lead Mountain (T. 4 N., R. 10 E., S.B.), Tucker (8) p. 95; **9,** Resting Springs, Tucker (4) p. 366; **10,** Oro Grande, Crossman (1) p. 233; **11,** Old Woman Mountains, ibid., p. 217; **12,** Clark Mountain (T. 17 N., R. 13 E., S.B.), Tucker (4) p. 340; **13,** Dale, Tucker and Sampson (27) p. 61, and **14,** Holcomb Valley, Tucker (4) p. 362.

Shasta County: **1,** Cerussite occurs with pyromorphite, tetrahedrite, etc., at the Chicago claim, 3 miles west of Igo, W. P. Blake (14) p. 125.

Sonoma County: **1,** Cerussite is found as a heavy yellow concentrate in sands near Healdsburg, W. W. Bradley (26) p. 608.

Tulare County: **1,** Cerussite occurs in the Silver Crown group (sec. 7, T. 23 S., R. 33 E., M.D.), Tucker and Sampson (29) p. 331.

CERVANTITE
Antimony dioxide, Sb_2O_4(?)

Inyo County: **1,** White or light-yellow cervantite is associated with valentinite in Wild Rose Canyon, D. E. White (1) p. 317, Mining and Scientific Press (38) p. 368. **2,** A specimen, CDMG (8585), shows probable cervantite from Cerro Gordo. **3,** Cervantite was found as an alteration product of stibnite in the Darwin Mining District, Kelley

(4) p. 544. **4,** The mineral was reported with metastibnite and valentinite $4\frac{1}{2}$ miles south of Bishop, Woodhouse (p.c. '45).

Kern County: **1,** Cervantite was reported from "San Amedio" Mountain by Hanks (12) p. 124. A specimen from this county in the American Museum of Natural History is a pseudomorph of cervantite after antimony, Frondel (1) p. 407.

Mono County: **1,** Cervantite was recorded from the Blind Spring Mining District, Loew (1) p. 654.

San Benito County: **1,** Coatings of cervantite on stibnite and matrix are found in a specimen from the Ambrose mine near Hollister, collected about 1900, now in the collection of Rocks and Minerals magazine in Peekskill, New York, Anon. (31) p. 575.

San Bernardino County: **1,** Clear yellow, colorless, or white coatings of cervantite in vugs in ore, with pyrostilpnite, was found in the California Rand mine, Red Mountain, Murdoch (12) p. 131.

San Luis Obispo County: **1,** Cervantite was found with stibiconite on antimony ores at the Marquart mine (T. 26 S., R. 9 E., M.D.), Eckel et al. (1) pp. 537, 543.

CHABAZITE
Hydrous calcium aluminum silicate, $Ca[Al_2Si_4O_{12}]\cdot 6H_2O$

Chabazite is a zeolite occurring as a secondary mineral in cavities of basic volcanic rock.

Mono County: **1,** Minute colorless or whitish crystals of chabazite line narrow fissures in biotite schist near the head of McGee Creek (approx. lat. 37°10' N, long. 118°50' W), Mayo (p.c. '32).

Nevada County: **1,** Colorless crystals of chabazite several mm across form coatings of fissures in diabase at the Star mine, Grass Valley, Lindgren (12) p. 120.

Plumas County: **1,** Pseudocubic crystals of chabazite occur in basalt at the Dodson mine, Mooreville Ridge, H. W. Turner (4) p. 490.

Riverside County: **1,** Chabazite has been found on the 330' level at Crestmore, Leavens (p.c. '62).

Santa Clara County: **1,** Chabazite is reported from the Cochran(e) Ranch, Coyote Creek, Kartchner (1) p. 18.

Shasta County: **1,** Chabazite is found with natrolite, tridymite, and analcime, in amygdaloidal basalt on Round Mountain, Melhase (3) no. 6, p. 1.

CHALCANTHITE—Blue Vitriol
Hydrous cupric sulphate, $CuSO_4\cdot 5H_2O$

Chalcanthite is common in mine workings where it results from the oxidation of copper sulphides.

Alameda County: **1,** Chalcanthite is abundant as massive coatings and crystals with melanterite, etc., at the Alma pyrite mine, Leona Heights, Schaller (1) p. 212.

Alpine County: **1,** Chalcanthite occurs in considerable amounts in mine openings at the Leviathan sulphur mine, 7 miles east of Markleeville, Gary (1) p. 488.

Calaveras County: **1,** "Cyanosite" (chalcanthite) was reported by Silliman (7) p. 351, from Quail Hills, **2,** Chalcanthite occurs in the

Jackson McCarthy (Old Calaveras) mine, W. B. Clark and Lydon (4) p. 26.

Fresno County: **1,** Chalcanthite was found at the Nieper copper mine (sec. 34, T. 11 S., R. 23 E., M.D.), Goldstone (1) p. 194.

Inyo County: **1,** Chalcanthite is found in minor amounts in the oxidized ores in the Darwin Mining District, Hall and MacKevett (4) p. 64.

Mono County: **1,** Chalcanthite was found in the Masonic Mining District, W. W. Bradley (26) p. 606.

Nevada County: **1,** Chalcanthite was reported from Sweetland, Mining and Scientific Press (3) no. 13, p. 5, Hanks (12) p. 124.

Placer County: **1,** Chalcanthite occurs with native silver, coquimbite, etc., at the Valley View mine, Whiskey Hill, 6 miles north of Lincoln, Silliman (7) p. 351, Logan (17) p. 40.

Shasta County: **1,** Chalcanthite is common at the Peck mine, Copper City, Hanks (12) p. 124.

Trinity County: **1,** Chalcanthite is found with other sulphates at the Island Mountain copper mine, Vonsen (p.c. '45). **2,** Considerable amounts of the mineral were found with chalcopyrite in the New River area, Aubury (4) p. 144.

CHALCOCITE—Copper Glance—Redruthite
Cuprous sulphide, Cu_2S

Chalcocite is common in many of the copper mines of the State, but large bodies of this valuable copper mineral are rare. Bornite and chalcopyrite are often intermixed with chalcocite, and malachite commonly coats the surfaces of specimens.

Bornite, chalcocite, chalcopyrite, cuprite, galena, marcasite, pyrite, pyrrhotite, stibnite, tenorite, tetrahedrite, and many other antimony, copper, iron, lead and zinc sulfides, and oxides are found in traces or in minor amounts in many localities. The entries listed reflect either mineralogical or historic interest, and the listings are not complete nor is all literature which mentions these minerals referenced.

Alpine County: **1,** Some chalcocite occurs in the ore from the old Billy Rogers claim in Hope Valley, reputed to be the earliest copper claim in California (1855), Woodhouse (p.c. '45). **2,** Chalcocite from the Globe mine (SW $\frac{1}{4}$ sec. 31, T. 10 N., R. 21 E., M.D.) carried some gold and silver, Logan (4) p. 404.

Calaveras County: **1,** Chalcocite was reported from Quail Hill, Silliman (7) p. 351.

Colusa County: **1,** Chalcocite was found massive at the American mine (N.R.).

Del Norte County: **1,** Chalcocite was found abundantly with magnetite in serpentine at the Cleopatra mine 18 miles east of Smith River, in the Diamond Creek Mining District, Hershey (4) p. 429; **2,** at the Alta mine, Copper Creek, Maxson (1) p. 148; **3,** near Low Divide, near Rockland, J. D. Whitney (7) p. 362; **4,** with carbonates and oxides in the Higgins Mountain group on the Siskiyou Fork, Smith River, 5 miles from North Monkey Creek, Aubury (1) p. 116.

El Dorado County: **1,** Chalcocite occurred with bornite and chalcopyrite in the old Cosumnes copper mine near Fairplay (N.R.), and **2,** at the Boston mine, Latrobe (N.R.)

Fresno County: **1,** A little chalcocite was found at the Fresno copper mine (T. 12 S., R. 21 E., M.D.), Aubury (1) p. 226.

Humboldt County: **1,** A vein of chalcocite up to 1 foot wide in schist occurred in the Horse Mountain mine (sec. 33, 34, T. 6 N., R. 4 E., H.), Averill (10) p. 508, and **2,** it was found in the Iron Mountain mine, Mad River area, CDMG (15686). **3,** Chalcocite, with cuprite and native copper, occurred as float at the Red Cap mine, 50 miles north of Eureka, on the divide between Red Cap and Boise Creeks, Hershey (4) p. 429.

Imperial County: **1,** Some secondary chalcocite is found in the Cargo Muchacho Mining District, Henshaw (1) p. 185.

Inyo County: **1,** Chalcocite occurs in all mines of the Ubehebe Mining District, and some excellent specimens have been collected, Aubury (4) p. 302. **2,** A small amount of chalcocite occurs in the Panamint Mining District, Murphy (2) p. 323. **3,** Some chalcocite was found with tetrahedrite and other sulphides at the Ashford (Golden Treasure) mine on the east side of Death Valley, Tucker and Sampson (25) p. 383. **4,** Chalcocite was found with oxides and carbonates at Greenwater, Black Mountains, Zalinski (1) p. 81. **5,** Chalcocite in small quantities is reported with covellite as a constituent of the silver-lead ores from the Darwin Mining District, Hall and MacKevett (1) p. 18.

Kern County: **1,** A little chalcocite is found with chalcopyrite in veins in granodiorite at the Greenback copper mine (sec. 1, etc., T. 26 S., R. 29 E., M.D.), Tucker (4) p. 308.

Lake County: **1,** Some chalcocite occurs with malachite at the Langtry Ranch (T. 10 N., R. 7 W., M.D.), 7 miles south of Middletown, CDMG (15727).

Lassen County: **1,** Fine chalcocite has come from the Lummis mine, Woodhouse (p.c. '45).

Los Angeles County: **1,** Irregular masses of chalcocite occurred in syenitic granite at the Maris mine, Soledad Canyon, W. P. Blake (9) p. 12. This may be the same locality described by W. P. Blake (7) p. 291, as "7 miles below the summit of Williamson's Pass, almost 90 feet above the bed of the stream."

Madera County: **1,** Chalcocite occurred with chalcopyrite in a small vein north of the Jessie Bell mine near Daulton, Forstner (4) p. 747.

Mariposa County: **1,** Small amounts of a "dark blue or blue-black sulphide," presumably chalcocite, were found in the Pocahontas mine (T. 7 S., R. 17 E., M.D.), Aubury (1) p. 210; **2,** it occurs at La Victoria mine (T. 4 S., R. 16 E., M.D.), ibid., p. 213, and **3,** with native copper at the Copper Queen mine (T. 5 S., R. 19 E., M.D.), ibid., p. 216.

Mono County: **1,** Chalcocite is found sparingly as secondary veinlets in the mines at Blind Spring Hill, A. L. Ransome (2) p. 172.

Napa County: **1,** Chalcocite occurs with covellite at the Jumper Mines (N.R.).

Nevada County: **1,** Chalcocite is found with bornite and covellite in the enriched zone on Mineral Hill near Spenceville (T. 15 N., R. 6 E., M.D.), Forstner (4) p. 745.

Placer County: **1,** Small amounts of chalcocite occur at the Valley View mine, Whiskey Hill, with sulphates, Silliman (7) p. 350.

Plumas County: **1,** Rich chalcocite-bornite ore has been mined in the Genesee Valley Mining District, J. D. Whitney (7) p. 309, Hanks (15) p. 100. **2,** Chalcocite was abundant in the Engels mine, intergrown with bornite, H. W. Turner and Rogers (32) p. 379. **3,** Chalcocite is found with bornite and chalcopyrite from the Gruss copper mine, Portola, Engineering and Mining Journal (25) p. 543. **4,** Chalcocite shows microscopic "graphic" intergrowth with bornite from Surprise Creek, A. F. Rogers (17) p. 593.

Riverside County: **1,** A little chalcocite is present in the limestone at Crestmore, Eakle (15) p. 353, and **2,** it occurs with cuprite in the Palen Mountains (secs. 29, 30, T. 4 S., R. 20 E., S.B.), F. J. H. Merrill (2) p. 526.

San Benito County: **1,** Small crystals of chalcocite occur scattered through the natrolite of the benitoite vein, near the headwaters of the San Benito River, Louderback and Blasdale (5) p. 359.

San Bernardino County: **1,** A considerable amount of pyrite-chalcocite ore came from the Pacific Mines Corp., 7 miles south of Ludlow, Cloudman et al. (1) p. 790. **2,** A little chalcocite is associated with bornite, chalcopyrite, and tetrahedrite in the Calico Mining District, Weeks (4) p. 534, and **3,** the mineral is found at Ivanpah and Ord, Loew (2) p. 186, Tucker and Sampson (17) p. 267. **4,** Chalcocite occurs as a secondary mineral in the new American Eagle mine (sec. 31, T. 3 N., R. 24 E., S.B.), L. A. Wright et al. (5) p. 65.

San Diego County: **1,** Massive chalcocite comes from Potrero, CDMG (10037).

Shasta County: **1,** Chalcocite is widespread but not abundant in the copper mines of the county: Bully Hill, Afterthought, Copper City, Iron Mountain, Balaklala, Silver King, Greenhorn, etc., as reported in Aubury (1) p. 65, Laizure (1) p. 528, Tucker (9) pp. 427, 445, Averill (9) p. 127, and the East Shasta copper-zinc area, Albers and Robertson (3) p. 70.

Sierra County: **1,** Chalcocite occurs in very minor amounts in the Alleghany Mining District, E. MacBoyle (3) p. 4.

Siskiyou County: **1,** Chalcocite has been reported from the Yellow Butte mine, 12 miles northeast of Weed, the Copper King mine, and the Bonanza mine near Honolulu (N.R.).

Trinity County: **1,** Chalcocite occurs as local enrichment in the Copper Queen lode, in the Carrville Mining District, D. F. MacDonald (2) p. 17. **2,** A small amount of "sooty chalcocite" is found in the Island Mountain mine, Vonsen (p.c. '45), and **3,** it occurs with native copper and carbonates on the North Fork, Trinity River, near the main stream, J. B. Trask (1) p. 24.

Tuolumne County: **1,** A considerable amount of chalcocite was found in the upper levels of the Oak Hill mine, Aubury (4) p. 250.

CHALCOPYRITE—Copper Pyrites
A sulphide of copper and iron, CuFeS₂

Chalcopyrite is the universal copper mineral, abundant in practically all copper ores, and present in nearly every mineral vein, and therefore in almost every county in the state. Good general references to copper ores are A. Knopf (2) and Aubury (1) and (4).

Bornite, chalcocite, chalcopyrite, cuprite, galena, marcasite, pyrite, pyrrhotite, stibnite, tenorite, tetrahedrite, and many other antimony, copper, iron, lead and zinc sulfides, and oxides are found in traces or in minor amounts in many localities. The entries listed reflect either mineralogical or historic interest, and the listings are not complete nor is all literature which mentions these minerals referenced.

Alameda County: **1,** Small amounts of chalcopyrite are present in the massive pyrite at the Alma mine, Leona Heights, Schaller (1) p. 194.

Alpine County: **1,** Chalcopyrite is found with enargite and other sulphides in the Mogul area, Eakle (16) p. 13.

Amador County: **1,** Chalcopyrite is the chief ore mineral at the Jackson (Newton) mine, 3 miles northeast of Ione, Storms (9) p. 87, and **2,** it occurs in minor amounts in some of the other mines of the county: Copper Hill (secs. 34, 35, T. 8 N., R. 9 E., M.D.), Ione City, Bull Run, etc., Aubury (1) pp. 185, 186.

Calaveras County: **1,** Many tons of chalcopyrite ore were mined in this county. The principal producers were the Copperopolis, Campo Seco, Lancha Plana, Union, and Keystone mines, Reid (3) p. 398, Aubury (1) p. 190. Minor amounts of chalcopyrite occur in the gold ores, Moss (1) p. 1011, Franke and Logan (4) p. 239.

Colusa County: **1,** Chalcopyrite is associated in small amounts with cinnabar, gold, and stibnite, at the Manzanita mine, Becker (4) p. 367.

Contra Costa County: **1,** Chalcopyrite occurs with gold and bornite at a prospect in a ravine, tributary to Mitchell Canyon on Mount Diablo, H. W. Turner (1) p. 391.

Del Norte County: **1,** Many mines in the Low Divide and Shelly Creek areas carry some chalcopyrite, Aubury (1) p. 27.

El Dorado County: **1,** Good specimens of chalcopyrite, with bornite, molybdenite, garnet, epidote, and axinite, have come from the old Cosumnes mine near Fairplay, Tucker and Waring (2) p. 276. **2,** Considerable chalcopyrite has been produced from other mines in the Foothill copper belt in this county: Alabaster Cave (secs. 10, 15, T. 11 N., R. 8 E., M.D.), Lilyama (sec. 3, T. 11 N., R. 9 E., M.D.), Cambrian (sec. 23, T. 11 N., R. 9 E., M.D.), Boston (sec. 22, T. 4 N., R. 9 E., M.D.), etc., Aubury (1) pp. 176–181.

Fresno County: **1,** Chalcopyrite is abundant in the Copper King mine (sec. 3, T. 12 S., R. 23 E., M.D.), Crawford (1) p. 66; **2,** at the Fresno copper mine, Aubury (4) p. 281, and **3,** massive at the Nieper copper mine (sec. 34, T. 11 S., R. 23 E., M.D.), Goldstone (1) p. 194.

Humboldt County: **1,** Boulders of massive pyrite and chalcopyrite occur on the seashore at Patrick's Point, 6 miles north of Trinidad, Aubury (4) p. 155. **2,** Chalcopyrite occurs on Horse Mountain (T. 6 N., R. 4 E., H), Lowell (1) p. 397, and **3,** a vein up to 7 feet in width was reported on the Hoopa Indian Reservation (sec. 2, T. 8 N., R. 4 E., H), Averill (10) p. 508.

Imperial County: **1,** Small amounts of chalcopyrite are present in the gold veins of the Picacho, Cargo Muchacho, and other areas in the county, Tucker (11) p. 252, Tucker and Sampson (27) pp. 16, 17, R. J. Sampson and Tucker (18) pp. 115, 125.

Inyo County: **1,** Chalcopyrite is found in many of the gold and lead-silver deposits in the Darwin, Argus, Coso, Inyo, Panamint, and other areas in the county, nowhere in considerable amount. Specific localities may be found listed in Aubury (1) p. 245, Tucker (11) pp. 469–473, Tucker and Sampson (25) pp. 383–413, Kelley (4) p. 543, Hall and MacKevett (4) p. 59.

Kern County: **1,** Some chalcopyrite is found in most of the gold mines of the county: Valley View, Rademacher, Goler, Woody, Mojave, and others: Tucker (4) p. 308, Tucker and Sampson (21) pp. 314, 360, E. C. Simpson (1) p. 409, and Tucker and Sampson (29) pp. 323, 329. **2,** Chalcopyrite is present as a minor mineral in the tin ores of the Gorman area, Troxel and Morton (2) p. 294.

Los Angeles County: **1,** Chalcopyrite is found with pyrrhotite, galena and sphalerite in veins in schist, at the property of the Denver Mining and Milling Company, 12 miles from the mouth of Pacoima Canyon, Tucker (4) p. 318. **2,** The mineral is found as veins and stringers in quartz, 7 miles below the summit of Soledad Pass (New Pass), 90 feet above the creek bed, W. P. Blake (3) p. 81. **3,** The mineral is found with marcasite and sphalerite on Mill Creek, near the Monte Cristo mine, R. J. Sampson (10) p. 187.

Madera County: **1,** Chalcopyrite occurs in small masses at the Buchanan mine (sec. 33, T. 8 S., R. 18 E., M.D.), Aubury (1) p. 218; **2,** at the Ne Plus Ultra and other mines near Daulton, ibid. **3,** The mineral is found in the Minarets Mining District, W. W. Bradley (9) p. 548, Erwin (1) pp. 66–71.

Marin County: **1,** Chalcopyrite occurs with pyrite in a number of veins in serpentine, near Bolinas Bay (sec. 1, T. 1 N., R. 8 W., M.D.), Aubury (1) p. 143.

Mariposa County: **1,** Massive chalcopyrite with pyrite is abundant at the Green Mountain copper group (secs. 31, 32, T. 7 S., R. 18 E., M.D.), **2,** Pocahontas (sec. 14, T. 7 S., R. 17 E., M.D.), **3,** Baretta (T. 3 S., R. 16 E., M.D.), **4,** near Hornitos (sec. 13, T. 3 S., R. 15 E., M.D.), and at other mines in small amounts, Aubury (1) pp. 206–215, (4) p. 268.

Mendocino County: **1,** Chalcopyrite is found with tetrahedrite at the Redwood Copper Queen (secs. 17, 20, T. 12 N., R. 13 W., M.D.), Aubury (1) p. 137.

Merced County: **1,** Small amounts of chalcopyrite occur in the Jose copper mine (sec. 4, T. 14 S., R. 9 E., M.D.) and Victor Bonanza mine (T. 13 S., R. 9 E., M.D.), Aubury (1) p. 146.

Modoc County: **1,** A little chalcopyrite is found in gold-quartz veins in the extreme northeast corner of the state, Hoag Mining District (T. 47, 48 N., R. 15, 16 E., M.D.), Stines (2) p. 386, Averill (6) p. 453.

Mono County: **1,** Chalcopyrite occurs sparingly on Blind Spring Hill, A. L. Ransome (2) p. 172, and **2,** with scheelite, molybdenite, etc., on the slope of Bloody Mountain above Laurel Lake, Mayo (4) pp. 83, 84.

Napa County: **1,** High-grade chalcopyrite ore was found 13 miles south of Middletown (sec. 17, T. 10 N., R. 5 W., M.D.), Aubury (1) p. 140.

Nevada County: **1,** Chalcopyrite has been mined in the Spenceville area, Aubury (1) p. 164. **2,** Good masses of pure chalcopyrite, associated with arsenopyrite, galena, etc., are found in the Meadow Lake Mining District, Wiskar (1) p. 194. **3,** The mineral was reported with pyrrhotite carrying platinum (?) values, at Liberty Hill, in greenish siliceous rock, Hill (3) p. 8. **4,** The mineral is widespread but not abundant in the Grass Valley mines, Lindgren (12) p. 118.

Placer County: Small amounts of chalcopyrite in pyrite are found at many localities in the county. Nowhere is it of much importance: Centennial (sec. 17, T. 12 N., R. 8 E., M.D.), Logan (4) p. 443; Valley View, Aubury (1) p. 174; Dairy Farm, Aubury (4) p. 208, and Baker (Whiskey Hill) near Lincoln, W. P. Blake (12) p. 290; Eclipse (sec. 17, T. 12 N., R. 8 E., M.D.), and Elder (sec. 4, T. 13 N., R. 8 E., M.D.), Aubury (4) pp. 207, 210, and Colfax (sec. 33, T. 15 N., R. 9 E., M.D.), C. A. Waring (4) p. 349.

Plumas County: **1,** Commercially valuable bornite-chalcopyrite ores have been mined at the Walker mine, Hanks (12) p. 94 and **2,** at the Engels and Superior mines, H. W. Turner and Rogers (32) p. 377. These have been the leading copper producers in the state since 1915. **3,** Chalcopyrite occurs with bornite and chalcocite at the Gruss copper mine, near Portola, Engineering and Mining Journal (25) p. 543. **4,** The mineral is present also in lesser amounts at a number of other properties, Logan (4) p. 470, Averill (8) pp. 93–95.

Riverside County: **1,** Chalcoyprite is one of the minor minerals at the Crestmore quarry, Eakle (15) p. 352.

San Benito County: **1,** A little chalcopyrite is found on Lewis Creek (secs. 2, 3, 4, T. 19 S., R. 10 E., M.D.), W. W. Bradley and Logan (7) p. 633, and **2,** at Copper Mountain (T. 16 S., R. 7 E., M.D.), L. L. Root (4) p. 233.

San Bernardino County: **1,** Chalcopyrite occurs in small amounts in practically all of the mining regions of the county: Aubury (1) pp. 249–255, (4) pp. 325–329, Cloudman et al (1) pp. 774–899, Tucker and Sampson (27) pp. 67, 69, (28) pp. 234–239. **2,** Chalcopyrite is the common ore mineral in the Ord Mountain deposits, Weber (3) p. 26.

San Diego County: **1,** Masses of chalcopyrite occur 8 miles east of Encinitas (T. 13 S., R. 3 W., S.B.), Aubury (1) p. 259, and **2,** also at the Barona copper claims (T. 14 S., R. 1 E., S.B.), 12 miles northeast of Lakeside, ibid., p. 260. **3,** The massive pyrrhotite of the Friday mine, 4 miles south of Julian, carries small amounts of chalcopyrite, with pentlandite and violarite, Calkins (2) p. 79, Hudson (1) p. 217.

San Luis Obispo County: Minor occurrences of chalcopyrite ores are scattered through the county. **1,** near Cayucas, and **2,** on Chorro Creek, Aubury (1) p. 148, and **3,** a few miles south and west from Santa Margarita at the summit of the Santa Lucia Mountains, Logan (3) p. 686.

Santa Barbara County: **1,** Small deposits carrying chalcopyrite occur northeast of Los Olivos (sec. 5, T. 7 N., R. 29 W., S.B.), Huguenin (2) p. 735.

Santa Clara County: **1,** A little chalcopyrite occurred in the New Almaden quicksilver mine, Randol (2) p. 180, E. H. Bailey and Everhart (12) p. 98; **2,** it is recorded from the Hooker Creek mine, 1 mile from Eva (T. 9 S., R. 1 W., M.D.), Hanks (14) p. 97, Huguenin and Castello (4) p. 184.

Shasta County: **1,** Chalcoyprite is the predominant mineral in the Shasta County copper belt, which includes the Iron Mountain, Bully Hill, Afterthought, Balaklala and other mines, Diller (7) pp. 126–132, (10) p. 12, Tucker (9) pp. 425–433, Kinkel et al. (2), Albers and Robertson (3) p. 70. **2,** Chalcopyrite was prominent in some of the veins in the Delta mine (T. 35 N., R. 5 W, M.D.), Ferguson (1) p. 72.

Sierra County: **1,** Chalcopyrite occurs in small amounts in the gold veins of the county, E. MacBoyle (3) p. 88, Averill (11) p. 17.

Siskiyou County: Some chalcopyrite, occasionally in considerable amount, is found, usually associated with pyrite and pyrrhotite, in nearly every ore deposit in the county. The occurrences are mostly in the western part, near Callahan, Dutch Creek, Happy Camp, Honolulu, and other areas. The principal source of detailed information as to localities is Aubury (1) pp. 105–111, (4) pp. 122–133.

Sonoma County: **1,** Cornucopia mine (secs. 33, 34, T. 12 N., R. 9 W., M.D.), produced chalcopyrite, W. W. Bradley (1) p. 320.

Tehama County: **1,** Pyrite and chalcopyrite form the ore of the California and Massachusetts copper mines (sec. 25, T. 27 N., R. 9 W., M.D.), Tucker (3) p. 261.

Trinity County: Chalcopyrite ores have been mined at a number of localities: **1,** Lambert group at the mouth of Rattlesnake Creek and **2,** on the Cold Fork of Indian Valley Creek, Aubury (1) pp. 118, 119; **3,** in the Copper Queen mine, Carrville Mining District, D. F. MacDonald (2) p. 17; **4,** with considerable chalcanthite in the New River area, Aubury (4) p. 144; **5,** in the pyrrhotite mass at Island Mountain, CDMG (15710) and **6,** at the Ralston mine (sec. 32, T. 35 N., R. 10 W., M.D.), Averill (10) p. 55. See also as a general reference Stinson (1).

Tulare County: **1,** Chalcopyrite occurs 7 miles northeast of Visalia, Tucker (2) p. 908; **2,** in Round Valley $2\frac{1}{4}$ miles east of Lindsay; **3,** with pyrrhotite on the north fork of the middle fork, Tule River (secs. 30, 32, T. 19 S., R. 31 E., M.D.), ibid., p. 909, and **4,** at the Hart (sec. 2, T. 15 S., R. 28 E., M.D.) and Powell (T. 19 S., R. 31 E., M.D.) properties, Franke (1) p. 435.

Tuolumne County: **1,** Considerable chalcopyrite ore was found at the Washington mine (secs. 20, 21, T. 2 N., R. 17 E., M.D.), and **2,** at the Oak Hill mine, Aubury (4) pp. 250, 251.

Ventura County: **1,** Chalcopyrite occurs in the White Mule group (sec. 13, T. 8 N., R. 20 W., S.B.), in gold quartz with marcasite and pyrite, Tucker (10) pp. 231, 232.

Yuba County: **1,** Chalcopyrite is a minor constituent in the gold quartz veins at the Golden Mary (W $\frac{1}{2}$ sec. 34, T. 19 N., R. 6 E., M.D.), C. A. Waring (4) p. 445; **2,** the mineral occurs at the Ayer mine (sec. 35, T. 16 N., R. 5 E., M.D.), ibid., p. 424, and **3,** in the Dobbins Mining District (sec. 23, T. 18 N., R. 7 E., M.D.), ibid., p. 447.

CHLORITES

The chlorites are a group of soft micaceous aluminosilicates of iron and magnesium. The species below grade into one another by continuous variations in composition. The chlorites are common constituents of metamorphic rocks and as such are often referred to by group name. It is frequently impossible to distinguish variety, or even species, without extensive chemical and optical examination.

Validity of varietal names in this group is sometimes subject to debate.

CHLORITE
Basic magnesium aluminum iron silicate, $(Mg,Al,Fe)_{12}[(Si,Al)_8O_{20}](OH)_{16}$
(general formula)

Humboldt County: **1**, Lateritic ores from this county carry chlorite and several varieties of serpentine, some nickeliferous, Montoya and Baur (1) p. 1228.

Riverside County: **1**, Chlorite occurs as a contact mineral in the Crestmore quarries, Woodford (11) p. 350.

San Bernardino County: **1**, Large plates of chlorite up to 6 inches across occur in abundance in chlorite schists in a newly exposed outcrop in Precambrian rocks in the Ivanpah Mountains. The locality is at the dead-end of a road entering a canyon from the east between the Clark Mountain fault and a parallel subordinate fault to the southwest, shown on the Kingman sheet of the Geologic map of California, (near center, T. 15 N., R. 14 E., S.B.), Norris and Webb (p.c. '63).

Sierra County: **1**, Crystals of chlorite associated with magnetite as replacement of dolomite occur at the Sierra iron mine at Upper Spencer Lake, Durrell (p.c. '45).

CLINOCHLORE
Basic magnesium iron aluminum silicate, $(Mg,Fe^{2+},Al)_6(Si,Al)_4O_{10}(OH)_8$

Clinochlore occurs as an alteration product of magnesium-iron minerals and is common in schists. *Kotschubeite* is a rose-red variety containing chromium, and is associated with chromite in serpentine rocks.

Amador County: **1**, Specimens from near Jackson are reported as probably kotschubeite, Lindgren (2) p. 5, although the material may be kämmererite.

El Dorado County: **1**, Coarsely crystalline chlorite, probably clinochlore, is found on the Stifle claim on Traverse Creek near Georgetown, Durrell (p.c. '44).

Fresno County: **1**, Large pseudo-hexagonal plates of clinochlore with some penninite occur in 1- to 6-inch veins (E $\frac{1}{2}$ sec. 11, T. 12 S., R. 23 E., M.D.), and **2**, also in road cuts along the highway on the north side of the north fork, Kings River, near Piedra, Durrell and MacDonald (1) p. 452. **3**, Clinochlore occurs as micaceous crusts in nodular masses near Humphreys (sec. 22, T. 11 S., R. 23 E., M.D.), Pabst (8) p. 582. **4**, Tabular crystals of clinochlore as much as $\frac{5}{16}$ of an inch in size are reported to be associated with andradite garnet in White Creek near the Archer mine, Watters (p.c. '51), Murdoch (p.c. '54).

Los Angeles County: **1**, Chlorite, probably clinochlore, occurs with clinozoisite and tourmaline on the north side of Sierra Pelona Valley (center sec. 2, T. 5 N., R. 14 W., S.B.), Neuerburg (p.c. '44).

Placer County: **1**, Rose-red kotschubeite occurs on chromite in the serpentine of Green Valley on the American River below Towle, Lindgren (2) p. 904; analysis by Melville, in Melville and Lindgren (1) p. 27.

Riverside County: **1**, Clinochlore occurs in pale-green flakes with idocrase in the limestone of the Wet Weather quarry at Crestmore, Eakle (15) p. 348, Woodford et al. (10) p. 370.

PENNINITE
Basic magnesium/iron/aluminum silicate, $(Mg,Fe^{2+},Al)_6(Si,Al)_4O_{10}(OH)_8$

Penninite is similar to clinochlore but has more iron in its composition. *Kämmererite* is a peach-blossom red variety associated with chromite. *Rhodochrome* is similar to kämmererite.

Alameda County: **1**, Reddish-violet kämmererite occurs with chromite on Cedar Mountain at the Mendenhall mine, A. F. Rogers (7) p. 380.

Amador County: **1**, Kämmererite (?) or kotschubeite occur near Jackson, Lindgren (2) p. 5.

Calaveras County: **1**, Abundant kämmererite is found in the chromite ores of the Mayflower property (NW $\frac{1}{4}$ sec. 9, T. 1 N., R. 13 E., M.D.), and in minor amounts in neighboring deposits, Cater (2) p. 50.

Del Norte County: **1**, Kämmererite with uvarovite has been observed coating chromite at the Camp 8 group (sec. 19, T. 16 N., R. 3 E., H.), J. E. Allen (2) p. 123. **2**, Kämmererite has come from the Brown mine at High Plateau (sec. 28, T. 18 N., R. 2 E., H.), Vonsen (p.c. '45).

El Dorado County: **1**, Kämmererite occurred with uvarovite at the Pilliken mine (sec. 21, T. 11 N., R. 8 E., M.D.), Averill (12) p. 90. **2**, Kämmererite has been found at Latrobe, CDMG (20511).

Monterey County: **1**, Kämmererite with uvarovite and chromite occurs west of King City, W. W. Bradley (26) p. 354. **2**, Kämmererite with uvarovite and chromite occurs at the South Slope mine, CDMG (21738). This may be the same as locality **(1)**.

Nevada County: **1**, *Rhodochrome* is abundant at the Red Ledge chrome mine near Washington (sec. 13, T. 17 N., R. 10 E., M.D.), E. M. Boyle (1) p. 77.

Placer County: **1**, Kämmererite occurs in chromite in Green Valley, above Dutch Flat, CDMG (9900). **2**, Shannon (3) p. 377, has analyzed a pale grayish-lavender chromiferous chlorite from the mine of the Placer Chrome Company, 6 miles south of Newcastle.

San Benito County: **1**, Red kämmererite occurs on chromite associated with uvarovite at New Idria, Brush (1) p. 268. **2**, Coarse flakes of kämmererite occur in massive chromite near the headwaters of the San Benito River (SW $\frac{1}{4}$ sec. 21, T. 18 S., R. 12 E., M.D.), Murdoch (p.c. '45).

Shasta County: **1**, Kämmererite coats chromite in the Little Castle Creek mine, near Dunsmuir (N.R.).

Siskiyou County: **1**, Kämmererite occurs with chromite and uvarovite at the Martin McKean mine near Callahan, Melhase (6) p. 23. **2**, Kämmererite occurs with uvarovite at the Youngs Valley group (T. 17 N., R. 5 E., H.), Rynearson and Smith (1) pp. 304, 306, J. E. Allen (2) p. 123. **3**, Kämmererite with uvarovite occurs north of Seiad (T.

46, 47 N., R. 11, 13 W., M.D.), Rynearson and Smith (1) pp. 304, 306, J. E. Allen (2) pp. 123, 124. **4,** Penninite is found with uvarovite at the Peg Leg mine, 14 miles southeast of Yreka, Symons (4) p. 101.

Tehama County: **1,** Kämmererite is found with chromite and uvarovite on North Elder Creek (T. 25 N., R. 7 W., M.D.), Rynearson (3) p. 200.

Yuba County: **1,** Kämmererite is found with uvarovite and chromite at the Red Ledge mine, Melhase (6) p. 23.

PROCHLORITE
Basic iron magnesium aluminum silicate, $(Mg,Fe^{2+},Al)_6(Si,Al)_4O_{10}(OH)_8$

Prochlorite forms large flaky masses in schists.

Butte County: **1,** Prochlorite is a constituent of the schists at Forbestown, specimens coming from the Gold Bank mine, Irelan (4) p. 47.

Contra Costa County: **1,** Prochlorite was described and analyzed from the schists near San Pablo by Blasdale (1) p. 341.

CHLORITOID
Basic iron magnesium manganese aluminum silicate,
$(Fe^{2+},Mg,Mn)_2Al_4Si_2O_{10}(OH)_4$

Ottrelite is used as a synonym for chloritoid and as a name for varieties rich in manganese.

Inyo County: **1,** The variety ottrelite occurs in dark-green oblong plates in schists on the west side of the Panamint Range, 5 to 10 miles east of Ballarat. The mineral comprises a considerable proportion of the schists in localized areas, Murphy (4) p. 347.

Kern County: **1,** Dark-green chloritoid occurs abundantly in schists, $2-2\frac{1}{2}$ miles northwest of Garlock, El Paso Mountains, Chesterman (p.c. '51).

Siskiyou County: **1,** A specimen of ottrelite schist has come from near Yreka, CDMG (12121).

CHLOROMAGNESITE
Magnesium chloride, $MgCl_2$

Magnesium chloride exists in solution in the waters of some springs and lakes, but its solubility prevents it from forming as a mineral except in the driest places. It is a doubtful species.

San Bernardino County: **1,** White efflorescences of chloromagnesite occur at Saratoga Springs, near the south end of Death Valley, G. E. Bailey (2) p. 106.

CHONDRODITE
Magnesium fluosilicate, $Mg_5(SiO_4)_2(OH,F)_2$

Riverside County: **1,** From Crestmore this mineral occurs in two environments: (a) in contact rock with brucite and periclase as rounded, but somewhat tabular, colorless crystals, A. F. Rogers (19) p. 583, (31) p. 463, Woodford et al. (10) p. 367; (b) more rarely in dark-green crystals up to one mm, in contact rock in Lone Star quarry, Woodford et al. (10) p. 367. **2,** Chondrodite was also found in the old City quarry, Riverside, A. F. Rogers (19) p. 582. **3,** Deep amber grains of chondrodite are abundant in some of the contact zone limestones of the Jensen quarry, Murdoch (p.c. '47).

San Bernardino County: **1,** Chondrodite is reported from the limestone quarries at Colton, Eakle (15) p. 333.

CHROMITE
Oxide of chromium and iron, FeCr$_2$O$_4$

Magnesium-chromite is a common variant, in which magnesium in part replaces chromium. *Trautwinite* was originally described in 1873 as a new mineral species from California, Goldsmith (1) p. 348, (5) p. 152. E. S. Dana (5) p. 447, suggested that it was a mixture of uvarovite garnet and chromite.

Chromite is an exceedingly widespread mineral in the state, notably in the Coast Ranges from Santa Barbara County northward, especially in the serpentine areas, Diller (18). Distribution of some of the localities is described in Bulletin 76 of the CDMG, W. W. Bradley et al. (4), Southern Coast Ranges, G. W. Walker and Griggs (4). Chromite occurs commonly as disseminated grains in basic and ultrabasic rocks, as irregular boulder-like masses, and seldom as individual crystals.

Alameda County: **1,** Massive chromite occurs in many mines in the Cedar Mountain area, 16 miles southeast of Livermore, Hanks (12) p. 136, (15) p. 100, Aubury (3) p. 267, W. W. Bradley et al. (4) p. 115; analysis by Kramm (1) p. 341.

Amador County: **1,** Chromite is found near Jackson, one mile south of Mountain Spring House, Hanks (12) p. 136, (15) p. 100. **2,** Some ore was shipped from properties near Ione (sec. 34, T. 6 N., R. 10 E., and sec. 2, T. 5 N., R. 10 E., M.D.), W. W. Bradley et al. (4) p. 116. **3,** Shipments have also been made from various properties occurring in serpentine on Cosumnes River 8 miles northeast of Carbondale (secs. 6, 29, T. 7 N., R. 10 E., M.D.), Hanks (12) p. 117. **4,** Many small deposits of chromite occur throughout the county (T. 5, 6, 7, 8, N., R. 10 E., M.D.), Cater (2) pp. 33–38, ibid. (3).

Butte County: **1,** Placer chromite is common and has been reported by Engineering and Mining Journal (12) p. 1259, (23) pp. 511, 597, 807, Diller (14) p. 11, Averill (13) p. 71. **2,** Deposits *in situ* are very numerous in small pockets in serpentine. Localities are mentioned or described by Hanks (12) p. 136, Aubury (3) p. 267, W. W. Bradley et al. (4) pp. 105, 118–121.

Calaveras County: Chromite is widespread in this county, mostly in lode but occasionally in placer deposits. Occurrences are reported from **1,** Tower Ranch, 9 miles east of Milton, and **2,** Wright Ranch in Salt Springs Valley, 10 miles northeast of Milton, Aubury (3) p. 267; **3,** from the Big Pine chrome mine (sec. 20, T. 4 N., R. 11 E., M.D.), Aubury (3) p. 267; **4,** near Murphys and at Campo Seco, Hanks (12) p. 136, and **5,** 5 miles southeast of Valley Springs and 4 miles north of Copperopolis on the road to Milton, Tucker (14) pp. 55, 56. **6,** W. W. Bradley et al. (4) p. 121, reported chromite 8 miles southwest of Angels Camp (secs. 3, 7, 10, T. 2 N., R. 12 E., M.D.); **7,** from 4 miles west of Fostoria (secs. 23, 30, T. 5 N., R. 10, 11 E., M.D.), ibid., p. 122; **8,** from 14 miles east of Milton Station (sec. 15, T. 2 N., R. 12 E., M.D.), ibid., p. 123, and **9**, from 10 miles northeast of Angels Camp at True Blue mine, ibid., p. 123. **10**, Large masses of chromite were reported from the south side of San Diego Gulch near Noble copper mine, J. R. Browne (4) p. 225. Other occurrences too numerous to list are in the serpentines of this county. Details of location of the many chromite deposits, mostly small, in the county (T. 1, 2, 3, 4, 5 N., R. 10, 11, 12, 13 E., M.D.) are given by Cater (2) pp. 33–58, L. D. Clark and Lydon (4) pp. 21–33, Cater (3).

Colusa County: **1**, Minor amounts of chromite were shipped from Chrome Wonder mine, near Stonyford, W. W. Bradley et al. (4) p. 123; **2**, near Wilbur Springs, ibid., p. 123, and **3**, from 1½ miles northwest of Cook Springs (T. 16 N., R. 6 W., M.D.), ibid., p. 124.

Contra Costa County: **1**, Chromite prospects were located in T. 1 N., R. 1 W., M.D., L. L. Root (5) p. 12. **2**, Occurrences have been reported from one mile northeast of North Peak, in the Mount Diablo range, and **3**, from east of San Antonio in the Contra Costa Hills, J. D. Whitney (7) p. 19.

Del Norte County: **1**, Black sands along Smith River carry chromite, Hanks (12) p. 136, and **2**, beach sands near Crescent City carry abundant chromite, Horner (1) p. 35. **3**, Lode occurrences are very numerous. Some important deposits occur in T. 15, 16, 17, 18 N., R. 2, 3 E., M.D.; these and other localities are described by Maxson (1) pp. 123–160 and J. C. O'Brien (1) pp. 77–84. Other references to chromite in this county are Hanks (12) p. 136, McGregor (1) p. 167, Aubury (1) p. 114, (3) pp. 267, 268, W. W. Bradley et al. (4) p. 125, Diller (18) p. 32 and F. G. Wells et al. (5).

El Dorado County: Serpentine rocks in this county carry chromite in disseminated irregular masses. Concentrations from which some sample shipments of ore were made are found in some parts of the county. Many localities are grouped about the following places: Volcanoville, Cummings, Newcastle, Clarksville, Georgetown and Folsom, W. W. Bradley et al. (4) pp. 132–143; near Coloma and Latrobe, ibid., p. 131, Hanks (12) p. 136, (15) p. 100; a 15-inch vein in slate is reported by Fairbanks (9) p. 479, from near the Fort Yuma mine. Occurrences in the Pilliken area (sec. 28, T. 11 N., R. 8 E., M.D.) are described by L. R. Page et al. (1) p. 433, and mentioned by W. W. Bradley et al. (4) p. 137, and Tucker (3) p. 274. Analysis of chromite from the Donnelly deposit, 10 miles northeast of Folsom (sec. 21, T. 11 N., R. 8 E., M.D.) is given by W. W. Bradley et al. (4) p. 133. Other references are Cater et al. (4) and W. B. Clark and Carlson (3).

Fresno County: Deposits of chromite occur in the Mount Diablo Range in the western part of the county. Many occurrences are mentioned in W. W. Bradley et al. (4) pp. 144–145, Goldstone (1) p. 189. J. D. Whitney (7) p. 59, reported chromite as a ". . . block 4' x 7'4" x 5'6" thought to be silver ore at first . . ." from near the New Idria mine.

Glenn County: Chromite occurrences are found **1**, near Millsaps (sec. 25, T. 22 N., R. 7 W., M.D.), Aubury (3) p. 268, W. W. Bradley et al. (4) p. 198, and **2**, on Big Stony Creek (T. 19 N., R. 6 W., M.D.), J. H. Rogers (1) p. 324. **3**, Claims are located 30 miles west of Orland (sec. 3, T. 22 N., R. 7 W., M.D.), W. W. Bradley et al. (4) p. 147. **4**,

Chromite also occurs near Newville, Boalich (1) p. 25, and **5**, 19 miles from Fruto (T. 19, 20 N., R. 5, 6 W., M.D.), Mining and Scientific Press (39) p. 454.

Humboldt County: **1**, Occurrences of chromite (sec. 24, T. 10 N., R. 5 E., H.) and (secs. 11, 13, T. 11 N., R. 4 E., H.) have been recorded by J. C. O'Brien (1) p. 78. **2**, Float was reported from Hoopa Indian Reservation and Little Wilder Creek, Averill (10) pp. 505, 506. **3**, Ore was shipped from deposits on Horse Mountain, 25 miles northeast of Eureka (secs. 33, 34, T. 6 N., R. 4 E., H.), W. W. Bradley et al. (4) p. 148.

Kings County: **1**, Float chromite has been found in the serpentine area at Table Mountain, W. W. Bradley (2) p. 527.

Lake County: Two general areas in this county have the largest number of reported prospects: **1**, east of Middletown (T. 10, 11, 12 N., R. 6, 7 W., M.D.) in decomposed serpentine, W. W. Bradley (1) p. 204, W. W. Bradley et al. (4) pp. 148, 149, and **2**, (sec. 36, T. 19 N., R. 10 W., M.D.) near Hullville, W. W. Bradley (1) p. 204, Laizure (9) p. 54. The serpentine rocks of the county carry disseminated chromite in many other areas.

Los Angeles County: **1**, Chromite is reported to occur 13 miles north of Saugus in Bouquet Canyon, in serpentine, Tucker (13) p. 288. **2**, Reports of occurrences from near Acton and Harold in Soledad Canyon, F. J. H. Merrill (2) p. 471, W. W. Bradley et al. (4) p. 151, are undoubtedly due to misidentification of ilmenite which is so abundant as float from the San Gabriel Mountains.

Madera County: **1**, Chromite is found near Madera in masses coated with zaratite, CDMG (13414).

Marin County: **1**, Chromite is reported from the Maillard Ranch in San Geronimo township, 8 miles northwest of San Rafael, Watts (2) p. 253.

Mariposa County: **1**, Chromite ore was shipped from Purcell-Griffin mine, southeast of Coulterville near Pleasant Valley Station, W. W. Bradley et al. (4) p. 151. **2**, Many small chromite deposits are in the region covered by T. 2 S., R. 16 E., M.D., Cater (1) pp. 1-32, O. E. Bowen and Gray (2).

Mendocino County: **1**, Chromite coated with uvarovite garnet is found 12 miles north of Willits, Melhase (6) p. 23, CDMG (12248). **2**, Many claims have been filed in vicinity of Big and Little Red Mountains (T. 24 N., R. 16 W., M.D.), W. W. Bradley et al. (4) p. 152 and **3**, 1½ miles west of Ukiah (sec. 24, T. 15 N., R. 13 W., M.D.), McGregor (1) p. 312. **4**, Several occurrences of chromite in the hills west of the Russian River are reported, Aubury (3) p. 268, Crawford (2) p. 49. The serpentine belts in the county carry chromite in many other places.

Monterey County: **1**, Goldsmith (1) p. 348, (2) p. 365, (5) p. 152, described trautwinite as a new mineral, but it appears to be a mixture of uvarovite garnet and chromite. **2**, Chromite is common in the serpentine belts of this county, reported occurrences being principally in the vicinity of Parkfield, Hanks (12) p. 136, W. W. Bradley (1) p. 527, W. W. Bradley and Waring (6) p. 599; analysis by Goldsmith (2) p. 365.

Napa County: **1,** Several chromite prospects are reported on the Knoxville road 12 miles from Middletown (secs. 32, 36, T. 10 N., R. 5 W., M.D.), Hanks (12) p. 136, Crawford (2) p. 50, W. W. Bradley et al. (4) p. 156, 157, Boalich (4) p. 158. **2,** 900 tons of chromite were shipped from Graves Ranch mine, 8 miles northwest of Monticello, Boalich (4) p. 158.

Nevada County: Chromite is found in the concentrates of many gold mines in this county. **1,** Fine octahedrons are reported to occur in serpentine near Indian Springs (N.R.). **2,** High grade chromium ore has been shipped from the Red Ledge and other mines, near Washington (T. 16, 17 N., R. 8, 9, 10 E., M.D.). The ore of the Red Ledge is commonly coated with uvarovite and kämmererite, J. B. Trask (1) p. 25, Hanks (12) p. 137, E. MacBoyle (1) p. 63, Averill (11) p. 141.

Placer County: Chromite is widespread in serpentine in this county. Many occurrences have been reported. Some references are: Hanks (12) p. 137, (15) p. 441, Aubury (3) p. 268, W. W. Bradley et al. (4) pp. 160-163, C. A. Waring (4) p. 326, Logan (4) p. 441, E. Sampson (3) p. 107, Averill (13) p. 75. **1,** 7 miles southeast of Newcastle, nodular masses of chromite coated with penninite, kämmerite, and good crystals of uvarovite are found, Melhase (6) p. 23. **2,** In Green Valley, 9 miles southeast of Towle, chromite occurs with uvarovite and clinochlore (kotschubeite), Lindgren (2) p. 5, Melville and Lindgren (1) p. 27.

Plumas County: **1,** Chromite occurrences in this county are similar to those of the other Mother Lode counties, in serpentines and as concentrates in placers. References are found in Hanks (15) p. 101, H. W. Turner (12) p. 590, (17) p. 6, W. W. Bradley et al. (4) p. 165, E. MacBoyle (2) p. 54, J. C. O'Brien (1) p. 79, Logan (21) p. 85.

Riverside County: **1,** Approximately one ton of chromite is reported to have been mined from the New City quarry, Victoria Ave., Riverside, Knowlton (p.c. '57).

Sacramento County: Chromite is reported **1,** in black sands of Sacramento River bars (N.R.), and **2,** from 7 miles east of Folsom on the South Fork of the American River, Hanks (12) p. 137.

San Benito County: **1,** Stream placers near Hollister have yielded chromite boulders with zaratite (?) coatings, W. W. Bradley et al. (4) p. 166. **2,** Chromite also occurs in the serpentine belts near Hernandez, L. L. Root (4) p. 228, and **3,** southeast of New Idria, Aubury (3) p. 269, W. W. Bradley and Logan (7) p. 630.

San Bernardino County: **1,** Chromite is reported from 28 miles west of Hesperia, Diller (14) p. 9, Dolbear (6) p. 359. (Murdoch and Webb suspect that this is another erroneous reference, based on the widespread ilmenite occurrences of the San Gabriel Mountains.)

San Francisco County: **1,** Chromite is found in the sands of Ocean Beach below the outlet of Lake Merced, CDMG (686), Hanks (12) p. 137.

San Luis Obispo County: Chromite occurs widespread in the serpentine of the county. **1,** Many marginal occurrences that have produced ore shipments from time to time are located around San Luis Obispo. Descriptions of some properties and localities are found in Hanks (12) p. 137, Irelan (3) p. 531, Crawford (1) p. 37, Aubury (3) p. 270, Harder (2) p. 167; analysis by H. Pemberton (1) p. 241.

San Mateo County: **1,** Scattered masses of chromite occur near Crystal Springs Lake west of San Mateo on the Pacific slope of the redwoods, in serpentine, Hanks (12) p. 137, Huguenin and Castello (4) p. 172.

Santa Barbara County: **1,** A small deposit of chromite occurs in the hills southwest of Point Sal, Huguenin (2) p. 735. **2,** Chromite also occurs (T. 8 N., R. 30 W., M.D.) near Santa Ynez, Tucker (4) p. 387. This is presumed to be the locality on the south slope of Figueroa Mountain.

Santa Clara County: As in other counties of the Coast Ranges, chromite occurs in the widespread serpentine rocks. Localities are mentioned by Hanks (12) p. 137, Irelan (3) p. 549, Crawford (1) p. 38, Carey and Miller (1) p. 162, Diller (20) p. 666, Huguenin and Castello (4) p. 183, and F. F. Davis and Jennings (6) p. 339.

Santa Cruz County: **1,** 70 tons of chromite were produced from this county in 1925, Furness (1) p. 139.

Shasta County: **1,** On Little Castle Creek (sec. 2, T. 38 N., R. 4 W., M.D.) occurs what is described as the largest chrome ore body on the Pacific Coast, at the Brown mine, 3 miles south of Dunsmuir, G. C. Brown (2) p. 755, W. W. Bradley et al. (4) pp. 183-188, Diller (16) p. 28. **2,** There are also deposits of chromite on Shotgun Creek (T. 37 N., R. 4 W., M.D.) in serpentine, Crawford (2) p. 50; **3,** on Boulder Creek, 4 miles west of Gibson (sec. 33, T. 37 N., R. 5 W., M.D.), Mining and Scientific Press (40) p. 66, and **4,** high-quality ore is reported 3 miles east of Sims Station (secs. 13, 24, T. 37 N., R. 5 W., M.D.), McGregor (1) p. 638, and Aubury (3) p. 270. **5,** Occurrences of chromite are mentioned near Round Bottom (sec. 5, T. 26 N., R. 10 W., M.D.), J. C. O'Brien (1) p. 81.

Sierra County: Dozens of placer and lode prospects have been explored in this county. Specific references are Hanks (1) p. 137, Crawford (1) p. 38, (2) p. 50, H. W. Turner (14) p. 8, Aubury (3) p. 271, E. MacBoyle (3) p. 29, Averill (11) pp. 14–16, (13) p. 76.

Siskiyou County: Chromite is widespread in serpentine rocks of the county. Prospects are too numerous to be recorded. Details, including an analysis of a chromite ore of unusual structure from Seiad Creek near the junction with the Klamath River (sec. 33, T. 47 N., R. 11 W., M.D.), appear in W. D. Johnston, Jr. (1) pp. 417–427. Other occurrences are described by: Hanks (12) p. 137, Aubury (3) p. 272, W. W. Bradley et al. (4) p. 190, Laizure (1) p. 530, Logan (8) p. 424, J. C. O'Brien (1) p. 82, F. G. Wells and Cater (6). For additional reference for numerous small occurrences throughout the county, see J. C. O'Brien (4) p. 419.

Solano County: Chromite is reported: **1,** from near Fairfield, CDMG (2772), Hanks (12) p. 137, and **2,** from near Culver-Baer quicksilver mine, Boalich (4) p. 248.

Sonoma County: This county is underlain in a large measure by the Franciscan serpentine rocks, in which chromite is widespread. Occurrences are reported from dozens of localities: Tyson (1) p. 19, Hanks (12) p. 137, Crawford (1) p. 38, W. W. Bradley (1) p. 319, W. W. Bradley et al. (4) pp. 201–203, Huguenin and Castello (1) p. 248, L. L. Root (4) p. 333, Laizure (9) p. 56.

Stanislaus County: **1,** Small deposits of chromite from which some ore has been shipped occur in Arroyo del Puerto, W. W. Bradley et al.

(4) p. 204, Hawkes and Wheeler (1) p. 1950, and **2,** one mile east of Camp Jones, Engineering and Mining Journal (23) p. 807.

Tehama County: Large deposits of chromite occur on the North Fork of Elder Creek (sec. 16, T. 25. N., R. 7 W., M.D.) and are described by several writers: Crawford (1) p. 38, Aubury (3) p. 121, W. W. Bradley et al. (4) pp. 206–209, Tucker (3) p. 260, L. L. Root (4) p. 12, J. C. O'Brien (1) p. 84. For additional reference to occurrences throughout the county, see J. C. O'Brien (3) pp. 186, 187.

Trinity County: **1,** Relatively unimportant but numerous occurrences of chromite are described by G. C. Brown (2) p. 877, Engineering and Mining Journal (23) p. 511, L. L. Root (4) p. 12, J. C. O'Brien (1) p. 84.

Tulare County: Several chromite prospects are reported near Porterville and Lindsay in and about T. 19 S., R. 27 E., M.D., Hanks (12) p. 138, W. W. Bradley et al. (4) p. 213, Tucker (3) p. 907.

Tuolumne County: The serpentine of the county carries much disseminated chromite. Localities are mentioned by Hanks (12) p. 138, H. W. Turner and Ransome (15) p. 7, W. W. Bradley et al. (4) p. 213, Averill (13) p. 76, and other localities are in the area of T. 1, 2, S., 1 N., R. 13, 14, 15 E., M.D., Cater (1) pp. 1–32, Logan (23) p. 52.

Yuba County: **1,** Placer chromite occurs in black sands along the Yuba River (N.R.). **2,** Chromite is found at the Woodleaf (Woodville) Canyon mine, Mining and Scientific Press (39) p. 569.

† * CHROMRUTILE, 1928

Nevada County: **1,** Chromrutile was described as a new mineral from California in 1928 as small brilliant black crystals with kämmererite on chromite from the Red Ledge mine in the Washington Mining District, Gordon and Shannon (1) p. 69, W. W. Bradley (29) p. 69, Palache et al. (10) p. 560. Strunz (1) in 1961 showed that the mineral from the Red Ledge mine identified as chromrutile is determined by x-ray study to be a magnesium chromium titano-silicate, not a chrome-bearing rutile, and the mineral has been renamed "redledgeite".

CHRYSOBERYL
Beryllium aluminum oxide, $BeAl_2O_4$

Butte County: **1,** Crysoberyl is reported to have been found near Stanwood and at Big Bar (N.R.)

CHRYSOCOLLA
Hydrous copper silicate, $CuSiO_3 \cdot 2H_2O$

Small amounts of chrysocolla occur in most, if not all, of the copper areas of the state, in the oxidized zone of ore bodies, as incrustations, coatings, and disseminated grains. It is also common in other types of ores, and is often an associate of other minerals when minute amounts of copper were in the mineralizing solutions. Only occurrences of mineralogical interest are specifically noted here.

Azurite, chrysocolla, malachite, and other blue, blue-green, and green minerals, mostly copper-bearing, are widespread in stringers, coatings, and alterations associated with other copper minerals referenced in this volume. No systematic effort to report all occurrences of these minerals is practical. However, many minor occurrences are reported, and others omitted, because early literature references were often to minor localities, and these have been retained for clarity of the historic record.

Inyo County: 1, Pseudomorphs of chrysocolla after calcite have been described from the Reward mine, 2 miles east of Manzanar, A. F. Rogers (3) p. 20, A. Knopf (5) p. 118. 2, Pseudomorphs of chrysocolla after cerussite are reported from the Aries mine in the Cerro Gordo Mining District, Kunz (24) p. 100; see also C. W. Merriam (1) p. 43. 3, Chrysocolla occurs in the Surprise mine, in the Modoc area, Hall and Stephens (3) p. 35. 4, Chrysocolla is common and widely distributed in the ores of the Darwin Mining District, Hall and MacKevett (4) p. 64.

Kern County: 1, Beautiful crystals (presumably pseudomorphs) mistaken for turquoise are supposed to occur near Randsburg, Kunz (24) p. 101. 2, Chrysocolla in small amounts is associated with the tin ores near Gorman, Troxel and Morton (2) p. 294.

Mono County: 1, Chrysocolla was formerly the chief ore mineral of deposits now worked for gold and silver at the Goleta Consolidated mine on Copper Mountain, Aubury (1) p. 243.

Plumas County: 1, Banded chrysocolla and malachite are important ore associates at the Engels mine in Copper Canyon, Kunz (24) p. 102, Graton and McLaughlin (4) p. 20.

Riverside County: 1, Chrysocolla is reported as a secondary mineral from Crestmore, Woodford et al. (10) p. 367.

San Bernardino County: 1, Chrysocolla is the principal mineral in the Horn mine (sec. 32, T. 2 N., R. 21 E., S.B.), L. A. Wright et al. (5) p. 64; 2, it also occurs abundantly in the Bagdad Chase gold mine, ibid, p. 60, and 3, it is abundant, with malachite, at the Blue Bell mine, 7 miles west of Baker (sec. 27 (?), T. 14 N., R. 7 E., S.B.), ibid., p. 101. 4, Chrysocolla is the most abundant copper mineral in the Ord Mountain mining area, Weber (3) p. 27.

Santa Clara County: 1, A. F. Rogers (3) p. 20, has described pseudomorphs of chrysocolla after cuprite from the Santa Margarita mine near New Almaden.

Chrysocolla is mentioned from other counties. Some references are: *Humboldt,* Laizure (3) p. 306; *Imperial,* Henshaw (1) p. 185; *Inyo,* Hanks (12) p. 139, Ball (2) p. 211, Zalinski (1) p. 81, A. Knopf (5) pp. 119, 120, C. A. Waring (4) p. 69, Tucker and Sampson (25) p. 399; *Los Angeles,* Storms (4) p. 244; *Madera,* Goudey (1) p. 8; *Mariposa,* J. R. Browne (4) p. 213, Aubury (1) p. 213; *Mendocino,* CDMG (15689); *Mono,* Hanks (12) p. 139, A. L. Ransome (2) p. 190; *Nevada,* Lindgren (4) p. 201; *Riverside,* Orcutt (2) p. 901; *San Benito,* Louderback and Blasdale (5) p. 359; *San Bernardino,* Hanks (12) p. 139, Lindgren (1) p. 724, Crawford (1) p. 69, (2) p. 60, Storms (8) p. 579, Aubury (1) p. 255, Kunz (24) p. 102, Tucker and Sampson (17) p. 344; *Tulare,* CDMG (14169).

CINNABAR
Mercuric sulphide, HgS

Cinnabar was known in the State long before the discovery of gold, and the old mine at New Almaden had been in operation when Lyman (2) p. 270 visited it in 1848. The most important quicksilver deposits lie in the Coast Ranges, extending from Del Norte County to Santa Barbara County. Those in the Sierra Nevada are of minor value. Lake, Napa, Santa Clara, and San Benito counties have been most important in the mining of cinnabar.

The quicksilver deposits of California have been described in Monograph XIII of the United States Geological Survey, Becker (4), and Bulletin 78 of the State Division of Mines, W. W. Bradley (5). The important producing areas are briefly described.

Lake-Napa-Sonoma area: The Mayacmas-Sulphur Bank deposits include hundreds of occurrences of cinnabar as well as other less important mercury minerals. The significant geological facts regarding occurrence and mineralogy, are described by C. P. Ross (3) and summarized as follows (pp. 327–328):

"The Mayacmas and Sulphur Bank quicksilver districts, in northern California have been active intermittently since the fifties and together have yielded about half a million flasks of quicksilver—more than a fifth of the total production of the State. Both districts are currently productive, * * *.

"In both districts the oldest formation is the Franciscan, whose beds are greatly deformed and are locally metamorphosed. Much ultrabasic rock, which has mainly been converted to serpentine, has been intruded into the Franciscan formation, most of it in irregular but more or less sill-like masses. The serpentine has locally been further changed to a silica-carbonate rock. Other intrusive rocks occur in small amount. The Franciscan formation and the intrusive rocks are overlain by Pliocene and later volcanic rocks.

"Most of the quicksilver deposits lie near the footwalls of the serpentine bodies, where they may be enclosed in serpentine, in silica-carbonate rock, or in the Franciscan formation; but the largest deposit, the Oat Hill, is in the Franciscan far from any exposed serpentine. Some deposits are in younger intrusive rocks, and a few are in Recent lava. The ore is localized where relatively abundant openings have been accessible to the solutions. Concentrations under impermeable bodies have locally aided in the formation of ore shoots, but in several mines no evidence of such a process has been recognized. Desposition may have been confined to the zone in which ascending solutions of magmatic origin mingled with ground water. This zone, though geologically shallow, probably extends beyond the depths to which it would be profitable to mine ore shoots that are so small and erratically distributed as those hitherto found in the area."

Santa Clara-San Benito area: Santa Clara and San Benito counties carry the two most famous cinnabar properties of the state—the New Almaden and the New Idria mines. The New Almaden, oldest of the many prospects now known in the Coast Ranges, is the oldest from which production has come. The New Idria, located farther south, though some 80 miles distant, has a similar geologic setting.

New Almaden, W. W. Bradley (5) p. 154

"The first known occurrence of quicksilver within the area of the United States, was that found at the New Almaden mine in Santa Clara County in 1824 by Antonio Suñol and Louis Chaboya. Though some occurrences had apparently been earlier noted in Mexico, the New Almaden was the first producing quicksilver mine in North America. Suñol and Chaboya built a mill nearby and endeavored to extract silver from the cinnabar. Late in 1845, the ore was shown to Andreas Castillero [Anonymous (3)], a Mexican officer, who identified it as cinnabar, and under whose direction development work was immediately begun. Gun barrels were utilized as their first retorts. The output was small, however, until after California became part of the United States, since which time more than a million flasks have been produced in this county, * * * the greatest portion of which came from the New Almaden mine * * *

"The quicksilver deposits of Santa Clara County are confined, with one exception, to what is known as the New Almaden district. This district lies east of south from San Jose, extending from the northeasterly foothills of the Gabilan Range on the west to the low foothills that lie between Coyote and Dry Creeks on the east. It also embraces the Santa Teressa Hills, a low spur ridge which lies between and in general parallel to the other two. The principal deposits are 8 to 13 miles from San Jose, on the ridge which forms the southwestern boundary of the Santa Clara Valley at this place, having a general NW-SE direction, and locally called the New Almaden Ridge.

"The geology of this district and particularly of the New Almaden Ridge and its orebodies has been described in considerable detail by various writers, especially by Becker (4) and by Forstner (1) p. 169, the latter of whom says:

'The three ridges in which the deposits occur are to a great extent formed by serpentine, especially the two first named. The serpentine is associated with metamorphic sandstone and jaspilites. Large bodies of croppings can be found in each of these ridges, having also a general northwestern trend, but not coinciding with the backbone of the ridges.

'In the New Almaden ridge the most extensive orebodies have been found in and close to Mine Hill, the highest peak of the ridge, lying in its southeastern part. From this point going northwestward the croppings, while not continuous, can be traced along the ridge into the territory of the Guadalupe mine, a distance of about 3½ miles. At the surface the serpentine shows in large detached bodies surrounded by the sandstones and shales of the Franciscan series and having a general northwestern trend. This general direction of the serpentine exposures is important in connection with its occurrence underground, proven in the New Almaden mine. The line of ore croppings runs from Mine Hill to the American shaft, passing about 600 feet southwest of the Randol shaft. The underground workings in this territory have shown that the fissures wherein the orebodies have formed have invariably a serpentine footwall; hence the serpentine must be considered to occur underground in a continuous body through this entire territory and to be in places covered by overlying sandstones and shales. Southwest of Capitancillos Creek lies another parallel exposure of serpentine, contiguous to which the outcrops of the Costello mines are found. The Santa Teresa and Bernal mines are located in the serpentine of the Santa Teresa hills, and the North Almaden or Silver Creek mine close to those of the most northern ridge. In the latter a great part of the serpentine is very highly altered by silicification, as also the sandstones, a great portion of the rocks being jaspilites. The western slope of the adjoining Mount Diablo range is nearly exclusively formed of shales.' "

New Idria. R. G. Yates and Hilpert (2) p. 12 describe the mercury deposits and the mines of central San Benito County as follows:

"Most of the quicksilver deposits described in this report lie in a fairly compact group about Panoche Valley in central San Benito County, California. One mine, the Mercy, is 5 miles north of this valley in northwestern Fresno County, and another, the Cerro Gordo, is about 9 miles to the west. Quicksilver was discovered in the region about 1859. Since then mining has been sporadic and the total output of quicksilver small. Discoveries since 1938 reawakened interest in the district and 1,741 flasks of quicksilver were produced between 1938 and 1944. This brought the total known production of the district to about 3,840 flasks.

"The quicksilver deposits are in a part of the Diablo Range characterized by northwestward-trending folds and by faults of diverse trends. Sedimentary rocks involved in these structures range in age from Jurassic to Recent, and the movements that produced the structures were probably recurrent during that time. Intrusive and extrusive igneous rocks formed at several periods. All but two of the quicksilver deposits are in the Jurassic Franciscan formation, which is the oldest, most widespread, and most diverse group of rocks in the area. Although the quicksilver deposits are of late Tertiary age, none have been found in the Tertiary rocks, and only two have been found in the Cretaceous rocks.

"The quicksilver deposits consist of irregular veins and disseminations of cinnabar or metacinnabar in silicified or kaolinized sandstone and fault breccia, and silicacarbonate rock formed by the hydrothermal alteration of serpentine. Prominent fault zones enclose, or are near, all the deposits except one. Most of the orebodies are irregular and of little horizontal or vertical extent and their positions and forms were controlled by minor faults and fractures or by the character of the wall rock. The deposits are characteristically spotty, consequently the grade of the ore varies between wide limits. Ore reserves in the district are not amenable to measurement. It is probable, however, that a small but wavering production will be maintained as long as the price of quicksilver exceeds $175 a flask.

"Further prospecting may disclose new deposits. Their universal association with faults and zones of hydrothermally altered rocks should be a valuable guide in prospecting."

For a specific discussion of the New Idria mine, the reader is referred to E. B. Eckel and Myers (2) pp. 81–124, from whom the following quotation is abstracted (p. 83):

"The New Idria District, third in all-time production among North American quicksilver mining districts, lies in the rugged Diablo Range, 140 miles southeast of San Francisco. The New Idria mine was discovered in 1853 and except for 1921–22, has been in continuous production ever since. Nearly 20 other deposits have been found, but of these only the San Carlos has yielded a large amount of quicksilver. Between 1858 and 1944 the district produced 437,195 flasks of quicksilver, valued at about 31 million dollars.

"The . . . area of about 135 square miles consists of a large oval body of strongly sheared serpentine, rimmed by sandstone of the Franciscan group and by the Upper Cretaceous Panoche formation and later sediments. The structure is that of an asymmetric anticlinal dome, marked on its northeast flank by overturned beds and by an irregular thrust fault, here termed the New Idria thrust fault, along the Franciscan-Panoche contact. On other sides of the dome, the contacts between Panoche and older rocks are steeply dipping faults, which encircle the core, and commonly dip away from it. The origin of the dome and of the faults is thought to be closely related to the emplacement of the serpentine mass, which has moved upward intermittently since pre-Panoche time.

"The quicksilver deposits consist predominantly of cinnabar as veins and stockworks that occupy fractures in altered rocks. The ones of greatest commercial importance, including the New Idria and San Carlos, lie in hydrothermally indurated beds of the Panoche formation beneath the New Idria thrust fault and associated tear faults which offset the thrust. Both rock alteration and ore deposition were localized primarily at abrupt changes in strike of the fault plane, though changes in dip were also locally important in controlling some of the ore shoots and deposits. Several minor deposits lie in altered Panoche rocks above the normal faults on the south side and below the reverse fault on the west side of the dome and still others occur in silica-carbonate rock derived from serpentine."

As is frequently the case with early mining operations, there is a history for the New Idria mine of poor records, legal and other battles, which have been described in an interesting and basically accurate fashion by Bret Harte (1) in his "Story of a mine".

San Luis Obispo area: Many prospects of cinnabar occur concentrated north of San Luis Obispo in the Coast Ranges east of and between Cambria and San Simeon. The deposits are described by E. B. Eckel et al. (1) p. 515 as follows:

"Most of the deposits * * * lie within an elongated area of about 75 square miles in northwestern San Luis Obispo County. Other deposits, most of them small, are scattered southeastward from southwestern Monterey County to the southern border of San Luis Obispo County. Quicksilver was first discovered in the region in 1862. Though mining since then has been intermittent, the output has been relatively large during or immediately after the periods of high quicksilver prices. Monterey County has produced very little quicksilver, but San Luis Obispo County, which ranks sixth among the quicksilver-producing counties of the State, produced 69,264 flasks between 1876 and the end of 1939, 70 percent of which came from the Oceanic and Klau mines.

"All but one of the known quicksilver deposits are in or closely associated with the Franciscan formation, of Jurassic (?) age. This formation, embodying the oldest and most widely distributed group of rocks in the mapped areas, consists mainly of highly contorted and metamorphosed shale, sandstone, and conglomerate and is overlain by Cretaceous and Tertiary sediments. Extrusive and intrusive igneous rocks, most of them basic in composition, were formed at several periods after the Franciscan formation was deposited. Many of the intrusive bodies are now represented by serpentine.

"This part of the Coast Range province is characterized by numerous strong, complex, northwestward-trending fault zones, many of which have been intermittently active since late Jurassic time. Bodies of silica-carbonate rock (quicksilver rock), composed of dense quartz and mixed carbonates, were formed in many places by solutions that rose along the major faults and replaced the country rocks. Most of the igneous rocks also are closely associated with these faults.

"The quicksilver deposits comprise not only irregular and discontinuous cinnabar-bearing veins but also rock masses that contain disseminated cinnabar. All are within or very near northwest-trending fault zones, and nearly all are intimately associated with silica-carbonate rock. Most of the ore shoots are small and irregular, though a few are several hundred feet in length and height and as much as 40 feet wide. The shoots are structurally controlled by local gouge zones or by changes in dip or strike of the enclosing vein matter. The quicksilver content of the ore has a wide range, but most of the ore mined in the past has probably contained 5 to 10 pounds of quicksilver to the ton."

Only occurrences of special mineralogical interest, and some commercial occurrences outside of the three regions discussed above, will be itemized by county.

Colusa County: **1,** Cinnabar is found with free gold at the Oriental mine, a quarter of a mile west of Simmins Spring near Sulphur Creek, Mining and Scientific Press (8) p. 287. **2,** At the Manzanita mine (sec. 29, T. 14 N., R. 5 W., M. D.), sufficiently important percentages of leaf and wire gold intergrown with cinnabar, calcite, marcasite, chalcopyrite, and stibnite to warrant mining for gold have been described, Becker (4) p. 367, Goodyear (4) p. 160, Fairbanks (6) p. 120, Aubury (2) p. 44, W. W. Bradley (1) p. 189. **3,** Near Wilbur Springs, according to Hanks (19) p. 284, cinnabar was observed in actual process of deposition as crystals forming by sublimation on walls of orifices.

Contra Costa County: **1,** Indians for years knew of deposits of cinnabar on the east side of Mount Diablo that they used for paint, Mining and Scientific Press (6) p. 280. What is probably the same occurrence is described (sec. 29, T. 1 N., R. 1 E., M. D.), by J. D. Whitney (7) p. 24, Irelan (3) p. 162, Aubury (2) p. 195, Becker (4) p. 378, C. P. Ross (2) p. 41. The mercury mineral in the Mount Diablo deposits is dominantly metacinnabar. The Ryne and Mt. Diablo mines are considered by Pampeyan (1) p. 24.

Inyo County: **1,** Cinnabar is found with metacinnabar at the Chloride Cliff mine in the Funeral Range southwest of Rhyolite, Nevada, Huguenin and Waring (1) p. 121. **2,** Fumaroles of the Coso Springs area near Little Lake show interesting mineral deposition including that of cinnabar and metacinnabar, T. Warner (2) pp. 59–63, A. L. Ransome and Kellogg (1) p. 378, C. P. Ross and Yates (6) p. 395. **3,** Cinnabar from Last Chance Mountain was used for paint by the Piutes, J. H. Steward (1) p. 276.

Kern County: **1,** Cinnabar crystals disseminated in a rhyolite dike occur in the Cuddeback (Cuddiback, Walabu, Walibu) mine (sec. 27, T. 31 S., R. 32 E., S.B.) 3 miles from Woodford, Gillan (1) p. 79, W. W. Bradley (5) p. 47, Tucker (4) p. 314, Troxel and Morton (2) p. 240. **2,** A similar deposit occurs 2½ miles west of Cinco, a quarter of a mile west of the Los Angeles aqueduct, W. W. Bradley (5) p. 49. **3,** Veinlets of cinnabar occur in rhyolite on the south side of Jawbone Canyon, Troxel and Morton (2) p. 38. This may be the same locality as **(2). 4,** Cinnabar is found in the metamorphic rocks on the south side of Chuckwalla Mountains, Troxel and Morton (2) p. 38.

Kings County: **1,** Cinnabar with native mercury is reported by W. W. Bradley (2) p. 529, in serpentine.

Lake County: **1,** The mineral was reported adhering to nuggets of gold from Sulphur Springs in Bear Valley 10 miles northeast of Borax Lake, J. A. Phillips (1) p. 326, D. E. White and Roberson (2) p. 405.

Lassen County: **1,** Cinnabar occurs with metacinnabar from Amedee Hot Springs, Dickson and Tunell (1) p. 484.

Marin County: **1,** Cinnabar was discovered in pods of fine-grained material in sandstone on the M. Gambonini Ranch on Salmon Creek, about 6 miles east of Marshall. Placer and float in abundance in Salmon Creek and its tributaries resulted in the lode discovery and some exploration was undertaken, Ver Planck (3) p. 263.

Mariposa County: **1,** Crystals of cinnabar in plates and bunches are reported by Becker (4) p. 383, H. W. Turner (12) p. 678, Lowell (1) p. 602, from the north shore of the Merced River at Horseshoe Bar, CDMG (12120).

Mendocino County: **1,** Cinnabar is reported with platinum, gold, iridium, and zircon from the Anderson Valley placer along Navarro River, Hanks (12) p. 310.

Mono County: **1,** Beautiful crystals of cinnabar have come from 4 or 5 miles northeast of Bodie, 3 miles west of a volcanic cone in this region, W. W. Bradley (5) p. 72, Whiting (1) p. 356, CDMG (10340).

Monterey County: **1,** Cinnabar is reported as occurring in calcite southeast of Jamesburg (SE $\frac{1}{4}$ sec. 31, T. 18 S., R. 5 E., M.D.), W. W. Bradley (p.c. '46).

Napa County: **1,** Cinnabar pseudomorphous after barite has been described from the Redington mine, Durand (1) p. 211. **2,** Fix and Swinney (1) pp. 31–46, report on an occurrence of cinnabar in the Oakville area.

Nevada County: **1,** Cinnabar with amalgam is found in small quantities at the Odin drift mine, near Nevada City, Lingren (20) p. 75. **2,** Other occurrences are described by W. P. Blake (10) p. 11, Lindgren (14) p. 6.

San Benito County: **1,** New Idria and New Almaden constitute the most important cinnabar deposits in the state, in Panoche Valley, R. G. Yates and Hilpert (2) p. 12, Eckel and W. B. Myers (2) pp. 81–124.

San Bernardino County: **1,** Cinnabar occurs in quartz veins 4 to 6 feet wide 9 miles northeast of Danby, W. W. Bradley (5) p. 123, Tucker (4) p. 356. **2,** Cinnabar occurring as inclusions in bluish-gray chalcedony near the southern end of Death Valley, 15 miles northeast of Lead Pipe Springs and 30 miles northeast of Johannesburg, colors the chalcedony with reddish blotches and streaks, forming the gem stone known as "myrickite," W. W. Bradley (5) p. 123. **3,** Cinnabar occurs in the Jack mine in the Clark Mountains in thin veins of wolframite, Hess (14) p. 47, and W. W. Bradley (5) p. 123. **4,** Cinnabar, with stibnite and possibly stibiconite, is reported from the Red Devil claim, Danby area (NW $\frac{1}{4}$, T. 6 N., R. 18 E., S.B.), about 12 miles southeast of Essex, G. W. Walker et al. (5) p. 24. This may be the same as locality **(2)**.

San Luis Obispo County: **1,** Cinnabar replaces fossil shells in the Oceanic mine (secs. 15, 21, T. 27 S., R. 9 E., M.D.), Aubury (2) p. 149, A. L. Ransome and Kellogg (1) p. 441. **2,** Small crystals of cinnabar occur sparingly, perched on marcasite needles, in the Klau quicksilver mine, Santa Lucia Range (sec. 33, T. 26 S., R. 10 E., M.D.), Woodhouse and Norris (6) p. 114, and **3,** from the Madrone mine, CDMG (21670).

San Mateo County: **1,** Cinnabar is reported with chlorides of mercury from the Corte de Madera Rancho near Searsville, west of Palo Alto, W. W. Bradley (5) p. 149, F. F. Davis (7) p. 415. **2,** Cinnabar occurs with mercury and metacinnabar, and possibly terlinguaite, from the Emerald Lake mine near Redwood City, CDMG (21669).

Santa Barbara County: **1,** The first discovery in California of cinnabar was apparently in this county as early as 1796, Hittel (3) vol. 2, p. 549. **2,** Cinnabar is described from the Cachuma area 23 miles northeast of Solvang, Everhart (5) pp. 509–532.

Santa Clara County: A general reference for New Almaden is W. W. Bradley (5) p. 154. **1,** Cinnabar pebbles have been recovered by panning from the gravels of Deep Gulch, close to the New Almaden mine, E. H. Bailey and Everhart (8) p. 27.

Siskiyou County: **1,** Perfect small crystals of cinnabar were found in placer gravels, Bixby (1) p. 154. **2,** Semitransparent crystals were found in the Minnehaha mine on the Klamath River 4 miles west of Oak Bar (sec. 22, T. 46 N., R. 10 W., M.D.), G. C. Brown (2) p. 870, Averill (3) p. 64. **3,** Cinnabar occurs at the Cowgill mine (sec. 34, T. 48 N., R. 9 W., M.D.), 12 miles from Gottville, as coarsely crystalline aggregates with metacinnabar, Hobson (1) p. 658, Aubury (2) p. 196, W. W. Bradley (5) p. 169. **4,** Small amounts of cinnabar occur in seams of hornblende schist at the Horse Creek mercury mine (secs. 15, 16, T. 46 N., R. 10 W., M.D.), J. C. O'Brien (4) p. 460.

Solano County: **1,** Cinnabar has been mined at the St. John's mine, near Vallejo, Carlton and Wichels (1) p. 35. **2,** Cinnabar occurs with metacinnabar at the Hastings mine near Benicia, W. W. Bradley (5) p. 172.

Sonoma County: **1,** Cinnabar is reported from the Culver-Baer mine in fine crystals with native mercury and metacinnabar, Aubury (2) p. 102. **2,** Crystals of cinnabar from the Great Eastern mine were described by Sachs (1) p. 17, and mentioned by Aubury (2) p. 108. **3,** Cinnabar from Skaggs Springs occurs with curtisite, metacinnabar, and realgar, F. E. Wright and Allen (3) p. 169. A report on geology of the Skaggs Springs occurrences of cinnabar, was made by Everhart (4) p. 385; **4,** an additional and recent report on the Mayacmas area was made by E. H. Bailey (6) pp. 199–230.

Stanislaus County: **1,** Cinnabar occurs in Del Puerto area, at the Adobe Valley, Summit and Winegar properties (T. 6 S., R. 5 E., M.D.), Hawkes et al. (2) p. 79.

Trinity County: **1,** Very large crystals of cinnabar are said to occur at the Altoona mine, Bixby (2) p. 168. The occurrence is sec. 22, T. 38 N., R. 6 W., M.D., Swinney (3) p. 395.

Yolo County: **1,** Crystals of cinnabar in "opalite" occur at Harrison mines (sec. 35, T. 12 N., R. 5 W., M.D.) in the Knoxville area, Aubury (2) p. 117. **2,** Cinnabar occurs with petroleum and sulphur at the New England mine, ibid.

CLAUDETITE
Arsenic oxide, As_2O_3

Imperial County: **1,** Kelley (1) p. 137, has described the occurrence of claudetite crystals in a vein of kaolin, gypsum, halloysite, and sulphur, at a sulphur prospect 6 miles north of the 4-S Ranch and $1\frac{1}{2}$ miles west of the Colorado River. Crystals from this locality are described by Palache (8) p. 194.

Trinity County: **1,** Claudetite is reported as crusts of well-formed monoclinic crystals in the pyrrhotite deposit at Island Mountain, Landon (1) p. 279, but the occurrence is probably arsenolite, Switzer (p.c. '49).

CLAUSTHALITE
Lead selenide, PbSe

Inyo County: **1,** Clausthalite is doubtfully reported in galena from the Darwin Mining District, Hall and MacKevett (1) p. 17, ibid. (4) p. 59.

CLINOHUMITE
Basic fluosilicate of magnesium, $Mg_9(SiO_4)_4(OH,F)_2$

Fresno County: **1,** Clinohumite is reported to occur in small yellowish-orange striated crystals in contact limestone of the Twin Lakes region by Chesterman (1) p. 254. **2,** Tiny (less than 1 mm) orange grains of clinohumite occur in a small outcrop of marble (sec. 33, T. 11 S., R. 25 E., M.D.), west of Big Creek. (Identification confirmed CDMG, by x-ray), John T. Alfors (p.c. '64).

Monterey County: **1,** Clinohumite is associated with geikielite in magnesian marbles in the Santa Lucia Mts., Wise (1), p. 879.

Riverside County: **1,** Clinohumite has been observed in the contact rocks at Crestmore, C. Wayne Burnham (1) p. 889.

CLINOPTILOLITE
Hydrous calcium/sodium/potassium/magnesium/aluminum silicate, $(Na_2O)_{0.7}(CaO)_{0.1}(K_2O)_{0.15}(MgO)_{.05}Al_2O_3 \cdot (SiO_2)_{8.5-10.5} \cdot 6\text{-}7H_2O$

The validity of clinoptilolite as a species has been questioned by Hey and Bannister (1) pp. 556–559, who suggest that it is a silica-rich heulandite.

Inyo County: **1,** Clinoptilolite and other zeolites, as well as gaylussite, occur in the lake bed deposits at Owens Lake, Hay and Moiola (2) p. 76A.

Kern County: **1,** A mineral, probably clinoptilolite, occurring as platy colorless grains, was reported by Kerr and Cameron (4) p. 234, from 5 miles east of the Tehachapi Pass at the property of the Filtrol Company. **2,** Clinoptilolite has been found associated with gay-lussite and other zeolites, in tuffaceous layers in China Lake, Moiola and Hay (1) 215.

San Luis Obispo County: **1,** Clinoptilolite was reported as a constitutent of altered fragmental volcanic rocks of Miocene age in the Highland monocline, Bramlette and Posnjak (1) p. 169.

San Bernardino County: **1,** Clinoptilolite is reported associated with hectorite in montmorillonite and saponite in the North Group of claims, six miles northwest of Hector Station on the Santa Fe Railroad east of Barstow, Ames et al. (1) p. 28. Material from this deposit has been used experimentally for the removal of radioactive material from atomic plant wastes, Ames (2) p. 868.

CLINOZOISITE
Basic calcium aluminum silicate, Ca$_2$Al$_3$(SiO$_4$)$_3$(OH)

Clinozoisite is a member of the epidote group, but nearly iron-free.

Inyo County: **1,** Clinozoisite is a common alteration product of igneous intrusives of the Darwin Mining District, Kelley (4) p. 541.

Los Angeles County: **1,** Clinozoisite occurs as a network of pure-white crystals up to 1½ cm with interstitial chlorite and tourmaline in the Pelona schists on the north side of Sierra Pelona Valley (NE ¼ sec. 12, T. 5 N., R. 14 W., S.B.), Neuerburg (p.c. '44). **2,** Quartz veins carrying clinozoisite crystals up to 3 or 4 inches and bundles of crystals up to 1 inch in diameter were abundant on the eastern edge of the old San Francisquito Canyon Reservoir, Murdoch and Webb (6) p. 354. **3,** The mineral occurs in lenses of greenish-gray radiating prisms as much as 4 inches in size, in albite amphibolite, in Pelona schist, on Bouquet Canyon highway near Bouquet Reservoir, (SW ¼ NE ¼ sec. 28, T. 6 N., R. 14 W., S.B.), Durrell (p.c. '49).

Mendocino County: **1,** Clinozoisite (or epidote) in gray blades is present with lawsonite and rutile on the new Covelo road, Vonsen (p.c. '45).

Monterey County: **1,** Boulders of crystalline masses of pinkish-gray clinozoisite occur on the beach north of Willow Creek, Crippen (p.c. '51).

Riverside County: **1,** Pale brownish-green crystals up to 15 mm, in divergent groups, occur in pegmatite at Crestmore, Daly (1) p. 650, Woodford et al. (10) p. 370. **2,** Clinozoisite is reported from the new City quarry, Richmond (1) p. 725.

San Bernardino County: **1,** Clinozoisite is found in veins in abundant pebbles of probable Pelona schist, west of the summit of Cajon Pass, in canyons north of the main highway, Murdoch and Webb (p.c. '43).

Sonoma County: **1,** Specimens of clinozoisite associated with glaucophane, CDMG (21318), came from 2½ miles east of Valley Ford.

COBALTITE
Sulpharsenide of cobalt, (Co,Fe)AsS

Calaveras County: **1,** Cobaltite has been observed in a number of mines in the Foothill Copper belt, W. B. Clark and Lydon (4) p. 24, who cite Heyl (2) p. 20.

Inyo County: **1,** Cobalt minerals are disseminated in small quantities in the metamorphic rocks of Chocolate Peak on the South Fork of Bishop Creek, near Bishop. The only established occurrence of cobaltite is on the west side of Chocolate Peak, 500 ft. east of Long Lake. Associated minerals are pyrrhotite, chalcopyrite, arsenopyrite, and pyrite; gossans carry erythrite, Bateman (3) p. 83.

Madera County: **1,** Cobaltite is reported to have formed more than 1½ percent of one lot of ore from the 200-foot level of the Jessie Bell mine (SE ¼ sec. 13, T. 9 S., R. 18 E., M.D.), Logan (24) p. 452.

Mariposa County: **1,** Good cobaltite crystals were found in the Copper Chieftain mine, CDMG (15481).

Mono County: **1,** Cobaltite occurred with gold in the Tioga mine, H. W. Turner (3) p. 469.

Nevada County: **1**, Small seams of cobaltite with chalcopyrite occur in a schist on Rattlesnake Creek south of Signal Peak (T. 17 N., R. 13 E., M.D.), Lindgren (19) p. 7, E. M. Boyle (1) p. 37. **2**, Cobaltite was reported from the Otis ledge, Meadow Lake (T. 18 N., R. 13 E., M.D.), C. W. Raymond (1) p. 48.

Placer County: **1**, Cobaltite was found with arsenopyrite in the Metallic mine, near Cisco, CDMG (1901), and 2, with chalcopyrite about 4 miles northeast of Alta, CDMG (13493).

COCCINITE
Mercury iodide, HgI_2

This compound has not as yet been identified with certainty in nature, but the name *coccinite* is reserved for it when it is established, Palache et al. (11) p. 42. The two occurrences reported below must be considered very doubtful.

Kern County: **1**, Coccinite is reported from San Emigdio Canyon (probably in the antimony mines), Hanks (12) p. 147, (15) p. 104.

Santa Barbara County: **1**, The mineral coccinite is reported by G. E. Moore, in Cronise (1) p. 593. C. D. Woodhouse (p.c. '63) considers it very doubtful that this mineral in fact was found in the county.

COFFINITE
A basic uranium silicate, probably $U(SiO_4)_{1-x}(OH)_{4x}$

Kern County: **1**, Coffinite has been identified from the Little Sparkler mine in Kern River Canyon, Troxel and Morton (2) pp. 327, 332.

*COLEMANITE, 1883
Hydrous calcium borate, $Ca_2B_6O_{11} \cdot 5H_2O$

Colemanite was first discovered in Death Valley in October 1882 by R. Neuschwander, Hanks (11) p. 86 (with analysis by Price) and later (April 1883) at the old ghost town of Borate in the Calico Mountains, A. W. Jackson (3) p. 358. Subsequently the deposits were described by many writers. A discussion of the origin of colemanite is found in H. S. Gale (3) p. 3.

Inyo County: **1**, Colemanite was discovered in the Death Valley region, where immense deposits occur along Furnace Creek in the Amargosa Range, A. W. Jackson (3) p. 358, G. E. Bailey (2) p. 46, M. R. Campbell (1) p. 16, Engineering and Mining Journal (10) p. 781, Foshag (10) p. 8. **2**, Colemanite occurs near Ryan, G. E. Bailey (2) p. 48, H. S. Gale (2) pp. 861–865, Cloudman et al. (1) p. 863, Foshag (10) p. 9. Analyses of material from occurrences **(1)** and **(2)** are presented by Whitfield (1) pp. 281–287. **3**, Some colemanite crystals from the Biddy McCarthy mine were shown by A. F. Rogers (20) p. 135, to be pseudomorphs after inyoite. The crystals were formed by dehydration of inyoite. **4**, Important deposits of colemanite with ulexite occur in clay-shale near Shoshone (T. 22 N., R. 7 E., S. B.), Noble (3) p. 63. **5**, Colemanite has been reported with ulexite and probertite from Resting Springs Range near Shoshone, Nolan (3) p. 11. This may be the same deposit referred to by Noble in **(4)** above. **6**, Colemanite has been reported from Bennetts Wells on the floor of Death Valley, as surface incrustations, G. E. Bailey (2) p. 45, but the samples were probably inaccurately identified. **7,** The atomic structure was determined on colemanite from the meyerhofferite tunnel, Twenty Mule Team Canyon, Christ et al. (3). **8,** Colemanite ore is mined on the 65 foot level of the Kern Borate mine near Ryan. The mineral is associated with ulexite and probertite, Anon. (47) p. 9.

Kern County: **1,** Colemanite occurs with kernite and borax near Boron in the deposits at Kramer (sec. 22, T. 11 N., R. 8 W., S. B.), Yale and Gale (4) p. 287, Noble (2) p. 47, Schaller (41) p. 24, (45) p. 138.

Los Angeles County: **1,** An important and extensive deposit of colemanite which Eakle (10) p. 179 (with analysis), described as a variety and called "neocolemanite," occurs at the Sterling borax mine near Lang. Hutchinson (1) p. 16 shows neocolemanite to be identical with colemanite. The colemanite occurs as thin and thick seams, and has considerable howlite associated with it; see also F. J. H. Merrill (2) p. 480, Armstrong and Van Amringe (1).

Riverside County: **1,** Colemanite reportedly occurs in the foothills of the San Bernardino Range northeast of Salton Sea (N. R.).

San Bernardino County: **1,** The extensive deposit of colemanite at Borate, in the Calico Mountains near Yermo, was discovered in the spring of 1883 and became the principal source of borax before the Death Valley colemanite deposits were worked. Beautiful crystals of colemanite in large geodal masses occur with celestite crystals. The colemanite is described by A. W. Jackson (1) p. 447, (2) p. 3, (3) p. 358, G. E. Bailey (2) p. 56, Eakle (2) p. 31, Foshag (9) p. 208; analyses are given by Hiortdahl (1) p. 25, Bodewig and Rath (1) p. 290. **2,** Colemanite is reported from 4 miles west of Lone Willow Springs on the south flank of Browns Mountain, G. E. Bailey (2) p. 12; **3,** from Lone Star Range (T. 18 N., R. 2 E., S. B.), in beds 2 to 3 feet thick, G. E. Bailey (2) p. 62, Cloudman et al. (1) p. 855. **4,** Cavities lined with slender colemanite crystals on calcite crystal crusts are found in old borax mines on the north side of Lead Mountain, northeast of Barstow, Durrell (p.c. '46). **5,** Colemanite is reported from Searles Lake, De Groot (2) p. 537 (probably an error). **6,** Colemanite was collected as float in the lower canyon of the Amargosa River, G. E. Bailey (2) p. 62, Cloudman et al. (1) p. 855; **7,** the mineral is reported from Owl Holes (T. 18 N., R. 3 E., S. B.) in niter beds with priceite (?), G. E. Bailey (2) p. 62, Cloudman et al. (1) p. 855; **8,** it is also reported from the Pilot beds at the south end of Slate Range southeast of Searles Lake under niter beds, G. E. Bailey (2) p. 63, Cloudman et al. (1) p. 856. **9,** Colemanite is found from southeast of Cave Springs on the south flank of the Avawatz Mountains on the road from Daggett, G. E. Bailey (2) p. 60, Cloudman et al. (1) p. 854. (Bailey notes this occurrence as "borate of lime," with sodium carbonates and sulphates, and it is probably ulexite.)

Ventura County: **1,** Deposits of colemanite, similar to those at Lang, in Los Angeles County, occur near Frazier Mountain, G. E. Bailey (2) p. 70, H. S. Gale (3) p. 5, (11) p. 440.

Additional references to literature on colemanite: Arzuni (1) p. 272, J. T. Evans (1) p. 57, (2) p. 37, Mülheims (1) p. 202, Braumhauer (1) p. 107, M. R. Campbell (1) p. 517, (2) p. 401, Foshag (7) p. 199.

An excellent general summary of the origin of borate deposits is found in Foshag (13) p. 419. A collecting expedition of interest to amateurs is described by Foshag (15) p. 39.

COLORADOITE
Mercuric telluride, HgTe

Calaveras County: **1**, Coloradoite is reported from the Stanislaus mine on Carson Hill, A. Knopf (11) p. 39.

Tuolumne County: **1**, Hillebrand (3) p. 62, found one specimen which he identified as coloradoite, associated with other tellurides from the Norwegian mine near Tuttletown; see also W. W. Bradley (5) p. 203.

COLUMBITE—Tantalite
Niobate and tantalate of iron and manganese, (Fe,Mn)(Nb,Ta)$_2$O$_6$

Columbite is the niobium-rich member.

Tantalite is the tantalum-rich member of a series in which these two elements are completely interchangeable.

Calaveras County: **1**, Tantalite has been reported near Milton, Irelan (4) p. 47.

Los Angeles County: **1**, Small crystals of columbite have been found in a pegmatite at the head of Rattlesnake Canyon (SW$\frac{1}{4}$ sec. 36, T. 4 N., R. 14 W., S. B.), Gregory (p.c. '51).

Madera County: **1**, Massive and crystalline black columbite (tantalum-rich?) has been found at the Reynolds mine, Kings Creek, Irelan (4) p. 46, CDMG (13546).

Riverside County: **1**, Columbite (30 percent tantalum-rich), high in manganese and poor in iron, is found at the Fano mine, in fan-shaped masses of radiating crystals up to 3 inches, in an albite-quartz mixture in pegmatite, Fisher (1) p. 75. **2**, Minute platy crystals of probable columbite occur in cleavelandite about 400 yards west-southwest of the northeast corner of sec. 16, T. 7 S., R. 2 E., S. B., Fisher (1) p. 67. **3**, Columbite is reported from the Anita mine 10 miles southeast of Hemet (west-southwest of center, sec. 22, T. 6 S., R. 12 E., S. B.) as minute wafers with garnet, lepidolite, and albite, ibid., p. 85.

San Diego County: **1**, A crystal of columbite from the Little Three mine, near Ramona was described by Eakle (7) p. 87, Schrader et al. (1) p. 53. **2**, Small imperfect crystals were found at the Victor mine, Rincon, A. F. Rogers (4) p. 217. **3**, Columbite occurs in the Clark vein at Rincon up to 2 inches, in well-formed crystals, Murdoch (p.c. '45), Hanley (1) p. 17; **4**, it is also reported from the Mack mine, Rincon (sec. 25, T. 10 S., R. 1 W., S. B.), Kunz (24) p. 50; **5**, from Pala, Kunz (23) p. 942; **6**, from the Mountain Lily mine on Aguanga Mountain in pegmatite, Kunz (24) p. 62; **7**, it occurs in good crystals associated with cassiterite, tourmaline, albite, and orthoclase in the Chihuahua Valley, 10 miles east of Oakgrove (SW$\frac{1}{4}$ sec. 12, T. 9 S., R. 3 E., S. B.), Schaller (36) p. 353. **8**, Columbite, rich in tantalum and manganese, from the Catharina (Katerina) mine, near Pala was analyzed by Schaller in F. W. Clarke (10 p. 345.

CONNELLITE
Basic hydrous chloride and sulphate of copper, $Cu_{19}(SO_4)Cl_4(OH)_{32} \cdot 3H_2O$?

Madera County: **1,** Radiating groups of blue-green acicular crystals occur up to 5 mm in diameter, and were found on cleavages of gray schist near the Buchanan copper mine, 5 miles northeast of Daulton by E. H. Oyler, Crippen (p.c. '57), CDMG (21703).

COOKEITE
Basic lithium aluminum silicate, $LiAl_4(Si,Al)_4O_{10}(OH)_8$

San Bernardino County: **1,** Cookeite has been reported from Oro Grande, CDMG (12826).

San Diego County: **1,** Cookeite from Pala has been reported by Kunz (23) p. 942, and analyzed by Schaller in F. W. Clarke (9) p. 288. **2,** Colorless and deep-pink cookeite is found in pockets at the Victor mine, Rincon, coating quartz, lepidolite, orthoclase, albite, and kunzite, and as pseudomorphs after kunzite, A. F. Rogers (4) p. 216.

COPIAPITE
Primarily a basic hydrous iron sulphate, perhaps $R^{2+}Fe^{3+}_4(SO_4)_6(OH)_2 \cdot nH_2O$
where R^{2+}=Fe,Mg,Al,Cu or Na_2

Alameda County: **1,** Copiapite was found as yellow needles at the Alma mine, Leona Heights, E. S. Larsen (11) p. 61, analysis by Schaller (1) p. 214.

Contra Costa County: **1,** Copiapite is reported from the Mount Diablo mine ($SE\frac{1}{4}$ sec. 29, T. 1 N., R. 1 E., M. D.), C. P. Ross (2) p. 42, Pampeyan (1) p. 24.

Kern County: **1,** Copiapite is reported as efflorescence in yellow balls as coatings, at the California borate property, Kramer Borate area, G. I. Smith et al. (1) p. 1074, Pemberton et al. (1) p. 38.

Lake County: **1,** Copiapite occurred at Sulphur Bank, Becker (4) p. 389, Everhart (1) p. 139, analysis by Melville and Lindgren (1) p. 25.

Napa County: **1,** Knoxvillite, described as a new mineral from the old Redington mine, Becker (4) p. 389, has been identified as magnesio-copiapite, Berry (1) p. 21. Some mineralogists consider magnesio-copiapite a variety of copiapite.

Riverside County: **1,** Specimens of copiapite as yellowish-brown crystalline masses, with amarantite have been described from the Santa Maria Mountains by Schairer and Lawson (1) p. 242, with analysis. This is probably identical with a locality mentioned as "near Blythe" by E. S. Larsen (11) p. 61. Magnesian copiapite has been analyzed from the Santa Maria Mountains near Blythe, Bandy (2) p. 737. It is reported as associated with amarantite, E. S. Dana (6) p. 626.

San Bernardino County: **1,** Copiapite occurs as pale-yellow scaly masses with krausite, coquimbite and alunite in the Calico Hills near Borate, about 6 miles northeast of Yermo, Foshag (19) p. 352.

Shasta County: **1,** Copiapite is reported as probably found in the gossan at the Iron Mountain mine, Kinkel et al. (2) p. 89.

Trinity County: **1,** Copiapite occurs with pyrrhotite as pale-brown scaly masses at the Island Mountain copper mine, Vonsen (p.c. '45), analysis by Foshag (p.c. '29).

COPPER
Native copper, Cu

Metallic copper has been found in most of the copper mines of the state, but no commercial deposits of native copper are known. It is frequently mixed with cuprite and malachite in the oxidized zone of copper deposits, or found as coatings along the walls of copper veins, or near intrusive dikes, which have brought about a natural reduction of the ores. Most occurrences of chalcopyrite have yielded some native copper.

Alameda County: **1,** Fine arborescent groups of native copper crystals were found in the Alma Pyrite mine at Leona Heights, East Oakland. The minerals of this mine have been described by Schaller (1) p. 195.

Amador County: **1,** Arborescent masses of copper occurred in the old Newton mine, Woodhouse (p.c. '45).

Calaveras County: Some of the mines along the Foothill copper belt, especially **1,** at Copperopolis, Irelan (3) p. 151, J. D. Whitney (7) p. 255, and **2,** at Campo Seco, Hanks (12) p. 152, CDMG (6049) have produced native copper. Other localities are mentioned: Aubury (1) p. 190; Hanks (12) p. 152, CDMG (1751).

Colusa County: **1,** Copper is found in serpentine with cuprite and tenorite at the Gray Eagle mine (sec. 20, T. 16 N., R. 6 W., M.D.), Aubury (4) p. 159. **2,** The mineral occurs at the Candace, CDMG (2439), and Lion mines (sec. 17, T. 17 N., R. 6 W., M. D.), with cuprite. Copper was first discovered in Colusa County in 1863, J. H. Rogers (1) p. 320, W. W. Bradley (1) p. 178.

Del Norte County: **1,** Some large pieces of native copper have come from the Diamond Creek Mining District, Aubury (1) p. 115; **2,** from the Keystone mine in the Rockland area in masses up to 300 pounds, J. D. Whitney (7) p. 362, Aubury (1) p. 115, and **3,** from near Crescent City, in serpentine (?), Richthofen (3) p. 44. **4,** Copper with native silver and tetrahedrite is reported from the Occidental mine (T. 18 N., R. 1 E., H.), Crawford (2) p. 58.

El Dorado County: Native copper occurs in numerous places in this county, wherever significant copper deposits are known. Some localities are mentioned by Hanks (12) p. 152, Tucker (3) pp. 276–278, Aubury (1) p. 177.

Glenn County: **1,** Large pieces of native copper float have been found near Peckville (sec. 18, T. 18 N., R. 6 W., M.D.), Aubury (1) p. 132.

Humboldt County: **1,** Copper occurs on Red Cap and Boise Creeks as float, Crawford (1) p. 66, Aubury (1) p. 127, W. P. Blake (14) p. 124; **2,** it is reported from Horse Mountain in masses up to 400 pounds as float (T. 6 N., R. 4 E., H.), Aubury (4) p. 153, Laizure (3) p. 305.

Imperial County: **1,** Native copper was reported from the Cargo Muchacho Mining District, Henshaw (1) p. 185.

Inyo County: **1,** The copper deposits in the Ubehebe Mountains contain native copper, Aubury (1) p. 245. **2,** Copper comes from Chloride Cliff, Death Valley, Ball (1) p. 73, (2) p. 174.

Kern County: **1,** Some native copper has been reported from near Gorman, Troxel and Morton (2) p. 294.

Lake County: **1,** Native copper was reported from the head of Little Indian Valley, as large pieces in rich oxide ores, Aubury (1) p. 138.

Lassen County: **1,** Native copper occurred in epidote rock at the Lummis mine, Woodhouse (p.c. '45), and **2,** in the Meadow Mountains (sec. 28, T. 28 N., R. 10 E., M.D.), 9 miles southeast of Westwood, Laizure (1) p. 508.

Los Angeles County: **1,** Copper was found in quartz at the Free Cuba mine, near Acton, F. J. H. Merrill (2) p. 471.

Madera County: **1,** Native copper was reported from north of the June Belle mine near Daulton (T. 9 S., R. 18 E., M.D.) in quartz veins, Forstner (4) p. 747.

Mariposa County: **1,** Massive copper occurred with malachite in the Copper Queen mine (sec. 19, T. 5 S., R. 19 E., M.D.), Aubury (1) p. 216. **2,** The mineral was reported from north fork of Chowchilla Creek (sec. 34, T. 6 S., R. 19 E., M.D.), Aubury (1) p. 216, and **3,** from Satellite mine, with melaconite, CDMG (12010).

Mendocino County: **1,** Sheets and grains of metallic copper occcur at Red Mountain, 15 miles southeast of Ukiah (sec. 23, T. 15 N., R. 11 W., M.D.), Aubury (4) p. 161, and **2,** in the serpentines in Lost Valley, Crawford (1) p. 67.

Merced County: **1,** Copper occurs with quartz and chalcopyrite in the Victor Bonanza mines, 16 miles from Dos Palos (T. 13 S., R. 9 E., M.D.), Lowell (1) p. 605.

Modoc County: **1,** Copper was observed with malachite and limonite at the Seitz mine 7 miles south of Fort Bidwell, Tucker (3) p. 241.

Mono County: **1,** Copper was found sparingly in the Detroit mine, Jordan Mining District, 6 miles northeast of Lundy, CDMG (7378).

Napa County: **1,** Copper was found near St. Helena with cuprite, Hanks (12) p. 158, and **2,** 6 miles west of Monticello, W. W. Bradley (28) p. 207, CDMG (20908).

Nevada County: **1,** Copper occurs with gold in quartz at Meadow Lake, John A. Veatch (2) p. 210; **2,** with chalcocite and graphite at Buckeye Hill, Sweetlands, Mining and Scientific Press (2) p. 5, (3) p. 5, and **3,** from South Yuba mine, Engineering and Mining Journal (14) p. 230.

Placer County: **1,** Copper occurred at the Algol mine near Spenceville (sec. 9, T. 13 N., R. 7 E., M.D.), Aubury (1) p. 173; **2,** at Valley View mine 6 miles from Lincoln (sec. 24, T. 13 N., R. 6 E., M.D.), Silliman (7) p. 351, C. A. Waring (4) p. 329. **3,** Lindgren (7) p. 272, reported native copper as one of the minerals of the Ophir Mining District, from the Gold Blossom shaft.

Plumas County: **1,** Copper occurs with rhodonite at Mumfords Hill, Hanks (12) p. 152. **2,** Large lumps of copper occurred with cuprite, malachite, and native silver in the old Pocohontas mine, Indian Valley, 20 miles from Susanville, Crawford (1) p. 69. **3,** Blackened grains and scales of copper were found in placers from North Fork of the Feather River, Edman (1) p. 372.

Riverside County: **1,** Copper occurs in the McCoy Mountains, 20 miles southwest of Blythe, F. J. H. Merrill (2) p. 525.

San Luis Obispo County: **1,** Copper is reported from the Tip Top mine 3 miles southwest of Santa Margarita, Aubury (1) p. 147; **2,** from Refugio claim on Chorro Creek, 7 miles north of San Luis Obispo, ibid., p. 148. **3,** Copper occurs as fine wires in serpentine southwest of Santa Margarita near the summit of the Santa Lucia Range, Logan (3) p. 686, Laizure (3) p. 512; **4,** with barite in the manganese property of the Noble Electric Company, Taliaferro and Hudson (3) p. 269.

Santa Barbara County: **1,** Hanks (12) p. 152 quotes Blake as recording copper in serpentine from the county.

Shasta County: Arborescent growths and compact masses of copper have been found in many of the copper mines of the county. Specimens have come from the Bully Hill and Copper City mines, Shasta King mine, Mountain Copper and Mammoth mines, Balaklala, Greenhorn, Kosk Creek, and other mines. Some localities are described in Aubury (1) p. 65, H. W. Turner (26) p. 276, F. M. Hamilton and Root (5) pp. 91–93, Tucker (9) p. 433, L. L. Root (4) p. 149.

Sierra County: **1,** Native copper is reported from Bassetts' Pride mine (sec. 11, T. 20 N., R. 12 E., M.D.) 5 miles northeast of Sierra City, E. MacBoyle (3) p. 30.

Siskiyou County: **1,** Copper is found in slate from Humbug Creek north of Yreka, CDMG (10600).

Tehama County: **1,** Small amounts of native copper occurred at Basler (sec. 4, T. 25 N., R. 7 W., M.D.), J. C. O'Brien (3) p. 189.

Trinity County: Native copper occurs **1,** with hausmannite, barite and copper carbonates in the Blue Jay mine (NW¼ sec. 17, T. 26 N., R. 12 W., M.D.), J. C. O'Brien (1) p. 84, Taliaferro and Hudson (3) p. 269; **2,** in crystals and masses from North Fork Trinity River (secs. 27, 28, 34, T. 34 N., R. 11 W., M.D.), J. B. Trask (1) p. 24.

Tulare County: **1,** Masses of copper have been found on the Middle Fork of Tule River, about 30 miles east of Porterville (sec. 30, T. 19 S., R. 31 E., M.D.), Aubury (1) p. 234.

COQUIMBITE
Hydrous iron sulphate, $Fe_2(SO_4)_3 \cdot 9H_2O$

Calaveras County: **1,** Coquimbite was found at Quail Hill, Silliman (7) p. 351.

El Dorado County: **1,** Coquimbite occurred in siliceous shales near Georgetown, CDMG (11249).

Inyo County: **1,** Yellow crystals of coquimbite have been found near Lone Pine, CDMG (7667).

Lake County: **1,** Coquimbite has been identified in opalized vein material at Sulphur Bank, D. E. White and Roberson (2) p. 407. Hanks (15) p. 104, originally reported this mineral from Sulphur Bank in 1886.

Napa County: **1,** Large masses of yellowish-green, granular coquimbite found at the old Redington cinnabar mine were described by Eakle (1) p. 322.

Placer County: **1,** Coquimbite is reported from Valley View mine (Whiskey Hill) 6 miles north of Lincoln, with chalcanthite, Silliman (7) p. 351, J. R. Browne (4) p. 111, Logan (17) p. 40. (This entry is incorrectly listed under Tuolumne County in older issues of this bulletin.)

San Bernardino County: **1,** Coquimbite occurs with krausite and alunite near Borate in the Calico Hills about 6 miles northeast of Yermo, Foshag (19) p. 352.

CORDIERITE—Iolite
Magnesium iron aluminum silicate, $(Fe,Mg)_2(Al,Fe)_4Si_5O_{18} \cdot H_2O$

Cordierite occurs chiefly as a microscopic constituent of highly alumi-nous metamorphic rocks.

Lake County: **1,** Purple cordierite occurs in a "gem stone" prospect ($SE\frac{1}{4} SE\frac{1}{4}$ sec. 20, T. 12 N., R. 7 W., M.D.). The material was originally described as amethystine quartz, Brice (1) p. 62.

Los Angeles County: **1,** Cordierite is a common constituent of the "spotted slates" of the Santa Monica Mountains, in megascopic sub-hedral crystals, Hoots (1) p. 88.

Mariposa County: **1,** Cordierite is reported from the Green Mountain Mining District with anthophyllite, W. W. Bradley (29) p. 311.

Riverside County: **1,** Cordierite is found in small grains in pegmatite with andalusite near Winchester, Murdoch (3) p. 69, Heinrich (2) p. 178.

Tulare County: **1,** Cordierite occurs with andalusite, biotite, quartz and orthoclase in a metamorphic rock on the north side of the South Fork of Kaweah River. about two-thirds of a mile southeast of Three Rivers (between secs. 25 and 36, T. 17 S., R. 28 E., M.D.), Durrell (p.c. '45).

CORONADITE
Hydrous oxide of lead and manganese, $PbMn^{2+}Mn^{4+}_7O_{16} \cdot H_2O$

Inyo County: **1,** Coronadite is reported by Charles Milton (p.c. '45) in massive form from an unknown locality. **2,** The mineral is also known from the Lookout (Modoc) Mining District, Fleischer and Rich-mond (1) p. 283. **3,** Hall and Stephens (3) pp. 24, 26, report coronadite from several mines in the Inyo-Argus Mountain area on the west side of the Panamint Valley. The mineral has been observed in ores of the Defense, Minietta and Big Four mines. It is likely that locality **(1)** and locality **(2),** as reported by Fleischer and Richmond, are from the mines listed by Hall and Stephens.

CORUNDUM
Aluminum oxide, Al_2O_3

Corundum-bearing rocks are rare in the state and no workable de-posits of this useful mineral are known. The gem varieties, ruby and sapphire, have not been found in good clear crystals.

Butte County: **1,** A few sapphires are said to have been found with diamonds in stream gravels in this county (N. R.).

Los Angeles County: **1,** The first mention of corundum in the state was of some sapphire-blue pebbles found in San Francisquito Pass, W. P. Blake (9) p. 10, Hanks (12) p. 157, Kunz (24) p. 45. **2,** Corundum was found on Santa Catalina Island in gneiss with kyanite, E. H. Bailey (1) p. 1955.

Mariposa County: **1,** Corundum occurs in pegmatite with andalusite from May Lake, Yosemite National Park, Rose (1) p. 635.

Mono County: **1,** Coarse nodular masses of corundum occur with andalusite at the mine of Champion Sillimanite, on the western slope of the White Mountains, north of Bishop, Peck (1) p. 151, Kerr (3) p. 633.

Plumas County: **1,** Large violet-blue crystals of corundum occur in the plumasite of Spanish Peak, A. C. Lawson (5) p. 219, Kunz (14) p. 436, (24) p. 45.

Riverside County: **1,** Large crystals of corundum have been found near the summit of the San Jacinto Mountains (sec. 5, T. 4 S., R. 1 E., S. B.), Murdoch and Webb (14) p. 328. **2,** Blue crystals up to half an inch in length were collected with andalusite from a pegmatite near Winchester (sec. 12, T. 5 S., R. 2 W., S. B.), Webb (11) p. 581.

San Bernardino County: **1,** Corundum was found in the Kingston Range, Kunz (24) p. 45. **2,** Pale-rose to deep-lilac crystals of corundum occur in metamorphosed limestone in Cascade Canyon, a branch of San Antonio Canyon, in the San Gabriel Mountains, Louderback and Blasdale (6) p. 793, R. H. Merriam and Laudermilk (1) p. 716. **3,** Corundum is found at the head of Cascade Canyon as $\frac{1}{8}$- to $\frac{1}{2}$-inch blue crystals disseminated in rock near the lapis lazuli occurrence [see lazurite, San Bernardino County **(1)**], Schmeltz (1) p. 69.

San Diego County: **1,** Corundum is a microscopic constituent of the dumortierite schist of Dehesa, Schaller (7) p. 97. **2,** Pink and gray crystals of corundum occur in a vein with garnet in mica schist on the northern slope of the San Miguel Mountains, 26 miles east of San Diego, Kunz (24) p. 45. **3,** Blue corundum is reported from Tule Mountain, north of Jacumba (N. R.).

Sierra County: **1,** Emery is reported sparsely in aggregates (sec. 1, T. 19 N., R. 8 E., M. D.), Crawford (1) p. 406.

COVELLITE
Cupric sulphide, CuS

Covellite is much rarer than chalcocite. It is usually associated with bornite, chalcocite, or chalcopyrite.

Calaveras County: **1,** Covellite has been found at the Satellite mine near Campo Seco, CDMG (14351). **2,** A. F. Rogers (6) p. 300, mentions specimens of covellite from the Poole mine at Nassua and from a prospect between Nassua and Copperopolis in which covellite formed by replacement of sphalerite.

Imperial County: **1,** Covellite is reported from the Cargo Muchacho Mining District, Henshaw (1) p. 185.

Inyo County: **1,** Covellite occurs as veinlets in sphalerite, and as blebs in galena, in the mines of the Panamint Mining District, Murphy (2) p. 323. **2,** Covellite occurs in some of the sulphide ores of the Darwin Mining District, Hall and MacKevett (1) p. 18.

Mono County: **1,** Small amounts of covellite have been found in Blind Spring Hill, A. L. Ransome (2) p. 172.

Nevada County: **1,** Covellite occurs with gold and chalcopyrite, from Spenceville, CDMG (13866).

Plumas County: **1,** Covellite occurs in blue needles as a marginal replacement of bornite and chalcopyrite at Engels, H. W. Turner and Rogers (32) p. 379.

Shasta County: **1,** Covellite occurs in the Balaklala mine, G. C. Brown (2) p. 762, Tucker (9) p. 427, and **2,** at the Bully Hill mine as an alteration of chalcopyrite, A. F. Rogers (6) p. 302. **3,** Covellite is found as a coating on pyrite at the Mountain Monarch prospect 2 miles south of Whiskeytown, Ferguson (1) p. 44.

Sierra County: **1,** Covellite was found at the Black Jack mine, Kanaka Creek (N.R.).

Siskiyou County: **1,** Small amounts of covellite occur with some bornite and chalcopyrite at the Preston Peak mine (sec. 22, T. 17 N., R. 5 E., H.), J. C. O'Brien (4) p. 428.

Tuolumne County: **1,** Covellite is reported from near Groveland, W. W. Bradley (26) p. 608.

CREDNERITE
Oxide of copper and manganese, $CuMn_2O_4$

Napa County: **1,** Massive crednerite occurs near Calistoga, CDMG (15349).

CREEDITE
Hydrous basic calcium aluminum sulfate with flourine, $Ca_3Al_2F_4(OH,F)_6SO_4 \cdot 2H_2O$

Inyo County: **1,** Creedite was first reported from California by Pabst (11a) p. 19. Excellent crystals were described from mineral specimens collected by Mr. Richard Thomssen from Darwin. Clusters of crystals occur embedded in pyrite and in linings in vugs. Hall and MacKevett (1) p. 18, (4) p. 64, report creedite from the Anaconda mine, Darwin Mining District, from what is presumed to be the same locality.

† * CRESTMOREITE, 1917
See riversideite and tobermorite

Riverside County: Crestmoreite was discovered at the Crestmore quarry, and was described and named as a new mineral by Eakle (15) p. 344. Subsequently, studies showed crestmoreite to be identical with tobermorite, H. F. W. Taylor (1).

CRISTOBALITE
Silicon dioxide, SiO_2

Imperial County: **1,** Cristobalite occurs with tridymite and feldspar in an obsidian metamorphosed by hot gases on Cormorant Island, Salton Sea, A. F. Rogers (30) p. 219, (42) p. 328.

Inyo County: **1,** Christobalite is associated with orthoclase, tridymite, opal, fayalite and magnetite in the linings of small spherical cavities in obsidian near Little Lake, about 8 miles west of Coso Hot Springs, A. F. Rogers (23) p. 213, W. W. Bradley (28) p. 494, M. B. Strong (7) p. 16, Stinson (4) p. 207, CDMG (20946).

Lake County: **1,** Cristobalite has been identified in the opal at Sulphur Bank, D. E. White and Roberson (2) p. 407.

Modoc County: **1,** Cristobalite occurs on the summit of Mount Hoffman in botryoidal masses lining cavities in dacite, Powers (1) p. 272.

Mono County: **1,** Cristobalite occurs in spherulites with feldspar from Casa del Diablo, A. F. Rogers (30) p. 82. **2,** Minor cristobalite has been identified in the clays of Little Antelope Valley, Cleveland (1) p. 19.

Nevada County: **1,** A specimen of cristobalite from Donner Lake is in the Stanford University Collections.

Plumas County: **1,** Cristobalite occurs with anauxite in cavities in pyroxene andesite, sometimes as paramorphs after tridymite, at Drakesbad, A. F. Rogers (38) p. 160, and **2,** in scattered minute crystals on fracture surfaces of basalt near Two Rivers, Murdoch (15) p. 500.

Riverside County: **1,** Cristobalite has been identified accompanying lechateliérite, in fulgurites near Indio, A. F. Rogers (50) p. 120.

Shasta County: **1,** A specimen of cristobalite from Black Butte, near Mount Shasta, is in Stanford University Collections.

Siskiyou County: **1,** Cristobalite occurs with fayalite in lithophysae in spherulitic obsidian, near Canyon Butte (sec. 13, T. 44 N., R. 43 E., M.D.), C. A. Anderson (p.c. '45). **2,** The mineral is reported from Shasta Springs, in Stanford University Collections.

Tehama County: **1,** Cristobalite is a constituent of volcanic rock near Tuscan Springs, A. F. Rogers (18) p. 222.

Tuolumne County: **1,** Distinct octahedral crystals of cristobalite occur in augite andesite, near Jamestown, A. F. Rogers (18) p. 224, (30) p. 85, (38) p. 160.

CROCOITE
Lead chromate, $PbCrO_4$

Inyo County: **1,** Crocoite was reported as early as 1923 from the Darwin mines, with wulfenite. The occurrence is confirmed by identification in ores by Hall and MacKevett (1) p. 18.

Riverside County: **1,** Crocoite is reported as occurring with wulfenite in the El Dorado mine, near Indio (N. R.).

CRYPTOMELANE
Essentially a hydrous oxide of manganese with potassium, near $KMn^{2+}Mn^{4+}_{7.25}O_{16} \cdot H_2O$

Cryptomelane was proposed by W. E. Richmond and Fleischer (2) p. 607 as the name to be used for "true psilomelane" of Ramsdell (1).

Inyo County: **1,** Cryptomelane is found in the Defense, Minietta and Modoc mines, Lookout (Modoc) Mining District, Hall and Stephens (3) p. 24.

San Bernardino County: **1,** Cryptomelane has been identified in the Logan mine, near Hector, Hewett (7) p. 1440. **2,** The mineral is also reported from the Van Dorn mine, ibid., p. 1452.

CUBANITE
Copper iron sulphide, $CuFe_2S_3$

Madera County: **1,** Cubanite is reported from Daulton mine, one mile southeast of Daulton Station, W. W. Bradley (32) p. 106.

Plumas County: **1,** Cubanite occurs with chalcopyrite and pyrrhotite in the Walker mine, 9 miles northeast of Spring Garden, A. Knopf (14) p. 244.

San Luis Obispo County: **1,** A large mass of cubanite (1,000 lbs.) is said to have been found on Santa Rosa Creek, near San Simeon. Hanks (12) p. 158, considers this doubtful.

MINERALS OF CALIFORNIA

CUPRITE—Red Copper Ore
Cuprous oxide, Cu₂O

Chalcotrichite is a delicate hair-like variety of cuprite.

Cuprite is an important ore of copper. It occurs in most of the copper localities as a secondary mineral in the oxidized portions of the deposits. Massive specimens have come from various counties, but no large bodies of cuprite are known in California. Only occurrences of mineralogical interest will be given specific references.

Calaveras County: **1,** Masses of cuprite as very rich ore with chalco-pyrite are occasionally found at Copperopolis, J. D. Whitney (7) p. 255, Reid (3) p. 398.

Colusa County: **1,** Chalcotrichite was found with massive cuprite in the Lion mine (sec. 17, T. 17 N., R. 6 W., M. D.), CDMG (13484), J. R. Browne (4) p. 210, W. W. Bradley (1) p. 178.

Del Norte County: **1,** Deposits in veins up to 4 feet wide are found in the Rockland area, McGregor (1) p. 167.

Riverside County: **1,** Abundant masses of cuprite occur in the Red Cloud mine, Chuckawalla Mountains, Orcutt (2) p. 901. **2,** Cuprite is reported as an oxidation coating on chalcopyrite from Crestmore, Woodford et al. (10) p. 367.

References to other localities by county are: *Calaveras,* Silliman (7) p. 349; *Colusa,* Hanks (12) p. 158, (15) p. 104; *Del Norte,* Hanks (12) p. 158, (15) p. 105, Aubury (1) p. 115; *El Dorado,* Aubury (1) p. 181, (4) p. 212, Tucker and Waring (2) p. 276; *Fresno,* Irelan (3) p. 209; *Humboldt,* W. P. Blake (14) p. 124; Laizure (3) p. 306; *Imperial,* Henshaw (1) p. 185; *Inyo,* Aubury (1) p. 245, (4) p. 301, Zalinski (1) p. 81, C. A. Waring and Huguenin (2) pp. 69, 70; *Kern,* Hanks (12) p. 158, Storms (13) p. 635, Troxel and Morton (2) p. 294; *Mariposa,* W. P. Blake (9) p. 20, Hanks (12) p. 158, Liebenam (1) p. 543, Aubury (1) pp. 204, 213; *Mendocino,* Aubury (1) p. 137; *Modoc,* Tucker (3) p. 241; *Mono,* Hanks (12) pp. 158, 159, 259, (15) p. 105, Whiting (1) p. 364, Aubury (1) p. 243; *Napa,* Hanks (12) p. 158, (15) p. 105; *Nevada,* Hanks (12) p. 158, Aubury (1) p. 27; *Placer,* Silliman (7) p. 351, Hanks (12) p. 158, (15) p. 105, Aubury (1) p. 173, (4) pp. 207, 210, C. A. Waring (4) p. 329; *Plumas,* Hanks (12) p. 158, Crawford (1) p. 69; *Riverside,* F. J. H. Merrill (2) p. 526, Tucker (8) p. 195, Woodford et al. (10) p. 371; *San Bernardino,* Aubury (1) p. 255, Tucker (4) p. 339, Weber (3) p. 27; *Shasta,* Hanks (12) p. 158, (15) p. 105, Diller (10) p. 12, Laizure (1) p. 519; *Siskiyou,* CDMG (15679); *Trinity,* Hanks (12) p. 158, (15) p. 105, CDMG (15116), (15149), (4223), (4556); *Ventura,* Tucker and Sampson (20) p. 257; *Yuba,* Aubury (1) p. 172.

CUPROPLUMBITE
See galena

Riverside County: Cuproplumbite was reported as a mineral species distinct from galena from Black Eagle mine, Eagle Mountains, Tucker (8) p. 195, CDMG (19939). The mineral was shown to be identical with galena, Palache et al. (10) p. 200.

CUPROSKLODOWSKITE
Basic hydrous copper uranyl silicate, $Cu(UO_2)_2(SiO_3)_2(OH)_2 \cdot 5H_2O$

Plumas County: **1,** Cuprosklodowskite is reported from Chilcoot area, CDMG (21610).

CUPROTUNGSTITE
Basic copper tungstate, $Cu_2WO_4(OH)_2$

Fresno County: **1,** A crystal of cuprotungstite of unusual size, originally described as cuproscheelite, was sent from an unknown locality in Fresno County to San Francisco in 1879, Hanks (12) p. 159, (15) p. 105. It may have come from the Kern County, locality **(1).**

Inyo County: **1,** Cuprotungstite is reported as a replacement of scheelite as light olive-green to greenish-yellow coloration in fractures in scheelite from the Cuprotungstite claim, 1.3 mi. N. 16° E. of Big Dodd Spring, Ubehebe Mining District, McAllister (4) p. 55.

Kern County: **1,** Material found with radiating black tourmaline at the Green Monster mine, 12 miles east of White River, was first reported as cuproscheelite, Hanks (2) p. 133. Later examination proved it to be scheelite with admixed cuprotungstite, Schaller (46) p. 237.

*CURTISITE, 1930—Idrialite
A hydrocarbon, $C_{24}H_{18}$

A specimen of curtisite from Skaggs Springs (Sonoma County, **1**) has been compared with curtisite from Czechoslovakia, and with idrialite from Idria, Yugoslavia, and the three appear to be identical in optical properties and x-ray powder patterns, according to Tuček and Kouřimský (1). Further study may result in the discrediting of curtisite as a species, since the name idrialite (idrialine) has priority.

Lake County: **1,** Curtisite occurs with cinnabar and dolomite in serpentine at the Mirabel (Standard) mine, near Middletown, Vonsen (p.c. '34). **2,** Curtisite is reported from the Helen and Research mines, R. G. Yates and Hilpert (4) p. 247.

Napa County: **1,** Curtisite has been found in the Knoxville mine, Averitt (1) p. 78.

San Francisco County: **1,** Curtisite occurs in a ledge of serpentine veined with chalcedony at Duboce Street, near Market Street, on the site of the United States Mint in San Francisco, W. W. Bradley (24) p. 71, CDMG (20746).

Sonoma County: **1,** Curtisite was found with realgar, metacinnabar, and opal at Skaggs Springs. It was described and named by F. E. Wright and Allen (3) p. 169 (with analysis); see also W. W. Bradley (24) p. 345, CDMG (20813), Everhart (4) p. 390.

Yolo County: **1,** Curtisite occurs at the Reed mine associated with cinnabar and a dark heavy oil, Michael A. Price (p.c. '62); written communication, January 1962, on file CDMG.

CUSPIDINE—Custerite
Basic calcium silicate with fluorine, $Ca_4Si_2O_7(OH,F)_2$

Riverside County: **1,** The custerite found by Tilley (1) p. 372, in a metamorphic rock from Crestmore, is identical with cuspidine, Tilley (2), p. 90.

CYANOTRICHITE
Basic hydrous copper, aluminum sulfate, $Cu_4Al_2(SO_4)(OH)_{12}\cdot2H_2O$

San Bernardino County: **1,** A specimen of cyanotrichite is in the Mineral Exhibit, CDMG (21704) from Clark Mountain.

CYRTOLITE
See zircon

Zirconium silicate, $ZrSiO_4$, but containing U, Y and other rare elements.

Kern County: **1,** Cyrtolite has been found in small amounts in pegmatite dikes of the Havilah area, Troxel and Morton (2) p. 27.

Riverside County: **1,** Cyrtolite occurs from the Southern Pacific quarry near Nuevo in radial clusters and individual crystals. Spectroscopic analysis shows zirconium and yttrium in large quantities. The mineral is associated with xenotime, monazite, and yttrocrasite (?) in pegmatite, Murdoch (19) p. 198. **2,** Cyrtolite occurs with monazite and xenotime in pegmatite, 4 miles east of Nuevo, Charles Seward (p.c. '60).

San Bernardino County: **1,** Cyrtolite occurs with betafite in a dark mass in pegmatite north of Hector, Hewett and Glass (3) p. 1048.

DANBURITE
Calcium borosilicate, $CaB_2Si_2O_8$

Riverside County: **1,** Danburite was identified by M. Vonsen on specimens from Crestmore, Eakle (20) p. 321.

DARAPSKITE
Hydrous sodium nitrate and sulphate, $Na_3(NO_3SO_4)\cdot H_2O$

Nitro-glauberite is probably a mixture of darapskite and soda niter, W. E. Ford (8) p. 740.

San Bernardino County: **1,** Darapskite occurs in the niter beds of Death Valley, according to G. E. Bailey (2) p. 170.

DATOLITE
Basic calcium borosilicate, $CaB(SiO_4)(OH)$

Colusa County: **1,** Datolite has been found with thomsonite, prehnite, and other minerals near Wilbur Springs, 2 miles east of the Lake County line, Vonsen (p.c. '33).

Inyo County: **1,** White massive datolite was found with idocrase and garnet at the San Carlos mine, 10 or 12 miles south of Fish Springs, Hanks (12) p. 159, Kunz (24) p. 97. The mineral was analyzed by J. L. Smith (1) p. 435. **2,** Datolite has been reported from the Slate Range, Kunz (24) p. 97.

Riverside County: **1,** Massive white glassy datolite, with a slight greenish tinge, occurs in a pegmatite at Crestmore, Eakle (15) p. 350, Foshag (12) p. 88, Anon. (42) p. 462.

San Bernardino County: **1,** Hanks (12) p. 97, reports datolite from the Calico Mountains.

San Francisco County: **1,** Glassy crystals and white veins of datolite occur in an altered diabase dike in the serpentine at Fort Point. Complex crystals were measured by Eakle (1) p. 317; see also Kunz (24) p. 97.

DAVIDITE

A multiple oxide of titanium and iron with uranium and rare earth metals, perhaps $Y_6Z_5O_{36}$, with $Y=Fe'',Ce,U,etc.$, and $Z=Ti,Fe''',V,Cr$

Davidite is mentioned on occasion in connection with reported radioactive mineral occurrences in the state. According to E. S. Dana (6) p. 542, it is ". . . apparently a mixture, largely ilmenite, magnetite, rutile, and a rare-earth mineral near chevkinite." Pabst and Thomssen (17) report hexagonal crystallization in a metamict occurrence from Arizona, which establishes davidite as a distinct species, Pabst (20).

DAWSONITE

Basic sodium aluminum carbonate, $NaAlCO_3(OH)_2$

Dawsonite is a very rare mineral, and occurs only in arid regions as white incrustations.

Inyo County: **1,** Dawsonite is reported to occur as a soft earthy incrustation in a dike in Amargosa Canyon, G. E. Bailey (2) p. 102.

* DEERITE, 1964

A complex silicate with manganese iron and aluminum, near $(Mg_{.09}Mn_{.95}-Fe''_{11.99})_{13.03}(Fe'''_{6.48}Al_{.42})_{6.90} \cdot Si_{13.04}O_{43.94}(OH)_{11.06}$

Mendocino County: **1,** Deerite is an important mineral in some of the Franciscan rocks near Laytonville, associated with the new minerals howeite and zussmanite, Agrell (1), p. 1507.

DESCLOIZITE

Basic lead zinc copper vanadate, $Pb(Zn,Cu)VO_4 \cdot OH$

Cuprodescloizite is a variety with about half of the zinc replaced by copper.

San Bernardino County: **1,** Minute colorless and yellowish plates of cuprodescloizite occur with cerussite and vanadinite at Camp Signal, Schaller (24) p. 149, (26) p. 88, Cloudman et al. (1) p. 849.

DEWEYLITE

A magnesium silicate near serpentine but with more water, perhaps hydrous magnesium silicate, $Mg_7Si_6O_{19}11H_2O$

Inyo County: **1,** Deweylite is mentioned by Hall and MacKevett (1) p. 16, as a gangue mineral of the ores of the Darwin Mining District; see also ibid. (4) p. 62.

Napa County: **1,** Deweylite occurs as a gangue mineral with the gold and silver ores of the Palisades mine, 2 miles north of Calistoga, Hulin (p.c. '36).

Riverside County: **1,** A. F. Rogers (19) p. 584 and Daly (1) p. 651, have described the occurrence of deweylite with chrysotile in the east Chino quarry at Crestmore. **2,** An opaline mineral closely resembling deweylite in x-ray pattern has been found on the 910' level of the Commercial quarry at Crestmore, Murdoch (p.c. '57). Some of the mineral forms an alteration zone around crude merwinite crystals.

San Bernardino County: **1,** Deweylite was mentioned from the Dewey mine, Clark Mountains, in a carbonate zone, Schaller (50) p. 816.

Santa Clara County: **1,** Crusts of deweylite have been found at the Western magnesite mine on Red Mountain, A. F. Rogers (7) p. 380.

DIADOCHITE
Hydrous ferric sulphate and phosphate, $Fe^{3+}_2(PO_4,SO_4)OH \cdot 5H_2O$

San Benito County: **1,** Diadochite has been found in the New Idria quicksilver mine, A. F. Rogers (43) p. 178.

DIAMOND
Native carbon, C

Bort is a hard rounded form without distinct cleavage. *Carbonado* is a hard black variety without cleavage.

Diamonds were found in California soon after placer mining began. As early as 1849, Lyman (3) p. 294, reported seeing a straw-yellow crystal about the size of a small pea, which came from one of the placers. A few years later diamonds were observed in the gold gravels at Cherokee, Butte County, and this locality has become the one most noted in the State for the number found.

Placer deposits elsewhere have also yielded diamonds from time to time, so their occurrence has not been limited to any one field. No record has been kept of the total number found, but it is probably between four and five hundred. Since all of them are chance finds, there can be no doubt that many more have been overlooked or destroyed.

A few of the stones found are over 2 carats in weight and of good quality, but the majority are small and mostly "off color," usually with a pale-yellow tinge. Most of these diamonds, now in the possession of different individuals, were found during the days when placer mining and hydraulicking were at their height, and since that time diamond finds have been less frequent.

In California, diamonds have been found only in placer gravels and in the black sands and concentrates of placer mines. Presumably their origin has been in the basic igneous rocks from which the serpentines of the gold regions have been derived. The discovery near Oroville of an apparent pipe of serpentinized rock bearing a resemblance to the diamond pipes of South Africa led to some active operations on the part of the United States Diamond Mining Company, and a shaft was sunk, which proved not successful, Sterrett (2) p. 1217. The rock is a hard eclogite differing in its character from the kimberlite of South Africa, Sterrett (2) p. 1217. Hanks (12) pp. 168-172, gives an interesting account of the diamonds found during the early days of gold mining, and H. W. Turner (20) and Storms (16) contribute short articles on California diamonds.

Occurrences of special mineralogical or commercial interest only are noted below.

Amador County: **1,** Among the 60 or 70 stones from Jackass Gulch near Volcano was found one single clear crystal of 1.57 carats and two small crystals showing the trapezohedron with curved faces, J. D. Whitney (7) p. 276. **2,** A stone (2.65 carats) with some crystal faces was found in 1934 near Plymouth, Sperisen (1) p. 39.

Fresno County: **1,** Small diamonds, reported to have been found near Coalinga, are probably quartz, and are popularly referred to as "Coalinga diamonds." No published references to this supposed occurrence have been found. (N.R.)

Nevada County: **1,** The largest diamond recorded from the state, weighing $7\frac{1}{4}$ carats, was found at French Corral sometime before 1867, Hanks (10) p. 251, (12) p. 169, Kunz (24) p. 44.

Trinity County: **1,** Hanks (1) p. 162, records a description by Wohler of minute diamonds occurring with finely divided platinum, from near the junction of Klamath and Trinity Rivers.

DIASPORE
Hydrous aluminum oxide, $Al_2O_3 \cdot H_2O$

Calaveras County: **1,** Diaspore occurs in good crystals from 5 to 6 miles east of Altaville on Janokis Ranch, with chlorite on chromite, University of California Collections, Berkeley.

Fresno County: **1,** Diaspore occurs in small crystals with spinel in metamorphosed limestone at Twin Lakes, Chesterman (p.c. '55).

Mono County: **1,** Diaspore occurs in compact masses with andalusite or in veins of pyrophyllite at the mine of Champion Sillimanite, on the western slope of the White Mountains, north of Bishop, Kerr (3) p. 626.

DIGENITE
Cuprous sulphide, $Cu_{9-x}S_5$, where x = 0.8 to 1.5

San Benito County: **1,** Small crystals of digenite associated with neptunite and benitoite, from the Dallas Gem mine, have been identified by x-ray methods, R. E. Desautels (p.c. '59).

DIOPTASE
Basic copper silicate, $CuSiO_2(OH)_2$

Mono County: **1,** Dioptase is tentatively identified from the Cornucopia mine in the Blind Spring Mining District, as crystals lining cavities in malachite. No tests have been made to confirm the identification, A. L. Ransome (2) p. 191

San Bernardino County: **1,** Dioptase occurs with linarite and caledonite on a specimen from a mine on Silver Lake Mountain, Murdoch (p.c. '49), CDMG (21350).

DOLOMITE
Carbonate of calcium and magnesium, $CaMg(CO_3)_2$

Dolomite is a common mineral, but is not as abundant as calcite. Much of the limestone and marble of the state is dolomitic. Dolomite is commonly associated with serpentine and other magnesian rocks, in which it is often found as white veins.

Dolomite is widespread in many parts of the state. Occurrences of the mineral are very numerous, but few have mineralogical significance. As a mineral resource, dolomite occurs in considerable quantity in many deposits. In the localities referenced below, no attempt has been made to systematically report commodity occurrences, nor to report the mineral wherever it is mentioned in the literature. Some localities of minor importance and of little general mineralogical interest are noted because they have been carried in early editions of *Minerals of California.* The authors consider it wise to retain these as part of the historical record, but newer and more important localities of the min-

Diamonds found in California

County	Location	Date	Total number of stones	Weight of large stones in carats	References
Amador	Jackass Gulch (near Volcano)		60–70	1–1.57	J. D. Whitney (7) p. 276, Hanks (10) p. 253, (12) p. 169, Kunz (24) p. 40
	Rancheria (near Volcano)		1		H. W. Turner (20) p. 183
	Loafer Hill (near Oleta)		1		H. W. Turner (20) p. 183
	Near Plymouth	1934	1	2.65	Sperisen (1) p. 39
	Indian Gulch (near Fiddletown)	1855–67	5		Silliman (8) p. 354, Hanks (10) p. 250, Kunz (24) p. 40
Butte	Cherokee Flat	from 1853 on	300+	1–2.25	Silliman (8) p. 355, (12) p. 133, Kunz (24) pp. 41, 42, Hanks (12) p. 170, C. A. Waring and Huguenin (2) p. 87, Eng. & Min. Jour. (21) p. 589
		1867		1–1 3/16 cut	
		1892–93		2	
		1910	1	2	Sterrett (6) p. 859
		1912	1	1.08+	Sterrett (8) p. 1040
		1913	Several	1–1¼	Sterrett (9) p. 651
		1915	3	1 each	
		1916	1	1.2	Schaller (38) p. 892
		1918	1	.75	Schaller (39) p. 9
	Oroville		10		Kunz (24) p. 43, Sterrett (2) p. 1217
	Thompsons Flat (2 miles from Oroville)	1915	9	3–1 each	
	Yankee Hill (1½ miles northwest of Oroville)	1916	2	Value $125, $52	C. A. Waring (4) p. 187
Del Norte	Smith River	1861	1	1½ cut	Hanks (10) p. 252, (12) p. 171, Kunz (24) p. 42, W. W. Bradley (10) p. 669, (25) p. 16
				Microscopic size	Hanks (12) p. 170, Kunz (24) p. 43

County	Locality	Date	No.	Size	References
El Dorado	Somewhere in county	Before 1873	12	1–1.5	Silliman (8) p. 355, Goodyear (2) p. 27
	Forest Hill	Before 1867	40–50		Silliman (5) p. 119, Kunz (24) p. 43
	White Rock Canyon, Cedar Ravine (near Placerville)		3–4	0.5, 1¼	Hanks (10) p. 250, (12) pp. 168, 169, Kunz (24) p. 44
	Webber Hill (south side)		3		Kunz (24) p. 169
	Smiths Flat	1859–1874	47+		B. Evans (1) p. 814
		1874	20	0.2, 0.12	
		1879	2	0.12	
			1	0.92	
		1894	1	1.88, 0.25, 1.62, 1.06	
		1896	4		
		1897	1	1.50	
		1899	1	0.65	
		1900	1	1.4+	
		1901	1	0.46	
		1912	1	0.95+	
Humboldt	Lower Trinity River				Min. & Sci. Press (13) p. 194
Imperial (?)	Along Mexican border				F. J. H. Merrill (1) p. 740
Nevada	French Corral		2	7¼, 1 3/5	Silliman (8) p. 355, Hanks (10) p. 251, (12) p. 169, Kunz (24) p. 44
Placer			Several	Small	Min. & Sci. Press (13) p. 194
Plumas	Gopher Hill and upper Spanish Creek		2		Kunz (24) p. 31, W. W. Bradley (10) p. 669
	Sawpit Flat		1		Sterrett (9) p. 651
	Nelson Point		1	2	Kunz (14) p. 423
Trinity	Near junction of Trinity and Klamath Rivers		Many, minute		Kunz (24) p. 44, Hanks (1) p. 162, (12) p. 310
Tulare	Alpine Creek	1895	1		Kunz (11) p. 896

eral as a mineral resource have not been added, and literature citations to articles on such localities have not necessarily been included.

Amador County: **1**, Narrow veins of dolomite traversing chloritic rocks carry free gold, Hanks (12) p. 177.

Calaveras County: **1**, White crystals of dolomite occurred in the gold-bearing schist of Carson Hill, CDMG (13140). **2**, Dolomite is found in fine crystals lining cavities and massive with free gold from Winter Hills mine near Angels Camp, Hanks (12) p. 177.

Inyo County: **1**, Well-formed microscopic crystals of dolomite are formed in sediments of Deep Springs Lake, M. N. A. Peterson et al. (1) p. 6494, B. F. Jones (1) p. 201.

Kern County: **1**, Dolomite was found replacing wood in Midway oil field, Adams (1) p. 357.

Lake County: **1**, Well-crystallized dolomite occurs as gangue of mercury ores in the Mirabel (Standard) mine (T. 10 N., R. 7 W., M. D.), W. W. Bradley (28) p. 393. **2**, Dolomite is a rare constituent of the ores at Sulphur Bank, D. E. White and Roberson (2) p. 408.

Los Angeles County: **1**, Crystals of dolomite occur with pyrite, marcasite (?), and other minerals in the Lomita quarry, Murdoch (p.c. '54).

Riverside County: **1**, Dolomite was found in 1942 as a few veinlets at Crestmore. These appear to be residuals of original dolomite most of which was lost during metamorphism, Woodford (11) p. 355.

San Bernardino County: **1**, Gold-bearing dolomite is reported from the Amargosa mine, Hanks (12) p. 177. **2**, Dolomite occurs as minute crystals in some of the mud layers at Searles Lake, G. I. Smith and Haines (3) p. 28.

Santa Clara County: **1**, Veins of coarsely bladed dolomite associated with opalized chalcedony and some cinnabar are reported from the Hillsdale (also called Oak Hill, San Juan Bautista, Chapman or Chaboya) mine, on the east slope of Oak Hills, 4 miles south of San José, Crittenden (1) p. 63. **2**, Dolomite veins occur occasionally in the New Almaden ores, E. H. Bailey and Everhart (12) p. 99.

DUFRENOYSITE
Lead arsenic sulphide, $Pb_2As_2S_5$

Inyo County: **1**, Dufrenoysite was reported to have been found in the Cerro Gordo Mining District, Hanks (12) p. 178.

DUFTITE
Basic copper lead arsenate, $[PbCu(AsO_4)(OH)]$

Inyo County: **1**, An olivine-green crust on a specimen from the Cerro Gordo area has been tentatively identified as duftite, Murdoch (p.c. '63).

San Bernardino County: **1**, Duftite has been identified in a specimen from the Mohawk mine, Mountain Pass area, Murdoch (p.c. '62).

DUMORTIERITE
Aluminum iron borosilicate, $(Al,Fe)_7BSi_3O_{18}$

Imperial County: **1**, Boulders of dark-blue dumortierite occur over a wide area about 18 miles northwest of Winterhaven, and 10 miles northwest of the now defunct station of Ogilby on the Southern Pacific Railroad, Kunz (10) p. 697, (24) p. 71, Tucker (11) p. 269, Wolff (1) p. 188. (The locality is described incorrectly in some of these references.)

Kern County: 1, Dumortierite has been reported in the heavy-mineral assemblage of drill cores from wells in the Lazard area of the Lost Hills (T. 27 S., R. 20 E., M.D.), R. D. Reed and Bailey (4) p. 363.

Riverside County: 1, Murphy (1) p. 80, reports dumortierite in quartz monzonite, a rock resembling granite, just west of the railroad trestle near the mouth of Temescal Wash, 2 miles southeast of Corona; see also E. S. Larsen (17) p. 106. 2, The occurrence of dumortierite in granodiorite near the Cajalco tin mine, 13 miles southwest of Riverside is also reported, ibid., p. 79. 3, Minute blue needles of dumortierite occur in the andalusite pegmatite at the magnesite mine, Winchester, Murdoch (p.c. '46).

San Diego County: 1, Violet-red dumortierite occurs near Dehesa, with sillimanite in quartz, Kunz (24) p. 71, Schaller (7) p. 211 with analysis by W. E. Ford (2) p. 427. Spectroscopic analysis of a specimen of dumortierite probably from this locality shows only trace elements besides the normal principal ones, Hey and Claringbull (2) p. 902. Previous analyses, W. E. Ford (2) p. 427, Schaller (7) p. 211, showed a noteworthy amount of titanium in addition to the normal principal constituents.

† * EAKLEITE, 1917
See xonotlite

Santa Barbara County: A mineral specimen collected years ago near Santa Ynez, labelled wollastonite, was found by E. S. Larsen (8) p. 465, to differ optically from that mineral. On the supposition that it was a new mineral, he proposed the name eakleite for it. E. S. Larsen (13) p. 181, later showed the specimen to be xonotlite.

ECDEMITE—Heliophyllite
Lead chloroarsenate, $Pb_6As_2O_7Cl_4$(?)(uncertain)

Inyo County: 1, Ecdemite was reported by Woodhouse (p.c. '56) as an alteration of mimetite from the Defense mine in the Inyo Range.

EDINGTONITE
Hydrous barium aluminum silicate, perhaps $BaAl_2Si_3O_{10}\cdot4H_2O$

Mendocino County: 1, Edingtonite was found on Ash Creek, 1 mile northeast of the highway on or near the Sonoma County line, with brewsterite, Vonsen (p.c. '45).

EGLESTONITE
Mercury oxychloride, Hg_4Cl_2O

San Benito County: 1, Eglestonite, as greenish-yellow coatings on silicate carbonate rock, is reported by E. H. Oyler (p.c. '62) from 3 miles south of the New Idria mine. It is associated with montroydite, calomel, native mercury and cinnabar.

San Mateo County: 1, Minute yellow crystals of eglestonite associated with cinnabar, mercury, calomel, dolomite, magnesite, opal and quartz occur about 5 miles west of Palo Alto. The mineral is found in seams and cavities in the siliceous material so common in the serpentine of the cinnabar areas of the State, A. F. Rogers (5) p. 48, W. W. Bradley (5) p. 149. **2,** Eglestonite is reported with montroydite, calomel and other mercury minerals from a locality in serpentine, 2 miles west of Redwood City, Woodhouse (3) p. 603.

*ELLESTADITE, 1937
An apatite-like sulphate-silicate, with SO_4 and SiO_4 as partial replacements of PO_4, $Ca_5(Si,S,P)_3O_{12}(Cl,F,OH)$

This mineral was noted in Murdoch and Webb (21) p. 134 as a variety of wilkeite, but it should have species rank.

Riverside County: **1,** Ellestadite occurs as pale rose stringers associated with wollastonite, vesuvianite and diopside at Crestmore. The mineral was originally described by D. McConnell (1) p. 977, with analysis by R. B. Ellestad, ibid., p. 983.

EMBOLITE
Silver chloro-bromide, $Ag(Br,Cl)$

Embolite has been found only in association with cerargyrite and in much smaller amounts.

Inyo County: **1,** Embolite is found with cerargyrite in the Indiana mine, near Swansea, Hanks (12) p. 178; **2,** at the Lee mine, 18 miles east of Keeler, Tucker (11) p. 488; **3,** from Panamint mines in Surprise Canyon 10 miles northeast of Ballarat, Tucker (10) p. 495, and **4,** from the Minnietta mine (T. 19 S., R. 42 E., M.D.), Tucker and Sampson (25) p. 445.

Mono County: **1,** Embolite is reported from the Minnie mine, Sweetwater Range, Hanks (12) p. 178, and **2,** from the Silver Reef mine in Long Valley (T. 3 S., R. 30 E., M.D.), R. J. Sampson (14) p. 146.

San Bernardino County: Embolite is reported **1,** from the Alhambra mine, Calico Mining District, Hanks (12) p. 178, (15) p. 107, and as well-formed crystals in Wall Street Canyon, Calico, D. J. Henry (1) p. 228; **2,** from the Death Valley mine, 3 miles east of Cima on the northeast slope of the New York Mountains, Tucker and Sampson (16) p. 275, (17) p. 349; **3,** from the Silver Reef Mining District, Storms (4) p. 367; **4,** from the Oro Plata mine in the Old Woman Mountains (sec. 23, T. 3 N., R. 19 E., S.B.), Tucker and Sampson (17) p. 354; **5,** from the War Eagle mine, Lead Mountains (T. 4 N., R. 10 E., S.B.), 9 miles south of Bagdad, Tucker (8) p. 95; **6,** from the Clark Mountains (T. 18 N., R. 13 E., S.B.), Tucker (8) p. 94; **7,** from Trojan Lake area, 22 miles northwest of Fenner, Tucker (4) p. 364, and **8,** reported by De Groot (2) p. 537 from Searles Lake.

EMMONSITE
Hydrated ferric tellurite, $Fe_2(TeO_3)_3 \cdot 2H_2O$

Frondel and Pough (1) p. 215, have shown that durdenite and emmonsite are identical and suggest the retention of the latter name.

Calaveras County: **1,** A specimen of telluride ore from this county, presumably from Carson Hill, contained along its fractures pale greenish-yellow spherulites, which on optical examination E. S. Larsen (5) p. 45 and (11) p. 71, identified as durdenite.

ENARGITE
Copper arsenic sulphide, Cu_3AsS_4, with Sb to 6 percent

Alpine County: **1,** Enargite was found in large masses associated with massive pyrite in the Mogul area, and formed the chief copper mineral of the Morning Star and a few other mines, E. W. Root (1) p. 201, Silliman (12) p. 126, Eakle (9) p. 232, (16) p. 12.

Del Norte County: **1,** Enargite has been reported with bornite from French Hill (N. R.).

El Dorado County: **1,** Enargite was found in the Ford mines, near Georgetown (N. R.).

Inyo County: **1,** Enargite may occur with famatinite as a constituent of the silver ore from the Thompson mine, Darwin Mining District, Hall and MacKevett (1) p. 17, ibid. (4) p. 59.

Plumas County: **1,** Small amounts of enargite occur with bornite and chalcopyrite at Engels, Graton and McLaughlin (4) p. 15.

Shasta County: **1,** Enargite, variety luzonite, has been identified in ores from the East Shasta copper-zinc mines, Albers and Robertson (3) p. 71.

EPIDOTE
Basic calcium/aluminum/iron silicate, $Ca_2(Al,Fe)_3(SiO_4)_3(OH)$

Epidote is a very common mineral in the State, especially as a secondary mineral in crystalline rocks. It is often found in aggregates of large crystals and columnar masses in veins with quartz and feldspar. It is abundant in contact-metamorphic deposits in limestone.

No attempt has been made to report all of the occurrences of epidote found in the State that are referenced in the literature. The mineral is widespread and is so common that only occurrences of mineralogical interest should be included. However, some localities of minor importance and of little mineralogical interest are noted for the historical record because they have been reported in early editions of *Minerals of California.*

Butte County: **1,** Epidote was mentioned by Silliman (13) p. 385, (12) p. 133, as a constituent of the gold washings at Cherokee.

Calaveras County: **1,** Epidote was found with garnet, quartz and idocrase at Garnet Hill, just above the confluence of Moore Creek and the Mokelumne River, H. W. Turner (12) p. 706, Melhase (6) p. 7. **2,** Large crystals of epidote were found at Bald Point on the Mokelumne River, Kunz (24) p. 99. **3,** Epidote was found in good crystals with quartz 7 miles north of Angels Camp, Woodhouse (p.c. '45).

Colusa County: **1,** Epidote is associated with hematite in a deposit 4 miles south of Lodoga (N. R.).

El Dorado County: **1,** Excellent large crystals of epidote, coated with axinite, occurred in a coarse vein with orthoclase, bornite, and molybdenite at the old Cosumnes copper mine, Schaller (18) p. 42. **2,** Granular aggregates of epidote occur in the schists at Mount Tallac and near Grass Lake, S. G. Clark (p.c. '35).

Fresno County: **1,** Epidote is common in Grub Gulch, CDMG (13525). **2,** Crystals of epidote up to 10 inches in length have been found in the north end of Clarks Valley, Noren (p.c. '35). Other occurrences: Tucker and Sampson (30) p. 565, Chesterman (1) p. 278.

Humboldt County: **1,** Large prisms of epidote with calcite occur in schists on the west side of Horse Mountain (N. R.).

Inyo County: **1,** Epidote is common in the contact zones of the tungsten deposits near Bishop, A. Knopf (6) pp. 233–238, Hess and Larsen (17) pp. 269, 276, Lemmon (5) p. 504; **2,** the mineral occurs abundantly in the contact zone at Darwin, Kelley (4) p. 539.

Kern County: **1,** Epidote was found with scheelite at the Cadillac claims in the Greenhorn Mining District, Storms (15) p. 768. **2,** Abundant crystals were found at the Aldridge mine (NW¼ sec. 27, T. 25 S., R. 32 E., M. D.), Durrell (p.c. '45). **3,** Coarsely crystalline epidote in quartz comes from Black Mountain, Durrell (p.c. '45).

Lassen County: **1,** Epidote occurs with native copper at the Lummis mine, Woodhouse (p.c. '45).

Los Angeles County: **1,** Epidote was found with bitumen and orthoclase at White Point, CDMG (8688). **2,** Epidote is disseminated through crystalline limestone in Pacoima Canyon, $3\frac{1}{2}$ miles from San Fernando, Goodyear (3) p. 340. **3,** Epidote and epidote group minerals are widely distributed in the Pelona schist, Ehlig (1) p. 170.

Madera County: **1,** Epidote is widespread in the Ritter Range, Erwin (1) p. 67. **2,** Epidote is the most abundant silicate mineral in the metamorphosed limestone of Shadow and Johnson Creeks, ibid; **3,** it occurred with quartz, hematite, and magnetite in the Hildreth Mining District, Erwin (p.c. '34). **4,** Specimens of epidote have come from Coarse Gold Kunz (24) p. 99.

Marin County: **1,** Epidote occurs with lawsonite near Reed Station, F. L. Ransome (3) p. 310. **2,** Epidote occurs as yellow, fairly well-formed crystals in glaucophane schist on the north side of Tiburon Peninsula, Watters (p.c. '58).

Mariposa County: **1,** Epidote occurs on the south side of Mount Hoffman, Kunz (24) p. 99.

Mendocino County: **1,** Gray-colored blades of epidote (or clinozoisite) up to 24 inches occur with lawsonite and rutile on the new Covelo road, Vonsen (p.c. '45).

Mono County: **1,** Crystals of epidote occur in veins at the Morris claims, Benton Range, Lemmon (6) p. 591, **2,** with garnet at Yellow-Jacket Spring, A. L. Ransome (2) p. 191, and **3,** at Black Rock mine (T. 3 S., R. 31 E., M. D.), R. J. Sampson (14) p. 147.

Nevada County: **1,** Epidote was found at Meadow Lake, Lindgren (5) p. 205.

Plumas County: **1,** Epidote occurs with bornite and chalcopyrite at Engels, Graton and McLaughlin (4) p. 20.

Riverside County: **1,** Deep-green epidote occurs in the calcite, and long prismatic epidote crystals, altered brown, occur in the pegmatite at Crestmore, Eakle (15) p. 349, Woodford et al. (10) p. 358. **2,** Epidote was found with specular hematite in the Monte Negro Mining District, Storms (4) p. 369; **3,** it occurs in gneiss on the Eagle Mountains, Harder (6) p. 48, F. J. H. Merrill (2) p. 545. **4,** Epidote crystals over six inches in length have been found in quartz near Allessandro, Foshag (p.c. '35). **5,** Epidote occurs with axinite and prehnite in the old City quarry in Fairmont Park, Riverside, A. F. Rogers (7) p. 380. **6,** Clear crystals of epidote 1 inch by ⅛ inch were found near Hemet, Kunz (23)

p. 942. **7,** Epidote, with scheelite and garnet, occurs at the Carr tungsten mine (sec. 31, T. 8 S., R. 3 E., S. B.), Tucker and Sampson (8) p. 48. **8,** Considerable massive epidote occurs in copper claims in the Palen Mountains, 2 miles south of Packards Well, Aubury (1) p. 256. **9,** Clear slender crystals of epidote occur with quartz in a pegmatite on Alder Creek, a tributary of Coyote Creek, Durrell (p.c. '44).

San Bernardino County: **1,** Epidote was found with garnet, magnetite and hematite in the iron-ore deposit near Dale, Harder and Rich (4) p. 237; **2,** it occurs in boulders in the lower part of Badger Canyon (secs. 4, 9, T. 1 N., R. 4 W., S. B.) about 5 miles north of San Bernardino, Garner and Wilkie (p.c. '36). **3,** Small amounts of epidote occur in vesicles of lava boulders on an alluvial fan south of Daggett, Murdoch and Webb (11) p. 553. **4,** Epidote occurs with garnet and scheelite in the Shadow Mountain mines (secs. 30, 31, T. 8 N., R. 6 W., S. B.), Tucker and Sampson (27) p. 78, and **5,** with scheelite in secs. 8, 9, T. 5 N., R. 17 E., S. B., Tucker and Sampson (32) p. 68.

San Diego County: **1,** Epidote occurs as a secondary mineral with black tourmaline at Rincon, A. F. Rogers (4) p. 213. **2,** Clear, transparent epidote crystals of gem quality occur at the McFall mine, $7\frac{1}{2}$ miles southeast of Ramona, Kunz (24) p. 99. **3,** Epidote in glassy transparent prisms can be found at the Lulubelle mine, Snyder (1) p. 23.

San Luis Obispo County: **1,** Epidote occurs with quartz, pyrite, and calcite near La Panza (N. R.).

Santa Barbara County: **1,** Epidote has been recorded in the heavy mineral content of the Alegria and Vaqueros formations of the Gaviota area, Grender (1) p. 269.

Siskiyou County: **1,** Epidote was found with dark-brown garnet and quartz on the South Fork of Coffee Creek (N. R.). **2,** Crystals of epidote occur in the ore of the King Solomon mine, Goudey (p.c. '36).

Sonoma County: **1,** Epidote occurs in glaucophane schist near Healdsburg (N. R.).

Trinity County: **1,** Green epidote associated with colorless garnet, sphene and zircon occurs in a soda granite porphyry at Iron Mountain, Weaverville quadrange (N. R.).

Tulare County: **1,** Epidote is common in the Mineral King Mining District, Goodyear (3) p. 646, Franke (1) p. 469. **2,** Large divergent columnar masses of epidote occur at Eber Flat, CDMG (11124), and **3,** in crystals up to 4 inches at Three Rivers, W. O. Jenkins (1) p. 172. **4,** Epidote is also common in Frazier Valley, Goodyear (3) p. 644. **5,** Massive epidote was found with quartz and garnet on a hill between Drum Valley and Slickrock Canyon, and on the west side of the valley of Sheep Creek, Durrell (p.c. '35).

Tuolumne County: **1,** Epidote occurs in contact rock in the Confidence area (secs. 11, 14, T. 2 N., R. 16 E., M. D.), Little (1) p. 287.

EPISTILBITE
Hydrous calcium aluminum silicate, $CaAl_2Si_6O_{16}\cdot5H_2O$

Riverside County: **1,** Flaky, feathery epistilbite occurs replacing feldspar at the Southern Pacific silica quarry near Nuevo, Murdoch (p.c. '45).

EPSOMITE—Epsom Salt
Hydrous magnesium sulphate, $MgSO_4 \cdot 7H_2O$

Efflorescences of epsomite are common in caves and tunnels where pyrite or other sulphides are decomposing in the presence of magnesian rocks. Long hair-like masses of epsomite are common in the cinnabar mines of the State. Commercial epsom salt is produced as a by-product in the evaporation of the bitterns of sea water.

Alameda County: **1,** Epsomite occurs as an efflorescence on the walls of the pyrite mines of Leona Heights, Schaller (1) p. 216.

Amador County: **1,** Epsomite was common in the mines on Copper Hill (N. R.).

Contra Costa County: **1,** Epsomite was found at the Mt. Diablo mine (SE¼ sec. 29, T. 1 N., R. 1 E., M. D.), C. P. Ross (2) p. 42, Pampeyan (1) p. 24.

Imperial County: **1,** Epsomite was mentioned by Emory (1) p. 102, as occurring in white crusts near the head of Cariso (Carrizo) Creek, on the west side of the Colorado Desert.

Inyo County: **1,** Epsomite occurs with alunogen in clay at the mine of the American Magnesium Company in the Wingate area, near Ballarat, Hewett et al. (1) p. 96.

Kings County: **1,** Epsomite is reported from old cinnabar mines at the head of Avenal Creek, Noren (p.c. '36).

Lake County: **1,** Epsomite was abundant in the old Abbott quicksilver mine, CDMG (15497). **2,** Epsomite, associated with copiapite, jarosite, and other minerals, is common at Sulphur Bank, Everhart (1) p. 136.

Los Angeles County: **1,** Epsomite has been found near Point Firmin, CDMG (8306). **2,** Epsomite occurs on the face of the cliff at Bluff Cove, Palos Verdes, Herzog (p.c. '56). This may be the same as locality **(1)**. **3,** Epsomite occurs as minute crystals and fine-grained efflorescences near the base of the sea cliffs at Castellamare, McGill (p.c. '57).

Mariposa County: **1,** Epsomite was found as fine fibers in the Purchase mine near Donovan (N. R.).

Napa County: **1,** Epsomite was abundant in long white fibers (up to one foot in length) in the tunnels of the old Redington mine, Friedrich (1) p. 22, Becker (4) p. 389, Kramm (1) p. 345. **2,** Extensive deposits of epsomite occur at the Oat Hill mines, Fairbanks (3) p. 66.

San Benito County: **1,** Crusts of long fibers of epsomite, occasionally cut by later cinnabar veinlets, occur at the New Idria mine, Becker (4) p. 306.

San Bernardino County: **1,** An extensive deposit of epsomite is described (approximately in T. 19 N., R. 3 E., S. B.), by Jahns (4).

San Luis Obispo County: **1,** Epsomite is reported as an alteration associated with morenosite, bieberite and other sulphates from the Klau quicksilver mine, Santa Lucia Range (sec. 33, T. 26 S., R. 10 E., M. D.), Woodhouse and Norris (6) p. 114.

Santa Barbara County: **1,** Colorless tufts and masses of epsomite have been found in a tunnel at Point Rincon, H. C. Ford (1) p. 55, Arnold and Anderson (3) p. 752.

Santa Clara County: **1,** Epsomite is abundant on the walls of the New Almaden and other cinnabar mines, CDMG (13449); see also E. H. Bailey and Everhart (12) p. 102.

Solano County: **1,** Epsomite (?) is reported in tunnels at the St. John mine (sec. 33, T. 4 N., R. 3 W., M. D.), Aubury (2) p. 95.

Sonoma County: **1,** Goldsmith (7) p. 265, reported epsomite as incrustations and stalactites, with boussingaultite at The Geysers; see also E. T. Allen and Day (2) p. 39, Vonsen (6) p. 290.

ERIONITE
Hydrous sodium calcium potassium magnesium aluminum silicate,
$$(Na_2,K_2,Ca,Mg)_{4.5}[Al_9Si_{27}O_{72}] \cdot 27H_2O$$

Kern County: **1,** Erionite is one of several zeolites which have been identified in tuffaceous layers, with gay-lussite, in the sediments of China Lake, Hay and Moiola (2) p. 76A, Moiola and Hay (1) p. 215.

ERYTHRITE—Cobalt Bloom
Hydrous cobalt arsenate, $Co_3As_2O_8 \cdot 8H_2O$

Coatings and incrustations of erythrite are common on primary cobalt minerals, and often serve to locate cobalt.

Calaveras County: **1,** Erythrite occurs with smaltite in a stringer between schist and quartzite (NW¼ sec. 21, T. 4 N., R. 14 E., M. D.), Logan (7) p. 4, Hess (19) p. 451.

Inyo County: **1,** Erythrite occurs with annabergite, argentite and other minerals at the Bishop silver-cobalt mine (sec. 14, T. 9 S., R. 31 E., M. D.), east of Long Lake, Tucker and Sampson (25) p. 378, Bateman (3) p. 83. **2,** The mineral was reported from the Cerro Gordo region, R. W. Raymond (1) p. 29. H. E. Pemberton (p.c. '64) notes that Cerro Gordo was not known until about 1868, and the reference given is dated 1869, making it unlikely that the citation is in fact to Cerro Gordo. The occurrence seems invalid.

Lassen County: **1,** Erythrite is reported with smaltite and annabergite from the county, CDMG (9981).

Los Angeles County: **1,** Coatings of erythrite with smaltite, argentite and barite occurred at the old Kelsey and O. K. mines near the San Gabriel Canyon, W. P. Blake (24) p. 207, (27) p. 163, Irelan (4) p. 47, Storms (4) p. 245. W. P. Blake (23) p. 376, reported erythrite from the "Bernardino Range," which is probably this same locality. This locality is reported erroneously as "near Compton" in some references.

Mariposa County: **1,** Erythrite was found in rock seams with danaite at the Josephine mine, Bear Valley, H. W. Turner (3) p. 468, (12) p. 679.

Mono County: **1,** Erythrite has been noted in the lower tunnel at the Goleta mine, associated with an unidentified cobalt mineral and sulphides, Michael A. Price (p.c. '62), written communication on file, CDMG.

Napa County: **1,** Erythrite occurs with smaltite in serpentine and chlorite in the Berryessa Valley (N. R.).

San Diego County: **1,** Erythrite occurs with limonite and morenosite at the Friday mine, in the Julian Mining District, Hudson (1) p. 214.

San Luis Obispo County: **1**, Cronise (1) p. 593, reports erythrite from near San Luis Obispo.

Siskiyou County: **1**, Erythrite is reported from Callahan, W. W. Bradley (28) p. 497, as coatings on smaltite.

Tuolumne County: **1**, Erythrite occurs associated with arsenopyrite in the Josephine mine, Logan (16) p. 189.

ETTRINGITE
Hydrous basic calcium aluminum sulphate, $Ca_6Al_2(SO_4)_3(OH)_{12}\cdot26H_2O$

Riverside County: **1**, Ettringite is reported from Crestmore, as a vein-filling in massive contact rock from the Commercial quarry, Murdoch and Chalmers (37) p. 1275. This occurrence was originally described as that of a new mineral "woodfordite", Murdoch and Chalmers (36) p. 1620, but the name has been withdrawn since the identity with ettringite is established. On the 910′ level of the Crestmore quarry, ettringite has been observed to be overgrown with a parallel oriented coating of thaumasite, A. B. Carpenter (2) p. 1394. The crystal chemistry of ettringite has been studied by McConnell and Murdoch (5) pp. 59–64.

EUCAIRITE
Selenide of copper and silver, CuAgSe

Calaveras County: **1**, "Gray copper" showing selenium instead of sulphur on analysis, may perhaps be referred to this species. It occurred at the Willard Mining Company property, in the Esmeralda (Murphy) Mining District, Irelan (1) p. 37.

EUXENITE
An oxide of rare earth elements including yttrium/cerium/uranium/thorium and calcium, $(Y,Ca,Ce,U,Th)(Nb,Ta,Ti)_2O_6$

Kern County: **1**, A mineral closely resembling euxenite has been found in a pegmatite in the Piute Mountains, 15 miles south of Weldon, Proctor (p.c. '56). **2**, Euxenite occurs in a few pegmatite dikes in small crystals in the Kern River uranium area, MacKevett (2) pp. 191, 197.

San Bernardino County: **1**, Euxenite occurs with ilmenite, monazite and allanite in the Pomona Tile quarry on the road between Old Woman Spring and Yucca Valley, Hewett and Glass (3) p. 1048. It appears in small tabular crystals 3–8 mm in diameter near the quartz nucleus of the pegmatite; see also Hewett et al. (4) p. 30.

Tulare County: **1**, Goodwin (1) p. 369, states: ". . . uranium- and thorium-bearing minerals which have been identified in Tulare County include xenotime, euxenite, torbernite, autunite and uraninite."

FAMATINITE—Luzonite
Copper antimony sulphide, Cu_3SbS_4
Luzonite is arsenical famatinite, $Cu_3(Sb,As)S_4$

Alpine County: **1**, Famatinite is found associated with enargite at the Morning Star mine, Eakle (16) p. 12, Harcourt (1) p. 521.

Inyo County: **1**, Microscopic grains of famatinite have been found in polished sections of ore from the Darwin Mining District, Kelley (4) p. 544, Hall and MacKevett (1) p. 17.

Shasta County: **1,** Luzonite is reported from two specimens in the ores of the East Shasta copper-zinc region, Albers and Robertson (3) p. 71.

FAYALITE
Iron silicate, Fe_2SiO_4
See also olivine and forsterite.

Imperial County: **1,** At Obsidian Butte, near Niland, lithophysae in the obsidian carry occasional crystals of fayalite, A. F. Rogers (42) p. 328.

Inyo County: **1,** Small brown crystals of fayalite occur with cristobalite, tridymite and orthoclase in spheroidal openings in obsidian, near Coso Hot Springs, Rutley (1) p. 427, A. F. Rogers (23) p. 215, Murdoch and Webb (11) p. 544 (crystal description), M. B. Strong (7) p. 16, Stinson (3) p. 207.

Riverside County: **1,** Fayalite in the Rubidoux Mountain leucogranite, has been partly altered to "iddingsite" and other minerals, Banks and Silver (1) p. 5.

Siskiyou County: **1,** Fayalite occurs with cristobalite in lithophysae in spherulitic obsidian near Cougar Butte (sec. 13, T. 44 N., R. 4 E., M. D.), C. A. Anderson (p.c. '35).

FELDSPARS

The name feldspar is given to a group of silicates of aluminum, sodium, calcium, potassium, or barium, similar in hardness, cleavage, specific gravity, and twinning.

The following classification of the feldspars shows the relationship of the varieties:

Orthoclase
   Soda orthoclase
Hyalophane
Celsian
Microcline
   Soda microcline
Anorthoclase
Plagioclase
   Albite molecule$=ab$ ($NaAlSi_3O_8$)
   Anorthite molecule$=an$ ($CaAl_2Si_2O_8$)

	ab	an
Albite	100–90	0– 10
Oligoclase	90–70	10– 30
Andesine	70–50	30– 50
Labradorite	50–30	50– 70
Bytownite	30–10	70– 90
Anorthite	10– 0	90–100

Feldspars are the most abundant and important of rock-forming silicates, and the classification of igneous rocks depends partly upon the feldspar of the rock. The albite-anorthite feldspars are commonly called the plagioclase feldspars, and in many petrographic descriptions this name is used, so that the particular kind of feldspar is not designated. As rock-forming minerals, the feldspars are too widely distributed to list all localities.

ALBITE
Sodium aluminum silicate, NaAlSi₃O₈
Cleavelandite is a platy variety of albite, common in pegmatite dikes.

Albite is a common constituent of granites, rhyolites, metamorphic gneisses and schists. It forms very prominent white veins in the crystalline schists of the Coast Ranges and the Sierra Nevada.

Calaveras County: **1,** Well-formed crystals of albite were found in the Winters vein, Angels Camp, analysis by Genth (3) p. 255. **2,** Crystals of albite line vugs at the Stanislaus mine, and are penetrated by crystals of millerite, A. W. Jackson (3) p. 365.

Contra Costa County: **1,** Veins of white albite cut the actinolite schists at San Pablo, Blasdale (1) p. 345.

Los Angeles County: **1,** Good transparent crystals of albite up to 1 inch across have been found in a pegmatite near Howlands Landing, Santa Catalina Island, Murdoch (p.c. '45). **2,** Well developed crystals of albite occur in chlorite-lawsonite schist at the western tip of Santa Catalina Island, Woodford (1) p. 55.

Marin County: **1,** Albite crystals up to 1 cm in size occur in lawsonite schist near Reed Station, Schaller (19) p. 48.

Mono County: **1,** Well-defined crystals of albite up to 4 inches in size occur with quartz at the Standard mine, Bodie. The crystals are often shells studded internally with fine quartz prisms, R. G. Brown (1) p. 344, H. W. Turner (30) p. 795.

Placer County: **1,** Fine crystals of albite were found in the Shady Run mine 8 miles east of Dutch Flat. Reid (1) p. 280.

Plumas County: **1,** White dikes in serpentine at Meadow Valley are composed wholly of albite, G. M. Wheeler (2) p. 379.

Riverside County: **1,** Pegmatites of the Crestmore quarry carry albite, Woodford et al. (10) p. 358.

San Benito County: **1,** Cleavelandite has been reported from Santa Rita Creek, W. W. Bradley (p.c. '44). **2,** Druses of some of the veins at the benitoite locality have yielded crystals of albite up to 10 millimeters in size, Louderback and Blasdale (5) p. 361.

San Diego County: **1,** Dark-colored manganese-bearing albite has been found in the Caterina mine, Pala, Kraus and Hunt (2) p. 466. **2,** Good small albite crystals are found in the pegmatites at Rincon, A. F. Rogers (4) p. 210. **3,** Well-crystallized cleavelandite occurs at the following gem-tourmaline localities: Pala, Donnelly (3) p. 10, Mesa Grande, Kunz (24) p. 137, Ramona, Kunz (24) p. 47, near Aguanga, Mountain Lily mine, Murdoch and Webb (p.c., '45).

ANDESINE
Sodium/calcium/aluminum silicate, mNaAlSi₃O₈ with nCaAl₂Si₂O₈, intermediate between albite and anorthite

Riverside County: **1,** Andesine is a common plagioclase feldspar in the country rock of the Crestmore quarry, Daly (1).

Yolo County: **1,** Sodic plagioclase (andesine) from the Nomlaki tuff on Putah Creek, has been observed and described by Emerson (1) p. 23.

ANORTHITE
Calcium aluminum silicate, $CaAl_2Si_2O_8$

Lake County: **1,** Fine cleavage fragments of anorthite have been collected 2 miles northeast of Middletown along the highway to Lower Lake (N. R.).

CELSIAN
Barium aluminum silicate, $BaAl_2Si_2O_8$

Fresno County: **1,** Fine-grained celsian associated with quartz, diopside, witherite and sanbornite occurs in quartzite near Rush Creek and Big Creek (secs. 16, 22, 27, T. 11 S., R. 25 E., M. D.), CDMG (21889). Celsian was also noted in a portion of a drill core taken near Rush Creek (CDMG identification, '64).

Mariposa County: **1,** Celsian was found with sanbornite and gillespite in veins in quartzite, 1 mile north of Trumbull Peak, near Incline, A. F. Rogers (39) p. 171.

Santa Cruz County: **1,** Celsian is reported in the mineral suite at the Pacific Limestone Products (Kalkar) quarry at Santa Cruz, C. W. Chesterman and Gross (p.c. '64).

LABRADORITE
Calcium/sodium/aluminum silicate, $mCaAl_2Si_2O_8$ with $nNaAlSi_3O_8$

Los Angeles County: **1,** Labradorite forms the principal part of anorthosite masses in the western San Gabriel Mountains (T. 4 N., R. 14 W., S. B.), Tucker and Sampson (4) pp. 417, 418, W. J. Miller (7) pp. 15–17, Higgs (1) p. 177.

Modoc County: **1,** Labradorite with inclusions of metallic copper has been found in this county, Andersen (1) p. 91.

Riverside County: **1,** Eakle (15) reports labradorite as a constituent of the country rock at Crestmore.

MICROCLINE
Potassium aluminum silicate, $KAlSi_3O_8$

Amazonite or *amazon stone* is a green microcline, and is sometimes used as a semi-precious gem.

Microcline has the same composition as orthoclase, but differs from it in its twinning structure and crystallization. It is a constituent of some granites and pegmatites. Much of the white feldspar of pegmatites is microcline rather than orthoclase.

Inyo County: **1,** Abundant green microcline[a] in poorly developed crystals, is found in pegmatite $1\frac{1}{2}$ miles east of Lone Pine Station, Murdoch (p.c. '45), M. B. Strong (4) p. 20. This may be the locality noted by Ward in Sterrett (10) p. 321. **2,** Microcline has been reported 6 miles west of Lone Pine, W. W. Bradley (29) p. 311. This may be the same as locality **(1)**, which is about 6 miles east of Lone Pine.

Riverside County: **1,** Graphic granite of the Southern Pacific silica quarry at Nuevo is quartz and microline, Wahlstrom (1) p. 694. **2,** Woodford et al. (10) p. 358, report microcline in the pegmatites that are common in the Crestmore quarry.

San Diego County: **1,** Graphic granite from the Ramona pegmatite area has been described by D. R. Simpson (1) pp. 1123–1138. Microcline perthite is the feldspar in this graphic intergrowth.

Tuolumne County: **1,** Phenocrysts of microcline up to 2 inches in length occur in granite porphyry at Tuolumne Meadows, Calkins (4) p. 127.

OLIGOCLASE
Sodium/calcium/aluminum silicate, mNaAlSi$_3$O$_8$ with nCaAl$_2$Si$_2$O$_8$

Riverside County: **1,** Oligoclase is found in the pegmatites of the Crestmore quarry, Woodford et al. (10) p. 358.

Tulare County: **1,** Large, well-formed crystals of oligoclase occur with quartz and black tourmaline in a pegmatite at Salt Creek, A. F. Rogers (32) p. 116.

ORTHOCLASE
Potassium aluminum silicate, KAlSi$_3$O$_8$

Adularia is a glassy, transparent variety, sometimes found in large crystals. *Moonstone* is a variety of adularia. *Sanidine*, a glassy feldspar, frequently occurs as crystals in rhyolite. *Valencianite* is a varietal name no longer used for vein orthoclase. *Perthite* is an intergrowth of orthoclase or microcline and albite. It is an important constituent of some granites and pegmatites.

Orthoclase is an essential constituent of many igneous rocks, granites, syenites, quartz porphyries, rhyolites, and trachytes. Large crystals often form the phenocrysts of porphyritic rocks, and these crystals are often Carlsbad twins. The color of granites is mainly due to the color of the orthoclase, red granites having orthoclase colored by ferric oxide. Granites, syenites, and diorites are often intersected by pegmatite dikes consisting of coarse crystals and massive orthoclase (or microcline) with quartz and mica, and these dikes vary greatly in width; some can be quarried for the feldspar.

Calaveras County: **1,** Valencianite occurs 5 miles east of Milton on the road to Copperopolis, A. F. Rogers (7) p. 376.

El Dorado County: **1,** Colorless crystals of adularia are found on the south side of Fallen Leaf Lake, A. F. Rogers (7) p. 376.

Inyo County: **1,** Adularia, variety moonstone, occurs as very small crystals in rhyolite near Rialto, in the Funeral Mountains, Kunz (23) p. 950, (24) p. 79. **2,** Distinct crystals of sanidine are common in the Bishop tuff, Gilbert (1) p. 1834. **3,** Orthoclase crystals of small size are associated with fayalite, cristobalite and tridymite in the obsidian near Coso Hot Springs, A. F. Rogers (23) p. 215, Stinson (4) p. 207.

Kern County: **1,** Large phenocrysts of orthoclase, usually as Carlsbad twins, occur in a dike-like mass of granite porphyry, 4 miles north of Cinco, by the aqueduct road, Murdoch and Webb (14) p. 325.

Madera County: **1,** Large Carlsbad twins of orthoclase occur in granite porphyry at Reds Meadows, Goudey (1) p. 8.

Monterey County: **1,** Orthoclase phenocrysts up to 10 cm in length occur in the Santa Lucia granite in the Carmelo Bay area, Lawson (1) p. 10. **2,** Orthoclase showing spectroscopic traces of germanium has come from Pacific Grove, Papish (2) p. 474. **3,** A large mass of pure creamy to white orthoclase has been quarried 4 miles east of Chualar (sec. 34, T. 15 S., R. 5 E., M.D.), W. W. Bradley and Waring (6) p. 601.

Riverside County: **1,** Orthoclase is generally distributed in the country rock of the Crestmore quarries, Woodford et al. (10) p. 368.

San Bernardino County: **1,** Orthoclase phenocrysts up to 7 inches in length are abundant, usually as Carlsbad twins, in monzonitic porphyry, $1\frac{1}{2}$ miles southwest of Twenty-Nine Palms, W. J. Miller (8) p. 428. **2,** Flesh-colored orthoclase phenocrysts as long as 2 inches occur 1 mile north of the Pines (sec. 5, T. 1 N., R. 1 E., S.B.), Baker (1) p. 338. **3,** Orthoclase (probably variety adularia) has been found in the Bottom Mud and the Mixed Layer, at Searles Lake, R. C. Erd (p.c. '58), confirmed by Hay and Moiola (1) p. 323. **4,** A monoclinic potash feldspar has been found as an authigenic mineral in Pleistocene beds of Searles Lake, Hay and Moiola (1) p. 168.

FERGUSONITE
An oxide of titanium with rare earth elements and other metals, (Y,Er,Ce,Fe)
$(Cb,Ta,Ti)O_4$

Riverside County: **1,** $1\frac{1}{2}$-inch crystals were reported to have come from Box Spring Mountain, Foshag (p.c. '46).

San Diego County: **1,** Two specimens of fergusonite from the southwest slope of Lawson Peak (sec. 1, T. 17 S., R. 2 E., S.B.), were presented to the California Division of Mines and Geology, CDMG (21701–21702).

FERRIERITE
A hydrous basic silicate of aluminum magnesium sodium potassium,
$(Na,K)_4Mg_2[Al_6Si_{30}O_{72}](OH)_2 \cdot 18H_2O$

Mono County: **1,** Ferrierite occurs at Leavitt Lake, Sonora Pass, Parnau (p.c. '63).

FERRIMOLYBDITE—Molybdite
Hydrous iron molybdate, $Fe_2Mo_4O_{15} \cdot 10H_2O$

El Dorado County: **1,** A specimen of ferrimolybdite in the University of California Collections, Berkeley, No. 278, is from the Cosumnes mine near Fairplay.

Del Norte County: **1,** Ferrimolybdite has been reported at French Hill, with bornite (N. R.).

Fresno County: **1,** Ferrimolybdite has been found near Palisade Creek, with molybdenite, W. W. Bradley (24) p. 345, CDMG (20311).

Kern County: **1,** Sulphur-yellow, fibrous crystals of ferrimolybdite have been found in Jawbone Canyon (secs. 10, 11, 14, 15, T. 30 S., R. 36 E., M.D.), W. W. Bradley (29) p. 107.

Madera County: **1,** Ferrimolybdite occurs with molybdenite on Red Mountain in the Ritter Range, Erwin (1) p. 71, Goudey (1) p. 8.

Mariposa County: **1,** Ferrimolybdite is reported with molybdenite from the Kinsley Mining District, 7 miles from El Portal (N. R.).

Mono County: **1,** Ferrimolybdite occurs in white quartz with molybdenite, 12 miles northwest of Bridgeport, J. H. Pratt (4) p. 265, and **2,** on Silverado Creek (T. 7 N., R. 25 E., M. D.), Whiting (1) p. 363. **3,** Beautifully crystallized ferrimolybdite from the Tiger claim, Patterson Mining District, is represented by a specimen in the University of California Collections, Berkeley.

Nevada County: **1,** Ferrimolybdite occurs mixed with limonite, at the Wisconsin and Illinois claim near Nevada City, D. D. Owen (1)

p. 108, Genth (3) p. 248. **2,** The mineral is found with molybdenite and gold at the Excelsior mine, Hanks (12) p. 274.

San Bernardino County: **1,** Ferrimolybdite was found near State Line (approx. T. 17 N., R. 16 E., S. B.), CDMG (16107).

San Diego County: **1,** Ferrimolybdite is found with feldspar near Ramona (sec. 11, T. 13 S., R. 1 W., S. B.), Calkins (1) p. 75.

Shasta County: **1,** The mineral is found with ilsemannite and molybdenite, 4 miles west of Gibson (sec. 33, T. 37 N., R. 5 W., M. D.), Cook (1) p. 50, and **2,** from Hazel Creek, CDMG (18569).

Sierra County: **1,** Ferrimolybdite is found in copper ore at the Sierra Buttes mine near Hurd's Ranch, J. R. Browne (4) p. 210, Burkart (2) p. 21.

Trinity County: **1,** The mineral occurs with molybdenite near Lewiston, CDMG (19433).

Tuolumne County: **1,** A specimen with minute canary-yellow needles, in the University of California Collections, Berkeley, is from the Stuart ledge, E. S. Larsen (11) p. 112.

Yuba County: **1,** Ferrimolybdite is reported with molybdenite near Camptonville (N. R.).

FIBROFERRITE
Hydrous basic ferric sulphate, $Fe^{3+}SO_4OH \cdot 5H_2O$

Napa County: **1,** Fibroferrite has been found with cinnabar, opal, sulphur and sulphates in the Redington mine at Knoxville, A. F. Rogers (35) p. 397.

San Bernardino County: **1,** Fibroferrite occurs with krausite, coquimbite and other sulphates in the Calico Hills near Borate, 6 miles northeast of Yermo, Foshag (19) p. 352.

Trinity County: **1,** Fibrous aggregates of yellow fibroferrite occur in the pyrrhotite deposit at Island Mountain, Landon (1) p. 279, Melhase (3) No. 6, p. 2.

FLUOBORITE
Basic magnesium borate with fluorine, $Mg_3(BO_3)(F,OH)_3$

Riverside County: **1,** Fluoborite occurs at the Crestmore quarries, 910' level, Segnit (p.c. '61).

San Bernardino County: **1,** In a contact zone fluoborite occurs as abundant sub-parallel prismatic crystals in matrix of calcite at the New Method mine (Hope uranium prospect), Bristol Mts., near Amboy, Chesterman and Bowen (6) p. 1678.

FLUORITE
Calcium fluoride, CaF_2

Fluorite is a common mineral, especially as gangue in lead deposits with galena. It sometimes forms thick veins.

No attempt has been made to report all of the occurrences of fluorite found in the State that are referenced in the literature. The mineral is widespread and is so common that only occurrences of mineralogical interest should be included. However, some localities of minor importance and of little mineralogical interest are noted for the historical record because they have been reported in early editions of *Minerals of California.*

Contra Costa County: **1,** Small cubes of white fluorite were found on Mount Diablo with some copper minerals, Hanks (12) p. 181, Kunz (24) p. 102.

Inyo County: **1,** Fluorite is found as a gangue mineral with argentiferous galena in the Cerro Gordo, Darwin, and other mining areas, A. Knopf (4) p. 7, C A. Waring and Huguenin (2) p. 95, Kelley (4) p. 543, A. L. Ransome and Kellogg (1) p. 483, Hall and MacKevett (4) p. 63. **2,** Purple veinlets of fluorite in marble are reported to carry gold values, at the Waterfall prospect, 3 miles north of Antelope Springs, Deep Spring Valley, A. Knopf (5) p. 113. **3,** An extensive deposit of fluorite is reported on Tin Mountain, Ubehebe Mining District, Anon. (5). **4,** Fluorite is reported as small purple veins from Warm Springs (T. 22 N., R. 1 E., S.B.), Crosby and Hoffman (1) p. 631.

Kern County: **1,** Fluorite is found (sec. 12, T. 29 S., R. 38 E., M.D.), in Last Chance Canyon, Crosby and Hoffman (1) p. 632.

Lake County: **1,** Massive green fluorite comes from a locality 4 miles southeast of Kelseyville, W. W. Bradley (29) p. 222.

Los Angeles County: **1,** Fine specimens of fluorite consisting of purple and green masses and cubes have come from the Felix mine north of Azusa, Murdoch (p.c. '45). **2,** Half-inch cubes of fluorite are found in cavities of a fault breccia at locality 20, west side of Higgins Canyon, Neuerburg (1) p. 159.

Mono County: **1,** Green and violet crystals and masses of fluorite occur in Ferris Canyon on the eastern slope of the Sweetwater Mountains, Kunz (24) p. 102. **2,** Fluorite occurs with andalusite in the mine of Champion Sillimanite, on the western slope of the White Mountains, north of Bishop, Jeffery and Woodhouse (3) p. 461.

Riverside County: **1,** Transparent crystals of fluorite were marketed for optical purposes in 1917-18, from the Floyd Brown mine, near Blythe, Aubury (1) p. 258. An additional reference, gives the location of Fluorspar group of mines (sec. 4, T. 10 S., R. 18 E., S. B.), Crosby and Hoffman (1) p. 632. A small tonnage was also shipped for industrial use. **2,** Large veins of fluorite are reported in quartzite (sec. 27, T. 3 S., R. 20 E., S. B.), Tucker and Sampson (35) p. 164. **3,** Fluorite is reported from the tin ore at Cajalco, West (3) p. 132.

San Bernardino County: **1,** Green and purple fluorite with some iceland spar comes from the Kings fluorspar mine, Cave Canyon Mining District, Tucker and Sampson (16) p. 301, Burchard (1) p. 373, Hewett et al. (1) p. 171. **2,** Fluorite is also found near Ludlow, CDMG (18952). **3,** Colored fluorite occurs in a vein on the McDermott deposit, 4 miles east of Nipton, Tucker and Sampson (16) p. 302. **4,** Numerous small veins of green and white fluorite occur near Baxter Station, near Soda Lake (T. 17 N., R. 13 E., S. B.), ibid., p. 302, Crosby and Hoffman (1) p. 625. **5,** Lenses of fluorite up to 2 feet in length are found in the Philadelphia fluorspar deposit in the Providence Mountains, 25 miles south of Cima (secs. 4, 5, 7, T. 10 N., R. 6 E., S. B.), Crosby and Hoffman (1) p. 633, Tucker (4) p. 343. **6,** Veins of fluorite, with sulphides, are found at the Live Oak mine (T. 14 N., R. 16 E., S. B.),

Crosby and Hoffman (1) p. 636. **7,** At the Green Hornet mine (secs. 7, 8, T. 6 N., R. 1 W., S. B.) fluorite occurs in veins with quartz, Crosby and Hoffman (1) p. 636. **8,** Dark purple fluorite is found in the Ivanpah Mountains (sec. 8, T. 14 N., R. 14 E., S. B.), Crosby and Hoffman (1) p. 636. **9,** Fluorite, colorless and purple, is common in the Ord Mountains, Weber (3) p. 26.

San Diego County: **1,** A small amount of fluorite is found at the Mountain Lily gem mine, Aguanga Mountain, F. J. H. Merrill (1) p. 705.

Santa Clara County: **1,** White crystals of fluorite were found near the Almaden mine, Hart (1) p. 138, Irelan (4) p. 46.

Tulare County: **1,** A deposit of massive fluorite occurs 18 miles east of Springville (sec. 34, T. 20 S., R. 31 E., M. D.), Franke (1) p. 439.

Yolo County: **1,** A fluorite deposit is reported from an unspecified locality in the county, Mining and Scientific Press (18) p. 370.

FORSTERITE
Magnesium silicate, Mg_2SiO_4
See also olivine and fayalite

Riverside County: **1,** Forsterite occurs with hydrotroilite in the new City quarry, Victoria Avenue, Riverside, W. W. Bradley (29) p. 456. **2,** Forsterite has been identified in the contact rocks of the Crestmore quarry, Burnham (p.c. '54).

San Bernardino County: **1,** Forsterite has been found on the northwest slope of Ontario Peak, at Cascade Canyon (SW¼ sec. 31, T. 2 N., R. 7 W., S. B.), W. W. Bradley (29) p. 456.

*FOSHAGITE, 1925
Hydrous basic calcium silicate, $Ca_5Si_3O_{10}(OH)_2 \cdot 2H_2O$

Riverside County: **1,** Foshagite was described as a new mineral from the Crestmore quarries by Eakle (23) p. 97, in 1925. Its validity as a species was questioned by Vigfussen (1) p. 76, who believed it to be a variety of hillebrandite. Flint et al. (1) p. 617, and Winchell (2) give foshagite separate status, and Heller and Taylor (1) p. 53, confirm the validity of the species. H. F. W. Taylor and Gard (7), (8) have determined the crystal structure of foshagite on material from Crestmore. Foshagite occurs primarily as fibrous masses and slip-veins in vesuvianite and monticellite-rich rocks, Woodford (11) p. 357.

FRANCKEITE
Lead tin antimony sulphide, $Pb_5Sn_3Sb_2S_{14}$

Inyo County: **1,** Franckeite was identified by Charles Milton of the U. S. Geological Survey from a rich silver ore body from the Thompson mine, Darwin Mining District, Hall and MacKevett (1) p. 17.

Santa Cruz County: **1,** This rare mineral occurs with meneghinite and stannite in the limestone contact rock of the Pacific Limestone (Kalkar) Products quarry, 2 miles northeast of Santa Cruz, Chesterman (p.c. '54).

* FRESNOITE, 1965
Barium titanium silicate, $Ba_2T_1Sl_2O_8$

Fresno County: **1,** Fresnoite, a new mineral from California, is described in a preliminary paper by Alfors and Stinson (5) p. 27, as tiny yellow grains disseminated widely in the sanbornite-bearing deposits of eastern Fresno County, at the Big Creek locality. This entry, first appearing in February 1965, after the cut-off date of this bulletin, is included because the article in which the preliminary description occurred is Part II of a report describing 3 new minerals in the same locality, Stinson and Alfors (6). See also "Seven new barium minerals from eastern Fresno County, California", by John T. Alfors, Melvin C. Stinson, Robert A. Matthews and Adolph Pabst: Am. Mineralogist, vol. 50, pp. 314–340, 1965.

GAHNITE
Zinc aluminate, $ZnAl_2O_4$

San Diego County: **1,** Small rounded patches of bright green gahnite occur in nodules of phosphate minerals from the Katerina mine, Heriart Hill, Pala, Jahns and Wright (5) p. 31, confirming Murdoch (p.c. '51).

* GALEITE, 1955
Sodium sulphate with fluorine and chlorine, $Na_3SO_4(F,Cl)$

San Bernardino County: **1,** A new mineral from Searles Lake was found in drill cores of the lake section in small nodular aggregates of minute crystals, embedded in clay and other salt minerals, Pabst et al. (15) p. 1658. The galeite is intergrown with schairerite, and associated with sulphohalite, Pabst et al. (21) p. 485, G. I. Smith and Haines (3) p. 27.

GALENA
Lead sulphide, PbS
Cuproplumbite is identical with galena.

Galena is a very common mineral, and occurs in nearly every ore deposit in the State. It is prominent in many mining regions, and occurs in considerable amounts in some of them. Much of it is accompanied by silver minerals, and such combinations form important sources of silver. Galena is present, usually in minor amount, with chalcopyrite or sphalerite in gold-quartz veins. Its common alteration products, cerussite and anglesite, frequently are associated. Only the more important or interesting occurrences can be noted in detail, but some references to those of lesser consequence will be listed under the counties. Hanks (12) p. 181, gives a rather extensive list of occurrences as known at that date.

Alameda County: **1,** Lumps of coarse crystalline galena, from an unknown source, weighing up to 100 pounds, have been found at Euclid Avenue and Cordonices Creek in Berkeley, A. C. Lawson (7) p. 23.

Alpine County: **1,** Argentiferous galena is common in the Loope area near Markleeville, Crawford (1) p. 373, Eakle (16) p. 11, Logan (4) p. 402, W. W. Bradley (15) p. 488, Gianella (1) p. 342.

Amador County: **1,** Galena is widespread in small amounts in the mines near Plymouth and along the Mother Lode, Josephson (1) p. 475.

Butte County: **1,** Galena is recorded at Butte Creek and other areas, C. A. Waring (4) p. 214.

Calaveras County: **1,** Galena is one of the universal minor vein minerals in the Mother Lode mines, Reid (3) p. 397, Moss (1) p. 1011.

El Dorado County: **1,** Galena is present in many of the mines of the county, Logan (9) p. 406.

Fresno County: **1,** Galena occurs in gold ores at a number of mines, Goldstone (1) p. 197.

Imperial County: **1,** Small amounts of galena occur in the Picacho and other areas, F. J. H. Merrill (1) p. 732, Tucker (11) p. 262, R. J. Sampson and Tucker (18) p. 128, Henshaw (1) p. 185.

Inyo County: Argentiferous galena has formed the important silver ore in the county. Extensive deposits occur in the Darwin, Cerro Gordo, Panamint, Ubehebe and other mining areas: **1,** Cerro Gordo, A. Knopf (8) p. 114, C. W. Merriam (1) p. 60; **2,** Darwin, Crawford (1) p. 24, A. Knopf (4) p. 7, Kelley (4) p. 543, Hall and MacKevett (4) p. 59; **3,** Panamint, fine crystals from the Blue Wing mine, CDMG (7616), Crawford (1) p. 373, Murphy (2) pp. 313, 321, Tucker (11) p. 488. Other lesser deposits in the county are referred to in the following: **4,** Mining and Scientific Press (1) p. 3; **5,** De Groot (2) p. 213; **6,** Crawford (2) p. 32; **7,** C. A. Waring and Huguenin (2) pp. 76, 84, 100, 101, 105; **8,** Tucker (4) pp. 284, 286, 291; **9,** Tucker (8) p. 33; **10,** Tucker (11) pp. 473, 489, 495, 507; **11,** R. J. Sampson (7) p. 369; **12,** R. J. Sampson (11) p. 266; **13,** Tucker and Sampson (25) pp. 383, 397, 413, 427, 429; **14,** Tucker and Sampson (27) p. 26; **15,** Tucker and Sampson (32) p. 59. **16,** Argentiferous galena formed the ore of mines on Kearsarge Peak, J. G. Moore (1) p. 148.

Kern County: **1,** Small amounts of galena are found in the Mojave Cove and other areas, Tucker and Sampson (21) p. 290, Simpson (1) p. 409, Prout (1) p. 413.

Los Angeles County: **1,** Galena was recorded from this county at a very early date. In 1792, Martinez (1) p. 42, reported Galena (?) from Santa Catalina Island. A "silver mine" was known here as early as 1847, Sloat (1) p. 366. Later references to this locality are in Mining and Scientific Press (5) p. 263, Preston (2) p. 280, Gieser (1) p. 245. **2,** Duflot de Mofras (1) p. 186, noted "silver ore," presumably argentiferous galena, at Rancho Cahuenga, 2 leagues north of Los Angeles. **3,** Galena occurs with fluorite at the Felix fluorite mine, Azusa, Murdoch (p.c. '45). Other references in the county to galena are: Preston (2) p. 204, Storms (4) p. 244, Tucker (4) p. 318, (8) p. 42, (13) p. 317.

Madera County: **1,** Large cubes of galena have come from the Star mine, in the Minarets Mining District, W. W. Bradley (9) p. 548, Erwin (1) pp. 66, 67.

Mariposa County: **1,** Minor amounts of galena occur in some of the gold-quartz veins, J. B. Trask (7) p. 52, J. D. Whitney (7) p. 238, Mining and Scientific Press (26) p. 24, Preston (2) p. 303.

Mono County: **1,** Argentiferous galena forms important bodies of ore in the Bodie, Blind Spring, Lundy and Sweetwater areas, Eakle and McLaughlin (17) pp. 141, 172, A. L. Ransome (2) p. 171.

Monterey County: **1,** One of the early mines in the State, at the Alisal Ranch, reported as early as 1802, carries galena, Duflot de Mofras

(1) p. 215, A. Robinson (1) p. 152, W. P. Blake (7) p. 295, W. W. Jenkins (1) p. 70.

Napa County: **1,** Galena is one of the minor minerals at the Palisades mine, 2 miles north of Calistoga, Hulin (p.c. '36).

Nevada County: **1,** Galena is one of the vein minerals in the gold ores of the county, W. P. Blake (9) p. 13, Hobson (1) pp. 384, 392–394, Lindgren (12) p. 118, Wisker (1) p. 194.

Orange County: **1,** "Leafy galena in narrow bands and solid bunches" occurs at the Alma mine (T. 5 S., R. 6 W., S.B.), Santiago Canyon, Fairbanks (4) pp. 115, 117, L. L. Root (3) p. 63.

Placer County: **1,** Galena is found in minor amounts in most of the gold mines of the county, Silliman (7) p. 351, Lindgren (7) p. 272, C. A. Waring (4) p. 331, Logan (4) p. 445, (17) pp. 16–39.

Riverside County: **1,** Galena was one of the minerals at the limestone quarry at Crestmore, Eakle (15) p. 352. **2,** The mineral occurs in various other localities in the county, Goodyear (3) p. 527, Irelan (5) p. 904, F. J. H. Merrill (2) pp. 532–541, Tucker (8) p. 195, R. J. Sampson (9) p. 514.

Sacramento County: **1,** Galena occurred with sphalerite and pyrite at Michigan Bar, Hanks (12) p. 181.

San Bernardino County: Galena, with its oxidation product cerussite, is widespread in relatively small amounts, in the silver and gold mines of the county. References follow: Crossman (1) p. 217 (Old Woman Mountains), p 231 (Lava Beds), p. 263 (Morongo); Storms (4) p. 366 (Silver Reef); Crawford (1) p. 25 (Silver Mountains); Cloudman et al. (1) p. 790 (New York Mountains), p. 805 (Goldstone), p. 821 (Ibex mine); Tucker (4) p. 340 (Kelso), p. 345 (Twenty-Nine Palms), p. 359 (Shadow Mountain), (7) p. 95 (Clark Mountain); Erwin and Gardner (3) p. 245 (Lead Mountain), p. 320 (Calico); Hulin (1) p. 83 (California Rand mine); Tucker and Sampson (17) p. 298 (Dale), (27) p. 61 (Dale), (32) p. 69 (Mohawk mine); Ord Mts. (Martha Prospect), Weber (3) p. 26.

San Diego County: **1,** A small deposit of galena occurs $2\frac{1}{2}$ miles north of Valley Center (NW$\frac{1}{4}$ sec. 1, T. 11 S., R. 2 W., S. B.), Tucker (10) p. 350; also **2,** in the Laguna Mountains, and **3,** Deer Park area, ibid. **4,** Galena is found at the Descanso mine (sec. 24, T. 15 S., R. 3 E., S. B.), Tucker (8) p. 371.

San Mateo County: **1,** A 30-inch vein of galena is reported half a mile south of Searsville Lake, Huguenin and Castello (4) p. 172.

Santa Clara County: **1,** A little galena has been reported in the New Almaden ores, E. H. Bailey and Everhart (12) p. 98.

Shasta County: **1,** Galena is abundantly present in the Woodrow Wilson mine (sec. 4, T. 33 N., R. 2 W., M. D.), Tucker (9) p. 447. Other deposits are listed by Logan (9) pp. 176–193, Averill (4) pp. 7, 57, Albers and Robertson (3) p. 76.

Sierra County: **1,** Ferguson (2) p. 165, describes an interesting occurrence of galena in the Alleghany district: ". . . frequently a small nucleus of solid cleavable galena, up to 2-3 mm, and radiating from it, delicate needles not over 2 mm, similar to rutile, so closely spaced as to give the effect of chestnut burrs." **2,** Masses of galena occur in a limestone cave near Downieville, Mining and Scientific Press (20) p. 23.

Siskiyou County: **1**, Galena is found at a number of localities, nowhere in great amount: Logan (7) p. 181, Averill (3) p. 60, (5) pp. 280, 298.

Tehama County: **1**, Galena occurs on Cow Creek, Hanks (12) p. 181.

Trinity County: **1**, Galena occurs widespread in the mines in the slates of the county, Ferguson (1) p. 44. Other references: W. P. Miller (1) p. 713, Logan (9) p. 16, Averill (10) pp. 28, 34, 36, 42, 64.

Tulare County: **1**, Galena occurs in minor amount in the mines of the Mineral King Mining District, Goodyear (3) p. 646, Tucker (3) pp. 947–954, Franke (1) p. 436.

Tuolumne County: **1**, Galena was reported at the Marble Springs mine by W. P. Blake (7) p. 295, and occurs at many other mines in the county, W. P. Blake (9) p. 13, Tucker (1) p. 138.

Ventura County: **1**, Galena has come from the Piru area, CDMG (384).

GANOPHYLLITE

Hydrous manganese aluminum silicate, $Mn_5Al_2Si_7O_{22} \cdot 5H_2O$

Santa Clara County: **1**, Ganophyllite was one of the minerals of the manganese boulder found near Alum Rock Park, 5 miles east of San Jose. The mineral occurred in seams with barite, as brownish-yellow tabular crystals, A. F. Rogers (21) p. 446.

GARNET GROUP

Grossular, Essonite, Hyacinth. Calcium-aluminum garnet, $Ca_3Al_2Si_3O_{12}$. These are common as contact minerals in crystalline limestone. They are generally a light shade of red or green, sometimes almost white, and when clear form a valued gem.

Pyrope. Magnesium-aluminum garnet, $Mg_3Al_2Si_3O_{12}$. It occurs usually in serpentine and peridotite. Deep blood-red color.

Almandite. Iron-aluminum garnet, $Fe_3Al_2Si_3O_{12}$. It is a common garnet of gneisses and schists. Color brownish red; sometimes of gem value.

Andradite. Calcium-iron garnet, $Ca_3Fe_2Si_3O_{12}$. It is a common garnet of gneisses and schists. It is rarely clear enough for gems. Color yellow, green, brown, to black. *Topazolite* is a calcium-iron garnet having the color and transparency of topaz. *Aplome* is a manganiferous variety of andracite. *Melanite* is black.

Spessartine. Manganese-aluminum garnet, $Mn_3Al_2Si_3O_{12}$. It occurs usually in pegmatite dikes. Dark-red color.

Uvarovite. Calcium-chromium garnet, $Ca_3Cr_2Si_3O_{12}$. It is generally found as crystals coating massive chromite. Color emerald green.

Garnet is one of the common minerals of the State and probably all of the known varieties occur here. Garnet is generally a product of metamorphism and is common in metamorphic rocks such as gneiss, schist, quartzite, and crystalline limestone. As a contact mineral it is formed by the intrusion of igneous rock into limestone and other rock. Garnet is often found in fine large crystals. Many pegmatites carry garnet crystals, sometimes of excellent form and quality. It is a common constituent of beach sands and of the concentrates from mining areas.

No attempt has been made to report all of the occurrences of garnet found in the State that are referenced in the literature. The mineral is widespread and is so common that only occurrences of mineralogical interest should be included. However, some localities of minor importance and of little mineralogical interest are noted for the historical record because they have been reported in early editions of *Minerals of California.*

Alpine County: **1,** The old Uncle Billy Rogers copper claim in Hope Valley was located in garnet rock. W. P. Blake (9) p. 13, reported fine green grossular from this valley; see also Hanks (12) pp. 182, 225. **2,** Uvarovite in small crystals has been reported from the Calaveras mine, Trainer (p.c. '46).

Butte County: **1,** Red and brown garnets were common in the sands of the gold washings at Cherokee, Silliman (13) p. 385.

Calaveras County: **1,** Good crystals of andradite occur in schist at the Shenandoah mine, Woodhouse (p.c. '45). **2,** Andradite is found with idocrase and epidote at Garnet Hill, just above the confluence of Moore Creek and the Mokelumne River, H. W. Turner (12) p. 706, Melhase (6) p. 7. **3,** Uvarovite is reported from an unidentified location in the county, Jarvis (p.c. '46). **4,** Numerous seams of uvarovite in chromite are reported (SW$\frac{1}{4}$ sec. 9, T. 1 N., R. 13 E., M.D.), Cater (2) p. 50. This may be a confirmation of locality (**3**) reported by Jarvis. **5,** Almandite is found at Bald Point, Mokelumne River, Kunz (24) p. 51.

Del Norte County: **1,** Uvarovite occurs with kämmererite on chromite at the Brown mine (sec. 28, T. 18 N., R. 2 E., H.), Vonsen (p.c. '45), and **2,** at Camp 8 (sec. 19, T. 16 N., R. 3 E., H.), J. E. Allen (2) p. 123.

El Dorado County: **1,** Large crystals of grossular have been found at the Old Cosumnes copper mine, Tucker and Waring (2) p. 276. **2,** Good crystals of garnet occurred 9 miles southeast of Placerville, CDMG (13937). **3,** At the Lilyama mine, Pilot Hill, crystals of garnet occurred with chalcopyrite, galena, calcite, and quartz (N. R.). **4,** Garnet occurs with quartz and epidote at Grass Lake, near Glen Alpine, S. G. Clark (p.c. '35). **5,** Garnet occurred at the Fairmount mine, 3 miles from Pilot Hill, in large blocks and masses 2 or more feet thick, Hanks (12) p. 181, Kunz (24) p. 52. **6,** Pure white grossular with idocrase has been described by Pabst (2) p. 2, from veins in serpentine along Traverse Creek about 2$\frac{1}{2}$ miles south-southeast of Georgetown. Some clear, perfect crystals were found there. **7,** Uvarovite occurs at the Pilliken mine (secs. 21, 22, T. 11 N., R. 8 E., M.D.), Averill (11) p. 90, and **8,** at the Placer chrome mine, 6 miles south of Newcastle, Shannon (3) p. 376.

Fresno County: **1,** Brown garnet is associated with green tourmaline on Spanish Peak in a ledge of white quartz, W. W. Bradley (2) p. 439; **2,** it was found in crystals near Dunlap, Irelan (3) p. 208. **3,** White opaque garnet occurs in calcite with green californite at San Ramon on the south side of Watts Valley, Kunz (24) p. 52, W. W. Bradley (2) p. 439. **4,** White garnet occurring with californite 35 miles east of Selma has been analyzed by Steiger, F. W. Clarke and Steiger (8) p. 72. **5,** Large crystals occur "frozen," in matrix on Squaw Creek, Melhase (6) p. 22.

Imperial County: **1,** Opaque white grossular is found with wollastonite near the highway a few miles west of El Centro, Melhase (6) p. 23.

Inyo County: **1,** Large semi-crystalline masses of light-yellow garnet are found in the Coso area, Hanks (12) p. 182, Kunz (24) p. 52. **2,** Fine large crystals of grossular occurred with massive white datolite and greenish-brown idocrase at the San Carlos mine, north of Mazourka Canyon, on the west slope of the Inyo Range, John L. Smith (1) p. 435. **3,** Garnet is one of the principal gangue minerals at the scheelite deposits about 7 miles west of Bishop, A. Knopf (6) p. 233, Lemmon (5) p. 504. **4,** An outcrop of dark-red rock, mostly garnet, with some crystals up to half an inch in size, occurs at New York Butte, near its summit, Goodyear (3) p. 256. **5,** Light-green grossular-andradite occurs in abundant large crystals (one nearly a foot across) in the contact zone at Darwin, A. Knopf (4) p. 7, Kelley (4) p. 538. **6,** Crystals of brown grossular showing the unusual form (210) have been collected near Bishop, Knowlton in Trainer (4) p. 811.

Kern County: **1,** Large crystals of almandite occur in diorite on a branch of Tunis Creek, about half a mile southwest of the Tejon Ranch headquarters, Melhase (6) p. 8, Schürmann (2) p. 225, Murdoch (8) p. 189. **2,** Fine crystals of green andradite occur in skarn on Erskine Creek (sec. 9, T. 27 S., R. 33 E., M.D.), Chesterman (p.c. '51).

Los Angeles County: **1,** Almandite in well-formed crystals up to 4 cm across occurs in a biotite-chlorite schist in a road cut of the Angeles Crest Highway near Georges Gap, Murdoch and Webb (6) p. 351. (This is incorrectly entered under Kern County, as locality **(2)** in both Bulletins 136 and 173 of CDMG.)

Madera County: **1,** Fair crystals of almandite have been found on the divide one mile east of Island Pass, Goudey (1) p. 7. **2,** Grossularite is abundant in limestone on Shadow and Johnston Creeks, and garnet rock occurs at Garnet Lake, Erwin (1) p. 67, Melhase (6) p. 8. **3,** Spessartite (?) has been found in small orange crystals in cavities near Shadow Lake, A. M. Short (1) p. 493.

Marin County: **1,** Almandite crystals are common in the schists of the Tiburon Peninsula, Kunz (24) p. 52, F. L. Ransome (3) p. 311.

Mendocino County: **1,** Uvarovite occurs coating chromite about 12 miles north of Willits, Melhase (6) p. 23.

Mono County: **1,** Uvarovite crystals occur locally in marble on the western side of Mt. Baldwin, S. J. Rice (p.c. '64).

Monterey County: Trautwinite, which was described as a new mineral by Goldsmith (1) p. 348, (2) p. 365, (5) p. 152, from this county, appears from the analysis to be a mixture of uvarovite and chromite, E. S. Dana (5) p. 447. **1,** Uvarovite is reported west of King City (probably Los Burros Mining District), with chromite and kämmererite, W. W. Bradley (28) p. 497. **2,** Garnet is abundant in the beach sand at the mouth of the Sur River, P. D. Trask (1) p. 165.

Nevada County: **1,** Fine green crystals of uvarovite occurred coating chromite at the Red Ledge mine, 2 miles southwest of Washington (sec. 13, T. 17 N., R. 10 E., M.D.), associated with rhodochrome and Kämmererite, E. MacBoyle (1) p. 77.

Orange County: **1,** Pale apple-green pebbles of grossular were found near El Toro and analyzed by Steiger, F. W. Clarke (5) p. 76.

Placer County: **1,** Essonite is found at Deer Park, Kunz (23) p. 925. **2,** Uvarovite has been found on chromite near Towle, Lindgren (2) p. 5,

Melville and Lindgren (1) p. 27. **3,** Fine uvarovite crystals have been found on chromite, 7 miles southeast of Newcastle at the Farmer Swanton mine, with rhodochrome and kämmererite, Melhase (6) p. 23. **4,** Uvarovite is found with chromite at the Placer chrome mine, 6 miles south of Newcastle, Shannon (3) p. 377.

Plumas County: **1,** Green grossular occurs at Good Hope mine, Kunz (24) p. 52.

Riverside County: **1,** Abundant grossular and some andradite garnet occurs in the crystalline limestone at Crestmore, associated with idocrase, diopside and wilkeite, Eakle (15) p. 339. Minute grains of uvarovite have been found on occasion in the limestones, A. B. Carpenter (p.c. '64). **2,** Essonite or hyacinth garnet occurs with tourmaline in fine crystals at Coahuila, Kunz (24) p. 52. **3,** Good crystals of garnet have been found in a pegmatite near the Southern Pacific silica quarry at Nuevo, J. W. Clark (p.c. '35). **4,** Garnet occurs in the old Riverside City quarry, Melhase (6) p. 23.

San Benito County: **1,** Fine green crystals of uvarovite were found coating chromite and rhodochrome at New Idria, Brush (1) p. 268, Hanks (12) p. 183. **2,** Topazolite has been reported near New Idria, Melhase (6) p. 22. **3,** Uvarovite has been found with kämmererite on chromite near the headwaters of San Benito River (SW¼ sec. 21, T. 18 S., R. 12 E., M.D.), Murdoch (p.c. '45). **4,** Black garnets (melanite), in well-formed small crystals, are abundant in chlorite schist, locally associated with spinel, 1 mile south and west of the benitoite mine, Williams (p.c. '49).

San Bernardino County: **1,** Garnet was found with epidote and calcite in the iron ores at Dale, Harder and Rich (4) p. 237. **2,** Showy green patches of uvarovite in rock have been found northeast of Yermo on the road to Coyote Lake, T. V. Little (p.c. '47).

San Diego County: **1,** Fine crystals of transparent essonite garnet are found in the tourmaline areas: Mesa Grande, Kunz (17) p. 745, (24) p. 53; Pala, Kunz (24) p. 128, and Rincon, A. F. Rogers (4) p. 212. Garnets have been cut into gems under the name "hyacinth." **2,** Essonite occurs about 10 miles east of Jacumba Hot Springs with idocrase and quartz, Kunz (24) p. 52. **3,** Garnet is found near Julian, ibid. p. 26. **4,** Fine-granular red garnet occurs at Rincon, Rogers (4) p. 212. **5,** Essonite or hyacinth in good crystals has come from Hercules, Surprise, Lookout and Prophet mines at Ramona, Kunz (24) p. 52. **6,** Garnet occurs near San Vicente, ibid., p. 52. **7,** Massive garnet occurs at the McFall mine, 7½ miles southeast of Ramona, F. T. H. Merrill (1) p. 705. **8,** Essonite is found near Banner (sec. 25, T. 13 S., R. 8 E., S.B.), ibid., p 765. **9,** Hyacinth garnet has come from Dos Cabezas, Kunz (24) p. 27, Sterrett (3) p. 810. **10,** Spessartine from the Katerina mine on Heriart Hill, near Pala, was analyzed by Schaller, R. C. Wells (3) p. 101. **11,** The first record of garnet in California was made at Point Loma in 1792 by Martinez (1) p. 40, **12,** Spessartine occurs with rhodonite in the Jacumba area (sec. 16, T. 18 S., R. 8 E., S.B.), P. D. Trask et al. (4) p. 85. **13,** Essonite garnet, sometimes of gem quality, is found at the Lulubelle mine, Snyder (1) p. 23.

Santa Barbara County: **1,** Beach sands produced from the Santa Barbara formation are locally rich in almandite along the Santa Barbara coast, Woodhouse (p.c. '63).

Santa Clara County: **1,** Garnet from the omphacite-eclogite of Coyote Creek was analyzed by W. O. Clarke, J. P. Smith (1) p. 203. Some of the small red garnets at this locality carry free gold, Holway (1) p. 347. **2,** Red garnets up to half an inch in size occur in the eclogites of Hilton Gulch, Oak Ridge, Holway (1) p. 353.

Shasta County: **1,** Uvarovite has been found on chromite on Shotgun Creek, Kunz (24) p. 52, Melhase (6) p. 23. **2,** Bands of garnet mixed with pyroxene occur on the McCloud River on a contact between diabase and carboniferous limestone, Prescott (2) p. 473.

Siskiyou County: **1,** Uvarovite coats chromite at the Martin McKean mine, near Callahan, Melhase (6) p. 23. **2,** Massive white to pale-green garnet occurs with californite on Indian Creek, ibid. **3,** Uvarovite occurs with chromite in Seiad Valley (T. 46, 47 N., R. 11, 12 W., M.D.), Rynearson and Smith (1) pp. 304, 306. **4,** Uvarovite with kämmererite is found in the Youngs Valley group (T. 17 N., R. 5 E., H.), J. E. Allen (2) p. 123. **5,** Uvarovite with kämmererite has been found 14 miles southeast of Yreka, Symons (4) p. 101.

Sonoma County: **1,** Large masses of garnet occur near Petaluma, W. P. Blake (9) p. 13, W. W. Bradley (1) p. 321. **2,** Almandite garnets occur abundantly with glaucophane and actinolite in schists at Camp Meeker and near Healdsburg, W. W. Bradley (1) p. 321.

Stanislaus County: **1,** Minute crystals of uvarovite, coating fractures and shear planes, are found in the Del Puerto area (T. 6 S., R. 5 E., M.D.), Hawkes et al. (2) p. 91.

Tehama County: **1,** Uvarovite is found with chromite and kämmererite on North Elder Creek (T. 25 N., R. 7 W., M.D.), Rynearson (3) p. 200.

Trinity County: **1,** Emerald-green crystals of uvarovite occur on chromite near Carrville, Kunz (24) p. 53.

Tulare County: **1,** Topazolite was found at the Old Soldier mine, Drum Valley, 12 miles northeast of Visalia, Kunz (24) p. 53, Melhase (6) p. 22. **3,** Aplome was found near Visalia (sec. 25, T. 17 S., R. 28 E., M.D.), Durrell (p.c. '35). **4,** Garnet occurs with tremolite on the North Fork of Tule River, Kunz (24) p. 53; **5,** it was found in good crystals with quartz and epidote on the Kaweah River, 25 miles northeast of Exeter, Goodyear (3) p. 644. **6,** Large crystals of grossular occur with diopside, quartz and epidote in metamorphic rock on a hill between Drum Valley and Slickrock Canyon, Durrell (p.c. '35). **7,** Essonite is abundant in the metamorphic rocks near Three Rivers, Kunz (12) p. 1204. **8,** Massive white grossular is found near the Fresno County line, 1½ miles from Hawkins schoolhouse, Kunz (24) p. 52.

Tuolumne County: **1,** A lens of spessartine occurs in a pegmatite one mile north of the town of Tuolumne. Some of the crystals are over 2 inches in diameter, Goudey (2) p. 10.

Ventura County: **1,** Garnet crystals occur in the Piru Mountains, Kunz (24) p. 54.

Yuba County: **1,** Uvarovite is found at the Red Lodge mine, Melhase (6) p. 23.

References to a number of other occurrences, not of special importance or interest, listed by counties, are: *Fresno,* Kunz (24) p. 52, Tucker and Sampson (30) pp. 565, 566; *Inyo,* A. Knopf, (5) p. 120;

Kern, CDMG (11388), Kunz (24) p. 52; *Lassen,* CDMG (2328); *Los Angeles,* Hanks (12) p. 182; *Mariposa,* Kunz (24) p. 52, Laizure (6) p. 146; *Monterey,* Kunz (24) p. 52; *Nevada,* Lindgren (20) p. 75, Logan (20) p. 380; *Plumas,* Hanks (12) p. 182; *San Bernardino,* Tucker and Sampson (16) p. 307, Murdoch and Webb (11) p. 553, Tucker and Sampson (27) p. 78; *San Diego,* Kunz (24) pp. 52, 53, (26) p. 1342, Hanks (12) p. 182; *Santa Clara,* Kunz (24) p. 53, Hanks (12) p. 182; *Sonoma,* Hanks (12) p. 182; *Tulare,* Kunz (24) p. 53, Melhase (6) p. 22; *Tuolumne,* Little (1) p. 286; *Ventura,* Hanks (14) p. 68, Kunz (11) p. 911.

GARNIERITE
Basic magnesium nickel silicate, $(Ni,Mg)_3Si_2O_5(OH)_4$

Del Norte County: **1,** Garnierite occurs as veins in serpentine associated with laterite at Pine Flat Mountain, Elk Camp Ridge and Red Mountain, Rice (p.c. '55), CDMG (21675).

El Dorado County: **1,** Garnierite has been reported near Lotus, W. W. Bradley (29) p. 222. **2,** Garnierite in laterite soils is found in the Pilliken Chrome mine, W. B. Clark and Carlson (3) p. 438.

Humboldt County: **1,** Lateritic ores from this county have been found by Montoya and Baur (1) p. 1228 to carry lizardite (nickel-bearing), garnierite, clinochrysotile, antigorite and nepouite.

Imperial County: **1,** Garnierite was found on the south slope of Coyote Mountain, F. J. H. Merrill (1) p. 732.

Mariposa County: **1,** Garnierite was reported with gerdsdorffite from the Pine Tree mine (sec. 9, T. 4 S., R. 17 E., M.D.), W. W. Bradley (30) p. 491.

San Benito County: **1,** Garnierite has come from the Aurora mine, near New Idria, W. W. Bradley (26) p. 608. **2,** The mineral has been tentatively reported from Clear Creek (sec. 15, T. 18 S., R. 11 E., M.D.), in a serpentine mass, K. G. Hines (p.c. '45).

Tulare County: **1,** A specimen from veins represented as crystalline garnierite associated with chrysoprase in altered serpentine, CDMG (21575), is in the collections of the CDMG. **2,** Garnierite occurs as irregular veins in silicified serpentine at Venice Hill and near Porterville, Rice (p.c. '55).

GAY-LUSSITE
Hydrous sodium calcium carbonate, $Na_2Ca(CO_3)_2 \cdot 5H_2O$

Inyo County: **1,** Gay-lussite is reported by B. F. Jones (1) p. B200 from muds of Deep Spring Lake. **2,** Gay-lussite appears in the lake bed deposits of Owens Lake, G. I. Smith and Pratt (2) p. 5.

Kern County: **1,** Gay-lussite has been found in the China Lake deposits, along with analcime, various zeolites, and other minerals, Hay and Moiola (2) p. 76A, G. I. Smith and Pratt (2) p 16, Moiola and Hay (1) p. 215.

Lake County: **1,** Gay-lussite was found with northupite and glauberite in the muds of Borax Lake, Vonsen (3) p. 22, Vonsen and Hanna (4) p. 103.

Mono County: **1,** The mineral was reported as present at Mono Lake, I. C. Russell (1) p. 297.

San Bernardino County: **1,** Gay-lussite was reported from Searles Lake by Hanks (18) p. 222, H. S. Gale (13) p. 306. Crystal forms were described by J. H. Pratt (1) p. 130, Murdoch (26) p. 360. A much more detailed description of the occurrence and relationships is reported in G. I. Smith and Haines (3) p. 27. Galeite is associated with gay-lussite in the Searles Lake occurrence, Pabst et al. (2) p. 489 and G. I. Smith and Pratt (2) p. 30. **2,** Gay-lussite was reported from the Owl Springs niter beds, G. E. Bailey (2) p. 102.

GEIKIELITE
Magnesium titanate, MgTiO₃

Monterey County: **1,** The second occurrence of geikielite in the State is reported from highly metamorphosed magnesian marbles in the Santa Lucia Mts., in place, as grains associated with spinel, clinohumite and other minerals, Wise (1).

Riverside County: **1,** Geikielite occurs in microscopic red grains and crystals disseminated in brucite limestone, at the Jensen quarry, Murdoch and Fahey (20) p. 1341, (23) p. 835. This was the second recorded locality in the world for this exceedingly rare mineral. It has previously been found only in Ceylon.

GEOCRONITE
Lead arsenic antimony sulphide, $Pb_{27}(As,Sb)_{12}S_{46}$

Inyo County: **1,** Geocronite was reported by Hanks (12) p. 182, (15) p. 110, with anglesite and argentiferous galena, from the Santa Maria and Eclipse mines, in the Inyo Mountains.

Mono County: **1,** Geocronite was reported from the Garibaldi mine, Prescott area, CDMG (4279), with argentiferous galena and sphalerite.

GERSDORFFITE
Sulpharsenide of nickel, NiAsS

Mariposa County: **1,** Gersdorffite is found with garnierite at the Pine Tree mine (sec. 9, T. 4 S., R 17 E., M.D.), W. W. Bradley (30) p. 491.

*GERSTLEYITE, 1956
Hydrous sodium lithium antimony arsenic sulphide, $(Na,Li)_4As_2Sb_8S_{17}·6H_2O$

Kern County: **1,** This new mineral is described by Frondel and Morgan (7) p. 839, from the Kramer borate region. It occurs in the workings of the Baker mine as cinnabar-red to blackish-red spherules, up to an inch in diameter, with a crudely radial fibrous structure. It also occurs as granular aggregates and groups of small thick plates.

GIBBSITE—Hydrargillite—Bauxite
Aluminum hydroxide, Al(OH)₃

The name "bauxite" was originally applied to a supposed species with the composition $Al_2O_3·2H_2O$ found at Les Baux, France. The original analysis was made on a mixture of minerals in a rock mass, and approached only by chance the ratio cited. Actually, $Al_2O_3·2H_2O$ has not been found either as a natural or as an artificial product, Palache et al. (10) p. 667.

Bauxite closely resembles clay and is distinguished at sight from clay only by its characteristic pea-shaped or pisolitic structure.

Clay and clay-like minerals such as bauxite, gibbsite, halloysite, montmorillonite, and others are widespread in many localities. Often, identification has been by field examination. This is especially true in early reported occurrences. Accordingly, few occurrences are included in the listings, some chosen for historic reasons, and some for mineralogic reasons. It is impractical to include all localities, especially since many important areas produce mineral commodities, and are not strictly mineral occurrences. Many reports may also in fact be in error as far as specific mineral identification is concerned. X-ray and optical examination is required for certain identification of most clay minerals.

Kern County: **1,** Pale to deep pink gibbsite was found in boulders of brecciated gray chert on the alluvial fans at the southern tip of the San Joaquin Valley, on the Tejon Ranch, Murdoch and Webb (6) p. 352.

Nevada County: **1,** Gibbsite has been doubtfully reported from the Brunswick mine at Grass Valley, Mining and Scientific Press (33) p. 271.

Riverside County: **1,** Pisolitic bauxite has been reported from the clay pits at Alberhill (sec. 26, T. 4 S., R. 6 W., S. B.), Richard (1) p. 13, but according to Bramlette (p.c. '45), this is a high-alumina clay.

GILLESPITE
Iron barium silicate, $BaFe_4Si_4O_{10}$

Fresno County: **1,** Gillespite is found sparingly in the Rush Creek sanbornite deposit (secs. 22, 27, T. 11 S., R. 25 E., M. D.), associated with witherite and taramellite, Matthews and Alfors (1) p. 2. **2,** Gillespite, sanbornite, and taramellite are found in sulphide-bearing quartz rock at Big Creek (sec. 16, T. 11 S., R. 25 E., M. D.), with a number of unidentified minerals, CDMG (21880); CDMG confirmed identification, 1964, Stinson and Alfors (3) p. 10.

Mariposa County: **1,** Gillespite was found with sanbornite and celsian in a vein in quartzite one mile north of Trumbull Peak, near Incline, A. F. Rogers (39) p. 161, Melhase (5) no. 9, p. 4. Its atomic structure was studied by Pabst (7) p. 372, ibid. (16).

GILSONITE
A variety of asphalt, a hydrocarbon

Santa Barbara County: **1,** Gilsonite was reported on the Goldtree Ranch, Sisquoc, Irelan (4) p. 47.

GINORITE
Hydrous calcium borate, $Ca_2B_{14}O_{23}\cdot8H_2O$

Inyo County: **1,** Ginorite is first reported from California from the head of Twenty Mule Team Canyon, Death Valley ($SW\frac{1}{4}$ sec. 9, T. 26 N., R. 2 E., S. B.), from the Mott open-cut colemanite prospect. The ginorite occurs in white pellets embedded in a pale yellow-brown matrix of sassolite and clay, R. D. Allen and Kramer (6) p. 56.

GLAUBERITE
Sodium calcium sulphate, $Na_2Ca(SO_4)_2$

Imperial County: **1,** Good crystals of glauberite have been found in the mud of the dry lake half a mile east of Bertram siding on the

Southern Pacific Railroad, near the east shore of the Salton Sea, Murdoch (p.c. '45), confirmed by M. F. Berkholz (18), p. 17.

Inyo County: 1, Glauberite is found with halite in the salt pools at Pluto Springs in the bottom of Death Valley, H. S. Gale (13) p. 303. It also appears here in drill cores down to a depth of 100 feet, ibid. 2, Specimens have been collected from the playa in Saline Valley, ibid, p. 303. 3, Glauberite is reported from saline crusts and efflorescences from Deep Spring Lake, B. F. Jones (1) p. B200.

Lake County: 1, Thin, flattened crystals of glauberite have been found in blue clay 40 feet below the surface at Borax Lake, Silliman (10) p. 399, Hanks (12) p. 182, Vonsen (3) p. 22.

San Bernardino County: 1, Glauberite is common at Searles Lake, in platy crystals, Rath (5) p. 233, De Groot (3) p. 535, H. S. Gale (13) p. 303.

GLAUCONITE
Essentially a hydrous iron aluminum and potassium silicate, $K_2(Mg,Fe)_2Al_6(Si_4O_{10})_2(OH)_{12}(?)$

Glauconite is found abundantly in ocean sediments near the continental shores. For central and southern California, see report in W. L. Pratt (1) p. 58.

Butte County: 1, A 2-foot layer of glauconite-anauxite sandstone occurs in Chambers Ravine, 4 miles north of Oroville, V. T. Allen (3) p. 369.

Los Angeles County: 1, Glauconite is found with glaucophane and crossite in siliceous shale at Malaga Cove, near Redondo, R. D. Reed (5) p. 347.

Merced County: 1, Glauconite occurs with jarosite in sandstone (sec. 35, T. 11 S., R. 10 E., M. D.), 10 miles south of Los Baños, Briggs (1) p. 902.

Monterey County: 1, Glauconite has been found in dredgings from Monterey Bay, Galliher (2) p. 1359, (3) p. 1580.

San Diego County: 1, The mineral occurs extensively with collophane on submarine banks off the coast, R. S. Dietz et al. (2) p. 819.

GOETHITE
Basic iron oxide (alpha-iron monohydrate), $FeO(OH)$

Goethite is usually found as slender prismatic crystals in masses of hematite, and resembles limonite so closely that it is often classed as such.

Inyo County: 1, Goethite has been found with chrysocolla and limonite at the St. Ignacio mine (N. R.).

Lake County: 1, Goethite pseudomorphs after pyrrhotite crystals have been found at Sulphur Bank, D. E. White and Roberson (2) p. 409.

Mariposa County: 1, Goethite is found in quartz on Burns Creek, Kunz (24) p. 105.

Riverside County: 1, A very small amount of goethite has been found in the Iron Age ore deposit near Dale, in the Eagle Mountains, Harder (6) p. 63.

GOLD
Native gold, Au

Native gold has a very wide distribution in California. It has been found in every county, and has been produced from two-thirds of them. It occurs either as free flakes or nuggets in sands and gravels, or in quartz veins, either alone, or more commonly with small amounts of pyrite, arsenopyrite and other sulphides. It is sometimes in such fine particles in quartz as to be invisible to the naked eye, or it may occur in minute grains in massive sulphides, or in the "limonite" gossans derived from their weathering. Less commonly it is finely disseminated in slates or greenstones. It has been found associated with any one of a long list of minerals, but is most common in quartz. A somewhat unusual association is with cinnabar, and occurrences of this type are listed below. Calcite, barite, arsenopyrite and pyrite are common gangue minerals, and gold and silver tellurides are occasionally found with the native metal.

Gold occurs in nuggets, flakes and stringers of a great variety of shapes: arborescent, spongiform, wires, plates and less commonly as well-formed crystals. Small octahedral crystals were described and figured by Alger (1) p. 102. C. U. Shepard (1) p. 231, has described some gold crystals two-fifths of an inch in diameter. W. P. Blake (11) p. 120, noted one cavernous crystal nearly 2 inches on its longest side (probably from Forest Hill, Placer County, ibid. (7) p. 299). Blake's report in November 1861 on the Mariposa Estate, quoted in J. R. Browne (4) p. 25, describes specimen gold ". . . crystals are bunches of tetrahedrons with perfectly flat and polished faces from $\frac{1}{8}$ to $\frac{3}{16}$ inches across, and are attached to masses of white quartz."

Numerous large nuggets and masses of gold and quartz have been found in the stream gravels and in the "pockets" of quartz veins. The first large nugget, weighing between 20 and 25 pounds, was found in 1848 on the Mokelumne River, by a soldier in Stevenson's regiment, Hanks (8) p. 148. A great number have been discovered since that time. A complete list would be too long to insert here, but probably well over 60 big finds, and hundreds of smaller ones, have been recorded, with the large ones ranging from 50 to 2300 ounces Troy weight. More detailed records of nuggets may be found by consulting the following references: Hittel (2) p. 492; Mining and Scientific Press (12) p. 178; ibid. (23) p. 162, Hanks (8) pp. 147–150; W. W. Allen and Avery *The California Gold Book* (1) p. 91; Hurley (1); Del Mar (1) p. 629.

The largest nugget on record, found at Carson Hill in 1854, weighed 2340 ounces. Several others nearly as large have been found at various times: Holden's Garden, El Dorado County, 1500 ounces (1850); Monumental mine, Sierra Buttes, 1596 ounces (1860), and 1893 ounces (1869). More large nuggets have come from Sierra County than from any other, with El Dorado County next. In Tuolumne County a great many nuggets weighing from 2 to 70 pounds were found between 1850 and 1858, in a 5-mile radius including Sonora, Columbia, and Springfield. A list of 25 or more of these is given by Hittel (2) p. 492. Coming down to more recent times, a $3,000 nugget was found in Siskiyou County in 1903, Engineering and Mining Journal (8) p. 49. Several large masses of practically pure crystallized gold have been found at various places within 3 years of 1935, Laizure (8) p. 29.

Primary deposits occur along the Mother Lode belt, at various points in the Sierra Nevada, east and north of the Lode, and in isolated ranges in the northwestern and southeastern parts of the state. The western slopes of the Sierra Nevada where the main streams leave their deep canyons to enter the valley, the large river courses in the northwest, and parts of the desert regions in the southeastern part of the state were important placer mining areas.

Some gold is found in the Coast Range and some has been mined in the southern counties, but the great bulk came from the northern half of the state and from counties along the Sierra Nevada.

Gold occurs in so many localities that it would be impossible to cite all of them. The literature on the gold deposits is also extensive. The gold placers of California have been described in Bulletin 92 of the CDMG, and the Mother Lode gold belt has been described in Bulletin 108. Professional Papers 73 and 157 of the United States Geological Survey are the best authorities on the Tertiary gravels of the Sierra Nevada and the Mother Lode gold belt, respectively.

The leading lode-gold producing counties of the state were: Amador. Calaveras, El Dorado, Kern, Mariposa, Nevada, Shasta, Siskiyou, Sierra, Trinity and Tuolumne.

The leading placer-gold producing counties of the state were: Butte, Merced, Placer, Sacramento, Stanislaus and Yuba.

Gold production has been curtailed significantly since about 1945.

For contemporary pictures and information concerning the early days of gold in California, see Egenhoff (1). See also Anon. (33) and Eric et al. (1).

Alameda County: **1,** Stringers of quartz with visible free gold were found on the west and north slopes of the Berkeley Hills, Lawson (7) p. 23.

Amador County: **1,** Talc filled with gold particles came from the Soapstone lode, Engineering and Mining Journal (2) p. 195. **2,** A ribbon of solid gold, three-eighths of an inch or more in thickness, was found in the old Eureka mine (sec. 8, T. 6 N., R. 11 E., M.D.), Logan (16) p. 101 (quotation from a report by John B. Trask, 1855).

Butte County: **1,** A nugget weighing 832 ounces came from the Willard claim near Magalia, J. D. Hubbard (1) p. 353. **2,** Gold in barite gangue came from Pinkstown Ledge, half a mile south of Big Bend Mountain, H. W. Turner (12) p. 588.

Calaveras County: **1,** The largest mass of gold-quartz ever reported in California came from the Morgan mine and was valued at $43,534, Logan (16) p. 129; see also Tuolumne County, **(3). 2,** F. L. Ransome (9) p. 8, records the presence of beautiful arborescent masses of crystallized gold associated with large arsenopyrite crystals in the Mother Lode belt.

Colusa County: **1,** Gold deposited on quartz crystals occurred in the Manzanita cinnabar mine on Sulphur Creek. This mine was worked for gold from 1865–92, Aubury (2) p. 44.

Contra Costa County: **1,** Gold is reported with sulphide minerals from Mitchell Canyon, Mt. Diablo, H. W. Turner (1) p. 391.

El Dorado County: **1,** Near Coloma, 3 miles from Sutter's Mill, a specimen was found weighing 31 ounces, a beautiful mass with a delicately marked surface consisting of a network of fibers, W. P. Blake (3) p. 79. **2,** A mass of gold in imperfect crystals was found 7 miles from Georgetown, in 1866, W. P. Blake (11) p. 120. **3,** A beautiful specimen of large crystalline plates studded with triangular markings was found at Spanish Dry Diggings, E. S. Dana (3) p. 138. **4,** Gold occurred in albite at the Shaw mine, Storms (6) p. 173.

Humboldt County: **1,** Gold washed out of the black sands of the sea cliffs at Upper Gold Bluffs was observed to form a nearly complete coating of the beach sands. This coating was temporary, and was dissipated with the next tide, S. Johnson (1) p. 536. R. W. Raymond (7) p. 145, described the bluff and presents a structure section.

Inyo County: **1,** Gold occurs in purple fluorite, producing an unusual ore, at the Waterfall prospect, 3 miles north of Antelope Springs, A. Knopf (5) p. 113. **2,** Microscopic octahedral crystals were found at the Ida mine, Hanks (12) p. 184. **3,** A nugget weighing 39½ ounces was reported from the Halleluja claim, at the north end of Death Valley, Los Angeles Times, July 30, 1945.

Kern County: **1,** Occurrences of gold, as shown by mines and prospects throughout the county, are listed by Troxel and Morton (2) pp. 92–196.

Lake County: **1,** Gold nuggets with attached cinnabar were found near Sulphur Springs, Bear Valley, 10 miles northeast of Borax Lake, J. A. Phillips (1) p. 326.

Los Angeles County: **1,** One of the early discoveries of gold was made on the San Francisquito Ranch in June 1841, J. J. Warner (1) p. 170.

Mariposa County: **1,** "Crystals [of gold] are bunches of octahedrons with perfectly flat and highly polished faces from $\frac{1}{8}''$ to $\frac{3}{16}''$ across," at the Princeton mine, Mariposa Estate, J. R. Browne (4) p. 25 quoting W. P. Blake's report of November 1861.

Nevada County: **1,** Gold associated with altaite occurred at the Providence mine, Lindgren (12) p. 116. **2,** Beautiful leaf gold occurred in cavities lined with quartz crystals, at the Granite Hill and North Gold Hill veins, ibid., p. 115. **3,** Wires of gold were found on large crystals of pyrite at the Pennsylvania mine, Nevada City, MacBoyle (1) p. 43. **4,** Beautiful plates and angular masses of gold in snow-white quartz, often associated with brilliant crystals of arsenopyrite, were found at the Lafayette and Helvetia mines, W. P. Blake (3) p. 76. **5,** A superb specimen of crystallized gold is reported to have been collected from a pocket in the Red Ledge mine, near Washington. The specimen was 1½ x 1½ inches, and is presumed to have been collected in September 1956, Anon. (32) p. 12.

Placer County: **1,** Several octahedral crystals three-eighths of an inch across, and a large "skeleton" crystal 1 by $\frac{7}{8}$ inches, came from Forest Hill, W. P. Blake (3) p. 78, (7) p. 299. One of these crystals of gold was used as the model for the drawing of the gold crystal in E. S. Dana (4), *System of Mineralogy,* and the specimen is in the collection of Dr. George Bain, of Amherst College, Amherst, Mass. The crystal was, in 1964, on display in the Amherst College Museum. **2,** Several beautiful arborescent specimens of gold were found on Irish Creek,

One (12 by 4 inches in dimensions) was in the form of a leaf, with one side arborescent and the other studded with 25 perfect octahedrons, W. P. Blake (3) p. 78. **3,** A mass, nearly all gold, weighing 187 ounces was found 2 miles above Michigan Bluff on American River, W. P. Blake (16) p. 166. **4,** The Golden Bear nugget, official insignia of the California Federation of Mineralogical Societies, was purchased by the Federation, and deposited for perpetuity in the CDMG Exhibit. The nugget was found in 1857.

San Bernardino County: **1,** Gold, in tremolite, is reported from the Wild Rose group of claims, 30 miles southeast of Victorville, H. W. Turner (31) p. 835.

San Joaquin County: **1,** Gold was discovered in specks from gravels of the San Joaquin River near Stockton in 1846, G. M. Evans (1) p. 385. The discovery went unnoticed by the general public.

Santa Clara County: **1,** Gold has been found in red garnets of the eclogite at Coyote Creek, 6 miles north of San Martin, Holway (1) p. 347.

Shasta County: **1,** A slab of gold nearly a quarter of an inch thick, weighing 100 ounces, came from the Mad Mule mine in Grizzly Gulch, northeast of Tower House, Ferguson (3) p. 251. Normally the gold here occurs as thin films or as dendritic forms in calcite.

Sierra County: **1,** A large nugget or mass from the vein, weighing about 95 pounds, came from the Monumental mine, near Sierra Buttes, Newberry (2) p. 10. The original mass was probably as much as 140 pounds. **2,** The Alleghany-Downieville region in 1956 was the only producing lode area in the state. A good discussion of this activity is found in Carlson and Clark (3).

Siskiyou County: **1,** Thin triangular plates of gold with a hexagonal pattern came from Yreka, E. S. Dana (3) p. 138. **2,** A mass of leaf gold from Quartz Valley, 25 miles from Yreka, was valued at $6,000, Engineering and Mining Journal (11) p. 828. **3,** Gold occurring in conglomerate was reported from the Cottonwood area, H. W. Turner (25) p. 653. **4,** Gold flakes in nephrite jade were found at Chan jade mine, Indian Creek, near Happy Camp, Kraft (1) p. 34.

Tuolumne County: **1,** A large nugget weighing 209¼ ounces was found at Sonora, Du Bois (1) p. 177, (2) p. 175. **2,** Numerous large nuggets have come from a small area including Sonora, Columbia, Springfield, and Shaws Flat, Hittel (2) p. 300. **3,** Small brilliant prisms of gold (distorted crystals) have come from Sonora and Angels Camp in Calaveras County, W. P. Blake (11) p. 57. **4,** Wire gold resembling a braided cord was found at the Golden Rule mine, CDMG (15176). **5,** Placer gold was reported as commonly coated with quicksilver, at Curtis Creek, J. S. Wilson (1) p. 315. **6,** A beautiful specimen of gold found in loose quartz crystals and talc measured 6 x 13 inches and weighed 67 ounces. It was found in 1946 on the Eureka and Grizzly claim (E½ E½ sec. 26, T. 1 S., R. 15 E., M.D.), Logan (23) p. 65.

GOLD, var. ARGENTIAN (ELECTRUM)
Alloy of gold and silver

Colusa County: **1,** Argentian gold was mined with cinnabar and sulphur from Sulphur Creek, E. S. Dana (5) p. 1096.

Fresno County: **1,** Electrum is reported from the Jeff Davis mine near Millerton, Hanks (3) p. 25.

Inyo County: **1,** Hanks (15) p. 135, reported electrum from the Kearsarge Mining District.

Kern County: **1,** Electrum has been found in the gold ores of the Cactus Queen mine, Mojave Mining District, Troxel and Morton (2) p. 44.

Lassen County: **1,** Electrum occurred with free gold from the Hayden Hill Mining District, Preston (1) p. 212.

Madera County: **1,** Wire argentian gold was found at the Hanover mine, Fine Gold Gulch, CDMG (1598), Hanks (14) p. 89.

Mono County: **1,** Electrum is reported from Bodie, Hanks (3) p. 25, (12) p. 190.

Placer County: **1,** Electrum occurred in the Moore and other mines of the Ophir Mining District, Lindgren (7) p. 271.

Tulare County: **1,** Angel (2) p. 732, reported electrum from the White River.

GOLD AMALGAM
A native alloy of gold and mercury very rarely found

Mariposa County: **1,** Gold amalgam was found in the region around Mariposa, noted first by Schmitz (1) p. 713, and analyzed by Sonnenschein (1) p. 244.

Nevada County: **1,** Gold amalgam was reported from the Odin drift mine near Nevada City Lindgren (12) p. 116.

GONNARDITE
Hydrous calcium sodium aluminum silicate, $Na_2Ca[(Al,Si)_5O_{10}]_2 \cdot 6H_2O$

Riverside County: **1,** Gonnardite was found in white, silky, radiated fibers with wollastonite and pyrite in the Commercial quarry at Crestmore, Foshag (p.c. '36).

GOSLARITE
Hydrous zinc sulphate, $ZnSO_4 \cdot 7H_2O$

Goslarite is formed through the decomposition of sphalerite and is sometimes found on mine walls.

Inyo County: **1,** Goslarite is mentioned as a component of silver-lead ores in the oxidized zone from the mines of the Darwin region, Hall and MacKevett (1) p. 18, ibid. (4) p. 64.

Kern County: **1,** Goslarite has been found in the Blackhawk mine, near Loraine, Troxel and Morton (2) p. 41.

Shasta County: **1,** Goslarite is reported from some of the copper deposits in the county, Graton (3) p. 100.

Trinity County: **1,** Goslarite occurs with other sulphate minerals in the alteration products at Island Mountain, Langdon (1) p. 279.

* GOWERITE, 1959
Hydrous calcium borate, $CaB_6O_{10} \cdot 5H_2O$

Inyo County: Gowerite, a new borate mineral, was described in 1959 by Erd et al. (1), from Death Valley. Several occurrences of gowerite have been noted: **1,** Mott open-cut colemanite prospect, Furnace Creek deposits, Erd et al. (1) p. 912; **2,** Hard Scramble claim on the west slope of the foothills of Black Mts., west of Ryan, Erd et al. (1) p. 912; **3**, 1.4 miles S. 43° E. of the Mott open-cut prospect, Erd et al. (1) p. 912, and **4**, 3000 ft. N. 72° W. of Ryan, Erd et al. (1) p. 912; see also Christ and Clark (6).

GRAPHITE—Plumbago—Black Lead
Native carbon, C

Graphite is prominent in some schists and gneisses and when present in considerable amount the graphitic gneiss or schist is sometimes mined for the graphite. In mining regions it is often seen coating the walls of veins and mixed with talcose gouge.

Graphite is a common constituent of crystalline limestones and is often disseminated through the limestone in minute flakes and in larger foliated masses.

No extensive deposits of high quality graphite are known to occur in the State, but a few small deposits have been worked for the manufacture of paints and lubricants. Much of the graphite of California is so intimately mixed with silica that its separation as pure material is an expensive operation. It is typically a constituent of metamorphic rocks.

Amador County: **1**, Graphite is rather abundant at the Argonaut mine, Josephson (1) p. 475.

Calaveras County: **1**, Graphite has been mined at Campo Seco, Bastin (1) p. 197.

Del Norte County: **1**, Foliated plates of graphite in limestone are found 18 miles northeast of Crescent City, Irelan (3) p. 164.

Fresno County: **1**, Graphite is prominent in the rocks on the Reeves Ranch, 3½ miles west of Dunlap, Crawford (2) p. 642, **2**, at Borer Hill, Hanks (12) p. 224, and **3**, at Sycamore Creek near Trimmer, W. W. Bradley (2) p. 451.

Imperial County: **1**, A large deposit of good graphite occurs on the southeast slope of Coyote Mountains 7 miles north of Coyote Wells, Tucker (4) p. 267.

Kern County: **1**, Graphite was noted near Fort Tejon, J. R. Browne (4) p. 254.

Los Angeles County: **1**, A large deposit of graphite occurs in the Verdugo Hills (sec. 4, T. 1 N., R. 13 W., S. B.), Aubury (3) p. 280. **2**, Graphite schist occurs in Kagel Canyon, 8 miles east of San Fernando, Beverly (1) p. 349. **3**, Two deposits of graphite are in Pacoima Canyon (sec. 17, T. 3 N., R. 15 W., S. B.), ibid., p. 351. **4**, Several deposits (graphitic schist) have been found near the head of San Francisquito Canyon (T. 6, 7 N., R. 15, 16 W., S. B.), ibid., p. 349. **5**, Crystalline graphite in a biotite-sillimanite schist occurs near Elizabeth Lake Canyon (T. 7 N., R. 15 W., S. B.), ibid., p. 351. **6**, A deposit of graphite in Bouquet Canyon (secs. 11, 12, T. 6 N., R. 15 W., S. B.), has been worked occasionally for a considerable period, E. C. Simpson (1) p. 410.

Marin County: **1**, A deposit of graphite has been reported from the border of Tomales Bay, J. A. Walker (1) p. 915.

Mendocino County: **1**, Graphite has been mined east of Point Arena (sec. 8, T. 12 N., R. 15 W., M. D.), Aubury (3) p. 280.

Monterey County: **1**, Graphite occurs in lustrous flakes in most of the limestones of the Sur series, P. D. Trask (2) p. 131.

Nevada County: **1**, A deposit of graphite carrying 26 percent carbon was reported at the Black. Quartz mine, near Washington, Mining and Scientific Press (42) p. 840.

Riverside County: **1**, Graphite flakes are abundant in the brucite limestone at Crestmore, Woodford et al. (10) p. 354. **2**, Crystals as much as 2–3 mm in size occur associated with wollastonite in the crystalline limestone at the Jensen quarry, Peebles (p.c. '44).

San Bernardino County: **1**, Large deposits of graphite are reported near the head of the Santa Ana River, 15 miles from East Highlands, Aubury (3) p. 280. **2**, Fine-grained graphite schist comes from Eva Canyon half a mile to one mile from its mouth, Bastin (2) p. 164. **3**, Graphitic schist occurs in Green Canyon, in the Big Bear Lake area (secs. 28, 29, 32, 33, T. 2 N., R. 2 E., S. B.), L. A. Wright et al. (5) p. 166.

San Diego County: **1**, Graphite in mica schist is reported near Mason (sec. 34, T. 13 S., R. 5 E., S. B.), Tucker (4) p. 378. **2**, ''Black mica,'' presumably graphite, was reported in 1792 by Martinez (1) p. 40, as occurring ''near San Diego.''

Sonoma County: **1**, Small deposits of graphite and graphitic schists occur southwest of Healdsburg, Aubury (3) p. 281; **2**, near Petaluma, ibid., p. 281, and 3, in Knights Valley, Hanks (12) p. 225.

Tulare County: **1**, A large low-grade deposit (Camp Nelson graphite) is described by (sec. 34, T. 20 S., R. 31 E., M. D.), Franke (1) p. 444. **2**, Graphite schist is found in Drum Valley, Aubury (3) p. 280.

Tuolumne County: **1**, Graphite was mined at an early date at the Eureka plumbago mine (discovered in 1853) (E. $\frac{1}{2}$ sec. 24, T. 2 N., R. 14 E., M. D.), J. R. Browne (4) p. 252, Logan (23) p. 75.

GREENOCKITE
Cadmium sulphide, CdS

A very rare mineral occasionally found coating sphalerite.

Xanthocroite has been shown to be identical with greenockite, Palache et al. (10) p. 230.

Inyo County: **1**, Orange yellow prismatic crystals of greenockite were found in a vein with hemimorphite at Cerro Gordo, Woodhouse (p.c. '45).

Mono County: **1**, Rock specimens from the South Forty claim (T. 8 N., R. 22 E., M. D.), near the Golden Gate mine, West Walker River area, were coated with brilliant yellow to orange greenockite (*xanthochroite*), Schaller (34) p. 137. Other specimens show as a coating on magnetite, CDMG (18924), Eakle and McLaughlin (17) p. 141.

Riverside County: **1**, Thin coatings of greenockite were reported on sphalerite at Crestmore, Eakle (15) p. 352. These coatings have been shown to be hawleyite, A. B. Carpenter (p.c. '62).

San Bernardino County: **1**, Thin coatings of greenockite were found on quartz from the San Bernardino Mountains (sec. 31, T. 1 N., R. 1 E., S. B.), W. W. Bradley (30) p. 194.

Santa Clara County: **1,** CDMG (18467) was sent in from this county.

Santa Cruz County: **1,** Greenockite is one of the minerals found by C. W. Chesterman (p.c. '64) at the Pacific Limestone Products (Kalkar) quarry at Santa Cruz.

Shasta County: **1,** Several thousand pounds of cadmium were produced at the Mammoth Copper Company plant, presumably from cadmium in the sphalerite. Logan (9) p. 130, reports that greenockite occurs in the copper-zinc ores as lemon yellow coatings on sphalerite. F. M. Hamilton (4) p. 241, also suggests that cadmium may in part occur as greenockite associated with sphalerite.

* GRIEGITE, 1964
Iron sulphide, Fe_3S_4.

San Bernardino County: **1,** Small grains and crystals occurring in clays from the Kramer-Four Corners area are identified as a new iron sulphide, described and named griegite by Skinner et al. (1) pp. 543–555. The occurrence in lake beds confirms in nature the synthesized iron sulphide which was predicted by chemical and crystallographic studies of laboratory products. The mineral was recovered from cores of test holes drilled in the lake beds. The geological relations are described by Dibblee (1) and precise location data are given by Benda et al. (1).

* GRIFFITHITE, 1917
Hydrous magnesium iron calcium sodium aluminum silicate,
$(Si_{6.38}Al_{1.62})(Mg_{3.76}Fe^{2+}_{1.04}Fe^{3+}_{0.88}Al_{.08})O_{20}(OH)_4Ca_{0.5}Na_{.22}$

Griffithite, originally placed as a member of the chlorite group, has been determined to be a trioctahedral member of the montmorillonite group, Faust (1) p. 66.

Los Angeles County: **1,** Griffithite, "a variety of chlorite," occurs in amygdules up to 1 inch in basalt of Cahuenga Pass. The mineral was described and named by E. S. Larsen and Steiger (6) p. 11. **2,** Griffithite occurs in the Pacific Electric quarry, Brush Canyon, locality 2, Neuerburg (1) p. 136.

GUADALCAZARITE
Variety of metacinnabar
Mercury zinc sulphide, $(HgZn)S$, Zn up to 5 percent

Santa Clara County: **1,** Minute rhombohedral-hemimorphic crystals from New Almaden described by Melville (2) p. 292 as metacinnabar, should be called guadalcazarite, Wherry (3) p. 37. According to Palache et al. (10) p. 216, however, guadalcazarite is simply a zinc-bearing metacinnabar. It is possible that these crystals were wrongly identified as to their form.

GUANAJUATITE
Bismuth sulpho-selenide, $Bi_2(Se,S)_3$

Inyo County: **1,** Irregular white inclusions (microscopic) in a polished surface of franckeite from silver ore of the Thompson mine, Darwin Mining District, are probably guanajuatite, Hall and Mac-Kevett (1) p. 17, ibid. (4) p. 61.

GÜMBELITE—Hydromuscovite

The composition is essentially the same as hydromuscovite, but the habit is fibrous instead of platy; see Aruja (1) p. 11.

San Bernardino County: **1,** Fine fibrous material from a locality between Bloomington and Jensen quarry (NE ¼ sec. 33, T. 1 S., R. 5 W., S. B.) has nearly the composition of muscovite, but is not micaceous. It is thought by Woodford (p.c. '45) to be gümbelite.

GUMMITE
Hydrous uranyl oxides

Gummite has the same relationship to well-defined secondary uranium oxides that limonite or wad have to oxides of iron or manganese. It may actually be largely one or more of the following minerals, fourmarierite, schoepite, becquerelite, clarkeite.

Kern County: **1,** Gummite is tentatively reported in quartzite float in the McKittrick-Taft area, Anon. (28) p. 2. **2,** The mineral is reported with autunite from the Buster Tom claims, 6 miles SSE of Tehachapi (sec. 8, T. 11 N., R. 14 W.), G. W. Walker et al. (5) p. 17; **3,** from the Embree property near Bodfish, but lacking positive identification, CDMG (21617), G. W. Walker et al. (5) p. 31; **4,** tentatively identified from the Jumpin claim, with autunite (secs. 9, 10, T. 9 N., R. 13 W., S. B.), 5½ miles WNW of Rosamond, G. W. Walker et al. (5) p. 15, and **5,** tentatively identified with autunite from the Rosamond prospect (SW ¼ sec. 25, T. 10 N., R. 13 W., S. B.), 10 miles S. of Mojave, as coatings in tuffaceous sedimentary rocks, G. W. Walker et al. (5) p. 15. **6,** Gummite was reportedly mined from the Miracle mine in the Kern River uranium area, MacKevett (2) p. 211. **7,** Gummite with pitchblende has been tentatively identified in quartzite at the Radiation property, Erskine Creek, Troxel and Morton (2) p. 34.

Sonoma County: **1,** Gummite has been questionably identified from Bodega Head, CDMG (21646).

GYPSUM
Hydrous calcium sulphate, $CaSO_4 \cdot 2H_2O$

Selenite, satin spar, alabaster and *gypsite* are varietal names. The granular, bedded and efflorescent deposits are the only ones of value in the state and the term "gypsite" is generally applied to the material of such deposits. Gypsum is a very common mineral. Since it is easily formed by the action of sulphate waters on limestone, small amounts of gypsum are common in mining regions where sulphides are decomposing. Larger bodies are generally bedded deposits formed by the evaporation of calcium sulphate waters. These are apt to be impure from admixtures of calcium carbonate and clay. The principal gypsum deposits of the State have been described by Hess (16) pp. 58–86, Ver Planck (2).

Gypsum is widespread in many parts of the state. Occurrences of the mineral are very numerous, but few have mineralogical significance. As a mineral resource, gypsum occurs in considerable quantity in many deposits. In the localities referenced below, no attempt has been made to systematically report commodity occurrences, nor to report the mineral wherever it is mentioned in the literature. Some localities of minor importance and of little general mineralogical interest are noted because they have been carried in early editions of *Minerals of California*. The authors consider it wise to retain these as part of the historical record, but newer and more important localities of the mineral as a mineral resource have not been added, and literature citations to articles on such localities have not necessarily been included.

Calaveras County: **1,** Platy aggregates of gypsum occur with quartz at the Utica mine, Angels Camp, A. Knopf (11) p. 37.

Fresno County: **1,** Gypsite of good quality occurs in beds 3–15 feet thick at the Paoli mine, Tumey Gulch (SW ¼ sec. 1, T. 16 S., R. 12 E., M. D.), and on adjacent lands, Hess (9) p. 9. **2,** Several deposits of gypsum are found near Coalinga (sec. 21, T. 19 S., R. 15 E., sec. 22, T. 20 S., R. 14 E., M. D.), ibid., p. 9. **3,** Satin spar has been found at the San Joaquin coal mine (sec. 26, T. 20 S., R. 14 E., M. D.), W. W. Bradley (2) p. 452. **4,** Gypsum encrusts nodules containing apatized wood in the Moreno formation, head of Escapardo Canyon (NW ¼ sec. 7, T. 15 S., R. 12 E., M. D.), Gulbrandson et al. (1) p. 101.

Imperial County: **1,** An extensive deposit of good quality gypsum, some of it in large cleavage plates, occurs with associated celestite, in the Fish Creek Mountains (T. 13 S., R. 8, 9 E., S. B.), Tucker (11) p. 271. The stratigraphic position of these layers has been determined by J. W. Durham and Allison (1) p. 22. **2,** Another extensive deposit occurs 3 miles northwest of Coyote Wells, Tucker (4) p. 267. Emory (1) p. 103, noted gypsum and mica crystals on the approaches to Carizzo Gorge, which may be near this deposit.

Inyo County: **1,** Several beds of pure white gypsum, 6 to 10 feet thick, are reported from China (Morrison) Ranch one mile northeast of Acme Station on the now abandoned Tonopah and Tidewater Railroad, Hess (16) p. 63. **2,** Six-inch veins of transparent selenite have been found in the Upper Canyon Bed niter deposits, G. E. Bailey (2) p. 172. **3,** Small crystals of gypsum are associated with glauberite and halite in the muds at Pluto Springs in the bottom of Death Valley, Webb (p. c. '45). **4,** Gypsum, in thin layers in shale, occurs in the Funeral Peak area, Drewes (1) p. 35.

Kern County: **1,** Gypsite has been found in extensive deposits at a number of localities on the west side of the San Joaquin Valley (T. 25, 26, 30, 32 S., R. 18, 22, 23, 24 E., M. D.), Hess (16) pp. 64, 65, Fairbanks (20) p. 123. **2,** Beds up to 10 feet thick are found southeast of Cane (Koehn) Springs (sec. 28, T. 30 S., R. 38 E., M. D.), Hess (16) p. 73. **3,** Good gypsum crystals have been found at the San Emigdio mine, W. P. Blake (5) p. 308. Two principal deposits of rock gypsum are: **4,** near Bitterwater Creek, and **5,** Cuddy Canyon west of Lebec, Troxel and Morton (2) pp. 198–208.

Lake County: **1,** Gypsum is abundant in efflorescences at Sulphur Bank, D. E. White and Robertson (2) p. 407.

Los Angeles County: **1,** Loose, well-formed crystals in sand and clay have been found half a mile from the shore, north of Sunset Boulevard, Murdoch (p.c. '45).

Mono County: **1,** Selenite crystals are occasionally found in the tubes of tufa at Mono Lake, I. C. Russell (1) p. 311.

Napa County: **1,** Good crystals of gypsum have been found in the Palisades mine, 2 miles north of Calistoga, Hulin (p.c. '36).

Nevada County: **1,** Gypsum in stellate radial groups up to 3 inches in diameter was found near Truckee Pass, Hanks (12) p. 226.

Riverside County: **1,** Good crystals of gypsum can be found in tunnels in Gypsum Canyon, 2 miles south of Corona, Hess (16) p. 77. **2,** Extensive deposits of gypsum associated with anhydrite occur at the Midland mine of the U.S. Gypsum Company, in the Little Maria Mountains, Ian Campbell (p.c. '36). **3,** Another large deposit of gypsum is 3 miles north of Packards Well, at the north end of Palen Mountains, F. J. H. Merrill (2) p. 579. **4,** Thick beds of gypsum occur in the Maria Mountains (T. 3, 4 S., R. 21 E., S. B.), F. J. H. Merrill (2) p. 577. **5,** Gypsum is reported as selenite from the Lone Star quarry at Crestmore, Woodford et al. (10) p. 368.

San Bernardino County: **1,** Crystals and cleavage slabs of selenite occur in veins in the borate beds of the Calico Hills, G. E. Bailey (2) p. 58, Hamilton (3) p. 352. **2,** Massive gypsum occurs (secs. 15, 22, etc., T. 18 N., R. 5 E., S. B.), in the Avawatz Mountains, Hess (16) p. 82. **3,** Extensive beds interstratified with salt are present in the Avawatz Mountains, Cloudman et al. (1) p. 869. **4,** Gypsum is one of the minor minerals at Searles Lake, H. S. Gale (13) p. 297; **5,** it occurs in Amboy sink at Bristol playa, H. S. Gale, (17) p. 5.

Santa Barbara County: **1,** Alabaster occurs on a branch of Santa Barbara Creek (SE¼ sec. 34, T. 9 N., R. 25 W., S. B.), Hess (16) p. 84. **2,** Crystals are reported from Santa Rosa Island, CDMG (12313). **3,** Large quantities of gypsum are found at Point Sal, Fairbanks (14) p. 16. **4,** Fishtail gypsum twins occur in clay shale of the Rincon formation, northward from the contact with the Vaqueros, approximately one mile north of Drake (Radio Tower) on the Hollister Ranch west of Gaviota Pass, in Cañada del Coyote. The crystals are well-formed individuals up to 3 inches in length. The locality was reported by Mr. Jerry McKey, Webb (p.c. '64).

Siskiyou County: **1,** Abundant gypsum crystals are found with crystallized sulphur at a spring at the summit of Mount Shasta, H. Williams (2) p. 240.

Ventura County: **1,** Massive gypsum is interbedded with diatomaceous shale 4 miles south of Fillmore (sec. 12, T. 3 N., R. 20 W., S. B.), Huguenin (2) p. 761. **2,** A 40-foot bed of pure gypsum is reported at French Point Hill, in the Cuyama Valley, Angel (2) p. 599. **3,** Selenite and massive gypsum are found at the Russell borax mine, north of Lockwood Valley, H. S. Gale (11) p. 446.

Occurrences of no particular commercial or mineralogic interest have been reported from the following counties: *Butte,* CDMG (7235); *Kings,* Hess (9) p. 14; *Los Angeles,* Hess (16) p. 75, E. C. Simpson (1) p. 412; *Merced,* Watts (1) p. 331; *Orange,* CDMG (12216); *San Benito,* Fairbanks (20) p. 120, W. W. Bradley and Logan (7) p. 639; *San Bernardino,* Hess (16) p. 81, Tucker and Sampson (17) p. 382; *San Francisco,* Eakle (1) p. 316; *San Joaquin,* CDMG (13885); *San Luis Obispo,* Hanks (12) p. 226, Crawford (1) p. 325; *Solano,* J. D. Dana (2) p. 656; *Stanislaus,* Hanks (12) p. 266; *Tulare,* Hanks (12) p. 226.

GYROLITE
Basic hydrous calcium silicate, $Ca_2Si_3O_7(OH)_2 \cdot H_2O$

Gyrolite is formed as a secondary mineral in crevices of rocks by the alteration of lime silicates.

San Francisco County: **1,** Gyrolite was found with apophyllite as spherical or massive, platy or plumose aggregates replacing wall rock in fissures of basalt at Fort Point, San Francisco, Schaller (8) p. 124.

Santa Clara County: **1,** A fibrous layer of gyrolite 1 to 3 cm thick was found associated with apophyllite and bitumen in veins at the New Almaden mine, F. W. Clarke (4) p. 128, E. H. Bailey and Everhart (12) p. 102.

* HAIWEEITE, 1959
Hydrous calcium uranyl silicate, $CaU_2Si_6O_{17} \cdot 5H_2O$

Inyo County: **1,** Haiweeite is described as a new mineral from the Coso Mts., near the Haiwee Reservoir, as spherulitic aggregates on fracture surfaces in granite, McBurney and Murdoch (1) p. 839, CDMG (21739).

HALITE—Common or Rock Salt
Sodium chloride, NaCl

Most of the salt produced in the State is obtained by the evaporation of the water of San Francisco Bay; also at San Diego and Monterey Bays. Extensive deposits of the mineral exist in the southern counties and some of them are mined. Salt is common in the desert regions, where former lakes existed and the deposits reach considerable thickness in some localities, often alternating with beds of sulphates, borates, carbonates and shales. Salt wells, salt springs, salt marshes and salt rivers occur in these arid plains, and white incrustations of salt are often found along their borders.

Almost all of the desert playas in Imperial, Inyo, Kern, Riverside, San Bernardino and San Luis Obispo Counties have incrustations, or sometimes considerable layers, of halite in the dry season. G. E. Bailey (2) pp. 110–134, records in detail many of these occurrences. A comprehensive discussion of all phases of salt (history, occurrence, mining, purification) is contained in Ver Planck (4).

Alpine County: **1,** Hopper-shaped crystals of halite have been found around pools, and in glacial potholes, at Hams Salt Springs, on the north fork of the Mokelumne River, H. W. Turner (1a) p. 453.

Inyo County: **1,** Cubes of halite up to one inch have been collected, as individuals and aggregates, from Pluto Springs salt pools on the floor of Death Valley, Webb (p.c. '28).

Lake County: **1,** Slender square prismatic crystals of halite were found at Borax Lake, Vonsen (3) p. 25.

San Bernardino County: **1,** Octahedral crystals of halite have been found at Searles Lake, where the main beds are solid halite, H. S. Gale (13) p. 298, G. I. Smith and Haines (3) p. 14. **2,** Extensive beds of rock salt occur on the north flank of the Avawatz Mountains, G. E. Bailey (2) p. 126, Phalen (3) p. 526. **3,** Large quantities of salt have been produced from Danby Dry Lake, G. E. Bailey (2) p. 128; **4,** from Amboy sink, Bristol playa, southeast of Amboy, Tucker (4) p. 357, H. S. Gale (17) p. 6.

HALLOYSITE
Hydrous aluminum silicate, $Al_2Si_2O_7 \cdot 4H_2O$

Clay and clay-like minerals such as bauxite, gibbsite, halloysite, montmorillonite, and others are widespread in many localities. Often, identification has been by field examination. This is especially true in early reported occurrences. Accordingly, few occurrences are included in the listings, some chosen for historic reasons, and some for mineralogic reasons. It is impractical to include all localities, especially since many important areas produce mineral commodities, and are not strictly mineral occurrences. Many reports may also in fact be in error as far as specific mineral identification is concerned. X-ray and optical examination is required for certain identification of most clay minerals.

Imperial County: **1,** Halloysite has been recorded in association with realgar and claudetite 6 miles north of the 4S Ranch, $1\frac{1}{2}$ miles west of the Colorado River, Kelley (1) p. 137.

Inyo County: **1,** Banded white and brown, and massive white, halloysite has been found at the Cerro Gordo mine, A. F. Rogers (7) p. 381, A. Knopf (8) p. 115.

Mono County: **1,** Halloysite from the Detroit copper mine near Mono Lake has been analyzed, F. W. Clarke and Chatard (1) p. 23, (2) p. 12.

San Diego: **1,** The so-called "pay streak" of pink clay in the pegmatite mines at Pala is halloysite, Schaller (3) p. 191. It occurs in large seams several inches thick and many feet in length.

HALOTRICHITE—Iron Alum
Hydrous aluminum iron sulphate, $Fe^{2+}Al_2(SO_4)_4 \cdot 24H_2O$

Alpine County: **1,** Halotrichite is found as incrustations and thin seams at the Leviathan sulphur mine, Gary (1) p. 488, Nichols (1) p. 172.

Alameda County: **1,** Halotrichite occurs as fibrous masses in the Eureka tunnel near Livermore (N. R.).

Contra Costa County: **1,** Halotrichite is found at the Diablo mine ($SE\frac{1}{4}$ sec. 29, T. 1 N., R. 1 E., M. D.), C. P. Ross (2) p. 42, Pampeyan (1) p. 24.

El Dorado County: **1,** The occurrence of halotrichite is reported by gift of specimen, CDMG (21343).

Los Angeles County: **1,** Halotrichite occurs with melanterite in altered boulders of a conglomerate, in a road cut on Cahuenga Peak ($S\frac{1}{2}$ $SW\frac{1}{4}$ sec. 25, T. 1 N., R. 14 W., S. B.), Neuerburg (1) p. 159.

Mono County: **1,** Halotrichite occurs with pyrophyllite at the Pacific Coast pyrophyllite mine, one mile north and 7 miles east of Mocalno, north of Bishop, at the west base of the White Mountains, Baur and Sand (1) p. 678, with analysis.

San Bernardino County: **1,** Halotrichite is found with other sulphates in the "sulphur hole" close to the borax mines, Calico Range, Foshag (19) p. 352.

Shasta County: **1,** Halotrichite is found as incrustations around springs on Lassen Peak, A. L. Day and Allen (1) p. 118.

Sonoma County: **1,** Halotrichite, reportedly rich in nickel, occurs sparingly at The Geysers, Vonsen (6) p. 290.

Trinity County: **1,** Halotrichite occurs in tufts at the Island Mountain pyrrhotite mass, Vonsen (p.c. '44).

HAMBERGITE
A basic beryllium borate, $Be_2(OH)BO_3$

San Diego County: **1,** This is the first reported occurrence of this rare beryllium mineral in the United States. Hambergite is reported from the workings of the Little Three mine near Ramona, and was discovered by Captain J. Sinkankas, U.S.N. The mine is owned by Louis B. Spaulding, who screened the dump after the discovery, and recovered some crystals. The crystals come from a pocket and range in size from slivers up to 2 inches, Anon. (36) p. 5. A new analysis of hambergite from the Little Three mine shows up to 6% fluorine, Switzer et al. (10) p. 1987, CDMG (21706). **2,** A second occurrence of this rare mineral at the Himalaya mine near Mesa Grande is reported by Switzer et al. (10) p. 1987.

* HANKSITE, 1884
Carbonate, sulphate and chloride of sodium and potassium, $Na_{22}K(SO_4)_9(CO_3)_2Cl$

Inyo County: **1,** Hanksite is reported from the borax fields of Death Valley by Hanks (17) p. 63.

Mono County: **1,** Hanksite in minute crystals has been found associated with trona on crusted deposits in salt pools on the east side of Mono Lake, Murdoch (26) p. 358.

San Bernardino County: **1,** Hanksite, the third most abundant mineral in the Searles Lake saline layers, was discovered in 1884, Hidden (1) pp. 230–241, with an analysis by MacKintosh, Hanks (17) p. 63. Another analysis was made by E. S. Dana and Penfield (2) p. 136, and again by J. H. Pratt (1) p. 133. Hanksite in euhedral crystals occurs chiefly in the upper salt in beds up to 5' thick and their varied habits are described by G. I. Smith and Haines (3) p. 17. The mineral is strongly luminescent, Melhase (4) p. 4; see also G. I. Smith and Pratt (2) p. 26.

San Luis Obispo County: **1,** Knowlton (p.c. '57) reports hanksite crystals showing the prism and pyramid, from Soda Lake.

HAUSMANNITE
Manganese oxide, Mn_3O_4

Manganese minerals like bementite, braunite, hausmannite, inesite, manganite, neotocite, psilomelane, pyrolusite, wad, and others are often not separable by field methods. It is apparent to the authors of this volume that many citations in the literature, especially those prior to 1940, may be incorrect identifications. Abundance of manganese minerals in the State in hundreds of localities makes systematic recording of all localities mentioned in the literature impractical. The following listings therefore may be incomplete, and many that are included are important only to reflect adequately the historic record.

Mariposa County: **1,** Hausmannite occurs with tephroite and bementite at the Caldwell (Daly) mine (NE¼ sec. 14, T. 3 S., R. 15 E., M. D.), Hewett et al. (6) p. 51.

Nevada County: **1,** Hausmannite occurs with tephroite at the Manga-Chrome (Duggan) mine (sec. 17, T. 14 N., R. 8 E., M. D.), Hewett et al. (6) p. 47, and **2,** at the Smith prospect (center sec. 2, T. 14 N., R. 8 E., M. D.), Hewett et al (6) p. 48.

Placer County: **1,** Hausmannite has been reported near Auburn, Fairbanks (1) p. 47.

Plumas County: **1,** Specimens of hausmannite have come from Meadow Valley, Miser and Fairchild (1) p. 6.

San Joaquin County: **1,** Hausmannite was found at the old Ladd mine, with bementite, W. W. Bradley (32) p. 98.

San Luis Obispo County: **1,** Hausmannite occurs as an alteration product of older manganese minerals at the Staneuch Ranch, Prefumo Canyon (sec. 6, T. 31 S., R. 12 E., M. D.), P. D. Trask et al. (4) p. 86. **2,** Hausmannite is abundant in the ore of the Noble Electric Company deposit, associated with barite and native copper, Taliaferro and Hudson (3) p. 269.

Santa Clara County: **1,** Hausmannite was abundant as crystals and subhedral grains in the manganese boulder at Alum Rock Park, A. F. Rogers (21) p. 444.

Stanislaus County: **1,** Hausmannite occurs with bementite and other manganese minerals at the Buckeye mine (secs. 2, 3, T. 5 S., R. 5 E., M. D.), P. D. Trask et al. (4) p. 59.

Trinity County: **1,** Hausmannite makes up 40–50 percent of the ore at the Blue Jay mine (NW$\frac{1}{4}$ sec. 17, T. 26 N., R. 12 W., M. D.), and occurs in neighboring mines in the Mad River area, P. D. Trask et al. (4) p. 59. **2,** Hausmannite occurs with tephroite at the Lucky Bill (Old Bill) prospect (sec. 9, T. 28 N., R. 11 W., M. D.), Hewett et al. (6) p. 45.

HAWLEYITE
Cadmium sulphide, CdS

Riverside County: **1,** An orange coating on fracture surfaces of specimens from the North Star dump, has been shown to be hawleyite instead of greenockite, A. B. Carpenter (p.c. '62).

HELVITE
A silicate of beryllium manganese iron and zinc with sulphur,
$(Mn,Fe,Zn)_8Be_6Si_6O_{24} \cdot S_2$

San Diego County: **1,** The first discovery of this rare mineral in the State is recorded from the Clark vein at Rincon, where it occurs in petalite-spodumene rock in small yellow grains and imperfect crystals, Murdoch (18) p. 198. **2,** Helvite is reported as very rare minute honey-colored tetrahedra in the Gem Star and Caterina mines, Pala, Jahns and Wright (5) p. 31.

HEMATITE—Red Ocher
Iron oxide, Fe_2O_3

Hematite forms the universal red coloring matter of rocks. It is commonly fine-grained, but occasionally occurs as flaky crystalline *specular hematite or specularite*. Much more rarely it may be in larger, well-formed crystals. Many of the magnetite ores in the state are partially changed to *martite*, a pseudomorph of hematite after magnetite. Many low-grade ''red ocher'' deposits of hematite in the state have been mined for pigment rather than for iron. It is possible to list only the more important occurrences of this mineral. H. Wilson (1) in Bulletin 370 of the U. S. Bureau of Mines, gives a good summary of the iron pigment ores of California.

Fresno County: **1,** A large vein of hematite and magnetite is found at the Magnetic and other mines in the Minaret Mountains, Goldstone (1) p. 191.

Humboldt County: **1,** A large quantity of hematite boulders, derived from several large veins, occur on the ocean beach 4 miles south of Centerville, Lowell (1) p. 408. Laizure (3) p. 295, describes what appears to be this deposit. Ogle (1) p. 79, was unable to verify the occurrence, although a large isolated fragment of altered volcanic rock that is probably limonite not hematite, was found at the locality.

Imperial County: **1,** Shiny, mirror-like plates of hematite are found in several veins in the Cargo Muchacho Mining District, Henshaw (1) p. 185.

Inyo County: **1,** Specular hematite occurs in considerable amount at the Roper iron mine 7 miles east of Kearsarge Station, Tucker (11) p. 475. **2,** A considerable body of hematite is reported 5 miles south of Shepherd Canyon, almost on the edge of Panamint Valley, Crawford (1) p. 326. **3,** Hematite of high grade occurs in the Millspaugh iron deposit, Argus Mountains (T. 22 S., R. 42 E., M.D.), Tucker (36) p. 319. Localities **(2)** and **(3)** may be identical. **4,** Specular hematite occurs in the Talc City Hills, six miles north of Darwin, Hall and MacKevett (4) p. 76.

Kern County: **1,** Specular hematite is found at Mount Breckenridge (sec. 4, T. 29 S., R. 31 E., M. D.), G. C. Brown (1) p. 516.

Lake County: **1,** Pseudomorphs of hematite after marcasite have been found at the Baker mine, 6 miles from Lower Lake, A. F. Rogers (3) p. 18.

Lassen County: **1,** An extensive deposit of hematite is reported 5 miles south of Susanville, J. C. O'Brien (1) p. 79. **2,** Micaceous hematite is found at Mountain Meadows, CDMG (13680).

Mono County: **1,** Specular hematite is locally abundant in the andalusite mine of Champion Sillimanite, A. Knopf (7) p. 551. **2,** The "red vein" in the Bodie mine was so called because of the bright red color produced by hematite, Whiting (1) p. 385. **3,** A contact metamorphic deposit occurs with magnetite northeast of the Black Rock mine, Casa Diablo Mt. quadrangle, Rinehart and Ross (1) p. 17.

Placer County: **1,** An important deposit of hematite, associated with magnetite, occurs at the Hotaling mine, 3½ miles west of Clipper Gap, Logan (4) p. 452.

Plumas County: Massive and specular hematite occurs in moderate abundance at several localities: **1,** Crescent Mills, **2,** Mumfords Hill, **3,** Lights Canyon, Hanks (12) p. 229; **4,** with magnetite near the Diadem Lode, E. MacBoyle (2) p. 12, and **5,** a large vein with magnetite near Moonlight, 11 miles north of Taylorsville, ibid., p. 36.

Riverside County: **1,** Considerable hematite has been formed by alteration of magnetite at Eagle Mountain (T. 4 S., R. 14 E., S. B.), Harder (6) p. 63, Powell (1) p. 481. **2,** Specular hematite with epidote is found in the Monte Negro Mining District, Storms (4) p. 369. **3,**

Hematite occurs as an alteration of chalcopyrite in the Lone Star quarry at Crestmore, Woodford et al. (10) p. 368.

San Bernardino County: **1**, At the Iron Age deposit, 6 miles east of Dale (sec. 29, T. 1 S., R. 13 E., S. B.), extensive deposits of hematite and magnetite occur, Harder and Rich (4) p. 237. **2**, Hematite-magnetite deposits, some of them rather sizeable, are found in the Kingston Mountains (T. 19 N., R. 11 E., S. B.), Tucker and Sampson (17) p. 335; **3**, at Iron Mountain (sec. 27, T. 6 N., R. 4 E., S. B.), Cloudman et al. (1) p. 819, and **4**, Cave Canyon (sec. 12, T. 11 N., R. 7 E., S. B.), ibid., p. 818. **5**, Soft hematite occurs near Kelso (T. 10 N., R. 13 E., S. B.), C. C. Jones (2) p. 1889, Lamey (5) p. 87. **6**, Massive hematite occurs at the Tiefort Mountains deposit (sec. 22 ?, T. 14 N., R. 4 E., S. B.), Tucker (36) p. 319. **7**, Hematite is found with magnetite in the Old Dad Mountains (secs. 13, 14 ?, T. 12 N., R. 10 E., S. B.), Lamey (3) p. 61. **8**, Hematite and magnetite occur in the Iron Mountain and Iron King deposits near Silver Lake (T. 15 N., R. 6, 7 E., S. B.), Lamey (2) p. 39. **9**, Hematite occurs with magnetite in the Iron Hat deposit (T. 6 N., R. 14 E., S. B.), Lamey (6) p. 99. **10**, Hematite is found in the Ship Mountains deposit (T. 5 N., R. 15 E., S. B.), Lamey (7) p. 113. **11**, Crystals and rosettes of specular hematite occur in metamorphic rocks at the Verde Antique quarry 15 miles northeast of Victorville; **12**, at Globerson Iron mine, 7 miles southeast of Hodge, and **13**, about 3 miles north of Barstow, found with yellow serpentine, epidote, green garnet and actinolite, O. E. Bowen (1) pp. 134, 135, 148. **14**, Hematite occurs in crystalline rosettes in the Marble Mountains south of Cadiz, M. F. B. Strong (3) p. 21.

San Luis Obispo County: **1**, An extensive deposit of hematite is found at the Harrington iron mine (T. 31 S., R. 11 E., M. D.), Franke (2) p. 423.

Shasta County: **1**, The Iron Mountain mine supplied a considerable amount of hematite to the smelter at Heroult, Hanks (12) p. 229.

Sierra County: **1**, Pure and abundant specular hematite was reported from Four Hills, 10 miles northeast of Downieville, J. R. Browne (4) p. 222.

Sonoma County: **1**, A large body of hematite was reported from the Hooper Ranch, 5 miles north of Nobles, near the west fork of the Gualala River, W. W. Bradley (1) p. 322.

HEMIMORPHITE—Calamine

Basic hydrous zinc silicate, $Zn_4Si_2O_7(OH)_2 \cdot H_2O$

Inyo County: **1**, A little hemimorphite has been found with willemite and smithsonite at the Ygnacio mine, Cerro Gordo, CDMG (8587), Siebenthal (1) p. 922. **2**, Hemimorphite occurs as colorless crusts with occasional crystals, at the Defiance mine, and in radial groups of crystals at the Christmas Gift mine, Darwin Mining District, A. Knopf (4) p. 12, Murdoch and Webb (14) p. 324, Hall and MacKevett (4) p. 64. **3**, Fine radial groups up to half an inch in diameter occur with wulfenite and chrysocolla from the Reward mine, 2 miles east of Manzanar Station, A. Knopf (5) p. 118. **4**, Hemimorphite occurs widely and in good crystals up to 5 mm and in coarse-grained aggregates in cavities in the Ubehebe mine, McAllister (4) p. 27. **5**, The mineral also occurs in the Lippincott mine, ibid., p. 39. **6,** Hemimorphite is found in the Big Four mine, northeast of Panamint Springs, Hall and Stephens (3) p. 36. **7,** The mineral is found in the ores of the Santa Rosa mine, Inyo Mountains, Hall and MacKevett (4) p. 64.

Kern County: **1,** A specimen (1231) in the University of California Collections at Berkeley is from the Jewett mine. **2,** The Blackhawk mine, near Loraine, has yielded some hemimorphite, Troxel and Morton (2) p. 41.

Riverside County: **1,** Abundant prismatic crystals of hemimorphite lining cavities, and accompanying massive material, has been found associated with smithsonite in sphalerite and galena-rich boulders on the old dump from the Lone Star quarry, Crestmore, Jenni (p.c. '57).

San Bernardino County: **1,** Hemimorphite is associated with smithsonite at the Cuticura mine, CDMG (11534). **2,** Crusts and radiating clusters of slender crystals of hemimorphite are found in cavities of barite at the Lead Mountain mine, Murdoch and Webb (14) p. 327. **3,** Hemimorphite is reported from ''Calico,'' E. S. Dana (5) p. 1097, but this may be questionable. **4,** Hemimorphite occurs with hydrozincite at the Carbonate mine (sec. 32, T. 15, 16 N., R. 14 E., S. B.), Tucker and Sampson (33) p. 128, Wiebelt (1) p. 1.

HESSITE
Silver telluride, Ag_2Te

Hessite generally contains gold and often grades into petzite, so the two tellurides are apt to be together in mines. They occur in most mines where gold tellurides are found, often associated with sylvanite or calaverite.

Calaveras County: **1,** Hessite was found with melonite and native tellurium at the Stanislaus mine on Carson Hill, Genth (5) p. 311, Logan (16) p. 133. **2,** Hessite, carrying some gold, occurs in the Ford mine half a mile east of San Andreas, A. Knopf (11) p. 39.

El Dorado County: **1,** One float specimen of hessite was found in 1854 near Georgetown, W. P. Blake (6) p. 270, (7) p. 302, Hanks (12) p. 229. Another was found 5 years later with native gold and galena, W. P. Blake (6) p. 270. **2,** Hessite was reported to occur in the Barnes Eureka mine, 3 miles northeast of Shingle Springs (N. R.).

Mono County: **1,** Hessite was found in the upper workings of the Silverado mine, Patterson Mining District, in the Sweetwater Range, Gianella (p.c. '37).

Nevada County: **1,** A specimen of soft gray hessite, with gold and sulphides, has come from the Nevada City mine, Lindgren (12) p. 117. **2,** Small specks of hessite associated with petzite and naumannite were found in the Idaho-Maryland mine, C. F. Tolman (p.c. '36).

Shasta County: **1,** Hessite was found in the Shearer and Rattler mine, 3 miles from Redding, Irelan (4) p. 47.

Siskiyou County: **1,** A specimen of hessite in gold ore has come from the Scott Bar mine, 3 miles from the mouth of Scott River, CDMG (10637).

Tuolumne County: **1,** Very small crystals of hessite were found in the Reist mine, Whiskey Hill, Silliman (9) p. 9, Schrader et al. (1)

p. 60, and **2**, it occurred in the Bonanza and Jumper mines near James-town, CDMG (13617). **3**, Hessite was associated with petzite and coloradoite in the Norwegian mine, Hillebrand (3) p. 62.

HEULANDITE

Hydrous calcium sodium aluminum silicate, $(Ca,Na_2)[Al_2Si_7O_{18}]\cdot 6H_2O$

Heulandite is a zeolite usually formed as a secondary mineral in cavities and seams of basic volcanic rock, with stilbite, chabazite and other zeolites.

Kern County: **1**, Heulandite occurs sparingly in amygdules in lava at Red Rock Canyon, associated with natrolite and analcite, Murdoch (p.c. '52).

Los Angeles County: **1**, Heulandite occurs with natrolite in vesicular basalts west of Cahuenga Pass, near Mulholland highway, Funk (1) p. 34. **2**, Neuerburg (1) p. 158, describes locality 9 where the mineral occurs with ptilolite in "pillow" basalt. **3**, Colorless crystals of heulandite in veins and cavities in basalt were found a quarter of a mile west of Acton, Murdoch and Webb (6) p. 352.

Madera County: **1**, Colorless plates of heulandite up to 2 mm across, associated with quartz, calcite and stilbite, occur in piemontite-bearing metavolcanic rock about 0.1 mile northeast of Shadow Lake, Alfors (p.c. '64).

Plumas County: **1**, Abundant heulandite replacing feldspar was found at the Engels mine, Graton and McLaughlin (4) p. 18.

San Bernardino County: **1**, Heulandite, as reported in Supplement 2 to *Minerals of California* for 1958–1961 from Amboy Crater, is in error.

San Diego County: **1**, Heulandite occurs sparingly as pale-brown crystals with stilbite, A. F. Rogers (4) p. 214, and rather abundantly replacing spodumene, associated with petalite, Murdoch (18) p. 198, both in the Rincon area. **2**, Heulandite occurs in buff-colored tabular crystals at Pala, in the gem pegmatites, Jahns and Wright (5) p. 42.

HILLEBRANDITE

Basic calcium silicate, $Ca_2SiO_3(OH)_2$

Riverside County: **1**, The original occurrence of hillebrandite was described as synonymous with foshagite. It is now known that the two names describe separate and distinct minerals, though they are inti-mately associated in the Crestmore limestone quarry, in irregular masses or veins of fibrous material, Eakle (23) p. 97, Vigfussen (1) p. 76, Woodford (11) p. 357. X-ray methods show hillebrandite to be distinct from foshagite and xonotlite, Heller and Taylor (1) p. 59.

HISINGERITE

A hydrated ferric silicate of doubtful composition, perhaps not a definite mineral

Sonoma County: **1**, Thin brown colloform crusts of hisingerite coat-ing tridymite have been found in vesicles of augite andesite ($NE\frac{1}{4}$ sec. 10, T. 7 N., R. 7 W., M. D.), Rose (p.c. '50).

HOHMANNITE
Basic hydrous iron sulphate, $Fe^{3+}SO_4OH \cdot 3\frac{1}{2}H_2O$

Ungemach (2) p. 115, shows that *castanite* is the same as hohmannite.

Napa County: **1,** Crystals of hohmannite, identified as castanite in brecciated opalite, have been described by A. F. Rogers (35) p. 396, from the Redington (Boston) quicksilver mine at Knoxville. This occurrence is reported also by Bandy (1) p. 534.

HOMILITE
Calcium iron borosilicate, $(Ca,Fe)_3B_2Si_2O_{10}$

A specimen of homilite from California (loc. uncited) was identified in 1957 by CDMG laboratory, O. P. Jenkins (4) p. 50.

* HOWIEITE, 1964
A complex silicate with iron, aluminum, sodium, calcium, titanium and manganese, near $(Na_{1.03}Ca_{.02})_{1.05}(Mg_{.45}Mn_{2.98}Fe''_{6.41})_{9.84}(Fe'''_{1.57}Al_{.62})_{2.19}$ $(Si_{11.96}Ti_{.40})_{12}O_{31}(OH)_{12.69}$

Mendocino County: **1,** Howieite occurs as a new and important mineral in Franciscan rocks near Laytonville, Agrell (1) p. 49. No description is yet available.

HOWLITE
Basic calcium borosilicate, $Ca_2B_5SiO_9(OH)_5$

Howlite is an associate of other borates, but owing to the silica present it is not utilized, although it contains a large amount of boric oxide. It has been mistaken for pandermite at several borate localities in California.

Inyo County: **1,** White micaceous masses of howlite have been found in Gower Gulch near Ryan, E. S. Larsen (11) p. 87.

Kern County: **1,** A small nodular mass of howlite was found on the 955' level of the Western borax mine at Kramer, H. S. Gale (16) p. 332.

Los Angeles County: **1,** Cauliflower-like masses of howlite are abundant in the colemanite deposit in Tick Canyon, Eakle (10) p. 187, Foshag (7) p. 204, Armstrong and Van Amringe (1). Microscopic crystals of howlite were recently found at the old Sterling borax mine, Tick Canyon, permitting determination of crystal data for this usually massive mineral, Murdoch (33) p. 521.

San Bernardino County: **1,** Howlite occurs in chalky white seams and nodules in the borate beds at Calico, and occasionally as delicate thin platy crystals encrusting celestite crystals, Giles (2) p. 353, Foshag (9) p. 208.

Ventura County: **1,** Masses of howlite, originally assumed to be priceite (pandermite) were found abundantly at the Russell and other borax mines north of Lockwood Valley, H. S. Gale (11) p. 442, Murdoch (p.c. '45).

HUNTITE
Magnesium calcium carbonate, $Mg_3Ca(CO_3)_4$

Riverside County: **1,** Huntite is noted as in incrustation on monticellite rock from Crestmore, A. B. Carpenter (1) p. 22A, p. 146.

HURÉAULITE
Hydrous manganese phosphate, $Mn_5H_2(PO_4)_4 \cdot 4H_2O$

San Diego County: **1,** Huréaulite is found at the Stewart mine, Pala, associated with lithiophilite and other phosphates, Schaller (29) p. 145. Minute, well-developed crystals from this locality were described by Murdoch (16) p. 19. Palaite and pseudopalaite are now considered to be identical with huréaulite, B. H. Mason (2) pp. 168, 175. Material from the Stewart mine has been studied by Fisher (2) p. 402.

HYDROBORACITE
Hydrous calcium magnesium borate, $CaMgB_6O_{11} \cdot 6H_2O$

Inyo County: **1,** Prismatic or needle-like crystals have been found near Ryan, in the Mount Blanco area of Death Valley, Foshag (10) p. 9; the crystals were measured by Schaller (43) p. 256.

Kern County: **1,** Hydroboracite from "the pit" at Boron occurs sparingly as fibrous crystalline masses, H. E. Pemberton et al. (1) p. 29.

Ventura County: **1,** Hydroboracite was reported in 1899 from the Frazier borax mine, CDMG (15347), (15446).

HYDROMAGNESITE
Basic hydrous magnesium carbonate, $Mg_5(CO_3)_4(OH)_2 \cdot 4H_2O$

Hydromagnesite is formed by the alteration of serpentine and other magnesian rocks.

Hydromagnesite and magnesite are widespread in many parts of the state. Occurrences are very numerous, but few have mineralogical significance. As a mineral resource, hydromagnesite occurs in considerable quantity in many deposits. In the localities referenced below, no attempt has been made to systematically report commodity occurrences, nor to report the mineral wherever it is mentioned in the literature. Some localities of minor importance and of little general mineralogical interest are noted because they have been carried in early editions of *Minerals of California.* The authors consider it wise to retain these as part of the historical record, but newer and more important localities of the mineral as a mineral resource have not been added, and literature citations to articles on such localities have not necessarily been included. It is emphasized that validation of correct mineral identification in the literature has not been undertaken, so early identifications may be incorrect.

Alameda County: **1,** Narrow veins in serpentine, at the south slope of Sugarloaf Butte, show minute crystals of hydromagnesite, Kramm (1) p. 344, A. F. Rogers (24) p. 38. **2,** Seams of hydromagnesite in serpentine, with calcite and aragonite, occur at Arroyo Mocho, 20 miles southeast of Livermore, A. F. Rogers (24) p. 46. **3,** Considerable hydromagnesite occurs at the Devil's Hole (sec. 3, T. 5 S., R. 3 E., M.D.), Dolbear (8) p. 238. **4,** Massive white hydromagnesite has been reported near Pleasanton, CDMG (8217).

Colusa County: **1,** Hydromagnesite occurs abundantly at Sulphur Creek, as a chalk-like alteration product of serpentine, Kramm (1) p.

344, A. F. Rogers (24) p. 47, and **2**, it occurs with thomsonite and datolite near Wilbur Springs, Pabst (p.c. '45).

Fresno County: **1**, Minute crystals of hydromagnesite occur in seams of serpentine east of Condon Peak, Watters (p.c. '51).

Inyo County: **1**, Hydromagnesite was reported as chalky or mealy crusts along the Amargosa River, G. E. Bailey (2) p. 102.

Marin County: **1**, Hydromagnesite is found at Bolinas (T. 1 N., R. 8 W., M.D.), CDMG (15763).

Merced County: **1**, A specimen of hydromagnesite in the Stanford University Collections came from the Bald Eagle mine, near Gustine.

Napa County: **1**, Hydromagnesite mixed with quartz is reported from Phillips Springs, E. S. Larsen (3) p. 3.

Riverside County: **1**, Hydromagnesite occurs as an alteration of brucite in the predazzite rock of the Wet Weather quarry at Crestmore, A. F. Rogers (19) p. 583, (31) p. 466. Measurable crystals have been found at Crestmore and x-ray determination of the unit cell was made by Murdoch (24) p. 1465, (29) p. 24. **2**, Hydromagnesite occurs with periclase and brucite in the crystalline limestone of the Jensen quarry, MacKevett (1) p. 6.

San Benito County: **1**, Hydromagnesite occurs in powdery white balls on Larious Creek, on the slope of Sampson Peak (W$\frac{1}{2}$ sec. 35, T. 17 S., R. 11 E., M.D.), H. S. Gale (12) p. 508; **2**, it was reported by J. D. Whitney (7) p. 59, between the San Carlos and New Idria mines, and **3**, minute crystals have been found in seams in serpentine near the benitoite locality, A. F. Rogers (24) p. 46.

San Bernardino County: **1**, Hydromagnesite altered from brucite is reported from Lucerne Valley (SE$\frac{1}{4}$ SE$\frac{1}{4}$ sec. 15, T. 6 N., R. 1 W., S.B.), Ian Campbell (1) p. 3.

San Diego County: **1**, Minute hollow spheres of hydromagnesite occur in the pyrrhotite ore of the Friday mine, Creasey (1) p. 27.

San Francisco County: **1**, Hydromagnesite occurs as botryoidal masses and veins 3 to 4 inches wide in the serpentines at Fort Point, Eakle (1) p. 316, Mining and Scientific Press (19) p. 28. **2**, Specimens have come from Market Street near Guerrero, CDMG (1320), (1321). **3**, Finely crystalline hydromagnesite occurs with xonotlite as veins in basalt at Marshall Beach, near Fort Point, Watters (p.c. '57).

San Luis Obispo County: **1**, Small veins of hydromagnesite were found near Port Harford (Port San Luis), CDMG (1175).

San Mateo County: **1**, Small white patches of hydromagnesite in serpentine occur near Searsville Lake, A. F. Rogers (24) p. 46.

Santa Barbara County: **1**, A specimen of hydromagnesite has come from near Santa Barbara, CDMG (13699). **2**, Massive hydromagnesite occurs on Figueroa Mountain, Woodhouse (p.c. '45).

Santa Clara County: **1**, Spherical nodules of finely crystalline hydromagnesite up to 4 cm in diameter, were found in serpentine at the lower end of Alum Rock Canyon, A. F. Rogers (24) p. 46, and **2**, microcrystalline masses come from the lower end of Calaveras Valley, ibid., p. 46.

Sonoma County: **1**, Chalky balls of hydromagnesite have been found in nickeliferous serpentine near Cloverdale, W. W. Bradley (29) p. 222.

Stanislaus County: **1,** A considerable quantity of hydromagnesite has been reported from Red Mountain, Dolbear (8) p. 238, and **2,** it has been found on the Pramberger.property 14 miles west of Patterson, Laizure (9) p. 57.

HYDROTROILITE
Hydrous iron sulphide, probably $FeS \cdot n H_2O$

Palache et al. (10) p. 236, suggest that the validity of hydrotroilite as a mineral species is doubtful.

Riverside County: **1,** Hydrotroilite has been found in the new City quarry, Victoria Avenue, Riverside, Laudermilk and Woodford (5) p. 418, and **2,** it occurs rather abundantly in the contact zone of the Lone Star quarry, Crestmore, Woodford et al. (10) p. 366.

San Bernardino County: **1,** Hydrotroilite has been found at the lapis lazuli occurrence in Cascade Canyon ($SW\frac{1}{4}$ sec. 31, T. 2 N., R. 7 W., S. B.), Laudermilk and Woodford (5) p. 418.

HYDROZINCITE
Basic zinc carbonate, $Zn_5(CO_3)_2(OH)_6$

Hydrozincite is of secondary origin, formed usually by the alteration of sphalerite.

Inyo County: **1,** Hydrozincite occurs associated with hemimorphite, aurichalcite, and smithsonite at the Cerro Gordo mine, A. F. Rogers (7) p. 374, A. Knopf (5) p. 106, C. W. Merriam (1) p. 43. **2,** Colorless or white blade-like crystals associated with linarite occur at the Defiance mine, Darwin Mining District, Murdoch and Webb (14) p. 324, Hall and MacKevett (4) p. 64. **3,** Hydrozincite is associated with ores at Minietta and Modoc mines, Argus Range, Woodhouse (p.c. '54). **4,** Colloform linings of fine-grained hydrozincite coat and fill cavities in the Ubehebe mine, McAllister (4) p. 27. **5,** Hydrozincite has been found in the Lemoigne mine, on the east slope of the Panamint Mountains, Death Valley National Monument, near Stovepipe Wells, Hall and Stephens (3) p. 37.

San Bernardino County: **1,** Hydrozincite is found with smithsonite and cerussite at the Carbonate King mine, 14 miles north of Cima (sec. 32, T. 16 N., R. 14 E., S. B.), Tucker and Sampson (33) p. 128, and **2,** it is found at Dale Lake, ibid. (34) p. 479.

* IDDINGSITE, 1893
Hydrous magnesium and iron silicate, $MgO \cdot Fe_2O_3 \cdot 3SiO_2 \cdot 4H_2O(?)$

Iddingsite was originally described as a new mineral from Monterey County by A. C. Lawson (1) p. 31. It is considered a doubtful species, P. Gay and Le Maitre (2) p. 92.

Alpine County: **1,** Iddingsite occurs abundantly as bright orange-yellow pseudomorphs after olivine phenocrysts, in the West Dardanelles flow, west of Dardanelles Cone on the border of Tuolumne County, F. L. Ransome (7) p. 52.

Inyo County: **1,** Iddingsite is found in the basalts about one kilometer southeast from the Russell borax mine, Mount Blanco area, Foshag (10) p. 10. **2,** Iddingsite occurs as a prominent alteration of olivine phenocrysts in the basalts of the Ubehebe quadrangle, McAllister (4) pp. 57, 59.

Kern County: **1,** Iddingsite occurs rather abundantly as pseudomorphs after olivine in basalt in the Bartolas country northeast of Isabella, Webb (9) p. 324. **2,** Iddingsite occurs at red-brown patches in the zeolitic lavas of Red Rock Canyon, Murdoch (p.c. '51).

Los Angeles County: **1,** Iddingsite has been found in the Santa Monica Mountains, E. S. Larsen (11) p. 91.

Monterey County: **1,** Iddingsite has been found as a prominent constituent of a basic rock called carmeloite. The mineral was recognized as new, and was described by A. C. Lawson (1) p. 31. It has been further discussed by C. S. Ross and Shannon (1) p. 13.

San Bernardino County: **1,** Iddingsite has been erroneously reported from Siberia crater, W. W. Bradley (30) p. 207, but all the material from here is olivine stained red by iron oxide, Foshag (p.c.), Murdoch (p.c. '45).

Siskiyou County: **1,** Yellow iddingsite has been doubtfully reported from the Hayes group (T. 44 N., R. 8 W., M. D.), W. W. Bradley (30) p. 128, and **2,** similarly from near Seiad Valley (T. 47 N., R. 11 W., M. D.), W. W. Bradley (28) p. 343.

Trinity County: **1,** Iddingsite is associated with olivine from this county, W. W. Bradley (29) p. 106.

IDOCRASE—Vesuvianite [1]
Calcium and aluminum silicate, $Ca_{10}(Mg,Fe^{2+},Fe^{+3}{}_2Al_4Si_9O_{34}(OH)_4$

Idocrase is characteristically formed in limestone near a contact with igneous rocks, and often is associated with grossular garnet. The variety *californite* is a compact, massive idocrase, sometimes called "California jade," occurring as streaks or nodules in serpentine. It was named and described from Happy Camp in Siskiyou County by Kunz (19) p. 397.

No attempt has been made to report all of the occurrences of idocrase found in the State that are referenced in the literature. The mineral is widespread and is so common that only occurrences of mineralogical interest should be included. However, some localities of minor importance and of little mineralogical interest are noted for the historical record because they have been reported in early editions of *Minerals of California.*

Butte County: **1,** Californite is found near Pulga (southwestern part of T. 25 N., R. 8 E., M. D.), Sterrett (6) p. 858. **2,** Californite occurs near Oroville, near the mouth of Feather River, as water-worn pebbles, A. F. Rogers (7) p. 377.

Calaveras County: **1,** Idocrase occurs with garnet and epidote at Garnet Hill, at the junction of Moore Creek and Mokelumne River, Melhase (6) p. 7.

El Dorado County: **1,** Brown crystals of idocrase were found in the Siegel lode near Georgetown, W. P. Blake (15) p. 16. **2,** Veins of idocrase have been found on Traverse Creek, 2½ miles southeast of George-

---

[1] The Commission on New Minerals and Mineral Names of the I.M.A. has failed to agree on change of vesuviante to idocrase, Anon. (55).

town (T. 12 N., R. 10 E., M. D.), L. L. Root (4) p. 409. Complex crystals of varied color have been described from this occurrence by Pabst (2) p. 1.

Fresno County: **1,** Californite has been produced from the south side of Watts Valley (sec. 5, T. 12 S., R. 24 E., M. D.), Kunz (24) p. 94, W. W. Bradley (2) p. 439. **2,** Californite occurs with white garnet near Selma, Kunz (24) p. 94, F. W. Clarke and Steiger (8) p. 72. **3,** Well-formed greenish-brown crystals of idocrase up to half an inch in diameter are widespread in a contact metamorphic limestone in the Twin Lakes region, Chesterman (1) p. 275.

Inyo County: **1,** Brownish-green idocrase intimately intergrown with garnet and white datolite, was found at San Carlos, about 12 miles south of Fish Springs, on the west slope of the Inyo Range, John L. Smith (1) p. 435. **2,** The mineral occurs with garnet in metamorphic rock in Round Valley, west of Bishop, A. Knopf (6) p. 244, Chapman (1) p. 866; **3,** with diopside and epidote about 5 miles east of Ballarat, Murphy (4) p. 349, and **4,** with blue calcite, half a mile north of Crystal Dome mine, North Fork Shepherd Canyon (T. 22 S., R. 42 E., M. D.), W. W. Bradley (26) p. 195. **5,** Idocrase occurs with scapolite and diopside in the contact zone at the Pine Creek Tungsten mine, Hess and Larsen (1) p. 276. **6,** Idocrase is common in the contact zone at Darwin, as dense green masses and crystals in calcite or wollastonite, Kelley (4) p. 539, Hall and MacKevett (4) p. 63. **7,** Idocrase occurs as coarse-grained crystalline masses and individuals in contact zones in marble in several places in the Ubehebe quadrangle, McAllister (4) p. 57.

Kern County: **1,** Idocrase occurs in a contact zone with garnet and wollastonite, as green and brown radial groups up to 6 inches across, 3 miles south of Havilah, O'Guinn (p.c. '35).

Mono County: **1,** Idocrase has been found in a contact zone with boulangerite and wollastonite, on the north side of Lee Vining Canyon (sec. 13, T. 1 N., R. 25 E., M. D.), Murdoch (p.c. '45).

Placer County: **1,** Small crystals of idocrase occur in metamorphic rock on the old highway about half a mile east of Cisco (T. 17 N., R. 13 E., M. D.), S. G. Clark (p.c. '36). **2,** Idocrase has been found in this county disseminated in massive garnet, A. F. Rogers (51) p. 1222.

Plumas County: **1,** Brownish-green crystals of idocrase have been found 5 miles from Portola, W. W. Bradley (28) p. 206.

Riverside County: **1,** Flat pyramidal crystals of idocrase up to 6 inches across, together with abundant smaller crystals and rounded grains, occur in the contact zone in the Crestmore limestone quarries, Eakle (15) p. 338, Kelley (2) p. 141. **2** Idocrase is found in the new City quarry, 2 miles south of Riverside, Richmond (1) p. 725.

San Bernardino County: **1,** Idocrase, massive and in crystals is associated with greenish garnet, green diopside and uvarovite on the east side of a hill which is west of a limestone quarry, 11 miles east of Victorville, O. E. Bowen (1) p. 32.

San Diego County: **1,** Crystals of idocrase of gem quality have been found near Jacumba and San Vicente, Kunz (24) p. 95.

Siskiyou County: **1,** The original discovery of californite was made 12 miles from Happy Camp (sec. 7, T. 17 N., R. 7 E., H.), Kunz (17)

p. 747, (19) p. 397, Averill (5) p. 291. White californite, which is almost indistinguishable from white garnet, has been described from this locality, Sterrett (6) p. 857.

Tulare County: **1,** Red porphyroblasts of idocrase have been found with wollastonite and diopside in Kaweah quarries (secs. 35, 36, T. 17 S., R. 27 E., M. D.), 2 miles northeast of Lemon Cove, Durrell (p.c. '35). **2,** Idocrase also occurs (sec. 25, T. 17 S., R. 28 E., M. D.), with wollastonite, ibid.

ILMENITE—Menaccanite
Oxide of iron and titanium, FeTiO₃

Ilmenite is very similar in appearance to magnetite, with which it is often confused. It is a common constituent of igneous rocks, and is frequently present in small grains in beach and river sands, accompanied by magnetite and other heavy minerals. In this form it is very widespread throughout the State, and only the most important occurrences can be noted.

Alpine County: **1,** Platy and massive ilmenite is found with lazulite and andalusite 10 miles south-southwest of Markleeville, Woodhouse (p.c. '45).

Calaveras County: **1,** Ilmenite is a common minor constituent of graphitic schists in the Calaveras formation in the Calaveritas quadrangle, L. D. Clark (1) p. 6.

El Dorado County: **1,** Ilmenite occurs in the placer sands near Georgetown, and from this locality, W. P. Blake (7) p. 303, records the occurrence of beautiful complex crystals, one as much as an inch across, with brilliant faces. This occurrence is quoted by Hanks (12) p. 260, Kunz (24) p. 105.

Kern County: **1,** Crystals of ilmenite up to 2 inches across have been found at the Greenback copper mine. H. W. Turner (23) p. 548.

Los Angeles County: **1,** A number of deposits of varying sizes of ilmenite occur in anorthosite in the San Gabriel Mountains (T. 3, 4 N., R. 12, 13, 14 w., S. B.), Tucker (13) p. 296. **2** Ilmenite sands have occurred in commercial quarry at Redondo Beach, Youngman (1) p. 20.

Madera County: **1,** Large platy masses of ilmenite are found with pyrophyllite and quartz at the low pass immediately east of the junction of Bench Creek and North Fork, San Joaquin River, Erwin (1) p. 29. **2,** Ilmenite is found as platy masses with epidote on Rush Creek Divide, west of Agnew Pass, ibid., p. 24, and 3, fine specimens have come from Taylors Ranch, near Buchanan, Hanks (12) p. 260.

Mono County: **1,** Ilmenite occurs very sparingly at the andalusite deposit in the White Mountains, 7 miles east of Mocalno, north of Bishop, Woodhouse (4) p. 4

Plumas County: **1,** Small amounts of ilmenite intergrown with magnetite and hematite, occur at the Engels mine, A. Knopf and Anderson (12) p. 27.

San Benito County: **1,** Rhombohedral crystals, 2-3 mm thick and 7 mm broad, were found with magnetite octahedrons in dark metamorphic rock near the Gem Mine by Watters, Crippen (p.c. '50).

San Bernardino County: **1,** Ilmenite in thin plates, 1-5 mm thick and extending up to 3 feet, occur in radial arrangement in quartz at the

Pomona Tile quarry, on the road between Old Woman Spring and Yucca Valley, Hewett & Glass (3) p. 1048. It is associated here with allanite, monazite and euxenite.

Santa Cruz County: **1,** Layers of black sand up to 6 inches in thickness occur at Aptos. They are largely magnetite and ilmenite, Hess (19) p. 463.

ILSEMANNITE
Molybdenum compound, formula uncertain, perhaps $Mo_3O_8 \cdot nH_2O(?)$

Inyo County: **1,** Ilsemannite is reported as a pigment on copiapite, in a molybdenite deposit near the north end of Death Valley, Palache et al. (10) p. 604.

Kern County: **1,** Ilsemannite was identified in sooty uraninite masses from the Kern River uranium area, MacKevett (2) p. 203. It has been identified, together with jordisite, in black radioactive material from the Kergon mine, Troxel and Morton (2) p. 330. **2,** Ilsemannite also occurs in the Miracle mine ($SE\frac{1}{4}$ sec. 17, T. 27 S., R. 32 E., M. D.), ibid., p. 333.

Shasta County: **1,** Blue zones surrounding molybdenite in quartz, with associated molybdenite, 4 miles west of Gibson, have been tentatively identified as ilsemannite, Cook (1) p. 50.

ILVAITE
Basic calcium iron silicate, $CaFe^{2+}_2Fe^{3+}Si_2O_8OH$

Fresno County: **1,** Slender black crystals of ilvaite have been reported in metamorphic limestone in the Twin Lakes area, Chesterman (p.c. '51).

Shasta County: **1,** Thin bands and long prisms of ilvaite occur on both sides of a narrow dike cutting limestone on Potter Creek, near Baird. The crystals occur on quartz and hedenbergite, and have been described by Prescott (1) p. 14. **2,** Small amounts of ilvaite have been found in the ore of the Shasta and California iron ore deposit (sec. 26, T. 34 N., R. 4 W., M. D.), Lamey (9) p. 149.

Sonoma County: **1,** A boulder of quartzite, colored black with ilvaite was found near Petaluma (N. R.).

INDERITE
Hydrous magnesium borate, $Mg_2B_6O_{11} \cdot 15H_2O$

Inyo County: **1,** A specimen submitted by M. Vonsen in 1941 was identified by Heinrich (1) p. 71, as inderite. It came from an unspecified locality in the county. The specimen was shown to be kurnakovite, not inderite, by Schaller and Mrose (56) p. 732, and the specimen was determined to have come not from Inyo County, but probably from South America, Frondel and Morgan (7).

Kern County: **1,** The rare borate mineral inderite was found in California in the Kramer borate mining area at Boron. When first reported in 1948, Mineral Notes and News (3) p. 12, it was the second American occurrence of the mineral, found elsewhere only in the Inder region of western Kazahkstan, USSR. Later, the first American occurrence was shown to be invalid (see Inyo County, **1**). Ward Smith (p.c. '64) has provided the following clarification of the occurrence: "At Kramer, inderite was reported first in core from a drill hole near the Baker mine. Later it was found underground in the Jenifer mine, and, in considerable quantities, in the Open Pit. All these localities fall within a square mile, and all the occurrences are in the hanging wall of the main sodium borate ore body, in a thin, discontinuous zone a foot or two above the ore. In this zone monoclinic inderite occurs with triclinic kurnakovite, which has the same composition. The nomenclature of these magnesium borate minerals became confused, chiefly because the Russian original descriptions do not provide adequate information, but has been clarified by Schaller and Mrose (56). As they point out, the crystals initially identified as "inderite" by Frondel and Morgan (7) p. 839 are kurnakovite, and those given the new name "lesserite" by Frondel, Morgan, and Waugh (8) p. 927 actually are "inderite." Thus, one occurrence of inderite to date is valid for the United States.

INESITE
Basic hydrous manganese calcium silicate, $Ca_2Mn_7Si_{10}O_{28}(OH)_2 \cdot 5H_2O$

P. D. Trask et al (4) p. 267, describe inesite in its California setting as " . . . of common occurrence in veins cutting the deposits [of manganese ores] that have been rather strongly recrystallized or subject to weak hydrothermal action. It is readily recognized under the microscope . . . " It is significant, however, that P. D. Trask reports only one occurrence of inesite, Trinity County (1), in his comprehensive bulletin on manganese in California. All of the reports of inesite entered below, except Trinity (1), are unvalidated. These entries appeared in *Minerals of California* between 1914 (CDMG, Bulletin 67), Eakle (12), and 1923 (Bulletin 91), Eakle (22). No references are available in the literature to support the entries. It is possible, therefore, that inesite has in fact been established as occurring only from Trinity County.

Alameda County: **1,** Rose-red veins of inesite with bementite intersect the rhodochrosite at the Newhall (Bailey mine, 10 miles southeast of Livermore, on the Arroyo Mocho (N. R.).

Mendocino County: **1,** Inesite veins with associated bementite and neotocite occurred in the rhodochrosite at Impassable Rock, Mount Sanhedrin, about 8 miles from Hearst (N. R.).

San Joaquin County: **1,** Inesite was common at the old Ladd mine (N. R.).

Stanislaus County: **1,** Gray rhodochrosite on the Cummings lease is intersected by veinlets of rose-red inesite with bementite. Crystals from this occurence have been described (N. R.).

Trinity County: **1,** Veins of silky radiating crystals of inesite, up to a quarter of an inch in diameter, occur with rhodochrosite and bementite at the Hale Creek mine (NW¼ sec. 23, T. 1 S., R. 6 E., H), P. D. Trask et al (4) p. 59.

* INYOITE, 1914
Hydrous calcium borate, $Ca_2B_6O_{11} \cdot 13H_2O$

Inyoite was one of the early discoveries of the many new borate minerals described to date from California.

Inyo County: **1,** Inyoite was found with meyerhofferite and colemanite in Corkscrew Canyon, Mount Blanco region, Death Valley. It was described and named by Schaller (33) p. 35. It is commonly altered to meyerhofferite, but occasionally a clear crystal may be found.

Kern County: **1,** Inyoite is reported from the Kramer borate area, Boron. The mineral is rare but in fine single crystals, E. H. Pemberton et al. (1) p. 25.

* IONITE, 1878
A hydrocarbon with about 50% H_2O

Amador County: **1,** Ionite was found in an argillaceous lignite in thin seams in Ione Valley. Purnell (1) p. 184, described it as a new mineral. It appears that the substance described as scales in the Ione sandstone as ''ionite'' is a varietal habit of the clay mineral anauxite, V. T. Allen (2) p. 145, E. S. Dana and Ford (8) p. 682. The name ''ionite'' is sometimes locally applied in California to clay-like scaly material of the Ione formation. It appears that the hydrocarbon to which the name ionite was assigned is still a valid identification; however, the use of the same name as the variety of clay, which is sanctioned by E. S. Dana and Ford, is not in fact used in this way elsewhere in the literature on California minerals.

IRIDIUM
Native iridium, Ir
(Probably iridosmine)

Mendocino County: **1,** Iridium was reported with platinum and gold from the Anderson Valley placer along Navarro River, Hanks (12) p. 310.

IRIDOSMINE—Siserskite
Native alloy of iridium and osmium, (Ir,Os)

The name *iridosmine* is applied to those mixtures with Ir>Os, and *siserskite* to those with Os>Ir. The alloy of these two metals is frequently found in gold placers, associated with platinum, and analysis shows the presence of the rarer elements rhodium and ruthenium, Deville and Debray (1) p. 449. Crystals were measured by Gladhill (1) p. 42.

Butte County: **1,** Iridosmine was found in the gold sands at Cherokee, Silliman (12) p. 132.

Del Norte or Humboldt County: **1,** The largest nugget of iridosmine found in California came from the lower Klamath River, Hittel (2) p. 61. It weighed $1\frac{1}{4}$ ounces.

Humboldt County: **1,** Iridosmine has been reported from China Flat, Horton (1) p. 874, and **2,** with platinum from Humboldt Bay, Richthofen (3) p. 46.

Placer County: **1,** Iridosmine is found on the North Fork, American River, Genth (1) p. 113.

Shasta County: **1,** Iridosmine occurs in placer concentrates at the headwaters of Cottonwood Creek, Mining and Scientific Press (28) p. 209.

Trinity County: **1,** A 27-ounce lot of nuggets of platinum and iridosmine from near Junction City, Trinity River, included one iridosmine nugget of $\frac{3}{4}$-ounce weight, Horton (1) p. 874.

Tuolumne County: **1,** Six-sided scales of siserskite were found by Genth (1) p. 113, (2) pp. 209, 247, after dissolving away the platinum and gold of concentrates, from near Stanislaus.

IRON
Native iron, Fe

Terrestrial iron, which sometimes occurs in basaltic rocks, has not so far been found in California. The only iron here is meteoritic, and to date 18 to 20 finds have been recorded. It is customary to locate these finds by means of coordinate numbers which give the longitude and the latitude to the nearest tenth of a degree. For example, 1181,349 is the coordinate designation of a find whose longitude is 118.1° W., and whose latitude is 34.9° N. Somewhat less than half the known finds are wholly or mainly iron, which invariably carries 5 to 30 percent nickel, usually a little cobalt, and other minor elements. Others are the stony meteorites, which usually carry some free iron, also nickeliferous, and which are largely composed of silicates of iron and magnesium.

A 1966 summary on "The Meteorites of California", by C. P. Butler, Calif. Div. Mines and Geology, Mineral Information Service, vol. 19, no. 7, pp. 103–108, 110–111, 1966, appeared after the cut-off date for entries in this volume.

Butte County: **1,** A 54-pound meteorite was found near Oroville (coord. + 1216,395) in 1893, Farrington (2) p. 16.

El Dorado County: **1,** The Shingle Springs meteorite was discovered in 1869 (coord. 1209,386), half a mile from Shingle Springs. It is a nickel-rich ataxite weighing 85 pounds, C. U. Shepard (2) p. 438, Silliman (11) p. 18, Farrington (2) p. 412.

Imperial County: **1,** A small stony meteorite (chondrite) weighing 4 grams was found in 1908 (coord. 1156,329), near Imperial, and is now in the U.S. National Museum in Washington, E. P. Henderson (p.c., '46).

Inyo County: **1,** About 22 miles northeast of Big Pine (coord. 1180,374 approx.), a medium octahedrite weighing 425 pounds was found in 1913 and is now in the U.S. National Museum and described by G. P. Merrill (3) p. 5. **2,** B. Mason (3) p. 229 reports a meteorite referred to without reference source as "Death Valley." Dr. C. A. Moore, Director of the Center for Meteorite Studies of Arizona State University indicates that this find is discredited. Apparently the specimen was established to be a piece of Plainview meteorite. The specimen is in the possession of the Arizona Center, C. A. Moore (p.c. '66).

Kern County: **1,** A stony meteorite, originally weighing about 80 pounds, was found in the San Emigdio Mountains in 1887 (coord. 1160,350 approx.). It was put through the crusher before its character was recognized, but it was definitely determined as a chrondrite by G. P. Merrill (1) p. 49, (2) p. 161. It was analyzed by Whitfield (3) p. 114. Another reference to this meteorite is Reeds (1) p. 618. **2,** In November 1940, an aerolite weighing 850 grams was discovered in Rosamond Dry Lake, W. T. Whitney (1) p. 387, (1) p. 291 (coord. 1181,349). **3, 4,** Finds of 3 stones were made in Muroc Dry Lake in 1936, Nininger and Cleminshaw (2) p. 273, p. 23. Two stones were found close together, and another at a little distance. They are all aerolites with nickel iron and have been designated as Muroc Dry Lake meteorites, weights 115 and 58 grams, and Muroc meteorite, weight 18.4 grams (coord. 1178,349). They may represent separate finds, but they are probably a single find, Leonard and Rowland (8) p. 447. **5,** The fifteenth meteorite of the California record was recovered on May 24, 1958, 5 miles east of Ridgecrest. It is an aerolite weighing 9.6 grams, Humiston (1) p. 50, Leonard (9) p. 52.

Los Angeles County: **1,** The Neenach stony meteorite (coord. +1185,348), was found by Mr. Elden Snyder in Antelope Valley in 1948. The stone was a gift to the University of California, Santa Barbara, by Mr. Snyder, Leonard (3) p. 28, Anon. (24) p. 80. The specimen has recently been transferred to the U.S. National Museum, Washington, D.C., as a part of the National Collection of the United States, and a facsimile of the stone is now on display at the University of California, Santa Barbara.

Modoc County: **1,** The largest known meteorite of California and the fourth largest in the United States was found October 13, 1938, near Goose Lake (coord. 1205,420). It is a siderite weighing 2573 pounds (1167 kilograms), and is probably an old find, Leonard (1) p. 508, (2) p. 3, Linsley (2) p. 308. The specimen now is in the U.S. National Museum, Washington, D.C. A sample is in the CDMG Museum (CDMG 21146).

Riverside County: **1,** The Pinto Mountains stony meteorite (chondrite) (coord. = 1161,337:), was recovered in November 1954 by V. Zimmerman while prospecting. The specimen weighed originally 39.5 lbs., and was the fourteenth verified meteorite from California. The specimen is preserved in the collections of the Institute of Meteoritics of the University of New Mexico, Albuquerque, N.M., La Paz (1), p. 295.

San Bernardino County: **1,** An aerolite, gray chondrite, was found June 10, 1929, half a mile north of Valley Wells (coord. 1157,355), Reeds (1) pp. 633, 634, Coulson (1) p. 220. This is clearly the same find as that called Windmill Station, recorded by Linsley (1) p. 472. Four pieces were found with weights 10.5, 13.5, 24, 81.9 grams, Leonard (6) p. 174. **2,** A siderite (medium octahedrite) was found in 1880, 8 miles from Ivanpah (coord. 1153,354). It weighed about 128 pounds and carried about 4½ percent nickel, C. U. Shepard (4) p. 381. It was analyzed by him, and also by Cohen and Weinschenk (1) pp. 131-165; and Cohen (2) p. 149. It is now in the CDMG Exhibit (CDMG 2339). **3,** An iron meteorite weighing 1524 grams (about 3 pounds), was found in 1899 lying on the surface of a quartz outcrop on the south slope of the Bullion Range, near Surprise Springs (coord. 1159,342), the specimen is in the Chicago Natural History Museum, Cohen (3) pp. 29-33, Farrington (2) p. 430. **4,** Two specimens of native iron are reported from a reputed new meteorite find near the California-Arizona border near Needles, Anonymous (38) p. 99. Dr. C. A. Moore, Director of the Center for Meteorite Studies of Arizona State University (p.c. '66) states that this report cannot be confirmed although it is asserted that one specimen is supposed to be at the University of Oklahoma or at Oklahoma State University, and another at the University of Arizona. These have not been verified. It is probable that this reported find is in error and should be discredited. **5,** Several aerolites were recovered in the vicinity of Lucerne Valley beginning in July 1963. To date, seven small pieces have been found ranging from 3.1 to 37.4 grams. The location is within an ellipse of 1.3 miles in sec. 26, T. 5. N., R. 1 W., S.B., Hartman and Oriti (1) p. 177. The specimens are located in the Griffith Observatory Collection in Los Angeles. **6,** Dale Dry Lake (coordinates 34°02'; 115°54') is a chondrite, and was found in 1957. There is no published reference describing this find, but it is recorded by B. Mason (3) p. 229. Dr. C. A. Moore, Director of the Center for Meteorite Studies of Arizona State University (p.c. '66) indicates that the stone was found by Mrs. Vincent Zimmerman of 29 Palms, about 2 miles north of the old Virginia Dale mine. One piece weighing 31.4 g. is in the collections of Arizona State; the balance of the original 300 g. stone is retained by the finder. **7,** The 29 Palms meteorite (34°04'; 115°57'), a white chondrite, was found as a partially encrusted stone, 4 miles west of the old Virginia Dale mine, by Mr. Vincent Zimmerman in 1955. The stone weighed 43 lbs. B. Mason (3) p. 229 records the find in his table of California meteorites, but no description is given. Dr. C. A. Moore, Director of the Center for Meteorite Studies of Arizona State University, in a personal communication (p.c. '66) reports that a small fragment of the stone is in the collection of the Institute of Meteoritics of the University of New Mexico. Presumably the main mass of the stone is held by the discoverer.

Trinity County: **1,** An oval-shaped piece of meteoritic iron weighing about 19 pounds was found in 1875 on a small tributary of Trinity River, 3 miles northeast of Canyon City (coord. 1231,409), C. U. Shepard (5) p. 469, Ward (1) p. 383.

JAMESONITE
Lead iron antimony sulphide, $Pb_4FeSb_6S_{14}$

Calaveras County: **1,** Jamesonite is recorded from Mokelumne Hill, Hanks (12) p. 244.

Inyo County: **1,** Compact massive specimens of jamesonite associated with argentiferous galena have come from the Cerro Gordo mine (N. R.).

Kern County: **1,** Jamesonite or bournonite is reported from Soledad Mountain, Mojave Mining District, with cerargyrite and argentite in the gold ores, Schroter (1) p. 185.

Napa County: **1,** Delicate capillary crystals of jamesonite ("feather ore") were found with cinnabar at the Manhattan mine, CDMG (15530).

Santa Cruz County: **1,** Jamesonite occurs at Pacific Limestone Products (Kalkar) quarry, E. H. Oyler (p.c. '60).

Sierra County: **1,** Small needles and clusters of jamesonite occur in vugs in quartz at the Rainbow and Plumbago mines, Forest (Alleghany) Mining District, Ferguson and Gannett (4) p. 30, (6) p. 49.

JAROSITE
Hydrous potassium iron sulphate, $KFe_3^{3+}(SO_4)_3 \cdot nH_2O$

Imperial County: **1,** Crusts of small brown crystals of jarosite are found at the American Girl mine, Cargo Muchacho Mountains, Murdoch (p.c. '49).

Inyo County: **1,** Jarosite is abundant in light-colored mica schists in Wild Rose Canyon, D. E. White (1) p. 318, and **2,** also in veins cutting across most other minerals in igneous rocks of the contact zone, Darwin Mining District, Kelley (4) p. 542. **3,** Yellow crusts of tungsten-bearing jarosite are found in the Yaney mine (SW cor. sec. 22, T. 7 S., R. 32 E., M. D.), with ferberite (reinite), Bateman (3) p. 76. **4,** Small crystals are reported in cavities in massive jarosite from the east shaft of the Lost Burro mine, Ubehebe quadrangle, McAllister (4) p. 58.

Kern County: **1,** A little jarosite occurs in the cassiterite ores of the deposit near Gorman, Troxel and Morton (2) p. 294. **2,** Jarosite is abundant in some of the oxidized veins of the Cactus Queen (Blue Eagle, Cactus) mine (SW$\frac{1}{4}$ NW$\frac{1}{4}$ sec. 17, T. 10 N., R. 13 W., S. B.), Mojave Mining District, Troxel and Morton (2) p. 104.

Lake County: **1,** Jarosite occurs associated with copiapite and epsomite at Sulphur Bank, Everhart (1) p. 139, D. E. White and Roberson (12) p. 406.

Merced County: **1,** Yellow-brown colloform crusts of jarosite have been found in a few antimony veins of the Stayton Mining District in this and San Benito Counties, E. H. Bailey and Myers (4) p. 418. **2,** Jarosite in microscopic grains occurs abundantly in glauconite-jarosite sandstone (sec. 35, T. 11 S., R. 10 E., M. D.), Briggs (1) p. 902.

Mono County: **1,** Jarosite has been reported by Hulin (p.c. '36) from the Blind Spring Mining District, near Benton. **2,** Some jarosite occurs with alunite and limonite at the andalusite deposit 7 miles east of Mocalno, north of Bishop, White Mountains, Tucker and Sampson (4) p. 461, Woodhouse (2) p. 4.

San Benito County: **1,** A. F. Rogers (7) p. 376, has found measurable jarosite crystals at the New Idria quicksilver mine. **2,** Jarosite was found in the Stayton Mining District (cf. Merced County), E. H. Bailey and Myers (4) p. 418.

San Bernardino County: **1,** Jarosite is abundant among the sulphates at the "sulphur hole," east of the borax mines in the Calico Hills, Foshag (19) p. 352. **2,** Jarosite occurs sparingly in the Keystone mine (SE$\frac{1}{4}$ sec. 18, T. 7 N., R. 4 W., S. B.), in Stoddard Mountain, 14 miles northeast of Victorville, in irregular microscopic crystals in clusters and aggregates, Hutton and Bowen (2) pp. 556–561.

Santa Clara County: **1,** Jarosite is present in the New Almaden mine, Irelan (4) p. 47, E. H. Bailey and Everhart (12) p. 102.

Shasta County: **1,** Jarosite is found in gangue of copper ore, Bully Hill mine, Anon. (44) p. 4.

JEFFERISITE
Basic hydrous magnesium iron aluminum silicate,
$(Mg,Fe^{3+},Fe^{2+},Al)_{6-7}(Si,Al)_8O_{20}(OH)_4 \cdot H_2O$

Jefferisite is a hydrated mica, a variety of vermiculite.

Lassen County: **1,** Large brown plates of jefferisite have been found at Susanville, Hanks (12) p. 244, CDMG (2126).

Mendocino County: **1,** A specimen of jefferisite, CDMG (13997), has come from this county.

Tulare County: **1,** Hanks (12) p. 244, reports jefferisite from the county—no precise location, CDMG (4911).

JEŽEKITE
Basic sodium calcium aluminum fluophosphate, $Na_4CaAl_2(PO_4)_2(OH)_2F_2O(?)$

San Diego County: **1,** Massive amblygonite in the Stewart mine at Pala carries thin veins with minute colorless grains of jezekite, associated with glassy wardite and fibrous carbonate-apatite, Murdoch (p.c. '53).

* JOAQUINITE, 1909
Sodium barium and iron titano-silicate, $NaBa(Ti,Fe)_3Si_4O_{15}$

San Benito County: **1,** Small brown crystals of the mineral joaquinite are found associated with benitoite and neptunite at the benitoite gem mine (sec. 25, T. 18 S., R. 12 E., M. D.). The mineral was described and named by Louderback and Blasdale (5) p. 376, Palache and Foshag (7) p. 308.

JORDISITE
Molybdenum sulphide, MoS_2

Kern County: **1,** Jordisite is associated with sooty pitchblende (uraninite) and ilsemannite in the ores from the Kern River uranium area, MacKevett (2) p. 203. The Kergon mine and its minerals are referenced in Troxel and Morton (2) p. 330.

† * JURUPAITE, 1921
See xonotlite

Jurupaite was described as a new mineral from the Crestmore quarries by Eakle (2) in 1921. Subsequent study has shown the mineral to be xonotlite, H. F. W. Taylor (2) p. 338.

KAOLINITE
Hydrous aluminum silicate, $Al_2Si_2O_5(OH)_4$

Miloschite, when it was reported [Sonoma County (**2**) below] was considered a chromian kaolinite. *Lithomarge* is a compact variety.

Kaolinite forms the base of most clays. It is formed by the alteration of rocks containing aluminum silicates, especially the feldspars, and most good clays come from the alteration of potash feldspar. The mineral is practically universal in occurrence, and only those localities which are of considerable importance are recorded. Common brick clay is found in every county. Detailed information as to deposits may be found in Dietrich (1), *Clay Resources and Ceramic Industry of California,* Bulletin 99 CDMG, and the references below are to this authority, unless otherwise specified.

Alameda County: **1,** High-grade clays were at one time mined near Tesla (p. 38).

Amador County: **1,** A number of clay deposits occur in the Ione formation, and have been mined in the vicinity of Carbondale and Ione (p. 51).

Calaveras County: **1,** The Ione formation near Valley Springs carries some high-grade clays (p. 68).

Orange County: **1,** A deposit of flint fire clay occurs on Goat Ranch, Santa Ana Canyon (p. 140).

Lake County: **1,** Kaolinite is relatively abundant at Sulphur Bank, D. E. White and Roberson (2) p. 407.

Placer County: **1,** Valuable clay deposits in the Ione formation are found near Lincoln (p. 147).

Riverside County: **1,** The Alberhill-Corona area is one of the three most important clay-producing areas in the state, and most of the better clays in the county have come from this region (pp. 162, 163). **2,** Kaolinite is reported with uncertainty as rare as an alteration product in the Crestmore quarries, Woodford et al. (10) p. 368.

San Bernardino County: Several deposits of high-grade clays occur in the county; **1,** those in the Hart Mountains are the most interesting (secs. 13, 24, T. 14 N., R. 17 E., S.B.), (p. 194), and **2,** another deposit in the same region is half a mile south of the now extinct mining town of Hart (p. 197).

Shasta County: **1,** Thick incoherent deposits of kaolinite occur with alunite and opal on the flanks of Brokeoff Mountain, Lassen National Park, H. Williams (1) p. 249.

Sonoma County: **1,** A deposit of white kaolin fire clay occurs (sec. 3, T. 6 N., R. 6 W., M. D.) east of Beltane Station (p. 227). **2,** Miloschite has been found at the Devils Pulpit, The Geysers, Vonsen (p.c. '45).

KASOLITE
Basic lead uranyl silicate, $Pb(UO_2)(SiO_3)(OH)_2$

San Bernardino County: **1,** Kasolite is reported from east of Twenty-nine Palms, CDMG (21630).

* KEMPITE, 1924
Basic manganese chloride, $Mn_2Cl(OH)_3$

Santa Clara County: **1,** Minute green crystals of kempite, a new mineral (1924), associated with pyrochroite, hausmannite, and other manganese minerals, were found in the manganese boulder in Alum Rock Park, near San Jose. The mineral was described and named by A. F. Rogers (27) p. 145. A. F. Rogers (53) p. 1944, notes the relationship of kempite to atacamite.

KERMESITE
Antimony oxysulphide, Sb_2S_2O

Kern County: **1,** Fine red needles of kermesite were found in 1899 on stibnite at the Mojave antimony mine, about 15 miles north of Mojave, CDMG (15346). **2,** Kermesite was reported from the Kramer area as small cherry red spherules with kramerite, Mineral Notes and News (4) p. 13. According to Frondel (p.c. '48) this is not kermesite but an unidentified and possibly new mineral; see under gerstleyite, described in 1956 as a new mineral, Frondel and Morgan (7) p. 839.

Mono County: **1,** Kermesite was found sparingly in early mining in the Blind Spring Mining District, W. J. Hoffman (1) p. 737.

* KERNITE, 1927
Hydrous sodium borate, $Na_2B_4O_7 \cdot 4H_2O$
Rasorite has been used as an alternative name.

Kern County: **1,** Kernite was described by Schaller (41) p. 24, as a new mineral from the Kramer area (sec. 22, T. 11 N., R. 8 W., S. B.), where it forms the principal ore mineral of the borate deposits. Its occurrence and crystallography have been treated fully by Schaller (45) p. 146, and the x-ray structure determined by Garrido (1) p. 469. Muessig and Allen (1), (2), describe a new borate (ezcurrite near kernite) from Argentina, and comment on similarities to the mineral suite at Kramer.

Kernite is also an associated mineral in the Argentine occurrence, as clusters of crystals in massive borax, Muessig and Allen (1) p. 429.

† * KNOXVILLITE, 1890
See magnesio-copiapite

Knoxvillite was described as a new mineral in 1890 by Becker (4) p. 389. E. S. Larsen (11) p. 61, considered knoxvillite to be a variety of copiapite, but its identity with magnesio-copiapite has been established by Whitmore et al. (1) p. 21.

KOBELLITE
Lead iron bismuth antimony sulfide, $Pb_6FeBi_4Sb_2S_{16}$

Mariposa County: 1, A specimen from the Eureka or Excelsior mines is perhaps this species, CDMG (16074).

KONINCKITE
Hydrous iron phosphate, $FePO_4 \cdot 3H_2O$

San Benito County: 1, A specimen of koninckite, CDMG (20781) came from the New Idria mercury mine, W. W. Bradley (24) p. 251.

* KRAUSITE, 1931
Hydrous iron potassium sulphate, $KFe^{3+}(SO_4)_2 \cdot H_2O$

San Bernardino County: 1, Krausite was discovered, described as a new mineral and named by Foshag (19) p. 352, from the "sulphur hole" east of the borax mines in the Calico Mountains. It is in yellow grains and crystals associated with alunite, coquimbite, voltaite and other minerals.

KRÖHNKITE
Hydrous copper sodium sulphate, $Na_2Cu(SO_4)_2 \cdot 2H_2O$

Alameda County: 1, Kröhnkite has been recorded from the Alma mine, Leona Heights, Schaller (1) p. 207.

* KRAUSKOPFITE, 1964
Hydrous barium silicate, presumably, $BaSi_2O_5 \cdot 3H_2O$

Fresno County: 1, Krauskopfite, a new mineral discovered in the Rush Creek sanbornite locality, is named in honor of Dr. Konrad B. Krauskopf of Stanford University. It is described by Stinson and Alfors (6) p. 238. The mineral is accompanied by two other new minerals, wahlstromite and macdonaldite, and is associated with taramellite, celsian and gillespite.

KURNAKOVITE
Hydrous magnesium borate, $Mg_2B_6O_{11} \cdot 13H_2O$

Kern County: 1, Kurnakovite is found abundantly in the Kramer borate area in roughly formed prismatic crystals. This mineral was described by Frondel and Morgan (7) p. 839 as inderite, but it has been shown by Schaller and Mrose (56) p. 732, to be kurnakovite, confirming Ward Smith (p.c. '58).

KYANITE—Disthene—Cyanite
Aluminum silicate, Al₂SiO₅

Kyanite is a metamorphic mineral found in schists and gneisses with andalusite, sillimanite, and dumortierite.

Imperial County: **1,** Kyanite occurs abundantly with quartz and black tourmaline at the property of the Vitrefrax Corporation, 10 miles west of Winterhaven and 3 miles north of the dismantled railroad station of Ogilby, on the west slope of the Cargo Muchacho Mountains, Tucker (11) p. 269, R. J. Sampson and Tucker (4) p. 455, Ian Campbell and Wright (2) p. 1520.

Inyo County: **1,** Kyanite occurred about 7 miles northwest of Death Valley Junction, in the Amargosa Range, W. W. Bradley (28) p. 343.

Los Angeles County: **1,** Kyanite was found with corundum in gneiss on Santa Catalina Island, E. H. Bailey (1) p. 1955.

Riverside County: **1,** Kyanite occurred in the Golden Charlotte mine west of Perris, W. W. Bradley (30) p. 194.

San Bernardino County: **1,** Crystals of kyanite have been found in a contact zone in marble, Furnace Creek Canyon, Baker (1) p. 337.

San Diego County: **1,** Kyanite has been reported from an unspecified locality in this county, Friederich (1) p. 22. This is probably the same locality as Imperial County **(1)** since Imperial was at the time of the report of Friederich part of San Diego County.

Tuolumne County: **1,** Kyanite is a constituent of the schists on Yankee Hill, R. J. Sampson and Tucker (4) p. 457.

LAUMONTITE
Hydrous calcium aluminum silicate, Ca[Al₂Si₄O₁₂]·4H₂O

An early name for laumontite is leonhardite which is partially dehydrated laumontite. This is not to be confused with leonhardtite, a hydrated magnesium sulphate. Laumontite is a zeolite occurring in cavities of basic volcanic rock, usually with other zeolites.

Inyo County: **1,** A large crumbly mass of interlocking prisms of laumontite was found in No. 4 glory hole of the Pine Creek tungsten mine, in the contact zone of the scheelite ore, Hess and Larsen (17) p. 276.

Kern County: **1,** Laumontite was reported with its alteration product, cementing a feldspathic sandstone from the Standard Oil Company of California well, C.C.M.O. 4, No. 35, Tejon field, 30 miles southwest of Bakersfield. The mineral was identified microscopically, Kaley and Hanson (1) p. 923.

Los Angeles County: **1,** Matted prismatic crystals and friable masses of laumontite in crevices in basalt, have been found at the south end of Cahuenga Pass, Neuerberg (1) p. 156, and **2,** on Mulholland Drive west of Cahuenga Pass, locality 4, ibid., p. 156. **3,** Large crumbly masses of very small crystals of laumontite occur in Soledad Canyon above the mouth of Agua Dulce Creek, Porter (p.c. '49).

Mendocino County: 1, Laumontite occurs as the cement of Cretaceous sandstone at Anchor Bay, Gilbert (2) p. 1517.

Plumas County: 1, Minor amounts of laumontite were identified at the Engels mine, Graton and McLaughlin (4) p. 18.

Riverside County: 1, Laumontite occurs in the Crestmore limestone quarries, as fibrous masses on green prehnite, Eakle (15) p. 352. At the same locality it is found in pegmatites or pegmatite-like masses, as white friable aggregates or interlacing crystals, and also as compact masses of radiating or columnar crystals 3 to 8 mm long, or in cavities, Woodford et al. (10) p. 371.

San Bernardino County: 1, Fibrous white laumontite in large veins has been found near the Grant mine, on the right slope of Cucamonga Canyon, CDMG (12479), Woodford (p.c. '44).

San Diego County: 1, Laumontite occurred in Moosa Canyon, near Bonsall, Schaller (18) p. 37, associated with axinite, and 2, it has been found in minute crystals at Rincon, A. F. Rogers (4) p. 214. 3, Rosettes and sprays of thin columnar crystals of laumontite have been found in the pegmatites at Pala, Jahns and Wright (5) p. 42.

Tulare County: 1, Veinlets of crystalline laumontite are associated with scheelite bearing tactite in the Tyler Creek (Bull Point, Vern Tyler) tungsten mine (N$\frac{1}{2}$ sec. 35, T. 23, S., R. 30 E., M. D.), Goodwin (1) p. 367.

* LAWSONITE, 1895
Basic calcium aluminum silicate, $CaAl_2Si_2O_6(OH)_4$

Lawsonite was discovered in 1895 as a new mineral and was described by F. L. Ransome (3) p. 301, in schists. It is widespread in the metamorphic rocks of the Coast Ranges.

Alameda County: 1, Lawsonite was found in seams of glaucophane schist near the head of Arroyo Mocho, A. F. Rogers (13) p. 106, in crystals up to 1 cm in length, and 2, as tabular crystals up to 5 mm across, in the extreme southeast corner of Tesla quadrangle, ibid., p. 109.

Contra Costa County: 1, Lawsonite was found in a chlorite boulder on the hillside north of Berkeley, Thelen (1) p. 221, Eakle (7) p. 84. 2, Lawsonite is found in schists with pumpellyite, on the private estate of Mrs. Anson Blake, G. A. Davis and Pabst (1) p. 692.

Humboldt County: 1, The northernmost recorded occurrence of lawsonite in the state is near Yager, A. F. Rogers (13) p. 111.

Los Angeles County: 1, Lawsonite is a microscopic constituent of the crossite schists of Santa Catalina Island, Woodford (1) p. 55. 2, The mineral is found in the San Pedro Hills, ibid.

Marin County: 1, The original discovery of lawsonite was made by F. L. Ransome (3) p. 301, in the schists of the Tiburon Peninsula, half a mile east of Reed Station. Crystals from the type locality were studied by Schaller and Hillebrand (4) p. 195. The destruction of this type locality for housing development is vividly described by Rice (3), p. 96. Analyses by Ransome (3), Schaller and Hillebrand (4). X-ray crystallography of lawsonite is reported by Pabst in G. A. Davis and Pabst (1) p. 697.

Mendocino County: 1, Lawsonite was found in a large glaucophane-schist outcrop on Burger Creek, 2 miles northwest of Dos Rios, Vonsen (p.c. '32.) **2**, Crystals of lawsonite occur in Franciscan schist near Covelo, at the headwaters of Jumpoff Creek, S. G. Clark (p.c. '32). The mineral occurs in fine euhedral tabular crystals of pale pink color, up to 2 inches in length, Chesterman (p.c. '51). **3**, Poorly developed lawsonite crystals occur with glaucophane in a quarry 5.1 miles north of Longvale on U.S. 101, together with riebeckite and stilpnomelane, Watters (p.c. '58).

Merced County: **1**, Lawsonite is associated with aragonite, pumpelly-ite and stilpnomelane in Franciscan rocks of the Pacheco Pass area, Bates McKee (2) p. 384; see also Santa Clara County **(6)**.

San Benito County: **1**, Lawsonite occurs with pumpellyite in the contact zone of jadeite on Clear Creek, Yoder and Chesterman (1) p. 3. **2**, Gray lawsonite occurs in veins in glaucophane schist (sec. 21, T. 14 S., R. 10 E., M. D.), at the north end of Glaucophane Ridge (N. R.).

San Diego County: **1**, Lawsonite is found in the San Onofre breccia, Woodford (2) p. 192.

San Luis Obispo County: **1**, Platy crystals of lawsonite in masses of green chlorite occur about 4 miles east of San Luis Obispo, Eakle (7) p. 86, A. F. Rogers (13) p. 111. **2**, Lawsonite is found in glaucophane-lawsonite schist near Cayucos, J. P. Smith (1) p. 213.

San Mateo County: **1**, Lawsonite-glaucophane schist has been found 3 miles southwest of Redwood, J. P. Smith (1) p. 212, Eakle (7) p. 86.

Santa Barbara County: **1**, Lawsonite is found sparingly in schist pebbles collected from Teritary sediments, at the northeast corner of Santa Rosa Island, T. L. Bailey and Woodford (1) p. 191.

Santa Clara County: A. F. Rogers (13) records lawsonite from the schists of many localities in the county: **1**, acicular crystals in cavities and seams of loose boulders, in the north end of Calaveras Valley, p. 108; **2**, in the Mount Hamilton area, crystals up to 4 mm, p. 108; **3**, Colorado Creek, p. 109; **4**, Smith Creek near Santa Clara Hotel, p. 111. **5**, Lawsonite-glaucophane schist, made up almost entirely of these two minerals, is reported by J. P. Smith (1) p. 212 from **(a)**, the San Juan mine, Oak Hill, near San Jose and **(b)**, one mile south of Coyote Canyon. **6**, Lawsonite occurs with aragonite, pumpellyite, and stilp-nomelane in Franciscan rocks of the Pacheco Pass area, McKee (2) p. 384; see also Merced County **(1)**.

Sonoma County: **1**, Veins of dull green lawsonite occur with pum-pellyite in glaucophane schist, at Mill Creek, Irving et al. (1) p. 338. **2**, Lawsonite occurs with pumpellyite at Camp Meeker, 2 miles north of Occidental (sec. 16 (?), T. 7 N., R. 10 W., M. D.), Vonsen (p.c. '23). **3**, Good crystals were found on the highway half a mile south of Cazadero (sec. 21, T. 8 N., R. 10 W., M. D.), Vonsen (p.c. '45). **4**, Lawsonite occurs with glaucophane 2 miles north of Valley Ford (sec. 15 (?), T. 6 N., R. 10 W., M. D.), Vonsen (p.c. '45). A specimen, CDMG (21317), from $2\frac{1}{2}$ miles northeast of Valley Ford, confirms Vonsen. **5**, Lawsonite-glaucophane schist occurs at Guerneville, J. P. Smith (1) p. 212. **6**, A specimen of lawsonite was identified from Buckeye Creek, CDMG (21737).

LAZULITE

Basic magnesium aluminum iron phosphate, $(Mg,Fe^{2+},Al_2(PO_4)_2(OH)_2$

Lazulite and lazurite are often difficult minerals to identify by field examination. It is evident in studying the literature that reports are often inaccurate. The user is reminded that all literature reports have not been validated for accuracy of identification.

Alpine County: **1,** Bands of lazulite with andalusite and rutile in garnetiferous quartzite occur 10 miles southwest of Markleeville, W. W. Bradley (28) p. 207.

Inyo County: **1,** Lazulite occurs in a vein in schist in Breyfogle Canyon, Chloride Cliff area (approx. T. 30 N., R. 1 E., S. B.), Cloudman et al. (1) p. 864. **2,** Lazulite is found in the Lee Mining District, 10 miles north of Darwin, CDMG (20758).

Kern County: **1,** Lazulite has been reported from an unspecified locality in this county, Pecora and Fahey (1) p. 14.

Madera County: **1,** Lazulite, originally identified as lazurite, has come from Wawona, in the Minarets Mining District, CDMG (18136). **2,** Scorzalite reported by Smerud and McDonald (1) p. 20, may be lazulite and, though unlikely, may be the same as the lazulite of locality **(1)**.

Mono County: **1,** Lazulite occurs in considerable amount in the andalusite mass in the White Mountains, Kerr (3) p. 629, Woodhouse (4) p. 38, Lemmon (2) p. 945, Jeffery and Woodhouse (4) p. 6, and **2,** as crystals up to 2 inches in size in the Vulcanus claim opposite the andalusite mine across Dry Creek Canyon, Kerr (3) p. 629. **3,** Large, deep-blue anhedrons of lazulite occur with rutile and andalusite 1 mile west of Green Lake (sec. 28 (?), T. 3 N., R. 24 E., M.D.), A. F. Rogers (7) p. 375.

San Bernardino County: **1,** Lazulite occurs crystalline and massive in veins associated with quartz, muscovite, talc, tremolite and specularite, 7 miles southeast of Hodge, 200 yards west of the Globerson Iron mine, O. E. Bowen (1) p. 135.

San Diego County: **1,** A specimen of lazulite, CDMG (13591), came from Oceanside, Kunz (24) p. 98.

LAZURITE—Lapis Lazuli
Sodium calcium aluminum silicate with sulphate, sulphur
$(Na,Ca)_8(Al,Si)_{12}O_{24}(SO_4,S_n)$

Lazurite and lazulite are often difficult minerals to identify by field examination. It is evident in studying the literature that reports are often inaccurate. The user is reminded that all literature reports have not been validated for accuracy of identification.

Madera County: **1,** A specimen of lazurite reported from the Minarets (Ritter Range) has been shown to be lazulite, Murdoch (p.c. '45).

Mono County: **1,** Lazurite has been doubtfully reported from the andalusite mine in the White Mountains, Peck (1) p. 152, but this was not confirmed by Kerr (3) p. 629. **2,** Lazurite is listed as occurring near Mono Lake, Kunz (24) p. 98, but this may refer to the Green Lake occurrence of lazulite **(3)**.

San Bernardino County: **1,** A small prospect pit (NE¼ sec. 6, T. 1 N., R. 7 W., S. B.), in Cascade Canyon, has produced a little lapis lazuli as patches and grains in a mica-diopside schist. It was first found as boulders in the bed of San Antonio Creek, and traced to the outcrop, Surr (6) p. 1153, A. F. Rogers (7) p. 377, (44) p. 111. Rogers considers the mineral to be a sulphide-bearing haüyne. Lazurite, presumably from this locality, was early (1867) mentioned by C. W. King (1) in a footnote on p. 273. A reference to lazurite from this county in Ostwald (1) pp. 84–101, is presumably from this same locality.

LEAD
Native lead, Pb

Native lead is an exceedingly rare mineral and its reported occurrence as a true mineral is sometimes open to doubt. Small bits of lead found in the placer gravels may be portions of lead bullets, but the occurrence of the metal in deep placer mines is indicative of its origin as a natural reduction product.

Butte County: **1,** Small, subangular fragments of lead, 3 to 4 mm in size, have been found 14 miles east of Chico, in the West Fork Feather River, A. F. Rogers (7) p. 373.

Kern County: **1,** Lead has been doubtfully reported from the dry placers at Goler (N. R.).

Placer County: **1,** Small pellets of lead, possibly native, have been found in a placer mine in North Ravine in the Edgewood area, near the Ophir Mining District (N. R.).

LEADHILLITE
Basic lead carbonate and sulphate, $Pb_4SO_4(CO_3)_2(OH)_2$

Inyo County: **1,** Small, imperfect crystals of leadhillite, of a pale sea-green tint, were found with linarite and caledonite at the Cerro Gordo mine, A. F. Rogers (1) p. 46.

LECHATELIÉRITE
Fused quartz, SiO_2

Riverside County: **1,** Fragments of fused quartz (lechateliérite), associated with some cristobalite, have been found in sand fulgurites near Indio, A. F. Rogers (50) p. 120.

LEPIDOCROCITE
Basic iron oxide, $FeO(OH)$ (γ-phase)

Lepidocrocite occurs under the same conditions as goethite, and is often associated with it.

Shasta County: **1,** Lepidocrocite has been recorded from Iron Mountain, Palache et al. (10) p. 644.

LEPIDOLITE—Lithia Mica
Hydrous potassium lithium and aluminum silicate, $K(Li,Al)_3(Si,Al)_4O_{10}(O,OH,F)_2$

This usually pink or lavender mica, characteristic of the lithia-tourmaline pegmatites, was first noted in California in 1856 by Antisell (1) p. 187, and then in 1881, by W. P. Blake (23) p. 376, who reported it with rubellite from the "Bernardino Range in Southern California."

Inyo County: **1,** White lepidolite is doubtfully reported from Surprise Canyon, R. W. Raymond (5) p. 34.

Riverside County: **1,** Lepidolite, with tourmaline, kunzite, and amblygonite, is abundant in the Fano mine (SW¼ sec. 33, T. 6 S., R. 2 E., S. B.), Kunz (23) p. 968, and **2,** it occurs in platy cleavelandite with colored tourmaline, on the southeast slope of Coahuila Mountain (NE¼ sec. 16, T. 7 S., R. 2 E., S. B.), Fisher (1) p. 67. **3,** Fine-grained, scaly, lilac lepidolite is found in moderate abundance in the Anita mine (sec. 22, T. 6 S., R. 1 E., S. B.), Fisher (1) p. 84.

San Bernardino County: **1,** Lepidolite from an unspecified locality, on analysis by Papish and Holt (1) p. 142, showed traces of gallium; see also W. P. Blake (23) p. 376.

San Diego County: The best general reference to lepidolite in this county is to be found in CDMG Bulletin 37, by Kunz (24). **1,** A large body of massive lepidolite, some with intergrown needles of pink tourmaline, occurs in the Stewart mine at Pala, Fairbanks (5) p. 36, Kunz (24) pp. 55, 100. Fine- to coarse-grained lepidolite associated with lithia tourmalines also occurs in all the other mines in the region. Analyses and spectroscopic tests have shown some unusual elements in these lepidolites: cesium, Kennard and Rambo (1) p. 454; cesium and rubidium, Stevens (1) p. 617; germanium, Papish (2) p. 473. Kennard and Rambo (2) p. 108, found .67 percent rubidium and .16 percent cesium with spectroscopic traces of gallium and thallium in lepidolite from the Sickler mine at Pala. **2,** Good crystals of lepidolite have been found in the pegmatites near Ramona (secs. 6, 9, T. 13 S., R. 2 E., S. B.), Schaller (8) p. 143, (7) p. 225. **3,** Lepidolite is abundant in the lithia pegmatites at Mesa Grande, Kunz (24) p. 100. Stevens (1) p. 617, found rubidium and cesium on analysis of material from here. **4,** Lepidolite occurs in the Victor mine at Rincon, A. F. Rogers (4) p. 214. The mineral occurs also in the southern extension of the Clark dike, with spodumene and beryl, Hanley (3) pp. 20, 23. **5,** Lepidolite is found with amblygonite at Granite Mountain (NW¼ sec. 18, T. 13 S., R. 5 E., S. B.), near Banner, J. H. Pratt (5) p. 314, Van Amringe (1) p. 1. **6,** Lepidolite occurs with cassiterite, columbite, and blue tourmaline in a small pegmatite on the east side of Chihuahua Valley (SW¼ sec. 12, T. 9 S., R. 3 E., S. B.), Schaller (36) p. 353. This lepidolite also shows cesium and rubidium, Stevens and Schaller (3) p. 531. **7,** Lepidolite occurs with tourmaline in the Pete Labat (French Pete, Elinor) mine (SW¼ sec. 36, T. 9 S., R. 3 E., S. B.), Tucker and Reed (26) p. 40. **8,** The mineral occurs with gem tourmaline at Oak Grove, Kunz (24) p. 100. Cesium and rubidium have been found in analyses, Stevens (1) p. 617. **9,** An early report by Antisell (1) p. 187, records lepidolite near San Felipe.

LEPIDOMELANE
Basic iron magnesium aluminum potassium silicate,
$$K_2(Fe^{3+},Fe^{2+},Mg)_{4-6}(Si,Al,Fe^{3+})_8O_{20}(OH)_4$$

Near biotite in composition, but characterized by a large amount of ferric iron, $(Fe^{2+} > Mg)$.

Kern County: **1,** A specimen of lepidomelane, CDMG (15674) came from Isabella.

Santa Cruz County: **1,** Lepidomelane has been identified in the mineral suite associated in the Pacific Limestone Products (Kalkar) quarry at Santa Cruz, C. W. Chesterman (p.c. '64).

† * LESSERITE, 1956
See inderite

Kern County: **1,** The mineral reported as the new California borate lesserite by Frondel et al. (8) p. 927, from the Kramer borate area has been shown to be inderite, Schaller and Mrose (56) p. 732, confirming Ward Smith (p.c. '58).

LEUCITE
Potassium aluminum silicate, $KAl(SiO_3)_2$

Inyo County: **1,** Leucite occurs in basalt plugs in Deep Spring Valley, Nash and Nelson (1) p. 47.

LEUCOPHOSPHITE
A hydrous potassium iron aluminum phosphate,
near $K_2(FeAl)_7(PO_4)_4(OH)_{11} \cdot 6H_2O$

Fresno County: **1,** Leucophosphite has been found as spherulites and pellets in nodules of apatized wood in the Moreno formation, head of Escarpado Canyon (NW¼ sec. 7, T. 15 S., R. 12 E., M. D.), Gulbrandsen et al. (1) p. 101.

LIBETHENITE
Basic copper phosphate, $Cu_2(PO_4)(OH)$

San Benito County: **1,** Libethenite is found in glaucophane schist, 4½ miles north of Llanada, E. H. Oyler (p.c. '59).

LIMONITE—Brown Hematite
Hydrous oxide of iron, $Fe_2O_3 \cdot nH_2O$ (α -monohydrate)

The name limonite formerly was given to a hydrous iron oxide with the supposed formula $2Fe_2O_3 \cdot 3H_2O$. It has been shown that "limonite" is usually cryptocrystalline goethite with absorbed or capillary water. The name is conveniently used for any natural hydrous iron oxide which is otherwise unidentified. It may occur in stalactitic, botryoidal or mammillary forms, and as spongy masses, or coatings. It varies quite widely in appearance, but always has a yellow-brown streak, and submetallic to dull luster.

Limonite is formed by the weathering of minerals containing iron, and is very common as the "gossan" or "iron hat" forming a surface capping of pyrite ore bodies. It may be used locally as an ore of iron, but is not as important as hematite or magnetite for this purpose. It is frequently abundant enough to be used as a mineral pigment, the "yellow ocher" corresponding to the "red ocher" of powdery or massive hematite. It is universally present in all parts of California, but only the most important · occurrences can be cited. The deposits used for mineral paints are listed and described by Symons (1) pp. 148–160, but none of these is of particular mineralogic interest, and most are of minor commercial importance.

Imperial County: **1,** Limonite pseudomorphs showing pyritohedrons occur in considerable abundance at the property of the Vitrefax Corporation, 10 miles west of Winterhaven, in the Cargo Muchacho area. The mineral occurs in massive quartzite in the Precambrian metamorphic rocks of the area, Murdoch and Webb (p.c. '64).

Inyo County: **1,** Pseudomorphs of limonite after long crystals of stibnite have been observed at the Cerro Gordo mine (N. R.).

Mariposa County: **1,** Pseudomorphs of limonite after pyrite have been found in Chowchilla Valley, Hanks (7) p. 200.

Placer County: **1,** The limonite gossan of some of the old mines— for example the Dairy Farm—in the Foothill copper belt have been mined in recent years for their gold content, Murdoch (p.c. '45).

Riverside County: **1,** Limonite pseudomorphous after pyrite occurs commonly in the Crestmore quarries, Eakle (15) p. 352, Woodford et al. (10) p. 368.

Shasta County: **1,** Beautiful stalactites of limonite have been found in the gossan at Bully Hill, Diller (7) p. 128. **2,** Iridescent limonite stalactites, up to 4 inches in length and 1 inch in diameter, have been collected at Iron Mountain, Lang (1) p. 561. **3,** Some stalactites from Charles Camden's mine were on display at the California Midwinter Fair in 1894, Benjamin (1) p. 153.

Trinity County: **1,** Very large cubes of limonite, pseudomorphous after pyrite, are found in the Golden Jubilee mine, Carrville Mining District, D. F. MacDonald (2) p. 31.

Tulare County: **1,** The Mineral King Mining District has furnished some good pseudomorphs of limonite after pyrite, CDMG (10865).

LINARITE
Basic lead copper sulphate, $(Pb,Cu)_2SO_4(OH)_2$

Inyo County: **1,** Beautiful, divergent, columnar masses of deep azure-blue linarite were obtained in the Cerro Gordo mines during the early days of mining. The specimens were sometimes banded with green caledonite and brochantite. Fine crystals were also obtained from pockets and cavities in the massive mineral, A. F. Rogers (12) p. 46, Eakle (9) p. 225, Waring and Huguenin (2) p. 97, C. W. Merriam (1) p. 43. **2,** Thin platy crystals of linarite were found with aurichalcite and malachite at the Defiance mine, Darwin Mining District, Murdoch and Webb (14) p. 323, and at the Wonder Prospect, with caledonite, in the same region, A. Knopf (4) p. 17. **3,** Linarite occurred in oxidized ores at the Reward mine, 2 miles east of Manzanar Station, A. Knopf (5) p. 118. **4,** Linarite, with caledonite and cerussite, was found at the Monster mine, on the east flank of the Inyo Range, northwest of Saline Valley, A. Knopf (5) p. 111. **5,** Linarite is occasionally present in the ores of the Big Four mine, northern Panamint Mountains, Hall and Stephens (3) p. 26.

Madera County: **1,** Linarite was found with anglesite on the Bliss claims near Davis Lake, Minarets Mining District, Erwin (1) p. 70.

Mono County: **1,** Hulin (p.c. '36) reports linarite from Blind Spring Hill.

San Bernardino County: **1,** Linarite occurs in the Ibex (Arcturus) mine, 6 miles north of Saratoga Springs, with argentiferous galena and cerussite, Waring and Huguenin (2) p. 96, Cloudman et al. (1) p. 821. **2,** Linarite is reported with caledonite and dioptase from near Baker in Soda Lake Mountains, CDMG (21350), Murdoch (p.c. '49).

Tulare County: **1,** Linarite was found with cerussite and anglesite at the Copper Queen mine, CDMG (18680).

LINNAEITE
Cobalt sulphide, Co_3S_4

San Luis Obispo County: **1**, Linnaeite is reported as microscopic isometric crystals in fractured vein quartz, altering to bieberite, from Klau quicksilver mine, Santa Lucia Range (sec. 33, T. 26 S., R. 10 E., M. D.), Woodhouse and Norris (6) p. 114.

LIROCONITE
Hydrous basic copper aluminum arsenate, $Cu_2Al(AsO_4)(OH)_4 \cdot 4H_2O$

Inyo County: **1**, Liroconite was found at the old Cerro Gordo mine associated with other rare copper minerals (N. R.).

LITHARGE
Lead monoxide, PbO

Inyo County: **1**, Litharge has been found 9 miles east of Big Pine, W. W. Bradley (29) p. 106. **2**, The mineral was reported in the Darwin (New Coso) Mining District, G. M. Wheeler (3) p. 57.

Kern County: **1**, Litharge has been recorded in plates bordered by massicot, from an unspecified locality in the county, E. S. Larsen (4) p. 18.

San Bernardino County: **1**, Brownish-orange-red scales of litharge bordered by massicot were found near Cucamonga Peak, Hanks (12) p. 256, E. S. Larsen (4) p. 18. Hanks (12) p. 256 suggests that this might have come from a prehistoric ore furnace.

LITHIOPHILITE
Lithium manganese phosphate, $LiMnPo_4$

San Diego County: **1**, Lithiophilite was found with purpurite and triphylite at Pala, Graton and Schaller (1) p. 146, Schaller (22) p. 79, (29) p. 145, Jahns and Wright (5) p. 40.

LÖLLINGITE
Iron diarsenide, $FeAs_2$

Amador County: **1**, Small crystals of löllingite were found in veins in slate at the Mayflower gold mine, Amador City, CDMG (14161).

Inyo County: **1**, A little löllingite was found with arsenopyrite and pyrrhotite at the Bishop Creek mine, 18 miles southwest of Bishop, Schroter (2) p. 53.

Riverside County: **1**, Löllingite forms the central part of lenses of sulphides in coarse-grained marble of the underground workings at Crestmore, Kelley (2) p. 141.

San Diego County: **1**, Löllingite is very rare, usually associated with phosphates, on Queen and Heriart Mountains, Pala, Jahns and Wright (5) p. 42.

LUDLAMITE
Hydrous ferric phosphate, $Fe_3^{3+}(PO_4)_2 \cdot 4H_2O$

San Diego County: **1**, Ludlamite is reported from the Pedro mine, Pala, Anon. (19) p. 265, Frondel (p.c. '51). It occurs as small greenish patches in lithiophilite.

LUDWIGITE
Magnesium iron borate, $(Mg,Fe^{2+})_2Fe^{3+}BO_5$

El Dorado County: **1,** Scaly masses originally identified as ludwigite, from the Cosumnes mine near Fair Play, A. F. Rogers (7) p. 375, have been shown to be biotite or some similar micaceous mineral, Schaller (p.c. '46).

Fresno County: **1,** Ludwigite occurs as needle-like crystals in metamorphosed dolomitic limestone in the Twin Lakes region, Chesterman (p.c. '55). **2,** Ludwigite occurs at Kaiser Peak, on the north side of Kaiser Ridge, Chesterman (7), p. 1712.

Kern County: **1,** Ludwigite was identified in some of the cassiterite ores at Gorman, 4 miles north of Quail Lake, Wiese and Page (1) p. 50, L. R. Page (3) p. 202; see also Riverside County **(1).**

Riverside County: **1,** A few black prisms in the margin of the limestone body at Crestmore have been tentatively identified as ludwigite, Woodford et al. (10) p. 365. Schaller (p.c. '46) suggests that the Kern and Riverside County occurrences may be paigeite rather than ludwigite; see also Schaller and Vlisidis (57).

San Bernardino County: **1,** Ludwigite is reported by Lamey (10) p. 673, from the Cave Canyon iron deposit, northeast of Yermo, and **2,** it occurs at Lava Bed iron deposit, south of Newberry Springs, Lamey (10) p. 673.

* MACALLISTERITE, 1964
Hydrous magnesium borate, $Mg_2B_{12}O_{20}\cdot15H_2O$

Inyo County: **1,** The new mineral macallisterite has been found in five different localities in the Death Valley region, California. The mineral is associated with ginorite, sassolite and gypsum, and is found as sugary white aggregates of minute crystals, intimately mixed with its associates, W. T. Schaller et al. (58) p. 173. No details of localities are given.

* MACDONALDITE, 1964 [1]
Hydrous barium calcium silicate, $Ba,Ca_4Si_{15}O_{35},11H_2O$

Fresno County: **1,** Macdonaldite, a new mineral discovered along Big and Rush Creeks in the eastern part of the county, is named in honor of Dr. Gordon Andrew Macdonald. The mineral is briefly described by Stinson and Alfors (6) p. 234. Macdonaldite occurs associated with the new minerals krauskopfite, walstromite and others along with sanbornite, gillespite, celsian and taramellite.

MAGHEMITE
Iron oxide, Fe_2O_3 (γ-ferric oxide)

Alameda County: **1,** Maghemite was reported from this county, but no detail of location is given, Newhouse and Glass (2) p. 701.

Kern County: **1,** Maghemite was identified from three claims in the tin deposits near Gorman, Wiese and Page (1): Upper Butler prospect, p. 47; Crowbar Gulch prospect, p. 49, and Gray Eagle prospect, p. 51.

---

[1] This new mineral is described in a paper which appeared in April, 1965, after the cutoff date (Dec. 31, 1964) for entries in this volume. "Seven new barium minerals from eastern Fresno County, California", by John T. Alfors, Melvin C. Stinson, Robert A. Matthews and Adolf Pabst: Am. Mineralogist, vol. 50, pp. 314–340, 1965.

Riverside County: **1,** Brown-coated lodestone from the Eagle Mountain iron mine contains maghemite, Crippen (p.c. '49).

Shasta County: **1,** Maghemite is reported from the gossan at Iron Mountain, Sosman and Posjak (1) p. 332; Newhouse and Glass (2) p. 701, Kinkel et al. (2) p. 119.

MAGNESIO-COPIAPITE
Basic hydrous magnesium iron sulfate, $Mg,Fe^{3+}_4(SO_4)_6(OH)_2 \cdot nH_2O$

Napa County: **1,** This complex mineral in greenish-yellow masses was described originally in 1890 as knoxvillite, and as a new mineral from California, Becker (4) p. 389. The mineral has been found with redingtonite and mercury minerals at the old Redington (Boston) mine at Knoxville, Melville and Lindgren (1) p. 24. It was considered by E. S. Larsen (11) p. 61, to be a variety of copiapite, and is established as magnesio-copiapite by Whitmore and Berry (1) p. 21.

MAGNESIOFERRITE
Oxide of iron and magnesium, $(Mg,Fe)Fe_2O_4$, $Mg > Fe^{3+}$

Riverside County: **1,** Black shiny crystals of this mineral, showing cube, octahedron and dodecahedron, have been found in the crystalline limestone of the Crestmore quarry, Schwartz (p.c. '53).

San Benito County: **1,** Brilliant black octahedrons, almost 1 mm across in chlorite schist from near the benitoite mine, were identified as magnesioferrite, Murdoch (p.c. '50).

MAGNESITE
Magnesium carbonate, $MgCO_3$

Magnesite is widespread in California because of the great areas of serpentine, of which it is often an alteration product. The serpentine is commonly intersected by veins and patches of snow-white to light-buff magnesite. Some of these veins are commercially important. The main deposits lie in the serpentine belts of the Coast Ranges, but deposits also occur in serpentines in the foothills of the Sierra Nevada and elsewhere. The mineral is mostly in cryptocrystalline masses with prominent conchoidal fracture, and the siliceous varieties are very hard. The magnesite deposits of California have been described in CDMG Bulletin No. 79, W. W. Bradley (8).

As a mineral resource, magnesite occurs in considerable quantity in many deposits. In the localities referenced below, no attempt has been made to systematically report commodity occurrences, nor to report the mineral wherever it is mentioned in the literature. Some localities of minor importance and of little general mineralogical interest are noted because they have been carried in early editions of *Minerals of California.* The authors consider it wise to retain these as part of the historical record, but newer and more important localities of the mineral as a mineral resource have not been added, and literature citations to articles on such localities have not necessarily been included. It is emphasized that validation of correct mineral identification in the literature has not been undertaken, so early identifications may be incorrect, especially regarding hydromagnesite and magnesite.

Alameda County: **1,** Several deposits of magnesite occur on Cedar Mountain, containing stringers of magnesite in serpentine (secs. 27, 35, T. 4 S., R. 3 E., M. D.), W. W. Bradley (8) pp. 41, 43. **2,** Magnesite occurs as boulders, none in place, at Hayes Ranch (SW¼ sec. 24, T. 4 S., R. 2 E., M. D.), ibid., p. 42.

Del Norte County: **1,** Stringers of magnesite up to 4 inches by 6 feet are found in serpentine at the Camp 7 group (sec. 7, T. 16 N., R. 3 E., H.), J. E. Allen (2) p. 121.

Fresno County: **1,** Massive white veins of magnesite occur in serpentine at the Piedra mine (secs. 5, 9, T. 13 S., R. 24 E., M. D.), Goldstone (1) p. 185, Hess (5) p. 50, W. W. Bradley (8) p. 44. **2,** Magnesite is reported from the Vance mine, Pine Flats, Yale and Stone (5) p. 7.

Humboldt County: **1,** Small veins of magnesite are found in a road cut between Willow and Hoopa, Laizure (3) p. 319.

Inyo County: **1,** Magnesite is reported from the J. E. Gould mine near Owenyo, Yale and Stone (5) p. 7.

Kern County: **1,** A deposit of bedded magnesite has been found 1½ miles north of Bissell (NE¼ sec. 11, T. 10 N., R. 11 W., S. B.), H. S. Gale (12) p. 512, W. W. Bradley (8) p. 47. **2,** Good specimens of magnesite have come from Walker Pass, Hess (5) p. 39.

Kings County: **1,** Boulders and segregations of magnesite in serpentine occur in a deposit which extends into Monterey County (sec. 20, T. 23 S., R. 16 E., M. D.), W. W. Bradley (8) p. 51.

Los Angeles County: **1,** A small deposit of magnesite occurs in serpentine 18 miles from Saugus (secs. 11, 12, T. 6 N., R. 15 W., S. B.), W. W. Bradley (8) p. 52.

Madera County: **1,** Magnesite in 3-foot veins is reported a quarter of a mile south of Grub Gulch, Laizure (6) p. 343.

Mariposa County: **1,** Magnesite occurs at Big Spring Hill (sec. 30, T. 5 S., R. 19 E., M. D.), Laizure (6) p. 148.

Mendocino County: **1,** Small deposits of magnesite in serpentine occur on the Hixon Ranch (sec. 11, T. 12 N., R. 11 W., M. D.), Hess (5) p. 21; **2,** Southard Ranch, W. W. Bradley (8) p. 52, and **3,** near Willits, Yale and Gale (4) p. 395.

Monterey County: **1,** A continuation of the magnesite deposit found in Kings County is about 3 miles east of Parkfield, W. W. Bradley (8) p. 53.

Napa County: A number of magnesite veins in serpentine occur in the county: **1,** at Pope Valley (sec. 2, T. 9 N., R. 5 W., M. D.), Hess (5) p. 28; **2,** Chiles Valley (sec. 28, T. 8 N., R. 4 W., M. D.), ibid., p. 29, and W. W. Bradley (19) p. 275, reports some crystalline pale to greenish vein magnesite; **3,** Soda Valley (secs. 25, 36, T. 8 N., R. 4 W., M. D.), Crawford (1) p. 328. An additional reference to segregations and veins in serpentine is in Weaver (1) p. 174.

Nevada County: **1,** Nearly pure magnesite in serpentine was found in the Idaho-Maryland mine, Lindgren (12) p. 115. **2,** Stringers and veins of magnesite occur in serpentine (secs. 25, 36, T. 18 N., R. 10 E., M. D.), Averill (13) p. 74.

Placer County: **1,** Magnesite, sometimes in considerable quantities, occurs in veins in serpentine in the central part of the county near

Towle, Gold Run, Iowa Hill, Michigan Bluff and Damascus (T. 15, 16 N., R. 10, 11 E., M. D.), Hanks (12) p. 257, G. E. Bailey (2) p. 103, H. S. Gale (12) p. 501, W. W. Bradley (8) p. 59.

Riverside County: **1,** A large deposit of magnesite veinlets in a mass of serpentine was mined near Winchester (NW¼ sec. 31, T. 5 S., R. 1 W., S. B.)., Hess (5) p. 38, W. W. Bradley (8) p. 61. **2,** Magnesite is tentatively identified as an alteration product from the Crestmore quarries, Woodford et al. (10) p. 368.

San Benito County: Magnesite veinlets occur widespread in the serpentines of the county. **1,** One large deposit is at the Sampson magnesite claims (secs. 34, 35, 36, T. 17 S., R. 11 E., M. D.), H. S. Gale (12) p. 503.

San Bernardino County: **1,** A bedded deposit of magnesite 10 to 20 feet thick occurs on the east side of Cave Canyon (sec. 21(?), T. 11 N., R. 6 E., S. B.), Hewett et al. (1) p. 117; and **2,** another bedded deposit, interstratified with dolomite, occurs southwest of Needles (secs. 15, 22, T. 8 N., R. 21 E., S. B.), Schlocker (1) p. 9, Tucker and Sampson (33) p. 138. For further description of several deposits near Needles, see Vitaliano (1) p. 363. **3,** Massive 2 to 4 foot veins of magnesite in dolomitic limestone occur 10 miles northwest of Cima in the Ivanpah Mountains, Tucker and Sampson (16) p. 314 (secs. 15, 16, T. 15 N., R. 14 E., S. B.), L. A. Wright et al. (5) p. 184. **4,** Thick beds of magnesite, interstratified with dolomitic clay and bentonite, occur 4 miles southeast of Kramer Station (secs. 3, 4, T. 9 N., R. 6 W., S. B.), Tucker and Sampson (32) p. 67, L. A. Wright et al. (5) p. 184. **5,** Veins of magnesite up to several feet in thickness occur 12 miles east of Victorville near the Victor Cement Company properties (sec. 2, T. 6 N., R. 2 W., S. B.), Yale and Gale (4) p. 581, L. A. Wright et al (5) p. 184.

San Francisco County: **1,** A little magnesite occurs with xonotlite on Army Street, San Francisco, Pabst (p.c. '44), and **2,** at Fort Point, as seams in serpentine, Eakle (1) p. 316.

San Luis Obispo County: **1,** Small veins of magnesite occur in serpentine on the Kiser Ranch about 9 miles northwest of Cambria, W. W. Bradley (8) p. 76, and **2,** a large deposit is reported on the Steele Ranch 7 miles east of Arroyo Grande, Franke (2) p. 426.

Santa Barbara County: **1,** Small stringers of magnesite in serpentine are found in Happy Canyon (sec. 15, T. 7 N., R. 29 W., S. B.), W. W. Bradley (8) p. 77.

Santa Clara County: **1,** An extensive deposit of magnesite occurs at the Sherlock and other mines, Red Mountain area (T. 6 S., R. 5 E., M. D.), Hess (5) p. 33, Bodenlos (1) p. 238. **2,** Many other deposits, all similarly veins in serpentine, are found in the county: near Edenville, Coyote Station, Madrone, W. W. Bradley (8) pp. 78, 79, 87. **3,** A. F. Rogers (25) p. 138, has described euhedral crystals of magnesite from a narrow vein in the San Juan quicksilver mine, 5 miles south of San Jose. **4,** Pods of magnesite occur with chromite in serpentine on the Smith property (sec. 35, T. 7 S., R. 1 E., M. D.), F. F. Davis and Jennings (6) p. 337.

Sonoma County: Many deposits, all as veins in serpentine, occur in the county: **1,** Kolling (Creon) deposit (sec. 32, T. 12 N., R. 10 W.,

M. D.), 2 miles north of Cloverdale, W. W. Bradley (1) p. 325; **2,** Yordi (Ekert) Ranch, 2 miles southeast of Cloverdale, Hess (5) p. 23; **3,** Gilliam Creek deposits (sec. 31, T. 9 N., R. 10 W., M. D.), ibid., p. 24; **4,** Red Slide (secs. 16, 17, 21, T. 9 N., R. 11 W., M. D.), 6 miles north of Cazadero, W. W. Bradley (1) p. 327. **5,** Small crystals of magnesite forming a crust with barite and dolomite are reported from the Great Eastern mine, Guerneville, Vonsen (p.c. '45).

Stanislaus County: **1,** The Bald Eagle and Quinto claims (sec. 32, T. 8 S., R. 7 E., M. D.), Perry and Kirwan (1) p. 1, Boalich (4) p. 254, have produced much magnesite. **2,** The Smith mine (T. 6 S., R. 6 E., M. D.), near Patterson, has produced some magnesite, Lowell (1) p. 629. **3,** Lenses of magnesite in serpentine occur at the Red Mountain mine (sec. 20, T. 6 S., R. 5 E., M. D.), W. W. Bradley (8) p. 98.

Tulare County: Very many deposits occur in the general area covered by townships 18–22 S., ranges 26–28 E., M. D., W. W. Bradley (8) pp. 106–135.

Tuolumne County: **1,** The Gray Eagle, Monarch and other claims near Chinese Camp (T. 1 S., R. 14 E., M. D.) have shipped some magnesite, W. W. Bradley (8) p. 138.

MAGNETITE
Iron oxide, Fe_3O_4

Lodestone is a variety possessing natural polarity.

Magnetite is one of the most abundant of the iron minerals, and several good deposits of it occur in the State. It is a minor constituent of most igneous rocks, and occurs in this manner in nearly all the counties. The black sands of streams and beaches have been derived from the weathering of igneous rocks and the subsequent concentration of magnetite grains, together with chromite, garnet, zircon and many other heavy, hard minerals. Only the more important or interesting occurrences can be listed.

Butte County: **1,** Lodestone has been found in a deposit near Chaparral Hill (T. 26 N., R. 5 E., M. D.), J. R. Browne (4) p. 224.

Calaveras County: **1,** Well-formed octahedrons of magnetite occur in talc schist at the Melones mine, Carson Hill, A. Knopf (11) p. 37. Massive magnetite has come from the Iron Rock mine, Carson Hill, CDMG (13696).

Del Norte County: **1,** Crystals of magnetite are reported from Gasquet, CDMG (21545).

El Dorado County: **1,** Veins of magnetite up to $4\frac{1}{2}$ feet in thickness have been reported from the Reliance mine (sec. 18, T. 10 N., R. 9 E., M. D.), Logan (9) p. 441, and **2,** large boulders were found by W. P. Blake (3) p. 82, (5) p. 289, at Volcanoville. **3,** Magnetite occurs with hematite at the Chaix prospect near Latrobe, in lenticular masses, W. B. Clark and Carlson (3) p. 437.

Fresno County: **1,** Magnetite is the principal vein mineral, with bornite, in the Uncle Sam mine opposite Tehipite dome, the Kings River, W. W. Bradley (2) p. 438. **2,** Magnetite is abundant in parts of the "skarn" of a scheelite deposit at Twin Lakes, Chesterman (1) p. 276.

Inyo County: **1,** Microscopic crystals of magnetite occur in lithophysae in obsidian, with tridymite, near Coso Hot Springs, Rutley (1) p. 426, A. F. Rogers (23) p. 215. **2,** A considerable quantity of lodestone was reported from the Slate Range, Hanks (12) p. 258.

Kern County: **1,** A mass of magnetite was reported 3 miles south of the San Emigdio mine, Angel (2) p. 226. **2,** A 3-foot vein of magnetite was reported near the summit of ''Cañada de las Uvas'' (Grapevine Canyon), W. P. Blake (3) p. 82, (5) p. 289.

Los Angeles County: **1,** Important masses of titaniferous magnetite (with intergrown ilmenite) have been found in the western San Gabriel Mountains, 1 mile southwest of the Monte Cristo mine (T. 3, 4 N., R. 12, 13, 14 W., S. B.), in anorthosite, Tucker (13) p. 296, W. J. Miller (5) p. 335, (7) p. 22. **2,** Masses of magnetite (ilmenite?) associated with cinnamon garnet, chlorite and hornblende were found in the New Pass (Soledad Canyon), W. P. Blake (3) p. 82, (5) p. 289.

Madera County: **1,** Large deposits of magnetite are found on the western slope of Iron Mountain, Minarets Mining District, Goldstone (1) p. 191, Erwin (1) p. 63. **2,** Extensive deposits of magnetite, with pyrite, are reported at Iron Creek (T. 5 S., R. 22, 23 E., M. D.), R. P. McLaughlin and Bradley (3) p. 554. **3,** Lodestone has been found at the Sparkling iron mine, Kings Creek, CDMG (12853).

Mono County: **1,** Magnetite occurs as an important mineral in the veins of the Benton, Lundy, and other areas, Whiting (1) p. 389, Rhinehart and Ross (1) p. 17. **2,** Magnetite was found coated with greenockite at the South 40 claim (T. 8 N., R. 22 E., M. D.), near the Golden Gate mine, West Walker River, Eakle and McLaughlin (17) p. 141.

Nevada County: **1,** Lodestone was found on Grouse Ridge, 14 miles north of Washington, J. R. Browne (4) p. 224, and **2,** a large deposit occurs at the contact of granodiorite and diabase 4 miles south of Indian Springs, Lindgren and Turner (10) p. 6, E. MacBoyle (1) p. 59.

Placer County: **1,** A large deposit of magnetite, which was worked from 1881–86 by blast furnace, occurs at Hotaling, 5 miles west of Clipper Gap, Lindgren (13) p. 3, C. A. Waring (4) p. 390.

Plumas County: **1,** A large deposit of magnetite occurs just west of Wades Lake, H. W. Turner (14) p. 8.

Riverside County: **1,** Magnetite is a very minor mineral at Crestmore, in the Lone Star quarry, Woodford et al. (10) p. 366. **2,** A very large mass of iron ore at Eagle Mountain (T. 4 S., R. 14 E., S. B.) is composed partly of magnetite, Harder (6) p. 63, and **3,** small crystals, separate or in clusters, and sometimes badly weathered, are found in the Southern Pacific silica quarry at Nuevo, Fisher (1) p. 34.

San Bernardino County: **1,** A large mass of magnetite-hematite ore occurs at the Iron Age mine (sec. 29, T. 1 S., R. 13 E., S. B.), 6 miles east of Dale, Tucker and Sampson (17) p. 334, and **2,** at Iron Mountain (secs. 27, 28, T. 6 N., R. 4 E., S. B.), in the Lava Beds Mining District, is a series of massive veins of magnetite and hematite, ibid., p. 335. **3,** There are other deposits of magnetite in the Providence Mountains (T. 10 N., R. 13 E., S. B.), Cave Canyon (T. 11 N., R. 7 E., S. B.), Kingston Mountains (T. 25 S., R. 11 E., M. D.), Crossman (1) p. 235,

Cloudman et al. (1) p. 820, Tucker and Sampson (17) p. 334, Lamey (5) p. 87. **4**, Magnetite and hematite occur in the Ship Mountain deposits (T. 5 N., R. 15 E., S. B.), Lamey (7) p. 113. **5**, Magnetite is found with hematite at Iron Hat (T. 6 N., R. 14 E., S. B.), Lamey (6) p. 99. **6**, Hematite and magnetite occur in the Old Dad Mountain deposit (secs. 13, 14(?), T. 12 N., R. 10 E., S. B.), Lamey (3) p. 61. **7**, Magnetite is found with hematite near the Silver Lake area Iron Mountain deposits (T. 15 N., R. 6, 7 E., S. B.), Lamey (2) p. 39.

Santa Cruz County: **1**, Layers of black sand up to 6 inches in thickness occur at Aptos; they are composed largely of magnetite and ilmenite, Katz (1) p. 463, Laizure (4) p. 75.

Shasta County: **1**, A large deposit of magnetite at Heroult was worked by electric smelter, Logan (7) p. 12. **2**, An extensive deposit occurs near the junction of McCloud and Pit Rivers, McGregor (1) p. 641. **3**, Magnetite occurs in quantity at Iron Mountain, Hanks (7) p. 195, and **4**, a large deposit, used mainly as heavy aggregate in naval construction, occurs at the Shasta Iron Company property (sec. 26, T. 34 N., R. 4 W., M. D.), J. C. O'Brien (1) p. 82. **5**, At the Black Diamond mine (secs. 2, 3, T. 33 N., R. 4 W., M. D.), magnetite occurs as a contact mineral with pyrrhotite and chalcopyrite, Tucker (11a) p. 146. **6**, A small deposit of magnetite, with garnet and epidote, occurs at the Hirz Mountains deposit (T. 35 N., R. 3 W., M. D.), Lamey (8) p. 131.

Sierra County: **1**, A large body of magnetite, some of it lodestone, is found at the Sierra iron mine (secs. 11, 12, T. 21 N., R. 11 E., M. D.), Hanks (7) p. 195, Aubury (3) p. 304. **2**, Perfect octahedral crystals in talcose slate have come from Forest City, CDMG (10443). **3**, Massive magnetite is found southeast of Spencer Lakes (T. 22 N., R. 10 E., M. D.), H. W. Turner (14) p. 8.

MALACHITE
Basic copper carbonate, $CuCO_3(OH)_2$

Azurite, chrysocolla, malachite, and other blue, blue-green, and green minerals, mostly copper-bearing, are widespread in stringers, coatings, and alterations associated with other copper minerals referenced in this volume. No systematic effort to report all occurrences of these minerals is practical. However, many minor occurrences are reported, and others omitted, because early literature was often to minor localities, and they have been retained for clarity of the historic record.

Amador County: **1**, Fine reniform masses have come from Volcano (N.R.).

Calaveras County: **1**, Fine specimens of massive malachite with crystallized copper have been found in the Union mine, Irelan (3) p. 151, Reid (3) p. 398. **2**, Fine specimens of malachite and azurite have been found in the Hughes mine, W. P. Blake (9) p. 17, Hanks (12) p. 259.

Humboldt County: **1**, Excellent specimens of malachite have come from the Horse Mountain mine, Laizure (3) p. 306.

Inyo County: **1**, Good drusy specimens of malachite have come from the Cerro Gordo mine, CDMG (18357). **2**, Malachite occurs with other copper carbonates in the Darwin Mining District, Hall and MacKevett (4) p. 64.

Kern County: **1,** A little malachite is present in the tin ores of a property near Gorman, Troxel and Morton (2) p. 294.

Mariposa County: **1,** Fine drusy coatings and excellent crystallized malachite occur at the White Rock Mine, CDMG (15741).

Mono County: **1,** Malachite is rather abundant in the Blind Spring Mining District, especially the Kerrick mine, Hanks (12) p. 259, A. L. Ransome (2) 190. **2,** Malachite occurs with cuprite and chrysocolla at the Detroit mine, in the Jordan Mining District, Whiting (1) p. 364.

Monterey County: **1,** J. B. Trask reported malachite from the old silver mine at Alisal Rancho, Hanks (12) p. 259.

Placer County: **1,** Malachite was abundant at the Algol mine (sec. 9, T. 13 N., R. 7 E., M. D.), Aubury (1) p. 173.

Plumas County: **1,** Alternating bands of malachite and chrysocolla were found at the Engels mine, Kunz (24) p. 102. **2,** Large masses of malachite in limestone occur in the Genesee Valley Mining District, Logan (4) p. 463.

Riverside County: **1,** Malachite occurs as an alteration product of copper sulphides at Crestmore, Eakle (17) p. 327, Woodford et al. (10) p. 368.

San Diego County: **1,** Excellent specimens of malachite have come from 3 miles south of Julian (perhaps from the Friday mine), CDMG (9980).

Santa Clara County: **1,** Malachite occurs with crystallized cinnabar in calcite from the Guadalupe mine, Kunz (24) p. 107, CDMG (4929).

Shasta County: **1,** Malachite is a minor mineral in the East Shasta copper-zinc mining area, Albers and Robertson (3) p. 71.

Tuolumne County: The reference to malachite, azurite, and other oxidation minerals at Whiskey Hill, in earlier editions of this bulletin, should be to Placer County, near Lincoln, see Silliman (7) p. 351.

MANGANITE
Basic manganese oxide, MnO(OH)

There are numerous small deposits of manganese oxides in the state, and much of the ore may be manganite mixed with psilomelane or pyrolusite. Unless crystals are present, it is impossible to identify manganite without x-ray methods, P. D. Trask et al. (4) p. 54.

In general, manganite may be present in any of these oxide deposits, so that its occurrences are possibly numerous. It has rarely been definitely identified in the state.

Imperial County: **1,** Minor amounts of manganite are found with pyrolusite and psilomelane in the Paymaster area (secs. 16, 18, 19, T. 11 S., R. 21 E., S. B.), Tucker (11) p. 266, Hadley (1) p. 465.

Madera County: **1,** Manganite, with rhodonite, rhodochrosite and psilomelane is reported by P. D. Trask et al (4) p. 130, from near Coarse Gold.

Riverside County: **1,** Manganite is tentatively reported as a rare oxide in the Crestmore quarries, Woodford et al. (10) p. 368.

San Diego County: **1,** Manganite is found associated with manganese-bearing albite at the Catherina mine, Pala, Schaller (29) p. 145, Kraus and Hunt (2) p. 465.

Shasta County: **1,** Minute crystals of manganite have been found in cavities and fractures in quartz at the Murray mine (sec. 1, T. 32 N., R. 6 W., M. D.), Raymond (p. c. '36).

MARCASITE
Iron disulphide, FeS₂

Bornite, chalcocite, chalcopyrite, cuprite, galena, marcasite, pyrite, pyrrhotite, stibnite, tenorite, tetrahedrite, and many other antimony, copper, iron, lead and zinc sulphides, and oxides are found in traces or in minor amounts in many localities. The entries listed reflect either mineralogical or historic interest, and the listings are not complete nor is all literature which mentions these minerals referenced.

Amador County: **1,** Marcasite is found with pyrrhotite and other sulphides at the Defender mine, 5 miles southeast of Volcano, Tucker (1) p. 27.

Calaveras County: **1,** Marcasite is reported from the West Point area, Franke and Logan (4) p. 239.

Colusa County: **1,** Marcasite occurs with stibnite, gold and cinnabar at the Manzanita mine, Becker (4) p. 367.

Contra Costa County: **1,** Marcasite is found with cinnabar and metacinnabar at the Mount Diablo (Ryne) mine (SE¼ sec. 29, T. 1 N., R. 1 E., M.D.), A. L. Ransome and Kellogg (1) p. 377, C. P. Ross (2) p. 41, Pampeyan (1) p. 24.

Del Norte County: **1,** Marcasite is found at Patrick Creek (T. 18 N., R. 3 E., H.), Laizure (3) p. 287.

Inyo County: **1,** Marcasite has been identified microscopically in massive pyrrhotite at the Curran mine, half a mile north of Panamint City, Murphy (2) p. 314, (4) p. 367.

Kern County: **1,** Marcasite occurs with gold quartz at the Bowman mine (sec. 20, T. 28 S., R. 34 E., M.D.), Tucker and Sampson (21) p. 293; **2,** in the Big Blue group (T. 25 S., R. 33 E., M.D.), Prout (1) p. 413, Troxel and Morton (2) p. 99; **3,** in the Green Mountain Mining District (T. 29 S., R. 34 E., M.D.), Tucker and Sampson (21) pp. 296, 307, and **4,** in small amounts in the gold veins of Soledad Mountain, Mojave Mining District, Tucker (23) p. 469.

Lake County: **1,** Marcasite occurs with cinnabar and metacinnabar at the Baker mine (sec. 16, T. 12 N., R. 6 W., M.D.), Becker (4) p. 368. **2,** Pseudomorphs of cinnabar and tiemannite after marcasite have been observed from the Abbott mine (sec. 32, T. 14 N., R. 5 W., M.D.), Watts (2) p. 240. **3,** Marcasite is found in the Red Elephant mine, near Knoxville, Averitt (1) p. 88. **4,** Considerable marcasite was found in some of the ores of the Helen mine (sec. 1, T. 10 N., R. 8 W., M.D.), Tucker (36) p. 276. **5,** Marcasite has been found at Sulphur Bank, D. E. White and Roberson (2) p. 404.

Los Angeles County: **1,** Marcasite occurs at the head of Mill Creek, near the Monte Cristo mine, R. J. Sampson (10) p. 187.

Mono County: **1,** Marcasite is found in quartz veins with pyrite and galena at the King group (T. 3 S., R. 31 E., M.D.), W. W. Bradley (29) p. 144.

Napa County: **1,** Marcasite occurs with metacinnabar at the Redington mine, Knoxville (secs. 6, 7, T. 11 N., R. 4 W., M.D.), A. L.

Ransome and Kellogg (1) p. 410. **2,** Botryoidal and stalactitic marcasite has come from the Palisades mine about 2 miles north of Calistoga, CDMG (20376).

Nevada County: **1,** Marcasite was reported by Lindgren (7) p. 231, as one of the minor minerals at Grass Valley, and **2,** it was found with copper sulphides in the Mineral Hill area (approximately T. 15 N., R. 8 E., M.D.), Forstner (4) p. 745.

Riverside County: **1,** Marcasite occurred at the Lucky Strike mine, between Perris and Elsinore, in a gold quartz vein, R. J. Sampson (9) p. 513.

San Bernardino County: Marcasite occurs in a number of gold mines in the county, in minor amounts: **1,** Colosseum (T. 17 N., R. 13 E., S.B.), **2,** Paymaster (T. 13 N., R. 10 E., S.B.), and **3,** Vanderbilt, 4 miles east of Ivanpah, Tucker and Sampson (17) pp. 292, 217, 330; also at **4,** Cumberland (sec. 25, T. 6 N., R. 2 E., S.B.), and **5,** Coarse Gold, east slope of Providence Mountains, Tucker and Sampson (27) p. 63, (28) p. 234. **6.** Cockscomb marcasite has been found at the Martha prospect, Ord mountains, Weber (3) p. 26.

San Diego County: **1,** Several mines in the Descanso region show a little marcasite, Tucker (8) p. 371.

San Luis Obispo County: **1,** Marcasite occurs as sheaves of slender crystals in chalcedony vugs, and with occasional cinnabar crystals perched on millerite needles, from the Klau quicksilver mine (sec. 33, T. 26 S., R. 10 E., M. D.), Woodhouse and Norris (6) p. 114.

Solano County: **1,** A small amount of marcasite occurs in the cinnabar ore at the St. John mine (NE¼ sec. 33, T. 4 N., R. 3 W., M. D.), Weaver (1) p. 170.

Tuolumne County: **1,** Marcasite occurs sparingly 2 miles northwest of Columbia, Tucker (1) p. 138.

Ventura County: **1,** Marcasite is found with gold at the White Mule mine on the north slope of Frazier Mountain, Tucker and Sampson (20) p. 257.

Yolo County: **1,** Marcasite is reported from the Reed mine, Averitt (1) p. 76.

MARGARITE
Basic calcium aluminum silicate, $CaAl_4Si_2O_{10}(OH)_2$

Margarite is prominent in glaucophane-bearing rocks and has been observed in several localities.

Calaveras County: **1,** Margarite has been found at the Gold Cliff mine, near Angels, CDMG (15483).

Marin County: **1,** The margarite mentioned by F. L. Ransome (3) p. 309, from Reed Station, Tiburon Peninsula, Eakle (22) p. 249, has been identified as muscovite, Eakle (7) p. 83.

Plumas County: **1,** Margarite occurs with corundum in the plumasite 1½ miles northwest of Meadow Valley post office, J. H. Pratt (6) p. 42.

Riverside County: **1,** Margarite is reported in contact rock with mineral "Z" at Crestmore, Ettinger (p.c. '59).

San Mateo County: **1,** Margarite is a microscopic constitutent of the schists at Belmont, Murgoci (1) p. 391.

Santa Clara County: **1,** Margarite occurs with garnet and glaucophane at Hilton Gulch, Oak Ridge, J. P. Smith (1) p. 203.

Sonoma County: **1,** Margarite is a microscopic constitutent of the glaucophane gneiss of Melitta, near Santa Rosa, Murgoci (1) p. 389.

* MARIPOSITE, 1868
Basic potassium aluminum chromium silicate,
$K(Al,Cr)_2(Al,Si)_4O_{10}(OH)_2$; up to 1% Cr

Mariposite is essentially muscovite, variety phengite characteristically colored green by the presence of some chromium. It is abundantly distributed in the gold belt of the Sierra Nevada, and was described as a new mineral by Silliman (9) p. 380. It is considered by some mineralogists to be identical with alurgite, Schaller (35) p. 139. A good general description of all Mother Lode occurrences is given by A. Knopf (11) p. 38.

Calaveras County: **1,** Mariposite occurs in schist at the Reserve and Golden Gate mines on Carson Hill, A. Knopf (11) p. 38.

El Dorado County: **1,** Green flakes of mariposite occur in the Pyramid mine, 4 miles north of Shingle Springs (N. R.).

Imperial County: **1,** Mariposite has been reported from this county, W. W. Bradley (28) p. 343.

Kern County: **1,** Mariposite occurs in the Randsburg schists, Hulin (1) p. 25. Location is NW$\frac{1}{4}$ sec. 10, T. 30 S., R. 40 E., M. D., Troxel (p.c. '57).

Los Angeles County: **1,** Mariposite occurs as nests and lenses in talc-sericite schists of the Sierra Pelona series, in San Francisquito Canyon, upstream from the old San Francisquito Canyon dam site, Murdoch and Webb (6) p. 353.

Mariposa County: **1,** The original mariposite was described and named from the Josephine mine, Silliman (9) p. 380, Hanks (12) p. 260; analysis, H. W. Turner (12) p. 679. It is common in the schists of this county.

Nevada County: **1,** Mariposite is found in the Idaho-Maryland mine at Grass Valley, Lindgren (12) p. 115. **2,** Mariposite is reported from the Red Ledge mine, Washington, with quartz and calcite in veins (N. R.).

Placer County: **1,** Mariposite was found at the Marguerite mine (N. R.).

Riverside County: **1,** Mariposite was reported on the west side of San Jacinto Mountain (N. R.).

San Diego County: **1,** Mariposite was reported near Oak Grove (N. R.).

Sierra County: **1,** Mariposite was found at the Rainbow mine, CDMG (10442); **2,** it occurs at the Alhambra mine, Poker Flats (sec. 10, T. 21 N., R. 10 E., M. D.), E. MacBoyle (3) p. 75, and **3,** in the Forest and other areas, ibid., Lindgren (20) p. 105.

Tuolumne County: **1,** Mariposite is common in quartz gangue of gold ores in the Rawhide and other mines near Tuttletown, H. W. Turner and Ransome (15) p. 6.

MASCAGNITE
Ammonium sulphate, $(NH_4)_2SO_4$

Sonoma County: **1,** Mascagnite has been found with boussingaultite and epsomite near The Geysers, Goldsmith (7) p. 265, Vonsen (6) p. 288. The mineral forms as incrustations and nodules during the early summer months, in the upper part of Geyser Creek Canyon.

MASSICOT
Lead monoxide, PbO

El Dorado County: **1,** Massicot was found at the Rescue mine, W. W. Bradley (26) p. 194, CDMG (20836).

Inyo County: **1,** Massicot was reported 9 miles southeast of Big Pine, W. W. Bradley (29) p. 106; **2,** it was found in the Darwin Mining District, Loew (2) p. 186, and **3,** it occurred abundantly in the first discovered ore bodies with minium, wulfenite and pyromorphite at Cerro Gordo, R. W. Raymond (9) pp. 29, 31, Loew (2) p. 186.

Kern County: **1,** Fine scales of massicot have been found near Fort Tejon, E. S. Larsen (11) p. 106. A specimen of this is in the University of California Collections, Berkeley. **2,** Another specimen of massicot occurring as borders on litharge has been recorded by E. S. Larsen (4) p. 18, from an unknown locality.

Mono County: **1,** Massicot has been found in the Blind Spring Mining District, probably mixed with minium, bindheimite and mimetite, A. L. Ransome (2) p. 189.

San Bernardino County: **1,** Massicot has been found near Cucamonga Peak in scales up to 1 mm across, and as borders on plates of litharge, E. S. Larsen (4) p. 18.

Trinity County: **1,** Massicot has been reported from the northern part of the county, CDMG (20193).

MATILDITE
Silver bismuth sulphide, $AgBiS_2$

Inyo County: **1,** Tiny lamellar, oriented inclusions found in polished surfaces of steel gray galena from the Essex mine, Darwin Mining District, are probably matildite, Hall and MacKevett (1) p. 17, ibid. (4) p. 61.

MELANTERITE—Copperas
Hydrous iron sulphate, $FeSO_4 \cdot 7H_2O$

Melanterite is a common alteration product in mines containing pyrite or marcasite.

Alameda County: **1,** Melanterite is abundant as crystals or fibrous masses on the walls of the mine workings at the Alma pyrite mine, Leona Heights. Complex crystals from this occurrence have been measured and described, Schaller (1) p. 195.

Alpine County: **1,** White brittle crusts and greenish stalactitic masses of melanterite have been found in the Leviathan sulphur mine, 7 miles east of Markleeville, Gary (1) p. 489, Nichols (1) p. 172.

Amador County: **1,** Melanterite occurred with mendozite on the walls of an old tunnel 1½ miles north of Volcano (N. R.).

Contra Costa County: **1,** Melanterite was found in the Mount Diablo mine (SE¼ sec. 29, T. 1 N., R. 1 E., M. D.), C. P. Ross (2) p. 42, Pampeyan (1) p. 24.

Inyo County: **1,** Melanterite was identified as a component of silver-lead ores from the oxidized zone in the Darwin Mining District, Hall and MacKevett (1) p. 18, ibid. (4) p. 64.

Kern County: **1,** Melanterite has been noted in the oxidized portion of veins of the Gold Peak and Cowboy mines, Mojave Mining District, Troxel and Morton (2) p. 281. **2,** Melanterite is common in the oxidized zones of silver ore bodies in the Loraine area, Troxel and Morton (2) p. 41.

Lake County: **1,** Melanterite is abundant as stalactites in the Sulphur Bank mine, near Clear Lake, Hanks (15) p. 104. **2,** Brilliant green stalactites have been found in the Bradford quicksilver mine, Friedrich (1) p. 22.

Los Angeles County: **1,** Colorless crusts of melanterite associated with halotrichite and gypsum occur in pyritiferous boulders in conglomerate on Cahuenga Peak, in a road-cut below the television station (sec. 25, T. 1 N., R. 14 W., S. B.), Neuerburg (1) p. 159, locality 10.

Napa County: **1,** Long pale-green stalactites of melanterite were abundant in the old Redington mine, Knoxville, Kramm (1) p. 345. **2,** Hulin (p.c. '36) has reported melanterite from the Palisades mine, 2 miles north of Calistoga.

Orange County: **1,** Fibrous crusts of melanterite up to 5 inches thick occur on the walls of old workings at the Santiago coal mine, Santiago Canyon, Van Amringe (p.c. '36).

San Benito County: **1,** Botryoidal masses and silky fibers of melanterite are found in the old tunnels of the New Idria mine, Wilkie (p. c. '36).

San Bernardino County: **1,** Melanterite was found in old drifts of the California Rand and other mines of the area, Hulin (1) p. 99.

San Diego County: **1,** Small green and white crystals of melanterite were reported 6 miles south of Escondido, W. W. Bradley (28) p. 207.

Santa Cruz County: **1,** Abundant white or greenish efflorescences of melanterite covered the sides and bottom of a ravine running to the sea northwest of Santa Cruz, J. B. Trask (2) p. 56, (4) p. 388.

Shasta County: **1,** Melanterite is fairly common in the copper mines of the county, Graton (3) p. 100.

Sonoma County: **1,** Drusy green melanterite has been found near Petaluma, CDMG (11832), and **2,** melanterite has been observed as occurring sparingly at The Geysers, Vonsen (6) p. 291, Irelan (3) p. 633.

Trinity County: **1,** Melanterite occurred with other sulphates at the Island Mountain mine, Vonsen (p.c. '17).

MELILITE

Melilite is a solid solution of three end-members: gehlenite, $Ca_2Al_2SiO_7$, åkermanite, $MgCa_2Si_2O_7$, and ferro-åkermanite $Ca_2FeSi_2O_7$. Its formula may be written $(Ca,Na_2)(Mg,Fe^{2+},Fe^{3+},Al)(Si,Al)_2O_7$.

Velardeñite is a granular variety of gehlenite described from Durango, Mexico.

Inyo County: **1**, A specimen of gehlenite, CDMG (21332), came from the Ubehebe Mining District, 2 miles east of Lost Burro Spring.

Riverside County: **1**, Gehlenite occurs in granular masses intimately intergrown with merwinite, spurrite and diopside, at the Crestmore limestone quarry, E. S. Larsen and Foshag (10) p. 144, Woodford (11) p. 358. The gehlenite at Crestmore is considered by C. Wayne Burnham (1), p. 880, to be about 60% gehlenite 40% åkermanite.

Tulare County: **1**, Dull-green gehlenite, variety velardeñite, occurs in this county, Shannon (4) p. 1.

* MELONITE, 1867
Nickel telluride, NiTe₂

Calaveras County: **1**, Melonite was discovered on Carson Hill in 1867 and described as a new mineral by Genth (4) p. 86, (5) p. 313. **2**, The mineral was also found in the Stanislaus mine associated with hessite (?) and native tellurium (?), Genth (5) p. 313; analysis by Hillebrand (3) p. 60.

MENDOZITE
Hydrous aluminum sodium sulphate, NaAl(SO₄)₂·11H₂O

Amador County: **1**, Crusts of mendozite and melanterite occur on the walls of an old tunnel 1½ miles north of Volcano (N. R.).

Napa County: **1**, Mendozite occurs on the Pritchard Ranch 9 miles southeast of St. Helena (N. R.).

San Bernardino County: **1**, Platy and fibrous white mendozite occurs 5 miles north of Hidden Springs, CDMG (18698).

MENEGHINITE
Sulfide of lead and antimony, CuPb₁₃Sb₇S₂₄

Santa Cruz County: **1**, This rare mineral has been found with franckeite and stannite in the contact rock of the Pacific Limestone Products (Kalkar) quarry, 2 miles west of Santa Cruz, Milton and Chesterman (p. c. '54).

MERCURY—Quicksilver
Native mercury, Hg

Liquid globules of mercury are common in most of the cinnabar mines, formed either by reduction of the sulphide or by sublimation of mercuric vapors. The mineral occurs in deep workings and in those parts of poorly ventilated mines where intense heat is developed by the decomposition of iron sulphides; it is also frequently found near the walls of cinnabar veins.

Del Norte County: **1**, Mercury was found in sec. 18, T. 18 N., R. 3 E., H., J. C. O'Brien (1) p. 78, and **2**, it was reported from the Rockland area (sec. 11, T. 18 N., R. 2 E., H.), Mining and Scientific Press (16). **3**, Plentiful mercury was found with cinnabar in the veins of the Webb mine (SE ¼ sec. 20, T. 18 N., R. 3 E., H.), J. C. O'Brien (9) p. 281.

Kings County: **1**, Mercury occurred in the Kings mine with cinnabar in serpentine, W. W. Bradley (2) p. 529.

Lake County: **1**, Mercury is abundant in the Wall Street mine, CDMG (63); **2**, in the Bradford mine, Friedrich (1) p. 22; **3**, at the

Great Western, Mirabel, and other mines west of Middletown, Crawford (1) p. 360, and **4**, at the Chicago mine (sec. 1, T. 10 N., R. 8 W., M. D.), Aubury (2) p. 51.

Mariposa County: **1**, Mercury was found with gold amalgam at an unspecified locality, Schmitz (1) p. 713.

Mendocino County: **1**, Mercury is found 5 miles west of Orr Springs, Watts (2) p. 256.

Mono County: **1**, Mercury was found with cinnabar in limonite in a canyon 4 miles north of Hammil Station (T. 2 S., R. 33 E., M. D.), Woodhouse (p.c. '45).

Napa County: **1**, Mercury occurs in La Joya and other mines in the vicinity of sec. 24, T. 7 N., R. 6 W., M. D., W. W. Bradley (5) p. 85, A. L. Ransome and Kellogg (1) p. 410, and **2**, it has been found in considerable amount in the mud of the hot springs on the east side of Napa Creek, near Calistoga, W. W. Bradley (5) p. 81.

Orange County: **1**, Small amounts of mercury have been reported at Red Hill, near Tustin, Fairbanks (4) p. 118. It seems probable from the description that this is not metallic mercury, but metacinnabar, which occurs at this locality with cinnabar.

San Benito County: **1**, Mercury occurred in very considerable amount in certain parts of the New Idria mine. In one instance as much as one pint of mercury was collected at a single spot, W. W. Bradley (5) p. 97; **2**, it is found in the Alpine and other mines, Stayton Mining District, ibid., and **3**, mercury globules have been found on cinnabar half a mile above the junction of Clear Creek and San Benito River, Watters (p.c. '51).

San Francisco County: **1**, Globules of mercury with cinnabar have been found in siliceous rock near Twin Peaks, San Francisco, J. D. Whitney (7) p. 78, W. W. Bradley (5) p. 124.

San Luis Obispo County: **1**, Mercury has been found with metacinnabar at La Libertad mine, Adelaide Mining District, Mining and Scientific Press (31) p. 323, and **2**, at the Oceanic mine, Von Leicht (1) p. 482.

San Mateo County: **1**, Mercury was found with montroydite and cinnabar on the McGarvey Ranch about 3 miles from Redwood City on the Searsville road, Woodhouse (3) p. 603, Mining and Scientific Press (10) p. 357. **2**, The mineral occurs on the Corte de Madera Rancho (?) 5 miles west of Palo Alto with cinnabar and calomel, W. W. Bradley (5) p. 149. **3**, Mercury came from the Emerald Lake mine near Redwood City, with cinnabar, metacinnabar and terlinguaite (?), (CDMG 21669).

Santa Clara County: **1**, Small amounts of mercury have been found in the New Almaden mine, Huguenin and Castello (4) p. 222, E. H. Bailey and Everhart (12) p. 96. **2**, The mineral occurs in the Vaughn mine (sec. 14, T. 11 S., R. 6 E., M. D.), with cinnabar, Crawford (1) p. 358.

Siskiyou County: **1**, Mercury is found sparingly at the Great Northern mine, A. L. Ransome and Kellogg (1) p. 459.

Sonoma County: **1**, Metallic mercury was the only ore mineral at the Rattlesnake mine (sec. 31, T. 11 N., R. 8 W., M. D.). The metal was so abundant that it would spurt out of the ore when a pick was sunk in, Egleston (1) p. 273, W. W. Bradley (5) p. 192. **2**, The main values were in metallic mercury in the Socrates (Pioneer) mine (sec. 32, T. 11 N., R. 8 W., M. D.), Aubury (2) p. 115, W. W. Bradley (5) p. 193. **3,** Considerable mercury occurred in the New Sonoma mine (secs. 4, 5, T. 10 N., R. 8 W., M. D.), W. W. Bradley (5) p. 191, and in other mines in the Pine Flat area, ibid. p. 187; **4,** at the Esperanza mine on Sulphur Creek, ibid., p. 186; **5,** at the Clear Quill mine, Greenville area, CDMG (61), and **6,** with metacinnabar at the Culver-Baer mine (sec. 23, T. 11 N., R. 9 W., M. D.), W. W. Bradley (5) p. 185. **7,** Aubury (1) p. 141, (4) p. 166, reported mercury from a 10-foot shaft on the Wall tract (sec. 30, T. 8 N., R. 9 W., M. D.), 5 miles southwest of Santa Rosa.

Trinity County: **1,** Mercury was found with stibnite and cinnabar at the Altoona mine (T. 38 N., R. 6 W., M. D.), W. P. Miller (1) p. 716. **2,** The mineral was reported with cinnabar and magnesite at the Integral mine (sec. 14, etc., T. 38 N., R. 6 W., M. D.), Mining and Scientific Press (25) p. 323.

* MERWINITE, 1921
Calcium magnesium silicate, $Ca_3Mg(SiO_4)_2$

Riverside County: **1,** Merwinite occurs as granular masses associated with gehlenite, spurrite and wollastonite in the limestone quarries at Crestmore. This new mineral was described and named by E. S. Larsen and Foshag (10) p. 143, in 1921. It alters to thaumasite and foshagite, Murdoch (p.c. '64).

MESOLITE
Hydrous sodium calcium aluminum silicate, $Na_2Ca_2[Al_2Si_3O_{10}]_3 \cdot 8H_2O$

Mesolite is a zeolite generally occurring as silky fibrous crusts in cavities of basaltic rock.

Kern County: **1,** Silky, fibrous aggregates of mesolite occur with other zeolites on fractures in basalt at Red Rock Canyon, Murdoch (p.c. '57).

Lassen County: **1,** Mesolite was observed in the lava of Lassen Peak, CDMG (10325).

Los Angeles County: **1,** The presence of mesolite in amygdules of lava on Frazier Mountain has been confirmed by H. E. Pemberton (p.c. '64).

Shasta County: **1,** Mesolite was found near Redding (N. R.).

Ventura County: **1,** Tufts of hair-like snow-white mesolite occur lining the hollow amygdules of the lavas of Lockwood Valley, H. E. Pemberton (p.c. '64).

* METACINNABAR, 1870
Mercuric sulphide, HgS

Colusa County: **1,** Metacinnabar was found with cinnabar and gold at the Manzanita mine near Sulphur Creek, Becker (4) p. 367.

Contra Costa County: **1,** Metacinnabar is the principal ore mineral mined, with subordinate cinnabar and stibnite at the Mount Diablo (Ryne) mine (sec. 29, T. 1 N., R. 1 E., M. D.), C. P. Ross (2) p. 41, Pampeyan (1) p. 24.

Inyo County: **1,** Metacinnabar has been found at Coso Hot Springs, T. Warner (2) p. 59. **2,** The mineral occurred in a small vein in limestone, with cinnabar, Chloride Cliff mine, C. A. Waring and Huguenin (2) p. 121. **3,** Metacinnabar occurs with stibnite at the Rocket claim, Argus Mountains (sec. 29, T. 22 S., R. 43 E., M. D.), Norman and Stewart (2) p. 84.

Lake County: **1,** Metacinnabar was prominent on the Great Western property, Hanks (84) p. 261; **2,** in the Baker mine, Becker (4) p. 286, and **3,** at the Abbott mine, Aubury (2) p. 47. **4,** The mineral occurs with mercury at the Mirabel mine (T. 10 N., R. 7 W., M. D.), A. L. Ransome and Kellogg (1) p. 392. **5,** Metacinnabar is reported from the northeast corner of the main dump, Sulphur Bank mine, CDMG (21744), D. E. White and Roberson (2) p. 405.

Lassen County: **1,** Metacinnabar occurs as thin coatings on calcareous tufa and lake sediments at Amedee Hot Springs, Dickson and Tunell (1) p. 484.

Monterey County: **1,** Metacinnabar occurs with cinnabar in the Parkfield area (sec. 35, T. 22 S., R. 14 E., M. D.), Aubury (2) p. 124.

Napa County: **1,** Metacinnabar was discovered in the Redington (Boston) mine, Knoxville. Durand (3) p. 220, Hanks (12) p. 261, and **2,** in the Aetna mine (T. 9 N., R. 6 W., M. D.), Melville and Lindgren (1) p. 22. It occurred there in black seemingly amorphous masses and was described as a new mineral by G. E. Moore (1) p. 319, (2) p. 380, (3) p. 36. Good crystals were later found in the same mine. Study showed the mineral to be isometric instead of amorphous, Penfield (1) p. 453. Analyses of metacinnabar from this mine were made by G. E. Moore (1) p. 319, and by Melville and Lindgren (1) p. 22. Metacinnabar formed a large part of the ore in the upper levels. **3,** Metacinnabar was found coated with white calomel in the Oat Hill mine, CDMG (16284).

Orange County: **1,** Metacinnabar was found at Red Hill on the San Joaquin Ranch, disseminated through a ferruginous barite, Genth and Penfield (10) p. 383. This occurrence was erroneously recorded as mercury in CDMG Bulletin 91, Eakle (22) p. 30.

San Benito County: **1,** Large pieces of metacinnabar have been found in the New Hope vein of the New Idria mine, Becker (4) p. 302, and **2,** it is found in black masses at the Picachos mine, A. F. Rogers (7) p. 373. **3,** Small amounts were found with cinnabar in the Bradford (Cerro Gordo) mine (sec. 3, T. 15 S., R. 8 E., M. D.), 11 miles west of Panoche, Becker (4) p. 380, Melville and Lindgren (1) p. 23, W. W. Bradley (5) p. 46. This occurrence has been mistakenly listed in Inyo County because of the identity in name of the mine with the Cerro Gordo mine of the latter county. **4,** Metacinnabar occurs on the Andy Johnsen claim, near Hernandez (Stanford·University Collections); **5,** with cinnabar in sandstone at Valley View (T. 15 S., R. 10 E., M. D.), near Llanada, A. L. Ransome and Kellogg (1) p. 430, and **6,** at the Butts mine (sec. 4, T. 16 S., R. 8 E., M. D.), W. W. Bradley (5) p. 101.

San Luis Obispo County: **1,** Metacinnabar has been found in the Adelaide (Klau) Mining District, Aubury (2) p. 160, CDMG (15860).

San Mateo County: **1,** Metacinnabar has been collected from the Emerald Lake mine near Redwood City, with mercury, cinnabar and terlinguaite (?), CDMG (21669).

Santa Clara County: **1,** Considerable amounts of metacinnabar have been found in the New Almaden and Guadalupe mines. Melville (3) p. 80, (1) p. 292, analyzed metacinnabar from the New Almaden mine and described the crystals as hexagonal, with some complex and doubtful forms. The occurrence has also been studied by G. E. Moore (3) p. 36. It is suggested by Wherry (3) p. 37, that at this occurrence the mineral is guadalcazarite (zincian metacinnabar) but the percentage of zinc appears too low; see also E. H. Bailey and Everhart (12) p. 97.

Solano County: **1,** Metacinnabar occurred with cinnabar in the Hastings mine near Benicia, (sec. 11, T. 3 N., R. 3 W., M. D.), W. W. Bradley (5) p. 172.

Sonoma County: **1,** Metacinnabar was found in the Culver-Baer mine (sec. 23, T. 11 N., R. 9 W., M. D.), east of Cloverdale, W. W. Bradley (5) p. 185. **2,** Metacinnabar occurs abundantly as small equant imperfect crystals, with cinnabar, curtisite and realgar in sandstone at Skaggs Springs, F. E. Wright and Allen (3) p. 169, Everhart (4) p. 390, and **3,** at the Commonwealth Consolidated mine, 2 miles from The Geysers, Crawford (1) p. 371. **4,** Metacinnabar was found in the Eureka mine (sec. 32, T. 11 N., R. 8 W., M. D.), Aubury (2) p. 106.

Yolo County: **1,** The ore of the California (Reed) mine was principally metacinnabar. Both crystals and massive metacinnabar occurred, Hanks (12) p. 261, (15) p. 122.

* METAHAIWEEITE, 1959
Hydrous calcium uranium silicate, $CaO \cdot 2UO_3 \cdot 6SiO_2 \cdot ?H_2O$

Inyo County: **1,** Spherulites of the new mineral haiweeite described by McBurney and Murdoch (1) p. 840, have inner cores of material with a higher index of refraction. Thus a similar relation is suggested to that of torbernite—metatorbernite, where difference in water content exists. The inner spheres are tentatively identified as the new mineral metahaiweeite, CDMG (21739).

METASTIBNITE
Antimony trisulphide, Sb_2S_3

Inyo County: **1,** Metastibnite has been reported with stibnite and oxides of antimony at the Bishop antimony mine, $4\frac{1}{2}$ miles south of Bishop, Woodhouse (p.c. '45).

Lake County: **1,** A little purple metastibnite has been observed in the boulder zone, Sulphur Bank, D. E. White and Roberson (2) p. 409.

Sonoma County: **1,** Metastibnite is reported to occur sparingly in siliceous sinter at The Geysers, Anon. (30) p. 426.

METASTRENGITE
Hydrous iron phosphate, $FePO_4 \cdot 2H_2O$

San Diego County: **1,** A violet-colored material from the Stewart mine, Pala, probably the one called strengite by Schaller (29) p. 145, has been identified by x-ray study as metastrengite, E. S. Dana (6) p. 771, confirming Mrose (p.c. '49) and Frondel (p.c. '48). The name metastrengite has replaced phosphosiderite, E. S. Dana (6) p. 769.

Metastrengite is associated here with yellow stewartite and oxides of manganese.

METATORBERNITE
Hydrous copper uranyl phosphate, $Cu(UO_2)_2(PO_4)_2 \cdot 8H_2O$

Imperial County: **1,** Metatorbernite has been tentatively identified from the Lucky Katy claims on the southwest flank of the Chocolate Mountains (sec. 7, T. 9 S., R. 14 E., S. B.). The mineral fills fractures, and is disseminated in country rock with quartz and iron oxides, G. W. Walker et al. (5) pp. 10, 26.

Inyo County: **1,** Metatorbernite is reported from an unspecified locality, CDMG (21619).

Kern County: **1,** Metatorbernite is tentatively identified from shear zones in volcanic and granitic rocks as coatings, with ferrimolybdite and molybdenite, from the Silver Lady claims in Jawbone Canyon, 20 miles north of Mojave (sec. 10, T. 30 S., R. 36 E., M. D.), G. W. Walker et al. (5) p. 32.

San Bernardino County: **1,** The mineral is reported from an uncertain locality, CDMG (21629).

Tuolumne County: **1,** Metatorbernite is reported from east of Yosemite Valley, CDMG (21620).

METAVOLTINE
Hydrous potassium sodium iron sulphate, $K_4Na_3Fe^{2+}Fe_5^{3+}(SO_4)_{12} \cdot 16H_2O$

San Bernardino County: **1,** Foshag (19) p. 352, has found metalvoltine with krausite, coquimbite, alunite and other sulphates at the "sulphur hole" east of the borate mines near Borate, in the Calico Mountains.

METAZEUNERITE
Hydrous copper uranium arsenate, $Cu(UO_2)_2(AsO_4)_2 \cdot 8H_2O$

Kern County: **1,** MacKevett (2) p. 205, suggests that arsenic and copper in the analyses of the uranium ores of the Kern River uranium area may be from metazeunerite. **2,** Metazeunerite is reported from the Little Sparkler prospect, Kern River uranium area, MacKevett (2) p. 214. **3,** Metazeunerite has been identified in the ore of the Kergon mine, Kern River Canyon, Troxel and Morton (2) p. 332.

Nevada County: **1,** A primary uranium mineral tentatively identified as metazeunerite occurs in the Truckee Canyon group of claims 13 miles E. of Truckee, near Highway 40 (sec. 13, T. 18 N., R. 17 E., M. D.), as minute cavity fillings in a shear zone in granodiorite, G. W. Walker et al. (5) p. 28.

Plumas County: **1,** Metazeunerite is reported from the Chilcoot area, CDMG (21608). G. W. Walker et al. (5) p. 28, describes the Perry Jones group of 61 claims (sec. 13, T. 24 N., 16 E.) and (sec. 18, T. 24 N., R. 17 E., M. D.), where "metazeunerite or torbernite" occurs in quartz vein material. The property is reached by road 4.6 miles north from Chilcoot.

*MEYERHOFFERITE, 1914
Hydrous calcium borate, $Ca_2B_6O_{11} \cdot 7H_2O$

Inyo County: **1,** Meyerhofferite occurs as an alteration of the glassy inyoite crystals in the colemanite deposit of Mount Blanco on Furnace

Creek. It was described, analyzed, and named by Schaller (33) p. 35; Foshag (7) p. 200, (10) p. 10.

Kern County: **1,** Meyerhofferite, pseudomorphous after inyoite, is found in the deposits at Boron, H. E. Pemberton et al. (1) p. 27.

MIARGYRITE
Silver antimony sulphide, $AgSbS_2$

San Bernardino County: **1,** Miargyrite is probably the most abundant silver mineral in the deposits from the Randsburg Mining District. Well-formed crystals are found in open drusy cavities in the veins, Hulin (1) p. 97. Shannon (7) pp. 1-10, has described and analyzed crystals from the California Rand silver mine. Murdoch (9) p. 773, has also studied complex crystals from this occurrence.

MICROLITE
Basic calcium sodium tantalum niobium oxide with fluorine,
$(Ca,Na)_2(Ta,Nb)_2(O,OH,F)_7 Ta > Nb$

Riverside County: **1,** The rare mineral microlite occurs on Queen Mountain, Pala, Jahns and Wright (5) p. 31. This may be the same locality referred to by A. F. Rogers (7) p. 375. **2,** Microlite is reported from the Fano mine, with lepidolite and quartz, Palache et al. (10) p. 753.

San Diego County: **1,** Microlite has been found, exact locality unknown, as a honey-yellow mineral associated with albite, lepidolite, tourmaline and colorless apatite. A few crystals are octahedral with narrow modifying faces, A. F. Rogers (7) p. 375.

MILLERITE
Nickel sulphide, NiS

Calaveras County: **1,** Crystals of millerite intergrown with albite are reported from the Stanislaus mine, A. W. Jackson (3) p. 365.

Humboldt County: **1,** Specimens of serpentine from this county occasionally contain needles of millerite (N. R.).

Lake County: **1,** Millerite occurs in the Great Western mine, in very small amount, R. G. Yates and Hilpert (4) p. 246.

Napa County: **1,** Small coatings of microscopic crystals of millerite were found with cinnabar at the Andalusia mine near Knoxville, Becker (4) p. 284. **2,** Minute millerite crystals were found at the Aetna mine (sec. 2, T. 9 N., R. 6 W., M. D.), Becker (4) p. 372, (6) p. 148. **3,** Millerite was found at the Oat Hill mine in Pope Valley (N. R.). **4,** Specimens of serpentine containing needles of millerite have come from Berryessa Valley (N. R.). **5,** Slender needle-like crystals which may be millerite found in microscopic sections from the Redington mine, Becker (4) p. 286, A. F. Rogers (35) p. 396. **6,** Millerite is found in the Twin Peaks mine, R. G. Yates and Hilpert (4) p. 246.

Placer County: **1,** Millerite was found with arsenopyrite near Cisco, Hanks (12) p. 264.

Plumas County: **1,** Millerite occurred as coatings in the Pocahontas mines at Mountain Meadow, Crawford (1) p. 69.

San Luis Obispo County: **1,** Bronze needle-like crystals of millerite up to $\frac{1}{2}$ inch, occur in the ore of La Libertad mine, Adelaide Mining

District (sec. 21, T. 27 S., R. 10 E., M. D.), F. F. Davis (p.c. '53). **2,** Millerite is reported with small euhedral cinnabar crystals in vugs in gouge and breccia in serpentine from the Klau quicksilver mine (sec. 33, T. 26 S., R. 10 E., M. D.), in the Santa Lucia Range. Linnaeite, marcasite (previously reported as pyrite), and alterations morenosite, bieberite, epsomite, and several iron sulphates are associated. The millerite occurs as sheaves of slender crystals, Woodhouse and Norris (6) pp. 113–115.

Santa Clara County: **1,** Millerite in fine needles is found occasionally in the mercury ores of the New Almaden mine, E. H. Bailey and Everhart (12) p. 99.

Ventura County: **1,** Millerite has been found with pyrrhotite and pentlandite at the Ventura mine (T. 1 N., R. 18 W., S. B.), Tucker and Sampson (20) p. 258.

MIMETITE
Lead chloro-arsenate, $Pb_5(AsO_4)_3Cl$

Inyo County: **1,** Mimetite is one of the numerous minerals occurring in the Cerro Gordo mines, Irelan (4) p. 47. This is probably an invalid entry. Specimen no. CDMG (8585), presented to CDMG about the time of Irelan's report, and alleged to be from Cerro Gordo, is not mimetite, and does not appear to be like other Cerro Gordo material, H. E. Pemberton (p.c. '64). **2,** The mineral is found in the Blind Spring Mining District, Loew (1) p. 657. **3,** Well-crystallized specimens of mimetite have come from the Anaconda mine at Darwin, Noren (p.c. '54). **4,** Mimetite occurs sparingly in small greenish crystals in the ores of the Minietta mines, Argus Range, Woodhouse (p.c. '64). **5,** Mimetite occurs occasionally in the lead-silver ores at the Big Four mine, Northern Panamint range, Hall and Stephens (3) p. 35. **6,** The mineral is also found in the Surprise and Defense mine, Lookout (Modoc) Mining District, ibid., p. 26. **7,** A specimen of mimetite, associated with shattuckite and planchéite, has been found in the Panamint Mountains, Freitag (p.c. '57).

Kern County: **1,** Mimetite was found with galena near Randsburg (N. R.).

Riverside County: **1,** Minute yellow needles of mimetite are found on fracture surfaces of pegmatite, Commercial quarry, 910' level, Crestmore, Murdoch (p.c. '59).

San Bernardino County: **1,** Small amounts of mimetite were found in the Morning Star mine, Lava Beds Mining District, near Lavic, CDMG (11394). **2,** A specimen of very pale mimetite, associated with pale wulfenite, in the University of California Collections at Berkeley, is probably from the Vanadium King mine near Goffs.

MINIUM—Red Lead
Lead oxide, Pb_3O_4

The red oxide of lead is rarely found native. It is an oxidation product of galena and other lead minerals, occurring as a powder.

Inyo County: **1,** Abundant minium was reported from Cerro Gordo, with massicot, wulfenite and pyromorphite, R. W. Raymond (9) pp. 29, 31.

Kern County: **1,** Minium has been found near Fort Tejon (N. R.).

Los Angeles County: **1,** Minium occurs as vivid red coatings on galena, with barite and fluorite in the Felix fluorite mine near Azusa, Clarke (p.c. '36).

Mono County: **1,** Minium has been recorded from the Rockingham mine, Blind Spring Mining District, W. J. Hoffman (1) p. 737.

San Bernardino County: **1,** Minium has been reported from the Bullion mine, probably in this county (T. 10 N., R. 1 E., or T. 14 N., R. 15 E., S. B.). The location is doubtful.

Tulare County: **1,** Minium is reported from the northern part of the county, Irelan (4) p. 47, CDMG (11420).

MIRABILITE—Glauber Salt
Hydrous sodium sulphate, $Na_2SO_4 \cdot 10H_2O$

Mirabilite is sometimes found on the walls of mines where sulphide ores are decomposing. It is also found as crusts about dry alkali lakes.

Imperial County: **1,** Mirabilite occurs with thenardite at Pope Siding (sec. 19, T. 9 S., R. 12 E., S. B.), Tucker (8) p. 87.

Kern County: **1,** Mirabilite is deposited as white coatings where moisture seeped through mine walls at the California borate property, Kramer borate area, G. I. Smith et al. (1) p. 1074, H. E. Pemberton et al. (1) p. 38.

Napa County: **1,** Mirabilite occurred on the walls of the tunnels in the old Redington cinnabar mine, Knoxville (N. R.).

San Bernardino County: **1,** Mirabilite occurs with gypsum and halite in the Chemahuevis Valley about 32 miles south of Needles, Graeff (1) p. 173. It is found here only by analysis of the soluble constituents of the clay. **2,** Mirabilite is abundant at Searles Lake, H. S. Gale (13) p. 297, but is found only in a zone 10 to 30 feet below the top of the Bottom mud, G. I. Smith and Haines (3) p. P30.

San Luis Obispo County: **1,** Mirabilite occurs with blödite in the white crystalline salts of Soda Lake (T. 31 S., R. 20, 21 E., M. D.), which receives the drainage of Carrizo Plain, H. S. Gale (10) p. 430, Franke (2) p. 455.

MIXITE
Basic hydrous copper bismuth arsenate, $Cu_{11}Bi(AsO_4)_5(OH)_{10} \cdot 6H_2O(?)$

Inyo County: **1,** Pale-blue needles in radiating clusters in specimens from the Cerro Gordo mine have been identified as mixite, Murdoch (p.c. '62).

MOLYBDENITE
Molybdenum disulphide, MoS_2

Molybdenite is the principal ore of molybdenum. The mineral is widely distributed in the State, occurring in small flakes and leaves in quartz veins and granites. It strongly resembles graphite but can generally be distinguished from that mineral by its lighter bluish lead-gray color and its occurrence with granitic rocks. It is of very common occurrence in contact metamorphic tungsten ores.

No attempt has been made to report all of the occurrences of molybdenite found in the State that are referenced in the literature. The mineral is widespread and is so common that only occurrences of mineralogical interest should be included. However, some localities of minor importance and of little mineralogical interest are noted for the historical record because they have been reported in early editions of *Minerals in California*.

Amador County: **1,** Molybdenite occurs in the gold ores of the Zeila mine near Jackson, F. L. Ransome (9) p. 8, A. Knopf (11) p. 39; **2,** in the Argonaut mine, Josephson (1) p. 475; **3,** in the Badger mine near Sutter, and **4,** in the Midian mine near Herbertville, J. B. Trask (7) pp. 35, 36.

Calaveras County: **1,** Molybdenite is common in the ores of the Melones mine, Carson Hill, A. Knopf (11) p. 39; **2,** it occurs at Garnet Hill, at the junction of Moore Creek and Mokelumne River, Melhase (6) p. 7, and **3,** it is found in sulphide-rich gold ore at the Hale mine near Angels Camp, J. A. Brown (1) p. 147. **4,** Molybdenite in coarse flakes is associated with scheelite at the Moore Creek mine (sec. 7, T. 7 N., R. 16 E., M. D.), W. B. Clark and Lydon (4) p. 123.

El Dorado County: **1,** Broad foliated plates of molybdenite occur in a pegmatite with axinite and copper sulphides at the old Cosumnes mine near Fairplay, Hanks (12) p. 274. **2,** Plates of molybdenite are found at Grizzly Flat, Mining and Scientific Press (37) p. 420, CDMG (15183). **3,** J. B. Trask (7) p. 28, reported molybdenite from the Pacific mine at Placerville.

Fresno County: **1,** Molybdenite is found at the Kings River Canyon copper mine, CDMG (16296). **2,** Good broad plates of molybdenite occur at Green Mountain on the South Fork, San Joaquin River, CDMG (14832). **3,** The mineral is reported with ferrimolybdite near Palisade Creek (approx. T. 10 S., R. 31, 32 E., M. D.), W. W. Bradley (24) p. 345. **4,** Small amounts of molybdenite occur with the tungsten ores in the Mt. Morrison quadrangle, Rinehart and Ross (2) p. 93. **5,** Some rich molybdenite specimens were found in the Hard Point prospect, Lee Lake, ibid., p. 96.

Inyo County: **1,** Large masses of molybdenite occur in the Pine Creek tungsten mine, south slope of Mount Morgan, Tucker (4) p. 296. **2,** The mineral is found in a 15-inch vein with quartz at the Lucky Boy prospect, 7 miles east of Kearsarge. (N.R.) **3,** A considerable deposit of molybdenite is reported south of Lida, in the west arm of Death Valley, Engineering and Mining Journal (9) p. 205. **4,** Molybdenite occurs disseminated in granite at the Coso molybdenite claim (T. 20 S., R. 38 E., M. D.), Tucker and Sampson (25) p. 459. **5,** Foliated molybdenite came from the Beveridge mine, Hanks (12) p. 274. Many other minor occurrences of molybdenite are found in the county: **6,** Panyo tungsten (T. 20 S., R. 40 E., M. D.), W. W. Bradley (30) p. 671; **7,** Wilshire gold mine, A. Knopf (6) p. 236; **8,** Deep Creek west of Bishop, Hess and Larsen (17) p. 269; **9,** Breakneck Canyon, The Mineralogist (5) p. 10, and **10,** $2\frac{1}{2}$ miles east of Willow (Wilson?), Funeral Range, CDMG (21022).

Kern County: **1,** Molybdenite is a minor mineral in the scheelite deposits around Hobo Hot Springs and Cedar Creek, Prout (1) p. 413, Hess and Larsen (17) p. 266; **2,** it occurs near Gorman with cassiterite and powellite, L. R. Page and Wiese (1) p. 36, Troxel and Morton

(2) p. 294; **3,** it is largely altered to powellite at Black Mountain, 15 to 20 miles northwest of Randsburg, Hess (14) p. 48, and **4,** it is abundant in the Amalie Mining District, Mining and Scientific Press (35) p. 868. **5,** Disseminated grains of molybdenite occur in granite between Hoffman and Butterbread Canyons, Murdoch (p.c. '50). **6,** 6. W. Walker et al. (5) p. 32, report molybdenite from the Silver Lady claims, probably confirming (5), Murdoch (p.c. '50). **7,** Molybdenite appears in the ores of the Big Blue group, near (new) Kernville, Troxel and Morton (2) p. 99.

Los Angeles County: **1,** Minor amounts of molybdenite have been found in the Winter Creek group, Santa Anita canyon, R. J. Sampson (10) p. 176; **2,** Lang Canyon, 6 miles north of Altadena, Tucker (13) p. 318, and **3,** at the junction of Coldwater and Franklin Canyon roads, Santa Monica Mountains, Neuerberg (p.c. '46). **4,** Coarse flakes of molybdenite occur in quartz and feldspar on the north side of Big Tujunga Canyon, 2 or 3 miles above its mouth, Murphy (p.c. '49).

Madera County: **1,** Molybdenite occurs at Speckerman's mine, 6 miles above Fresno Flat, Hanks (12) p. 274; **2,** a small deposit is found at Sugar Pine, R. P. McLaughlin and Bradley (3) p. 559, and **3,** it occurs in cavities in quartz with ferrimolybdite, on the west slope of Red Top Mountain on the Minaret-Kings Creek trail, Erwin (1) p. 71.

Mariposa County: **1,** A little molybdenite occurs in a lens of garnet, epidote and quartz on the southeast slope of Mount Hoffman, H. W. Turner (19) p. 426. **2,** The mineral is found with ferrimolybdite in the Kinsley Mining District, 7 miles from El Portal (N.R.).

Mono County: **1,** Molybdenite is found in a number of localities in the Sweetwater Range, north of Bridgeport, Whiting (1) p. 362, J. H. Pratt (4) pp. 199, 265, Boalich (4) p. 154; **2,** it also occurs on Bloody Mountain, above Laurel Lakes, Mayo (4) p. 83, and **3,** in the Benton and Payote areas, Loew (2) p. 186.

Monterey County: **1,** Abundant molybdenite was found in a series of quartz veins on the Westcott Ranch, 8 miles east of Soledad, Boalich (4) p. 157.

Nevada County: **1,** Molybdenite occurs sparingly in the Grass Valley and Nevada City areas, Lindgren (12) p. 119, W. D. Johnston (4) p. 39.

Placer County: **1,** Molybdenite is abundant in some of the mines of the Ophir Mining District, Lindgren (7) p. 273.

Plumas County: **1,** Some high-grade molybdenite ore was produced near Chilcoot, E. MacBoyle (2) p. 180.

Riverside County: **1,** Molybdenite occurs with other sulphides in shear zones of quartz, at the southeast base of Mt. Hole (sec. 10 ?, T. 3 S., R. 6 W., S. B.), E. S. Larsen (17) p 96. **2,** Molybdenite occurs in the sheeting planes of an aplitic granite 3½ miles NE of Corona, east of the small gulch that heads east of Mt. Hole, E. S. Larsen et al. (18) p. 49. **3,** Molybdenite is found in garnet rock at Crestmore, Woodford et al. (10) p. 368.

San Bernardino County: **1,** There are several small occurrences of molybdenite on the South Fork of Lytle Creek, Tucker (4) p. 356, Tucker and Sampson (16) p. 266. **2,** Molybdenite occurs with wolframite and hübnerite in the New York Mountains (sec. 35, T. 14 N., R. 15 E., S. B.), Tucker and Sampson (30) p. 584, (34) p. 497. **3,**

Strongly fluorescing molybdenite is found in garnet-epidote contact zones (NE¼ sec. 32, T. 3 N., R. 2 E., S. B.), Guillou (1) p. 16. **4,** Molybdenite is an important constituent of the quartz veins in the Red Hill area, Ord Mountains, Weber (3) p. 26.

San Diego County: **1,** A large deposit of molybdenite in granite occurs near Campo (sec. 8, T. 18 S., R. 5 E., S. B.), Orcutt (1) p. 71, Tucker (4) p. 379. **2,** Molybdenite occurs in quartz veins 4 miles southeast of Dulzura, on the north side of Cottonwood Creek, Engineering and Mining Journal (22) p 1017, Tucker (4) p. 380; **3,** it occurs as masses and flakes in aplite (secs. 3, 11, T. 13 S., R. 1 W., S. B.), 6 miles west of Ramona, Calkins (1) p. 73, and **4,** it occurs with pyrrhotite at the Echo mine near Lakeside, W. W. Bradley (28) p. 495, CDMG (20948).

Shasta County: **1,** A considerable deposit of molybdenite in aplite or alaskite, is found on Boulder Creek (sec. 33, T. 37 N., R. 5 W., M. D.), F. M. Hamilton and Root (5) p. 126, Averill (9) p. 168, J. B. Trask (7) p. 50.

Sierra County: **1,** Molybdenite was found with molybdite in copper ore at the Sierra Buttes mine, Burkart (2) p 21, J. R. Browne (4) p. 210.

Siskiyou County: **1,** Molybdenite and chalcopyrite have been recorded from the Yellow Butte mine (sec. 25, T. 43 N., R. 4 W., M. D.), Averill (5) p. 273. **2,** The mineral was found in a quartz vein with gold and tetradymite at the Quartz Hill mine (sec. 16, T. 45 N., R. 10 W., M. D.), Averill (p.c. '45).

Trinity County: **1,** Molybdenite was found with ferrimolybdite near Lewiston, CDMG (19433).

Tulare County: **1,** Molybdenite occurs with ferrimolybdite in the Mineral King Mining District (approx. T. 16 N., R. 31 E., M. D.), Laizure (2) p. 47. **2,** Fine large foliated plates of molybdenite occur in granodiorite at the head of Kaweah River, F. M. Hamilton and Root (5) p. 126, and **3,** it has been reported from Cow Mountain, Hot Springs area, Engineering and Mining Journal (16) p. 228.

Tuolumne County: **1,** Molybdenite with pyrite in a quartz vein occurs on the south side of Knights Creek, near Big Trees, H. W. Turner (12) p. 707, H. W. Turner and Ransome (18) p. 8, and **2,** in quartz veins with epidote and garnet, 3 miles west of Tower Peak (secs. 16, 17, T. 3 N., R. 15 E., M. D.), Logan (23) p. 81, H. W. Turner (19) p. 427. **3,** A good specimen of molybdenite has come from the Norwegian mine, CDMG (19525).

Ventura County: **1,** Small kidney-like deposits of molybdenite, with copper minerals, occur on Frazier Mountain (sec. 11, T. 6 N., R. 19 W., S. B.), Tucker and Sampson (20) p. 257, and **2,** on McDonald Peak (Alamo Mountain), J. H. Pratt (4) p. 266, Tucker and Sampson (20) p. 257.

Yuba County: **1,** Plates of molybdenite with yellow ferrimolybdite have been reported near Camptonville (N. R.).

MONAZITE
Phosphate of rare earth elements, $(Ce,La,Pr,Nd)PO_4$

Minute grains of monazite are not uncommon in small amounts in beach and river sands of the State. Other occurrences are in pegmatites. Small amounts have been found in the sands of Butte, El Dorado, Humboldt, Nevada, Placer, Plumas and Yuba Counties, D. T. Day and Richards (7) pp. 1185, 1186, 1187, Lindgren (20) p. 74.

Del Norte County: **1,** Monazite was observed in the black sands at Crescent City in amounts up to 56 pounds per ton of concentrates, D. T. Day and Richards (7) p. 74.

Riverside County: **1,** Monazite in small crystals associated with xenotime and cyrtolite is a conspicuous constituent of a pegmatite in the Southern Pacific silica quarry near Nuevo, Dykes (1) p. 161, Melhase (7) p. 11, Patchick (3), p. 323. **2,** Monazite is also found in pegmatites, about 2 miles north of Winchester, W. W. Bradley (23) p. 117, and **3,** east of Riverside, at the foot of the Box Springs Mountains, Dykes (1) p. 161. **4,** Crystals of monazite have been found with albite in a pegmatite, about 200 yards west of the Jensen limestone quarry in the Jurupa Mountains, J. W. Clark (p.c. '36). It seems probable that the monazite crystals reported from west of the Jensen quarry are sphene instead, as this mineral is abundant there, Murdoch (p.c. '47). **5,** Rosettes of monazite (?) have been found with rose quartz in the Williamson silica mine (sec. 20, T. 7 S., R. 2 E., S. B.), Fisher (1) p. 54. **6,** Monazite has been reported from fine-grained granite, on the west side of Mt. Rubidoux, E. S. Larsen (p.c. '46). **7,** Monazite has been reported as a minor constituent of tonalite, together with anatase and zircon, from a tunnel south of Val Verde, R. W. Wilson (1) p. 124. **8,** The Mountain View pegmatite has yielded small crystals of monazite, Murdoch (p.c. '54). **9,** Monazite is reported from a pegmatite in the magnesite mine near Winchester, Chesterman (5) p. 362. **10,** An unidentified mineral, probably monazite, is sparsely distributed in biotite gneiss at the Desert View claim (secs. 31, 32, T. 5 S., R. 10 E., S. B.), about 2 miles N. 25° W. of Cactus City, G. W. Walker et al. (5) p. 26. **11,** Monazite is found in sands near Live Oak Tank in the Joshua Tree National Monument, 12 miles south of Twenty-Nine Palms, G. W. Walker et al. (5) p. 25. **12,** Well-formed crystals of monazite occur with cyrtolite and xenotime in pegmatite, 4 miles east of Nuevo, Charles Sewart (p.c. '60). **13,** Monazite occurs with xenotime in a northwest-trending belt of Precambrian gneiss, southern Music Valley area, J. R. Evans (1) p. 38. **14,** Minor amounts of the mineral have been identified in the area at the Ajax, Uranus No. 4, and U-Thor prospects, ibid., pp. 10–15.

San Bernardino County: **1,** Monazite occurs in crystals and grains in the bastnaesite deposit at Mountain Pass, Olson (2), quoted in L. A. Wright et al. (5) p. 125. **2,** Monazite, with ilmenite, allanite and euxenite, is found in the borders of the quartz nucleus of the pegmatite in the Pomona tile quarry, on the road between Old Woman Spring and Yucca Valley, Hewett and Glass (3) p. 1048. **3,** Monazite is suggested as the mineral which causes radioactivity in the Uranus claims SW of Pinto Basin (sec. 6, T. 2 S., R. 10 E., S. B.), occurring in biotite-rich portions of the Pinto gneiss, G. W. Walker et al. (5) p. 25. **4,** Thorium-bearing monazite is tentatively identified as occurring in the Homestretch group of claims near Copper Mt. (secs. 19, 30, T. 1 N., R. 8 E., S. B.), in granitic rocks, ibid. **5,** Anamalous radioactivity in the Lucky Seven claim (sec. 18, T. 2 N., R. 4 E., S. B.), is attributed to thorium-bearing allanite and monazite in biotite pods in granitic rocks, ibid., p. 24. **6,** Abnormally high radioactivity in the Mountain Pass area is largely due to thorium in thorite and monazite in the bedrock of the area, ibid., p. 22. **7,** Monazite is tentatively identified from the Original and Pack Saddle claims in granitic rocks (T. 6 N., R. 13 E., S. B.), ibid., p. 13. **8,** Irregular crystals of iron-stained monazite occur in a pegmatite at the Rainbow group of claims in the Solo area, 12 miles S. 69° E. of Baker, with thorite crystals, ibid., p. 22. **9,** Monazite is suggested by G. W. Walker et al. (5) p. 24, as the source of radioactivity in the Steiner claims (sec. 31, T. 2 N., R. 7 E., S. B.).

San Diego County: **1,** Occasional well-developed monazite crystals, often enclosed in garnet, occur in the old Garnet Ledge (center sec. 19, T. 11 S., R. 2 E., S. B.) at Mesa Grande, Fisher (1). **2,** Monazite has been reported from the A. B. C. mine, Ramona, Dawson (p.c. '50). **3,** Crystals as much as half an inch in size have been found in the Caterina mine, Heriart Mountain, Pala, Jahns and Wright (5) p. 31. **4,** Age determinations have been made on monazite from Woodson Mountain and Descanso, Bushee (1) p. 29.

MONTICELLITE
Calcium magnesium silicate, CaMgSiO$_4$

Monticellite is a rare mineral formed by contact metamorphism in magnesian limestone.

Riverside County: **1,** Monticellite is one of the many minerals occurring in the crystalline limestone at Crestmore. It was found massive, A. F. Rogers (46) p. 192, and in isolated grains in blue calcite, associated with xanthophyllite, Eakle (14) p. 335, (15) p. 342. Woodford et al. (10) p. 365, report prisms up to 8 cm in length. Moehlman and Gonyer (1) p. 474, describe the occurrence of monticellite with garnet and diopside at Crestmore.

San Bernardino County: **1,** Monticellite occurs as very pure, round greenish granular masses in metamorphosed dolomite at the Dewey mine in the Clark Mountain Mining District, 6 miles east of Valley Wells, Schaller (50) p. 815.

MONTMORILLONITE—Saponite, Hectorite
Basic magnesium aluminum silicate, $(Si_{7.67}Al_{0.33})^{IV}(Al_{3.67}Mg_{0.33})^{VI}O_{20}(OH)_4$

The clay known as *bentonite* which has been derived from the alteration of volcanic ash or tuff, is usually composed of montmorillonite. Griffithite, described as a new mineral from California in 1917, E. S. Larsen and Steiger (6) p. 11, is a member of the montmorillonite series, Faust (1) p. 66.

Clay and clay-like minerals such as bauxite, gibbsite, halloysite, montmorillonite, and others are widespread in many localities. Often, identification has been by field examination. This is especially true in early reported occurrences. Accordingly, few occurrences are included in the listings, some chosen for historic reasons, and some for mineralogic reasons. It is impractical to include all localities, especially since many important areas produce mineral commodities, and are not strictly mineral occurrences. Many reports may also in fact be in error as far as specific mineral identification is concerned. X-ray and optical examination is required for certain identification of most clay minerals.

Inyo County: **1,** Montmorillonite is mined under the name of "amargosite" along the Amargosa River, near Tecopa, Shoshone and Ash Meadows, Melhase (2) p. 838. Montmorillonite from Amargosa Valley was analyzed by Fairchild, R. C. Wells (3) p. 101.

Kern County: **1,** A fullers earth deposit, largely bentonite, has been developed 5 miles southeast of Tehachapi Pass, Kerr and Cameron (4) p. 231. **2,** The mineral has been reported from Bissell, W. W. Bradley (30) p. 602.

Lake County: **1,** Minor amounts of montmorillonite occur with other clay minerals at Sulphur Bank, D. E. White and Roberson (2) p. 408.

Los Angeles County: **1,** Waxy montmorillonite, apparently formed by the alteration of feldspar, occurs in an abandoned quarry in pegmatite, 2 miles north of Claremont, Laudermilk and Woodford (3) p. 260.

Riverside County: **1,** Soft, white clay-like montmorillonite occurs with prehnite on the 700' level below the Chino quarry, Crestmore, Woodford et al. (10) p. 372.

San Bernardino County: **1,** Large deposits of montmorillonite are reported about 7 miles east of Barstow on the north side of the Mojave River, Melhase (2) p. 837, C. W. Davis and Vacher (1) p. 6. **2,** Magnesium-rich bentonite (probably saponite), locally called hectorite, is found between Barstow and Ludlow beyond Newberry Springs, Foshag and Woodford (22) p. 238. This may be the same locality as **(1)**. The quarry is $3\frac{1}{2}$ miles south of Hector (secs. 26, 27, T. 8 N., R. 6 E., S. B.). Saponite from Hector has been analyzed by Fairchild and by Stevens, R. C. Wells (3) p. 110. A comprehensive review of the occurrence of hectorite is provided in Ames et al. (1) pp. 22-37. Infra-red spectra of this mineral from the type locality show isomorphous substitution of lithium for magnesium, and fluorine for hydroxyl, Farmer (1) p. 858.

San Diego County: **1,** Fairchild analyzed: (a) montmorillonite from this county; (b) pink montmorillonite from pegmatite from this county, R. C. Wells (3) p. 107 (probably from Pala or Mesa Grande). **2,** Under the local name of "otaylite", commercial shipments of montmorillonite have been made from a deposit 3 miles southeast of Otay, Irelan (4) p. 139, Hertlein and Grant (1) p. 57, Kerr (7) p. 51.

Ventura County: **1,** Montmorillonite is the essential constituent of the bentonite clay beds along Los Sauces Creek, 2 miles south of the Ventura Avenue oil field and 2 miles north of the Rincon oil field, Kerr (1) p. 157; **2,** at the mouth of Rincon Creek, and **3,** near Oakview, ibid.

MONTROYDITE
Mercuric oxide, HgO

Lake County: **1,** Montroydite has been found at the Red Elephant mine, near Lower Lake, W. W. Bradley (26) p. 608.

San Benito County: **1,** Bladed crystals of montroydite on mercury globules in cavities are reported from Clear Creek, Oyler (p.c. '59). **2,** Montroydite is associated with calomel, mercury, cinnabar and eglestonite in a silicate-carbonate rock 3 miles south of the New Idria mine, Oyler (p.c. '62).

San Mateo County: **1,** Montroydite has been found in long prismatic and bent crystals with eglestonite, calomel, native mercury and cinnabar in joints and fissures in a siliceous rock replacing serpentine, about 2 miles west of Redwood City, Woodhouse (3) p. 603.

Sonoma County: 1, Montroydite, with mercury and cinnabar, has come from the Esperanza mine, Sulphur Creek, W. W. Bradley (26) p. 608. 2, Montroydite crystals occur on globules of native mercury at the Socrates mine, Cureton (p.c. '63).

MORDENITE—Ptilolite
A calcium/potassium/sodium silicate, $(Na_2,K_2,Ca)(Al_2Si_{10}O_{24})\cdot7H_2O$

Los Angeles County: 1, Mordenite (described as ptilolite) occurs in clusters of capillary crystals, with heulandite, locality 9, Cahuenga Pass, Neuerberg (1) p. 158.

Riverside County: 1, Mordenite (described as ptilolite) occurs as radiating clusters of slender needles and thin blades, coating calcite on fracture surfaces of diopside-wollastonite contact rock in the 910' level at Crestmore, Murdoch (p.c. '51). Another occurrence in lath-like crystals, also on broad fracture surfaces in the contact rock of the 910' level at Crestmore, was reported by Murdoch (p.c. '53).

MORENOSITE
Hydrous nickel sulphate, $NiSO_4\cdot7H_2O$

Napa County: 1, Morenosite was reported by Becker (4) p. 389, as a coating on a specimen of millerite from the Phoenix cinnabar mine.

San Diego County: 1, Morenosite occurs with limonite and erythrite in the oxidized part of the ore in the Friday copper mine, near Julian, Hudson (1) p. 214.

San Luis Obispo County: 1, Morenosite is reported with marcasite from the Klau quicksilver mine, Woodhouse and Norris (6) p. 114.

Trinity County: 1, Morenosite has been found with associated secondary minerals at the Island Mountain copper mine, Landon (1) p. 279.

MOTTRAMITE
Basic copper/zinc/lead vanadate, $(Cu,Zn)Pb(VO_4)(OH)$

Riverside County: 1, The yellow-green coatings (probably mineral "N" of Woodford) at Crestmore (Lone Star and other locations) are mottramite, Murdoch (p.c. '61).

* MUIRITE, 1965 [1]
Basic barium calcium titanium chlorosilicate, $Ba_{10}Ca_2Mn\cdot TiSi_{10}O_{30}(OH,Cl)_{10}$

Fresno County: 1, The new mineral muirite, named for John Muir, the famous Sierran naturalist, is found in association with several other new minerals in the eastern Fresno County sanbornite deposits. The mineral occurs disseminated in sanbornite-quartz rock. Muirite is an orange mineral, generally anhedral but occasionally in minute crystals, Alfors and Stinson (6). This entry, first appearing in February 1965 after the cut-off date for this bulletin, is included because the article in which the preliminary description occurred is part II of a report describing three new minerals in the same locality, Stinson and Alfors (6).

---

[1] This new mineral described in a paper which appeared in April, 1965, after the cutoff date (Dec. 31, 1964) for entries in this volume. "Seven new barium minerals from eastern Fresno County, California", by John T. Alfors, Melvin C. Stinson, Robert A. Matthews and Adolf Pabst: Am. Mineralogist, vol. 50, pp. 314–340, 1965.

MUSCOVITE—Potash Mica
Basic potassium aluminum silicate, $KA_3Si_3O_{10}(OH)_2$

Sericite, margarodite, damourite, are fine-grained, greasy-feeling types of muscovite forming sericitic schists. Sericite is common in the Mother Lode mines, and a good general description of its occurrence is given by A. Knopf (11) p. 40. *Fuchsite* is an emerald-green chrome-muscovite.

Muscovite is a common constituent of granites, pegmatites, gneisses, and schists. It is generally called mica or isinglass, and is of special economic value when in large transparent sheets. Extensive areas of mica schists occur in the state, in which muscovite is a principal constituent and gives the rock its schistose structure. Muscovite is so widespread that only the most interesting occurrences can be listed.

Imperial County: **1,** A very large deposit of nearly pure sericite has been worked by the Western Non-Metallic Company in the Cargo Muchacho Mountains, 4 miles northeast of Ogilby. It is associated with kyanite, R. J. Sampson and Tucker (18) p. 139.

Kern County: **1,** Muscovite, variety fuchsite, occurs as scaly masses of brilliant green plates, two miles south of Randsburg, M. F. Strong (1) p. 21. This may be the same as mariposite locality **(1)** of Kern County, this bulletin.

Marin County: **1,** Much of the material called margarite in the schists near Reed Station has been shown to be muscovite, Eakle (7) p. 83.

Orange County: **1,** The variety fuchsite has been found at Arch Beach. **2,** A specimen of chrome mica (fuchsite) was found among the beach pebbles at San Juan Capistrano. Irelan (4) p. 46, Preston (1) p. 210.

Riverside County: **1,** Muscovite and the variety sericite are common in the Crestmore quarries, Woodford et al. (10) p. 368.

San Bernardino County: **1,** Fuchsite occurs in the schist at Cascade Canyon, near the lapis lazuli locality, R. H. Merriam and Laudermilk (1) p. 716. **2,** The "alurgite" described by Webb (6) p. 124, from boulders and pebbles of quartz-mica schist, with piemontite, from the alluvial gravels north of Cajon Pass, and west of the highway is shown to be ferrian muscovite by Heinrich and Levinson (3) p. 41.

San Diego County: **1,** Well-formed crystals of muscovite from the Mack mine, Rincon, have been measured by A. F. Rogers (4) p. 214. **2,** Muscovite, carrying small amounts of cesium and rubidium, has been analyzed from Pala, Stevens and Schaller (3) p. 526. **3,** A. F. Rogers (3) p. 19, has observed pseudomorphs of muscovite after tourmaline at Pala. **4,** Muscovite pseudomorphs after radiating clusters of dumortierite have been found near Alpine, Murdoch (p.c. '45). **5,** Pink muscovite was collected from the lithia pegmatites at Mesa Grande, Heinrich (3) p. 34; the mineral was analyzed by F. W. Clarke (10) p. 330.

Sierra County: **1,** Margarodite has been found at Table Rock, CDMG (16290).

Trinity County: **1,** A large deposit of muscovite has been reported from the Salmon Mountains, F. W. Clarke (3) p. 911.

Ventura County: **1,** Sheets of muscovite up to 10 inches across have been shipped from a pegmatite on Mount Alamo (sec. 12, T. 7 N., R. 20 W., S. B.), Sterett (3) p. 743, (11) p. 48.

NAGYAGITE
Sulpho-telluride of lead and gold, $Pb_5Au(Te,Sb)_4S_{5-8}$

Calaveras County: **1,** Nagyagite has been tentatively reported from the Stanislaus mine, J. D. Whitney (7) p. 263.

Shasta County: **1,** A sulpho-telluride of lead has been doubtfully reported from Sugar Loaf, 3 miles south of Mount Pleasant, C. J. O'Brien (1) p. 349.

Trinity County: **1,** Nagyagite was observed with hessite at the Dorleska mine (sec. 16 (?), T. 38 N., R. 9 W., M. D.), Coffee Mining District, Hershey (2) p. 689, Osborne (1) p. 252, Stines (1) p. 25.

NAHCOLITE
Sodium hydrogen carbonate, $NaHCO_3$

Inyo County: **1,** Nahcolite was identified from the muds of Deep Spring Lake, B. F. Jones (1) p. B200, ibid. (2) p. 88A.

San Bernardino County: **1,** Large amounts of nahcolite have been found at various horizons in the lake beds in Searles Lake. It is relatively uncommon, but may form beds up to two feet in thickness. The mineral was discovered by Foshag (26) p. 769. A detailed description of its occurrence and associated minerals is contained in G. I. Smith and Haines (3) p. 18, G. I. Smith and Pratt (2) p. 38.

*NAPALITE, 1888
A hydrocarbon, C_3H_4

Napa County: **1,** Napalite occurred with pyrite and millerite at the old Phoenix cinnabar mine, Pope Valley, and was described as a new mineral by Becker (4) p. 372, with analyses by Melville. **2,** The mineral was found also at the Silver Bar mine. CDMG (13935). **3,** Napalite is reported from the Aetna mine, R. G. Yates and Hilpert (4) p. 247.

Sonoma County: **1,** Napalite has been found at Skaggs Springs, W. W. Bradley (24) p. 345, CDMG (20814).

NASONITE
A lead calcium chlorine silicate, $Ca_4Pb_6Si_6O_{21}Cl_2$

Riverside County: **1,** Thin coatings of massive nasonite, with a few recognizable crystals, appear on fracture surfaces in compact garnet-wollastonite rock in the contact zone, on the 910' level of the Commercial quarry, Crestmore, Murdoch (28) p. 1341. The color varies, probably due to minor differences in composition, and is sometimes yellow, sometimes blue-green.

NATROLITE
Hydrous sodium aluminum silicate, $Na_2Al_2Si_3O_{10} \cdot 2H_2O$

Natrolite is a zeolite formed as a secondary mineral in cavities of igneous rock and sometimes as veins in such rock. It usually occurs in fibrous or acicular form, associated with stilbite and other zeolites.

Alameda County: **1,** Needles of natrolite occur with analcime in the amygdules of the andesitic rock in the Berkeley Hills, A. C. Lawson and Palache (4) p. 417.

Fresno County: **1,** Natrolite occurs as an alteration product of soda-nepheline at the head of White Creek, Arnold and Anderson (8) p. 158.

Inyo County: **1,** Foshag (10) p. 10, reports the occurrence of natrolite in radiating groups with analcime in cavities in lava near the Russell borax mine, Mount Blanco, in Death Valley.

Kern County: **1,** Fibrous bunches of natrolite occur with analcime in small cavities in a lava flow at Red Rock Canyon, Baker (2) p. 125, Murdoch and Webb (14) p. 330.

Los Angeles County: **1,** Natrolite was found in vesicular basalts at the Pacific Electric quarry, Brush Canyon (sec. 35, T. 1 N., R. 14 W., S. B.), Neuerberg (1) p. 158; **2,** west of Cahuenga Pass with heulandite, Schürmann (1) p. 12, Funk (1) p. 34, and **3,** as compact nodules with analcime at Lake Malibu, Schwartz (1) p. 414. **4,** The mineral occurs as hair-like radiating crystals in amygdaloidal cavities in lava at the head of Tick Canyon, near Lang, Anon. (20) p. 382, Armstrong and Van Amringe (1). **5,** Amygdules of natrolite, up to the size of a hen's egg, are found west of Laurel Canyon, locality 8, Neuerburg (1) p. 158. **6,** Radiating needles of the mineral in vesicles in basalt of Brush Canyon (locality 5) have pink bases, changing to white out from the center, Neuerburg (1) p. 156.

Modoc County: **1,** Slender needles of natrolite occur with stilbite in the lava of this county, CDMG (10258).

Plumas County: **1,** Natrolite occurs in druses of pegmatite at Engels, Graton and McLaughlin (4) p. 18.

San Benito County: **1,** A large vein of white natrolite in which crystals of benitoite and neptunite are included occurs near the headwaters of the San Benito River. The locality is on the west side of the Diablo Range about 25 miles north of Coalinga. The natrolite is mostly granular, although some crystals occur. The occurrence has been described by Louderback and Blasdale (2) p. 153, (5) p. 357, with analysis by Blasdale. **2,** Unusually large and complex crystals of natrolite were found in veins in serpentine near the headwaters of San Benito River (sec. 29, T. 18 S., R. 12 E., M. D.), Murdoch (15) p. 504. **3,** Well-crystallized natrolite has come from Clear Creek (sec. 12, T. 18 S., R. 11 E., M. D.), W. W. Bradley (p.c. '44).

San Luis Obispo: **1,** Natrolite has been found in an analcime diabase on the north side of the Cuyama Valley, Fairbanks (12) p. 277.

Santa Clara County: **1,** Natrolite in serpentine has been found west of the Cochrane Ranch, Kartchner (1) p. 22.

Shasta County: **1,** Natrolite occurs with chabazite and tridymite in basalt near Round Mountain, Melhase (3) No. 6, p. 1.

Sierra County: **1,** Natrolite was found on Herkin's Ranch, north of Sierra (N. R.).

Sonoma County: **1,** Natrolite occurs in the rocks of the Sonoma Mountains, near Petaluma (N. R.).

Ventura County: **1,** Natrolite occurs with analcime in cavities of an amygdaloidal lava at the Frazier Mountain borax deposit (T. 8 N., R. 21 W., S. B.), Bowers (2) p. 680, H. S. Gale (11) p. 439.

NATRON
Hydrous sodium carbonate, $Na_2CO_3 \cdot 10H_2O$

Inyo County: **1,** Crystals of natron mixed with sodium bicarbonate are obtained by evaporating the water of Owens Lake, and other soda lakes. The waters of Owens Lake have been analyzed by Chatard (4) p. 75.

San Bernardino County: **1**, Natron has been found at Searles Lake, H. S. Gale (13) p. 297.

NAUMANNITE
Silver selenide, Ag_2Se

Nevada County: **1**, Microscopic specks of naumannite have been found with petzite and hessite at the Idaho-Maryland mine, Grass Valley, Tolman (p.c. '37).

* NEKOITE, 1956
Hydrous calcium silicate, $Ca_3Si_6O_{15} \cdot 8H_2O$

Riverside County: **1**, A white fibrous mineral from Crestmore, determined by Eakle and Rogers (13) p. 266, as okenite, has been shown by Gard and Taylor (1) p. 5, to be a new mineral, which was named nekoite.

†* NEOCOLEMANITE, 1911
See colemanite

Los Angeles County: Neocolemanite was described from Tick Canyon, near Lang, as a variety of colemanite or as a new mineral by Eakle (10) p. 179. Hutchinson (1) p. 16, showed neocolemanite to be identical with colemanite.

NEOTOCITE
Hydrous manganese iron silicate, near $Mn_2Fe_2Si_4O_{13} \cdot 6H_2O(?)$

What is called neotocite is in general a manganiferous opal, from which the manganese may sometimes be removed by solution, leaving a spongy framework of opal. Taliaferro and Hudson (3) p. 257, mention the appearance of veins of neotocite in the Sierra, but give no specific locality. The mineral has apparently been found at a few widely scattered places in the Coast Ranges, P. D. Trask et al. (4) p. 70.

Humboldt County: **1**, Neotocite has been found in the Charles Mountain deposit (sec. 2, T. 1 S., R. 4 E., H.), P. D. Trask et al. (4) p. 59.

Mendocino County: **1**, Neotocite is supposed to occur with bementite at the Thomas mine, 6 miles northeast of Redwood (N. R.), and **2**, with inesite at the Mount Sanhedrin deposits (N. R.).

Riverside County: **1**, Some neotocite is present in the Elsinore area, P. D. Trask et al. (4) p. 83.

San Luis Obispo: **1**, The principal ore mineral at the Johe Ranch mine (sec. 35, T. 30 S., R. 11 E., M. D.) is neotocite, P. D. Trask et al. (4) p. 59.

NEPHELINE—Nephelite
Sodium/potassium/aluminum silicate, $(Na,K)AlSiO_4$

Inyo County: **1**, Nepheline is a constituent of syenite at a contact with dolomite, at Tin Mountain in the Panamint Range, McAllister (1) p. 1961, (3).

NEPOUITE
A basic nickel magnesium silicate, near $(Ni,Mg)_3Si_2O_5(OH)_4$

Humboldt County: **1**, Montoya and Baur (1) p. 1228, report the presence of nepouite with garnierite, clinochrysotile and antigorite in lateritic ores from the county.

NEPTUNITE
Sodium/potassium/iron/manganese titano-silicate, $(Na,K)(Fe^{2+},Mn,Ti)Si_2O_6$, with $Fe>Mn$

San Benito County: **1**, Black crystals of neptunite occur with benitoite in a natrolite vein in schist about 4 miles south of New Idria near the headwaters of the San Benito River. The crystals were first described by Louderback and Blasdale (2) p. 150, (5) p. 354; analyses by Blasdale and later by W. M. Bradley (1) p. 16. Further notes on neptunite are in Arnold (4) p. 312, W. E. Ford (5) p. 235, Schaller (20) p. 55, Buttgenbach (2) p. 325. Neptunite was originally erroneously identified and named carlosite.

NESQUEHONITE
Hydrous magnesium carbonate, $MgCO_3 \cdot 3H_2O$

San Benito County: **1**, Nesquehonite is reported as occurring with hydromagnesite near the Florence Mack quicksilver mine, south of New Idria (N. R.).

NICCOLITE
Nickel arsenide, NiAs

Calaveras County: **1**, Niccolite was reported with tellurides, tellurium, and native gold in specimens from the Stanislaus mine, Küstel (2) p. 128.

Inyo County: **1**, Niccolite is reported from Long Lake, on the head of Bishop Creek, Woodhouse (p.c. '60).

NITER—Saltpeter
Potassium nitrate, KNO_3

Niter is even less common in nature than soda niter. Its occurrences in California are closely associated with the latter, but it has been reported from only a few places. In none of these occurrences is the mineral visible as such, but its presence is revealed by analysis.

Imperial County: **1**, A trace of niter has been observed near Volcano Station, F. J. H. Merrill (1) p. 741. The occurrence along the former high levels of the Salton Sea is soda niter.

Inyo County: **1**, Crusts of niter and soda niter along the Amargosa River and the old shorelines of Death Valley are reported by G. E. Bailey (2) p. 69. **2**, The mineral has been reported with soda niter near Shoshone, Noble (4) p. 71, but the occurrence has been shown to be sodium nitrate.

Kern County: **1**, A sample of potassium nitrate is said to have come from sec. 16, T. 32 S., R. 34 E., M. D., Mansfield and Boardman (4) p. 25.

Modoc County: **1**, Incrustations of niter have been found near Cedarville (N. R.).

Riverside County: **1**, G. E. Bailey (2) p. 169, mentions saltpeter as occurring in the desert northeast of Salton. **2**, Small amounts of potassium nitrate are found in salts from Mud Hill, Twentynine Palms, Noble (4) p. 31. **3**, A very little niter has been found with soda niter in the Vivet Eye area, in the extreme northeast corner of the county, H. W. Turner (28) p. 636.

San Bernardino County: **1,** G. E. Bailey (2) p. 181, Phalen (2) p. 894, report niter in the Upper Canyon beds. All other nitrate occurrences in the county are apparently sodium nitrate.

* NOBLEITE, 1961
Hydrous calcium borate, $CaB_6O_{10} \cdot 4H_2O$

Inyo County: **1,** Nobleite occurs in seven places in Death Valley. It is found at Corkscrew Canyon, Ryan, and other well known areas associated with the other borates of the region, Erd et al. (2) p. 560. It is described as another of the several newly validated minerals of the borate group.

NONTRONITE—Chloropal
Basic hydrous iron aluminum silicate, $(Fe^{3+},Al)_9(Si,Al)_{16}O_{40}(OH)_8 \cdot nH_2O$

Alpine County: **1,** Nontronite is reported from this county, CDMG (18857).

El Dorado County: **1,** Nontronite altering to limonite occurs near Georgetown, CDMG (1613).

Inyo County: **1,** A yellowish-green mineral identified as a ferric silicate, doubtfully classed as nontronite, is reported from the Green Monster mine, $1\frac{1}{2}$ miles north of Citrus (Kearsarge), A. Knopf (5) p. 120.

Kern County: **1,** Nontronite occurring as veinlets in garnet-pyroxene rock near Woody has been analyzed by Steiger, E. S. Larsen and Steiger (6) p. 4, R. C. Wells (3) p. 108, Storms (13) p. 635. **2,** The mineral is briefly described from Kelso Creek near Weldon, in a contact zone with scheelite, Hess and Larsen (17) p. 266.

Mariposa County: **1,** Nontronite is reported from Hites Cove, Hanks (15) p. 100.

Modoc County: **1,** A specimen CDMG (19569) from near Alturas is recorded, F. M. Hamilton (4) p. 129.

Mono County: **1,** Nontronite has been tentatively identified from oxidized scheelite ore bodies from the Black Rock mine in the Benton Range, Lemmon (6) p. 590.

Nevada County: **1,** CDMG (8215) is nontronite from the Blue Gravel lead.

Placer County: **1,** Nontronite is reported from Bath, Hanks (15) p. 100.

Riverside County: **1,** Nontronite from the new City quarry, 2 miles south of Riverside, occurs as an alteration product of pyroxene in a labradorite-hedenbergite rock. The material is greenish-yellow, earthy, fibrous and micaceous, G. M. Richmond (1) p. 726; **2,** also at Crestmore, Woodford et al. (10) p. 368.

* NORTHUPITE, 1895
Sodium magnesium carbonate chloride, $Na_3Mg(CO_3)_2Cl$

Lake County: **1,** Northupite occurs with gay-lussite and pirssonite in trona at Borax Lake, Vonsen (3) p. 22, Vonsen and Hanna (4) p. 103.

San Bernardino County: **1,** Northupite, first discovered as small octohedral crystals at Searles Lake and named by Foote (1) p. 480, in 1895, is perhaps the most abundant magnesium-bearing mineral in the lake beds. It is associated with galeite, tychite and trona, Pabst et al. (21) p. 487. It is relatively common in the Lower Salt, Bottom Mud, and Mixed Layer. The mineral occurs as nodules of microscopic octahedral crystals, and layers or veins of aggregates of fine crystals, G. I. Smith and Haines (3) p. P30. It has been analyzed by J. H. Pratt (1) p. 123. Other references are H. S. Gale (13) p. 291, Foshag (21) p 51, G. I. Smith and Pratt (2) p. 31.

†*NUEVITE, 1946
See samarskite

Riverside County: Nuevite was described as a new mineral, Murdoch (19) p. 1219, from Riverside County. The mineral was shown, also by Murdoch (26) p. 358, to have been erroneously identified, and to be samarskite.

OLIVENITE
Basic copper arsenate, $Cu_2(AsO_4)(OH)$

A specimen of olivenite, submitted from California (locality uncited), was identified by CDMG in 1957, O. P. Jenkins (4) p. 50.

OLIVINE—Chrysolite—Peridot
Magnesium iron silicate, $(Mg,Fe)_2SiO_4$

See also *fayalite* and *forsterite.*

Olivine is a rock-forming mineral which is practically limited to basic rocks like diabase, basalt, andesite, gabbro, and peridotite. It occurs occasionally in clear crystals large enough to cut into gems. It is so common in the basic igneous rocks, and stream sands derived from them, that only the following occurrences seem worthy of mention.

San Bernardino County: **1,** Massive granular olivine forms the core of many of the bombs found at Siberia (Dish Hill) crater, near Amboy, Brady and Webb (1) p. 406. C. S. Ross et al. (3) p. 700, report olivine bombs from Ludlow (U. S. Nat. Mus. specimen #94430) collected by W. F. Foshag. Correspondence with Foshag established the identity of the Siberia crater and the "Ludlow" locality.

Shasta County: **1,** Massive coarse-grained peridotite showing very good cleavage on the olivine grains, has been observed near the Little Creek chromite mine, Hawkes (3) p. 277.

OPAL
Silicon dioxide, with a varying amount of water, $SiO_2 \cdot nH_2O$

Common opal occurs in white, yellow, brown, bluish or greenish masses having a prominent conchoidal fracture. *Fire opal* is opal with fire-like reflections. *Hyalite* is transparent glassy opal found in the cavities of volcanic rock. *Chrysopal* or *prase opal* is a greenish opal found with chrysoprase. *Moss opal* is common opal with moss-like inclusions of pyrolusite or chlorite. *Wood opal* is petrified wood. *Geyserite* is a hydrous silica formed about the vents of geysers and hot springs. *Diatomaceous earth* and *infusorial earth* are deposits of opaline silica formed by diatoms.

Opal is colloidal silica containing from 2 to 10 percent water. It occurs as veins, nodules and coatings.

The occurrences of opal are too numerous to list in detail, except in cases where the deposit is of particular interest. Petrified wood has been found in a few important localities, and in small amounts in the following counties: Alpine, Amador, Butte, Calaveras, Lassen, Nevada, Plumas, Riverside, Sierra, Sonoma, Tulare and Tuolumne.

Diatomaceous earth has been found in Fresno, Inyo, Lake, Lassen, Los Angeles, Merced, Mono, Napa, Orange, Placer, San Luis Obispo, San Mateo, Santa Barbara, Shasta, Sonoma and Tulare counties.

Calaveras County: 1, Considerable amounts of rich white opal, none of gem character, were found in a buried gravel in Chile Gulch, near Mokelumne Hill, J. R. Browne (4) p. 56, Kunz (24) p. 76, Lewis (1) p. 37.

Fresno County: 1, Moss opal has come from the mountains east of Fresno, Woodhouse (p.c. '45).

Kern County: 1, Canary-colored moss opal has been found 18 miles southwest of Johannesburg, Stoddard (2) p. 217. 2, "Milk" or "resin" opal occurs near Rosamond, Lewis (1) p. 37. 3, Some precious opal has been mined east of Red Rock Canyon, Lewis (4) p. 116. 4, Wood opal occurs in the petrified forest, Last Chance Canyon, Murdoch (p.c. '45).

Lake County: 1, Pale-blue opal occurs as irregular masses in hydrothermally altered andesite at the Sulphur Bank mine, Brice (1) p. 62, D. E. White and Roberson (2) p. 403.

Los Angeles County: 1, An extensive deposit of diatomaceous earth has been mined near Lomita, F. J. H. Merrill (2) p. 507.

Mono County: 1, Fluorescent hyalite occurs as thin coatings on joint surfaces in the Morris claims, Blind Spring Mining District, Lemmon (6) p. 591.

Napa County: 1, Gem quality "prase" has been found in a 10-inch vein at the Lone Pine chromite mine, 3½ miles from Knoxville, CDMG (20676).

Riverside County: 1, Common opal and the variety hyalite occur at Crestmore, Woodford et al. (10) p. 368.

San Bernardino County: 1, Semi-precious opal, amber and pink in color, occurs in an eastern branch of Black Canyon about 25 miles northwest of Barstow (T. 32 S., R. 44 E., M. D.), Kunz (21) p. 76, Sterrett (7) p. 1050, Baker (1) p. 347.

Santa Barbara County: 1, A very large and pure deposit of diatomaceous earth has been mined near Lompoc, Huguenin (1) p. 737, Mulryan (1) p. 133. 2, Opalized termite pellets have been found near Santa Maria, A. F. Rogers (45) p. 389.

Siskiyou County: 1, Fire opal has been found near Dunsmuir, Kunz (21) p. 76. 2, Greenish stalactitic and coralloidal opal has been found in "the Catacombs," Lava Beds National Monument (secs. 28, 33, T. 45 N., R. 4 E., M. D.), Swartzlow and Keller (1) p. 101.

Sonoma County: 1, Fire opal has been found in kaolin on the Weise Ranch, between Glen Ellen and Kenwood, W. W. Bradley (2) p. 321. 2, Large trees of petrified wood are found in the petrified forest west of Calistoga, Kunz (24) p. 78. 3, Crusts of delicate capillary fibers of opal have been found at The Geysers, Vonsen (6) p. 291.

Tehama County: 1, Stalactites and stalagmites of opal are found in a lava tunnel on the north side of Inskip Hill (T. 29 N., R. 1 W., M. D.), C. A. Anderson (3) p. 22, (6) p. 310.

Tulare County: **1**, Green "chrysopal" comes from the chrysoprase mine near Lindsay, Kunz (24) p. 76.

ORPIMENT
Arsenic sulphide, As_2S_3

Kern County: **1**, A foliated massive specimen of orpiment has come from this county, W. W. Bradley (31) p. 97. **2**, Orpiment occurs with realgar at Boron in borate minerals, H. E. Pemberton et al. (1) p. 33.

Lake County: **1**, Orpiment, with realgar, is said to have been found on the Eel River, about 15 miles northwest of Bartlett Springs (N. R.).

Siskiyou County: **1**, Foliated orpiment has come from this county, W. W. Bradley (31) p. 97.

Sonoma County: **1**, Orpiment occurs with curtisite and realgar at Skaggs Springs (T. 10 N., R. 11 W., M. D.), W. W. Bradley (28) p. 469, Everhart (4) p. 390.

Trinity County: **1**, Yellow orpiment occurs in the decomposition of the iron sulphides at the Island Mountain copper mine, Vonsen (p.c. '45).

* PABSTITE, 1965
Barium tin titanium silicate, Ba $(Sn_{0.77}Ti_{0.23})Si_3O_9$

Santa Cruz County: **1**, Gross and Wainwright (1) p. 36, reported an unnamed new silicate mineral associated with taramellite in the contact zone of the limestones at the Kalkar quarry near Santa Cruz. After the cut-off date for this volume, the name *pabstite* was assigned and the mineral identified as the tin analogue of benitoite. (E. B. Gross, John E. N. Wainwright and Bernard W. Evans: Pabstite, the tin analogue of benitoite: Am. Mineralogist, vol. 50, pp. 1164–1169, 1965). The mineral occurs as disseminated grains with stannite, franckeite and cassiterite. Each is found in small amounts.

PAIGEITE
Hydrous iron magnesium tin borate, $30FeO \cdot 5Fe_2O_3 \cdot SnO_2 \cdot 6B_2O_3 \cdot 5H_2O$

Kern County: **1**, Ludwigite is reported from the Gorman tin property by Wiese and Page (1) p. 50. They comment that, based on work of Miss Jewell Glass of the U.S. Geological Survey, ". . . . the ludwigite may contain some of the tin reported. . . ." in the cassiterite deposit at Gorman. This supports the view of Schaller (p.c. '46) who considers paigeite and ludwigite to be identical. This view, if supported, will invalidate ludwigite as a mineral species; see Riverside County **(1)**.

Riverside County: **1**, Vonsenite was described as a new mineral from the old City quarry at Riverside, in 1920. Since vonsenite is a member of the same group of minerals as paigeite, with paigeite tin-bearing, Schaller (p.c. '46) considers the Riverside material to be paigeite because tin was overlooked in the first analysis of vonsenite. The matter has not been finally settled. Accordingly, see vonsenite, this bulletin.

†* PALACHEITE, 1903
See botryogen

Napa County: Palacheite was described by Eakle (3) p. 231, in 1903, as a new mineral. Eakle (4), p. 379 later showed it to be a misidentification of botryogen.

†* PALAITE, 1912
See huréaulite

San Diego County: Schaller (29) p. 145, 1912, described a manganese phosphate as the new mineral, palaite. Murdoch (16) p. 19, studied crystals of huréaulite from the San Diego County area, and it is concluded that palaite was misidentified as a new mineral, and is huréaulite, Schaller (p.c. '46), letter to R. C. Crippen, 4/21/58 (unpublished).

PARAVEATCHITE
Hydrous strontium calcium borate, $(Sr,Ca)_3B_{16}O_{27} \cdot 5H_2O$

Los Angeles County: 1, Paraveatchite occurs at the Sterling borax mine. Crystals of veatchite originally described by Murdoch (7) have been shown by J. R. Clark and Mrose (4) p. 1221, to be identical with the paraveatchite described by Braitsch (1) p. 352, and with different crystallography from the original veatchite from Lang, Switzer (2) p. 409. Thus, both forms, veatchite and paraveatchite occur at Lang.

PARISITE
A fluocarbonate of calcium and rare earth elements, $Ca(Ce,La)_2(CO_3)_3F_2$

San Bernardino County: 1, Parisite in small amounts has been identified in the ores of the bastnaesite deposite at Mountain Pass, Olson (2), quoted in L. A. Wright et al. (5) p. 125.

* PARTZITE, 1867
Hydrous oxide of antimony, copper and other bases,
$[Cu_{2-y}Sb_{2-x}(O,OH,H_2O)_{6-7}](?)$ x—0 to 1, y to $\frac{1}{2}$

Stetefeldite is similar to partzite but with more silver. According to Palache et al. (10) p. 599, partzite is a mixture of oxides, and does not warant species rank.

Mono County: 1, Partzite has been reported from various mines in the Blind Spring Mining District, W. P. Blake (13) p. 119, Arents (1) p. 362, Loew (2) p. 185, A. L. Ransome (2) p. 192. Partzite from Blind Spring has been shown to be possibly a hydrated copper antimonate, with the pyrochlore structure, Mason and Vitaliano (1) p. 106. Its formula is probably Cu_ySb_{2-x} $(O,OH,H_2O)_{6-7}$.

PECTOLITE
Basic sodium calcium silicate, $NaCa_2Si_3O_8(OH)$

Colusa County: 1, Pectolite occurs with calcite and zeolites in serpentine near Wilbur Springs, Vonsen (p.c. '33).

Lake County: 1, Extensive veins of fibrous pectolite occur with calcite in serpentine $1\frac{1}{2}$ miles east of Middletown in a cut on the highway to Lower Lake, Vonsen (p.c. '34).

Mono County: 1, Pectolite was doubtfully reported by Aaron in a boulder near Montgomery, at the foot of the White Mountains, Hanks (12) p. 277.

San Benito County: 1, Radiating masses of compact pectolite occur in veins in basalt (sec. 32, T. 18 S., R. 12 E., M. D.), along the trail to the benitoite gem mine, Murdoch (p.c. '45).

San Francisco County: **1,** Fibrous pectolite occurs as veins in an altered dike which intersects the serpentine at Fort Point. It was described and analyzed by Eakle (1) p. 316, Kunz (24) p. 96.

Santa Barbara County: **1,** A large quantity of fibrous crystalline material called pectolite, which phosphoresces when broken in the dark, was found on the J. C. Keyes claim, 7 miles north of Santa Ynez, Hanks (16) p. 44, Irelan (4) p. 47. Woodhouse (p.c. '63) suggests that perhaps this is the same material that was labelled "wollastonite" [see Murdoch and Webb (39) p. 348, wollastonite, Santa Barbara County **(1)**], which was studied by E. S. Larsen (8) p. 465, and thought to be a new mineral, which he named eakleite. Subsequently E. S. Larsen (13) p. 181, showed the material to be xonotlite. **2,** Pectolite has been reported from the Santa Barbara Islands, E. S. Dana (5) p. 1097.

Sonoma County: **1,** Narrow veins of pectolite are widely distributed at The Geysers, Vonsen (p.c. '45).

Tehama County: **1,** A large vein of pectolite occurred in serpentine on Elder Creek (sec. 16, T. 25 N., R. 7 W., M. D.), Kunz (3) p. 561. It was analyzed by Eitel, in Preston (2) p. 693.

PENTAHYDRITE
Hydrous magnesium sulphate, $MgSO_4 \cdot 5H_2O$

Sonoma County: **1,** An unnamed substance, which upon analysis proved to be hydrated magnesium sulphate, was described as a constituent of efflorescent salts at The Geysers, E. T. Allen and Day (2) p. 45. It was called pentahydrite by Frondel, Palache et al. (11) p. 492.

PENTLANDITE
Nickel iron sulphide, $(FeNi)_9S_8$

San Diego County: **1,** Hudson (1) p. 219, has reported the probable occurrence of pentlandite with pyrrhotite and chalcopyrite in the nickel ore of the Friday mine near Julian; see also Donnelly (1) p. 370. Residual cores of pentlandite altering to violarite are common in the massive pyrrhotite ore of this mine, Murdoch (p.c. '45).

Ventura County: **1,** Pentlandite has been found with millerite and pyrrhotite at the Ventura mine (T. 1 N., R. 18 W., S. B.), Tucker and Sampson (20) p. 258.

PERICLASE
Magnesium oxide, MgO

Riverside County: **1,** Periclase was found altering to brucite, in the old City quarry at Riverside, A. F. Rogers (19) p. 581. **2,** The mineral was reported by A. F. Rogers (19) p. 583, (31) p. 462, from the Wet Weather quarry at Crestmore. **3,** Periclase occurs in the contact zone at the new City quarry south of Riverside, G. M. Richmond (1) p. 725. **4,** Good residual cores of periclase, up to 1 mm in diameter, have been found in the brucite pseudomorphs of the Jensen quarry, MacKevett (1) p. 6, confirming Murdoch (p.c. '51).

PEROVSKITE
Calcium titanium oxide, with rare earth metals, $CaTiO_3$

Riverside County: **1,** Small bright amber crystals, octahedral in habit, have been found in the contact zone at Crestmore, on the 910′ level,

Murdoch (25) p. 573. An additional variety of perovskite, in dead black cubes and cubo-octahedra, has been found in the 910' level of the Commercial quarry, Crestmore, associated with brown octahedra of spinel, and colorless diopside, in calcite, Murdoch (p.c. '57). **2,** Minute deep-red grains of perovskite, associated with chondrodite and spinel occur in contact zone at the new City quarry, Morton (p.c. '59).

San Benito County: **1,** Shiny black crystals of perovskite as much as a quarter of an inch in size, with the cubic form dominant, occur in chloritic schist with black spinel and melanite garnet near the benitoite locality. This locality was reported by Grigsby (p.c. '49), and published validation appeared later, Bolander (1) p. 65, Murdoch (25) p. 573. Colorless and honey-colored octahedral crystals of perovskite associated with melanite garnet occur one mile from Dallas Gem mine, Murdoch (p.c. '61). This is the same locality as the black cubic crystals.

PETALITE
Lithium aluminum silicate, $LiAlSi_4O_{10}$

Petalite is a rare mineral occurring occasionally in lithia pegmatites.

San Diego County: **1,** Petalite occurs in quartz-spodumene masses, as groups of radiating and divergent needle-like grains, in the Clark vein at Rincon, Murdoch (18) p. 198. **2,** Rare petalite, in white cleavage masses up to 1 inch maximum size, has been found on Queen and Heriart Mountains, Pala, Jahns and Wright (5) p. 42.

PETZITE
Silver gold telluride, $(Ag,Au)_2Te$

Petzite is usually associated with hessite, sylvanite and calaverite. It is the commonest gold telluride found in the State.

Calaveras County: **1,** Petzite was found with hessite in the Stanislaus and Melones mines on Carson Hill, W. P. Blake (18) p. 178. Specimens from the Stanislaus mine have been analyzed by Genth (5) p. 310, Küstel (1) p. 306. **2,** The mineral occurs in the Ford mine, half a mile east of San Andreas, F. L. Ransome (9) p. 9, Storms (7) p. 108, A. Knopf (11) p. 39. **3,** Petzite occurs with altaite at the Frenchwood mine, Robinsons Ferry (sec. 25, T. 2 N., R. 13 E., M. D.), Hanks (12) p. 68, and **4,** at the Morgan mine with calaverite and sylvanite on the north slope of Carson Hill, Hanks (12) pp. 309, 388.

El Dorado County: **1,** Petzite was found with calaverite at the Darling mine, about 3 miles northeast of American Flat (N. R.).

Nevada County: **1,** Petzite occurs in the Idaho-Maryland mine, Farmin (2) p. 173.

San Diego County: **1,** Petzite has been doubtfully reported in microscopic grains from the Julian Mining District, Donnelly (1) p. 359.

Siskiyou County: **1,** Petzite is recorded with gold at the Porphyry Dike mine, near Callahan, F. M. Hamilton (4) p. 246, CDMG (19621), and **2,** it has been found in the northern part of the county near the State line, with calaverite and free gold. (N. R.).

Trinity County: **1,** Petzite occurs in some of the gold ores of the Dorleska mine (sec. 16 (?), T. 38 N., R. 9 W., M. D.), Coffee Mining District, Osborne (1) p. 252, Stines (1) p. 25.

Tuolumne County: **1**, Petzite is one of the tellurides that occurred in the Golden Rule mine, analysis by Genth (5) p. 309, Stines (1) p. 25; **2**, at Rawhide Ranch, and **3**, at Norwegian mines near Tuttletown, Silliman (9) p. 379, analysis by Hillebrand (2) p. 297. **4**, Petzite was found in the Bonanza mine, Sonora, CDMG (10019). **5**, Petzite, with sylvanite and beautifully crystallized gold, was reported in the early days from Sugarman and Nigger mines (sec. 30, T. 2 N., R. 15 E., M. D.), Logan (23) p. 72.

PHARMACOLITE
Acid hydrous calcium arsenate, $HCaAsO_4 \cdot 2H_2O$

A product of surface alteration of mineral deposits carrying arsenopyrite or similar minerals.

Los Angeles County: **1**, Pharmacolite is reported with erythrite and smaltite, at the O.K. mine, San Gabriel Canyon, Irelan (4) p. 47.

PHENAKITE
Beryllium silicate, Be_2SiO_4

San Diego County: **1**, Flat, colorless crystals of phenakite, none over half an inch, occur in the Vandenberg Catherina mine on Heriart Hill, Pala, associated with blue topaz on cleavelandite, Jahns and Wright (5) p. 31.

PHILLIPSITE
Hydrous sodium potassium calcium aluminum silicate, $(\frac{1}{2}Ca,Na,K)_3(Al_3Si_5O_{16}) \cdot 6H_2O$

Inyo County: **1**, The beds of Owens Lake have been found to carry phillipsite and other zeolites, Hay and Moiola (2) p. 76A.

Kern County: **1**, Occasional cavities in basalt at Red Rock Canyon have been found to contain pale salmon-pink phillipsite in poor crystals, Murdoch (p.c. '47). **2**, Phillipsite, with gay-lussite and other zeolites, has been found in tuffaceous layers in China Lake, Hay and Moiola (2) p. 76A, Moiola and Hay (1) p. 215.

Plumas County: **1**, Phillipsite is probably one of the zeolites occurring in very minor amount at the Engels mine, Graton and McLaughlin (1) p. 18.

Riverside County: **1**, Phillipsite occurs as secondary radial aggregates in garnet rock, at the Crestmore limestone quarry, Woodford et al. (10) p. 362.

San Bernardino County: **1**, Phillipsite is found as an authigenic mineral in the Pleistocene sediments of Searles Lake, Hay and Moiola (1) p. 323, G. I. Smith and Haines (3) p. P31.

PHLOGOPITE
Basic potassium/magnesium/aluminum silicate, $KMg_3AlSi_3O_{10}(OH)_2$

Phlogopite is a mica similar to biotite, but containing little or no iron.

Fresno County: **1**, Phlogopite is found as isolated crystals or aggregates in contact limestones of the Twin Lakes area, Chesterman (1) p. 271.

Inyo County: **1**, Phlogopite occurs with scheelite in calc-hornfels at Round Valley and Deep Canyon, west of Bishop, A. Knopf (6) p. 247, Hess and Larsen (17) p. 273, Lemmon (5) p. 504.

Madera County: **1,** Phlogopite occurs in minor amounts with the magnetite deposit at Iron Mountain, Erwin (1) p. 65.

Riverside County: **1,** A few flakes of phlogopite have been observed in the white limestone of Chino Hill, at Crestmore, Eakle (15) p. 334, and **2,** in crystals up to 5 mm in calcite of the Lone Star quarry, Crestmore, Woodford et al. (10) p. 366. **3,** Abundant crystals of phlogopite, up to one inch, have been found in the contact zone at the Jensen quarry, Murdoch (p.c. '47).

PHOSGENITE
Chlorocarbonate of lead, (PbCl)$_2$CO$_3$

Inyo County: **1,** Phosgenite as acicular, straw-yellow crystals in quartz came from the Silver Sprout mine, Hanks (12) p. 309.

PICKERINGITE—Magnesia Alum
Hydrous aluminum magnesium sulphate, MgAl$_2$(SO$_4$)$_4$·22H$_2$O

Inyo County: **1,** Pickeringite was reported as an efflorescence in the mountains west of Bishop (N. R.).

San Bernardino County: **1,** Pickeringite occurs as a coating on quartzite along the South Fork of Barrett Canyon, a tributary of San Antonio Canyon (sec. 31, T. 2 N., R. 7 W., S. B.), R. H. Merriam (p.c. '36).

Shasta County: **1,** Pickeringite (?) has been found as incrustations around the hot springs of the Mount Lassen area, A. L. Day and Allen (1) p. 118.

Sonoma County: **1,** The name "sonomaite", no longer recognized as a species, E. S. Dana (6) p. 523, was given by Goldsmith (6) p. 263, to a mineral from near The Geysers having a composition similar to pickeringite. E. T. Allen and Day (2) p. 45, have reported pickeringite from this locality.

PIEMONTITE—Piedmontite
Basic calcium/aluminum/manganese/iron silicate, Ca$_2$(Al,Fe,Mn^{3+})$_3$(SiO$_4$)$_3$(OH)

Kern County: **1,** Piemontite, with benitoite and other heavy minerals, has been identified in sediments penetrated by drill holes in the Lazard area, west of Lost Hills, R. D. Reed and Bailey (4) p. 363.

Lassen County: See Sierra County **(1).**

Los Angeles County: **1,** Piemontite has been found in quartz-sericite schist near the junction of Bouquet and Texas Canyons, Simonson (1) p. 737, and **2,** in a ravine entering the Prairie Fork of San Gabriel River from the south, about 3 miles above the mouth of the fork (approx. sec. 22, T. 3 N., R. 8 W., S. B.), Woodford (p.c. '36). **3,** Piemontite occurs in quartz schist with crossite and lawsonite on Santa Catalina Island, E. H. Bailey (1) p. 1955. **4,** The mineral occurs in the Pelona schist derived from calcareous manganiferous chert, Ehlig (1) p. 170.

Madera County: **1,** Piemontite occurs in minute needles in a sericite schist 100 yards downstream from the outlet of Shadow Lake, Mayo (2) p. 240, (3) p. 239, Alfors (3) p. 210, and **2,** as small tablets in a metamorphosed extrusive rock at the summit of the east end of Volcanic Ridge, Mayo (2) p. 244, (3) p. 239. A. M. Short (1) p. 495, has published an analysis by T. Kameda of the piemontite from Shadow Lake. **3,** Needles and crystals up to half an inch are found in metarhyolite at Garnet Lake in the Minarets Mining District, Chesterman (p.c. '51).

Monterey County: **1,** Piemontite grains have been found in the sediments of Monterey Bay, W. W. Bradley (18) p. 243.

Orange County: **1,** Woodford (2) p. 192, has reported the occurrence of piemontite in a boulder of San Onofre breccia near San Juan Capistrano Point.

Plumas County: **1,** Piemontite in considerable quantity is associated with braunite in the Braito (Iron Dike) mine (sec. 37, T. 26 N., R. 9 E., M. D.), Taliaferro and Hudson (3) p. 62.

Riverside County: **1,** Boulders and pebbles of quartz-piemontite schist occur in sedimentary rocks on the south side of the Painted Hills about 3 miles north of Whitewater, W. W. Bradley (31) p. 276. **2,** Piemontite occurs abundantly in meta-tuff of the Palen Mountains, Alfors (3) p. 210.

San Bernardino County: **1,** Quartz-piemontite schist is found in a ravine entering Lytle Creek from the northeast upstream from the mouth of Coldwater Canyon, Mayo (3) p. 243, confirming Woodford (p.c. '36). **2,** Piemontite-schist pebbles occur in the alluvial fans immediately north of the Cajon Pass summit, Webb (6) p. 124. **3,** Crystals to 5 mm long occur in groups in vugs in metavolcanic rocks 12 miles east of Victorville, O. E. Bowen (1) pp. 51, 52.

San Diego County: **1,** Piemontite has been found in a boulder of quartz porphyry from the gravels at Pacific Beach, A. F. Rogers (7) p. 378.

Sierra County: **1,** Piemontite in slender crystals up to one inch has been found in quartz veins in quartz-latite country rock that also contains some piemontite. along the state border, between Lassen and Sierra Counties, Gianella (p.c. '45), Frey (p.c. '53).

Tulare County: **1,** Piemontite occurs in a quartz-sericite schist $2\frac{1}{2}$ miles east of Lindsay, and **2,** in a metachert 2 miles east of Lindsay. At both localities the piemontite is a minor constituent and the piemontite-bearing rock is of limited extent, Alfors (3) p. 210.

PILINITE
Hydrous calcium aluminum silicate, near $Ca_2Al_2Si_5O_{15}\cdot1\frac{1}{2}H_2O$

Santa Clara County: **1,** Pilinite is reported from near New Almaden, CDMG (11956), (18243), E. H. Bailey and Everhart (12) p. 102.

Yuba County: **1,** Pilinite is represented from Smartsville by CDMG (11525).

*PIRSSONITE, 1896
Hydrous double carbonate of calcium and sodium, $Na_2Ca(CO_3)_2\cdot2H_2O$

Inyo County: **1,** Pirssonite occurs with other saline minerals as efflorescences from Deep Spring Lake, B. F. Jones (1) p. B200.

Lake County: **1,** Pirssonite occurs with gay-lussite and northupite in trona at Borax Lake, Vonsen and Hanna (4) p. 104.

San Bernardino County: **1,** Pirssonite was discovered at Searles Lake as good crystals in the New Well. It was named by J. H. Pratt (1) p. 126. Crystals were described by H. S. Gale (13) p. 305, Foshag (21) p. 51, G. I. Smith and Pratt (2) p. 28. Pirssonite is perhaps the next mineral in abundance after gay-lussite at Searles Lake, and occurs in most of the mud layers. Details of its occurrence are given in G. I. Smith and Haines (3) pp. P31–2.

PISANITE
Hydrous iron and copper sulphate, $(Fe,Cu)SO_4 \cdot 7H_2O$

Pisanite is thought to be a variety of melanterite.

Alameda County: **1,** Pisanite was one of the secondary sulphates formed with melanterite and chalcanthite on the walls of the Alma pyrite mine at Leona Heights. The mineral was described and analyzed by Schaller (1) p. 199.

Monterey County: **1,** Pale-blue crystals of pisanite from near Gonzales were analyzed by Schaller (8) p. 123.

Trinity County: **1,** The mineral was found with goslarite in the pyrrhotite mass at Island Mountain, Vonsen (p.c. '17).

PITTICITE
Basic hydrous arsenate and sulphate of ferric iron, formula variable, $Fe_2^{3+}AsO_4SO_4OH \cdot nH_2O$

Mariposa County: **1,** Dark-brown amorphous pitticite, resembling limonite was found with scorodite as an alteration product of arsenopyrite, on the South Fork of Merced River near the mouth of Devils Gulch, A. F. Rogers (7) p. 375.

Tuolumne County: **1,** Brown colloidal material from the Carlin mine, near Jamestown, has been referred to this species, Goudey (3) p. 12.

PLANCHÉITE
Basic copper silicate, $Cu_8(Si_4O_{11})_2(OH)_4 \cdot H_2O$

Inyo County: **1,** Planchéite has been identified, with mimetite and shattuckite, in a specimen from the Panamint Mountains, Freitag (p.c. '57).

PLATINIRIDIUM
Native alloy of platinum and iridium, (Pt,Ir)

Much of the so-called platinum of the State is really this alloy; several nuggets of a few ounces have been found along the Trinity River.

Trinity County: **1,** Nuggets from the Enright claim, 3 miles above Trinity Center, are in the CDMG Exhibit, CDMG (1892).

PLATINUM
Native platinum, Pt

Native platinum has been found most frequently in gold-bearing sands, and in this State has not been found otherwise. On account of its weight it remains in the sluices with gold and other heavy material. The native platinum is usually very impure. Occasionally it contains so much iron and other impurities as to be dark in color and not easily distinguished from grains of chromite with which it is very frequently associated. Platinum is often accompanied by iridosmine, which occurs as flat angular scales, while platinum grains are usually rounded like gold dust. Analyses of California platinum show the presence of all other members of the platinum group, Genth (2) p. 209, Deville and Debray (1) p. 496, Weil (1) p. 354. Many of the black sands have been investigated by D. T. Day and Richards (6) p. 152.

Gray metallic grains and small nuggets of platinum were early observed in some of the gold-bearing black sands of the streams and beaches, and in the concentrates from the gold washings. R. B. Mason (1) p. 536, in a letter from Monterey dated August 7, 1848, records the presence of a small piece of "platina" mixed with gold. Teschemacher (2) p. 121, notes 50 granules of platinum in an ounce of gold dust. R. M. Patterson (1) p. 61, comments on the presence of platinum in California gold sands. J. B. Trask (1) p. 23, gives a number of occurrences of platinum from gold sands.

Generally, platinum grains are smaller than gold grains, and large nuggets are unknown. Some of the largest nuggets have come from the Junction City Mining District, along the Trinity and lower courses of its tributaries from Weaverville to North Fork, Logan (1) p. 82.

References to platinum occurrences not specifically mentioned in the county descriptions below are: D. T. Day (5) p. 410, Hanks (12) p. 310, Kunz (24) p. 42, Silliman (12) p. 132, F. M. Hamilton (4) p. 759, Angel (2) p. 598, Laizure (1) p. 497, Logan (1) p. 50.

The occurrence of platinum in the gold sands of the State is widespread, and has been described in detail by Logan (1). The principal production of platinum has come from Butte, Del Norte, Humboldt, Placer, Siskiyou, Stanislaus and Trinity counties. It has also been found in the gold sands of the following counties: Calaveras, El Dorado, Inyo (?), Kern, Mendocino, Merced, Nevada, Plumas, Santa Barbara, Santa Cruz, Shasta, Tehama, Ventura and Yuba.

Mariposa County: **1,** A reported occurrence of platinum at Devils Gulch, Castello (5) p. 142, is highly doubtful.

Mendocino County: **1,** Platinum has been found associated with cinnabar, zircon and gold in some of the sands of the Navarro River, Anderson Valley, Hanks (12) p. 310.

Plumas County: **1,** Platinum, almost always with grains of cinnabar, has been found in the North Fork, Feather River, at and below Rich Bar, Edman (2) p. 401. **2,** Several pieces of platinum up to the size of a large bean have been found on Nelson Creek, Hanks (12) p. 310.

Trinity County: **1,** Nuggets of platinum up to $2\frac{1}{2}$ ounces Troy weight have been found on Hay Fork branch of Trinity River, Hanks (1) p. 162, (12) p. 310. **2,** Nuggets up to 1 ounce have come from Junction City, Bixby (1) p. 154. **3,** A nugget weighing about $\frac{2}{3}$ of an ounce (310 grains) was found at the Old Eagle mine (sec. 9, T. 33 N., R. 11 W., M. D.), CDMG (11959), and **4,** another just over 1 ounce (484.4 grains) came from sec 9, T. 33 N., R. 10 W., M. D., CDMG (11958).

<h3 style="text-align:center">*PLAZOLITE, 1920</h3>
Basic calcium aluminum silicate, $Ca_3Al_2Si_2O_8(OH)_4$

Riverside County: **1,** Plazolite occurred as minute crystals with idocrase in the limestone quarry at Crestmore. Only a few specimens were found. It was named, analyzed and described by Foshag (3) p. 183. Tetrahedral crystals up to $\frac{3}{4}$ inch, with the forms 211, possibly also 211 and 221, are reported by Schwartz and Murdoch (p.c. '54). Massive white plazolite with black gehlenite occurred in Commercial quarry, Crestmore, Woodford et al. (10) p. 367.

PLOMBIÈRITE
A hydrated calcium silicate, near $Ca_5Si_6O_{16}(OH)_2 \cdot 11(?)H_2O$

Riverside County: **1,** Calcium silicate hydrate 14 Å has been detected by x-ray methods in specimens from Crestmore, intergrown with tobermorite and wilkeite, Heller and Taylor (1) p. 32, who consider the substance to be plombièrite, although they state that the character of the original plombièrite is uncertain. In any case, the x-ray powder pattern of the Crestmore mineral does not match that of plombièrite from Scawt Hill, Ireland, which does physically agree well with the description of the original mineral. The identity of the Crestmore material with type plombièrite must thus still be considered dubious.

PLUMBOGUMMITE
Basic hydrous lead aluminum phosphate, $PbAl_3(PO_4)_2(OH)_5 \cdot H_2O$

Inyo County: **1,** Plumbogummite has been reported from the Cerro Gordo mine (N. R.).

PLUMBOJAROSITE
Basic lead iron sulphate, $PbFe_6(OH)_{12}(SO_4)_4$

Inyo County: **1,** Plumbojarosite is found as a secondary alteration product in the Darwin Mining District, Kelley (4) p. 545.

Kern County: **1,** Plumbojarosite occurs frequently in the oxidized zone of veins of the Cactus Queen mine, Mojave Mining District, Troxel and Morton (2) p. 104; see also jarosite.

POLLUCITE
Hydrous caesium sodium aluminum silicate, $(Cs,Na)AlSi_2O_6 \cdot nH_2O$

San Diego County: **1,** Massive pollucite occurs in small amounts in the gem-bearing pegmatites near Pala and Mesa Grande, W. T. Schaller (p.c. '35), CDMG (20623). **2,** Massive pollucite occurs with lepidolite, albite, and tourmaline in a small pegmatite, southern part of Vulcan Mountain, Chesterman (p.c. '64).

POLYBASITE
Silver antimony sulphide, $Ag_{16}Sb_2S_{11}$

Polybasite closely resembles stephanite (Ag_5SbS_4), and the two are often mixed and are seldom differentiated. When in good crystals they can be distinguished, but when massive, their separate identification is difficult.

Alpine County: **1,** Specimens of polybasite have come from the Pennsylvania mine, Silver Mountain (N. R.). **2,** Hanks (12) p. 311 and Eakle (16) p. 13, observed polybasite in microscopic crystals from the Morning Star and Monitor mines.

San Bernardino County: **1,** Polybasite has been found with pyrargyrite and stephanite in the Carlyle mine, near Dale (sec. 11, T. 1 S., R. 12 E., S. B.), Tucker and Sampson (27) p. 61.

*POSEPNYTE, 1877
An oxygenated hydrocarbon

Lake County: **1,** Posepnyte was found at the Great Western mine and was described and named by von Schröckinger (1) p. 129, with analyses by Dietrich. Part of the mineral was soluble in ether, and part insoluble, the latter corresponding to ozocerite. Becker (4) p. 360, gives an analysis by Melville of similar material; see also Wagoner (2) p. 334.

Napa County: **1,** Posepnyte was found with aragotite at the Redington (?) mine, Rolland (1) p. 101.

POTASH ALUM
Hydrous aluminum potassium sulphate, $KAl(SO_4)_2 \cdot 12H_2O$

Alpine County: **1,** Potash alum was found in the mines of Silver Mountain, A. Williams (1) p. 606, as an efflorescence on argillaceous rocks.

Calaveras County: **1,** Potash alum was observed at Quail Hill, Silliman (7) p. 351.

Contra Costa County: **1,** Fine specimens of crystallized potash alum have come from the old coal mine at Nortonville (N. R.).

Fresno County: **1,** Potash alum was common with sulphur in the oil fields at Coalinga (N. R.).

Inyo County: **1,** Potash alum was found on the shores of Owens Lake (N. R.). **2,** The mineral occurred as white crusts on the sides of a steaming vent 2 miles east of Coso Hot Springs, A. F. Rogers (7) p. 376.

Lake County: **1,** Potash alum occurs as thick incrustations with other sulphates at the Sulphur Bank cinnabar mine, A. Williams (2) p. 949.

Los Angeles County: **1,** Potash alum was reported near Newhall by Hanks (12) p. 68.

Mono County: **1,** Potash alum occurred sparingly as coatings on rock about 5 miles NE from Bodie, Whiting (1) p. 356. **2,** The mineral occurs with alunite and sulphur in the andalusite deposits of the White Mountains, Woodhouse (4) p. 37.

Napa County: **1,** Potash alum occurs on Howell Mountain, 5 miles north of St. Helena, A. Williams (1) p. 606.

Placer County: **1,** Potash alum was found in slates near Auburn, Hanks (12) p. 68. **2,** The mineral accompanied by coquimbite occurs at Whiskey Hill, near Lincoln, Silliman (7) p. 351.

San Bernardino County: **1,** A specimen associated with pickeringite or halotrichite, in the U.S. National Museum, is labelled as coming from this county, E. S. Larsen (11) p. 94.

San Diego County: **1,** A specimen, CDMG (12066), of potash alum is from the Ready Relief mine, near Banner; it is reported as abundant at mine openings in the area, Donnelly (1) p. 362.

Santa Barbara County: **1,** Potash alum was reported in 1792 as a coating with sulphur at the "Fire Volcano" between Santa Barbara Channel and La Purisima, Martinez (1) p. 39.

Sonoma County: **1,** Potash alum was abundant at The Geysers, Hanks (12) p. 68. **2,** Massive, stony alum occurs on Hoods Mountain, 4 miles from Guilicos Ranch, between Sonoma and Santa Rosa, Mining and Scientific Press (11) p. 264.

POWELLITE
Calcium molybdate, CaMoO$_4$

El Dorado County: **1,** Powellite is reported with molybdenite from the Cosumnes copper mine, W. B. Clark and Carlson (3) p. 437.

Fresno County: Powellite is associated with scheelite in most of the tungsten occurrences in the Mt. Morrison quadrangle, Rinehart and Ross (2) p. 93.

Inyo County: **1,** Powellite occurs in the Pine Creek tungsten mine at the head of Pine Creek in the Sierra Nevada west of Bishop, Young (6) p. 605, Bateman (1) p. 236. **2,** Powellite is found with scheelite at the Powell tungsten property (sec. 24, T. 19 S., R. 40 E., M. D.), and **3,** at the Panyo tungsten mine with molybdenite (T. 20 S., R. 40 E., M. D.), Tucker and Sampson (30) p. 570. **4,** Powellite is reported on scheelite as greenish-yellow crusts, Anon. (41) p. 304.

Kern County: **1,** Powellite occurs in veins in the El Paso Mountains, about 12 miles northwest of Randsburg, Hess (14) p. 48. The powellite is pseudomorphous after molybdenite, and occurs in dikes, Troxel and Morton (2) p. 31. **2,** Powellite is found in minor amount in the tin ores at Gorman, Wiese and Page (1) p. 39, Troxel and Morton (2) p. 294. **3,** Powellite with scheelite, is locally abundant in a tactite zone in the Lake Isabella area, R. L. Engel (1) p. 24.

Mono County **1,** Powellite is found with molybdenite on the Morris claims, Benton Range (sec. 23, T. 35 S., R. 31 E., M. D.), Lemmon (6) p. 591.

San Bernardino County: **1,** Powellite occurs as an alteration product of molybdenite in the Red Hill region, Ord Mountains, Weber (3) p. 27.

Tulare County: **1,** Powellite has been found near Lemon Cove, pseudomorphous after molybdenite, Stanford University Collections. This may be the same as Hill Bros. prospects (sec. 14, T. 15 S., R. 28 E., M. D.), W. O. Jenkins (1) p. 175.

PREHNITE
Basic calcium aluminum silicate, Ca$_2$Al$_2$Si$_3$O$_{10}$(OH)$_2$

Prehnite is sometimes present as green drusy coatings and veins in altered diabase and lavas, but it is not common in the State.

Colusa County: **1,** Prehnite has been found in veins with calcite and pectolite in serpentine near Wilbur Springs, Vonsen (p.c. '33).

El Dorado County: **1,** Prehnite is found in veinlets with diopside at Traverse Creek, 2½ miles west of Georgetown, Pabst (2) p. 3.

Inyo County: **1,** Prehnite occurs in veinlets with epidote at the Pine Creek tungsten mine, Hess and Larsen (17) p. 276. **2,** White prehnite in crystalline grains up to 2 mm occurs with contact metamorphic minerals in a contaminated border zone in the Nelson Range, Ubehebe quadrangle, McAllister (4) p. 59.

Los Angeles County: **1,** The mineral is found in botryoidal crusts on fracture surfaces in basalt at the Pacific Electric quarry, Brush Canyon (sec. 35, T. 1 N., R. 14 W., S. B.), Neuerburg (1) p. 158, locality 2. **2,** Veins of calcite and prehnite occur in basalt at locality 3, south end of Cahuenga Pass, ibid., p. 158.

Marin County: **1**, Prehnite occurs in crystals with crystallized axinite, in the hills around Stinson Beach, Vonsen (p.c. '45).

Plumas County: **1**, Prehnite occurs as a hydrothermal product at the Engels mine, Graton and McLaughlin (4) p. 18.

Riverside County: **1**, Green drusy and light-brown prehnite occur in cavities of white feldspar in the pegmatic veins of the limestone at Crestmore, Eakle (15) p. 351. Foshag (12) p. 88, also reports orange crystals associated here with wollastonite and datolite, in pegmatite. **2**, Prehnite occurs in bands of radiating prismatic clusters in massive contact rock at the Jensen quarry, Schwartz (p.c. '57). **3**, Prehnite occurs in small vugs with quartz in a pegmatic dike in Bautista Canyon, Filer (p.c. '61).

San Diego County: **1**, Prehnite from Smiths Mountain, near Oak Grove, has been analyzed by Schaller, F. W. Clarke (9) p. 273.

San Luis Obispo County: **1**, Prehnite occurs in the analcite diabase of Cuyama Valley, Fairbanks (12) p. 289.

PRICEITE—Pandermite
Hydrous calcium borate, $Ca_5B_{12}O_{23}\cdot 9H_2O$

A general reference on priceite is Kramer and Allen (5).

Inyo County: **1**, Priceite was found as nodules and irregular masses in soft gray shale in the second wash to the west of the Russell mine, Mount Blanco area, Foshag (10) p. 10, (11) p. 11. **2**, Priceite was found in extensive massive veins or narrow lenses in shale, filling cracks in altered basalt near the mouth of Corkscrew Canyon, and as amygdule fillings, sometimes large, Foshag (25) p. 728. In the veins it is partly altered to delicate radiating needles of ulexite, or crystals of colemanite. **3**, The mineral is doubtfully reported as incrustations at Bennetts Well and Furnace Creek, G. E. Bailey (2) pp. 45, 46.

San Bernardino County: **1**, Priceite is reported from Owl (Hole) Springs with colemanite in the niter beds (T. 18 N., R. 3 E., S. B.), G. E. Bailey (2) p. 62, Cloudman et al. (1) p. 855. **2**, Hanks (12) p. 313, reports priceite from Calico.

*PROBERTITE—Kramerite, 1929
Hydrous sodium calcium borate, $NaCaB_5O_9\cdot 5H_2O$

Inyo County: **1**, Probertite, locally known as "boydite", occurs with colemanite and ulexite as translucent satiny needles in the Widow and Upper Biddy McCarthy mines near Ryan, Foshag (18) p. 338. **2**, Probertite is abundant enough to be mined as ore in the Kern borate mine near Ryan, associated with colemanite and ulexite, Anon. (47) p. 9. **3**, Probertite, ulexite and colemanite from the Resting Springs Range, near Shoshone, are reported by Nolan (3) p. A-11.

Kern County: **1**, Probertite was described by Eakle (26) p. 427, as a new mineral from the Kramer borate area where it occurs in clay with borax and kernite. Schaller (45) p. 139, described the crystals and occurrence under the name of "kramerite." Other references for the Kramer occurrences are Murdoch (17) p. 720, H. S. Gale (16) p. 362.

Los Angeles County: **1**, Probertite is abundant at the Sterling borax mine, Tick Canyon, as compacted rosettes of rather coarse needles, in the borax ore, Murdoch (17) p. 719.

PROUSTITE—Ruby Silver Ore
Silver arsenic sulphide, Ag_3AsS_3

The term "ruby silver" is given indiscriminately to proustite and pyrargyrite. Both minerals usually contain arsenic and antimony. The metallic gray pyrargyrite is more common than the transparent red proustite, but the two are often associated.

Alpine County: **1,** Proustite has been reported from the Exchequer mine, Silver Mountain, R. W. Raymond (10) p. 23.

Kern County: **1,** Specimens of proustite with pyrargyrite have come from the Amalie Mining District, Dyke (1) p. 764, Troxel and Morton (2) p. 41. **2,** Proustite is the principal silver mineral in the Cactus Queen and Blue Eagle (sec. 17, T. 10 N., R. 13 W., S. B.), Tucker et al. (37) p. 216, Troxel and Morton (2) p. 44. **3,** Proustite occurs, but is rare, in the veins of the Elephant (Elephant Eagle, Lodestar) group of claims, Mojave Mining District, A. G. Nelson, cited by Troxel and Morton (2) p. 107.

Mariposa County: **1,** Proustite occurred with pyrargyrite and argentite in the Bryant silver mine, Laizure (6) p. 123, (8) p. 44.

Mono County: **1,** Proustite was found in the Oro and Bodie mines, Bodie Mining District, Hanks (12) p. 314.

Napa County: **1,** Proustite has been found in the Palisades mine, about 2 miles north of Calistoga, Crawford (2) p. 414.

San Bernardino County: **1,** Proustite is a minor constituent of the silver ores of the Randsburg silver mines, Hulin (12) p. 98.

Shasta County: **1,** Proustite occurred with galena, pyrite and quartz in the Chicago mine, near Igo, Hanks (12) p. 314.

PSEUDOMALACHITE
Basic hydrous copper phosphate, $Cu_{10}(PO_4)_4(OH)_8 \cdot 2H_2O$

Inyo County: **1,** Pseudomalachite is reported associated with the lead-silver ores in the oxidized zone of the Darwin lead mine, Woodhouse (p.c. '51).

PSILOMELANE
A basic barium manganese oxide, usually impure, $(Ba,Mn^{2+})Mn^{4+}_4O_8(OH)_2$

The massive fine-grained oxides of manganese form a group whose members are impossible to separate by physical means of identification. They may be distinguished usually by x-ray determination. It is recommended, Fleischer and Richmond (1) p. 271, that massive, hard, heavy material not specifically identified should be referred to as belonging to the *"psilomelane type,"* and massive, soft material of apparent low specific gravity should be referred to as "wad." *Asbolite* is a wad containing cobalt. In the following notation of occurrences, the word "psilomelane" must be considered as meaning "psilomelane type," unless specific determination is indicated; see also cryptomelane, this volume, W. E. Richmond and Fleischer (2), p. 607.

Most of the manganese deposits are composed of the oxides at and near the surface, changing to the primary minerals with depth.

Detailed reports on the manganese deposits of California have been issued by CDMG as bulletin 76, W. M. Bradley et al. (4), and bulletin 125, P. D. Trask et al. (4).

Alameda County: **1,** Psilomelane is the chief mineral in the manganese deposits near Corral Hollow and the Arroyo Mocho, Watts (2) p. 121, Huguenin and Castello (4) pp. 26–28, Laizure (9) p. 53.

Amador County: **1,** Deposits of psilomelane mixed with pyrolusite occur 1½ miles south of Volcano, W. W. Bradley et al. (4) p. 29, Laizure (9) p. 71; **2,** 4 miles east of Pine Grove, W. W. Bradley et al. (4) p. 31, and **3,** about half a mile southeast of Defender, ibid., p. 29.

Butte County: **1,** Psilomelane occurs in several localities near Clipper Mills (sec. 35, T. 20 N., R. 7 E., M. D.), C. A. Waring (4) p. 224, W. W. Bradley et al. (4) p. 30.

Calaveras County: **1,** Deposits of psilomelane occur 2 miles northeast of San Andreas, W. W. Bradley et al. (4) p. 31. **2,** Asbolite is reported 6 miles southeast of Valley Springs, W. W. Bradley (23) p. 500. **3,** Asbolite came from 1 mile east of Mokelumne Hill, F. M. Hamilton (4) p. 760, Logan (8) p. 142.

Colusa County: **1,** Psilomelane occurs in small amounts on the eastern slope of St. Johns Mountain, east of Stonyford, Harder (1) p. 164, W. W. Bradley (1) p. 180.

Contra Costa County: **1,** Psilomelane was formerly mined on Red Rock in San Francisco Bay, A. C. Lawson (2) p. 423, (7) p. 23, W. W. Bradley et al. (4) p. 31, Huguenin and Castello (4) p. 55.

Fresno County: **1,** Psilomelane occurs on Pine Flat, near Piedra, W. W. Bradley et al. (4) p. 32.

Glenn County: **1,** The mineral occurred with pyrolusite at the Black Diamond and Rattlesnake mines (sec. 14, T. 18 N., R. 7 W., M. D.), about 30 miles southwest of Fruto, W. W. Bradley et al. (4) p. 32.

Humboldt County: **1,** Psilomelane occurs with pyrolusite as massive ore on the Porter Ranch (sec. 32, T. 3 N., R. 4 E., H.), W. W. Bradley et al. (4) p. 33, and **2,** on Charles Mountain (sec. 2, T. 1 S., R. 4 E., H.), Averill (10) p. 519.

Imperial County: **1,** Psilomelane deposits have been reported in the Chocolate Mountains, W. W. Bradley et al. (4) pp. 34, 35, and **2,** as filling of basalt breccia (T. 9, 10 S., R. 19, 20 E., S. B.), E. L. Jones (1) p. 201. **3,** Psilomelane is found in the Paymaster area (secs. 16, 18, 19, T. 11 S., R. 21 E., S. B.), Hadley (1) p. 465, and **4,** there are many other minor occurrences in the county, R. J. Sampson and Tucker (18) pp. 128–130.

Inyo County: **1,** Psilomelane is found at the southeast end of the Panamint Range, 25 miles south of Bennetts Wells on the Death Valley slope, W. W. Bradley et al. (4) p. 36.

Kern County: **1,** Wad has been found as a pseudomorph after calcite at the Echo mine near Mojave, A. F. Rogers (3) p. 18.

Lake County: **1,** Psilomelane occurs on the Phillips Ranch, about 1½ miles south of Laurel Dell, Huguenin and Castello (4) p. 78; **2,** on Dry Creek about 3 miles west of Middletown, W. W. Bradley et al. (4) p. 37, and **3,** a large deposit occurs about 10 miles north of Upper Lake on the southwestern slope of the Horse Mountains (sec. 10, T. 16 N., R. 10 W., M. D.), ibid., p. 37.

Los Angeles County: **1,** Asbolite occurred in the O.K. mine, San Gabriel Canyon, CDMG (11599). **2,** Deposits of siliceous psilomelane occur about 5 miles west of Palmdale, W. W. Bradley et al. (4) p. 38, F. J. H. Merrill (2) p. 479.

Marin County: **1,** Psilomelane occurs near Sausalito and Fort Baker, A. C. Lawson (7) p. 23. **2,** Psilomelane is found in masses on the Mailliard Ranch, about 8 miles northwest of San Rafael, W. W. Bradley et al. (4) p. 39.

Mendocino County: **1,** Large deposits of psilomelane occur in Potter Valley (sec. 3, T. 17 N., R. 12 W., M. D.), W. W. Bradley et al. (4) p. 40. **2,** Deposits of psilomelane occur at the Cleveland mine, 3 miles east of Calpella, W. W. Bradley et al. (4) pp. 42, 43; **3,** at the Independent mine, 14 miles east of Willits, ibid., pp. 42, 43; **4,** it occurs in the hills east of the Middle Fork of Eel River, ibid., p. 40, and **5,** psilomelane with rhodochrosite occurs on Mount Sanhedrin, ibid., p. 44. **6,** Psilomelane in jasper is found at the Thomas and Wild Devil mines, about 6 miles northeast of Redwood Station, ibid., p. 46.

Merced County: **1,** Manganese ore deposits occur about 26 miles east of Tres Piños (sec. 13, T. 13 S., R. 9 E., M. D.), W. W. Bradley et al. (4) p. 49.

Monterey County: **1,** Some small occurrences of psilomelane are found in the county, W. W. Bradley et al. (4) pp. 50, 51.

Napa County: **1,** Several small deposits of psilomelane occur near Oakville and Mount St. Helena, W. W. Bradley et al. (4) p. 51.

Nevada County: **1,** A large body of psilomelane occurs in the Limekiln area, E. MacBoyle (1) p. 262. **2,** Psilomelane is widespread but not abundant in the Grass Valley mines, W. D. Johnston (4) p. 44.

Placer County: **1,** Deposits of psilomelane occur about 9 miles north of Colfax, near Yankee Jims, W. W. Bradley et al. (4) p. 52.

Plumas County: **1,** Small amounts of psilomelane occur on Mumford Hill, W. W. Bradley et al. (4) pp. 53, 54. **2,** Psilomelane, manganite and rhodonite occur in the Diadem and Penrose lodes, near Edmanton, in the Edmanton (Meadow Valley) Mining District, W. W. Bradley et al. (4) pp. 53, 54. **3,** Deposits of psilomelane occur near Crescent Mills, ibid. For other localities, see J. C. O'Brien (1) pp. 80, 87.

Riverside County: **1,** Many small deposits of psilomelane occur in the McCoy Mountains, in the Palen Mountains, near Perris and Elsinore, Palo Verde, and Little Maria Mountains, W. W. Bradley et al. (4) pp. 54–59, E. L. Jones (1) pp. 195, 199. **2,** Botryoidal psilomelane is reported from near Tadpole Tanks, Anon. (13) p. 15.

San Benito County: **1,** Minor stringers and coatings of psilomelane occur with benitoite near the headwaters of the San Benito River, Louderback and Blasdale (5) p. 363; **2,** it occurs in cherts on the Fries and Lewis Ranches about 18 miles east of Tres Piños, Crawford (1) pp. 644, 645, and **3,** it is found at the McCreary Ranch (sec. 29, T. 14 S., R 9 E., M. D.), I. F. Wilson (2) p. 265.

San Bernardino County: **1,** Massive asbolite has been found with gypsum in clay near Borate, 7 miles north of Yermo (N. R.). References to other localities are W. W. Bradley et al. (4) pp. 61–64, Cloudman et al. (1) p. 822, E. L. Jones (1) pp. 189, 190, Tucker and Sampson (17) p. 337, (8) p. 241, (32) pp. 67, 132.

San Diego County: **1,** Fine specimens of psilomelane have come from Campo (N. R.).

San Joaquin County: **1,** Psilomelane is found in the manganese ore deposits of the Diablo Range, notably at the Ladd mine in Corral Hollow, Watts (1) p. 564, P. D. Trask et al. (4) p. 86.

San Luis Obispo County: **1,** Psilomelane occurs on the Staneuch Ranch, 8 miles west of San Luis Obispo, W. W. Bradley et al. (4) p. 72.

Santa Clara County: **1,** The outer crust of the manganese ore boulder near Alum Rock Park, 5 miles east of San Jose, was psilomelane, A. F. Rogers (21) p. 447. Other occurrences are referenced in W. W. Bradley et al. (4) pp. 75–81.

Shasta County: **1,** A deposit of psilomelane occurs on the Pit River, 1 mile south of Heroult, G. C. Brown (2) p. 807.

Siskiyou County: **1,** Many small occurrences are listed by W. W. Bradley et al. (4) p. 82.

Sonoma County: **1,** A deposit of high-grade psilomelane occurs on the Shaw Ranch, 7 miles northwest of Cloverdale, Crawford (1) p. 330. Other small deposits are recorded in W. W. Bradley et al. (4) pp. 82, 83.

Stanislaus County: **1,** Psilomelane occurs on Arroyo del Puerto, west of Patterson, W. W. Bradley et al. (4) p. 84, and **2,** in the manganese ore deposits of the Diablo Range, notably at the Buckeye mine, west of Vernalis, L. A. Smith (1) p. 213.

Trinity County: **1,** A number of small prospects are listed by W. W. Bradley et al. (4) p. 89, Averill (10) pp. 67, 68, J. C. O'Brien (1) p. 84.

Tulare County: **1,** Melhase (3) no. 7, p. 23, has reported the occurrence of asbolite from the King C. Gillette Farm, near Lindsay. **2,** Asbolite has been reported from the chrysoprase workings near Deer Creek, F. M. Hamilton (4) p. 247.

Tuolumne County: **1,** Psilomelane occurs massive with pyrolusite near Columbia, D. T. Day (1) p. 554.

PUCHERITE
Bismuth vanadate, $BiVO_4$

San Diego County: **1,** Pucherite occurs at the Pala Chief mine, near Pala. It was analyzed by Schaller (25) p. 230. **2,** The mineral occurred at the Victor mine, Rincon, with bismite and bismutite (?) Palache et al. (10) p. 600.

PUMPELLYITE
Basic hydrous calcium aluminum iron silicate,
$Ca_4(Al,Fe,^{2+}Fe,^{3+}Mg)_6Si_6O_{23}(OH)_3 \cdot 2H_2O$

Contra Costa County: **1,** Pumpellyite is found in schists with lawsonite on the private estate of Mrs. Anson Blake, G. A. Davis and Pabst (1) p. 692.

Marin County: **1,** Crystalline pumpellyite has come from 2 miles east of Novato, Vonsen (p.c. '45).

Merced County: **1,** Pumpellyite is sometimes associated with brown stilpnomelane, lawsonite and aragonite in the Franciscan rocks of the Pacheco Pass region, McKee (2) p. 384; see also Santa Clara County **(1).**

San Benito County: **1,** Pumpellyite occurs in association with jadeite and lawsonite on Clear Creek, Yoder and Chesterman (1) p. 3.

San Mateo County: **1,** Pumpellyite has been reported in quartzofeldspathic rocks, Hutton (1) p. 1373.

Santa Clara County: **1,** Pumpellyite is sometimes associated with brown stilpnomelane, lawsonite and aragonite in the Franciscan rocks of the Pachaco Pass area, McKee (2) p. 384; see also Merced County (1).

Sonoma County: 1, Pumpellyite was reported as dull green material with lawsonite in veins in glaucophane schist at Porter Creek (not at Mill Creek), 2 miles northwest of River Road, 8½ miles southwest of Healdsburg, Irving et al (1) p. 338. 2, Brown fibrous pumpellyite occurs in tufts or radiating aggregates in glaucophane schist near Skaggs, ibid., p. 338. 3, Pumpellyite is reported from Mill Creek, Combs (1) p. 119. This may be the same locality as (1).

Trinity County: 1, Pale-green veinlets of fibrous pumpellyite have been found in NW¼ sec. 21, T. 28 N., R. 11 W., M. D., Simons (p.c. '41).

PURPURITE—Heterosite
Manganese iron phosphate, $(Mn^{3+},Fe^{3+})PO_4$

San Diego County: 1, Purpurite was found with lithiophilite and triphylite in a pegmatite dike on Heriart Hill at Pala, Graton and Schaller (1) p. 146, Kunz (26) p. 1344, Schaller (22) p. 79. 2, A purple alteration product, either purpurite or heterosite (called heterosite by Jahns and Wright (5) p. 31), is the same occurrence reported by Schaller from Heriart Hill, Pala. Heterosite is considered to be the iron-rich end member of the purpurite-heterosite series. 3, Purpurite is doubtfully reported in pegmatites carrying beryl crystals, near Tule Mountain, Weber (1) p. 11.

PYRARGYRITE—Dark Ruby Silver Ore
Silver antimony sulphide, Ag_3SbS_3

Pyrargyrite is found in silver veins with argentite, polybasite, stephanite, tetrahedrite and other silver minerals. It is often embedded in quartz and good crystals of pyrargyrite may occur in cavities in quartz.

Alpine County: 1, Pyrargyrite occurred in the old I X L and Exchequer mines of the Silver Mountain area, R. W. Raymond (6) p. 13, Wheeler (4) p. 184, Hanks (15) p. 129, Lindgren (20) p. 184, Eakle (16) p. 13. 2, The mineral was observed at the Morning Star mine, Eakle (16) p. 13.

Kern County: 1, Pyrargyrite was found with argentite at the Amalie mine, CDMG (14831); 2, at the Reform mine (sec. 6, T. 29 S., R. 33 E., M. D.), Tucker and Sampson (21) p. 323, and 3, 1 mile north of (Old) Kernville, Wheeler (3) p. 65. 4, Pyrargyrite is found in small amounts in the Mojave Mining District, Troxel and Morton (2) p. 44.

Mariposa County: 1, Pyrargyrite was found with argentite and proustite in the Bryant Silver and Silver Lane mines (sec. 15, T. 6 S., R. 19 E., M. D.), Laizure (6) p. 123. 2, The mineral is reported from the Washington and Georgia mines, Quartzburg, J. B. Trask (1) p. 24.

Mono County: 1, Pyrargyrite and stephanite were abundant in the Oro, Addenda, Fortuna and other mines south of Bodie, Hanks (12) p. 315. Crystals of pyrargyrite were found in a vug in the Bodie mine, Whiting (1) p. 392. 2, The mineral also occurred in the Blind Spring Hill mines, in the Tower mine, and in other mines near Benton, Whiting (1) p. 392, R. J. Sampson (14) p. 140. 3, Pyrargyrite was found at the Dunderberg mine, Castle Peak, Conkling (1) p. 184.

Napa County: **1,** Pyrargyrite is a constituent of the gold and silver ore in the Palisades mine, 2 miles north of Calistoga, W. W. Bradley (26) p. 195, and **2,** it occurs with cinnabar at the Elephant vein 1½ miles north of Calistoga, Becker (4) p. 370.

Nevada County: **1,** Pyrargyrite was found with pyrite, chalcopyrite and galena in the Allison Ranch mine, Lindgren (12) p. 119, W. D. Johnston (3) p. 27. **2,** Pyrargyrite occurs in the Central mine of the Lava Cap Company, south of Banner Hill, and is probably present in other mines of the Grass Valley and Nevada City areas as indicated by the silver-rich concentrates, W. W. Bradley (30) p. 364, W. D. Johnston (3) p. 216, CDMG (21054).

Placer County: **1,** Pyrargyrite occurs in gold quartz at the Three Stars mine, Ophir Mining District, CDMG (16416).

San Bernardino County: **1,** Pyrargyrite occurs with miargyrite in the silver ores of the Randsburg area, Hulin (1) p. 98; **2,** with wolframite in Cliff Canyon, 2 miles southeast of Brant, New York Mountains, Tucker (4) p. 373; **3,** at the Carlyle mine, near Dale, with polybasite and stephanite, Tucker and Sampson (27) p. 61, and **4,** sparingly in the Calico Mining District, Weeks (4) p. 533.

Shasta County: **1,** Small amounts of pyrargyrite were occasionally found in the mines near Igo (N. R.).

Tulare County: **1,** Pyrargyrite occurred in minor amounts in the Empire mine, Mineral King Mining District, Engineering and Mining Journal (6) p. 8.

PYRITE—Iron Pyrites
Iron disulphide, FeS$_2$

Melnikovite is a cryptocrystalline variety of pyrite.

Pyrite is the commonest of the sulphide minerals and is found in all kinds of rock. It is commonly found in distinct crystals and in granular masses. Cubes several inches in diameter are frequent in gold areas, but in general the smaller crystals and granular masses are more highly auriferous. All of the localities given for chalcopyrite and many more, might be cited for pyrite since the mineral is present in every county. The oxidation of pyrite produces limonite and hematite, and the gossan of mineral veins is mostly formed by its alteration. Limonite as pseudomorphs after pyrite are exceedingly common.

Alameda County: **1,** Well-developed crystals from the Alma mine, Leona Heights, have been measured by Schaller (1) p. 191. C. W. Clark (1) p. 374, gives a list of minerals, including pyrite from the Alma mine.

Alpine County: **1,** Melnikovite occurs at the Leviathan mine, Pabst (6) p. 425.

Calaveras County: **1,** Cubes and pyritohedrons of pyrite occur with gold on Carson Hill, A. Knopf (11) p. 39, and **2,** slender needles from the Stanislaus mine are described as distorted pyrite crystals by A. W. Jackson (3) p. 365.

Colusa County: **1,** Hexagonal plates of pyrite occur as pseudomorphs after pyrrhotite at the Sulphur Creek deposit, Genth (9) p. 40.

El Dorado County: **1,** Blake reported brilliant cubes of pyrite at the Mameluke mine near Georgetown, Hanks (12) p. 317.

Lake County: **1,** Pyrite is sometimes abundant at Sulphur Bank, D. E. White and Roberson (2) p. 405.

Madera County: **1,** Large cubes of pyrite associated with wolframite occur in a quartz vein at the head of Iron Creek, Ritter Range, Minarets Mining District, Hess (18) p. 938, Erwin (1) p. 73, Krauskopf (1) p. 72.

Mariposa County: **1,** Large and perfect crystals of pyrite occur in the slates near Princeton Hill, Hanks (12) p. 317.

Nevada County: **1,** Pyrite forms the substance of fossilized trees at French Corral, J. A. Phillips (2) p. 408.

Riverside County: **1,** Pyrite is present in the Crestmore limestone as grains cubes and pyritohedra; some of the crystals are large. Limonite pseudomorphs after the pyrite are common, Eakle (15) p. 352.

San Diego County: **1,** Veins of compact botryoidal pyrite occur cutting the pyrrhotite mass at the Friday mine, Creasey (1) p. 27.

Santa Clara County: **1,** Slender prismatic crystals from the New Almaden cinnabar mine were measured by A. W. Jackson (3) p. 371, E. H. Bailey and Everhart (12) p. 97.

Shasta County: **1,** Pyrite was found by A. L. Day and Allen (1) pp. 121, 137, in the hot springs and mud pots of Lassen Volcanic National Park. **2,** Pyrite used for sulphuric acid occurs in commercial quantities and is produced at the Hornet mine (NE$\frac{1}{4}$ sec. 34, T. 33 N., R. 6 W., M. D.), Aubury (1) p. 68, Tucker (9) p. 441. **3,** Pyrite is the most abundant sulphide in the ores of the Iron Mountain mine, associated with chalcopyrite and sphalerite, Kinkel and Albers (1) p. 9.

Sonoma County: **1,** Large octahedrons have been found on Austin Creek near Healdsburg (N. R.).

Tuolumne County: **1,** Fine crystals of pyrite were found in the Patterson mine, Tuttletown, Hanks (12) p. 318.

PYROCHLORE
Niobate of the cerium group elements, calcium and other bases, with titanium, thorium and fluorine, (Ca,Na,Ce)(Nb,Ti,Ta)$_2$(O,OH,F)$_7$

Lassen County: **1,** Tiny (1 mm or less) black grains of pyrochlore are found disseminated in metavolcanic rocks at the Madonna Mia claim (sec. 19, T. 22 N., R. 17 E.), (CDMG X-ray identification, 1964).

San Diego County: **1,** A dark-brown isotropic mineral, presumably pyrochlore, surrounded by microlite, came from some locality in the county, A. F. Rogers (7) p. 375.

PYROCHROITE
Manganese hydroxide, Mn(OH)$_2$

Santa Clara County: **1,** Pyrochroite was a prominent constituent of a boulder of manganese ore near Alum Rock Park, 5 miles east of San Jose, A. F. Rogers (21) p. 445.

PYROLUSITE
Manganese dioxide, MnO$_2$

Pyrolusite is the commonest of the manganese minerals, but may readily be confused with "wad," or if in compact form, with other minerals of the "psilomelane type." Pyrolusite is common in the surface portions of manganese deposits, and very pervasive as coatings on fracture surfaces, and as an associate with other oxides. Its occurrences are practically the same as those of manganese ores or prospects, and are treated in considerable detail in Bulletins 76 [W. W. Bradley (4)] and 125 [P. D. Trask et al (4)] of the CDMG. Hanks (12) p. 316, also gives an extensive list of localities.

Manganese minerals like bementite, braunite, hausmannite, inesite, manganite, neotocite, psilomelane, pyrolusite, wad, and others are often not separable by field methods. It is apparent to the authors of this volume that many citations in the literature, especially those prior to 1940, may be incorrect identifications. Abundance of manganese minerals in the State in hundreds of localities makes systematic recording of all localities mentioned in the literature impractical. The following listings therefore may be incomplete, and many that are included are important only to reflect adequately the historic record.

Alameda County: **1,** Pyrolusite occurs with psilomelane in the Corral Hollow and Arroyo Mocho manganese deposits, Huguenin and Castello (4) pp. 26-28.

Calaveras County: **1,** Good specimens of pyrolusite have come from San Andreas (N. R.).

Colusa County: **1,** Pyrolusite is found with cinnabar at Stonyford, CDMG (9133).

Contra Costa County: **1,** Pyrolusite occurs with psilomelane on Red Rock in San Francisco Bay, J. D. Whitney (1) p. 79.

Del Norte County: **1,** Pyrolusite occurs with manganite on the North Fork, Smith River, Maxson (1) p. 160.

El Dorado County: **1,** Masses of pyrolusite occur in Greenwood, CDMG (12153).

Glenn County: **1,** Pyrolusite and psilomelane are associated at the Black Diamond and Rattlesnake mines about 30 miles southwest of Fruito, W. W. Bradley et al. (4) p. 32.

Humboldt County: **1,** Pyrolusite occurs on the Porter Ranch, Fort Baker, W. W. Bradley et al. (4) p. 33.

Imperial County: **1,** Pyrolusite is found with manganite at Tolbard (T. 11 S., R. 21 E., S. B.), Tucker (11) p. 226, Hadley (1) p. 465.

Inyo County: **1,** Some pyrolusite is present in the oxidized mineral zone of the Darwin Mining District, Hall and MacKevett (4) p. 64. **2,** Pyrolusite occurs in the Big Four mine, northern Panamint range, Hall and Stephens (3) p. 24. **3,** The mineral occurs in the Minietta and Modoc mines, Argus Range, ibid., pp. 32, 34.

Lake County: **1,** Pyrolusite occurs with psilomelane at the Phillips mine near Laurel Dell, Huguenin and Castello (4) p. 79.

Lassen County: **1,** Pyrolusite is rather abundant in the gold ores of the Hayden Hill Mining District, Hill (2) p. 36.

Madera County: **1,** Pyrolusite occurs with limonite 14 miles from Fresno Flat, Laizure (9) p. 55, **2,** near Coarse Gold with psilomelane, manganite, rhodochrosite, and rhodonite, P. D. Trask et al. (4) p. 130.

Marin County: **1,** Small amounts of pyrolusite were found in the rock at Sausalito, Hanks (12) p. 316.

Mariposa County: **1,** Small masses of pyrolusite occur in Hunters Valley, CDMG (467).

Mendocino County: **1,** Pyrolusite is found at Red Mountain; **2,** it occurred with psilomelane at the Independence manganese mine, Potter Valley; **3,** near Covelo; **4,** 4 miles west of Hopland with psilomelane; **5,** in Redwood Valley; **6,** near Willits; **7,** at the Long mine near Woodman Station; **8,** in chert at Westport, and **9,** at the Cleveland mine, Ukiah. For these localities and as a general reference for the county, see W. W. Bradley et al. (4) pp. 39-49.

Napa County: **1,** Pyrolusite occurred as radiating concentric masses with cinnabar at the old Redington and Manhattan mines, Knoxville (N. R.).

Placer County: **1,** Pyrolusite occurs with rhodonite 12 miles from Auburn on Wolf Creek road, CDMG (12152).

Plumas County: **1,** Pyrolusite is common near the Diadem lode, Meadow Valley Mining District, H. W. Turner (17) p. 6.

Riverside County: **1,** Pyrolusite occurs with manganite and psilomelane in the McCoy Mountains, E. L. Jones (1) p. 197.

San Benito County: **1,** Pyrolusite replaces jasper at the Cleveland manganese mine, 20 miles east of Tres Pinos, Crawford (1) p. 330.

San Bernardino County: **1,** Pyrolusite occurs in the Calico and Barstow areas, Erwin and Gardner (3) p. 301, and **2,** it occurred with psilomelane in the Emma and Owls Hole mines, in the Owl (Hole) Mountains, Cloudman et al. (1) p. 823. Other references to this county are E. L. Jones (1) p. 199, Tucker and Sampson (28) p. 241, (33) pp. 132, 135.

San Joaquin County: **1,** Pyrolusite is found in the manganese deposits of the Diablo Range, Watts (1) p. 564.

San Luis Obispo County: **1,** Pyrolusite is found with psilomelane in the manganese deposits on the Staneuch Ranch, 8 miles west of San Luis Obispo, W. W. Bradley et al. (4) p. 72.

Santa Clara County: **1,** Pyrolusite was found at the Washington mine, and in the mines of the Diablo Range, W. W. Bradley et al. (4) pp. 75-80.

Sonoma County: **1,** Pyrolusite occurred at the Shaw mine, Crawford (1) p. 330.

Stanislaus County: **1,** Pyrolusite occurs with rhodochrosite at the Buckeye mine on Hospital Creek, Laizure (3) p. 213.

PYROMORPHITE
Lead chloro-phosphate, $Pb_5(PO_4)_3Cl$

Pyromorphite is found as an alteration product of galena and cerussite.

Calaveras County: **1,** Green crystals of pyromorphite have been found in gold quartz at the Reliance mine (N. R.).

El Dorado County: **1,** Pyromorphite occurred as yellowish-green coloring matter in botryoidal chalcedony and as a crystalline coating at Mosquito Gulch, 6 miles northeast of Placerville, H. W. Turner (22) p. 343.

Inyo County: **1,** Pyromorphite was found in small amounts in the Cerro Gordo Mining District, R. W. Raymond (10) p. 29. **2,** Euhedral crystals of pyromorphite have been found at Darwin, in oxidized lead ore, in the Surprise mine (sec. 20, T. 19 S., R. 42 E., M. D.), confirming Woodhouse (p.c. '47), Norman and Stewart (2) p. 81, Hall and Stephens (1) p. 35.

Mariposa County: **1,** A small amount of pyromorphite was found in the mines near Coulterville, and is represented by a specimen in the University of California Collections at Berkeley.

Mono County: **1,** Prisms of pyromorphite on quartzite have come from the property of the Log Cabin Mining Company, 3 miles west of Mono Lake, W. W. Bradley (29) p. 311. **2,** Minute crystals lining a cavity have been found in the Blind Spring Mining District, W. W. Bradley (29) p. 191.

Nevada County: **1,** Pyromorphite occurs with galena in quartz at the Rocky Glen mine, Whiting (1) p. 450, Irelan (4) p. 47.

Riverside County: **1,** The mineral reported from the El Dorado mine as pyromorphite, Eakle (22), was proved to be vanadinite, Pabst (p.c. '45). **2,** Minute yellow crystals of pyromorphite have been reported as collected at the old City quarry, Riverside, Jenni (p.c. '57). This material is now known to have been collected from the Wet Weather quarry dump at Crestmore.

San Bernardino County: **1,** Pyromorphite has been found with vanadinite at the Vanadium King mine, near Kleinfeldter, Tucker (4) p. 375.

Shasta County: **1,** W. P. Blake (14) p. 125, reported the occurrence of pyromorphite with tetrahedrite, galena and cerussite on the Chicago claim, 3 miles west of Igo.

Tulare County: **1,** Pyromorphite was found in the White Chief mine, Mineral King Mining District, Goodyear (3) p. 646, Schrader et al. (1) p. 71.

PYROPHYLLITE
Hydrous aluminum silicate, $Al_2Si_4O_{10}(OH)_2$
Agalmatolite is a varietal name for pyrophyllite

Alameda County: **1,** A specimen from Irvington is in the CDMG Exhibit, CDMG (16214).

Amador County: **1,** Pyrophyllite (or damourite?) is one of the gangue minerals of the Central Eureka and Kennedy mines, Logan (16) p. 78.

El Dorado County: **1,** Pyrophyllite is reported from the county, CDMG (1811).

Imperial County: **1,** Pyrophyllite occurs in veins with kyanite and andalusite at the mine of the Vitrefax Corporation, 10 miles west of Winterhaven, near the abandoned railroad station of Ogilby, Tucker (11) p. 280.

Inyo County: **1,** Pyrophyllite has been found near Sheephead Pass, 7 miles west of Shoshone, W. W. Bradley (30) p. 194.

Madera County: **1,** Radiating and massive pyrophyllite occurs in schist near the junction of the North Fork of San Joaquin River and Bench Creek, Erwin (1) p. 29.

Mariposa County: **1,** Pyrophyllite occurs in beautiful radiating tufts of golden yellow color with quartz at Tres Cerritos, Hanks (12) p. 318, H. W. Turner (12) p. 685, O. E. Bowen and Gray (2) p. 219.

Mono County: **1,** Pyrophyllite occurs abundantly in radiating masses and veinlets in andalusite at the mine of Champion Sillimanite, on the western slope of the White Mountains, 7 miles east of Mocalno, north of Bishop, Peck (1) p. 151, Kerr (3) p. 627. **2,** Pyrophyllite has been shipped from a deposit 17 miles north of Laws, CDMG Mineral Information Service, April 7, 1947. This is incorrectly reported as Inyo County **(2)**, Murdoch and Webb (39) p. 269.

Plumas County: **1,** Massive pyrophyllite occurs in the Diadem Lode, Meadow Valley, Schrader et al. (1) p. 71.

San Bernardino County: **1,** A considerable deposit of pyrophyllite occurs in a hydrothermally altered zone in volcanic rock on the Victorite pyrophyllite property (secs. 24, 25, T. 7 N., R. 3 W., S. B.), near Victorville, L. A. Wright et al. (5) p. 243.

San Diego County: **1,** Agalmatolite occurs near Encinitas, A. F. Rogers (7) p. 381, Sanford and Stone (1) p. 24. **2,** A large commercial deposit of massive pyrophyllite occurs near Escondido at the Pioneer mine, 7½ miles southwest of Escondido, Jahns and Lance (3) pp. 1-32, D. F. Palmer (1) p. 5.

San Luis Obispo County: **1,** Massive pyrophyllite from the county is represented by CDMG (4060).

PYROSTILPNITE—Fireblende
Silver antimony sulphide, Ag_3SbS_3

San Bernardino County: **1,** A few minute crystals of pyrostilpnite have been found in cavities of the rich silver ores at the California Rand mine, Murdoch (12) p. 130, W. W. Bradley (30) p. 194.

PYROXENES

In this group is a series of complex silicates of magnesium, iron, calcium and aluminum, or varying combinations of these elements with others. The pyroxenes are very common rock-forming minerals and are found both in igneous and metamorphic rocks. They are so common that only the most interesting occurrences can be mentioned.

The validity of varietal names in this group are sometime subject to debate.

The identification of the varieties of pyroxene in the older literature was often based on physical inspection. Confirmation of the identification requires optical, chemical, or crystallographic data. Validation of identification in locality reports has not been undertaken in the entries given below.

ENSTATITE
Magnesium silicate, $MgSiO_3$

Bronzite is a variety in which part of the magnesium is replaced by iron. It occurs in bronze-brown reticulated masses.

Enstatite is a rock-forming mineral which is characteristic of gabbros, and rocks that have been derived from gabbros, like much of the serpentinized rocks of the Coast Ranges and Sierra Nevada. It is a common mineral, but has seldom been mentioned.

Alameda County: **1**, Bronzite occurs in some of the rocks of the Berkeley Hills, Hanks (12) p. 178.

Contra Costa County: **1**, Massive enstatite is found in the Diablo Range in this and other counties to the south, Kunz (24) p. 81.

Kern County: **1**, Bronzite was one of the constituents of the San Emigdio meteorite, and was analyzed by Whitfield (3) p. 114.

Nevada County: **1**, Enstatite is an important constituent of the gabbros of Nevada City, Lindgren (12) p. 53.

San Francisco County: **1**, Enstatite occurs abundantly in the serpentine of San Francisco, W. P. Blake (7) p. 307, Palache (2) p. 166, Eakle (1) p. 316, Kunz (24) p. 81.

Santa Barbara County: **1**, Enstatite in large crystals has been collected on the north slope of Figueroa Mountain, Woodhouse (p.c. '63).

HYPERSTHENE
Iron and magnesium silicate, $(Fe,Mg)SiO_3$

Hypersthene is a constituent of basic eruptive rocks, especially gabbros and andesites.

Plumas County: **1**, Hypersthene is a constituent of the hypersthene andesite at La Porte, H. W. Turner (4) p. 488.

Riverside County: **1**, Hypersthene is reported from Crestmore by J. W. Daly (1), but its presence in the quarries at Crestmore has not been confirmed, Woodford et al. (10) p. 368.

San Diego County: **1**, Hypersthene is one of the minerals in the orbicular gabbro at Dehesa, A. C. Lawson (6) p. 386.

Siskiyou County: **1**, Hypersthene is mentioned by J. D. Dana (3) p. 254, as a constituent of the hypersthene andesite of Mount Shasta.

Trinity County: **1**, Hypersthene with magnetite is abundant on the northwest side of Chuachelulla Mountain, G. C. Brown (2) p. 920.

CLINOENSTATITE
Magnesium silicate, $MgSiO_3$

San Bernardino County: **1**, Red-brown clinoenstatite occurs with green forsterite at Dish Hill (Siberia) crater near Amboy (CDMG identification 1964).

CLINOFERROSILITE
Iron silicate, $FeSiO_3$

Clinoferrosilite is characteristic of lithophysae in obsidians.

Inyo County: **1**, Clinoferrosilite is found as needles in lithophysae in obsidian from Coso Mountains, N. L. Bowen (1) p. 491, W. W. Bradley (29) p. 107.

DIOPSIDE
Calcium magnesium silicate, $CaMg(SiO_3)_2$

Omphacite is a variety commonly occurring in contact metamorphic rocks. *Violan* is purple diopside.

Contra Costa County: **1**, Diopside is common with albite in the schists near San Pablo, Blasdale (1) p. 343.

El Dorado County: **1**, Fine, dark-green crystals of diopside occur near Mud Springs, Hanks (12) p. 318, Kunz (4) p. 80. **2**, Fine crystals of diopside have come from the old Cosumnes copper mine, near Fairplay, Hanks (12) p. 319, Kunz (24) p. 80. **3,** Massive white diopside, resembling idocrase, and lath-like crystals up to 7 mm occur with prehnite on West Hill, Traverse Creek, 2½ miles southeast of George-town, Pabst (2) p. 3.

Fresno County: **1,** Pink, white and dull-gray crystals of diopside occur in limestone in the Twin Lakes area, Chesterman (1) p. 254.

Inyo County: **1,** Pale-green diopside is found in a contact zone at Round Valley, 6 miles west of Bishop, Chapman (1) p. 866. **2,** Color-less diopside, with scapolite and idocrase, is found at the Pine Creek tungsten mine, Hess and Larsen (17) p. 276.

Lake County: **1,** Violan is reported from Big Canyon (N. R.).

Madera County: **1,** Diopside is common in contact zones in limestone on Shadow and Johnson Creeks, in the Minarets Mining District, Erwin (1) p. 30.

Placer County: **1,** Diopside, showing crystals in cavities, is found associated with axinite and black tourmaline near the summit of Wards Peak, Wilkie (p.c. '36).

Riverside County: **1,** Diopside is abundant in the contact zones at Crestmore, Eakle (15) p. 340, R. H. Merriam and Laudermilk (1) p. 715, Woodford (11) p. 359. Complex crystals were measured by Eakle (15) p. 340. **2,** Large green crystals of diopside appear in the contact zone at the new City quarry, south of Riverside, E. S. Larsen (17) p. 34. **3,** Coarse-grained diopside, with garnet, occurs at a limestone-gabbro contact 1½ miles northeast of Winchester, ibid., p. 35.

San Bernardino County: **1,** Snow-white, fine-grained diopside occurs near the mouth of Cascade Canyon (SE¼ sec. 36, T. 2 N., R. 8 W., S. B.), R. H. Merriam and Laudermilk (1) p. 716. **2,** Granular pale-blue diopside is found in a contact zone above the main adit of the Ball magnesite mine 12 miles east of Victorville, O. E. Bowen (p.c. '55).

San Francisco County: **1,** Lilac-colored diopside in fibrous and co-lumnar radial groups occurs in seams of serpentine near San Fran-cisco, Sterrett (6) p. 864.

DIALLAGE
Near diopside in composition, but usually with more or less aluminum

Contra Costa County: **1,** Gabbro, containing a high proportion of pure diallage, occurs on Bagley Creek about 1½ miles due north of the summit of Mt. Diablo, H. W. Turner (1) p. 391.

Nevada County: **1,** Diallage is common at Grass Valley and Nevada City, Lindgren (12) p. 52.

Riverside County: **1,** A little diallage occurs in the garnet contact rock, and in the quartz monzonite, at Crestmore, J. W. Daly (1) p. 649.

San Francisco County: **1,** Grains of diallage occur in the serpentine one-half mile south of Fort Point in the city of San Francisco, with residual olivine and enstatite, Palache (2) p. 166, A. C. Lawson (2) p. 447.

Trinity County: **1,** Diallage is reported from T. 40 N., R. 6 W., M. D., CDMG (21708).

HEDENBERGITE
Calcium iron silicate, $CaFe^{2+}Si_2O_6$

Fresno County: **1,** Hedenbergite is the principal skarn mineral with scheelite, magnetite and garnet, in a contact deposit near Twin Lakes, Chesterman (1) p. 277.

Shasta County: **1,** Green, fibrous hedenbergite, associated with ilvaite, occurs at Potters Creek, in an iron-ore deposit, Prescott (1) p. 14, (2) p. 473.

AUGITE
Calcium, magnesium, aluminum, iron silicate, $(Ca,Mg,Fe^{2+},Fe^{3+},Ti,Al)_2(Si,Al)_2O_6$

Augite is a dark-green to black aluminous pyroxene. It is the commonest of all the pyroxenes, and is an important constituent of diorites, gabbros, diabases, basalts, andesites, and pyroxenites. It is mentioned in most petrographic descriptions of basic igneous rocks.

No occurrences are of sufficient interest to warrant a separate entry.

AEGIRINE—Acmite
Sodium iron silicate, essentially $NaFe^{3+}(SiO_3)_2$

Aegirine is a rock-forming mineral prominent in some syenites.

Fresno County: **1,** Aegirine occurs with analcime and barkevikite in cavities of a soda syenite, near the head of White Creek ($SE\frac{1}{4}$ sec. 4, T. 19 S., R. 13 E., M. D.), Arnold and Anderson (8) p. 158.

San Benito County: **1,** Aegirine occurs in stellate groups with benitoite and natrolite in the albite at the benitoite locality near the headwaters of the San Benito River, Louderback and Blasdale (5) p. 363.

San Diego County: **1,** Aegirine occurs with quartz, crossite and garnet in schist boulders in the San Onofre breccia on the state highway due west of San Onofre Mountain, Woodford (2) p. 186.

Sonoma County: **1,** Black, stumpy crystals of aegirine occur with riebeckite in cavities of soda rhyolite, near Glen Ellen on the east side of Sonoma Valley, Chesterman (p.c. '51).

JADEITE
Sodium aluminum silicate, $NaAl(SiO_3)_2$

General reference: The occurence of jadeite in Franciscan cherts and graywackes has been reported from Contra Costa, Sonoma, and San Benito counties. The conclusion is offered that jadeite-bearing rocks may be widespread in California in the Franciscan series, Bloxam (1) p. 488.

Marin County: **1,** Jadeite occurs as an important constituent of weakly metamorphosed graywacke at Massa Hill nephrite locality, Chesterman (p.c. '55).

Mendocino County: **1,** Jadeite occurs in stream boulders, with nephrite and with crocidolite, on the north fork, Eel River, near Mina, Yoder and Chesterman (1) p. 6, Anon. (12) p. 2. **2,** Stream boulders of jadeite are found in Williams Creek, Yoder and Chesterman (1) p. 6. **3,** Doubly terminated crystals of jadeite occur along Russian River near Cloverdale, Wolfe and Riska (1) p. 1491, Wolfe (3).

San Benito County: **1,** Boulders of jadeite, and nodules in serpentine associated with pumpellyite and lawsonite, have been found on

Clear Creek (NW¼ sec. 12, T. 18 S., R. 11 E., M. D.), Anon. (9) p. 2. The description of the original find, Bolander (2) p. 186, with comments, is found in Dake (1) p. 188; see also Yoder and Chesterman (1) p. 1, Coleman (1) p. 11. Prewitt and Burnham (1) p. 156, have described the crystal structure of jadeite from a single natural crystal from Santa Rita Peak from the locality as described by Yoder and Chesterman (1). op. cit.

San Luis Obispo County: **1,** Stream boulders of jadeite have been found near Paso Robles, Yoder and Chesterman (1) p. 6.

Sonoma County: **1,** Jadeite occurs in schist at Valley Ford, Yoder and Chesterman (1) p. 6.

Trinity County: **1,** Stream boulders of jadeite with nephrite are reported from the north fork of the Eel River, Anon. (8) p. 16.

PYROXMANGITE
Iron manganese silicate, (FeMn)SiO₃

Kern County: **1,** Pyroxmangite occurs in the contact zone of manganese ores at the Big Indian deposit two miles south of Randsburg (sec. 11, T. 30 S., R. 40 E., M. D.), as small yellowish grains in quartzite, Hewett et al. (6) p. 54.

PYRRHOTITE—Magnetic Pyrites
Iron sulphide, Fe₁₋ₓS

Pyrrhotite is often associated with pyrite, chalcopyrite and arsenopyrite, and is sometimes found in large lenticular masses. It is common in gold and copper regions although usually in small amounts. Occasionally it is accompanied by nickel minerals. Many occurrences exist besides those listed below.

Alpine County: **1,** Pyrrhotite occurs with other sulphides in a quartz vein near Red Lake Peak, 13 miles west of Woodfords, W. W. Bradley (15) p. 488.

Amador County: **1,** Pyrrhotite was found in albite veinlets at the Treasure mine near Amador City, A. Knopf (11) p. 39; **2,** it occurs at the Defender mine 5 miles southeast of Volcano, Tucker (1) p. 27, and **3,** it is found at the Argonaut mine, L. L. Root (2) p. 67.

Calaveras County: **1,** Pyrrhotite occurs in the Westpoint and other areas, H. W. Turner (3) p. 470, Franke and Logan (4) p. 239. **2,** Pyrrhotite is disseminated in diorite at the Easy Bird mine, northeast of Mokelumne Hill, A. Knopf (11) p. 39; **3,** it is found in the Lockwood mine 1½ miles northeast of Woodcocks Mill, H. W. Turner and Ransome (18) p. 6, and **4,** is occurs with tetrahedrite at Carson Hill, Moss (1) p. 1011.

Del Norte County: **1,** Pyrrhotite is found in copper ores on Diamond Shelly and Copper Creeks, and at Low Divide and other localities, Aubury (1) p. 112, (4) pp. 136, 139, Maxson (1) p. 148.

Fresno County: **1,** A very large mass of sulphide ore, mainly pyrrhotite, occurred on the 200-foot level of the Fresno copper mine (sec. 10, T. 12 S., R. 21 E., M. D.), Aubury (4) p. 281.

Humboldt County: **1,** Large masses of pyrrhotite occur at Elk Ridge, CDMG (12195).

Inyo County: **1,** Many small occurrences of pyrrhotite are found in the Panamint Range, R. J. Sampson (7) pp. 349, 367, 371, 373, Murphy (2) pp. 313, 317. **2,** West of Bishop, in Tungsten Hills and vicinity, pyrrhotite is associated with scheelite, Hess and Larsen (17) p. 269, Tucker and Sampson (32) p. 60. **3,** Pyrrhotite is found at the Bishop and Wilshire Bishop Creek mines, Tucker (11) p. 474, Schroter (2) p. 53, Lenhart (1) p. 4. **4,** Pyrrhotite is present in small quantities in the ores of the Darwin Mining District, Hall and MacKevett (4) p. 62.

Kern County: **1,** Pyrrhotite occurs in contact deposits with scheelite in the Green Mountains (sec. 19, T. 25 S., R. 32 E., M. D.), Storms (15) p. 768, Hess and Larsen (17) p. 262, and **2,** in the Big Blue group (T. 25 S., R. 33 E., M. D.), Prout (1) p. 413. **3,** Pyrrhotite (troilite?) was one of the constituents of the San Emigdio meteorite, Whitfield (3) p. 114.

Los Angeles County: **1,** Pyrrhotite occurs with other sulphides, siderite and annabergite, in Pacoima Canyon, 12 miles northeast of San Fernando, Tucker (4) p. 318, (8) p. 42, R. J. Sampson (10) p. 176, D'Arcy (3) p. 269.

Madera County: **1,** Pyrrhotite was found in the old Buchanan mine, H. W. Turner (12) p. 696. **2,** Large masses of pyrrhotite, reported to carry several percent of cobalt and nickel, occur about 12 miles northeast of Madera, R. P. McLaughlin and Bradley (3) p. 559. **3,** Pyrrhotite occurred at the Ne Plus Ultra mine near Daulton, Forstner (4) p. 747.

Marin County: **1,** Tabular crystals have been found on Mount Tamalpais (N. R.).

Mariposa County: **1,** Thick bodies of pyrrhotite occur in the Green Mountain mine, Forstner (4) p. 747. **2,** The mineral occurs abundantly in the ore at the Croesus prospect on Merced River, 2 miles north of Bagby, A. Knopf (11) p. 39, and **3,** 1 mile north of Trumbull Peak, near Incline, W. W. Bradley (13) p. 84. **4,** The mineral is present in the Iona Copper Company tunnel on Merced River, Hanks (12) p. 316.

Mono County: **1,** Pyrrhotite is abundant in quartz at the Tioga mine, H. W. Turner (4) p. 469; and **2,** it is found at Laurel Creek and upper Mammoth Valley, Mayo (4) pp. 84, 85.

Nevada County: **1,** Pyrrhotite was found in the mines of Grass Valley and Nevada City, Lindgren (12) p. 118, Knaebel (1) p. 393. **2,** The mineral was also found in the Meadow Lake Mining District, Conkling (1) p. 184, Lindgren (5) p. 205. **3,** The mineral occurred massive at the Yuba mine, Washington Mining District, Irelan (4) p. 47, and **4,** it was reported in considerable quantity and said to carry platinum in the Liberty Hill area, Hill (3) p. 8.

Orange County: **1,** Pyrrhotite is found with sphalerite on the north bank of San Juan creek in the south southwest part of the Elsinore quadrangle, about 1½ miles east of the western quadrangle boundary, E. S. Larsen et al. (18) p. 48.

Plumas County: **1,** Pyrrhotite occurs in masses between sandstone and serpentine about 1½ miles south of Taylorsville, Diller (9) p. 47, (11) p. 115.

Riverside County: **1,** Minor amounts of pyrrhotite occur at Long Canyon (sec. 7, T. 6 S., R. 5 W., S. B.), R. J. Sampson (9) p. 514,

2, in the old City quarry, Riverside, A. F. Rogers (19) p. 582, and **3,** at Crestmore, Kelley (2) p. 141. **4,** The mineral occurs with siderite in the Old Dominion mine in the Santa Ana Mountains, E. S. Larsen et al. (18) p. 48.

San Diego County: **1,** A large body of nickel-bearing pyrrhotite associated with chalcopyrite, pyrite and violarite occurs on a contact of gabbro and fine-grained schist, at the Friday copper mine (sec. 15, T. 13, S., R. 4 E., S. B.), Julian Mining District, Calkins (2) p. 78, Hudson (1) p. 219, Creasey (1) p. 27. **2,** Pyrrhotite has been found near Descanso, Tucker (8) p. 371, and **3,** at the Echo mine near Lakeside, W. W. Bradley (28) p. 495.

Santa Clara County: **1,** Pyrrhotite occurs in the ore of the Hooker Creek mine (sec. 10, T. 9 S., R. 1 W., M. D.), 7 miles south of Los Gatos, F. F. Davis (p.c. '53).

Shasta County: **1,** Pyrrhotite was found with pyrite at some of the copper mines, and noticed at the Black Diamond copper mine and Sutro mines, Tucker (9) pp. 428, 433, L. L. Root (4) pp. 146, 149.

Sierra County: **1,** Pyrrhotite occurred with chalcopyrite at the Lost Cabin prospect (N. R.).

Siskiyou County: **1,** Pyrrhotite is prominent with chalcopyrite at Callahan, Aubury (1) p. 105, and **2,** the mineral is said to be nickel-iferous at the Hummer mine, ibid.

Trinity County: **1,** A large mass of pyrrhotite associated with chalcopyrite occurs at Island Mountain on the South Fork of Eel River, Landon (1) p. 279.

Tulare County: **1,** Pyrrhotite occurs in some of the contact deposits near Mineral King, Tucker (3) pp. 910, 917.

Tuolumne County: **1,** Pyrrhotite occurs in gneiss on the North Fork of Beaver River, H. W. Turner (22) p. 344; **2,** it occurs with sphalerite and galena at the Soulsby mine, Irelan (5) p. 744, Storms (17) p. 873, and **3,** with galena and sphalerite in quartz at the Montgomery, Cherokee, Carlotta, Densmore, Draper and Louisiana mines, Tucker (1) p. 138: **4,** The mineral is found on the north bank of the Tuolumne River east of Jawbone Creek, Mining and Scientific Press (36) p. 974.

Ventura County: **1,** Pyrrhotite occurs with nickel minerals and chalcopyrite at the Ventura mine (T. 1 N., R. 18 W., S. B.), Tucker and Sampson (20) p. 258.

QUARTZ
Silicon dioxide, SiO_2

Common quartz is an essential constituent of granites, granodiorites, quartz porphyries, rhyolites, gneisses, schists, quartzites, and sandstones, and is an accessory mineral in many other kinds of rock, either volcanic, metamorphic, or sedimentary. Veins, ledges, seams and pockety masses of white quartz are common in volcanic and metamorphic rocks. *Rock crystal* is a clear, colorless variety which is found as hexagonal crystals. *Amethyst* is a violet-colored variety sometimes used as a gem. It occurs in groups of crystals. Very little good amethyst has been found in the State. *Rose quartz* is a massive pink variety. *Smoky quartz* or *cairngorm stone* is a hair-brown transparent variety occurring as crystals. The color is readily discharged or converted to citrine yellow by heat. This is a common variety of quartz and some excellent large crystals have been found. *Thetis hairstone* is rock crystal containing long hair-like fibers of asbestos or actinolite. *Phantom crystals* show the outlines of one crystal within another; they are caused often by inclusions of green chloritic matter or brownish earthy material arranged about the boundaries of the crystal during growth. Inclusions of other minerals in quartz are common.

No attempt has been made to report all of the occurrences of quartz found in the State that are referenced in the literature. The mineral is widespread and is so common that only occurrences of mineralogical interest should be included. However, some localities of minor importance and of little mineralogical interest are noted for the historical record because they have been reported in early editions of *Minerals of California*.

Alameda County: **1,** Yellow crystals of quartz occur with glassy albite at the Newman mine on Cedar Mountain, 12 miles southeast of Livermore, Symons (3) p. 41.

Alpine County: **1,** Rose quartz has been found in Hope Valley, CDMG (3706).

Amador County: **1,** Fine, large specimens of rock crystal, many of them rounded stream boulders, have come from Volcano and Oleta, Durrell (p.c. '45). **2,** The Volcano and Oleta areas have also produced good specimens of amethyst, smoky and rose quartz, Symons (3) p. 41. **3,** Quartz carrying carbonaceous inclusions comes from the New York mine (sec. 6, T. 5 N., R. 11 E., M. D.), Preston (4) p. 140. **4,** Durrell (p.c. '45) has reported the occurrence of quartz crystals near Fiddletown, confirmed by Carlson and Clark (2) p. 214. **5,** Interesting quartz crystals are found near the town of Mokelumne Hill, off the road to Glencoe, as clear crystals, individually and in groups. A detailed description of the locality is found in Owens (1) p. 578.

Butte County: **1,** Fine rose quartz occurs near Forbestown, Sterrett (10) p. 324.

Calaveras County: **1,** Good rock crystal in fine large aggregates has been found in many of the gold mines. Mokelumne Hill, Green Mountain gravel mine near Murphy, Angels Camp, and Westpoint have produced large crystals, Storms (9) p. 124, F. L. Ransome (9) p. 11, G. E. Bailey (2) p. 468, Kunz (24) p. 65. Kunz (13) p. 587, reports quartz as enormous clusters of crystals in gravels, and cites a 5-inch flawless sphere cut from the quartz, and one flawed sphere $7\frac{1}{2}$ inches. **2,** Quartz colored green by pyroxene inclusions has been found on Garnet Hill, Moore Creek, H. W. Turner (12) p. 706. **3,** Quartz crystals occur in a buried deposit of gold gravel at Chili Gulch, $2\frac{1}{2}$ miles south of Mokelumne Hill, Ver Planck (5) p. 5. This may be the same locality as **(1)** above, as reported by Storms (9) and others.

El Dorado County: **1,** The best rock crystal, phantom crystal and smoky quartz in the State have come from near Placerville, Hanks (12) p. 65, Kunz (5) p. 329, (6) p. 395, (8) p. 547. **2,** A blue variety of quartz occurring in pegmatite in this county has been named "eldoradoite" by Watkins (1) p. 26. **3,** Quartz in good clear crystals is reported from the Josephine mine, near Volcanoville, Hanks (1) p. 361.

Fresno County: **1,** Smoky quartz crystals were reported from miarolitic cavities in an alaskite (granite), from the Dinkey Lakes region by W. B. Hamilton (1). The mineral has been studied further by A. J. Cohen (1) p. 570, Marshall (1), p. 535.

Inyo County: **1,** Good rock crystal and smoky quartz have been found in the Cerro Gordo Mining District, CDMG (11137). **2,** Crystal Hill, in Deep Spring Valley, has supplied many good specimens of quartz crystals, Webb (p.c. '45). **3,** Good quartz crystals, frequently coated with specular hematite or chlorite, up to 3 inches, are found on "crystal ridge", 10 miles northeast of Independence, M. F. B. Strong (8) p. 16.

Kern County: **1,** Rose quartz has been reported north of Kernville, Sterrett (4) p. 837. **2,** Large smoky quartz crystals occur in pegmatite on Black Mountain (S$\frac{1}{2}$ sec. 22, T. 25 S., R. 32 E., M. D.), Durrell (p.c. '45). **3,** Quartz crystals up to 10 pounds, some colored greenish by epidote inclusions, are found at the Aldridge (Zelner) mine (NW$\frac{1}{4}$ sec. 27, T. 25 S., R. 32 E., M. D.), Durrell (p.c. '45). **4,** Rose quartz is reported from the western slope of Breckenridge Mt., Paul (1), p. 26.

Lake County: **1,** Quartz inclusions in basalt near Clear Lake Highlands have been called "Clear Lake diamonds," Hanks (15) p. 125, C. A. Anderson (9) p. 635. Localities showing these quartz fragments and crystalline grains are referenced as "hyalite" in earlier editions of *Minerals of California,* Pabst (4), Murdoch and Webb (21), (39). One locality, the Manke Ranch, is available for collecting, reported to be good. The quartz is now referred to as "Lake County diamonds", Anon. (49) p. 45. **2,** "Amethystine quartz" has been mined for gems near Howard Springs (secs. 10, 20, 21 T. 12 N., R. 7 W., M. D.), Averill (2) p. 342, Symons (3) p. 41. The amethystine quartz is purple cordierite, Brice (1) p. 62.

Los Angeles County: **1,** Pseudomorphs of quartz after fluorite have been found in sandstone and breccia near Encino, and near the head of Higgins Canyon on the northern slope of the Santa Monica Mountains, Murdoch (2) p. 18. **2,** Good bipyramids of quartz in basalt are abundant over the tunnel east of the Griffith Observatory, Webb (p.c. '45). **3,** Quartz showing a strong blue color occurs in graphic granite in Pacoima Canyon (NE$\frac{1}{4}$ sec. 6, T. 3 N., R. 13 W., S. B.), Neuerburg (p.c. '49).

Mariposa County: **1,** A. F. Rogers (41) p. 327, has described the occurrence of a large mass of quartz showing prominent parting, at White Rock on the Helm Ranch, about 25 miles east of Merced; see also R. J. Sampson and Tucker (4) p. 439.

Mono County: **1,** Rock crystal, amethyst and tabular drusy quartz (pseudomorphs after feldspar) have come from the Bodie Mining District, Kunz (24) p. 67, R. G. Brown (1) p. 344, H. W. Turner (30) p. 795. **2,** Quartz crystals up to 3 inches in diameter, with bubbles and cavities, occur abundantly half a mile southwest of the west end of Parker Lake, Durrell (p.c. '44).

Napa County: **1,** Fine groups of crystals came from the Silverado mine, L. L. Palmer (1) p. 29. **2,** Quartz pseudomorphs after barite, colored red with cinnabar, were found at the Redington mine, Durand (1) p. 211. **3,** Quartz crystals in float from a lava flow are found on the H and M Ranch, north of the ranch house, on the flat above Putah Creek, F. Nelson (1), p. 40.

Placer County: **1,** Quartz crystals, many with inclusions of green chlorite, and phantoms occur at Shady Run, Durrell (p.c. '44).

Plumas County: **1,** Deep-colored rose quartz has come from Meadow Valley, (N. R.). **2,** Veins of blue quartz in serpentine are found southeast of Meadow Valley, H. W. Turner (11) p. 388. **3,** Quartz in pegmatitic granite, with quasi-cleavage, has been described from Plumas National Forest, 3 miles east of the junction of Indian and Squaw Creeks, Halden (1) p. 38.

Riverside County: **1,** Rock crystal, smoky and pink quartz are associated with the gem tournaline at Coahuila, Kunz (14) pp. 66, 70. **2,** Quartz, much of it showing asterism, is obtained from a pegmatite at the Southern Pacific silica quarry near Nuevo, Wahlstrom (1) p. 694. **3,** Smoky quartz occurs in a pegmatite near Tripp Flats (sec. 2, T. 7 S., R. 2 E., S. B.), Durrell (p.c. '44). **4,** Quartz is common in the Crestmore quarry mineral suite, Woodford et al. (10) p. 368.

Sacramento County: **1,** Rock crystal of fine quality is found at Folsom, CDMG (18996).

San Benito County: **1,** Amethyst crystals were found in vugs in the San Carlos mine of the New Idria Quicksilver Company, Symons (3) p. 41.

San Bernardino County: **1,** Quartz with rutile needles has been found in the San Bernardino Range, Kunz (16) p. 763, (24) p. 70; **2,** it is found as pseudomorphs after calcite at Hart, A. F. Rogers (3) p. 19; **3,** it occurs with specular hematite and with chlorite phantoms in the San Bernardino Mountains about 30 miles northeast of San Bernardino, Kunz (16) p. 763, and **4,** it has been found pseudomorphous after glauberite at Searles Lake, Frondel (1) p. 420. **5,** Milky white quartz, showing a strong lamellar cleavage (?), occurred in an outcrop about 5 miles south of Twenty-Nine Palms, on the road to White Tank, Murdoch and Webb (6) p. 354. **6,** Quartz pseudomorphs after natrolite, from 3 miles north of Calico, are represented by CDMG (21313).

San Diego County: **1,** Rock crystal, smoky and pink quartz are associated with green and pink tourmaline of the county. Large groups of crystals of a deep-rose color occur in the pegmatite dikes which carry the tourmaline at Pala, G. A. Waring (2) p. 362, **2,** at Mesa Grande, and **3,** at Rincon, Kunz (24) p. 661. Rock crystal with long and almost black needles of tourmaline occurs at Pala. Crystals from Pala and Rincon show complex forms, G. A. Waring (2) p. 362. Smoky and ordinary quartz from Rincon have been spectroscopically examined by Kennard (3) p. 393. **4,** An opalescent rose quartz occurs at Escondido, Kunz (24) p. 68. **5,** Some large crystals or rolled cobbles of quartz have been found on the Santa Margarita Ranch, Kunz (2) p. 749. **6,** A large mass of rose quartz is found near the Mexican border, 29 miles from Tijuana on the public road from San Diego to Ensenada, Kunz (24) p. 68. **7,** A rose quartz mass is reported from the quartz deposit $3\frac{1}{2}$ miles WNW from Mesa Grande, Ver Planck (5) p. 5.

San Francisco County: **1,** Quartz pseudomorphs after apophyllite have been found with datolite and pectolite at Fort Point, San Francisco, Schaller (3) p. 194, (8) p. 121, E. H. Bailey (3) p. 566.

Santa Clara County: **1,** A. F. Rogers (30) p. 81 (33) p. 316, has described paramorphs of quartz after tridymite in rhyolite at Lone Hill, near Los Gatos. **2,** Quartz psudomorphous after apophyllite has been found at Mine Hill, New Almaden, E. H. Bailey and Everhart (12) p. 102.

Shasta County: **1,** Diller in 1883 collected bipyramids of quartz showing the rare basal cleavage plane, in granite porphyry at Salt Creek, 26 miles north of Redding, Foshag (p.c. '36).

Sierra County: **1,** A few large, clear yellow quartz crystals have been found in a pegmatite at Crystal Peak, on the west side of Dog Valley, 5 miles west of Verdi, Nevada, Symons (3) p. 41.

Sonoma County: **1,** Radial, spherulitic quartz is found in Alexander Valley, Symons (p.c. '46). **2,** Small clear pseudo-cubic crystals of quartz occur 3 miles northeast from Cloverdale, Vonsen (p.c. '45).

Tulare County: **1,** Rock crystal occurs at Three Rivers and in Drum Valley, Kunz (24) p. 66. **2,** Rose quartz is found at Bull Run Meadows, CDMG (7345), and **3,** at Yokohl, Kunz (24) p. 68. **4,** Beautiful rose quartz occurs at the Summer rose quartz claim, 8 miles southeast of California Hot Springs near the Kern County line, Tucker (3) p. 910. **5,** Rose quartz occurs on the west side of Bull Run Ridge, near Badger, Melhase (p.c. diary), and **6,** in pegmatite on the ridge west of Dry Creek, about 5 miles north of Lemon Cove, Stoddard (1) p. 178. **7,** Rose quartz occurs in a pegmatite with massive black allanite on the Casenberger Ranch near Exeter, CDMG (19659). **8,** Rose quartz occurs on the west side of Tobias Mountain, Symons (3) p. 41.

CHALCEDONY
Silicon dioxide, SiO_2

Many names are given to the varieties of cryptocrystalline quartz that may be classed under chalcedony, most of them based on color and structure. They include *chalcedony, agate, carnelian, sard, prase, heliotrope* or *bloodstone, chrysoprase, onyx, sardonyx, jasper* and *flint,* all of which are found in the State. Ordinary petrified wood is largely agate or chalcedony. *Myrickite* is a local name applied to chalcedony having blood-red spots and patches of cinnabar. *Kinradite* is a local name given to a spherulitic jasper.

Chalcedony occurs in dense masses and layers, often banded. Many large masses of chalcedony and jasper have been deposited by springs. Chalcedony is a common secondary filling of cavities and fissures in volcanic rock, and may form large geodes.

It would be impracticable to list all occurrences of chalcedony in the State. The following is a selection of some of the more interesting or unusual.

Amador County: **1,** Chrysoprase is reported in serpentine at the Mooney claims 6 miles southeast of Ione (sec. 34, T. 6 N., R. 10 E., M. D.), L. L. Root (5) p. 149, Carlson and Clark (2) p. 11. **2,** Bluish chalcedony occurs at Volcano, CDMG (813).

Butte County: **1,** Chrysoprase is reported near Magalia, Engineering and Mining Journal (13) p. 653.

Calaveras County: **1,** Moss agate was found at Stockton Hill, Mining and Scientific Press (7) p. 146.

Fresno County: **1,** Large masses of white, delicately-veined chalcedony are found at Panoche, W. P. Blake (9) p. 9.

Inyo County: **1,** Pebbles of red jasper and bloodstone are found at the south end of Death Valley, on the road between Shoshone and Ashford Mill, on the west slope of Jubilee Pass, Wolff (p.c. '35), confirmed by Symons (3) p. 41.

Kern County: **1,** Sapphirine chalcedony was reported near Kane (Koehn or Desert) Springs, probably in the hills to the north, Kunz (24) p. 73. **2,** Petrified wood is common in Last Chance Canyon, Murdoch (p.c. '45). **3,** Semi-opal and variegated chalcedony are found near Rademacher, about 14 miles south of Inyokern, Kunz (14) p. 54. **4,** Excellent jasper and petrified wood occur on Gem Hill (sec. 18, T. 10 N., R. 12 W., S. B.), Lewis (4) p. 116.

Los Angeles County: **1,** The so-called moonstones found at Redondo Beach are chalcedony, Kunz (17) p. 755.

Marin County: **1,** A spherulitic jasper, kinradite, has been found 1 mile south of Sausalito, Sterrett (6) p. 870.

Modoc County: **1,** Abundant and varied agates occur on the shore of the south end of Goose Lake, according to J. A. Edman in Sterrett (4) p. 807.

Monterey County: **1,** Brecciated jasper occurs in Stone Canyon, Nelson Creek, Symons (p.c. '46).

Napa County: **1,** Petrified wood is abundant near Calistoga, Goodyear (4) p. 356.

Placer County: **1,** Fine geodal masses of chalcedony have been found at the Spanish mine, Ophir Mining District (N. R.).

Plumas County: **1,** Chrysoprase occurs in the gravels at Meadow Valley, Kunz (17) p. 755.

Riverside County: **1,** Chalcedony, with high iridescence when cut and polished, has been found near Blythe. Specimens are botryoidal, with interlaminated minute layers of chalcedonic quartz alternating with limonitic and hematitic iridescent bands, which show upon polishing a beautiful color and a near fiery play of colors. A mining parcel is owned by Mr. Frank Ross of Blythe, who is developing the prospect for gem material as precious chalcedony, to be marketed under the name "Rossjewel", Webb (p.c. '57). **2,** Fire agate has been collected in the Mule Mountains west of Palo Verde, M. F. B. Strong (6) p. 16. **3,** Chalcedony is reported from Crestmore, Woodford, et al. (10) p. 367.

San Benito County: **1,** Bluish-gray chalcedony occurred as pseudomorphs after barite crystals in the Phipps quicksilver mine east of Emmett (N. R.).

San Bernardino County: **1,** Large masses of moss agate have been collected in the San Bernardino Mountains, Kunz (16) p. 763. **2,** Geodes of fine blue chalcedony occur 2 miles northeast of Leadpipe Springs (approx. T. 29 S., R. 45 E., M. D.), Sterrett (9) p. 650, Melhase (3) No. 7, p. 8. **3,** Agate with bright-red inclusions of cinnabar (myrickite) is found about 15 miles northeast of Leadpipe Springs, Sterrett (9) p. 651. **4,** Myrickite also occurs 15 miles east of Indian Springs (sec. 4, T. 30 S., R. 46 E., M. D.), Sterrett (9) p. 651. **5,** Chalcedony pseudomorphs after calcite, was collected from the Barium

Queen mine, near Lead Mountain, Durrell (p.c. '45). **6,** Excellent pseudomorphs of chalcedony after barite come from the Mud Hills (sec. 20, T. 11, N., R. 1 W., S. B.), Durrell (p.c. '45). **7,** Some bloodstone is reported from Brown Mountain, south of Wingate Pass, Sterrett (8) p. 1050. **8,** Red and green jasper, in part bloodstone, is reported from Canyon Springs, Sterrett (6) p. 872.

San Diego County: **1,** Red, yellow and gray chalcedony from southeast of Dulzura is said to polish beautifully, Kunz (26) p. 1346.

San Francisco County: **1,** Kinradite is found near Land's End Station, 1 mile northeast of the Cliff House, San Francisco, Kunz (24) p. 75, Sterrett (6) p. 870.

San Luis Obispo County: **1,** Myrickite has come from the Rinconada mine, CDMG (18838).

San Mateo County: **1,** Hollow chalcedony geodes, with liquid and a moving bubble, have been found in the beach gravels at Pescadero, Kunz (24) p. 71.

Santa Clara County: **1,** Decorative orbicular jasper comes from Paradise Valley near Morgan Hill, Melhase (3) No. 7, p. 7; The Mineralogist (1) p. 34. **2,** Myrickite is reported from Coyote, CDMG (18832).

Siskiyou County: **1,** Bloodstone is found at Bogus Mountain, 18 miles northeast of Yreka, Symons (3) p. 41.

Sonoma County: **1,** At the petrified forest west of Calistoga, the petrified wood is largely chalcedony (N. R.).

Tulare County: Chrysoprase has been mined at several localities in the county: **1,** 1 mile east of Lindsay, **2,** Venice Hill, **3,** near Visalia (T. 18 S., R. 26 E., M. D.), **4,** Stokes Mountain (secs. 9, 10, T. 16 S., R. 26 E., M. D.), and **5,** Deer Creek (sec. 20, T. 22 S., R. 28 E., M. D.), Kunz (13) p. 589, (24) pp. 12, 74, Tucker (3) p. 911.

RAMSDELLITE
Manganese dioxide, MnO$_2$

Riverside County: **1,** Ramsdellite has been identified in veins of manganese oxides at the Tolbard mine, Hewett (7) p. 1440. This is the first reported occurrence of this mineral in California.

REALGAR
Arsenic monosulphide, AsS

Alpine County: **1,** Deep-red realgar coating pyrite, with minute white octahedrons of arsenolite, occurred in the Monitor mine, Hanks (12) p. 344.

Imperial County: **1,** Kelley (1) p. 137, has reported the occurrence of realgar with sulphur and claudetite at a sulphur prospect 6 miles north of the 4S Ranch and 1½ miles west of the Colorado River.

Inyo County: **1,** Realgar has been found in the Cerro Gordo Mining District, Loew (2) p. 186. Restudy now under way of Cerro Gordo minerals makes it likely that this is an invalid occurrence. Realgar is not a mineral typical of Cerro Gordo type occurrences. This may be an inadvertent error due to the name, since a Cerro Gordo (later Bradford) mine of San Benito County was prominent in production of cinnabar, where realgar might be predicted as a minor associate; see metacinnabar, San Benito County (3), H. E. Pemberton (p.c. '64).

Kern County: 1, A small amount of realgar occurs with borax and kernite in the borate mines of the Kramer area, Schaller (45) p. 165.

Lake County: 1, Realgar and orpiment are presumed to occur on the Eel River, about 15 miles northwest of Bartlett Springs (N. R.).

Los Angeles County: 1, Very thin films and crystals of realgar appear on fracture surfaces in massive colemanite from the Sterling borax mine, Tick Canyon, Stager (p.c. '47).

Riverside County: 1, Realgar is reported with brown monticellite from Crestmore, Woodford et al. (10) p. 368.

San Bernardino County: 1, Small crystals of realgar have been found with hanksite, pirssonite, and halite in the salt beds of Searles Lake (N. R.). 2, Weeks (2) p. 763, has reported that realgar occurs in the mines of the Calico Mining District. 3, The mineral has been reported 40 miles from the Needles, E. S. Dana (5) p. 1097, CDMG (10338). (This may be from Arizona, or even Imperial County (1).)

Siskiyou County: 1, Realgar has come from Scott Bar, Klamath River, W. W. Bradley (29) p. 311.

Sonoma County: 1, Realgar occurs in small prismatic crystals with metacinnabar and curtisite in the cracks and interstices of sandstone at Skaggs Springs (T. 10 N., R. 11 W., M. D.), F. E. Wright and Allen (3) p. 169, A. L. Ransome and Kellogg (1) p. 469, Everhart (4) p. 390.

Trinity County: 1, Realgar has been reported from Deadwood (T. 33 N., R. 8 W., M. D.), Bixby (2) p. 169. 2, A specimen of realgar, CDMG (11391), came from the northwestern part of the county.

* REDINGTONITE, 1890
Hydrous chromium aluminum iron and magnesium sulphate, $(Fe,Mg)(Cr,Al)_2(SO_4)_4 \cdot 22H_2O$

Napa County: 1, Redingtonite is a pale-purple sulphate which was mixed with knoxvillite from the Redington mine at Knoxville. The mineral was first discovered by Becker (4) p. 279 and was described as a new mineral by Melville and Lindgren (1) p. 23. It was also noted by W. W. Bradley (5) p. 83.

* REDLEDGEITE, 1961
Magnesium and chromium titano-silicate, $Mg_8Cr_{12}Ti_{48}Si_4O_{130}(?)$

Nevada County: 1, The Red Ledge mine in the Washington Mining District contributed some unusual brilliant black crystals with chromite and kämmererite, which were described in 1928 as the new mineral chromrutile. Strunz (1) p. 107, has shown the identification to be incorrect. The crystals are a new species to which the name redledgeite is assigned. The small brilliant black crystals, with kämmererite on chromite at the Red Ledge mine, were originally described by Gordon and Shannon (1) p. 69; see also W. W. Bradley (29) p. 69, and Palache et al. (10) p. 560. Strunz (1) p. 107, has shown by x-ray studies, that redledgeite is a definite mineral and not an impure chromian rutile. The atomic structure of redledgeite has been shown by Strunz (2) p. 116 to be the same as that of cryptomelane.

RHODOCHROSITE
Manganese carbonate, MnCO₃

Rhodochrosite is one of the important primary minerals in deposits of manganese ores, and is typical of those of the Franciscan type, which occur in the Coast Ranges.

Alameda County: **1,** Rhodochrosite, both gray and pink, occurs commonly in the manganese mines of the Livermore (Tesla) Mining District, southeast of Livermore, W. W. Bradley et al. (4) p. 24. **2,** Rhodochrosite occurs with oxides on the Arroyo Mocho road (NW¼ sec. 9, T. 4 S., R. 3 E., M. D.), ibid., p. 26.

Alpine County: **1,** Pink crystals of rhodochrosite were found in the Colorado mine no. 2, Monitor area, Hanks (12) p. 159, Irelan (1) p. 105, Eakle (16) p. 25, Gianella (1) p. 342. **2,** Rhodochrosite is also found in other mines in the region, Mining and Scientific Press (9) p. 151, Logan (4) p. 401, Partridge (1) p. 264.

Amador County: **1,** Rhodochrosite occurs in several mines (sec. 10, T. 7 N., R. 11 E., M. D.), P. D. Trask et al. (4) pp. 102, 103.

Calaveras County: **1,** Rhodochrosite occurs with bementite at the Big Little Bear and Kellog mines (sec. 24, T. 3 N., R. 11 E., M. D.), P. D. Trask et al. (4) p. 60.

Humboldt County: **1,** Rhodochrosite occurs with bementite at the Woods (Charles Mountain) manganese claim (sec. 2, T. 1 S., R. 4 E., H.), P. D. Trask et al. (4) p. 77.

Madera County: **1,** Rhodochrosite occurs in a replacement deposit with rhodonite and specular hematite at Agnew Meadows (T. 3 S., R. 26 E., M. D.), P. D. Trask et al. (4) p. 79, M. F. B. Strong (2) p. 23. **2,** P. D. Trask et al. (4) p. 130, also report rhodochrosite, rhodonite, manganite and psilomelane from a locality near Coarse Gold

Mariposa County: **1,** Rhodochrosite occurs with rhodonite and spessartite at the Surprise claim (sec. 23, T. 3 S., R. 17 E., M. D.), P. D. Trask et al. (4) p. 132.

Mendocino County: **1,** Rhodochrosite occurs in the Mount Sanhedrin group at Impassible Rock (sec. 30, T. 20 N., R. 11 W., M. D.), W. W. Bradley et al. (4), P. D. Trask et al. (4) p. 136 ; **2,** Cinco de Mayo (sec. 27, T. 24 N., R. 11 W., M. D.), ibid., (1) p. 134; **3,** Thomas (sec. 22, T. 17 N., R. 12 W., M. D.), ibid., p. 141, and **4,** Brereton (sec 31, T. 23 N., R. 11 W., M. D.), Taliaferro and Hudson (3) p. 238.

Placer County: **1,** Small druses of rhodochrosite have been found in some of the mines of the county (N. R.).

San Bernardino County: **1,** Rhodochrosite has been reported as a vein mineral in quartz at the Sagamore mine, New York Mountains, Cloudmen et al. (1) p. 790.

San Joaquin County: **1,** Rhodochrosite occurs in the Ladd mine at Corral Hollow, W. W. Bradley et al. (4) p. 65, P. D. Trask et al. (4) p. 86.

Santa Clara County: **1,** Rhodochrosite occurred as pink crystals showing unusual faces in the manganese boulder near Alum Rock Park, 5 miles east of San Jose, A. F. Rogers (21) p. 446. **2,** The mineral is found in the Jones group (sec. 27, T. 6 S., R. 5 E., M. D.), P. D. Trask et al. (4) p. 87, and **3,** from the manganese property on the Miller

Ranch, on the Sierra Road on the extreme southeast point of Los Buellis Hills, Crittenden (1) p. 64.

Siskiyou County: **1,** Rhodochrosite occurs in quartzite at the Oro Fino no. 2 (sec. 17, T. 43 N., R. 9 W., M. D.), P. D. Trask et al. (4) p. 60.

Sonoma County: **1,** Massive gray rhodochrosite occurs with bementite of the Aho property (sec. 15, T. 8 N., R. 12 W., M. D.), 6 miles west of Cazadero, P. D. Trask et al. (4) p. 89.

Stanslaus County: **1,** Rhodochrosite was found with calcite and pyrolusite in the Buckeye manganese mine, Hospital Creek, Laizure (3) p. 213, Taliaferro and Hudson (3) p. 239.

Tuolumne County: **1,** Rhodochrosite occurs with bementite at the Hughes mine (sec. 17, T. 2 S., R. 15 E., M. D.), P. D. Trask et al. (4) p. 91.

Trinity County: There are at least a dozen localities at which manganese ores, carrying more or less rhodochrosite with bementite and oxides, are found in the southern half of the county. The detail of these localities is given by P. D. Trask et al. (4) pp. 194–206. The names of the properties are: Armstrong, Bertha, Blue Jay, Dahrman, Emma, Hale Creek, Lucky Bill, Manganese Queen, Rainy Day, Shell View, and Spider. W. W. Bradley et al. (4) pp. 89–91, describe some of these also.

RHODONITE
Manganese silicate, $MnSiO_3$

Rhodonite is one of the important primary minerals of manganese ores, and is typical of strongly metamorphosed areas, such as those in the deposits on the west side of the Sierra Nevada. A summary of collecting localities for rhodonite is found in Anon. (45) p. 18.

Alameda County: **1,** Rhodonite occurs in the Corral Hollow manganese deposits, Wilke (p.c. '36).

Amador County: **1,** Rhodonite is present in several of the manganese deposits of the county: Alexander, Custer, Du Frene, Everett, Jones, Perini, Peyton, and Stirnaman. The exact locations are given by P. D. Trask et al. (4) pp. 102, 103.

Butte County: **1,** Rhodonite occurs in several deposits (T. 20 N., R. 7 E., M. D.), P. D. Trask et al. (4) pp. 104, 105.

Calaveras County: **1,** Rhodonite is found in the following deposits: Airola, Callahan, Daniels, Gorham, Harrington, Hauselt, and Pescia, P. D. Trask et al. (4) pp. 106, 107.

El Dorado County: **1,** Rhodonite occurs in the Martinez gold claim (sec. 13, T. 9 N., R. 10 E., M. D.), P. D. Trask et al. (4) p. 111.

Fresno County: **1,** Rhodonite occurs in the Crisle, Harper, McMurtry, Price, Trewick and Woods claims, P. D. Trask et al. (4) p. 112.

Humboldt County: **1,** Rhodonite is found in the Sam Brown claim (sec. 15, T. 8 N., R. 4 E., H.), P. D. Trask et al. (4) p. 116, and **2,** at the Woods (Charles Mountain) manganese claim (sec. 2, T. 2 S., R. 4 E., H.), CDMG (18766).

Kern County: **1,** Rhodonite in large crystals was found at the O. K. mine (sec 27(?), T. 26 S., R. 34 E., M. D.), P. D. Trask et al. (4) p. 123. **2,** Other occurrences in the county include the Big Indian, Culbert Manganese Queen and Midlothian, ibid., pp. 123, 124. **3**, Small amounts of rhodonite suitable for cutting have been found in the Rand Mining District, Troxel and Morton (2) p. 50. **4**, Rhodonite of fine cutting quality is found on the Tejon Ranch in a locality described as "west of Rosamond", Anon. (45) p. 20.

Los Angeles County: **1**, Massive deep-pink rhodonite occurs on Portal Ridge, near Lancaster. Several deposits are found here (T. 5, 6 N., R. 12, 13, 14 W., S. B.), P. D. Trask et al. (4) p. 128.

Madera County: **1**, Rhodonite occurs with rhodochrosite, pyrolusite, manganite and psilomelane near Coarse Gold, P. D. Trask et al. (4) p. 130. **2**, The mineral occurs with garnet and epidote in crystalline limestone on the south side of Shadow Creek Canyon in the Ritter Range, Erwin (1) p. 67, Goudey (1) p. 26, and **3**, on the Garnet Lake side of Shadow-Garnet divide, ibid., p. 26. **4**, At the Agnew Meadows deposit, P. D. Trask et al. (4) p. 63, reports rhodonite.

Mariposa County: **1**, Rhodonite is found at the Donnelly, Robie and Surprise properties, P. D. Trask et al. (4) p. 132.

Monterey County: **1**, Beach boulders of gem-quality rhodonite have been found at Lime Kiln Creek, Crippen (p.c. '51). **2**, Rhodonite has been collected along the beaches near Jade Cove, south of Monterey, Anon. (45) p. 20.

Nevada County: **1**, P. D. Trask et al. (4) pp. 147, 148, locate 15 occurrences of rhodonite in the county. Averill (13) p. 141, notes one of these, Manga-Chrome or Stearns and Owens.

Placer County: **1**, Several rhodonite deposits are in the vicinity of Forest Hill, P. D. Trask et al. (4) p. 149.

Plumas County: **1**, Good red rhodonite has come from Genesee Valley (T. 25, 26 N., R. 11 E., M. D.), P. D. Trask et al. (4) p. 153. **2**, Rare but good material occurred with copper at the Diadem lode, Meadow Valley, H. W. Turner (12) p. 590, (9) p. 6. **3**, Good gem rhodonite has been reported to occur near Taylorsville, Sterrett (4) p. 837. **4**, Several localities are listed by P. D. Trask et al. (4) pp. 151–153. These include Benner, Burch and Woody, Cannon, Crystal Lake, Dickie Bird, Iron Queen, Liberty, Lost Soldier, Rush Creek, Sunset and Valley View.

Riverside County: **1**, Rhodonite was found with pyrolusite and psilomelane near Elsinore (secs. 23, 24, T. 5 S., R. 4 W., S. B.), W. W. Bradley et al. (4) p. 58.

San Bernardino County: **1**, Minor amounts of rhodonite have been found near Colton, Hanks (12) pp. 316, 345, Mining and Scientific Press, (22) p. 152, and **2**, in pebbles at the summit of Cajon Pass, Murdoch and Webb (11) p. 552. **3**, The Grafton Hills rhodonite property has produced beautiful specimens of rhodonite, Anon. (45) p. 18.

San Diego County: **1**, Beautiful specimens of rhodonite have come from the Anza State Park, near the Riverside County line, Tucker and Reed (26) p. 29. **2**, The Ruby deposit (sec. 16, T. 18 S., R. 8 E., S. B.) has rhodonite with spessartite, P. D. Trask et al. (4) p. 85. **3**, The mineral occurs with manganese oxides near Jacumba, Berkholz (15a) p. 26.

Shasta County: **1**, Rhodonite-bearing deposits are found in Goat Camp, Nigger Hill and Victor claims, P. D. Trask et al. (4) p. 182.

Siskiyou County: **1,** Excellent rhodonite occurs at Sawyers Bar, CDMG (15180). **2,** Massive red rhodonite occurs on Indian Creek, near Happy Camp, W. W. Bradley (23) p. 217. Many other occurrences are listed by P. D. Trask et al. (4) pp. 183–185.

Trinity County: **1,** Rhodonite occurs with rhodochrosite at the Manganese Queen claim (sec. 26, T. 30 N., R. 12 W., M. D.), P. D. Trask et al. (4) p. 200. **2,** The mineral also occurs at the Shell View claim (sec. 16, T. 4 S., R. 6 E., H.), ibid., p. 202, and **3,** at the Spider claim (sec. 20, T. 28 N., R. 11 W., M. D.), ibid., p. 203.

Tulare County: **1,** Coarse, massive rhodonite occurs as a contact metamorphic mineral near Lemon Cove (secs. 22, 34, T. 16 S., R. 27 E., M. D.), Tucker (3) p. 911, Sterrett (7) p. 1063. **2,** Occasional layers of rhodonite, formed by metamorphism of manganiferous cherts, are found near Greasy Creek and on the west side of Dry Creek, Durrell (2) p. 32.

Tuolumne County: **1,** Rhodonite was found with pyrolusite on Rose Creek near Columbia, P. D. Trask et al. (4) p. 207. **2,** The mineral occurs as veins altering to manganese oxides 2 miles north of Sonora, Hanks (12) p. 345, W. W. Bradley et al. (4) p. 91. Other occurrences are listed (Flaming Arrow, Hog Mountain, Hughes, Pedro, West Wonder) by P. D. Trask et al. (4) pp. 207, 208.

Yuba County: **1,** Rhodonite occurs in the Clemens claim (sec 29, T. 19 N., R. 7 E., M. D.), P. D. Trask et al. (4) p. 208.

*RIVERSIDEITE, 1917
Hydrous calcium silicate, near $xCaO \cdot SiO_2 \cdot \frac{1}{2}H_2O$

Riverside County: **1,** Riversideite was described in 1917 by Eakle (15) p. 327, as a new mineral. It was associated with a second new mineral named by Eakle, ibid., crestmoreite. Subsequently restudy of the original specimens showed the riversideite to have been the mineral tobermorite, H. F. W. Taylor (1), p. 155. Thus riversideite was a discredited species. More recently, a white fibrous compound called calcium silicate hydrate 9Å has been considered by Heller and Taylor (1) p. 39, to be most likely the same as the material described by Eakle as riversideite, and accordingly they believe it should be given this name. It has so far been identified from Crestmore only in admixture with residual wilkeite. It appears that riversideite should be reinstated as a new species.

RÖMERITE
Hydrous iron sulphate, near $Fe^{2+}Fe^{3+}_2(SO_4)_4 \cdot 12H_2O$

Alpine County: **1,** Römerite occurs as brittle, chestnut-brown crystals in masses and on stalactites of melanterite, at the Leviathan sulphur mine, 7 miles east of Markleeville, Gary (1) p. 489, Nichols (1) p. 172.

Contra Costa County: **1,** A little römerite has been found in the Mount Diablo mine (SE¼ sec. 29, T. 1 N., R. 1 E., M. D.), C. P. Ross (2) p. 42, Pampeyan (1) p. 24.

Napa County: **1,** Tiny, light-brown crystals of römerite occur with other hydrous iron sulphates at the Corona mercury mine, CDMG identification, 1964.

San Benito County: **1,** Römerite occurs as stalactitic masses in the Stayton mine, Lone Tree, two miles south of Antimony Peak near Hollister, Anon. (39), p. 195.

San Bernardino County: **1,** Römerite occurs with alunite, coquimbite, krausite and other sulphates in the Calico Hills near Borate, about 6 miles northeast of Yermo, Foshag (19) p. 352.

Trinity County: **1,** Small brown crystals of römerite, showing complex forms, occurring on altered pyrrhotite from Island Mountain, were described by Landon (1) p. 279.

ROSASITE
Basic copper zinc carbonate, $(Cu,Zn)_2(OH)_2CO_3$

Inyo County: **1,** Rosasite is reported as relatively common at Cerro Gordo, occurring as botryoidal crusts or individual spherules on smithsonite and hemimorphite, H. E. Pemberton (2) p. 16.

*ROSCOELITE—Vanadium Mica, 1875
Basic potassium/aluminum/vanadium silicate, near $K(V,Al)_3Si_3O_{10}(OH)_2$

Vanadium is a rare constituent of some igneous rocks, and is occasionally found in small amounts in biotite. Roscoelite is unique in having a large percentage of vanadium in place of iron, thus forming a vanadium-mica.

El Dorado County: **1,** Layers of a dark-green micaceous mineral, up to half an inch in thickness, interlaminated with gold, found at the Stuckslager or Sam Sims mine (sec. 24, T. 11 N., R. 9 E., M. D.) on Granite Creek, near Coloma, proved to be a new mineral which was named roscoelite by James Blake (2) p. 31. It was later described and analyzed by Genth (7) p. 32, Roscoe (1) p. 110, Hillebrand et al. (2) p. 456, Hillebrand (3) p. 70. **2,** Several hundred pounds of roscoelite were found in Big Red Ravine, near the old Sutter Mill, (sec. 31, T. 11 N., R. 10 E., M. D.), but were destroyed to obtain the interlaminated gold, Hanks (4) p. 428, (7) p. 263. **3,** Roscoelite was reported by Kimble (1) pp. 343, 344, from the surface soil at the eastern base and part of the slope of Mount Thompson. The mineral occurred also in pockets. Determination of the optical properties was made by F. E. Wright (1) p. 305. **4,** An occurrence of roscoelite in quartz was found also in the Tip Top vein (sec. 7, T. 11 N., R. 10 E., M. D.), Hanks (12) p. 349. This is represented by a beautiful specimen, CDMG (5768). Hillebrand et al. (2) pp. 457, 458, described in detail 5 occurrences of roscoelite in this locality.

Kern County: **1,** Subordinate amounts of roscoelite have been found in the Miracle mine, Kern River Uranium area (SE¼ sec. 17, T. 27 S., R. 32 E., M.D.) Troxel and Morton (2) p. 333.

Los Angeles County: **1,** Roscoelite has been doubtfully reported near Los Angeles, W. W. Bradley (28) p. 498.

ROZENITE
Hydrous ferrous sulphate, $FeSO_4 \cdot 4H_2O$

Napa County: **1,** Pale blue-green rozenite occurs with römerite, melanterite and coquimbite as a coating on black chert and silicified shale fragments at the Corona mercury mine, CDMG identification by x-ray '64.

Santa Cruz County: **1,** Chesterman (p.c. '64) reports rozenite in the mineral suite from the Pacific Limestone Products (Kalkar) quarry at Santa Cruz, x-ray identification.

RUTILE
Titanium dioxide, TiO$_2$

Strüverite is tantalian rutile. *Sagenite* is rutilated quartz.

Rutile, as a rock constituent occurring in microscopic crystals, is common in many of the metamorphic rocks of the State. Small grains and crystals are frequently found in beach and river sands.

Alpine County: **1,** Granular and subhedral rutile occurs with lazulite and andalusite about 10 miles SSW from Markleeville, W. W. Bradley (29) p. 311.

Amador County: **1,** Needles of rutile in quartz, forming sagenite, have been reported to occur at Tylers Ranch near Oleta (N.R.).

Butte County: **1,** Rutile was a constituent of the gold washings at Cherokee, Silliman (12) p. 133.

Contra Costa County: **1,** Irregular patches of brown rutile occur with sphene in glaucophane schist near the south end of the Berkeley Country Club, Coats (p.c. '36).

Fresno County: **1,** Brownish-red rutile crystals occur with ilmenite near Friant (N.R.). **2,** Striated prismatic crystals of rutile have been found in glaucophane schist near Panoche, Foshag (p.c. '36).

Marin County: **1,** Fair-sized prismatic crystals of rutile have been found in a boulder of glaucophane schist on the beach of the Tiburon Peninsula, about 150 yards north of California Point, Vonsen (p.c. '36). **2,** Rutile occurs sparingly at the Hein Bros. quarry near Petaluma, Watters (p.c. '62).

Mendocino County: **1,** Long prismatic crystals of rutile embedded in chlorite occur in glaucophane schist in a highway cut about 3½ miles north of Longvale on the new Covelo road, Vonsen (p.c. '37).

Mono County: **1,** Abundant minute specks of rutile occur in andalusite at the mine of Champion Sillimanite, on the western slope of the White Mountains, 7 miles east of Mocalno, north of Bishop, Pack (1) p. 151, Kerr (3) p. 627. **2,** Crystals of rutile up to an inch in Length are found on the Moreau Claim about a mile from locality **(1),** Kerr (3) p. 627. **3,** Rutile occurs in small reddish-brown crystals in white quartzite with bands of blue lazulite on Green Creek one mile west of Green Lake (sec. 28 (?), T. 3 N., R. 24 E., M.D.), Woodhouse (p.c. '35).

Placer County: **1,** Rutile has been reported at Michigan Bluff (N.R.).

Riverside County: **1,** A small mass of strüverite was found at the Anita mine (sec. 22, T. 6 S., R. 1 E., S.B.), Fisher (1) p. 86. **2,** Rutile is found in the Wet Weather quarry, Crestmore, Woodford et al. (10) p. 368.

San Benito County: **1,** Slender, doubly-terminated red crystals of rutile (?) as much as a quarter of an inch in size appear in altered serpentine, associated with perovskite and andradite garnet, half a mile south of the Gem mine, Watters (p.c. '51). This occurrence has subsequently turned out to be a possible new mineral. The material is still under study, Murdoch (p.c. '64).

San Bernardino County: 1, Discontinuous concentrations of rutile occur in thin beds of quartzite near the Mojave River southwest of Barstow (SE¼ SW¼ sec. 21, T. 9 N., R. 3 W., S.B.), W. H. Grant (p.c. '47).

San Diego County: 1, Abundant minute crystals of rutile occur scattered through the quartz of the dumortierite dike near Alpine, Schaller (7) p. 211.

Santa Clara County: 1, Rough crystals of rutile occur in glaucophane schist in the Coyote Valley about 6 miles east of Morgan Hill, The Mineralogist (4) p. 41.

SABUGALITE
Hydrous uranium aluminum phosphate, $HAl(UO_2)_4(PO_4)16H_2O$

Lassen County: 1, Sabugalite is reported from the Western Mining Corporation lease near Doyle, CDMG (21659).

* SAHAMALITE, 1954
Magnesium iron carbonate, with rare earth elements, $(Mg,Fe)(Ce,La,Nd,Pr)_2(CO_3)_4$

San Bernardino County: 1, Minute tabular crystals, almost microscopic in size, were discovered in barite-dolomite rock in the bastnaesite deposit at Mountain Pass, and were named as a new mineral and described by Jaffe et al. (2) p. 721.

SAL AMMONIAC
Ammonium chloride, NH_4Cl

Imperial County: 1, Sal ammoniac (?) was found as a crust in fissures near the mud volcanoes at Niland, J. L. Le Conte (1) p. 5.

Inyo County: 1, According to G. E. Bailey (2) p. 106, sal ammoniac is found as efflorescences at some of the fissure springs in Death Valley.

Los Angeles County: 1, A white crystalline incrustation of sal ammoniac was found in the Monterey shale of Burning Mountain (at the Bernheimer Gardens), A. F. Rogers (7) p. 373, Clearwater (1) p. 2.

Santa Barbara County: 1, Crusts of sal ammoniac, 5 mm thick, associated with sulphur, came from burning oil-shales on the Hope Ranch, A. F. Rogers (7) p. 373.

*SALMONSITE, 1912
Hydrous iron and manganese phosphate, $Mn_9^{2+}Fe_2^{3+}(PO_4)_8 \cdot 14H_2O$

San Diego County: 1, Salmonsite is a buff-yellow alteration product of huréaulite, associated with fibrous "palaite" and blue strengite, which was discovered in the Stewart mine at Pala. It was described as a new mineral and analyzed by Schaller (29) p. 144, E. S. Larsen (11) p. 129.

SAMARSKITE
A niobate and tantalate of the rare earth elements probably AB_2O_6 with A=Y,Er,Ce,La,U,Ca,Fe,Pb,Th; B=Nb,Ta,Ti,Sn,W,Zr

Riverside County: 1, Samarskite (?) has been reported from the Southern Pacific silica quarry near Nuevo, W. W. Bradley (28) p. 207.

An aggregate of poorly formed crystals and grains, found associated with cyrtolite in quartz and feldspar at the Southern Pacific silica quarry, was named nuevite for the locality, Murdoch (19) p. 1219. The mineral has since been shown by x-ray pattern to be samarskite, Murdoch (26) p. 358.

*SANBORNITE, 1931
Barium silicate, $BaSi_2O_5$

Fresno County: **1,** Sanbornite occurs at Rush Creek (sec. 16, T. 11 S., R. 25 E.), Big Creek mining area, CDMG (21751), Anon. (41) p. 11. The deposit appears to be the largest yet known. The mineral occurs as tabular bodies of sanbornite-bearing rock, paralleling the bedding of the enclosing metamorphic rock. The sanbornite is associated with taramellite, witherite, and rare gillespite, together with several unidentified minerals, Matthews and Alfors (1) p. 2, CDMG (21769). **2,** Sanbornite occurs in quartzite with taramellite, gillespite, quartz, and pyrrhotite near Big Creek (secs. 22 27, T. 11 S., R. 25 E.), Alfors and Stinson (5) p. 27.

Mariposa County: **1,** Sanbornite was first found in California with celsian and gillespite in a metamorphic rock 1 mile north of Trumbull Peak, near Incline. It was described and named by A. F. Rogers (39) p. 161, (36) p. 84, W. W. Bradley (17) p. 82, with analysis by O. C. Shepard. Douglass (1) shows sanbornite which was originally discovered in California to be orthorhombic in crystallization instead of triclinic as first described. Melhase (5) p. 3, gives details of its first discovery and exact location.

SASSOLITE
Boron hydroxide, $B(OH)_3$

Inyo County: **1,** Sassolite with ginorite is reported by R. D. Allen and Kramer (6) p. 56, from the Mott prospect near the head of Twenty Mule Team Canyon in Death Valley. The mineral occurs as pale yellowish-brown masses with embedded ginorite.

Kern County: **1,** Sassolite occurs as thin, small, colorless flakes as crystals in the California Borate Company property in the Kramer borate area (Western borax mine of earlier references) with other borate minerals, G. I. Smith et al. (1). **2,** Sassolite is found as an efflorescence at the exposed contact of shale and basalt in the Pacific Coast Borax Company mine, Kramer borate area, G. I. Smith et al. (1) p. 1070.

Lake County: **1,** Sassolite was found as an efflorescence at Siegler Springs, John A. Veatch (2) p. 180, G. E. Bailey (2) p. 54.

Sonoma County: **1,** Sassolite is reported by R. L. Smith (1) p. 1204, in a specimen collected from The Geysers.

Tehama County: **1,** Sassolite occurred as an efflorescence at Tuscan (Lick) Spring, G. E. Bailey (2) p. 69.

SBORGITE
Hydrous sodium borate, $NaB_5O_8 \cdot 5H_2O$

Inyo County: Sborgite is found at three separate places in Twenty Mule Team Canyon, as surficial growths by alteration from other borate minerals, McAllister (7) p. B300. **1,** The mineral occurs at Widow No.

3 mine, 10 miles southeast of Twenty Mule Team Canyon, in stalactites, and **2,** at two other localities near Twenty Mule Team Canyon,
McAllister (7) p. B300. In each case thermonatrite is an associated
mineral.

SCAPOLITE

Scapolite is the name given to a group of rock-forming silicates consisting of
isomorphous mixtures of marialite, $Na_4(Al_3Si_9O_{24})Cl$; intermediate member,
wernerite; meionite, $Ca_4(Al_6Si_6O_{24})CO_3$

The scapolites are in general formed by contact metamorphism.

Inyo County: **1,** Scapolite was found at the Pine Creek tungsten
mine in a contact zone with idocrase and wollastonite, Hess and Larsen
(1) p. 276. **2,** A specimen of scapolite with chrysocolla, CDMG (21326),
has been received from 3 miles east of Dodd Spring, Ubehebe Mining
District. The scapolite occurrences are described by McAllister (4)
p. 60.

Kern County: **1,** Scapolite occurs in a contact zone of scheelite ore
at Weldon, Kelso Creek, Hess and Larsen (17) p. 266.

Nevada County: **1,** Scapolite was doubtfully identified on a schist
contact at Nevada City and Grass Valley, Lindgren (12) p. 91.

Riverside County: **1,** Scapolite occurs at Crestmore as white radiating aggregates of fine needles in contact rock with wollastonite and
diopside, Eakle (15) p. 350, J. W. Daly (1) p. 649, and as long prisms
in blue calcite, Woodford et al. (10) p. 362. **2,** The mineral occurs predominantly in small dikes with pyroxene, apatite and sphene, at the
iron-ore deposit in the Eagle Mountains, Harder (6) p. 54. **3,** Scapolite
is found also in the contact rocks of the new City quarry, south of
Riverside, G. M. Richmond (1) p. 725.

Tulare County: **1,** Scapolite occurs in a metamorphic rock with
wollastonite, calcite and diopside southwest of Three Rivers ($S\frac{1}{2}$ sec.
25, T. 17 S., R. 28 E., M.D.), Durrell (p.c. '35).

SCAWTITE
Basic silicate and carbonate of calcium, $Ca_7Si_6O_{16}CO_3(OH)_4$

Riverside County: **1,** Small tabular crystals of scawtite have been
found lining veins in massive diopside-wollastonite-spurrite rock on the
910' level of the Commercial quarry at Crestmore, Murdoch (30) p.
1347, (31) p. 505, Murdoch and Duncan McConnell (34) p. 498, J. D.
C. McConnell (2) p. 510.

*SCHAIRERITE, 1931
Sodium sulphate with fluorine, chlorine, $Na_3SO_4(F,Cl)$

San Bernardino County: **1,** Schairerite was discovered as a new mineral in drill samples from Searles Lake. The minute crystals were described by Foshag (17) p. 133. The mineral, associated with galeite and
sulphohalite, is discussed by Pabst et al. (21) pp. 485–510. The mineral
occurs in a saline layer near the base of the Lower Salt, G. I. Smith and
Haines (3) p. P32. Shairerite has been reported from other parts of
the deposit, but in most of these occurrences galeite has been misidentified as schairerite, ibid. The mineral has also been reported in nepheline
syenites from the Kola Peninsula, USSR, Kogarko (1) p. 839.

SCHEELITE
Calcium tungstate, CaWO$_4$

Scheelite is the principal tungsten mineral of the State, and a vast number of deposits exist, some of them important. A comprehensive compilation of occurrences was published in Volume 38 of the California Journal of Mines and Geology, numbers 3 and 4, 1942. Prospecting with ultraviolet light has been responsible for the discovery of many occurrences. The principal producing areas are in Inyo, Kern, and San Bernardino counties, but smaller deposits occur in many of the others, and references will be given to these, by counties. General references are Jenkins (1) and Krauskopf (1), the latter covering Madera, Fresno, and Tulare counties; see also Bateman (3).

No attempt has been made to report all of the occurrences of scheelite found in the State that are referenced in the literature. The mineral is widespread and is so common that only occurrences of mineralogical interest should be included. However, some localities of minor importance and of little mineralogical interest are noted for the historical record because they have been reported in early editions of *Minerals of California*.

Calaveras County: **1,** Crystals of scheelite up to two inches in length have been found in the tactite of Garnet Hill, W. B. Clark and Lydon (4) p. 121.

Fresno County: **1,** Scheelite occurs one mile southwest of Dunlap (sec. 3, T. 14 S., R. 26 E., M.D.), Kerr (6) p. 139. **2,** Scheelite is the common tungsten mineral in the Mt. Morrison quadrangle, and occurs in many prospects. In some of these production has occurred, Rinehart and Ross (2) p. 92; see also Mono County **(4).**

Inyo County: **1,** The most important occurrence of scheelite is at the Pine Creek tungsten mine, at an elevation of 11,000 feet, where the scheelite is accompanied by considerable molybdenite, and occurrs at the contact of granite and metamorphic rocks, Hess and Larsen (17) p. 275, Tucker (4) p. 301. **2,** Another important area is in the Tungsten Hills, northwest of Bishop, where a number of deposits occur, A. Knopf (6) pp. 238, 247, Tucker (4) pp. 302, 303, Tucker and Sampson (25) pp. 462, 466, Lemmon (5) pp. 507, 511, Bateman et al. (2) pp. 31–42. Other references are as follows: Engineering and Mining Journal (17) p. 186, (30) p. 84, A. Knopf (6) pp. 247, 248, Tucker (4) p. 301, Tucker and Sampson (25) pp. 463–467, Ridgway and Davis (1) p. 569, Lemmon (7) pp. 79–104, Tucker and Sampson (30) pp. 567–571. **3,** Scheelite is found at the Copper Queen, 4 miles south of Oasis (sec. 7, T. 6 S., R. 37 E., M.D.), Kerr (6) p. 141; **4,** on the northeast flank of the Inyo Mountains (sec. 19, T. 8 S., R. 37 E., M.D.), ibid., p. 141, and **5,** in Trail Canyon, Sheephead claim (T. 19 S., R. 46 E., M.D.), ibid., p. 147. **6,** Scheelite occurs in the Darwin mines in well-formed crystals, Butner (1) pp. 1–6, Hall and MacKevett (4) pp. 62, 76. **7,** Scheelite has been mined in Armstrong Canyon, north of Division Creek, J. G. Moore (1) p. 146.

Kern County: **1,** Translucent to transparent crystals of scheelite up to 1 inch across have been found at the Aldridge mine (NW$\frac{1}{4}$ sec. 27, T. 25 S., R. 32 E., M.D.), Durrell (p.c. '45). **2,** Schaller (46) p. 237, has shown so-called cuproscheelite from the Green Monster mine 12 miles east of White River to be a mixture of scheelite and cuprotungstite. **3,** A number of deposits occur in the neighborhood of Cedar Creek and Isabella, Storms (15) p. 768, Mining and Scientific Press (41) p. 887, Hess and Larsen (17) pp. 263, 265, Tucker (4) p. 315, Tucker and Sampson (29) pp. 332, 333, (30) pp. 575–579, Dale (1) p. 1896, Tucker and Sampson (32) pp. 61–64, 121, Troxel and Morton (2) pp. 294–326. Other localities: Hess (10) p. 35, (12) p. 988, (14) p. 48, Hulin (1) pp. 70, 97. **4,** In the Gorman area, scheelite occurs with cassiterite and ludwigite, L. R. Page (3) p. 202, Troxel and Morton (2) p. 294; **5,** Cottonwood Canyon (T. 30 S., R. 35 E., M.D.), Kerr (6) p. 151, and **6,** Indian Creek, 12 miles east of Caliente (T. 30 S., R. 33 E., M.D.), ibid., p. 151. **7,** Scheelite occurs in disseminated grains in tactite and in quartz veins near Havilah, Troxel and Morton (2) p. 27. **8,** The principal mineral mined in the deposits in Indian Wells Canyon is scheelite, ibid., p. 37. **9,** Scheelite with some wolframite, occurs in the High-low mine in Jawbone Canyon, ibid., p. 37. **10,** Large crystals of scheelite have been found in a gold vein at the Minnehaha mine, near Loraine, ibid., p. 41. **11,** Small pods of scheelite have been mined in the Piute mining area, ibid., p. 46. **12,** Scheelite has been mined from small leases in quartz veins 4 miles south of Tehachapi, ibid., p. 52. **13,** Scheelite in tactite occurs in the Weldon tungsten area southwest of Weldon, ibid., p. 52. **14,** Scheelite is an associated mineral in the Baltic gold mine (SE¼ sec. 1, T. 30 S., R. 40 E., M.D.), ibid., p. 94, and **15,** in the Black Mountain King mine (center of sec. 27, T. 25 S., R. 32 E., M.D.), clear scheelite crystals occur in a gouge zone, ibid., p. 296. **16,** Scheelite and powellite are locally important in a tactite zone in the Lake Isabella region, R. L. Engel (1) p. 24.

Madera County: **1,** Many occurrences of scheelite are found in the Jackass Creek area (T. 4 S., R. 24, 25 E., M.D.), Kerr (6) p. 157, Trengrove (1) p. 4; **2,** North Fork, San Joaquin River (T. 8 S., R. 23, 24 E., M.D.), ibid., p. 156, and **3,** Yellowjacket (secs. 3, 4, 10, T. 5 S., R. 23 E., M.D.), ibid., p. 157, Trengrove (1) p. 4. **4,** Scheelite has been reported since 1947 in various localities in the following areas: sec. 10, T. 9 S., R. 22 E., M.D., and secs. 4, 5, T. 7 S., R. 22 E., M.D., Logan (24) p. 466.

Marin County: **1,** Scheelite has been found in the Tomales Bay area, Anon. (17) p. 4. **2,** Scheelite-bearing alluvium and scheelite in place on contacts of metamorphic rocks with quartz diorite have been found on Inverness Ridge on the Point Reyes Peninsula. Two properties have been explored. The first, known as the Bender deposit is ¾ mile west of Sir Frances Drake highway on the banks of the stream that enters Tomales Bay at Willow Point, where some scheelite crystals up to a quarter of an inch across have been found in place. The second property is known as the Noren deposit, at the junction of the Bear Valley Road and Sir Frances Drake highway, one mile from Point Reyes Station. These two alluvial occurrences and their bedrock associates probably are the same as the reported occurrence **(1),** Ver Planck (3) p. 265.

Mono County: **1,** Scheelite is found in tactite north of Tioga Pass (sec. 6, T. 2 N., R. 25 E., M.D.), Kerr (6) p. 160, and **2,** near Topaz Lake (T. 7, 8, 9 N., R. 22, 23 E., M.D.), ibid., p. 160. **3,** Scheelite is widely distributed in the metamorphic rocks of the Casa Diablo Mountain quadrangle, north of Bishop. The Black Rock mine is the most productive of the mineral, Rinehart and Ross (1) p. 11. **4**, Scheelite is the common tungsten mineral in the Mt. Morrison quadrangle, especially at the Hilton Creek and other mines in the area, Rinehart and Ross (2) p. 92; see also Fresno County **(2)**.

Placer County: **1**, Scheelite in tactite zones has been reported from 11 miles west of Lake Tahoe on the upper reaches of the Rubicon River, Anon. (14) p. 2.

Riverside County: **1**, Scheelite is found in the Alice group (secs. 25, 36, T. 1 S., R. 23 E., S.B.), Kerr (6) p. 162; **2**, six miles southwest of Perris, ibid., p. 161, and **3**, Beatty claims, 6 miles west of Perris (secs. 32, 33, 34, T. 4 S., R. 4 W., S.B.), ibid., p. 161. **4**, Considerable scheelite, associated with radiating black tourmaline needles, has been found in Temescal Canyon, near Corona, Knowlton (p.c. '57).

San Bernardino County: **1**, Very important deposits of scheelite occur in the Atolia and Stringer areas, near Randsburg, G. C. Brown (1) p. 522, Cloudman et al. (1) p. 830, Hulin (1) pp. 70, 97. **2**, The mineral occurs with bismutosphaerite (?) in the Morongo Mining District,. Hess and Larsen (17) p. 262, Tucker (4) p. 374, and **3**, with cassiterite in the Ivanpah Mountains (sec. 30, T. 15 N., R. 14 E., S.B.), Tucker and Sampson (30) p. 585, (15) p. 498. Other occurrences: Surr (3) p. 9, J. H. Williams (1) p. 545, Engineering and Mining Journal (24) p. 730, Cloudman et al (1) p. 839, W. W. Bradley (26) p. 345, Tucker and Sampson (27) p. 78, (30) pp. 584, 585, (32) p. 68, Gardner (1) p. 261, **4**, Scheelite occurs in tactite at the Starbright tungsten mine, 25 miles northwest of Barstow (sec. 19, T. 12 N., R. 1 E., S.B.), Anon. (16) p. 1, L. A. Wright et al. (5) p. 152, Hazenbush (1) p. 201.

San Diego County: **1**, Scheelite occurs in aplite dikes in Mason Valley, 60 miles east of San Diego, close to the Mexican border, Kerr (6) p. 165, and **2**, in tactite, in the Laguna Mountains (sec. 28, T. 15 S., R. 4 E., S.B.), ibid., p. 165.

Trinity County: **1**, Scheelite occurs at Stewart Fork, 10 miles northwest of Minersville (sec. 10, T. 35 N., R. 9 W., M.D.), Kerr (6) p. 166.

Tulare County: **1**, The mineral is found at Mineral King, near Empire mine (secs. 11, 16, T. 17 S., R. 31 E., M.D.), Kerr (6) p. 167; **2**, near Middle Fork, Kaweah River (sec. 13, T. 16 S., R. 29 E., M.D.), ibid., p. 167; **3**, Brush Creek near Fairview (sec. 36, T. 22 S., R. 32 E., M.D.), ibid., p. 168, and **4**, Tule Indian Reservation (sec. 7, T. 22 S., R. 30 E., M.D.), ibid., p. 168. **5**, Large quantities of well-formed crystals have been discovered at the Tyler Creek tungsten mine near California Hot Springs, Anon. (37) p. 6. Goodwin (1) pp. 336-367, 369, describes the Tyler Creek occurrence, including diagrams of the scheelite crystals (N½ sec. 35, T. 23 S., R. 30 E., M.D.).

Tuolumne County: **1**, Scheelite occurs at Dorothy Lake, Yosemite National Park (sec. 20, T. 4 N., R. 22 E., M.D.), Kerr (6) p. 168. An additional reference to the county is Logan (23) p. 81.

Yuba County: **1**, Scheelite has been observed at Stephens, Dobbins Ranch (sec. 7, T. 17 N., R. 7 E., M.D.), Kerr (6) p. 169.

References to other localities of lesser commercial importance are listed as follows: *Alpine,* Tucker and Sampson (30) p. 565; O. P. Jenkins (1) p. 311; *Amador,* W. W. Bradley (28) p. 498; *Calaveras,*

W. W. Bradley (30) p. 491; *El Dorado*, W. W. Bradley (32) p. 318; *Fresno*, Engineering and Mining Journal (19) p. 1045, W. W. Bradley (2) p. 470, Tucker and Sampson (30) pp. 565, 566, Chesterman (1) p. 276, Laizure (9) p. 54, Thickstun (1) p. 29; *Humboldt*, Forstner et al. (3) p. 372; *Madera*, Tucker and Sampson (30) p. 580, W. W. Bradley (31) p. 294, Laizure (9) p. 55, Thickstun (1) p. 79; *Mariposa*, W. W. Bradley (29) p. 311, Tucker and Sampson (30) p. 580; *Mono*, Loew (1) p. 656, Hess and Larsen (17) p. 277, Mayo (4) pp. 83, 84, R. J. Sampson (14) p. 147, Lemmon (6) pp. 581–593; *Nevada*, Mining and Scientific Press (22) p. 124 (first discovery of the mineral in California), Hanks (12) p. 353, E. MacBoyle (1) p. 29, Farmin (3) p. 224; *Plumas*, Tucker and Sampson (30) p. 581; *Riverside*, Hess and Larsen (17) p. 260, Tucker and Sampson (30) p. 587, (33) p. 125; *San Diego*, Tucker (10) p. 353, Tucker and Sampson (30) p. 587, (35) pp. 155–157, Symons (4) p. 364; *Shasta*, Partridge (1) p. 318, Tucker and Sampson (30) p. 587; *Sierra*, CDMG (20198); *Trinity*, J. C. O'Brien (2) p. 142; *Tulare*, Franke (1) p. 464, Tucker and Sampson (30) p. 588, Partridge (1) p. 319, Laizure (9) p. 57, O. P. Jenkins (1) pp. 172–179; *Tuolumne*, Hamilton (4) p. 130, W. W. Bradley (31) p. 286, L. A. Wright et al. (5) p. 139.

SCHROECKINGERITE
Hydrous sodium calcium uranyl carbonate sulphate with fluorine
$NaCa_3UO_2(CO_3)_3SO_4F \cdot 10H_2O$

Kern County: **1,** Schroeckingerite is noted as one of the uranium minerals in the Miller Ranch deposit (SE¼ sec. 1 T. 30 S., R. 30 E., M.D.), 6 miles north of Cantil, Troxel and Morton (2) pp. 327, 333.

San Luis Obispo County: **1,** Schroeckingerite occurs as scaly aggregates in a decomposed plutonic rock from the Pozo area, Woodhouse (p.c. '57).

Ventura County: **1,** The mineral is reported from the northwest portion of the county, CDMG (21613).

* SCHUETTEITE, 1959
Mercury oxy-sulphate, $Hg_3SO_4O_2$

Contra Costa County: **1,** Schuetteite has been found in small amount in the Mt. Diablo mine, Pampeyan (1) p. 24.

Lake County: **1,** Schuetteite, a new mineral described first from Lake County, occurs as coatings on cinnabar-bearing basalt at the Sulphur Bank mine, E. H. Bailey et al. (10) p. 1034. Several localities where schuetteite has been artifically formed, on the bricks of mercury furnaces, are also reported in California, ibid.

SCOLECITE
Hydrous calcium aluminum silicate, $CaAl_2Si_3O_{10} \cdot 3H_2O$

Scolecite is a zeolite formed as a secondary mineral in cavities of igneous rocks and sometimes as veins in such rock.

Plumas County: **1,** Scolecite occurs as a hydrothermal mineral in small veinlets of finely radial fibers at the Engels mine, Graton and McLaughlin (4) p. 18.

Riverside County: **1,** The CDMG has identified scolecite from Crestmore.

SCORODITE
Hydrous ferric arsenate, $FeAsO_4 \cdot 2H_2O$

Imperial County: **1,** Scorodite from this county is represented by CDMG (19794).

Inyo County: **1,** Scorodite occurred in the Noonday mine, near Tecopa, Woodhouse (p.c. '45).

Kern County: **1,** Scorodite is reported to occur with arsenopyrite at the Contact mine (sec. 10, T. 10 N., R. 15 W., S.B.), Tucker (37) p. 207.

Mariposa County: **1,** Pale-green crystals of scorodite were found as an alteration product of arsenopyrite associated with pitticite on the South Fork of Merced River, near the mouth of Devils Gulch, A. F. Rogers (7) p. 375.

San Diego County: **1,** Scorodite was found with arsenopyrite near Moreno Lake, F. M. Hamilton (4) p. 759, CDMG (19699).

Sierra County: **1,** Small quantities of scorodite have been found in the Forest (Alleghany) Mining District, Lindgren (20) p. 52.

Tuolumne County: **1,** Scorodite has been reported from Jamestown as druses and crusts of gray-green octahedral crystals, Goudey (3) p. 12.

SCORZALITE
Basic phosphate of aluminum magnesium and ferrous iron, $(Fe^{2+},Mg)Al_2(PO_4)_2(OH)_2$ (an iron-rich lazulite)

Madera County: **1,** Scorzalite is reported from the west side of the Ritter Range as gem material, Smerud and McDonald (1) p. 20. This may be identical with lazulite, Madera County **(1).**

Mono County: **1,** Scorzalite occurs associated with hematite and quartz in a pegmatite-like mass in the lower group of patented claims of the Mono County andalusite mine on the west slope of White Mountains, Woodhouse (p.c. '54).

* SEARLESITE, 1914
Hydrous sodium borosilicate, $NaB(SiO_3)_2 \cdot H_2O$

Kern County: **1,** Searlesite is cited as an associate of sassolite and probertite at the California Borate Company mine, Kramer borate area, G. I. Smith et al. (1) p. 1070, H. E. Pemberton et al. (1) p. 31.

San Bernardino County: **1,** Searlesite was found as a new mineral in a drill core of the Searles Deep Well, at a depth of 540 feet, E. S. Larsen and Hicks (1) p. 438. It was described and named by them, with an analysis by Hicks. H. S. Gale (13) p. 292, also comments on the occurrence. The mineral occurred as spherulites of radiating fibers embedded in mud. It has since been found at other horizons in the Upper Salt, Bottom Mud, and Mixed Layer, Hay and Moiola (1) p. 324, G. I. Smith and Haines (3) p. P33. Further study of the chemistry of searlesite shows that material from rhyolitic tuffs and brines combine to form searlesite, phillipsite and potash feldspar, Hay and Moiola (2) p. P76A.

SENARMONTITE
Antimony trioxide, Sb_2O_3

Inyo County: **1,** Senarmontite was found with cervantite and stibnite at the property of the Skidoo Mining Company, Mining and Scientific Press (38) p. 368.

Santa Clara County: **1,** Possible crystals of senarmontite were reported from the county by Goldsmith (3) p. 369.

SEPIOLITE—Meerschaum
Hydrous basic magnesium silicate, $Mg_8Si_{12}O_{30}(OH)_4(OH_2)_4 \cdot 8H_2O$

Inyo County: **1,** Sepiolite was mentioned by Hanks (12) p. 353, as possibly occurring at the Half Dollar mine.

Riverside County: **1,** Sepiolite occurs as fine interlocking fibers in small veins in calcite at Crestmore, J. W. Daly (1) p. 651. The mineral has been found as brown-stained pellets in limestone in the Commercial quarry, Murdoch (p.c. '57).

SERENDIBITE
Calcium magnesium aluminum borosilicate, $(Ca,Mg)_5Al_5BSi_3O_{20}$

Riverside County: **1,** A massive granular aggregate of dark-blue, glassy serendibite occurs in thin bands in limestone at the new City quarry, 2 miles south of Riverside, G. M. Richmond (1) p. 725. **2,** The mineral occurs at Commercial quarry, Crestmore, as irregular grains in calcite and colorless idocrase (?), Morton (p.c. '58).

SERPENTINE

Serpentine as a name is appropriately applied to a group of minerals, and is also used loosely as a rock name. The mineral and rock occurrences of frequency in California described as "serpentine" in the literature usually cannot be separated, and the localities given must be so viewed. As used in the literature, serpentine as a mineral is in fact composed of one or more of the minerals chrysotile, lizardite or antigorite. Bastite, marmolite, picrolite and williamsite are varieties which are reported to have been found in California, but several of these names have been discredited and should be discarded. The rock serpentine or serpentinite is an alteration product of basic igneous rocks rich in magnesium silicates. The only variety of commercial importance is the fibrous or asbestiform variety known as chrysotile, which occurs in narrow veins in massive serpentine. Massive serpentine rock ranges in color from light-green to greenish-black, but very little of it can be utilized as an ornamental stone on account of its foliated and sheared structure. The serpentine group of minerals has been studied and classification and nomenclature clarified by Faust and Fahey (2), pp. 1–91.

Serpentine is abundant in the Coast Ranges from Del Norte County to San Diego County, and on the west flank of the Sierra Nevada. Some important or interesting localities are:

Amador County: **1,** Veins of chrysotile occur in a dark-green serpentine at the Mace mine, $2\frac{1}{2}$ miles east of Ione, Tucker (1) p. 5.

Calaveras County: **1,** Veins of short-fiber chrysotile occur in the serpentine on the ridge northwest of the Stanislaus River, about 6 miles southeast of Copperopolis (secs. 21, 22, T. 1 N., R. 13 E., M.D.), Tucker (1) p. 55, Diller (17) p. 53. **2,** Veinlets of chrysotile asbestos up to 1 mm thick are found in serpentine ($S\frac{1}{2}$ $NE\frac{1}{4}$ sec. 2, T. 4 N., R. 13 E., M.D.), L. D. Clark (1) p. 17.

El Dorado County: **1,** Veins of fibrous chrysotile are found at French Hill, 6 miles north of Greenwood (sec. 36, T. 13 N., R. 9 E., M.D.), Logan (9) p. 404, (19) p. 207. **2,** A good quality of fibrous chrysotile occurs near Georgetown (sec. 24, T. 12 N., R. 10 E., M.D.), Logan (19) p. 207.

Fresno County: **1,** Serpentine containing veinlets of chrysotile occurs in the Dinuba quadrangle (sec. 22, T. 11 S., R. 23 E., M.D.), as cores in nodules, altered outwardly to talc and actinolite, G. A. Macdonald (4) p. 276. **2,** Serpentine is found near Hernandez, E. Sampson (1) p. 138, and **3,** at the head of Los Gatos Creek in fine crude fibers, Diller (19) p. 551.

Inyo County: **1,** Veins of cross-fiber asbestos (chrysotile) occur in dolomite in Death Valley, at the Indian Camp asbestos mine, Murdoch (p.c. '51). .

Kern County: **1,** Chrysotile veins occur in serpentine in Jawbone Canyon (sec. 7, T. 30 S., R. 36 E., M.D.), G. C. Brown (1) p. 476.

Humboldt County: **1,** Lateritic ores from this county carry nickel-bearing serpentine (lizardite), garnierite, clinochrysotile and antigorite, Montoya and Baur (1) p. 1228.

Lake County: **1,** Becker (4) p. 111, gives analyses by Melville of the serpentine at Sulphur Bank. **2,** Fibrous chrysotile in serpentine occurs north of Middletown, Bowles and Stoddard (1) p. 300.

Los Angeles County: **1,** Serpentine marble has been quarried commercially on Santa Catalina Island in Potts Valley, F. J. H. Merrill (2) p. 483.

Mariposa County: **1,** "Bastite" occurs in considerable amount in the Mary Harrison mine south of Coulterville, A. Knopf (11) p. 36, and **2,** at Three Buttes (secs. 8, 16, 17, T. 6 S., R. 16 E., M.D.), California Academy of Sciences Proceedings (1) p. 110.

Monterey County: **1,** Fibrous chrysotile occurs in $1\frac{1}{2}$-foot veins in Burro Gorge near Jolon, Laizure (3) p. 28.

Napa County: **1,** Chrysotile asbestos in short fibers occurs in Steel Canyon, L. L. Root (2) p. 26.

Nevada County: **1,** "Picrolite" occurred in the Maryland mine, Grass Valley, CDMG (7464).

Placer County: **1,** Long fibers of chrysotile occur at Iowa Hill (secs. 28, 33, T. 15 N., R. 10 E., M.D.), L. L. Root (5) p. 237. **2,** Broad sheets and long fibers of chrysotile occur in the American River Canyon near Towle, Diller (17) p. 53.

Plumas County: **1,** Diller (6) p. 374, gives an analysis of serpentine from Greenville by Melville.

Riverside County: **1,** Small grains of serpentine (probably mixed with "deweylite," J. W. Daly (1) p. 650) occur in the white crystalline limestone at Crestmore, Eakle (15) p. 334. **2,** Antigorite (platy serpentine) occurs with magnesite near Winchester, Murdoch (p.c. '36).

San Benito County: **1,** Becker (4) p. 110, gives an analysis by Melville of a light-green "marmolite" from New Idria. **2,** Serpentine occurs on Clear Creek, near Hernandez (secs. 10, 15, T. 18 S., R. 11 E., M.D.), Laizure (4) p. 223.

San Bernardino County: **1,** Good fibers of serpentine asbestos occur in an undeveloped property near Cronise, Tucker and Sampson (16) p. 296.

San Francisco County: **1,** Newberry (1) p. 66, gives an analysis of the serpentine of San Francisco.

Shasta County: **1,** Large fibrous masses of chrysotile asbestos occur near Sims Station, Logan (7) p. 7, E. Sampson (2) p. 316, Averill (9) p. 113.

Sierra County: **1,** Serpentine asbestos occurs on the west bank of Goodyear Creek, and elsewhere in Sierra County, W. W. Bradley (11) p. 154.

Siskiyou County: **1,** "Williamsite," or gem serpentine, occurs near Indian Creek, north of Happy Camp on the Klamath River, Melhase (3) p. 8.

Trinity County: **1,** Chrysotile has been mined at the Jones Brothers asbestos mine, 2 miles northwest of Carrville, Averill (3) p. 26, J. E. Allen (2) p. 117. Localities are also mentioned in Logan (7) p. 7, (9) p. 128.

Tulare County: **1,** Chrysotile is found in the serpentine east of Lindsay on Tule River (T. 20 S., R. 29 E., M.D.), Tucker (3) p. 905.

SEYBERTITE—Xanthophyllite
Basic magnesium/calcium/aluminum silicate, $Ca(Mg,Al)_3(Al,Si)_4(O,OH)_{12}$

Imperial County: **1,** Seybertite, described as xanthophyllite, variety "zyberdite," is reported from the Turtle Mts., Anon. (43) p. 22.

Riverside County: **1,** Abundant, platy crystals of seybertite (xanthophyllite) occur in the blue calcite at Crestmore, intimately associated with monticellite, and scattered through the inner contact zone, Eakle (14) p. 333, Woodford et al. (10) p. 375. **2,** Seybertite (xanthophyllite) occurs in minor amounts in a contact zone $1\frac{1}{2}$ miles northeast of Winchester, E. S. Larsen (17) p. 36.

SHATTUCKITE
Basic copper silicate, $Cu_5(SiO_3)_4(OH)_2$

Inyo County: **1,** A specimen from the Panamint Mountains has been found to carry shattuckite, mimetite and planchéite, along with another undetermined mineral, Freitag (p.c. '57).

*SICKLERITE, 1912
Lithium manganese iron phosphate, $(Li,Mn^{2+},Fe^{3+})PO_4$

San Diego County: **1,** Sicklerite, resulting from the alteration of lithiophilite, occurs in cleavable masses at the Vanderburg-Naylor mine on Heriart Hill near Pala. It was described as a new mineral from California and was analyzed and named by Schaller (29) p. 144.

SIDERITE
Ferrous carbonate, $FeCO_3$

Siderite is occassionally found in mining regions in drusy crystallizations associated with pyrite and galena, but does not appear to be common in California.

Calaveras County: **1,** Siderite occurs with albite, calcite and quartz at Campo Seco (N.R.).

El Dorado County: **1,** The mineral occurs with calcite and albite at the Red Hill mine, Kelsey Mining District (N.R.).

Imperial County: **1,** Siderite occurs with specular hematite in quartz near Bard (N.R.).

Inyo County: **1,** Masses of siderite have been found at the Custer mine, Coso area, CDMG (7618). **2,** Siderite occurs with pyrite, pyrrhotite and chalcopyrite in a quartz vein at the Curran mine, half a mile northeast of Panamint, Murphy (2) p. 314, R. J. Sampson (7) p. 367, and **3,** at the Mountain Girl, 4 miles south of Panamint, R. J. Sampson (7) p. 371.

Los Angeles County: **1,** Massive siderite occurs in the Tujunga Canyon, Hanks (12) p. 354, and **2,** it has been found with pyrrhotite and annabergite in Pacoima Canyon 12 miles east of San Fernando, D'Arcy (3) p. 269.

Mariposa County: **1,** Siderite was found with calcite at Devils Gulch (N.R.).

Mono County: **1,** The mineral occurs with limonite and hematite near Benton, A. L. Ransome (2) p. 190.

Plumas County: **1,** The mineral was found with copper minerals at the Engels mine, Graton and McLaughlin (4) p. 19.

Riverside County: **1,** Siderite occurs with pyrrhotite in the old Dominion mine, E. S. Larson et al. (18) p. 48. **2,** Siderite occurs at Crestmore, underground, as honey-colored rhombohedrons, in cavities, Keller (p.c. '59).

San Diego County; **1,** Siderite has been recognized from Pala, Kunz (23) p. 942.

Santa Clara County: **1,** A deposit of siderite occurs on the Weber Ranch, in Los Animos Hills, 3 miles northeast of Madrone (N.R.). **2,** Siderite occurs in large masses on Red Mountain (N.R.).

SIDEROTIL
Hydrous ferrous sulphate, $FeSO_4 \cdot 5H_2O$

Contra Costa County: **1,** Siderotil is found in the Mount Diablo quicksilver mine ($SE\frac{1}{4}$ sec. 29, T. 1 N., R. 1 E., M.D.) as a dehydration product of melanterite, C. P. Ross (2) p. 44, Pampeyan (1) p. 24.

SILLIMANITE—Fibrolite
Aluminum silicate, Al_2SiO_5

Sillimanite is a constituent of metamorphic gneiss and schist, often with kyanite, andalusite and staurolite.

Inyo County: **1,** Random fibers of sillimanite are found abundantly in schist at the scheelite deposit in Deep Canyon, west of Bishop, A. Knopf (6) p. 233. **2,** Sillimanite occurs massive near Laws (N.R.). This unconfirmed report may refer to andalusite from the Champion Sillimanite mine in Mono County, and not to the mineral sillimanite.

Kern County: **1,** Sillimanite occurs in schists of the Kernville series, near Cook peak, W. J. Miller (6) p. 338.

Los Angeles County: **1,** The mineral occurs in schists in the San Rafael Hills, W. J. Miller (7) p. 5, and **2,** it was observed by Beverly (1) pp. 344, 351, at the graphite deposits in San Francisquito, Kagel and Elizabeth Lake Canyons, in the western part of the San Gabriel Mountains.

Mariposa County: **1,** Sillimanite occurs in the schists near Mariposa in minute silvery prisms, H. W. Turner (12) p. 690.

San Bernardino County: **1,** Sillimanite occurs in schist at Ord Mountain, 15 miles southeast of Daggett (N. R.). **2,** Sillimanite probably occurs in the corundum gneiss at Cascade Canyon, Foshag (p.c. '46).

San Diego County: **1,** Sillimanite is a constituent of the dumortierite gneiss at Dehesa, Schaller (7) p. 96; **2,** it occurs 4 miles southeast of Fallbrook, G. A. Waring (2) p. 359; **3,** abundant sillimanite up to 2 cm in size occurs in schists south and east of Ramona, and **4,** 2 miles south of Mesa Grande, R. H. Merriam (p.c. '46). **5,** Abundant and widespread occurrences of sillimanite as needles in quartz-muscovite-sillimanite schist are found south and east of Ramona (T. 12 S., R. 2 E., S.B.), R. H. Merriam (4) p. 228. **6,** In the Mesa Grande area needles of sillimanite as much as 1 to 2 cm in size occur in the schists, ibid., p. 228. **7,** Sillimanite occurs in gneiss at the entrance to Palm Canyon, Borego Valley, Durrell (p.c. '48). **8,** Sillimanite is abundant in blocks of breccia in Split Mountain Canyon, Durrell (p.c. '48).

Tuolumne County: **1,** Sillimanite from this county has been analyzed by H. N. Stokes, F. W. Clarke (10) p. 317.

SILVER
Native silver, Ag

Native silver has not been found in any large masses in the State, yet it is present in many gold and copper regions, and occasionally arborescent crystal groups, wires and thin sheets are found. It is more common in silver-lead areas, where it often occurs near the walls of veins and intrusive dikes.

Alpine County: **1,** Good specimens of native silver have come from the Silver Mountain Mining District, W. P. Blake (9) p. 21, R. W. Raymond (6) p. 12.

Calaveras County: **1,** Silver occurred in arborescent forms with the copper ore at Quail Hill, Mining and Scientific Press (4) p. 5.

Del Norte County: **1,** Silver was found with tetrahedrite at the Occidental mine, Crawford (2) p. 58.

Fresno County: **1,** Silver occurred at Millerton, Hanks (15) p. 135.

Imperial County: **1,** Silver is reported with argentite in a 'gold quartz vein in the Mary Lode mine, R. J. Sampson and Tucker (18) p. 122.

Inyo County: **1,** Occasional sprinklings of native silver occur with argentite in the quartz-calcite veins of Saline Valley, about 30 miles northeast of Mount Whitney, T. Warner (1) p. 938, and **2,** at the Eclipse mine, near Mazourka Canyon, Goodyear (3) p. 263. **3,** Thin sheets of silver occur at the Sorba mine, near Darwin, Kelley (4) p. 543; **4,** it occurred in the Cerro Gordo mines, G. M. Wheeler (3) p. 62, and **5,** it was found in the Panamint Mining District, Stetefeldt (1) p. 259.

Kern County: **1,** Silver is reported with other silver minerals in the Amalie Mining District (N. R.). Argentite and pyrargyrite are noted by Crawford (2) p. 605, and proustite by Dyke (1) p. 764, but neither of these references mention native silver. **2,** Near Garlock (N. R.). This may have reference to the silver minerals from the Kelly Rand property near Randsburg, [see miargyrite, San Bernardino County **(1)**] to the east rather than to Garlock. **3,** A little native silver appears in the Cactus Queen ores, Mojave Mining District, Troxel and Morton, (2) p. 49.

Los Angeles County: **1,** Native silver was associated with argentite, and with cobalt and nickel minerals, at the Kelsey mine, near San Gabriel Canyon, Storms (4) p. 244, and **2,** at the O. K. mine, Irelan (4) p. 47. **3,** Native silver is found at the Maria mine, Soledad Canyon, W. P. Blake (9) p. 21.

Madera County: **1,** Silver occurs in quartz veins at the Sullenger property, 3 miles northwest of Agnew Meadows on the eastern slope of Middle Fork Canyon, Erwin (1) p. 71.

Mariposa County: **1,** Silver occurs with proustite at the Silver Lane (sec. 15, T. 6 S., R. 19 E., M.D.), Laizure (8) p. 44.

Mono County: **1,** Silver occurs in narrow veins cutting granitic rocks on Blind Spring Hill, Benton. Good specimens have come from the Diana and Comanche mines of this region, Hanks (15) p. 135. **2,** Some native silver occurs in the Silverado mine in the Patterson Mining District, Whiting (1) p. 359. **3,** At Bodie silver has been found in wire and flake form with crystallized argentite, with the copper-gold ores, Hanks (15) p. 135, Whiting (1) p. 391. **4,** Native silver has been found at the Dunderberg and Napoleon mines, on Castle Peak, G. M. Wheeler (4) p. 184.

Napa County: **1,** Silver occurs with argentite and cerargyrite at the Calistoga mines, L. L. Palmer (1) p. 28.

Placer County: **1,** Silver occurred at the Gold Blossom and the California mines in the Ophir Mining District, Lindgren (7) p. 272. **2,** The mineral also occurred at the Valley View mine, 6 miles south of Lincoln, as films on a talcose mass, Silliman (7) p. 351.

Plumas County: **1,** Native silver has been found in the old Pocahontas mine, associated with millerite, native copper and cuprite, Crawford (1) p. 69.

San Bernardino County: **1,** Silver was first discovered in the Calico Mining District about 1874. The ore carried cerargyrite and native silver, Mining and Scientific Press (21) p. 98, Lindgren (1) p. 717, Storms (2) p. 382, (4) p. 337. **2,** The mineral occurred in the Grapevine Mining District, CDMG (4234). **3,** Native silver with gold occurs in the Avawatz Mountains, Irelan (3) p. 501. **4,** Native silver was reported from the San Gabriel mine, Mining and Scientific Press (22) p. 152. **5,** Silver was found with cerargyrite and embolite at the Alta mine, 1¼ miles east of Riggs, Tucker (4) p. 359, Tucker and Sampson (16) p. 267. **6,** Small flecks of silver were noted on the 150-foot level of the Kelly Rand mine near Randsburg, J. A. Carpenter (2) p. 135. **7,** Native silver and cerargyrite are found in the Waterman mine (sec. 3, T. 10 N., R. 2 W., S.B.), 4 miles north of Barstow, L. A. Wright et al. (5) p. 139.

San Mateo County: **1,** Native silver is recorded from a well 478 feet deep at the Redwood City mine, Hanks (14) p. 94.

Shasta County: **1,** Native silver is rare in the copper deposits of this county, but a few arborescent specimens have come from the Bully

Hill, Afterthought and other mines, Aubury (1) p. 65, A. C. Boyle (1) p. 98. **2,** Fine crystallized silver occurred in the old Excelsior mine, Copper City, Fairbanks (2) p. 32. **3,** Native silver in arborescent crystal groups, associated with stephanite, tetrahedrite, galena and sphalerite, in a calcite-quartz gangue, occurs at the Igo Consolidated mines (secs. 17, 18, T. 31 N., R. 6 W., M.D.), Becker (2) p. 24, Laizure (1) p. 526. **4,** Native silver occurs occasionally in the East Shasta copper-zinc area, Albers and Robertson (2) p. 71.

SJOGRENITE
Hydrous basic magnesium iron carbonate, $Mg_6Fe_2(OH)_{16}CO_3 \cdot 4H_2O$

San Francisco County: **1,** Sjogrenite occurs as a thin coating with hydromagnesite on fractures in serpentine at Fort Point, CDMG X-ray identification, 1964.

SMALTITE
Cobalt nickel arsenide, $(Co,Ni)As_{3-x}$ where $x \approx 0.5$–1.0

Calaveras County: **1,** Smaltite has been found with erythrite in a small stringer at the Mar John mine near Sheepranch (NW¼ sec. 21, T. 4 N., R. 14 E., M.D.), Logan (7) p. 4.

Los Angeles County: **1,** Smaltite coated with erythrite occurred with native silver and argentite at the Kelsey and O.K. mines near San Gabriel Canyon, Irelan (4) p. 47.

Inyo County: **1,** Smaltite has been found with erythrite, annabergite and argentite at the Bishop silver and cobalt mine, near Long Lake (sec. 14, T. 9 S., R. 31 E., M.D.), Woodhouse (p.c. '36).

Lassen County: **1,** Smaltite is recorded from this county, with annabergite, Irelan (4) p. 47, CDMG (9981).

Napa County: **1,** Smaltite has been found in thin seams with erythrite in the serpentine rock of Berryessa Valley (N.R.).

Nevada County: **1,** Smaltite occurs in the Meadow Lake Mining District (N.R.).

Siskiyou County: **1,** Smaltite has been reported from Callahan with erythrite, W. W. Bradley (28) p. 497.

SMITHSONITE
Zinc carbonate, $ZnCO_3$

Smithsonite is a secondary mineral ofter found in silver-lead mining areas. It is usually associated with galena, sphalerite, hemimorphite (calamine) and cerussite.

Inyo County: **1,** Smithsonite was found with cerussite at the Modoc mine (sec. 34, T. 19 S., R. 42 E., M.D.), Hanks (12) p. 368, CDMG (2177). **2,** The mineral was also present at the Ignacio mine at Cerro Gordo with hemimorphite and willemite, Irelan (4) p. 47, A. Knopf (5) p. 97. An unusual stalactitic form of smithsonite occurs at Cerro Gordo, CDMG (19287), and it was found in abundance in the limestone footwall of the Cerro Gordo mine, C. W. Merriam (1) p. 43. Yellow cadmium-bearing smithsonite was obtained in the Cerro Gordo mine, CDMG (19297). **3,** Smithsonite occurred with cerussite and galina in limestone at the Redwing and Noonday mines, Resting Springs, C. A. Waring and Huguenin (2) p. 104. **4,** Smithsonite occurred with galena and cerussite in limestone at the Ophir mine 10 miles northeast of Trona, C. A. Waring and Huguenin (2) p. 105. **5**, Smithsonite has been found at the Swansea mine, 2½ miles northeast of Keeler, Tucker (11) p. 501, and **6**, in the Leadfield area, ibid. p. 507. **7**, Small amounts of smithsonite are present in the Darwin Mining District, Tucker (4) p. 294, Kelley (4) p. 546, Hall and MacKevett (4) p. 64; **8**, in the Wild Rose Mining District, Tucker and Sampson (32) p. 59, and **9**, in the Panamint Mining District, Murphy (2) p. 322. **10**, Smithsonite occurs with galena at the Lippincott lead mine (sec. 13, T. 15 S., R. 40 E., M.D.), McAllister (2) pp. 1–10.

Kern County: **1**, Smithsonite occurred in drusy veins at the Jewett mine on Cottonwood Creek (N.R.), and **2**, it was found on the Tejon Ranch (T. 9 N., R. 18 W., S.B.), Tucker and Sampson (32) p. 65.

Riverside County: **1**, Smithsonite occurs with copper and lead minerals at the Palisade zinc property, 2 miles from English siding on the California Southern Railroad, Tucker (4) p. 332. **2**, Smithsonite, in globular grains and poorly developed crystals, has been found with galena and sphalerite in boulders, associated with hemimorphite, on the old dump of the Lone Star quarry, Crestmore, Jenni (p.c. '57).

San Bernardino County: **1**, Smithsonite occurred with hemimorphite at the Cuticura mine, near Daggett, CDMG (11534); **2**, it occurred with cerussite, anglesite, linarite and galena in dolomite at the Ibex mine, Black Mountains, 6 miles north of Saratoga Springs, Cloudman et al. (1) p. 821; **3**, at the Carbonate King mine (sec. 4, T. 15 N., R. 14 E., S. B.), Tucker and Sampson (33) p. 128, Wiebelt (1) p. 1; **4**, in the Clark Mountains, 5 miles northeast of Valley Wells (T. 17 N., R. 13 E., S. B.), Tucker (8) p. 95, and **5**, with galena in the Ivanpah Mining District, Tucker (4) p. 363.

Tulare County: **1**, Smithsonite has been found in the Silver Crown group (sec. 7, T. 23 S., R. 33 E., M. D.), Tucker and Sampson (29) p. 331.

SODA NITER—Chile Saltpeter
Sodium nitrate, NaNO$_3$

Nitrates can exist in solid form only in arid regions, and are therefore peculiar to desert lands, where they are sometimes left as white incrustations by evaporation. Some of these white crusts may be found in the California desert land, but no important deposits are known, Mansfield and Boardman (4) pp. 23–30.

Imperial County: **1**, Soda niter has been found along the shoreline of the old Salton Sea, near the Mud Volcanoes, H. S. Gale (1) p. 27.

Inyo County: **1**, Crusts containing soda niter and niter, occurring along the Amargosa River and along shore lines and old beaches of Death Valley, were reported by G. E. Bailey (2) p. 169. **2**, Crusts of soda niter and niter occur near Shoshone, Noble (4) p. 71. **3**, The Confidence, Upper Canyon, Zabriskie, Ratcliff claims, and Furnace Creek nitrate fields contain small amounts of soda niter, Noble et al. (1) pp. 22–88.

Merced County: **1**, Soda niter occurs in crusts with other sodium salts, from Merced Bottom, Hilgard (1) p. 25, Laizure (3) p. 182.

Riverside County: **1,** Minor amounts of soda niter are found in the Vivet Eye area (T. 1 S., R. 23, 24 E., S. B.), H. W. Turner (28) p. 636, Noble (4) p. 54.

San Bernardino County: **1,** White incrustations containing soda niter and niter occur along the Amargosa River, G. E. Bailey (2) p. 169. **2,** Small amounts of soda niter have been found in the Calico Mining District, A. Williams (1) p. 599. **3,** The Lower Canyon, Saratoga, Upper Canyon, Barstow syncline, Coolgardie Lake, Pilot, Leach Lake, Owl Spring, Twenty-Nine Palms, West Well, Beal, Vidal and Danby Lake nitrate fields contain small amounts of soda niter, Noble (4) pp. 10–32.

Tulare County: **1,** Alkaline crusts containing soda niter with other soda salts occur in the San Joaquin Valley, near Tulare, Hilgard (1) p. 25.

† * SONOMAITE, 1877
See pickeringite

Sonoma County: The name sonomaite was assigned to samples from The Geysers which were thought to be a new mineral by Goldsmith (6) p. 263. Subsequently the mineral was identified as pickeringite, E. S. Dana (6) p. 523.

SPHALERITE—Zincblende—Black Jack
Zinc sulphide, ZnS

Sphalerite is very common and is prevalent in most mining regions. It varies from clear light-brown to very dark-brown, almost black masses. Its typical associate is galena, but it is also often intimately mixed with pyrite, chalcopyrite, tetrahedrite, arsenopyrite and lead-silver minerals.

Only the more interesting occurrences can be listed in any detail. For other occurrences, references will be given by counties.

Inyo County: **1,** Cleavage pieces of sphalerite up to 3 inches across, with fluorite and galena, have been found in the Darwin Mining District, Defiance and other ore bodies, A. Knopf (4) p. 7, Kelley (4) p. 543, Hall and MacKevett (4) p. 62. **2,** Sphalerite is present in the Cerro Gordo ores, C. W. Merriam (1) p. 43.

Kern County: **1,** Sphalerite has been mined from the Blackhawk mine (SW$\frac{1}{4}$ sec. 5, T. 31 S., R. 33 E., M.D.), near Loraine, Troxel and Morton (2) p. 345.

Los Angeles County: **1,** The lead mines on Santa Catalina Island were rich in sphalerite, Hanks (12) p. 371, Tucker (12) pp. 33–38. **2,** Massive sphalerite, with galena and pyrrhotite, occurs at the Indicator mine, 12 miles from the mouth of Pacoima Canyon, Tucker (4) p. 318.

Mariposa County: **1,** Triboluminescent sphalerite, a mixture of fine-grained sphalerite, barite, chalcopyrite and kaolinite, which glows when rubbed, occurs at the Fitch mine (secs. 9, 10, T. 4 S., R. 15 E., M.D.), Eakle (5) p. 30, Eakle and Sharwood (6) p. 1000, Headden (1) p. 177.

Merced County: **1,** Triboluminescent sphalerite with barite has been found near Merced Falls, Laizure (3) p. 175.

Nevada County: **1,** Large masses of sphalerite, with other sulphides, are found in the Washington Mining District, Meadow Lake, Wisker

(1) p. 194. **2,** The mineral is quite abundant in several of the mines in Grass Valley, Lindgren (12) p. 118.

Orange County: **1,** Sphalerite is plentiful in the Blue Light mine (secs. 11, 14, T. 5 S., R. 7 W., S.B.), Fairbanks (4) p. 115. **2,** Sphalerite is found with pyrrhotite and chalcopyrite on the north bank of San Juan Creek, in the southwest part of the Elsinore quadrangle, about 1½ miles east of the western quadrangle boundary. Veins several feet wide occur as irregular replacement in Triassic sediments, E. S. Larsen et al. (18) p. 48.

Placer County: **1,** Yellowish transparent zincblende occurs in the Ophir Mining District (NE¼ sec. 17, T. 12 N., R. 8 E., M.D.), Lindgren (7) p. 273.

Riverside County: **1,** Sphalerite is one of the minerals at Crestmore, Kelly (2) p. 141.

San Bernardino County: **1,** Large masses of sphalerite carry the silver values in some of the mines of the Silver Mountain Mining District, 5 miles north of Adelanto and 1 mile west of US 395, Tucker and Sampson (16) p. 267.

Shasta County: **1,** An extensive ore body of finely divided sphalerite is found at the Hobbs mine, 6 miles southwest of Round Mountain, Crawford (1) p. 411. **2,** Sphalerite is abundant in the East Shasta copper-zinc ores, Albers and Robertson (3) p. 71.

Other references are to minor occurrences, listed by counties as follows: *Alpine:* Crawford (1) p. 373, Gianella (1) p. 342, W. W. Bradley (15) p. 488; *Amador:* Hulin (3) p. 352; *Calaveras:* Hanks (12) p. 371, Franke and Logan (4) p. 239; *El Dorado:* Logan (9) p. 406; *Fresno:* Aubury (4) p. 281; *Imperial:* Tucker (11) p. 267, Henshaw (1) p. 185; *Inyo:* A. Knopf (5) p. 104, Tucker (11) pp. 471, 473, Murphy (2) p. 321, Lemmon (5) p. 505, Tucker and Sampson (32) p. 59; *Kern:* Hulin (1) p. 84, Tucker and Sampson (21) pp. 290, 329, Simpson (1) p. 409, Engineering and Mining Journal (28) p. 62; *Los Angeles:* Storms (4) p. 243, R. J. Sampson (10) p. 187; *Madera:* W. W. Bradley (9) p. 548, Erwin (1) pp. 66, 70; *Mariposa:* J. B. Trask (8) p. 52; *Mono:* CDMG (7273), Mayo (4) p. 84, R. J. Sampson (14) pp. 139, 140; *Orange:* Fairbanks (4) p. 117; *Placer:* Logan (11) p. 286, (17) pp. 16, 23; *Plumas:* Preston (2) p. 467, Graton and McLaughlin (4) p. 15; *Sacramento:* W. P. Blake (9) p. 9; *San Bernardino:* Cloudman et al. (1) p. 790, Tucker and Sampson (17) p. 341, Erwin and Gardner (3) p. 302, Tucker and Sampson (32) p. 69, (33) p. 128; *San Diego:* F. J. H. Merrill (1) pp. 667, 668; *San Mateo:* Hanks (12) p. 371, (15) p. 135; *Shasta:* Aubury (4) p. 102, G. C. Brown (2) p. 808, Averill (4) pp. 7, 14, 50, 57; *Sierra:* E. MacBoyle (3) p. 4; *Siskiyou:* Averill (5) p. 280; *Trinity:* Averill (9) pp. 28, 34; *Tulare:* Hanks (12) p. 371, Franke (1) p. 436; *Tuolumne:* Tucker (1) p. 138, Oak Hill mine (sec. 30, T. 2 S., R. 14 E., M.D.), Logan (23) p. 54.

SPHENE—Titanite
Calcium titano-silicate, $CaTiSiO_5$

Sphene is a common accessory mineral of the granites, gneisses and schists of the State. It has been mentioned by many writers in their petrographical descriptions as a microscopic constituent of rocks. It is a characteristic heavy mineral of the granitic rocks of the Coast Range batholith, Spotts (1) pp. 1236–1237.

Contra Costa County: **1,** Sphene is mentioned as an associate of crossite in the schists near San Pablo, Palache (3) p. 184.

El Dorado County: **1,** Sphene was first observed in the State by W. P. Blake (17) p. 193, in the granite of Slippery Ford and other places of the Sierra Nevada.

Fresno County: **1,** Sphene is a constituent of the rocks at Fine Gold Gulch, Hanks (15) p. 138.

Inyo County: **1,** Sphene occurs in small amount at the Wilshire gold mine west of Bishop, H. W. Turner (34) p. 888. **2,** The mineral occurs in fair-sized crystals in the tactite at Darwin, Kelly (4) p. 540. **3,** Sphene occurs rather abundantly in large well-formed crystals (up to 2 inches in length), at the foot of the Palisade Glacier, Axelrod (p.c. '46).

Imperial County (?): **1,** Chromiferous sphene from the "southern California desert area," was examined by Jaffe (1) p. 640.

Kern County: **1,** Sphene occurs with garnet, quartz and feldspar in a contact-metamorphic limestone 200 yards east of Hobo Springs, near Havilah, Melhase (p.c. '36).

Los Angeles County: **1,** Green, brown and yellow sphene crystals up to ⅛ inch are found in large boulders of diorite in alluvial fan material in Sierra Madre Canyon, Sierra Madre, Metzer (1) p. 56.

Marin County: **1,** Sphene occurs as one of the minerals of the lawsonite schists on the Tiburon Peninsula, F. L. Ransome (3) p. 311.

Mendocino County: **1,** Pale yellowish crystals of sphene occur with lawsonite at Syke rock, 3 miles east of Longvale on the new Covelo road (T. 20 N., R. 14 W., M.D.), Chesterman (p.c. '51).

Mono County: **1,** Minute grains of sphene are scattered through the andalusite at the mine of Champion Sillimanite on the western slope of the White Mountains, 7 miles east of Malcalno, north of Bishop, Woodhouse (2) p. 4.

Plumas County: **1,** Sphene occurs as numerous irregular grains with apatite in the diorite country rock of the Superior mine, Graton and McLaughlin (4) p. 34.

Riverside County: **1,** Granular sphene in pale-brown grains is abundant in the quartz monzonite at Crestmore, Eakle (15) p. 330, and in some of the pegmatites, Woodford (11) p. 360. **2,** Small crystals of sphene occur in the gangue of the Eagle Mountain iron ores, Harder (6) p. 54. **3,** Sphene occurs as large yellow crystals with black tourmaline and quartz at a contact of granodiorite and quartzite in the West Riverside Hills, Eggleston (p.c. '36). **4,** Crystals up to 1 by ½ by ½ inches appear in granodiorite on the northwest side of Deep Canyon (sec. 36, T. 6 S., R. 5 E., S.B.), Webb (7) p. 344.

San Bernardino County: **1,** Considerable sphene appears in the Iron Age ore deposit near Dale, Harder and Rich (4) p. 234.

San Diego County: **1,** Sphene is a minor associate of dumortierite at Dehesa, Schaller (7) p. 211.

San Mateo County: **1,** Sphene is a notable constituent of the Montara granite near San Francisco, A. C. Lawson (2) p. 411.

Santa Barbara County: **1**, Sphene is one of the heavy minerals present in the Alegria and Vaqueros formations in the Gaviota area, Grenden (1) p. 269.

Santa Clara County: **1**, Excellent large crystals of sphene occur in the eclogites of Calaveras Valley, Murgoci (1) p. 388, and **2**, in the quartzite and diorite of Oak Hill, near San Jose, ibid., p. 390.

Sonoma County: **1**, Sphene is a conspicuous constituent of glaucophane schists near the mouth of the Russian River, Pabst (1) p. 333. **2**, Crystals up to 1 cm in size, often concentrated along crevices in eclogite, have been found at the W. P. A. quarry, Mill Creek, Switzer (5) p. 83.

Trinity County: **1**, Sphene was found with epidote, colorless garnet and zircon in a soda granite-porphyry in the Iron Mountain region, Weaverville quadrangle (N. R.).

SPINEL
Magnesium/aluminum oxide, $MgAl_2O_4$

Picotite is a brown spinel containing chromium and iron; it occurs in serpentine rocks. *Pleonaste* is a dark-green iron-magnesium spinel. Spinel occurs only as a rock constituent and appears in some of the gold-placer sands as ruby-red grains resembling red garnet.

Butte County: **1**, Small crystals of ruby spinel have been found in the rock of the "diamond mine" near Oroville (N. R.).

Fresno County: **1**, Colorless, red, and black crystals of spinel 1 to 4 mm in diameter are present in the contact metamorphosed limestone of the Twin Lakes area, Chesterman (1) p. 254.

Humboldt County: **1**, Ruby spinel occurs in the beach sands at Gold Bluff, Kunz (24) p. 47.

Inyo County: **1**, Spinel, variety pleonaste, has been found in the south end of Butte Valley, Ubehebe Mining District, CDMG (21329), McAllister (4) p. 61.

Lassen County: **1**, Microscopic brown octahedral crystals of picotite have been found in quartz basalt at Cinder Cone, Lassen Volcanic National Park, Diller (3) p. 23, Finch and Anderson (1) p. 261.

Monterey County: **1**, Grains of ruby spinel have been found near Jolon, CDMG (15855).

Placer County: **1**, Picotite has been found at Rocklin, Hanks (12) p. 309, Schrader et al. (1) p. 75.

Riverside County: **1**, Specimens of spinel have come from northwest of Anza, and on Thomas Mountain, W. W. Bradley (29) p. 107. **2**, Spinel, both pale and dark blue-green, has been found in minor amount at Crestmore, A. F. Rogers (31) p. 466, W. W. Bradley (28) p. 498. **3**, Spinel has come from the old City quarry, Riverside, A. F. Rogers (19) p. 581, and **4**, from the new City quarry, south of Riverside, G. M. Richmond (1) p. 725.

San Benito County: **1**, Pale crystals and grains of spinel have been found in altered serpentine half a mile downstream from the benitoite locality, Woodhouse (p.c. '45), Williams (p.c. '49), Watters (p.c. '51).

San Bernardino County: **1**, Black spinel occurs in the basalt flows south of Pipes Canyon (secs. 21, 22, T. 1 N., R. 4 E., S.B.) (N. R.); **2**, in basalt near Quail Springs (T. 1 S., R. 7 E., S.B.) (N. R.), and **3**, black granular masses and small crystals of spinel have been found at the Dewey mine, Clark Mountain Mining District, Schaller (50) p. 816.

San Diego County: **1**, Blue spinel was reported to occur in the Mack mine near Rincon. The deep-green, pleonaste variety, in small octahedrons, occurs there with garnet, Kunz (24) p. 48, A. F. Rogers (4) p. 209.

San Luis Obispo County: **1**, Ruby spinel has been observed near San Luis Obispo, Kunz (1) p. 486, (24) p. 47. Some of the crystals were half a carat each, and of gem quality.

Santa Barbara County: **1**, Nearly perfect crystals of spinel are found in microscopic sizes, but quite abundantly, in the beach sands of the Santa Barbara coast, Norris and Woodhouse (4) p. 55. **2**, Picotite is found in the Franciscan rocks of the San Rafael Mountains, Woodhouse (p.c. '63).

Siskiyou County: **1**, Picotite occurs in the basalts of Mount Shasta, Wadsworth (1) p. 314, Hanks (12) p. 309.

Tulare County: **1**, Granular green spinel occurs in metamorphosed serpentine on the southwest side of Rocky Hill, and in metamorphosed basic volcanic rocks on the southern slope of Woodlake Mountain, Durrell (p.c. '35).

SPODUMENE
Lithium aluminum silicate, LiAl(SiO$_3$)$_2$

Kunzite is a beautiful transparent variety, lilac or amethystine in color. It is sometimes called *California iris*. *Hiddenite* is an emerald-green spodumene. *Triphane* is colorless to yellow. Spodumene is found in large crystals and cleavage masses in pegmatites, commonly associated with lepidolite and lithia tourmaline.

Kern County: **1**, Grains of spodumene have been identified in the heavy minerals from drill cores in the Lazard area, west of Lost Hills, R. D. Reed and Bailey (4) p. 363.

Riverside County: **1**, The variety kunzite, has been found in the Fano (Simmons) mine (sec. 33, T. 6 S., R. 2 E., S.B.), on Cahuila Mountain. Kunz (23) p. 967, (24) p. 25. This kunzite shows spectroscopic traces of germanium, Papish (2) p. 477.

San Diego County: **1**, The variety kunzite was first discovered in the White Queen mine, Pala in 1902, Kunz (26) p. 1345, and was described from the Pala Chief mine, Kunz (18) p. 264, (24) p. 83. The largest crystal found was 23 by 4 by 2 cm in dimensions. This kunzite showed 0.043 percent gallium by spectroscopic methods, Gabriel et al. (1) p. 119. Schaller (2) p. 265, has also recorded hiddenite and white spodumene from Pala; other references: Baskerville (1) p. 303, Baskerville and Kunz (2) pp. 25–28, R. O. E. Davis (1) p. 29, Sinkankas (1), p. 50. Spodumene associated with lithia-beryl and purpurite (?) was found at the Naylor-Vanderberg mine, Pala, Kunz (26) p. 1344. Kunzite and hiddenite in crystals up to 7½ by 2 by 1½ inches are reported in the gem pegmatites at Pala, Jahns and Wright (5) pp. 19, 30, 36. **2**, Kunzite was found in small amounts at the Victor mine, Rincon, A. F. Rogers (4) p. 210. In the Clark vein, in the same locality, large rough crystals of spodumene occur in quartz, altering to petalite and heulandite, Murdoch (18) p. 198, Hanley (1) p. 23. **3**, Kunzite was found in the Mountain Lily mine, Aguanga Mountain, Kunz (24) pp. 25, 62. **4,** Small, clear pieces of spodumene have come from the Himalaya mine, Mesa Grande, Kunz (24) p. 135. **5,** An unverified report records kunzite from the Vista Chief and Mountain Belle mines, Moosa Canyon (E$\frac{1}{2}$ sec. 27, T. 10 S., R. 3 W., S.B.), Kunz (24) p. 62, F. J. H. Merrill (1) p. 702. **6,** Kunz (18) p. 280, has reported kunzite from near Menchoir.

SPURRITE
Calcium silicate and carbonate, $Ca_5Si_2O_8CO_3$

Riverside County: **1,** Spurrite occurs intimately associated with merwinite and gehlenite in the limestone at Crestmore, Foshag (2) p. 80, Woodford (11) p. 360.

STANNITE
Copper iron tin sulphide, Cu_2FeSnS_4

Inyo County: **1,** The rich silver ore of the Thompson mine, Darwin Mining District, includes stannite, Hall and MacKevett (1) p. 17, ibid. (4) p. 62.

Santa Cruz County: **1,** Stannite occurs in crystalline limestone, associated with franckeite and meneghinite, in the Pacific Limestone Products (Kalkar) quarry, 2 miles northeast of Santa Cruz, Milton and Chesterman (p.c. '54).

STAUROLITE
Basic iron magnesium aluminum silicate, $(Fe,Mg)_4Al_{18}Si_8O_{46}(OH)_2$

Staurolite occurs only in metamorphic rocks rich in aluminum.

Inyo County: **1,** Microscopic grains of staurolite have been found in quartz-mica schist on the west side of the Panamint Range near Ballarat, Murphy (4) p. 345.

STEPHANITE—Brittle Silver Ore
Silver antimony sulphide, Ag_5SbS_4

Stephanite is an important and usually prominent silver mineral in silver areas, but it is not common in California. It is often associated with argentite and polybasite as an original mineral of veins.

Alpine County: **1,** Stephanite has been reported from the Morning Star mine, Hanks (12) p. 371, Eakle (16) p. 13, and **2,** with hübnerite from the Zaca mine, Gianella (1) p. 342, Partridge (1) p. 264.

Inyo County: **1,** Stephanite was found with argentite in the Cliff mine, northwest of the head of Deep Spring Valley, Goodyear (3) p. 237, and **2,** it occurred with tetrahedrite and argentite at the Belmont mine, Cerro Gordo Mining District, Tucker (4) p. 283.

Mono County: **1,** Stephanite occurred in the Blind Spring (Benton) Mining District, Whiting (1) p. 378, and **2,** it was abundant, with pyrargyrite, in the Oro, Addenda and Fortuna mines, Bodie Mining District, Whiting (1) p. 392. **3,** Stephanite is found in the Patterson Mining District, Sweetwater Range (N. R.).

Nevada County: **1,** Stephanite was found in the Allison Ranch mine, Grass Valley, Lindgren (12) p. 119.

San Bernardino County: **1,** Stephanite occurred in the St. Lawrence Rand mine (sec. 1, T. 30 S., R. 40 E., M. D.), F. M. Hamilton and

Root (5) p. 170, and **2**, in the Carlyle mine, near Dale (sec. 11, T. 1. S., R. 12 E., S. B.), Tucker and Sampson (27) p. 61.

Shasta County: **1**, Stephanite occurs with native silver, galena and sphalerite in a calcite-quartz gangue at the Igo Consolidated mines (N. R.).

STERNBERGITE
Silver iron sulphide, $AgFe_2S_3$

Riverside County: **1**, The Colorado School of Mines has identified sternbergite in material collected from Crestmore (p.c. '61).

*STEWARTITE, 1912
Hydrous manganese phosphate, $Mn_3(PO_4)_2 \cdot 4H_2O(?)$

San Diego County: **1**, The new mineral stewartite was found as an abundant alteration product of lithiophilite in the Stewart mine at Pala. It was described and named by Schaller (29) p. 144.

STIBICONITE
Hydrous antimony oxide, $Sb^{3+}Sb^{5+}_2(O,OH,H_2O)_7$, Ca replacing Sb^{3+}

Stibiconite occurs as an alteration product of stibnite or native antimony.

Inyo County: **1**, The bright- or orange-yellow alteration product of stibnite in Wild Rose Canyon may be stibiconite, D. E. White (1) p. 317, and **2**, it has been doubtfully reported from Cerro Gordo, CDMG (8584).

Kern County: **1**, Stibiconite has been found with native antimony at Little Caliente Springs, CDMG (11671), and **2**, on Erskine Creek, Behre (1) p. 332.

San Benito County: **1**, Stibiconite has been reported from the Stayton mine, W. W. Bradley (28) p. 343, Anon. (39) p. 195.

San Bernardino County: **1**, An occurrence of stibiconite has been reported from the Old Woman Mountains, W. W. Bradley (28) p. 207. **2**, Stibiconite is questionably identified, with stibnite and cinnabar, from the Red Devil claim near Danby ($NW\frac{1}{4}$ T. 6 N., R. 18 E., S.B.), about 12 miles SE of Essex, G. W. Walker et al. (5) p. 24.

San Luis Obispo County: **1**, Stibiconite has been found with cervantite at the Marquart mine (T. 26 S., R. 9 E., M.D.), Eckel et al. (1) pp. 537, 543.

* STIBIOFERRITE—Stibiaferrite, 1873
Hydrous antimony/iron oxide and silicate, $Sb_2O_5 \cdot Fe_2O_3 \cdot SiO_2 \cdot H_2O \cdot$

Santa Clara County: **1**, A substance described as a new antimony mineral was found as a coating on stibnite at an unidentified location in the county, Goldsmith (3) p. 366. It was studied and named stibioferrite. See also Palache et al. (10) p. 599.

STIBIOTANTALITE
Niobate and tantalate of antimony, $Sb(Ta,Nb)O_4$

San Diego County: **1**, Stibiotantalite was found in small amounts in the pegmatite veins at Mesa Grande associated with gem tourmaline, pink beryl, quartz, orthoclase, lepidolite and cassiterite. It was described and analyzed by Penfield and Ford (8) p. 61. It was noted by Schaller (25) p. 352. Ungemach (1) p. 92, observes that stibiotantalite is not ismorphous with columbite. Stibiotantalite is listed as specimen No. 53-84-2 in University of Wisconsin Collections, and is reported in a paper on general investigation of columbium and tantalum minerals as "from Mesa Verde" (Table, p. 436), Hutchinson (1) p. 432. The correct locality is Mesa Grande (letter, Hutchinson to University of Wisconsin to Webb, from Harvard Collection, specimen No. 87843, 7/22/58). **2,** Stibiotantalite is very rare, but present in the pegmatites of Heriart Hill, Pala, Jahns and Wright (5) p. 31.

STIBNITE—Antimonite
Antimony sulphide, Sb₂S₃

Stibnite is the common ore of antimony, and numerous deposits of it exist in the State. It occurs generally as veins in granitic rocks and schists. In gold and copper regions stibnite is a common associate of galena, sphalerite, chalcopyrite, pyrite and tetrahedrite. It is characteristically associated with cinnabar.

Alameda County: **1,** Large masses of stibnite occur at Mount Oso, in the Mount Diablo Range, J. B. Trask (2) p. 94, (4) p. 390.

Alpine County: **1,** Stibnite occurs with pyrargyrite and proustite at the Exchequer mine, Silver Mountain, R. W. Raymond (9) p. 22.

Calaveras County: **1,** Stibnite has been observed with gold at Mokelumne Hill (N.R.), and **2,** with cinnabar at the Oro y Plata mine near Murphy, H. W. Turner and Ransome (18) p. 6.

Colusa County: **1,** Stibnite occurs with cinnabar and gold at the Manzanita mine, Becker (4) p. 367, Anon. (54) p. 30.

Contra Costa County: **1,** Stibnite occurs at the Mount Diablo quicksilver mine, with metacinnabar, C. P. Ross (2) p. 41, Pampeyan (1) p. 24. The mineral occurs as fine thread-like crystals associated with valentinite at the Mount Diablo quicksilver mine, Oyler (p.c. '61).

Inyo County: **1,** In the Cerro Gordo Mining District, stibnite was found with the silver-lead ores, and some limonite specimens from there seem to be pseudomorphs after long prismatic stibnite crystals (N.R.). The confirmation of stibnite at Cerro Gordo still is unobtained. It may be that this report, like metacinnabar, San Benito **(3),** is actually from San Benito County, and the locality is the Bradford (Cerro Gordo) mine, and that the entry was misplaced in Inyo County. **2,** Large bodies of stibnite with cervantite occur on the western slope of the Panamint Range near Wild Rose Springs, Crawford (1) p. 21. **3,** A large outcrop of stibnite occurs on the eastern slope of the Argus Mountains, between Revenue and Shepards Canyons, C. A. Waring and Huguenin (2) p. 60. **4,** Blades of stibnite up to 4 inches in length, partly oxidized to cervantite, are found in the Darwin Mining District, Kelley (4) p. 544, Hall and MacKevett (4) p. 79. **5,** Stibnite has been mined 4½ miles south of Bishop, Tucker and Sampson (32) p. 58. Bateman (3) p. 82, reports stibnite as "3½ miles SW of Bishop (SE cor. sec. 23, T. 7 S., R. 32 E., M.D.)". This is probably confirmation of the occurrence given by Tucker and Sampson (32). The stibnite occurs as localized stringers in a fault zone, sometimes with quartz and pyrite. **6,** Stibnite occurs as lenses and pods in limestone at the Old Dependable antimony mine (NE¼ T. 19 S., R. 45 E., M. D.), Norman and Stewart (2) p. 29, and 7, at the Rocket claim (sec. 29, T. 22 S., R. 43 E., M. D.), ibid., p. 84.

Kern County: 1, The deposits of stibnite in the San Emigdio Mountains at the head of San Emigdio Canyon (sec. 10, T. 9 N., R. 21 W., S.B.) have long been known and were the first worked in the state, W. P. Blake (7) p. 292, Angel (2) p. 225. 2, Veins of stibnite are plentiful in the mountains in the northeastern part of the county. On Erskine Creek stibnite has been found with native antimony, W. W. Bradley (11) pp. 21, 22. 3, Stibnite also occurs near Caliente, Boalich and Castello (2) p. 11; 4, in the Tom Moore mine, Clear Creek, W. W. Bradley (11) pp. 21, 22; 5, near Tehachapi, W. W. Bradley (11) p. 21; 6, near Kernville, Hanks (12) p. 375; 7, at Hot Springs; and 8, near Havilah, Watts (2) p. 237. 9, Minute spherulites of stibnite occur in kernite and borax near Kramer, Schaller (45) p. 165; 10, 30 miles west of Koehn (Cane) (secs. 5, 6, T. 30 S., R. 31 E., M. D.), G. C. Brown (1) p. 476; 11, near Amalie (sec. 34, T. 30 S., R. 32 E., M. D.), Tucker and Sampson (32) p. 61, and 12, rarely in Golden Queen mine, near Mojave, J. W. Bradley (p.c. '45) confirmed by Troxel and Morton (2) p. 54.

Lake County: 1, Stibnite has been found with cinnabar at Sulphur Bank on Clear Lake, W. P. Blake (29) p. 642, D. E. White and Roberson (2) p. 405. It is being deposited now, C. P. Ross (3) p. 339, (5) p. 451, Everhart (1) p. 139.

Los Angeles County: 1, Stibnite has been found in the mountains south of Lancaster, Aubury (3) p. 359, and 2, in Pacoima Canyon, with cobalt-nickel ores, Tucker (13) p. 288.

Merced County: 1, Fine specimens of prismatic stibnite have come from the Stayton (McLeod) Mining District (sec. 32, T. 11 S., R. 7 E., M. D.), Laizure (3) p. 175, and 2, from the Red Metal mine (sec. 32, T. 11 S., R. 7 E., M. D.), Irelan (3) p. 350.

Mono County: 1, Stibnite is common in the Blind Spring Mining District, associated with the silver-lead ores, and good specimens have come from the Comanche, Comet and Diana mines, Loew (1) p. 653. 2, Stibnite occurs in Bloody Canyon (T. 1 S., R. 25 E., M. D.), Hanks (12) p. 375.

Monterey County: 1, Stibnite occurs at Los Burros mines (sec. 1, T. 24 S., R. 5 E., M. D.), Preston (4) p. 261.

Napa County: 1: Fibrous bands of stibnite occurred with cinnabar at the Manhattan and the Boston or old Redington mines at Knoxville, W. W. Bradley (5) p. 86.

Nevada County: 1, Stibnite occurs with galena in quartz at the Red Ledge mine, E. MacBoyle (1) p. 67, and 2, in the Mohawk antimony mine near Nevada City, ibid., pp. 13, 67.

Orange County: 1, Stibnite occurs with galena and sphalerite in the Dunlap mine, head of Santiago Canyon, Hanks (14) p. 119.

Placer County: 1, Stibnite occurs with gold-bearing quartz in the St. Laurence mine, Ophir Mining District, C. A. Waring (4) p. 350.

Riverside County: 1, Stibnite is reported from the Wet Weather quarry, Crestmore, Woodford et al. (10) p. 369. 2, Fine-grained stibnite was found near Corona, F. J. H. Merrill (2) p. 524. **3,** Stibnite occurs in Mabey Canyon, Tucker and Sampson (32) p. 65.

San Benito County: **1,** There are numerous veins of stibnite in association with the cinnabar deposits, especially in the northeastern part of the county. Fine crystallized specimens have come from the Rip Van Winkle, Alta, Gleason and Shriver claims on Antimony Peak, northeast of Hollister, Hanks (12) p. 374, Crawford (1) p. 22. Some of the good crystals were measured by Eakle (9) p. 231. **2,** Long divergent prisms of stibnite have come from the Blue Wing vein of the Stayton quicksilver mine, Aubury (2) p. 148.

San Bernardino County: **1,** Stibnite was found in a boulder at the Centennial mine, Hanks (12) p. 375, De Groot (1) p. 461. **2,** A small vein of stibnite associated with wolframite was found on Clark Mountain, Hess (14) p. 49, Tucker and Sampson (16) p. 204; **3,** it occurred with scheelite at Atolia, Hess (14) p. 49, Lemmon and Dorr (4) p. 219, and **4,** in large crystals in the silver ores of the Rand Mining District, Hulin (1) p. 99. **5,** Stibnite is present with wolframite at the Sagamore mine, New York Mountains, Aubury (4) p. 332. **6,** The mineral is found occasionally at the Calico mines with realgar, Weeks (2) p. 768. **7,** Stibnite is reported from the Desert Antimony mine (sec. 18, T. 16 N., R. 14 E., S. B.), $2\frac{1}{2}$ miles east of Mountain Pass, L. A. Wright et al. (5) p. 60.

San Luis Obispo County: **1,** Stibnite occurs near the head of the San Simeon Creek, Logan (3) p. 676. **2,** Radiating prisms of stibnite in quartz occur near Cambria, CDMG (13827). **3,** Beautiful crystalline stibnite with pyrite in quartz occurs on the South Fork of San Simeon Creek, near the summit of the Santa Lucia Range (N. R.).

Santa Clara County: **1,** Large divergent columnar masses of stibnite have come from near Gilroy, Hanks (12) p. 375. **2,** Stibnite is an associate of cinnabar at the New Almaden quicksilver mines (Stanford Collection), E. H. Bailey and Everhart (12) p. 98, and **3,** the mineral occurs at Pacheco Pass, Hanks (12) p. 375.

Sierra County: **1,** Stibnite occurs with the gold ores at Downieville, CDMG (7101).

Trinity County: **1,** Stibnite is found near T. 38 N., R. 6 W., M. D., W. P. Miller (1) p. 716.

Tulare County: **1,** Stibnite is found in the Mineral King Mining District as an associate of argentiferous galena in quartz with pyrite in the Dennison Mountains, and **2,** in a quartz vein cutting slate at the Lady Alice mine, a quarter of a mile south of Mineral King, Hanks (12) p. 375, Franke (1) p. 431.

STILBITE
Hydrous sodium calcium potassium aluminum silicate,
$(Ca,Na_2K_2)(Al_2Si_7O_{18}) \cdot 7H_2O$

Stellerite and *epidesmine* are varietal names of certain types of stilbite. Stilbite is a common zeolite occurring usually as sheaf-like aggregates in cavities and seams of volcanic rock.

Inyo County: **1,** Stilbite crystals occur in platy calcite from the Cardinal mine, Middle Fork, Bishop Creek, Murdoch (p.c. '51).

Los Angeles County: **1,** Stilbite occurs with heulandite, as sheaves and platy crystals up to 8 cm long, a quarter of a mile west of Acton, Murdoch and Webb (6) p. 352. **2,** Sheaf-like aggregates of tabular crystals of stilbite occur at locality 6, Coldwater Canyon, Neuerburg (1) p. 158. **3,** Stilbite is very widespread on fractures in dioritic rocks in the region of the Vincent cutoff, Angeles Crest Highway, Neuerburg (p.c. '53).

Madera County: **1,** Straw-yellow radiating aggregates of stilbite up to 6 mm long occur in piemontite-bearing metavolcanic rock about 0.1 mile northeast of Shadow Lake. The stilbite is associated with heulandite, calcite and quartz. The identification is confirmed by x-ray methods, Alfors (p.c. '64).

Modoc County: **1,** Specimens of lava with amygdules filled with stilbite and natrolite have come from this county, CDMG (10258).

Plumas County: **1,** White and brown stilbite occurs with chabazite and natrolite in the cavities of basic rock at Engles, A. Knopf and Anderson (12) p. 30. **2,** Stilbite occurs as coatings or sheaves, in veins with apatite, south of and near the Superior mine, C. A. Anderson (6) p. 313.

Riverside County: **1,** Translucent stilbite occurs with phillipsite in garnet rock at Crestmore, Woodford et al. (10) pp. 362, 374.

San Bernardino County: **1,** Tabular stilbite crystals in lava cavities occur on Opal Mountain (T. 32 S., R. 45 E., M. D.), Lackie (p.c. '43).

San Diego County: **1,** Stilbite occurs as sheaf-like aggregates of small brown crystals at the Victor mine near Rincon, A. F. Rogers (4) p. 213. **2,** Stilbite appears occasionally in some of the gem-bearing pegmatites at Pala, Schaller (p.c. '35) confirmed by Jahns and Wright (5) p. 42. **3,** Stellerite, which according to Pabst (5) p. 271, is the same as stilbite, has been found in cavities of the igneous rock at the Calavera quarry, E. S. Larsen and Switzer (16) p. 567. **4,** Stellerite has been recorded as abundant in irregular veins in a quartz latite stock at the head of the south fork of San Onofre Creek, E. S. Larsen (17) p. 111. **5,** Stilbite is found in veins in granodiorite boulders in Fish Creek wash, 2 or 3 miles south of the Fish Creek Mountains gypsum deposit, Murdoch (p.c. '48).

Santa Barbara County: **1,** Stilbite was found in the San Pablo Mountains of Santa Rosa Island, CDMG (12295).

Sonoma County: **1,** Stellerite is reported from near the Devil's Pulpit, The Geysers, on the ridge above the bluff, Vonsen (6) p. 292.

Tulare County: **1,** Stilbite occurs in volcanic rock at Mount Kaweah (N. R.).

STILPNOMELANE

Hydrous basic iron magnesium calcium potassium sodium manganese aluminum silicate, $(K,Na,Ca)_{0-1.4}(Fe^{3+},Fe^{2+},Mg,Al,Mn)_{5.9-8.2}Si_8O_{20}(OH)_4$-$(O,OH,H_2O)_{3.6-8.5}$

Chalcodite is a rare brown variety, occurring in minute scales, often with a bronze luster.

Inyo County: **1,** Stilpnomelane has been reported to occur as bronze-brown flakes on analcite and natrolite in the amygdules of an andesite in the Furnace Creek wash, 2 miles west of Ryan. Foshag (p.c. '47), however, thinks its identiy is quite doubtful, and suggests that the material is celadonite or chlorite.

Kern County: **1,** Stilpnomelane is reported by Hewett et al. (6) p. 54, in the manganese ores of the Big Indian deposit (sec. 11, T. 30 S., R. 40 E., M. D.).

Marin County: **1,** Stilpnomelane is a common constituent of meta-cherts on Tiburon Peninsula, Rice (p.c. '55).

Mendocino County: **1,** Golden-brown stilpnomelane occurs rather abundantly in a quarry 5.1 miles north of Longvale on U.S. 101, in glaucophane schist with riebeckite and lawsonite, Watters (p.c. '58).

Merced County: **1,** Stilpnomelane is commonly associated with law-sonite and aragonite as brown flakes in Franciscan rocks of the Pacheco Pass area. It is sometimes found with pumpellyite, McKee (2) p. 384; see also Santa Clara County **(3)**.

San Benito County: **1,** Stilpnomelane occurs as bronze-colored plates in metamorphosed chert at the north end of Glaucophane ridge, Chesterman (p.c. '55).

Santa Barbara County: **1,** Brown crystals of "chalcodite" have come from this county, CDMG (11533).

Santa Clara County: **1,** Stilpnomelane has been reported in some of the glaucophane schists of the New Almaden region, Hutton (1) p. 1373. **2,** The mineral is reported by Hutton (4) p. 608, from the San Juan Bautista mine (Hillsdale mine) southeast of San Jose, Oak Hill area. **3,** Brown stilpnomelane is occasionally associated with pumpel-lyite, aragonite and lawsonite in Franciscan rocks of the Pacheco Pass area, McKee (2) p. 384; see also Merced County **(1)**.

Tulare County: **1,** Brown plates of stilpnomelane occur in metachert associated with a pale-blue amphibole (sec. 18, T. 19 S., R. 27 E., S. B.), 0.3 mile east of Lindsay Peak. The identification is confirmed by x-ray methods, Alfors (p.c. '64).

STOLZITE
Lead tungstate, $PbWO_4$

Inyo County: **1,** Bunches of crystals of stolzite, coated with tungstite, were found in the Thompson mine at Darwin, Tucker and Sampson (30) p. 567, CDMG (21074). The validity of this occurrence of stolzite is questioned, since a study of ore which appears to be from the Darwin locality shows no stolzite, but only scheelite, Hall and MacKevett (1) p. 59.

STRENGITE
Hydrous iron phosphate, $FePO_4 \cdot 2H_2O$

See also *metastrengite.*

Amador County: **1,** Strengite was described by Hulin (3) p. 351 as occurring with apatite in the deep levels of the Kennedy mine.

San Diego County: **1,** Blue fibrous strengite (?) occurred with sal-monsite in the Stewart mine at Pala, Schaller (29) p. 145.

STROMEYERITE
Silver copper sulphide, $(Ag,Cu)_2S$

Alpine County: **1,** Stromeyerite was observed in the Monitor mining region, Crawford (1) p. 373, Eakle (16) p. 13.

El Dorado County: **1,** Stromeyerite was tentatively identified in the Winton and Threlkil prospect (SE¼ sec. 17, T. 11 N., R. 8 E., M. D.), Logan (19) p. 225.

Inyo County: **1,** The Silver Queen and other mines of the Panamint Range contained stromeyerite associated with tetrahedrite and cerargyrite (N. R.). The mineral was found: **2,** in the Cerro Gordo, Irelan (4) p. 47, **3,** Wild Rose area, Crawford (1) pp. 373, 374, and **4,** in the White Mountains and the Inyo Range, at various places, according to Aaron, Hanks (12) p. 375.

Kern County: **1,** Stromeyerite has been reported from the gold ores of the Mojave Mining District, Troxel and Morton (2) p. 44.

Mono County: **1,** Stromeyerite occurs with tetrahedrite in the silver ores of the Blind Spring Mining District, where it is the principal secondary silver mineral, Fairbanks (15) p. 151, R. J. Sampson (14) p. 172.

Riverside County: **1,** "Copper-silver glance," perhaps stromeyerite, was found at the Homestake group 8 miles northwest of McCoy Springs, Palen Mountains, Aubury (1) p. 257.

San Bernardino County: **1,** Stromeyerite occurred as one of the numerous minerals of the Calico Mining District and an analysis of it from the Silver King mine was made by Melville and Lindgren (1) p. 27. **2,** The mineral occurred with cerargyrite and oxidized ores in the Clarke Mountains, G. M. Wheeler (3) p. 53.

Sierra County: **1,** A specimen of stromeyerite came from the original 16 to 1 mine, Alleghany (N. R.).

STRONTIANITE
Strontium carbonate, $SrCO_3$

Inyo County: **1,** A deposit of brown massive strontianite occurs 3 miles west of Shoshone, CDMG (19440-D).

Kern County: **1,** Strontianite occurs in the tin deposits of the Gorman area, Troxel and Morton (2) p. 294.

Los Angeles County: **1,** Strontianite, as compact masses and slender needles in colemanite, has been found at the Sterling borax mine, Tick Canyon, Murdoch (p.c. '63).

Plumas County: **1,** Large masses of divergent columnar strontianite were found in the Genessee Valley, CDMG (15350).

Riverside County: **1,** Strontianite occurs sparsely as white tufted fibers in minute balls, on a joint surface of rock in the Lone Star quarry at Crestmore, Woodford et al. (10) p. 374.

San Bernardino County: **1,** Large deposits of strontianite occur as brown fibrous and gray granular masses in limestone in the Mud Hills (Strontium Hills) (secs. 20, 30, T. 11 N., R. 1, 2 W., S. B.), 10 miles north of Barstow, A. Knopf (9) p. 257, B. N. Moore (1) p. 376, Durrell (8) p. 23. Celestite and gypsum are associated in this deposit. It also occurs here in fan-shaped or spherical aggregates up to 3 inches in size, in clay beds. **2,** Strontianite is relatively common as yellow-brown drusy coatings lining cavities in limestone which carry celestite and colemanite, at Borate in the Calico Hills, Murdoch (p.c. '45). This is probably the same material mentioned by Silliman (12) p. 130, as aragonite, presumably from Calico. **3,** A small deposit of strontianite is found also in the Calico Hills about halfway down hill on the road from Borate to Yermo, Murdoch (p.c. '45).

San Diego County: **1,** Strontianite is reported from the Lost Canyon mine 5 miles northwest of Jacumba, Tucker and Reed (26) p. 52.

*SULPHOHALITE, 1888
Sodium sulphate with chlorine and fluorine, $Na_6(SO_4)_2ClF$

San Bernardino County: **1,** Sulphohalite was first discovered in 1888, as small crystals implanted on hanksite at Searles Lake, and was described and named by Hidden and MacKintosh (2) p. 464. It was analyzed by Penfield (5) p. 425, and by Hicks, H. S. Gale and Hicks (7) p. 273. The crystals are cubo-octahedrons, Foshag (21) p. 51, or occasionally simple octahedrons, H. S. Gale and Hicks (7) p. 273, H. S. Gale (13) p. 307, Foshag (4) p. 76, Pabst et al. (21) pp. 485–510, G. I. Smith and Pratt (2) p. 27, G. I. Smith and Haines (3) p. P19.

SULPHUR
Native sulphur, S

Yellow sulphur is common in the vicinity of geysers, hot springs and volcanoes. It is also found in gypsum beds, and in association with borax.

Alpine County: **1,** Sulphur occurs in brecciated tuff and is commercially produced at the Leviathan mine, 7 miles east of Markleeville, W. W. Bradley (21) p. 183, Gary (1) p. 495, Pabst (6) p. 425.

Colusa County: **1,** On the banks of Sulphur Creek, solfataric action has produced fine crystallized masses and granular coatings of sulphur, sometimes in association with cinnabar, Fairbanks (6) p. 121. **2,** Good specimens have come from the Manzanita mine, W. W. Bradley (19) p. 196, and **3,** from the Elgin mine, Goodyear (4) pp. 157, 159, Fairbanks (6) p. 121, W. W. Bradley (10) p. 678; the latter mine also produced a small commercial output of sulphur.

Imperial County: **1,** The solfataric vents near Niland have rims of sulphur crystals and salt. They have been described by Hanks (9) p. 231. **2,** A small sulphur deposit occurs on the eastern slope of Coyote Mountain (SE¼ sec. 6, T. 16 S., R. 10 E., S. B.), F. J. H. Merrill (1) p. 741, Tucker (11) p. 284, and **3,** another is 8 miles north of Iris siding on the Southern Pacific Railroad, Tucker (11) p. 285. **4,** Sulphur is found with claudetite and realgar 6 miles north of the 4S Ranch, Kelley (1) p. 137.

Inyo County: **1,** A deposit of sulphur occurs at Sulphur Bank on Owens Lake, near Olancha, Loew (1) p. 652. **2,** Sulphur has been found with fluorite and gypsum is the Defiance mine, Darwin, CDMG (7601), Hall and MacKevitt (4) p. 64. **3,** Sulphur deposited by solfataric action occurs in an area of several acres, 9 miles east of Coso Junction, Loew (3) p. 195, Tucker (11) p. 523. **4,** A small deposit of sulphur is reported in the mountains east of Big Pine, Tucker and Sampson (25) p. 487, Lynton (1) p. 575. **5,** A number of deposits of sulphur in limestone occur in the Last Chance Range (sec. 15, T. 9 S., R. 34 l., M. D.), Tucker (4) p. 300.

Kern County: **1,** On both sides of the San Joaquin Valley impure beds of gypsum and limestone occur, having considerable sulphur intermixed, Watts (2) p. 233. **2**, Sulphur occurs with alum in the Sunset area, Watts (3) p. 33.

Lake County: **1**, An interesting deposit of sulphur at the Sulphur Bank quicksilver mine on Clear Lake was described by J. Le Conte and Rising (1) p. 26, Becker (4) p. 255. The black basaltic rock which outcrops on the lake has been bleached white and altered to a porous mass of silica by the action of fumes coming from several vents. Brilliant crystals of sulphur and acicular crystals of cinnabar have formed in the pores and cavities of this altered mass of rock. Stalactites of sulphur were found in crevices, J. A. Phillips (1) p. 422. Sulphur was obtained in considerable quantity commercially from this deposit before it was found to overlie a richer deposit of cinnabar, D. E. White and Roberson (2) p. 403. **2**, Sulphur also occurred with borax at Little Borax Lake, just south of Clear Lake (N. R.).

Mariposa County: **1**, Crystals of sulphur have been found with cinnabar on Horseshoe Bend Mountain, near Coulterville (N. R.).

Mono County: **1**, Sulphur occasionally occurs in large balls filling cavities in the andalusite ore at the mine of Champion Sillimanite on the western slope of the White Mountains, 7 miles east of Mocalno, north of Bishop, Melhase (1) p. 92, R. J. Sampson and Tucker (4) p. 461.

Monterey County: **1**, Sulphur occurs with cinnabar in pockets in sandstone at the Parkfield mine (sec. 35, T. 22 S., R. 14 E., M. D.), Aubury (2) p. 123. **2**, "Large mines or beds" of sulphur were reported in 1847, 25 miles north of Monterey, Sloat (1) p. 366.

San Bernardino County: **1**, Sulphur occurs at Searles Lake as one of the many minerals associated with borax, J. H. Pratt (1) p. 124. **2**, Sulphur occurs in lenticular masses of mixed sulphates in the Calico Hills, at the "sulphur hole," Borate, Foshag (19) p. 352.

Santa Barbara County: **1**, Sulphur crystals occur at Point Rincon, and on the north side of Graciosa Ridge, south of the Santa Maria Valley, at openings caused by the escape of gases from burnt shales, Martinez (1) p. 39, Duflot de Mofras (1) p. 196, Antisell (1) p. 67, H. C. Ford (1) p. 53, Arnold (2) p. 13, Arnold and Anderson (3) p. 751. **2**, Free sulphur is found in sediments of the Channel Islands, P. D. Trask and Wu (3) p. 89. **3**, Sulphur deposits are reported in the Azur Mountains, D. T. Day (2) p. 864.

Shasta County: **1**, Sulphur occurs in the gossans of the copper belt, L. C. Raymond (1) p. 414, and **2**, at Bumpass Hell and Supan Springs in Lassen Volcanic National Park, A. L. Day and Allen (1) p. 120.

Siskiyou County: **1**, Crystals of sulphur and gypsum are abundant at the spring near the summit of Mount Shasta, H. Williams (2) p. 240.

Sonoma County: **1**, Sulphur is found at The Geysers, Laizure (4) p. 365. **2**, As early as 1847, pure masses of sulphur weighing as much as 1 pound were found near the town of Sonoma, Sloat (1) p. 366.

Ventura County: **1**, Deposits of sulphur occur on Sulphur Mountain 3 miles east of Fillmore, CDMG (14592).

Yolo County: **1**, Sulphur occurs with cinnabar in decomposed serpentine at the New England mine (sec. 26, T. 12 N., R. 5 W., M. D.), Aubury (2) p. 117.

SVANBERGITE
Basic strontium aluminum sulphate phosphate, $SrAl_3PO_4SO_4(OH)_6$

Mono County: **1,** Brown svanbergite associated with lazulite and quartz occurs at the White Mountain andalusite deposit, north of Bishop. Identification was confirmed by x-ray, CDMG.

SYLVANITE
Gold silver telluride, $(Au,Ag)Te_4$

Though sylvanite may be present in many of the gold areas where tellurium is found, it has been identified from few localities in California.

Calaveras County: **1,** Sylvanite was one of the tellurides occurring in the Carson Hill mines and was especially prominent in the Melones and Stanislaus mines, and also occurred in the Morgan mine, Silliman (9) p. 378, J. R. Browne (4) p. 62, Hanks (12) pp. 384, 388. An analysis of sylvanite from the Stanislaus mine was made by Mathewson (1) p. 274.

Siskiyou County: **1,** Sylvanite was incorrectly identified from the Quartz Hill mine by Averill (3) p. 49; he later identified the mineral as tetradymite.

Trinity County: **1,** Sylvanite has been found with gold in the Yellow Jacket mine (N. R.); **2,** with nagyagite at the Dorleska mine, Coffee Mining District, Stines (1) p. 25; **3,** in the Gold Jubilee mine, 5 miles northwest of Carrville, Averill (3) p. 39; and **4,** at the Yellow Aster mine, with petzite, Mining and Scientific Press (34) p. 473.

Tuolumne County: **1,** Sylvanite occurs with petzite in the Sugarman and Nigger mine, 2 miles north of Sonora (sec. 30 T. 2 N., R. 15 E., M. D.), Logan (23) p. 72. **2,** Brilliant crystalline plates of sylvanite have come from the Rawhide Ranch near Junction, Silliman (9) p. 378, and **3,** from the Golden Rule mine, ibid.

Yuba County: **1,** Sylvanite occurs with gold in the Red Ravine mine, Dobbins Mining District (sec. 30 T. 18 N., R. 7 E., M. D.), C. A. Waring (4) p. 453.

SYLVITE
Potassium chloride, KCl

Inyo County: **1,** Sylvite was identified in saline crusts and from efflorescences in Deep Spring Lake, B. F. Jones (1) p. B200.

SZAIBELYITE
Basic magnesium borate, $MgBO_2OH$

Marin County: **1,** Szaibelyite occurs as impregnations and coatings on serpentine near Stinson Beach. It was first observed and analyzed by Eakle (24) p. 100, who considered it to be camsellite. Schaller (44) p. 230, suggested the identity of camsellite and szaibelyite, and Watanabe (1) p. 454, has reported the identity of camsellite from California, with szaibelyite from Leopoldshall, Germany. Schaller (53) p. 470, has shown definitely that szaibelyite =(ascharite, camsellite, beta ascharite).

SZOMOLNOKITE—Ferropallidite
$FeSO_4 \cdot H_2O$

Trinity County: **1,** Brown pyramidal crystals of szomolnokite have been found at the Island Mountain copper deposit, Foshag (p.c. '46).

TALC
Basic magnesium silicate, $Mg_3Si_4O_{10}(OH)_2$

Soapstone (steatite) is a compact to coarse granular, grayish-green to brownish-gray variety.

Talc is common in the metamorphic rocks of the State, forming talc schists. It occurs as a hydration product in the alteration of magnesian silicates, and is often associated with serpentine and with actinolite.

Talc is widespread in many parts of the state. Occurrences of the mineral are very numerous, but few have mineralogical significance. As a mineral resource, talc occurs in considerable quantity in many deposits. In the localities referenced below, no attempt has been made to systematically report commodity occurrences, nor to report the mineral wherever it is mentioned in the literature. Some localities of minor importance and of little general mineralogical interest are noted because they have been carried in early editions of *Minerals of California*. The authors consider it wise to retain these as part of the historical record, but newer and more important localities of the mineral as a mineral resource have not been added, and literature citations to articles on such localities have not necessarily been included.

Alameda County: **1,** Talc pseudomorphs after actinolite occur on Apperson Creek, southeast of Sunol, A. F. Rogers (3) p. 19.

Amador County: **1,** Pure steatite is abundant on the Van Dusen Ranch near Newtonville, Engineering and Mining Journal (4) p. 148.

Calaveras County: **1,** Talc occurs in many parts of the Calaveritas quadrangle, and from some areas it has been marketed in very small amounts, L. D. Clark (1) p. 17.

El Dorado County: **1,** Good-quality steatite was worked for the first time in the county near Webber Creek (Darlington soapstone), J. R. Browne (4) p. 82, Logan (9) p. 45.

Imperial County: **1,** A selvage of talc occurs along the kyanite deposit of the Vitrefax Corporation 4 miles northeast of Ogilby, an abandoned railroad station 10 miles west of Winterhaven, Melhase (1) p. 94. This is thought to be mica schist from the Bluebird mine and not talc as reported, Foster (p.c. '58).

Inyo County: **1,** A number of valuable deposits of talc occur in this county, along the contact of limestones and intrusive rocks: Sierra and Acme Talc (secs. 32, 33, T. 18 S., R. 40 E., M. D.), Tucker (4) p. 300, R. J. Sampson (11) p. 269; **2,** Simonds, 17 miles southeast of Keeler, C. A. Waring and Huguenin (2) p. 126; **3,** Tramway, 3½ miles northwest of Keeler, Tucker (4) p. 301, and **4,** 8 miles southwest of Zabriskie, Diller, (13) p. 158. Detailed discussion of talc deposits in Inyo County is found in B. M. Page (1), L. A. Wright (7), Chidester et al. (1) p. 27, Bateman (3) p. 83. **5,** Massive talc (variety *amesite*) is mined as "pyrophyllite" at the Frisco mine near Darwin, Hall and MacKevett (4) p. 81. **6,** Talc deposits occur from the southern end of Death Valley eastward to the Kingston Range, Chidester et al. (1) p. 26. **7,** Talc is mined six miles north of Darwin, in the Talc City Hills, Hall and MacKevett (4) p. 80. This may be the same locality as **(2)** above.

Los Angeles County: **1,** A deposit of steatite on Santa Catalina Island was used by the Indians to make soapstone kettles and other artifacts, Schumacher (2) pp. 117–121.

Madera County: **1,** Talc schists, which can be sawed into blocks, occur on the north side of the San Joaquin River above Friant, R. P. McLaughlin and Bradley (3) p. 559.

Riverside County: **1,** Talc is tentatively identified from the Wet Weather quarry, Crestmore, Woodford et al. (10) p. 369.

San Bernardino County: **1,** A large deposit of talc occurs near Silver Lake (T. 17 N., R. 10 E., S. B.), Diller (13) p. 159, Tucker (4) p. 368. **2,** The southern end of a series of talc deposits occurs near Yucca Grove, Chidester et al. (1) p. 25. A general discussion of occurrences is found in L. A. Wright (6).

Shasta County: **1,** A good grade of white talc occurs $2\frac{1}{2}$ miles north of Whiskeytown (secs. 5, 8, 15, T. 32 N., R. 6 W., M. D.), Logan (9) p. 210.

Sierra County: **1,** Blocks of soapstone for hoist foundations have been quarried at the Alaska mine near Pike City, Averill (11) p. 49.

References to other less important occurrences of talc, listed by counties, are: *Amador,* Tucker (1) p. 53; *Butte,* Stoddard (3) p. 162, L. L. Root (6) p. 210; *Calaveras,* H. W. Turner (4) p. 471, Tucker (1) p. 131; *El Dorado,* Logan (4) pp. 432, 433; *Glenn,* W. W. Bradley (1) p. 199; *Inyo,* Tucker and Sampson (25) pp. 492, 493, 495, Diller (13) p. 159; *Los Angeles,* E. C. Simpson (1) p. 414; *Mariposa,* Hanks (15) p. 137; *Riverside,* (with tremolite asbestos) F. J. H. Merrill (2) p. 552; *San Bernardino,* Tucker (4) p. 367, Tucker and Sampson (33) p. 131, E. Sampson (1) p. 98; *Siskiyou,* G. C. Brown (2) p. 871; *Trinity,* G. C. Brown (2) p. 924; *Yuba,* C. A. Waring (4) p. 458.

TARAMELLITE
Basic barium iron magnesium titano-silicate,
$Ba_2(Fe^{3+},Fe^{2+},Ti,Mg)_2O_2(Si_4O_{10})(OH)_2$

Fresno County: **1,** Reddish-brown crystals of taramellite, associated with coarse-grained sanbornite, quartz, witherite, pyrrhotite and diopside, occur near Rush Creek (sec. 16, T. 11 S., R. 25 E., S. B.), Matthews and Alfors (1) p. 2, CDMG (21782). **2,** At Big Creek (sec. 22, T. 11 S., R. 25 E., S. B.), taramellite with gillespite and sanbornite, together with eight or more unidentified, possibly new, minerals, occurs in quartz sulphide-bearing rocks, Anon. (48) p. 11, Stinson and Alfors (6) p. 235, Alfors and Stinson (5) p. 27, CDMG (21881).

Mariposa County: **1,** Taramellite has been identified at the sanbornite locality near Incline, Matthews and Alfors (1) p. 1.

Santa Cruz County: **1,** Taramellite has been found at the Pacific Limestone Products (Kalkar) quarry near Santa Cruz. Chesterman (p.c. '64).

TARANAKITE—Minervite
Hydrous basic potassium aluminum phosphate, near $KAl_3(PO_4)_3(OH)\cdot8\frac{1}{2}H_2O$

San Francisco County: **1,** Taranakite (reported as minervite), a phosphate not heretofore reported from California, occurs in a cave on the South Farallon Island off the Golden Gate, Hanna (2) p. 308.

*TEEPLEITE, 1938
Hydrous sodium borate with chlorine, $Na_2BO_2Cl\cdot2H_2O$

Lake County: **1,** Teepleite, a new California mineral, occurs with trona and halite in Borax Lake, near Clear Lake. It was found and named by W. A. Gale and Vonsen, W. W. Bradley (26) p. 297, W. A. Gale et al. (1) p. 48, analysis by Foshag, ibid., p. 50.

San Bernardino County: **1,** Teepleite has been recently found in lower layers of the beds at Searles Lake, Sawyer, cited by G. I. Smith and Haines (3) p. 20.

TELLURIUM
Native tellurium, Te

Native tellurium is sometimes found in association with the tellurides of gold, silver, lead and bismuth. It is occasionally found in the gold concentrates when not visible in the ore, and has been thus reported from some of the mining regions of the State.

Butte County: **1,** Tellurium was reported to have occurred in a cavity in a fragment of unrounded coarse gold washed from gravel, H. W. Turner (19) p. 424.

Calaveras County: **1,** Foliated masses of native tellurium with the gold tellurides occurred in the old Stanislaus and Melones mines, Genth (5) p. 312, Silliman (9) p. 379, Küstel (2) p. 128. **2,** Foliated tellurium was reported to have been found in one of the mines at Angels Camp, Genth (5) p. 312, Silliman (9) p. 379.

Mariposa County: **1,** Tellurium has been found at the Josephine and Pine Tree mines at Mariposa, Silliman (9) p. 9.

Shasta County: **1,** Native tellurium was found in the Eureka mine, near Redding (N. R.).

Tuolumne County: **1,** Some native tellurium has been found associated with tellurides of gold and silver in the mines near Tuttletown and Jamestown, Silliman (9) p. 379, Hanks (12) p. 388, H. W. Turner (19) p. 427.

TENORITE—Melaconite
Copper oxide, CuO

The massive material is frequently called *melaconite*.

Bornite, chalcocite, chalcopyrite, cuprite, galena, marcasite, pyrite, pyrrhotite, stibnite, tenorite, tetrahedrite, and many other antimony, copper, iron, lead and zinc sulfides, and oxides are found in traces or in minor amounts in many localities. The entries listed reflect either mineralogical or historic interest, and the listings are not complete nor is all literature which mentions these minerals referenced.

Alpine County: **1,** Melaconite was reported by Conkling (1) p. 184, from the Monitor area, Aubury (1) p. 115.

Calaveras County: **1,** Tenorite is a common alteration product of chalcopyrite at Copperopolis, J. D. Whitney (7) p. 255. **2,** The mineral occurs at Campo Seco, Hanks (12) p. 260.

Colusa County: **1,** Tenorite was found in serpentine with native copper and cuprite at the Gray Eagle mine, Aubury (4) p. 159.

Del Norte County: **1,** Tenorite occurred with chalcopyrite at the Alta and Pearl mines, Diamond Creek Mining District, Aubury (1) p. 115.

El Dorado County: **1,** "Gray oxide" was found on the Bryant Ranch (sec. 2, T. 8 N., R. 9 E., M.D.), Aubury (1) p. 180.

Fresno County: **1,** Tenorite has been reported from Pine Flat, 10 miles east of Letcher, Crawford (2) p. 58.

Inyo County: **1,** Tenorite has been found in the mines of the ghost town of Greenwater on the east slope of the Black Mountains, C. A. Waring and Huguenin (2) p. 70. **2,** Tenorite has been identified in the oxidized ores of the Darwin mines, Hall and MacKevett (4) p. 64.

Kern County: **1,** Tenorite was found with sulphides at the Greenback mine, Woody Mining District, Storms (13) p. 635, and **2,** it is reported from the San Emidio (Emigdio) Ranch, Hanks (12) p. 259.

Mariposa County: **1,** A large mass of melaconite was mined at the White Rock Copper King (sec. 14, T. 7 S., R. 17 E., M.D.), Aubury (1) p. 210. **2,** Considerable "black oxide" came from the Buchanan mine, Hunters Valley, J. R. Browne (4) p. 213.

Mendocino County: **1,** Tenorite occurs with sulphides and carbonates at the Redwood Copper Queen (secs. 17, 20, T. 12 N., R. 13 W., M.D.), Aubury (1) p. 137.

San Bernardino County: **1,** Melaconite has been found at several localities: Silver Mountain, Old Dad Mountains, New York Mountains, Cloudman et al. (1) pp. 784, 790.

San Diego County: **1,** Some melaconite was found at the Barona copper mine (T. 14 S., R. 1 E., S.B.), Aubury (1) p. 260.

Shasta County: **1,** Tenorite has been recorded from the Afterthought mine, Hanks (12) p. 260.

TEPHROITE
Manganese silicate, Mn$_2$SiO$_4$

Amador County: **1,** Tephroite occurs with other manganese minerals, including alleghanyite, at the Germolis prospect near Fiddletown (SE$\frac{1}{4}$ sec. 9, T. 7 N., R. 11 E., M.D.), Hewett et al. (6) p. 49. **2,** The mineral is in nodules with other manganese ores at the Lubanko prospect (SE$\frac{1}{4}$ sec. 10, T. 7 N., R. 11, E., M.D.). Alleghanyite is also associated, Hewett et al. (6) p. 49.

Butte County: **1,** Tephroite was observed in specimens from the Benet prospect (sec. 34, T. 20 N., R. 7 E., M.D.), and **2,** from the nearby Bear Canyon mine (S$\frac{1}{2}$ sec. 34, T. 20 N., R. 7 E., M.D.), with other manganese minerals, Hewett et al. (6) pp. 45–46.

Calaveras County: **1,** Tephroite occurs in the Kellogg mine (sec. 4, T. 2 N., R. 12 E., M.D.), seven miles west of Altaville, Hewett et al. (6) p. 51.

Kern County: **1,** Tephroite occurs in the Big Indian manganese deposit (sec. 11, T. 30 S., R. 40 E., M.D.), two miles south of Randsburg, Hewett et al. (6) p. 52, CDMG (21736).

Mariposa County: **1,** Microcrystals of plumose tephroite occur with bementite and other manganese minerals at the Caldwell (Daly) mine (NE$\frac{1}{4}$ sec. 14, T. 3 S., R. 15 E., M.D.), six miles southwest of Coulterville and one mile north of the Merced River, Hewett et al. (6) p. 51.

Nevada County: **1,** Tephroite was observed in the ores of the Manga-Chrome (Duggan) mine (sec. 17, T. 14 N., R. 8 E., M.D.), Hewett et al. (6) p. 47, and **2,** it occurs on the dumps with hausmannite at the Smith prospect (center sec. 2, T. 14 N., R. 8 E., M.D.), Hewett et al. (6) p. 48.

San Diego County: **1,** Tephroite has been found with quartz and garnet in a quartzite boulder near the summit of San Onofre Mountain, Woodford (2) p. 194.

Santa Clara County: **1,** Grayish-red tephroite in small residual masses occurred in the manganese boulder found near Alum Rock Park, 5 miles east of San Jose, A. F. Rogers (21) p. 444.

Siskiyou County: **1,** Tephroite is found in the National Defense manganese claim (sec. 16, T. 40 N., R. 10 W., M.D.), in quartzite, Hewett et al. (6) p. 44.

Trinity County: **1,** Tephroite also occurs at the Lucky Bill (Old Bill) property with hausmannite (sec. 9, T. 28 N., R. 11 W., M.D.), Hewett et al. (6) p. 45.

TERLINGUAITE
Mercury oxychloride, Hg_2OCl

San Mateo County: **1,** Terlinguaite is reported, but with questionable identification, from the Emerald Lake mine near Redwood City, with mercury, cinnabar and metacinnabar, CDMG (21669).

TETRADYMITE
Bismuth telluride-sulphide, Bi_2Te_2S

Calaveras County: **1,** Tetradymite was found with gold in the Melones and Morgan mines on Carson Hill, associated with other tellurides of this famous telluride locality, Hanks (12) p. 388.

Inyo County: **1,** Tetradymite was found with rutile, chalcopyrite and bismutite in a brecciated quartz vein in the Cerro Gordo Mining District, Webb (2) p. 399.

Nevada County: **1,** Tetradymite occurred at the old Murchie mine near Nevada City, Hanks (12) p. 388, and **2,** as brilliant scales at Grass Valley, W. P. Blake (6) p. 97.

Siskiyou County: **1,** Sylvanite, reported from the Quartz Hill mine (sec. 16, T. 45 N., R. 10 W., M.D.), Averill (3) p. 49, has been shown by him (p.c. '45) to be tetradymite.

Tuolumne County: **1,** Tetradymite was found with free gold in calcite and dolomite in the Jumper and Golden Rule mines near Jamestown, Sharwood (5) p. 28. **2,** Bismuth telluride is reported from the Soulsby mine, Sharwood (2) p. 118.

TETRAHEDRITE—Tennantite
Copper antimony sulphide, $(Cu)_{12}Sb_4S_{13}$ to
Copper arsenic sulphide, $Cu_{12}As_4S_{13}$

Arsenic may replace antimony in all proportions, and when the ratio As:Sb is more than 1:1, the mineral is called tennantite. *Freibergite* (argentian tetrahedrite) is the argentiferous variety and is perhaps the most common form of the mineral in California. *Schwatzite* is mercury-bearing tetrahedrite.

Tetrahedrite is common in many of the gold and copper mines of the State. It is, however, seldom prominent but occurs in small amounts mixed with galena, sphalerite, chalcopyrite and other sulphides.

Alpine County: **1,** Considerable tetrahedrite has been found in the Silver Mountain Mining District, Woodhouse (p.c. '45). **2,** The mineral was observed in the Monitor mining area, Eakle (16) p. 13, Gianella (1) p. 342, Partridge (1) p. 264.

Amador County: **1**, Tetrahedrite has been found with chalcopyrite and pyrrhotite at the Argonaut mine, Logan (16) p. 67.

Calaveras County: **1**, Small amounts of tetrahedrite were found in the mines on Carson Hill, Hanks (12) p. 388. **2**, The mineral was present in the ore at the Jones mine, Carson Creek, Woodhouse (p.c. '45). **3**, Freibergite occurs disseminated in quartz at the Live Oak mine, Hanks (15) p. 138; **4**, it was found with stibnite at the Blue Wing (secs. 5, 6, T. 3 N., R. 14 E., M.D.), Franke and Logan (4) p. 280, and **4**, it occurred at the Ilex mine, H. W. Turner (3) p. 468.

Del Norte County: **1**, The mineral occurred with native silver and copper at the Occidental mine (T. 18 N., R. 1 W., H.), Crawford (2) p. 58.

Imperial County: **1**, Tetrahedrite appeared in the Bluejacket and other mines of the Picacho Mining District (N.R.).

Inyo County: **1**, Tetrahedrite, containing a large percentage of silver, was an important mineral in the Cerro Gordo Mining District, C. A. Waring and Huguenin (2) p. 108, Tucker and Sampson (25) p. 432, C. W. Merriam (1) p. 60. **2**, The mineral also occurred in some of the mines of the White Mountains and the Dutton Range, Hanks (12) p. 388, and **3**, it was found in the old San Carlos mine, Goodyear (3) p. 263. **4**, Freibergite is the principal sulphide in the silver ores of the Panamint Mining District, Stetefeldt (1) p. 259, Crawford (1) p. 374, Murphy (2) p. 321. **5**, Tennantite has been reported from the Darwin Mining District, Kelley (4) p. 544, Hall and MacKevett (4) p. 62. **6**, Schwatzite is reported from the western part of Ubehebe Peak, McAllister (4) p. 61. References to other occurrences in the county are as follows: Tucker and Sampson (25) pp. 383, 397, 427, 428, A. Knopf (5) pp. 109, 110, Aubury (1) p. 245, Crawford (1) p. 373.

Kern County: **1**, Tetrahedrite occurs with ruby silver and argentite at the Amalie mine, Crawford (2) p. 605. **2**, Small amounts of tetrahedrite and proustite occur in a vein in the Lorraine area, Troxel and Morton (2) p. 41. **3**, Tetrahedrite is present in some of the gold ores of the Mojave Mining District, ibid., p. 44.

Los Angeles: **1**, The mineral was found in the Zapata mine in San Gabriel Canyon, W. P. Blake (9) p. 23.

Mariposa County: **1**, Freibergite was found in large masses in white quartz, at the Live Oak mine, near Mariposa (N.R.) ; **2**, it also occurred in the Pine Tree mine, Hanks (12) p. 388, and **3**, near Coulterville, ibid. **4**, Tetrahedrite occurs at La Victoria mine (sec. 4, T. 4 S., R. 16 E., M.D.), Aubury (1) p. 213. **5**, Tetrahedrite was found with tribolu-minescent sphalerite at the Fitch mine (sec. 9, T. 4 S., R. 15 E., M.D.), Laizure (6) p. 143. **6**, Tetrahedrite was reported at Piñon Blanco, Storms (7) p. 92.

Mendocino County: **1**, Tetrahedrite was found with chalcopyrite, gold and silver, in the Redwood Copper Queen mine, Aubury (1) p. 137.

Mono County: **1**, The mineral occurred massive as the principal primary copper mineral, and the source of most of the silver, in the Diana, Comet, Comanche and other mines of the Blind Spring Mining District, Whiting (1) p. 378, A. L. Ransome (2) p. 189. **2**, Tetrahedrite was also found in the Bodie Mining District, Woodhouse (p.c. '45).

Nevada County: **1,** A heavy mass of tetrahedrite associated with sphalerite and chalcopyrite was found in the Osborn Hill vein, Lindgren (12) p. 119. **2,** Tetrahedrite was found in small quantities at the North Banner and other mines of the Banner Hill and Willow Valley areas, ibid. **3,** Argentiferous tetrahedrite is abundant in the Central mine of the Lava Cap Gold Mining Corporation at Nevada City, W. D. Johnston (3) p. 216.

Placer County: **1,** Dark steel-gray tetrahedrite, associated with other sulphide minerals and with electrum, was common in the Ophir Mining District, having been noticed in the Boulder, Gold Blossom, Pine Tree and Golden Stag mines, Lindgren (7) p. 273. **2,** The mineral is reported from Whiskey Hill, with native silver, Silliman (7) p. 351 (this occurrence was placed in Tuolumne County in earlier editions of *Minerals of California*).

Plumas County: **1,** Tetrahedrite was found at the Irby Holt mine in Indian Valley, Hanks (12) p. 28. **2,** Argentiferous tetrahedrite was found at the Trask and Coffer mine (sec. 24, T. 27 N., R. 10 E., M.D.), Logan (4) p. 470; **3,** it was observed in small amounts in the ore at Engels, C. A. Anderson (6) p. 321, and **4,** it was found 4 miles from Genessee (sec. 11, T. 25 N., R. 11 E., M.D.), Logan (4) p. 463.

Riverside County: **1,** A small amount of tetrahedrite was found with chalcopyrite, pyrite and galena, at Crestmore, Eakle (15) p. 352. **2,** Tennantite altering to a green copper arsenate (?) has been collected from the Commercial quarry, Crestmore, Nieburger (p.c. '63).

San Bernardino County: **1,** Tetrahedrite has been found at Calico, with cerargyrite, Weeks (4) p. 534; **2,** at Harrison Gulch, Kramm (2) p. 238; and **3,** as freibergite, with argentite, at the Big Dike (sec. 17, T. 31 S., R. 6 W., M. D.), Laizure (1) p. 526. **4,** Freibergite, in crystals and in massive ore, is found in the California Rand mine, Murdoch (p.c. '45). This is the material considered by Hulin (1) p. 98, to be stylotypite ($(Cu, Ag, Fe)_{12}Sb_4S_{13}$).

Shasta County: Tetrahedrite is common in the copper mines of the county, although it occurs only in small amounts, Tucker (7) p. 315. **1,** The mineral has been found in a barite gangue in the Bully Hill mine, Aubury (1) p. 65; **2,** it occurs with pyromorphite and cerussite at the Chicago claim, 3 miles west of Igo, Hanks (14) p. 125, and **3,** tetrahedrite-tennantite occur in the ores of the East Shasta copper-zinc area, Albers and Robertson (3) p. 71.

Sierra County: **1,** Tetrahedrite occurs massive and in tetrahedral crystals with crystallized gold in the mines at Alleghany, Ferguson (2) p. 166, E. MacBoyle (3) p. 4.

Siskiyou County: **1,** Tetrahedrite occurs at the Isabella mine (sec. 34, T. 41 N., R. 7 W., M. D.), Laizure (1) p. 532.

Tuolumne County: **1,** Massive tetrahedrite was found in the Golden Rule mine, near Jamestown, Hanks (12) p. 388. **2,** Tennantite has been reported from the Rawhide mine (T. 1 N., R. 14 E., M. D.), F. L. Ransome (9) p. 9, Logan (16) p. 171. **3,** Tetrahedrite comes from the Tioga mine, 3 miles north west of Mount Dana, H. W. Turner (12) p. 715, and **4,** from the Alameda mine, Storms (7) p. 92.

THAUMASITE
Basic hydrous calcium silicate, carbonate, and sulphate,
$Ca_6(CO_3)_2(SO_4)_2Si_2O_4(OH)_4 \cdot 27H_2O$

Riverside County: **1,** Thaumasite occurred as veinlets and silky coatings in spurrite at Crestmore. It was observed, described, and analyzed, Foshag (2) p. 80. It has also been observed in parallel overgrowth on ettringite at Crestmore, on the 910' level, A. B. Carpenter (2) pp. 1394–96. It is also very common as veinlets in massive brown monticellite rock, and in other types of contact zone material, Murdoch (p.c. '60).

THENARDITE
Sodium sulphate, Na_2SO_4

Imperial County: **1,** A large deposit of thenardite occurs about $2\frac{1}{2}$ miles northeast of Bertram (sec. 9, T. 9 S., R. 12 E., S. B.), in the Salton sink, Tucker (4) p. 271, (8) p. 87, Ver Planck (3) p. 5.

Inyo County: **1,** White masses of thenardite occur in the Funeral Range and in the dry depressions of Death Valley, G. E. Bailey (2) pp. 45, 46, Bodewig and Rath (3) p. 181. **2,** Large, blue-gray crystals of thenardite, some twinned, occur at Deep Spring Valley, F. M. Hamilton (4) p. 129. The mineral has recently been observed with burkeite, nahcolite and other salines in layered salt-pan deposits from Deep Spring Lake, B. F. Jones (2) p. 88A, ibid. (1) p. B201.

Kern County: **1,** Thenardite collected by D. G. Thompson from near Buckhorn Springs, 6 miles south of Muroc, was analyzed by R. C. Wells (3) p. 19. **2,** Thenardite is reported from the California borate mine (Western Borate mine of earlier references), H. E. Pemberton et al. (1) p. 38.

San Bernardino County: **1,** Thenardite forms layers several feet thick at Searles Lake, Robottom (1) p. 82, H. S. Gale (13) p. 292, De Groot (3) p. 535. Large crystals often occur as cruciform twins. The crystals were described by Ayres (1) p. 235, G. I. Smith and Pratt (2) p. 40, G. I. Smith and Haines (3) p. P20. **2,** Thenardite has been found pure or mixed with halite at Dale Lake (sec. 26, etc., T. 1 N., R. 12 E., S. B.), Tucker and Sampson (34) p. 541, L. A. Wright et al. (5) p. 220.

San Luis Obispo County: **1,** Soda Lake on the Carrizo Plain, a depression between the Caliente and Temblor Ranges, is a dry lake with crusts of thenardite, Arnold and Johnson (7) p. 370, Tucker (4) p. 386.

THERMONATRITE
Hydrous sodium carbonate, $Na_2CO_3 \cdot H_2O$

Thermonatrite occurs as an efflorescence in dry regions.

Inyo County: **1,** Thermonatrite forms white efflorescent coatings in Death Valley, according to G. E. Bailey (2) p. 102. **2,** Efflorescences from Deep Spring Lake contain thermonatrite, B. F. Jones (1) p. B200. **3,** Thermonatrite is associated with sborgite near Twenty Mule Team Canyon, McAllister (7) p. 300. **4,** The mineral is also found 10 miles southeast of locality **(3),** ibid., p. 300.

Lake County: **1,** Clusters of platy needles of thermonatrite occur between halite crystals in specimens from Borax Lake, Murdoch (p.c. '53).

THOMSONITE
Hydrous sodium/calcium/aluminum silicate, $NaCa_2[(Al,Si)_5O_{10}]_2·6H_2O$

Colusa County: **1,** Thomsonite occurs with calcite, pectolite, datolite, prehnite and hydromagnesite as veins in serpentine in a road quarry near Wilbur Springs, about 2 miles east of the Lake County line, Pabst (p.c. '44).

Kern County: **1,** Thomsonite occurs in veins of radiating clusters in the lavas of Red Rock Canyon, associated with analcime and natrolite, Murdoch (p.c. '51).

Los Angeles County: **1,** Thomsonite occurs as platy crystals in basalt in the Pacific Electric quarry, Brush Canyon, Neuerberg (p.c. '45). **2,** Specimens of thomsonite have been collected from the Sir' Kegian gem beds, Escondido Canyon near Acton, Bensusan (p.c. '57).

Plumas County: **1,** Thomsonite has been found at the Engels mine, Graton and McLaughlin (4) p. 18.

Riverside County: **1,** Thomsonite occurs as clusters of prismatic and bladed crystals in cavities in quartz and prehnite from the 910' level, Commercial quarry, Crestmore, Murdoch (p.c. '59).

San Bernardino County: **1,** Abundant amygdules of thomsonite occur in lava in the Black Canyon-Opal Mountain area north of Hinkley, M. F. B. Strong (9) p. 30.

THORITE
Thorium silicate, $ThSiO_4$, usually with H_2O from alteration. Orangite is altered thorite. Uranothorite is a variety carrying uranium. $(Th,U)SiO_4$.

Thorite has been reported as a minor constituent of placer sands along the Feather, Yuba, American, Mokelumne, Tuolumne and Merced Rivers, from Oroville in Butte County to Snelling in Merced County. It has also been observed in placer sands on Scott River near Callahan in Siskiyou County and at Atolia in San Bernardino County, George (1) pp. 129-132.

Los Angeles County: **1,** Thorite is found in small amount in one part of the zircon-allanite pegmatite in Pacoima Canyon (sec. 17, T. 3 N., R. 13 W., S.B.), Neuerburg (2) p. 834.

Riverside County: **1,** Orangite has been found in small irregular patches in the contact zone at Crestmore on the 910' level, Murdoch (p.c. '51).

San Bernardino County: **1,** The Atomic Energy Commission collected samples of this mineral with uranothorite from the Copper Mt. claim, 8 miles NE of Twentynine Palms (sec. 19, T. 1 N., R. 8 E., S.B.), G. W. Walker et al. (5) p. 24. **2,** Thorite is reported as irregular crystals in a pegmatite in the Solo area, 12 miles S 69° E of Baker, with monazite, G. W. Walker et al. (5) p. 22. **3,** Radio-activity in the Mt. Pass area is largely attributed to thorium in thorite and monazite, according to G. W. Walker et al. (5) p. 22. **4,** Prospects east of Forest Home on Mill Creek, in tributaries known as Lost, Alger and Falls Creek, have yielded uranothorite in small dark brown grains and subhedral crystals in magnetite, biotite and allanite aggregates, Hewett and Stone (5) p. 104.

THOROGUMMITE
Hydrous thorium silicate, $Th(SiO_4)_{1-x}(OH)_{4x}$

Riverside County: **1,** Small, powdery-white, square crystals in the Southern Pacific Silica quarry at Nuevo, test for thorium and silica, and give the x-ray powder pattern of thorogummite, Murdoch and Hawley (p.c. '54).

TIEMANNITE
Mercuric selenide, HgSe

Lake County: **1,** According to W. P. Blake (9) p. 21, tiemannite occurred in large masses near Clear Lake, in the Abbott mine associated with cinnabar and petroleum, Watts (2) p. 240. **2,** Tiemannite is reported in the ore of the Helen mine (sec. 1, T. 10 N., R. 8 W., M.D.), R. G. Yates and Hilpert (4) p. 278, Watts (2) p. 240.

Orange County: **1,** Tiemannite was doubtfully reported to occur with cinnabar and metacinnabar at the San Joaquin Ranch mine, CDMG (12220).

Santa Clara County: **1,** Tiemannite was found with cinnabar at the old Guadalupe mine near New Almaden (N. R.).

Sonoma County: **1,** Tiemannite occurred with native mercury at the Socrates mine (sec. 32, T. 11 N., R. 8 W., M.D.), W. W. Bradley (5) p. 195.

* TILLEYITE, 1933
Calcium silicate carbonate, $Ca_5Si_2O_7(CO_3)_2$

Riverside County: **1,** Tilleyite was discovered in the contact zone at Crestmore, and named by E. S. Larsen and Dunham (15) pp. 469–473 with analysis by Gonyer. Analysis of excellent material from Ireland, Nockolds (1) p. 151, indicates that the formula should be $2CaCO_3 \cdot Ca_3Si_2O_7$, instead of $CaCO_3 \cdot Ca_2SiO_4$.

TIN
Tin, Sn

Metallic tin is a great mineralogic rarity, and its occurrence in California may be considered doubtful.

Humboldt County: **1,** A small round nugget, CDMG (15100), from Orleans Bar hydraulic mine, is said to be tin.

Tuolumne County: **1,** Tin is doubtfully reported also from Columbia, CDMG (13082).

* TINCALCONITE—Mohavite, 1878
Hydrous sodium borate, $Na_2B_4O_7 \cdot 5H_2O$

The name tincalconite was given by C. U. Shepard (3) p. 144, to a pulverulent and efflorescent sodium borate from California containing 32 percent water. It is rapidly formed wherever borax is exposed to dry air.

Kern County: **1,** Tincalconite occurs as a coating on borax and kernite in the Kramer area, Vonsen (1) p. 76, Schaller (45) p. 163.

San Bernardino County: **1,** Well-formed crystals of tincalconite up to 4 mm across have been found in drill cores at Searles Lake, associated with trona and borax, Pabst and Sawyer (10) p. 472, in the

Lower Salt. The mineral has also been noted as coarsely crystalline material in saline layers within the overburden mud, G. I. Smith and Haines (3) p. P21, Bowser (2) p. 1507.

TOBERMORITE
Hydrous calcium silicate, $XC_aO \cdot SiO_2 \cdot H_2O \cdot$

Tobermorite was named for its locality, Tobermory, Island of Mull, by Heddle, 1880, E. S. Dana (4). The name was discredited later when tobermorite was thought to be the same as gyrolite. Recently, the mineral has been reinstated as a result of x-ray diffraction analysis. By the same method, tobermorite has been found to be identical with crestmoreite, and with the material in old specimens labeled riversideite, now hydrated by air moisture to crestmoreite, H. F. W. Taylor (1). Optical and chemical properties of riversideite reported by Eakle (15) are like those of a substance of a lowered hydration produced in tobermorite by heating, J. D. C. McConnell (1); see also Gard and Taylor (2).

Riverside County: **1,** Crestmoreite and riversideite were described from Crestmore by Eakle (15), crestmoreite as soft, white grains, crystals and masses pseudomorphic after wilkeite. Tobermorite has been identified as pseudomorphous after wilkeite, at Crestmore, Heller and Taylor (1) p. 34. This is the material called crestmoreite by Eakle (15).

TOPAZ
Basic aluminum silicate with flourine, $Al_2(F,OH)_2SiO_4$

Butte County: **1,** Topaz was mentioned by Silliman (13) p. 385 as minute crystals in the sands at Cherokee; the occurrence is noted also in Silliman (12) p. 133, Hanks (12) p. 42.

El Dorado County: **1,** Topaz is reported from this county, location not given, Ball (4) p. 1387.

Fresno County: **1,** Topaz is said to occur with beryl at the feldspar deposit, 5 miles northeast of Trimmer, Tucker (1) p. 43. The location for this mineral in Fresno County probably is not authentic, Noren (p.c. '54).

Inyo County: **1,** A single topaz crystal is reported to have come from near Saratoga Springs, editorial note, in M. F. B. Strong (17) p. 17.

Mono County: **1,** A small amount of granular topaz occurs in andalusite at the mine of Champion Sillimanite on the western slope of the White Mountains, 7 miles east of Mocalno, north of Bishop, Jeffery and Woodhouse (3) p. 461, Kerr (3) p. 620.

San Diego County: **1,** Fine large crystals of colorless and aquamarine-colored topaz occurred at the Little Three and Surprise mines, near Ramona, Hanks (12) p. 46, Snyder (2) p. 24. Some of them resemble topaz from the Ural Mountains, U.S.S.R. **2,** Fine crystals of topaz, light green in color, occur in the Aguanga Mountains, Sterrett (10) p. 327, Snyder (5) p. 32. **3,** Good bluish topaz, resembling Ural Mt. topaz, has been found at the Mountain Lily mine, near Oak Grove, CDMG (18621).

TORBERNITE

Hydrous copper uranyl phosphate, $Cu(UO_2)_2(PO_4)_2 \cdot 10H_2O$

Imperial County: **1**, Torbernite or autunite occurs with carnotite in the Lucky Star claims, 10 miles northeast of Glamis (sec. 36 (?), T. 12 S., R. 19 E., S.B.), G. W. Walker et al. (5) pp. 10, 26. **2**, Torbernite (?) is reported from the Tenn-Cal group of claims (sec. 14, T. 12 S., R. 19 E., S.B.) in altered metamorphic rocks, associated with other yellow uranium minerals, ibid., pp. 10, 26.

Inyo County: **1**, Gianella (p.c. '37) has identified thin green tetragonal scales from near Oasis as torbernite.

Kern County: **1**, G. W. Walker et al. (5) p. 19, report green platy torbernite with autunite from the Summit Range 6 miles north of Randsburg, in Red Mt. volcanics, Chilson Property (sec. 36 (?), T. 28 S., R. 40 E., M.D.), confirming Woodhouse (p.c. '45). **2**, Torbernite occurs with autunite on the property of the Miracle Mining Company, near Miracle Hot Springs, in Kern Canyon, Min. Inf. Service (9) p. 18. **3**, Torbernite is reported with minor amounts of autunite in a shear zone on a granite contact with metasedimentary rocks (sec. 23, T. 27 S., R. 35 E., M.D.), $9\frac{1}{2}$ miles SE of Weldon, G. W. Walker et al. (5) p. 31. **4**, Torbernite has been doubtfully reported from the Kergon mine, Kern Canyon, Troxel and Morton (2) p. 332.

Plumas County: **1**, Torbernite or metazeunerite is described from the Perry Jones group of claims, 4.6 miles north of Chilcoot, G. W. Walker et al. (5) p. 28.

Tulare County: **1**, Goodwin (1) p. 369, states: ". . . uranium and thorium-bearing minerals which have been identified in Tulare County include xenotime, euxenite, torbernite, autunite, and uraninite." Specific localities are not given, and torbernite is not heretofore reported from this county.

TOURMALINE

Aluminum borosilicate with various bases, $(Na,Ca)(Li,Mg,Fe^{2+}Al)_3(Al,Fe^{3+})_6$- $B_3Si_6O_{27}(O,OH,F)_4$, composition variable

Pink or red tourmaline is often called *rubellite*. Black tourmaline is called *schorl* or *schorlite*.

Black tourmaline is a very common mineral, and large areas of tourmaline granites exist in the Sierra Nevada. The richly colored red and green tourmalines of San Diego County are the finest in the world, and have become widely known and used as gems. Tourmaline always occurs in prismatic crystals, often bunched into radiating groups and usually much fractured. The common black tourmaline is characteristic of granites and quartz veins in granites. Brown tourmaline is found in crystalline limestone near contacts with intrusive igneous rock. Translucent pink or green tourmaline contains lithium and is found only in pegmatites.

The best description of the discovery and occurrence of lithia tourmalines in California, is to be found in Bulletin 37 of the CDMG, Kunz (24). An early note (1881) on rubellite reports the mineral as needles in white lepidolite, but gives no locality beyond the "Bernardino Range in Southern California," W. P. Blake (23) p. 376, (24) p. 207.

Alpine County: **1**, Black tourmaline is common in Hope Valley in pegmatite dikelets of the area, Woodhouse (p.c. '45).

Calaveras County: **1,** Black tourmaline occurs in quartz in Sheepranch, Hanks (12) p. 390.

El Dorado County: **1,** Black tourmaline occurs with orthoclase at Bucks Bar (N.R.). **2,** Black tourmaline occurs at Emerald Bay, Lake Tahoe (N.R.).

Fresno County: **1,** Red and green tourmaline occur in quartz on the White Divide, south of Mount Goddard, W. W. Bradley (2) p. 439. **2,** Green tourmaline with brown garnet occurs on Spanish Peak, ibid. **3,** Green radiating clusters of tourmaline came from a road cut east of Trimmer, on the north side of Kings River, Noren (p.c. '45). **4,** Black crystals up to 6 inches in size were found in feldspar on a hill in the southwest corner of Clarks Valley, Noren (p.c. '35).

Imperial County: **1,** Fine-grained black tourmaline is found in veinlets 6 miles north of 4S Ranch, $1\frac{1}{2}$ miles west of the Colorado River, Kelley (1) p. 137.

Inyo County: **1,** Black tourmaline occurs in the Lee Mining District, CDMG (7878), and **2,** in a metamorphosed sandstone at Deep Canyon, west of Bishop, A. Knopf (6) p. 233. **3,** Small crystals of tourmaline occur in contact rock at Darwin, Kelley (4) p. 540.

Kern County: **1,** Black tourmaline occurs in a schist 2 miles south of Randsburg, Murdoch (p.c. '45). **2,** Small amounts of black tourmaline with cassiterite occur in the Gorman area, Troxel and Morton (2) p. 294.

Lassen County: **1,** Tourmaline is reported by Melhase (p.c. '40) with beryl at the Mount Thompson gem mine (T. 28 N., R. 13 E., M.D.) north and east of Milford.

Los Angeles County: **1,** Numerous small occurrences of tourmaline in slender black crystals are recorded at localities 21, 22, 23, 24 and 25 in the Santa Monica Mountains, Neuerburg (1) p. 160.

Madera County: **1,** Black tourmaline occurs in pegmatites on Iron Mountain near Raymond, Goudey (1) p. 27, and **2,** in Fine Gold Gulch, Hanks (15) p. 138.

Marin County: **1,** Brown tourmaline, with quartz in altered Franciscan sediments, and white needles and brown prisms in vugs, occurs at the East Peak of Mt. Tamalpais, Rice (1) p. 2073.

Modoc County: **1,** Black tourmaline crystals occur in quartz near Cedarville (N.R.).

Mono County: **1,** A small amount of black tourmaline is found in the andalusite mine in the White Mountains, Woodhouse (4) p. 38.

Nevada County: **1,** Dark-brown tourmaline was found 2 miles northwest of Colfax, Lukesh and Buerger (1) p. 143, and analyzed by Melville (5) p. 39. **2,** Tourmaline is reported from Meadow Lake, Lindgren (18) p. 258.

Orange County: **1,** Black tourmaline is found at the Santa Ana tin mine, Santa Ana Mountains (N. R.).

Placer County: **1,** Black tourmaline occurs at Soda Springs (N. R.); **2,** with quartz near Blue Canyon (N. R.); **3,** at the Excelsior mine near Cisco (N. R.), and **4,** black tourmaline with white feldspar and glassy quartz occurs in granitic rock near Rocklin (N. R.).

Plumas County: **1,** Small crystals of tourmaline occur in the Diadem lode south of Meadow Valley, H. W. Turner (17) p. 6. **2,** Doubly terminated black tourmaline crystals as much as 3″ in size have been found in chlorite schists between Oroville and Quincy, near Feather River, Williams (p.c. '49).

Riverside County: **1,** Fine gem tourmaline occurs near Coahuila and in the San Jacinto Mountains. The first discovery of gem tourmalines in California was made in 1872, on the south slope of Thomas Mountain (sec. 28, T. 6 S., R. 3 E., S. B.), by Henry Hamilton, Hanks (12) p. 21, F. J. H. Merrill (2) p. 577. **2,** The San Jacinto gem mine (sec. 1, T. 7 S., R. 3 E., S. B.), was discovered in 1893—from "float" crystals of colored tourmaline, some as large as 9 inches long, ibid., Kunz (9) p. 765. **3,** The Columbia mine (SW¼ sec. 1, T. 7 S., R. 3 E., S. B.), on Coahuila Mountain, is one of the oldest gem mines in the state, Kunz (23) p. 968. **4,** Black tourmaline occurs in the pegmatite veins at Crestmore, Eakle (15) p. 350. **5,** Black tourmaline occurs with cassiterite in the Cajalco tin mine about 11 miles southwest of Riverside, Fairbanks (4) p. 111, West (3) p. 131. **6,** A pegmatite dike containing a tourmaline-bearing pocket from which about half a pound of gem quality red and green tourmaline was collected is reported from the Jensen quarry, Crestmore, Anon. (29) p. 141, Jenni (p.c. '62). **7,** Tourmaline, in dikes and as massive tourmaline-quartz plugs, have been reported in the Lake Mathews area, R. J. Proctor (1) p. 50.

San Bernardino County: **1,** Black tourmaline occurs in a schist with clinozoisite in the Sierra Pelona Valley (center sec. 12, T. 5 N., R. 14 W., S. B.), Neuerburg (p.c. '44). **2,** Well-formed crystals of tourmaline occur abundantly in a muscovite schist near Wrightwood, Schwartz (p.c. '54).

San Diego County: A series of pegmatite dikes, consisting mainly of white albite with quartz and lepidolite, cut through the diorite hills in the northwestern part of the county from Mesa Grande northward through Pala. These dikes have been prolific in their yield of beautiful transparent tourmalines in many shades of rose-red and green. The first material obtained was the lavender and lilac lepidolite containing radiating clusters of bright-red rubellite prisms, which form beautiful museum specimens and can be seen in most mineral collections. The gem varieties were found later, Fairbanks (5) p. 35, and since 1893 a number of mines have been located and many beautiful large crystals obtained. At present the best tourmalines come from Mesa Grande. Analyses of the tourmaline of the county have been made by Schaller, F. W. Clarke (9) p. 278. **1,** Sterrett (1) p. 459, measured and described a number of interesting crystals of tourmaline from Damarons Ranch, 4 miles northwest of Mesa Grande. **2,** Black, pink, blue, violet, green and colorless tourmaline occurs at Rincon in the Victor and other claims, A. F. Rogers (4) p. 213. **3,** Bluish-green tourmaline is found in the Mountain Lily mine near Oak Grove, Hanks (12) p. 124, Sterrett (9) p. 688. **4,** Fine blue and pink tourmaline occurs at the Peter Cabat mine, about 6 miles north of Warner Hot Springs, Schaller (37) p. 856. **5,** A deposit of green tourmaline occurs south of Banner, Sterrett (2) p. 1240, Schaller (37) p. 856. **6,** Good blue and green tourmaline occurs on the east side of Chihuahua Valley, Schaller (36) p. 353. The occurrences: **7,** at Mesa Grande are described by Kunz (24) p. 59, Fairbanks (5) p. 36, and **8,** at Pala, by Kunz (18) p. 264, (24) p. 60,

Fairbanks (5) p. 36. Tourmaline from Pala shows spectroscopic traces of germanium, Papish (2) p. 475. **9**, Tourmaline is found with axinite and smoky quartz in Moosa Canyon (E¼ sec. 27, T. 10 S., R. 3 E., S. B.), Hanks (12) p. 62. **10**, Slender dark prisms of tourmaline occur with quartz on Elder Creek (sec. 27, T. 9 S., R. 4 E., S. B.), Durrell (p.c. '44). **11**, Antisell (1) p. 119, reported schorl between Warners Ranch and San Felipe. **12**, Martinez (1) p. 39 mentioned schorl near San Diego as early as 1792. **13**, Snyder (2) p. 25, reports tourmaline from the Little Three mine.

Shasta County: **1**, Small rosettes of black tourmaline occur at the Mountain Monarch prospect, Weaverville quadrangle, Ferguson (1) p. 43.

Tulare County: **1**, Black tourmaline occurs in Frazier Valley, CDMG (10320); **2**, Drum Valley, Angel (2) p. 732, and **3**, at Mineral King with pyromorphite, Goodyear (3) p. 646. **4**, Large crystals of tourmaline are found in Griffiths Canyon (sec. 9, T. 17 S., R. 28 E., M. D.), Goodyear (3) p. 644. **5**, Large crystals, up to 2 feet long, occur with rose quartz in pegmatite (W½ sec. 15, T. 17 S., R. 27 E., M. D.), Durrell (p.c. '35).

Tuolumne County: **1**, Tourmaline occurs as black prisms with quartz about 8 miles south of Sonora (N. R.).

*TRASKITE, 1965 [1]
Basic barium iron titanium silicate, $Ba_5FeTiSi_6O_{18}(OH)_4$

Fresno County: **1**, Traskite, named as a new mineral from California for John B. Trask, the first state geologist of California, is found in the sanbornite deposits around Rush and Big Creeks in eastern Fresno County, as reddish brown grains sporadically distributed in the country rock. Alfors and Stinson (5) p. 30. This entry, first appearing in February 1965 after the cut-off date for entries for this bulletin, is included because the article in which the preliminary description occurred is part II of a report describing three new minerals in the same locality, Stinson and Alfors (6).

† * TRAUTWINITE, 1873

Trautwinite was described in 1873 as a new mineral from Monterey County by Goldsmith (1) p. 348, (2) p. 365, (5) p. 152. It has since been shown to be a mixture of chromite and uvarovite, E. S. Dana (5) p. 447.

TRIDYMITE
Silicon dioxide, SiO_2

Tridymite is a form of silica which is found in volcanic rocks. It is generally in crystals of microscopic size and therefore is rarely seen, except in thin sections of rocks.

Imperial County: **1**, Tridymite with cristobalite and feldspar is a principal constituent of an altered rhyolite obsidian which makes up Cormorant Island in the Salton Sea, A. F. Rogers (29) p. 219, (42) p. 328.

---

[1] This new mineral is described in a paper which appeared in April, 1965, after the cutoff date (Dec. 31, 1964) for entries in this volume. "Seven new barium minerals from eastern Fresno County, California", by John T. Alfors, Melvin C. Stinson, Robert A. Matthews and Adolf Pabst: Am. Mineralogist, vol. 50, pp. 314–340, 1965.

Inyo County: **1**, Tridymite occurs in lithophysae in obsidian at Coso Hot Springs near Little Lake, F. E. Wright (2) p. 368, A. F. Rogers (23) p. 215, M. F. B. Strong (7) p. 16, Stinson (4) p. 207.

Lake County: **1**, Druses and groups of sharp tridymite crystals occur in vugs and seams in andesite in Seigler Canyon, near Lower Lake, Wilke (p.c. '36), and **2**, as coronas about quartz inclusions in the basalts of the area, C. A. Anderson (9) p. 637.

Los Angeles County: **1**, Tridymite has been identified in the volcanics of Santa Catalina Island, A. F. Rogers (30) p. 80. **2**, The mineral occurs as white hexagonal plates in lava between Pomona and Spadra at the south foot of the Puente Hills, Foshag (p.c. '46).

Marin County: **1**, Tridymite has been found in specimens from the Heim Bros. quarry, Petaluma, Watters (p.c. '62).

Mono County: **1**, Schaller (8) p. 128 has described small plates of tridymite with complex forms, in the cavities of lava 8 miles west of Bridgeport.

Plumas County: **1**, Crystals of tridymite in andesite have been found north of Portola on the Smith Peak road (sec. 4, T. 23 N., R. 13 E., M. D.), Durrell (2) p. 501, and **2**, in cavities of pyroxene andesite with anauxite at Drakesbad (T. 30 N., R. 5 E., M. D.), A. F. Rogers (38) p. 160.

San Diego County: **1**, Tridymite constitutes up to 25 percent of a dacite volcanic neck at Morro Hill, 6 miles south of Fallbrook (sec. 23, T. 10 S., R. 4 W., S. B.), E. S. Larsen (17) p. 111.

San Luis Obispo County: **1**, Tridymite is found in lithophysae in rhyolite on Black Mountain in the southern Santa Lucia Range, Taliaferro and Turner (2) p. 237.

Shasta County: **1**, Tridymite has been described by C. A. Anderson (8) p. 242, as a secondary mineral at Bumpass Hell and other hot springs in Lassen Volcanic National Park. **2**, The mineral occurs abundantly in vesicular basalts on the road to Terrys Mill, east of Round Mountain, Melhase (3) No. 6, p. 1.

Sonoma County: **1**, Tridymite occurs in cavities of andesite, coated by hisingerite (sec. 10, T. 7 N., R. 7 W., M. D.), in Los Alamos Canyon, Rose (p.c. '50).

Tuolumne County: **1**, Tridymite occurs as very thin, white plates in cavities of an andesite near Jamestown, A. F. Rogers (7) p. 374, (38) p. 160.

TRIPHYLITE
Lithium iron phosphate, $LiFePO_4$

This rare phosphate usually contains manganese and grades into lithiophilite.

San Diego County: **1**, Triphylite was found with lithiophilite and purpurite in the lithia mines at Pala, Hanks (12) p. 125, Graton and Schaller (1) p. 146.

TRIPLITE
Manganese iron phosphate with fluorine, $(Mn,Fe)_2PO_4F$

Triplite is a rare mineral found with tungsten minerals in pegmatite veins.

San Bernardino County: **1,** Triplite was found with hübnerite on specimens from a deposit at Camp Signal, about 9 miles north of Goffs, Hess (14) p. 57.

San Diego County: **1,** Triplite, derived from lithiophilite, was found at Pala, Hanks (12) p. 125, G. A. Waring (2) p. 363, Schaller (29) p. 145.

TROILITE
Ferrous sulphide, FeS

Del Norte County: **1,** Troilite was found massive in a sheared zone of serpentine, in a copper claim northeast of Crescent City. It was analyzed and described by Eakle (9) p. 77. It contains inclusions of magnetite from which it has probably been derived. This is the only known terrestrial occurrence of troilite. It has been observed previously in meteorites.

TRONA
Acid hydrous sodium carbonate, $Na_3H(CO_3)_2 \cdot 2H_2O$

Trona is found in the deposits of saline lakes or is produced by the evaporation of their waters. It is common in playa lakes in Kern, Inyo, San Bernardino and Riverside counties, G. E. Bailey (2) p. 102.

Inyo County: **1,** Trona was reported from the borax deposits of Death Valley by Bodewig and Rath (3) p. 181, G. E. Bailey (2) pp. 45, 46. **2,** White layers of trona occur along the shores of Owens Lake, Chatard (3) p. 59, (4) p. 75. Analysis of material formed by evaporation at the edge of the lake shows it to be nearly pure trona, F. W. Clarke (9) p. 256. **3,** Trona occurs as saline crusts and efflorescences from Deep Spring Lake, B. F. Jones (1) p. B200, ibid. (2) p. 88A.

Lake County: **1,** Trona occurs at Borax Lake with gaylussite, pirssonite, and northupite, Vonsen and Hanna (4) p. 103.

Mono County: **1,** Trona, in layers of well-formed crystals, occurs with hanksite, in evaporation crusts of halite on the east edge of Mono Lake, Murdoch (25) p. 358.

San Bernardino County: **1,** Thick layers of solid trona occur with borax, hanksite, thenardite, glauberite and other salts at Searles Lake, Ayres (2) p. 65, G. E. Bailey (2) p. 102, H. S. Gale (13) p. 294. Lath-like crystals are very common, Foshag (21) p. 51, G. I. Smith and Pratt (2) p. 27. The mineral is the second most abundant mineral at Searles Lake. It occurs in every saline unit in the deposit, G. I. Smith and Haines (3) pp. P21–P24.

TSCHERMIGITE—Ammonium Alum
Hydrous aluminum ammonium sulphate, $NH_4Al(SO_4)_2 \cdot 12H_2O$

Lake County: **1,** Tschermigite was mentioned by Becker (4) p. 389 as an efflorescence at Sulphur Bank.

Sonoma County: **1,** Tschermigite is found at numerous places in upper Geyser Creek Canyon, The Geysers, E. T. Allen and Day (2) p. 45, as brilliant octahedral crystals, and crusts and crystalline masses, Vonsen (6) p. 289.

*TUNELLITE, 1961
Hydrous strontium borate, $SrB_6O_{10} \cdot 4H_2O$

Kern County: **1,** Tunellite, a new mineral, is found at the Jennifer mine, Kramer borate area. It has been described by Erd et al. (3) p. 294. The crystal structure has been studied by J. R. Clark (7) p. 1178, (8) pp. 1549–1568.

Inyo County: **1,** Tunellite has been identified from the Furnace Creek borate area by McAllister, reported in Erd et al. (3) p. 294.

TUNGSTITE
Tungstic acid, H_2WO_4

Inyo County: **1,** Tungstite has been found on scheelite at the Margarita claim, Shepherd Canyon, W. W. Bradley (32) p. 271, CDMG (21114). **2,** The mineral occurs as a coating on stolzite at the Darwin mine, W. W. Bradley (30) p. 602. The validity of the occurrence of stolzite has been questioned by Hall and MacKevett (1) p. 59.

TURGITE—Hydrohematite
α - Fe_2O_3 with adsorbed water

Inyo County: **1,** CDMG (19597), labelled turgite, is from near Shoshone.

Kern County: **1,** A specimen of turgite has come from the Golden Queen mine, near Mojave, J. W. Bradley (p.c. '45).

TURQUOISE
Basic copper aluminum phosphate, $CuAl_6(PO_4)_4(OH)_8 \cdot 5H_2O$

Imperial County: **1,** Bluish-green turquoise in pockets and nodules, has been found about 2 miles east of Midway Well on the trail to the True Friend and Silver Mom mines, on the east slope of the Chocolate Mountains, Tucker (11) p. 270.

Madera County: **1,** A specimen of turquoise having a hexagonal form, from the Taylor Ranch, was described as a pseudomorph after apatite, J. D. Whitney (4) p. 5, G. E. Moore and von Zepharovich (4) p. 240, Kunz (24) p. 107.

San Benito County: **1,** Narrow veins of turquoise appear cutting glaucophane schist about $4\frac{1}{2}$ miles north of Llanada (sec. 33, T. 14 S., R. 10 E., M.D.), Chesterman (p.c. '51).

San Bernardino County: **1,** Turquoise mines, worked by the prehistoric Indians, whose stone hammers and inscriptions still remained, were rediscovered in 1897. In 1898, the *San Francisco Call* sent an expedition under Dr. Gustav Eisen to explore them. A most interesting account of this expedition was published in *The Call* of March 18, 1898, Eisen (1) p. 2, and has been extensively quoted by Kunz (24) p. 107. This area is in the Turquoise Mountains (T. 16 N., R. 10, 11, E., (S.B.), along the southern edge of the township. The turquoise mines were visited by Sterrett (9) p. 695, Himalaya (Toltec) in 1911, East Toltec in 1913. H. E. Pemberton (3) has retraced Sterrett's routes on the Halloran Springs quadrangle map, and suggests that the names of the mines were confused on the map prepared by M. J. Rogers (1), and reproduced by Murdoch and Webb (39) p. 14. H. E. Pemberton's map is reproduced in the historical section of this volume. Two groups of claims, the Toltec and Himalaya, have been worked, with considerable production of light-green gem material, Kunz (24) p. 107. **2,** Turquoise has been mined in the Solo mining area (approx. T. 16 N., R. 8 E., S.B.), Tucker and Sampson (16) p. 307. **3,** Turquoise in black matrix has come from Goldstone Camp, 30 miles north of Barstow. An occurrence described as near Granite Wells, 22 miles east of Johannesburg, M. J. Rogers (1), may be the same. **4,** The Gove turquoise mine, 2 miles east of Cottonwood siding on the Santa Fe Railroad, has been fully described by Sterrett (5) p. 780, Pogue (1) p. 47. **5,** Specimens have come from near Goffs, Kunz (24) p. 107. **6,** Martin (2) p. 317, reports turquoise near Barnwell in the New York Mountains.

San Luis Obispo County: **1,** Nodular earthy masses of turquoise have been found near Paso Robles, Gregory (p.c. '51).

* TYCHITE, 1905
Sodium magnesium sulphate carbonate, $Na_6Mg_2SO_4(CO_3)_4$

San Bernardino County: **1,** A few small octahedrons of tychite were mixed with the northupite crystals discovered at Searles Lake. They were analyzed and named by Penfield and Jamieson (7) p. 217, H. S. Gale (13) p. 308. Foshag (21) p. 51 found minute, sharp, clear crystals; see also G. I. Smith and Pratt (2) p. 31, Pabst et al. (21) p. 487. Tychite is the least abundant of the three magnesium-bearing minerals at Searles Lake, and is found at several horizons in the Bottom Mud and the Mixed Layer, G. I. Smith and Haines (3) p. P33.

TYUYAMUNITE
Hydrous calcium uranyl vanadate, $Ca(UO_2)_2(VO_4)_2 \cdot 5\text{-}8H_2O$

Kern County: **1,** Tyuyamunite may be a mineral occurring in the Miracle mine, Kern River Canyon, Troxel and Morton (2) p. 333.

Madera County: **1,** This mineral was reported 28 miles from Mid Pine in Yosemite National Park by Dr. F. E. Tiffany of Mid Pine, in a clay seam between granite and slate. This was reported by the *Mariposa Gazette* on October 6, 1949, G. W. Walker et al. (5) p. 38.

San Bernardino County: **1,** Tyuyamunite is reported from near Adelanto, CDMG (21626).

ULEXITE—Boronatrocalcite—Natroborocalcite
Hydrous sodium calcium borate, $NaCaB_5O_9 \cdot 8H_2O$

White silky balls of ulexite are frequently found at some of the desert depressions, often with borax.

Inyo County: **1,** Surface incrustations of ulexite are found at some of the sinks in Death Valley (Furnace Creek, Bennetts Wells, etc.), Hanks (12) p. 394, Bodewig and Rath (3) p. 181, G. E. Bailey (2) pp. 45, 46. **2,** Ulexite occurs in large compact masses with colemanite at Mount Blanco, Foshag (13) p. 420. **3,** The mineral is found in great abundance with colemanite and probertite in the Widow and Biddy McCarthy mines near Ryan, Foshag (18), p. 338. **4,** Ulexite with colemanite has been found near Shoshone (one mile west of center T. 22

N., R. 7 E., S.B.), Noble (3) p. 72. **5**, A specimen of ulexite has been found in Mesquite Valley, CDMG (14595). **6**, Ulexite, colemanite and probertite have been found in the Resting Springs Range, near Shoshone, Nolan (3) p. A-11. **7**, Ulexite is abundant in the workings of the 124 ft. level of the Kern borate mine near Ryan, associated with colemanite and probertite, Anon. (47) p. 9.

Kern County: **1**, Ulexite was mentioned from the Cane Spring [Kane (Koehn) Spring, Mesquite Spring, Desert Spring, Desert Well] area (T. 30 S., R. 38 E., M.D.), Silliman (12) p. 130, J. A. Phillips (4) p. 637 (boronatrocalcite), W. P. Blake (23) p. 323, G. E. Bailey (2) p. 50. **2**, Ulexite occurs abundantly as compact fibrous veins in clay-shale in the Kramer area, Schaller (4) p. 24, (45) p. 138. Crystals from the Suckow mine have been described by Murdoch (10) p. 754; chemical analysis, Baur and Sand (1) p. 678; on optical properties, Baur et al. (2) p. 697; and R. W. Dietz (2) p. 16. R. D. Allen and Almond (8) p. 169, describe a strontian-bearing nonfibrous variety.

Lake County: **1**, Ulexite from Lake Hachinhama was mentioned in Hanks (11) p. 38.

Los Angeles County: **1**, Ulexite is found in compact divergent masses with probertite at Lang, Foshag (1) p. 35, (7) p. 200.

Riverside County: **1**, Ulexite is reported by G. E. Bailey (2) p. 54 from the foothills of the San Bernardino Range, northeast of the Salton Sea.

San Bernardino County: **1**, Small amounts of ulexite occur with colemanite at Borate, near Yermo, Foshag (9) p. 209. **2**, Float ulexite, with colemanite, was reported from the Lower Canyon, Amargosa River, G. E. Bailey (2) p. 62, Cloudman et al. (1) p. 855. **3**, The mineral has been reported from the playa at Coyote Holes (Willow Springs Lake) (T. 11 N., R. 2 E., S.B.), Hanks (11) p. 28, G. E. Bailey (2) p. 62, Cloudman et al. (1) p. 855.

Shasta County: **1**, An incrustation at Lick Springs, called "borocalcite of Hayes" by J. B. Trask (7) p. 61, may be either ulexite or bechilite.

† URACONITE
Hydrous uranium sulphate, SO_3,UO_3,H_2O

"Uraconite" is one of the names used in early literature for yellow uranium-bearing ochres. It is discredited as a name. For summary see Frondel (9) p. 147.

Calaveras County: **1**, Uraconite—"yellow uranium ochre"—occurs as an alteration product of pitchblende in coatings in contact with gold at the Rathgeb mines, near San Andreas, Rickard (1) p. 329, G. W. Walker et al. (5) pp. 10, 28.

URANINITE—Pitchblende
Uranium dioxide, UO_2 (usually oxidized so that it is nearer U_3O_8)

Calaveras County: **1**, Uraninite was reported in acicular crystals in a pocket with a spongy gold, quartz, and clay at the Rathgeb mine, near San Andreas, Rickard (1) p. 329, (2) p. 215, Logan (16) p. 147, G. W. Walker et al. (5) pp. 10, 28.

Kern County: **1**, Uraninite is reported in uncertain identification with gummite (?) and secondary yellow stains of other uranium minerals from the Embree property near Bodfish, G. W. Walker et al. (5) p. 31. **2**, Uraninite is reported in several prospects in the Kern River uranium area, MacKevett (2) pp. 203, 211. Uraninite has been identified in ore from the Little Sparkler mine, and possibly from the Kergon and Miracle mines in this area, Troxel and Morton (2) pp. 327, 332. **3**, Uraninite as pitchblende and gummite, has been tentatively identified at the Radiation property, Erskine Creek, ibid., p. 34.

Madera County: **1**, A radioactive mineral in minute quantities, possibly uraninite, is reported from the Rainbow claim, Jackass area, (T. 4 S., R. 24 E., M. D.), 16 miles SE of Camp Curry, G. W. Walker et al. (5) p. 29.

Mono County: **1**, Pitchblende, altering to uranophane, has been found in talus near Emerald Lake, Mt. Morrison quadrangle, Rinehart and Ross (2) p. 100.

Riverside County: **1**, Uraninite is reported from near Twenty-Nine Palms, CDMG (21637, 21639, 21640).

San Bernardino County: **1**, Pitchblende has been found in the Scotty Wilson mine, VanDusen Canyon (sec. 4, T. 2 N., R. 1 E., S. B.). The mineral occurs in a pod-like mass of metallic sulphides in limestone, L. A. Wright et al. (5) p. 112. **2**, Uraninite is reported from the county, CDMG (21642). **3**, It has been suggested that pitchblende may be the source of radioactivity in the St. Patrick claim (secs. 7, 8, T. 1 S., R. 1 E., S. B.), G. W. Walker et al. (5) p. 23. **4**, Uraninite is probably the uranium-bearing mineral erratically distributed in masses of sulphide minerals at the Yerih group of claims (secs. 3, 4, T. 2 N., R. 1 E., S. B.), in crushed zones in limestone, in the Holcomb Valley area, ibid.

San Luis Obispo County: **1**, Uraninite is associated with schroeckingerite and zippeite from the Pozo area, Woodhouse (p.c. '57).

Tuolumne County: **1**, Uraninite is reported from Radium no. 1, CDMG (21643).

Tulare County: **1**, Goodwin (1) p. 396, states: ". . . uranium and thorium-bearing minerals which have been identified in Tulare County include xenotime, euxenite, torbernite, autunite, and uraninite."

URANOPHANE

Basic hydrous calcium uranyl silicate, $Ca(UO_2)_2(SiO_3)(OH)_2 \cdot 5H_2O$

Imperial County: **1**, Uranophane is reported from near Niland, CDMG (21625).

Inyo County: **1**, Uranophane occurs in fracture coatings on granite at an uranium prospect up slope from the Haiwee Reservoir in the Coso Mts., with weeksite and haiweeite, Outerbridge et al. (1) p. 43. It is likely that the uranium deposits reported to carry uranophane by Cureton (p.c. '63) at the Haiwee Reservoir in the Coso Mts. are the same as these referred to by Outerbridge.

Kern County: **1**, A specimen of uranophane was submitted to the CDMG, CDMG (21621) as "from near Jawbone Canyon." Troxel and Morton (2) p. 333, report uranophane from the Miller Ranch deposit (SE¼ sec. 1, T. 30 S., R. 36 E., M.D.), as 6 miles south of Cantil. It is probable that the specimen comes from this locality. **2**, Uranophane occurs associated with autunite at the Kergon mine, Kern River Canyon uranium area, Troxel and Morton (2) pp. 330, 332. **3**, The mineral also occurs in the Miracle mine, Kern River area, ibid., p. 333.

Mono County: **1,** Uranophane, in one specimen altering from pitchblende (uraninite), has been found near Emerald Lake, in a coarse talus, Rinehart and Ross (2) p. 100.

Riverside County: **1,** Uranophane is reported from near Twenty-Nine Palms, CDMG (21638).

San Bernardino County: **1,** Uranophane is reported from Kramer Hills, CDMG (21618). **2,** Uranophane occurs with fluoborite and betauranotil from the New Method mine (Hope uranium prospect), Bristol Mts. near Amboy, Chesterman and Bowen (6) p. 1679.

VALENTINITE
Antimony oxide, Sb_2O_3

Valentinite is an oxidation product of antimony minerals, especially of stibnite, and probably is present in most of the antimony mines of the state.

Contra Costa County: **1,** Valentinite occurs at the Mt. Diablo mine as clusters of slender, colorless needles, with threads of stibnite, Oyler (p.c. '61).

Inyo County: **1,** Valentinite is reported to occur with stibnite and cervantite at the Bishop antimony mine $4\frac{1}{2}$ miles south of Bishop, Woodhouse (p.c. '45). **2,** Valentinite probably occurs in Wild Rose Canyon, as a brownish crust on stibnite, D. E. White (1) p. 317.

Kern County: **1,** Valentinite occurs with antimony and stibiconite along Erskine Creek, Behre (1) p. 331. **2,** Tabular crystals, and coatings of valentinite, have been found in Lone Tree Canyon, Murdoch (13) p. 613.

San Benito County: **1,** Lemon-yellow bladed aggregates of valentinite, probably pseudomorphs after stibnite, with cinnabar, quartz and chalcedony, occur at the Picahotes (Picachos) mine, A. F. Rogers (7) p. 374.

San Bernardino County: **1,** Valentinite (?) occurs sparsely as yellow coatings at the Martha prospect, Ord Mountains, Weber (3) p. 27.

Santa Clara County: **1,** Goldsmith (3) p. 369, notes small crystals of valentinite with stibioferrite, from this county.

VANADINITE
Lead chloro-vanadate, $Pb_5(VO_4)_3Cl$

Kern County: **1,** Vanadinite has been found 2 miles north of Searles Lake (N. R.), and **2,** it was found with galena and mimetite near Randsburg (N. R.).

Inyo County: **1,** Vanadinite occurs as small reddish crystals in crevices from the Emperor mine, Darwin, Hall and MacKevett (1) p. 18, confirming Woodhouse (p.c. '54). **2,** Crusts and clusters of small crystals lining cavities in limonite, commonly associated with wulfenite, are reported from the Ubehebe mine, McAllister (4) p. 62.

Mono County: **1,** Vanadinite has been reported near Coleville, W. W. Bradley (29) p. 106.

Riverside County: **1,** Vanadinite has been found at Gold Park, near Twenty-Nine Palms, in this and San Bernardino Counties, Tucker and Sampson (16) p. 295. **2,** The mineral is reported with galena and car-

bonate minerals from the Black Eagle mine (sec. 30, T. 3 S., R. 14 E.,
S. B.), Tucker (8) p. 195, Tucker and Sampson (27) p. 47. **3,** Good
crystals have come from the El Dorado mine near Indio, J. S. Brown
(1) p. 63. (This occurrence was listed as pyromorphite in CDMG Bulletin 113, Pabst (4) p. 209).

San Bernardino County: **1,** Vanadinite occurs with cerussite and
cuprodescloizite in the Vanadium King mine at Camp Signal, near
Goffs, Schaller (24) p. 149, Cloudman et al. (1) p. 849. **2,** The mineral
was found near Moore Station on the Union Pacific Railroad, CDMG
(18743).

VANTHOFFITE
Sodium magnesium sulphate, $Na_6Mg(SO_4)_4$

Imperial County: **1,** Vanthoffite has been identified from Bertram
siding ($N\frac{1}{2}$ sec. 19, T. 9 S., R. 12 E., and $S\frac{1}{2}$ sec. 13, T. 9 S., R. 11 E.,
S. B.), Gricius (p.c. '64). This is associated with massive blödite reported by R. J. Sampson and Tucker (8) p. 140, but is much coarsergrained.

VARISCITE
Hydrous aluminum phosphate, $AlPO_4 \cdot 2H_2O$

El Dorado County: **1,** Variscite was dubiously reported to have been
found in Pleasant Valley. The specimen is in the collections of University of California, Berkeley. This occurrence has been verified by a
specimen collected from the west slope of Slate Mountain, near Placerville, Parnau (p.c. '63).

VAUQUELINITE
Lead copper phospho-chromate, near $(Pb,Cu)_3[(Cr,P)O_4]_2$

San Bernardino County: **1,** Fine crystals, doubtfully identified as
vauquelinite, were reported as associated with chromic iron ore from
this county, J. R. Browne (4) p. 225.

* VEATCHITE, 1938
Hydrous strontium borate, $Sr_3B_{16}O_{27} \cdot 5H_2O(?)$, with some Ca

Los Angeles County: **1,** Veatchite occurs in small amount with howlite and colemanite at the old Sterling borax mine at Lang. It was
named and described, with analysis by F. A. Gonyer, by Switzer (2)
p. 409. Crystals were described by Murdoch (7) p. 130. A new find
in the same locality shows a platy instead of fibrous habit, Switzer and
Brannock (6) pp. 90–92. Most of the material here is paraveatchite
(which see) but some corresponds to veatchite as identified from occurrence in San Bernardino County (1).

San Bernardino County: **1,** Veatchite was identified from drill core
No. 5, Four Corners area, Kramer region, collected by Richard C. Erd,
and reported by J. R. Clark et al. (1) p. 1142.

VERMICULITE
Basic hydrous magnesium calcium iron aluminum silicate,
$(Mg,Ca)_{0.7}(Mg,Fe^{3+},Al)_6(Al,Si)_8O_{20}(OH)_4 \cdot 8H_2O$

The name vermiculite is applied to a group of micaceous minerals,
all hydrated silicates, in part closely related to the chlorites, but varying somewhat widely in composition. Some alternate names used (but

which should be abandoned) are: *jefferisite, culsageeite*. They do not in general merit species rank.

Fresno County: **1**, Vermiculite is reported in nodules with talc near Humphreys (sec. 22, T. 11 S., R. 23 E., M. D.), Pabst (8) p. 577.

Kern County: **1**, Vermiculite is reported in the Meeke tin mine as an associate of the ore, with other minerals, in the Gorman tin region, Jewell Glass in Wiese and Page (1) p. 39.

Riverside County: **1**, Brown to black plates up to 15 mm in diameter have been found in pegmatite at Crestmore, Woodford et al. (10) p. 374. **2**, Vermiculite has been observed in a biotite-rich intrusive in the Little San Bernardino Mountains (sec. 9, T. 3 S., R. 6 W., S. B.), R. Proctor (p.c. '57). This occurrence produced a small amount commercially in 1940. **3**, The mineral also occurs on the property of the Asbestos King mine, 15 miles southeast of Indio, R. Proctor (p.c. '57).

San Diego County: **1**, Vermiculite has been observed as an alteration of mica, **1**, at Pala, and **2**, at Rincon, G. A. Waring (4) pp. 363, 368.

* VERPLANCKITE, 1965 [1]
Basic barium manganese chlorosilicate, $Ba_2(Mn,Fe,Ti)Si_2O_6(O,OH,Cl)_2 \cdot 3H_2O$

Fresno County: **1**, At the Big Creek locality in the sanbornite-bearing rocks, the rarest of several new minerals, verplanckite, is found in brownish-orange clots and individual crystals from the deposits. The mineral is named for William E. Ver Planck, deceased member of the CDMG staff, Alfors and Stinson (5) p. 27. This entry, first appearing in February 1965 after the cut-off date for entries for this bulletin, is included because the article in which the preliminary description occurred is part II, of a report describing three new minerals in the same locality, Stinson and Alfors (6).

VIOLARITE
Iron nickel sulphide, $FeNi_2S_4$

San Diego County: **1**, Violarite occurs with pyrrhotite and chalcopyrite in the nickel ores of the Friday mine at Julian, M. N. Short and Shannon (1) p. 8, Donnelly (1) p. 370. This occurrence was earlier considered to be polydymite, Hess (15) p. 747, Donnelly (1) p. 370, Creasey (1) p. 27.

VIVIANITE
Hydrous ferrous phosphate, $Fe_3(PO_4)_2 \cdot 8H_2O$

Vivianite is frequently formed in sedimentary rocks, from phosphatic matter such as bones, in the presence of iron.

Alameda County: **1**, Small pieces of earthy blue vivianite were found in the hills behind Berkeley, CDMG (12983).

Butte County: **1**, Vivianite was doubtfully identified near Oroville, Hanks (12) p. 395.

Calaveras County: **1**, Vivianite has been found at Copperopolis (N. R.).

[1] This new mineral is described in a paper which appeared in April, 1965, after the cutoff date (Dec. 31, 1964) for entries in this volume. "Seven new barium minerals from eastern Fresno County, California", by John T. Alfors, Melvin C. Stinson, Robert A. Matthews and Adolf Pabst: Am. Mineralogist, vol. 50, pp. 314–340, 1965.

Humboldt County: **1,** Vivianite occurs at Yager, Lowell (1) p. 408, and **2,** it is reported to have been found on Maple Creek, ibid.

Inyo County: **1,** Vivianite, in crystals on quartz, is reported from the Darwin mines, Woodhouse (p.c. '47).

Los Angeles County: **1,** Vivianite, was early observed as earthy blue masses in the asphalt bed of the Rancho la Brea, where it formed by the decomposition of the bones of extinct animals. It was mentioned by W. P. Blake in Hanks (7) p. 265, Hanks (12) p. 395, H. W. Turner (22) p. 344.

Madera County: **1,** Dark-blue earthy masses of vivianite have been found near Raymond, CDMG (16493).

San Benito County: **1,** Vivianite was identified from the Sulphur Spring ore body of the New Idria mine, W. W. Bradley (p.c. '44), CDMG (21197).

San Mateo County: **1,** Chalky blue nodules of vivianite in siliceous rock have been found one mile north of Point Año Nuevo, Chesterman (p.c. '51).

Santa Barbara County: **1,** Vivianite was found at Concepcion, CDMG (18114).

Shasta County: **1,** Vivianite concretions were found near Burney, in diatomite of a Tertiary lake bed, W. W. Bradley (29) p. 107.

Yuba County: **1,** Good crystals of vivianite occurred near Camptonville and were described by A. W. Jackson (3) p. 371.

VOLBORTHITE
Hydrous copper vanadate, $Cu_3(VO_4)_2 \cdot 3H_2O$

Glenn County: **1,** Volborthite was reported to have been found at the Mammoth copper mine on Grindstone Creek (T. 22 N., R. 9 W., M. D.), CDMG (15139), E. S. Larsen (11) p. 154.

VOLTAITE
Hydrous potassium iron aluminum sulphate, $3(K_2Fe)O \cdot 2(Al,Fe)_2O_3 \cdot 6SO_3 \cdot 9H_2O$

Contra Costa County: **1,** Voltaite is reported from the Mount Diablo mine, in association with metallic sulphates, Watters (p.c. '57).

Napa County: **1,** Black isometric crystals of voltaite were found with knoxvillite and redingtonite at the Redington mine, Melville and Lindgren (1) p. 23.

San Benito County: **1,** Voltaite has been reported from the no. 4 level of the New Idria mine, W. W. Bradley (p.c. '44), CDMG (21166).

San Bernardino County: **1,** Voltaite was found by Foshag (19) p. 352, with krausite, copiapite, coquimbite and other sulphates in a lenticular mass near the ghost town of Borate, about 6 miles northeast of Yermo.

Shasta County: **1,** A. L. Day and Allen (1) p. 118, C. A. Anderson (1) p. 290, observed voltaite with melanterite on some altered pyrite from the Mount Lassen area.

Sonoma County: **1,** Dark-green voltaite occurs sparingly at The Geysers, E. T. Allen and Day (2) p. 40, and **2,** as black crusts in Geyser Creek Canyon, near the Witches Cauldron, Vonsen (6) p. 291.

* VONSENITE—Paigeite, 1920
Ferrous ferric borate, $Fe^{2+}_2Fe^{3+}BO_5$

Monterey County: **1,** Vonsenite is associated with magnetite and hedenbergite at a contact between granite and limestone in the Gabilan Range of eastern Monterey County, Chesterman (p.c. '64).

Riverside County: **1,** Vonsenite was discovered by M. Vonsen in the old City quarry at Riverside and described and named as a new mineral by Eakle (18) p. 141. Schaller (p.c. '46) considers vonsenite to be paigeite, since the mineral carries some tin which was missed in the first analysis.

WAIRAKITE
Hydrous calcium aluminum silicate, $CaAl_2Si_4O_{12}\cdot2H_2O$

Sonoma County: **1,** Wairakite is reported by Steiner (1) p. 781, from a greywacke fragment erupted from a new steam well at The Geysers. The mineral lines cavities and fractures in the specimen. Wairakite was first described as a mineral in 1955, and this occurrence is the first reported for California.

WALPURGITE
Hydrous bismuth uranyl arsenate, probably $Bi_4(UO_2)(AsO_4)_2O_4\cdot3H_2O$

Kern County: **1,** Walpurgite has been identified in the ore of the Miracle mine ($SE\frac{1}{4}$ sec. 17, T. 27 S., R. 32 E., M. D.), Troxel and Morton (2) p. 333.

* WALSTROMITE, 1964 [1]
Barium calcium silicate, $BaCa_2Si_3O_9$

Fresno County: **1,** Walstromite, a new mineral discovered in the sanbornite deposits along Big Creek and Rush Creek in the eastern part of the county, is named in honor of its discoverer, Robert E. Walstrom of Fresno. The mineral is described in a preliminary paper by Stinson and Alfors (6) p. 238. It is accompanied by the new minerals krauskopfite and macdonaldite, and is associated with gillespite, taramellite, celsian and other minerals.

WARDITE
Hydrous basic sodium calcium aluminum phosphate, $Na_4CaAl_{12}(PO_4)_8(OH)_{18}\cdot6H_2O$

San Diego County: **1,** Wardite occurs with jezekite in narrow veins in massive amblygonite in the Stewart mine, Pala, Murdoch (p.c. '53).

WATER—Ice
H_2O

Modoc and Siskiyou Counties: **1,** Permanent ice is found in lava tunnels in the Lava Bed National Monument, Swartzlow (1) p. 440.

WAVELLITE
Basic hydrous aluminum phosphate, $Al_6(PO_4)_4(OH)_6\cdot9H_2O$

El Dorado County: **1,** Wavellite occurs as veins and crusts in quartz, in well-formed colorless prisms and pale-green massive material, near Slate Mountain, Cureton (p.c. '59).

---

[1] This new mineral is described in a paper which appeared in April, 1965, after the cutoff date (Dec. 31, 1964) for entries in this volume. "Seven new barium minerals from eastern Fresno County, California," by John T. Alfors, Melvin C. Stinson, Robert A. Matthews and Adolf Pabst: Am. Mineralogist, vol. 50, pp. 314–340, 1965.

WEEKSITE
Hydrous potassium uranyl silicate, $K_2(UO_2)_2(Si_2O_5)_3 \cdot 4H_2O$

Inyo County: **1,** Weeksite occurs at a uranium prospect up slope from the Haiwee Reservoir in the Coso Mts., associated with haiweeite and uranophane, in fracture coatings on granite, Outerbridge et al. (1) p. 43.

WHITLOCKITE
Calcium phosphate, $Ca_3(PO_4)_2$

Trinity County: **1,** Whitlockite, with hydroxyapatite, has been identified in phosphate-bearing rocks near Hyampom (sec. 13, T. 3 N., R. 6 E., H.), Lydon (2) p. 67.

* WIGHTMANITE, 1962
Hydrous magnesium borate, $Mg_9B_2O_{12} \cdot 8H_2O$

Fresno County: **1,** Wightmanite occurs in metamorphosed dolomitic limestone in the Twin Lake region, associated with ludwigite, Chesterman (p.c. '64).

Riverside County: **1,** The new mineral wightmanite was found as single prisms or radiating clusters of crystals in crystalline limestone in the contact zone, 910′ level, Crestmore. It was first reported by Segnit (p.c. '61). It is associated with coarse grains of dolomite, occasional fluoborite and ludwigite (?). Wightmanite was named for Mr. R. H. Wightman, Director of Exploration and Mining, Riverside Cement Co., Murdoch (41) pp. 718–722.

* WILKEITE, 1914
Basic silicate/phosphate/carbonate/and sulphate of calcium with fluorine, $Ca_5(Si,P,S)_3O_{12}(O,OH,F)$

This rare mineral of the apatite group is unlike any other in having four acid radicals. It resembles apatite in physical properties.

Riverside County: **1,** Wilkeite, discovered at Crestmore and described as a new mineral in 1914, occurs in blue calcite associated with diopside, idocrase, garnet and its alteration product, crestmoreite, and was analyzed and named by Eakle and Rogers (13) p. 263, A. F. Rogers (31) p. 465. The crystal forms were described by Eakle (20) p. 343.

WILLEMITE
Zinc orthosilicate, Zn_2SiO_4

Inyo County: **1,** Willemite is found with hemimorphite and hydrozincite at the Ygnacio and Cerro Gordo mines, CDMG (8587), C. W. Merriam (1) p. 43.

WITHERITE
Barium carbonate, $BaCO_3$

Fresno County: **1,** Witherite is finely disseminated in quartzite with quartz, sanbornite, celsian, taramellite, gillespite, diopside, barite and pyrrhotite near Rush Creek (secs. 16, 17, T. 11 S., R. 25 E., M. D.), Matthews and Alfors (1) p. 2. **2,** The mineral is also found near Big Creek (secs. 22, 27, T. 11 S., R. 25 E., M. D.), CDMG (21890).

Mariposa County: **1,** Massive witherite occurs with barite in the deposit near El Portal, W. W. Bradley (12) p. 6, (13) p. 173, Fitch (2)

p. 461. According to Dolbear (9) p. 611, the barite of this deposit changes to witherite in the deeper levels. **2**, Witherite is also found with barite in the Devil's Gulch (secs. 17, 20, T. 4 S., R. 20 E., M. D.) (N. R.). **3**, Witherite, originally described as alstonite, is found with sanbornite and gillespite 1 mile north of Trumbull Peak, near Incline, A. F. Rogers (39) p. 171.

WOLFRAMITE
Iron manganese tungstate, (Fe,Mn)WO₄

Reinite is a varietal name for iron-rich wolframite (ferberite), pseudomorphous after scheelite. The iron-poor variety is called *hübnerite*, the iron-rich *ferberite*.

Alpine County: **1**, Hübnerite is found in the Zaca mine, Loope (Monitor) area, south of Markleeville, Gianella (1) p. 342.

Inyo County: **1**, Boulders of black wolframite have been found at the Monarch tungsten mine (T. 15 S., R. 41 E., M. D.), Ubehebe Mining District, C. A. Waring and Huguenin (2) p. 129, Partridge (1) p. 311. The tungsten mineral from the Monarch mine is probably ferberite, McAllister (4) p. 56. **2**, Wolframite has been reported from the Tin Mountain (T. 12 S., R. 41 E., M. D.), Hess (8) p. 724. **3**, Small pseudomorphs of wolframite after scheelite have been found at the Yaney tungsten mine near Bishop, McAllister (4) p. 76. The pseudomorphs are known by the varietal name reinite, and are associated with jarosite rich in WO_3, confirming Bateman (p.c. '49).

Kern County: **1**, Wolframite occurs in a pipe in granodiorite near Woody, Kerr (5) p. 421. **2**, Hübnerite (?) occurs in Jawbone Canyon about half a mile from the Granite King mine, Hess (12) p. 988, (13) p. 354, Partridge (1) p. 313, Troxel and Morton (2) p. 37. **3**, Wolframite occurs with scheelite at the Blue Point deposits (secs. 10, 11, T. 30 S., R. 31 E., M. D.), ibid., p. 312.

Madera County: **1**, Large crystals and masses of wolframite weighing several pounds occur in a quartz vein in andalusite schist on the I.X.L. claim, about 12 miles north of Raymond, R. P. McLaughlin and Bradley (3) p. 568. Pyrite is an accessory mineral, Hess (4) p. 271, Krauskopf (1) p. 73. **2**, Brownish-black crystals of wolframite associated with large cubes of pyrite occur in a quartz vein in micro-pegmatitic granite at the head of Iron Creek, Ritter Range, Minaret Mining District, Hess (18) p. 938, Erwin (1) p. 73, Krauskopf (1) p. 72. **3**, Wolframite has been found near Buchanan, Hanks (15) p. 140. **4**, Wolframite has been reported with tellurides, from Chiquita Ridge (sec. 28, T. 6. S., R. 23 E., M. D.), Laizure (2) p. 306.

Mono County: **1**, Wolframite occurs one mile east of Highway 395 and seven miles north of Mono Lake, CDMG (21709).

San Bernardino County: **1**, Wolframite has been found with scheelite and cinnabar, at the Jack claim, near Nipton, in the Clark Mountains, Hess (8) p. 724, (14) p. 47, and **2**, it occurs in a quartz vein with chalcopyrite, sphalerite and galena at the Sagamore mine, New York Mountains, Hess (8) p. 724, Cloudman et al. (1) p. 790. **3**, Wolframite and hübnerite were found in the Confidence mine (sec. 5, T. 11 N., R. 14 E., S. B.), near Kelso, Tucker (4) p. 340. **4**, Small crystals of wolframite occur in quartz stringers in a pegmatite at the Mojave Annex tungsten mine, north slope of the New York Mountains, 2 miles southeast of Brant, ibid., p. 373. **5,** Hübnerite and wolframite occur in sec. 35, T. 14 N., R. 15 E., S. B., Tucker and Sampson (30) p. 584. **6,** Fine crystals of wolframite, with some hübnerite, occur near Camp Signal, 6 miles north of Goffs, Hess (8) p. 724, Cloudman et al. (1) p. 843. **7,** Wolframite came from 15 miles northwest of Victorville, Hess (8) p. 724; and **8,** from the Ivanpah Mountains, Hess (6) p. 712. **9,** Hübnerite occurs in quartz veins with sulphide minerals in the Sagamore (New York) mine (secs. 33, 34, T. 13 N., R. 16 E., S. B.), L. A. Wright et al. (5) p. 67.

Tulare County: **1,** Wolframite occurs sparingly with molybdenite and scheelite southwest of Tamarack Lake, Sequoia National Park (approx. secs. 35, 36, T. 15 S., R. 31 E., S. B.), Tehipite quadrangle, Krauskopf (1) p. 81.

WOLLASTONITE
Calcium silicate, CaSiO₃

Wollastonite is formed as a metamorphic mineral in limestone near contacts with intrusive rocks.

No attempt has been made to report all of the occurrences of wollastonite found in the State that are referenced in the literature. The mineral is widespread and is so common that only occurrences of mineralogical interest should be included. However, some localities of minor importance and of little mineralogical interest are noted for the historical record because they have been reported in early editions of *Minerals of California.*

Alameda County: **1,** Wollastonite has been found in the Berkeley Hills (N. R.).

Amador County: **1,** Wollastonite was found massive on the Mokelumne River, near Bear Creek, and analyzed by Hillebrand, H. W. Turner (12) p. 703.

Del Norte County: **1,** White divergent masses of wollastonite were found near Crescent City (N. R.).

Fresno County: **1,** Wollastonite has been found about 3 miles southeast of Dunlap, Noren (p.c. '35), and **2,** it occurs in contact-metamorphosed limestone of the Twin Lakes area, Chesterman (1) p. 254.

Imperial County: **1,** Wollastonite was reported to occur with white grossularite near the state highway, a few miles west of El Centro, Melhase (6) p. 23.

Inyo County: **1,** Wollastonite occurs at the Wilshire gold mine, 25 miles southwest of Laws, H. W. Turner (35) p. 172; **2,** it occurs as bunches of radiating fibers with diopside in metamorphosed limestone at Round Valley on the north side of Tungsten Hills, 9 miles west of Bishop, Chapman (1) p. 866 and **3,** it occurs in the gangue of the cobalt veins at Long Lake (sec. 14, T. 9 S., R. 31 E., M. D.), Tucker and Sampson (25) p. 378. **4,** A very large deposit of wollastonite is said to occur in the Panamint Range northwest of Warm Springs, Vonsen (p.c. '45); **5,** it is abundant at the Christmas Gift mine at Darwin, A. Knopf (4) p. 12, and in large crystals in the contact limestones of that area, Kelley (4) p. 538, Hall and MacKevett (4) p. 63, and **6,** it occurs at the Cardinal Gold property (sec. 19, T. 8 S., R. 31

E., M. D.), Lenhart (1) p. 3. **7**, Wollastonite occurs in a contact zone at Birch Creek, Deep Spring Valley, Nash (1) pp. 48, 216.

Kern County: **1**, A deposit of wollastonite occurs near Code siding in the Rademacher area, W. W. Bradley (21) p. 183, Murdoch and Webb (11) p. 553, Tucker (24) p. 19, Troxel and Morton (2) p. 344; **2**, it was found outcropping in fibrous aggregates up to 6 inches, along the canyon of Clear Creek between the Kern River and Walker Basin, Melhase (8) p. 7, and **3**, it is found with scheelite in a contact deposit at the Rand group, Greenhorn Mountains (secs. 19, 20, T. 25 S., R. 32 E., M. D.), Hess and Larsen (17) p. 263.

Lake County: **1**, White drusy wollastonite has come from Dry Creek, near Middletown, CDMG (14012). **2**, Specimens of wollastonite have come from near Glenbrook, Irelan (4) p. 47.

Marin County: **1**, Wollastonite occurs as crystals and layers in schist on the shore of Tomales Bay, $1\frac{1}{2}$ miles northwest of Inverness, F. M. Anderson (1) p. 132.

Mono County: **1**, The mineral occurs with boulangerite in contact limestone in Leevining Canyon (sec. 13, T. 1 N., R. 25 E., M.D.), Murdoch (p.c. '45).

Napa County: **1**, White massive wollastonite occurs in Hunting Creek Canyon, near Knoxville, CDMG (13229).

Nevada County: **1**, White and pink wollastonite are found as contact minerals at Grass Valley (N. R.).

Riverside County: **1**, Wollastonite occurs in fibrous, columnar, and fine granular forms in the crystalline limestone at Crestmore as one of the contact-metamorphic minerals, Eakle (15) p. 334, Foshag (12) p. 88. Complex crystals were studied by Eakle. The triclinic character of some wollastonite was confirmed on excellent crystals from Crestmore, Peacock (3) p. 495. **2**, Pink granular wollastonite occurs at a contact of limestone and granodiorite in the new City quarry, Riverside, Eggleston (p.c. '36). **3**, The mineral was found at the scheelite deposit about 9 miles east of Aguanga, Hess and Larsen (17) p. 261. **4**, Wollastonite occurs with scapolite in the iron ores at Eagle Mountain, Hadley (1) p. 4.

San Diego County: **1**, Wollastonite occurs at Carrizo Gorge, near Jacumba, CDMG (21224), Symons (5) p. 62.

San Francisco County: **1**, A specimen of wollastonite has come from Fort Point, CDMG (205).

Santa Barbara County: **1**, A specimen of a divergent fibrous mineral labelled wollastonite, and having a pale-rose color, was found at Santa Ynez many years ago. It was studied by E. S. Larsen (8) p. 465, who thought it a new mineral and named it eakleite. Later studies showed the specimen to be xonotlite and the name eakleite was withdrawn, E. S. Larsen (13) p. 181.

Sierra County: **1**, Bands of wollastonite and wollastonite-quartz schist occur near Sierra City, on the small north tributary of the South Fork of the North Fork of Yuba River, opposite Milton Creek, S. G. Clark (p.c. '35).

Siskiyou County: **1**, Fine divergent specimens of wollastonite have come from the limestone on the Salmon River, 3 miles above Somes Bar (N. R.).

Tehama County: **1,** Wollastonite occurs in sec. 16, T. 25 N., R. 7 W., M. D., E. S. Dana (5) p. 1097, CDMG (9753).

Trinity County: **1,** White fibrous wollastonite occurs near Hyampam (N. R.).

Tulare County: **1,** Massive wollastonite is found in metamorphosed limestone near Three Rivers (sec. 16. T. 16 S., R. 28 E., M. D. and sec. 25, T. 17 S., R. 28 E., M. D.) and near Lemon Cove (secs. 11, 14, T. 16 S., R. 27 E., M. D.), Durrell (p.c. '35).

† * WOODFORDITE, 1958

Riverside County: **1,** This mineral, described from Crestmore as a new mineral by Murdoch and Chalmers (36), has been shown by the same authors (37) to be ettringite.

* WOODHOUSEITE, 1937
Basic calcium aluminum phosphate sulphate, $CaAl_3PO_4SO_4(OH)_6$

Mono County: **1,** Woodhouseite occurs in veins with quartz, topaz, lazulite and augelite in the andalusite deposit at the mine of Champion Sillimanite, on the western slope of the White Mountains, 7 miles east of Mocalno, north of Bishop. It was described and named by Lemmon (2) p. 939. An analysis of woodhouseite by A. Rautenberg has been reported by Lemmon (2) p. 943.

WULFENITE
Lead molybdate, $PbMoO_4$

El Dorado County: **1,** Wulfenite occurs in small grains near Garden Valley (N. R.).

Imperial County: **1,** Fine crystals of wulfenite have been found north of Salton, Orcutt (4) p. 26.

Inyo County: **1,** Crystals of wulfenite occurred with the linarite and caledonite at the Cerro Gordo mine, R. W. Raymond (1) p. 29. **2,** Wulfenite has been observed in the Darwin mines, Murdoch and Webb (14) p. 325, and **3,** it has been reported from the Ophir and other mines in the Slate Range, Tucker (11) p. 510. **4,** Wulfenite occurs as thin seams and crusts on malachite at the Empire mine (T. 21 S., R. 45 E., M. D.), W. P. Blake (14) p. 125. **5,** Well-formed crystals of wulfenite have been found at the Brown Monster mine, 2 miles east of Manzanar station, G. M. Wheeler (1) p. 45, A. Knopf (5) p. 118. **6,** Wulfenite occurs widely distributed with other lead minerals in the Ubehebe mine, as thinly tabular, and minute elongate crystals, McAllister (4) p. 24. **7,** Wulfenite is an important mineral at the Lippincott mine, McAllister (4) p. 39. **8,** Crystals of wulfenite have been found at the Big Four and Lemoigne mines, northern Panamint Mountains, Hall and Stephens (3) p. 26.

Kern County: **1,** Wulfenite was found 6 miles northeast of Kane Springs, Hanks (12) p. 395, and **2,** it has been tentatively identified in the gold ores of the Yellow Aster mine, Hess (10) p. 35.

Mono County: **1,** Crystals of wulfenite have been noted on a specimen of pyromorphite from Blind Spring Hill, A. L. Ransome (2) p. 192. **2,** Crystals of wulfenite have been found in an oxidized lead vein 6 miles east of Hammil station, Woodhouse (p.c. '45).

Plumas County: **1,** Wulfenite was found at the Diadem lode on Mumford Hill (N. R.). **2,** Wulfenite occurs in an oxidized zone in the Granite Basin Mining District, H. W. Turner (12) p. 589.

Riverside County: **1,** Wulfenite occurs at the El Dorado mine near Indio, Webb (p.c. '45), and **2,** it was reported to occur in the gold mines of the Chuckawalla Mountains, Orcutt (2) p. 901.

San Bernardino County: **1,** Wulfenite was found with cerussite in the Blackhawk (Silver Reef) Mining District, and **2,** at Holbergs gold mine in the Lava Beds Mining District, Storms (4) pp. 366, 359. **3,** Crystals of wulfenite from Lavic were described by Guild and Wartman (2) p. 167. **4,** The mineral occurs with vanadinite at the Vanadium King mine, near Goffs, University of California Collections, Berkeley; **5,** it was observed in limestone in the upper part of Black Hawk Canyon, Woodford and Harriss (4) p. 268, and **6,** it is found in the Calico Mining District, Cloudman et al. (1) p. 829. **7,** A considerable mass of wulfenite was shipped from near Tipton, Mining and Scientific Press (32) p. 171. **8,** Wulfenite is a minor constituent of the bastnaesite deposit at Mountain Pass, Pray (p.c. '51).

San Luis Obispo County: **1,** Wulfenite was found at the Fairview mine (N. R.).

WURTZITE
Zinc sulphide, ZnS

Mono County: **1,** Wurtzite was found in small, orange-brown grains, in contact limestone, with boulangerite and wollastonite (S$\frac{1}{2}$ sec. 13, T. 1 N., R. 25 E., M. D.), Milton (p.c. '44).

XENOTIME
Yttrium phosphate, YPO$_4$

Kern County: **1,** Xenotime is reported as a probable primary mineral from the pegmatite dikes in the Kern River uranium area, MacKevett (2) pp. 197, 206. This mineral is suggested as the source for the secondary uranium concentrations for the Kern River uranium field, ibid, p. 216.

Riverside County: **1,** Xenotime was found in well-formed crystals in pegmatite at the Southern Pacific silica quarry near Nuevo, Melhase (7) p. 11. It occurs here also in parallel growth with cyrtolite, Murdoch (p.c. '45). **2,** The mineral was reported from a pegmatite 2 miles north of Winchester (sec. 9, T. 5 S., R. 2 W., S. B.), W. W. Bradley (23) p. 117, Patchick (3). **3,** Xenotime occurs four miles due east of Nuevo as parallel intergrowths with cyrtolite in pegmatite, Seward (p.c. '60). **4,** Xenotime is reported in sands with monazite from Live Oak Tank area, 12 miles south of Twenty-Nine Palms, G. W. Walker et al. (5) p. 25. **5,** Xenotime occurs, usually in pods or lenses, in the Pinto gneiss of southern Music Valley, in a number of deposits: Ajax and Baby Blue (Dixie Girl) prospects with monazite; Hansen No. 2; Uranus No. 2; Uranus No. 4, with monazite; Uranus No. 6; U-Thor, with monazite and allanite (?), J. R. Evans (1) pp. 10–15.

Tulare County: **1,** Goodwin (1) p. 369, states: "... uranium and thorum-bearing minerals which have been identified in Tulare County include xenotime, euxenite, torbernite, autunite, and uraninite."

XONOTLITE
Hydrous calcium silicate, $CaSiO_3 \cdot \frac{1}{4}H_2O$

Mendocino County: **1,** Pale pink xonotlite occurs with pectolite, nephrite, and calcite in sheared serpentine at Leech Lake Mountain, Chesterman (p.c. '55).

Monterey County: **1,** Xonotlite associated with thomsonite occurs in veins from $\frac{1}{8}$ to 2 inches in width in metamorphic rocks in a stream bed 3 miles west of Priest Valley, CDMG, identification '64.

Riverside County: **1,** Jurupaite from Crestmore has been shown to be identical with xonotlite, H. F. W. Taylor (2) p. 338. Radiating white fibers up to 2 cm in length, associated with blue calcite and cinnamon-brown grossularite were described as a new mineral, Eakle (15) p. 347, (20) p. 107, named jurupaite. It is now a discredited species.

San Francisco County: **1,** Xonotlite occurred with brucite in veins in serpentine exposed by excavations of the Western Pacific Railroad on Army Street, San Francisco, Pabst (p.c. '44). **2,** Xonotlite occurs with hydromagnesite at Marshall Beach, near Fort Point, Watters (p.c. '57).

Santa Barbara County: **1,** A mineral specimen collected years ago near Santa Ynez, labelled wollastonite, was found by E. S. Larsen (8) p. 465 to differ optically from that mineral, and on the supposition that it was a new mineral, he proposed the name eakleite for it. E. S. Larsen (13) p. 181 later showed this material to be xonotlite.

YTTROCRASITE
A rare earth type mineral, near YTi_2O_5OH, Th to 9 percent

Riverside County: **1,** A few minute tabular crystals from the pegmatite of the Southern Pacific silica quarry at Nuevo, gave on spectroscopic analysis by Kennard and Drake: Fe, Ti,Y, large; Mn,Si, small. The crystals may be referred to this species, Murdoch (p.c. '45).

ZARATITE
Hydrous basic nickel carbonate, $Ni_3CO_3(OH)_4 \cdot 4H_2O$

Zaratite is always accompanied by chromite. The mineral occurs as incrustations on massive chromite. Most of the green coatings on the chromite of the State, however, consist of small uvarovite garnet crystals or green chlorite. J. B. Trask (2) p. 57, notes the occurrence of zaratite in fractures of chromite in the Coast Range counties from Contra Costa southward.

Alameda County: **1,** Green coatings of zaratite (?) occur on the chromite at the Mendenhall mine on Cedar Mountain, Woodhouse (p.c. '45).

Contra Costa County: **1,** "Nickel green," perhaps zaratite, was observed by J. B. Trask (4) p. 388, in this county.

Del Norte County: **1,** Zaratite coating chromite and with Kämmererite is reported in good specimens from the Blue Creek Mts. mine. Anon. (53) p. 153.

Madera County: **1,** Zaratite was found as a coating on chromite near Madera, CDMG (13414).

Mendocino County: **1,** Hanks (15) p. 140, reports zaratite on boulders of chromite (T. 20 N., R. 14 W., M. D.).

Monterey County: **1,** Zaratite was found on the chromite in this county, W. P. Blake (3) p. 82, (7) p. 303, (9) p. 13, Hanks (12) p. 396.

San Benito County: **1,** Zaratite was found on chromite near Hollister and near Panoche, Hanks (12) p. 396.

San Luis Obispo: **1,** Zaratite has been reported near San Luis Obispo, Cronise (1) p. 593.

Santa Clara County: **1,** Zaratite is a minor mineral in the New Almaden area, E. H. Bailey and Everhart (12) p. 102.

Shasta County: **1,** Zaratite was observed on the chromite at Castella (N. R.).

Siskiyou County: **1,** Green coatings of zaratite occur on the chromite near Callahan (N. R.).

ZINC
Zn

Shasta County: **1,** Several pieces of metallic zinc were reported by Fairbanks (2) p. 30, as coming from 5 miles southwest of Round Mountain. He is dubious of their truly natural character, but says that a fragment of rock was attached to one piece, and therefore considers that the occurrence may be authentic.

ZINNWALDITE
An iron lithia mica near biotite in composition and appearance,
$$K_2(Fe^{2+}_{2-1},Li_{2-3}Al_2)(Si_{6-7}Al_{2-1}O_{20})[F_{3-2}(OH)_{1-2}]$$

Riverside County: **1,** Greenish-gray flakes of zinnwaldite occur with calcite and vesuvianite at Crestmore, CDMG identification '64.

San Diego County: **1,** Zinnwaldite in dark-gray to reddish-brown flakes and crystals, up to a quarter of an inch in size, is associated with beryl, cleavelandite and other minerals in pockets of the pegmatites at Pala, Jahns and Wright (5) p. 31.

ZIPPEITE
Hydrous uranyl sulphate, $2UO_3 \cdot SO_3 \cdot 5H_2O(?)$ or $(UO_2)_2SO_4 \cdot 5H_2O$

San Luis Obispo County: **1,** Associated as orange yellow crusts with schroeckingerite, zippeite is reported from near Pozo, Woodhouse (p.c. '57).

ZIRCON
Zirconium silicate, $ZrSiO_4$

Zircon is a very common minor constituent in intrusive rocks, especially granites and syenites. Accordingly, the sands derived from the weathering of these rocks contain grains of zircon, and they are sometimes quite abundant in the black sands and gold placers from such sources. It is seldom a conspicuous mineral, but it occurs in small grains in many of the sands of the State. Zircon is also abundant in the granites, quartz-diorites, and mafic inclusions as a minor accessory mineral in the Coast Ranges in such areas as Bodega Head, Point Reyes Peninsula, Montara Mountain, Ben Lomond Mountain, and Farallon Islands, Spotts (1) pp. 1226–1234. *Cyrtolite* is a zircon with rare earth elements.

Alameda County: **1,** Zircon was mentioned by Palache (3) p. 184, as one of the constituents of the soda rhyolite of North Berkeley.

Butte County: **1,** Zircon was first mentioned in this state by Silliman (13) p. 385 as a constituent of the gold washings at Cherokee.

Fresno County: **1,** Splendid crystals of zircon have been found in the sands at Picayune Flat, Hanks (15) p. 141.

Inyo County: **1,** Lead-alpha ratios have been determined on zircons from Paleozoic rocks in the White Mountains, De Lisle (1) p. 33. **2,** Zircons of contact zones in the Pahrump formation, in the southern end of Death Valley, have been studied by Gastil (1) p. 180.

Kern County: **1,** Cyrtolite has been noted in a pegmatite dike in the Clear Creek area, Troxel and Morton (2) p. 290.

Los Angeles County: **1,** Abundant, clear, pinkish crystals of zircon have been found in a pegmatite in Pacoima Canyon (sec. 17, T. 3 N., R. 13 W., S.B.), Neuerburg (2) p. 833. Patchik (2) p. 237, gives detailed location diagrams.

Marin County: **1,** Zircon is present in vugs of the igneous rock in Heim Bros. quarry, Petaluma, Watters (p.c. '62).

Mono County: **1,** Minor amounts of zircon have been observed in the andalusite deposit 7 miles east of Mocalno, north of Bishop, R. J. Sampson and Tucker (4) p. 461, Woodhouse (4) p. 4.

Nevada County: **1,** Zircon is an abundant accessory mineral in the granodiorite of Nevada City, Lindgren (12) p. 37. Black sands from this area have yielded 928 pounds of zircon per ton, ibid. (20) p. 74.

Orange County: **1,** Age determinations have been made on detrital zircons from Bedford Canyon, Bushee (1) p. 30.

Placer County: **1,** Hyacinthine zircon is mentioned by Genth (1) p. 113, in sands with platinum and iridosmine on the North Fork, American River, and **2,** it has been produced commercially from the sands near Lincoln, Woodhouse (p.c. '45).

Plumas County: **1,** Zircon was a principal constituent of heavy sands from placer diggings at Spanish Ranch (Eagle Gulch), H. W. Turner (19) p. 426.

Riverside County: **1,** Zircon crystals of moderate size occur in some of the pegmatites at Crestmore, Eakle (15) p. 349, Woodford et al. (10) p. 375. **2,** Zircon crystals of the variety crytolite occur in a pegmatite four miles due east of Nuevo, intergrown with xenotime, Seward (p.c. '61); see crytolite. **3,** The age of zircons from the Rubidoux Mountain granite has been determined by Banks and Silver (1) p. 6.

San Bernardino County: **1,** Cyrtolite occurs with betafite in a lens of platy biotite in a pegmatite in the Cady Mountains, north of Hector, Hewett and Glass (3) p. 1044.

San Diego County: **1,** Zircon occurs in a pegmatite near Ramona, J. W. Patton (1) p. 116. **2,** Age determinations have been made from zircons from a number of localities in this county, Bushee (1) p. 30.

Santa Barbara County: **1,** Zircon occurs prominently as near-perfect crystals in microscopic sizes in the beach sands in the vicinity of Santa Barbara, Norris and Woodhouse (4) p. 21, confirming Woodhouse (p.c. '57). **2,** Pink zircon is recorded among the heavy minerals of the Alegria and Vaqueros formations in the Gaviota area, Grenden (1) p. 269.

References to a few of the other minor occurrences follow listed by county: *Amador,* CDMG (4892); *Mendocino,* Hanks (15) p. 141; *Plumas,* Graton and McLaughlin (4) p. 6; *Riverside,* Harder (6) p. 45; *San Diego,* Schaller (7) p. 211; *Siskiyou,* Eakle (1) p 319. Zircon is found in addition, in minor amounts, in sands of the following counties: Calaveras, Del Norte, El Dorado, Humboldt, Marin, Nevada, Sacramento, San Luis Obispo, San Mateo, Santa Cruz, Shasta, Trinity, and Yuba.

ZOISITE
Basic calcium aluminum silicate, $Ca_2Al_3(SiO_4)_3(OH)$

Thulite is a pink variety containing a small amount of manganese. *Saussurite* is a mixture of zoisite, calcite and plagioclase feldspar formed in gabbros and plutonic rocks by alteration. Zoisite is often developed by the metamorphism of gabbros and diorites.

Inyo County: **1,** Thulite occurs in large irregular patches in boulders on the east side of Saline Valley near the south end, Murdoch and Webb (4) p. 69 (called bustamite by them), Schaller and Glass (54) p. 519, McAllister (4) p. 63.

Kern County: **1,** Zoisite crystals up to one inch in length occur in schist about 2 miles south of Randsburg, Hulin (1) p. 25, M. F. B. Strong (1) p. 21. **2,** Zoisite is a minor mineral with cassiterite ores in the property near Gorman, Troxel and Morton (2) p. 294.

Lake County: **1,** The zoisite mentioned by Becker (4) p. 79 as common in the metamorphic rocks at Sulphur Bank is probably pale epidote. It is common in the Coast Range, ibid., p. 79.

Los Angeles County: **1,** White veinlets of fine-grained zoisite occur cutting albitized rock in many places in the Santa Monica Mountains, localities 27, 28, 29, 30, 31, 32, Neuerburg (1) p. 160. **2,** The occurrence and relationships of zoisite in the Pelona schist is discussed by Ehlig (1) p. 170.

Mendocino County: **1,** Very large radiating crystal clusters of zoisite have been found at Syke Rock (T. 20 N., R. 14 W., M. D.), 3 miles east of Longvale on the new Covelo road, Vonsen (p.c. '45).

Mono County: **1,** Zoisite, variety thulite, has been found near Baldwin Mountain, associated with scheelite in a contact zone, Ķerr (6) p. 159.

Plumas County: **1,** Zoisite was reportedly found with rhodonite in the Diadem lode, Meadow Valley, H. W. Turner (12) p. 590.

Riverside County: **1,** Thulite is found in bright-pink crystals in quartz monzonite pegmatite at Crestmore, Woodford et al. (10) p. 214.

San Bernardino County: **1,** Zoisite occurs with axinite in the Henshaw quarry (SE¼ sec. 33, T. 1 S., R. 5 W., S. B.), Cooney (p.c. '53).

San Diego County: **1,** Zoisite occurs with actinolite in boulders of sausserite gabbro in the San Onofre breccia, Woodford (2) p. 193.

Santa Clara County: **1,** Zoisite was mentioned by Murgoci (1) p. 359, and J. P. Smith (1) p. 193, as a microscopic constituent in the eclogite of Oak Ridge.

Sonoma County: **1,** Zoisite occurs near Healdsburg (N. R.).

Tulare County: **1,** Large masses of zoisite occur in a metamorphosed gabbro west and south of Rocky Hill, near Exeter (secs. 18, 20, T. 19 S., R. 27 E., M. D.), Durrell (p.c. '35).

*ZUSSMANITE, 1964

A complex silicate with sodium, potassium, magnesium, iron, aluminum and titanium, near $(Na_{.07}K_{.92})_{.99}(Mg_{1.33}Mn_{.46}Fe''_{10.85})_{10.85}$-
$(Fe'''Al_{.34}Ti_{.01})_{13.1}(Si_{16.6}Al_{1.4})_{18}O_{42.2}(OH)_{13.8}$

Mendocino County: **1,** Zussmanite occurs as an important mineral in Franciscan rocks near Laytonville (51) p. 138, Agrell (1) p. 1507.

UNNAMED MINERALS

Riverside County: Crestmore: 10 Å hydrate, $xCaO \cdot SiO_2 \cdot 10H_2O$. Heller and Taylor (1) p. 37, describe one of the calcium silicate hydrates of the tobermorite series, occurring locally in the crusts in the contact zone at Crestmore, but they do not assign a name to the material.

Santa Cruz County: Kalkar quarry: Unknown silicate. Gross and Wainwright (1) p. 36, describe a mineral associated with taramellite in the contact metamorphic limestone at the Kalkar quarry near Santa Cruz. They do not assign a name to the mineral. (Ed. note: Too late for the December 1964 cutoff date for this volume, this mineral was named pabstite $(Ba[Sn_{78}Ti_{22}]Si_3O_9)$ by Gross, E. B., Wainwright, J. E., and Evans, B. W., in "Pabstite, the tin analogue of benitoite", Am. Mineralogist, vol. 50, pp. 1164–1169, 1965.)

BIBLIOGRAPHY

SERIALS CONSULTED

Acad. Sci. Paris. Académie des sciences, Paris.
Comptes rendus hebdomadaires des séances. 1835+

Acad. Nat. Sci. Philadelphia. Academy of Natural Sciences of Philadelphia.
Proceedings. 1841+
Journal. 1817–1918.
Notulae Naturae. 1939+

Acad. Sci. St. Louis. Academy of Science of St. Louis.
Transactions. 1856+

Am. Acad. Arts. Sci. American Academy of Arts and Sciences, Boston.
Proceedings. 1846+
Memoirs. 1821+

Acta Crystallographica. 1948+

Akademiia Nauk, USSR, Leningrad.
Doklady (Comptes Rendus) 1934+

Am. Anthropologist. American Anthropologist, Washington, D.C. 1888+

Am. Assoc. Advancement Sci. American Association for the Advancement of Science, New York.
Proceedings. 1848+

Am. Assoc. Petroleum Geologists. American Association of Petroleum Geologists.
Bulletin. 1917+

Am. Ceramic Soc. American Ceramic Society.
Bulletin.

Am. Chem. Soc. American Chemical Society.
Journal. 1879+
Proceedings. 1876+

Am. Geologist. American Geologist, Minneapolis. 1888–1905.

Am. Inst. Min. Met. Eng. American Institute of Mining and Metallurgical Engineers.
Transactions. 1871+
Bulletins. 1905–19.
Technical Publications. 1927+

Am. Jour. Sci. American Journal of Science, New Haven. 1818+

Am. Mineralogist. American Mineralogist, Lancaster, Penn. 1916+

Am. Min. Rev. American Mining Review. See Los Angeles Mining Review.

Am. Mus. Nat. History. American Museum of Natural History, New York.
Bulletin. 1881+
Memoirs. 1893+
Novitates.

Am. Naturalist. American Naturalist, Boston, New York. 1867+

Am. Petrol. Inst. American Petroleum Institute.
Preliminary Reports.

Am. Philos. Soc. American Philosophical Society, Philadelphia.
Memoirs. 1935+
Proceedings. 1838+
Transactions. 1769+

Annalen der Chemie und Pharmazie (von Justus Liebig), Heidelberg. 1832+

Annalen der Physik, Halle, Leipzig. 1799+ (Poggendorff's)

Annales Chimie Physique. Annales de Chimie et de Physique, Paris. 1789–1913.

Annales des mines, Paris. 1816–1918.

Annotated Bibliography Econ. Geology. Annotated Bibliography of Economic Geology, Lancaster, Penn. 1929+

Archiv für wiss. Kunde von Russland. Archiv für wissenschaftliche Kunde von Russland, Berlin. 1841–67.

Arizona Min. Jour. Arizona mining Journal, Phoenix. 1917+

Berg- u. hüttenm. Zeit. Berg—and hüttenmänische Zeitung, Freiberg, Leipzig. 1842–1904.

Blackwood's Mag. Blackwood's Magazine, Edinburgh ; London. 1817+

Boston Soc. Nat. History. Boston Society of Natural History.
Memoirs. 1862+
Proceedings. 1841+

California Acad. Sci. California Academy of Sciences, San Francisco.
Bulletin. 1884–87.
Memoirs. 1868+
Proceedings. 1854+
Occasional Papers. 1890–1931.

California Div. Mines and Geology. California Div. Mines. California State Division of Mines (California State Mining Bureau).
Reports. 1880+
Bulletins. 1880+
County Reports. 1962+
Mineral Information Service. 1948+
Preliminary Reports. 1913+
Special Reports. 1950+
Miscellaneous Publications. 1881+

California Geological Survey.
Reports. 1851–80.

California Jour. Technology. California Journal of Technology, Berkeley. 1903–14.

Canadian Jour. Sci. Canadian Journal of Science, Literature, and History, Toronto. 1852–78.

Canadian Min. Jour. Canadian Mining Journal, Ottawa ; Toronto ; Montreal. 1882+

Carnegie Inst. Washington. Carnegie Institution of Washington.
Publications. 1902+
Yearbook. 1902+

Centralbl. Mineralogie. Centralblatt für Mineralogie, Geologie, und Palæontologie, Stuttgart. 1900–24. Abt. A,B, 1925–40, in combination with Neues Jahrbuch.

Chem. Abstracts. Chemical Abstracts, Easton, Penn. 1907+

Chem. Eng. and Min. Rev. Chemical Engineering and Mining Review, Melbourne. 1908+

Chem. Gazette. Chemical Gazette (Journal of Practical Chemistry), London, 1842–59. Continued as Chemical News ; later as Chemical News and Journal of Industrial Science.

Chem. News. Chemical News and Journal of Industrial Science, London, 1859–1932. Preceded by Chemical Gazette, 1842–59.

Chem. Soc. London. Chemical Society, London.
Journal. 1847+

Colliery Eng. Colliery Engineer, Pottsville ; Scranton, Penn.

Colorado Sci. Soc. Colorado Scientific Society.
Proceedings, Denver. 1883+

Columbia Univ., School of Mines Quart. Columbia University, School of Mines Quarterly. 1879–1915.

Congrès international des Mines, de la Metallurgie, de la Mechanique, et de la Géologie appliquées.

Dana Mag. The Dana Magazine, Los Angeles. 1940+

Deutsche geol. Gesell. Zeitschr. Deutsche geologische Gesellschaft, Berlin Zeitschrift. 1848+

Dinglers Polytech. Jour. Dinglers Polytechnisches Journal, Berlin ; Stuttgart. 1820–1931.

Econ. Geology. Economic Geology, Lancaster, Penn. 1905+

Eng. and Min. Jour. Engineering and Mining Journal, New York. 1866+

Engineering and Science Monthly, California Institute of Technology, Pasadena, California. 1938+

Eng. Index. Engineering Index, New York. 1895+

Eng. Mag. Engineering Magazine (now Factory and Industrial Management), New York, 1891–1933.

Field Mus. Nat. History. Field Museum of Natural History (Field Columbian Museum), Chicago.
Publications, Geological Series. 1895+

Fortschr. Mineralogie. Fortschritte der Mineralogie, Kristallographie, und Petrographie, Berlin; Jena. 1911+

Franklin Inst. Franklin Institute, Philadelphia.
Journal. 1826+

Gems and Gemology.
1934+

Gems and Minerals (formerly Mineral Notes and News), Palmdale, California.
September 1953+

Geol. Mag. Geological Magazine, London. 1864+

Geol. Rec. Geological Record, London. 1874–84.

Geol. Soc. America. Geological Society of America, New York. 1888+
Bulletins. 1888+
Proceedings. 1933+
Programs of Meetings. 1888+
Special Papers. 1961+

Geol. Soc. London. Geological Society of London.
Quarterly Journal. 1845+

K. geol. Reichsanstalt. Geologische Bundesanstalt (Kaiserlich-königlich geologische Reichsanstalt, Geologische Staatsanstalt), Vienna.
Verhandlungen. 1867+
Jahrbuch. 1850+
Abhandlungen. 1851+

Geol. Rundschau. Geologische Rundschau, Zeitschrift für Allgemeine Geologie, Leipzig. 1910+

Geol. Zentralbl. Geologisches Zentralblatt, Leipzig; Berlin. 1901+

Geologist. The Geologist, London (superseded by Geological Magazine). 1858+

Griffith Observer, Los Angeles. 1937+

Harvard Univ. Mus. Comp. Zoology. Harvard University, Museum of Comparative Zoology.
Memoirs. 1864+
Bulletin. 1863+

Heidelberger Beiträge. 1947+

Hist. Soc. Southern California. Historical Society of Southern California, Los Angeles.
Publications. 1884+

Hobbies, Buffalo Society of Natural Sciences. 1920+

Hunts Merchants Mag. See Merchants Magazine and Commercial Review.

India, Geol. Survey. India, Geological Survey of.
Memoirs. 1859+

L'Institut. L'Institut de Sciences Mathématiques, Physiques, et Naturelles, Paris.
Journal general des societés et traveaux scientifiques de la France et de L'Etranger.

Inst. Min. Eng. Institution of Mining Engineers, Newcastle-upon-Tyne.
Transactions. 1889+

Inst. Min. Metallurgy. Institution of Mining and Metallurgy, London.
Transactions. 1892+

Inst. Petroleum Technologists. Institution of Petroleum Technologists, London.
Journal. 1914+

Internat. Geol. Cong. International Geological Congress.
Guide des excursions, Comptes rendus, Report, Guide-book.

Jour. Chemical Physics. Journal of Chemical Physics, New York. 1933+

Jour. Gemmology. Journal of Gemmology, London. 1947+

Jour. Geology. Journal of Geology, Chicago. 1893+

Jour. Geophysical Res. Journal of Geophysical Research.

Jour. Petrology. Journal of Petrology, London. 1960+

Jour. Physical Chemistry. Journal of Physical Chemistry, Ithaca. 1896+

Jour. prakt. Chemie. Journal für praktische Chemie, Leipzig. 1834+

Jour. Res. Natl. Bur. Standards. Journal of Research of the National Bureau of Standards, Washington, D.C. 1934+

Jour. Sed. Petrology. Journal of Sedimentary Petrology, Tulsa, Oklahoma. 1931+

K. geol. Reichsanstalt. Kaiserliche-königliche geologische Reichsanstalt, Vienna.

K. Naturh. Hofmuseum. Kaiserliche-königliche Naturhistorisches Hofmuseum, Vienna.

Kansas City Rev. Sci. and Ind. Kansas City Review of Science and Industry (Western Review of Science and Industry) Kansas City, Mo.

Lapidary Journal.

Living Age, Boston. 1844+

Los Angeles Junior College. Los Angeles Junior College Publication, Geology Series.

Los Angeles Mining Rev. Los Angeles Mining Review (American Mining Review). Los Angeles 1896–1913.

Los Angeles Times.

Lyceum Nat. History New York. Lyceum of Natural History of New York (New York Academy of Sciences)
Annals. 1823+

Manchester Geol. and Min. Soc. Manchester Geological and Mining Society. Transactions. 1841–1902.

Merchants Magazine and Commercial Review (Hunts Merchants Magazine), New York. 1839–70.

Meteoritical Soc. Cont. Meteoritical Society, Contributions. Contributions of the Society for Research on Meteorites, 1946–1953.

Meteoritics. The journal of the Meteoritical Society and the Institute of Meteoritics of the University of New Mexico. 1953+

Mineral Collector, New York. 1894–1909.

Mineral Industry, New York, London. 1892+

Mineral Notes and News—See Gems and Minerals.

Mineralog. Abstracts. Mineralogical Abstracts, London. 1920+

Mineralog. Mag. Mineralogical Magazine and Journal of the Mineralogical Society, London. 1876+

Mineralog. Mitt. Mineralogische und petrographische Mitteilungen, Vienna.

Mineral. Soc. Southern California. Mineralogical Society of Southern California, Altadena.
Bulletin. 1931–34.

Mineralogist, The (Oregon Mineralogist), Portland. 1934–1937. See Gems and Minerals.

Mines and Methods, Salt Lake City. 1909–20.

Mines and Minerals (Colliery Engineer), Scranton, Penn. 1881–1915.

Min. American. Mining American, Denver.

Min. and Eng. World. Mining and Engineering World (Mining World, Western Mining World), Butte, Chicago.

Min. and Oil Bull. Mining and Oil Bulletin, Los Angeles. 1914–32.

Min. Cong. Jour. Mining Congress Journal, American Mining Congress, Washington; Denver. 1915+

Min. Jour. Mining Journal, London. 1835+

Min. Mag. Mining Magazine, London. 1909+

Min. Mag. and Jour. Mining Magazine and Journal of Geology, Mineralogy, Metallurgy, Chemistry, etc., New York. 1853–61.

Min. Met. Soc. America. Mining and Metallurgical Society of America, New York. Bulletin. 1908+

Min. Sci. Press. Mining and Scientific Press, San Francisco. 1860–1922.

Min. World. Mining World (Mining and Engineering World), Butte; Chicago. 1894–1917.

Mining and Metallurgy, American Institute of Mining and Metallurgical Engineers, New York. 1905+

Mining Investor, Colorado Springs; Denver. 1894–1918.

Mining Reporter (Mining American, Mining Science), Denver. 1898–1907.

Mining Science (Mining American, Mining Reporter), Denver. 1908–12.

Montan. Rundschau. Montanistische Rundschau, Berlin; Vienna. 1908+

Nat. Acad. Sci. National Academy of Sciences, Washington.
Memoirs. 1866+
Proceedings. 1915+

Nat. Geog. Mag. National Geographic Magazine, Washington. 1888+

Nature, London. 1869+

Naturh. Ver. preuss. Rheinlande u. Westfalens. Naturhistorischer Verein der Preussischen Rheinlande und Westfalens, Bonn.
Verhandlungen. 1849+

Naturh. Mus. Wien. Naturhistorisches Hofmuseum, Wien.
Annalen. 1886+

Naturwiss. Ver. für Neu-Vorpommern und Rügen Greifswald. Naturwissenschaftlicher Verein von Neu-Vorpommern und Rügen, Greifswald.
Mitteilungen. 1869+

Neues Jahrb. Neues Jahrbuch für Mineralogie, Geologie und Paleontologie, Heidelberg; Stuttgart. 1830+
Beilage. 1881+
Monatschäfte. 1950+

New York Acad. Sci. New York Academy of Sciences (Lyceum of Natural History of New York).
Annals. 1877+
Proceedings. 1870+
Transactions. 1881+

Niederrheinische Gesell. Sitzungsber. Niederrheinische Gesellschaft für Natur- und Heilkunde, Bonn.
Sitzungsberichte. 1854–1905.

Oil Bull. Oil Bulletin (Mining and Oil Bulletin), Los Angeles; New York.

Oregon Mineralogist. 1933–34. See Gems and Minerals.

Overland Monthly, San Francisco. 1868–1935.

Pacific Coast Ann. Min. Rev. Pacific Coast Annual Mining Review, San Francisco. 1878–89.

Pacific Min. News. Pacific Mining News, San Francisco (supplement to Engineering and Mining Journal-Press). 1922–23.

Pacific Mineralogist, Los Angeles. 1934+

Paleontologisches Zentralblatt, Leipzig; Berlin. 1932+

Palisadian, The, Pacific Palisades, California.

Pan-Am. Geologist. Pan-American Geologist, Des Moines. 1922–1942.

Petermanns Mitt. Petermanns geographische Mitteilungen aus Justus Perthes geographischer Anstalt, Gotha. 1855+
Beilage.
Ergänzungsheft. 1861+

Petroleum Times, London. 1919+

Pharmaceutical Journal, London. 1841+

Philos. Mag. Philosophical Magazine (London, Edinburgh, and Dublin Philosophical Magazine and Journal of Science), London, 1798+

Pioneer. Pioneer, or California Monthly Magazine, San Francisco, 1854–55.

Pit and Quarry, Chicago. 1916+

Poggendorffs Annalen der Physik. See Annalen der Physik, Leipzig. 1799+

Popular Astron. Popular Astronomy. Northfield, Minn. 1893–1951.

Popular Sci. Monthly. Popular Science Monthly, New York. 1872+

Popular Sci. Rev. Popular Science Review, London. 1861–81.

Rev. des Deux Mondes. Revue des deux Mondes, Paris. 1831+

Rev. géologie et sci. Connexes. Revue de géologie et des sciences connexes, Liége. 1920+

Rocks and Minerals, Peekskill, New York. 1926+

Royal Micr. Soc. Royal Microscopical Society, London.
Journal. 1878+

Royal Soc. London. Royal Society of London.
Proceedings. 1800+

San Diego Department of Agriculture. Division of Natural Resources, San Diego, Calif.
Annual Reports. 1945+

San Diego Mus. Archeology. San Diego Museum, Archeology.
Papers. 1929+

San Diego Soc. Nat. History. San Diego Society of Natural History.
Transactions. 1905+
Memoirs. 1931+

Santa Barbara Mus. Nat. History. Santa Barbara Museum of Natural History.
Occasional Papers. 1932+
Bulletins.

Sci. Am. Scientific American, New York. 1845+

Science, Cambridge, Mass.; New York; etc. 1883+

Scottish Geog. Mag. Scottish Geographical Magazine, Edinburgh. 1885+

Sedimentology. Journal of the International Association of Sedimentologists.
London. 1962+

Siskiyou County Historical Society. Yreka, California, Siskiyou Pioneer.

Smithsonian Inst. Smithsonian Institution, Washington.
Annual Reports. 1846+
Miscellaneous Papers. 1862+
Contributions to Knowledge. 1848–1916.
Scientific Series. 1929–32.

Soc. franç. minéralogie. Société français de Minéralogie, Paris.
Bulletin. 1878+

Soc. geol. Belgique. Société geologique de Belgique, Liége.
Annales. 1874+

Soc. California Pioneers. Society of California Pioneers, San Francisco.
Quarterly. 1924–33.

Soc. Res. Meteorites, Cont. Contributions of the Society for Research on Meteorites, Northfield, Minnesota. 1937–1951. See Meteoritics.

Southern California Acad. Sci. Southern California Academy of Sciences, Los Angeles.
Bulletin. 1902+

Southwest Mus. Masterkey. Southwest Museum, The Masterkey, Los Angeles. 1926+

Stanford University, University Publications, Dept. Geology.
Contributions. 1930+

Uebersicht der Resultate Mineralog. Forschungen. Uebersicht der Resultate Mineralogischer Forschungen, Wein.
Jahrgang. 1844–65.

U.S. Bur. Mines. United States Bureau of Mines, Washington.
Bulletins, 1910+
Technical Papers, 1911+
Information Circulars. 1925+
Minerals Yearbook. 1932+
Mineral Resources. 1924–31.

U.S. Census Rept. United States Census Report, Washington.

U.S. Coast Geod. Survey. United States Coast and Geodetic Survey, Washington.

U.S. Dept. Agr., Bur. Soils. United States Department of Agriculture, Bureau of Soils, Washington.
Circulars.
Bulletin.

U.S. Geog. Survey W. 100th Mer. United States Geographical Surveys West of the 100th Meridian.

U.S. Geol. Survey. United States Geological Survey, Washington.
  Professional Papers. 1902+
  Bulletins. 1883+
  Water-Supply Papers. 1896+
  Monographs. 1890+
  Folios. 1894+
  Annual Reports. 1880+
  Mineral Resources. 1882–1927.

U.S. Nat. Mus. United States National Museum, Washington.
  Bulletin. 1875+
  Proceedings. 1878+

Univ. California, Berkeley.
  Department of Geological Sciences Bulletin. 1893+
  Publications in American Archeology and Ethnology. 1903+

Univ. California, Los Angeles.
  Publications in Mathematical and Physical Sciences, 1934+
  Publications in Astronomy. 1934+

Univ. Nevada.
  Mackay School of Mines Staff Bulletin. 1904+

Univ. Toronto.
  Studies, Geological Series. 1900+

Vidensk, selsk. Kristiania. Videnskabs-selskabet i Kristiania (Norske Videnskaps-Akademie i Oslo).
  Forhandlinger. 1857+

Volcano Letter, The, Honolulu, 1925+

Washington Acad. Sci. Washington Academy of Sciences, Washington, D.C.
  Journal. 1911+
  Proceedings. 1899–1911.

West Am. Sci. West American Scientist, San Diego. 1884–1921.

Western Rev. Sci. Ind. Western Review of Science and Industry (Kansas City Review of Science and Industry), Kansas City, Mo. 1877–85.

Zeitschr. Berg-, Hüttenm- u. Salinenwesen preuss. Staate. Zeitschrift für das Berg– Hütten– und Salinenwesen in preussischen Staate, Berlin. 1853+

Zeitschr. für die gesamte Naturwiss. Zeitschrift für die gesamte Naturwissenschaft, Brunswick. 1935+

Zeitschr. Krystallographie. Zeitschrift für Mineralogie, Krystallographie und Petrologie, Leipzig. 1877+

Zeitschr. prakt. Geol. Zeitschrift für praktische Geologie, Berlin. 1893+

Zeitschr. Vulkanologie. Zeitschrift für Vulkanologie, Berlin. 1914–38.

Zoe; a Biological Journal, San Francisco. 1890–1908.

REFERENCES

A

Abbott, Charles Conrad
1. Steatite cooking pots, plates, and food vessels, in Wheeler, George M., Geographical and geological explorations and surveys west of the 100th meridian . . . VII (archeology), pp. 93–214, 1879.

Abbott, James W.
1. The Greenwater district: Min. Sci. Press, vol. 94, pp. 52–53, 1907.

Adams, Sidney F.
1. A replacement of wood by dolomite: Jour. Geology, vol. 28, pp. 356–365, 1920.

Agey, W. W.
1. (and **Shibler, B. K.**) Concentration of oxide manganese ores from the Turtle claims and Pacific Coast manganese properties, Paymaster district, Imperial County, California: U.S. Bur. Mines Dept. Invest. 4441, 9 pp., April 1949.

Agrell, Stuart Olof
1. Deerite, howieite and zussmanite, three new minerals from the Franciscan of the Laytonville district, Mendocino County, California: (title only) Am. Mineralogist, vol. 49, p. 1507, 1964.

Albers, John P.
1. See Kinkel, Arthur Rudolph, Jr. (1).
2. See Kinkel, Arthur Rudolph, Jr. (2).
3. (and **Robertson, Jacques F.**) Geology and ore deposits of East Shasta copper-zinc district, Shasta County, California: U.S. Geol. Survey Prof. Paper 338, 107 pp., 1961.
4. Geology of the French Gulch quadrangle, Shasta and Trinity Counties, California: U.S. Geol. Survey Bull. 1141-J, pp. J1–J70, 1964.

Alfors, John Theodore
1. (**Stinson, Melvin Clarence, Matthews, Robert Alfred,** and **Pabst, Adolf**): (title only). Seven new barium minerals from eastern Fresno County, California: Am. Mineralogist, vol. 49, p. 1507, 1964. (Note: A paper of this title appearing after the cutoff date for this volume is Am. Mineralogist, vol. 50, pp. 314–340, 1965.)
2. See Matthews, Robert Alfred (1).
3. Piemontite from Shadow Lake: California Div. Mines and Geol., Mineral Information Service, vol. 17, p. 210, 1964.
4. See Stinson, Melvin Clarence (3).
5. See Stinson, Melvin Clarence (6).
6. (and **Stinson, Melvin Clarence**). New minerals from Fresno County—II: California Div. Mines and Geol., Mineral Information Service, vol. 18, pp. 27–30, 1965.

Alger, Francis
1. Crystallized gold from California: Am. Jour. Sci., 2d ser., vol. 10, pp. 101–106, 1850.
2. On specimens of crystallized gold from California: Boston Soc. Nat. History Proc., vol. 3, pp. 266–267, 1850.
3. Remarks on several very remarkable crystals of gold from California: Am. Acad. Arts Sci. Proc., vol. 2, pp. 246–249, 1852.

Allen, Eugene Thomas
1. See Day, Arthur Louis (1).
2. (and **Day, Arthur Louis**) Steam wells and other thermal activity at "The Geysers," California: Carnegie Inst. Washington Pub. 378, 106 pp., 1927 . . . (abstract): Geol. Zentralbl., Band 38, pp. 176–177, 1928 . . . Neues Jahrb., Referate 2, pp. 634–636, 1928 . . . Scottish Geog. Mag., vol. 44, pp. 230–231, 1928.
3. See Wright, Fred Eugene (3).

Allen, John Eliot
1. Geologic features of west coast chromite deposits: Mining and Metallurgy, vol. 20, no. 386, p. 100, Feb. 1939.
2. Geologic investigation of the chromite deposits of California: Calif. Div. Mines Rept. 37, pp. 101–167, 1941.
3. Geology of the San Juan Bautista quadrangle, California: California Div. Mines Bull. 133, 75 pp., 1946 . . . (abstract) Geol. Soc. America Bull. 56, p. 1143, 1945.

Allen, Robert D.
1. (and **Kramer, Henry C.**) Occurrence of bassanite in two desert areas in southeastern California: Am. Mineralogist, vol. 38, pp. 1266–1268, 1953.
2. See Kramer, Henry C. (1).
3. (and **Kramer, Henry C.**). Hornblende in diorite pegmatite near Camp Irwin, San Bernardino County, California: Am. Mineralogist, vol. 40, pp. 527–29, 1955.
4. See Kramer, Henry C. (5).
5. See Muessig, Siegfried (1).
6. (and **Kramer, Henry C.**). Ginorite and sassolite from Death Valley, California: Am. Mineralogist, vol. 42, pp. 56–61, 1957.
7. See Muessig, Siegfried (2).
8. (and **Almond, Hy**) Non-fibrous ulexite from the Kramer district, California: Am. Mineralogist, vol. 43, pp. 169–70, 1958.

Allen, Victor Thomas
1. Ionite, a hydrous silicate of aluminum (abstract): Am. Mineralogist, vol. 12, p. 78, 1927 . . . Mineralog. Abstracts, vol. 3, p. 370, 1927.
2. Anauxite from the Ione formation of California: Am. Mineralogist, vol. 13, pp. 145–152, 1928 . . . Annotated Bibliography Econ. Geology, vol. 1, p. 57 . . . (abstract): Neues Jahrb. 1929, Referate I, p. 365 . . . Mineralog. Abstracts, vol. 2, p. 487, 1928.
3. The Ione formation of California: Univ. California, Dept. Geol. Sci. Bull., Vol. 18, pp. 347–448, 1929 . . . (abstract): Geol. Soc. Am. Bull., vol. 40, pp. 175–176, 1929 . . . Pan-Am. Geologist, vol. 49, p. 313, 1928 . . . Annotated Bibliography Econ. Geology, vol. 1, p. 57, 1928.
4. Andalusite in California Eocene sediments (abstract): Geol. Soc. America Bull., vol. 51, p. 1919, 1940.
5. Eocene anauxite clays and sands in the Coast Range of California: Geol. Soc. America Bull., vol. 52, pp. 271–294, 1941.
6. Sedimentary and volcanic processes in the formation of high alumina clays: Econ. Geology, vol. 41, pp. 124–138, 1946.
7. Some United States boehmite localities: (abstract) Geol. Soc. America Bull. vol. 57, p. 1173, 1946.

Allen, W. W.
1. (and **Avery, R. B.**) California gold book, San Francisco and Chicago, 1893.

Alling, Mark N.
1. Ancient auriferous gravel channels of Sierra County, California: Am. Inst. Min. Met. Eng. Bull., vol. 91, pp. 1709–1728, 1914 . . . Trans., vol. 49, pp. 238–257, 1915.
2. Ancient river-bed deposits in California: Pacific Min. News, vol. 1, pp. 134–140, 161–166, 1922.

Allison, Edwin Chester
1. See Durham, John Wyatt (1).

Almond, Hy
1. See Allen, Robert D. (8).
2. See Smith, George Irving (1), and Sawyer, Dwight Lewis, Jr. (3).
3. See Erd, Richard Clarkson (1), and McAllister, James Franklin (5).

American Journal of Science
1. On colemanite, the new borate of lime: Am. Jour. Sci., 3d ser., vol. 29, pp. 341–342, 1885.

Ames, Lloyd Leroy, Jr.
1. (**Sand, Leonard B.** and **Goldich, Samuel Stephen**) A contribution on the Hector, California bentonite deposit: Econ. Geology, vol. 53, pp. 22–37, 1958.
2. Mass reactions of some zeolites in the region of high competing cation concentrations, Am. Mineralogist, vol. 48, pp. 868–882, 1963.

Andersen, Olaf
1. Aventurine laboradorite from California: Am. Mineralogist, vol. 2, p. 91, 1917 . . . Mineralog. Abstracts, vol. 1, p. 392, 1922.

Anderson, A. D.
1. The silver country of the great southwest, 221 pp., New York, 1877.

Anderson, Charles Alfred

1. Voltaite from Jerome, Arizona: Am. Mineralogist, vol. 12, pp. 287–290, 1927.
2. Dumortierite: Univ. Nevada Bull., vol. 22, p. 10, 1928.
3. Opal stalactites and stalagmites from a lava tube in northern California: Am. Jour. Sci. 5th ser., vol. 20, pp. 22–26, 1930 . . . (abstract): Pan-Am. Geologist, vol. 54, p. 155, 1930.
4. See Finch, Ruy Herbert (1).
5. See Knopf, Adolph (12).
6. The geology of the Engels and Superior mines, Plumas County, California, with a note on the ore deposits of the Superior mine: Univ. California, Dept. Geol. Sci. Bull., vol. 20, pp. 293–330, 1931 . . . Annotated Bibliography Econ. Geology, vol. 4, p. 40, 1931.
7. Opal stalactites from a lava tube in northern California (abstract): Geol. Soc. America Bull., vol. 42, p. 310, 1931.
8. Alteration of the lavas surrounding the hot springs in Lassen Volcanic National Park: Am. Mineralogist, vol. 20, pp. 240–252, 1935.
9. Volcanic history of the Clear Lake area, California: Geol. Soc. America Bull., vol. 47, pp. 629–664, 1936.

Anderson, E. T.

1. See White, Donald Edward (3).

Anderson, Frank Marion

1. The geology of Point Reyes peninsula: Univ. California, Dept. Geol. Sci. Bull., vol. 2, pp. 119–153, 1899 . . . (abstract): Petermanns Mitt. 1900 (Beil zum 46), p. 126.
2. Ore deposits of Shasta County, California (abstract): Science, new ser., vol. 15, p. 412, 1902 . . . Geol. Zentralbl., vol. 9, p. 346, 1907.

Anderson, George Harold

1. (and **Maclellan, Donald D.**) An unusual feldspar from the northern Inyo Range (abstract): Am. Mineralogist, vol. 22, p. 208, 1937.

Anderson, Robert

1. See Arnold, Ralph (3).
2. See Arnold, Ralph (8).

Andrews, Philip

1. Geology of the Pinnacles National Monument: Univ. California, Dept. Geol. Sci. Bull., vol. 24, pp. 1–38, 1936.

Angel, Myron

1. History of San Luis Obispo County, Oakland, 1883.
2. Kern, Monterey, San Benito, San Luis Obispo, Santa Barbara, Tulare Counties: California Min. Bur. Rept. 10, pp. 219–226, 345–348, 515–517, 567–585, 595–599, 728–733, 1890.

Anonymous

1. Mercury (pamphlet), 29 pp., New York, American Quicksilver Company of California, 1849.
2. The Mariposas Estate (includes reports by J. Adelberg, Frederick Claudet, and letters from J. D. Whitney), 63 pp., London, 1861.
3. The United States vs. Andreas Castillero, Black's Supreme Court Reporter, vol. 2, 1862.
4. The Mariposa Company (contains reports of Board of Directors, L. A. Garnett, H. P. Wakelee, J. Adelberg, and T. C. Allyn), 81 pp., New York, 1863.
5. Fluorite: Los Angeles Times, August 30, 1949.
6. History and geology of Horse Canyon in the heart of Kern County: Mineral Notes and News no. 151, pp. 4–6, April, 1950.
7. Jade and chrysoprase in Tulare County: California Div. Mines Mineral Information Service, vol. 3, no. 1, p. 2, 1950.
8. Jade find in Trinity County: Mineral Notes and News no. 159, pp. 1–2, December, 1950.
9. Jadeite from Clear Creek, San Benito County: California Div. Mines, Mineral Information Service, vol. 3, no. 4, p. 2, 1950.
10. Large pocket of kunzite found: Mineral Notes and News no. 168, p. 11, 1951.
11. Nephrite near Porterville: Mineral Notes and News no. 150, p. 1, March, 1950.
12. New jade occurrence in California: California Div. Mines, Mineral Information Service, vol. 3, no. 11, p. 2, 1950.

13. New products: Mineral Notes and News no. 158, pp. 1–18, 1950.

14. New tungsten find in Placer County: California Div. Mines, Mineral Information Service, vol. 3, no. 11, p. 2, 1950.

15. Rare earth deposits found in California: California Div. Mines, Mineral Information Service, vol. 3, no. 1, p. 1, 1950.

16. Scheelite, San Bernardino County, Starbright deposit: California Div. Mines, Mineral Information Service, vol. 4, no. 2, p. 1, 1951.

17. Scheelite, Tomales Bay region, Marin County: California Div. Mines, Mineral Information Service, vol. 4, no. 7, p. 4, 1951.

18. World news on mineral occurrences: Rocks and Minerals, vol. 25, pp. 496–507, 1950.

19. World news on mineral occurrences: Rocks and Minerals, vol. 26, pp. 265–279, 1951.

20. World news on mineral occurrences: Rocks and Minerals, vol. 26, pp. 382–385, 1951.

21. California Div. Mines, Mineral Information Service, vol. 5, p. 4, May 1952.

22. Carson Hill, gem of the Mother Lode: Mineral Notes and News p. 6, June 1952.

23. California Div. Mines, Mineral Information Service, vol. 6, p. 1, June 1953.

24. The Neenach, Los Angeles County, aerolite: Griffith Observer, vol. 17, pp. 80–82, 1953.

25. Notes on Uranium. Gems and Minerals, pp. 14–17, September 1954.

26. California Div. Mines, Mineral Information Service, vol. 7, p. 18, October 1954.

27. California Div. Mines, Mineral Information Service, vol. 7, p. 5, November 1954.

28. California Div. Mines, Mineral Information Service, vol. 7, pp. 2, 18, December 1954.

29. World news on mineral occurrences: Rocks and Minerals, vol. 30, pp. 141–142, 1955.

30. World news on mineral occurrences: Rocks and Minerals, vol. 31, p. 462 (on metastibnite), 1955.

31. World news on mineral occurrences: Rocks and Minerals, vol. 31, p. 575, 1956 (Letter to editor on cervantite).

32. World news on mineral occurrences: Rocks and Minerals, vol. 32, p. 12, 1957 (gold).

33. California Division of Mines, Mineral Information Service, vol. 8, no. 5, 1955.

34. California Division of Mines, Mineral Information Service, vol. 9, no. 10, 1956.

35. The Siskiyou Pioneer: Guidebook to Siskiyou's gold fields, vol. 2, no. 10, pp. 1–88, 1957. (Publications of the Siskiyou County Historical Society.)

36. Rare mineral found in California: California Div. Mines, Mineral Information Service, vol. 10, no. 9, 1957.

37. California Division of Mines, Mineral Information Service, vol. 10, no. 5, 1957, pp. 6–7.

38. World news on mineral occurrences: Rocks and Minerals, vol. 33, p. 99, 1958.

39. World news on mineral occurrences: Rocks and Minerals, vol. 33, pp. 195–6, 1958.

40. World news on mineral occurrences: Rocks and Minerals, vol. 34, p. 210, 1959.

41. World news on mineral occurrences: Rocks and Minerals, vol. 34, p. 304, 1959.

42. World news on mineral occurrences: Rocks and Minerals, vol. 35, p. 462, 1960.

43. Collecting rare minerals: Gems and Minerals, no. 271, p. 22, April 1960.

44. Lead and zinc in California: California Div. Mines, Mineral Information Service, vol. 9, p. 4, July 1956.

45. Rhodonite: Gems and Minerals, no. 294, pp. 18–20, 57, March 1962.

46. Kunzite: Gems and Minerals, no. 295, pp. 18–20, April 1962.

47. California Mineral Production 1962: California Div. Mines and Geol., Mineral Information Service, vol. 16, no. 1, p. 9, 1963.

48. Core drilling at Rush Creek completed: California Div. Mines and Geol. Mineral Information Service, vol. 16, no. 1, p. 11, 1963.

49. Field trip vignette, California: Gems and Minerals, no. 322, p. 45, July 1964.

50. (O.E.B.) New jade deposit found by Division: California Div. Mines and Geol., Mineral Information Service, vol. 17, p. 21, 1964.

51. Three new minerals from California (deerite, howieite, and zussmanite): California Div. Mines and Geol., Mineral Information Service, vol. 17, p. 138, 1964.
52. World news on mineral occurrences: Rocks and Minerals, vol. 37, p. 590, 1962.
53. World news on mineral occurrences: Rocks and Minerals, vol. 37, p. 153, 1962.
54. World news on mineral occurrences: Rocks and Minerals, vol. 39, p. 30, 1964.
55. Work of the commission on new minerals and mineral names, I.M.A.: Am. Mineralogist, vol. 49, pp. 223–224, 1964.
56. New mineral names: Am. Mineralogist, vol. 46, pp. 241–245, 1961.

Anten, Jean
1. Sur la composition lithologiques des psammites du Condroz: Soc. Geologique de Belgique, Annales, vol. 51, pp. B330–331, 1928.

Antisell, Thomas
1. Reports of explorations and surveys: 33d Cong., 2d sess., H. Doc. 91, vol. 7, pt. 2, 204 pp., 1853–56.

Appleman, Daniel Everett
1. See Clark, Joan Robinson (6).

Arcienega, Victor M.
1. San Diego County's pegmatites: Mineral Notes and News, p. 30, 32, 69, December 1954.

Arents, Albert
1. Partzite, a new mineral: Am. Jour. Sci., 2d ser., vol. 43, p. 362, 1867 . . . Min. Sci. Press, vol. 14, p. 34, 1867 . . . Berg. and Hütten, Zeit 26, p. 119, 1867.
2. Notes on partzite: Eng. and Min. Jour., vol. 4, p. 162, 1867.

Armstrong, V. L.
1. (and Van Amringe, Edwin Verne) Tick Canyon field trip: reprinted from Grieger's "Encyclopedia and Super-Catalog of the Lapidary and Jewelry Arts," Pasadena, 1948.

Arnold, Ralph
1. See Haehl, Harry Lewis (1).
2. Geology and oil resources of the Summerland district, Santa Barbara County, California: U.S. Geol. Survey Bull. 321, 93 pp., 1907.
3. (and Anderson, Robert) Metamorphism by combustion of the hydrocarbons in the oil-bearing shale of California: Jour. Geol., vol. 15, pp. 750–758, 1907 . . . (abstract): Geol. Zentralbl. 12, p. 6, 1909.
4. Notes on the occurrence of the recently described gem mineral, benitoite: Science, new ser., vol. 27, pp. 312–314, 1908.
5. (and Johnson, Harry Roland) The so-called volcano in the Santa Monica Mountains near Los Angeles, California: Science, new ser., vol. 27, pp. 553–554, 1908.
6. See Branner (1), John Casper (1).
7. (and Johnson, Harry Roland) Sodium sulphate in Soda Lake, Carriso Plain, San Luis Obispo County, California: U.S. Geol. Survey Bull. 380, pp. 369–371, 1909 . . . (abstract): Geol. Zentralbl. 14, p. 125, 1910.
8. (and Anderson, Robert) Geology and oil resources of the Coalinga district, California: U. S. Geol. Survey Bull. 398, 354 pp., 1910 . . . (reprinted) 1911.

Aruja, Endel
1. An x-ray study on the crystal structure of gümbelite: Mineralog. Mag., vol. 27, pp. 11–15, 1944.

Arzuni, A.
1. Ueber einen Colmanit Krystall: Zeitschr. Kristallographic 10, p. 272, 1884.

Aubury, Lewis E.
1. The copper resources of California: California Min. Bur. Bull. 23, 282 pp., 1902. Includes contributions by P. C. DuBois, F. M. Anderson, J. H. Tibbetts, and G. A. Tweedy.
2. The quicksilver resources of California: California Min. Bur. Bull. 27, 273 pp., 1903.
3. The structural and industrial materials of California: California Min. Bur. Bull. 38, pp. 13–378, 1906 . . . (abstract): Geol. Zentralbl. 9, p. 13, 1907.
4. The copper resources of California: California Min. Bur. Bull. 50, 366 pp., 1908. Includes contributions by A. Hausmann, J. Kruttschnitt, W. E. Thorne, and J. A. Edman.

Averill, Charles Volney
1. Redding field division, Tehama and Plumas Counties: California Div. Mines and Mining Rept. 24, pp. 211–216, 261–316, 1928.
2. Redding field division, Lassen and Modoc, Napa, Lake, Glenn, Mendocino Counties: California Div. Mines Rept. 25, pp. 2–19, 213–242, 337–365, 418–426, 456–467, 1929.
3. Preliminary report on economic geology of the Shasta quadrangle: California Div. Mines Rept. 27, pp. 3–65, 1931 . . . Annotated Bibliography Econ. Geology, vol. 4, p. 10, 1931.
4. Gold deposits of the Redding-Weaverville quadrangles: California Div. Mines Rept. 29, pp. 3–73, 1933 . . . Annotated Bibliography Econ. Geology, vol. 6, p. 223, 1934.
5. Mines and mineral resources of Siskiyou County: California Division Mines Rept. 31, pp. 255–338, 1935.
6. Mineral resources of Modoc County: California Div. Mines Rept. 32, pp. 445–457, 1936.
7. (and **Erwin, Homer D.**) Mineral resources of Lassen County: California Div. Mines Rept. 32, pp. 405–443, 1936.
8. Mineral resources of Plumas County: California Div. Mines Rept. 33, pp. 79–143, 1937.
9. Mineral resources of Shasta County: California Div. Mines Rept. 35, pp. 108–190, 1939.
10. Mineral resources of Trinity and Humboldt Counties: California Div. Mines Rept. 37, pp. 8–89, 499–528, 1941.
11. Mines and mineral resources of Sierra County: California Div. Mines Rept. 38, pp. 7–67, 1942.
12. Chromium: California Div. Mines Rept. 38, pp. 70–93, 1942.
13. Current notes on activity in the strategic minerals, Sacramento field district: California Div. Mines Rept. 39, pp. 71–76, 139–141, 1943.
14. Mines and mineral resources of Lake County, California: California Div. Mines Rept. 43, pp. 15–40, 1947.
15. Mines and mineral resources of San Benito County, California: California Div. Mines Rept. 43, pp. 41–60, 1947.
16. (**King, C. R., Symons, Henry Heilbronner,** and **Davis, Fenelon Francis**) California mineral production for 1946: California Div. Mines Bull. 139, 76 pp., 1948.

Averitt, Paul
1. Quicksilver deposits of the Knoxville district, Napa, Yolo, and Lake Counties, California: California Div. Mines Rept. 42, pp. 65–90, 1945.

Avery, R. B.
1. See Allen, W. W. (1).

Ayers, William O.
1. Borax in America: Popular Sci. Monthly, vol. 21, pp. 350–361, 1882 . . . California Min. Bur. Rept. 3, pp. 20–24, 1882–83.

Ayres, Edward F.
1. Mineralogical notes (thenardite, pyrite): Am. Jour. Sci., 3d ser., vol. 37, pp. 235–236, 1889.
2. Notes on the crystallization of trona (urao): Am. Jour. Sci., 3d ser., vol. 38, pp. 65–66, 1889.

B

Bacon, Charles Sumner
1. Geology of Riverside area, California (abstract): Pan-Am. Geologist, vol. 59, pp. 313–314, 1933 . . . Geol. Soc. America, Proc. 1933, vol. 1, pp. 311–312, 1934.

Bailey, Edgar Herbert
1. Piedmontite and kyanite from the Franciscan of Santa Catalina Island (abstract): Geol. Soc. America Bull. 51, p. 1955, 1940.
2. See Woodford, A. O., (9) and Laudermilk, J. D. (6).
3. Skeletonized apophyllite from Crestmore and Riverside, California: Am. Mineralogist, vol. 26, pp. 565–567, 1941.
4. (and **Myers, W. Bradley**) Quicksilver and antimony deposits of the Stayton district, California: U. S. Geol. Survey Bull. 931Q, pp. 405–434, 1942.

5. Quicksilver deposits of the Parkfield district, California: U. S. Geol. Survey Bull. 936-F, pp. 143–169, 1942.

6. Quicksilver deposits of the western Mayacmas district, Sonoma County, California: California Div. Mines Rept. 42, pp. 199–230, 1946.

7. (and **Swinney, Chauncey Melvin**) Walibu quicksilver mine, Kern County, California: California Div. Mines Rept. 43, pp. 9–14, 1947.

8. (and **Everhart, Donald Lough**) Almaden placer yields cinnabar-rich gravels: Eng. Min. Jour., vol. 148, pp. 77–79, 1947.

9. See Switzer, George S. (8).

10. (**Hildebrand, Fred Adelbert, Christ, Charles Louis**, and **Fahey, Joseph John**) Schuetteite, a new supergene mercury mineral: Am. Mineralogist, vol. 44, pp. 1026–1038, 1959.

11. Metamorphic facies of the Franciscan Formation of California, and their geologic significance. Geol. Soc. America Spec. Paper 68, p. 4–5, 1962.

12. (and **Everhart, Donald Lough**) Geology and quicksilver deposits of the New Almaden district, Santa Clara County, California: U. S. Geol. Survey Prof. Paper 360, 206 pp., 1964.

Bailey, Gilbert Ellis

1. Minerals of California: California Min. Bur., 56 pp., illus., 1902.

2. The saline deposits of California: California Min. Bur. Bull. 24, 216 pp., 1902 . . . (abstract): Eng. and Min. Jour., vol. 74, p. 452, 1902.

3. California as a gem state: Overland Monthly, new ser., vol. 40, pp. 468–470, 1902.

Bailey, J. P.

1. See Reed, Ralph Daniel (4).

Bailey, Thomas Laval

1. (and **Woodford, Alfred Oswald**) Northwestern continuation of the San Onofre breccia: Calif. Univ., Dept. Geol. Sci. Bull., vol. 17, pp. 187–191, 1928 . . . (abstract): Geol. Zentralbl. 39, p. 48, 1929.

Baker, Charles Laurence

1. Notes on the later Cenozoic history of the Mojave Desert region in southeastern California: Calif. Univ., Dept. Geol. Sci. Bull., vol. 6, pp. 333–383, 1911.

2. Physiography and structure of the western El Paso Range and the southern Sierra Nevada: Calif. Univ., Dept. Geol. Sci. Bull., vol. 7, pp. 117–142, 1912.

Ball, Sydney Hobart

1. Notes on ore deposits of southwestern Nevada and eastern California: U. S. Geol. Survey Bull. 285, pp. 53–73, 1906.

2. A geologic reconnaissance in southwestern Nevada and eastern California: U. S. Geol. Survey Bull. 308, 218 pp., 1907.

3. Molybdenite and its occurrences: Eng. and Min. Jour., vol. 104, p. 333, 1917.

4. Gem stones: Minerals Yearbook, 1939, pp. 1385–1396, 1939.

5. The mining of gems and ornamental stones by American Indians: Smithson. Inst., Bur. Am. Ethnol., Anthropological Papers, Bull. 128, no. 13, xii, 77 pp., 1941.

Bancroft, Hubert Howe

1. History of California, vol. 2, 795 pp., San Francisco, History Company, 1884.

Bandy, Mark Chance

1. Castanite from Chuquicamata, Chile: Am. Mineralogist, vol. 17, pp. 534–537, 1932.

2. Mineralogy of three sulphide deposits of northern Chile: Am. Mineralogist, vol. 23, pp. 669–760, 1938.

Banks, Philip O.

1. (and **Silver, Leon Theodore**) Petrological and geochronological observations on the Roubidoux Mountain leucogranites, Riverside County, California (abst.): Geol. Soc. America Spec. Paper 68, p. 5–6, 1962.

Bannister, F. A.

1. See Hey, M. H. (1).

Barber, William Burton

1. See Nutter, Edward Hoit (1).

Barker, Daniel S.

1. Ammonium in alkali feldspars: Am. Mineralogist, vol. 49, pp. 851–858, 1964.

Barnes, William H.

1. The unit cell and space group of probertite: Am. Mineralogist, vol. 34, pp. 19–25, 1949.

Baskerville, Charles
 1. Kunzite, a new gem: Science, new ser., vol. 18, pp. 303–304, 1903.
 2. (and **Kunz, George Frederick**) Kunzite and its unique properties: Am. Jour. Sci., 4th ser., vol. 18, pp. 25–28, 1904.

Bassett, Allen Mordorf
 1. (and **Kupfer, Donald Harry**) A geologic reconnaissance in the southeastern Mojave Desert; California Div. Mines and Geol. Spec. Rept. 83, 43 pp., 1964.

Bastin, Edson Sunderland
 1. Graphite: Mineral Resources U. S., 1913, pp. 181–251, 1914.
 2. Graphite: Mineral Resources U. S., 1914, pt. 2, pp. 159–174, 1916.

Bateman, Paul Charles
 1. Pine Creek and Adamson tungsten mines, Inyo County, California: California Div. Mines Rept. 42, pp. 231–250, 1945.
 2. (**Erickson, Max Perry** and **Proctor, Paul Dean**) Geology and tungsten deposits of the Tungsten Hills, Inyo County, California: California Jour. Mines and Geology, vol. 46, pp. 23–42, 1950.
 3. Economic geology of the Bishop Tungsten district, California: California Div. Mines, Special Rept. 47, 87 pp., 1956.
 4. (**Clark, Lorin Delbert, Huber, Norman King, Moore, James Gregory,** and **Rinehart, Charles Dean**) The Sierra Nevada batholith: A synthesis of recent work across the central part: U. S. Geol. Survey Prof. Paper 414-D, 46 pp., 1963.
 5. (and **Irwin, William Porter**) Tungsten in southeastern California: California Div. Mines and Geol. Bull. 170, Ch. VIII, pp. 31–40, 1954.

Bateson, Charles E. W.
 1. The Mojave mining district of California: Am. Inst. Min. Met. Eng., Bull. 7, pp. 65–82, 1905 . . . Trans., vol. 37, pp. 160–177, 1907 . . . (abstract): Geol. Zentralbl. 12, p. 12, 1909 . . . (abstract): Eng. Index 1906, p. 281, 1907.

Baumhauer, H.
 1. Ueber sog. anomale Aetzfiguren an monoklinen krystallen, ibesondere am colemanit: Zeitschr. Kristallographie, Band 30, pp. 97–117, 1899.
 2. Ueber die winkelverhältnisse des benitoit: Zentralbl. Min., pp. 592–594, 1909.

Baur, Gretta S.
 1. (and **Sand, Leonard B.**) X-ray powder data for ulexite and halotrichite: Am. Mineralogist, vol. 42, pp. 676–678, 1957.
 2. (**Larsen, Willard N.,** and **Sand, Leonard B.**) Image projection by fibrous minerals: Am. Mineralogist, vol. 42, pp. 697–699, 1957.
 3. See Montoya, J. W. (1).

Baverstock, R. S.
 1. A California scheelite deposit: Min. World, vol. 24, pp. 414–415, 1906.

Bealey, A.
 1. Zinnober-Erz aus Neu-Almaden in Californien: Chem. Soc. London Jour., vol. 4, p. 180, 1852 . . . (abstract): Neues Jahrb., p. 183, 1854 . . . p. 686, 1856.

Bean, Edwin F.
 1. History and directory of Nevada County, California: Daily Gazette Book and Job Office, Nevada, 1867.

Becker, George Ferdinand
 1. Reconnaissance of the San Francisco, Eureka, and Bodie districts: U. S. Geol. Survey 1st Ann. Rept., pp. 29–35, 1880.
 2. Geological sketch of the Pacific division: U. S. 10th Census, vol. 13, pp.. 5–59, 1885.
 3. Geology of the quicksilver deposits of the Pacific slope: U. S. Geol. Survey 7th Ann. Rept., pp. 93–94, 96, 1888.
 4. Geology of the quicksilver deposits of the Pacific slope: U. S. Geol. Survey Mon. 13, 486 pp., atlas, 1888 . . . Petermanns Mitt. (Beil zum 38), p. 53, 1892.
 5. Summary of the geology of the quicksilver deposits of the Pacific slope: U. S. Geol. Survey 8th Ann. Rept., pp. 961–985, 1889.
 6. Quicksilver ore deposits: Mineral Resources U. S., 1892, pp. 139–168, 1893.
 7. See Turner, Henry Ward (13).

Behre, Charles Henry, Jr.
 1. Native antimony from Kern County, California: Am. Jour. Sci., 5th ser., vol 2, pp. 330–333, 1921 . . . Mineralog. Abstracts, vol. 2, p. 364, 1924.

Bekeart, P. B.
  1. James Wilson Marshall, discoverer of gold: Soc. California Pioneers, Jour., vol. 1, no. 3, 1924.

Belov, N. V.
  1. See Mamedov, Kh. S. (1).

Belyankin, D. S.
  1. (and **Petrov, V. P.**) The grossularoid group (hibschite, plazolite) : Am. Mineralogist, vol. 26, pp. 450–453, 1941.

Benda, William K.
  1. (and **Erd, Richard Clarkson,** and **Smith, Ward Conwell**) Core logs from five test holes near Kramer, California: U. S. Geol. Survey Bull. 1045F, pp. 319–393, 1960.

Benedict, William de L.
  1. The San Jacinto (California) tin mines: Eng. and Min. Jour., vol. 50, pp. 447, 450–453, 1890.

Benjamin, E. H.
  1. Mining exhibit California Midwinter Fair: Eng. and Min. Jour., vol. 57, p. 153, 1894.

Bennett, William Alfred Glenn
  1. Saline lake deposits in Washington: Washington Div. of Mines Bull. 49, p. 129, 1962.

Berkholz, Mary Frances (See also Mary Frances Berkholz Strong)
  1. Turquoise of the desert Mojaves: Mineral Notes and News, p. 7, December 1952.
  2. Magnesite and a ghost town: Mineral Notes and News, p. 5, February 1953.
  3. Guide to the Toltec mine: Mineral Notes and News, p. 7, March 1953.
  4. Green gems of the San Gabriel Mountains: Mineral Notes and News, p. 14, May 1953.
  5. Magic gems, a San Diego County field trip: Mineral Notes and News, p. 12, June 1953.
  6. Crystals by the sea: Mineral Notes and News, p. 12, July 1953.
  7. Fresno goes after chiastolite: Gems and Minerals, p. 7, September 1953.
  8. Gems from the sea: Gems and Minerals, p. 9, October 1953.
  9. Black Canyon opal: Gems and Minerals, p. 7, December 1953.
  10. Minerals at Mountain View: Gems and Minerals, p. 16, January 1954.
  11. Gems of the Rosamonds: Gems and Minerals, p. 28, April 1954.
  12. Garnet and epidote: Gems and Minerals, p. 22, May 1954.
  13. Gems near Mount Tule: Gems and Minerals, p. 28, June 1954.
  14. The Greenhorn mountains: Gems and Minerals, p. 11, September 1954.
  15. Stifle Memorial collecting areas: Gems and Minerals, p. 20, October 1954.
  15a. Rhodonite at Jacumba: Gems and Minerals, p. 26, December 1954.
  15b. Aragonite crystals in San Luis Obispo County, California: Gems and Minerals, no. 212, pp. 25–26, May 1955.
  16. Actinolite at Wrightwood: Gems and Minerals, no. 228, pp. 21, 71, Sept. 1956.
  17. Smoky quartz: Gems and Minerals, no. 233, pp. 16–17, Feb. 1957.
  18. Salton Sea glauberite: Gems and Minerals, no. 245, pp. 17–19, Feb. 1958.
  19. Aragonite in Holcomb Valley: Gems and Minerals, no. 287, pp. 14–16, Aug. 1961.

Bergland, Eric
  1. Temescal tin mines, California: U.S. Geog. Surveys W. 100th Mer. Rpt. 1876, pp. 68–69 . . . 44th Cong., 2d sess., H. Doc. 1, pt. 2, vol. 2, pt. 3, ap. J. J., pp. 288–289, 1876.

Berg- und Hüttenmanische Zeitung
  1. Neue Goldquelle: Berg- u. hütten. Zeit. 7, pp. 791–792, 1848.
  2. Die Goldminen in Californien (nach originalberichten): Berg- u. hütten. Zeit. 8, pp. 94–96, 109–112, 1849.

Berman, Harry
  1. (and **Harcourt, George Alan**) Natural amalgams: Am. Mineralogist, vol. 23, pp. 761–764, 1938.
  2. See Palache, Charles (10).
  3. See Palache, Charles (11).

Berner, Robert A.
  1. See Petersen, Melvin N. A. (1).

Berry, Leonard Gascoigne
  1. See Whitmore, Duncan Richard Elmer (1).
  2. The unit cell of ettringite: Am. Mineralogist, vol. 48, p. 939, 1963.

Bertrand, Emile
1. Zinnober von Californien : Zeitschr. Kristallographie, Band 2, p. 199, 1878.
2. Étude optique de différent mineraux, aragotite : Soc. Min. de France, Bull. 4, p. 87, 1881.

Best, Myron G.
1. (and **Weiss, Lionel Edward**) Mineralogical relations in some pelitic hornfels from the southern Sierra Nevada, California : Am. Mineralogist, vol. 49, pp. 1240–1266, 1964.

Beverly, Burt, Jr.
1. Graphite deposits in Los Angeles County, California : Econ. Geol., vol. 29, pp. 346–355, 1934 . . . Annotated Bibliography. Econ. Geology, vol. 7, p. 68, 1935 . . . (abstract) : Rev. geologie et sci. connexes, tome 14, p. 491, 1934 . . . Neues Jahrb., Referate 2, p. 682, 1934.

Bien, George Sung-Nien
1. See Peterson, Melvin N. A. (1).

Bixby, Maynard
1. Notable minerals in western mines, I : Mineral Collector, vol. 1, pp. 153–154, 1895.
2. Notable minerals in western mines, II : Mineral Collector, vol. 1, pp. 168–169, 1895.

Blackwood's Magazine
1. Romance of the mines ; California gold discoveries : Blackwood's Mag., vol. 165, pp. 272–282, 1899.

Blake, James
1. Nickeliferous sand from Frazer River : Am. Jour. Sci., 3d ser., vol. 7, p. 238, 1874 . . . California Acad. Sci., Proc., vol. 5, p. 200, 1874.
2. Roscoelite, a vanadium mica : California Acad. Sci. Proc., vol. 6, p. 150, 1875 . . . Am. Jour. Sci., 3d ser., vol. 12, pp. 31–32, 1876 . . . (abstract) : Geol. Rec., 1876, p. 224, 1878.

Blake, John Marcus
1. On the crystallization of natural hydrated terpin from California : Am. Jour. Sci., 2d ser., vol. 43, p. 202, 1867.

Blake, Milton C., Jr.
1. Petrology and magnetic properties of the Cazadero ultramafic mass, northern Coast Ranges, California : Geol. Soc. America Spec. Paper 76 (abstract) p. 191, 1964.

Blake, William Phipps
1. Quicksilver mine of Almaden, California : Am. Jour. Sci., 2d ser., vol. 17, pp. 438–440, 1854.
2. On gold and platinum of Cape Blanco, California : Am. Jour. Sci., 2d ser., vol. 18, p. 156, 1854.
3. Observations on the extent of the gold region of California and Oregon, with notices of mineral localities in California and of some remarkable specimens of crystalline gold : Am. Jour. Sci., 2d ser., vol. 20, pp. 72–85, 1855.
4. Observations on the physical geography and geology of the coast of California, from Bodega Bay to San Diego : U. S. Coast Survey, Rept. 1855 [1856].
5. Reports of explorations and surveys to ascertain the most practical and economical route for a railroad from the Mississippi River to the Pacific Ocean : 33d Cong., 2d sess., H. Doc. 91, vol. 5, pt. 2, geological report, 310 pp., 1856.
6. Note on the occurrence of telluret of silver in California : California Acad. (Nat.) Sci. Proc., vol. 1, pp. 96–97, 1857 . . . 2d ed., pp. 107–108, 1873 . . . Am. Jour. Sci., 2d ser., vol. 23, pp. 270–271, 1857.
7. Report of a geological reconnaissance in California. 370 pp., New York, 1858.
8. Report on the minerals of the Mechanics' Fair Exposition of California : Min. Sci. Press, vol. 9, p. 264, 1864.
9. Annotated catalogue of the principal mineral species hitherto recognized in California and the adjoining states and territories ; being a report to the Califorina State Board of Agriculture (and notes on the geographical distribution and geology of the precious metals and valuable minerals on the Pacific slope of the United States), 31 pp., Sacramento, 1866 . . . California State Board Agr., St. Agr. Soc., Trans. 1864–65, pp. 335–363, 1866 . . . in Browne, J. R., and Taylor, J. W., Re-

sources of the states and territories west of the Rocky Mountains, pp. 200–211, 1867 . . . California Legislature, App. to Journals, 16th sess., 3, pp. 335–363, 1866 . . . (notice). Am. Jour. Sci., 2d ser., vol. 42, p. 125, 1866.

10. Note on the geographical distribution and geology of the precious metals and valuable minerals of the Pacific slope: Calif. Sen. and Assembly Jour., vol. 3, p. 314, 1886.

11. Crystallized gold in California: Am. Jour. Sci., 2d ser., vol. 41, p. 120, 1866.

12. Miscellaneous notices, IV, Quarry of gold bearing rock: California Acad. Sci., Proc., vol. 3, pt. 1, pp. 289–291, 1866.

13. Note upon "partzite": Am. Jour. Sci., 2d ser., vol. 44, p. 119, 1867.

14. Mineralogical notices II: Am. Jour. Sci., 2d ser., vol. 43, pp. 124–125, 1867 . . . California Acad. (Nat.) Sci., Proc. vol. 3, pp. 297–298, 1867.

15. Annotated catalogue of the principal mineral species hitherto recognized in California and the adjoining states and territories, in Browne, J. R., and Taylor, J. W., Mineral resources of the states and territories west of the Mississippi, pp. 200–211, 1867.

16. Note on a large lump of gold found on the middle fork of the American River: California Acad. (Nat.) Sci. Proc., vol. 3, p. 166, 1868.

17. Note upon the occurrence of sphene in the granite of the Sierra Nevada: California Acad. (Nat.) Sci. Proc., vol. 3, p. 193, 1868.

18. The melones tellurides; letter to G. Küstel: Min. Sci. Press, vol. 16, p. 178, 1868.

19. Notes upon some of the mineralogical curiosities of the Paris Exposition of 1867: Am. Jour. Sci., 2d ser., vol. 43, pp. 194–198, 1868.

20. Note sur les gisments de cinabre de la Californie et du Nevada: Soc. Franç. mineralogie, Bull. 1, pp. 81–84, 1878.

21. Contributions to the geology and mineralogy of California: Calif. Min. Bur., 15 pp., Sacramento, 1881.

22. Ulexite in California. Am. Jour. Sci., 3d ser., vol. 22, p. 323, 1881.

23. Contributions to the geology of California: Min. Sci. Press, vol. 42, p. 376, 1881.

24. Rare minerals recently found in the state: California Min. Bur., Rept. 2, appendix, pp. 207–223, 1882.

25. Crystallized gold (in California): U. S. Mint, Rept. of Director, 1884.

26. Crystallized gold in prismatic forms: Am. Jour. Sci., 3d ser., vol. 28, pp. 57–58, 1884.

27. New localities of erythrite: Am. Jour. Sci., 3d ser., vol. 30, p. 163, 1885 . . . Neues Jahrb., Band 2 (Ref.), p. 282, 1887.

28. Tin ores and deposits: Mineral Resources U. S., 1883–84, pp. 592–640, 1885.

29. Antimony: Mineral Resources U. S., 1883–84, pp. 641–653, 1885.

30. Gold in granite and plutonic rocks: Am. Inst. Min. Eng., Trans. 1896, vol. 26, pp. 290–298, 1897.

Blank, Eugene W.

1. Diamond finds in the United States: Rocks and Minerals, vol. 9, pp. 147–150, 163–166, 179–182, 1934.

Blasdale, Walter Charles

1. Contributions to the mineralogy of California: Univ. Calif., Dept. Geol. Sci. Bull., vol. 2, pp. 327–348, 1901 . . . (abstract): Geol. Zentralbl., Band 3, p. 33, 1903 . . . Neues Jahrb. Band 1 (Ref. 7), pp. 402–405, 1903.

2. See Louderback, George Davis (2).

3. See Louderback, George Davis (4).

4. Chemical formula of the mineral benitoite: Science, new ser., vol. 28, pp. 233–234, 1908.

5. See Louderback, George Davis (5).

6. See Louderback, George Davis (6).

Bloxam, T. W.

1. Jadeite-bearing metagraywackes in California: Am. Mineralogist, vol. 41, pp. 488–496, 1956.

2. Glaucophane schists and associated rocks near Valley Ford, California; Am. Jour. Sci., vol. 257, pp. 95–112, 1959.

3. Jadeite rocks and glaucophane schists from Angel Island, San Francisco Bay, California: Am. Jour. Sci., vol. 258, pp. 555–573, 1960.

Boalich, Edwin Snow
1. Manganese and chromium: California Min. Bur. Preliminary Rept. 3, 2d ed., 46 pp., 1918.
2. (and **Castello, W. O.**) Tungsten, molybdenum, and vanadium: California Min. Bur. Preliminary Rept. 4, 34 pp., 1918 . . . (abstract): Geol. Zentralbl., Band 29, p. 425, 1923.
3. (and **Castello, W. O.**) Antimony, graphite, nickel, potash, strontium, tin: California Min. Bur. Preliminary Rept. 5, 44 pp., 1918 . . . (abstract): Geol. Zentralbl., Band 29, p. 425, 1923.
4. Mendocino, Monterey, Mono, Napa, Solano, Stanislaus Counties: California Min. Bur. Rept. 17, pp. 144–161, 242–247, 253–255, 1921.
5. Notes on iron occurrences in California: California Min. Bur. Rept. 18, pp. 110–113, 1922.

Boardman, Leona
1. See Mansfield, George Rogers (3).
2. See Mansfield, George Rogers (4).

Bodenlos, Alfred John
1. Geology of the Red Mountain magnesite district, Santa Clara and Stanislaus Counties, California: California Jour. Mines and Geology, vol. 46, pp. 224–278, 1950.

Bodewig, C.
1. (and **vom Rath, G.**) Mineralogische Notizen: Naturh. Ver. preuss, Rheinlande u. Westfalens Verh., Band 290, 1884 . . . (abstract): Mineralog. Mag., vol. 6, p. 147, 1886.
2. (and **vom Rath, G.**) Colmanit aus Californien: Niederrheinische Gesell für Natur- u. Heilkunde in Bonn, in Naturh. Ver. preuss. Rheinlande u. Westfalens Verh., Band 41, pp. 333–342, 1884.
3. (and **vom Rath, G.**) Colmanit aus Californien: Zeitschr. Kristallographie, Band 10, pp. 179–186, 1885.
4. Notes on Hanksite: Am. Jour. Sci., 3d ser., vol. 38, p. 164, 1889.

Bolander, L. Ph., Jr.
1. New California mineral: perovskite: The Mineralogist, vol. 18, p. 65, 1950.
2. First jadeite discovery in America: The Mineralogist, vol. 18, pp. 186–188, 1950.

Borg, Iris Y.
1. Glaucophane schists and eclogite near Healdsburg, California: Geol. Soc. America Bull., vol. 67, pp. 1563–1584, 1956.

Boundey, E. S.
1. See Rogers, Austin Flint (8).

Bowen, Norman Levi
1. Ferrosilite as a natural mineral: Am. Jour. Sci., 5th ser., vol. 30, p. 481, 1935.

Bowen, Oliver Earle, Jr.
1. Geology and mineral deposits of Barstow quadrangle, San Bernardino County, California: California Div. Mines Bull. 165, pp. 7–185, 1954.
2. (and **Gray, Cliffton Herschel, Jr.**) Mines and mineral deposits of Mariposa County, California: California Jour. Mines and Geology, vol. 53, pp. 34–343, 1957.
3. See Chesterman, Charles Wesley (6).
4. See Hutton, Colin Osbourne (2).
5. (and **Gray, Cliffton Herschel, Jr.**) Geology and economic possibilities of the limestone and dolomite deposits of the northern Gabilan Range, California: Calif. Dept. Nat. Res., Div. Mines and Geol. Spec. Rept. 56, 40 pp., 1959.

Bowers, Stephen
1. Geology of Santa Rosa Island: Smithsonian Inst., Ann. Rept., 1877, pp. 316–320, 1878.
2. Ventura County, California: California Min. Bur. Rept. 8, pp. 679–690, 1888.
3. San Nicolas Island: California Min. Bur. Rept. 9, pp. 57–61, 1890.
4. Orange, Ventura Counties: California Min. Bur. Rept. 10, pp. 399–409, 758–772, 1890.
5. Reconnaissance of the Colorado Desert mining district: California Min. Bur. Bull., 12 pp. 1901.

Bowles, Oliver
1. (and **Stoddard, B. H.**) Asbestos: Mineral Resources U. S., 1927, pp. 299–311, 1930.

2. (and **Cornthwaite, M. A.**) Asbestos: Minerals Yearbook 1937, pp. 1363–1370, 1937.

Bowman, Amos

1. Geology of the Sierra Nevada in its relation to vein mining: in Raymond, Rossiter W., Statistics of mines and mining in the states and territories west of the Rocky Mountains, 7th Ann. Rept., pp. 441–470, 1875 . . . 43d Cong., 2d sess., H. Ex. Doc. 177, 1874.

Bowser, Carl J.

1. Mechanism of borax deposition and the chemical composition of Pliocene lake waters at Kramer, California (abst.) : Geol. Soc. America program New York Ann. Meeting, p. 19A, 1963.

2. The origin of tincalconite at Searles Lake, California: (title) Am. Mineralogist, vol. 49, p. 1507, 1964.

Boyd, Julian

1. The saline deposits of Death Valley, California: Chem. Eng. and Min. Rev., vol. 21, pp. 287–290, 1929 . . . Annotated Bibliography Econ. Geology, vol. 2, p. 92, 1929 . . . Arizona Min. Jour., vol. 13, no. 11: pp. 7–9, 14–16, October 30, 1929.

Boyle, Albert C., Jr.

1. The geology and ore deposits of the Bully Hill mining district, California: Am. Inst. Min. Met. Eng. Bull. 85, pp. 57–105, 1914 . . . Trans., vol. 48, pp. 67–117, 1915 . . . (abstract) : Eng. Index 1914, p. 407, 1915.

Boyle, O. M., Jr.

1. The Greenwater mining district, California: California Jour. Technology, vol. 10, pp. 29–32, 1907.

Bradley, P. R.

1. Pyrites deposit in Plumas County, California: Min. Met. Soc. America Bull. 6, pp. 276–277, 1913.

Bradley, Walter Minor

1. On the analysis of the mineral neptunite from San Benito County, California: Am. Jour. Sci., 4th ser., vol. 28, pp. 15–16, 1909 . . . Zeitschr. Kristallographie, Band 46, pp. 516–517, 1909.

Bradley, Walter Wadsworth

1. Colusa, Glenn, Lake, Marin, Napa, Solano, Sonoma, Yolo Counties: California Min. Bur. Rept. 14, pp. 175–370, 1916; issued separately July 1915 under title Mines and mineral resources of the counties of Colusa, Glenn, Lake, Marin, Napa, Solano, Sonoma, Yolo . . . (abstract) : Geol. Zentralbl. Band 27, p. 393, 1922 . . . 29, p. 425, 1923.

2. Fresno and Kings Counties: California Min. Bur. Rept. 14, pp. 429–470, 525–530, 1916, issued separately July 1915 under title Mines and mineral resources of the counties of Fresno, Kern, Kings, Madera, Mariposa, Merced, San Joaquin, Stanislaus . . . (abstract) : Geol. Zentralbl. Band 27, p. 393, 1922.

3. See McLaughlin, R. P. (3).

4. (and others) Manganese and chromium in California: California Min. Bur. Bull. 76, 248 pp., 1918 . . . (abstract) : Geol. Zentralbl. Band 29, p. 425, 1923 . . . (abstract) : Min. Sci. Press, vol. 118, p. 369, 1919 . . . (abstract) : Eng. Index 1919, p. 293, 1920.

5. Quicksilver resources of California, with a section on metallurgy and ore dressing: California Min. Bur. Bull. 78, 389 pp., 1918.

6. (and **Waring, Clarence Alm**) Monterey County: California Min. Bur. Rept. 15, pp. 595–615, 1919; issued separately under title Mines and mineral resources of the counties of Monterey, San Benito, 1916 . . . (abstract) : Eng. Index 1918, p. 325, 1919.

7. (and **Logan, Clarence August**) San Benito County: California Min. Bur. Rept. 15, pp. 616–673, 1919; issued separately under title Mines and mineral resources of the counties of Monterey, San Benito, San Luis Obispo, Santa Barbara, Ventura . . . (abstract) : Geol. Zentralbl. Band 27, p. 393, 1922.

8. Magnesite in California: California Min. Bur. Bull. 79, 147 pp. 1925 . . . Mineralog. Abstracts, vol. 3, p. 77, 1926.

9. The Minarets district, Madera County: California Min. Bur. Rept. 22, pp. 539–557, 1926.

10. California's commercial nonmetallic minerals: Min. Cong. Jour., vol. 14, pp. 669–678, 718, 1928 . . . (abstract) : Mining and Metallurgy, vol. 9, p. 404, 1928.

11. Twenty-fifth report, State Mineralogist: California Min. Bur. Rept. 25, 588 pp., 1929.

12. Barite in California: Am. Inst. Min. Met. Eng., Tech. Pub. 266, 9 pp., 1929 . . . (abstract) : Mining and Metallurgy, vol. 11, p. 18, 1930 . . . California Min. Bur. Rept. 26, pp. 45–47, 1930.

13. Twenty-sixth report of the State Mineralogist: California Min. Bur. Rept. 26, 535 pp., 1930.

14. Barite in California: Am. Inst. Min. Met. Eng., Trans. 1931, pp. 170–176, 1931 . . . Annotated Bibliography Econ. Geology, vol. 4, p. 272, 1931.

15. Twenty-seventh report of the State Mineralogist: California Min. Bur. Rept. 27, 582 pp., 1931.

16. Twenty-eighth report of the State Mineralogist: California Min. Bur. Rept. 28, 429 pp., 1932.

17. Sanbornite, a newly described mineral from California: California Min. Bur. Rept. 28, pp. 82–83, 1932.

18. Twenty-ninth report of the State Mineralogist: California Div. Mines Rept. 29, 411 pp., 1933.

19. Thirtieth report of the State Mineralogist: California Div. Mines Rept. 30, 487 pp., 1934.

20. The nonmetallic minerals of California: Pit and Quarry, vol. 26, pp. 35–40, 1934 . . . Annotated Bibliography Econ. Geology, vol. 7, p. 56, 1935.

21. Recent nonmetallic mineral development in California: Mining and Metallurgy, vol. 16, pp. 181–184, 1935.

22. Thirty-first report of the State Mineralogist: California Div. Mines Rept. 31, 583 pp., 1935.

23. Thirty-second report of the State Mineralogist: California Div. Mines Rept. 32, 563 pp., 1936.

24. Thirty-third report of the State Mineralogist: California Div. Mines Rept. 33, 385, pp., 1937.

25. California's commercial minerals: Min. Cong. Jour., vol. 24, pp. 16–20, 1938.

26. Thirty-fourth report of the State Mineralogist: California Div. Mines Rept. 34, 669 pp., 1938.

27. Mineral highlights of California: California Div. Mines Rept. 34, pp. 292–297, 1938.

28. Thirty-fifth report of the State Mineralogist: California Div. Mines Rept. 35, 552 pp., 1939.

29. Thirty-sixth report of the State Mineralogist: California Div. Mines Rept. 36, 494 pp., 1940.

30. Thirty-seventh report of the State Mineralogist: California Div. Mines Rept. 37, 636 pp., 1941.

31. Thirty-eighth report of the State Mineralogist: California Div. Mines Rept. 38, 414 pp., 1942.

32. Thirty-ninth report of the State Mineralogist: California Div. Mines Rept. 39, 609 pp., 1943.

33. Fortieth report of the State Mineralogist: California Div. Mines Rept. 40, 509 pp., 1944.

34. Forty-first report of the State Mineralogist: California Div. Mines Rept. 41, 401 pp., 1945.

35. Observations at "The Geysers," Sonoma County, California: California Div. Mines Rept. 42, pp. 295–298, 1946.

Bradley, William Frank
1. See Grim, Ralph Early (1).
2. See Graf, Donald Lee (1).

Brady, Lionel Francis
1. (and **Webb, Robert Wallace**) Cored bombs from Arizona and California volcanic cones: Jour. Geology, vol. 51, pp. 398–410, 1943.

Braitsch, Otto
1. Über p—Veatchit, eine neue Veatchit—Varietät aus dem Zechsteinsalz: Beit zur Mineralogie and Petrographie, vol. 6, pp. 352–356, 1959.

Bramlette, Milton Nunn
1. (and **Posnjak, Eugen**) Zeolitic alteration of pyroclastics: Am. Mineralogist, vol. 18, pp. 167–171, 1933 . . . Mineralog. Abstracts, vol. 5, pp. 357, 1933.

2. Heavy mineral studies on correlation of sands at Kettleman Hills, California: Am. Assoc. Petroleum Geologists. Bull., vol. 18, pp. 1559–1576, 1934.

3. See Woodring, Wendell Phillips (1).

4. The Monterey formation of California and the origin of its siliceous rocks: U. S. Geol. Survey Prof. Paper 212, 57 pp., 1946.

Branner, John Caspar

1. (**Newsom, John Flesher,** and **Arnold, Ralph**) Description of the Santa Cruz quadrangle, California: U. S. Geol. Survey Geol. Atlas, Santa Cruz, Calif. folio (no. 163) 11 pp., 1909.

Brannock, Walter Wallace

1. See Switzer, George S. (6).

Braun, Lewis Timothy

1. See Logan, Clarence August (25).

2. See O'Brien, John Charles (7).

Bredemeyer, W.

1. San Francisco and Pine Grove mining districts: Min. Sci. Press, vol 48, p. 18, 1884.

Breithaupt, A.

1. Gediegen Gold aus Austrialien und Californien: Berg.-u. hüttenm. Zeit. Band 12, p. 613, 1853.

Bremner, Carl St. J.

1. Geology of Santa Cruz Island, Santa Barbara County, California: Santa Barbara Mus. Nat. History, Occ. Paper 1, 33 pp., 1932.

Brice, James Coble

1. Geology of Lower Lake quadrangle, California: California Div. Mines Bull. 166, 72 pp., 1953.

Briggs, Louis Isaac, Jr.

1. Jarosite from the California Tertiary: Am. Mineralogist, vol. 36, p. 902, 1951.

Brindley, George William

1. Structural mineralogy of clays: California Div. Mines Bull. 169, pp. 33–43, 1955.

2. The x-ray identification and crystal structures of clay minerals (ed. by G. Brown): Mineralogical Soc. England (2nd Ed.), 1961.

Brooks, E. F.

1. Platinum in California: Min. Sci. Press, vol. 114, p. 116, 1917.

Brothers, R. N.

1. Glaucophane schists from the North Berkeley Hills, Calif.: Am. Jour. Sci., vol. 252, pp. 614–626, 1954.

Brown, G. Chester

1. Kern County: California Min. Bur. Rept. 14, pp. 471–523, 1916; issued separately July 1915 under title, Mines and mineral resources of the counties Fresno, Kern, Kings, Madera, Mariposa, Merced, San Joaquin, Stanislaus . . . (abstract): Geol. Zentralbl., Band 27, p. 393, 1922.

2. Shasta, Siskiyou, Trinity Counties: California Min. Bur. Rept. 14, pp. 745–925, 1916; issued separately under title Mines and mineral resources of the counties Shasta, Siskiyou, Trinity, 1915 . . . (abstract): Geol. Zentralbl., Band 27, p. 393, 1922.

Brown, J. A.

1. Amador, Calaveras Counties: California Min. Bur. Rept. 10, pp. 98–123, 147–152, 1890.

Brown, John Stafford

1. The Salton Sea region, California: U. S. Geol. Survey, Water-Supply Paper 497, 292 pp., 1923.

Brown, R. Gilman

1. The vein system of the Standard mine, Bodie, California: Am. Inst. Min. Met. Eng., Bull. 16, pp. 587–601, 1907 . . . Trans., vol. 38, pp. 343–357, 1908 . . . (abstract): Geol. Zentralbl., Band 12, pp. 12–13, 1909.

Brown, Will L.

1. Chiastolite crystals, Madera, California: Mineralogist, vol. 4, no. 7, p. 9, 1936.

Browne, E. F.

1. Explorations in Death Valley: Min. World, vol. 24, pp. 58–60, 1906.

Browne, John Ross
1. (and **Taylor, James W.**) Mineral resources of the states and territories west of the Rocky Mountains for 1866, 360 pp., 1867.
2. Mineral resources of the states and territories west of the Rocky Mountains: 40th Cong. 2d Sess., H. Ex. Doc. 202, 674 pp. [1867], 1868.
3. The Mariposa Estate; its past, present and future, 62 pp., New York, Russell's American Steam Printing House, 1868.
4. Report of J. Ross Browne on the mineral resources of the states and territories west of the Rocky Mountains: (U. S. Treas. Dept.), 674 pp., H. H. Bancroft and Co., San Francisco, 1869. [reprint of 2]
5. Resources of the Pacific Slope, 678 pp., San Francisco, 1869; New York, 1887 [reprint of 2 with addition of report on Lower California, 200 pp.]

Browne, Ross E.
1. Ancient river beds of the Forest Hill Divide: California Min. Bur. Rept. 10, pp. 435–465, 1890.

Brush, George Jarvis
1. New mineral localities; ouvarovite: Am. Jour. Sci., 2d ser., vol. 42, p. 268, 1866.

Bryant, Edwin
1. Reports of bitumen near Santa Barbara and Los Angeles, in What I saw in California, pp. 385, 411, 451, D. Appleton and Co., 1849.

Buckland, William
1. The zoology of Captain Beechey's voyage, London, 1839.

Buerger, Martin Julian
1. See Lukesh, Joseph (1).

Burch, Stephen H.
1. Relationship of rock magnetism to petrologic properties in a Franciscan peridotite, Burro Mountain, California: (abst.) Geol. Soc. America Spec. Paper 76, pp. 192–193, 1964.

Burchard, Ernest Francis
1. Fluorspar deposits in western United States: Am. Inst. Min. Eng., Tech. Pub. 500, 26 pp., 1933 . . . Trans., vol. 109, pp. 370–396, 1934.

Burkart, Herman Joseph
1. Gediegenes Gold und Zinnober aus Californien, so wie Manganblende und Fahlerz aus Mexico: Niederrheinische Gesell. für Natur- und Heilkunde in Bonn, Sitzungsber., in Naturh. Ver. preuss. Rheinlande, Verh. Band 13, pp. xv-xx, 1856.
2. Der Mineralreichthum Californiens und der angrenzenden Staaten und Territorien: Berg- u. hüttenm. Zeit., Band 28, pp. 3–5, 21–22, 51–52, 83–85, 94–95, 103–104, 198–199, 212–215, 221–223, 1869.
3. Die Goldlagerstätten Californiens: Neues Jahrb., 1870, pp. 21–50, 129–182.
4. Ueber das Vorkommen verschiedener, Tellur-Minerale in den Vereinigten Staaten von Nordamerika: Neues Jahrb., 1873, pp. 476–495.
5. Das Borax-Vorkommen in den westlichen Staaten von Nordamerika: Neues. Jahrb., 1874, pp. 716–720 . . . (abstract): Geol. Rec., 1874, p. 225, 1875.

Burley, Gordon
1. See Clark, Joan Robinson (1).

Burnham, Charles Wilson
1. See Prewitt, C. T. (1).

Burnham, Clifford Wayne
1. Contact metamorphism of magnesian limestones at Crestmore, California: Geol. Soc. America Bull., vol. 70, pp. 879–920, 1959.
2. Contact metamorphism at Crestmore, California: California Div. Mines and Geol. Bull. 170, Ch. VII, pp. 61–70, 1954.

Bushee, Jonathan
1. Lead alpha ages for zircons from batholithic and prebatholithic rocks, San Diego and Orange Counties, California: (abst.) Geol. Soc. America Spec. Paper 73, pp. 29–30, 1963.

Butler, C. P.
1. The Goose Lake fragments: The Meteoritical Society, Program of the 27th Ann. Meeting, pp. 5–6, 1964.

Butler, Robert Dexter
1. See Stoiber, Richard Edwin (1).

Butner, D. W.
1. Investigation of tungsten occurrences in Darwin district, Inyo County, California: U. S. Bur. Mines Rept. Invest, no. 4475, 6 pp., June, 1949.

Buttgenbach, H.
1. Notes minéralogiques: Soc. géol. Belgique Annales 55, pp. B165–178, 1932.
2. Sur un cristal de neptunite: Soc. géol. Belgique Annales 61, pp. 324–325, 1937–38.

C

California Academy of (Natural) Sciences
1. Specimens presented to the California Academy, Donations to the Cabinet to January 1, 1858: California Acad. Sci. Proc., vol. 1, pt. 2, p. 110 [1856] 1858.

California Miners' Association
1. California mines and minerals, 450 pp., San Francisco, 1899.

California State Mining Bureau (California Division of Mines and Geology)
1. Register of mines and minerals, with map (of each of the following counties, issued separately): Amador, 17 pp., 1903; Butte, 13 pp., 1903; Calaveras, 50 pp., 1900; El Dorado, 32 pp., 1902; Inyo, 24 pp., 1902; Kern, 37 pp., 1904; Lake, 14 pp., 1901; Mariposa, 19 pp., 1903; Nevada, 18 pp., 1898; Placer, 21 pp., 1902; Plumas, 36 pp., 1900; San Bernardino, 35 pp., 1902; San Diego, 15 pp., 1902; Santa Barbara, 12 pp., 1906; Shasta, 27 pp., 1902; Sierra, 24 pp., 1903; Siskiyou, 50 pp., 1900; Tuolumne, 24 pp., 1903: Yuba, 20 pp., 1905.

Calkins, Frank Cathcart
1. Molybdenite near Ramona, San Diego County, California: U. S. Geol. Survey Bull. 640, pp. 73–76, 1916 . . . (abstract): Washington Acad. Sci. Jour., vol. 7, p. 78, 1917.
2. An occurrence of nickel ore in San Diego County, California: U. S. Geol. Survey Bull. 640, pp. 77–82, 1916 . . . (abstract): Washington Acad. Sci. Jour., vol. 7, p. 78, 1917 . . . Geol. Zentralbl., Band 28, p. 134, 1922.
3. See Mansfield, George Rogers (1).
4. The granitic rocks of the Yosemite region: U. S. Geol. Survey Prof. Paper 160, pp. 120–129, 1930.

Cameron, Eugene Nathan
1. See Kerr, Paul Francis (4).

Campbell, Donald F.
1. The iron ore of Shasta County, California: Min. Sci. Press, vol. 93, p. 603, 1906.
2. The copper of Shasta County, California: Min. Sci. Press, vol. 94, pp. 28–30, 55–58, 1907 . . . (abstract): Eng. Index, 1907, p. 306, 1908.

Campbell, Ian
1. Magnesium metasomatism in dolomite from Lucerne Valley, California: Internat. Geol. Cong. Rept., 18th Sess., Great Britain, 1948, part III, pp. 1–8, 1950.
2. (and **Wright, Lauren Albert**) Kyanite paragenesis at Ogilby, California: Geol. Soc. America Bull. vol. 61, pp. 1520–1521, 1950.
3. (and **staff**) Fifty-sixth report of the State Mineralogist: California Div. Mines, 219 pp., 1960.
4. (and **staff**) Fifty-seventh report of the State Mineralogist: California Div. Mines, 206 pp., 1961.
5. State mineralogy: why, whence and whither. Am. Mineralogist, vol. 48, pp. 227–240, 1963.

Campbell, Marius Robison
1. Reconnaissance of the borax deposits of Death Valley and Mojave Desert: U. S. Geol. Survey Bull. 200, 23 pp., 1902 . . . (abstract): Eng. and Min. Jour., vol. 74, pp. 517–518, 1902.
2. Borax deposits of eastern California: U.S. Geol. Survey Bull. 213, pp. 401–405, 1903 . . . (abstract): Geol. Zentralbl., Band 5, p. 466, 1904.

Caras, Alice
1. See Wolfe, Caleb Wroe. (2).

Carey, Everett P.
1. (and **Miller, William John**) The crystalline rocks of Oak Hill area, near San Jose, California: Jour. Geology, vol. 15, pp. 152–169, 1907.

Carl, Howard Frederick
1. See Gabriel, Alton. (1), and Slavin, Morris. (1).

Carlisle, Donald
1. (**Davis, Dudley L., Kildale, Malcolm Brus,** and **Stewart, Richard M.**) Base metal and iron deposits in southern California: California Div. Mines and Geol. Bull. 170, Ch. VIII, pp. 41–50, 1954.

Carlson, Denton W.
1. See Davis, Fenelon Francis. (5).
2. (and **Clark, William Bullock**) Mines and Minerals of Amador County, California: California Jour. Mines and Geology vol. 50, pp. 149–285, 1954.
3. (and **Clark, William Bullock**) Lode gold mines of the Alleghany-Downieville area, Sierra County, California: California Jour. Mines and Geology, vol. 52, pp. 237–291, 1956.
4. See **Clark, William B.** (3).

Carlton, S. J.
1. (and **Wichels, Ernest**) Cinnabar of northern California: Gems and Minerals, No. 321, pp. 35–36, June 1964.

Carman, Max Fleming, Jr.
1. Geology of the Lockwood Valley area, Kern and Ventura Counties, California: California Div. Mines and Geol., Special Rept. 81, 66 pp., 1964.

Carnall, V.
1. Verbreitung des Goldes in Californien: Deutsche Geol. Gesell. Zeitschr., Band 3, p. 376, 1851.
2. Ueber Zinnobergruben in Californien: Deutsche Geol. Gesell. Zeitschr., Band 4, pp. 210, 218, 1852.

Carpenter, Alden B.
1. Mineral assemblage, magnesium calcite-aragonite-huntite at Crestmore, California (abst.): Geol. Soc. America, Program of Annual Meeting, 1961, Nov. 2-4, Cincinnati, Ohio, p. 22A; ibid., Spec. Paper 68, p. 146, 1962.
2. Oriented overgrowths of thaumasite on ettringite: Am. Mineralogist, vol. 48, pp. 1394–1395, 1963.

Carpenter, Jay A.
1. The Kelly silver mine at Randsburg, California: Eng. and Min. Jour., vol. 108, pp. 940–943, 1919.
2. A sagebrush silver producer (the Kelly mine development to 1921): Eng. and Min. Jour., vol. 112, pp. 132–135, 1921.

Carron, Maxwell Kenneth
1. See Glass, Jewell Jeannette (4).
2. See Glass, Jewell Jeannette (5).

Castello, W. O.
1. See Boalich, Edwin Snow (2).
2. See Boalich, Edwin Snow (3).
3. The commercial minerals of California, with notes on their uses, distribution, properties, ores, field tests, and preparation for the market: California Min. Bur., Bull. 87, 124 pp., 1920.
4. See Huguenin, Emile (4).
5. Mariposa County: California Min. Bur. Rept. 17, pp. 86–143, 1921.

Cater, Frederick William, Jr.
1. Chromite deposits of Tuolumne and Mariposa Counties, California: California Div. Mines Bull. 134, pt. III, Chap. 1, pp. 1–32, 1948.
2 and 3. Chromite deposits of Calaveras and Amador Counties, California: California Div. Mines Bull. 134, pt. III, Chap. 2, pp. 33–60, 1948.
4. (**Rynearson, Garn Arthur** and **Dow, Donald Huse**) Chromite deposits of El Dorado County, California: California Div. Mines Bull. 134, pt. III, Chap. 4, pp. 108–167, 1951.
5. See Wells, Francis Gerritt (5).
6. See Wells, Francis Gerritt (6).

Chalmers, R. A.
1. See Stuart, F. H. (1).
2. See Murdoch, Joseph (36).
3. See Murdoch, Joseph (37).

Chandler, J. W.

1. Mining methods and costs of the Lava Cap Gold Mining Corporation: U. S. Bur. Mines Inf. Circ. 7164, May 1941.

Chapman, Randolph Wallace

1. The contact metamorphic deposit of Round Valley, California: Jour. Geology, vol. 45, pp. 859–871, 1937.

Charles, Abbott

1. Mines and minerals of Stanislaus County: California Division Mines Rept. 43, pp. 85–100, 1947.

Chase, A. W.

1. On the Klamath River mines; remarkable gravel deposits of the lower Klamath—a sketch of their geology: Am. Jour. Sci., 3d ser., vol. 6, pp. 57–59, 1873.

2. Auriferous sands of Gold Bluff (Klamath County): California Acad. Sci. Proc., vol. 5, p. 246, 1874.

3. The auriferous gravel deposits of Gold Bluff: Am. Jour. Sci., 3d ser., vol. 7, pp. 379–384, 1874.

Chatard, Thomas Marean

1. See Clarke, Frank Wigglesworth (2)
2. See Clarke, Frank Wigglesworth (1).
3. On urao: Am. Jour. Sci., 3d ser., vol. 38, pp. 59–64, 1889 . . . U. S. Geol. Survey Bull. 60, pp. 75–78, 1890.
4. Natural soda; its occurrence and utilization: U. S. Geol. Survey Bull. 60, pp. 27–101, 1890.
5. The natural soda deposits of the United States: Franklin Inst. Jour., vol. 139, pp. 271–283, 341–351, 1895.

Chesterman, Charles Wesley

1. Contact metamorphic rocks of the Twin Lakes region, Fresno County, California: California Div. Mines Rept. 38, pp. 243–281, 1942.

2. Jadeite in San Benito County, California: Lapidary Jour., vol. 4, pp. 204–208, 1950.

3. Nephrite in Marin County, California: (abstract) Geol. Soc. America Bull., vol. 62, p. 1517, 1951 . . . California Div. Mines Special Rept. 10-B, 11 pp., 1951.

4. See Yoder, Hatten Schuyler, Jr. (1).

5. Uranium, thorium, and rare-earth elements: California Div. Mines Bull. 156, pp. 361–363, 1950.

5a. See Wright, Lauren Albert (9).

6. (and **Bowen, Oliver Earle, Jr.**) Fluoborite from San Bernardino County, California (abst.): Geol. Soc. America Bull., vol. 69, pp. 1678–79, 1958.

7. Ludwigite from Fresno County, California (abst.): Geol. Soc. America Bull., vol. 70, pp. 1712–1713, 1959.

8. See Hewett, Donnel Foster (6).

9. (and **Gross, Eugene Bischoff**) Mineralogy of the Kalkar quarry, Santa Cruz, California: Am. Mineralogist, vol. 49, p. 1507, 1964.

Chidester, Alfred Herman

1. (**Engel, Albert Edward John,** and **Wright, Lauren Albert**) Talc resources of the United States: U. S. Geol. Survey Bull. 1167, 61 pp., 1964.

Christ, Charles Louis

1. Studies of borate minerals I—X-ray crystallography of colemanite: Am. Mineralogist, vol. 38, pp. 411–415, 1953.

2. Studies of borate minerals II—X-ray crystallography of inyoite and meyerhofferite: X-ray and morphological crystallography of $2CaO \cdot 3B_2O_3 \cdot 9H_2O$: Am. Mineralogist, vol. 38, pp. 912–918, 1953.

3. (**Clark, Joan Robinson,** and **Evans, Howard Tasker, Jr.**) The crystal structure of colemanite, $CaB_3O_4(OH)_3 \cdot H_2O$, in Studies of Borate Minerals (III): Acta Crystallographica, vol. 11, pp. 761–770, 1958.

4. (and **Garrels, Robert Minard**) Relations among sodium borate hydrates at the Kramer deposit, Boron, California: Am. Jour. Sci., vol. 257, pp. 516–528, 1959.

5. See Bailey, Edgar Herbert (10).

6. (and **Clark, Joan Robinson**) X-ray crystallography and crystal chemistry of gowerite, $CaO \cdot 3B_2O_3 \cdot 5H_2O$: Am. Mineralogist, vol 45, pp. 230–234, 1960.

7. See Clark, Joan Robinson (6).

Christy, Samuel Benedict
1. The ocean placers of San Francisco: Eng. and Min. Jour., vol. 26, p. 279, 1878.
2. On the genesis of cinnabar deposits: Am. Jour. Sci., 3d ser., vol. 17, pp. 453–463, 1879.

Chromy, Ben J.
1. Lawsonite crystals on Tiburon Peninsula, California: Rocks and Minerals, vol. 3, nos. 3 and 4, pp. 130–132, 1955.

Cissarz, Arnold
1. Überganslagerstätten innerhalb der Intrusiv-Magmatischen Abfolge, I, Zinn-Wolfram- und Molybdanformationen: Neues Jahrb., Beilage-Band 56 A, pp. 185–274, 1927–28.

Claringbull, Gordon Frank
1. See Hey, M. H. (2).

Clark, Clifton W.
1. The geology and ore deposits of the Leona rhyolite, California: Univ. California Dept. Geol. Sci. Bull., vol. 10, pp. 361–382, 1917 . . . (abstract): Geol. Zentralbl., Band 29, p. 424, 1923.

Clark, Joan Robinson
1. (**Mrose, Mary Emma, Perloff, Alvin,** and **Burley, Gordon**) Investigation of veatchite in Studies of Borate Minerals (VI): Am. Mineralogist, vol. 44, pp. 1141–1149, 1959.
2. See Christ, Charles Louis (3).
3. See Erd, Richard Clarkson (3).
4. (and **Mrose, Mary Emma**) Veatchite and p-veatchite: Am. Mineralogist, vol. 45, pp. 1221–1229, 1960.
5. See Christ, Charles Louis (6).
6. (**Christ, Charles Louis,** and **Appleman, Daniel Everett**) Studies of borate minerals (X): the crystal structure of $CaB_3O_5(OH)$: Acta. Cryst., vol. 15, pp. 207–213, 1962.
7. Boron-oxygen polyion in the crystal structure of tunellite, Science, vol. 141, p. 1178, 1963.
8. The crystal structure of tunellite, $SrB_6O_9(OH)_2 \cdot 3H_2O$: Am. Mineralogist, vol. 49, pp. 1549–1568, 1964.

Clark, Lorin Delbert
1. Geology and mineral deposits of the Calaveritas quadrangle, Calaveras County, California: California Div. Mines, Special Rept. 40, 23 pp., 1954.
2. See Bateman, Paul Charles (4).

Clark, Samuel Gilbert
1. Milton formation of Sierra Nevada: Unpub. Ph.D. thesis in Library of University of Calif. . . . (abstract): Pan-Am. Geologist, vol. 59, pp. 314–315, 1933

Clark, William Bullock
1. See Carlson, Denton W. (2).
2. See Carlson, Denton W. (3).
3. (and **Carlson, Denton W.**) Mines and mineral resources of El Dorado County, California: California Jour. Mines and Geology, vol. 52, pp. 369–591, 1956.
4. (and **Lydon, Philip Andrew**) Mines and mineral resources of Calaveras, County, California: California Div. Mines and Geol. County Rept. 2, 217 pp., 1962. . . . Geol. Soc. America Proc., 1933, pp. 312–313, 1934.

Clarke, Frank Wigglesworth
1. (and **Chatard, Thomas Marean**) Mineralogical notes from the laboratory of the U. S. Geological Survey: Am. Jour. Sci., 3d ser., vol. 28, pp. 20–25, 1884.
2. (and **Chatard, Thomas Marean**) Halloysite from California: U. S. Geol. Survey Bull. 9, pp. 12–13, 1884.
3. Mica: Mineral Resources U.S., 1883–84, pp. 906–912, 1885.
4. A new occurrence of gyrolite: U. S. Geol. Survey Bull. 64, pp. 22–23, 1890 . . . Am. Jour. Sci., 3d ser., vol. 38, pp. 128–129, 1889.
5. Note on garnet from California: Am. Jour. Sci., 3d ser., vol. 50, pp. 76–77, 1895.
6. See Hillebrand, William Francis (1).
7. Mineral analyses from the laboratories of the U.S. Geological Survey, 1880–1903; U. S. Geological Survey Bull. 220, 119 pp., 1903.
8. (and **Steiger, George**) On "californite": U.S. Geol. Survey Bull. 262, pp. 72–74, 1905.

9. Analyses of rocks and minerals from the laboratory of the United States Geological Survey, 1880–1908; U. S. Geological Survey, Bull. 419, 323 pp., 1910.

10. Analyses of rocks and minerals from the laboratory of the U.S. Geological Survey, 1880–1914: U.S. Geological Survey Bull. 591, 376 pp.. 1915.

Clarke, Roy S., Jr.
1. See Switzer, George S. (10), and Sinkankas, John (2).

Clearwater, C. D.
1. "Burning canyon": Palisadian, vol. 16, no. 49, p. 2, April 14, 1944.

Clements, Thomas
1. Some of the world's great gold mining districts: Pacific Mineralogist, vol. 1, no. 1, pp. 3–4, 1934.
2. The geology of gem stones: Pacific Mineralogist, vol. 2, no. 1, pp. 3–4, 17, 1935.

Cleminshaw, Clarence Higbee
1. See Nininger, Harvey Harlow. (2).

Cleveland, George Barrie
1. Geology of the Little Antelope Valley clay deposits, Mono County, California: California Div. Mines and Geol., Spec. Rept. 72, 28 pp., 1962.

Cloudman, H. C.
1. (Merrill, Frederick James Hamilton, and Huguenin, Emile) San Bernardino County: California Min. Bur. Rept. 15, pp. 774–899, 1919; issued separately under title Mines and mineral resources of San Bernardino County, Tulare County, 1916 . . . (abstract): Geol. Zentralbl., Band 27, p. 394, 1922 . . . Eng. Index 1918, p. 325, 1919.

Cohen, Alvin Jerome
1. Regularity of the F center maxima in fused silica and alpha quartz: Jour. of Chemical Physics, vol. 22, p. 570, 1955.

Cohen, E.
1. (and Weinschenk, E.) Meteoreisen-Studien: K. Naturh. Hofmuseum Annales, Band 6, pp. 131–165, 1891.
2. Meteoreisen-Studien II: K. Naturh. Hofmuseum Annales, Band 7, pp. 143–162, 1892.
3. Das Meteoreisen von Surprise Springs, Bagdad, San Bernardino County, Sud-Californien: Naturwiss. Ver für Neuvorpommern und Rügen Greifswald, Mitt., Band 33, pp. 29–33, 1 taf., 1901.

Coleman, Robert Griffin
1. Optical and chemical study of jadeite from California: Geol. Soc. America, Bull. 65, p. 1241, 1954.
2. (and Lee, Donald Edward) Metamorphic aragonite in the glaucophane schists of Cazadero, California (abst.): Geol. Soc. Amer. Spec. Paper 68, p. 16, 1962; Am. Jour. Sci., vol. 260, pp. 577–595, 1962.
3. (and Lee, Donald Edward) Glaucophane-bearing metamorphic rocks of the Cazadero area, California: Jour. Petrol., vol. 4, pp. 260–301, 1963.
4. See Lee, Donald Edward (3).
5. See Lee, Donald Edward (4).
6. See Lee, Donald Edward (5).

Collins, Elizabeth
1. See Murdoch, Joseph (40).

Combs, D. S.
1. The pumpellyite mineral series: Mineral. Mag. vol. 30, pp. 113–135, 1953.

Compton, Robert Ross
1. Charnockitic rocks of Santa Lucia Range, California: Am. Jour. Sci., vol. 258, pp. 609–636, 1960.

Conkling, Alfred Ronald
1. Annual report upon geographical survey west of the 100th meridian in California, Nevada, Utah, Colorado, Wyoming, New Mexico, Arizona, and Montana, App. I, pp. 167–183, App. I, 1, p. 184, 1878.

Cook, Charles Wilford
1. A new occurrence of ilsemannite (Gibson, Shasta County, California): Am. Jour. Sci., 5th ser., vol. 4, pp. 50–52, 1922 . . . Mineralog. Abstracts, vol. 2, p. 42, 1923.

Corning, Frederick Gleason
1. The gold quartz mines of Grass Valley, Nevada County, California: Eng. and Min. Jour., vol. 42, pp. 418–420, 1886.

Cornthwaite, M. A.
1. See Bowles, Oliver (2)

Cornwall, Henry Rowland
1. (and **Kleinhampl, Frank Joseph**) Geology of Bullfrog quadrangle and ore deposits related to Bullfrog Hills caldera, Nye County, Nevada and Inyo County, California: U.S. Geol. Survey Prof. Paper 454-J, pp. J1-J25, 1964.

Coulson, A. L.
1. Catalogue of meteorites: India Geol. Survey Mem., vol. 75, p. 220, 1940.

Cowan, John L.
1. Tourmaline in California: Min. Sci. Press, vol. 100, pp. 864–865, 1910

Coy, Owen C.
1. California County boundaries: California Historical Survey Commission, Berkeley, California, 335 pp., 1923.

Crampton, F. R.
1. Auriferous gravel channels of Nevada County, California: Min. Jour., vol. 16, no. 6, pp. 5–7, 1932.

Crandall, Roderic
1. The geology of the San Francisco peninsula: Am. Philos. Soc. Proc., vol. 46, no. 185, pp. 3–58, 1907.

Crawford, James John (see also John Jones Crawford)
1. Twelfth report of the State Mineralogist: California Min. Bur. Rept. 12, 412 pp., Sacramento, 1894.
2. Thirteenth report of the State Mineralogist: California Min. Bur. Rept. 13, 726 pp., Sacramento, 1896.

Creasey, Saville Cyrus
1. Geology and nickel mineralization of the Julian-Cuyamaca area, San Diego County, California: California Div. Mines Rept. 42, pp. 15–30, 1946.

Crippen, Richard A., Jr.
1. See Woodford, Alfred Oswald, (10).
2. Nephrite jade and associated rocks of the Cape San Martin region, Monterey County, California: (abstract) Geol. Soc. America Bull. 60, p. 1938, 1949 . . . California Div. Mines Special Rept. 10-A, 14 pp., 1951.

Crittenden, Max Dermont, Jr.
1. Geology of the San Jose-Mount Hamilton area, California. California Div. Mines. Bull. 157, 74 pp., 1951.

Cronise, Titus Fey
1. The natural wealth of California, 696 pp., H. H. Bancroft Co., San Francisco, 1868.

Crook, Theo H.
1. Occurrence and minerals of manganese: California Div. Mines, Bull. 125, pp. 41-49, 1943.

Crosby, James W., III
1. (and **Hoffman, Samuel R.**) Fluorspar in California: California Jour. Mines and Geology, vol. 47, pp. 619–638, 1951.

Crossman, James H.
1. San Bernardino County: California Min. Bur. Rept. 9, pp. 214–239, 1890.
2. San Bernardino County, its mineral and other resources XXI: Min. Sci. Press, vol. 61, p. 347, 1890.

Cuthbert, J. D.
1. See Petch, Howard Earl (1).

D

Dake, Henry Carl
1. The jadeite locality: The Mineralogist, vol. 18, pp. 188–190, 1951.

Dale, Nelson Clark
1. Scheelite deposits in the Greenhorn Mountains of the southern Sierras (abstract): Geol. Soc. America, Bull., vol. 52, p. 1896, 1941.

Daly, John W.

1. Paragenesis of mineral assemblages at Crestmore, California (abstract): Pan-Am. Geologist, vol. 59, pp. 312–313, 1933 . . . Geol. Soc. America, Proc. 1933, vol. 1, p. 311, 1934 . . . Am. Mineralogist, vol. 20, pp. 638–659, 1935.

2. The Crestmore locality: Pacific Mineralogist, vol. 4, no. 1, pp. 29–32, 1937.

Dana, Edward Salisbury

1. A crystallographic study of the thinolite of Lake Lahonton: U. S. Geol. Survey Bull. 12, 34 pp. 1884.

2. (and **Penfield, Samuel Lewis**) Mineralogical notes: Am. Jour. Sci., 3d ser., vol. 30, pp. 136–139, 1885 . . . California Min. Bur. Rept. 5, pp. 65–66, 1885.

3. On the crystallization of gold: Am. Jour. Sci., 3d ser., vol. 32, pp. 132–138, 1886 . . . Zeitschr. Kristallographie, Band 12, pp. 275–281, 1886 . . . (abstract): Neues Jahrb., 1889, pp. 226–227.

4. System of mineralogy, 6th ed., 1134 pp., Wiley and Sons, New York, 1892.

5. System of mineralogy, 6th ed., App. I, 75 pp., 1903, App. II, 114 pp., Wiley and Sons, New York, 1914.

6. See Palache et al. (10).

7. See Palache et al. (11).

8. (and **Ford, William Ebenezer**) Textbook of mineralogy with an extended treatise on crystallography and physical mineralogy, by E. S. Dana, 4th ed., revised and enlarged by W. E. Ford, xi, 851 pp., New York, John Wiley & Sons, 1932.

Dana, James Dwight

1. Gold in California: Am. Jour. Sci., 2d ser., vol. 7, pp. 125–126, 1849.

2. Geology: in Charles Wilkes, U. S. Exploring Expedition during the years 1838–1842, vol. X, 756 pp., 1849.

3. Notes on upper California: Am. Jour. Sci., 2d ser., vol. 7, pp. 247–264, 1849.

4. System of mineralogy, 5th ed., 877 pp., New York, Wiley and Sons, 1868.

D'Arcy, Nicholas A., Jr.

1. The William B. Pitts collection of semi-precious stones: Pacific Mineralogist, vol. 4, no. 2, pp. 16, 17, 40, 1937.

2. Rocks and minerals outing to Owens Valley: Rocks and Minerals, vol. 14, pp. 67–75, 1939.

3. Geology of a field trip to San Fernando Valley and Pacoima Canyon, California: Rocks and Minerals, vol. 14, pp. 267–269, 1939.

Darrow, Richard L.

1. Age and structural relationships of the Franciscan formation in the Montara Mountain quadrangle, San Mateo County, California: California Div. Mines and Geol., Spec. Rept. 78, 23 pp., 1963.

Daviess, Steven Norman

1. Mineralogy of late Upper Cretaceous, Paleocene and Eocene sandstones of Los Banos district, west border of San Joaquin Valley, California: Am. Assoc. Petroleum Geologist Bull., vol. 30, pp. 63–83, 1946.

Davis, Charles H.

1. The Los Burros mining district, California: Min. Sci. Press, vol. 104, pp. 696–698, 1912 . . . (abstract): Eng. Index 1912, p. 388, 1913.

Davis, C. W.

1. (and **Vacher, H. C.**) Bentonite: U. S. Bur. Mines Tech. Paper 438, p. 51, 1928.

Davis, D. L.

1. (and **Peterson, E. C.**) Anaconda's operation at Darwin mines, Inyo County, California: Am. Inst. Mining Eng. Trans. Tech. Pub. 2407, 11 pp., 1948.

Davis, Dudley L.

1. See Carlisle, Donald (1).

Davis, Fenelon Francis

1. Mines and mineral resources of Napa County, California: California Div. Mines Rept. 44, pp. 159–188, 1948.

2. See Averill, C. V. (16).

3. Mines and mineral resources of Alameda County, California: California Jour. Mines and Geology, vol. 46, pp. 280–346, 1950.

4. (and **Vernon, James W.**) Mines and mineral resources of Contra Costa County, California: California Jour. Mines and Geology, vol. 47, pp. 561–618, 1951.

5. (and **Carlson, Denton W.**) Mines and mineral resources of Merced County, California: California Jour. Mines and Geology, vol. 48, pp. 207–251, 1952. '
6. (and **Jennings, Charles William**) Mines and mineral resources of Santa Clara County, California: California Jour. Mines and Geology, vol. 50, pp. 301–430, 1954.
7. Mines and mineral resources of San Mateo County, California: California Jour. Mines and Geology, vol. 51, pp. 401–458, 1955.
8. Highlights in California Mining, 1962. California Div. Mines and Geol., Mineral Information Service, vol. 16, pp. 1–8, 1963.

Davis, Gregory A.
1. (and **Pabst, Adolf**) Lawsonite and pumpellyite in glaucophane schists, North Berkeley Hills, California, with notes on x-ray crystallography of lawsonite by A. Pabst: Am. Jour. Sci., vol. 258, pp. 689–704, 1960.

Davis, H. E.
1. Molybdenum in San Diego: Eng. and Min. Jour., vol. 20, pp. 28–29, 1918.

Davis, H. W.
1. See Ridgeway, Robert H. (1).

Davis, R. O. E.
1. Analyses of kunzite: Am. Jour. Sci., 4th ser., vol. 18, p. 29, 1904.

Dawson, E. J.
1. See Schenck, W. E. (1).

Dawson, N. E.
1. Gem minerals of San Diego County: Mineral Notes and News, p. 6, June 1953.

Day, Arthur Louis
1. (and **Allen, Eugene Thomas**) The volcanic activity and hot springs of Lassen Peak, California: Carnegie Inst. Washington Pub. 360, 190 pp., 1925 . . . Volcano Letter no. 293, pp. 1–3, 1930.
2. See Allen, Eugene Thomas (2).

Day, David Talbot
1. Manganese: Mineral Resources U. S., 1883–84, pp. 550–566, 1885.
2. Sulphur: Mineral Resources U. S., 1883–84, pp. 864–876, 1885.
3. Mineral resources of the United States, 1894; non-metallic products: U. S. Geol. Survey 16th Ann. Rept., pt. 4, 735 pp., 1895.
4. Black sands of the Pacific coast: 59th Cong., 1st sess., S. Doc. 65, 24 pp., 1905.
5. Platinum in black sands from placer mines: Am. Jour. Sci., 4th ser., vol. 20, p. 410, 1905.
6. (and **Richards, R. H.**) Investigation of the black sands from placer mines: U. S. Geol. Survey Bull. 285, pp. 150–164, 1906.
7. (and **Richards, R. H.**) Useful minerals in the black sands of the Pacific slope: Mineral Resources, U. S., 1905, pp. 1175–1258, 1906.

De Groot, Henry
1. Mining resources of California: Overland Monthly, vol. 9, pp. 455–462, 1887.
2. Alpine, El Dorado, Inyo, Mono, San Bernardino Counties: California Min. Bur. Rept. 10, pp. 96–97, 169–182, 209–218, 336–344, 518–533, 1890.
3. The Searles borax marsh: California Min. Bur. Rept. 10, pp. 534–539, 1890.
4. The San Francisco ocean placer—the auriferous beach sands: California Min. Bur. Rept. 10, pp. 545–547, 1890.
5. The mining region east of the Sierra: some of the borax deposits: Min. Sci. Press, vol. 64, p. 404, 1892.

De Kalb, Courtenay
1. Onyx marbles: Eng. and Min. Jour., vol. 60, p. 368, 1895 . . . Am. Inst. Min. Met. Eng. Trans., vol. 10, p. 573, 1896.
2. Geology of the Exposed Treasure Lode, Mojave, California: Am. Inst. Min. Met. Eng. Bull. 13, pp. 15–24, 1907 . . . Trans., vol. 38, pp. 310–319, 1908 . . . (abstract): Geol. Zentralbl., Band 12, p. 13, 1909.
3. Guadalupe quicksilver works: Min. Sci. Press, vol. 100, pp. 446–447, 1910.

De Lisle, Mark
1. Lead retention of zircons under conditions of hydrothermal contact metamorphism, White Mountains, California (abst.): Geol. Soc. Amer., Spec. Paper 73, p. 33, 1963.

De Schulten, A.
1. Sur l'isomorphisme de la northupite avec la tychite: Acad. Sci. Paris Comptes Rendus, tome 143, p. 405, 1906.

De Tregoborski, Louis
1. Essai sur les consequences eventualles de découvert des gites aurifers en Californie et en Australie, 199 pp., Paris, 1853.

De Violini, R.
1. See Leonard, Frederick Charles (10).

Debray, H.
1. See Deville, H. St. C. (1).

Delessert, B.
1. Les mines d'or de la Californie: Revue des Deux Mondes, n. p. 1, pp. 468–484, Feb., 1849.

Del Mar, Alexander
1. Gold nuggets of California: Min. Sci. Press, vol. 102, p. 629, 1911.

Denny, Marion Vaughn
1. See Huggins, Charles W. (1).

Dent, L. S.
1. (and **Taylor, H. F. W.**) The dehydration of xonotlite: Acta Crystallographica, vol. 9, pp. 1002–1004, 1956.

Deville, H. St. C.
1. (and **Debray, H.**) Du platine et des métaux qui l'accompagnent: Annales de Chimie et de Physique, tome 56, pp. 385–496, 1859.

Dibblee, Thomas Wilson, Jr.
1. Geologic map of the Boron quadrangle, Kern and San Bernardino Counties, California: U. S. Geol. Survey Mineral Invest. Field Studies Map MF–204, 1958.

Dickson, Frank Wilson
1. (and **Tunell, George**) Stability relations of cinnabar and metacinnabar: Am. Mineralogist, vol. 44, pp. 471–487, 1959.

Dietrich, Waldemar Fenn
1. The clay resources and the ceramic industry of California: California Min. Bur. Bull. 99, 383 pp. 1928.

Dietz, Robert Sinclair
1. (and **Emery, Kenneth Orris**) Marine phosphate deposits off the coast of California: . . . (abstract): Geol. Soc. America Bull., vol. 49, p. 1878, 1938.
2. (**Emery, Kenneth Orris** and **Shepard, Francis Parker**) Phosphorite deposits on the sea floor off southern California: Geol. Soc. America Bull., vol. 53, pp. 815–848, 1942.
3. See Bradley, William Frank (3).
4. See Emery, Kenneth Orris (3).

Dietz, Ralph W.
1. Crystals of jade from California: Gems and Minerals, no. 213, pp. 20–22, June 1955.
2. Television ulexite: Gems and Minerals, no. 232, pp. 16–17, Jan. 1957.

Diller, Joseph Silas
1. Geology of the Lassen Peak district, California: U. S. Geol. Survey 8th Ann. Rept., pp. 395–432, 1889 . . . (abstract): Petermanns Mitt. 1891 (Beil zum 37), pp. 114–115.
2. Native gold in calcite: Am. Jour. Sci., 3d ser., vol. 39, p. 160, 1890.
3. A late volcanic eruption in northern California and its peculiar lava: U. S. Geol. Survey Bull. 79, 33 pp., 1891.
4. Geology of the Taylorsville region of California: Geol. Soc. America Bull., vol. 3, pp. 369–394, 1892 . . . (abstract): Am. Geologist, vol. 9, p. 215, 1892 . . . Nature, vol. 47, pp. 39–40, 1892.
5. Description of the Lassen Peak quadrangle, California: U. S. Geol. Survey Geol. Atlas, Lassen Peak folio (no. 15), 4 pp., 1895; prelim. ed. 1892 . . . (abtract): Jour. Geology, vol. 3, pp. 974–976, 1895.
6. The educational series of rock specimens collected and distributed by the United States Geological Survey: U. S. Geol. Survey Bull. 150, 400 pp., 1898.
7. Copper deposits of the Redding region, California: U. S. Geol. Survey Bull. 213, pp. 123–132, 1903 . . . (abstract): Geol. Zentralbl., Band 5, pp. 394–395, 1904 . . . Eng. and Min. Jour., vol. 77, p. 729, 1904.
8. Iron ores of the Redding quadrangle, California: U. S. Geol. Survey Bull. 213, pp. 219–220, 1903 . . . (abstract): Geol. Zentralbl., Band 5, p. 196, 1904.

9. Mineral resources of the Indian Valley region, California: U. S. Geol. Survey Bull. 260, pp. 45–49, 1905.

10. Description of the Redding quadrangle: U. S. Geol. Survey Geol. Atlas, Redding folio (no. 138), 14 pp. 1906.

11. Geology of the Taylorsville region, California: U. S. Geol. Survey Bull. 353, 128 pp., 1908.

12. Auriferous gravels in the Weaverville quadrangle, California: U. S. Geol. Survey Bull. 540, pp. 11–21, 1914.

13. Talc and soapstone: Mineral Resources U. S., 1913, pt. II, non-metals, pp. 153–163, 1914.

14. Chromic iron ore: Mineral Resources U. S., 1914, pt. I, metals, pp. 1–15, 1914.

15. (and others) Guidebook of the western United States, Pt. D, The Shasta route and Coast line: U. S. Geol. Survey Bull. 614, 142 pp., 1915.

16. Chromite: Mineral Resources U. S., 1916, pt. I, metals, pp. 21–37, 1919.

17. Asbestos: U. S. Geol. Survey Bull. 666, pp. 51–56, 1919.

18. Chromite in the Klamath Mountains, California and Oregon: U. S. Geol. Survey Bull. 725, pp. 1–35, 1921 . . . (abstract): Washington Acad. Sci. Jour., vol. 12, p. 72, 1922 . . . Geol. Zentralbl., Band 31, p. 330, 1925 . . . Rev. Geologic et sci. connexes, tome 3, p. 67, 1922.

19. Asbestos: Mineral Resources U. S., 1918, pt. II, non-metals, pp. 545–556, 1921.

20. Chromite: Mineral Resources U. S., 1918, pt. I, metals, pp. 657–725, 1921.

Dodd, James Robert

1. Shell mineralogy and structure as evidence for two subspecies of *Mytilus edulis* on the Pacific Coast of North America (abst.): Geol. Soc. America Spec. Paper 68, p. 20, 1962.

2. Paleoecological implications of shell mineralogy in two West Coast pelecypod species (abst.): Geol. Soc. America Spec. Paper 68, p. 163, 1962.

Dolbear, C. E.

1. The Searles Lake potash deposit, California: Eng. and Min. Jour., vol 95, pp. 259–261, 1913.

Dolbear, Samuel H.

1. Dry placer mining in California: Eng. and Min. Jour., vol. 89, p. 359, 1910.

2. Tungsten in California in 1910: Mineral Industry, vol. 19, pp. 661–662,• 1911 . . . Eng. and Min. Jour., vol. 91, p. 86, 1911.

3. The saline deposits of Searles Lake, California: Min. World, vol. 41, pp. 797–800, 1914.

4. Magnesite deposits and possibility in California: Min. Sci. Press, vol. 110, pp. 105–108, 1915 . . . (abstract): Eng. Index, 1915, p. 355, 1915.

5. The manganese industry in California: Min. Sci. Press, vol. 110, p. 172, 1915.

6. Chromite possibilities in California: Min. Sci. Press, vol. 110, pp. 358–359, 1915.

'7. Magnesite production and markets: Min. Sci. Press, vol. 113, pp. 234–235, 1916.

8. The origin and geochemistry of magnesite: Min. Sci. Press, vol. 114, pp. 237–238, 1917.

9. Possible sources of barium carbonate: Min. Sci. Press, vol. 116, pp. 611–612, 1917.

Donnay, Gabrielle

1. (and **Donnay, Joseph Désiré Hubert**) The crystallography of bastnaesite, parasite, roentgenite and synchosite: Am. Mineralogist, vol. 38, pp. 932–965, 1953.

Donnay, Joseph Désiré Hubert'

1. Genesis of the Engels copper deposit; a field study and microscopic investigation of a late magmatic deposit: Congrés internat. des Mines, de la Metallurgie, de la Mechanique, et de la Géologie appliquées, sess. 6, pp. 99–111, 1931 . . . (abstract): Annotated Bibliography Econ. Geology, vol. 4, p. 233, 1931 . . . Rev. geologie et sci. connexes, tome 15, pp. 69–70, 1934.

2. See Donnay, Gabrielle (1).

Donnelly, Maurice

1. Geology and mineral deposits of the Julian district, San Diego County, California: California Div. Mines Rept. 30, pp. 331–370, 1934 . . . (abstract): Geol. Soc. America, Proc. 1934, p. 321, 1934.

2. The lithia pegmatites of Pala and Mesa Grande, California: Appendix unpubl., Ph.D. thesis, California Inst. Technology, 1935.

3. Notes on the lithium pegmatites of Pala, California: Pacific Mineralogist, vol. 3, no. 1, pp. 8–12, 1936.

Dorr, John Van Nostrand
1. See Lemmon, Dwight Moulton, (4).

Dougherty, E. Y.
1. Magnetite deposits of Madera County, California, constitute important reserves: Eng. and Min. Jour., vol. 123, pp. 765–770, 1927 . . . (abstract): Geol. Zentralbl., Band 36, p. 122, 1927.

Douglass, Robert Marshall
1. Crystal structure of sanbornite (abstract): Geol. Soc. America Bull. 65, p. 1246, 1954.

2. The crystal structure of sanbornite, $BaSi_2O_5$: Am. Mineralogist, vol. 43, pp. 517–536, 1958.

Dow, Donald Huse
1. (and Thayer, Thomas Prence) Chromite deposits of the northern Coast Ranges of California: California Div. Mines Bull. 134, pt. 2, pp. 1–38, 1946.

2. See Rynearson, Garn Arthur (5).

Downer, S. A.
1. The quicksilver mine of New Almaden: The Pioneer, vol. 2, pp. 220–228, 1854.

Drewes, Harald
1. Geology of the Funeral Peak quadrangle, California, on the east flank of Death Valley: U. S. Geol. Survey Prof. Paper 413, 78 pp., 1963.

Droste, John Brown
1. (and Gates, Gary Rickey) Attapulgite in lacustrine sediments of southern California (abst.): Geol. Soc. America Bull., vol. 70, p. 1593, 1959.

2. Clay mineral composition of sediments in some desert lakes in Nevada, California, and Oregon: Science, vol. 133, p. 1928, 1961.

Du Bois, W. E.
1. Large specimen of gold from California (verbal communication): Am. Philos. Soc. Proc., vol. 5, no. 46, p. 177, 1851.

2. Grosster Gold-Klumpen in Kalifornien: L'Institut, Sciences Math., Phys., et Nat., Jour. General des Societes et Traveaux Scientifiques de la France et de l'Etranger, 21 p. 175, 1853 . . . (abstract): Neues Jahrb. 1853, pp. 696–697, 1853.

Duflot de Mofras, Eugene
1. Travels on the Pacific coast; exploration du territoire de l'Oregon, des Californies et de la mer Vermeille, 1840–1842, translated by Marguerite E. Wilbur, Pasadena, 2 vols., 1937.

Dufrenoy, A.
1. Ueber die Zusammensetzung des Goldsandes von Californien, Sudamerika, von Ural und von Rhein: Berg-u. hüttenm. Zeit., Band 9, pp. 52–54, 1850 . . . Acad. sci. Paris Comptes rendus, 1849, pp. 193–203.

Dunham, Kingsley Charles
1. See Larsen, Esper Signius (15).

2. A note on the texture of the Crestmore contact rocks: Am. Mineralogist, vol. 18, pp. 474–477, 1933.

Dunn, Joseph Avery
1. Andalusite in California and kyanite in North Carolina: Econ. Geology, vol. 28, pp. 692–695, 1933 . . . (abstract): Annotated Bibliography Econ. Geology, vol. 6, p. 244, 1934.

Dunn, Russell L.
1. Siskiyou, Trinity Counties: California Min. Bur. Rept. 11, pp. 420–449, 480–484, 1893.

2. Auriferous conglomerate in California: California Min. Bur. Rept. 12, pp. 459–471, 1894.

Durand, F. E.
1. Note on crystals of quartz of a red color by the interposition of cinnabar: California Acad. Sci., Proc., vol. 4, p. 211, 1873.

2. Description of a new mineral from the New Almaden mine : California Acad. Sci., Proc., vol. 4, 218, 1873.

3. Notes on the crystallization of metacinnabarite : California Acad. Sci., Proc., vol. 4, pp. 219–220, 1873.

Durham, David Leon
1. See Winterer, Edward L. (1).

Durham, John Wyatt
1. (and **Allison, Edwin Chester**) Stratigraphic position of the Fish Creek gypsum at Split Mountain gorge, Imperial County, California (abst.) : Geol. Soc. America Spec. Paper 68, p. 22, 1962.

Durrell, Cordell
1. (and **MacDonald, Gordon Andrew**) Chlorite veins in serpentine near Kings River, California : Am. Mineralogist, vol. 24, pp. 452–456, 1939.

2. Metamorphism in the southern Sierra Nevada, northeast of Visalia, California : Univ. California, Dept. Geol. Sci. Bull., vol. 25, pp. 1–118, 1940.

3. New data on the optical properties of tridymite : Am. Mineralogist, vol. 25, pp. 501–502, 1940.

4. Geology of the Sierra Nevada, northeast of Visalia, Tulare County, California : California Div. Mines Rept. 39, pp. 153–168, 1943.

5. Strontium deposits of southern California (abstract) : Geol. Soc. America Bull. 58, p. 1250, 1947.

6. (and **Proctor, Paul Dean**) Iron ore deposits near Lake Hawley and Spencer Lakes, Sierra County, California : California Div. Mines Bull. 129, pp. 165–192, 1948.

7. Barite deposits near Barstow, San Bernardino County, California : California Div. Mines Special Rept. 39, 8 pp., 1954.

8. Geological investigations of strontium deposits in southern California : California Div. Mines Special Rept. 32, 48 pp., 1953.

Dyke, L. H.
1. The Amalie district of California : Min. Sci. Press, vol. 94, p. 764, 1907.

Dykes, Leland H.
1. Occurrence of monazite in a granodiorite pegmatite in Riverside County, California . . . (abstract) : Pan-Am. Geologist, vol. 58, p. 74, 1932 . . . Geol. Soc. America Bull., vol. 44, p. 161, 1933 . . . Annotated Bibliography Econ. Geology, vol. 6, p. 72, 1934.

E

Eakle, Arthur Starr
1. Mineralogical notes; with chemical analyses by W. T. Schaller : Univ. California, Dept. Geol. Sci. Bull., vol. 2, pp. 315–325, 1901.

2. Colemanite from southern California : Univ. California, Dept. Geol. Sci. Bull., vol. 3, pp. 31–50, 1902 . . . (abstract) : Science, new ser., vol. 15, p. 417, 1902.

3. Palacheite : Univ. California, Dept. Geol. Sci. Bull., vol. 3, pp. 231–236, 1903.

4. Note on the identity of palacheite and boytryogen : Am. Jour. Sci., 4th ser., vol. 16, pp. 379–380, 1903.

5. Phosphorescent sphalerite (Mariposa County, California) : California Jour. Technology, vol. 3, pp. 30–31, 1904.

6. (and **Sharwood, William J.**) Luminescent zinc blende (Mariposa County, California) : Eng. and Min. Jour., vol. 77, p. 1000, 1904.

7. Notes on lawsonite, columbite, beryl, barite, and calcite : Univ. California, Dept. Geol. Sci. Bull., vol. 5, pp. 81–94, 1906 . . . (abstract) : Neues Jahrb., Referate 2, pp. 29–30, 1908.

8. California minerals : Min. Sci. Press, vol. 96, pp. 98–99, 1908 . . . (abstract) : Eng. Index, 1908, p. 371, 1909.

9. Notes on some California minerals : Univ. California, Dept. Geol. Sci. Bull., vol. 5, pp. 225–233, 1908.

10. Neocolemanite, a variety of colemanite, and howlite from Lang, Los Angeles County, California : Univ. California, Dept. Geol. Sci. Bull., vol. 6, pp. 179–189, 1911 . . . (abstract) : Geol. Soc. America Bull., vol. 23, p. 70, 1912.

11. Some contact metamorphic minerals in crystalline limestone at Crestmore, near Riverside, California . . . (abstract) : Geol. Soc. America Bull., vol. 25, p. 125, 1914.

12. Minerals of California: California Div. Mines Bull. 67, 226 pp., 1914 . . . (abstract): Geol. Zentralbl., Band 27, p. 226, 1922.

13. (and **Rogers, Austin Flint**) Wilkeite, a new mineral of the apatite group, and okenite, its alteration product, from southern California: Am. Jour. Sci., 4th ser., vol. 37, pp. 262–267, 1914.

14. Xanthophyllite in crystalline limestone: Washington Acad. Sci. Jour., vol. 6, pp. 332–335, 1916.

15. Minerals associated with the crystalline limestone at Crestmore, Riverside County, California: Univ. California, Dept. Geol. Sci. Bull., vol. 10, pp. 327–360, 1917 . . . (abstract): Mineralog. Abstracts, vol. 1, p. 20, 1920 . . . Geol. Zentralbl., Band 29, p. 514, 1923.

16. Alpine County: California Min. Bur. Rept. 15, pp. 5–27, 1919; issued separately under title Mines and mineral resources of Alpine County, Inyo County, Mono County, 1916 . . . (abstract): Geol. Zentralbl., Band 27, p. 394, 1922.

17. (and **McLaughlin, R. P.**) Mono County: California Min. Bur. Rept. 15, pp. 135–175, 1919; issued separately under title Mines and mineral resources of Alpine County, Inyo County, Mono County, 1916 . . . (abstract): Eng. Index, 1918, p. 325, 1919.

18. Vonsenite; a preliminary note on a new mineral from Riverside, California; Am. Mineralogist, vol. 5, pp. 141–143, 1920 . . . Mineralog. Abstracts, vol. 1, p. 122, 1920.

19. New rare minerals formed in limestone by contact metamorphism . . . (abstract): Geol. Soc. America Bull., vol. 31, pp. 162–163, 1920.

20. Jurupaite, a new mineral: Am. Mineralogist, vol. 6, pp. 107–109, 1921 . . . Mineralog. Abstracts, vol. 1, pp. 253–254, 1922.

21. Massive troilite from Del Norte County. California: Am. Mineralogist, vol. 7, pp. 77–80, 1922 . . . Mineralog. Abstracts, vol. 2, p. 43, 1923.

22. Minerals of California: California Min. Bur. Bull. 91, 328 pp., 1923 . . . (abstract): Eng. Index, 1923, p. 448, 1924 . . . Mineralog. Abstracts, vol. 3, p. 29, 1926.

23. Foshagite, a new silicate from Crestmore, California: Am. Mineralogist, vol. 10, pp. 97–99, 1925 . . . Mineralog. Abstracts, vol. 2, p. 520, 1925.

24. Camsellite from California: Am. Mineralogist, vol. 10, pp. 100–102, 1925 . . . Mineralog. Abstracts, vol. 2, p. 565, 1925.

25. Famous mineral localities, Crestmore, Riverside County, California: Am. Mineralogist, vol. 12, pp. 319–321, 1927 . . . Mineralog. Abstracts, vol. 3, p. 446, 1928.

26. Probertite, a new borate: Am. Mineralogist, vol. 14, pp. 427–430, 1929 . . . Mineralog. Abstracts, vol. 4, p. 245, 1930.

Eckel, Edwin Butt

1. (**Yates, Robert Giertz** and **Granger, Arthur Earle**) Quicksilver deposits in San Luis Obispo County and southwstern Monterey County, California: U. S. Geol. Survey Bull. 922-R, pp. 515-580, 1941.

2. (and **Myers, W. Bradley**) Quicksilver deposits of the New Idria district, San Benito and Fresno Counties, California: California Div. Mines Rept. 42, pp. 81–124, 1946.

Eddy, Lewis H.

1. Forbestown district, California: Eng. and Min. Jour., vol. 94, pp. 167–169, 1017, 1912 . . . (abstract): Eng. Index, 1912, p. 388, 1913.

2. Sonoma magnesite mines, California: Eng. and Min. Jour., vol. 102, pp. 225–226, 1916.

Edman, J. A.

1. Notes on the gold-bearing black sands of California: Min. Sci. Press, vol. 69, pp. 294, 356, 372, 1894.

2. The platinum metals of Plumas County, California: Min. Sci. Press, vol. 77, p. 401, 1898.

3. The auriferous black sands of California: Eng. and Min. Jour., vol. 83, pp. 1047–1048, 1907 . . . Mines and Minerals, vol. 27, p. 563, 1907 . . . Min. Reporter, vol. 55, p. 397, 1907 . . . California Min. Bur. Bull. 45, pp. 5–10, 1907.

Egenhoff, Elisabeth Lee

1. The elephant as they saw it: California Jour. Mines and Geology, vol. 45, supplement, 1949.

2. Fabricas: California Jour. Mines and Geology, vol. 48, 189 pp., suppl. 1952.

Eggleston, Thomas
1. Notes on the treatment of mercury in north California: Am. Inst. Min. Met. Trans., vol. 3, pp. 273–274, 1874–75.

Ehlig, Perry Lawrence
1. Epidote group minerals in the Pelona Schist, southern California (abst.): Geol. Soc. America Program of Annual Meeting, Nov. 2–4, Cincinnati, Ohio, p. 45A, 1961; Geol. Soc. Amer. spec. paper 68, p. 170, 1962.

Ehrreich, Albert L.
1. Multiple metamorphism of aluminous rocks in the foothills of the Sierra Nevada, Madera, Mariposa and Merced Counties, California (abst.): Geol. Soc. America Spec. Paper 76, p. 199, 1964.

Eidel, J. James
(and **Tunell, George**) Genesis of antimony-mercury deposits (abst.) Geol. Soc. America Program of Cordilleran Section Meeting, Berkeley, California, Apr. 1963, p. 31; Geol. Soc. America Spec. Paper 76, pp. 199–200, 1964.

Eilers, A.
1. A new occurrence of the telluride of gold and silver: Am. Inst. Min. Met. Eng. Trans., vol. 1, pp. 316–320, 1871–73.

Eisen, Gustav
1. Long lost mines of precious gems are found; the prehistoric turquoise mines of California and the ancient Indian workers: San Francisco Call, March 18, 1898, p. 2; March 19, 1898, p. 6; March 27, 1898, p. 17.

Ellis, W. H.
1. A California borax deposit: Canadian Jour. Sci., new ser., vol. 15, pp. 328–329, 1877 . . . (abstract): Geol. Rec., 1877, pp. 232–233, 1880.

Emerson, Donald Orville
1. Sodic plagioclase of intermediate temperature state in the "Nomlaki Tuff", near Winters, California (abst.): Geol. Soc. America Spec. Paper, p. 23, 1962.

Emery, Kenneth Orris
1. See Dietz, Robert Sinclair (1)
2. See Dietz, Robert Sinclair (2),
3. (and **Dietz, Robert Sinclair**) Submarine phosphorite deposits off California and Mexico: California Jour. Mines and Geology, vol. 46, pp. 7–16, 1950.

Emory, William Hemsley
1. Notes of a military reconnaissance from Fort Leavenworth in Missouri to San Diego in California, including part of the Arkansas, Del Norte, and Gila Rivers: 30th Cong., 1st Sess., S. Ex. Doc. 7, pp. 5–126, 1848 .'. . H. Ex. Doc. 41, pp. 5–126, 1848.

Endlich, Frederick Miller
1. The Randsburg mining district, California: Eng. and Min. Jour., vol. 63, p. 209, 1897.

Engel, Albert Edward John
1. See Chidester, Alfred Herman (1).

Engel, René Laurent Henri
1. Granitization and contact metamorphism in the Kern River Basin, California (abst.): Geol. Soc. America Spec. Paper 68, p. 24, 1962.

Engineering and Mining Journal
1. Mining summary: vol. 1, p. 66, 1866.
2. Mining summary: vol. 1, p. 195, 1866.
3. The first gold mining in California: vol. 6, p. 18, 1868.
4. Miscellaneous: vol. 6, p. 148, 1868.
5. Quoting from the Inyo Independent: vol. 11, p. 183, 1871.
6. Letter to Mining and Scientific Press, June 21, 1879: vol. 28, p. 8, July, 1879.
7. The California tin mines: vol. 53, p. 49, 1892.
8. $3000 nugget from Siskiyou County: vol. 76, p. 749, 1903.
9. General mining news: vol. 81, p. 205, 1906.
10. General mining news: vol. 83, p. 781, 1907.
11. Mining news: vol. 83, p. 828, 1907.
12. Mining news: vol. 38, p. 1259, 1907.
13. Mining news: vol. 84, p. 653, 1907.
14. Mining news: vol. 85, p. 230, 1908.

15. Mining news: vol. 91, p. 1176, 1911.
16. Mining news: vol. 92, p. 228, 1911.
17. Amargosa Valley nitrate prospects: vol. 95, p. 236, 1913.
18. Mining news: vol. 96, p. 186, 1913.
19. Mining news: vol. 96, pp. 855, 1045, 1913.
20. Mining news: vol. 97, p. 589, 1914.
21. Mining news: vol. 98, p. 187, 1914.
22. Editorial correspondence: vol. 104, p. 1017, 1917.
23. Mining news: vol. 106, pp. 511, 597, 807, 1918.
24. Mining summary: vol. 95, p. 730, 1913.
25. Mining news: vol. 110, p. 543, 1920.
26. Kempite, a new manganese mineral from California: vol. 119, p. 3, 1925
. . . (abstract): Geol. Zentralbl., Band 36, p. 319, 1928.
27. Beryl occurrences in California: vol. 120, p. 890, 1925 . . . Geol. Zentralbl.,
Band 37, p. 375, 1928.
28. News: vol. 139, p. 62, June, 1938.
29. News: vol. 142, p. 82, April, 1941.
30. News: vol. 143, p. 84, June 1942.
31. Salute to the Golden State: vol. 149, no. 1, pp. 52–55, 1948.

English, Walter Atheling
1. Geology and oil prospects of Cuyama Valley, California: U. S. Geol. Survey,
Bull. 621, pp. 191–215, 1916.

Erd, Richard Clarkson
1. (McAllister, James Franklin, and Almond, Hy) Gowerite, a new hydrous
calcium borate from Death Valley, California: Am. Mineralogist, vol. 44, pp. 911–
919, 1959.
2. (McAllister, James Franklin, and Vlisidis, Angelina Calomeris) Nobleite,
another new hydrous calcium borate from the Death Valley region, California: Am.
Mineralogist, vol. 46, pp. 560–571, 1961.
3. (Morgan, Vincent, and Clark, Joan Robinson) Tunellite, a new hydrous
strontium borate from the Kramer borate district, California. U. S. Geol. Survey
Prof. Paper 424-C, article No. 255, pp. C294–C297, 1961.
4. See Benda, William K. (1).
5. See Skinner, Brian John (1).
6. (White, Donald Edward, Fahey, Joseph John, and Lee, Donald Edward)
Buddingtonite, an ammonium feldspar with zeolitic water: Am. Mineralogist, vol. 49,
pp. 831–850, 1964.

Eric, John Howard
1. (Stromquist, Arvid A., and Swinney, Chauncey Melvin) Geology and mineral deposits of the Angels Camp and Sonora quadrangles, Calaveras and Tuolumne
Counties, California: California Div. Mines Special Rept. 41, 55 pp., 1955.

Erickson, Max Perry
1. See Bateman, Paul Charles (2).

Erman, A.
1. Bemerkungen über das Clima und die geologischen Verhältnisse dieses Landes,
in Hoppe, J., Californiens Gegenwart und Zukunft: Archiv für wissenschaftliche
Kunde von Russland, Band 7, pp. 615–750, 1849.

Erwin, Homer D.
1. Geology and mineral resources of northeastern Madera County, California:
Calif. Div. Mines, Rept. 30, pp. 7–78, 1934.
2. See Averill, Charles Volney (7).
3. (and Gardner, Dion L.) Notes on the geology of a portion of the Calico Mountains, San Bernardino County, California: Calif. Div. Mines, Rept. 36, pp. 293–304,
1940.

Eugster, Hans Peter
1. See Wise, William Stewart (2).

Evans, Burr
1. Diamonds of Smiths Flat: Eng. and Min. Jour., vol. 102, p. 814, 1916.

Evans, George M.
1. A history of the discovery of gold in California: Hunt's Merchants' Mag.,
vol. 31, pp. 385–386, 1854.

Evans, Howard Tasker, Jr.
1. See Jaffe, Howard William (2).
2. See Glass, Jewell Jeannette (4).
3. See Glass, Jewell Jeannette (5).
4. See Christ, Charles Louis (3).

Evans, J. T.
1. Colemanite: California Acad. Sci. Bull. 1, pp. 57–59, 1884.
2. The chemical properties and relations of colemanite: California Acad. Sci. Bull. 1, no. 2, pp. 37–42, 1885.

Evans, James Roy
1. Xenotime mineralization in the southern Music Valley area, Riverside County, California: California Div. Mines and Geol. Spec. Rept. 79, 24 pp., 1964; (abst.), Geol. Soc. America Spec. Paper 73, pp. 38–39, 1963.

Everhart, Donald Lough
1. Quicksilver deposits at the Sulphur Bank mine, Lake County, California: California Div. Mines Rept. 42, pp. 125–153, 1946.
2. See Bailey, Edgar Herbert (8).
3. See Myers, W. Bradley (3).
4. Skaggs Springs quicksilver mine, Sonoma County, California: California Jour. Mines and Geology, vol. 46, pp. 385–394, 1950.
5. Quicksilver deposits of the Cachuma district, Santa Barbara County, California: California Jour. Mines and Geology, vol. 46, pp. 509–532, 1950.
6. See Larsen, Esper Signius Jr. (17), and Merriam, Richard (5).
7. See Bailey, Edgar Herbert (12).

F

Fahey, Joseph John
1. See Murdoch, Joseph (20).
2. See Murdoch, Joseph (22).
3. See Bailey, Edgar Herbert (10).
4. See Pecora, William Thomas (1).
5. See Faust, George Tobias (2).

Fairbanks, Harold Wellman
1. Geology of the Mother Lode region: California Min. Bur. Rept. 10, pp. 23–90, 1890.
2. Geology and mineralogy of Shasta County, California: California Min. Bur. Rept. 11, pp. 24–53, 1893.
3. Notes on the geology and mineralogy of portions of Tehama, Colusa, Lake, and Napa Counties: California Min. Bur. Rept. 11, pp. 54–75, 1893.
4. Geology of San Diego County; also portion of Orange and San Bernardino Counties: California Min. Bur. Rept. 11, pp. 76–120, 1893.
5. Notes on the occurrences of rubellite and lepidolite in southern California: Science, vol. 21, pp. 35–36, 1893.
6. Some remarkable hot springs and associated mineral deposits in Colusa County, California: Science, vol. 23, pp. 120–121, 1894.
7. Red Rock, Goler, and Summit mining districts in Kern County; California Min. Bur. Rept. 12, pp. 456–458, 1894.
8. Preliminary report on the mineral deposits of Inyo, Mono, and Alpine Counties: California Min. Bur. Rept. 12, pp. 472–478, 1894.
9. Geology of a section of El Dorado County: California Min. Bur. Rept. 12, pp. 479–481, 1894.
10. Geology of northern Ventura, Santa Barbara, San Luis Obispo, Monterey and San Benito Counties: California Min. Bur. Rept. 12, pp. 493–526, 1894.
11. A remarkable folded vein in the Ready Relief mine, Banner district, San Diego, California: Eng. and Min. Jour., vol. 57, pp. 321–322, 1894.
12. On analcite diabase from San Luis Obispo County, California: Univ. California, Dept. Geol. Sci. Bull., vol. 1, pp. 273–300, 1895.
13. Auriferous conglomerate in California: Eng. and Min. Jour., vol. 59, pp. 389–390, 1895.
14. The geology of Point Sal, Santa Barbara, California: Univ. California, Dept. Geol. Sci. Bull., vol. 2, pp. 1–91, 1896.
15. The mineral deposits of eastern California: Am. Geologist, vol. 17, pp. 144–158, 1896 . . . Min. Sci. Press, vol. 73, pp. 480–481, 501, 1896 . . . (abstract): Eng. Index, vol. 3, p. 639, 1901.

16. The great Mother Lode of California: Eng. and Min. Jour., vol. 62, pp. 248–250, 1896.
17. Ore deposits with special reference to the Mother Lode: California Min. Bur. Rept. 13, pp. 665–672, 1895–96.
18. The tin deposits at Temescal, southern California: Am. Jour. Sci., 4th ser., vol. 4, pp. 39–42, 1897 . . . Min. Sci. Press, vol. 75, p. 362, 1897 . . . (abstract): Nature, vol. 56, p. 286, 1897.
19. Description of the San Luis quadrangle: U. S. Geol. Survey Geol. Atlas, San Luis folio (no. 101), 14 pp., 1904.
20. Gypsum deposits in California: U. S. Geol. Survey Bull. 223, pp. 119–123, 1904 . . . (abstract): Geol. Zentralbl., Band 6, p. 330, 1905.

Fairchild, John Gifford
1. See Miser, Hugh Dinsmore (1).
2. See Schaller, Waldemar Theodore (48).

Farmer, Victor Colin
1. The infra-red spectra of talc, saponite and hectorite: Mineralog. Mag., vol. 31, pp. 829–845, 1958.

Farmin, Rollin
1. Dislocated inclusions in gold-quartz veins at Grass Valley, California: Econ. Geology, vol. 33, pp. 579–599, 1938.
2. Host-rock inflation by veins and dikes at Grass Valley, California: Econ. Geology, vol. 36, pp. 143–174, 1941.
3. Occurrence of scheelite in Idaho-Maryland mines at Grass Valley, California: California Div. Mines Rept. 37, p. 224, 1941.

Farrington, Oliver Cummings
1. Mineralogical notes: Am. Jour. Sci., 4th ser., vol. 10, pp. 83–84, 1900 . . . Field Mus. Nat. History, Geol. Ser., Pub. 1, no. 7, pp. 221–240, 1900.
2. Catalogue of the meteorites of North America to January 1, 1909: Nat. Acad. Sci. Mem. 13, 1915.

Faucher, Lèon
1. De la production et de la démonétisation de l'or: Rev. des Deux Mondes, tome 15, pp. 751–752, August 1852.

Faust, George Tobias
1. Thermal analysis and X-ray studies of griffithite: Washington Acad. Sci. Jour., vol. 45, pp. 66–70, 1955.
2. (and **Fahey, Joseph John**) The Serpentine-group minerals: U. S. Geological Surv. prof. paper 384A, pp. 1–91, 1962.

Ferguson, Henry Gardiner
1. Gold lodes of the Weaverville quadrangle, California: U. S. Geol. Survey Bull. 540, pp. 22–79, 1914.
2. Lode deposits of the Alleghany district, California: U. S. Geol. Survey Bull. 580, pp. 153–182, 1914 . . . (abstract): Geol. Zentralbl., Band 28, p. 76, 1922.
3. Pocket deposits of the Klamath Mountains, California: Econ. Geology, vol. 10, pp. 241–261, 1915.
4. (and **Gannett, Roger W.**) Gold quartz veins of the Alleghany district, California: Am. Inst. Min. Met. Eng., Tech. Pub. 211 (class 1 Mining geology 24), 40 pp. May 1929 . . . (abstract): Mining and Metallurgy, vol. 10, p. 252, 1929 . . . Annotated Bibliography Econ. Geology, vol. 2, p. 64, 1929.
5. Vein quartz of the Alleghany district, California . . . (abstract): Washington Acad. Sci. Jour., vol. 20, pp. 151–152, 1930.
6. (and **Gannett, Roger W.**) Gold quartz veins of the Alleghany district, California: U. S. Geol. Survey Prof. Paper 172, 139 pp., 1932 . . . (abstract): Annotated Bibliography Econ. Geology, vol. 5, p. 54, 1932 . . . Rev. géologie et sci. connexes tome 13, p. 587, 1933 . . . Econ. Geology, vol. 28, pp. 399–401, 1933 . . . Geol. Zentralbl., Abt. A, 48, pp. 362–363, 1932 . . . Neues Jahrb., Refrate 2, pp. 186–187, 1933 . . . Eng. Index 1932, p. 632, 1932.

Finch, Ruy Herbert
1. (and **Anderson, Charles Alfred**) The quartz-basalt eruptions of Cinder Cone, Lassen Volcanic National Park, California: Univ. California, Dept. Geol. Sci. Bull., vol. 19, pp. 245–273, 1930.

Fishburn, Randolph E.
1. Copper deposits in the Saline Valley, California: Eng. and Min. Jour., vol. 82, p. 546, 1906.

Fisher, Daniel Jerome
1. Some southern California pegmatites: unpubl. manuscript, U. S. Geol. Survey, 1944.
2. Lithian hureaulite from the Black Hills: Am. Mineralogist, vol. 49, pp. 398–406, 1964.

Fitch, Albert Alfred
1. The geology of Ben Lomond Mountain, California: Univ. California Dept. Geol. Sci. Bull., vol. 21, pp. 1–13, 1931.
2. Barite and witherite from near El Portal, Mariposa County, California: Am. Mineralogist, vol. 16, pp. 461–468, 1931 . . . (abstract): Annotated Bibliography Econ. Geology, vol. 4, p. 272, 1931.

Fix, Philip Forsyth
1. (and **Swinney, Chauncey Melvin**) Quicksilver deposits of the Oakville district, Napa County, California: California Jour. Mines and Geology, vol. 45, pp. 31–46, 1949.

Flaherty, G. F.
1. See Newhouse, Walter Harry (1).

Fleischer, Michael
1. (and **Richmond, Wallace Everett, Jr.**) The manganese oxide minerals; a preliminary report: Econ. Geology, vol. 38, pp. 269–286, 1943.
2. See Richmond, Wallace Everett, Jr. (2).

Fleming, E. L.
1. California borax: Chem. News, vol. 63, pp. 74–75, 1891 . . . Berg-u. hüttenm. Zeit. 46, pp. 248–249, 1892.

Flint, Einar Philip
1. (**McMurdie, Howard Francis**, and **Wells, Lansing S.**) Formation of hydrated calcium silicates at elevated temperatures and pressures: Natl. Bur. of Standards, vol. 21, pp. 617–638.

Flint, Richard Foster
1. (and **Gale, William Alexander**) Stratigraphy and radiocarbon dates at Searles Lake, California: Am. Jour. Sci., vol. 256, pp. 689–714, 1958.

Foote, Warren Mathews
1. Preliminary note on a new alkali mineral: Am. Jour. Sci., 3d ser., vol. 50, pp. 480–481, 1895.

Ford, Henry Chapman
1. Solfataras in the vicinity of Santa Barbara: Santa Barbara Mus. Nat. History, Bull. 1, no. 2, pp. 53–56, October 1890.

Ford, William Ebenezer
1. See Penfield, Samuel Lewis (6).
2. On the chemical composition of dumortierite: Am. Jour. Sci., 4th ser., vol. 14, pp. 426–430, 1902 . . . Zeitschr. Kristallographie, Band 37, pp. 417–421, 1903.
3. See Penfield, Samuel Lewis (8).
4. Some interesting beryl crystals and their association: Am. Jour. Sci., 4th ser., vol. 22, pp. 217–223, 1906.
5. Neptunite crystals from San Benito, California: Am. Jour. Sci., 4th ser., vol. 27, pp. 235–240, 1909 . . . Zeitschr. Kristallographie, Band 46, pp. 321–325, 1909.
6. The effect of the presence of alkalies in beryl upon its optical properties: Am. Jour. Sci., 4th ser., vol. 30, pp. 128–130, 1910.
7. Note on some analyses of stibiotantalite: Am. Jour. Sci., 4th ser., vol. 32, pp. 287–288, 1911.
8. See Dana, Edward Salisbury (8).

Forney, J. M.
1. The niter beds of the United States, privately published, Los Angeles, 1892.

Forstner, William
1. The quicksilver resources of California: California Min. Bur. Bull. 27, 273 pp., 1903.
2. The quicksilver deposits of California: Eng. and Min. Jour., vol. 78, pp. 385–386, 426–428, 1904.

3. (and others) The structural and industrial materials of California: California Min. Bur. Bull. 38, 412 pp., 1906.

4. Copper deposits in the western foothills of the Sierra Nevada: Min. Sci. Press, vol. 96, pp. 743–748, 1908.

5. The genesis of the copper ores in Shasta County, west of the Sacramento River: Min. Sci. Press, vol. 97, pp. 261–262, 1908.

Foshag, William Frederick

1. Ulexite from Lang, California: Am. Mineralogist, vol. 3, p. 35, 1918 . . . Mineralog. Abstracts, vol. 1, p. 341, 1922.

2. Thaumasite (and spurrite) from Crestmore, California: Am. Mineralogist, vol. 5, pp. 80–81, 1920 . . . Mineralog. Abstracts, vol. 1, p. 102, 1920.

3. Plazolite, a new mineral from Riverside, California: Am. Mineralogist, vol. 5, pp. 183–185, 1920 . . . Mineralog. Abstracts, vol. 1, p. 151, 1921.

4. Sulphohalite from Searles Lake, California: Am. Jour. Sci., 4th ser., vol. 49, pp. 76–77, 1920 . . . Mineralog. Abstracts, vol. 1, p. 424, 1922 . . . (abstract): Rev. géologie et sci. connexes, tome 4, p. 301, 1922.

5. Apthitalite (glaserite) from Searles Lake, California: Am. Jour. Sci., 4th ser., vol. 49, pp. 367–368, 1920 . . . Mineralog. Abstracts, vol. 1, p. 74, 1920 . . . (abstract): Rev. géologie et sci. connexes, tome 4, p. 300, 1922.

6. See Larsen, E. S. (10).

7. The origin of the colemanite deposits of California: Econ. Geology, vol. 16, pp. 199–214, 1921 . . . Mineralog. Abstracts, vol. 2, p. 454, 1925 . . . (abstract): Rev. géologie et sci. connexes, tome 2, pp. 504–505, 1921.

8. (and **Wherry, Edgar Theodore**) Notes on the composition of talc: Am. Mineralogist, vol. 7, pp. 167–171, 1922.

9. Calico Hills, San Bernardino County, California: Am. Mineralogist, vol. 7, pp. 208–209, 1922.

10. Famous mineral localities: Furnace Creek, Death Valley, California: Am. Mineralogist, vol. 9, pp. 8–10, 1924.

11. Priceite from Furnace Creek, Inyo County, California: Am. Mineralogist, vol. 9, pp. 11-13, 1924 . . . Mineralog. Abstracts, vol. 2, pp. 318–319, 1924.

12. Centrallasite from Crestmore, California: Am. Mineralogist, vol. 9, pp. 88–90, 1924 . . . Mineralog. Abstracts, vol. 3, p. 217, 1926.

13. The world's biggest borax deposits (California and Nevada): Eng. and Min. Jour., vol. 118, pp. 419–421, 1924.

14. Gems and gem minerals: Smithsonian Inst. Sci. ser. 3, pt. 2, pp. 238–243, 1929.

15. Collecting boron minerals in Death Valley: Smithsonian Inst., explorations and field work in 1929, pp. 39–46, 1930.

16. A new sulfate of iron and potash from California . . . (abstract): Am. Mineralogist, vol. 16, p. 115, 1931.

17. Schairerite, a new mineral from Searles Lake, California: Am. Mineralogist, vol. 16, pp. 133–139, 1931.

18. Probertite from Ryan, California: Am. Mineralogist, vol. 16, pp. 338–341, 1931 . . . (abstract): Annotated Bibliography Econ. Geology, vol. 5, p. 35, 1932.

19. Krausite, a new sulphate from California: Am. Mineralogist, vol. 16, pp. 352–360, 1931 . . . (abstract): Annotated Bibliography Econ. Geology, vol. 5, p. 34, 1932 . . . (abstract): Am. Mineralogist, vol. 16, p. 115, 1931.

20. See Palache, Charles (7).

21. Burkeite, a new mineral species from Searles Lake, California: Am. Mineralogist, vol. 20, pp. 50–56, 1935.

22. (and **Woodford, Alfred Oswald**) Bentonitic magnesian clay-mineral: Am. Mineralogist, vol. 21, pp. 238–244, 1936.

23. Sodium bicarbonate from Searles Lake, California . . . (abstract): Am. Mineralogist, vol. 23, p. 169, 1938.

24. See Gale, William Alexander (1) and Vonsen, Magnus (5).

25. New Mineral names—priceite: Am. Mineralogist, vol. 24, p. 728, 1939.

26. Sodium bicarbonate (nahcolite) from Searles Lake, California: Am. Mineralogist, vol. 25, pp. 769–778, 1940.

Foster, E. B.

1. Mineral resources of the Malibu Ranch, California: Eng. and Min. Jour., vol. 120, p. 308, 1925.

Foster, G. G.
1. Gold regions of California, 80 pp., New York, 1849.

Foster, Margaret Dorothy
1. See Ross, Clarence Samuel (3).

Foster, Robert K.
1. Howlite from Borate: Pacific Mineralogist, vol. 7, no. 1, p. 27, 1940.
2. Minerals on Bluebird Hill: Mineral Notes and News, p. 4, Nov. 1952.

Franke, Herbert A.
1. Santa Clara, Nevada, Kings, Tulare Counties: California Min. Bur. Rept. 26, pp. 2–39, 413–471, 1930.
2. Mines and mineral resources of San Luis Obispo County, California: California Div. Mines Rept. 31, pp. 402–461, 1935.
3. Mineral resources of portions of Monterey and Kings Counties: Calif. Div. Mines Rept. 31, pp. 462–464, 1935.
4. (and **Logan, Clarence August**) Mines and mineral resources of Calaveras County: California Div. Mines Rept. 32, pp. 226–364, 1936.

Fraser, Donald McCoy
1. Geology of San Jacinto quadrangle south of Gorgonio Pass, California: California Min. Bur. Rept. 27, pp. 494–540, 1931 . . . (abstract): Geol. Soc. America, Bull. 42, p. 235, 1931 . . . Pan-Am. Geologist, vol. 55, pp. 318–319, 1931 . . . Eng. Index, 1932, p. 612, 1932.

Fraser, Horace John
1. (**Wilson, Harry David Bruce,** and **Hendry, N. W.**) Hot springs deposits of the Coso Mountains: California Div. Mines Rept. 38, pp. 223–242, 1942.

Frazer, John F.
1. Report on minerals from Oregon and California forwarded by General Persifor F. Smith, in Report of the Secretary of War: 31st Cong., 1st sess., S. Ex. Doc. 47, pp. 116–117, 1850 . . . reprinted, Baltimore, 1851.

Free, E. E.
1. Nitrate prospects in the Amargosa Valley, near Tecopa, California: U. S. Bur. Soils, Circ. 73, 6 pp., 1912.

Frémont, John Charles
1. Report of the exploring expedition to the Rocky Mountains in 1842, and in Oregon and north California in the years 1843–44: 28th Cong., 2d sess., S. Ex. Doc. 174, 693 pp., 1845.
2. Geographical memoir upon Upper California, address to U. S. Senate, 1848, 80 pp., Philadelphia, Wm. McCarthy, 1849.
3. The Mariposa Estate, reports by the company, T. C. A. Allyn, Garnett, and Waklee, J. Adelberg, 1861.

Friedrich, James J.
1. Stalactitic melanterite and other minerals from California: New York Acad. Sci. Trans., vol. 8, p. 22, 1888.
2. Silicified woods from California: New York Acad. Sci. Trans., vol. 8, pp. 29–30, 1889.

Frondel, Clifford
1. Catalogue of mineral pseudomorphs in the American Museum: Am. Mus. Nat. Hist. Bull. 67, art. IX, pp. 389–426, 1935.
2. Redefinition of tellurobismuthite and vandiestite: Am. Jour. Sci., 5th ser., pp. 238, 880–888, 1940.
3. The mineralogy of the oxides and carbonates of bismuth: Am. Mineralogist, vol. 28, pp. 521–535, 1943.
4. See Palache, C. (10), and Berman, H. (2).
5. (and **Pough, Frederick Harvey**) Two new tellurites of iron; mackayite and blakeite, with new data on emmonsite and "durdenite": Am. Mineralogist, vol. 29, pp. 211–225, 1944.
6. See Palache, Charles (11), and Berman, Harry (3).
7. (and **Morgan, Vincent**) Inderite and gerstleyite from the Kramer borate district, Kern County, California: Am. Mineralogist, vol. 41, pp. 839–843, 1956.
8. (and **Morgan, Vincent,** and **Waugh, J. L. T.**) Lesserite, a new borate mineral: Am. Mineralogist, vol. 41, pp. 927–928, 1956.
9. Systematic mineralogy of uranium and thorium: U. S. Geological Surv. Bull. 1064, 400 pp., 1958.

Fry, C. H.
1. The story of Randsburg: Pacific Mining News, Eng. Min. Jour.-Press, vol. 113, pp. 101–103, 1922.

Funk, Benjamin Gordon
1. What we found in the Santa Monica Mountains: Pacific Mineralogist, vol. 6, no. 2, pp. 33–34, 1940.

Furness, James W.
1. Chromite: Mineral Resources U. S., 1925, pt. 1, pp. 127–147, 1928.

G

Gabriel, Alton
1. (**Slavin, Morris,** and **Carl, Howard Frederick**) Minor constituents in spodumene: Econ. Geology, vol. 37, pp. 115–125, 1942.

Gale, Hoyt Stoddard
1. Nitrate deposits: U. S. Geol. Survey Bull. 523, 36 pp., 1912.
2. The Lila C. borax mine at Ryan, California: Mineral Resources U. S., 1911, pp. 861–865, 1912.
3. The origin of colemanite deposits: U. S. Geol. Survey Prof. Paper 85, pp. 3–9, 1914 . . . (abstract): Washington Acad. Sci. Jour., vol. 4, pp. 165–166, 1914.
4. The search for potash in the desert basin region: U. S. Geol. Survey Bull. 530, pp. 295–312, 1913.
5. See Yale, Charles Gregory (4).
6. Searles Lake, California (potash): Mineral Resources U. S., 1912, pt. 2, pp. 884–890, 1913.
7. (and **Hicks, W. B.**) Octahedral crystals of sulphohalite: Am. Jour. Sci., 4th ser., vol. 38, pp. 273–274, 1914.
8. Prospecting for potash in Death Valley, California: U. S. Geol. Survey Bull. 540, pp. 407–415, 1914.
9. Salt, borax, and potash in Saline Valley, Inyo County, California: U. S. Geol. Survey Bull. 540, pp. 416–421, 1914.
10. Sodium sulphate in the Carrizo Plain, San Luis Obispo County, California: U. S. Geol. Survey Bull. 540, pp. 428–433, 1914.
11. Borate deposits in Ventura County, California: U. S. Geol. Survey Bull. 540, pp. 434–456, 1914.
12. Late developments of magnesite deposits in California and Nevada: U. S. Geol. Survey Bull. 540, pp. 483–520, 1914.
13. Salines in the Owens, Searles, and Panamint basins, southeastern California: U. S. Geol. Survey Bull. 580, pp. 251–323, 1915 . . . (abstract): Geol. Zentralbl., Band 27, p. 172, 1921.
14. Borate deposits near Kramer, California: Am. Inst. Min. Met. Eng. Trans., vol. 73, pp. 449–463, 1926.
15. A new borate mineral: Eng. and Min. Jour., vol. 123, p. 10, 1927.
16. Geology of the Kramer borate district, Kern County, California: California Div. Mines Rept. 42, pp. 325–378, 1946.
17. Geology of the saline deposits Bristol dry lake, San Bernardino County, California: California Div. Mines Special Rept. 13, 21 pp., 1951.

Gale, William Alexander
1. (**Foshag, William Frederick,** and **Vonsen, Magnus**) Teepleite, a new mineral from Borax Lake, California: Am. Mineralogist, vol. 24, pp. 48–52, 1939.
2. See Flint, Richard Foster (1).

Gallagher, David
1. Albite and gold: Econ. Geology, vol. 35, pp. 698–736, 1940.

Galliher, Edgar Wayne
1. Collophane from Miocene brown shales of California: Am. Assoc. Petroleum Geologists Bull., vol. 15, pp. 257–269, 1931 . . . (abstract): Rev. Geologie et sci. connexes, tome 12, p. 544, 1932 . . . Annotated Bibliography Econ. Geology, vol. 4, p. 27, 1931 . . . Geol. Zentralbl., Band 45, p. 163, 1931 . . . Eng. Index, 1931, p. 655, 1931.
2. Glauconite genesis: Geol. Soc. America Bull., vol. 46, pp. 1351–1366, 1935.
3. Geology of glauconite: Am. Assoc. Petroleum Geologists Bull., vol. 19, pp. 1569–1601, 1935.

Gannett, Roger W.
1. See Ferguson, Henry Gardiner (4).
2. See Ferguson, Henry Gardiner (6).

Gard, John Alan
1. (and **Taylor, H. F. W.**) Okenite and nekoite: Mineralog. Magazine, vol. 31, pp. 5–20, 1956.
2. (and **Taylor, H. F. W.**) A further investigation of tobermorite from Loch Eynort, Scotland: Mineralog. Magazine, vol. 31, pp. 361–370, 1956.
3. See Taylor, H. F. W. (7).
4. See Taylor, H. F. W. (8).

Gardner, Dion Lowell
1. Geology of the Newberry and Ord Mountains, San Bernardino County, California: California Div. Mines Rept. 36, pp. 257–292, 1940.
2. See Erwin, Homer D. (3).
3. Gold and silver mining districts in the Mojave Desert region of southern California: California Div. Mines and Geol., Bull. 170, ch. VIII, pp. 51–58, 1954.

Garner, Kenneth B.
1. See Woodford, Alfred Oswald (10), and Crippen, Richard A., Jr. (1).

Garrels, Robert Minard
1. See Christ, Charles Louis (3).

Garrido, J.
1. Symmetrie und Raumgruppe des Kernits: Zeitschr. Kristallographie, Band 82, pp. 468–470, 1932.

Gary, George L.
1. Sulphate minerals at the Leviathan sulphur mine, Alpine County, California: California Div. Mines Rept. 35, pp. 488–489, 1939.

Gastil, Russell Gordon
1. Effect of contact metamorphism on the lead content of detrital zircon at Owlshead Peak, California (abst.): Geol. Soc. America Spec. Paper 68, p. 180, 1962.

Gates, Gary Rickey
1. See Droste, John Brown (1).

Gay, Peter
1. The crystallography of cerite: Am. Mineralogist, vol. 42, pp. 429–432, 1957.
2. (and **Le Maitre, Robert W.**) Observations on "iddingsite": Am. Mineralogist, vol. 46, pp. 92–111, 1961.

Gay, Thomas Edwards, Jr.
1. See Wright, Lauren Albert (5).

Genth, Frederick Augustus
1. On some minerals which accompany gold in California: Acad. Nat. Sci. Philadelphia Proc., vol. 6, pp. 113–114, 1852 . . . (abstract): Neues Jahrb., pp. 68–69, 1855.
2. On a probably new element with iridosmine and platinum from California: Acad. Nat. Sci. Philadelphia Proc., vol. 6, pp. 209–210, 1852 . . . Am. Jour. Sci., 2d ser., vol. 15, pp. 246–248, 1853.
3. Contributions to mineralogy: Am. Jour. Sci., 2d ser., vol. 28, pp. 246–255, 1859 . . . Min. Mag., 2d ser., vol. 1, pp. 147–150, 1859 . . . Philos. Mag., 4th ser., vol. 18, pp. 318–320, 1859 . . . in Cotta, B. von, und Müller, Hermann, Gangstudien oder Beiträge zur Kenntniss der Erzgänge 3, pp. 508–511, Freiberg, 1860.
4. Observations on certain doubtful minerals: Acad. Nat. Sci. Philadelphia Proc., vol. 19, p. 86, 1867.
5. Contributions to mineralogy, no. 7: Am. Jour. Sci., 2d ser., vol. 45, pp. 305–321, 1868.
6. Tin ores in the United States: Eng. and Min. Jour., vol. 9, p. 322, 1870.
7. On some American vanadium minerals: Am. Jour. Sci., 3d ser., vol. 12, pp. 32–36, 1876 . . . Chem. News, vol. 34, pp. 78–79, 1876.
8. Ueber einige Tell- und Vanad-Mineralian: Zeitschr. Kristallographie, Band 2, pp. 1–13, 1878.
9. Contributions to mineralogy, no. 29: Am. Philos. Soc. Proc., vol. 24, pp. 23–44, 1887.
10. (and **Penfield, Samuel Lewis**) Contributions to mineralogy, no. 54, with crystallographic notes: Am. Jour. Sci., 3d ser., vol. 44, pp. 381–389, 1892.

George, D'Arcy Roscoe
1. Thorite from California: Am. Mineralogist, vol. 36, pp. 129–132, 1951.

Ghent, Edward
1. Low grade regional metamorphism in northern Coast Ranges of California (abst.): Geol. Soc. America Spec. Paper 76, pp. 201–202, 1964.

Gianella, Vincent Paul
1. Epithermal hübnerite from the Monitor district, Alpine County, California: Econ. Geology, vol. 33, pp. 339–348, 1938.

Gibbs, Wolcott
1. Researches on the platinum metals: Am. Jour. Sci., 2d ser., vol. 31, pp. 63–71, 1861.

Gieser, H. S.
1. Mining and milling on Santa Catalina Island: Eng. and Min. Jour., vol. 124, pp. 245–247, 1927 . . . (abstract): Geol. Zentralbl., 36, pp. 215–216, 1927.

Gifford, E. W.
1. The kamia of Imperial Valley: Smithsonian Inst., Bur. Am. Ethnol., Bull. 97, 1931.

Gilbert, Charles Merwin
1. Welded tuff in eastern California: Geol. Soc. America Bull., vol. 49, pp. 1829–1862, 1938.
2. Laumontite from Anchor Bay, Mendocino County, California: (abstract) Geol. Soc. America Bull., vol. 62, p. 1517, 1951.

Giles, W. B.
1. Mittheilungen über Howlite und andere Borosilikate aus den Ablagerungen von Bormineralien in Californien: Centralbl. Mineralogie, 1903, p. 334.
2. Bakerite (a new borosilicate of calcium) and howlite from California: Mineralog. Mag., vol. 13, pp. 353–355, 1903.

Gillan, S. L.
1. Cinnabar in the Sierra Nevada: Min. Sci. Press, vol. 114, p. 79, 1917.

Gillespie, Charles B.
1. Marshall's account of gold discovery: Century Mag., new ser. 19, vol. 41, pp. 537–538, 1891.

Gillson, Joseph Lincoln
1. Titanium in industrial minerals and rocks: Am. Inst. Min. Met. Eng. 2d ed., pp. 1042–1073, 1949.

Gladhill, T. L.
1. Iridosmine crystals from Ruby Creek, Atlin district, B. C.: Univ. Toronto Studies, Geol. ser., vol. 12, pp. 40–42, 1921 . . . Mineralog. Abstracts, vol. 1, p. 410, 1922.

Glass, Jewell Jeannette
1. See Schaller, Waldemar Theodore (54).
3. See Hewett, Donnel Foster (3).
4. (and **Evans, Howard Tasker, Jr., Carron, Maxwell Kenneth,** and **Rose, Harry, Jr.**) Cerite from Mountain Pass, San Bernardino County, California: Am. Mineralogist, vol. 41, p. 665, 1956.
5. (**Evans, Howard Tasker, Jr., Carron, Maxwell Kenneth,** and **Hildebrand, Frederick Adelbert**) Cerite from Mountain Pass, San Bernardino County, California: Am. Mineralogist, vol. 43, pp. 460–480, 1958.

Glass, J. P.
1. See Newhouse, Walter Harry (2).

Gluskoter, Harold J.
1. Orthoclase distribution and authigenesis in a portion of the Franciscan formation, California (abst.): Geol. Soc. America Program of meeting, Houston, Texas 1962, p. 60A.

Goddard, G. H.
1. Report of a survey of portions of the eastern boundary of California: California Legislature, 7th sess., A. Doc. 5, pp. 91–186, 1856.

Goldich, Samuel Stephen
1. See Ames, Lloyd Leroy Jr. (1)

Goldschmidt, Victor

1. (**Palache, Charles** and **Peacock, Martin Alfred**) Über Calaverit: Neues Jahrb. f. Min. etc. B.B. 63, Abt. A., pp. 1–58, 1931.

Goldsmith, E.

1. Trautwinite, a new mineral: Acad. Nat. Sci. Philadelphia Proc., vol. 25, pp. 1–2, 348–349, 1873.

2. Analysis of chromite from Monterey County, California: Acad. Nat. Sci. Philadelphia Proc., vol. 25, pp. 365–366, 1873 . . . (abstract): Geol. Rec. 1874, p. 233, 1875.

3. Stibioferrite, a new mineral from Santa Clara County, California: Acad. Nat. Sci. Philadelphia Proc. vol. 25, pp. 366–369, 1873 . . . (abstract): Geol. Rec. 1874, p. 234, 1875 . . . Am. Jour. Sci., 3d ser., vol. 7, p. 152, 1874.

4. The blue gravel of California: Acad. Nat. Sci. Philadelphia Proc., vol. 26, pp. 73–74, 1874.

5. Chromite and trautwinite from Monterey County, California: Acad. Nat. Sci. Philadelphia Proc., vol. 25, p. 365, 1873 . . . Am. Jour. Sci., 3d ser., vol. 7, p. 152, 1874.

6. On sonomaite: Acad. Nat. Sci. Philadelphia Proc., vol. 28, pp. 263–264, 1877.

7. On boussingaultite and other minerals from Sonoma County, California: Acad. Nat. Sci. Philadelphia Proc., vol. 28, pp. 264–266, 1877 . . . (abstract): Geol. Rec., 1877, p. 234, 1880.

Goldstone, L. P.

1. Fresno County, California Min. Bur. Rept. 10, pp. 183–204, 1890.

Gonyer, Forest A.

1. See Irving, John (1).

2. See Moehlman, Robert Stevens (1).

Goodwin, Joseph Grant

1. Mines and mineral resources of Tulare County, California: California Jour. Mines and Geology, vol. 54, pp. 317–492, 1958.

Goodyear, Watson Andrews

1. Salt Springs Valley and the adjacent region in Calaveras County: California Acad. Sci. Proc., vol. 3, pp. 387–399, 1867.

2. Diamonds in El Dorado County, in Raymond, R. W., Fourth report on mineral resources of the states and territories west of the Mississippi, 1871, p. 27, 1873 . . . 42d Cong., 2d sess., H. Ex. Doc. 211, 1873.

3. Inyo, Kern, Los Angeles, San Bernardino, San Diego, Tulare Counties: California Min. Bur. Rept. 8, pp. 224–324, 335–342, 504–512, 516–528, 643–652, 1888.

4. Alameda, Colusa, Contra Costa, Lake, Marin, Mendocino, Napa, Yolo Counties: California Min. Bur. Rept. 10, pp. 91–95, 153–164, 165, 227–271, 299, 314, 322, 349–363, 793–794, 1890.

5. San Diego County: California Min. Bur. Rept. 9, pp. 139–154, 1890.

6. Santa Cruz Island: California Min. Bur. Rept. 9, pp. 155–170, 1890.

Gordon, Samuel G.

1. (and **Shannon, Earl Victor**) Chromrutile, a new mineral from California: Am. Mineralogist, vol. 13, p. 69, 1928.

2. Results of the Chilean mineralogical expedition, 1938, pt. IV, The identity of salvadorite with kroehnkite: Acad. Nat. Sci. Philadelphia, Notulae Naturae, vol. 72, 4 pp., 1941.

Gottfriend, David

1. (and **Waring, C. L.**) Hafnium content and Hf/Zr ratio in zircon from the southern California batholith. U. S. Geol. Survey Prof. Paper 501B, pp. 88–91, 1964.

Goudey, Hatfield

1. Minerals—Ritter Range, California: Mineralogist, vol. 4, no. 5, pp. 7–8, 26–28, 1936.

2. Spessartite near Tuolumne, California: Mineral Notes and News, Bull. 114, p. 10, March 1947.

3. Scorodite near Jamestown, California: Mineral Notes and News, Bull. 114, p. 12, March 1947.

Graeff, F. W.
1. Nitrate deposits of southern California: Eng. and Min. Jour., vol. 90, p. 173, 1910.

Graf, Donald Lee
1. (and **Bradley, William Frank**) The crystal structure of huntite, $Mg_3Ca(CO_3)_4$: Acta Cryst., vol. 15, pp. 238–242, 1962.

Granger, Arthur Earle
1. See Eckel, Edwin Butt (1).

Grant, Ulysses S., IV
1. See Hertlein, Leo George (1).

Graton, Louis Caryl
1. (and **Schaller, Waldemar Theodore**) Purpurite, a new mineral: Am. Jour. Sci., 4th ser., vol. 20, pp. 146–151, 1905 . . . Zeitschr. Kristallographie, Band 41, pp. 433–438, 1905.
2. (and **Hess, Frank L.**) Occurrence and distribution of tin: U. S. Geol. Survey Bull. 260, pp. 161–187, 1905.
3. The occurrence of copper in Shasta County, California: U. S. Geol. Survey Bull. 430, pp. 71–111, 1910 . . . (abstract): Eng. Index, 1910, p. 364, 1911.
4. (and **McLaughlin, Donald Hamilton**) Ore deposition and enrichment at Engels, California: Econ. Geology, vol. 12, pp. 1–38, 1917.

Graves, A. W.
1. The identification of dumortierite as grains; dumortierite in Cornish granite: Mineralog. Mag., vol. 21, pp. 489–492, 1928.

Gray, Cliffton Herschel, Jr.
1. See Bowen, Oliver Earle, Jr. (2).
2. California tin mine producing again: California Div. Mines and Geol., Mineral Information Service, vol. 17, pp. 205–206, 1964.
3. See Bowen, Oliver Earle, Jr. (5).

Greene, C. S.
1. The California Rand: Overland Monthly, new ser., vol. 29, pp. 546–561, 1897.

Gregory, J. W.
1. The ore deposits of Mount Lyell, California: Min. Sci. Press, vol. 91, pp. 40–41, 58, 75–76, 90–91, 1905.

Grender, Gordon Conrad
1. Alegria-Vaqueros (Oligocene-Miocene) sequence near Gaviota, California: Geol. Soc. America Bull., vol. 73, pp. 267–272, 1962.

Grieger, J. M.
1. San Diego County, California, gem mines not exhausted: Mineralogist, vol. 2, no. 10, pp. 7–8, 20, 1934.

Griggs, Allan Bingham
1. See Smith, Clay Taylor (2).
2. See Walker, George Walton (4).

Grim, Ralph Early
1. (**Dietz, Robert Sinclair, and Bradley, William Frank**) Clay mineral composition of some sediments from the Pacific Ocean off the California coast and the Gulf of California: Geol. Soc. America Bull., vol. 60, pp. 1785–1808, 1949.

Grimaldi, Frank Saverio
1. See Skinner, Brian John (1).

Grimsley, George Perry
1. The gold deposits of Nevada County: Eng. and Min. Jour., vol. 68, p. 487, 1899.

Gross, Eugene Bischoff
1. (and **Wainwright, John E. N.**) Barium-tin-titanium silicate having the benitoite structure (abst.): Geol. Soc. America, Cordilleran Section Meeting Program, Seattle, March 1964, p. 36.
2. See Chesterman, Charles Wesley (9).

Grubbs, Donald K.
1. See White, Donald Edward (3).

Guild, Frank Nelson
1. Mineralogische Notizen: Zeitschr. Kristallographie, Band 49, pp. 321–331, 1911.
2. See Wartman, Franklin Secord (1).

Guillemin-Tarayre, Edmond
1. Description des anciennes possessions mexicaines du nord: France, Expedition scientifique au Mexique et dans l'Amerique centrale, Geologie pt. 2, 216 pp., Paris, 1868.
2. Exploration mineralogique des regions Mexicaines: Imprimerie Imperiale, Paris ix (1), 304 pp., 1869.

Guillou, Robert B.
1. Geology of the Johnson Grade area, San Bernardino County, California: California Div. Mines Spec. Rept. 31, 18 pp., 1953.

Gulbrandsen, Robert Allen
1. (Jones, David Lawrence, Tagg, Kathleen McQ., and Reeser, D. W.) Apatitized wood and leucophosphite in nodules in the Moreno formation, California: U. S. Geol. Survey Prof. Paper 475-C, pp. 100–104, 1963.

Gutzkow, F.
1. Hydromagnesite from Livermore, California: California Min. Bur. Rept. 6, pt. 2, p. 74, 1886.

H

Hadley, Jarvis Bardwell
1. Manganese deposits in the Paymaster mining district, Imperial County, California: U. S. Geol. Survey Bull. 931 S, pp. 459–473, 1942.
2. Iron-ore deposits in the eastern part of the Eagle Mountains, Riverside County, California: California Div. Mines Bull. 129, pp. 1–24, 1948.

Haehl, Harry Lewis
1. (and Arnold, Ralph) The Miocene diablase of the Santa Cruz Mountains in San Mateo County, California: Am. Philos. Soc. Proc., vol. 43, pp. 16–53, 1904.

Haines, David Vincent
1. Core logs from Searles Lake, San Bernardino County, California: U. S. Geol. Surv. Bull. 1045E, pp. 139–317, 1959.

Halbouty, Michel Thomas
1. See Lonsdale, John Tipton (1).

Haldeman, S. S.
1. La Patera and Dos Pueblos—near Santa Barbara: U. S. Geog. Surveys W. 100th Mer., 1879, vol. 7, Archeology, pp. 263–276, 1879.

Halden, G. H.
1. Quasi-cleavable quartz: Rocks and Minerals, vol. 30, nos. 1 and 2, pp. 38–40, 1955.

Hall, Wayne Everett
1. (MacKevett, Edward Malcolm, Jr., and others) Economic geology of the Darwin quadrangle, Inyo County, California: Calif. Div. Mines Special Rept. 51, 77 pp., 1958.
2. See Kinkel, Arthur Rudolph, Jr. (2).
3. (and Stephens, Hal G.) Economic geology of the Panamint Butte quadrangle and Modoc district, Inyo County, California: California Div. Mines and Geol. Spec. Rept. 73, 39 pp., 1963.
4. (and MacKevett, Edward Malcolm, Jr.) Geology and ore deposits of the Darwin quadrangle, Inyo County, California: U. S. Geol. Survey Prof. Paper 368, 87 pp., 1963.

Halse, Edward
1. California mercury deposits: Inst. Min. Met. Eng. Trans., vol. 30, pp. 79–80, 1922.
2. Mercury ores: Imperial Inst., Monograph, Murray, London, 1923.

Hamilton, Fletcher McNab
1. Administrative statement: California Min. Bur. Rept. 14, xix–xxiii, 1916.
2. Administrative statement: California Min. Bur. Rept. 15, xxiii–xxx, 1919.
3. Seventeenth report of the State Mineralogist: California Min. Bur. Rept. 17, 562 pp., 1921.
4. Eighteenth report of the State Mineralogist: California Min. Bur. Rept. 18, 767 pp., 1922.
5. (and Root, Lloyd L.) Nineteenth report of the State Mineralogist: California Min. Bur. Rept. 19, 258 pp., 1923.

Hamilton, Warren Bell
1. Granitic rocks of the Huntington Lake area, Fresno County, California, Ph.D. thesis, University of California, Los Angeles, 1951.

Hamilton, W. R.
1. See Kessler, H. H. (1).

Hamman, William David
1. The Searles Lake potash deposit: Eng. and Min. Jour., vol. 93, pp. 975–976, 1912.

Hammond, John Hays
1. Auriferous gravels of California: California Min. Bur. Rept. 9, pp. 105–138, 1890.

Hanke, Adolph G. E.
1. World news on mineral occurrences: Rocks and Minerals, vol. 28, pp. 361–2, 1953.

Hanks, Henry Garber
1. Diamonds in California: Min. Sci. Press, vol. 20, p. 162, 1870.
2. Notes on cuproscheelite: California Acad. Sci. Proc., vol. 5, pp. 133–134, 1873.
3. Annual report of the State Mineralogist: California Min. Bur. Rept. 1, 43 pp., 1881.
4. Notes on roscoelite: Min. Sci. Press, vol. 42, p. 428, 1881.
5. Notes on mica: Min. Sci. Press, vol. 44, pp. 113, 129, 1882.
6. On the occurrence of vivianite in Los Angeles County: Min. Sci. Press, vol. 44, p. 160, 1882 . . . Am. Jour. Sci., 3d ser., vol. 24, p. 155, 1882.
7. Second report of the State Mineralogist: California Min. Bur. Rept. 2, 226 pp., 1882.
8. Gold nuggets: California Min. Bur. Rept. 2, pp. 147–150, 1882.
9. Mud volcanoes and Colorado Desert: California Min. Bur. Rept. 2, pp. 227–240, 1882.
10. Diamonds in California: California Min. Bur. Rept. 2, pp. 241–254, 1882.
11. Report on borax deposits: California Min. Bur. Rept. 3, pt. 2, 111 pp., 1883.
12. Fourth report of the State Mineralogist: California Min. Bur. Rept. 4, 410 pp., 1884; includes catalog of minerals of California (pp. 63–410), and miscellaneous observations on mineral products.
13. Cassiterite: California Min. Bur. Rept. 4, pp. 115–123, 1884.
14. Fifth report of the State Mineralogist: California Min. Bur. Rept. 5, 235 pp., 1885.
15. Sixth report of the State Mineralogist: California Min. Bur. Rept. 6, pt. 1, 145 pp., 1886; includes catalogue of minerals . . . (abstract): Neues Jahrb., 1887, Band 2, p. 474.
16. Pectolite: Min. Sci. Press, vol. 56, pp. 37, 44, 1888.
17. On the occurrence of hanksite in California: Am. Jour. Sci. 3d ser., vol. 37, pp. 63–66, 1889.
18. Gaylussite (new variety, San Bernardino County, California): Min. Sci. Press, vol. 64, p. 222, 1892.
19. The mineral hydrocarbons: Min. Sci. Press, vol. 70, pp. 38–39, 56, 71, 88, 109, 136, 150, 189, 263, 284, 320, 393, 1895 . . . vol. 71, p. 14, 1895.
20. Notes on "aragotite," a rare California mineral: Royal Micr. Soc. Jour., 1905, pp. 673–676.

Hanley, John Bernard
1. Economic geology of the Rincon pegmatites, San Diego County, California: California Div. Mines Special Rept. 7-B, 24 pp., 1951.

Hanna, G. Dallas
1. See Vonsen, Magnus (4).
2. Geology of the Farallon Islands: California Div. Mines Bull. 154, pp. 301–310, 1951.

Hanson, R. F.
1. See Kaley, Mary Elizabeth (1).

Harcourt, George Alan
1. The distinction between enargite and famatinite (luzonite): Am. Mineralogist, vol. 22, pp. 517–525, 1937.
2. See Berman, Harry (1).

Harder, Edmund Cecil
  1. Manganese deposits of the United States: U. S. Geol. Survey Bull. 427, 298 pp., 1910.
  2. Some chromite deposits in western and central California: U. S. Geol. Survey Bull. 430, pp. 167–183, 1910.
  3. Some iron ores of western and central California: U. S. Geol. Survey Bull. 430, pp. 219–227; 1910.
  4. (and **Rich, John Lyon**) The Iron Age iron-ore deposit, near Dale, San Bernardino County, California: U. S. Geol. Survey Bull. 430, pp. 228–239, 1910.
  5. The gypsum deposits of the Palen Mountains, Riverside County, California: U. S. Geol. Survey Bull. 430, pp. 407–416, 1910.
  6. Iron-ore deposits of the Eagle Mountains, California: U. S. Geol. Survey Bull. 503, 81 pp., 1912.

Harker, Robert Ian
  1. Synthesis and stability of tilleyite, $Ca_5Si_2O_7(CO_3)_2$: Am. Jour. Sci., vol. 257, pp. 656–667, 1959.

Harris, R. P.
  1. On borax in California: Am. Philos. Soc. Proc., vol. 9, p. 450, 1864.

Harriss, Trewhitt Fairman
  1. See Woodford, Alfred Oswald (4).

Hart, T. S.
  1. Notes on the Almaden mine, California: Am. Jour. Sci., 2d ser., vol. 16, p. 137, 1853.

Harte, Bret
  1. The story of a mine, 172 pp., Boston, Mass., 1910.

Hartman, Ronald M.
  1. (and **Oriti, Ronald A.**) A preliminary report on the Lucerne Valley, San Bernardino County, California, aerolites (CN 1169, 345): Meteoritics: vol. 2, no. 2, pp. 177–178, 1964.

Hasse, T. L.
  1. Neue Goldquelle: Letter from New York to correspondent in Germany, Sept. 26, 1848: Berg- u. Hüttenm. Zeit. vol. 7, pp. 791–792, 1848.

Hawkes, Herbert Edwin, Jr.
  1. (and **Wheeler, Dooley P., Jr.**) Chromite deposits of the Del Puerto area, California . . . (abstract): Geol. Soc. America Bull. vol. 52, p. 1950, 1941.
  2. (**Wells, Francis Gerritt** and **Wheeler, Dooley P., Jr.**) Chromite and quicksilver deposits of the Del Puerto area, Stanislaus County, California: U. S. Geol. Survey Bull. 936-D, pp. 79–110, 1942.
  3. Olivine from northern California showing perfect cleavage: Am. Mineralogist vol. 31, pp. 276–283, 1946.

Hawley, James Edwin
  1. See Whitmore, Duncan Richard Elmer (1).

Hay, Richard Le Roy
  1. (and **Moiola, Richard J.**) Authigenic silicate minerals in Pleistocene sediments of Searles Lake, California (abst.): Geol. Soc. America Spec. Paper 73, p. 168, 1963; Sedimentology, vol. 2, pp. 312–332, 1962.
  2. (and **Moiola, Richard J.**) Authigenic silicate minerals in three desert lakes of eastern California (abst.): Program, New York Meeting, Geol. Soc. America, p. 76A, 1963.
  3. See Moiola, Richard J. (1).
  4. Phillipsite of saline lakes and soils: Am. Mineralogist, vol. 49, pp. 1366–1387, 1964.

Hayden, Ferdinand Vandiveer
  1. U. S. Geological and geographical survey of the territories, vol. IV, 908 pp., 1878.

Hayes, A. A.
  1. Heavy sands of Australia and California: Boston Soc. Nat. History Proc., vol. 6, p. 228, 1857.

Hayton, J. D.
  1. The constitution of davidite: Econ. Geology, vol. 55, pp. 1030–1038, 1960.

Hazenbush, George C.

1. Geology of the Starbright tungsten mine, San Bernardino County, California: California Jour. Mines and Geology, vol. 48, pp. 201–206, 1952.

2. See Wright, Lauren Albert (5).

Headden, William Parker

1. Mineralogic notes, III, phosphorescent zinc blendes: Colorado Sci. Soc., Proc., vol. 8, pp. 167–182, 1906.

Heikkila, Henry Herman

1. (and MacLeod, George Marshall) Geology of Bitterwater Creek area, Kern County, California: California Div. Mines Special Rept. 6, 21 pp., 1951.

Heinrich, Eberhardt William

1. A second discovery of inderite (from California): Am. Mineralogist, vol. 31, pp. 71–76, 1946.

2. Cordierite in pegmatite near Micanite, Colorado: Am. Mineralogist, vol. 35, pp. 173–184, 1950.

3. (and Levinson, Alfred Abraham) Studies in the mica group: mineralogy of the rose muscovites: Am. Mineralogist, vol. 38, pp. 25–49, 1953.

Heizer, Robert Fleming

1. (and Treganza, Adan E.) Mines and quarries of the Indians of California: California Div. Mines Rept. 40, pp. 291–359, 1944.

2. Jade artifacts in prehistoric shellmounds, Willow Creek, Monterey County: California Div. Mines, Mineral Inf. Service, vol. 4, no. 8, p. 6, 1951.

Heller, L.

1. (and Taylor, H. F. W.) Crystallographic data for the calcium silicates, H. M. Stationery Office, 79 pp., 1956.

Helmhacker, R.

1. Das Vorkommen der Goldgänge in Amador County, Californien, verglichen mit Eule in Böhman: Berg- u. Hüttenm. Zeit., Band 56, pp. 380–382, 1897.

Hendry, N. W.

1. See Wilson, Harry David Bruce (1).

2. See Fraser, Horace John (1).

Henley, R. F.

1. Jade in California: Rocks and Minerals, vol. 22, pp. 1114–1115, 1947.

Henry, D. J.

1. The California Calico Mountains: The Mineralogist, vol. 14, pp. 225–233, 1946.

2. The northeast portion of Eagle Crags: The Mineralogist, vol. 14, pp. 339–342, 1946.

3. Collecting Kern County, California: The Mineralogist, vol. 15, pp. 3–7, 1947.

4. Wiley Well district a mecca for the collector: The Mineralogist, vol. 15, pp. 171–176, 1947.

5. Black Hills, California: The Mineralogist, vol. 15, pp. 451–453, 1947.

6. Gem Trail Journal, 2d ed., 93 pp., Long Beach, California, 1952.

Henry, John L.

1. Silver-gold deposits of Alpine County, California: Eng. and Min. Jour., vol. 121, p. 936, 1926.

Henry T. H.

1. Composition of gold from California: Philos. Mag., 3d ser., vol. 34, pp. 205–207, 1849.

Henshaw, Paul Carrington

1. Geology and mineral resources of the Cargo Muchacho Mountains, Imperial County, California: California Div. Mines Rept. 38, pp. 147–196, 1942.

Hershey, Oscar H.

1. Origin and age of certain gold "pocket" deposits in northern California: Am. Geologist, vol. 24, pp. 38–43, 1899.

2. The upper Coffee Creek mining district, California: Min. Sci. Press, vol. 79, p. 689, 1899.

3. Gold-bearing lodes of the Sierra Costa Mountains in California: Am. Geologist, vol. 25, pp. 76–96, 1900.

4. Primary chalcocite in California: Min. Sci. Press, vol. 96, pp. 429–430, 1908.

5. Foothill copper belt of the Sierra Nevada: Min. Sci. Press, vol. 96, pp. 591–592 . . . vol. 97, pp. 322–323, 1908.
6. Origin of gold "pockets" in northern California: Min. Sci. Press, vol. 101, pp. 741–742, 1910.

Hertlein, Leo George
1. (and **Grant, Ulysses S., IV**) The geology and paleontology of the marine Pliocene of San Diego, California; pt. I, geology: San Diego Soc. Nat. History Mem., vol. 2, 72 pp., 1944.

Hess, Frank L.
1. See Graton, Louis Caryl (2).
2. Some magnesite deposits of California: U. S. Geol. Survey Bull. 285, pp. 385–392, 1906 . . . Eng. Mag., vol. 31, pp. 691–704, 1906.
3. Some molybdenum deposits of Maine, Utah, and California: U. S. Geol. Survey Bull. 340, pp. 231–240, 1908.
4. Notes on a tungsten-bearing vein near Raymond, California: U. S. Geol. Survey Bull. 340, p. 271, 1908.
5. The magnesite deposits of California: U. S. Geol. Survey Bull. 355, 67 pp., 1908.
6. Tungsten, nickel, cobalt, titanium, etc.: Mineral Resources U. S., 1907, pp. 711–722, 1908.
7. Selenium: Mineral Resources U.S., 1908, pp. 715–717, 1909.
8. Tungsten, nickel, cobalt, etc.: Mineral Resources, U. S., 1908, pp. 721–749, 1909.
9. A reconnaissance of the gypsum deposits of California, with a note on errors in the chemical analysis of gypsum by George Steiger: U. S. Geol. Survey Bull. 413, 37 pp., 1910.
10. Gold mining in the Randsburg quadrangle, California: U. S. Geol. Survey Bull. 430, pp. 23–47, 1910.
11. Gypsum deposits near Cane Springs, Kern County, California: U. S. Geol. Survey Bull. 430, pp. 417–418, 1910.
12. Tungsten: Mineral Resources U. S., 1912, pt. 1, pp. 987–1001, 1913.
13. Tungsten: Mineral Resources U. S., 1913, pt. 1, pp. 353–361, 1914.
14. Tungsten minerals and deposits, U. S. Geol. Survey Bull. 652, 85 pp., 1917.
15. Nickel: Mineral Resources U. S., 1915, pt. 1, pp. 743–766, 1917.
16. Gypsum deposits of California, in Stone, R. W., Gypsum deposits of the United States: U. S. Geol. Survey Bull. 697, pp. 58–86, 1920.
17. (and **Larsen, Esper Signius**) Contact-metamorphic tungsten deposits of the United States: U. S. Geol. Survey Bull. 725, pp. 245–309, 1922.
18. Tungsten: Mineral Resources U. S., 1917, pt. 1, pp. 931–954, 1921.
19. Rare metals—cobalt: Mineral Resources U. S., 1924, pt. 1, pp. 451–476, 1927.

Hewett, Donnel Foster
1. (and others) Mineral resources of the region around Boulder Dam: U. S. Geol. Survey Bull. 871, 323 pp., 1936.
2. Iron deposits of the Kingston Range, San Bernardino County, California: California Div. Mines Bull. 129, pp. 193–206, 1948.
3. (and **Glass, Jewel Jeannette**) Two uranium-bearing pegmatite bodies in San Bernardino County, California: Am. Mineralogist, vol. 38, pp. 1040–1050, 1953.
4. (and **Stone, Jerome,** and **Levine, Harry**) Brannerite from San Bernardino County, California: Am. Mineralogist, vol. 42, pp. 30–38, 1957.
5. (and **Stone, Jerome**) Uranothorite near Forest Home, San Bernardino County, California: Am. Mineralogist, vol. 42, pp. 104–107, 1957.
6. (**Chesterman, Charles Wesley,** and **Troxel, Bennie Wyatt**), Tephroite in California manganese deposits: Econ. Geology, vol. 56, pp. 39–58, 1961.
7. Veins of hypogene manganese oxide minerals in the southwestern United States: Econ. Geol., vol. 59, pp. 1429–1472, 1964.

Hey, M. H.
1. (and **Bannister, F. A.**) Clinoptilolite: Mineralog. Mag., vol. 23, pp. 556–559, 1934.
2. (and **Claringbull, Gordon Frank**) New data for dumortierite (read March 27, 1952): Mineralog. Mag., vol. 31, pp. 901–907, 1958.

Heyl, George Richard
1. Foothill copper-zinc belt of the Sierra Nevada (abstract): Geol. Soc. America Bull. 58, p. 1253, 1947.

2. Foothill copper-zinc belt of the Sierra Nevada: California Div. Mines Bull. 144, pp. 11–29, 1948.

3. Ore deposits of Copperopolis, Calaveras County, California: California Div. Mines Bull. 144, pp. 93–110, 1948.

Hicks, W. B.

1. See Gale, Hoyt Stoddard (7).
2. See Larsen, Esper Signius (1).

Hidden, William Earl

1. On hanksite, a new anhydrous sulphato-carbonate of sodium from San Bernardino County, California: New York Acad. Sci. Annals, vol. 3, pp. 238–241, 1885 . . . Am. Jour. Sci., 3d ser., vol. 30, pp. 133–135, 1885 . . . Min. Sci. Press, vol. 50, p. 1, 1885.

2. (and **MacKintosh, James B.**) Sulphohalite, a new sodium sulphato-chloride: Am. Jour. Sci., 3d ser., vol. 36, p. 463, 1888 . . . Zeitschr. Kristallographie, Band 15, p. 294, 1889.

3. (and **MacKintosh, James B.**) Mineralogical notes: Am. Jour. Sci., 3d ser., vol. 41, p. 438, 1891.

Hietanen, Anna

1. Metamorphic and igneous rocks of the Merrimac area, Plumas national forest, California: Geol. Soc. America Bull., vol. 62, pp. 565–608, 1951.

Higgins, Charles Graham

1. Significance of some fossil wood from California: Science, vol. 134, p. 473, 1961.

Higgs, Donald Val

1. Anorthosite and related rocks of the western San Gabriel Mountains, southern California: Univ. California Dept. Geol. Sci., vol. 30, pp. 172–222, 1954.

2. Anorthosite complex of the western San Gabriel Mountains, southern California: California Div. Mines and Geol. Bull. 170, ch. VII, pp. 71–75, 1954.

Hildebrand, Fred Adelbert

1. See Glass, Jewell Jeannette (5).
2. See Bailey, Edgar Herbert (10).

Hilgard, Eugene Woldemar

1. Alkali lands, irrigation and drainage in their mutual relations: Rept. Univ. California, College of Agriculture, Appendix for 1890, pp. 25–26, 1892.

Hill, James Madison

1. The mining districts of the Western United States: U. S. Geol. Survey Bull. 507, 309 pp., 1912 . . . (abstract): Geol. Zentralbl., Band 18, p. 631, 1913.

2. Some mining districts in northeastern California and northwestern Nevada: U. S. Geol. Survey Bull. 594, 200 pp., 1915.

3. Platinum and allied metals: Mineral Resources U. S., 1916, pt. 1, pp. 1–20, 1919.

4. The Los Burros district, Monterey County, California: U. S. Geol. Survey Bull. 735, pp. 323–336, 1923 . . . Pacific Min. News, p. 234, 1923.

Hillebrand, William Francis

1. (Turner, Henry Ward and Clarke, Frank Wigglesworth) On roscoelite, with a note on its chemical composition: Am. Jour. Sci., 4th ser., vol. 7, pp. 451–458, 1899.

2. Mineralogical notes: melonite (?), coloradoite, petzite, hessite: Am. Jour. Sci., 4th ser., vol. 8, pp. 295–298, 1899.

3. Mineralogical notes: U. S. Geol. Survey Bull. 167, pp. 57–76, 1900.
4. See Schaller, Waldemar Theodore (4).
5. See Schaller, Waldemar Theodore (6).

Hilpert, Lowell Sinclair

1. See Yates, Robert Giertz (2).
2. See Yates, Robert Giertz (4).

Hiortdahl, Th.

1. Colemanit, ein krystallisirtes Kalkborat aus Californien: Vidensk, selsk. Christiania Forh., 1884, no. 10, 8 pp., 1885 . . . Zeitschr. Kristallographie, Band 10, pp. 25–31, 1885.

Hittell, John Sherzer

1. Mining in the Pacific states of North America, 224 pp., San Francisco, H. H. Bancroft & Co., 1861.

2. The resources of California, 494 pp. San Francisco, A. Roman & Co., 1868.

3. History of California, vol. 1, 799 pp., vol. 2, 823 pp., San Francisco, Pacific Press Publishing House, 1885.

4. Discovery of gold in California: Century Mag., new ser., vol. 19, p. 525, 1891.

Hlawatsch, C.

1. Bemerkungen, von über die Krystallklasse des Benitoit: Tschermak's Mitt., Band 28, pp. 178–181, 1909 . . . (abstract): Zeitschr. Kristallographie, Band 50, p. 617, 1912.

2. Bemerkung zum Aragonit von Rohitsch, Natrolit, und Neptunit von S. Benito: Tschermak's Mitt., Band 28, pp. 293–296, 1909.

3. Bemerkungen über den Benitoit: Zeitschr. Kristallographie, Band 46, p. 602, 1909.

4. Die Kristalform des Benitoit: Centralbl. Mineralogie, 1909, pp. 293–302, 410.

Hobson, John B.

1. Nevada, Placer, Siskiyou Counties: California Min. Bur. Rept., 10, pp. 364–398, 410–434, 655–658, 1890.

2. (and **Wiltsee, E. A.**) Nevada County: California Min. Bur. Rept. 11, pp. 263-318, 1893.

Hodson, W. G.

1. Shasta County: California Min. Bur. Rept. 11, pp. 395–399, 1893.

Hoffman, Samuel R.

1. See Crosby, James W., III (1).

Hoffman, W. J.

1. On the mineralogy of Nevada: U. S. Geol. and Geog. Survey of the Territories, vol. IV, art. XXXI, pp. 731–745, 1878.

Hoffmann, Wolfgang

1. See Schröder, Alfred (1).

Hofmann, Dr.

1. California gold: Am. Jour. Sci., 2d ser., vol. 8, p. 449, 1849.

Holdaway, Michael J.

1. Mafic metamorphic rocks in a portion of the Klamath Mountains, northern California (abst.): Geol. Soc. America, Spec. Paper 73, pp. 172–173, 1963.

Holder, Charles Frederick

1. A remarkable salt deposit, Salton, California: Sci. Am. vol. 84, p. 217, 1901 . . . Nat. Geog. Mag., vol. 12, p. 391, 1901.

Holt, Donald Aubrey

1. See Papish, Jacob (1).

Holway, Ruliff S.

1. Eclogites in California: Jour. Geology, vol. 12, pp. 344–358, 1904 . . . (abstract): Geol. Zentralbl., Band 9, p. 515, 1907.

Honke, Martin T., Jr.

1. (and **Ver Planck, Wm. E., Jr.**) Mines and mineral resources of Sonoma County, California: California Jour. Mines and Geology, vol. 46, pp. 83–141, 1950.

Hoots, Harold William

1. Geology of the eastern part of the Santa Monica Mountains, Los Angeles County, California: U. S. Geol. Survey Prof. Paper 165C, pp. 83–134, 1931.

Hoppe, J.

1. Californiens Gegenwart und Zukunft; nebst Beitragen von A. Erman ueber die Klimatologie von Californien und ueber der Geographischen verbreitung des Goldes: Archiv für Wiss. Kunde von Russland, Band 7, pp. 615–750, 1849.

Hoppin, Richard Arthur

1. (and **Norman, L. A.**) Commercial "black granite" of San Diego County, California: California Div. Mines Special Rept. 3, 19 pp., 1950.

2. Palen Mountains gypsum deposit, Riverside County, California: (abstract) Geol. Soc. America Bull. vol. 62, p. 1518, 1951.

Horner, R. R.

1. Notes on the black sand deposits of southern Oregon and northern California: U. S. Bur. Mines Tech. Paper 196, 39 pp., 1918.

Horton, F. W.

1. See Julihn, C. E. (1).

Horton, Frederick W.

1. Iridium in American placer platinum: Eng. and Min. Jour., vol. 94, pp. 873–875, 1912.

Hoskold, C. A. L.

1. Deposits of hydroborate of lime, its exploitation and refination: Inst. Min. Eng. Trans., vol. 23, pp. 456–471, 1901–02.

Hotz, Preston Enslow

1. Nickeliferous laterites in southwestern Oregon and northwestern California: Econ. Geol., vol. 59, pp. 355–396, 1964.

Howard, Arthur David

1. Microcrystals of barite from Barstow, California: Am. Mineralogist, vol. 17, p. 120, 1932 . . . (abstract): Annotated Bibliography Econ. Geology, vol. 5, p. 33, 1932.

Howe, Ernest

1. The gold ores of Grass Valley, California (with discussion by A. M. Bateman, Waldemar Lindgren, J. E. Spurr, and the author): Econ. Geology, vol. 19, pp. 595–622, 1924.

Hubbard, Henry G.

1. Mines and mineral resources of Santa Cruz County: California Div. Mines, Rept. 39, pp. 11–52, 1943.

2. Manganese discovery in San Mateo County: California Div. Mines Rept. 39, p. 117, 1943.

Hubbard, J. D.

1. The quartz veins of Butte County, California: Eng. and Min. Jour., vol. 102, pp. 352–353, 1916.

Huber, Norman King

1. See Bateman, Paul Charles (4).

Hudson, Frank Samuel

1. Geology of the Cuyamaca region of California with special reference to the origin of the nickeliferous pyrrhotite: Univ. California, Dept. Geol. Sci. Bull., vol. 13, 175–252, 1922.

2. See Taliaferro, Nicholas Lloyd (3).

Huey, Arthur Sidney

1. Geology of the Tesla quadrangle, California: California Div. Mines Bull. 140, 75 pp., 1948.

Huggins, Charles W.

1. (**Denny, Marion Vaughn** and **Shell, Haskell Roy**) Properties of palygorskite, an asbestiform mineral: U.S. Bur. Mines, Rept. of investigations no. 6071, 17 pp., 1962.

Hughes, H. Herbert

1. Iceland spar and optical fluorite: U. S. Bur. Mines, Inf. Circ. 6468, pp. 1–18, 1931.

Huguenin, Emile

1. See Waring, Clarence Alm (2).

2. Santa Barbara, Ventura Counties: California Div. Mines, Rept. 15, pp. 727–769, 1919.

3. See Cloudman, H. C. (1).

4. (and **Castello, W. O.**) Alameda, Contra Costa, San Francisco, San Mateo, Santa Clara, Santa Cruz Counties: California Min. Bur., Rept. 17, pp. 17–42, 48–67, 163–165, 167–241, 1921.

Hulin, Carlton D.

1. Geology and ore deposits of the Randsburg quadrangle, California: California Min. Bur. Bull. 95, 152 pp., 1925 . . . (review by J. E. Spurr): Eng. and Min. Jour., vol. 121, pp. 463–464, 1929.

2. Mineralization in the vicinity of Randsburg, California: Eng. and Min. Jour., vol. 119, pp. 407–411, 1925.

3. A Mother Lode gold ore: Econ. Geology. vol. 25, pp. 348–355, 1930 . . . (abstract): Annotated Bibliography Econ. Geology, Vol. 3, p. 67, 1930.

Humiston, Lee E.

1. A preliminary report on the Ridgecrest, California, meteorite, a new aerolite (C-1176,356): Meteoritics, vol. 2, pp. 50–51, 1963.

Hunt, Walter Frederick
   1. See Kraus, Edward Henry (2).

Hurley, T. J.
   1. Famous gold nuggets of the world, 64 pp., 1900.

Hutchinson, A.
   1. On the identity of neocolemanite with colemanite: Mineralog. Mag., vol. 16, pp. 239–246, 1912.

Hutchinson, Richard W.
   1. Preliminary report on investigations of minerals of columbium and tantalum and of certain associated minerals: Am. Mineralogist, vol. 40, pp. 432–452, 1955.

Huttl, John B.
   1. New Almaden today: Eng. and Min. Jour., vol. 144, pp. 59–61, 1943.
   2. Spud patch tungsten placer proves commercial venture: Eng. and Min. Jour., vol. 144, pp. 94–95, 1943.
   3. Neglected copper-zinc belt revived under war demand: Eng. and Min. Jour., vol. 145, pp. 60–63, 1944.
   4. Guadaloupe mercury mine has new treatment plant: Eng. and Min. Jour., vol. 145, pp. 86–87, 1944.

Hutton, Colin Osborne
   1. Stilpnomelane and pumpellyite, constituents of the Franciscan series (abstract): Geol. Soc. America Bull. 59, pp. 1373–1374, 1948.
   2. (and **Bowen, Oliver Earle, Jr.**) An occurrence of jarosite in altered volcanic rocks of Stoddard Mt., San Bernardino County, California: Am. Mineralogist, vol. 35, pp. 556–561, 1950.
   3. Allanite from Yosemite national park: (abstract) Geol. Soc. America Bull., vol. 61, p. 1525, 1950 . . . Am. Mineralogist vol. 36, pp. 233–248, 1951.
   4. Further data on the stilpnomelane mineral group: Am. Mineralogist, vol. 41, pp. 608–615, 1956.

I

Ingerson, Earl
   1. Some features of origin of quartz veins at Grass Valley, California . . . (abstract): Geol. Soc. America Bull. 51, p. 1931, 1940.

Irelan, William, Jr.
   1. Sixth annual report of the State Mineralogist: California Min. Bur. Rept. 6, pt. 2, 222 pp., 1887.
   2. Seventh annual report of the State Mineralogist: California Min. Bur. Rept. 7, 315 pp., 1888.
   3. Eighth annual report of the State Mineralogist [includes Mineral resources of the State, with contributions by W. A. Goodyear, H. A. Whiting, and Stephen Bowers]: California Min. Bur. Rept. 8, 946 pp., 1888.
   4. Ninth annual report of the State Mineralogist: California Min. Bur. Rept. 9, 352 pp., 1890.
   5. Tenth annual report of the State Mineralogist [includes county reports by W. A. Goodyear, Henry De Groot, J. A. Brown, J. A. Miner, Alexander McGregor, L. P. Goldstone, Myron Angel, E. B. Preston, W. L. Watts, J. B. Hobson, Stephen Bowers, W. P. Miller]: California Min. Bur. Rept. 10, 983 pp., 1890.
   6. Eleventh report of the State Mineralogist [includes county reports by W. L. Watts, E. B. Preston, W. H. Storms, J. B. Hobson, E. A. Wiltsee, W. G. Hodson, R. L. Dunn, H. W. Fairbanks]: California Min. Bur. Rept. 11, 612 pp., 1893.

Irving, John
   1. (**Vonsen, Magnus,** and **Gonyèr, Forest A.**) Pumpellyite from California: Am. Mineralogist, vol. 17, pp. 338–342; correction, p. 456, 1932.

Irwin, William Porter
   1. See Bateman, Paul Charles (5).

J

Jackson, Abraham Wendell, Jr.
   1. On colemanite, a new borate of lime: Am. Jour. Sci., 3d ser., vol. 28, pp. 447–448, 1884.
   2. On the morphology of colemanite: California Acad. Sci., 1st ser., Bull. 2, pp. 3–36, 1885.
   3. Mineralogical contributions: California Acad. Sci., 1st ser., Bull. 4, pp. 358–374, 1886 . . . (abstract): Neues Jahrb., 1888, pp. 179–181.

Jackson, Charles Thomas

1. ——————————————: Boston Soc. Nat. History Proc., vol. 7, p. 152, 1859.

2. "Decouverte de minerals d'etain en Californie et de fer meteorique dans l'Oregon": Acad. sci. Paris, vol. 50, p. 105, 1860.

Jaffe, Howard William

1. Re-examination of sphene: Am. Mineralogist, vol. 32, pp. 637–642, 1947.

2. (**Meyrowitz, Robert** and **Evans, Howard Tasker, Jr.**) Sahamaite, a new rare earth carbonate mineral: Am. Mineralogist, vol. 38, pp. 721–754, 1953.

Jahns, Richard Henry

1. Internal structure of the Pala pegmatites, San Diego County, California (abstract): Geol. Soc. America Bull. 58, p. 1254, 1947.

2. Gem deposits of southern California: Gems and Gemology, vol. 6, pp. 6–9, 28, 30, 1948.

3. (and **Lance, John Franklin**) Geology of the San Dieguito pyrophyllite area, San Diego County, California: California Div. Mines, Special Rept. 4, 32 pp., 1950.

4. The Epsom salts mine: Engineering and Science Monthly, April, 1951.

5. (and **Wright, Lauren Albert**) Gem and lithium bearing pegmatites of the Pala district, San Diego County, California: California Div. Mines, Special Rept. 7-A, 72 pp., 1951.

6. Geology, mining and uses of strategic pegmatites: Am. Inst. Min. Met. Eng., Trans., vol. 190, pp. 45–59, 1951.

7. The genesis of pegmatites, I, Occurrence and origin of giant crystals: Am. Mineralogist, vol. 38, pp. 563–598, 1953.

8. Pegmatites of southern California: California Div. Mines and Geol. Bull. 170, ch. VII, pp. 37–50, 1954.

James, Howard Lloyd

1. See Wells, Francis Gerritt (1).

Jameson, Robert

1. A system of mineralogy, 2d ed., Edinburgh, 1816.

Jamieson, George S.

1. On the natural iron-nickel alloy, awaruite: Am. Jour. Sci., 4th ser., vol. 19, pp. 413–415, 1905 . . . Zeitschr. Kristallographie, Band 41, pp. 157–160, 1905.

2. See Penfield, Samuel Lewis (7).

Jamison, C. E.

1. Santa Clara River placers: Min. Sci. Press, vol. 100, pp. 360–361, 1910.

Jeffery, Joseph Arthur

1. Discovery of andalusite in California: Eng. and Min. Jour., vol. 120, p. 663, 1925.

2. Andalusite in California: Eng. and Min. Jour., vol. 120, p. 982, 1925.

3. (and **Woodhouse, Charles Douglas**) Note on a deposit of andalusite in Mono County, California: its occurrence and technical importance: California Min. Bur. Rept. 27, pp. 459–464, 1931 . . . (abstract): Annotated Bibliography Econ. Geology, vol. 4, p. 271, 1931.

4. (and **Woodhouse, Charles Douglas**) Mining andalusite in Mono County, California: Arizona Min. Jour., vol. 15, no. 16, pp. 5–6, 43–44, 1932.

Jenkins, Olaf Pitt

1. Tabulation of tungsten deposits of California to accompany Economic Minerals Map no. 4: California Div. Mines Rept. 38, pp. 303–364, 1942.

2. Manganese in California: California Div. Mines Bull. 125, 387 pp., 1943.

3. Annual report of the State Mineralogist: California Div. Mines Rept. 45, pp. 7–29, 1949.

4. Annual Report of the State Mineralogist: California Jour. Mines and Geology, vol. 54, pp. 9–66, 1958.

Jenkins, William O.

1. Tungsten deposits northeast of Visalia, California: California Div. Mines Rept. 39, pp. 169–182, 1943.

Jenkins, W. W.

1. History of the development of placer mining in California: Historical Soc. Southern California, Ann. Pub., vol. 7, 1906.

Jenni, Clarence M.
1. Crestmore and its minerals: Gems and Minerals, no. 236, pp. 24, 25, 63–67, May, 1957 . . . no. 237, pp. 38–40, June 1957 . . . no. 238, pp. 34–79, July 1957 . . . no. 239, pp. 50, 52, 64, Aug. 1957 . . . no. 240, pp. 46, 48, Sept. 1957.

Jennings, Charles William
1. Mines and minerals of Kings County, California: California Jour. Mines and Geology, vol. 49, pp. 273–296, 1953.
2. See Davis, Fenelon F. (6).

Jermain, G. D.
1. (and Ricker, S.) Investigation of Antimony Peak, Kern County, California: U. S. Bur. Mines Rept. Invest. 4505, 5 pp., July, 1949.

Johnson, Fremont T.
1. (and Ricker, Spangler) Investigation of Oat Hill mercury mine, Napa County, California: U. S. Bur. Mines Rept. Invest. 4542, 1949.

Johnson, Harry Roland
1. See Arnold, Ralph (5).
2. See Arnold, Ralph (7).

Johnson, Solomon
1. The Gold Coast of California and Oregon: Overland Monthly, vol. 2, pp. 534–537, 1869.

Johnston, T. J.
1. Discovery of gold in California: Eng. and Min. Jour., vol. 79, p. 472, 1905.

Johnston, William Drumm
1. Nodular, orbicular, and banded chromite in northern California: Econ. Geology vol. 31, pp. 417–427, 1936.
2. Native arsenic from Grass Valley, California: California Div. Mines Rept. 33, p. 340, 1937.
3. Vein filling at Nevada City, California: Geol. Soc. America Bull., vol. 49, pp. 23–24, 1938 . . . (abstract): Am. Mineralogist, vol. 22, p. 216, 1937.
4. The gold quartz veins of Grass Valley, California: U. S. Geol. Survey Prof. Paper 194, 101 pp., 1940.

Jones, Blair Francis
1. Zoning of saline minerals at Deep Spring Lake, California: U. S. Geol. Survey Prof. Paper 424B, Article 83, pp. B199–B202, 1961.
2. Layer sequence of saline minerals at Deep Spring Lake, California (abst.): Geol. Soc. America Program, New York Meeting, p. 88A, 1963.

Jones, Charles Colcock
1. An iron deposit in the California desert region: Eng. and Min. Jour., vol. 87, pp. 785–788, 1909.
2. The Pacific coast iron situation: Am. Inst. Min. Met. Eng., Bull. 105, pp. 1887–1898, 1915.

Jones, David Lawrence
1. See Gulbrandsen, Robert Allen (1).

Jones, Edward Leroy, Jr.
1. Deposits of manganese ore in southeastern California: U. S. Geol. Survey Bull. 710, pp. 185–208, 1919.

Jones, W. R.
1. California tin and tungsten deposits: Inst. Min. Met. Trans., vol. 29, pp. 330, 344, 1921.

Josephson, W. G.
1. Argonaut mine of today: Min. and Met., vol. 13, pp. 475–476, 1932 . . . (abstract): Eng. Index 1932, p. 634, 1932.

Julihn, C. E.
1. (and Horton, F. W.) Mineral industries survey of the United States: California: Kern County, Mojave District: The Golden Queen and other mines of the Mojave District, California: U. S. Bur. Mines Inf. Circ. 6931, 42 pp., 1937.

K

Kaley, Mary Elizabeth
1. (and Hanson, R. F.). Laumontite and leonhardite cement in Miocene sandstone from a well in San Joaquin Valley, California: Am. Mineralogist, vol. 40, pp. 923–925, 1955.

Kartchner, Wayne E.
1. Minerals in Santa Clara County: Gems and Minerals, no. 308, pp. 17, 22, May 1963.

Katz, F. J.
1. ——————————: Mineral Resources U. S., 1924, pt. I, VII, 112A, 589 pp., 1927.

Keller, Walter David
1. See Swartzlow, Carl Robert (2).

Kelley, Vincent Cooper
1. Occurrence of claudetite in Imperial County, California: Am. Mineralogist, vol. 21, pp. 137–138, 1936.
2. Notes on mineralization at Crestmore, California: Am. Mineralogist, vol. 22, pp. 140-141, 1937.
3. Origin of the Darwin silver-lead deposits: Econ. Geology, vol. 32, pp. 987-1008, 1937.
4. Geology and ore deposits of the Darwin silver-lead mining district, Inyo County, California: California Div. Mines Rept. 34, pp. 503-562, 1938.

Kellog, J. L.
1. See Ransome, Alfred Leslie (1).

Kellogg, A. E.
1. Origin of flour gold in black sands: Arizona Min. Jour., vol. 14, no. 20, pp. 3–4, 49–50, 1931.

Kennard, Theodore Gladden
1. (and **Rambo, A. I.**) Occurrence of rubidium, gallium, and thallium in lepidolite from Pala, California: Am. Mineralogist, vol. 18, pp. 454, 455, 1933 . . . (abstract): Annotated Bibliography Econ. Geology, vol. 6, p. 194, 1934.
2. (and **Rambo, A. I.**) The extraction of rubidium and cesium from lepidolite: Am. Jour. Sci., 5th ser., vol. 28, pp. 102–109, 1934.
3. Spectrographic examination of smoky and ordinary quartz from Rincon, California: Am. Mineralogist, vol. 20, pp. 392–399, 1935 . . . (abstract): Neues Jahrb., 1935, Referate 1, p. 445.
4. See Merriam, Richard Holmes (3).

Kengott, A.
1. Magnesite from Pitch (or Pit) River, near Sacramento, California: Uebersicht der Resultate mineralog. Forschungen, Jahrg. 1853, p. 38, 1855.

Kerr, Paul Francis
1. Bentonite from Ventura, California: Econ. Geology, vol. 26, pp. 153–168, 1931 . . . (abstract): Annotated Bibliography Econ. Geology, vol. 4, p. 68, 1931.
2. See Ross, Clarence Samuel (2).
3. Occurrence of andalusite and related minerals at White Mountain, California: Econ. Geology, vol. 27, pp. 614–643, 1932 . . . (abstract): Annotated Bibliography Econ. Geology, vol. 5, p. 299, 1932.
4. (and **Cameron, Eugene Nathan**) Fuller's earth of bentonitic origin from Tehachapi, California: Am. Mineralogist, vol. 21, pp. 230–237, 1936.
5. Tungsten mineralization at Oreana, Nevada: Econ. Geology, vol. 33, pp. 390–427, 1938.
6. Tungsten mineralization in the United States: Geol. Soc. America Mem. 15, 241 pp., 1946.
7. (and **Kulp, John Laurence**) Clay localities in the United States: Am. Petrol. Inst. Project 49 Prelim. Rept. No. 2 on clay mineral standards, Columbia University, 101 pp., 1949.
8. Formation and occurrence of clay minerals: California Div. Mines Bull. 169, pp. 19–32, 1955.

Kessler, H. H.
1. (and **Hamilton, W. R.**) The orbicular gabbro of Dehasa, California: Am. Geologist, vol. 34, pp. 133–140, 1904.

Kew, William Stephen Webster
1. See Woodring, Wendell Phillips (1).

Keyes, Charles Rollin
1. Death Valley borax deposits: Am. Inst. Min. Met. Eng. Trans., vol. 34, p. 870, 1910.

Keyes, Winfield Scott
1. Borax Lake and sulphur and quicksilver deposits near Clear Lake, California:
Eng. and Min. Jour., vol. 22, p. 118, 1876.

Kildale, Malcolm Brus
1. See Carlisle, Donald (1).

Kimble, George W.
1. Pockets in the upper portion of gold veins: Min. Sci. Press, vol. 94, pp. 343–344, 1907.

King, C. R.
1. See Averill, Charles Volney (16).

King, Charles W.
1. The natural history of gems or decorative stones, London, 1867.

King, Clarence
1. Silver contained in placer gold, California: U. S. Geol. Survey 2d Ann. Rept., pp. 379–380, 1882.

King, T. Butler
1. Appendix, in Taylor, Bayard, El Dorado, pp. 201–247, 1854.

Kinkel, Arthur Rudolph, Jr.
1. (and Albers, J. P.) Geology of the massive sulphide deposits at Iron Mountain, Shasta County, California: California Div. Mines Special Rept. 14, pp. 19, 1951.
2. (Hall, Wayne Everett and Albers, John P.) Geology and base-metal deposits of west Shasta copper-zinc district, Shasta County, California: U.S. Geol. Survey Prof. Paper 285, 156 pp. 1956.

Kirivan, G. M.
1. See Perry, Joseph B. (1).

Kleinhampl, Frank Joseph
1. See Cornwall, Henry Rowland (1).

Knaebel, John Ballantine
1. The veins and crossings of the Grass Valley district, California: Econ. Geology, vol. 26, pp. 375–398, 1931 . . . (abstract): Annotated Bibliography Econ. Geology, vol. 4, p. 49, 1931.

Knight, C. Y.
1. A curious occurrence of copper near Shingle Springs, El Dorado County, California: Min. Sci. Press, vol. 94, p. 242, 1907.

Knight, Enoch
1. Temescal tin mines: Eng. and Min. Jour., vol. 53, p. 276, 1892.

Knopf, Adolph
1. (and Thelen, Paul) Sketch of the geology of Mineral King, California: Univ. California, Dept. Geol. Sci. Bull., vol. 4, pp. 227–262, 1905 . . . (abstract): Geol. Zentralbl., Band 8, pp. 275–276, 1906.
2. Notes on the foothill copper belt of the Sierra Nevada: Univ. California, Dept. Geol. Sci. Bull., vol. 4, pp. 411–423, 1906 . . . (abstract): Geol. Zentralbl., Band 10, p. 391, 1908.
3. An alteration of Coast Range serpentine: Univ. California, Dept. Geol. Sci. Bull. 4, pp. 425–430, 1906 . . . (abstract): Geol. Zentralbl., Band 10, p. 386, 1908.
4. The Darwin silver-lead mining district, California: U. S. Geol. Survey Bull, 580, pp. 1–18, 1914 . . . (abstract): Geol. Zentralbl., Band 21, p. 597, 1915.
5. Mineral resources of the Inyo and White Mountains, California: U. S. Geol. Survey Bull. 540, pp. 81–120, 1914.
6. Tungsten deposits of northwestern Inyo County, California: U. S. Geol. Survey Bull. 640, pp. 229–249, 1917 . . . (abstract): Washington Acad. Sci. Jour., vol. 7, p. 357, 1917 . . . Geol. Zentralbl., Band 28, p. 165, 1922.
7. An andalusite mass in the pre-Cambrian of the Inyo Range, California: Washington Acad. Sci. Jour., vol. 7, pp. 549–552, 1917.
8. A geologic reconnaissance of the Inyo Range and the eastern slope of the southern Sierra Nevada, California; with a section on the stratigraphy of the Inyo Range, by Edwin Kirk: U. S. Geol. Survey Prof. Paper 110, 130 pp., 1918 . . . (abstract): Washington Acad. Sci. Jour., vol. 9, p. 414, 1919.
9. Strontianite deposits near Barstow, California: U. S. Geol. Survey Bull. 660, pp. 257–270, 1918 . . . (abstract): Washington Acad. Sci. Jour., vol. 8, pp. 94–95, 1918 . . . Geol. Zentralbl., Band 28, p. 166, 1922.

10. Discovery of andalusite in California: Eng. and Min. Jour., vol. 120, p. 778, 1925.

11. The Mother Lode system of California: U. S. Geol. Survey Prof. Paper 157, 88 pp., 1929 . . . (abstract): Eng. and Min. Jour., vol. 128, p. 24, 1929 . . . Jour. Geology, vol. 38, pp. 377–378, 1930 . . . Annotated Bibliography Econ. Geology, vol. 2, p. 64, 1929 . . . Rev. geologie et sci. connexes, tome 10, p. 325, 1929 . . . Geol. Zentralbl., Band 41, pp. 364–367, 1930 . . . Geol. Mag., vol. 67, p. 36, 1930.

12. (and **Anderson, Charles Alfred**) The Engels copper deposits, California: Econ. Geology, vol. 25, pp. 14–35, 1930 . . . (abstract): Annotated Bibliography Econ. Geology, vol. 3, p. 60, 1931 . . . Geol. Zentralbl., Band 42, p. 366, 1930 . . . Eng. Index, 1930, p. 450, 1931.

13. Pyrometasomatic deposits, in Ore deposits of the western states: Am. Inst. Min. Met. Eng., Lindgren vol., pp. 537–557, 1933 . . . (abstract): Neues. Jahrb., 1934, Referate 2, p. 679.

14. Copper resources of the world; Plumas County copper belt, California: 16th Internat. Geol. Cong., I, pp. 241–245, 1935.

Knopf, E. C.
1. Santa Catalina Island minerals and geology: Pacific Mineralogist, vol. 5, no. 2, pp. 3–5, 1938.

Koenig, George Augustus
1. Mountain soap of California: Acad. Nat. Sci. Philadelphia Proc., 1878, pp. 405–406, 1879.

Kouřimský, J.
1. See Tucek, K. (1)

Kogarko, L. N.
1. Lovozero massif, Kola Peninsula: Doklady Akad. Nauk, U.S.S.R., vol. 139 (Engl. translation), pp. 839–841, 1963.

Kouvo, O.
1. A variety of monticellite from Crestmore, California: Bull. Comm. Geol. Finlande, no. 157, pp. 7–11, 1952.

Kracek, Frank Charles
1. (and **Neuvonen, Kalle J.**) Thermochemistry of plagioclase and alkali feldspars: Am. Jour. Sci., vol. 230 (Bowen volume) 1952, (suppl.) pp. 293–318.

Kraft, James L.
1. Adventure in jade. 1947.

Kramer, Henry C.
1. (and **Allen, Robert D.**) Analyses and indices of refraction of tourmaline from fault gouge near Barstow, San Bernardino County, California: Am. Mineralogist, vol. 39, pp. 1020–1022, 1954.
2. See Allen, Robert D. (1)
3. See Allen, Robert D. (3)
4. See Allen, Robert D. (6)
5. (and **Allen, Robert D.**) A restudy of bakerite, priceite, and veatchite: Am. Mineralogist, vol. 41, pp. 689–700, 1956.

Kramm, H. E.
1. Serpentines of the central coast ranges of California: Am. Philos. Soc., Proc., vol. 49, pp. 315–349, 1910 . . . (abstract): Science, new ser., vol. 32, p. 31, 1910 . . . Geol. Soc. America Bull., vol. 21, p. 793, 1910.
2. Geology of Harrison Gulch, in Shasta County, California: Am. Inst. Min. Met. Eng., Bull. 67, pp. 709–715, 1912 . . . Trans., vol. 43, pp. 233–239, 1913 . . . (abstract): Geol. Zentralbl., Band 18, p. 695, 1913 . . . Eng. Index, 1912, p. 449, 1913.

Kraus, Edward Henry
1. Interpretation of the chemical composition of the mineral benitoite: Science, new ser., vol. 27, pp. 710–711, 1908.
2. (and **Hunt, Walter Frederick**) Manganhaltiger Albit von Kalifornien: Zentralbl. Mineralogie , 1915, pp. 465–467 . . . Mineralog. Abstracts, vol. 2, p. 62, 1923.

Krauskopf, Konrad Bates
1. Tungsten deposits of Madera, Fresno, and Tulare Counties, California: California Div. Mines Special Rept. 35, 83 pp., 1953.

Kroeber, Alfred L.
1. Handbook of the Indians of California: Smithsonian Inst., Bur. Am. Ethnol., Bull. 78, 1925.

Kulp, John Laurence
   1. See Kerr, Paul Francis (7).

Kunz, George Frederick
   1. American gems and precious stones : Mineral Resources U. S., 1882, pp. 483–499, 1883.
   2. Precious stones : Mineral Resources U. S., 1883–1884, pp. 723–782, 1885.
   3. Precious stones : Mineral Resources U. S., 1887, pp. 555–579, 1888.
   4. Apophyllite from California : Soc. franc. mineralogie, Bull. 12, p. 27, 1889.
   5. Mineralogical notes on brookite, octahedrite, quartz, and ruby : Am. Jour. Sci., 3d ser., vol. 43, pp. 329–330, 1892.
   6. Octahedrite (anatase) near Placerville, El Dorado County : Mineralog. Mag., vol. 9, p. 395, 1892.
   7. Mineralogical notes on brookite, octahedrite, and quartz : California Min. Bur. Rept. 11, pp. 207–209, 1893.
   8. Precious stones : Mineral Resources U. S., 1891, pp. 539–551, 1893.
   9. Precious stones : Mineral Resources U. S., 1892, pp. 756–781, 1893.
   10. Precious stones : Mineral Resources U. S., 1893, pp. 680–702, 1894.
   11. Precious stones : Mineral Resources U. S., 1895, pp. 895–926, 1896.
   12. Precious stones : Mineral Resources U. S., 1896, pp. 1183–1217, 1897.
   13. Precious stones : Mineral Resources U. S., 1898, pp. 557–600, 1899.
   14. Precious stones : Mineral Resources U. S., 1899, pp. 419–462, 1900.
   15. Octahedrite (anatase) from Placerville, El Dorado County : Mineralog. Mag., vol. 9, p. 394, 1901.
   16. Precious stones : Mineral Resources U. S., 1900, pp. 744–778, 1901.
   17. Precious stones : Mineral Resources U. S., 1901, pp. 729–771, 1902.
   18. On a new lilac-colored spodumene, San Diego County, California : Am. Jour. Sci., 4th ser., vol. 16, pp. 264–267, 1903 . . . (abstract) : Science, new ser., vol. 18, p. 280, 1903.
   19. Californite (vesuvianite) ; a new ornamental stone : Am. Jour. Sci., 4th ser., vol. 16, pp. 397–398, 1903.
   20. Native bismuth and bismite from Pala, California : Am. Jour. Sci., 4th ser., vol. 16, p. 398, 1903.
   21. Precious stones : Mineral Resources U. S., 1902, pp. 813–866, 1903.
   22. See Baskerville, Charles (2).
   23. Precious stones : Mineral Resources U. S., 1903, pp. 911–977, 1904.
   24. Gems, jewelers' materials, and ornamental stones of California : California Div. Mines Bull. 37, 171 pp., 1905.
   25. Precious stones : Mineral Resources U. S., 1904, pp. 941–987, 1905.
   26. Precious stones : Mineral Resources U. S., 1905, pp. 1323–1358, 1906.
   27. Morganite, a rose-colored beryl : Am. Jour. Sci., 4th ser., vol. 31, pp. 81–82, 1911.

Kupfer, Donald Harry
   1. See Bassett, Allen Mordorf (1).

Kuss, M. H.
   1. Memoire sur les mines et usines d'Almaden : Annales des mines, 1876–78, p. 47.

Küstel, Guido
   1. Tellurite of gold and silver : Min. Sci. Press, vol. 10, p. 306, 1865.
   2. Communication : Berg-u. hüttenm. Zeit., Band 25, p. 128, 1866.

L

La Croix, Alfred
   1. A propos de la plumasite, roche à corindon : Soc. franç. mineralogie, Bull. 26, pp. 147–150, 1903.

Ladoo, Raymond Bardeen
   1. Wollastonite—a new industrial material : Eng. and Min. Jour., vol. 151, no. 11, pp. 95–97, Nov., 1950.

Laizure, Clyde McK
   1. Redding field division : California Min. Bur. Rept. 17, pp. 491–544, 1921.
   2. San Francisco field division : California Min. Bur. Rept. 18, pp. 45–47, 101–103, 1922.

3. San Francisco field division: California Min. Bur. Rept. 21, pp. 23–57, 173–222, 281–324, 499–538, 1925.

4. Marin, San Benito, Santa Cruz, and Sonoma Counties: California Min. Bur. Rept. 22, pp. 68–93, 217–247, 314–365, 1926.

5. Contra Costa, Solano Counties: California Min. Bur. Rept. 23, pp. 2–31, 203–213, 1927.

6. Mariposa, Madera Counties: California Min. Bur. Rept. 24, pp. 72–153, 317–345, 1928.

7. Fresno, Alameda, and San Francisco Counties: California Min. Bur. Rept. 25, pp. 242–245, 301–336, 427–456, 1929.

8. Mining activities in the San Francisco district: California Min. Bur. Rept. 31, pp. 24–48, 1935.

9. Discoveries in the strategic minerals; San Francisco field district: California Div. Mines Rept. 39, pp. 53–57, 1943.

Lamey, Carl Arthur

1. Iron Mountain iron-ore deposits, Lava Beds district, San Bernardino County, California: California Div. Mines Bull. 129, pp. 25–38, 1948.

2. Iron Mountain and Iron King iron-ore deposits, Silver Lake district, San Bernardino County, California: California Div. Mines Bull. 129, pp. 39–58, 1948.

3. Old Dad Mountain iron-ore deposit, San Bernardino County, California: California Div. Mines Bull. 129, pp. 59–68, 1948.

4. Cave Canyon iron-ore deposits, San Bernardino County, California: California Div. Mines Bull. 129, pp. 69–84, 1948.

5. Vulcan iron-ore deposit, San Bernardino County, California: California Div. Mines Bull. 129, pp. 85–96, 1948.

6. Iron Hat (Iron-Clad) iron-ore deposits, San Bernardino County, California: California Div. Mines Bull. 129, pp. 97–110, 1948.

7. Ship Mountains iron-ore deposit, San Bernardino County, California: California Div. Mines Bull. 129, pp. 113–116, 1948.

8. Hirz Mountain iron-ore deposits, Shasta County, California: California Div. Mines Bull. 129, pp. 129–136, 1948.

9. Shasta and California iron-ore deposits, Shasta County, California: California Div. Mines Bull. 129, pp. 137–164, 1948.

10. Contact metasomatic iron deposits of California: Geol. Soc. America Bull., vol. 72, pp. 669–678, 1961.

Lance, John Franklin

1. See Jahns, Richard Henry (3)

Lancucki, C. J.

1. See Segnit, E. Ralph (1).

Landon, Robert Emmanuel

1. Roemerite from California: Am. Mineralogist, vol. 12, pp. 279–283, 1927 . . . Mineralog. Abstracts, vol. 3, p. 456, 1928.

Lang, Herbert

1. Copper resources of California: Eng. and Min. Jour., vol. 67, pp. 442, 470, 561, 619–620 . . . vol. 68, p. 5, 1899.

2. Black sand of the Pacific coast: Min. Sci. Press, vol. 113, pp. 811–813, 1916.

La Paz, Lincoln

1. A preliminary report on the Pinto Mountains, Riverside County, California, chondrite (CN = 1161, 337): Meteoritics, vol. 1, pp. 295–99, 1955.

Larsen, Esper Signius

1. (and Hicks, W. B.) Searlesite, a new mineral, San Bernardino County, California: Am. Jour. Sci., 4th ser., vol. 38, pp. 437–440, 1914 . . . (abstract): Washington Acad. Sci. Jour., vol. 4, pp. 397–398, 1914 . . . Rev. geologie et sci. connexes, tome 1, p. 135, 1920 . . . Neues. Jahrb., 1917, Referate, pp. 27–28.

2. Proof that priceite is a distinct mineral species: Am. Mineralogist, vol. 2, p. 1, 1917.

3. Optical evidence that "hydrogiobertite" is a mixture: Am. Mineralogist, vol. 2, p. 3, 1917 . . . Mineralog. Abstracts, vol. 1, p. 261, 1922.

4. Massicot and litharge, the two modifications of lead monoxide: Am. Mineralogist, vol. 2, pp. 18–19, 1917 . . . Mineralog. Abstracts, vol. 1, p. 120, 1921 . . . (abstract): Rev. geologie et sci. connexes, tome 1, pp. 134–135, 1920.

5. Durdenite from California: Am. Mineralogist, vol. 2, pp. 45–46, 1917 . . . Mineralog. Abstracts, vol. 2, p. 475, 1925.

6. (and **Steiger, George**) Mineralogical notes; griffithite, a new member of the chlorite group: Washington Acad. Sci. Jour., vol. 7, pp. 6–12, 1917.

7. Hydrogioberite—evidence that it is a mixture: Am. Jour. Sci., 4th ser., vol. 43, p. 3, 1917.

8. Eakleite, a new mineral from California: Am. Jour. Sci., 4th ser., vol. 43, pp. 464–465, 1917 . . . Mineralog. Abstracts, vol. 1, p. 206, 1921 . . . (abstract): Rev. geologie et sci. connexes, tome 1, p. 221, 1920.

9. (and **Shannon, Earl Victor**) Boussingaultite from South Mountain near Santa Paula, California: Am. Mineralogist, vol. 5, pp. 127–129, 1920.

10. (and **Foshag, William Frederick**) Merwinite, a new calcium magnesium orthosilicate from Crestmore, California: Am. Mineralogist, vol. 6, pp. 143–148, 1921 . . . Mineralog. Abstracts, vol. 1, p. 254, 1922.

11. The microscopic determination of nonopaque minerals: U. S. Geol. Survey Bull. 679, 294 pp., 1921.

12. See Hess, Frank L. (17).

13. The identity of eakleite and xonotlite: Am. Mineralogist, vol. 8, pp. 181–182, 1923.

14. (and **Steiger, George**) Dehydration and optical studies of alunogen, nontronite, and griffithite: Am. Jour. Sci., 5th ser., vol. 15, pp. 1–19, 1928.

15. (and **Dunham, Kingsley Charles**) Tilleyite, a new mineral from the contact zone at Crestmore, California: Am. Mineralogist, vol. 18, pp. 469–473, 1933.

16. (and **Switzer, George S.**) An obsidian-like rock formed from the melting of a granodiorite: Am. Jour. Sci., 5th ser., vol. 237, pp. 562–568, 1939.

17. Batholith and associated rocks of Corona, Elsinore, and San Luis Rey quadrangles, southern California: Geol. Soc. America Mem. 29, 182 pp., 1948.

18. (**Everhart, Donald Lough,** and **Merriam, Richard Holmes**) Crystalline rocks of southwestern California: California Div. Mines Bull. 159, 136 pp., 1951.

Larsen, Willard N.
1. See Baur, Gretta S. (2).

Laudermilk, Jerome Douglas
1. (and **Woodford, Alfred Oswald**) Soda-rich anthophyllite asbestos from Trinity County: Am. Mineralogist, vol. 15, pp. 259–262, 1930.

2. A mineralogical occurrence of iron tannate: Rocks and Minerals, vol. 6, pp. 24–25, 1931.

3. (and **Woodford, Alfred Oswald**) Secondary montmorillonite in a California pegmatite: Am. Mineralogist, vol. 19, pp. 260–267, 1934.

4. See Merriam, Richard Holmes (1).

5. (and **Woodford, Alfred Oswald**) Hydrous iron sulfide in California crystalline limestone: Am. Mineralogist, vol. 25, pp. 418–424, 1940.

6. See Woodford, Alfred Oswald (9).

Laur, P.
1. Observations sur l'origine et la distribution de l'or dans les divers terrains de la Californie: Acad. sci. Paris, vol. 53, pp. 1096–1099, 1861.

2. De la production des métaux precieux en Californie, 132 pp., Paris, 1862.

Lawson, Andrew Cowper
1. The geology of Carmelo Bay: Univ. California, Dept. Geol. Sci. Bull., vol. 1, pp. 1–59, 1893 . . . (abstract): Petermanns Mitt., 1894, (Beil zum 40), pp. 119–120.

2. Sketch of the geology of the San Francisco peninsula: U. S. Geol. Survey 15th Ann. Rept., pp. 399–476, 1895.

3. Feldspar corundum rock from Plumas County, California . . . (abstract): Geol. Soc. America Bull., vol. 12, pp. 501–502, 1901 . . . Jour. Geology, vol. 9, p. 78, 1901 . . . Am. Geologist, vol. 27, p. 132, 1901 . . . Geol. Zentralbl., Band 4, p. 1, 1903.

4. (and **Palache, Charles**) The Berkeley Hills, a detail of Coast Range geology: Univ. California, Dept. Geol. Sci. Bull., vol. 2, pp. 349–450, 1902.

5. Plumasite, an oligoclase corundum rock, near Spanish Peak, California: Univ. California, Dept. Geol. Bull., vol. 3, pp. 219–229, 1903 . . . (abstract): Geol. Zentralbl., Band 9, p. 514, 1907.

6. The orbicular gabbro at Dehesa, San Diego County, California: Univ. California, Dept. Geol. Sci. Bull., vol. 3, pp. 383–396, 1904 . . . (abstract): Science, new ser., vol. 15, p. 415, 1902.

7. Description of the San Francisco district; Tamalpais, San Francisco, Concord, San Mateo, and Hayward quadrangles: U. S. Geol. Survey Geol. Atlas, San Francisco folio (no. 193), 24 pp., 1914.

Lawson, C. C.
1. See Schairer, John Frank (1).

Le Conte, John Lawrence
1. Account of some volcanic springs in the desert of the Colorado, in southern California: Am. Jour. Sci., 2d ser., vol. 19, pp. 1–5, 1855.

Le Conte, Joseph
1. (and **Rising, W. B.**) The phenomena of metalliferous vein formation now in progress at Sulphur Bank, California: Am. Jour. Sci., 3d ser., vol. 24, pp. 23–33, 1882 . . . (abstract): Eng. and Min. Jour., vol. 34, pp. 109–110, 1882.
2. Mineral vein formation in progress at Steamboat Springs and Sulphur Bank: Am. Jour. Sci., 3d ser., vol. 25, pp. 424–428, 1883.

Lee, Donald Edward
1. See Coleman, Robert Griffin (2).
2. See Coleman, Robert Griffin (3).
3. (**Coleman, Robert Griffin** and **Erd, Richard Clarkson**) Garnet types from the Cazadero area, California: Jour. of Petrology, vol. 4, pp. 460–492, 1963.
4. (**Thomas, H. H., Marvin, R. F.,** and **Coleman, Robert Griffin**) Isotope ages of glaucophane schists from Cazadero, California (abst.): Program, Geol. Soc. America Cordilleran Section, Berkeley, April 1963, p. 42.
5. (**Thomas, H. H., Marvin, R. F.** and **Coleman, Robert Griffin**) Isotope ages of glaucophanne schists from Cazadero, California (abst.): Geol. Soc. America Spec. Paper 76, pp. 210–211, 1964.

Lehmann, W. M.
1. Rontgenographische Untersuchungen an naturlichem and synthetischem Meta-cinnabarit (HgS): Zeitschr. Kristallographie, Band 60, pp. 379–413, 1924 . . . Mineralog. Abstracts, vol. 2, pp. 510–511, 1925.

Leith, Carlton James
1. Mineralogy and petrology of the Quien Sabe volcanics, California: (abstract) Geol. Soc. America Bull., vol. 61, p. 1527, 1950.

Le Maitre, Robert W.
1. See Gay, Peter (2).

Lemmon, Dwight Moulton
1. Augelite from Mono County, California: Am. Mineralogist, vol. 20, pp. 664–668, 1935.
2. Woodhouseite, a new mineral of the beudantite group: Am. Mineralogist, vol. 22, pp. 939–948, 1937.
3. Woodhouseite, a new mineral of the beudantite group: Pacific Mineralogist, vol. 5, no. 2, p. 6, 1938.
4. (and **Dorr, John Van Nostrand, II**) Tungsten deposits of the Atolia district, San Bernardino and Kern Counties, California: U. S. Geol. Survey Bull. 922-H, pp. 205–245, 1940.
5. Tungsten deposits in the Tungsten Hills, Inyo County, California: U. S. Geol. Survey Bull. 922-Q, pp. 497–514, 1941.
6. Tungsten deposits of the Benton Range, Mono County, California: U. S. Geol. Survey Bull. 922-S, pp. 581–593, 1941.
7. Tungsten deposits in the Sierra Nevada near Bishop, California: U. S. Geol. Survey Bull. 931-E, pp. 79–104, 1941.

Lenhart, W. B.
1. Milling methods and costs of the Cardinal Gold Mining Company, Bishop Creek, California: U. S. Bur. Mines Inf. Circ. 7012, 1938.

Leonard, Frederick Charles
1. Preliminary announcement of the Goose Lake, California, meteorite: Science, new ser., vol. 89, p. 508, 1939.
2. The Goose Lake siderite; California's largest known meteorite: Pacific Mineralogist, vol. 6, no. 1, pp. 3–4, 1939 . . . Popular Astron., vol. 47, pp. 322–324, 1939 . . . Griffith Observer, vol. 4, no. 1, pp. 1–8, 1940.
3. (and **Norris, Robert Matheson**) Preliminary note on the Neenach, Los Angeles County, California, aerolite: Meteoritics, vol. 1, p. 28, 1953.
4. The Goose Lake siderite: California's largest known meteorite: Contributions of the Society for Research on Meteorites, vol. 2, pp. 113–114, 1941.
5. Note on the surroundings of the Goose Lake, California, siderite *in situ:* Contributions of the Society for Research on Meteorites, vol. 2, p. 202, 1941.

6. The identity of the Windmill Station with that of the "Valley Wells", California aerolite fall: Contributions of the Society for Research on Meteorites, vol. 3, pp. 174–175, 1944.

7. On the identification and recovery of the Goose Lake, California siderite (ECN = +1205,420): Meteoritical Society, Contributions, vol. 4, pp. 323–324, 1950.

8. (and **Rowland, Gerald L.**) Catalog of the multiple meteoritic falls of the world: Meteoritics, vol. 1, pp. 440–458, 1955.

9. Further remarks on the Ridgecrest, California, aerolite (CB — 1176,356): Meteoritics, vol. 2, pp. 52–53, 1963.

10. (and **DeViolini, R.**) Classificational catalog of the meteoritic falls of the world: Univ. Calif. (Los Angeles) Publ. in Astronomy, vol. 2, pp. 1–80, 1956.

Levine, Harry
1. See Hewett, Donnel Foster (4).

Levinson, Alfred Abraham
1. See Heinrich, Eberhardt William (2).

Lewis, W. Scott
1. Occurrences of opal in California: Rocks and Minerals, vol. 8, pp. 36–37, 1933.

2. California jasper: Pacific Mineralogist, vol. 5, no. 2, pp. 8–9, 1938.

3. A little known mineral locality: Pacific Mineralogist, vol. 9, no. 2, pp. 8–9, 1941.

4. Gem collecting in California: Hobbies, vol. 47, pp. 116–117, 1942.

Liebenam, W. A.
1. Kupfervorkommen in Kalifornien und ihre wirtschaftliche Bedeutung: Zeitschr. Berg-, Hütten- u. Salinenwesen preuss. Staate, Band 55, pp. 522–546, 1907 . . . (abstract): Geol. Zentralbl., Band 11, p. 250, 1908.

Lindgren, Waldemar
1. The silver mines of Calico, California: Am. Inst. Min. Met. Eng. Trans., vol. 15, pp. 717–734, 1887.

2. Contributions to the mineralogy of the Pacific coast: California Acad. Sci. Proc., 2d ser., vol. 1, pp. 1–6, 1888.

3. See Melville, William Harlow (1).

4. The gold deposit at Pine Hill, California: Am. Jour. Sci., 3d ser., vol. 44, pp. 92–96, 1892.

5. The auriferous veins of Meadow Lake, California: Am. Jour. Sci., 3d ser., vol. 46, pp. 201–206, 1893 . . . (abstract): Min. Sci. Press., vol. 68, p. 118, 1894.

6. An auriferous conglomerate of Jurassic age from the Sierra Nevada: Am. Jour. Sci., 3d ser., vol. 48, pp. 275–280, 1894.

7. The gold-silver veins of Ophir, California: U. S. Geol. Survey 14th Ann. Rept., pt. 2, pp. 243–284, 1894 . . . (abstract): Min. Sci. Press, vol. 71, pp. 216, 233, 1895 . . . Jour. Geology, vol. 4, pp. 373–374, 1896 . . . Nature, vol. 53, p. 466, 1896.

8. (and **Turner, Henry Ward**) Description of the gold belt, California; description of the Placerville sheet: U. S. Geol. Survey Geol. Atlas, Placerville folio (no. 3), 3 pp., 1894; reprint, 1914 . . . (abstract): Jour. Geology, vol. 4, pp. 248–250, 1896.

9. (and **Turner, Henry Ward**) Description of the Marysville sheet, California: U. S. Geol. Survey Geol. Atlas, Marysville folio (no. 17), 2 pp., 1895 . . . (abstract): Jour. Geology, vol. 3, pp. 976–977, 1895.

10. (and **Turner, Henry Ward**) Description of the gold belt; description of the Smartsville sheet, California: U. S. Geol. Survey Geol. Atlas, Smartsville folio (no. 18), 6 pp., 1895.

11. Characteristic features of California gold quartz veins: Geol. Soc. America Bull., vol. 6, pp. 221–240, 1895 . . . (abstract): Min. Sci. Press, vol. 70, pp. 181–182, 213–214, 244, 1895 . . . Science, new ser., vol. 1, p. 68, 1895 . . . Zeitschr. prakt. Geologie, Jahrg. 3, pp. 423–426, 1895.

12. The gold-quartz veins of Nevada City and Grass Valley districts, California: U. S. Geol. Survey 17th Ann. Rept. pt. 2, pp. 1–262, 1896 . . . (abstract): Inst. Min. Eng. Trans., vol. 14, pp. 667–668, 1897–98 . . . (abstract): Zeitschr. prakt. Geologie, Jahrg. 7, pp. 210–213, 1899.

13. Description of the gold belt; description of the Sacramento sheet: U. S. Geol. Survey Geol. Atlas, Sacramento folio (no. 5), 3 pp., 1894 . . . (abstract): Jour. Geology, vol. 4, pp. 250–251, 1896.

14. Description of the Nevada City, California, special sheet: U. S. Geol. Survey Geol. Atlas, Nevada City special folio (no. 29), 7 pp., 1896 . . . (abstract): Jour. Geology, vol. 5, pp. 409–411, 1897.

15. Description of the gold belt; description of the Pyramid Peak sheet: U. S. Geol. Survey Geol. Atlas, Pyramid Peak folio (no. 31), 8 pp., 1896.

16. Description of the gold belt; description of the Truckee sheet: U. S. Geol. Survey Geol. Atlas, Truckee folio (no. 39), 8 pp., 1897.

17. See Turner, Henry Ward, (13), and Becker, George Ferdinand, (7).

18. The primary gold deposits of the Sierra Nevada: Min. Sci. Press, vol. 76, pp. 258–259, 1898.

19. Description of the Colfax sheet, California: U. S. Geol. Survey Geol. Atlas, Colfax folio (no. 66), 10 pp., 1900.

20. The Tertiary gravels of the Sierra Nevada of California: U. S. Geol. Survey Prof. Paper 73, 226 pp., 1911.

21. The mining districts of the western United States: U. S. Geol. Survey Bull. 507, pp. 5–43, 1912.

Linsley, Earle Garfield

1. A description of the meteorites available for public inspection in the San Francisco Bay region: Popular Astron., vol. 47, pp. 472–477, 1934.

2. The giant Goose Lake meteorite from Modoc County, California: California Div. Mines Rept. 35, pp. 308–312, 1939.

Lipman, Peter W.

1. Mineralogy and paragenesis of amphiboles from Gibson Peak pluton, northern California: Am. Mineralogist, vol. 49, pp. 1321–1330, 1964.

Lisle, T. O.

1. Amethysts of the Bullfrog mine and Death Valley onyx: Rocks and Minerals, vol. 21, pp. 200–204, 1946.

Little, James Macfarlane

1. Tungsten deposits of the Confidence mining district, Tuolumne County, California: California Div. Mines Rept. 38, pp. 283–290, 1942.

2. Geology of the Welsh tungsten deposits, Madera County, California: California Div. Mines Rept. 38, pp. 291–294, 1942.

3. Ghost Canyon tungsten claims, Madera County, California: California Div. Mines Rept. 38, pp. 295–302, 1942.

Loew, Oscar

1. Investigation of mineralogical and agricultural conditions: U.S. Geog. Surveys W 100th Mer. Rept. 1875, pt. 3, pp. 573–661.

2. Report on the geological and mineralogical character of southeastern California and adjacent regions: U.S. Geog. Surveys W. 100th Mer. Rept. 1876, ap. H 2, pp. 173–189.

3. Report on the alkaline lakes, thermal springs, mineral springs, and brackish waters of southern California and adjacent country: U.S. Geog. Surveys W. 100th Mer. Rept. 1876, pp. 188–199 . . . 44th Cong., 2d sess., H. Ex. Doc. 1, pt. 2, vol. 2, pt. 3, app. J. J., pp. 408–419, ap. H 3, p. 189, 1876.

Logan, Clarence August

1. Platinum and allied metals in California: California Min. Bur. Bull. 85, 120 pp., 1918.

2. See Bradley, Walter Wadsworth. (7).

3. San Luis Obispo County: California Min. Bur. Rept. 15, pp. 674–726, 1919.

4. Auburn field division: California Min. Bur. Rept. 17, pp. 391–490, 1921.

5. Notes on the West Point district, Calaveras County: California Min. Bur. Rept. 18, pp. 15–21, 1922.

6. Quartz mining in the Alleghany district: California Min. Bur. Rept. 18, pp. 499–519, 1922.

7. Sacramento field division: California Min. Bur. Rept. 20, pp. 1–23, 73–84, 177–183, 355–367, 1924.

8. Sacramento field division: California Min. Bur. Rept. 21, pp. 1–22, 135–172, 275–280, 414–498, 1925.

9. El Dorado, Shasta and Trinity Counties: California Min. Bur. Rept. 22, pp. 1–67, 121–216, 397–452, 1926.

10. Copper in California: California Min. Bur. Rept. 22, pp. 372–376, 1926.

11. Amador County, Placer County: California Min. Bur. Rept. 23, pp. 131–202, 235–286, 1927.

12. Tuolumne County, Butte County: California Min. Bur. Rept. 24, pp. 3–53, 173–210, 1928.

13. Sierra County, Colusa County: California Min. Bur. Rept. 25, pp. 151–211, 284–300, 1929.

14. Nevada, Yuba Counties: California Min. Bur. Rept. 26, pp. 90–136, 186–200, 1930.

15. Yuba County: California Min. Bur. Rept. 27, pp. 246–261, 1931.

16. Mother Lode gold belt of California: California Div. Mines Bull. 108, 221 pp., 1934.

17. Gold mines of Placer County: California Div. Mines Rept. 32, pp. 7–96, 1936.

18. See Franke, Herbert A. (4).

19. Mineral resources of El Dorado County: California Div. Mines Rept. 34, pp. 206–280, 1938.

20. Mineral resources of Nevada County: California Div. Mines Rept. 37, pp. 374–408, 1941.

21. Current mining activity in Plumas County: California Div. Mines Rept. 39, pp. 85–87, 1943.

22. Limestone in California: California Div. Mines Rept. 43, pp. 177–357, 1947.

23. Mines and mineral resources of Tuolumne County, California: California Jour. Mines and Geology, vol. 45, pp. 47–83, 1949.

24. Mines and mineral resources of Madera County, California: California Jour. Mines and Geology, vol. 46., pp. 445–482, 1950.

25. (and **Braun, Lewis Timothy,** and **Vernon, James W.**) Mines and mineral resources of Fresno County, California: California Jour. Mines and Geology, vol. 47, pp. 485–552, 1951.

Lonsdale, John Tipton
1. (**Metz, M. S.** and **Halbouty, Michel Thomas**) The petrographic character of some Eocene sands from southwest Texas: Jour. Sed. Petrol. vol. 1, pp. 73–81, 1931.

Los Angeles Times
1. [Gold nugget from Death Valley]: Los Angeles Times, July 30, 1945.

Louderback, George Davis
1. Study of the basin range structure and glaucophane and associated schists of California and Oregon: Carnegie Inst. Washington yearbook, vol. 4, p. 191, 1906.

2. (and **Blasdale, Walter Charles**) Benitoite, a new California gem mineral, with chemical analysis by Walter C. Blasdale: Univ. California, Dept. Geol. Sci. Bull., vol. 5, pp. 149–153, 1907.

3. (and **Sharwood, William J.**) Crocidolite-bearing rocks of the California coast ranges . . . (abstract): Geol. Soc. America Bull., vol. 18, p. 659, 1908.

4. (and **Blasdale, Walter Charles**) Benitoite, its mineralogy, paragenesis, and geological occurrence (abstract): Science, new ser., vol. 27, p. 411, 1908.

5. (and **Blasdale, Walter Charles**) Benitoite, its paragenesis and mode of occurrence: Univ. California, Dept. Geol. Sci. Bull., vol. 5, pp. 331–380, 1909.

6. (and **Blasdale, Walter Charles**) Ruby corundum from San Bernardino fornia (abstract): Science, new ser., vol. 32, p. 31, 1910 . . . Geol. Soc. America Bull., vol. 21, p. 793, 1910.

Lovering, Tom Seward
1. See Walker, George Walton (5).

Lowell, F. L.
1. Mines and mineral resources of the counties of Del Norte, Humboldt, Mendocino, Mariposa, Merced, San Joaquin, and Stanislaus: California Min. Bur. Rept. 14, pp. 371–425, 569–604, 627–634, 1916.

Luce, John W.
1. A field trip to Tick and Red Rock Canyons: Pacific Mineralogist, vol. 2, no. 1, pp. 14–17, 1935.

2. Los Angeles mineralogical society field trips, 1935–36: Pacific Mineralogist, vol. 3, no. 1, pp. 4–6, 1936.

Lukesh, Joseph
1. (and **Buerger, Martin Julian**) The tridymite problem (abstract): Am. Mineralogist, vol. 27, p. 143, 1942.

Lydon, Philip Andrew
1. See Clark, William Bullock. (4).

2. Unusual phosphatic rock: Calif. Div. Mines and Geol., Mineral Information Service, vol. 17, pp. 66–74, 1964.

3. "Silicate slag" from Trinity County: Calif. Div. Mines and Geol., Mineral Information Service, vol. 17, pp. 96–101, 1964.

Lyle, D. A.

1. Notes on mining districts in Nevada, California, and Arizona: 42d Cong., 2d sess., S. Ex. Doc. 65, pp. 42–43, 45–46, 49–51, 1872.

Lyman, C. S.

1. Ueber die Zinnoberminen in Ober-Californien und die Quecksilbergewinnung aus diesen Erzen: Berg- u. hüttenm. Zeit, Band 10, pp. 125–127, 1848 . . . Chem. Gazette, no. 44, Oct. 1848 . . . Dinglers Polytech. Jour., Band 112, Heft 2, p. 116, 1848.

2. Mines of cinnabar in Upper California: Am. Jour. Sci., 2d ser., vol. 6, pp. 270–271, 1848.

3. Platinum and diamonds in California: Am. Jour. Sci., 2d ser., vol. 8, p. 294, 1849.

4. Observations on California: Am. Jour. Sci., 2d ser., vol. 7 pp. 290–292, 305–309, 1849.

5. Notes on the California gold region: Am. Jour. Sci., 2d ser., vol. 8, pp. 415–419, 1849 . . . Philos. Mag., 3d ser., vol. 35, pp. 470–474, 1849.

6. Gold of California: Am. Jour. Sci., 2d ser., vol. 9, pp. 126–127, 1850.

Lynton, Edward Dale

1. Sulphur deposits of Inyo County, California: California Div. Mines Rept. 34, pp. 563–590, 1938.

M

McAllister, James Franklin

1. Melanite-nepheline syenite from the Panamint Range, California . . . (abstract): Geol. Soc. America Bull., vol. 51, p. 1961, 1940.

2. Geology of the Lippincott lead area, Mono County, California: U.S. Geol. Survey, open file release, 10 pp., Sept. 1949.

3. Rocks and structure of the Quartz Spring area, northern Panamint Range, California: California Div. Mines Special Rept. 25, 38 pp., 1952.

4. Geology of mineral deposits in the Ubehebe Peak quadrangle, Inyo County, California: California Div. Mines, Special Rept. 42, 63 pp., 1955.

5. See Erd, Richard Clarkson. (1).

6. See Erd, Richard Clarkson. (2).

7. Sborgite in the Furnace Creek area, California: U.S. Geol. Survey Prof. Paper 424B, Article 129, pp. B299–B301, 1961.

McBurney, Thomas Chester

1. (and **Murdoch, Joseph**) Haiweeite, a new uranium mineral from California: Am. Mineralogist, vol. 44, pp. 839–843, 1959.

McCaskey, H. D.

1. The New Idria quicksilver mine, California: Min. World, vol. 32, p. 104, 1910.

McColl, R. S.

1. Geochemical and structural studies in batholithic rocks of southern California: Part I, Structural geology of Rattlesnake Mountain pluton: Geol. Soc. America Bull., vol. 75, pp. 805–822, 1964.

McConnell, Duncan

1. The substitution of SiO_4 and SO_4 groups for PO_4 groups in the apatite structure; ellestadite, the end-member: Am. Mineralogist, vol. 22, pp. 977–986, 1937.

2. A structural investigation of the isomorphism of the apatite group: Am. Mineralogist, vol. 23, pp. 1–19, 1938.

3. X-ray data on several phosphate minerals: Am. Jour. Sci., 5th ser., vol. 240, pp. 649–657, 1942.

4. See Murdoch, Joseph (34).

5. (and **Murdoch, Joseph**) Crystal chemistry of ettringite, Mineralog. Mag., vol. 33, pp. 59–64, 1962.

McConnell, James Desmond Caldwell

1. The hydrated calcium silicates riversideite, tobermorite and plombierite, Mineralog. Mag. 30, pp. 293–305, 1954.

2. A chemical, optical, and X-ray study of scawtite from Ballycraigy, Larne, N. Ireland: Am. Mineralogist, vol. 40, pp. 510–514, 1955.

McDonald, William H.

1. See Smerud, Sara K. (1).

McGregor, A.
1. Del Norte, Humboldt, Mendocino, Shasta Counties: California Min. Bur. Rept. 10, pp. 166–168, 205–208, 311–314, 627–641, 1890.

McIntosh, F. G.
1. Two rare and beautiful California gems: Oregon Mineralogist, vol. 2, no. 1, p. 10, 1934.
2. Rare gem minerals of America: Oregon Mineralogist, vol. 2, no. 7, pp. 3–4, 30 . . . no. 8, pp. 5–6, 21, 1934.

McIver, Edward J.
1. The structure of bultfonteinite, $Ca_4Si_2O_{10}F_2H_6$: Acta. Cryst. vol. 16, pp. 551–558, 1963.

McKee, Bates
1. Widespread distribution of aragonite in the Pacheco Pass area, California (abst.): Geol. Soc. America Spec. Paper 68, p. 43, 1962.
2. Aragonite in the Franciscan rocks of the Pacheco Pass, California: Am. Mineralogist, vol. 47, pp. 379–387, 1962.

McLaughlin, Donald Hamilton
1. See Graton, Louis Caryl (4).

McLaughlin, R. P.
1. Geology of the Bodie district, California: Min. Sci. Press, vol. 94, pp. 795–796, 1907.
2. Masonic mining district, Mono County, California: Min. Sci. Press, vol. 110, pp. 27–29, 1915 . . . (abstract): Eng. Index, 1915, p. 367, 1915.
3. (and **Bradley, Walter Wadsworth**) Madera County, California: California Min. Bur. Rept. 14, pp. 531–568, 1916 . . . issued as separate chapter with title Mines and mineral resources of counties of Fresno, Kern, Kings, Madera, Mariposa, Merced, San Joaquin, Stanislaus, July, 1915.
4. See Eakle, Arthur Starr (17).

McLennan, John F.
1. Gold-quartz replacements in intrusive rocks (geology and ores of the Feather River region, northern California): Min. World, vol. 44, pp. 389–392, 1916.

McMurdie, Howard Francis
1. See Flint, Einar Philip (1).

MacBoyle, Errol
1. Mines and mineral resources of Nevada County: California Min. Bur. Rept. 16, 270 pp., 1919 (published as separate chapter).
2. Mines and mineral resources of Plumas County: California Min. Bur. Rept. 16, 188 pp., 1920 (published as separate chapter).
3. Mines and mineral resources of Sierra County: California Min. Bur. Rept. 16, 144 pp., 1920 (published as separate chapter).

MacDonald, Donald Francis
1. The Weaverville-Trinity Center gold gravels, Trinity County, California: U. S. Geol. Survey Bull. 430, pp. 48–58, 1910.
2. Notes on the gold lodes of the Carrville district, Trinity County, California: U. S. Geol. Survey Bull. 530, pp. 9–41, 1913.

Macdonald, Gordon Andrew
1. (and **Merriam, Richard Holmes**) Andalusite in pegmatite from Fresno County, California: Am. Mineralogist, vol. 23, pp. 588–594, 1938.
2. An intrusive pépérite at San Pedro Hill, California: Univ. California, Dept. Geol. Sci. Bull., vol. 24, pp. 329–338, 1939.
3. See Durrell, Cordell (1).
4. Progressive metasomatism of serpentine in the Sierra Nevada of California: Am. Mineralogist, vol. 2, pp. 276–287, 1941.

MacKevett, Edward Malcolm, Jr.
1. Geology of Jurupa Mountains, San Bernardino and Riverside Counties, California: California Div. Mines, Special Rept. 5, 14 pp., 1951.
2. Geology and ore deposits of the Kern River uranium area, California: U. S. Geol. Survey Bull. 1087-F, pp. 169–222, 1960.
3. See Hall, Wayne Everett (1).
4. See Hall, Wayne Everett (4).

Mackintosh, James B.
1. See Hidden, William Earl (2).
2. See Hidden, William Earl (3).

MacLachlan, D.
1. Gold, the history maker: Min. Notes and News, p. 4, June 1952.

Maclellan, Donald D.
1. See Anderson, George Harold (1).

MacLeod, Geo. Marshall
1. See Heikkila, Henry Herman (1).

Mace, Clement H.
1. Genesis of Leona Heights deposit, California: Min. World, vol. 35, p. 1320, 1911.

Macre-Patton, P.
1. The revival of the Meadow Lake mining district: Arizona Min. Jour., vol. 20, no. 12, pp. 5–6, 1936.

Mallery, Willard
1. A discovery of celestite (Lavic Station, San Bernardino County, California): Min. Sci. Press, vol. 113, p. 952, 1916.
2. Tin in California: Dana Mag., vol. 2, pp. 8–11, 18–20 . . . vol. 3, pp. 6–8, 1944.

Mamedov, Kh. S.
1. (and **Belov, N. V.**) The crystal structure of foshagite: Doklady Akad. Nauk SSSR *121*, p. 901, 1958.

Mann, R. L.
1. Owl Head manganese deposit, San Bernardino County, California: Min. and Eng. World, vol. 44, pp. 743–744, 1916.

Mansfield, George Rogers
1. (and **Calkins, Frank Cathcart**) Confidence field, Zabriskie field: U. S. Geol. Survey Bull. 724, pp. 51–58, 61–66, 1922.
2. See Noble, L. F., and others (1).
3. (and **Boardman, Leona**) Potash: Mineral Resources U. S., 1923, pt. 2, pp. 167–204, 1927.
4.' (and **Boardman, Leona**) Potash: Mineral Resources U. S., 1924, pp. 27–61, 1927.
5. (and **Boardman, Leona**) Nitrate deposits of the United States: U. S. Geol. Survey Bull. 838, vi, 107 pp., 1932 . . . (abstract): Geol. Zentralbl., Abt. A, Band 48, pp. 413–414, 1932.

Marcou, Jules
1. Geology of North America, with two reports on the prairies of Arkansas and Texas, the Rocky Mountains of New Mexico, and the Sierra Nevada of California, 148 pp., Zurich, 1858.

Marryat, F. S.
1. Mountains and molehills, 393 pp., New York and London, 1855.

Marshall, Royal R.
1. Absorption spectra of smoky quartz from an Arkansas vein deposit and from a Sierran miarolitic granite: Am. Mineralogist, vol. 40, pp. 535–537, 1955.

Martin, Al. H.
1. Gem mining in California a profitable industry: Min. World, vol. 33, pp. 1227–1228, 1910.
2. Mining for precious stones in California: Min. Sci. Press, vol. 66, pp. 316–317, 1911.

Martinez, José Longinos
1. California in 1792 (trans. L. B. Simpson, San Marino, California): 111 pp., 1938.

Marvin, R. F.
1. See Lee, Donald Edward (4).
2. See Lee, Donald Edward (5).

Masimer, George
1. See Pemberton, H. Earl (1), Moller, William (1), and Swartz, Jack (1).

Mason, Brian Harold
　　1. (and **Vitaliano, Charles Joseph**) The mineralogy of the antimony oxides and antimonites: Mineralog. Mag., vol. 30, pp. 100, 112, 1953.
　　2. Minerals of the Varuträsk pegmatite: XXII. Some iron-manganese phosphate minerals and their alteration products, with special reference to material from Varuträsk: Geol. Fören Förhandl., vol. 63, H 2, pp. 117–175, 1941.
　　3. Meteorites: John Wiley and Sons, Inc., New York, 274 pp., 1962.

Mason, R. B.
　　1. Letter from Monterey, dated Aug. 17, 1848: 31st Cong., 1st sess., H. Doc. 17, pp. 528–536, 1850.

Mathewson, H. D.
　　1. A day at the Mirabel and Sulphur Bank mines: Rocks and Minerals, vol. 23, pp. 312–315, 1948.

Mathewson, J. D.
　　1. Vorkommen von Tellurerzen in Californien: Berg- u. hüttenm. Zeit., Band 24, p. 374, 1865.

Matson, E. J.
　　1. See Volin, M. E. (1).
　　2. Investigation of Little Castle Creek chromite deposit, Shasta County, California: U.S. Bur. Mines Rept. Invest. 4516, 16 pp., July, 1949.

Matthews, Robert Alfred
　　1. (and **Alfors, John Theodore**) Sanbornite from Rush Creek, Fresno County: California Div. Mines and Geol. Mineral Information Service, vol. 15, No. 6, pp. 1–3, 1962.
　　2. See Alfors, John Theodore (1).

Maxson, John Haviland
　　1. Economic geology of portions of Del Norte and Siskiyou Counties, northwesternmost California: California Div. Mines Rept. 29, pp. 123–160, 1933.

Maynard, George W.
　　1. Remarks on a gold specimen from California: Am. Inst. Min. Met. Eng. Trans., vol. 8, pp. 451–457, 1879.

Mayo, Evans Blakemore
　　1. Preliminary report on the geology of southwestern Mono County, California: California Min. Bur. Rept. 26, pp. 475–482, 1930.
　　2. Two new occurrences of piedmontite in California: Am. Mineralogist, vol. 17, pp. 238–248, 1932 . . . (abstract) Rev. géologie et sci. connexes, tome 13, p. 264, 1933 . . . Am. Mineralogist, vol. 17, p. 117, 1932 . . . Mineralog. Abstracts, vol. 5, p. 222, 1932.
　　3. Discovery of piedmontite in the Sierra Nevada: California Div. Mines Rept. 29, pp. 239–243, 1933.
　　4. Geology and mineral deposits of Laurel and Convict Basins, southwestern Mono County, California: California Div. Mines Rept. 30, pp. 79–90, 1934.

Mead, Roy Gibbons
　　1. Kramer borax deposit in California and the development of other borate ores: Mining and Metallurgy, vol. 14, pp. 405–409, 1933.

Melhase, John
　　1. Andalusite in California (Inyo Range): Eng. and Min. Jour., vol. 120, pp. 91–94, 1925 . . . (abstract): Geol. Zentralbl., Band 37, p. 73, 1928.
　　2. Mining bentonite in California: Eng. and Min. Jour., vol. 121, pp. 837–842, 1926.
　　3. A diversity of many fine minerals available in California for collectors: Oregon Mineralogist, vol. 2, no. 6, pp. 1–2, 4 . . . vol. 7, pp. 7–8, 23, 1934.
　　4. Fluorescent minerals of California: Mineralogist, vol. 3, no. 1, pp. 4, 38, 1935.
　　5. Sanbornite in California: Mineralogist, vol. 3, no. 9, pp. 3–4, 28–29, 1935.
　　6. Some garnet localities of California: Mineralogist, vol. 3, no. 11, pp. 7–8, 22–24, 1935.
　　7. A new occurrence of rare-earth minerals in California: Mineralogist, vol. 4, no. 1, p. 11, 1936.
　　8. Industrial uses of non-metallic minerals: Mineralogist, vol. 4, no. 8, pp. 7–8, 1936.

Melville, William Harlow

1. (and **Lindgren, Waldemar**) Contributions to the mineralogy of the Pacific coast: U.S. Geol. Survey Bull. 61, 40 pp., 1890.

2. Metacinnabarite from New Almaden, California: Am. Jour. Sci., 3d ser., vol. 40, pp. 291–295, 1890.

3. Metacinnabarite from New Almaden, California: U.S. Geol. Survey Bull. 78, pp. 80–83, 1891.

4. The chemistry of the Mount Diablo rocks: Geol. Soc. Am. Bull., vol. 2, pp. 402–414, 1891.

5. Tourmaline from Nevada County, California: U.S. Geol. Survey Bull. 90, p. 39, 1892.

Merriam, Charles Warren

1. Geology of the Cerro Gordo Mining District, Inyo County, California: U.S. Geol. Survey Prof. Paper 408, 83 pp., 1963.

Merriam, Richard Holmes

1. (and **Laudermilk, Jerome Douglas**) Two diopsides from southern California: Am. Mineralogist, vol. 21, pp. 715–718, 1936.

2. See Macdonald, Gordon Andrew (1).

3. (and **Kennard, Theodore Gladden**) An unidentified mineral in the quartz basalt of Lassen Volcanic National Park, California: Am. Mineralogist, vol. 28, pp. 602–604, 1943.

4. Igneous and metamorphic rocks of the southwestern part of the Ramona quadrangle, San Diego County, California: Geol. Soc. America Bull. 57, pp. 223–260, 1946.

5. See Larsen, Esper S., Jr. (18).

Merrill, Charles White

1. Strategic minerals in California: California Div. Mines. Rept. 34, pp. 283–291, 1938.

Merrill, Frederick James Hamilton

1. San Diego, Imperial Counties: California Min. Bur. Rept. 14, pp. 635–743, 1916 . . . issued as separate chapter, with title Mines and mineral resources of the counties of San Diego, Imperial, December 1914 . . . (abstract): Geol. Zentralbl., Band 27, p. 395, 1922.

2. Los Angeles, Orange and Riverside Counties: California Min. Bur. Rept. 15, pp. 461–589, 1919.

3. See Cloudman, H. C. (1).

Merrill, George Perkins

1. On a new meteorite from the San Emigdio Range, San Bernardino County, California: Am. Jour. Sci., 3d ser., vol. 35, pp. 490–491, 1888.

2. On the San Emigdio meteorite: U.S. Nat. Mus. Proc., vol. 11, pp. 161–167, 1889.

3. A meteoric iron from Owens Valley, California: Nat. Acad. Sci. Mem. 19, 4th Mem., 7 pp. 1922 . . . (abstract) Rev. géologie et sci. connexes, tome 3, pp. 701–702, 1922.

Metz, M. S.

1. See Lonsdale, John Tipton (1).

Metzer, Stephen

1. Sphene locality in Sierra Madre Canyon: Gems and Minerals, no. 206, pp. 56–57, 1954.

Meyrowitz, Robert

1. See Jaffe, Howard William (2).

2. See Outerbridge, William F. (1).

Mielenz, R. C.

1. Geology of the southwestern part of San Benito County, California: Univ. California, Berkeley, unpublished thesis, 59 pp., 1936.

Miller, Franklin Stuart

1. Anorthite from California: Am. Mineralogist, vol. 20, pp. 139–146, 1935.

Miller, William John

1. See Carey, Everett P. (1).

2. Anorthosite in Los Angeles County, California . . . (abstract): Pan-Am. Geologist, vol. 49, pp. 73–74, 1928 . . . Geol. Soc. Am. Bull., vol. 39, pp. 164–165, 1928.

3. Geology of Deep Spring Valley, California: Jour. Geology, vol. 36, pp. 510–525, 1928 . . . (abstract): Geol. Soc. America Bull., vol. 39, pp. 190-191, 1928 . . . Pan-Am. Geologist, vol. 49, p. 144, 1928 . . . Geol. Zentralbl., Band 39, p. 327, 1929 . . . Rev. geologie et sci. connexes, tome 9, pp. 343-344, 1928.

4. Geologic section across the southern Sierra Nevada (abstract): Geol. Soc. America Bull., vol. 41, pp. 49–50, 1930 . . . Pan-Am. Geologist, vol. 53, p. 74, 1930.

5. Anorthosite in Los Angeles County, California: Jour. Geology, vol. 39, pp. 331-344, 1931.

6. Geologic section across the southern Sierra Nevada of California: Univ. California, Dept. Geol. Sci. Bull., vol. 20, pp. 331–360, 1931.

7. Geology of the western San Gabriel Mountains; Univ. California Los Angeles, Pub. Math. and Physical Sci., vol. 1, pp. 1–114, 1934.

8. Pre-Cambrian and associated rocks near Twenty-Nine Palms, California: Geol. Soc. America Bull., vol. 49, pp. 417–446, 1938.

9. Crystalline rocks of southern California: Geol. Soc. America Bull. 57, pp. 457–542, 1946.

Miller, William P.
1. Trinity County: California Min. Bur. Rept. 10, pp. 695–727, 1890.

Miner, J. A.
1. Butte County, California: California Min. Bur. Rept. 10, pp. 124–146, 1890.

Mineral Notes and News (See also Gems and Minerals; vol. 1–)
1. Underwood discovers new benitoite deposit: Mineral Notes and News, Bull. 96, p. 3, 1945.
2. Ramona yields fine specimens: Mineral Notes and News, Bull. 104, p. 7, 1946.
3. Inderite discovered at Boron: Mineral Notes and News, Bull. 127, p. 12, 1948.
4. Kermesite at Boron: Mineral Notes and News, Bull. 127, p. 13, 1948.

Mineralogist, The
1. _____: Mineralogist, vol. 3, no. 3, p. 34, 1935.
2. California minerals: Mineralogist, vol. 3, no. 8, p. 23, 1935.
3. News of the societies: Mineralogist, vol. 3, no. 9, p. 20, 1935.
4. "Showy California minerals" (advertisement): Mineralogist, vol. 4, no. 3, p. 41, 1936.
5. Unique occurrence in Breakneck Canyon, Inyo County: Mineralogist, vol. 4, no. 4, p. 10, 1936.

Mining and Scientific Press
1. Summary of mining news, California [selected counties]: Min. Sci. Press, vol. 2, no. 38, p. 3, 1860.
2. Summary of mining news, California [selected counties]: Min. Sci. Press, vol. 3, no. 13, p. 5, 1861.
3. Summary of mining news, California [selected counties]: Min. Sci. Press, vol. 3, no. 14, p. 5, 1861.
4. Summary of mining news, California [selected counties]: Min. Sci. Press, vol. 4, no. 2, p. 5, 1862.
5. Santa Catalina Island: Min. Sci. Press, vol. 8, p. 263, 1864.
6. Quicksilver at Mount Diablo: Min. Sci. Press, vol. 10, p. 280, 1865.
7. The "opal claims" of Stockton Hill: Min. Sci. Press, vol. 12, p. 146, 1866.
8. Letter by "miner" to Press—mineral developments of Colusa County: Min. Sci. Press, vol. 12, p. 287, 1866.
9. Mining summary: Min. Sci. Press, vol. 15, p. 151, 1867.
10. Quicksilver in San Mateo County (from San Mateo Gazette): Min. Sci. Press, vol. 16, p. 357, 1868.
11. Mineralogical and geological notices: Min. Sci. Press, vol. 18, p. 264, 1869.
12. California gold nuggets: Min. Sci. Press, vol. 20, p. 178, 1870.
13. California diamonds: Min. Sci. Press, vol. 20, p. 194, 1870.
14. Silver in Placer County: Min. Sci. Press, vol. 23, p. 241, 1871.
15. Nugget of crystallized gold: Min. Sci. Press, vol. 26, p. 273, 1873.
16. Quicksilver in Del Norte County: Min. Sci. Press, vol. 29, p. 104, 1874.
17. Quicksilver in El Dorado County: Min. Sci. Press, vol. 31, p. 118, 1875.
18. Fluor-spar in Yolo County: Min. Sci. Press, vol. 39, p. 370, 1879.
19. Formation of the San Francisco peninsula: Min. Sci. Press, vol. 42, p. 28, 1881.
20. A silver cave: Min. Sci. Press, vol. 45, p. 23, 1882.

21. Calico district: Min. Sci. Press, vol. 45, p. 98, 1882.
22. The mineral exposition: Min. Sci. Press, vol. 47, pp. 121, 124, 136, 152, 1883.
23. Gold nuggets: Min. Sci. Press, vol. 60, p. 162, 1890.
24. California tin: Min. Sci. Press, vol. 64, p. 261, 1892.
25. The Integral quicksilver mine: Min. Sci. Press, vol. 67, p. 323, 1893.
26. Mining districts of Mariposa County: Min. Sci. Press, vol. 69, pp. 24–25, 1894.
27. A Los Angeles County, California, mine: Min. Sci. Press, vol. 79, p. 173, 1899.
28. Tin in California: Min. Sci. Press, vol. 82, p. 209, 1901.
29. The Dewey mine: Min. Sci. Press, vol. 87, p. 9, 1903.
30. Tin in the United States: Min. Sci. Press, vol. 87, p. 117, 1903.
31. Cinnabar in San Luis Obispo County, California: Min. Sci. Press, vol. 89, p. 323, 1904.
32. General mining news: Min. Sci. Press, vol. 98, p. 171, 1909.
33. General mining news: Min. Sci. Press, vol. 98, p. 271, 1909.
34. General mining news: Min. Sci. Press, vol. 107, p. 473, 1913.
35. General mining news: Min. Sci. Press, vol. 107, p. 868, 1913.
36. The mining summary: Min. Sci. Press, vol. 109, p. 974, 1914.
37. The mining summary: Min. Sci. Press, vol. 110, p. 420, 1915.
38. The mining summary: Min. Sci. Press, vol. 111, p. 368, 1915.
39. The mining summary: Min. Sci. Press, vol. 112, pp. 454, 569, 1916.
40. The mining summary: Min. Sci. Press, vol. 113, pp. 28, 66, 1916.
41. The mining summary: Min. Sci. Press, vol. 113, p. 887, 1916.
42. The mining summary: Min. Sci. Press, vol. 115, p. 840, 1917.

Mining World

1. Late news from busy mining camps, California: Min. World, vol. 26, p. 514, 1907.
2. Prospecting for potash in Death Valley, California: Min. World, vol. 38, pp. 855–856, 1913 . . . (transl. by G. Bentz) Zietschr. prakt. Geologie, Jahrg. 21, pp. 419–422, 1913.

Miser, Hugh Dinsmore

1. (and **Fairchild, John Gifford**) Hausmannite in the Batesville district, Arkansas: Washington Acad. Sci. Jour., vol. 10, pp. 1–8, 1920.

Moddle, D. A.

1. See Peacock, Martin Alfred (1).

Moehlman, Robert Stevens

1. (and **Gonyer, Forest A.**) Monticellite from Crestmore, California: Am. Mineralogist, vol. 19, pp. 474–476, 1934.

Moiola, Richard J.

1. (and **Hay, Richard L.**) Zeolite zones in pleistocene and recent sediments of China Lake, California (abst.): Geol. Soc. America, Cordilleran Section Meeting, Berkeley, California, p. 47, April 1963; Geol. Soc. America Spec. Paper 76, p. 215, 1964.
2. See Hay, Richard L. (1).
3. See Hay, Richard L. (2).

Moller, William

1. See Pemberton, H. Earl (1).

Möllmann, W.

1. Jungste Entdeckungen von Asbest in Californien: Berg- u. huttenm. Zeit., Band 61, pp. 601–602, 1902.

Montoya, J. W.

1. (and **Baur, Gretta S.**) Nickeliferous serpentines, chlorites, and related minerals found in two lateritic ores: Am. Mineralogist, vol. 48, pp. 1227–1238, 1963.

Moore, Bernard Nettleton

1. Some strontium deposits of southeastern California and western Arizona: Am. Inst. Min. Met. Eng. Tech. Pub. 599, 24 pp., 1935 . . . Trans., vol. 115, pp. 356–377, 1935.

Moore, Gideon E.

1. Ueber das Vorkommen des amorphen Quecksilbursulfids in der Natur: Jour. prakt. Chem., Bank 110, new ser. 2, pp. 319–329, 1870.

2. On native amorphous mercuric sulphide: Am. Jour. Sci., 3d ser., vol. 1, p. 380, 1871.
3. On the occurrence in nature of amorphous mercuric sulphide: Am. Jour. Sci., 3d ser., vol. 3, p. 36, 1872.
4. (and von **Zepharovich, V.**) Kallait pseudomorph nach Apatit aus Californien: Zeitschr. Kristallographic, Band 10, pp. 240–251, 1885.

Moore, James Gregory
1. Geology of the Mount Pinchot quadrangle, southern Sierra Nevada, California: U.S. Geol. Survey Bull. 1130, 152 pp. 1963.
2. See Bateman, Paul Charles (4).

Morgan, Vincent
1. See Frondel, Clifford (7).
2. See Frondel, Clifford (8).
3. See Erd, Richard Clarkson (3).

Moorhouse, Walter Wilson
1. Some titaniferous magnetites of the San Gabriel Mountains, Los Angeles County, California: Econ. Geology, vol. 33, pp. 737–748, 1938.

Morton, Paul Kenneth
1. See Troxel, Bennie Wyatt (2).

Moss, Frank A.
1. The geology of Carson Hill, California: Eng. and Min. Jour., vol. 124, pp. 1010–1012, 1927.

Mott, A. S.
1. Hakluyt's voyages (arranged by Mott), 317 pp., Boston, 1929.

Mrose, Mary Emma
1. See Clark, Joan Robinson (1).
2. See Schaller, Waldemar Theodore (56).
3. See Clark, Joan Robinson (4).
4. See Schaller, Waldemar Theodore (58).

Muessig, Siegfried
1. (and **Allen, Robert D.**) Ezcurrite ($2Na_2O \cdot 7H_2O$), a new sodium borate from Argentina; occurrence, mineralogy, and associated minerals: Econ. Geology, vol. 52, pp. 426–437, 1957.
2. (and **Allen, Robert D.**) The hydration of kernite ($Na_2B_4O_7 \cdot 4H_2O$): Am. Mineralogist, vol. 42, pp. 699–701, 1957.

Mülheims, A.
1. Ueber eine neue Art der Axenwinkelmessung und ueber die Bestimmung von Brechungsexponenten nach der Methode der Totalreflexion—Colemanit von Californien: Zeitschr. Kristallographic, Band 14, pp. 202–236, 1888.

Mulryan, Henry
1. Geology, mining and processing of diatomite at Lompoc, Santa Barbara County, California: Am Inst. Min. Met. Eng., Tech. Pub. 687, 30 pp., 1936 . . . Trans., vol. 129, pp. 469–500, 1938 . . . California Div. Mines Rept. 32, pp. 133–166, 1936.

Mumford, Russell W.
1. Deposits of saline minerals in southern California: California Div. Mines and Geol. Bull. 170, Ch. VIII, pp. 15–22, 1954.

Murdoch, Joseph
1. Amber in California: Jour. Geology, vol. 42, pp. 309–310, 1934 . . . (abstract): Annotated Bibliography Econ. Geology, vol. 7, p. 66, 1935.
2. Silica-fluorite pseudomorphs: Am. Mineralogist, vol. 21, pp. 18–32, 1936.
3. Andalusite in pegmatite: Am. Mineralogist, vol. 21, pp. 68–69, 1936.
4. (and **Webb, Robert Wallace**) Bustamite from Inyo County, California: Am. Mineralogist, vol. 21, pp. 69–70, 1936.
5. Adamite from Chloride Cliff, California: Am. Mineralogist, vol. 21, pp. 811–813, 1936.
6. (and **Webb, Robert Wallace**) Notes on some minerals from southern California: Am. Mineralogist, vol. 23, pp. 349–355, 1938.
7. Crystallography of veatchite: Am. Mineralogist, vol. 24, pp. 130–135, 1939.
8. Some garnet crystals from California: Jour. Geology, vol. 47, pp. 189–197, 1939.

9. Miargyrite crystals from Randsburg, California: Am. Mineralogist, vol. 24, pp. 772–781, 1939.

10. The crystallography of ulexite: Am. Mineralogist, vol. 25, pp. 754–762, 1940 . . . (abstract): Am. Mineralogist, vol. 25, pp. 210–211, 1940.

11. (and **Webb, Robert Wallace**) Notes on some minerals from southern California, II: Am. Mineralogist, vol. 25, pp. 549–555, 1940.

12. Pyrostilpnite from Randsburg, California: Am. Mineralogist, vol. 26, pp. 130–132, 1941.

13. Valentinite crystals from California: Am. Mineralogist, vol. 26, pp. 613–616, 1941.

14. (and **Webb, Robert Wallace**) Notes on some minerals from southern California, III: Am. Mineralogist, vol. 27, pp. 323–330, 1942.

15. Crystallographic notes, cristobalite, stephanite, natrolite: Am. Mineralogist, vol. 27, pp. 500–506, 1942.

16. Crystallography of hureaulite: Am. Mineralogist, vol. 28, pp. 19–24, 1943 . . . (abstract): Am. Mineralogist, vol. 27, p. 228, 1942.

17. Probertite from Los Angeles County, California: Am. Mineralogist, vol. 30, pp. 719–721, 1945.

18. Progress on revision of Bulletin 113 "Minerals of California," with notes on some new mineral occurrences: California Div. Mines Rept. 42, pp. 197–198, 1946. . . . (abstract): Geol. Soc. America Bull. 57, p. 1256, 1946.

19. Nuevite, a new rare-earth mineral from California (abstract): Geol. Soc. America Bull. 57, p. 1219, 1946.

20. (and **Fahey, Joseph John**) Geikielite, a new find from California (abstract): Geol. Soc. America Bull. 59, pp. 1341–1342, 1948.

21. (and **Webb, Robert Wallace**) Minerals of California: California Div. Mines Bull. 136, 402 pp., 1948.

22. Minerals of California: supplement No. 1 to Bulletin 136: California Jour. Mines and Geology, vol. 45, pp. 521–540, 1949.

23. (and **Fahey, Joseph John**) Geikielite, a new find from California: Am. Mineralogist, vol. 34, pp. 835–838, 1949.

24. Unit cell of hydromagnesite: (abstract) Geol. Soc. America Bull., vol. 62, p. 1465, 1951.

25. Perovskite from California: (abstract) Geol. Soc. America Bull., vol. 60, p. 1911, 1949. . . . (abstract) Am. Mineralogist, vol. 35, p. 287, 1950. . . . Am. Mineralogist, vol. 36, pp. 573–580, 1951.

26. Notes on California minerals: nuevite = samarskite; trona, and hanksite; gaylussite: Am. Mineralogist, vol. 36, pp. 358–361, 1951.

27. (and **Webb, Robert Wallace**) Minerals of California, 1952 supplement to Bulletin 136: California Div. Mines, 46 pp., 1952.

28. Nasonite from Crestmore, California: (abstract) Geol. Soc. America Bull., vol. 63, p. 1341, 1952.

29. The unit cell of hydromagnesite: (abstract) Am. Mineralogist, vol. 37, pp. 296–297 . . . Am. Mineralogist, vol. 39, pp. 24–29, 1954.

30. Scawtite and bultfonteinite from Crestmore, California: (abstract) Geol. Soc. America Bull., vol. 65, pp. 1347–1348, 1954.

30a. (and **Webb, Robert Wallace**) Minerals in southern California: California Div. Mines and Geol. Bull. 170, Ch. VII, pp. 5–12, 1954.

31. Scawtite from Crestmore, California: Am. Mineralogist, vol. 40, pp. 505–509, 1955.

32. Bultfonteinite from Crestmore, California: Am. Mineralogist, vol. 40, pp. 900–906, 1955.

33. Crystallography and X-ray measurements of howlite from California: Am. Mineralogist, vol. 42, pp. 521–524, 1957.

34. (and **McConnell, Duncan**) Crystal chemistry of scawtite: Am. Mineralogist, vol. 43, pp. 498–502, 1958.

35. See McBurney, Thomas Chester (1).

36. (and **Chalmers, Robert A.**) Woodfordite a new mineral from Crestmore, California: (abstract) Geol. Soc. America Bull., vol. 69, pp. 1620–1621, 1958.

37. (and **Chalmers, Robert A.**) Ettringite ("woodfordite") from Crestmore, California: Am. Mineralogist, vol. 45, pp. 1275–1278, 1960.

38. Crestmore, past and present: Am. Mineralogist, vol. 46, pp. 245–257, 1961.

39. (and **Webb, Robert Wallace**) Minerals of California: California Div. Mines Bull. 173, 452 pp., 1956.

40. (and **Webb, Robert Wallace**) Supplement to minerals of California for 1955 through 1957, with index to minerals of California arranged by counties, prepared by Elizabeth Collins, California Div. Mines, 64 pp., 1960.
41. Wightmanite, a new borate mineral from Crestmore, California: Am. Mineralogist, vol. 47, pp. 718–722, 1962.
42. Bakerite crystals: Am. Mineralogist, vol. 47, pp. 919–923, 1962.
43. See McConnell, Duncan (5).
44. (and **Webb, Robert Wallace**) Supplement 2 to Minerals of California for 1958 through 1961, California Div. Mines and Geol., 28 pp., 1964.

Murgoci, G. M.
1. Contribution to the classification of the amphiboles; on some glaucophane schists, syenites, etc.: Univ. California, Dept. Geol. Sci. Bull., vol. 4, pp. 359–396, 1906.

Murphy, Franklin Mac
1. Dumortierite in Riverside County: Am. Mineralogist, vol. 15, pp. 79–80, 1930 . . . Mineralog. Abstracts, vol. 4, p. 331, 1930.
2. Geology of the Panamint silver district, California: Econ. Geology, vol. 25, pp. 305–325, 1930 . . . (abstract): Rev. geologie et sci. connexes, tome 11, p. 438, 1930 . . . Geol. Soc. America Bull., vol. 41, p. 152, 1930 . . . Pan-Am. Geologist, vol. 51, pp. 370–371, 1929 . . . Mineralog. Abstracts, vol. 51, pp. 370–371, 1929 . . . Geol. Zentralbl., Band 43, pp. 407–408, 1931 . . . Zeitschr. prakt. Geologie, Band 39, p. 48, 1931.
3. Geology and ore deposits of a part of the Panamint Range, Inyo County, California (abstract): Geol. Soc. America Bull., vol. 41, p. 152, 1930 . . . Pan-Am. Geologist, vol. 51, pp. 370–371, 1929 . . . Neues Jahrb., 1931, Referate 2, p. 447.
4. Geology of a part of the Panamint Range, California: California Min. Bur. Rept. 28, pp. 329–356, 1932.

Muter, A. F.
1. Placer scheelite: Min. Cong. Jour., vol. 30, no. 8, pp. 36–37, 46, 1944.

Myers, Alfred Tennyson
1. See Ross, Clarence Samuel (3).

Myers, T. R.
1. Green lazulite from Stoddard, New Hampshire: Am. Mineralogist, vol. 33, pp. 366–368, 1948.

Myers, W. Bradley
1. See Bailey, Edgar Herbert (4).
2. See Eckel, Edwin Butt (2).
3. (and **Everhart, Donald Lough**) Quicksilver deposits of the Guerneville district, Sonoma County, California: California Div. Mines Rept. 44, pp. 255–277, 1948.

N

Nash, Douglas B.
1. Metamorphism along a composite granitic-sedimentary contact zone at Birch Creek, Deep Spring Valley, California (abst.): Geol. Soc. America, Cordilleran Section Meeting, Program, Berkeley, p. 48, April 1963; Geol. Soc. America Spec. Paper 76, p. 216, 1964.
2. (and **Nelson, Clemens Arvid**) Leucite-bearing volcanic plugs, Deep Spring Valley, California (abst.): Geol. Soc. America, Cordilleran Section Meeting, Program, p. 47, March 1964.

Nelson, A. G.
1. Geology of the northwest part of Soledad Mountain, Kern County, California: Unpublished M.S. Thesis, University of Southern California, 1940.

Nelson, Clemens Arvid
1. See Nash, Douglas B. (2).

Nelson, Frank
1. Crystals at the H. and M. Ranch: Gems and Minerals, no. 248, p. 40, May 1958.

Neuerberg, George Joseph
1. Minerals of the eastern Santa Monica Mountains, Los Angeles city: Am. Mineralogist, vol. 36, pp. 156–160, 1951.

2. Allanite pegmatite, San Gabriel Mountains, Los Angeles County, California: Am. Mineralogist, vol. 39, pp. 831–834, 1954.

Neuvonen, Kalle J.
1. See Kracek, Frank Charles (1).
2. Heat of' formation of merwinite and monticellite: Am. Jour. Sci., Bowen volume, pp. 373–380, 1952.

Nevius, J. Nelson
1. Notes on the Randsburg tungsten district, California: Min. World, vol 45, no. 1, pp. 7–8, 1916.

Newberry, John Strong
1. On the occurrence of chromic iron and serpentine in California: Lyceum Nat. Hist. New York Proc., vol. 2, no. 3, p. 66, 1874.
2. Genesis and distribution of gold: Columbia Univ., School of Mines Quart., vol. 3, pp. 5–15, 1881.

Newhouse, Walter Harry
1. (and **Flaherty, G. F.**) The texture and origin of some banded or schistose sulphide ores: Econ. Geology, vol. 25, pp. 600–620, 1930.
2. (and **Glass, J. P.**) Some physical properties of certain iron oxides: Econ. Geology, vol. 31, pp. 699–711, 1936.

Newman, M. A.
1. Nonmetallic minerals of southern California: California Min. Bur. Rept. 18, pp. 13–14, 230–234, 1922 . . . (abstract): Geol. Zentralbl., Band 29, p. 425, 1923.

Newsom, John Flesher
1. See Branner, John Casper (1).

Nicholas, Francis Child
1. Recent developments at Furnace Creek copper mines: Min. World, vol. 27, pp. 1087–1088, 1907 . . . (abstract): Eng. Index, 1908, p. 308, 1909.

Nichols, J. B.
1. Collecting minerals in Alpine County, California: The Mineralogist, vol. 14, pp. 171–175, 1946.
2. Collecting minerals in northern California: Mineral Notes and News, no. 152, pp. 8–9, May, 1950.

Nickles, John Milton
1. Geologic literature on North America, 1785–1918, pt. 1, bibliography: U. S. Geol. Survey Bull. 746, 1167 pp., 1923.
2. Bibliography of North American geology, 1919–1928: U. S. Geol. Survey Bull. 823, 1005 pp., 1931.

Nicol, B. A.
1. Practical mineralogy in the schools; and minerals of Mint Canyon, California: Pacific Mineralogist, vol. 9, no. 2, pp. 5–7, 19–20, 1941.

Nininger, Harvey Harlow
1. Our stone pelted planet, xxv, 235 pp., Boston, 1933.
2. (and **Cleminshaw, Clarence Higbee**) Some new California aerolites, Muroc and Muroc Dry Lake: Soc. Research on Meteorites, Contr., vol. 1, no. 3, pp. 24–25, 1937 . . . Popular Astron., vol. 45, pp. 273–275, 1937.

Nisson, William H.
1. (and **Switzer, George S.**) Skiing for specimens: Mineralogist, vol. 3, no. 2, p. 20, 1935.

Noble, Levi Fatzinger
1. (**Mansfield, George Rogers,** and others) Nitrate deposits in the Amargosa region, southeastern California: U. S. Geol. Survey Bull. 724, 99 pp., 1922.
2. Borate deposits in the Kramer district, Kern County, California: U. S. Geol. Survey Bull. 785, pp. 45–61, 1926 . . . (abstract): Geol. Zentralbl., Band 37, p. 185, 1928 . . . Rev. geologie et sci. connexes, tome 8, p. 78, 1927.
3. Note on a colemanite deposit near Shoshone, California, with a sketch of the geology of a part of Amargosa Valley: U. S. Geol. Survey Bull. 785, pp. 63, 73, 1926 . . . (abstract): Geol. Zentralbl., Band 37, p. 129, 1928 . . . Rev. geologie et sci. connexes, tome 8, pp. 78–79, 1927.
4. Nitrate deposits in southeastern California, with notes on deposits in southeastern Arizona and southwestern New Mexico: U. S. Geol. Survey Bull. 820, 108 pp., 1931.

Nockolds, Stephen Robert
1. On tilleyite and its associated minerals from Carlingford, Ireland: Mineralog. Mag., vol. 28, pp. 151–158, 1947.

Nolan, Thomas Brennan
1. Mother Lode district, in Ore deposits of the western States: Am. Inst. Min. Met. Eng., Lindgren vol., p. 579, 1933.
2. Epithermal precious-metal deposits, in Ore deposits of the western States: Am. Inst. Min. Met. Eng., Lindgren vol., pp. 623–641, 1933.
3. Geological Survey Research 1963, Summary of investigations: U. S. Geol. Survey Prof. Paper 475A, 300 pp., 1964.

Norman, Lewis Arthur, Jr.
1. See Hoppin, Richard Arthur (1).
2. (and **Stewart, Richard Maclin**) Mines and mineral resources of Inyo County, California: California Jour. Mines and Geology, vol. 47, pp. 18–223, 1951.
3. See Wright, Lauren Albert (9).

Norris, Robert Matheson
1. See Leonard, Frederick Charles (3).
2. See Woodhouse, Charles Douglas (6).
3. See Woodhouse, Charles Douglas (7).
4. (and **Woodhouse, Charles Douglas**) Minerals from the beach at Santa Barbara: Gems and Minerals, no. 279, pp. 21, 54–55, December, 1960.
5. See Vedder, John Graham (1).

Nutter, Edward Hoit
1. (and **Barber, William Burton**) On some glaucophane and associated schists in the Coast Ranges of California: Jour. Geology, vol. 10, pp. 738–744, 1902.

O

Oakeshott, Gordon Blaisdell
1. Geology and mineral deposits of the western San Gabriel Mountains, Los Angeles County, California: California Div. Mines, Rept. 33, pp. 215–249, 1937.
2. Titaniferous iron-ore deposits of the western San Gabriel Mountains, Los Angeles County, California: California Div. Mines Bull. 129, pp. 243–266, 1948.
3. Titano-magnetite rocks of the western San Gabriel Mountains, California: (abstract) Geol. Soc. America Bull., vol. 60, pp. 1942–43, 1949.
4. See Sampson, R. G. (23) and Tucker, W. B. (37).
5. Guide to the geology of Pfeiffer Big Sur state park, Monterey County, California: California Div. Mines, Special Rept. 11, 16 pp., 1951.
6. (and **staff**) Fifty-fifth annual report of the State Mineralogist. California Div. of Mines and Geology, 244 pp., 1959.

O'Brien, Charles John
1. Geology of the district west of Redding, California: Min. Sci. Press, vol. 86, p. 349, 1903 . . . (abstract): Geol. Zentralbl., Band 9, p. 640, 1907.

O'Brien, J. C.
1. Current notes on activity in the strategic minerals, Redding field district: California Div. Mines. Rept. 39, pp. 77–84, 1943.
2. Clerbus-Mae tungsten prospect, Trinity County: California Div. Mines. Rept. 39, p. 142, 1943.
3. Mines and mining in Tehama County, California: California Div. Mines Rept. 42, pp. 183–195, 1946.
4. Mines and mineral resources of Siskiyou County: California Div. Mines Rept. 43, pp. 413–468, 1947.
5. Current and recent mining activities in the Redding district: California Div. Mines Rept. 44, pp. 336–378, 1948.
6. Mines and mineral resources of Butte County, California: California Jour. Mines and Geology, vol. 45, pp. 417–454, 1949.
7. (and **Braun, Lewis Timothy**) Mines and mineral resources of Glenn County, California: California Jour. Mines and Geology, vol. 48, pp. 29–45, 1952.
8. Mines and mineral resources of Yuba County, California: California Jour. Mines and Geology, vol. 48, pp. 143–179, 1952.
9. Mines and minerals of Del Norte County, California: California Jour. Mines and Geology, vol. 48, pp. 261–309, 1952.
10. Mines and mineral resources of Mendocino County, California: California Jour. Mines and Geology, vol. 49, pp. 347–398, 1953.

Ochsenius, Carl
1. Natronsaltpeter in California: Zeitschr. prakt. Geologie, Jahrg. 10, pp. 337–339, 1902.

Ogle, Burdette Adrian
1. Geology of Eel River Valley Area, Humboldt County, California: California Div. Mines Bull. 164, 128 pp., 1953.

Olson, Jerry Chipman
1. (and **Sharp, William N.**) Geologic setting of the Mountain Pass bastnaesite deposits, San Bernardino County, California: (abstract) Geol. Soc. America Bull., vol. 62, p. 1467, 1951.
2. Preliminary report to accompany the geologic map of the Mountain Pass district, San Bernardino County, California: U. S. Geol. Survey, open file report, 1952.
3. (**Shawe, Daniel Reeves, Pray, Lloyd Charles,** and **Sharp, William N.**) Rare-earth mineral deposits of the Mountain Pass district, San Bernardino County, California: U. S. Geol. Survey Prof. Paper 261, 75 pp., 1954.
4. (and **Pray, Lloyd Charles**) The Mountain Pass rare earth deposit: California Div. Mines and Geol. Bull. 170, ch. VIII, pp. 23–30, 1954.

Orcutt, Charles Russell
1. Minerals and mines of San Diego County, California: West Am. Sci., vol. 3, pp. 69–72, 1887.
2. The Colorado Desert: California Div. Mines Rept. 10, pp. 899–919, 1890.
3. Note on the occurrence of tourmaline in California (abstract): Am. Assoc. Advancement Sci. Proc., vol. 47, p. 306, 1898 . . . Am. Geologist, vol. 22, p. 265, 1898 . . . Science, new ser., vol. 8, p. 505, 1898.
4. Minerals: West Am. Sci., vol. 12, no. 102, pp. 15–26, 1901.
5. Mohave Desert iron mines: West Am. Sci., vol. 12, no. 105, pp. 73–74 . . . no. 106, pp. 91–92, 1901.
6. Tourmaline: West Am. Sci., vol. 12, no. 108, pp. 113–115, 1901.

Oriti, Ronald A.
1. See Hartman, Ronald M. (1).

Osborne, H. Z.
1. The Dorleska gold mine: Min. Sci. Press, vol. 87, p. 252, 1903.

Ostwald, Joseph
1. Some notes on the mineralogy of lapis lazuli: Jour. Gemology, vol. 9, pp. 84–101, 1963.

Outerbridge, William F.
1. (**Staatz, Mortimer Hay, Meyrowitz, Robert,** and **Pommer, Alfred Michael**) Weeksite, a new uranium silicate from the Thomas Range, Juab County, Utah: Am. Mineralogist, vol. 45, pp. 39–52, 1960.

Owen, David Dale
1. Notice of a new mineral from California: Acad. Nat. Sci. Philadelphia Proc., vol. 6, pp. 108–109, 1852.

Owens, George W.
1. An interesting quartz crystal location: Rocks and Minerals, vol. 30, nos. 11–12, pp. 578–579, 1955.

P

Pabst, Adolf
1. The garnets in the glaucophane schists of California: Am. Mineralogist, vol. 16, pp. 327–333, 1931.
2. Vesuvianite from Georgetown, California: Am. Mineralogist, vol. 21, pp. 1–10, 1936.
3. The crystal structure of plazolite: Am. Mineralogist, vol. 22, pp. 861–868, 1937.
4. Minerals of California: California Div. Mines Bull. 113, 344 pp., 1938.
5. The relation of stellerite and epidesmine to stilbite: Mineralog. Mag., vol. 25, pp. 271–276, 1939 . . . (abstract): Am. Mineralogist, vol. 24, p. 63, 1939.
6. Cryptocrystalline pyrite from Alpine County, California: Am. Mineralogist, vol. 25, pp. 425–431, 1940.
7. The unit cell and space group of gillespite: Am. Mineralogist, vol. 28, pp. 372–390, 1942 . . . (abstract): Am. Mineralogist, vol. 26, p. 199, 1941.

8. The mineralogy of metamorphosed serpentine at Humphreys, Fresno County, California: Am. Mineralogist, vol. 27, pp. 570–585, 1942.

9. Some computations on svanbergite, woodhouseite and alunite: Am. Mineralogist, vol. 31, pp. 16–30, 1947.

10. (and **Sawyer, Dwight Lewis, Jr.**) Tincalconite crystals from Searles Lake, San Bernardino County, California: Am. Mineralogist, vol. 33, pp. 472–481, 1948.

11. Minerals of the serpentine area in San Benito County, California: Rocks and Minerals, vol. 26, pp. 478–485, 1951.

11a. A new locality for creedite: Rocks and Minerals, vol. 27, p. 19, 1952.

12. Manganese content of garnets in the Franciscan schists (abstract): Geol. Soc. America Bull., vol. 65, p. 1292, 1954 . . . (abstract): Mineralog. Soc. America, 35th ann. meeting, Nov. 1954, p. 28.

13. Brannerite from California, Am. Mineralogist, vol. 39, pp. 109–117, 1954.

14. Manganese content of garnets from the Franciscan schists: Am. Mineralogist, vol. 40, pp. 919–923, 1955.

15. (**Sawyer, Dwight Lewis, Jr.**, and **Switzer, George S.**) Galeite, a new mineral from Searles Lake, California (abst.): Geol. Soc. America, vol. 66, p. 1658, 1955.

16. The structure of leached gillespite: Am. Mineralogist, vol. 43, pp. 970–980, 1958.

17. (and **Thomssen, Richard Wyatt**) Davidite from the Quijotoa Mountains, Pima County, Arizona (abst.): Geol. Soc. America Bull., vol. 70, p. 1739, 1959.

18. (and **Stinson, Melvin Clarence**) Brannerite with gold from Plumas County, California, (abst.) Geol. Soc. America Bull., vol. 71, p. 2071, 1960.

19. See Davis, Gregory A. (1).

20. X-ray crystallography of davidite: Am. Mineralogist, vol. 46, pp. 700–718, 1961.

21. (**Sawyer, Dwight Lewis, Jr.**, and **Switzer, George S.**) Galeite and related phases in the system $Na_2SO_4 \cdot NaF \cdot NaCl$: Am. Mineralogist, vol. 48, pp. 485–510, 1963.

22. See, Alfors, John Theodore (1).

Pack, Robert Wallace
1. Ornamental marble near Barstow, California: U. S. Geol. Survey Bull. 540, pp. 363–368, 1914.

2. Reconnaissance of the Barstow-Kramer region, California: U. S. Geol. Survey Bull. 541, pp. 141–154, 1914.

Page, Benjamin Markham
1. Talc deposits of steatite grade, Inyo County, California: California Div. Mines, Special Rept. 8, 35 pp., 1951.

Page, Lincoln Ridler
1. See Wells, Francis Gerritt (1).

2. See Wiese, John Herbert (1).

3. Contact metamorphic deposits of cassiterite in California: (abstract) Geol. Soc. America Bull. 56, p. 1187, 1945 . . . : (abstract) Am. Mineralogist, vol. 31, p. 202, 1946.

Pagliuchi, F. D.
1. The mineral resources of the Johnsville district in Plumas County, California: Pacific Min. News, vol. 2, pp. 1–5, 1923.

Palache, Charles
1. The soda rhyolite north of Berkeley, California: Univ. California, Dept. Geol. Sci. Bull., vol. 1, pp. 61–72, 1893.

2. The lherzolite serpentine and associated rocks of the Potrero, San Francisco: Univ. California, Dept. Geol. Sci. Bull., vol. 1, pp. 161–179, 1894.

3. On a rock from the vicinity of Berkeley containing a new soda amphibole: Univ. California, Dept. Geol. Sci. Bull., vol. 1, pp. 181–192, 1894.

4. See Ransome, Frederick Leslie (4).

5. See Lawson, Andrew Cowper (4).

6. Note on a crystal form of benitoite: Am. Jour. Sci., 4th ser., vol. 27, p. 398, 1909 . . . (abstract): Zeitschr. Kristallographie, Band 46, p. 379, 1909.

7. (and **Foshag, William Frederick**) The chemical nature of joaquinite: Am. Mineralogist, vol. 17, pp. 308–312, 1932.

8. Contributions to crystallography; claudetite, minasragrite, samsonite, native selenium, indium: Am. Mineralogist, vol. 19, pp. 194–205, 1934 . . . (abstract): Am. Mineralogist, vol. 19, p. 128, 1934.

9. Crystallography of meyerhofferite: Am. Mineralogist, vol. 23, pp. 644–648, 1938.
10. (**Berman, Harry,** and **Frondel, Clifford**) A system of mineralogy, 7th ed., vol. 1, 834 pp., New York, John Wiley & Sons, 1944.
11. (**Berman, Harry** and **Frondel, Clifford**) A system of mineralogy, 7th ed., vol. 2, 1124 pp., New York, John Wiley and Sons, 1951.
12. See Goldschmidt, Victor (1).

Palmer, Allison Ralph
1. Miocene arthropods from the Mojave Desert, California: U. S. Geol. Survey Prof. Paper 294G, pp. 237–280, 1957.

Palmer, D. F.
1. Second Ann. Rept. San Diego County Dept. Agriculture, Div. Nat. Res., vol 2, no. 2, 1946.

Palmer, Leroy A.
1. Ore occurrence at the Cloverdale mine, Sonoma County, California: Min. Sci. Press, vol. 108, p. 812, 1914.
2. A sedimentary magnesite deposit, Bissell, California: Eng. and Min. Jour., vol. 102, pp. 965–967, 1916.
3. The Calico district, California: Min. Sci. Press, vol. 116, pp. 755–758, 1918 . . . (abstract): Eng. Index, 1918, p. 326, 1919.
4. The eastern portion of the Mohave Desert, a region of diversified mineral possibilities: Pacific Min. News, vol. 1, pp. 234–235, 1922.
5. Magnesite mining in California: Min. Cong. Jour., vol. 13, pp. 180–184, 1927 . . . Am. Inst. Min. Met. Eng. Trans. (reprint, 1629-H), pp. 743–756, 1927 . . . (abstract): Mining and Metallurgy, vol. 8, p. 86, 1927 . . . Mineralog. Mag., vol. 36, pp. 250–251, 1927.
6. Kernite or rasorite?: Eng. and Min. Jour., vol. 123, p. 494, 1927 . . . vol. 125, pp. 207–208, 1928.

Palmer, Lyman L.
1. History of Napa and Lake Counties, 291 pp., San Francisco, Slocum, Bowen and Co., 1881.

Pampeyan, Earl Haig
1. Geology and mineral deposits of Mount Diablo, Contra Costa County, California: Calif. Div. Mines and Geol., Spec. Rept. 80, 31 pp., 1963.

Papish, Jacob
1. (and **Holt, Donald Aubrey**) Gallium; I. Arc spectographic detection of gallium; II. Extraction of gallium from lepidolite: Jour. Physical Chemistry, vol. 32, pp. 142–147, 1928.
2. New occurrences of germanium; II. The occurrence of germanium in silicate minerals; Econ. Geology, vol. 24, pp. 470–480, 1929.

Parsons, A. B.
1. The California Rand silver mine: Min. Sci. Press, vol. 123, pp. 667–675, 855–859, 1921 . . . vol. 124, pp. 11–17, 1922.

Partridge, John F., Jr.
1. Tungsten resources of California: California Div. Mines Rept. 37, pp. 225–326, 1941.

Pask, Joseph Adam
1. (and **Turner, Mortimer Darling**) Clays and clay technology: California Div. Mines Bull. 169, 326 pp., 1955. (Especially part 1, Geology and mineralogy of clays, containing papers by Kerr, Paul F., "Formation and occurrence of clay minerals," pp. 19–32, and Brindley, George W., "Structural mineralogy of clays," pp. 33–43).

Patchick, Paul F.
1. Mineral collecting at Crestmore, California: Rocks and Minerals, vol. 27, pp. 130–135, 1952.
2. A remarkable occurrence of allanite and zircon crystals from a southern California pegmatite: Rocks and Minerals, vol. 30, no. 5–6, pp. 237–246, 1955.
3. A rare-earth pegmatite near Nuevo, California: Rocks and Minerals, vol. 35, pp. 323–327, 1960.

Patterson, L. B.
1. Twelve years in the mines of California, 108 pp., Cambridge, Massachusetts, 1862.

Patterson, R. M.
1. Ueber die Beschaffenheit und das Vorkommen des Goldes, Platins und der Diamanten in den Vereinigten Staaten : Deutsche geol. Gesell. Zeitschr., Band 2, pp. 60–64, 1850.

Patton, J. W.
1. Gems in California : Rocks and Minerals, vol. 9, pp. 116–117, 1934.
2. The Mint Canyon agate beds in California : Rocks and Minerals, vol. 11, pp. 156–159, 1936.

Patton, William
1. Geology of a portion of Calaveras County ; California Surveyor General, Ann. Rept. 1854 : California Legislature, 6th sess., A. Jour. ap. F, pp. 86–88, 1855.

Paul, Jan S.
1. Mt. Breckinridge rose quartz : Gems and Minerals, no. 268, pp. 26–27, January 1960.

Payne, Max B.
1. Type Moreno formation and overlying Eocene strata on the west side of the San Joaquin Valley, Fresno and Merced Counties, California : California Div. Mines, Special Rept. 9, 29 pp., 1951.

Peacock, Martin Alfred
1. (and **Moddle, D. A.**) On a crystal of augelite from California : Mineralog. Mag., vol. 26, pp. 105–115, 1941.
2. See Goldschmidt, Victor (1).
3. On wollastonite and parawollastonite : Am. Jour. Sci. 5th ser., vol. 30, pp. 495–529, 1935.

Peck, Albert B.
1. Note on andalusite from California ; a new use and some thermal properties : Am. Mineralogist, vol. 9, pp. 123–129, 1924 . . . California Min. Bur. Rept. 20, pp. 149–154, 1924 . . . Mineralog. Abstracts, vol. 3, p. 51, 1926.

Pecora, William Thomas
1. (and **Fahey, Joseph John**) The lazulite-scorzalite isomorphous series : Am. Mineralogist, vol. 35, pp. 1–18, 1950.

Peikert, E. W.
1. Three-dimensional mineralogical variation in the Glen Alpine stock, Sierra Nevada, California (abst.) : Geol. Soc. America Program, Houston Meeting, p. 114A, 1962.

Pemberton, H.
1. Chromite : Chem. News, vol. 63, p. 241, 1891.

Pemberton, H. Earl (Editor)
1. (**Moller, William, Schwartz, Jack,** and **Masimer, George**) The minerals of Boron, California : 40 pp., 1960. (Published by the Mineral Research Society of California, Box 106, Montebello, California).
2. Minerals new to California : The Mineralogist, vol. 32, p. 16, Aug. 1964.
3. Place names in the Turquois Mountains : The Mineralogist, vol. 32, pp. 10–13, Oct. 1964.

Penfield, Samuel Lewis
1. Crystallized tiemannite and metacinnabarite : Am. Jour. Sci., 3d ser., vol. 29, pp. 449–454, 1885 . . . Yale Univ., Bicen. Pub., Contr. Mineralogy, pp. 130–133, 1901.
2. See Dana, Edward Salisbury (2).
3. See Genth, Frederick Augustus (10).
4. Notes on the crystallography of metacinnabarite : Am. Jour. Sci., 3d ser., vol. 44, p. 383, 1892.
5. On the chemical composition of sulphohalite : Am. Jour. Sci., 4th ser., vol. 9, pp. 425–428, 1900.

6. (and **Ford, William Ebenezer**) Ueber den Calaverit: Zeitschr. Kristallographie, Band 35, pp. 430–451, 1902.

7. (and **Jamieson, George S.**) On tychite, a new mineral from Borax Lake, California, and on its artificial production and its relations to northupite: Am. Jour. Sci., 4th ser., vol. 20, pp. 217–224, 1905 . . . Zeitschr. Kristallographie, Band 41, pp. 235–242, 1905.

8. (and **Ford, William Ebenezer**) On stibiotantalite: Am. Jour. Sci., 4th ser., vol. 22, pp. 61–77, 1906 . . . Zeitschr. Kristallographie, Band 43, pp. 334–350, 1906.

Pennington, K. S.

1. See Petch, Howard Earl (1).

Perloff, A.

1. See Clark, Joan Robinson.

Perry, Joseph B.

1. (and **Kirivan, G. M.**) Bald Eagle magnesite mine: Am. Inst. Min. Met. Eng., Tech. Pub. 861, pp. 1–15, 1938.

Petar, Alice V.

1. Beryllium and beryl: California Min. Bur. Rept. 27, pp. 83–97, 1931.

Petch, Howard Earl

1. (**Pennington, K. S.,** and **Cuthbert, J. D.**) On Christ's postulated boron-oxygen polyions in some hydrated borates of unknown crystal structures: Am. Mineralogist, vol. 47, pp. 401–404, 1962.

Petersen, Melvin N. A.

1. (**Bien, George Sung-Nien,** and **Berner, Robert A.**) Radiocarbon studies of recent dolomite from Deep Spring Lake, California: Jour. Geophysical Research, vol. 68, pp. 6493–6505, 1963.

Peterson, E. C.

1. See Davis, D. L. (1).

Petrascheck, W.

1. Die Magnesit von Kalifornien und Nevada: Montan. Rundschau, Wien, Band 12, pp. 344–345, 1920.

Petrov, V. P.

1. See Belyankin, D. S. (1).

Phalen, William Clifton

1. Prospecting for chromium ore: Min. Sci. Press, vol. 105, pp. 400–401, 1912.

2. Potash salts; summary for 1912: Mineral Resources U. S., 1912, pt. 2, pp. 877–908, 1913.

3. Celestite deposits in California and Arizona: U. S. Geol. Survey Bull. 540, pp. 521–533, 1914.

Phillips, John Arthur

1. Notes on the chemical geology of the gold fields of California: Philos. Mag., 4th ser., vol. 36, pp. 321–336, 422–433, 1868 . . . (abstract): Royal Soc. London Proc., vol. 16, pp. 294–299, 1868 . . . Am. Jour. Sci., 2d ser., vol. 47, pp. 134–139, 1869.

2. On the connexion of certain phenomena with the origin of mineral veins: Philos. Mag., 4th ser., vol. 42, pp. 401–413, 1871.

3. Note on the silicified woods of California: Geol. Mag., vol. 10, pp. 98–99, 1873.

4. The alkaline and boracic lakes of California: Living Age, vol. 133, pp. 632–638, 1877 . . . Popular Sci. Rev., new ser., vol. 16, pp. 153–163, 1877 . . . Western Rev. Sci. and Ind., vol. 1, pp. 225–235, 1887 . . . (abstract): Geol Rec., 1877, p. 272, 1880.

5. A contribution to the history of mineral veins: Geol. Soc. London Quart. Jour., vol. 35, pp. 390–395, 1879.

Phillips, R.

1. See Stuart, F. H. (1).

Phillips, William

1. Lectures on mineralogy, London, 1818.

Pogue, Joseph Ezekiel

1. The turquoise: Nat. Acad. Sci. Mem. 12, pt. 2, no. 3, 162 pp., 1915.

2. The aboriginal use of turquois in North America: Amer. Anthropologist, n.s., vol. 14, pp. 437–456, 1912.

Pommer, Alfred Michael

1. See Outerbridge, William F. (1).

Pošepný, Franz
1. Geologisches aus dem Hochlande im western Nordamerikas: K. geol. Reich-sanstalt, verh. 1877, pp. 61–66.

Posnjak, Eugen
1. See Bramlette, Milton Nunn (1).
2. See Sosman, Robert Browning (1).

Pough, Frederick Harvey
1. Crystallographic notes on powellite and augelite (abstract): Am. Mineralogist, vol. 21, p. 536, 1936.
2. See Frondel, Clifford (5).

Powell, Kenneth B.
1. How Eagle Mountain helps Kaiser supply growing steel needs: Min. Eng., vol. 5, pp. 478–483, 1953.

Powers, Howard Adorno
1. The lavas of the Modoc Lava Bed quadrangle, California: Am. Mineralogist, vol. 17, pp. 253–294, 1932.

Pratt, Joseph Hyde
1. On northupite; pirssonite, a new mineral; gaylussite and hanksite from Borax Lake, San Bernardino County, California: Am. Jour. Sci., 4th ser., vol. 2, pp. 123–135, 1896 . . . Zeitschr. Kristallographie, Band 27, pp. 416–429, 1896 . . . Yale Univ., Bicen. Pub., Contr. Mineralogy, pp. 261–274, 1901 . . . (abstract): Neues Jahrb., Band 2, pp. 451–455, 1897.
2. The occurrence and distribution of corundum in the United States: U. S. Geol. Survey Bull. 180, 98 pp., 1901.
3. Roscoelite: Mineral Resources U. S., 1900, pp. 257–265, 1901.
4. Tungsten, molybdenum, uranium and vanadium: Mineral Resources U. S., 1901, pp. 261–270, 1902.
5. Lithium: Mineral Resources U. S., 1903, pp. 313–315, 1904.
6. Corundum and its occurrence and distribution in the United States: U. S. Geol. Survey Bull. 269, 175 pp., 1906.

Pratt, Walden Penfield
1. See Smith, George Irving (2).

Pratt, Willis L.
1. Glauconite from the sea floor of central and southern California (abst.): Geol. Soc. America Spec. Paper 73, p. 58, 1963.

Pray, Lloyd Charles
1. (and **Sharp, William N.**) Bastnaesite discovered near Mountain Pass, California: (abstract) Geol. Soc. America Bull., vol. 62, p. 1519, 1951.
2. See Olson, Jerry Chipman (3).
3. See Olson, Jerry Chipman (4).

Prescott, Basil
1. Ilvaite from Shasta County, California: Am. Jour. Sci., 4th ser., vol. 26, pp 14–16, 1908.
2. The occurrence and genesis of the magnetite ores of Shasta County, California: Econ. Geology, vol. 3, pp. 465–480, 1908 . . . (abstract): Geol. Zentralbl., Band 12, p. 615, 1909.

Preston, E. B.
1. Los Angeles, Lassen Counties: California Min. Bur. Rept. 9, pp 189–213, 1890.
2. Tehama, Plumas, Los Angeles, Mariposa Counties: California Min. Bur. Rept. 10, pp. 272–283, 300–310, 466–495, 692–694, 1890.
3. North Fork mining district of Fresno County, California: California Min. Bur. Rept. 11, pp. 218–223, 1892.
4. Amador, Butte, Calaveras, El Dorado, Lassen, Monterey, Plumas, San Benito, Sierra, Tuolumne Counties, also Salton Lake: California Min. Bur. Rept. 11, pp. 139–178, 200–209, 241–242, 259–262, 323–333, 370–373, 387–393, 400–419, 493–513, 1893.

Prewitt, C. T.
1. (and **Burnham, Charles Wilson**) Crystal structure of jadeite, $NaAlSi_2O_6$ (abst.): Geol. Soc. American Program, Miami, Florida, Meeting, p. 156, November 1964.

Prichard, William A.

1. Observation on Mother Lode gold deposits, California (with discussion by H. W. Turner) : Am. Inst. Min. Met. Eng. Trans., vol. 34, pp. 454–466, 973–974, 1904 . . . (abstracts) : Eng. and Min. Jour., vol. 76, pp. 125–127, 1903.

Proctor, Paul Dean

1. See Durrell, Cordell (6).

2. See Bateman, Paul Charles (2).

Proctor, Richard J.

1. Engineering geology of Lake Mathews enlargement (abst.) : Geol. Soc. America Spec. Paper 68, p. 50, 1962.

Prout, John W., Jr.

1. Geology of the Big Blue group of mines, Kernville, California ; California Div. Mines Rept. 36, pp. 379–421, 1940.

Purington, C. W.

1. Copper in serpentine : Min. Sci. Press, vol. 94, pp. 719–720, 1907.

Purnell, S.

1. On ionite, a new mineral : Min. Sci. Press, vol. 34, p. 184, 1877 . . . Am. Jour. Sci., 3d ser., vol. 16, p. 153, 1878 . . . (abstract) : Geol. Rec. 1872, p. 247, 1880.

R

Ralston, William C.

1. The Greenwater copper district, California : Eng. and Min. Jour., vol. 82, pp. 1105–1106, 1906 . . . (abstract) : Eng. Index, 1907, p. 306, 1908.

Rambo, A. I.

1. See Kennard, Theodore Gladden (1).

2. See Kennard, Theodore Gladden (2).

Ramsdell, Lewis Stephen

1. An X-ray study of psilomelane and wad : Am. Mineralogist, vol. 17, pp. 143–149, 1932.

Rand, William Whitehill

1. Preliminary report of the geology of Santa Cruz Island, Santa Barbara County, California : California Min. Bur. Rept. 27, pp. 214–219, 1931 . . . (abstract) : Rev. Géologie et sci connexes, tome 13, p. 289, 1933 . . . Geol. Zentralbl., Band 46, p. 244, 1932 . . . Eng. Index, 1931, p. 655, 1931.

Randol, J. B.

1. Mines and mining—quicksilver : California Min. Bur. Rept. 10, pp. 920–929, 1890.

2. Quicksilver : U. S. Census Rept. 11, Mineral Industries in the U. S., pp. 179–245, 1892.

Randolph, Gladys C.

1. Turquoise trails : Mineralogist, vol. 2, no. 2, pp. 3–4, 20–21, 1934.

2. Santa Catalina Island : Mineralogist, vol. 3, no. 8, pp. 7–8, 1935.

Ransome, Alfred Leslie

1. (and **Kellogg, J. L.**) Quicksilver resources of California : California Div. Mines Rept. 35, pp. 353–486, 1939.

2. General geology and ores of the Blind Spring Hill mining district, Mono County, California : California Div. Mines Rept. 36, pp. 159–197, 1940.

Ransome, Frederick Leslie

1. The eruptive rocks of Point Bonita (Marin County, California) : Univ. California, Dept. Geol. Sci. Bull., vol. 1, pp. 71–114, 1893.

2. The geology of Angels Island, California : Univ. California, Dept. Geol. Sci. Bull., vol. 1, pp. 193–234, 1894.

3. On lawsonite, a new rock-forming mineral from the Tiburon Peninsula, Marin County : Univ. California, Dept. Geol. Sci. Bull., vol. 1, pp. 301–312, 1895.

4. (and **Palache, Charles**) Ueber Lawsonit ein neues gesteinsbildendes Mineral aus Californien : Zeitschr. Kristallographie, Band 25, pp. 531–537, 1896.

5. See Turner, Henry Ward (16).

7. Some lava flows of the western slope of the Sierra Nevada, California : U. S. Geol. Survey Bull. 89, 74 pp., 1898 . . . (abstract) : Am. Jour. Sci., 4th ser., vol. 5, pp. 355–375, 1898 . . . Nature, vol. 58, p. 117, 1898 . . . Neues Jahrb., 1900, Band 1, pp. 69–72.

8. See Turner, Henry Ward (18).
9. Description of the Mother Lode district, California: U. S. Geol. Survey Geol. Atlas, Mother Lode (no. 63), 11 pp., 1900.

Rath, Gerhart vom
1. See Bodewig, C. (2).
2. Ueber Colemanit (Dry Lake, southern California): Neues Jahrb., 1885, Band 1, pp. 77–78.
3. See Bodewig, C. (3).
4. See Bodewig, C. (1)
5. Ueber Glauberit und Hanksit von San Bernardino County; Niederrheinische Gesell. Sitzungsber., Band 44, p. 233, 1887.

Rau, A. E.
1. The Goldstone district: Min. and Oil Bull., June 1916.

Raymond, Charles W.
1. Meadow Lake mining district: Min. Sci. Press, vol. 84, pp. 46–48, 1902 . . . (abstract): Eng. Index, vol. 4, pp. 576, 1906.

Raymond, Louis C.
1. Small native sulphur deposits associated with gossans: Mining and Metallurgy, vol. 16, p. 414, 1935.

Raymond, Rossiter Worthington
1. The mines of the West, Report to the Secretary of the Treasury, 256 pp., New York, 1869.
2. Resources of the states and territories west of the Rocky Mountains: 40th Cong., 3d sess., H. Ex. Doc. 54, 1868.
3. Resources of the states and territories west of the Rocky Mountains: 41st Cong., 2d sess., H. Ex. Doc. 207, 256 pp., 1869.
4. Statistics of mines and mining in the states and territories west of the Rocky Mountains: 41st Cong., 2d sess., H. Ex. Doc. 10, 805 pp., 1870.
5. Statistics of mines and mining in the states and territories west of the Rocky Mountains: 42d Cong., 2d sess., H. Ex. Doc. 211, 566 pp., 1871.
6. Mines and mining in the states and territories west of the Rocky Mountains: 42d Cong., 3d sess., H. Ex. Doc. 210, 550 pp., 1872.
7. Mines and mining in the states and territories west of the Rocky Mountains: 43d Cong., 1st sess., H. Ex. Doc. 141, 585 pp., (1873) 1874.
8. Mariposa County, Hite's Cave mine: Eng. and Min. Jour., vol. 18, pp. 52–53, 1874.
9. Statistics of the mines and mining in the states and territories west of the Rocky Mountains: 43d Cong., 2d sess., H. Ex. Doc. 177, (1874) 1875.
10. Mines and mining in the states and territories west of the Rocky Mountains: 44th Cong., 1st sess., H. Ex. Doc. 159, 519 pp., 1875.

Reed, Charles H.
1. See Tucker, W. Burling (26).

Reed, Ralph Daniel
1. See Rogers, Austin Flint (28).
2. Aragonite concretions from the Kettleman Hills, California: Jour. Geology, vol. 34, pp. 829–833, 1926 . . . (abstract): Geol. Zentralbl., Band 36, p. 540, 1928 . . . Rev. géologie et sci. connexes, tome 8, p. 31, 1937.
3. Phosphate beds in the, Monterey shales (abstract): Geol. Soc. America Bull., vol. 38, pp. 195–196, 1927.
4. (and **Bailey, J. P.**) Subsurface correlation by means of heavy minerals: Am. Assoc. Petroleum Geologists Bull., vol. 11, pp. 359–372, 1927 . . . (abstract): Rev. géologie et sci. connexes, tome 8, pp. 584–585, 1927.
5. A siliceous shale formation from southern California: Jour. Geology, vol. 36, pp. 342–361, 1928 . . . (abstract): Annotated Bibliography Econ. Geology, vol. 1, p. 184, 198 . . . Geol. Zentralbl., Band 38, p. 171, 1928 . . . 39, p. 497, 1929 . . . Rev. géologie et sci. connexes, tome 9, pp. 186–187, 1928 . . . Eng. Index, 1928, p. 176, 1929 . . . Neues Jahrb., 1931, Referate 3, pp. 571–572.
6. Geology of California, Am. Assoc. Petroleum Geologists, 355 pp., 1933 . . . (review): Econ. Geology, vol. 28, pp. 697–700, 1933 . . . Inst. Petroleum Technologists Jour., vol. 19, p. 815, 1933 . . . Petroleum Times, vol. 30, p. 21, 1933 . . . Geol. Mag., vol. 71, pp. 92–93, 1934 . . . (abstract): Paleont. Zentralbl., Band 4, p. 268, 1934.

Reeds, Chester Albert
1. Catalog of meteorites: Am. Mus. Nat. History Bull. 73, Art. 6, pp. 117–672, 1937.

Reeser, D. W.
1. See Gulbrandsen, Robert Allen (1).

Reiche, Parry
1. Geology of part of the Delta-Mendota canal near Tracy, California: California Div. Mines, Special Rept. 2, 12 pp., 1950.

Reid, John A.
1. The country east of the Mother Lode (in Placer County, California): Min. Sci. Press, vol. 94, pp. 279–280, 1907.
2. Some ore deposits in the Inyo Range, California: Min. Sci. Press, vol. 95, pp. 80–82, 1907.
3. The ore deposits in Copperopolis, Calaveras County, California: Econ. Geology, vol. 2, pp. 380–417, 1907 . . . (abstract): Geol. Zentralbl., Band 11, p. 350, 1908.
4. Note on the geology of the Coso Range, Inyo County, California: Jour. Geology, vol. 16, pp. 64–72, 1908 . . . (abstract): Geol. Zentralbl., Band 12, pp. 720–721, 1909.
5. The ore deposits of Copperopolis, California: Econ. Geology, vol. 3, pp. 340–342, 1908 . . . (abstract): Geol. Zentralbl., Band 12, pp. 168–169, 1909 . . . Eng. Index, 1907, p. 306, 1908.
6. Foothill copper belt of the Sierra Nevada: Min. Sci. Press, vol. 96, pp. 388–393 . . . vol. 97, pp. 48–49, 1908 . . . (abstract): Eng. Index, 1908, p. 308, 1909.

Rice, Salem Jewell
1. Tourmalinized Franciscan sediments at Mt. Tamalpais, Marin County, California (abst.): Geol. Soc. America Bull., vol. 71, p. 2073, 1960.
2. California asbestos industry: California Div. Mines and Geol., Mineral Information Service, vol. 16, pp. 1–6, 1963.
3. A trip to the lawsonite type locality: California Div. Mines and Geol., Mineral Information Service, vol. 17, pp. 96–7, 1964.

Rich, John Lyon
1. See Harder, Edmund Cecil (4).

Richard, L. M.
1. Californian clays require special treatment to meet metallurgical demands: Pacific Min. News, vol. 1, no. 1, p. 13, 1922.
2. Pyrophyllite in San Diego County, California: Am. Ceramic Soc. Bull., vol. 14, pp. 123–129, 1930.

Richards, R. H.
1. See Day, David Talbot (6).
2. See Day, David Talbot (7).

Richardson, J. Frederick
1. The Rand mining district: Min. and Oil Bull., vol. 9, pp. 45–47, 1923.

Richmond, Gerald Martin
1. Serendibite and associated minerals from the New City Quarry, Riverside, California: Am. Mineralogist, vol. 24, 725–726, 1939.

Richmond, Wallace Everett, Jr.
1. See Fleischer, Michael (1).
2. (and Fleischer, Michael) Cryptomelane, a new name for the commonest "psilomelane" minerals: Am. Mineralogist, vol. 27, pp. 607–610, 1942.

Richthofen, Ferdinand [Baron von]
1. Reisebericht aus Californien: Deutsche geol. Gessell., Zeitschr., Band 16, pp. 331–340, 1864.
2. Ueber Californien: Deutsche geol. Gessell., Zeitschr., Band 16, pp. 606–610, 1864.
3. Die Metall-Produktion Californiens und der angrenzenden Länden: Petermanns Mitt. Erganzungsband III, Erganzung Heft 14, 58 pp., 1865.
4. Ueber das Alter der goldführenden Gänge und der von ihnen durchsetzten Gesteine: Deutsche geol. Gessell., Zeitschr., Band 21, pp. 723–740, 1869 . . . (abstract): Zeitschr. Gessell. Naturwiss. Band 35, pp. 223–226, 1870.

Rickard, Thomas Arthur
1. Certain dissimilar occurrences of gold-bearing quartz (with discussion by Philip Argall): Colorado Sci. Soc. Proc., vol. 4, pp. 323–339, 1895 (separate ed. 23 pp., 1893).
2. The formation of bonanzas in the upper portions of gold veins: Am. Inst. Min. Met. Eng. Trans., vol. 31, pp. 198–220, 1902 . . . Min. Sci. Press, vol. 83, pp. 6–7, 15, 26, 36, 1901.
3. The later Argonauts: Inst. Min. Metallurgy Trans., vol. 36, pp. 14–37, 1926.

Ricker, Spangler
1. See Sanborn, W. C. (1).
2. See Jermain, G. D. (1).
3. See Johnson, Fremont T. (1).

Ridgeway, Robert H.
1. (and **Davis, H. W.**) Molybdenum, tungsten, and vanadium: Minerals Yearbook, 1938, pp. 563–576, 1938.

Riehr
1. Goldausbringung in Californien: Deutsche geol. Gesell. Zeitschr., Band 4, pp. 722–724, 1852.

Ries, Heinrich
1. Note on the occurrence of allanite in the Yosemite Valley, California . . . (abstract): Science, new ser., vol. 11, pp. 229–230, 1900 . . . New York Acad. Sci. Annals, vol. 13, pp. 438–439, 1901.

Rinehart, Charles Dean
1. (and **Ross, Donald Clarence**) Economic geology of the Casa Diablo Mountain quadrangle, California: California Div. Mines Special Rept. 48, 17 pp., 1956.
2. (and **Ross, Donald Clarence**) Geology and mineral deposits of the Mount Morrison quadrangle, Sierra Nevada, California: U. S. Geol. Survey Prof. Paper 385, 106 pp., 1964.
3. See Bateman, Paul Charles (4).

Rising, W. B.
1. See Le Conte, Joseph (1).

Riska, Daphne
1. See Wolfe, Caleb Wroe (1).

Rivot, M.
1. Analysis of California gold: Annales des mines, tome 14, p. 67, 1849 . . . Philos. Mag., 3d ser., vol. 34, p. 394, 1849 . . . Am. Jour. Sci., 2d ser., vol. 8, p. 128, 1849.

Roberson, Charles Elmer
1. See White, Donald Edward (2).

Robertson, Jacques F.
1. See Albers, John P. (3).

Robinson, Alfred
1. Life in California, 182 pp. San Francisco, 1891.

Robinson, Gershon Duvall
1. The Leona rhyolite, Alameda County, California: Am. Mineralogist, vol. 38, pp. 1204–1217, 1953.

Robinson, Samuel
1. A catalogue of American minerals with their localities, 316 pp., Boston, 1825.

Robinson, Thomas William, Jr.
1. See Stearns, Harold Thornton (1).

Robottom, Arthur
1. Borax deposits in California—an interesting discovery: Eng. and Min. Jour., vol. 18, p. 82, 1874.

Rocks and Minerals
1. Rocks and Minerals first national outing; California (southern California): Rocks and Minerals, vol. 8, no. 3, p. 120, 1933.
2. Recent finds of interest: Rocks and Minerals vol. 11, no. 3, p. 46, 1936.
3. Luminescent reactions under the cold-quartz lamp: Rocks and Minerals, vol. 11, no. 5, pp. 69–72, 1936.

Roe, H. P.
1. American potash: Min. Sci. Press, vol. 119, pp. 195–202, 1919.

Roessler, A. R.
1. New California tin mine: Eng. and Min. Jour., vol. 8, pp. 371, 1869 . . . [Editorial] p. 377.
2. The San Jacinto tin ore: Eng. Min. Jour., vol. 9, pp. 105, 1870.

Rogers, Austin Flint
1. Mineralogical notes: Am. Jour. Sci. 4th ser., vol. 12, pp. 42–48, 1901.
2. Note on the crystal form of benitoite: Science, vol. 28, p. 616, 1908.
3. Notes on some pseudomorphs, petrifactions and alterations: Am. Philos. Soc. Proc., vol. 49, pp. 17–23, 1910.
4. Minerals from the pegmatite veins of Rincon, San Diego County, California: Columbia Univ., School of Mines Quart., vol. 31, pp. 208–218, 1910.
5. Eglestonite from San Mateo County, California: Am. Jour. Sci., 4th ser., vol. 32, pp. 48–50, 1911.
6. A new synthesis and new occurrences of covellite: Columbia Univ., School of Mines Quart., vol. 32, pp. 298–304, 1911.
7. Notes on rare minerals from California: Columbia Univ., School of Mines Quart., vol. 33, pp. 373–381, 1912 . . . (abstract): Min. World, vol. 37, pp. 105–106, 1912 . . . Eng. Index, 1912, p. 446, 1913.
8. (and **Boundey, E. S.**) Occurrence of free gold in granodiorite in Siskiyou County (abstract): Geol. Soc. America Bull., vol. 25, p. 124, 1914.
9. A new locality for voelckerite, Santa Clara County, California, and the validity of voelckerite as a mineral species: Mineralog. Mag., vol. 17, pp. 155–162, 1914.
10. See Eakle, Arthur Starr (13).
11. See Turner, Henry Ward (32).
12. Secondary sulphide enrichment of copper ores with special reference to microscopic study: Min. Sci. Press., vol. 109, pp. 680–686, 1914.
13. Lawsonite from the central Coast Ranges of California: Am. Jour. Sci. 4th ser., vol. 39, pp. 105–112, 1915 . . . Mineralog. Abstracts, vol. 1, p. 353, 1922 . . . Neues Jahrb., 1916, Band 2, pp. 25–26.
14. Notes on the occurrence of anhydrite in the United States: Columbia Univ., School of Mines Quart., vol. 36, pp. 123–142, 1915.
15. See Tolman, Cyrus Fischer, Jr. (1).
16. Sericite, a low temperature hydrothermal mineral: Econ. Geology, vol. 11, pp. 118–150, 1916.
17. The so-called graphic intergrowth of bornite and chalcocite: Econ. Geology, vol. 11, pp. 582–593, 1916.
18. The occurrence of cristobalite in California: Am. Jour. Sci., 4th ser., vol. 45, pp. 222–226, 1918 . . . Mineralog. Abstracts, vol. 2, p. 410, 1925.
19. An American occurrence of periclase and its bearing on the origin and history of calcite brucite rocks: Am. Jour. Sci., 4th ser., vol. 46, pp. 581–586, 1918.
20. Colemanite pseudomorphous after inyoite from Death Valley, California: Am. Mineralogist, vol. 4, pp. 135–139, 1919 . . . Mineralog. Abstracts, vol. 1, p. 241, 1921.
21. An interesting occurrence of manganese minerals near San Jose, California: Am. Jour. Sci., 4th ser., vol. 48, pp. 443–449, 1919 . . . Mineralog. Abstracts, vol. 1, p. 46, 1920 . . . Rev. géologie et sci connexes, tome 2, p. 145, 1921.
22. Tridymite-orthoclase rock, a new metamorphic rock type from Imperial County, California . . . (abstract): Geol. Soc. America Bull., vol. 33, p. 129, 1922.
23. A new occurrence of cristobalite in California: Jour. Geology, vol. 30, pp. 211–216, 1922 . . . Mineralog. Abstracts, vol. 2, p. 410, 1925.
24. The crystallography of hydromagnesite: Am. Jour. Sci., 5th ser., vol. 6, pp. 37–47, 1923 . . . Mineralog. Abstracts, vol. 2, p. 320, 1924.
25. Euhedral magnesite crystals from San Jose, California: Am. Mineralogist, vol. 8, pp. 138–140, 1923 . . . Mineralog. Abstracts, vol. 2, p. 238, 1924.
26. The crystallography of searlesite: Am. Jour. Sci., 5th ser., vol. 7, pp. 498–502, 1924.
27. Kempite, a new manganese mineral from Santa Clara County, California: Am. Jour. Sci., 5th ser., vol. 8, pp. 145–150, 1924 . . . (abstract): Geol. Soc. America Bull., vol. 36, p. 206, 1925 . . . Mineralog. Abstracts, vol. 2, p. 338, 1924 . . . Rev. géol. et sci. connexes, tome 6, p. 301, 1925.
28. (and **Reed, Ralph Daniel**) Sand-calcite crystals from Monterey County, California: Am. Mineralogist, vol. 11, pp. 23–28, 1926 . . . Mineralog. Abstracts, vol. 3, p. 316, 1927.

29. Geology of Cormorant Island, Salton Sea, Imperial County, California . . . (abstract) : Geol. Soc. America Bull., vol. 37, p. 219, 1925 . . . Pan-Am., Geologist, vol. 45, pp. 249–250, 1926.

30. Natural history of the silica minerals : Am. Mineralogist, vol. 13, pp. 73–92, 1928 . . . Mineralog. Abstracts, vol. 4, p. 95, 1929.

31. Periclase from Crestmore near Riverside, California, with a list of minerals from this locality : Am. Mineralogist, vol. 14, pp. 462–469, 1929 . . . Mineralog. Abstracts, vol. 4, p. 240, 1930.

32. Granite pegmatite from Salt Creek, Tulare County, California . . . (abstract) : Am. Mineralogist, vol. 16, p. 116, 1931.

33. Geological history of Lone Hill, Santa Clara County, California . . . (abstract) : Geol. Soc. America Bull., vol. 42, p. 316, 1931.

34. Chromite in the dunite of northwestern Siskiyou County, California . . . (abstract) : Pan-Am. Geologist, vol. 55, pp. 368–369, 1931 . . . Geol. Soc. America Bull., vol. 43, p. 232, 1932 . . . Annotated Bibliography Econ. Geology, vol. 5, p. 287, 1932.

35. Castanite, a basic ferric sulphate from Knoxville, California : Am. Mineralogist, vol. 16, pp. 396–404, 1932 . . . (abstract) : Annotated Bibliography Econ. Geology, vol. 4, p. 217, 1931.

36. Sanbornite, a new barium disilicate mineral from Mariposa County, California : California Min. Bur. Rept. 28, p. 84, 1932 . . . (abstract) : Am. Mineralogist, vol. 17, p. 117, 1932.

37. Euhedral gold crystals from Mariposa County, California (abstract) : Am. Mineralogist, vol. 17, p. 115, 1932.

38. Anauxite as a secondary mineral in some volcanic rocks of California and Arizona (abstract) : Pan-Am. Geologist, vol. 58, pp. 72–73, 1932 . . . Geol. Soc. America Bull., vol. 44, pp. 159–160, 1933 . . . Annotated Bibliography Econ. Geology, vol. 6, p. 244, 1934.

39. Sanbornite, a new barium silicate mineral from Mariposa County, California : Am. Mineralogist, vol. 17, pp. 161–172, 1932 . . . (abstract) : Annotated Bibliography Econ. Geology, vol. 5, p. 35, 1932.

40. Cleavage and parting in quartz (abstract) : Am. Mineralogist, vol. 18, pp. 111–112, 1933.

41. Unique occurrence of vein quartz in Mariposa County, California (abstract) : Geol. Soc. America, Proc., 1934, pp. 327–328, 1935.

42. Salton volcanic domes of Imperial County, California (abstract) : Geol. Soc. America, Proc., 1934, p. 328, 1935.

43. Diadochite, a mineraloid from the New Idria mine, San Benito County, California . . . (abstract) : Am. Mineralogist, vol. 22, no. 12, pt. 2, p. 13, 1937 . . . vol. 23, p. 178, 1938.

44. Lapis lazuli from San Bernardino County, California : Am. Mineralogist, vol. 23, pp. 111–114, 1938.

45. Fossil termite pellets in opalized wood from Santa Maria, California : Am. Jour. Sci., 5th ser., vol. 36, pp. 389–392, 1938.

46. Monticellite rock from Crestmore, California (abstract) : Am. Mineralogist, vol. 24, p. 192, 1939.

47. Nephrite jade from Monterey County, California (abstract) : Geol. Soc. America Bull., vol. 51, p. 1941, 1940.

48. Nephrite jade from Monterey County, California (abstract) : Am. Mineralogist, vol. 26, p. 202, 1941.

49. (and **Sperisen, Francis J.**) American synthetic emerald : Am. Mineralogist, vol. 27, pp. 762–768, 1942 . . . (abstract) : Am. Mineralogist, vol. 27, p. 232, 1942.

50. Sand fulgurites with enclosed lechateliérite from Riverside County, California : Jour. Geology, vol. 54, pp. 117–122, 1946 . . . (abstract) : Am. Mineralogist, vol. 31, p. 206, 1946.

51. Garnet-idocrase rock, a pseudo-jade from Placer County, California (abstract) : Geol. Soc. America Bull. 58, p. 1222, 1947.

52. Blue agate of Lead Pipe Springs, San Bernardino County, California (abstract) : Geol. Soc. America Bull. 58, p. 1256, 1947.

53. Chemical formula of kempite : (abstract) Geol. Soc. America Bull., vol. 60, p. 1944, 1949.

Rogers, J. H.
1. Colusa County, its history and resources, 473 pp., Orland, California, 1891.

Rogers, Malcolm J.
1. Report of an archeological reconnaissance in the Mohave sink region: San Diego Mus. Arch., vol. 1, no. 1, 13 pp., 1929.

Rolker, Charles M.
1. The late operations of the Mariposa estate (gold veins, Mariposa County, California) : Am. Inst. Min. Met. Eng. Trans., vol. 6, pp. 145–164, 1879.

Rolland, G.
1. Les gisements de mercure de Californie: Soc. franc. mineralogie, Bull. 1, pp. 98–104, 1878 . . . Annales des Mines, 7th ser., vol. 14, pp. 384–432, 1878.

Rolston, Jack W.
1. See Trask, Parker Davies (6).

Roney, F. B.
1. Hemet magnesite: Min. Sci. Press, vol. 118, p. 531, 1919.

Root, Edward W.
1. On enargite from the ‚Morning Star mine, California: Am. Jour. Sci., 2d ser., vol. 46, pp. 201–203, 1868.

Root, Lloyd L.
1. See Hamilton, Fletcher McNab (5).
2. Twentieth report of the State Mineralogist: California Min. Bur. Rept. 20, 473 pp., 1924.
3. Twenty-first report of the State Mineralogist: California Min. Bur. Rept. 21, 595 pp., 1925.
4. Twenty-second report of the State Mineralogist: California Min. Bur. Rept. 22, 610 pp., 1926.
5. Twenty-third report of the State Mineralogist: California Min. Bur. Rept. 23, 456 pp., 1927.
6. Twenty-fourth report of the State Mineralogist: California Min. Bur. Rept. 24, 405 pp., 1928.

Root, W. A.
1. The Furnace Creek mining district, California: Min. World, vol. 25, pp. 719–721, 1906.

Roscoe, H. E.
1. On two new vanadium minerals: Royal Soc. London Proc., vol. 25, pp. 109–112, 1876.

Rose, Harry, Jr.
1. See Glass, Jewell Jeannette (4).

Rose, Robert Leon
1. Andalusite and corundum-bearing pegmatites in Yosemite National Park, California : Am. Mineralogist, vol. 42, pp. 635–647, 1957.
2. "Franciscan" metamorphic rocks near Novato, Marin County, California (abst.) : Geol. Soc. America Spec. Paper 68, pp. 52–53, 1962.

Rosenholtz, Joseph Leon
1. (and **Smith, Dudley Thompson**) Crestmore sky blue marble, its linear thermal expansion and color: Am. Mineralogist vol. 35, pp. 1049–1054, 1950.

Ross, Clarence Samuel
1. (and **Shannon, Earl Victor**) The origin, occurrence, composition, and physical properties of the mineral iddingsite: U. S. Nat. Mus. Proc. 2579, vol. 67, art. 7, pp. 1–19, 1926.
2. (and **Kerr, Paul Francis**) Manganese mineral of a vien near Bald Knob, North Carolina: Am. Mineralogist, vol. 17, pp. 1–18, 1932.
3. (**Foster, Margaret Dorothy, and Myers, Alfred Tennyson**) Origin of dunites in basaltic rocks: Am. Mineralogist, vol. 39, pp. 693–737, 1954.

Ross, Clyde Polhemus
1. Quicksilver deposits, in Ore deposits of the western states: Am. Inst. Min. Met. Eng., Lindgren vol., pp. 652–658, 1933.
2. Quicksilver deposits of the Mount Diablo region, Contra Costa County, California : U. S. Geol. Survey Bull. 922-B, 54 pp., 1940.
3. Quicksilver deposits of the Mayacmas and Sulphur Bank districts, California : U. S. Geol. Survey Bull., 922-L, pp. 329–353, 1940.

4. Some quicksilver prospects in adjacent parts of Nevada, California, and Oregon: U. S. Geol. Survey Bull. 931-B, pp. 23–37, 1941.

5. Some concepts on the geology of quicksilver deposits in the United States: Econ. Geology, vol. 37, pp. 439–465, 1942.

6. (and **Yates, Robert Giertz**) The Coso quicksilver district, Inyo County, California: U. S. Geol. Survey Bull. 936-Q, pp. 395–416, 1943.

Ross, Donald Clarence
1. See Rinehart, Charles Dean (1).
2. See Rinehart, Charles Dean (2).

Rowland, Gerald L.
1. See Leonard, Frederick Charles (8).

Rühl, Karl
1. Californien, 283 pp., New York, 1867.

Russell, Israel Cook
1. Quaternary history of Mono Valley, California: U. S. Geol. Survey, 8th Ann. Rept., pp. 261–394, 1889 . . . (abstract): Petermanns Mitt., 1891 (Beil zum 37): p. 115, 1891.

Russell, Richard Dana
1. Fossil pearls from the Chico formation of Shasta County, California: Am. Jour. Sci., 5th ser., vol. 18, pp. 416–428, 1929.

Rutley, Frank
1. On composite spherulites in obsidian from Hot Springs, near Little Lake, California: Geol. Soc. London Quart. Jour., vol. 46, pp. 423–428, 1890 . . . (abstract): Geol. Mag., 3d ser., vol. 7, pp. 233–234, 1890.

Rynearson, Garn Arthur
1. (and **Smith, Clay Taylor**) Chromite deposits in the Seiad quadrangle, Siskiyou County, California: U. S. Geol. Survey Bull. 922-J, pp. 281–306, 1940.
2. (and **Wells, Francis Gerritt**) Geology of the Grey Eagle and some nearby chromite deposits, in Glenn County, California: U. S. Geol. Survey Bull. 945-A, pp. i–iv, 1–22, 1944.
3. Chromite deposits of the North Elder Creek area, Tehama County, California: U. S. Geol. Survey Bull. 945 G, pp. 191–210, 1946.
4. Chromite deposits of Tulare and eastern Fresno Counties, California: California Div. Mines Bull. 134, pt. 3, chap. 3, pp. 61–104, 1948.
5. See Cater, Frederick William (4).
6. Geological investigations of chromite in California: California Div. Mines Bull. 134, pt. 3, chap. 3, pp. 171–321, 1953.
7. See Cater, Frederick William (5).

S

Sachs, A.
1. Zinnoberkristalle aus Sonoma County, in Kalifornien; Gips- und Kalkspatkristalle von Terlingua in Texas: Zentralbl., Mineralogie, pp. 17–19, 1907.

Sampson, Edward
1. Talc and soapstone, asbestos: Mineral Resources U. S. 1921, pt. 2, pp. 97–103, 135–142, 1924.
2. Asbestos: Mineral Resources U. S., 1920, pt. 2, pp. 309–322, 1923.
3. Chromite: Mineral Resources U. S., 1922, pt. 1, pp. 107–112, 1925.

Sampson, Reid J.
1. See Tucker, W. Burling (15).
2. See Tucker, W. Burling (16).
3. See Tucker, W. Burling (17).
4. (and **Tucker, W. Burling**) Feldspar, silica, andalusite, and cyanite deposits of California: California Min. Bur. Rept. 27, pp. 407–464, 1931 . . . (abstract): Annotated Bibliography Econ. Geology, vol. 4, p. 264, 1931.
5. Economic mineral deposits of the San Jacinto quadrangle: California Min. Bur. Rept. 28, pp. 3–11, 1932 . . . (abstract): Annotated Bibliography Econ. Geology, vol. 5, p. 12, 1932.
6. See Tucker, W. Burling (20).
7. Mineral resources of a part of the Panamint Range: California Min. Bur. Rept. 28, pp. 357–376, 1932 . . . (abstract): Annotated Bibliography Econ. Geology, vol. 6, p. 9, 1934.
8. See Tucker, W. Burling (21).

9. Mineral resources of a portion of the Perris block, Riverside County, California: California Div. Mines Rept. 31, pp. 507–521, 1935.

10. Mineral resources of Los Angeles County, California: California Div. Mines Rept. 33, pp. 173–213, 1937.

11. Mineral resources of the Resting Springs region, Inyo County: California Div. Mines Rept. 33, pp. 264–270, 1937.

12. See Tucker, W. Burling (25).

13. See Tucker, W. Burling (27).

14. Mineral resources of Mono County: California Div. Mines Rept. 36, pp. 117–156, 1940.

15. See Tucker, W. Burling (28).

16. See Tucker, W. Burling (29).

17. See Tucker, W. Burling (30).

18. (and **Tucker, W. Burling**) Mineral resources of Imperial County: California Div. Mines Rept. 38, pp. 105–145, 1942.

19. See Tucker, W. Burling (32).

20. See Tucker, W. Burling (33).

21. See Tucker, W. Burling (34).

22. See Tucker, W. Burling (35).

23. See Oakeshott, Gordon Blaisdell (4).

Sanborn, W. C.

1. (and **Ricker, S.**) Investigation of French Hill chromite mine, Del Norte County, California: U. S. Bur. Mines Rept. Invest. 4365, 9 pp., Oct., 1948.

Sand, Leonard B.

1. See Baur, Gretta S. (1).

2. See Baur, Gretta S. (2).

3. See Ames, Lloyd Leroy, Jr. (1).

Sanford, Samuel

1. (and **Stone, Ralph Walter**) Useful minerals of the United States: U. S. Geol. Survey Bull. 585, 250 pp., 1914.

2. See Schrader, Frank Charles (1).

San Francisco Bulletin

1. ————————: San Francisco Bulletin, July 16, 1884.

Santmeyers, R. M.

1. See Tyler, P. M. (1).

Sawyer, Dwight Lewis, Jr.

1. See Pabst, Adolf (10).

2. See Pabst, Adolf (15).

3. See Smith, George Irving (1).

4. See Pabst, Adolf (21).

Schairer, John Frank

1. (and **Lawson, C. C.**) Copiapite from the Santa Maria Mountains, eastern Riverside County, California: Am. Mineralogist, vol. 9, pp. 242–244, 1924 . . . Mineralog. Abstracts, vol. 3, p. 214, 1926.

Schaller, Waldemar Theodore

1. Minerals from Leona Heights, Alameda County, California: Univ. California, Dept. Geol. Sci. Bull., vol. 3, pp. 191–217, 1903.

2. Spodumene from San Diego County, California: Univ. California, Dept. Geol. Sci. Bull., vol. 3, pp. 265–275, 1903.

3. Notes on some California minerals: Am. Jour. Sci., 4th ser., vol. 17, pp. 191–194, 1904.

4. (and **Hillebrand, William Francis**) Crystallographical and chemical notes on lawsonite: Am. Jour. Sci., 4th ser., vol. 17, pp. 195–197, 1904.

5. The tourmaline localities of southern California: Science, new ser., vol. 19, pp. 266–268, 1904.

6. (and **Hillebrand, William Francis**) Notes on lawsonite: U. S. Geol. Survey Bull. 262, pp. 58–60, 1905.

7. Dumortierite: Am. Jour. Sci., 4th ser., vol. 19, pp. 211–224, 1905 . . . U. S. Geol. Survey Bull. 262, pp. 91–120, 1905.

8. Mineralogical notes: U. S. Geol. Survey Bull. 262, pp. 121–144, 1905.

9. Crystallography of lepidolite: Am. Jour. Sci., 4th ser., vol. 19, pp. 225–226, 1905.

10. See Graton, Louis Caryl (1).

11. Ueber Dumortierit: Zeitschr. Kristallographie, Band 41, pp. 19–47, 1906.

12. The chemical composition of molybdic ocher: Amer. Jour. Sci., 4th ser., vol. 23, pp. 297–303, 1907 . . . Zeitschr. Kristallographie, Band 43, pp. 331–337, 1907.

13. Mineralogical notes: Am. Jour. Sci., 4th ser., vol. 24, pp. 152–158, 1907 . . . Zeitschr. Kristallographie, Band 44, pp. 1–8, 1907.

14. Some calcite crystals with new forms: Washington Acad. Sci. Proc., vol. 11, pp. 1–16, 1909 . . . Zeitschr. Kristallographie, Band 44, pp. 321–331, 1908.

15. Axinit von Californien: Zeitschr. Kristallographie, Band 48, pp. 148–157, 1910.

16. Some pegmatites from southern California (abstract): Science, new ser., vol. 31, pp. 516–517, 1910.

17. Mineralogical notes, series 1: U. S. Geol. Survey Bull. 490, 109 pp., 1911.

18. Axinite from California: U. S. Geol. Survey Bull. 490, pp. 37–47, 1911.

19. Albite from lawsonite schist, Marin County: U. S. Geol. Survey Bull. 490, pp. 48–52, 1911.

20. Notes on neptunite: U. S. Geol. Survey Bull. 490, pp. 55–57, 1911.

21. Orbicular gabbro from Pala, San Diego County, U. S. Geol. Survey Bull. 490, pp. 58–59, 1911.

22. Notes on purpurite and heterosite: U. S. Geol. Survey Bull. 490, p. 79, 1911.

23. Calcite from San Francisco, California: U. S. Geol. Survey Bull. 490, pp. 103–104, 1911.

24. Cuprodescloizite from California: Washington Acad. Sci. Jour., vol. 1, pp. 149–150, 1911.

25. Bismuth ochers from San Diego County, California: Am. Chem. Soc. Jour., vol. 33, pp. 162–166, 1911 . . . Zeitschr. Kristallographie, Band 49, pp. 229–232, 1911 . . . (abstract): Washington Acad. Sci. Jour., vol. 1, p. 37, 1911.

26. Krystallographische Notizen ueber Albit, Phenakit und Neptunit: Zeitschr. Kristallographie, Band 48, pp. 550–558, 1911 . . . U. S. Geol. Survey Bull. 490, pp. 53–56, 1911.

27. Mineralogical notes, series 2: U. S. Geol. Survey Bull. 509, 115 pp., 1912 . . . (abstract); Washington Acad. Sci. Jour., vol. 2, p. 349, 1912.

28. Cuprodescloizite from California: U. S. Geol. Survey Bull. 509, p. 88, 1912.

29. New manganese phosphates from the gem tourmaline field of southern California: Washington Acad. Sci. Jour., vol. 2, pp. 143–145, 1912.

30. Immense bloedite crystals: Washington Acad. Sci. Jour., vol. 3, pp. 75–76, 1913.

31. The refractive indices of strengite: Washington Acad. Sci. Jour., vol. 3, p. 249, 1913.

32. Mineralogic notes, 3d ser.: U. S. Geol. Survey Bull. 610, 164 pp., 1916 . . . (abstract): Washington Acad. Sci. Jour., vol. 6, pp. 453–454, 1916.

33. Inyoite and meyerhofferite, two new calcium borates: U. S. Geol. Survey Bull. 610, pp. 35–55, 1916.

34. New occurrences of some rare minerals: U. S. Geol. Survey Bull 610, p. 137, 1916.

35. The probable identity of mariposite and alurgite: U. S. Geol. Survey Bull. 610, pp. 139–140, 1916.

36. Cassiterite in San Diego County, California: U. S. Geol. Survey Bull. 620, pp. 351–354, 1916 . . . Mineralog. Abstracts, vol. 1, p. 414, 1927 . . . Geol. Zentralbl., Band 28, p. 101, 1922.

37. Gems and precious stones: Mineral Resources U. S., 1915, pt. 2, pp. 843–858, 1917.

38. Gems and precious stones: Mineral Resources U. S., 1916, pt. 2, pp. 887–899, 1919.

39. Gems and precious stones: Mineral Resources U. S., 1918, pt. 2, pp. 7–14, 1921.

40. The genesis of lithium pegmatites: Am. Jour. Sci., 5th ser., vol. 10 pp. 269–279, 1925 . . . Mineralog. Abstracts, vol. 3, p. 36, 1926 . . . Rev. Géologie et sci. connexes, tome 8, p. 285, 1927.

41. Kernite, a new sodium borate: Am. Mineralogist, vol. 12, pp. 24–25, 1927 . . . Mineralog. Abstracts, vol. 3, p. 271, 1927.

42. Mineral replacements in pegmatites: Am. Mineralogist vol. 12, pp. 59–63, 1927.

43. Hydroboracite from California: Festschrift Victor Goldschmidt, pp. 256–262, Heidelberg, 1928.

44. The probable identity of camsellite with szaibelyite: Am. Mineralogist, vol. 13, pp. 230–232, 1928.

45. Borate minerals from the Kramer district, Mohave Desert, California: U. S. Geol. Survey Prof. Paper 158-I, pp. 137–170, 1930 . . . Mineralog. Abstracts, vol. 4, pp. 245–246, 1930 . . . Mineralog. Mag., vol. 22, p. 622, 1931.

46. Chemical composition of cuprotungstite: Am. Mineralogist, vol. 17, pp. 234–237, 1932.

47. The refractive indices of bloedite: Am. Mineralogist, vol. 17, pp. 530–533, 1932.

48. (and **Fairchild, John Gifford**) Bavenite, a beryllium mineral, pseudomorphous after beryl, from California: Am. Mineralogist, vol. 17, pp. 409–422, 1932 . . . (abstract) : Annotated Bibliography Econ. Geology, vol. 5, p. 255, 1932 . . . Am. Mineralogist, vol. 17, p. 114, 1932.

49. Pegmatites, in Ore deposits of the Western States (Lindgren volume), pp. 144–151, Am. Inst. Min. Met. Eng., 1933 . . . (abstract): Neues Jahrb., 1934, Referate 2, pp. 206–207.

50. Monticellite from San Bernardino County, California, and the monticellite series: Am. Mineralogist, vol. 20, pp. 815–827, 1935.

51. The origin of kernite and borax in the Kramer borate field, California (abstract) : Am. Mineralogist, vol. 21, p. 192, 1936.

52. (and **Stevens, Rollin Elbert**) The validity of paragonite as a mineral species: Am. Mineralogist, vol. 26, pp. 541–545, 1941.

53. The identity of ascharite, camsellite and B-ascharite with szaibelyite; and some relations of the magnesium borate minerals: Am. Mineralogist, vol. 27, pp. 467–486, 1942.

54. (and **Glass, Jewell Jeannette**) Occurrence of pink zoisite (thulite) in the United States: Am. Mineralogist, vol. 27, pp. 519–524, 1942.

55. See Stevens, Rollin Elbert (3).

56. (and **Mrose, Mary Emma**) The naming of the hydrous magnesium borate minerals from Boron, California—a preliminary note: Am. Mineralogist, vol. 45, pp. 732–734, 1960.

57. (and **Vlisidis, Angelina Calomeris**) The composition of aluminian ludwigite from Crestmore, California: Am. Mineralogist, vol. 46, pp. 335–339, 1961.

58. (**Vlisidis, Angelina Calomeris,** and **Mrose, Mary Emma**) Macallisterite, $2MgO \cdot 6B_2O_{36} \cdot 15H_2O$, a new hydrous magnesium borate mineral from the Death Valley region, Inyo County, California (abst.): Geol. Soc. America Program, Miami, Florida Meeting, p. 173, Nov. 1964.

Schenck, W. E.
1. (and **Dawson, E. J.**) Archeology of the northern San Joaquin Valley: Univ. California, Pub. Arch. and Ethnol., vol. 25, pp. 289–413, 1929.

Schlocker, J.
1. Magnesium bearing minerals in the Boulder Dam area for the production of magnesium metal: U. S. Bur. Mines Inf. Circ. 7216, 16 pp., 1942.

Schmeltz, Fred W.
1. Lapis-lazuli in California: Rocks and Minerals, vol. 7, p. 69, 1932.

Schmitz
1. Goldamalgan in Californien, letter to V. Gerolt: Deut. Geol. Ges., Zeitschr. 4, pp. 712–714, 1852.

Scholl, David W.
1. (and **Taft, William H.**) Deposition, mineralogy, and C14 dating of tufa, Mono Lake, California (abst.) : Geol. Soc. America Cordilleran Section Meeting Program, p. 56, March 1964.

Schrader, Frank Charles
1. (and **Stone, Ralph Walter,** and **Sanford, Samuel**) Useful minerals of the United States (a revision of Bulletin 585) : U. S. Geol. Survey, Bull. 624, 412 pp., 1917 . . . (abstract) : Geol. Zentralbl. 28, p. 229, 1922.
2. Epithermal antimony deposits: In Ore deposits of the western states, Am. Inst. Min. Eng., Lindgren Volume, pp. 658–665, 1933.

Schrauf, A.
1. Aphorismen über Zinnober: Zeitschr. Prak. Geol., pp. 10–18, 1894.

Schröckinger, J. von
1. Pošephit, ein neues Harg aus Californien: K. geol. Reichsanstalt, Verh. 8, 1877, pp. 128–130 . . . (abstract) : Geol. Rec. 1877, p. 251, 1880.

Schröder, Alfred
1. (and **Hoffmann, Wolfgang**) Zur optik des Colemanits: Neues del Jahr. Min., pp. 265–271, 1956.

Schroter, G. A.
1. A geologist visits the Mohave mining district: Eng. Min. Jour., vol. 136, pp. 185–188, 1935.
2. Some hypothermal gold deposits near Bishop, California: Eng. Min. Jour., vol. 139, pp. 42–45, April 1938; vol. 139, pp. 52–54, May 1938.

Schuette, Curt Nicolaus
1. Occurence of quicksilver orebodies: Am. Inst. Met. Eng., Tech. Publ. 335, 87 pp., 1931.

Schumacher, Paul
1. Ancient graves and shell-heaps of California: Smithsonian Inst. Ann. Rept. 1874, pp. 335–350, 1874.
2. Method of manufacture of soapstone pots, in Wheeler, George, Geographical survey of the territory west of the 100th meridian . . . VII (Archeology), pp. 117–121, 1879.

Schürmann, H. M. E.
1. Beitrag zur Petrographie der Hollywood Hills (Santa Monica Gebirge) in Los Angeles, Süd-Kalifornien; Centralbl. Mineralogie, Abt. A, pp. 7–13, 1928.
2. Granatführender Diorit aus der Sierra Nevada, Kalifornien: Neues Jahrb., Beilage Band 74, Abt. A, pp. 225–250, 1938.

Schwartz, Jack
1. Southern California localities, 2, Lake Malibu: Rocks and Minerals, vol. 17, p. 414, 1942.
2. Southern California localities, 10, Redondo Beach and Palos Verdes: Rocks and Minerals, vol. 18, p. 243, 1943.
3. Obtainable minerals of Los Angeles County, California: Rocks and Minerals, vol. 31, nos. 1–2, pp. 39–41, 1956.
4. See Pemberton, H. Earl (1).

Scientific American
1. California borax mines: Sci. Am., vol. 71, p. 60, 1894.

Scott, W.
1. Diamond quest in California; Cherokee mine may become a diamond mine: Sci. Am., vol. 134, p. 312, 1925.

Segerstrom, R. J.
1. Tin in California: California Div. Mines Rept. 37, pp. 531–557, 1941.

Segnit, E. Ralph
1. (and **Lancucki, C. J.**) Fluoborite from Crestmore, California: Am. Mineralogist, vol. 48, pp. 278–282, 1963.

Shannon, Earl Victor
1. The occurrence of bindheimite as an ore mineral: Econ. Geology, vol. 15, pp. 88–93, 1920 . . . (abstract): Rev. géologie et sci. connexes, vol. 5, p. 135, 1924.
2. See Larsen, Esper Signius (9).
3. Analyses and optical properties of amesite and corundophilite from Chester, Massachusetts, and chromium-bearing chlorites from California and Wyoming: U. S. Nat. Mus. Proc., vol. 58, pp. 371–379, 1920 . . . Mineralog. Abstracts, vol. 1, p. 214, 1921.
4. Velardeñiite from a new locality in Tulare County, California: U. S. Nat. Mus. Proc., vol. 60, art. 22, 4 pp., 1922 . . . Mineralog. Abstracts, vol. 2, p. 190, 1923.
5. See Ross, Clarence Samuel (1).
6. See Gordon, Samuel G. (1).
7. Miargyrite silver ore from the Randsburg district, California; U. S. Nat. Mus. Proc., vol. 74, no. 21, pp. 1–10, 1929 . . . (abstract): Annotated Bibliography Econ. Geology, vol. 2, p. 64, 1929 . . . Mineralog. Abstracts, vol. 4, p. 142, 1929.
8. See Short, Maxwell Naylor (1).

Sharp, W. N.
1. See Olson, Jerry Chipman (1).
2. See Pray, Lloyd Charles (1).
3. See Olson, Jerry Chipman (3).

Sharwood, William J.
1. See Eakle, Arthur Starr (6).
2. Some associations of gold with pyrite and tellurides: Min. Sci. Press, vol. 94, p. 117, 1907.
3. See Louderback, George Davis (3).
4. The O'Harra pocket mine: Min. Sci. Press, vol. 96, p. 782, 1908.
5. Notes on tellurium-bearing gold ores: Econ. Geology, vol. 6, pp. 22–36, 1911.

Shawe, Daniel Reeves
1. See Olson, Jerry Chipman (3).

Shedd, Solon
1. Bibliography of the geology and mineral resources of California: California Div. Mines Bull. 104, 376 pp., 1933.
2. Bibliography of the geology and mineral resources of California for the years 1931 to 1936 inclusive: California Div. Mines Bull. 115, 125 pp., 1938.

Shell, Haskell Roy
1. See Huggins, Charles W. (1).

Shelvocke, Capt. George
1. A voyage around the world, 468 pp., London, 1726.

Shenon, Philip John
1. A massive sulphide deposit of hydrothermal origin in serpentine: Econ. Geology, vol. 27, pp. 597–613, 1932.

Shepard, Charles Upham
1. Notice of several American minerals: Am. Acad. Sci. Proc., vol. 6, pp. 230–232, 1852.
2. On a meteoric iron lately found in El Dorado County, California: Am. Jour. Sci., 3d ser., vol. 3, p. 438, 1872.
3. Tincalconite (borax): Soc. franç mineralogie, Bull. 1, p. 144, 1878.
4. On the Ivanpah, California, meteoric iron: Am. Jour. Sci., 3d ser., vol. 19, pp. 381–382, 1880.
5. On meteoric iron from Trinity County, California: Am. Jour. Sci., 3d ser., vol. 29, p. 469, 1885.

Shepard, Francis Parker
1. See Dietz, Robert Sinclair (2).

Shibler, B. K.
1. See Agey, W. W. (1).

Shinn, C. H.
1. Mining camps of California: Overland Monthly, new ser., vol. 4, p. 173, 1870.

Short, Allan McIlroy
1. A chemical and optical study of piedmontite from Shadow Lake, Madera County, California: Am. Mineralogist, vol. 18, pp. 493–500, 1933.

Short, Maxwell Naylor
1. (and **Shannon, Earl Victor**) Violarite and other rare nickel sulfides: Am. Mineralogist, vol. 15, pp. 1–22, 1930.

Siebenthal, C. E.
1. Zinc: Mineral Resources U. S., 1915, pt. 1, pp. 851–978, 1917.

Silliman, Benjamin, Jr.
1. Notes on the New Almaden quicksilver mine: Am. Jour. Sci., 2d ser., vol. 38, pp. 190–194, 1864.
2. On the deep placers of the south and middle Yuba, Nevada County, California: Am. Jour. Sci., 2d ser., vol. 40, pp. 1–19, 1865.
3. Report on Church Union Gold Company (included in a description of its resources), 16 pp., New York, 1865.
4. Notes on the quartz mines of the Grass Valley district, quoted from Bean, History and directory of Nevada County, California: Eng. and Min. Jour., vol. 4, p. 9, 1867.
5. On new localities of diamonds in California: Am. Jour. Sci., 2d ser., vol. 44, p. 119, 1867.
6. Notes on the Grass Valley gold-mining district, California: Am. Jour. Sci., 2d ser., vol. 44, pp. 236–244, 1867.
7. A notice of the peculiar mode of the occurrence of gold and silver in the foothills of the Sierra Nevada, and especially at Whiskey Hill, in Placer County, and

Quail Hill, in Calaveras County, California: California Acad. Nat. Sci. Proc., vol. 3, pp. 349–351, 1867 . . . Am. Jour. Sci., 2d ser., vol. 45, pp. 92–95, 1868.

8. Notice of new localities of diamonds in California: California Acad. Nat. Sci. Proc., vol. 3, pp. 354–355, 1867.

9. Note on three new localities of tellurium minerals in California and on some mineralogical features of the mother vein: California Acad. Nat. Sci. Proc., vol. 3, pp. 378–382, 1868 . . . Min. Sci. Press, vol. 16, p. 9, 1868.

10. On the occurrence of glauberite at Borax Lake, California: California Acad. Nat. Sci. Proc., vol. 3, p. 399, 1868.

11. On the meteoric iron found near Shingle Springs, El Dorado County, California: Am. Jour. Sci., 3d ser., vol. 6, pp. 18–22, 1873.

12. Mineralogical notes on Utah, California, and Nevada, with a description of priceite, a new borate of lime: Am. Jour. Sci., 3d ser., vol. 6, pp. 126–133, 1873 . . . Eng. and Min. Jour., vol. 16, pp. 82, 98–99, 1873.

13. On the probable existence of microscopic diamonds with zircons and topaz, in the sands of hydraulic washings in California: Am. Inst. Min. Met. Eng., Trans., vol. 1, pp. 371–373, 1873 . . . (abstract): Am. Jour. Sci., 3d ser., vol. 5, pp. 384–385, 1873 . . . 6, p. 133, 1873 . . . Eng. and Min. Jour., vol. 15, p. 184, 1873 . . . Geol. Rec., 1874, p. 251, 1875.

Silver, Leon Theodore
1. See Banks, Philip O. (1).

Simkins, William A.
1. The Alleghany district of California: in Pacific Min. News, Eng. and Min. Jour., vol. 2, pp. 288–291, 1893 . . . (abstract): Eng. Index 1923, p. 336, 1924.

Simonin, L.
1. Observations sur les gisements aurifères de la Californie: Acad. Sci. Paris Comptes rendus, tome 50, pp. 389–392, 1860.
2. Les mines d'or et d'argent aux Etats Unis: Rev. des Deux Mondes, 9th ser., tome 12, pp. 285–314, 1875.

Simons, Frank Stanton
1. See Trask, Parker Davies (4).
2. See Trask, Parker Davies (5).

Simonson, Russell Ray
1. Piedmontite from Los Angeles County, California: Am. Mineralogist, vol. 20, pp. 737–738, 1935.

Simoons, F. J.
1. Nineteenth century mines and mineral spring resorts of Lake County, California: California Jour. Mines and Geology, vol. 50, pp. 295–319, 1954.

Simpson, Dale R.
1. Graphic granite from the Ramona pegmatite district, California: Am. Mineralogist, vol. 47, pp. 1123–1138, 1962.

Simpson, Edward Cannon
1. Geology and mineral deposits of the Elizabeth Lake quadrangle, California: California Div. Mines Rept. 30, pp. 371–415, 1934.

Sinkankas, John
1. Naming California's spodumene: Gems and Minerals, no. 219, pp. 50–52, Dec. 1955.
2. See Switzer, George S. (10).

Skinner, Brian John
1. (Erd, Richard Clarkson, and Grimaldi, Frank Saverio) Greigite, the thiospinel of iron, a new mineral: Am. Mineralogist, vol. 49, pp. 543–555, 1964.

Slavin, Morris
1. See Gabriel, Alton (1).

Sloat, L. W.
1. The mines of Upper California: Merchants Mag. and Commercial Rev., vol. 16, pp. 365–367, 1847.

Smerud, Sara K.
1. (and McDonald, Wm. H.) Scorzalite and lazulite: Gems and Minerals, no. 224, pp. 20–21, 86, May 1956.

Smith, Clay Taylor

1. See Rynearson, Garn Arthur (1).

2. (and **Griggs, Allan Bingham**) Chromite deposits near San Luis Obispo, San Luis Obispo County, California: U. S. Geol. Survey Bull. 945-B, pp. i–iv, 23–44, 1944.

Smith, Dudley Thompson

1. See Rosenholtz, Joseph Leon (1).

Smith, George Frederick Herbert

1. Ueber das bemerkenswerthe Problem der Entwickelung der Krystallformen der Calaverit: Zeitschr. Kristallographie, Band 37. pp. 209–234, 1903.

Smith, George Irving

1. (**Almond, Hy,** and **Sawyer, Dwight Lewis, Jr.**) Sassolite from the Kramer borate district, California: Am. Mineralogist, vol. 43, pp. 1068–1078, 1958.

2. (and **Pratt, Walden Penfield**) Core logs from Owens, China, Searles and Panamint Basins, California: U. S. Geol. Survey Bull. 1045A, 62 pp., 1957.

3. (and **Haines, David Vincent**) Character and distribution of non-clastic minerals in the Searles Lake evaporite deposit, California: U. S. Geol. Surv. Bull, 1181-P, pp. P1–P58, 1964.

4. Subsurface stratigraphy of late quaternary deposits, Searles Lake, California— a summary: Article 88 in U. S. Geol. Surv. Prof. Paper 450-C, pp. C65–69, 1962.

Smith, James Perrin

1. The paragenesis of the minerals in the glaucophane-bearing rocks of California: Am. Philos. Soc. Proc., vol. 45, pp. 183–242. 1906.

Smith, John Lawrence

1. Curious association of garnet, idocrase and datolite: Am. Jour. Sci., 3d ser., vol. 8, pp. 434–436, 1874.

Smith, Lewis A.

1. Manganese and manganiferous ores: Mineral Resources U. S., 1928, pt. 1, pp. 205–259, 1931.

Smith, Robert Leland

1. Some new occurrences of sassolite in the United States: Am. Mineralogist, vol. 43, pp, 1204–5, 1958.

Smith, Ward Conwell

1. See Benda, William K. (1).

Smith, William Sidney Tangier

1. The geology of Santa Catalina Island: California Acad. Sci. Proc., 3d ser., vol. 1, pp. 1–71, 1897 . . . (abstract): Petermanns Mitt. 1897 (Beil zum 43), p. 121, 1897.

2. A geological sketch of San Clemente Island, California: U. S. Geol. Survey 18th Ann. Rept. pt. 2, pp. 459–496, 1898 . . . (abstract): Nature, vol. 60, p. 182, 1899.

Snyder, Doris

1. Epidote and garnet in San Diego County: Gems and Minerals, no. 292, pp. 22–23, Jan. 1962.

2. Wonderful world of pegmatite minerals: Part I: Gems and Minerals, no. 293, pp. 24–26, Feb. 1962.

3. ――――――――――: Part II: Gems and Minerals, no. 294, pp. 6, 29, Mar. 1962.

4. ――――――――――: Part III: Gems and Minerals, no. 295, pp. 16–17, April 1962.

5. Blue topaz from San Diego County: Gems and Minerals, no. 297, p. 32, June 1962.

Solari, A. J.

1. See Taliaferro, Nicholas Lloyd (4).

Sonnenschein, F.

1. Ueber das Vorkommen der natürlichen Goldamalgams in Californien: Deutsche geol. Gesell., Zeitschr., Band 6, pp. 243–244, 1854.

Sosman, Robert Browning

1. (and **Posnjak, Eugen**) Ferromagnetic ferric oxide, artificial and natural: Jour. Washington Acad. Sci., vol. 15, pp. 329–342, 1925.

Sovereign, L. Douglas
1. Gems and rare minerals of southern California : Southern California Acad. Sci. Bull. 4, pp. 85–90, 1905 . . . (abstract) : Geol. Zentralbl., Band 10, p. 445, 1908.

Sperisen, Francis J.
1. Gem minerals of California : California Div. Mines Rept. 34, pp. 34–78, 1938.
2. See Rogers, Austin Flint (49).

Sperry, Edwin A.
1. Investigation of Feather River black sands, California : Min. Sci. Press., vol. 105, pp. 624–626, 1912.

Spotts, John H.
1. Zircon and other accessory minerals, Coast Range batholith, California : Geol. Soc. America Bull., vol. 73, pp. 1221–1240, 1962.

Staatz, Mortimer Hay
1. See Outerbridge, William F. (1).

Stanley-Brown, Joseph
1. Bernardinite; is it a mineral or fungus? : Am. Jour. Sci., 3d ser., vol. 42, pp. 46–50, 1891.

Stanton, Robert B.
1. The discovery of gold in California : Eng. and Min. Jour., vol. 79, p. 376, 1905.

Staples, Lloyd William
1. Ilsemannite and jordisite : Am. Mineralogist, vol. 36, pp. 609–614, 1951.

Stearns, Harold Thorton
1. (**Robinson, Thomas William, Jr.,** and **Taylor, George Holmes**) Geology and water resources of the Mokelumne area, California : U. S. Geol. Survey, Water-Supply Paper 619, 402 pp., 1930.

Steiger, George
1. See Clarke, Frank Wigglesworth (8).
2. See Larsen, Esper Signius (6).
3. See Larsen, Esper Signius (14).

Steiner, A.
1. Occurrence of wairakite at The Geysers, California : Am. Mineralogist, vol. 43, p. 781, 1958.

Stephens, Hal G.
1. See Walker, George Walton (5).
2. See Hall, Wayne Everett (3).

Sterrett, Douglas Bovard
1. Tourmaline from San Diego County, California : Am. Jour. Sci., 4th ser., vol. 17, pp. 459–465, 1904 . . . (abstract) : Geol. Zentralbl., Band 9, p. 677, 1907.
2. Precious stones : Mineral Resources U. S., 1906, pt. 2, pp. 1213–1252, 1907.
3. Gems and precious stones : Mineral Resources U. S., 1907, pt. 2, pp. 795–842, 1908.
4. Precious stones : Mineral Resources U. S., 1908, pt. 2, pp. 805–859, 1909.
5. Gems and precious stones : Mineral Resources U. S., 1909, pt. 2, pp. 739–808, 1911.
6. Gems and precious stones : Mineral Resources U. S., 1910, pt. 2, pp. 847–900, 1911.
7. Gems and precious stones : Mineral Resources U. S., 1911, pt. 2, pp. 1037–1078, 1912.
8. Gems and precious stones : Mineral Resources U. S., 1912, pt. 2, pp. 1023–1060, 1913.
9. Gems and precious stones : Mineral Resources U. S., 1913, pt. 2, pp. 649–708, 1914.
10. Gems and precious stones : Mineral Resources U. S., 1914, pt. 2, pp. 307–346, 1916.
11. Mica deposits of the United States : U. S. Geol. Survey Bull. 740, 342 pp., 1923.

Stetefeldt, C. A.
1. Extract from a report on the Panamint mining district : Eng. and Min. Jour., vol. 18, pp. 242–243, 259, 262, 1874.

Stevens, Rollin Elbert

1. New analyses of lepidolites and their interpretation: Am. Mineralogist, vol. 23, pp. 607–628, 1938.

2. See Schaller, Waldemar Theodore (52).

3. (and **Schaller, Waldemar Theodore**) The rare alkalies in micas: Am. Mineralogist, vol. 27, pp. 525–537, 1942.

Steward, Julian H.

1. Ethnography of the Owens Valley Paiute: Univ. California, Pub. Arch. and Ethnol., vol. 33, pp. 233–338, 1933.

Stewart, Richard Maclin

1. See Norman, Lewis Arthur, Jr. (2).

2. See Wright, Lauren Albert (5).

3. See Carlisle, Donald (1).

Stillman, J. M.

1. Bernardinite, a new mineral resin from San Bernardino County, California: Am. Jour. Sci., 3d ser., vol. 18, pp. 57–59, 1879.

2. Bernardinite, its nature and origin: Am. Jour. Sci., 3d ser., vol. 20, pp. 93–94, 1880.

Stines, Norman S.

1. The geology of the Coffee Creek mining district, California: Min. Sci. Press, vol. 95, pp. 25–26, 1907.

2. Hoag district, Modoc County, California: Min. Sci. Press, vol. 100, pp. 384–386, 1910.

3. The camp of High Grade in northern California; historical facts and a description of the geology of the Hoag district in Modoc County: Mining Sci., vol. 65, pp. 27–29, 1912.

4. Geology of High Grade district, California: Mining Investor, vol. 66, pp. 192–193, 1912.

Stinson, Melvin Clarence

1. Geology of the Island Mountain copper mine, Trinity County, California: California Jour. Mines and Geology, vol. 53, pp. 9–33, 1957.

2. See Pabst, Adolph (18).

3. (and **Alfors, John Theodore**) Unusual minerals from Fresno County: Calif. Div. Mines and Geol., Mineral Information Service, vol. 16, no. 1, pp. 10–11, 1963.

4. Fayalite in obsidian: Calif. Div. Mines and Geol., Mineral Information Service, vol. 17, pp. 207–208, 1964.

5. See Alfors, John Theodore (1).

6. (and **Alfors, John Theodore**) New Minerals from Fresno County—I: Calif. Div. Mines and Geol., Mineral Information Service, vol. 17, pp. 235–238, 1964.

Stoddard, B. H.

1. Gems and precious stones: Mineral Resources U. S., 1919, pt. 2, pp. 165–180, 1922.

2. Gems and precious stones: Mineral Resources U. S., 1920, pt. 2, pp. 215–218, 1923.

3. Talc and soapstone: Mineral Resources U. S., 1923, pt. 2, pp. 161–163, 1926.

4. See Bowles, Oliver (1).

5. Barite and barium products: Minerals Yearbook, 1935, pp. 1125–1135, 1935.

Stoiber, Richard Edwin

1. (**Tolman, Carl**, and **Butler, Robert Dexter**) Geology of quartz crystal deposits: Am. Mineralogist, vol. 30, pp. 245–268, 1945.

Stone, Jerome

1. See Hewett, Donnel Foster (4).

2. See Hewett, Donnel Foster (5).

Stone, Ralph Walter

1. See Sanford, Samuel (1).

2. See Schrader, Frank Charles (1).

3. See Yale, Charles Gregory (5).

Storms, William H.

1. Acton mines: Min. Sci. Press, vol. 55, p. 2, 1887.

2. The mines of Calico district, San Bernardino County, California: Eng. and Min. Jour., vol. 49, pp. 382–383, 1890.

3. Certain ore deposits (Daggett, San Bernardino County, California) : Min. Sci. Press, vol. 64, p. 18, 1892.

4. Los Angeles, San Bernardino, San Diego Counties: California Min. Bur. Rept. 11, p. 243–248, 337–369, 376–387, 1893.

5. Occurrence of diamonds: Min. Sci. Press, vol. 66, pp. 117–118, 1893.

6. The wall rocks of California gold mines: Eng. and Min. Jour., vol. 59, pp. 172–173, 1895.

7. Characteristic mines of the California gold belt: Min. Sci. Press, vol. 79, p. 92, 1899.

8. The Vanderbilt mining district, San Bernardino County, California : Min. Sci. Press, vol. 79, pp. 579–580, 1899.

9. The Mother Lode region of California : California Min. Bur. Bull. 18, 154 pp., 1900.

10. Geology of the Yellow Aster mine, California : Eng. and Min. Jour., vol. 87, pp. 1277–1280, 1909.

11. Mineral deposits of the Sierra Nevada, California : Min. World, vol. 36, pp. 121–122, 1912 . . . (abstract) : Eng. Index, 1912, p. 449, 1913.

12. The High Grade mining district (Modoc County, California) : Min. Sci. Press, vol. 105, pp. 273–275, 1912 . . . Mines and Methods, vol. 4, no. 1, pp. 22–24, 1912 . . . (abstract) : Eng. Index, 1912, p. 387, 1913.

13. Geology of the Woody copper district, California : Eng. and Min. Jour., vol. 96, p. 635, 1913.

14. The Trinity-Balaklala-Vulcan mines, Shasta County, California : Min. Sci. Press, vol. 107, pp. 408–411, 1913 . . . (abstract) : Eng. Index, 1913, p. 375, 1914.

15. New scheelite discovery (Greenhorn Mountains), Kern County, California : Min. Sci. Press, vol. 113, p. 768, 1916.

16. Diamonds in California : Min. Sci. Press, vol. 114, pp. 273–275, 1917.

17. The Black Oak mine : Min. Sci. Press, vol. 114, pp. 873–875, 1917.

Stose, George Willis
1. Barytes and barium products: Mineral Resources U. S., 1919, pt. 2, pp. 335–347, 1922.

Stromquist, Arvid A.
1. See Eric, John Howard (1).

Strong, A. M.
1. Andalusite in California : Eng. and Min. Jour., vol. 120, p. 899, 1925.

Strong, Mary Frances Berkholz (See also Berkholz, Mary Frances)
1. Minerals in the Rand district: Gems and Minerals, no. 308, pp. 21–22, May 1963.

2. A high Sierra field trip : Gems and Minerals, no. 309, pp. 22–24, June 1963.

3. Marble Mountains minerals: Gems and Minerals, no. 314, pp. 20–21, Nov. 1963.

4. Gem valley in the Inyo Mountains: Gems and Minerals, no. 317, pp. 18–20, Feb. 1964.

5. Gem hollow in the Little Chuckwallas: Gems and Minerals, no. 318, pp. 22–23, March 1964.

6. Fire agate in the Mule Mountains: Gems and Minerals, no. 319, pp. 16–18, Apr. 1964.

7. Obsidian ridge in Coso Range: Gems and Minerals, no. 320, pp. 16–18, May 1964.

8. Crystal ridge in the Inyo Mountains: Gems and Minerals, no. 325, pp. 16–18, Oct. 1964.

9. Thomsonite at Black Mountain: Gems and Minerals, no. 326, pp. 30–32, Nov. 1964.

Strunz, Hugo
1. "Chromrutil" von der Red Ledge mine ist kein rutil. Redledgeite : Neues Jahrb. Mineral., Monatsh., pp. 107–111, 1961.

2. Redledgeite, eine TiO_2-einlagerungestruktur analog kryptomelan : Neues. Jahrb. Min. mh. 5, pp. 116–119, 1963.

Stuart, F. H.
1. (Chalmers, R. A. and Phillips, R.) Veatchite from the Permian evaporites of Yorkshire : Mineralog. Mag., vol. 30, pp. 389–392, 1953.

Stuiver, Minze
1. Carbon isotopic distribution and correlated chronology of Searles Lake sediments : Am. Jour. Sci., vol. 262, pp. 377–392, 1964.

Surr, Gordon
1. Tungsten near Randsburg: Am. Mining Rev., vol. 22, pp. 7–8, November 1907.
2. A new tungsten find: Am. Mining Rev., vol. 23, p. 9, March 1908.
3. Tungsten at Victorville: Am. Mining Rev., vol. 24, pp. 8–9, July 1908.
4. Gypsum in the Maria Mountains of California: Mining World, vol. 34, pp. 787–790, 891, 1911.
5. Note on occurrence, origin, and uses of gypsum: Mining World, vol. 34, pp. 1283–1284, 1911.
6. Lapis lazuli in southern California: Mining World, vol. 39, pp. 1153–1154, 1913 . . . (abstract): Eng. Index, 1914, p. 467, 1915.

Swartzlow, Carl Robert
1. Ice caves in northern California: Jour. Geology, vol. 43, pp. 440–442, 1935.
2. (and **Keller, Walter David**) Coralloidal opal: Jour. Geology, vol. 45, pp. 101–108, 1937.

Swinney, Chauncey Melvin
1. See Bailey, Edgar Herbert (7).
2. See Fix, Philip Forsyth (1).
3. The Altoona quicksilver mine, Trinity County, California: California Jour. Mines and Geology, vol. 46, pp. 395–404, 1950.
4. See Eric, John Howard (1).

Switzer, George S.
1. See Nisson, William H. (1).
2. Veatchite, a new calcium borate from Lang, California: Am. Mineralogist, vol. 23, pp. 409–411, 1938.
3. See Larsen, Esper Signius (16).
4. Eclogite from the California glaucophane schists: Am. Jour. Sci., vol. 243, pp. 1–8, 1945.
5. Glaucophane schists of the central California Coast Ranges: Unpublished thesis, Harvard University, 1942.
6. (and **Brannock, Walter Wallace**) Composition of veatchite: Am. Mineralogist, vol. 35, pp. 90–92, 1950.
7. "The Geysers," Sonoma County, California: Rocks and Minerals, vol. 26, pp. 504–509, 1951.
8. (and **Bailey, Edgar Herbert**) Afwillite from Crestmore, California: Am. Mineralogist, vol. 38, pp. 629–633, 1953.
9. See Pabst, Adolf (15).
10. (**Clarke, Roy S., Jr.,** and **Sinkankas, John**) Fluorine in hambergite (abst.): Geol. Soc. America Bull., vol. 71, p. 1987, 1960.
11. See Pabst, Adolf (21).

Symons, Henry Heilbronner
1. Mineral-paint materials in California: California Min. Bur. Rept. 26, pp. 148–160, 1930.
2. Museum of the California State Division of Mines: Pacific Mineralogist, vol. 4, no. 2, pp. 9–10, 1937.
3. Quartz gem stones of California: Rocks and Minerals, vol. 15, pp. 39–44, 1940.
4. Accessions to the exhibit: California Div. Mines Rept. 42, pp. 101, 195, 364, 1945.
5. Accessions to the exhibit: California Div. Mines Rept. 42, pp. 61–62, 1946.
6. See Averill, Charles Volney (16).

T

Taft, William H.
1. See Scholl, David W. (1).

Tagg, Kathleen McQ.
1. See Gulbrandsen, Robert Allen (1).

Taliaferro, Nicholas Lloyd
1. Analcite diabase and related rocks in California (abstract): Pan-Am. Geologist, vol. 54, p. 73, 1930 . . . Geol. Soc. America Bull., vol. 42, pp. 296–297, 1931.
2. (and **Turner, R. E.**) Lithophysae-bearing rhyolites in the southern Santa Lucia Range (abstract): Pan-Am. Geologist, vol. 55, p. 374, 1931 . . . Geol. Soc. America Bull., vol. 43, p. 237, 1932.
3. (and **Hudson, Frank Samuel**) Genesis of the manganese deposits of the Coast Ranges of California: California Div. Mines Bull. 125, pp. 217–275, 1943.

4. (and **Solari, A. J.**) Manganese deposits of the Sierra Nevada: their genesis and metamorphism: California Div. Mines and Geol. Bull. 125, pp. 277–332, 1943.

5. Franciscan-Knoxville problem: Am. Assoc. Petroleum Geologists Bull. 27, pp. 109–219, 1943.

Taylor, Bayard
1. Metallischer und Mineral-Reichthum in Californien: Berg- u. hüttenm. Zeit., Band 10, pp. 9–11, 27–31, 44–48, 59–61, 1851.
2. El Dorado, appendix by T. Butler King, pp. 201–247, 1854.

Taylor, George Holmes
1. See Stearns, Harold Thornton (1).

Taylor, H. F. W.
1. Crestmoreite and riversideite: Mineralog. Mag., vol. 30, pp. 155–165, 1953.
2. The identity of jurapaite and xonolite: Mineralog. Mag., vol. 30, pp. 338–341, 1953.
3. See Dent, L. S. (1).
4. See Gard, John Alan (1).
5. See Gard, John Alan (2).
6. See Heller, L. (1).
7. (and **Gard, John Alan**) Crystal structure of foshagite, $Ca_4Si_3O_9(OH)_2$: Nature (London), vol. 183, pp. 171–173, 1959.
8. (and **Gard, John Alan**) The crystal structure of foshagite: Acta Crystallographica 13, II, pp. 785–793, 1960.

Taylor, James W.
1. See Browne, John Ross (1).

Teschemacher, J. E.
1. Platinum grains from Feather River: Boston Soc. Nat. History Proc., vol. 3, p. 280, 1848.
2. Platinum of California: Am. Jour. Sci., 2d ser., vol. 10, p. 121, 1850.
3. Gold in California: Boston Soc. Nat. History Proc., vol. 3, p. 287, 1850.

Thayer, Thomas Prence
1. Preliminary chemical correlation of chromite with the containing rocks: Econ. Geology, vol. 41, pp. 202–217, 1946.
2. See Dow, Donald Huse (1).

Thelen, Paul
1. The differential thermal conductivities of certain schists: Univ. California, Dept. Geol. Sci. Bull., vol. 4, pp. 201–226, 1905.
2. See Knopf, Adolph (1).

Thickstun, Andrew
1. A new tungsten area in California: Eng. and Min. Jour., vol. 144, pp. 78–81, 1943.

Thom, Emma Mertins
1. Bibliography of North American geology for 1940 and 1941: U. S. Geol. Survey Bull. 938, 479 pp., 1942.
2. Bibliography of North American geology, 1929–1939; U. S. Geol. Survey Bull. 937, 1546 pp., 1944.

Thomas, H. H.
1. See Lee, Donald Edward (4).
2. See Lee, Donald Edward (5).

Thomas, W. J.
1. Minerals of Inyo County: Min. Notes and News, p. 9, Nov. 1952.

Thomssen, Richard Wyatt
1. See Pabst, Adolf (17).

Thorndyke, J. T.
1. Mineral wool from wollastonite: Mining and Metallurgy, vol. 17, pp. 133–135, 1936.

Tilley, Cecil Edgar
1. On a custerite-bearing contact rock from California: Geol. Mag., vol. 65, pp. 371–372, 1928 . . . Mineralog. Abstracts, vol. 4, p. 84, 1929.
2. Cuspidine from dolomite contact skarns, Broadford, Skye: Min. Mag., vol. 28, pp. 90–95, 1947.

Tolman, Carl
1. See Stoiber, Richard Edwin (1).

Tolman, Cyrus Fischer, Jr.
1. (and **Rogers, Austin Flint**) A study of the magmatic sulfid ores: Stanford Univ. Pub., Univ. Ser., 76 pp., 1916.
2. Ore deposition and enrichment at Engels, California: Econ. Geology, vol. 12, pp. 379–386, 1917.

Tompkins, E. E.
1. Tourmaline: Pacific Mineralogist, vol. 5, no. 2, pp. 10–11, 1938.

Trainer, John N.
1. Pseudomorphism and zonal growth of garnets from Garnet Hill, California: Rocks and Minerals, vol. 20, no. 8, pp. 359–363, August 1945.
2. Green garnets—uvarovites: Rocks and Minerals, vol. 21, no. 10, pp. 652–655, Oct. 1946.
3. More on uvarovite garnets: Rocks and Minerals, vol. 22, no. 6, pp. 506–509, June 1947.
4. Eight recent garnet finds: Rocks and Minerals, vol. 22, no. 9, pp. 811–818, Sept. 1947, containing a section entitled "Grossularite from near Bishop, Inyo County, California."
5. Vicinal forms on garnets: Rocks and Minerals, vol. 23, no. 2, pp. 105–107, Feb. 1948.

Trask, John Boardman
1. Report on the geology of the Sierra Nevada, or California Range: California Legislature, 4th sess., Ap. to Jour., S. Doc. 59, 30 pp., 1853.
2. Report on the geology of the Coast mountains and part of the Sierra Nevada: California Legislature, 5th sess., Ap. to Jour., S. Doc. 9, 95 pp. 1854.
3. Mineral district of central California: Mineralog. Mag., vol. 3, pp. 121–136, 239–250, 1854.
4. (Extracts from) Geology of California, appendix in F. S. Marryat, Mountains and molehills, pp. 383–393, New York and London, 1855.
5. Report on the geology of the Coast Mountains: California Legislature, 6th sess., Ap. to Jour., S. and A. Doc. 14, 93 pp. 1855.
6. Geology of the Sierra Nevada: Pharmaceutical Jour., Trans., vol. 14, pp. 20–24, 1855.
7. Report on the geology of northern and southern California: California Legislature, 7th sess., Ap. to Jour., S. Doc. 14, 66 pp., 1856.
8. Mines and mining in California: Mineralog. Mag., vol. 5, p. 193, 1856.

Trask, Parker Davies
1. Unique garnet sand forming along the beach at the mouth of the Sur river, Monterey County, California . . . (abstract): Geol. Soc. America Bull., vol. 35, p. 165, 1924.
2. Geology of Point Sur quadrangle, California: Univ. California, Dept. Geol. Sci. Bull., vol. 16, pp. 119–186, 1926 . . . (abstract): Geol. Zentralbl., Band 36, pp. 136–137, 1927.
3. (and **Wu, Chin Chuan**) Free sulphur in recent sediments (abstract): Geol. Soc. America Bull., vol. 41, pp 89–90, 1930 . . . Pan-Am. Geologist, vol. 53, p. 132, 1930.
4. (and **Wilson, Ivan Franklin** and **Simons, Frank Stanton**) Manganese deposits of California—a summary report: California Div. Mines Bull. 125, pp. 51–215, 1943.
5. (and **Simons, Frank Stanton**) Minarets magnetite deposits of Iron Mountain, Madera County, California: California Div. Mines Bull. 129, pp. 117–128, 1948.
6. (and **Rolston, Jack W.**) Engineering geology of San Francisco Bay: Geol. Soc. America Bull., vol. 62, pp. 1079–1110, 1951.

Treganza, Adan E.
1. See Heizer, Robert Fleming (1).

Trengrove, R. R.
1. Investigation of the Strawberry tungsten deposit, Madera County, California; U. S. Bur. Mines Rept. Invest. 4543, 24 pp., Sept. 1949.
2. Investigation of New Idria mercury deposit, San Benito, California: U. S. Bur. Mines Rept. Invest. 4525, 24 pp., Aug. 1949.

Troxel, Bennie Wyatt
1. See Hewett, Donnel Foster (6).
2. (and **Morton, Paul Kenneth**) Mines and mineral resources of Kern County, California: California Div. Mines and Geol. County Report No. 1, 370 pp., 1962.
3. Mineral resources and geologic features of the Trona sheet, California Div. Mines and Geol. Mineral Information Service, vol. 16, pp. 1–7, 1963.

Tuček, K.
1. (and **Kouřimský, J.**) The occurrence of curtisite in Czechoslovakia and its identity with idrialine. Čezk. Akad. Věd, Rozpravy, vol. 63, no. 3, pp. 1–18, 1953.

Tucker, W. Burling
1. Amador, Calaveras, Tuolumne Counties: California Min. Bur. Rept. 14, pp. 1–172, 1916; issued separately under title Mines and mineral resources of Amador County, Calaveras County, Tuolumne County, 1915 ... (abstract): Geol. Zentralbl., Band 27, p. 396, 1922.
2. (and **Waring, Clarence Alm**) El Dorado County: California Min. Bur. Rept. 15, pp. 271–308, 1919.
3. El Dorado, Lassen, Modoc, Tehama, and Tulare Counties: California Min. Bur. Rept. 15, pp. 226–253, 258–266, 271–308, 900–954, 1919.
4. Los Angeles field division: California Min. Bur. Rept. 17, pp. 263–390, 1921.
5. Economic minerals of the Avawatz Mountains: California Min. Bur. Rept. 18, pp. 114–117, 1922.
6. Gold lodes of the East Fork mining district, Trinity County, California: California Min. Bur. Rept. 18, pp. 270–273, 1922.
7. Silver lodes of the South Fork mining district, Shasta County: California Min. Bur. Rept. 18, pp. 313–321, 1922.
8. Imperial, Inyo, Kern, Los Angeles, Riverside, San Bernardino, San Diego, Ventura Counties: California Min. Bur. Rept. 20, pp. 33–50, 87–97, 185–200, 367–374, 1924.
9. Copper resources of Shasta County: California Min. Bur. Rept. 20, pp. 419–447, 1924.
10. San Diego, Ventura Counties: California Min. Bur. Rept. 21, pp. 223–245, 325–382, 1925.
11. Imperial, Inyo Counties: California Min. Bur. Rept. 22, pp. 248–285, 453–530, 1926.
11a. Copper: California Min. Bur. Rept. 22, pp. 138–162, 1926.
12. Mineral resources of Santa Catalina Island: California Min. Bur. Rept. 23, pp. 32–39, 1927.
13. Los Angeles, Mono Counties: California Min. Bur. Rept. 23, pp. 287–345, 374–406, 1927.
14. Kern County: California Min. Bur. Rept. 25, pp. 20–81, 1929.
15. (and **Sampson, Reid J.**) Riverside County: California Min. Bur. Rept. 25, pp. 468–526, 1929.
16. (and **Sampson, Reid J.**) Los Angeles field division: California Min. Bur. Rept. 26, pp. 202–325, 1930.
17. (and **Sampson, Reid J.**) San Bernardino County: California Min. Bur. Rept. 27, pp. 262–401, 1931.
18. See Sampson, Reid J. (4).
19. Notes on mining activity in Inyo and Mono Counties in July, 1931: California Min. Bur. Rept. 27, pp. 543–545, 1931.
20. (and **Sampson, Reid J.**) Ventura County: California Min. Bur. Rept. 28, pp. 247–277, 1932.
21. (and **Sampson, Reid J.**) Gold resources of Kern County: California Div. Mines Rept. 29, pp. 271–339, 1933 ... (abstract): Annotated Bibliography Econ. Geology, vol. 7, p. 41, 1935.
22. South of the Tehachapi gold mining makes new gain: Eng. and Min. Jour., vol. 135, pp. 518–521, 1934.
23. Mining activity at Soledad Mountain and Middle Buttes, Mojave mining district, Kern County: California Div. Mines Rept. 31, pp. 465–485, 1935.
24. Mineral development and mining activity in southern California during the year 1937: California Div. Mines Rept. 34, pp. 8–19, 1938.
25. (and **Sampson, Reid J.**) Mineral resources of Inyo County: California Div. Mines Rept. 34, pp. 368–500, 1938.

26. (and **Reed, Charles H.**) Mineral resources of San Diego County: California Div. Mines Rept. 35, pp. 8–55, 1939.

27. (and **Sampson, Reid J.**) Current mining activity in southern California: California Div. Mines Rept. 36, pp. 9–82, 1940.

28. (and **Sampson, Reid J.**) Economic mineral deposits of the Newberry and Ord Mountains, San Bernardino County: California Div. Mines Rept. 36, pp. 232–254, 1940.

29. (and **Sampson, Reid J.**) Mineral resources of the Kernville quadrangle: California Div. Mines Rept. 36, pp. 322–333, 1940.

30. (and **Sampson, Reid J.**) Recent developments in the tungsten resources of California: California Div. Mines Rept. 37, pp. 565–588, 1941.

31. See Sampson, Reid J. (18).

32. (and **Sampson, Reid J.**) Current notes on activities in the strategic minerals, Los Angeles field district: California Div. Mines Rept. 39, pp. 58–70, 1943.

33. (and **Sampson, Reid J.**) Current mining activity in southern California: California Div. Mines Rept. 39, pp. 118–138, 1943.

34. (and **Sampson, Reid J.**) Mineral resources of San Bernardino County: California Div. Mines Rept. 39, pp. 427–550, 1943.

35. (and **Sampson, Reid J.**) Mineral resources of Riverside County: California Div. Mines Rept. 41, pp. 121–182, 1945.

36. Current notes—Inyo County, San Bernardino County: California Div. Mines Rept. 42, p. 319, 1946.

37. (**Sampson, Reid J.** and **Oakeshott, Gordon Blaisdell**) Mineral resources of Kern County, California: California Jour. Mines and Geology, vol. 45, pp. 297–302, 1949.

Tunell, George

1. See Dickson, Frank Wilson (1).

2. See Eidel, J. James (1).

Turner, Henry Ward

1. The geology of Mount Diablo, California: Geol. Soc. America Bull., vol. 2, pp. 383–402, 1891 ... (abstract): Am. Geologist, vol. 8, pp. 117–118 ... Am. Naturalist, vol. 25, pp. 822–823, 1891 ... Petermanns Mitt., 1892 (Beil zum 38), pp. 115–116, 1892.

1a. Glacial pot-holes in California: Am. Jour. Sci., 3d ser., vol. 44, pp. 453–454, 1892.

2. Geological atlas, Jackson (California) folio (no. 11), pp. 1–6, 1894 ... (abstract): Jour. Geology, vol. 3, pp. 969–970, 1895.

3. Notes on the gold ores of California: Am. Jour. Sci., 3d ser., vol. 47, pp. 467–473, 1894 ... (abstract): Zeitschr, prakt. Geologie, Jahrg. 4, p. 275, 1896.

4. The rocks of the Sierra Nevada: U. S. Geol. Survey, 14th Ann. Rept., pt. 2, pp. 435–495, 1894 ... (abstract): Jour. Geology, vol. 3, pp. 985–986, 1895 ... Nature, vol. 53, p. 466, 1896.

5. See Lindgren, Waldemar (8).

6. See Lindgren, Waldemar (9).

7. See Lindgren, Waldemar (10).

8. Further notes on the gold ores of California: Am. Jour. Sci., 3d ser., vol. 49, pp. 374–380, 1895 ... (abstract): Min. Sci. Press, vol. 70, p. 344, 1895.

9. Gold in serpentine: Am. Jour. Sci., 3d ser., vol. 49, p. 478, 1895.

10. Description of the gold belt; description of the Jackson sheet: U. S. Geol. Survey, Geol. Atlas Jackson folio (no. 11), 6 pp., 1894 (reprinted 1914) ... (abstract): Jour. Geology, vol. 3, pp. 969–970, 1895.

11. Notice of some syenite rocks from California: Am. Geologist, vol. 17, pp. 375–388, 1896.

12. Further contributions to the geology of the Sierra Nevada: U. S. Geol. Survey, 17th Ann. Rept. pt. 1, pp. 521–762, 1896.

13. (**Lindgren, Waldemar** and **Becker, George Ferdinand**) Description of the gold belt: U. S. Geol. Survey Geol. Atlas Sonora folio (no. 41), 2 pp., 1897 ... Bidwell Bar folio (no. 43), 2 pp., 1898 ... Downieville folio (no. 37), 8 pp., 1897.

14. Description of the gold belt; description of the Downieville sheet: U. S. Geol. Survey Geol. Atlas Downieville folio (no. 37), 8 pp., 1897.

16. (and **Ransome, Frederick Leslie**) Description of the gold belt; description of the Sonora sheet: U. S. Geol. Survey Geol. Atlas, Sonora folio (no. 41), 7 pp., 1897.

17. Description of the gold belt; description of the Bidwell Bar sheet: U. S. Geol. Survey Geol. Atlas, Bidwell Bar folio (no. 43), 6 pp., 1898.

18. (and **Ransome, Frederick Leslie**) Description of the gold belt; description of the Big Trees sheet, California: U. S. Geol. Survey Geol. Atlas, Big Trees folio (no. 51), 8 pp., 1898.

19. Notes on rocks and minerals from California: Am. Jour. Sci., 4th ser., vol. 5, pp. 421–428, 1898.

20. The occurrence and origin of diamonds in California: Am. Geologist, vol. 23, pp. 182–191, 1899 . . . (abstract): Min. Sci. Press, vol. 78, p. 586, 613, 1899.

21. See Hillebrand, William Francis (1), and Clarke, F. W. (6).

22. Notes on unusual minerals from the Pacific states: Am. Jour. Sci., 4th ser., vol. 13, pp. 343–346, 1902 . . . (abstract): Min. Sci. Press, vol. 84, p. 296, 1902.

23. The Greenback copper mine, Kern County, California: Eng. and Min. Jour., vol. 74, pp. 547–548, 1902.

24. Observations on Mother Lode gold deposits, California: Am. Inst. Min. Met. Eng. Trans., 2 pp., October 1903.

25. The Cretaceous auriferous conglomerate of the Cottonwood mining district, Siskiyou County, California: Eng. and Min. Jour., vol. 76, pp. 653–654, 1903 . . . (abstract): Geol. Zentralbl, Band 9, p. 681, 1907.

26. Native copper in greenstone from the Pacific slope: Eng. and Min. Jour., vol. 77, p. 276, 1904 . . . (abstract): Geol. Zentralbl., Band 9, p. 681, 1907.

27. Notes on contact-metamorphic deposits in the Sierra Nevada Mountains: Am. Inst. Min. Met. Eng. Trans., vol. 34, pp. 666–668, 1904 . . . (abstract): Geol. Zentralbl., Band 9, p. 708, 1907 . . . Min. Sci. Press, vol. 88, p. 97, 1904.

28. The sodium nitrate deposits of the Colorado: Min. Sci. Press, vol. 94, pp. 634–636, 1907.

29. The ore deposits of Copperopolis, California: Econ. Geology, vol. 2, pp. 797–799, 1907 . . . (abstract): Geol. Zentralbl., Band 12, p. 18, 1909.

30. The vein system of the Standard mine, Bodie, California: Am. Inst. Min. Met. Eng., Bull. 22, pp. 623–624, 1908 . . . Trans., vol. 39, pp. 795–797, 1909 . . . (abstract): Geol. Zentralbl., Band 12, p. 167, 1909.

31. Unusual gold ore: Min. Sci. Press, vol. 97, p. 835, 1908.

32. (and **Rogers, Austin Flint**) A geologic and microscopic study of a magmatic copper sulphide deposit in Plumas County, California, and its modification by ascending secondary enrichment: Econ. Geology, vol. 9, pp. 359–391, 1914.

33. The magmatic origin of the chalcopyrite and bornite at Engels (Plumas County, California): Min. Sci. Press, vol. 123, pp. 333–334, 1924.

34. The Wilshire gold mine: Eng. and Min. Jour., vol. 114, pp. 888–890, 1922.

35. Origin of Wilshire gold ore (California): Eng. and Min. Jour., vol. 118, p. 172, 1924.

Turner, Mortimer Darling
1. See Pask, Joseph Adam (1).

Turner, R. E.
1. See Taliaferro, Nicholas Lloyd (2).

Turrentine, J. W.
1. The occurrence of potassium salts in the salines of the United States: U. S. Dept. Agr., Bur. Soils Bull. 94, 96 pp., 1913.

Tyler, P. M.
1. (and **Santmyers, R. M.**) Platinum: U. S. Bur. Mines Inf. Circ. 6389, 24 pp., 1931.

Tyson, Philip T.
1. Report on the geology of California: 31st Cong., 1st sess., S. Ex. Doc. 47, pp. 3–74, 1850 (republished by Wm. Minifie and Co., Baltimore, 1851).

U

Ungemach, H.
1. Sur la stibiotantalite: Soc. franç. mineralogie, Bull. 32, pp. 92–103, 1909.
2. Sur certains mineraux sulfates du Chili: Soc. franç. mineralogie, Bull. 58, pp. 97–221, 1935.

V

Vacher, H. C.
1. See Davis, C. W. (1).

Valeton, J. J. P.

1. Über die Struktur des Benitoits: Fortschr. Mineralogie, Band 12, pp. 91–92, 1927.

Van Amringe, Edwin Verne

1. The gem minerals of San Diego County, California: Mineralog. Soc. Southern California Bull. 2, no. 7, pp. 1–4, 1933 . . . Mineralog. Abstracts, vol. 5 p. 281, 1933.

2. Benitoite, neptunite, and joaquinite: Oregon Mineralogist, vol. 2, no. 11, pp. 9–10, 1934.

3. Fine colemanite specimens found in California: Mineralogist, vol. 3, no. 1, p. 51, 1935.

4. See Armstrong, V. L. (1).

Vaughan, Francis Edward

1. Geology of the San Bernardino Mountains north of San Gorgonio Pass: Univ. California, Dept. Geol. Sci. Bull., vol. 13, pp. 319–411, 1922 . . . (abstract): Geol. Zentralbl., Band 30, p. 396, 1924.

Veatch, J. Allen

1. The genesis of the mercury deposits of the Pacific coast: Am. Inst. Min. Met. Eng., Bull. 86, pp. 209–226, 1914.

Veatch, John A.

1. Notes on a visit to the "mud volcanoes" in the Colorado Desert, in the month of July, 1857: California Acad. Sci. Proc., vol. 1, pt. 2, pp. 104–108, 1857 . . . Am. Jour. Sci., 2d ser., vol. 26, pp. 288–295, 1858.

2. Discovery of borax in California, in Browne and Taylor, Mineral resources of the states and territories west of the Mississippi, pp. 179–185, 1867.

Vedder, John Graham

1. (and **Norris, Robert Matheson**) Geology of San Nicolas Island, California: U. S. Geol. Survey Prof. Paper 369, 65 pp., 1963.

Vernon, James W.

1. See Logan, Clarence August (25).

2. See Davis, Fenelon F. (4).

Ver Planck, Wm. E., Jr.

1. See Honke, Martin T., Jr. (1)

2. Gypsum in California: California Div. Mines Bull. 163, 151 pp., 1952.

2a. Salines in southern California: California Div. Mines and Geol. Bull. 170, ch. VIII, pp. 5–14, 1954.

3. Mines, mineral resources and mineral industries of Marin County, California: California Jour. Mines and Geology, vol. 51, pp. 221–289, 1955.

4. Salt in California: California Div. Mines Bull. 175, 168 pp., 1958.

5. Vitreous silica: Calif. Div. Mines and Geol., Mineral Information Service, vol. 15, pp. 1–5, 10, 1962.

Vigfussen, V. A.

1. The system $CaO-SiO_2-H_2O$, hillebrandite and foshagite: Am. Jour. Sci., 5th ser., vol. 21, pp. 67–78, 1931.

Vitaliano, Charles Joseph

1. Needles magnesite deposit, San Bernardino County, California: California Jour. Mines and Geology, vol. 46, pp. 357–372, 1950.

2. See Mason, Brian Harold (1).

Vlisidis, Angelina Calomeris

1. See Schaller, Waldemar Theodore (57).

2. See Erd, Richard Clarkson (2).

3. See Schaller, Waldemar Theodore (58).

Vodges, Anthony Wayne

1. A bibliography relating to the geology, paleontology, and mineral resources of California: California Min. Bur. Bull. 30, 290 pp., 1904.

Volin, M. E.

1. (and **Matson, E. J.**) Investigation of the Ladd manganese deposits, San Joaquin County, California: U. S. Bur. Mines Rept. Invest. 4580, 14 pp., Dec., 1949.

Von Leicht, F.

1. Cinnabar in San Luis Obispo County, California: Min. Sci. Press, vol. 78, p. 482, 1899.

Von Petersdorff, F. C.
1. Meteorites: California Min. Bur. Rept. 10, pp. 946–951, 1890.
2. The mineral resources of Kern County, California, 51 pp., Bakersfield, California, 1895.

Vonsen, Magnus
1. Death Valley and the borates of California: Rocks and Minerals, vol. 3, pp. 73–77, 1929.
2. See Irving, John (1).
3. The discovery of borates in California: Mineralogist, vol. 3, no. 12, pp. 3–4, 21–25, 1935.
4. (and **Hanna, G. Dallas**) Borax Lake, California: California Div. Mines Rept. 32, pp. 99–108, 1936.
5. See Gale, William Alexander (1).
6. Minerals at "The Geysers," Sonoma County, California: California Div. Mines Rept. 42, pp. 287–293, 1946.
7. Borates of California: Rocks and Minerals, vol. 26, pp. 494–503, 1951.

Voy, C. D.
1. Geology of Santa Rosa Island (abstract): Am. Geologist, vol. 20, pp. 226–227, 1897.

W

Wadsworth, Marshman Edward
1. [On picotite from Mt. Shasta, California]: Boston Soc. Nat. History Proc., vol. 21, pp. 314–315, 1882.

Wagoner, Luther
1. Report on Guadalupe quicksilver mine, California: Eng. and Min. Jour., vol. 34, pp. 185–186, 1882.
2. The geology of the quicksilver mines of California: Eng. and Min. Jour., vol. 34, p. 334, 1882.

Wahlstrom, Ernest Eugene
1. Graphic granite: Am. Mineralogist, vol. 24, pp. 681–698, 1939.

Wainewright, Wilfrid B.
1. Borate deposits of California: Manchester G. M. Soc., Trans., vol. 31, pp. 60–66, 1909 . . . Inst. Min. Eng. Trans., vol. 37, pp. 156–162, 1909 . . . (abstract): Geol. Zentralbl. 16, p. 552, 1911.

Wainwright, John E. N.
1. See Gross, Eugene Bischoff (1).

Walenta, K.
1. Haiweeit (gastunit) von Badgastein: Neues Jahrb. Mineral., Monatsh., pp. 37–47, 1960.

Walker, Edwin F.
1. A Yokuts cemetery at Elk Hills: Southwest Mus. Masterkey, vol. 9, no. 5. 1935.

Walker, John A.
1. Graphite: Mineral Resources U. S., 1883–84, pp. 915–919, 1885.

Walker, George Walton
1. Sierra Blanca limestone in Santa Barbara County, California: California Div. Mines, Special Rept. 1-A, 5 pp. 1950.
2. The Calera limestone, San Mateo and Santa Clara Counties, California: California Div. Mines, Special Rept. 1-B, 8 pp., 1950.
3. Rosamond uranium prospect, Kern County, California: California Div. Mines Special Rept. 37, 8 pp., 1953.
4. (and **Griggs, Allan Bingham**) Chromite deposits of the southern Coast Ranges of California: California Div. Mines Bull. 134, pt. 2, chap. 2, pp. 40–88, 1953.
5. (**Lovering, Tom Seward,** and **Stephens, Hal G.**) Radioactive deposits in California: California Div. Mines Special Rept. 49, 38 pp., 1956.

Wallace, Robert Earl
1. Structure of a portion of the San Andreas rift in southern California: Geol. Soc. America Bull., vol. 60, pp. 781–806, 1949.

Ward, Henry L.
1. The Canyon City meteorite from Trinity County, California: Am. Jour. Sci., 4th ser., vol. 17, pp. 383–384, 1904.

Waring, Clarence Alm
1. Geological map of Inyo County, California, with notes on geology: California Min. Bur., 1917.
2. (and **Huguenin, Emile**) Inyo County: California Min. Bur. Rept. 15, pp. 29–134, 1919.
3. See Tucker, W. Burling (2).
4. Butte, Placer, Sacramento, Yuba Counties: California Min. Bur. Rept. 15, pp. 181–225, 309–459, 1919.
5. See Bradley, Walter Wadsworth (6).

Waring, C. L.
1. See Gottfried, David (1).

Waring, Gerald Ashley
1. Quartz from San Diego County, California: Am. Jour. Sci., 4th ser., vol. 20, pp. 125–127, 1905 . . . (abstract): Geol. Zentralbl., Band 10, p. 536, 1908.
2. The pegmatite veins of Pala, San Diego County (California): Am. Geologist, vol. 35, pp. 356–369, 1905 . . . (abstract): Geol. Zentralbl., Band 8, p. 642, 1906.

Warner, J. J.
1. The first California gold (letter to San Francisco Bulletin): Eng. and Min. Jour., vol. 32, p. 170, 1881.

Warner, Thor
1. Silver discovery in Saline Valley, Inyo County, California: Eng. and Min. Jour., vol. 121, p. 938, 1926 . . . (abstract): Geol. Zentralbl., Band 36, p. 10, 1927.
2. Mercury deposit in Coso range, Inyo County, California: California Min. Bur. Rept. 26, pp. 59–63, 1930.

Wartman, Franklin Secord
1. (and **Guild, Frank Nelson**) Wulfenite from Lavic, California: Am. Mineralogist, vol. 6, pp. 167–168, 1921 . . . Mineralog. Abstracts, vol. 1, p. 420, 1922.

Washington, Henry Stephens
1. A chemical study of the glaucophane schists: Am. Jour. Sci., 4th ser., vol. 11, pp. 47–52, 1901.

Wasson, Joseph
1. Bodie and Esmeralda: 60 pp., San Francisco, 1878 (abstract): Min. Sci. Press, vol. 36, pp. 345, 377, 1878.
2. An account of San Ygnacia and the leading mines of the Cerro Gordo district, California, New York, 1880.

Watanabe, T.
1. Kotoit, ein neues gesteinsbildendes magnesiumborat: Min. p. Petr. Mitth. vol. 50, pp. 441–463, 1939.

Watkins, S. L.
1. El Doradoite: Am. Mineralogist, vol. 2, p. 26, 1917.

Watters, Lucius
1. Notes on some shoreline minerals of San Francisco, California: Rocks and Minerals, vol. 28 nos. 11–12, pp. 563–566, Nov.–Dec. 1953.
2. Notes on the glaucophane schists of the California Coast Ranges: Rocks and Minerals, vol. 30, nos. 11–12, pp. 572–577, 1955.

Watts, William L.
1. Merced, Sacramento, San Joaquin, San Mateo, Santa Clara, Santa Cruz, Solano, Stanislaus, Yolo Counties: California Min. Bur. Rept. 10, pp. 324–331, 496–514, 548–566, 586–594, 604–605, 620–626, 659–671, 680–690, 773–793, 1890.
2. Alameda, Colusa, Del Norte, Fresno, Glenn, Humboldt, Marin, Mendocino Merced, Placer, Sacramento, Santa Clara, San Joaquin, Sonoma, Stanislaus, Sutter, Kern, Lake, Contra Costa, Tehama, Tulare Counties: California Min. Bur. Rept. 11, pp. 121–138, 179–199, 210–240, 249–258, 319–322, 334–336, 374–375, 394, 453–479, 485–492, 1893.
3. Gas and petroleum yielding formations of the central valley of California: California Min. Bur. Bull. 3, 100 pp., Sacramento, 1894.
4. Oil and gas yielding formations of California: California Min. Bur. Bull. 19, 236 pp., Sacramento, 1901.

Waugh, J. L. T.
1. See Frondel, Clifford (8).

Weaver, Charles Edwin
1. Geology of the Coast Ranges immediately north of the San Francisco Bay region, California: Geol. Soc. America, Mem. 35, 242 pp., 1949.

Webb, Robert Wallace
1. The Cerro Gordo mining district: Pacific Mineralogist, vol. 2, no. 1, pp. 9–11, 1935.
2. Tetradymite from Inyo Mountains, California: Am. Mineralogist, vol. 20, pp. 399–400, 1935.
3. See Murdoch, Joseph (4).
4. Gold mining and gold discovery in California: Pacific Mineralogist, vol. 4, no. 2, pp. 5–7, 1937.
5. See Murdoch, Joseph (6).
6. Investigation of a new occurrence of alurgite from California: Am. Mineralogist, vol. 24, pp. 123–129, 1939.
7. Large sphene crystals from San Jacinto Mountains, California: Am. Mineralogist, vol. 24, pp. 344–346, 1939 . . . (abstract): Am. Mineralogist, vol. 24, p. 193, 1939.
8. See Murdoch, Joseph (11.)
9. Quartz xenocrysts in olivine basalt, from the southern Sierra Nevada of California: Am. Mineralogist, vol. 26, pp. 321–337, 1941.
10. See Murdoch, Joseph (14).
11. Two andalusite pegmatites from Riverside County, California: Am. Mineralogist, vol. 28, pp. 581–593, 1943.
12. See Brady, Lionel Francis (1).
13. See Murdoch, Joseph (21).
14. See Murdoch, Joseph (27).
15. See Murdoch, Joseph (39).
16. See Murdoch, Joseph (40).
17. See Murdoch, Joseph (44).
18. See Murdoch, Joseph (30a).

Weber, A. H.
1. Santa Clara County: California Min. Bur. Rept. 9, pp. 48–56, 1890.

Weber, Frank Harold, Jr.
1. A beryl discovery in southeastern San Diego County, California. California Div. Mines and Geol., Mineral Information Service, vol. 15, no. 2, pp. 8–11, 1962.
2. Barite in California: California Div. Mines and Geol., Mineral Information Service, vol. 16, pp. 1–10, 1963.
3. Geology and mineral deposits of the Ord Mountain district, San Bernardino County, California: California Div. Mines and Geol. Spec. Rept. 45, pp., 1964.

Weeks, Fred Boughton
1. The Minaret iron deposit, Madera County: California Min. Bur. Rept. 14, pp. 555–558, 1913–14.
2. Possibilities of the Calico mining district (San Bernardino County, California): Eng. and Min. Jour., vol. 119, pp. 757–763, 1925 . . . (abstract): Geol. Zentralbl., Band 37, pp. 7–8, 1928.
3. Mineralized breccias at Calico, California: Eng. and Min. Jour., vol. 121, p. 484, 1926 . . . (abstract): Geol. Zentralbl., Band 35, pp. 445–446, 1927.
4. The Calico mining district: Mining and Metallurgy, vol. 10, pp. 531–534, 1929.

Weil, F.
1. Neues Platinerz aus Californien: Dinglers Polytech. Jour., Band 153, p. 41, 1860 . . . (abstract): Neus Jahrb., 1860, p. 354.

Weinschenk, E.
1. See Cohen, E. (1).

Weiss, Lionel Edward
1. See Best, Myron G. (1).

Wells, Francis Gerritt
1. (**Page, Lincoln Ridler** and **James, Harold Lloyd**) Chromite deposits of the Pilliken area, El Dorado County, California: U. S. Geol. Survey Bull. 922-O, pp. 417–460, 1940.
2. See Rynearson, Garn Arthur (2).
3. See Hawkes, Herbert Edwin, Jr. (2).
4. (et al.). Chromite deposits near Seiad and McGuffy Creeks, Siskiyou County, California: U. S. Geol. Survey Bull. 948-B, 62 pp., 1949.

5. (and **Cater, Frederick William, Jr.,** and **Rynearson, Garn Arthur**) Chromite deposits of Del Norte County, California: California Div. Mines. Bull. 134, pt. 1, chap. 1, pp. 1–76, 1946.

6. (and **Cater, Frederick William, Jr.**) Chromite deposits of Siskiyou County, California: California Div. Mines Bull. 134, pt. 1, chap. 2, pp. 77–127, 1950.

Wells, Lansing S.
1. See Flint, Einar Philip (1).

Wells, Roger Clark
1. A new occurrence of hydrogioberite (Chiles Valley, Napa County, California): Am. Jour. Sci., 4th ser., vol. 30, pp. 189–190, 1910.
2. Sodium sulphate; its sources and uses: U. S. Geol. Survey Bull. 717, 43 pp., 1923.
3. Analyses of rocks and minerals: U. S. Geol. Survey Bull. 878, 134 pp., 1937.

Wells, W. V.'
1. A visit to the quicksilver mines of New Almaden; reprinted from Harper's New Monthly Magazine, pp. 25–40, June 1863.

West, H. E.
1. Tin in California: Eng. and Min. Jour., vol. 79, pp. 852–853, 1905.
2. Early tin mining in California: Eng. and Min. Jour., vol. 117, pp. 55–57, 1924.
3. New attempt to develop Temescal tin deposit in southern California: Eng. and Min. Jour., vol. 126, pp. 131–132, 1928 . . . (abstract): Annotated Bibliography Econ. Geology, vol. 1, p. 105, 1928 . . . Geol. Zentralbl., Band 40, p. 423, 1929.

Wheeler, Dooley P., Jr.
1. See Hawkes, Herbert Edwin, Jr. (1).
2. See Hawkes, Herbert Edwin, Jr. (2).

Wheeler, George Montague
1. Preliminary report of explorations in Nevada, California and Arizona: 42d Cong., 2d sess., S. Ex. Doc. 65, pp. 42–43, 45–46, 48, 1872.
2. Geographical and geological explorations and surveys west of the 100th meridian, III (geology), 681 pp., 1875.
3. Annual report upon the geographical surveys west of the 100th meridian in California, Nevada, Utah, Colorado, Wyoming, New Mexico, Arizona, and Montana: 44th Cong., 2d sess., H. Ex. Doc. 1, pt. 2, vol. 2, pt. 3 app. J. J., 355 pp., 1876.
4. Annual report upon the geographical surveys west of the 100th meridian in California, Nevada, Utah, Colorado, Wyoming, New Mexico, Arizona, and Montana: Appendix of U. S. War Dept. Chief Eng., Ann. Rept. 1878, 234 pp., 1878.
5. Geographical and geological explorations and surveys west of the 100th meridian, VII (archeology), 497 pp., 1879.

Wherry, Edgar Theodore
1. Notes on alunite, psilomelanite and titanite: U. S. Nat. Mus. Proc., vol. 51, pp. 81–88, 1916 . . . Mineralog. Abstracts, vol. 1, pp. 378–379, 1922.
2. Neodymium as the cause of the red-violet color in certain minerals: Washington Acad. Sci. Jour., vol. 7, pp. 143–146, 1917 . . . Mineralog. Abstracts, vol. 1, p. 230, 1921.
3. The species rank of guadalcazarite: Am. Mineralogist, vol. 5, p. 37, 1920.
4. See Foshag, William Frederick (8).

White, Donald Edward
1. Antimony deposits of the Wildrose Canyon area, Inyo County, California: U. S. Geol. Survey Bull. 922-K, pp. 307–325, 1940.
2. (and **Roberson, Charles Elmer**) Sulphur Bank, California. Geological Soc. America Buddington Memorial Volume: Petrologic studies: pp. 397–428, 1962.
3. (**Anderson, E. T.,** and **Grubbs, D. K.**) Geothermal brine well: mile deep drill hole may tap ore-bearing magmatic water and rock undergoing metamorphism: Science, vol. 139, pp. 919–922, 1963.

White, W. A.
1. The mineralogy of desert sands: Am. Jour. Sci., 5th ser., vol. 237, pp. 742–747, 1939.

Whitfield, James Edward
1. Analyses of some natural borates and borosilicates: Am. Jour. Sci., 3d ser., vol. 34, pp. 281–287, 1887.
2. Analyses of natural borates and borosilicates: U. S. Geol. Survey Bull. 55, pp. 56–62, 1889.

3. Analyses of six new meteorites: U. S. Geol. Survey Bull. 60, pp. 103–114, 1890.
4. Analyses of borates: U. S. Geol. Survey Bull. 419, p. 300, 1910.

Whiting, H. A.
1. Mono County, California: California Min. Bur. Rept. 8, pp. 352–401, 1888.

Whitmore, Duncan Richard Elmer
1. (**Berry, Leonard Gascoigne**, and **Hawley, James Edwin**) Chrome micas: Am. Mineralogist, vol. 31, pp. 1–23, 1946.

Whitney, Josiah Dwight
1. Metallic wealth of the United States, 510 pp., Philadelphia, 1854.
2. First annual report of the State Geologist for 1862: App. Jour. Senate and Assembly, 14th sess., 12 pp., 1863.
3. Lecture on geology delivered before the legislature of California: App. Jour. Senate and Assembly, 14th sess., 17 pp., 1863.
4. Second annual report of the State Geologist for 1863: App. Jour. Senate and Assembly, 15th sess., 7 pp., 1864.
5. On borax in California: Am. Jour. Sci., 2d ser., vol. 41, pp. 255–258, 1866 . . . California Geol. Survey, vol. 1, pp. 96–100, 1865.
6. Tin in Temescal range: California Geol. Survey, vol. 1, pp. 180–181, 1865.
7. Geological survey of California, Geology, 1, Report of progress and synopsis of the field work from 1860 to 1864, xxvii, 498 pp., 1865 . . . (abstract): Am. Jour. Sci., 2d ser., vol. 41, pp. 124, 231–246, 351–368, 1866.
8. ——————————: California Acad. Sci. III, p. 354, 1867.
9. (Minerals in California and Westcoast America), in von Richthofen, F., Mittheilungen von der Westküste Nordamerika's: (Fortsetzung) Deutsche geol. Gesell, Zeitschr., Band 21, pp. 2–4, 1869.
10. The auriferous gravels of the Sierra Nevada of California: Harvard Coll. Mus. Comp. Zoology Mem., vol. 6, 569 pp., 1879.
11. The Coast Ranges: Appendix to California geological survey, vol. 2 (geology), 143 pp., Cambridge, 1882.

Whitney, Walter T.
1. A recently discovered aerolite from Rosamond Dry Lake, California: Popular Astron., vol. 49, p. 387, 1941 . . . Contrib. Soc. Res. Meteorites, vol. 2, p. 291, 1941.

Wichels, Ernest
1. See Carleton, S. J. (1).

Wicks, Frank R.
1. Crystalline talc. Operations in California of the Pacific Coast Talc Co.; Eng. and Min. Jour., vol. 130, pp. 319–321, 1930 . . . California Min. Bur. Rept. 27, pp. 100–104, 1931.

Wiebelt, F. J.
1. Investigation of the Mohawk lead-zinc mine, San Bernardino County, California: U. S. Bur. Mines Rept. Invest. 4478, 7 pp., June, 1949.
2. Investigation of Carbonate King zinc mine (Crystal Cave group), San Bernardino County, California: U. S. Bur. Mines Rept. Invest. 4522, 12 pp., Aug., 1949.

Wiese, John Herbert
1. (and **Page, Lincoln Ridler**) Tin deposits of the Gorman district, Kern County, California: California Div. Mines Rept. 42, pp. 31–52, 1946.
2. Geology and mineral resources of the Neenach quadrangle, California: California Div. Mines Bull. 153, 53 pp., 1950.

Wilke, R. M.
1. Benitoite and neptunite: Mineral Collector, vol. 14, pp. 167–168, 1908.

Wilkes, Charles
1. United States exploring expedition during the years 1838–1842, vol. X (Geology, by J. D. Dana), 756 pp., 1849.

Williams, Albert, Jr.
1. Mineral resources of the United States: Mineral Resources U. S., 1882, XI, 813 pp., 1883.
2. Mineral resources of the United States: Mineral Resources U. S., 1883–84, vol. 14, 1016 pp., 1885.

Williams, Howel
1. Geology of the Lassen Volcanic National Park, California: Univ. California, Dept. Geol. Sci. Bull., vol. 21, pp. 195–386, 1932.
2. Mount Shasta, California: Zeitschr. Vulkanologie, Band 15, pp. 225–253, 1934.

Williams, John H.
1. Tungsten deposits in San Bernardino County, California: Min. Sci. Press, vol. 103, p. 545, 1911.

Wilson, A. D.
1. The great California diamond mines: Overland Monthly, vol. 291, 1904.

Wilson, F. L.
1. The Seneca mining district, California: Min. Sci. Press, vol. 103, pp. 682–683, 1911 . . . (abstract): Eng. Index, 1912, p. 388, 1913.

Wilson, Hewitt
1. Iron oxide mineral pigments of the United States: U. S. Bur. Mines Bull. 370, 198 pp., 1933.

Wilson, Harry David Bruce
1. (and **Hendry, N. W.**) Geology and quicksilver deposits of Coso Hot Springs area (abstract): Geol. Soc. America Bull., vol. 51, p. 1965, 1940.
2. See Fraser, Horace John (1).

Wilson, Ivan Franklin
1. See Trask, Parker Davies (4).
2. Geology of the San Benito quadrangle, California: California Div. Mines Rept. 39, pp. 183–270, 1943.

Wilson, James S.
1. On the gold regions of California: Geol. Soc. London Quart. Jour., vol. 10, pp. 308–321, 1854.

Wilson, L. Kenneth
1. Tungsten deposits of the Darwin Hills, Inyo County, California: Econ. Geology, vol. 38, pp. 543–560, 1943.

Wilson, Robert Warren
1. Heavy accessory minerals of the Val Verde tonalite: Am. Mineralogist, vol. 22, pp. 122–132, 1937.

Wiltsee, E. A.
1. See Hobson, John B. (2).
2. Some additional Sierra County mines: California Min. Bur. Rept. 11, pp. 413–420, 1893.

Winchell, Alexander Newton
1. Camsellite and szaibelyite: Am. Mineralogist, vol. 14, pp. 48–49, 1929.
2. Elements of optical mineralogy, 4th ed., 1951.

Winston, W. B.
1. Barium: California Jour. Mines and Geology, vol. 45, pp. 85–97, 1949.

Winterer, Edward L.
1. (and **Durham, David Leon**) Geology of southeastern Ventura Basin, Los Angeles County, California: U. S. Geol. Survey Prof. Paper 334-H, pp. 275–366, 1962.

Wise, William Stewart
1. An occurrence of geikielite: Am. Mineralogist, vol. 44, pp. 879–882, 1959.
2. (and **Eugster, Hans Peter**) Celadonite: synthesis, thermal stability and occurrence: Am. Mineralogist, vol. 49, pp. 1031–1083, 1964.

Wisker, A. L.
1. The gold-bearing veins of Meadow Lake district, Nevada County: California Div. Mines Rept. 32, pp. 189–204, 1936.

Wolfe, Caleb Wroe
1. (and **Riska, Daphne**) Crystallography of jadeite from near Cloverdale, California: (abstract) Geol. Soc. America Bull., vol. 62, p. 1491, 1951.
2. (and **Caras, Alice**) Unit cell of schairerite: (abstract) Geol. Soc. America Bull., vol. 62, p. 1491, 1951. . . . Am. Mineralogist, vol. 36, pp. 912–915, 1951.
3. Crystallography of jadeite crystals from near Cloverdale, California: Am. Mineralogist, vol. 40, nos. 3–4, pp. 248–260, 1955.

Wolff, John Eliot
1. Dumortierite from Imperial County: Am. Mineralogist, vol. 15, pp. 188–193, 1930.

Woodford, Alfred Oswald
1. The Catalina metamorphic facies of the Franciscan series: Univ. California, Dept. Geol. Sci. Bull., vol. 15, pp. 49–68, 1924 . . . (abstract): Geol. Zentralbl., Band 33, p. 98, 1926.
2. The San Onofre breccia; its nature and origin: Univ. California, Dept. Geol. Sci. Bull., vol. 15, pp. 159–280, 1925 . . . (abstract): Geol. Zentralbl., Band 33, p. 109, 1926.
3. See Bailey, Thomas Laval (1).
4. (and **Harriss, Trewhitt Fairman**) Geology of Blackhawk Canyon, San Bernardino Mountains, California: Univ. California, Dept. Geol. Sci. Bull., vol. 17, pp. 265–304, 1928 . . . (abstract): Geol. Soc. America Bull., vol. 39, p. 268, 1928 . . . Geol. Zentralbl., Band 41, p. 151, 1930 . . . Eng. Index, 1928, p. 868, 1929.
5. See Laudermilk, Jerome Douglas (1).
6. See Laudermilk, Jerome Douglas (3).
7. See Foshag, William Frederick (22).
8. See Laudermilk, Jerome Douglas (5).
9. (**Laudermilk, Jerome Douglas,** and **Bailey, Edgar Herbert**) Treanorite, a new mineral from Crestmore, California (abstract): Geol. Soc. America Bull., vol. 51, p. 1965, 1940.
10. (**Crippen, Richard A.,** and **Garner, Kenneth B.**) Section across Commercial quarry, Crestmore, California: Am. Mineralogist, vol. 26, pp. 351–381, 1941.
11. Crestmore minerals: California Div. Mines Rept. 39, pp. 333–365, 1943.

Woodhouse, Charles Douglas
1. See Jeffery, Joseph Arthur (3).
2. See Jeffery, Joseph Arthur (4).
3. A new occurrence of montroydite in California: Am. Mineralogist, vol. 19, pp. 603–604, 1934.
4. Change them every 10,000 miles: Mineralogist, vol. 4, no. 3, pp. 3–4, 37–38, 1936.
5. The Mono County andalusite mine: Rocks and Minerals, vol. 34, pp. 486–493, 1951.
6. (and **Norris, Robert Matheson**), A new occurrence of millerite: Am. Mineralogist, vol. 42, pp. 113–115, 1957.
7. (and **Norris, Robert Matheson**), Nickel and mercury minerals at Klau: Gems and Minerals, no. 234, pp. 18–20, March 1957.
8. See Norris, Robert Matheson (4).

Woodring, Wendell Phillips
1. (**Bramlette, Milton Nunn,** and **Kew, William Stephen Webster**) Geology and paleontology of Palos Verdes Hills, California: U. S. Geol. Survey Prof. Paper 207, 125 pp., 1946.

Woodward, Arthur
1. Fluorite beads in California: Southern California Acad. Sci. Bull. 36, pp. 1–56, 1937.

Woolsey, W. J.
1. Asbestos in California: Pacific Min. News, vol. 1, pp. 104–106, 1922.

Wright, Fred Eugene
1. The optical properties of roscoelite: Am. Jour. Sci., 4th ser., vol. 38, pp. 305–308, 1914.
2. Note on the lithophysae in a specimen of obsidian from California: Washington Acad. Sci. Jour., vol. 6, pp. 367–369, 1916 . . . Mineralog. Abstracts, vol. 2, p. 78, 1923 . . . Geol. Zentralbl., Band 25, p. 515, 1921.
3. (and **Allen, Eugene Thomas**) Curtisite, a new organic mineral from Skaggs Springs, Sonoma County, California (abstract): Am. Mineralogist, vol. 11, p. 67, 1925 . . . Am. Mineralogist, vol. 15, pp. 169–173, 1930 . . . Mineralog. Abstracts, vol. 2, p. 239, 1927; vol. 4, p. 348, 1930.

Wright, J. W. A.
1. Fresno County mines: Min. Sci. Press, vol. 39, p. 121, 1879.

Wright, Lauren Albert
2. Geology of the Silver Lake talc area, San Bernardino County, California: Geol. Soc. America Bull., vol. 60, p. 1932, 1949.
3. See Campbell, Ian (2).
4. See Jahns, Richard Henry (5).

5. (Stewart, Richard Maclin, Gay, Thomas Edwards, Jr., and Hazenbush, George C.) Mines and mineral resources of San Bernardino County, California: California Jour. Mines and Geology, vol. 49, pp. 49–192, 1953.

6. Geology of Silver Lake talc deposits, San Bernardino County, California: California Div. Mines Special Rept. 38, 30 pp., 1954.

7. Geology of the Superior talc area, Death Valley, California: California Div. Mines Special Rept. 20, 22 pp., 1952.

8. See Chidester, Alfred Herman (1).

9. (Chesterman, Charles W., and Norman, L. A.) Occurrence and use of non-metallic commodities in southern California: California Div. Mines and Geol. Bull. 170, ch. VIII, pp. 59–70, 1954.

Wright, Lawrence Boynton
1. Geology of Santa Rosa Mountain area, Riverside County, California: California Div. Mines Rept. 42, pp. 9–14, 1946.

Wright, Randall
1. Magnetic iron sulphide of Pliocene of Ventura Basin, California: Am. Assoc. Petroleum Geologists Bull., vol. 21, pp. 627–629, 1937.

Wright, W. G.
1. Rubellite in California: Mineral Collector, vol. 1, no. 2, pp. 18–20, 1894.
2. Cinnabar in California: Mineral Collector, vol. 2, no. 2, pp. 24–27, 1895.

Wu, Chin Chuan
1. See Trask, Parker Davies (3).

Wyld, James
1. Guide to the gold country of California, London, 1849.
2. Notes on distribution of gold throughout the world, 44 pp., London, 1852.

Y

Yale, Charles Gregory
1. California diamonds: West Am. Sci., vol. 2, p. 60, 1885.
2. Borax: Mineral Resources U. S., 1903, pp. 1017–1028, 1904.
3. California mines and minerals: California Min. Bur. Bull. 41, 56 pp., Sacramento, 1905.
4. (and Gale, Hoyt Stoddard) Borax: Mineral Resources U. S., 1912, pt. 2, pp. 839–846, 1913.
5. Borax: Mineral Resources U. S., 1913, pt. 2, pp. 521–536, 1914.
6. Borax: Mineral Resources U. S., 1914, pt. 2, pp. 285–296, 1916.
7. Borax: Mineral Resources U. S., 1916, pt. 2, pp. 387–389, 1919.
8. (and Stone, Ralph Walter) Magnesite: Mineral Resources U. S., 1920, pt. 2, pp. 1–16, 1923.

Yates, Lorenzo Gordin
1. Catalogue of minerals in Lorenzo G. Yates' collection, Santa Barbara, California, 71 pp., Santa Barbara, 1886.
2. Allanite: Santa Barbara Soc. Nat. History Bull. 1887, pp. 11–12, 1887.
3. Notes on the geology and scenery of the islands forming the southern line of the Santa Barbara Channel: Am. Geologist, vol. 5, pp. 43–52, 1890.
4. Stray notes on the geology of the Channel Islands: California Min. Bur. Rept. 9, pp. 171–174, 1890.
5. Prehistoric California: Southern California Acad. Sci. Bull. 4, pp. 26–27, 1905.

Yates, Robert Giertz
1. See Eckel, Edwin Butt (1).
2. (and Hilpert, Lowell Sinclair) Quicksilver deposits of central San Benito and northwestern Fresno Counties, California: California Div. Mines Rept. 41, pp. 11–35, 1945.
3. See Ross, Clyde Polhemus (6).
4. (and Hilpert, Lowell Sinclair) Quicksilver deposits of eastern Mayacmas district, Lake and Napa Counties, California: California Div. Mines Rept. 42, pp. 231–286, 1946.

Yoder, Hatten Schuyler, Jr.
1. (and Chesterman, Charles Wesley) Jadeite of San Benito County, California: California Div. Mines, Special Rept. 10-C, 8 pp., 1951.

Young, George Joseph
1. Potash salts and other salines in the Great Basin region: U. S. Dept. Agr., Bull. 61, 96 pp., 1914.

2. The sink of the Amargosa (Death Valley, Inyo County, California): Eng. and Min. Jour., vol. 105, pp. 985–986, 1918.

3. Gold mining in Carson Hill, California: Eng. and Min. Jour., vol. 112, pp. 725–729, 1921.

4. Magnesite mining at Red Mountain, California: Eng. and Min. Jour., vol. 120, pp. 178–180, 1925.

5. Mines and minerals of Inyo County, California: Eng. and Min. Jour.-Press, vol. 120, pp. 969–972, 1925 . . . (abstract): Geol. Zentralbl., Band 37, p. 228, 1928.

6. Mining tungsten at Pine Creek: Eng. and Min. Jour., vol. 121, pp. 605–606, 1926 . . . (abstract): Rev. geologie et sci. connexes, tome 7, pp. 455–456, 1926.

7. Mining and milling barite: Eng. and Min. Jour., vol. 130, pp. 70–71, 1930.

8. Mining and processing magnesite: Eng. and Min. Jour., vol. 133, pp. 422–426, 1932.

Youngman, E. P.

1. Titanium: U. S. Bur. Mines Inf. Circ. 6365, 20 pp., 1930.

Z

Zachariasen, W. H.

1. The crystal structure of benitoite, $BaTiSi_3O_9$: Zeitschr. Kristallographie, Band 74, pp. 139–146, 1930.

Zalinski, E. R.

1. Some notes on Greenwater: Eng. and Min. Jour., vol. 83, pp. 77–82, 1907.

Zepharovich, V. von

1. See Moore, Gideon E. (4).

COUNTIES OF CALIFORNIA: MINERALS AND MINERAL LISTS

In this section, minerals reported from California through 1964 are listed by counties, with some commentary on each county's mineral economics. Acknowledgment is given of the earlier indices of minerals by counties of California prepared by Miss Elizabeth Collins, California Division of Mines and Geology, in Supplement to Bulletin 173, Minerals of California, 1955 through 1957, published in 1960; to the late Rita Matson of the Santa Barbara Mineral and Gem Society, Santa Barbara, Calif.; and to Professor Donald O. Emerson, University of California, Davis.

ALAMEDA COUNTY

Alameda County, one of the populous counties on the east side of San Francisco Bay, produced mineral commodities in 1964 valued in excess of 20 million dollars. The county has grown at a fast rate, with increasing industrialization and consequent urbanization of its lands, at the expense of at least one famous mineral locality. The Alma mine, in the Leona rhyolite, a collector's locality of note, contributed one new mineral to mineralogical knowledge, boothite, Schaller (1) p. 195. Today the mine area is so urbanized that the locality is inaccessible. The only occurrence of the mineral krohnkite in the state is also from the Alma mine. Over 40 minerals are reported from this county: actinolite, alunogen, analcime, anauxite, aragonite, barite, bementite, boothite, calcite, chalcanthite, chalcopyrite, chromite, copiapite, copper, enstatite, epsomite, galena, glaucophane, gold, halotrichite, hydromagnesite, inesite, kaolinite, krohnkite, lawsonite, maghemite, magnesite, melanterite, natrolite, penninite, pisanite, psilomelane, pyrite, pyrolusite, quartz, rhodochrosite, rhodonite, stibnite, talc, vivianite, wollastonite, zaratite, and zircon.

ALPINE COUNTY

Alpine County, situated near the crest of the Sierra Nevada is the least populous of California's 58 counties. Its mineralogical richness however, is attested by several well-known mines producing silver, copper, and sulfur. More silver minerals come from Alpine County than any other, including native silver, argentite, polybasite, proustite, pyrargyrite, stephanite, and stromeyerite. Good crystals of arsenolite and arsenopyrite are reported, and the relatively uncommon (to California) copper mineral enargite formed the chief copper ore mineral in the Mogul region, where it occurred in large quantity. The county is also reported to have been the site of the earliest copper claim (1855) in the state. Over 40 minerals reported through December 1964 from the county are: andalusite, argentite, arsenolite, arsenopyrite, barite, calcite, chalcanthite, chalcocite, chalcopyrite, chloropal, enargite, famatinite, galena, garnet, halite, halotrichite, iddingsite, ilmenite, lazulite, melanterite, polybasite, potash alum, proustite, pyrargyrite, pyrite, pyrrhotite, quartz, realgar, rhodochrosite, romerite, rutile, silver, stephanite, stibnite, stromeyerite, sulfur, tenorite, tetrahedrite, tourmaline, and wolframite.

AMADOR COUNTY

"A ribbon of solid gold ⅜ of an inch or more in thickness . . ." is an early description of an occurrence of gold in this famous gold-producing county of the Mother Lode. Amador County, in the foothills of the Sierra Nevada, is crossed by the Mother Lode belt, in which there are many interesting mineralogical occurrences. Arsenopyrite crystals intergrown with arborescent gold, quartz (variety rock crystal), and the interesting variety of tremolite known as mountain leather and mountain cork are reported. Diamonds were found in the early days of California mining (1850–1865), one locality yielding 60–70 stones from placers. As late as 1934, one stone of 2.65 carats was recovered. In addition, Amador County contributed one new substance, ionite, a hydrocarbon, described in 1878 by Purnell (1).

Minerals reported through 1964 from Amador County are: alleghany-ite, anauxite, ankerite, apatite, arsenopyrite, axinite, cassiterite, chalced-ony, chalcopyrite, chromite, clinochlore, copper, diamond, dolomite, epsomite, galena, gold, graphite, ionite, kaolinite, löllingite, malachite, marcasite, melanterite, mendozite, molybdenite, penninite, psilomelane, pyrophyllite, pyrrhotite, quartz, rhodochrosite, rhodonite, rutile, scheel-ite, serpentine, sphalerite, strengite, talc, tephroite, terahedrite, tremol-ite, wollastonite, and zircon.

BUTTE COUNTY

Butte County, situated on the western flank of the north-central Sierra Nevada, is noted for its large production of mineral commodities from placer deposits. In the gold rush, the placer deposits yielded, in addition to commercial gold, such rare minerals as iridosmine and tel-lurium. In addition in the extensive placers, garnet, epidote, axinite, cassiterite, corundum (sapphire), rutile, topaz, and zircon are reported. Axinite in good crystals, only slightly water-worn, were also noted. In addition over 300 diamonds were recovered from 1853 to 1867 from the Cherokee flat placers. This county has the distinction of having pro-duced the largest number of diamonds of any California county. Dia-monds were collected from 1853 to the latest reported in 1918. One meteorite, an iron and one 832-ounce gold nugget from the Willard claim near Magalia, J. D. Hubbard (1) p. 253, are also of mineralogical interest. Minerals reported from this county are: andalusite, antimony, axinite, barite, bournonite, cassiterite, chalcedony, chromite, chryso-beryl, corundum, diamond, epidote, galena, garnet, glauconite, gold, gypsum, idocrase (vesuvianite), iridosmine, iron (meteorite), lead, mag-netite, prochlorite (chlorite), psilomelane, quartz, rhodonite, rutile, spinel, talc, tellurium, tephroite, topaz, vivianite, and zircon.

CALAVERAS COUNTY

Almost 100 minerals have been reported from this famous gold-pro-ducing county of the Mother Lode Belt. Home of discovery of two new minerals, the tellurides melonite, discovered in 1867, and calaverite in 1868, the gold deposits carried other rich and interesting telluride minerals such as altaite, coloradoite, hessite, petzite, sylvanite, and tetradymite. The iron tellurite emmonsite is reported from California only in this county. The second California occurrence of the mineral boothite, which was first discovered in Alameda County in 1903, was in this county. From the Morgan Mine in the Mother Lode gold belt in Calaveras County, came the largest gold nugget from California valued at \$43,534 on the pre-1930 gold standard. Chalcopyrite in large masses has been mined for its copper. Pyrite and quartz in good crystals are widely spread in the gold mines, and many other minerals are reported of fine quality from this continuous contributor to the mineral wealth, both scientific and economic, of the State of California.

The minerals reported through 1964 as occurring in Calaveras County are: albite, allanite, altaite, alunite, ankerite, aragonite, arsenopyrite, azurite, barite, bementite, boothite, bornite, brochantite, calaverite, calcite, cerargyrite, chalcanthite, chalcedony, chalcocite, chalcopyrite, chromite, chrysotile, cobaltite, coloradoite, columbite, copper, coquimbite, covellite, cuprite, diaspore, dolomite, emmonsite, epidote, erythrite, eucairite, galena, garnet, glaucophane, gold, graphite, gypsum, hessite, hornblende, idocrase (vesuvianite), ilmenite, jamesonite, kaolinite, magnetite, malachite, marcasite, margarite, mariposite, melonite, molybdenite, nagyagite, niccolite, opal, orthoclase, penninite, petzite, potash alum, psilomelane, pyrite, pyrolusite, pyromorphite, pyrrhotite, quartz, rhodochrosite, rhodonite, scheelite, serpentine, siderite, silver, smaltite, sphalerite, stibnite, sylvanite, talc, tellurium, tenorite, tephroite, tetradymite, tetrahedrite, tourmaline, tremolite, uraconite, uraninite, vesuvianite, vivianite, and zircon.

COLUSA COUNTY

Colusa County, like all counties of the Sacramento Valley, has much of its bedrock geology buried under the gravel, sands, and muds deposited by the Sacramento River and its tributaries. Though unconsolidated sedimentary rocks are often rich in mineral commodities, they do not normally develop widely varied and unique minerals of special mineralogical significance. However, Colusa County embraces foothill belts of the Coast Range Mountains on its western margin, and here, at Sulfur Creek, most interesting mineral assemblages have been found. Gold and argentian gold (electrum) was mined, and the Manzanita mine was a gold producer from 1865 to 1892. Leaf and wire gold came from this mine in specimen quality. Cinnabar with gold has been collected, and the unusual variety of cuprite, chalcotrichite, is also found. Native copper was discovered as early as 1863, and copper minerals of several types are reported. Sulfur in excellent crystals has been collected. The Sulfur Creek locality accounts for over half of the minerals reported in the county.

The minerals recorded from Colusa County through 1964 are: alunite, aragonite, argentian gold, chalcocite, chalcopyrite, chromite, cinnabar, copper, cuprite, datolite, epidote, gold, hydromagnesite, marcasite, metacinnabar, pectolite, prehnite, psilomelane, pyrite, pyrolusite, stibnite, sulfur, tenorite, and thomsonite.

CONTRA COSTA COUNTY

Contra Costa County includes the Mt. Diablo block of the Coast Ranges and the Mt. Diablo Mining District from which, for many years, mercury was produced from the black sulfide, metacinnabar, in the Mt. Diablo mine. The county is in close proximity to the University of California, Berkeley, and the minerals of the Mt. Diablo (Ryne) mine were collected repeatedly and reported upon. From this Mining District are noted 14 minerals, of which one, siderotil, is reported to date from no other localities in California. The soda-rich amphibole, crossite, was first described from this county in 1894, Palache (3) p. 181. Currently Contra Costa County is feeling the effects of the urban expansion of the San Francisco Bay area, and many of its lands are being removed from future mineralogical study.

The minerals reported from Contra Costa County are: actinolite, albite, anauxite, anthophyllite, apatite, barite, bornite, chalcopyrite, chromite, cinnabar, copiapite, crossite, diallage, diopside, enstatite, epsomite, fluorite, halotrichite, jadeite, lawsonite, marcasite, melanterite, metacinnabar, potash alum, prochlorite, psilomelane, pumpellyite, pyrolusite, römerite, rutile, schuetteite, siderotil, sphene, stibnite, tremolite, valentinite, voltaite, and zaratite.

DEL NORTE COUNTY

The number of reported mineral occurrences in Del Norte County, in view of the geologic setting of the county, is small indeed. This is probably a reflection of accessibility and location. However, Del Norte County reports 29 minerals, of which two, awaruite (terrestrial nickel-iron) and troilite are reported only from this county. Troilite, when described in 1908, was the first known occurrence of this mineral under terrestrial conditions, having been found before only in meteorites. In addition, chromite, native mercury, and the relatively rare (in California) nickel mineral garnierite, are reported from this county. The largest copper nugget (300 pounds) from the state also comes from this county, and such unusual minerals as iridosmine, monazite, and diamonds of microscopic size are found in the placers of the county.

Minerals reported to date are: arsenopyrite, awaruite, bornite, chalcocite, chalcopyrite, chromite, copper, cuprite, diamond, enargite, ferrimolybdite, garnet, garnierite, graphite, iridosmine, magnesite, magnetite, marcasite, mercury, monazite, penninite, pyrolusite, pyrrhotite, silver, tenorite, tetrahedrite, troilite wollastonite zaratite, and zircon.

EL DORADO COUNTY

El Dorado County, of Mother lode fame, has 67 mineral species reported within its boundaries. In the early mineral history of the county, gold in excellent crystals was found and several of the specimens preserved in museums in the state and elsewhere are among the finest ever recovered in the world. The first meteorite found in California, the Shingle Springs iron, weighing 85 pounds was found in this county. Quartz, as rock crystal as phantom quartz, and as smoky quartz occurs and fine specimens are still being discovered. The only occurrences reported to date in California of bismuth-gold is from El Dorado, and the new mineral roscoelite a vanadium-bearing mica, was discovered in 1875, J. Blake (2).

Roscoelite occurs laminated with gold between the mica flakes. Unfortunately, few specimens have been preserved from the original find because the gold content was so high that the specimen material became ore. Three localities are known in El Dorado County for this mineral. Roscoelite has not been confirmed from any other California locality, although it is doubtfully reported from Los Angeles County.

The minerals reported from El Dorado County are: anatase, ankerite, antimony, arsenopyrite, axinite, azurite, barite, bismuth-gold, bornite, brookite, calaverite, calcite, carnotite, chalcocite, chalcopyrite, chloropal, chromite, clinochlore, copper, coquimbite, cuprite, diamond, diopside, enargite, epidote, ferrimolybdite, galena, garnet, garnierite, gold, halotrichite, hematite, hessite, hornblende, idocrase (vesuvianite), ilmenite, iron (meteorite), magnetite, mariposite, massicot, molybdenite, orthoclase, penninite, petzite, powellite, prehnite, pyrite, pyrolusite, pyromorphite, pyrophyllite, quartz, rhodonite, roscoelite, scheelite, serpentine, siderite, sphalerite, sphene, stromeyerite, talc, tenorite, topaz, tourmaline, variscite, wavellite, wulfenite, and zircon.

FRESNO COUNTY

Fresno County lies astride the San Joaquin Valley. Its geologic setting, unlike most California counties, includes three geologic provinces: The Coast Ranges, the Central Valley, and the Sierra Nevada, extending to the crestline of this great range. Consequently the mineral occurrences are widely varied, including minerals associated with serpentine rocks and consolidated sedimentary rocks of the Coast Ranges, those characteristic of alluvial deposits of the Great Valley, and those of the crystalline igneous and metamorphic complex of the granites, marbles, and schists of the Sierra Nevada. Many localities of the nearly 90 minerals reported show minerals in individual crystals. The new mineral fresnoite, with several other new minerals, is described from Big Creek. One of the first reports (if not the first) of chrome in California came from this county where in 1865 J. D. Whitney, (7) p. 59, recounted the discovery of a block of chromite nearly 150 cubic feet in size, thought at first to be silver ore. Two general localities have special interest from the standpoint of variety and number of minerals: the Twin Lakes and Minaret Regions, Chesterman (1), and the Kings Canyon copper belt mines.

Fresno County produced in 1964 mineral products whose value exceeded 80 million dollars. In that year, production value was exceeded in the State of California by only 7 other counties of the 58 in California.

Mineral occurrences in Fresno County as reported to date are: acmite, analcime, anauxite, andalusite, apatite, aragonite, arsenopyrite, artinite, barite, barkevikite, bassanite, benitoite, beryl, bindheimite, bismuthinite, bismutite, bornite, brucite, calcite, celsian, chalcanthite, chalcedony, chalcocite, chalcopyrite, chromite, clinochlore, clinohumite, collophane, cuprite, cuprotungstite, diamond, diaspore, diopside, epidote, ferrimolybdite, fresnoite, galena, garnet, gillespite, gold (argentian), graphite, gypsum, hedenbergite, hematite, hornblende, hydromagnesite, idocrase (vesuvianite), ilvaite, krauskopfite, leucophosphite, ludwigite, macdonaldite, magnesite, magnetite, molybdenite, muirite, natrolite, opal, phlogopite, potash alum, powellite, psilomelane, pyrrhotite, quartz, rhodonite, rutile, sanbornite, scheelite, serpentine, silver, sphalerite, sphene, spinel, talc, taramellite, tenorite, topaz, tourmaline, traskite, tremolite, vermiculite, verplanckite, walstromite, witherite, wollastonite, and zircon.

GLENN COUNTY

Glenn County is located in the north central Sacramento Valley. Geologically, the county is underlain by the unconsolidated sediments of the lower Sacramento River drainage, and by the sedimentary section of largely Cretaceous rocks that crop out on the western edge of the county. A small area includes Coast Range materials in which chromite has been found and claims staked. Native copper as float is reported from three localities, and the only California occurrence known to date of the rare hydrous vanadate of copper, volborthite, comes from the Mammoth copper mine on Grindstone Creek, Larsen (11) p. 154.

The minerals reported from Glenn County are chromite, copper, psilomelane, pyrolusite, and volborthite.

HUMBOLDT COUNTY

Humboldt County of northern coastal California has deposits of chromium, copper, and manganese in several areas from which interesting minerals have been collected. Systematic mineralogical studies have not been undertaken to date, however, on any of the deposits. Manganese minerals reported include bementite, braunite, psilomelane, pyrolusite, rhodochrosite, and rhodonite. A 400 lb. block of native copper as float is recorded from Humboldt County, and chromite has been shipped commercially from this county. One of the two occurrences of native tin, a true mineralogical rarity, is asserted to be at Orleans Bar. The placer deposits that are extensive along the rivers of the county have yielded the rare iridosmine from two placers. In 1850, an interesting gold find was made of Gold Bluff Beach, where travelers reported that the beach was literally paved with gold. The samples collected were confirmed to be gold, but upon return to the beach, the waves and tide had dispersed "the deposit," S. Johnson (1) p. 536, R. W. Raymond (7) p. 145.

Humboldt County is credited with occurrences of 36 minerals as follows: apatite, barite, bementite, bornite, braunite, chalcocite, chalcopyrite, chlorite, chromite, chrysocolla, collophane, copper, cuprite, dahllite, diamond, epidote, garnierite, gold, hematite, idocrase (vesuvianite), iridosmine, lawsonite, magnesite, malachite, millerite, neotocite, nephrite, psilomelane, pyrolusite, pyrrhotite, rhodochrosite, rhodonite, scheelite, spinel, tin, vivianite, and zircon.

IMPERIAL COUNTY

Imperial, one of the counties bordering Mexico, is a rich desert county, spanning the Salton Sink and the Colorado-Imperial Desert. Irrigation makes it one of the most productive land areas in the world per acre. About 60 minerals are reported from the county. Two mining areas, the Cargo Muchacho and the Paymaster, have produced gold, and also have mineralogical variety in manganese, copper, and silver compounds. Dumortierite in large placer boulders of dark blue color are found in a unique alluvial deposit in the Cargo Muchacho Mountains. The rare arsenic oxide claudetite in good crystals occurs near the Colorado River in northeastern Imperial County and is the only verified find of the mineral in California. One of two reported occurrences of blödite, and the interesting kyanite deposit of the Vitrefax Corporation, with its excellent specimen material, are in this county. A bedded deposit of very pure gypsum is interesting collecting because of the many varieties of gypsum found there. In the Fish Creek Mountains, this deposit produces commercial gypsum.

The more than 60 minerals reported are: andalusite, anhydrite, argentite, arsenopyrite, autunite, azurite, barite, blödite, bornite, calcite, carnotite, celestite, cerussite, chalcocite, chalcopyrite, chrysocolla, claudetite, copper, covellite, cristobalite, cuprite, diamond, dumortierite, epsomite, fayalite, galena, garnet, garnierite, glauberite, graphite, gypsum, halloysite, hematite, iron (meteorite), jarosite, kyanite, limonite, manganite, mariposite, metatorbernite, mirabilite, muscovite, niter, psilomelane, pyrolusite, pyrophyllite, realgar, sal ammoniac, scorodite, siderite, silver, soda niter, sphalerite, sphene, sulfur, talc, tetrahedrite, thenardite, torbernite, tourmaline, tridymite, turquoise, uranophane, vanthoffite, wollastonite, and wulfenite.

INYO COUNTY

Inyo County, in eastern California, spans the Sierra Nevada and Basin Ranges geological provinces, and is a most prolific county from the standpoint of number and variety of mineral occurrences that have unique or unusual mineralogical significance. It is exceeded in number of occurrences only by larger San Bernardino County. Over 150 different mineral species have been reported, including several minerals new to mineralogy and 16 minerals reported with only one occurrence each in the state, all in Inyo County. Many noted Mining Districts are found in this county, such as Cerro Gordo, Darwin, Modoc, Panamint, Ubehebe and others, each with many mines in which common and unusual minerals have been found. The famous Twenty-Mule Team borax localities in Death Valley, and the many associated borate and saline minerals of the valley, come from this county. The legendary Cerro Gordo mine, with more than 30 minerals, was working when the Yanqui arrived. An occurrence of obsidian with lithophysae of cristobalite, tridymite, fayalite, clinoferrosilite, and magnetite has such beautiful and abundant specimen material that it is valued the world over. Mineral production in the county is still important. Over 126,000 ounces of silver were produced in 1964, and talc is shipped in quantity from several mines.

The minerals reported from Inyo County are: adamite, allanite, alunite, alunogen, analcime, andalusite, andorite, anglesite, anhydrite, annabergite, antlerite, apatite, aphthitalite, aragonite, argentite, arsenic, arsenopyrite, atacamite, aurichalcite, autunite, axinite, azurite, bakerite, barite, bassanite, beryl, beta-uranotil, bindheimite, bismuth, bismuthinite, bismutite, blödite, borax, bornite, boulangerite, bournonite, brochantite, burkeite, calcite, caledonite, cassiterite, celestite, cerargyrite, cerussite, cervantite, chalcanthite, chalcedony (quartz), chalcocite, chalcopyrite, chiastolite, chloritoid, chloropal, chrysocolla, cinnabar, clausthalite, clinoferrosilite, clinoptilolite, clinozoisite, cobaltite, colemanite, copper, coquimbite, coronadite, covellite, creedite, cristobalite, crocoite, cryptomelane, cuprite, cuprotungstite, datolite, dawsonite, deweylite, diopside, dolomite, dufrenoysite, duftite, ecdemite, embolite, enargite, epidote, epsomite, erythrite, famatinite, fayalite, ferberite, fluorite, franckeite, galena, garnet, gay-lussite, gehlenite, geocronite, ginorite, glauberite, goethite, gold, gold (argentian), goslarite, gowerite, greenockite, grossularite, guanajuatite, gypsum, halloysite, hanksite, haiweeite, halite, heliophyllite, hematite, hemimorphite, hornblende, howlite, hydroboracite, hydromagnesite, hydrozincite, iddingsite, idocrase (vesuvianite), ilsemannite, inyoite, iron (meteorite), jamesonite, jarosite, kyanite, laumontite, lazulite, leadhillite, lepidolite, leucite, limonite, linarite, liroconite, litharge, löllingite, macallisterite, magnesite, magnetite, malachite, marcasite, massicot, matildite, melanterite, metacinnabar, metahaiweeite, metastibnite, metatorbernite, meyerhofferite, microcline, mimetite, minium, mixite, molybdenite, montmorillonite, nahcolite, natrolite, natron, nepheline, niccolite, niter, nobleite, orthoclase, phillipsite, phlogopite, phosgenite, pickeringite, pirssonite, plancheite, plumbogummite, plumbojarosite, potash alum, powellite, prehnite, priceite, probertite, pseudomalachite, psilomelane, pyrite, pyrolusite, pyromorphite, pyrophyllite, pyrrhotite, quartz, realgar, reinite, rosasite, sal ammoniac, sassolite, sborgite, scapolite, scheelite, schwatzite, scorodite, senarmontite, sepiolite, serpentine, shattuckite, siderite, sillimanite, silver, smaltite, smithsonite, soda niter, sphalerite, sphene, spinel, stannite, staurolite, stephanite, stibiconite, stibnite, stilbite, stilpnomelane, stolzite, stromeyerite, strontianite, sulfur, sylvite, talc, tenorite, tetradymite, tetrahedrite, thenardite, thermonatrite, topaz, tobernite, tourmaline, tremolite, tridymite, trona, tungstite, tunellite, turgite, ulexite, uranophane, valentinite, vanadinite, vivianite, weeksite, willemite, wolframite, wollastonite, wulfenite, zircon, and zoisite.

KERN COUNTY

Kern County, one of California's largest counties, is the leading mineral-producing county in the state. Petroleum products are prolific, and there is a great variety in its mineralogical material. Some of the earliest mining activities in the state were in Kern County. The county includes nearly all the geological variety of the state, including parts of the Coast Range, Transverse Range, Basin Range, Sierra Nevada, and San Joaquin Valley geological provinces. The antimony deposits of the Havilah and Amalie mining areas have been worked sporadically since 1880, and nuggets of native antimony up to 300 pounds are reported. Cassiterite in one of the two known deposits of California has been developed commercially in this county, and nodular masses of tin oxide up to 3 tons have been processed. In the county are the localities of three of California's 19 meteorite falls to date, and the giant borax-producing deposit at Boron on the eastern edge of the county has contributed several new minerals as "firsts" for California. In addition, several minerals are reported in California only from Kern County. Extensive recent prospecting for uranium has resulted in the discovery of eight or more radioactive minerals in the county from several localities. The literature on mining in the county features several prolific mining areas such as Amalie, Soledad, Greenhorn, Rand, Kernville, and others. In addition, large well-formed crystals are abundant in several localities. There are large scheelite crystals in the Greenhorn Mountain tungsten area, giant garnets (almandine) on Tejon Ranch, and sharp, large, near-perfect orthoclase twinned crystals from Cinco. The lavas of Red Rock Canyon contain excellent small crystals of minerals of the zeolite family suitable for micromount mineralogical collections.

The more than 130 reported minerals of Kern County are: actinolite, allanite, alunite, analcime, andalusite, antimony, apatite, aragonite, argentite, argentojarosite, arsenopyrite, attapulgite, aurichalcite, autunite, axinite, azurite, barite, benitoite, berthierite, biotite, bismuth, bismuthinite, borax, bornite, bournonite, bromyrite, brookite, calcite, carnotite, cassiterite, celadonite, cerargyrite, cervantite, chalcedony, chalcocite, chalcopyrite, chloritoid, chloropal, chrysocolla, cinnabar, clinoptilolite, coccinite, coffinite, colemanite, copiapite, copper, cuprite, cuprotungstite, cyrtolite, dolomite, dumortierite, electrum, enstatite, epidote, erionite, euxenite, ferrimolybdite, fluorite, galena, garnet, gay-lussite, gerstleyite, gibbsite, gold, goslarite, graphite, gummite, gypsum, hematite, hemimorphite, heulandite, howlite, hydroboracite, iddingsite, idocrase (vesuvianite), ilmenite, ilsemannite, inderite, inyoite, iron (meteorite), jamesonite, jarosite, jordisite, kermesite, kernite, kurnakovite, laumontite, lazulite, lead, leonhardite, lepidomelane, litharge, ludwigite, maghemite, magnesite, magnetite, malachite, marcasite, mariposite, massicot, melanterite, mesolite, meta-autunite, metatorbernite, metazeunerite, meyerhofferite, mimetite, minium, mirabilite, molybdenite, montmorillonite, muscovite, natrolite, niter, opal, orpiment, orthoclase, paigeite, phillipsite, piemontite, plumbojarosite, powellite, probertite, proustite, psilomelane, pyrargyrite, pyrite, pyroxmangite, pyrrhotite, quartz, realgar, rhodonite, roscoelite, sassolite, searlesite, scapolite, scheelite, schroeckingerite, scorodite, serpentine, sillimanite, silver, smithsonite, sphalerite, sphene, spodumene, stibiconite, stibnite, stilpnomelane, stromeyerite, strontianite, sulfur, tenorite, tephroite, tetrahedrite, thenardite, thomsonite, tincalconite, torbernite, tourmaline, tremolite, tunellite, turgite, tyuyamunite, ulexite, uraninite, uranophane, valentinite, vanadinite, vermiculite, walpurgite, wolframite, wollastonite, wulfenite, xenotime, and zoisite.

KINGS COUNTY

Kings County is situated in the southwestern part of the San Joaquin Valley. Part of the Central Valley geological province of the state, the county is underlain entirely by sedimentary rocks, with unconsolidated gravels and sands composing most of the surface geology. Accordingly, the variety of mineralogical products is small in number, although high in value for the area of the county. Anapaite is found in this county, the only California occurrence to date.

The minerals reported from Kings County are anapaite, atacamite, chromite, cinnabar, epsomite, gypsum, magnesite, and mercury.

LAKE COUNTY

Borax Lake and Sulfur Bank in Lake County are two of the most famous mineral collecting areas in the state. Known to be mineralized since the gold rush days, the two areas have yielded unique and new minerals, as well as several rare minerals. Teepleite was discovered as a new mineral species from Borax Lake in 1938, where it occurs with at least a dozen other saline and borate compounds. The rare mineral northupite, described first from San Bernardino County, also occurs at Borax Lake, making two known occurrences to date in the world. The Sulfur Bank and Mayacmas areas are also noted for the abundance of common and uncommon mercury minerals, and from this highly volcanic and recently active region over 20 minerals are reported. The region has also been a continuous producer of mercury since its discovery in the middle of the last century. Over a half-million flasks of mercury have been marketed. The substance posepnyte, a hydrocarbon, was first described from the county in 1877.

Minerals reported from Lake County to date are: alunite, ammoniojarosite, anatase, anorthite, aragonite, azurite, borax, bornite, buddingtonite, calcite, chalcocite, chromite, cinnabar, copiapite, copper, coquimbite, cordierite, cristobalite, curtisite, diopside, dolomite, epsomite, fluorite, gay-lussite, glauberite, glaucophane, goethite, gold, gypsum, halite, hematite, jarosite, kaolinite, marcasite, melanterite, mercury, metacinnabar, metastibnite, millerite, montmorillonite, montroydite, northupite, opal, orpiment, pectolite, pirssonite, posepnyte, potash alum, psilomelane, pyrolusite, quartz, realgar, riebeckite, sassolite, serpentine, schuetteite, stibnite, sulfur, teepleite, thermonatrite, tiemannite, tridymite, trona, tschermigite, ulexite, wollastonite, and zoisite.

LASSEN COUNTY

Lassen County, in northeastern California, is a sparsely populated, rich agricultural and stock-raising county, with superb scenery and forest resources. The county is almost entirely underlain by volcanic rocks, and its mineralogical localities are not prolific. Interesting specimens of native copper and chalcocite have been collected from the Lummis mine, and, in the most recent accelerated prospecting for uranium sources, the only occurrence in the state of sabugalite, a hydrous phosphate of uranium and aluminum, has been reported.

Minerals reported to date from Lassen County are: annabergite, autunite, beryl, carnotite, chalcocite, cinnabar, copper, epidote, erythrite, garnet, gold (argentian), hematite, jefferisite, mesolite, metacinnabar, pyrochlore, pyrolusite, sabugalite, smaltite, spinel, tourmaline.

LOS ANGELES COUNTY

Los Angeles County has two important mountain ranges within its borders whose variety and diversity of geology provide for mineralogical occurrences in large numbers. The Santa Monica Mountains and the San Gabriel Range, the former of volcanic and sedimentary rocks with plutonic igneous and metamorphic basement beneath the volcanic-sedimentary cover, and the latter a dominantly igneous and metamorphic terrain, contribute most of the 103 reported minerals. The Santa Monica Mountains have many occurrences of zeolites in the vesicular lavas, but many of these localities are no longer accessible because of urban development. The San Gabriel Mountains are especially notable because the mineral labradorite, found in the rock-type anorthosite, occurs in abundance in the western half of the range. Associated with the labradorite are large masses of ilmenite and titaniferous magnetite in several hundred localities, some of which have been mined commercially. The county contributed two new minerals to mineralogical literature, griffithite (1917) and a rare borate, veatchite (1938). Four localities are of classic interest: (1) Sterling Borax at Tick Canyon, (2) Felix Mine near Azusa, with its brilliant green fluorite, (3) Kelsey and O K mines in San Gabriel Canyon, with cobalt-silver minerals, and (4) Palos Verdes Hills barite.

The minerals from Los Angeles County are: albite, allanite, almandine, analcime, andalusite, annabergite, apophyllite, aragonite, argentite, autunite, azurite, bakerite, barite, barkevikite, beidellite, bismutite, bornite, calcite, celestite, cerargyrite, chalcedony, chalcocite, chalcopyrite, chromite, chrysocolla, clinochlore, clinozoisite, colemanite, columbite, copper, cordierite, corundum, crossite, dolomite, epidote, epsomite, erythrite, fluorite, galena, garnet, glaucophane, gold, graphite, griffithite, gypsum, halotrichite, heulandite, howlite, iddingsite, ilmenite, iron (meteorite), kyanite, labradorite, laumontite, lawsonite, magnesite, magnetite, marcasite, mariposite, melanterite, mesolite, minium, molybdenite, montmorillonite, natrolite, opal, paraveatchite, pharmacolite, piemontite, potash alum, prehnite, probertite, psilomelane, ptilolite, pyrrhotite, quartz, realgar, rhodonite, roscoelite, sal ammoniac, serpentine, siderite, sillimanite, silver, smaltite, sphalerite, sphene, stibnite, stilbite, strontianite, talc, tetrahedrite, thomsonite, thorite, tourmaline, tridymite, ulexite, veatchite, vivianite, zircon, and zoisite.

MADERA COUNTY

Madera County, one of several counties in the southern Central Valley of California, extends its geographic boundaries from the alluvial geology of the valley floor through the complete rock sequence of the Sierra Nevada Mountains (the eastern boundary of the county is the crest of the Sierra Nevada). One of the most interesting minerals in mineralogical literature is the variety of andalusite whose crystal structure is outlined by inclusions of organic matter. This variety, known as chiastolite, occurs abundantly in fine showy crystals at several localities in the schists of the lower slopes of the Sierra Nevada. Crystals from Madera County are found in collections throughout the United States. The mineral connellite is reported in its first and to date only California occurrence from Madera County.

The minerals reported to date from this county are: actinolite, altaite, andalusite, anglesite, antlerite, aragonite, argentian gold, axinite, azurite, bismuthinite, bornite, bustamite, calcite, cerussite, chalcocite, chalcopyrite, chromite, chrysocolla, cobaltite, columbite, connellite, copper, cubanite, diopside, epidote, ferrimolybdite, galena, garnet, gold, heulanite, ilmenite, lazulite, lazurite, linarite, magnesite, magnetite, manganite, molybdenite, orthoclase, phlogopite, piemontite, pyrite, pyrolusite, pyrophyllite, pyrrhotite, rhodochrosite, rhodonite, scheelite, scorzalite, silver, sphalerite, stilbite, talc, tourmaline, tremolite, turquoise, tyuyamunite, uraninite, vivianite, wolframite, and zaratite.

MARIN COUNTY

Marin County, on the north shore of San Francisco Bay, has many interesting mineral localities reported within its boundaries. Several of the minerals were first observed by M. Vonsen, an amateur mineralogist of Petaluma, who for nearly 50 years provided information that led to identification and discovery both of new minerals and new mineral localities in the state. As a partial reward for his efforts, the mineral vonsenite was named for him from a discovery he made from Riverside County. The new mineral lawsonite was first described from Marin County in 1895 from a locality on the Tiburon Peninsula. The mineral has since been found in many localities elsewhere in California. The type locality for the mineral has been obliterated by grading for homes, as Marin County is strategically located in the path of the population explosion in California, Rice (3) p. 96. Progress seems to include the erasure or removal from accessibility of many mineral localities in Marin County. The only occurrence in California of the mineral szaibelyite has been recorded from this county and a recent discovery of tungsten has yielded interesting scheelite crystals.

The minerals reported from Marin County are: actinolite, albite, alunogen, apophyllite, axinite, calcite, chalcedony, chalcopyrite, chromite, cinnabar, epidote, garnet, glaucophane, graphite, hydromagnesite, jadeite, lawsonite, margarite, muscovite, nephrite, prehnite, psilomelane, pumpellyite, pyrolusite, pyrrhotite, rutile, scheelite, sphene, stilpnomelane, szaibelyite, tremolite, tridymite, tourmaline, wollastonite, and zircon.

MARIPOSA COUNTY

Mariposa County, one of the southernmost of the counties of the Mother Lode belt, was the source of discovery of interesting minerals very early in the settlement of California, and has been a continuous contributor since of new and "one of a kind for California" occurrences. The first new mineral described from the county was named "mariposite", in 1868. It is a chromium-bearing mica. The mineral has since been found in several occurrences in the Mother Lode belt and in other metamorhic rocks in the state. A number of closely related localities around El Portal in which barium-bearing minerals were discovered is also of mineralogical interest. The new mineral sanbornite was described in 1932 (or 1931) from Mariposa barium properties. It occurs with celsian, witherite, gillespite, and other minerals. One locality famous for its gold crystals, and one occurrence of crystals of cobaltite are reported from this County.

The minerals from Mariposa County are: alunite, alunogen, andalusite, ankerite, argentite, arsenopyrite, azurite, barite, bementite, bornite, bromlite, celsian, chalcocite, chalcopyrite, chloropal, chromite, chrysocolla, cinnabar, cobaltite, copper, cordierite, corundum, cuprite, epidote, epsomite, erythrite, ferrimolybdite, galena, garnet, garnierite, gersdorffite, gillespite, goethite, gold, gold amalgam, kobellite, limonite, magnesite, malachite, mariposite, mercury, molybdenite, nephrite, pitticite, platinum, proustite, pyrargyrite, pyrite, pyrolusite, pyromorphite, pyrophyllite, pyrrhotite, quartz, rhodochrosite, rhodonite, sanbornite, scheelite, scorodite, serpentine, siderite, sillimanite, silver, sphalerite, sulfur, taramellite, tellurium, tenorite, tephroite, tetrahedrite, and witherite.

MENDOCINO COUNTY

Mendocino County, in the northern Coast Range of California, has wide surface exposures of the Franciscan formation. Associated with the Franciscan are large serpentine bodies, which as part of the basement, contain many interesting minerals of special interest to collectors. Mendocino County has many localities for minerals like lawsonite, chromite, epidote, actinolite, crossite, glaucophane, garnet, and a wide variety of common, but interesting, manganese minerals. Many of the localities have yielded large and good crystals. The minerals brewsterite and edingtonite are reported from this county only. Three new minerals, deerite, howieite, and zussmanite, were described in 1964 from Mendocino County.

Minerals known from Mendocino County are: actinolite, azurite, bementite, bornite, brewsterite, chalcopyrite, chromite, chrysocolla, cinnabar, clinozoisite, copper, crossite, cuprite, deerite, edingtonite, epidote, garnet, graphite, glaucophane, howieite, inesite, iridium, iridosmine, jadeite, jefferisite, laumontite, lawsonite, magnesite, mercury, neotocite, nephrite, platinum, psilomelane, pyrolusite, rhodochrosite, riebeckite, rutile, sphene, stilpnomelane, talc, tenorite, tetrahedrite, xonotlite, zaratite, zircon, zoisite, and zussmanite.

MERCED COUNTY

Merced County is situated in a great agricultural belt, producing primarily from unconsolidated sedimentary rocks and their rich soils, and from the alluvial sediments of the flood plains of several of the great rivers of the Sierra Nevada tributary to the San Joaquin River. The mineralogical occurrences of the county are therefore less numerous, although gold is still being produced, copper is represented by several different minerals, and gypsum and other sedimentary minerals also occur.

The minerals reported from Merced County are: aragonite, calcite, chalcopyrite, copper, glauconite, gold, gypsum, hydromagnesite, jarosite, lawsonite, pumpellyite, soda niter, sphalerite, stibnite, and stilpnomelane.

MODOC COUNTY

The northeasternmost county in the state is Modoc County. Its geology is almost entirely that of the great Columbian andesitic and basaltic lava province. Volcanic rocks carry many zeolitic minerals. An occurrence of calcite, variety iceland spar, was of sufficient quality to have been mined commercially. Sixty-pound masses were extracted. Modoc County also contributed the Goose Lake meteorite, a siderite of 2,573 pounds. the largest meteorite known from the state. This fall was recovered in 1938.

Minerals from Modoc County are: azurite, calcite, chalcedony, chalcopyrite, chloropal, copper, cristobalite, cuprite, iron (meteorite), labradorite, natrolite, niter, stilbite, tourmaline, and water (permanent ice).

MONO COUNTY

Mono County is one of the most prolific mineral counties in California. There are over 100 localities, many of them of mineralogical importance, including some of the earliest known occurrences of minerals in the state. In addition several mining districts such as Blind Spring Hill, Bodie, and Patterson, are old producers of lead, silver, and gold. The important Champion Sillimanite Incorporated developed the andalusite deposit near the north end of the White Mountains on the western flank of the range. This locality is one of the most famous mineral localities in the west. Over 20 different mineral species are reported to date, including the rare mineral augelite and the new mineral woodhouseite, which was named and described in 1937. Other new minerals may yet be found as further mineralogical study progresses. Several mineral localities are firsts for the state from Mono County. The sparse population of the county and its many outdoor tourist attractions make it likely that many more interesting mineral localities will be discovered.

The recorded occurrences in Mono County have produced the following mineral species: albite, alunite, analcime, andalusite, anglesite, anhydrite, apatite, aragonite, argentite, arsenopyrite, augelite, aurichalcite, axinite, azurite, barite, bismuth, bismuthinite, bismutite, bornite, boulangerite, brannerite, calcite, caledonite, carnotite, cerargyrite, cerussite, cervantite, chabazite, chalcanthite, chalcocite, chalcopyrite, chloropal, chrysocolla, cinnabar, cobaltite, copper, corundum, covellite, cristobalite, cuprite, diaspore, dioptase, embolite, epidote, erythrite, ferrierite, ferrimolybdite, fluorite, galena, gay-lussite, geocronite, gold (argentian), greenockite, gypsum, halloysite, halotrichite, hanksite, hematite, hessite, hornblende, idocrase (vesuvianite), ilmenite, jarosite, kermesite, lazulite, lazurite, linarite, magnetite, malachite, marcasite, massicot, mercury, minium, molybdenite, opal, partzite, pectolite, potash alum, powellite, proustite, pyrargyrite, pyromorphite, pyrophyllite, pyrrhotite, quartz, rutile, scheelite, scorzalite, siderite, silver, sphalerite, sphene, stephanite, stibnite, stromeyerite, sulfur, svanbergite, tetrahedrite, topaz, tourmaline, tridymite, trona, uraninite, uranophane, uvarovite, vanadinite, wolframite, wollastonite, woodhouseite, wulfenite, wurtzite, zircon, and zoisite.

MONTEREY COUNTY

Monterey County was known for its minerals as early as 1802, when, according to Duflot de Mofras, in *Travels on the Pacific Coast* (1840–42), galena was discovered at Alisal. The mineral iddingsite was described as a new species from Carmelo Bay in 1893, by A. C. Lawson, professor of geology at the University of California, Berkeley. In the past ten years, mineral collectors have flocked to Monterey County's Pacific coastline where nephrite jade of high quality is found in beach gravels along the rugged serpentine coastline. Boulders of very large size and of good gem quality are uncovered by tidal and wave action from time to time. The rare mineral geikielite is also found in this county.

Minerals reported from Monterey County are: apatite, aragonite, arsenic, arsenopyrite, axinite, azurite, calcite, carnotite, cerussite, chalcedony, chromite, cinnabar, clinohumite, clinozoisite, collophane, galena, garnet, geikielite, glauconite, graphite, iddingsite, magnesite, malachite, metacinnabar, molybdenite, nephrite, orthoclase, penninite, piemontite, pisanite, psilomelane, rhodonite, serpentine, spinel, stibnite, sulfur, uvarovite, vonsenite, xonotlite, and zaratite.

NAPA COUNTY

Seven new minerals have been found and described from Napa County, this number being exceeded only by Riverside and San Bernardino counties. Almost all seven are from the Redington (Boston) mine near Knoxville and were described between 1873 and 1903. Three, aragotite, napalite, and posepnyte, are hydrocarbons, and by modern classification not minerals. Palacheite, described in 1903 as a new mineral, has since been shown to be botryogen. The occurrence of botryogen, however, is still exclusive to Napa County. One other locality in the county has been discovered, but no others in the state. Knoxvillite, described as new in 1890, has since been shown to be magnesiocopiapite, which has not been reported elsewhere in the state. Crednerite and hohmannite occur only in Napa County. Metacinnabar has, since its discovery in 1870, been found in many other areas, but redingtonite, discovered in 1890 and named for the famous Redington mine, has yet to be found elsewhere. The Redington mine contributed at least a dozen of the 57 minerals reported in the county. Important production of mercury and chromium has come from Napa County.

Minerals reported from Napa County to date are: aragotite, argentite, arsenopyrite, barite, botryogen, calomel, cassiterite, cerargyrite, chalcedony, chalcocite, chalcopyrite, chromite, cinnabar, copiapite, copper, coquimbite, crednerite, cuprite, curtisite, deweylite, epsomite, erythrite, fibroferrite, galena, gypsum, hohmannite, hydromagnesite, jamesonite, magnesiocopiapite, magnesite, marcasite, melanterite, mendozite, mercury, metacinnabar, millerite, mirabilite, morenosite, napalite, opal, posepnyte, potash alum, proustite, psilomelane, pyrargyrite, pyrolusite, quartz, redingtonite, römerite, rosenite, serpentine, silver, smaltite, stibnite, voltaite, wollastonite.

NEVADA COUNTY

Several counties of the central Sierra Nevada were the focal areas for lode gold production in California's Mother Lode gold rush. Nevada County, with such famous gold mines as the Empire and Idaho-Maryland, made history in terms of quantity and quality of gold. Though gold production in the county has been depressed, some gold specimen material of note continues to come from the county. In 1956, crystals of gold with leaf and wire gold were on pyrite and quartz crystals in the Red Ledge mine. The same mine produced a mineral, chromrutile, described as new in 1928. In 1961, the chromrutile was shown to be incorrectly identified, and the material has been renamed redledgeite by Strunz (1) p. 107 as a new mineral from the state. The largest diamond found in California, weighing $7\frac{1}{2}$ carats, was recovered in Nevada County before 1867, and three minerals of rarity are found in the county, gold amalgam, metazeunerite, and naumannite, the last found in California only at the Nevada County occurrence.

The minerals from Nevada County are: altaite, alunogen, anatase, andalusite, ankerite, argentite, arsenic, arsenopyrite, azurite, barite, bismuth, bornite, calcite, carnotite, chabazite, chalcanthite, chalcocite, chalcopyrite, chloropal, chromite, chrysocolla, cinnabar, cobaltite, copper, covellite, cristobalite, cuprite, diallage, diamond, enstatite, epidote, ferrimolybdite, galena, garnet, gibbsite, gold, gold amalgam, graphite, gypsum, hessite, magnesite, magnetite, marcasite, mariposite, metazeunerite, molybdenite, naumannite, penninite, petzite, psilomelane, pyrargyrite, pyrite, pyromorphite, pyrrhotite, redledgeite, rhodonite, scapolite, scheelite, serpentine, smaltite, sphalerite, stephanite, stibnite, tephroite, tetradymite, tetrahedrite, tourmaline, wollastonite, and zircon.

ORANGE COUNTY

Orange County, now almost completely a suburban county of the Metropolitan Los Angeles area, has had the largest population increase of any county in California, with resultant reduction in land available for mineral finds. It is to be expected therefore that the present list of 24 minerals from the county will not increase significantly. The mineral arcanite, an uncommon sulfate of potassium, was first described from Orange County in 1908.

Minerals known to date from Orange County are: alunite, anhydrite, aragonite, arcanite, argentite, barite, calomel, cassiterite, cerrussite, crossite, galena, garnet, gypsum, kaolinite, melanterite, mercury, metacinnabar, muscovite, piemontite, pyrrhotite, sphalerite, stibnite, tiemannite, tourmaline, and zircon.

PLACER COUNTY

Placer County, of Mother Lode gold rush fame, produced what appears to have been the second largest single gold mass known, a 187-ounce nugget from near Michigan Bluff on the American River. In addition, arborescent gold specimens and near-perfect octahedral crystals of gold up to $\frac{3}{8}''$ on an edge came from mines in this county. Of those preserved, one of unusual perfection served as the model for Dana's *System of Mineralogy,* and the type specimen is in the Amherst College Museum, Amherst, Mass., on loan from the private collection of Dr. George W. Bain. Cerargyrite with intergrown wire gold also was found in beautiful, large masses in several places during the early days of mining in the county. Uvarovite is to be found in many places, usually in excellent crystals.

The minerals from Placer County are: albite, alunogen, aragonite, argentian gold, argentite, arsenopyrite, axinite, azurite, barite, cassiterite, cerargyrite, chalcanthite, chalcedony, chalcocite, chalcopyrite, chloropal, chromite, clinochlore, cobaltite, copper, coquimbite, cuprite, diamond, diopside, galena, garnet, gold, hausmannite, hematite, idocrase (vesuvianite), iridosmine, kaolinite, lead, limonite, magnesite, magnetite, malachite, mariposite, millerite, molybdenite, penninite, potash alum, psilomelane, pyrargyrite, pyrolusite, quartz, rhodochrosite, rhodonite, rutile, scheelite, serpentine, silver, sphalerite, spinel, stibnite, tetrahedrite, tourmaline, tremolite, and zircon.

PLUMAS COUNTY

Plumas County, a beautiful county located in the Sierra Nevada, has long been known for variety in the minerals it has within its boundaries. North of the Mother Lode gold belt, copper has been the chief metal mined, especially from the long-lived and well-known Engels mine. From this mine and its near surroundings almost two dozen minerals are reported. Copper minerals, including both primary sulfide minerals like bornite, covellite, and chalcocite, and secondary minerals like azurite and malachite, have been abundant. Many zeolites have come from the country rocks and gangue of the mines, including the zeolite scolecite along with cuprosklodowskite which are reported for California from this county only.

Minerals from Plumas County are: albite, analcime, anauxite, anglesite, ankerite, apatite, apophyllite, azurite, barite, bornite, brannerite, braunite, brochantite, chabazite, chalcedony, chalcocite, chalcopyrite, chromite, chrysocolla, copper, corundum, covellite, cristobalite, cubanite, cuprite, cuprosklodowskite, diamond, enargite, epidote, garnet, hausmannite, hematite, heulandite, hornblende, hypersthene, idocrase (vesuvianite), ilmenite, laumontite, magnetite, malachite, margarite, metazeunerite, millerite, molybdenite, natrolite, phillipsite, piemontite, platinum, prehnite, psilomelane, pyrolusite, pyrophyllite, pyrrhotite, quartz, rhodonite, scheelite, scolecite, serpentine, siderite, silver, sphalerite, sphene, stilbite, strontianite, tetrahedrite, thomsonite, torbernite, tourmaline, tremolite, tridymite, wulfenite, zircon, and zoisite.

RIVERSIDE COUNTY

Riverside County is one of California's most prolific mineral counties. It contains the world renowned Crestmore quarries, which have yielded more than 145 different mineral species, including ten minerals new to science and other compounds not yet identified. Besides Crestmore, there are many other localities of exceptional mineralogical interest, such as the pegmatite belt of the Coahuila area, where several mines contained unusually high quality gem beryl and gem tourmaline, as well as such rare minerals as microlite. One of the two commercially developed tin mines in the state was in Riverside County; it is now under the waters of Lake Mathews. North Hill, the new City quarry, Box Springs, the Southern Pacific silica quarry at Nuevo, the Eagle Mountain iron deposits currently producing the raw material for Kaiser Steel, have all contributed interesting minerals including some rare specimens.

The minerals reported from Riverside County include more than 175 species, as follows: actinolite, afwillite, allanite, amarantite, amblygonite, anatase, andalusite, andesine, anglesite, anhydrite, anthophyllite, antimony, apatite, apophyllite, aquamarine, aragonite, argentite, arsenopyrite, autunite, axinite, azurite, bayldonite, barite, bementite, beryl, biotite, bismuth, bismuthinite, boehmite, bornite, brucite, bultfonteinite, calcite, carnotite, cassiterite, centrallasite, cerussite, chabazite, chalcedony, chalcocite, chalcopyrite, chlorite, chloropal, chondrodite, chromite, chrysocolla, clinochlore, clinohumite, clinozoisite, colemanite, columbite, copiapite, copper, cordierite, corundum, crestmoreite, cristobalite, crocoite, cuprite, cuproplumbite, custerite, cyrtolite, danburite, datolite, deweylite, diallage, diopside, dolomite, dumortierite, ellestadite, epidote, epistilbite, ettringite, fayalite, fergusonite, fluoborite, fluorite, forsterite, foshagite, galena, garnet, gehlenite, geikielite, gibbsite, goethite, gonnardite, graphite, greenockite, gypsum, hawleyite, hematite, hemimorphite, hillebrandite, hornblende, huntite, hydromagnesite, hydrotroilite, hypersthene, idocrase (vesuvianite), iron (meteorite), jurupaite, kaolinite, kyanite, labradorite, laumontite, lechatelierite, lepidolite, limonite, loellingite, ludwigite, maghemite, magnesioferrite, magnesite, magnetite, malachite, manganite, marcasite, margarite, mariposite, meerschaum, merwinite, microline, microlite, mimetite, molybdenite, monazite, monticellite, montmorillonite, mottramite, muscovite, nasonite, nekoite, neotocite, nephrite, niter, nuevite, oligoclase, okenite, opal, orthoclase, paigeite, parawollastonite, periclase, perovskite, phillipsite, phlogopite, piemontite, plazolite, plombierite, prehnite, psilomelane, ptilolite, pyrite, pyrolusite, pyromorphite, pyrrhotite, quartz, ramsdellite, realgar, rhodonite, riversideite, rutile, samarskite, scapolite, scawtite, scheelite, scolecite, sepiolite, serendibite, serpentine, siderite, smithsonite, soda niter, sphalerite, sphene, spinel, spodumene, spurrite, sternbergite, stibnite, stilbite, stromeyerite, strontianite, talc, tetrahedrite, thaumasite, thomsonite, thorite, thorogummite, tilleyite, tobermorite, tourmaline, tremolite, ulexite, uraninite, uranophane, vanadinite, vermiculite, vonsenite, wightmanite, wilkeite, wollastonite, wulfenite, xanthophyllite, xenotime, xonotlite, yttrocrasite, zinnwaldite, zircon, and zoisite.

SACRAMENTO COUNTY

Sacramento County has a substantial annual production of mineral resources peculiar to a region of unconsolidated sedimentary rocks and alluvial plains. However, for mineralogical variety and unique mineralogical occurrences, bed rock exposures are almost a necessity. Thus, few minerals come from the capital county of California. These are chromite, galena, pyrite, quartz, sphalerite, zircon, and gold, which is still found in commercial quantities on occasion along the rivers of the county.

SAN BENITO COUNTY

San Benito County is the home of the famous New Idria mercury mine, a producer of mercury since about the middle of the last century, and of the world-famous locality for the new mineral benitoite, discovered in 1907 and not yet reported elsewhere in the world. At least 20 other minerals are found with the benitoite, including the new mineral joaquinite, discovered in 1909, and the unusual mineral neptunite. Since the discovery, the "benitoite locality" has been a "must" for mineralogists and lay collectors alike. The locality, in recent years, has yielded little benitoite, but other interesting minerals are still collected from the area. California's only occurrence of several other minerals are in San Benito County. Over 50 mineral species are reported as follows: acmite, actinolite, albite, analcime, anatase, apatite, aragonite, artinite, barite, barkevikite, bementite, benitoite, brucite, calomel, celestite, cervantite, chalcedony, chalcocite, chalcopyrite, chrysocolla, chromite, cinnabar, diadochite, digenite, eglestonite, epsomite, fluoborite, garnet, garnierite, glaucophane, gypsum, hydromagnesite, ilmenite, jadeite, jarosite, joaquinite, koninckite, lawsonite, libethenite, magnesioferrite, magnesite, melanterite, mercury, metacinnabar, montroydite, natrolite, neptunite, nesquehonite, pectolite, penninite, perovskite, psilomelane, pumpellyite, pyrolusite, quartz, römerite, rutile, serpentine, spinel, stibiconite, stibnite, stilpnomelane, turquoise, valentinite, vivianite, voltaite, and zaratite.

SAN BERNARDINO COUNTY

San Bernardino County, the largest county in California, is also the most prolific in variety and number of new minerals reported. Famous Searles Lake, discovered in 1862, was early recognized as a store-house not only of valuable mineral products, but as a potential source of new minerals. Since the inception of production and study, this locality alone has yielded over 25 minerals, including ten new species. The first new mineral was described in 1884 (hanksite) and the latest was described in 1955 (galeite). Four other new minerals have been described from the county, one from the Calico Mountains from the mines at the now defunct town of Borate, one from the "Sulphur Hole" near Borate, one from the rare earth deposit at Mountain Pass, and one from the Kramer-Four Corners area. Sixteen minerals are reported in this county in single occurrence in the state. Five meteorites have been found, and the expanse of terrain with much varied geology makes it a safe prediction that many more mineralogical finds will be made in the county. The value of mineral products from the county continues among the highest in the state, in a wide variety of commercial materials.

Over 200 minerals are reported from San Bernardino County: actinolite, adamite, allanite, allophane, alunite, amblygonite, analcime, anatase, anglesite, anhydrite, anthophyllite, ankerite, apatite, aphthitalite, aragonite, argentite, arsenosiderite, arsenolite, arsenopyrite, atacamite, attapulgite, autunite, axinite, azurite, bakerite, barite, bassanite, bastnaesite, bayldonite, betafite, betauranophane, bindheimite, biotite, bismuthinite, bismutite, boltwoodite, boracite, borax, bornite, brannerite, brochantite, brucite, burkeite, calciovolborthite, calcite, caledonite, carnotite, cassiterite, celestite, cerargyrite, cerite, cerrussite, cervantite, chabazite, chalcedony, chalcocite, chalcopyrite, chlorite, chloromagnesite, chondrodite, chromite, chrysocolla, cinnabar, clinoptilolite, clinozoisite, colemanite, cookeite, copiapite, coquimbite, corundum, cryptomelane, cummingtonite, cuprite, cyanotrichite, cyrtolite, darapskite, datolite, descloizite, deweylite, diopside, dioptase, dolomite, duftite, embolite, epidote, epsomite, euxenite, ferrimolybderite, fibroferrite, fluorite, forsterite, galeite, galena, garnet, gay-lussite, glauberite, gold, graphite, greigite, greenockite, gümbelite, gypsum, halite, halotrichite, hanksite, hematite, hemimorphite, heulandite, hornblende, howlite, hydromagnesite, hydrotroilite, hydrozincite, iddingsite, idocrase (vesuvianite), ilmenite, iron (meteorite), jarosite, kaolinite, kasolite, krausite, kyanite, laumontite, lazulite, lazurite, lepidolite, linarite, litharge, ludwigite, magnesite, magnetite, marcasite, massicot, melanterite, mendozite, metatorbernite, metavoltine, miargyrite, mimetite, minium, mirabilite, molybdenite, monazite, monticellite, montmorillonite, muscovite, nahcolite, natron, niter, northupite, olivine, opal, orthoclase, pargasite, parisite, phillipsite, pickeringite, piemontite, pirssonite, pitchblende, polybasite, potash alum, powellite, priceite, proustite, psilomelane, pyrargyrite, pyrolusite, pyromorphite, pyrophyllite, pyrostilpnite, quartz, realgar, rhodochrosite, rhodonite, römerite, rutile, sahamalite, saponite, schairerite, scheelite, searlesite, serpentine, sillimanite, silver, smithsonite, soda niter, sphalerite, sphene, spinel, stephanite, stibiconite, stibnite, stilbite, stromeyerite, strontianite, stylotypite, sulphohalite, sulphur, talc, teepleite, tenorite, tetrahedrite, thaumasite, thenardite, thomsonite, thorite, tincalconite, tourmaline, tremolite, triplite, trona, turquoise, tychite, tyuyamunite, ulexite, uraninite, uranophane, uranothorite, valentinite, vanadinite, vauquelinite, veatchite, voltaite, wolframite, wulfenite, zircon, and zoisite.

SAN DIEGO COUNTY

San Diego County is the gem county of California. Home of a world-famous pegmatite belt which has attracted geological attention for nearly a century, study has been extensive and prospecting vigorous. Discovery of the gem-bearing pockets in the pegmatites has led to identification of several new minerals and to recovery of giant crystals and crystal aggregates of tourmaline, spodumene (gem variety kunzite), garnet, beryl, and topaz. Specimens are in all major mineral collections in the world and in most minor ones. Famous localities are Mesa Grande, Pala, Rincon, Ramona, and Oak Grove, with many minor but equally interesting prospects in the gem region. Of the nearly 125 mineral occurrences, at least half are related to the pegmatite gem belt. Eighteen minerals are reported in California only from San Diego County.

The minerals recorded to date are: acmite, alabandite, albite, allanite, amblygonite, andalusite, apatite, aragonite, arsenopyrite, axinite, azurite, bavenite, bertrandite, beryl, beyerite, biotite, bismite, bismuth, bismuthinite, bismutite, calcite, cassiterite, celestite, cerargyrite, chalcedony, chalcocite, chalcopyrite, columbite, cookeite, corundum, crossite, dumortierite, epidote, erythrite, essonite, fergusonite, ferrimolybdite, fluorite, francolite, gahnite, galena, garnet, glauconite, glaucophane, gold, graphite, halloysite, hambergite, helvite, heulandite, hureaulite, hydromagnesite, hypersthene, idocrase (vesuvianite), jezekite, kyanite, laumontite, lawsonite, lazulite, lepidolite, lithiophilite, löllingite, ludlamite, malachite, manganite, marcasite, mariposite, melanterite, metastrengite, microcline, microlite, molybdenite, monazite, montmorillonite, morenosite, muscovite, pentlandite, petalite, petzite, phenakite, piemontite, pollucite, potash alum, prehnite, psilomelane, pucherite, purpurite, pyrite, pyrochlore, pyrophyllite, pyrrhotite, quartz, rhodonite, rutile, salmonsite, scheelite, scorodite, sicklerite, siderite, sillimanite, sphalerite, sphene, spinel, spodumene, stewartite, stibiotantalite, stilbite, strengite, strontianite, talc, tenorite, tephroite, topaz, tourmaline, tremolite, tridymite, triphylite, triplite, vermiculite, violarite, wardite, wollastonite, zinnwaldite, zircon, and zoisite.

SAN FRANCISCO COUNTY

The city of San Francisco occupies the territory of San Francisco County. Because it is an urban area, mineral development is minimal. However, one locality of very considerable interest, Fort Point, has reported 14 minerals, including sjögrenite, found nowhere else in the state to date. Fort Point also accounts for most of the 24 occurrences from this county. Taranakite, a rare phosphate, is reported in the state only from the Farallon Islands, in San Francisco County.

The following minerals are known: apophyllite, aragonite, barite, brucite, calcite, chalcedony, chromite, curtisite, datolite, diallage, diopside, enstatite, gypsum, gyrolite, hydromagnesite, magnesite, mercury, pectolite, quartz, serpentine, sjögrenite, taranakite, wollastonite, and xonotlite.

SAN JOAQUIN COUNTY

The bedrock of San Joaquin County is almost exclusively concealed by the alluvium deposited by the San Joaquin River. Accordingly, although its mineral products have continuing and considerable value, the minerals of the county are few. Except for six manganese minerals reported from a single mine on the western edge of the county where a bedrock fringe of the Coast Range mountains enters county boundaries, no minerals are reported. Interestingly, however, gold was observed and reported from San Joaquin River channels in 1846 by G. M. Evans (1), p. 385, but, like the discoveries of gold in southern California in 1842 and 1843, it went unnoticed.

Minerals reported from San Joaquin County are: bementite, gold, gypsum, hausmannite, inesite, psilomelane, pyrolusite, and rhodochrosite.

SAN LUIS OBISPO COUNTY

San Luis Obispo County, located in the heart of the southern Coast Ranges, has been a consistent producer of mercury among California counties. As early as 1876 commercial mercury production began and has continued intermittently since. The Oceanic and Klau mines are important, each having provided interesting specimens and groups of minerals. Fossil shells petrified in cinnabar were found in the Oceanic mine, and minerals such as bieberite, linnaeite, millerite, and morenosite are reported, with mercury minerals, from the Klau mine. Soda Lake, on the eastern edge of the county, has yielded good crystals of saline minerals. Mineral products continue to form an important part of the economy of the county.

Minerals reported from San Luis Obispo County are: allophane, alunogen, analcime, aragonite, autunite, barite, bieberite, blödite, cervantite, chalcedony, chalcopyrite, chromite, cinnabar, clinoptilolite, copper, cubanite, epidote, epsomite, erythrite, gypsum, hanksite, hausmannite, hematite, hydromagnesite, jadeite, lawsonite, linnaeite, magnesite, marcasite, mercury, metacinnabar, millerite, mirabilite, morenosite, natrolite, neotocite, prehnite, psilomelane, pyrolusite, pyrophyllite, schroeckingerite, spinel, stibiconite, stibnite, thenardite, tridymite, turquoise, uraninite, wulfenite, zaratite, zippeite, and zircon.

SAN MATEO COUNTY

San Mateo County, extending from the Pacific Ocean to San Francisco Bay, has produced few minerals, but several are of special interest in California mineralogy. Four unusual mercury minerals are reported from San Mateo. A locality near Redwood City gives the state its only representation of the mineral terlinguaite and two localities, both in San Mateo, yield calomel, the rare chloride of mercury. Montroydite, an oxychloride of mercury, is also found here. Two localities for eglestonite are known in the state, both in this county.

Mineral occurrences noted in the county are of the following varieties: analcime, apophyllite, calomel, celadonite, chalcedony, chromite, cinnabar, eglestonite, galena, hydromagnesite, lawsonite, margarite, mercury, metacinnabar, montroydite, pumpellyite, silver, sphalerite, sphene, terlinguaite, vivianite, and zircon.

SANTA BARBARA COUNTY

Some of the earliest references to minerals in California are from Santa Barbara County. In 1792, potash alum and sulfur were found, and cinnabar is first mentioned in 1796. One new mineral, eakleite, later found to be misidentified, was described from the county. Minerals reported are: allanite, analcime, apatite, apophyllite, aragonite, azurite, barite, boothite, calcite, cassiterite, chalcopyrite, chromite, cinnabar, coccinite, collophane, copper, enstatite, epsomite, epidote, garnet, gilsonite, gypsum, hydromagnesite, lawsonite, magnesite, nephrite, opal, pectolite, potash alum, sal ammoniac, sphene, spinel, stilbite, stilpnomelane, sulfur, vivianite, wollastonite, xonotlite, and zircon.

SANTA CLARA COUNTY

Santa Clara County is the site of the New Almaden quicksilver mine, oldest producing mercury mine in the United States. This locality may have been the earliest known occurrence of mercury in the United States. The county has produced three new minerals, aragotite and stibioferrite in 1873, and kempite in 1924. In addition, several localities represent a mineral found only once in California. Santa Clara County's production of mineral products is quite large every year, and is of continuing importance in the mineral economy of the state.

Minerals noted are: albandite, alleghanyite, analcime, apatite, apophyllite, aragonite, aragotite, arsenopyrite, azurite, barite, bementite, bornite, braunite, cassiterite, chabazite, chalcedony, chalcopyrite, chromite, chrysocolla, cinnabar, deweylite, dolomite, epsomite, fluorite, galena, ganophyllite, garnet, glaucophane, gold, greenockite, guadalcazarite, gyrolite, hausmannite, hydromagnesite, jarosite, kempite, lawsonite, magnesite, malachite, margarite, mercury, metacinnabar, millerite, natrolite, pilinite, psilomelane, pumpellyite, pyrite, pyrochroite, pyrolusite, pyrrhotite, quartz, rhodochrosite, riebeckite, rutile, senarmontite, siderite, sphene, stibioferrite, stibnite, stilpnomelane, tephroite, tiemannite, valentinite, zaratite, zoisite.

SANTA CRUZ COUNTY

Santa Cruz County has produced very few minerals. From the Kalkar quarry, however, have come the rare minerals frankeite, meneghinite, rosenite, and stannite, each in the first occurrence recorded in this state.

The minerals listed from Santa Cruz County are: adamite, annabergite, arsenopyrite, bindheimite, bismuth, boulangerite, calcite, cassiterite, celsian, chromite, franckeite, greenockite, ilmenite, jamesonite, lepidomelane, magnetite, melanterite, meneghinite, pabstite, rosenite, stannite, taramellite, tremolite, and zircon.

SHASTA COUNTY

Shasta County has produced copper and iron, and a little chromium from its many mines. Four minerals described from the county are found nowhere else in the state. Many minerals (over 75) have been reported, but none is of unusual mineralogical importance.

Occurrences noted from Shasta County are: alunite, alunogen, analcime, anhydrite, anthophyllite, antlerite, argentite, arsenopyrite,

azurite, barite, bechilite, bornite, calcite, cerargyrite, cerrussite, chabazite, chalcanthite, chalcocite, chalcopyrite, chromite, copiapite, copper,
covellite, cristobalite, cuprite, enargite, ferrimolybdite, galena, garnet,
gold, goslarite, greenockite, halotrichite, hedenbergite, hematite, hessite,
ilsemannite, ilvaite, iridosmine, jarosite, kaolinite, lepidocrocite, limonite, luzonite, maghemite, magnetite, malachite, manganite, melanterite, mesolite, molybdenite, nagyagite, natrolite, olivine, penninite, pickeringite, proustite, psilomelane, pyrargyrite, pyrite, pyromorphite,
pyrrhotite, quartz, rhodonite, scheelite, serpentine, silver, sphalerite,
stephanite, sulphur, talc, tellurium, tenorite, tetrahedrite, tourmaline,
tridymite, ulexite, vivianite, voltaite, zaratite, zinc, and zircon.

SIERRA COUNTY

Sierra County, in the Mother Lode belt of the western Sierran foothills, is the county with the record of longest significant gold production from mines largely in the Alleghany district. Early in the mining
history, very large gold nuggets were common, including a famous
strike in the Monumental mine involving a mass of 95 pounds that was
presumed to have weighed 140 pounds originally.

Thirty-four minerals are reported from the county: apatite, arsenopyrite, beidellite, bismuth, chalcocite, chalcopyrite, chlorite, chromite,
copper, corundum, covellite, ferrimolybdite, galena, gold, hematite,
jamesonite, magnetite, mariposite, molybdenite, muscovite, natrolite,
piemontite, pyrrhotite, quartz, scheelite, scorodite, serpentine, sphalerite, stibnite, stromeyerite, talc, tetrahedrite, tremolite, wollastonite.

SISKIYOU COUNTY

The rugged terrain and varied geology of Siskiyou County, northernmost county of central California, includes many of the famous early
mining regions in California gold history. The Klamath River crosses
the county approximately from east to west, and hydraulic mining
of its gold gravels yielded many values. Several interesting mineral
occurrences are reported among the more than 50 minerals known from
the county. An unusual variety of the mineral idocrase enjoyed a brief
flurry of interest in a special gem-quality occurrence on Indian Creek,
near Happy Camp on the middle Klamath River. The gem was marketed
under the varietal name "californite."

The minerals from Siskiyou County are: actinolite, aragonite, arsenopyrite, axinite, azurite, barite, borax, bornite, calaverite, cassiterite,
chalcedony, chalcocite, chalcopyrite, chloritoid, chromite, cinnabar,
copper, covellite, cristobalite, cuprite, epidote, erythrite, fayalite, galena, garnet, gold, gypsum, hessite, hornblende, hypersthene, iddingsite, idocrase (vesuvianite), mercury, molybdenite, nephrite, opal, orpiment, penninite, petzite, psilomelane, pyrrhotite, realgar, rhodochrosite, rhodonite, serpentine, smaltite, sphalerite, spinel, sulfur, sylvanite,
talc, tephroite, tetradymite, tetrahedrite, water (permanent ice) wollastonite, zaratite, and zircon.

SOLANO COUNTY

Solano County currently markets substantial quantities of mineral
products, but few minerals are reported from the county, only seven

being on formal record: aragonite, chromite, cinnabar, epsomite, gypsum, marcasite, and metacinnabar.

SONOMA COUNTY

Sonoma County is an important county mineralogically because of the variety of minerals found at the hot springs known as The Geysers. This locality has recently become almost world-famous because of the completion of a steam power plant using nature's stored energy.

As early as 1847, sulfur was known in this area in large quantity, and the fact reported that minerals were being formed currently from the hot gases and hot waters from the geysers. Two new substances were described, sonomaite in 1877 and curtisite in 1930, the former subsequently being discredited when the supposed new mineral was identified as an already known species. Several minerals occurring only from California are also known in this county.

Minerals reported to date are: acmite, aenigmatite, alunite, alunogen, aragonite, azurite, boussingaultite, cassiterite, cerussite, chalcedony, chalcopyrite, chromite, cinnabar, clinozoisite, curtisite, epidote, epsomite, garnet, glaucophane, graphite, gummite, halotrichite, hematite, hisingerite, hydromagnesite, ilvaite, jadeite, kaolinite, lawsonite, magnesite, margarite, mascagnite, melanterite, mercury, metacinnabar, metastibnite, montroydite, napalite, natrolite, opal, orpiment, pectolite, pentahydrite, pickeringite, potash alum, psilomelane, pumpellyite, pyrite, pyrolusite, quartz, realgar, rhodochrosite, riebeckite, sassolite, sphene, stilbite, sulphur, talc, tiemannite, tremolite, tridymite, tschermigite, voltaite, wairakite, and zoisite.

STANISLAUS COUNTY

Stanislaus County is not prolific in its mineral resources. Some magnesite has been produced commercially, and attempts have been made to market the not inconsiderable variety of manganese minerals found in one part of the county. Chromite has also been prospected.

The minerals reported from Stanislaus County are: bementite, braunite, chromite, cinnabar, garnet, gypsum, hausmannite, hydromagnesite, inesite, magnesite, psilomelane, pyrolusite, and rhodochrosite.

TEHAMA COUNTY

Tehama County has produced very few minerals. Only those from the interesting Tuscan Springs have significance, although mineral products of some importance are produced annually from the county.

The minerals reported to date are: aragonite, borax, chalcopyrite, chromite, copper, cristobalite, galena, garnet, opal, pectolite, penninite, sassolite, and wollastonite.

TRINITY COUNTY

Trinity County, a landscape wonderland of California often billed as "the Alps" of the state, is a county in which early mining for gold is historic. Many minerals have been noted from the county, and copper mining has been sporadic since gold declined. One meteorite has been recovered in the county.

Minerals reported from Trinity County are: analcime, anthophyllite, apatite, arsenolite, arsenopyrite, autunite, azurite, barite, bementite, beryl, bieberite, bornite, braunite, cassiterite, chalcanthite, chalcocite, chalcopyrite, chromite, cinnabar, claudetite, copiapite, copper, cuprite, diallage, diamond, epidote, ferrimolybdite, fibroferrite, galena, garnet, goslarite, halotrichite, hausmannite, hypersthene, iddingsite, inesite, iridosmine, iron (meteorite), jadeite, limonite, massicot, melanterite, mercury, molybdenite, morenosite, muscovite, nagyagite, nephrite, orpiment, petzite, pisanite, platiniridium, platinum, psilomelane, pumpellyite, pyrrhotite, realgar, rhodochrosite, rhodonite, romerite, scheelite, serpentine, sphalerite, sphene, stibnite, sylvanite, szomolnokite, talc, tephroite, tremolite, whitlockite, wollastonite, and zircon.

TULARE COUNTY

Many minerals are reported from Tulare County, but only chrysoprase, a semiprecious gem variety of chalcedony, and an occurrence of exceptionally fine scheelite crystals are worthy of special note.

The minerals from the county to date are: allanite, andalusite, annabergite, apatite, aragonite, argentian gold, arsenopyrite, autunite, axinite, azurite, barite, bornite, calcite, cerussite, chalcedony, chalcopyrite, chromite, chrysocolla, chrysoprase, copper, cordierite, diamond, epidote, euxenite, fluorite, galena, garnet, garnierite, gehlenite, gold, graphite, gypsum, hornblende, idocrase (vesuvianite), jefferisite, laumontite, limonite, linarite, magnesite, minium, molybdenite, nephrite, oligoclase, opal, piemontite, powellite, psilomelane, pyrargyrite, pyromorphite, pyrrhotite, quartz, rhodonite, riebeckite, scheelite, scorodite, sillimanite, sphalerite, stilpnomelane, sylvanite, talc, tellurium, tetradymite, tetrahedrite, tin, torbernite, tourmaline, tremolite, tridymite, uraninite, and xenotime.

TUOLUMNE COUNTY

Tuolumne County, one of the Mother Lode counties sharing early mining excitement in the California Gold Rush, produced unusual mineralogical finds of tellurides of gold, silver, mercury, and lead from several famous mines around Jamestown and Sonora. Gold nuggets of large size, wire gold, and gold crystals of note were found, and more recently, in 1946, a spectacular gold specimen. The county produced graphite commercially as early as 1853. Current mineral products of the county are copper, gold, silver, tungsten, clay, and stone.

Minerals reported from Tuolumne County are: allanite, altaite, anauxite, ankerite, aragonite, argentite, arsenopyrite, autunite, azurite, bementite, berthierite, beryl, bornite, calaverite, calcite, chalcocite, chalcopyrite, chromite, coloradoite, covellite, cristobalite, epidote, erythrite, ferrimolybdite, galena, garnet, gold, graphite, hessite, iridosmine, kyanite, magnesite, malachite, marcasite, mariposite, metatorbernite, microcline, molybdenite, petzite, pitticite, psilomelane, pyrite, pyrrhotite, rhodochrosite, rhodonite, riebeckite, scheelite, scorodite, sillimanite, sphalerite, sylvanite, talc, tellurium, tetradymite, tetrahedrite, tin, tourmaline, tremolite, tridymite, uraninite.

VENTURA COUNTY

Ventura County is one of the state's five leading counties of mineral commodity production. The county is the only one reporting amber, and in early development interesting mineralogical occurrences of borate minerals and others were found in the Frazier Mountain region.

Minerals reported to date are: amber, analcime, azurite, boussingaultite, chalcopyrite, colemanite, cuprite, galena, garnet, gypsum, howlite, hydroboracite, marcasite, mesolite, millerite, molybdenite, montmorillonite, muscovite, natrolite, pentlandite, pyrrhotite, schroeckingerite, sulfur, and talc.

YOLO COUNTY

The minerals reported from Yolo County are andesine, aragotite, cinnabar, curtisite, fluorite, marcasite, metacinnabar, and sulfur, and these are found primarily in a single prospect area. The county is almost entirely on an alluvial plain.

YUBA COUNTY

Yuba County, with its county seat at the junction of two large California rivers, shared in gold rush activity in placer mining. Minerals reported from Yuba County are: arsenopyrite, chalcopyrite, chromite, cuprite, ferrimolybdite, garnet, molybdenite, penninite, pilinite, rhodonite, scheelite, sylvanite, talc, tremolite, vivianite, and zircon.

MINING DISTRICTS OF CALIFORNIA

Apparently no formal recognition of mining districts was ever made by statute in California at the state level. Study of the written record, however, suggests that many early geologists, mining engineers, and prospectors expected that formal requirements would be legislated, and, in anticipation, terms like "Bonanza Mining District" were coined and widely used in early literature. The usage soon became "district," with "mining" understood. Since there was no law defining "mining district," the coinage of names without definitive location created confusion that still exists, and becomes worse as time erases old sites, old mines, and old towns, or changes names. In addition, the California literature since 1920 (which seems to be about the date that references to mining districts disappeared) refers to "district" primarily as a synonym for "region" or "area." The confusion that results for a volume such as this is understandably unfortunate.

An attempt has been made to regularize the usage of "district." In *Minerals of California*, California Division of Mines and Geology Bulletin 173 for 1956, Murdoch and Webb (39), used "district" about 600 times. The word has been evaluated in each entry. An alphabetical list has been prepared of those referenced localities which appear to be in what was intended as a "Mining District." These are now indexed and their geography given in 1964 terms. The U.S. Geological Survey Bulletin 507, Lindgren (21), J. M. Hill (1), published in 1912, has been used as a guide. Where a mining district is recorded therein, usage in this volume has continued. In addition, all use of the word "district" (outside of editorial error) is deleted in text except where reference is to "Mining District," and then the entire designation is used with initial capital letters, viz: "*Darwin Mining District*." It is hoped to avoid the use of the word "district" in the future, except when mining district is the desired meaning, and then only if the mining district is appropriately entered on the index list.

The compilers believe it is wise not to use the term "mining district" any longer. New coinage in this volume will be discouraged. Locations for new entries should be sufficiently precise that the addition of the qualification "mining district" or "district" is unnecessary.

MINING DISTRICTS REFERRED TO IN THIS VOLUME

Preferred official name (from U.S.G.S. Bulletin 507)	Synonyms, if any	County in which located	Nearest "permanent" town or settlement
Adelaida	Adelaide Klau	San Luis Obispo	16 miles W. of Paso Robles
Adelaide	See Adelaida		
Alleghany	See Forest		
Amalie	Paris	Kern	15 miles E. of Caliente
Atolia		San Bernardino	4 miles S.E. of Randsburg
Auburn	See Ophir		
Badger Hill	See North San Juan		
Ballarat	See Panamint		
Ben Hur	See Green Mountain		
Benton	See Blind Spring		
Blackhawk	Silver Reef	San Bernardino	30 miles E. of Victorville

MINING DISTRICTS REFERRED TO IN THIS VOLUME—Continued

Preferred official name (from U.S.G.S. Bulletin 507)	Synonym, if any	County in which located	Nearest "permanent" town or settlement
Blind Spring	Blind Spring Hill Benton	Mono	Benton
Blind Spring Hill	See Blind Spring		
Bodie		Mono	Bodie
Bullion	Standard	San Bernardino	14 miles N. of Cima
Bully Hill	Winthrop	Shasta	Winthrop (?)
Calico	Daggett	San Bernardino	Yermo
Canada Hill		Nevada	40 miles E. of Colfax
Cargo Muchacho	Hedges, Ogilby	Imperial	10 miles N.W. of Winterhaven
Carrville		Trinity	Trinity Center
Cave Canyon		San Bernardino	
Cerro Gordo		Inyo	15 miles E. of Lone Pine
Chip Flats	See Forest		
Clark Mountain		San Bernardino	Mt. Pass (35 miles E. of Baker)
Coffee	Coffee Creek	Trinity	40 miles N.W. of Trinity Center
Coffee Creek	See Coffee		
Copper World	See Ivanpah		
Coso	New Coso	Inyo	15 miles N.E. of Little Lake
Daggett	See Calico		
Darwin		Inyo	Darwin
Diamond Creek		Del Norte	California-Oregon border. 65 miles S.W. of Grants Pass
Dobbins		Yuba	30 miles N.E. of Marysville
Dutch Flat	Gold Run, Towle	Placer	25 miles E. of Colfax
Eagle Mountain	See Monte Negro		
Edmanton	Meadow Valley	Plumas	12 miles S.W. of Quincy
Esmeralda	Murphy, Sperry	Calaveras	10 miles S.E. of San Andreas
Forest	Alleghany, Chips Flats, Minnesota	Sierra	5–10 miles S. of Downieville
Frasier (Fraser) Mountain		Ventura	10 miles W. of Gorman
French Gulch		Shasta	21 miles N.W. of Redding
Genesee	See Genesee Valley		
Genesee Valley	Genesee	Plumas	20 miles E.N.E. of Quincy
Gold Run	See Dutch Flat		
Granite Basin		Plumas	57 miles N.E. of Oroville
Grapevine		San Bernardino	10 miles N. of Barstow
Grass Valley	See Nevada City		
Green Mountain	Ben Hur	Mariposa	30 miles E. of Merced
Green Mountain		Kern	S. of Onyx
Greenhorn	See Greenhorn Mountains		
Greenhorn Mountains	Greenhorn	Kern	W. of New Kernville
Hayden Hill		Lassen	20 miles S. of Adin
Hedges	See Cargo Muchacho		
Hildreth		Madera	35 miles E. of Madera
Hoag		Modoc	5 miles N. of Fort Bidwell
Ivanpah	Copper World	San Bernardino	10 miles S. of Mountain Pass
Jordan		Mono	12 miles N.E. of Lee Vining
Julian		San Diego	Julian
Junction City		Trinity	5 miles W. of Weaverville
Kearsarge		Inyo	5 miles W. of Independence
Kelsey		El Dorado	5 miles N. of Placerville
Kelso		San Bernardino	Kelso
Kinsley		Mariposa	10 miles W. of El Portal
Klau	See Adelaida		
Lake	See Lakes		
Lakes	Lake, Mammoth	Mono	Mammoth
Lava Beds	Newberry	San Bernardino	Newberry
Lee		Inyo	10 miles N. of Darwin
Leviathan	See Silver Mountain (Alpine)		
Leviathan Peak	See Silver Mountain (Alpine)		
Livermore	Tesla	Alameda	Livermore
Lone Valley	See Morongo		

MINING DISTRICTS REFERRED TO IN THIS VOLUME—Continued

Preferred official name (from U.S.G.S. Bulletin 507)	Synonym, if any	County in which located	Nearest "permanent" town or settlement
Lookout	Modoc	Inyo	10 miles S. of Panamint Springs
Loraine	See Amalie		
Los Burros		Monterey	45 miles W. of King City
Low Divide		Del Norte	30 miles N.E. of Crescent City
Mammoth	See Lakes		
Masonic		Mono	10 miles N.E. of Bridgeport
McLeod	See Stayton		
Meadow Lake		Nevada	25 miles W. of Truckee
Meadow Valley	See Edmanton		
Minaret	See Minarets		
Minarets	Mountain, Raymond, Minaret	Madera	10 miles N.W. of Mammoth
Mineral King		Tulare	Mineral King
Minnesota	See Forest		
Modoc	See Lookout		
Mohave		Kern	Mojave
Monte Negro	Eagle Mountain	Riverside	Eagle Mountain
Morongo	Lone Valley	San Bernardino	Morongo Valley
Mount Raymond	See Minarets		
Murphy	See Esmeralda		
Nevada City	Grass Valley	Nevada	Nevada City
Newberry	See Lava Beds		
New Coso		Inyo	12 miles S.E. of Olancha
North Fork		Trinity	45 miles E.N.E. of Madera
North San Juan	Badger Hill	Nevada	13 miles N. of Nevada City
Ogilby	See Cargo Muchacho		
Omega	See Washington		
Ophir	Auburn	Placer	Auburn
Ord		San Bernardino	15 miles S. of Barstow
Oro Grande		San Bernardino	Oro Grande
Panamint	Ballarat	Inyo	Panamint City
Panoche	See Stayton		
Paris	See Amalie		
Patterson		Mono	5 miles N.W. of Bridgeport
Picacho		Imperial	20 miles N.W. of Winterhaven
Pine Grove		Amador	8 miles E. of Amador
Poker Flat	Table Rock	Sierra	15 miles W.S.W. of Clio
Providence	See Trojan		
Rademacher		Kern	10 miles S. of Inyokern
Russ		Inyo	20 miles E.S.E. of Independence
Signal	Vontrigger	San Bernardino	30 miles N.W. of Needles
Silver Mountain	Leviathan, Leviathan Peak	Alpine	3 miles S. of Markleeville
Silver Mountain		San Bernardino	10 miles E. of Victorville
Silver Reef	See Blackhawk		
Sperry	See Esmeralda		
Standard	See Bullion		
Stayton	McLeod, Panoche	San Benito	8 miles E.N.E of Hollister
Stringer		San Bernardino	8 miles S. of Johannesburg
Sulphur Creek		Colusa	25 miles S.W. of Williams
Saratoga	Tecopa Mountain	Inyo	Tecopa
Table Rock	See Poker Flat		
Tecopa Mountain	See Saratoga		
Tesla	See Livermore		
Tioga		Mono	Summit Tioga Pass
Towle	See Dutch Flat		
Trojan	Providence	San Bernardino	20 miles W. of Essex
Ubehebe		Inyo	10 miles W. of Death Valley Scotty's Castle
Vontrigger	See Signal		
Washington	Omega	Nevada	19 miles E.N.E. of Nevada City
West Point		Calaveras	15 miles N.E. of Jackson
Wild Rose	Wildrose	Inyo	20 miles S.E. of Panamint Springs
Winthrop	See Bully Hill		
Woody		Kern	40 miles N.E. of Bakersfield

UNVALIDATED ENTRIES IN THE MINERAL LOCALITIES

Every effort has been made to provide either (1) a literature source (2) a personal communication or (3) an identification report through labelled specimens for all entries in the section of this volume on "Description of California Minerals and Mineral Localities." The best efforts to date still leave 196 entries unvalidated. Over one-third of these are reports from the Mother Lode belt of counties and represent entries collated apparently almost exclusively prior to 1900. No entries remain unless the writers are reasonably satisfied that there was originally a valid basis for their inclusion.

Localities for which confirmation has not been found are marked (N.R.). The writers have continued such entries for the completeness of the historic record. Many of these (N.R.) entries are of long standing in the volumes of *Minerals of California* since 1866.

In an effort to encourage the users of this volume to report information that might provide validation of these localities for future volumes on *Minerals of California*, an alphabetical list of such entries follows.

Mineral	County and Entry Number in Catalog
Alabandite	San Diego (1)
Allophane	San Luis Obispo (1)
Actinolite	Mendocino (2)
Anthophyllite	Riverside (1)
Hornblende	El Dorado (1)
Tremolite	Kern (1)
Anhydrite	Inyo (1)
Antimony	El Dorado (1)
	Kern (5) and (7)
Aragonite	Tuolumne (1)
Argentite	Orange (1)
Azurite	Mariposa (2)
Bementite	Alameda (1) and (2)
	Humboldt (1)
	Mendocino (1) and (2)
	Stanislaus (1)
Bismuth	Inyo (1) and (2)
	Mono (1)
Bismuthinite	Fresno (2)
	Riverside (1)
Brochantite	Plumas (1)
	San Bernardino (1)
Calaverite	Siskiyou (1)
Calcite	Alameda (2)
	Alpine (1)
	Calaveras (1)
	El Dorado (1) and (2)
	Marin (1)
	Nevada (1) and (2)
	Santa Cruz (1)
Cassiterite	Siskiyou (1)
Chalcocite	Colusa (1)
	El Dorado (1) and (2)
	Napa (1)
	Siskiyou (1)
Chlorite-Penninite	Shasta (1)
Chromite	Nevada (1)
	Sacramento (1)
	Yuba (1)

Mineral	County and Entry Number in Catalog
Chrysoberyl	Butte (1)
Colemanite	Riverside (1)
Corundum	Butte (1)
	San Diego (3)
Covellite	Sierra (1)
Crocoite	Riverside (1)
Diamond	Fresno (1)
Enargite	Del Norte (1)
	El Dorado (1)
Epidote	Colusa (1)
	Humboldt (1)
	San Luis Obispo (1)
	Siskiyou (1)
	Sonoma (1)
	Trinity (1)
Epsomite	Amador (1)
	Mariposa (1)
Erythrite	Napa (1)
Feldspar-Anorthite	Lake (1)
Ferrimolybdite	Del Norte (1)
	Mariposa (1)
	Yuba (1)
Garnet	El Dorado (3)
Goethite	Inyo (1)
Halotrichite	Alameda (1)
Hessite	El Dorado (2)
Ilvaite	Sonoma (1)
Inesite	Alameda (1)
	Mendocino (1)
	San Joaquin (1)
	Stanislaus (1)
Jamesonite	Inyo (1)
Lawsonite	San Benito (2)
Lead	Kern (1)
	Placer (1)
Limonite	Inyo (1)
Liroconite	Inyo (1)
Malachite	Amador (1)

Mineral	County and Entry Number in Catalog	Mineral	County and Entry Number in Catalog
Mariposite	El Dorado (1)	Rutile	Amador (1)
	Nevada (2)		Fresno (1)
	Placer (1)		Placer (1)
	Riverside (1)	Siderite	Calaveras (1)
	San Diego (1)		El Dorado (1)
Melanterite	Amador (1)		Imperial (1)
Mendozite	Amador (1)		Mariposa (1)
	Napa (1)		Santa Clara (1) and (2)
Mesolite	Shasta (1)	Sillimanite	Inyo (2)
Millerite	Humboldt (1)		San Bernardino (1)
	Napa (3) and (4)	Silver	Kern (1) and (2)
Mimetite	Kern (1)	Smaltite	Napa (1)
Minium	Kern (1)		Nevada (1)
Mirabilite	Napa (1)	Smithsonite	Kern (1)
Molybdenite	Inyo (2)	Sphene	Trinity (1)
	Mariposa (1)	Spinel	Butte (1)
	Yuba (1)		San Bernardino (1) and (2)
Natrolite	Sierra (1)	Stephanite	Mono (3)
	Sonoma (1)		Shasta (1)
Neotocite	Mendocino (1) and (2)	Stibnite	Calaveras (1)
Nesquehonite	San Benito (1)		Inyo (1)
Niter	Modoc (1)		San Luis Obispo (3)
Orpiment	Lake (1)	Stilbite	Tulare (1)
Petzite	El Dorado (1)	Stromeyerite	Inyo (1)
	Siskiyou (2)		Sierra (1)
Pickeringite	Inyo (1)	Sulphur	Lake (2)
Plumbogummite	Inyo (1)		Mariposa (1)
Polybasite	Alpine (1)	Sylvanite	Trinity (1)
Potash alum	Contra Costa (1)	Tellurium	Shasta (1)
	Fresno (1)	Tetrahedrite	Imperial (1)
	Inyo (1)		Mariposa (1)
Psilomelane-Asbolite		Tiemannite	Santa Clara (1)
	San Bernardino (1)	Tourmaline	El Dorado (1) and (2)
	San Diego (1)		Modoc (1)
Pyrargyrite	Shasta (1)		Orange (1)
Pyrite	Sonoma (1)		Placer (1), (2), (3) and (4)
Pyrolusite	Calaveras (1)		Tuolumne (1)
	Napa (1)	Vanadinite	Kern (1) and (2)
Pyromorphite	Calaveras (1)	Vivianite	Calaveras (1)
Pyroxene-Diopside	Lake (1)	Witherite	Mariposa (2)
Pyrrhotite	Marin (1)	Wollastonite	Alameda (1)
	Sierra (1)		Del Norte (1)
Quartz	Plumas (1)		Nevada (1)
Chalcedony	Plumas (1)		Siskiyou (1)
	San Benito (1)		Trinity (1)
	Sonoma (1)	Wulfenite	El Dorado (1)
Realgar	Lake (1)		Plumas (1)
	San Bernardino (1)		San Luis Obispo (1)
Rhodochrosite	Placer (1)	Zaratite	Shasta (1)
			Siskiyou (1)
		Zoisite	Sonoma (1)

CONTRIBUTORS OF UNPUBLISHED INFORMATION ON CALIFORNIA MINERAL LOCALITIES

Individuals who have contributed personal communications on entries in the Mineral Catalog of this bulletin are named after each contribution, followed by "p.c." and the year the contribution was received. If the mineralogy of the locality has been subsequently published, the reference also follows.

The index lists last addresses, or professional connections, if known. "(D)" means deceased, and the address is usually the last known professional address of the contributor. Addresses may have changed any time since this manuscript was submitted in June 1965.

Name, address, deceased (D)

Alfors, John T., California Division of Mines and Geology, San Francisco.
Averill, Charles V., California Division of Mines and Geology, San Francisco. (D)
Axelrod, Daniel I., Dept. of Geology, University of California, Davis.
Bateman, Paul C., U.S. Geological Survey, Menlo Park, California.
Bensusan, Kilian, 8615 Columbus Ave., Sepulveda, California.
Bowen, Oliver E., Jr., California Division of Mines and Geology, San Francisco.
Bradley, J. W., Unknown. (See for example, stibnite, Kern County.)
Bradley, W. W., California Division of Mines and Geology, San Francisco. (D)
Bramlette, M. N., Dept. of Geology, University of California, San Diego.
Burnham, C. Wayne, Dept. of Geology, Pennsylvania State University, College Park.
Carpenter, Alden B., Dept. of Geology, University of Missouri, Columbia.
Campbell, Ian, California Division of Mines and Geology, San Francisco.
Carter, Unknown. (See for example, azurite, Ventura County.)
Chelikowsky, Joseph R., Dept. of Geology, Kansas State University, Manhattan, Kansas
Chesterman, Charles W., California Division of Mines and Geology, San Francisco.
Clark, J. W., Unknown. (See for example, hornblende, Riverside County.)
Clark, S. G., c/o Dept. of Geology, University of California, Berkeley. (D)
Clarke, Unknown. (See for example, minium, Los Angeles County).
Coats, Robert R., U.S. Geological Survey, Menlo Park, California.
Cooney, Robert, Dept. of Geology, Fullerton City College, Fullerton, California.
Crippen, R. C., California Division of Mines and Geology, San Francisco.
Cureton, Forrest, 328 Canterbury Dr., Stockton, California.
Davis, Fenelon F., California Division of Mines and Geology, San Francisco.
Dawson, Unknown. (See for example, monazite, San Diego County.)
Desautels, Paul E., United States National Museum, Washington, D.C.
Dickson, Frank W., Dept. of Geology, University of California, Riverside.
Dunning, Gail, Rt. 2, Box P10, Morgan Hill, California.
Durrell, Cordell, Dept. of Geology, University of California, Davis.
Eggleston, J. W., c/o Dept. of Geology, Riverside City College, Riverside, Calif. (D)
Erwin, Homer D., 940 S. Concord St., Los Angeles, California. (D)
Ettinger, L. J., Unknown. (See for example, margarite, Riverside County.)
Filer, Russ, P.O. Box 372, Redlands, California.
Foshag, William F., U.S. Geological Survey, Washington, D.C. (D)
Foster, Robert K., 4821 Pacific Avenue, Venice, California.
Frey, Richard C., P.O. Box 7, Richvale, California.
Frondel, Clifford, Geological Museum, Harvard University, Cambridge, Massachusetts.
Garner, Kenneth B., c/o Dept. of Geology, Pomona College, Claremont, California. (D)
Guillou, Robert B., 802 St. Lukes Dr., Richardson, Texas. (D)
Goudey, Hatfield, American Exploration & Mining Co., Russ Building, San Francisco, California.
Gianella, Vincent P., Dept. of Geology, University of Nevada, Reno.
Grant, W. H., Unknown. (See for example, rutile, San Bernardino County.)
Gregory, Unknown. (See for example, columbite, Los Angeles County.)
Gricius, Anthony, 4426 W. Montana St., Chicago, Illinois.
Grigsby, Donald B., 1724 University Ave., Berkeley, California.
Hawley, A. E., 5938 E. Turnergrove Dr., Long Beach, California.

Name, address, deceased (D)

Henderson, Edward P., U.S. National Museum, Washington, D.C.

Herzog, Unknown. (See for example, epsomite, Los Angeles County.)

Hines, K. G., P.O. Box 368, Elsinore, California.

Hulin, Carleton D., c/o Dept. of Geology, University of California, Berkeley. (D)

Jarvis, A. L., Unknown. (See for example, garnet, Calaveras County.)

Jenni, Clarence M., Dept. of Geology, University of Missouri, Columbia.

Keller, Unknown. (See for example, siderite, Riverside County.)

Knowlton, Charles S., c/o West Coast Mineral Society, Fullerton, California (D)

Lackie, Opal Marie, c/o Dept. Geology, University of California, Los Angeles (D)

Larsen, Esper S., c/o Dept. Geology, Harvard University, Cambridge, Massachusetts. (D)

Leavens, Unknown. (See for example, chabazite, Riverside County.)

Lemmon, Dwight M., U.S. Geological Survey, Menlo Park, California.

Leonard, Frederick C., c/o Department of Astronomy, University of California, Los Angeles. (D)

Little, T. V., Unknown. (See for example, garnet, San Bernardino County.) (D)

Mayo, Evans P., Dept. of Geology, University of Arizona, Tucson.

McGill, John T., Department of Geology, University of California, Los Angeles.

Melhase, John, Formerly Geologist, Southern Pacific Railroad. (D)

Merriam, Richard H., Dept. of Geology, University of Southern California, Los Angeles.

Milton, Charles, U.S. Geological Survey, Washington, D.C.

Morton, Douglas, 16515 Mallory Dr., Fontana, California.

Murdoch, Joseph, Dept. of Geology, University of California, Los Angeles.

Murphy, Michael A., Dept. of Geology, University of California, Riverside.

Neuerburg, George, U.S. Geological Survey, Denver, Colorado.

Nieburger, Jack, 22740 Allesandro, Riverside, California.

Noren, Carl A., 2256 S. Peach Ave., Fresno, California.

O'Guinn, W. D., Unknown. (See for example, idocrase, Kern County.)

Oke, William C., Dept. of Geology, California Institute of Technology, Pasadena (D)

Over, Edwin C., Box 596, Woodland Park, California.

Oyler, E. H., 765 Camino Escuela, San Jose, California.

Pabst, Adolph, Dept. of Geology, University of California, Berkeley.

Parnau, J. L. Unknown. (See for example, ferrierite, Mono County.)

Patterson, Robert O., Pacific Oil Well Logging Company, P.O. Box 2985, Los Angeles, California (D)

Peebles, E. H., Unknown. (See for example, tremolite, Riverside County.)

Pemberton, H. Earl, Mineral Research Society of California, P.O. Box 106, Montebello, California.

Porter, P. W. Unknown. (See for example, laumontite, Los Angeles County.) (D)

Pray, Lloyd C., Ohio Oil Company, Denver Research Center, Littleton, Colorado.

Price, Michael A., Box 1067, Riverton, Wyoming.

Proctor, Richard, 420 Punahaull, Altadena, California.

Raymond, L. C., Unknown. (See for example, manganite, Shasta County.)

Rice, Salem J., California Division of Mines and Geology, San Francisco.

Rogers, Austin F., c/o Dept. of Geology, Stanford University, California. (D)

Rose, Robert L., Dept. of Geology, San Jose State College, San Jose, California.

Schaller, Waldemar T., U.S. Geological Survey, Washington, D.C.

Schwartz, Jack, 656 So. Hendricks, Los Angeles, California.

Seward, Charles, 9223 Dorothy Ave., South Gate, California.

Simons, Frank S., U.S. Geological Survey, Denver, Colorado.

Smith, Ward C., U.S. Geological Survey, Menlo Park, California.

Snidecor, John C., Dept. of Speech, University of California, Santa Barbara, California.

Stager, Harold, U.S. Geological Survey, Washington, D.C.

Stinson, Melvin C., California Division of Mines and Geology, San Francisco.

Switzer, George S., United States National Museum, Washington, D.C.

Symons, Henry H., California Division of Mines and Geology, San Francisco.

Tolman, Cyrus F., c/o School of Mineral Sciences, Stanford University, California (D)

Trainer, J. M., Unknown. (See for example, garnet, Alpine County.)

Troxel, Bennie W., California Division of Mines and Geology, Los Angeles.

Tucker, W. Burling, c/o California Division of Mines and Geology, Los Angeles (D)

Van Amringe, Edwin, c/o Dept. of Geology, Pasadena City College, Pasadena, California (D)

Name, address, deceased (D)

Vonsen, Magnus, Unknown. (D)

Watters, Lou, P.O. Box 88, Cotati, California.

Webb, Robert W., Dept. of Geology, University of California, Santa Barbara.

Wilkie, R. M., Unknown, Former mineral collector and dealer, Palo Alto, California (D)

Williams, Unknown. (See for example, tourmaline, Plumas County.)

Wolff, John E., c/o Dept. of Geology, Harvard University, Cambridge, Massachusetts. (D)

Wood, Harry O., c/o Dept. of Geology, California Institute of Technology, Pasadena. (D)

Woodford, A. O., Dept. of Geology, Pomona College, Claremont, California.

Woodhouse, C. D., Dept. of Geology, University of California, Santa Barbara.

INDEX TO MINERAL SPECIES

INDEX TO MINERAL SPECIES—Continued

INDEX TO MINERAL SPECIES—Continued

INDEX TO MINERAL SPECIES—Continued

INDEX TO MINERAL SPECIES—Continued

INDEX TO MINERAL SPECIES—Continued

INDEX TO MINERAL SPECIES—Continued

o

printed in CALIFORNIA OFFICE OF STATE PRINTING

△ 75135—650   7-66   5M